KT-364-487

With amazing culture, beaches, activities and weather – not to mention the rum – the Caribbean is a joyous riot of islands offering the ultimate escape.

(left) Island in the Tobago Cays (p754). St Vincent & the Grenadines
(below) The striking Caribbean flamingo

spot the accents of red orchids and yellow parrots.

Even the food is colorful, with rainbows of produce brightening up the local markets. You'll also see every color but dull at intense, costume-filled festivities like Carnival, celebrated throughout the region.

And all this color is infectious. Like birds shedding dull adolescent plumage, visitors leave their wardrobes of gray and black behind when they step off the plane and don the Caribbean palette.

Your Kind of Trip

No matter what you're looking for in an island adventure, you'll find it here. Zero in on one perfect place or mix and match from a banquet of islands.

With so many islands, beaches, cultures, flavors and waves to choose from you are bound to have a fabulous time. Doing nothing on the sand, partying at a resort, exploring a new port of call, hopping between islands, discovering wonders under the water or catching a perfect wave above, reveling in a centuries-old culture, and finding your inner pirate are all possible.

Go on, take the plunge.

❯ Caribbean Islands

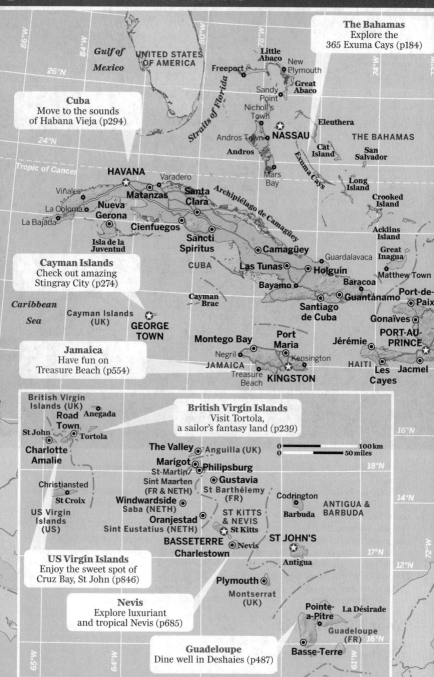

The Bahamas
Explore the
365 Exuma Cays (p184)

Cuba
Move to the sounds
of Habana Vieja (p294)

Cayman Islands
Check out amazing
Stingray City (p274)

Jamaica
Have fun on
Treasure Beach (p554)

British Virgin Islands
Visit Tortola,
a sailor's fantasy land (p239)

US Virgin Islands
Enjoy the sweet spot of
Cruz Bay, St John (p846)

Nevis
Explore luxuriant
and tropical Nevis (p685)

Guadeloupe
Dine well in Deshaies (p487)

Gulf of
Mexico

UNITED STATES
OF AMERICA

Freeport

Little
Abaco

New
Plymouth

Great
Abaco

Sandy
Point

Nicholl's
Town

Eleuthera

Andros Town

NASSAU

THE BAHAMAS

Andros

Cat
Island

San
Salvador

Mars
Bay

Exuma Cays

Long
Island

Tropic of Cancer

HAVANA

Varadero

Matanzas

Santa
Clara

Archipiélago de Camagüey

Crooked
Island

Viñales

La Coloma

Nueva
Gerona

Cienfuegos

Acklins
Island

La Bajada

Isla de la
Juventud

Sancti
Spíritus

Camagüey

Great
Inagua

CUBA

Las Tunas

Holguín

Guardalavaca

Matthew Town

Cayman
Brac

Bayamo

Baracoa

Port-de-
Paix

Caribbean
Sea

Cayman Islands
(UK)

GEORGE
TOWN

Santiago
de Cuba

Guantánamo

Gonaïves

PORT-AU-
PRINCE

Montego Bay

Port
Maria

Jérémie

Negril

Kensington

HAITI

Les
Cayes

Jacmel

JAMAICA

Treasure
Beach

KINGSTON

British Virgin
Islands (UK)

Road
Town

Anegada

St John

Tortola

Charlotte
Amalie

The Valley

Anguilla (UK)

Marigot

Philipsburg

0   100km
0   50 miles

Christiansted

St Croix

St-Martin/
Sint Maarten
(FR & NETH)

Gustavia

St Barthélemy
(FR)

Codrington

ANTIGUA &
BARBUDA

US Virgin
Islands
(US)

Windwardside

Saba (NETH)

Oranjestad

Sint Eustatius (NETH)

ST KITTS
& NEVIS

St Kitts

Barbuda

BASSETERRE

Charlestown

Nevis

ST JOHN'S

Antigua

Plymouth

Montserrat
(UK)

Pointe-
a-Pitre

La Désirade

Guadeloupe
(FR)

Basse-Terre

PAGE
88

ON THE ROAD

YOUR COMPLETE DESTINATION GUIDE
In-depth reviews, detailed listings
and insider tips

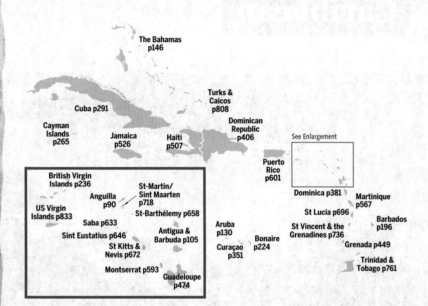

The Bahamas
p146

Turks &
Caicos
p808

Cuba p291

Dominican
Republic
p406

See Enlargement

Cayman
Islands
p265

Jamaica
p526

Haiti
p507

Puerto
Rico
p601

British Virgin
Islands p236

St-Martin/
Sint Maarten
p718

Anguilla
p90

US Virgin
Islands p833

St-Barthélemy p658

Saba p633

Sint Eustatius p646

Antigua &
Barbuda p105

St Kitts &
Nevis p672

Montserrat p593

Guadeloupe
p474

Dominica p381

Martinique
p567

St Lucia p696

Aruba
p130

St Vincent & the
Grenadines p736

Barbados
p196

Curaçao
p351

Bonaire
p224

Grenada p449

Trinidad &
Tobago p761

WITHDRAWN
FROM
STOCK

THIS EDITION WRITTEN AND RESEARCHED BY

Ryan Ver Berkmoes

Jean-Bernard Carillet, Nate Cavalieri, Paul Clammer, Michael Grosberg,
Adam Karlin, Tom Masters, Emily Matchar, Brandon Presser, Brendan Sainsbury,
Andrea Schulte-Peevers, Polly Thomas, Karla Zimmerman

welcome to the Caribbean

One Region, 7000 Islands

Rocked by music, rolled by change, lapped by turquoise water, blown by hurricanes – the Caribbean is not a place anyone could call static. It's a lively and intoxicating profusion of people and places spread over 7000 islands (fewer than 10% are inhabited). But, for all they share, there's also much that makes them different. Forming a huge swath around the Caribbean Sea, the namesake islands contradict in ways big and small. Can there be a greater contrast than between socialist Cuba and its neighbor, the bank-packed Cayman Islands? Or between booming British-oriented St Kitts and its sleepy, Dutch-affiliated neighbor Sint Eustatius, just across a narrow channel?

Travel long enough in this region and you'll soon discover there is no typical Caribbean.

Every Color Everywhere

Azure seas, white beaches, green forests so vivid they actually hurt the eyes – there is nothing subtle about the bold colors of the Caribbean. Swim below the waters for a color chart of darting fish and corals. Wander along the sand and stop at the paint-factory explosion that is a beach bar, from the garish decor to the rum punch in your glass. Hike into emerald wilderness and

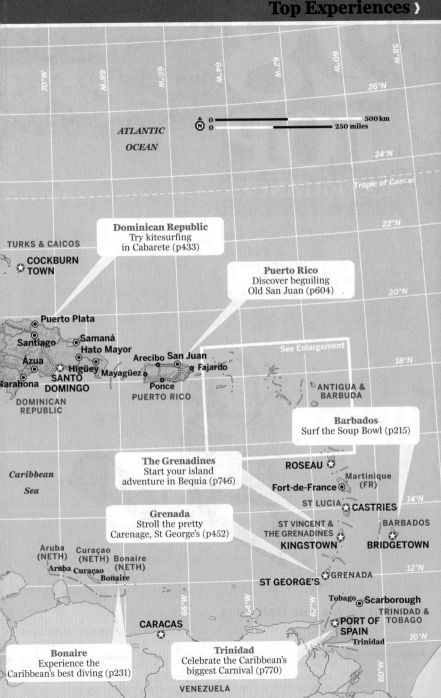

ATLANTIC
OCEAN

0   500 km
0   250 miles

Tropic of Cancer

Dominican Republic
Try kitesurfing
in Cabarete (p433)

Puerto Rico
Discover beguiling
Old San Juan (p604)

TURKS & CAICOS

COCKBURN
TOWN

Puerto Plata

Santiago   Samaná
Hato Mayor

Ázua   Arecibo   San Juan
Higüey   Mayagüez   Fajardo
Barahona   SANTO
DOMINGO   Ponce
PUERTO RICO

DOMINICAN
REPUBLIC

See Enlargement

ANTIGUA &
BARBUDA

Barbados
Surf the Soup Bowl (p215)

Caribbean
Sea

The Grenadines
Start your island
adventure in Bequia (p746)

ROSEAU

Martinique
(FR)

Fort-de-France

Grenada
Stroll the pretty
Carenage, St George's (p452)

ST LUCIA   CASTRIES

BARBADOS

ST VINCENT &
THE GRENADINES

Aruba
(NETH)   Curaçao
(NETH)   Bonaire
(NETH)
Aruba   Curaçao
Bonaire

KINGSTOWN

BRIDGETOWN

ST GEORGE'S   GRENADA

Tobago   Scarborough

TRINIDAD &
TOBAGO

CARACAS

PORT OF
SPAIN

Trinidad

Bonaire
Experience the
Caribbean's best diving (p231)

Trinidad
Celebrate the Caribbean's
biggest Carnival (p770)

VENEZUELA

28 TOP EXPERIENCES

Hidden Coves, the Bahamas

1 With nearly 700 islands spread across 100,000 sq miles of ocean, the Bahamas has enough secluded beaches and tempting hidden coves for a lifetime of exploration. For ethereal rosy-hued sands, hit up Eleuthera and Harbour Island, where beaches are tinted pink by crushed coral. The 365 Exuma Cays (p184) are a wonderland of cerulean waters and uninhabited islets, while Grand Bahama (p165) offers luscious sands just a few minutes from bustling downtown Freeport. It's fair to say the Bahamas' ugliest beach would still be a beauty queen in most other places in the world.

The Carenage, St George's, Grenada

2 One of the prettiest water-fronts in the Caribbean, this buzzing little horseshoe-shaped harbor (p452) is the perfect place to get a flavor of Grenada, with bobbing boats, busy cafes and a sprinkling of shady spots where you can watch the world go by or admire the lineup of gorgeous old waterside buildings. Spreading up from the bay, the hillside hodgepodge of brightly colored rooftops and a glowering stone fort get a scenic backdrop courtesy of the green, misty peaks of the Grand Etang National Park.

Seafarer's Joy, British Virgin Islands

3 Endowed with steady trade winds, tame currents and hundreds of protected bays, the British Virgin Islands (p236) are a sailor's fantasyland. Many visitors come expressly to hoist a jib and dawdle among the multiple isles, trying to determine which one serves the best rum-pineapple-and-coconut Painkiller. Tortola (p239), known as the charter boat capital of the world, is the launching pad, so it's easy to get geared up. Don't know how to sail? Learn on the job with a sailing school

Fishing Villages, Martinique

4 The remedy to Martinique's often rampant development can be found in its charming fishing villages, where life goes on much as it always has and the tourist dollar has still not made much of an impact. Surrounded by majestic forested hillsides and framed by crescent sand beaches, there's a particular string of these beauties on the island's southwestern corner – don't miss lovely Anse d'Arlet (p583), friendly Petite Anse (p583) or stunning Grande Anse (p582).

J-L BELLURGET/PHOTOLIBRARY

JUSTIN FOULKES/PHOTOLIBRARY

Wild Wonder, Dominica

5 Before you die, spend some time in Dominica (p381), one of the least developed and most unusual islands in the region. Covered almost entirely by thick, virgin rainforest, it has a landscape quilted with innumerable shades of green. Stagger into beautiful scenes of misty waterfalls, chilly and boiling lakes, hot sulfur springs steaming through the earth, and valleys and gorges chiseled by time and the elements. It's a natural mosaic that will tug mightily at the hearts of artists, wanderers, romantics and anyone with an eco bent.

GARDEL BERTRAND/PHOTOLIBRARY

Tiny Islands, the Grenadines

6 It's heard in office cubicles the world over daily: 'I'm chucking it all in and going to tramp around tropical islands!' In a world of package tourism, huge cruise ships and mega-resorts, the very idea seems lost in another, simpler time. Until, that is, you reach the Grenadines. Starting with Bequia (p746), multiple tiny islands stretch south, still mostly linked by wooden fishing boats and poky mail boats. Hitch a ride, feel the wind in your face and head off to adventure.

Music & Culture, Havana, Cuba

7 Few come to Cuba without visiting Havana (p294), a hauntingly romantic city, ridden with ambiguity and imbued with shabby magnificence. A stroll around the mildewed but atmospheric streets of Habana Vieja reveals rusting American Buicks, kids playing stickball with rolled-up balls of plastic, and a mishmash of architecture that mirrors the nation's diverse history. Underlying it all is the musical soundtrack for which Cuba is famous – rumba, salsa, *son*, reggaeton and *trova*. Tropicana Nightclub, Havana, right

SCHULER BERND/PHOTOLIBRARY

Surfing the Soup, Barbados

8 Like a monster wave breaking, Barbados (p196) has crashed onto the world surf scene. Although long the haunt of surf-happy locals, only recently has Barbados' east-side surf break, called the Soup Bowl (p215), gone supernova. Sets travel thousands of miles across the rough Atlantic and form into huge waves that challenge the world's best. From September to December, faces found in surfing magazines stare wistfully out to sea from the very mellow beach village of Bathsheba. A slight calming from January to May brings out the hopefuls.

RICK DOYLE/PHOTOLIBRARY

Spellbinding Views, Nevis

9 Nevis (p685) is tailor-made for trading the beach lounger for the nature trail. Hit the higher ground on a ramble through luxuriant tropical forest, colorful gardens and cane fields clinging to the slopes of volcanic Mt Nevis. Walk through air perfumed by exotic flowers and along paths shaded by fruit-laden trees while keeping an eye out for the elusive vervet monkey. Panoramic views opening up between the foliage extend to other islands, including neighboring St Kitts, and will have you burning up the bytes in your digicam, fast. View from Pinney's Beach, Nevis, right

Historic Cockburn Town, Turks & Caicos

10 Look no further for the old Caribbean than Cockburn Town (p822), the tiny national capital of the Turks and Caicos islands, where brightly painted colonial buildings line the roads and life goes on at a wonderfully slow pace miles away from the resorts of Providenciales. Wander down Duke St and Front St and pass whitewashed stone walls, traditional streetlamps and creaking old buildings, some of which have miraculously survived for over two centuries in this charming backwater.

Stingray City, Cayman Islands

11 Otherworldly-looking stingrays languidly cruise the warm and shallow waters just off Grand Cayman's shore at famous Stingray City (p274). Years of free food have stoked a population of these creatures, who flit about cheerfully accepting handouts of squid from giggling, delighted onlookers. You can just stand in the water and stroke their astonishingly smooth and velvety skin while they swim around you, or go snorkeling and see them in their true habitat.

GREG JOHNSTON/LONELY PLANET IMAGES ©

Treasure Beach, Jamaica

12 Down in Treasure Beach (p554), miles from the urban chaos of Kingston, you'll find a quiet stretch of sand where visitors, expats and Jamaican locals kick back every evening. Beers are passed around, reggae cracks over the air and a supreme sense of chilled-out-ed-ness – oh, let's just say it: 'irie' – descends onto the crowd. Music, food, Red Stripe, smiles – it all comes together here to create the laid-back Jamaican scene that many travelers dream of. Pelican Bar, Treasure Beach, above

JEAN-PIERRE DEGAS/CORBIS

Runway Bars, St-Martin/Sint Maarten

13 Most island-goers would consider careening jumbo jets and large tracts of concrete runway to be noisy eyesores, but not on St-Martin/Sint Maarten (p718). Clustered around Juliana International Airport – the area's transportation hub – you'll find a handful of bumpin' bars that cling to the sides of the runway while also abutting the turquoise waters. At Sunset Beach Bar (p724), arrival times are posted in chalk on a surfboard and aircraft landings are awaited with much anticipation as beach bums get blown into the blue from the backlash of jet propulsion.

Willemstad Reborn, Curaçao

15 Curaçao's capital Willemstad (p354) is a bit of a holiday black hole: once you get sucked in, you might never leave. There's the Sint Annabaai ship channel, which cleaves the town in two and leads to one of the world's great harbors. Pause while strolling the Unesco-recognized colonial-era neighborhoods and watch huge freighters pass meters away. Old sailors' and workers' districts are being restored and reenergized, and Pietermaai – a faded area of old Dutch traders mansions – is getting edgy new cafes and bars.

Best Caribbean Diving, Bonaire

14 Almost the entire coast of Bonaire (p224) is ringed by some of the healthiest coral reefs in the region. Sometimes it seems like half the population of the island are divers – and why shouldn't they be? The Unesco-recognized shore reefs (p231) can be reached right off your room's back deck at oodles of low-key diver-run hotels. All-you-can-breathe-in-a-week tank specials are common. Beyond the exquisite shore diving (more than half the 90 named sites are right off the beach) are more challenging sites for advanced divers.

Upscale Resorts, St Lucia

16 Swim-up bars, lavish spas, infinity pools, gourmet restaurants... When it comes to upscale resorts, St Lucia (p696) is hard to beat and there's something for everybody. Some venues are straight from the pages of a glossy magazine, with luxurious units that ooze style and class, such as Ladera, Hotel Chocolat and Jade Mountain, near Soufrière, while others specialize in all-inclusive packages. You don't need to remortgage the house to stay in one of them; special rates can be found on the hotels' websites or on booking sites. Reduit Beach, St Lucia, left

Carnival, Trinidad

17 Home to one of the world's biggest and best Carnivals (p770), Trinidad is party central, and its two days of festival fabulousness have inspired the most creative and dynamic music and dance culture in the Caribbean. Visit a panyard and let the rhythmic sweetness of steel pan vibrate through your body, check out the fireworks and drama of a soca concert or, best of all, don a spangly, feathery band costume and learn to 'wine your waist' like the locals during the two-day street parade.

Food & French Vibe, St-Barthélemy

18 It's easy to dismiss St-Barth (p658) as the Caribbean's capital of jet-setterdom, but there's so much more to this hilly island. Cradled within its craggy coves are small towns with stone walls that look as though they've been plucked directly from the French countryside. This counterpoint of cultures plays out in the local cuisine as well – scores of world-class restaurants dish out expertly crafted meals that meld the savoir faire and mastery of French cuisine with vivid bursts of bright island flavors. View over the village of Corossol, St-Barthélemy, left

Kitesurfing, Dominican Republic

19 Do your part for the environment: use wind-powered transportation. Year-round strong offshore breezes make Cabarete (p433), on the north coast of the DR, one of the undisputed capitals for the burgeoning sport of kitesurfing. Harnessing the wind's power to propel you over the choppy surface of the Atlantic isn't like another day at the beach. It takes training and muscles, not to mention faith, before you can try the moves of the pros from around the world who ply their trade here.

GREG JOHNSTON/LONELY PLANET IMAGES ©

Old San Juan, Puerto Rico

20 Even those limited to a quick visit find it easy to fall under the beguiling spell of Old San Juan's cobblestone streets, pastel-painted colonial buildings and grand fortresses (p604). Atop the ramparts of El Morro, the allure of this place is evident in every direction – from the labyrinth of crooked lanes to the endless sparkle of the Atlantic. By day, lose yourself in historical stories of blood and bombast; by night float along in crowds of giggling tourists, rowdy locals and syncopated salsa rhythms.

CHRISTOPHER GROENHOUT/LONELY PLANET IMAGES ©

Deshaies, Guadeloupe

21 This Basse-Terre village (p487) strikes just the right balance between working fishing port and sophisticated dining destination to keep its well-heeled visitors happy. The setting is like a colonial-era painting, with wooden houses lining the tidy sand beach and colorful fishing boats bobbing up and down in the turquoise waters. Only the odd yacht in the distance gives you any indication of the smart crowd that flocks to Deshaies for its great restaurants, lively bars and fabulous nearby beaches.

COLIN DUTTON/CORBIS

Oranjestad Ruins, Sint Eustatius

22 Like monuments to fallen empires, the ruins of Oranjestad (p648) are the whispers of a forgotten age, when rum, gold and slaves moved around the world with great alacrity. Sint Eustatius' naturally deep harbor was doorway to the New World, and during its golden era there were over 25,000 inhabitants representing a diverse spread of cultures and religions. Today, all that's left of this time are the stone skeletons of several imposing forts, mansions, a synagogue and a church. Remains of the Dutch Reformed Church, Oranjestad, above

JOCHEM WIJNANDS/PHOTOLIBRARY

Amazing Hiking, Saba

23 Rising dramatically out of the ocean, tiny Saba's volcanic peak (p633) can only be fully appreciated in person. Even the craftiest photographers can't correctly capture its beauty, especially ethereal when the setting sun casts flickering shadows across the forested terrain. Sign up for a trek with Crocodile James and wend your way through fascinatingly different climate zones as you make your way from the crashing waves up into the lazy clouds. From the top, you can stare out over the island's trademark white-green-brown architecture in the valleys below.

Hot & Sandy Party, Aruba

24 Hit the beach with 10,000 of your new best friends on Aruba (p130). Two legendary beaches, Eagle (pictured below) and Palm, stretch for miles and fulfill the sun-drenched fantasies of shivering hordes every winter. Wide, white and powdery, they face water that has enough surf to be interesting but not so much you'll be lost at sea. The beaches are backed by shady palms, and cheery holidaymakers stay at the long row of resorts just behind. The scene here is pulsing, vibrant and happy, with action that extends well into the night.

Beach Time, Anguilla

25 It's hard to go past the sandy coast and glistening water of Anguilla (p90). There's nothing better to do than spend days under the bright tropical sun on the beach, swinging in hammocks, splashing in the sea, and licking your fingers after gorging on ribs barbecued by limin' locals under windswept tents nearby. On weekends don't be surprised to find local artists jammin' at their favorite seaside haunts, like the world-famous Dune Preserve (p98), home to Bankie Banx.

Beach at Meads Bay, Anguilla, left

Cruz Bay, US Virgin Islands

26 Nowhere embodies the territory's vibe better than Cruz Bay, St John (p846). As the gateway to Virgin Islands National Park, it has trails right from town that wind by shrub-nibbling wild donkeys and drop onto secluded beaches prime for snorkeling. All the activity can make a visitor thirsty, so it's a good thing Cruz Bay knows how to host a happy hour. Hippies, sea captains, retirees and reggae devotees all clink glasses at daily parties that spill out into the street.

Resilient Haiti

27 You want beaches and seafood? Check. A lively culture, music and arts? Haiti (p507) has those too, and rum punches aplenty. But people don't come to Haiti for the traditional Caribbean scene. This is Africa in the West, raw and up close. Haitians are sadly used to adversity – the most recent tragedy being the devastating January 2010 earthquake. But their resilience, dignity, and pride in their rich history, can still make this one of the most welcoming countries in the Caribbean.

Historic Harbor, Antigua

28 Antigua (p105) has been blessed with many off-the-charts splendors, including gorgeous beaches, crystalline waters and a deeply indented coastline with natural harbors. English Harbour (p116) boasts one of the preeminent historic sites in the Caribbean: Nelson's Dockyard. Travel back to the 18th century as you wander along cobbled lanes and past meticulously restored old buildings. Still a working marina, it's also one of the world's key yachting centers and attracts an international flotilla to its regattas. *Historic building at Nelson's Dockyard, left*

need to know

Planes

» Essential for island hopping between destinations without ferries, and for reaching the region in the first place

Ferries

» You'll wish there were more between islands but where they run (eg St Kitts to Nevis, Dominica to Martinique) you'll love 'em

When to Go

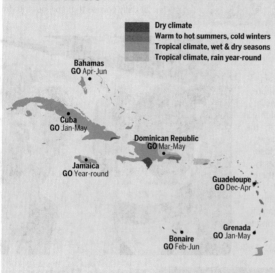

Dry climate
Warm to hot summers, cold winters
Tropical climate, wet & dry seasons
Tropical climate, rain year-round

Bahamas GO Apr-Jun

Cuba GO Jan-May

Dominican Republic GO Mar-May

Jamaica GO Year-round

Guadeloupe GO Dec-Apr

Bonaire GO Feb-Jun

Grenada GO Jan-May

High Season
(Dec–Apr)

» People fleeing the northern winter arrive in droves and prices peak

» The region's driest time

» Can be cold in the northern Caribbean from Cuba to the Bahamas

Shoulder
(May–Jun & Nov)

» The weather is good, rains are moderate

» Warm temperatures elsewhere reduce visitor numbers

» Best mix of affordable rates and good weather

Low Season
(Jul–Oct)

» Hurricane season; odds of being caught are small, but tropical storms are like clockwork

» Good for Eastern Caribbean's surf beaches, eg Barbados

» Room prices can be half or less than in high season

Your Daily Budget

Budget less than
US$150

» Divers hotels often best value

» Look for rooms off the beach – save US$10 for every minute you walk

» Eat what the locals eat

Midrange
US$150 –300

» Double room in the action: US$200

» Eschew hyped activities; rent bikes, walk, visit parks

» Stay at the best places... in low season

Top end over
US $300

» Beautiful rooms at the best resorts in high season: US$400 and over

» Get private surfing lessons

» Buy the posh bar a round of champagne

Cruise Ship
» Not a viable way to independently island hop; itineraries are set and you're on for the duration

Sailing
» With time, skills and a boat you can set your own schedule in the islands; rentals are easy

Mail Boats
» Aging tubs that take passengers; they're still found in back corners of the region, such as Grenada to the Grenadines

Bumming
» With a winning smile and some pluck, you might meet somebody at a marina who's looking for a deckhand, a cook or just a companion

Websites
» **Lonely Planet** (www.lonelyplanet.com/caribbean) Destination information, hotel bookings, travelers forums and more.

» **Caribbean Broadcasting Corp** (www.cbc.bb) Regional news.

» **Caribbean Travel+Life** (www.caribbeantravelmag.com) Features on regional travel and events.

» **Pirate Jokes** (www.piratejokes.net) How does a pirate keep fit? Aarrrrobics.

Money
See the opening pages of each chapter for details on which currencies are used on each island. The main currencies in the region:
» Eastern Caribbean dollar (EC$)
» US dollar (US$) – accepted almost everywhere
» Euro (€)
» Netherlands Antillean guilder (NAf/ANG) – there are plans to replace this currency (see p732)

Visas
» Citizens of most Western countries (Canada, the EU, the US etc) don't need visas for visits of under 90 days throughout the region
» Cuba requires a tourist card (CUC$15/US$25), usually included with your airline ticket and issued upon check-in
» Immigration officials may ask to see proof of a ticket out of the country

What to Take
The Caribbean islands are casual, so bring light, comfy clothes: a bathing suit, T-shirt and shorts will be your wardrobe. Add long pants or a dress for nights out. A few essentials:
» sun hat
» a small quick-dry towel, for when the whim to swim hits
» flashlight with batteries (nighttime reading, blackouts)
» plastic resealable bags – essential for keeping things (cameras, air tickets, passports) dry on boat trips

Get in the Mood
Books and movies can fuel your Caribbean desires. Think James Bond movies: *Dr No* as Ursula Andress emerges from the water (Jamaica) or *Thunderball*'s Junkanoo parade (the Bahamas). *Pirates of the Caribbean*, partly shot on St Vincent, captures the region's exciting past. For literary inspiration: *The Firm* by John Grisham, about financial shenanigans in the Cayman Islands; *The Slave Ship: A Human History* by Marcus Rediker, looking at the transportation of 12 million Africans to the US and Caribbean during slavery; and Dan Koeppel's *Banana: The Fate of the Fruit that Changed the World*, which explores the enormous impact of this ubiquitous fruit.

if you like...

Diving

The Caribbean is a diver's dream. The wide variety of dive sites are easily accessible with excellent local dive operators, and many resorts cater just to divers. See p39 for more details.

Bloody Bay Wall Little Cayman has fine wall diving, with sheer cliff drops to make you gasp; the shallow tops of the walls – some just 18ft (5.5m) below the surface – are almost as impressive (p285)

Saba Marine Park The collection of pinnacles, which peak at about 80ft (24m) below, offer deep and spectacular dives (p637)

Bonaire The island's perimeter is a protected marine park and Bonaire is dedicated to diving tourism; the gently sloping reef is adorned with gorgeous sights (p231)

St Lucia You'll wonder if Picasso came along with his paintbrush to coat St Lucia's corals with splashes of vibrant color (p710)

White-sand Beaches

After the color of the water, white-sand beaches may be the second-biggest cliché of the Caribbean. But what a cliché! Almost every island has at least one perfect stretch of powdery sand.

Anse de Gouverneur Wide and blissfully secluded, St-Barthélemy's beautiful beach lines a U-shaped bay with high cliffs at both ends (p666)

Grace Bay Beach A world-famous long stretch of sand in the Turks and Caicos, big enough that you can easily find your own patch of paradise (p812)

White Bay Bask on the dazzling white sand, sip a cocktail and watch people coming in off yachts in the British Virgin Islands (p254)

Barbuda There is no such thing as a bad beach on this island (p120)

Family Fun

Taking the kids on their first-ever boat ride. Digging on a sandy beach. Wandering rainforest trails. Meeting local children. It's simple adventures like these that make the Caribbean such a great region for travel with kids. See p79 for more.

Aruba Large resorts have lots of kids programs and the island offers activities geared towards children, from submarine rides to beach playgrounds (p130)

Dominican Republic Bávaro and Punta Cana are tops for family tourism and all-inclusive resorts, where scads of activities are available on the beach, in the pool and on day trips (p420)

US Virgin Islands Tropical family fun with a North American accent

St-Martin/Sint Maarten There are busy beaches popular with European families and lots of water sports for the kids (p718)

The Bahamas Paradise Island: the name says it all. Kids love waterslides, walk-through shark tanks and more (p154)

FRANK CARTER/LONELY PLANET IMAGES ©

» A restaurant band performing, Cuba

Beautiful Scenery

The Caribbean has a lot more than beaches. Green volcanic peaks rise out of the ocean, valleys are cleaved by waterfalls, and palm trees and flowers are everywhere you look.

Dominica This island doesn't have mountains – it *is* a mountain. Dominica has some of the most striking scenery in the Caribbean: a lake that boils, the aptly named Valley of Desolation and waterfalls splashing down everywhere (p381).

Mt Scenery, Saba Rising dramatically out of the ocean, tiny Saba's volcanic peak has an ethereal beauty, which is particularly stunning at dusk (p640)

Cascada El Limón, Dominican Republic This 170ft-high waterfall is rough, rugged and surrounded by forest-covered peaks (p429)

Northern Range, Trinidad & Tobago This chain of small coastal mountains hosts rich rainforests and stunning beaches (p779)

Music

Reggae, calypso, salsa, soca and more – the music of the Caribbean is as ingrained in perceptions of the region as beaches and fruity drinks. Vibrant and ever changing, the Caribbean's beat is its soul and reason alone to make the trip.

Trinidad & Tobago Electrifying, mesmerizing and embodying the creativity of Trinidad and Tobago, steel-pan music is infectious. Panorama, the pinnacle competition for steel bands, takes place during Carnival season (p802).

Santiago de Cuba Cuba's most Caribbean city grinds to its own rhythm in sweaty bars and open-air *trova* and rumba clubs (p335)

British Virgin Islands When the sun sets and the moon waxes full, the fungi music begins at Tortola's Aragorn's Studio (p247)

Dominican Republic Test out your merengue moves with seriously talented dancers at one of Santo Domingo's nightclubs (p417)

Puerto Rico Music and dance are part of daily life from the smallest village to the streets of San Juan (p614)

Romantic Getaways

With 7000 islands, the Caribbean has no shortage of places to get away to and shut out the world. People have been flocking here for steamy, sultry times for decades and everybody's in on it.

Barbuda Enjoy total privacy with that special person at Lighthouse Bay, a luxe boutique hotel on an endless stretch of white beach, reachable only by boat or helicopter (p123)

Dominica Fall asleep to the sounds of the rainforest in a wooden cottage on stilts deep in the jungle at River Rush Eco Retreat (p398)

Grenada Petite Anse has an isolated beach, fragrant with the natural perfumes the island is known for (p462)

The Grenadines Pick a tiny island like Bequia, Mustique or Canouan, hole up with someone special and let love blossom (p736)

Leabharlann
5304259
Contae na Mí

» A red hind among the coral

Snorkeling

Many of the top dive spots in the region are also rewarding for snorkelers, and there are some sites that are best enjoyed sporting only a mask and fin. See p39 for more details.

Buccoo Reef This fringing reef in Tobago has five flats, separated by deep channels, hosting a great variety of sponges, hard corals and tropical fish (p790)

Buck Island A St Croix, US Virgin Islands gem, Buck Island 18,800 acres (29 sq miles) of coral reef system that is so impressive it's a National Monument (p857)

Exuma Cays Land & Sea Park With 112,640 acres (175 sq miles) of protected land and sea, you won't know which shallows to explore first at this Bahamas 'replenishment nursery' (p184)

Stingray City In waters off Grand Cayman, dozens of alien-looking stingrays glide about accepting handouts from snorkelers (p274)

Old Colonial Towns

French, British and Spanish ships carrying explorers and colonizers once prowled the Caribbean waters. They established some of the hemisphere's oldest and enduringly charming towns.

Havana Crumbling and vast, the Cuban capital can steal days of your life as you wander this metropolitan time capsule, finding surprise and delight around every corner (p294)

Willemstad, Curaçao Little changed in a century, this old Dutch city dates back 300 years and is being beautifully restored (p354)

Sint Eustatius Once the busiest seaport in the world, it has over 600 archaeological sites and ruins (p646)

Cockburn Town, Turks & Caicos The real old Caribbean, Cockburn Town is undeveloped and absolutely charming (p822)

Old San Juan Half of it is in collapsing shambles – but that only adds to the appeal; the huge forts, crooked streets and pastel facades are amazing (p604)

Outdoor Adventure

The biggest problem with getting outside for an adventure in the Caribbean is choosing a location: you can surf the waves, hike a volcano, mountain bike the trails and more. See also p46.

Surfing, Puerto Rico Rincón throws expats among wacky locals in a laid-back wave-riding scene that was immortalized in a song by the Beach Boys (p626)

Windsurfing, Barbados The southern surf isn't too rough, the wind blows well and one of the world's great windsurf shops is here (p208)

Hiking, Martinique Hike along the base of the still-smoldering Mont Pelée, a volcano that wiped out Martinique's former capital in 1902 (p578)

Cycling, St Lucia The purpose-built cycling tracks are some of the best you'll find anywhere (p709)

Hiking, US Virgin Islands Feral donkeys watch as you hike along St John's trails to petroglyphs, sugar-mill ruins, and beaches (p846)

If you like a wild ride, taptap buses weave through the traffic of Port-au-Prince, Haiti, embellished with extra bumpers and mirrors and repainted until they look like a fairground attraction (p524)

Nightlife

Sipping a glass of wine on a beach with someone special while yachts gently clank offshore, making a hundred new friends at a raucous strip of bars, losing yourself in intoxicating island culture: all ways you'll relish the hours after dark.

Havana A music and culture scene unmatched in the Caribbean – cabarets, rumba, jazz, cutting-edge ballet and more (p313)

Jost Van Dyke, British Virgin Islands Head to Foxy's and many other party-hearty beach bars, one of which invented the Painkiller cocktail (p253)

South Frigate Bay, St Kitts Compare the potency of the rum punches poured at the string of funky beach bars making up the 'Strip' (p680)

Fortaleza, San Juan The heart of nightlife in Old San Juan – a lively mix of tourists and locals out for their evening stroll (p614)

Gosier, Guadeloupe A festive international scene of carousing (p481)

Pirates, Forts & Ruins

It could be a movie set. Wait, it was! Old forts and other crumbling ruins date from the days when buccaneers owned the waters.

Brimstone Hill Fortress, St Kitts This huge fort was seized after a month-long battle between French and British troops (p683)

The Citadelle, Haiti A vast mountaintop fortress completed in 1820, the Citadelle was built to repel French invasions; with the ruined palace Sans Souci at its base, it is one of the most inspiring sights in the Caribbean (p518)

Wallilabou, St Vincent The beaches and bay here were the setting for much of the first *Pirates of the Caribbean* (p745)

Port Royal, Jamaica Wander the fascinating historic sites, including old Fort Charles, of what was once the pirate capital of the Caribbean (p533)

Relaxing at a Resort

The very idea of a Caribbean resort – beautiful beach, warm water, lots of activities, pools, buffets, romantic dining, room service, sunset drinks and more – has people counting down to their holiday all year.

Aruba Dozens of resorts sit right on the sand along a string of lovely beaches fronted by classically azure waters (p130)

Virgin Gorda, British Virgin Islands A very laid-back place with dreamy resorts, especially around North Sound (p247)

The Bahamas It has more resorts than islands – family-friendly ones on Lucaya Beach, Grand Bahama; the world's biggest resort, Atlantis, on Paradise Island; and the rather exclusive Pink Sands on Harbour Island (p146)

St Lucia There are dozens of lovely resorts on the beach around Rodney Bay; and magnificent inns and boutique hotels nestled in the hillside, far from the crowds, in the Soufrière area (p696)

If you like... rum
Jamaica's overproof is a clear white rum and an eye-popping 151 proof; it's best enjoyed mixed with Ting, a local grapefruit drink (p527)
If you like... history
Curaçao's restored plantation houses tell tragic tales of the slave era (p362)

Shopping

Ports of call filled with stores selling luxury items and souvenirs at duty-free prices, local crafts and artwork, and wonderful specialty items are all part of the region's shopping scene. For more on shopping in the Caribbean, see p68.

The Bahamas Nassau's Bay St is lined with duty-free stores that were some of the first in the Caribbean (p164)

Puerto Rico Old San Juan has great arts and crafts shopping; head to San Francisco and Fortaleza, the two main arteries in the old city (p614)

St Lucia There are silk-screen paintings, woodcarvings, batik and clothing in Castries, plus excellent duty-free shopping (p700)

US Virgin Islands Charlotte Amalie has plenty of the jewelry and electronics shops that cruisers love, and the USVI has the highest duty-free allowance ($1600) for Americans (p842)

Cuba Two legendary items to seek out: rum, in the shop of Havana's Museo del Ron (p295); and cigars, from Havana's Partagás cigar factory (p299)

Sailing

The Caribbean is one of the world's prime yachting locales, offering diversity, warm weather and fine scenery. The many small islands and relatively calm sailing waters make this region great to explore by sea.

The Grenadines The 31 cays and islands of the Grenadines, stretching between St Vincent and Grenada, have long been known as a yachters' haven. Sparsely inhabited islands and pristine bays shelter boats on adventures from a week to a year; Bequia is a fab port island (p746).

Tortola One of the globe's premier places to set sail and the charter boat capital of the Caribbean, with hundreds of protected bays in the Virgin Islands (p239)

Abacos Yachties love this glittering crescent of islands and cays, which stretches south for 200 miles just east of Grand Bahama (p173)

Pampered Luxury

In the Caribbean you can find places to simply surrender yourself to total pampering. Resorts that are among the world's best sit back from beautiful beaches and offer every service imaginable.

West Coast, Barbados Not called the Platinum Coast for nothing, these gentle shores welcome old and new money alike at cloistered old resorts (p210)

Anguilla The preferred retreat for those needing an escape from the spotlight (p90)

Mustique The exclusive Grenadines island where rock stars weary from being rolling stones come to get reenergized (p750)

Pine Cay, Turks & Caicos The bastion of the wealthy, the famous and the infamous (p819)

Caneel Bay, St John Lovebirds like Angelina Jolie and Brad Pitt come to this resort when they need a total escape (p851)

UNITED ARCHIVES GMBH/ALAMY

» Boats taking part in Antigua Sailing Week (p27)

Watching Wildlife

We don't mean the folks partying one bar over. When it comes to watching wildlife, divers don't have all the fun. There's plenty of wildlife to spot above the water in some of the remote corners of the Caribbean.

Barbuda Observe magnificent birds up close in one of the world's largest frigate bird colonies, off the west coast of Barbuda (p122)

Cuba Parque Nacional Alejandro de Humboldt in Guantánamo Province is home to the world's smallest frog and largest surviving tract of Caribbean rainforest (p340)

Turks & Caicos Salt Cay is one of the best places on earth to see whales during the annual humpback migration (p825)

Bonaire Take a break from the underwater thrills to spot pink flamingos across the island (p224)

Secluded Coves

Finding a pristine natural masterpiece in an extremely remote corner of some beautiful green dot amid the blue waters is a fantasy that draws scores to the islands.

Happy Bay, St-Martin Follow a dirt path that twists over a bumpy headland onto this deserted spot, where the sand and the sunbathers are bare (p726)

Rendezvous Bay, Antigua So remote, it takes a rugged 4WD or a long hike through the rainforest to get to this beach (p117)

Bahía de Las Águilas, Dominican Republic Those who make the effort to come here get to enjoy 10km of slowly arcing, nearly deserted beach (p419)

Water Island, US Virgin Islands Sometimes called the 'Fourth Virgin,' it features Honeymoon Beach, with fine swimming and snorkeling and hidden behind a hill of sand (p843)

Partying

The Caribbean is home to some legendary bars, neighborhoods and towns where you can cut loose and just simply party your holiday away.

Oistins Fish Fry, Barbados There's barbecued fish and plenty of rum drinking at this legendary weekly town festival, where the bars are open 24/7 and locals and tourists party (p209)

Elvina's, the Bahamas On Friday nights, every surfer, yachtie and Eleutheran within a 50-mile radius comes here for the rotating sets of roof-blowing jams (p181)

Runway beach bars, St-Martin/Sint Maarten Join the beach bums at bars between the runway and the water and get blown into the sea by the jet propulsion of the arriving planes (p724)

Carnival, Trinidad One of the world's biggest and best celebrations sees two days of festival fabulousness (p770)

Negril, Jamaica Party till the sun comes up and goes back down again (p551)

month by month

Top Events

1. **Trinidad's Carnival** February
2. **Junkanoo** December
3. **Spring Break** March
4. **Pirates Week** November
5. **Crop-Over Festival** July

January

New Year's is celebrated with huge gusto in the Caribbean since it is the peak of high season on every island. Hotels and resorts are full, and people are partying. Weather across the region is balmy, although there is the odd cool day in the north.

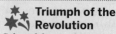 Triumph of the Revolution

Cuba celebrates the new year, the revolution and the nation's birth. Sure there are speeches – often long ones – but this is really an excuse for people to take to the streets with a passion.

☆ Jamaica Jazz & Blues Festival

Internationally acclaimed acts jam Jamaica's Montego Bay in late January for three nights of mellow music under the stars (www.jamaica jazzandblues.com). It starts the jazz festival season across the region.

Festival San Sebastián

Puerto Rico's famous street party, Festival San Sebastián, draws big crowds to Old San Juan for a week in mid-January. See p610 for details.

February

Carnival is a huge event in many Caribbean countries, where it is tied to the Lenten calendar. No country has a bigger Carnival than Trinidad, which prepares all year for its exuberant explosion. It's sunny and nearly ideal across the region.

☆ Bob Marley Birthday Bash

The love for the sound that plays in beach bars worldwide brings acolytes and reggae fans to the Bob Marley Museum (p530) in Jamaica, on Bob Marley's birthday, February 6 (www.bobmarley.com).

 Master of the Ocean

Called a 'triathlon of the waves', this thrilling competition has the world's best windsurfers, kitesurfers and surfers going board to board on Playa Encuentro in the Dominican Republic during the last week in February (www.masteroftheocean.com).

Holetown Festival

A week of celebration, the Holetown Festival (p220) marks the anniversary of the first English settlers' arrival on Barbados.

⋆ Trinidad's Carnival

It's the biggest party in the Caribbean. Trinidad spends all year gearing up for its legendary, pre-Lent street party, with steel-pan bands, blasting soca and calypso music, and outrageous costumes. Ecstatic revelers indulge their most hedonistic inclinations as they welcome in Carnival (p770).

⋆ Republic of Fun

The Dominican Republic celebrates its Carnival with great fervor every Sunday in February, culminating in a huge blowout in Santo Domingo on the last weekend of the month or the first weekend of March. Santiago hosts an international *careta* (mask) competition.

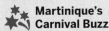 St-Barthélemy
Bash

St-Barth's five-day Carnival
(p669) includes costumes,
street dancing and a grand
finale at Shell Beach.

 Martinique's
Carnival Buzz

Fort-de-France, Martinique,
explodes with Carnival energy in the five days running
up to Ash Wednesday.

 Party Puerto
Rico

Ponce's Carnival festivities
are some of the best on
Puerto Rico and are a
chance to see traditional
masks, music and lots of
drunken parades.

 Parading in
Dominica

Dominica's Carnival runs
for two weeks leading up
to Ash Wednesday, with a
costume parade among its
highlights.

 Dancing in
Curaçao

Curaçao's Carnival begins
right after New Year's Day
and continues through to
Lent.

Haiti Unmasked
Jacmel, on Haiti's
south coast, is known for
its fantastic, papier-mâché
masks, which are made
especially for Carnival.

March

**It's high season through-
out the Caribbean. On
Barbados, American
college students invade
for spring break. The late-
winter influx of visitors is
greeted by lovely weather
everywhere.**

 St Patrick's
Week

It's not a day, it's a week
on Montserrat. There's a
lot of Irish heritage here so
the day o' green has always
been huge. Costumes, food,
drink, dance and concerts
by the much-lauded Emer-
ald Community Singers are
highlights.

Spring Break
In March and April,
thousands of American
college students descend on
Montego Bay in Jamaica for
all-day, all-night bacchana-
lia. Other huge destinations
are St Thomas in the US
Virgin Islands and Nassau
in the Bahamas.

Moonsplash
At this Anguilla
music festival, reggae
greats gather for late-night
jam sessions. See p102 for
details.

April

**Easter signals more
Carnivals. High season
continues but the winds
of change are blowing and
some visitors are starting
to pack for a return north.
Rates begin to fall at
resorts. Temperatures are
climbing in the south but
the Caribbean is
mostly dry.**

Simadan
Bonaire's harvest
festival is held in the small
town of Rincon in early
April. This is only proper
as this was the historic
home of the slaves who
were brought to the island
to make salt and harvest
food. The celebrations
include traditional dance
and food.

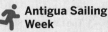 Antigua Sailing
Week

The Caribbean's largest regatta, Antigua Sailing Week
follows the Antigua Classic
Yacht Regatta and involves
a range of sailing and social
events around Nelson's
Dockyard and Falmouth
Harbour.

Easter Regatta
The Grenadines may
be the most boat-friendly
region in the Caribbean,
with natural moorings
throughout. And Bequia is
the star of the Grenadines
so it makes sense that
SVG's top sailing event is
here.

 Séu Parade
Curaçao's 'Feast
of the Harvest' features
parades replete with folk
music and dancing on
Easter Monday. People in
rural areas go a little nuts,
and for them it outclasses
Carnival.

Oistins Fish
Festival

On the southern coast of
Barbados, the Oistins Fish
Festival commemorates
the signing of the Charter
of Barbados and celebrates
the skills of local fishermen. It's held over Easter
weekend and features boat
races, fish-filleting competitions, local foods and
dancing.

 Jamaica's
Carnival

The Easter Carnival in
Kingston brings people into
the streets for music and an
impressive costume parade
(www.jamaicacarnival.com).
See p531 for details.

Carnival

The two-week Sint Maarten Carnival (p732), on the Dutch side, outclasses its counterpart on the French side. Activities begin in the second week after Easter.

Family Island Regatta

This regatta draws hundreds of yachts to Elizabeth Harbour, in the Bahamas, during the last week of April (p184).

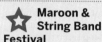 Maroon & String Band Festival

Held late in the month, this music festival draws hordes of partiers from Grenada for big-drum music and dancing, string bands, Shakespeare Mas, and every other Carriacou tradition at venues around the tiny island. (www.carriacou maroon.com)

June

June remains dry and relatively storm-free. Like May, it's not a peak time for visitors, except the savvy ones who value dry, sunny days and low hotel rates.

St Kitts Music Festival

Top-name calypso, soca, reggae, salsa, jazz and gospel performers from throughout the Caribbean gather on the small island during the four-day St Kitts Music Festival and pack out every venue – plus parks, stadiums and more. Reserve a room way in advance.

(above) Sailboat in the Antigua Classic Yacht Regatta, April
(below) Colorful mask at the Ponce Carnival, Puerto Rico, February

July

A busy month! Summer holiday crowds start arriving, as do the very first tropical storms of the hurricane season. There's another tranche of carnivals and other special events.

Crop-Over Festival

Beginning in mid-July and running until early August, the Crop-Over Festival (p220) is Barbados' top event and features fairs, activities and a parade.

Reggae Sumfest

Die-hard Rastafarians and Marley followers come to Jamaica from all over the world to jam with the masses at this reggae festival in Montego Bay. Although everyone is feelin' mellow, be sure to book in advance.

St Lucia Carnival

St Lucia's biggest show takes place in Castries. See p699 for details.

Vincy Mas

St Vincent's Carnival and biggest cultural event for the year, Vincy Mas, is held in late June and early July. See p748 for details.

Saba Summer Festival

Saba's Summer Festival runs for one activity-filled week in late July. See p644 for details.

Statia Carnival

Sint Eustatius celebrates for 10 days in late July, with music and local food. See p646 for highlights.

Cuban Carnival

Santiago de Cuba throws Cuba's oldest, biggest and wildest celebration in the last week of July.

Santo Domingo Merengue Festival

Santo Domingo hosts the Dominican Republic's largest and most raucous merengue festival. Late in the month, the world's top merengue bands play for the world's best merengue dancers all over the city.

BVI Emancipation Festival

Held on Tortola, the nation's premier cultural event features beauty pageants, horse racing and 'rise and shine tramps' (3am parades led by reggae bands). The celebration marks the end of slavery (1834).

August

The summer high season continues and you can expect the first real storms of the hurricane season, although mostly that means heavy rains as opposed to big blows.

Anguilla Summer Festival

Anguilla's week-long Summer Festival (p102) takes place around the first week of August and is celebrated with boat races, music, dancing and more.

Latin Music Festival

The Dominican Republic's huge, three-day Latin Music Festival, held at Santo Domingo's Olympic Stadium, attracts the top names in Latin music, including players of jazz, salsa, merengue and *bachata* (popular guitar music based on bolero rhythms). Dates vary – check ahead.

More Carnival!

The famous 10-day Carnival on Antigua is a grand affair. Its parade takes place on the first Tuesday in August, with calypso music, steel bands, masks, floats and street parties all adding to the excitement.

Grenada Carnival

Grenada's big annual event may be later than most islands' but that doesn't dim its festivities. The celebration is spirited and includes calypso and steel-pan competitions, costumed revelers, pageants and a big, grand-finale jump-up (nighttime street party).

September

Crowds are down and the weather tends to be wet. This is the low season and it might be a good time to rent a beach house for a month and write that book.

Martinique Heritage Days

One of the few large events for the month, Martinique's Journées du Patrimoine

(Heritage Days) celebrates local heritage and culture, and features museum open houses, storytelling, lectures, and workshops on local crafts, clothing and more.

October

Dominica comes to the rescue of what is otherwise a quiet month (other than a few passing squalls).

⭐ World Creole Music Festival

Dominica's ode to Creole music attracts big-name Caribbean music and dance acts, and food vendors sell much spicy goodness.

November

Hurricane season has mostly blown itself out and Christmas decorations are going up. Baseball season arrives in Cuba and the Dominican Republic.

⭐ Tranquility Jazz Festival

Attracting big names as well as local talent, and culminating with a free jazz concert on the beach, Anguilla's Tranquility Jazz Festival draws jazz fans from far and wide (p103; www.anguillajazz.org).

✹ Statia Day

Ceremonies are held on November 16 to commemorate the date in 1776 that Sint Eustatius became the first foreign land to salute the US flag after the revolution. Celebrations, including the Golden Rock

(above) Elaborate costume at Trinidad's Carnival, February
(below) Street performance during the Festival San Sebastián in Puerto Rico, January

Regatta (p646), take place in the week prior.

Route du Rhum

It only happens every four years (next up: 2014) but the Route du Rhum sailing race (St-Malo to Pointe-à-Pitre) is a huge deal on the island of Guadeloupe. Book rooms a year or more in advance and prepare for one long party.

Pirates Week

This wildly popular family-friendly extravaganza on Grand Cayman features a mock pirate invasion, music, dances, costumes, games and controlled mayhem. Book hotels in advance or you'll be out on your booty (www .piratesweekfestival.com).

December

High season begins mid-month and incoming flights are full. Rates are up and everything is open. Down backstreets Carnival prep is reaching fever pitch on many islands.

Junkanoo

The Bahamas national festival takes over Nassau, starting in the twilight hours of Boxing Day (December 26). It's a frenzied party with marching 'shacks,' colorful costumes and music. Crowds prepare much of the year for this Carnival-like happening (p164).

Foxy's New Year's Eve Party

Hundreds of boats show up in Jost Van Dyke's harbors on December 31. Party Central is Foxy's, which swings all night with live reggae and calypso, but every beach bar at this end of the British Virgin Islands is hopping.

St Kitts Carnival

Carnival is the biggest event on St Kitts. Starting around mid-December, it offers a couple of weeks of music, dancing and steel pan (p672).

itineraries

Whether you've got six days or 60, these itineraries provide a starting point for the trip of a lifetime. Want more inspiration? Head online to lonelyplanet .com/thorntree to chat with other travelers.

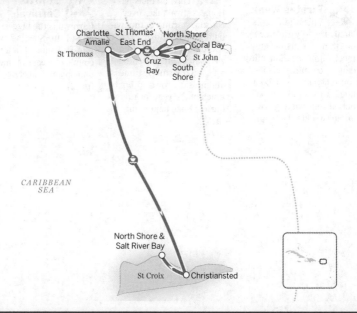

One Week
The Accessible Virgin Islands

Scads of nonstop flights put the US Virgin Islands in easy reach of the US and Canada. Subtract stops if you have less than a week.

Start on **St John**. Spend day one at the **North Shore** beaches: Cinnamon Bay with windsurfing and trails through mill ruins; Maho Bay, where sea turtles swim; or Leinster Bay/Waterlemon Cay, where snorkelers can jump in amid rays and barracudas. Raise a toast to your beach in rollicking **Cruz Bay**.

Spend day two on the **South Shore** at Salt Pond Bay, where cool hikes, groovy beachcombing and turtle-and-squid snorkeling await. Drink, dance and dine with the colorful characters in **Coral Bay** afterward.

Devote day three to hiking the Reef Bay trail, kayaking along coastal reefs or another favorite activity. Hop on a ferry on day four to check out **St Thomas' East End**.

Spend part of day five in **Charlotte Amalie**, St Thomas, then take the ferry to **Christiansted**, **St Croix**. Over the next two days drink at old windmills turned gin mills, dive the **North Shore** wall and paddle through **Salt River Bay**'s glowing water.

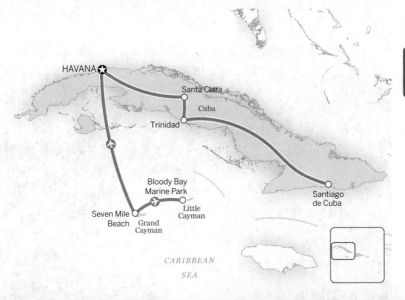

Two Weeks
Cuba & the Cayman Islands

Grand Cayman is a major transit point for people visiting Cuba and there are daily flights between the two.

The contrasts of this itinerary make it appealing – enjoy a bastion of socialism and a citadel of capitalism. Cuba can be mind-blowing while the Cayman Islands are anything but.

Begin in **Grand Cayman**. There are flights here from across North America. Stay on **Seven Mile Beach** and prepare for your trip north with a read of the Cuba chapter. Fly to **Havana**, the extraordinary capital city, and stay at one of the venerable old luxury hotels for a price that hasn't changed in years. Marvel at block after block of gloriously dissolving buildings, listen to some music and drink with locals. Just wander around: every block holds a surprise and the seawall is world-famous. Head to **Santa Clara** and the venerable monument to Ernesto Che Guevara, the city's adopted son. Plunge into the city's youth-oriented culture. Push on from here to **Trinidad**, a Unesco World Heritage site. You can easily spend a week in this colonial town, hiking in Topes de Collantes, horseback riding in Valle de los Ingenios or lazing at Playa Ancón. Push east to **Santiago de Cuba** and its many attractions, including the Castillo de San Pedro del Morro, the Cuartel Moncada and, of course, the vibrant music scene.

Return to Havana and fly back to **Grand Cayman**. Return to **Seven Mile Beach** and do purely fun things like snorkeling at Stingray City. The glitzy hotels, drinkable tap water and First World excess may give you a cultural hangover after Cuba, which can be both absorbing and exhausting. Beat this with an excursion to **Little Cayman**, where the 120 residents will be happy to see you. Laze on its deserted beaches and consider a world-class wall dive at **Bloody Bay Marine Park**. Choose from its several excellent yet low-key resorts, and have the best ice cream of the trip at the National Trust Visitors Centre. Feeling all chilled? Return to Grand Cayman and fly home.

» (above) Eagle Beach, Aruba
» (left) Inquisitive iguana, Aruba

HOLGER LEUE/LONELY PLANET IMAGES ©

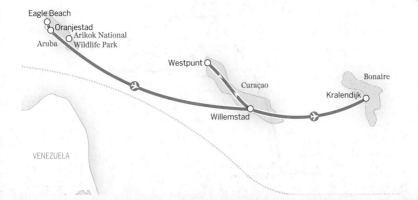

One to Two Weeks
Aruba, Curaçao & Bonaire

You can do any two of the three ABCs in a week but trying to do all three of these small islands would mean more time in airports than at the beach. The small size of all three islands means that even the most peripatetic vacationer will require little time for complete explorations, meaning there'll be plenty of time to simply plop down and relax.

Most places to stay, eat and even play on **Aruba** are in the north. Stay on relaxed **Eagle Beach**, Aruba's best. Assuming you're here for the sand – that's Aruba's real charm – then besides a day to explore the wet and wild northeast coast, **Arikok National Wildlife Park** and interesting **Oranjestad**, you should just play on the beach. And given the vast stretches of sand on the island, it won't be too hard to find the ideal plot for your beach blanket.

Unlike its neighbors, **Curaçao** is all about exploring. Stay in colonial **Willemstad**, which is one of the region's most interesting towns, then wander the coasts north to **Westpunt**, where national parks, restored plantations and a bevy of hidden beaches await. Count on three days at least to enjoy it all at a leisurely pace. You might even want to try some snorkeling or head to Spaanse Water, where the windsurfing will blow you away.

You may not see much of **Bonaire** above sea level as you'll be underwater much of the time. One of the world's great diving locations, Bonaire's underwater splendor and 90 named dive sites will keep you busy. Exploring the island, which has stark beauty, spotting flamingos and learning about an easily accessed past will also take about a day. The island's second city – a village really – Rincon, has a slow and inviting pace, while at the horizon-spanning salt flats in the south you can still see evidence of slavery and colonial trade. In the middle of it all, cute little **Kralendijk** combines eating, sleeping and fun.

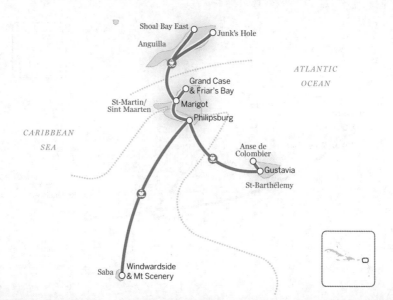

ATLANTIC
OCEAN

CARIBBEAN
SEA

One Week
St-Martin/Sint Maarten to Neighbor Islands

> Once off the plane in **St-Martin/Sint-Maarten**, you can hop your way around some of the Caribbean's cutest islands by ferry and never see another plane until it's time to go home. St-Martin/Sint Maarten will be your hub for this ferry fantasy.

Head to the French side of the island and hang out in **Grand Case**, where your dining choices range from beach-shack casual to fine-French bistro. For beach time try the local favorite **Friar's Bay**. From **Marigot**, make the 25-minute ferry run to **Anguilla**. Once there, choose between two beaches: popular **Shoal Bay East** or the quieter, windswept **Junk's Hole**.

Back on St-Martin/Sint Maarten, head down to **Philipsburg**, which allows time for some retail therapy. Get a ferry to **Saba**, and enjoy the view of the volcano that acts as a beacon during the 90-minute trip. Explore the small town of **Windwardside**, then head out into the bush for a rugged hike up the aptly named **Mt Scenery**. Rent some diving gear and explore submerged pinnacles that teem with nurse sharks. Head back to Philipsburg, then take the 45-minute ferry to **St-Barthélemy**, famous for being a wild ride. Have lunch at the gorgeous French village of **Gustavia**, and then sun yourself on white-sand **Anse de Colombier**. Although St-Barth is fabled as a playground of the rich and famous, the beauty of the island is that this matters little once everybody's in T-shirts and shorts – and all enjoy the exquisite tropical restaurants at night.

» (above) View of a cruise ship,
St-Martin/Sint Maarten
» (left) Colorful boats, Anguilla

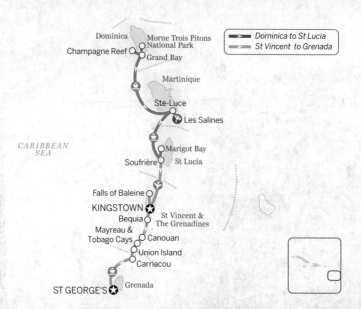

Dominica to St Lucia
St Vincent to Grenada

Dominica
Morne Trois Pitons National Park
Champagne Reef
Grand Bay

Martinique

Ste-Luce
Les Salines

CARIBBEAN SEA

Marigot Bay
Soufrière   St Lucia

Falls of Baleine
KINGSTOWN
Bequia   St Vincent & The Grenadines
Mayreau & Tobago Cays   Canouan
Union Island
Carriacou
ST GEORGE'S   Grenada

One Week
St Vincent to Grenada

You can add the Dominica to St Lucia itinerary to this one for a real island-hopping adventure. Just get a connecting flight from St Lucia to St Vincent and the Grenadines. **St Vincent** is an island of boundless energy that is far removed from affluent islands such as neighboring Barbados. Market days in **Kingstown** are chaotic as the streets teem with people. The scenes have changed little in decades. See some of the lush countryside that lured the makers of the *Pirates of the Caribbean* movies on a boat excursion to the **Falls of Baleine**.

Catch a ferry for the one-hour ride to **Bequia**, the center of beach fun and nightlife in the Grenadines and quite possibly the best all-around little island in the Caribbean. Choose between fast and slow ferries and head down the Grenadines, stopping at **Canouan**, **Mayreau** and **Union Island**. Take a day trip to snorkel amazing **Tobago Cays**.

Catch a mail boat or hire a fishing boat and cross the aquatic border to **Carriacou**, the pint-sized sister island to **Grenada**, which you will reach by ferry. Once there, immerse yourself in **St George's**, one of the Caribbean's most charming capital cities. Smell the local nutmeg in the air.

One Week
Dominica to St Lucia

Hopscotch your way south through some of the least visited, least developed Caribbean islands. Begin at **Dominica**, which many people consider the wildest and most natural of the bunch. Start by getting on local time at the comfy properties of **Grand Bay**. Then lose yourself in the rainforest at **Morne Trois Pitons National Park**, a Unesco World Heritage site. On an island laced with waterfalls, the walk in the park to Middleham Falls is splendid. It can be enjoyed in less than half a day. Celebrate with a glass of bubbly – or at least the natural bubbles that tickle you while diving at **Champagne Reef**.

It's a quick hop to **Martinique**, where you should hit the beach at **Les Salines**, followed by diving and drinking in the lively fishing village of **Ste-Luce**.

Skip the airport and take the scenic ferry to **St Lucia**, which emerges like a virescent monolith from the Caribbean as you home in. Stay in **Soufrière**, which has a dramatic position on a bay that's shadowed by the iconic peaks of the Pitons. You can hike these in the morning and dive in the afternoon. For a jaunt, head over to **Marigot Bay**, with its small beach and beautiful surrounds.

Diving & Snorkeling

Best Places to Take a Nondiving Travel Mate

Puerto Rico
Jamaica
St Lucia
Guadeloupe
Cuba

Best for Wreck Diving

Martinique
Sint Eustatius
Aruba
US Virgin Islands
Grenada

Best for Getting Certified

The Bahamas
Barbados
Cayman Islands
Bonaire
St Vincent & the Grenadines

Best for Underwater Photographers

Bonaire
The Bahamas
Dominica
Tobago
British Virgin Islands

Whether you're an experienced diver or slapping on fins for the first time, few places offer such perfect conditions for underwater exploration. The Caribbean Sea is consistently warm – temperatures average 80°F (27°C) – and spectacularly clear waters mean visibility can exceed 100ft (30m). Professional dive operators are as prolific as the postcard-worthy beaches and, whether you skim the surface or plunge far below, the colorful, active marine world delivers an amazing show.

The diversity of dive sites is almost endless. You'll find shallow, fringing reefs that curve into protected bays, sheer walls and coral-covered pinnacles, exciting drift dives and remnants of ancient shipwrecks on the seafloor.

Come face-to-face with fish the size of small cars, or moray eels longer than your armspan. Peer into sea grass and find tiny sea horses, or watch translucent shrimp scratch along the coral. Caribbean waters harbor colorful sponges, and both soft and hard coral, including gorgonian fans and gemlike black coral.

See the individual island chapters for more on dive areas and dive shops.

Sites
Antigua & Barbuda

Antigua has excellent diving, with coral canyons, wall drops and sea caves hosting a range of marine creatures, including turtles, sharks and barracuda. Popular sites include the 2-mile-long (3km) Cades Reef and Ariadne Shoal. A fun spot for divers and

ISLANDS	MAIN DIVE AREAS	WRECK DIVES	FISH LIFE	COSTS
Antigua & Barbuda	Cades Reef, Great Bird Island	✓✓	✓✓	US$60-120
Aruba	South coast	✓✓	✓✓	US$60-110
The Bahamas	All major islands	✓✓	✓✓✓	US$80-105
Barbados	West coast	✓✓	✓✓	US$60-100
Bonaire	West coast and around Klein Bonaire	✓	✓✓✓	US$60-100
British Virgin Islands	Out Islands, south of Tortola, Virgin Gorda	✓✓	✓✓	US$85-110
Cayman Islands	Seven Mile Beach, West Bay, Little Cayman	✓	✓✓✓	US$60-100
Cuba	Bay of Pigs, María la Gorda, Península de Guanahacabibes	✓	✓✓	US$50-80
Curaçao	Willemstad, Playa Lagún	✓	✓✓	US$60-100
Dominica	Soufriere, Douglas Bay, Salisbury	✓	✓✓	US$60-80
Dominican Republic	Península de Samaná	✓	✓✓	US$50-80
Grenada	Southwest coast	✓✓✓	✓✓	US$50-105
Guadeloupe	Réserve Cousteau, Les Saintes	✓	✓✓	US$70-110
Jamaica	Negril, Ocho Rios, Runaway Bay	✓	✓✓	US$40-90
Martinique	St-Pierre, Grande Anse, Diamant	✓✓✓	✓✓	US$70-110
Puerto Rico	Vieques, Culebra, Fajardo, Rincón	✓	✓✓	US$50-90
Saba	South and west coasts	None	✓✓✓	US$70-120
Sint Eustatius	West and south coasts	✓✓✓	✓✓	US$70-120
St Kitts & Nevis	West coast	✓	✓✓	US$70-95
St Lucia	Soufrière, Pigeon Island	✓	✓✓	US$80-120
St Vincent & the Grenadines	St Vincent, Canouan, Bequia, Tobago Cays	None	✓✓✓	US$60-100
Trinidad & Tobago	Crown Point, Speyside, Little Tobago	✓	✓✓✓	US$50-90
Turks & Caicos	Salt Cay, Grand Turk	✓	✓✓✓	US$55-80
US Virgin Islands	St Thomas (south coast, northern cays), St John (south coast), St Croix (north coast)	✓✓✓	✓✓	US$75-125

snorkelers is the wreck of the *Jettias*, a 310ft (94m) steamer that sank in 1917 and now provides habitat for fish and coral.

And Barbuda? It's still a secret, word-of-mouth destination, with scores of shipwrecks along its surrounding reef.

Aruba

There is fine diving and snorkeling around the southern shores, with elaborate, shallow reefs and coral gardens ablaze with colorful critters. Wreck fans will love it here too, with a series of plane- and shipwrecks, some of which were sunk intentionally as artificial reefs. Of particular interest is the large German WWII freighter, *Antilla*.

The Bahamas

This is Caribbean diving heaven. The Bahamas' great success as a diving hub is due to its unbeatable repertoire of diving adventures. Pristine reefs, shipwrecks, blue holes, vertigo-inducing drop-offs, abundant tropical fish, rays, sharks and dolphins are the reality of diving here. Where else in the world can you join a shark feed, then mingle with dolphins, visit movie-set shipwrecks, descend along bottomless walls and explore a mysterious blue hole – all in the same area? A bonus is state-of-the-art dive operations.

Almost all islands offer diving, from Walker's Cay in the north down to Long Island in the south.

Barbados

Barbados cannot compete with its neighboring heavyweights, but it boasts excellent diving nonetheless. The west coast is blessed with lovely reefs, wreathed with soft corals, gorgonians and colorful sponges. There are also a dozen shipwrecks. The largest and most popular, the 111m freighter *Stavronikita*, sits upright off the central west coast in 138ft (42m) of water, with the rigging reaching to within 20ft (6m) of the surface. In Bridgetown's Carlisle Bay, a series of coral-encrusted wrecks lie in only 23ft (7m) of water, making for good snorkeling as well as diving.

Bonaire

Bonaire is the stuff of legend, and one of the most charismatic dive areas in the Caribbean. What's the pull? Since 1979 the crystal-blue canvas that wraps around the island has been a protected haven and its excellent administration has paid off. Dive boats are required to use permanent moorings and popular dive sites are periodically closed to

let the reefs recover. Good news for novice divers (and snorkelers) in search of excitement: with the exception of Klein Bonaire sites, most dive sites are accessible from shore. Diving is absurdly easy; drive up, wade in, descend, explore. The gently sloping reefs are positively festooned with hard and soft corals, sponges, gorgonians and a dizzying array of tropical fish. A couple of wrecks, including the *Hilma Hooker*, spice up the diving.

British Virgin Islands

The islands huddle to form a sheltered paradise of secluded coves, calm shores and crystal-clear water, which in turn provide outstanding visibility, healthy coral and a wide variety of dive and snorkeling sites. Conservation is taken seriously, and there are lots of permanent mooring buoys.

Salt Island offers one of the Caribbean's best wreck dives: the monster-sized RMS *Rhone* – 310ft (94m) long and 40ft (12m) abeam – sunk in 1867. Amazingly, it's still in good shape and is heavily overgrown with marine life. The stern, with its propeller, lies in only 20ft to 40ft (6m to 12m) of water, making it suitable for snorkelers and novice divers.

Another drawcard is the seascape – expect giant boulders, canyons, tunnels, caverns and grottoes.

Cayman Islands

Diving is the most popular activity in the Cayman Islands, and rightly so. An extensive marine-park system and fascinating dive sites make it perfect for all skill levels. With more than 250 moored sites, and plenty of shore diving and snorkeling possibilities, the only question is where to start. All three islands have fine-tuned dive operations ready to submerse you, although Little Cayman has the finest Caribbean wall diving – along Bloody and Jackson's Bays, sheer cliffs drop so vertically they'll make you gasp in your

---

BOOKS

» *Best Dives of the Caribbean* by Joyce Huber

» *The Complete Diving Guide: The Caribbean* series by Colleen Ryan and Brian Savage

» *Diving & Snorkeling Bonaire* and *Diving & Snorkeling Cayman Islands*, Lonely Planet

» *Reef Fish Identification: Tropical Pacific* and *Reef Creature Identification: Florida Caribbean Bahamas*, by Paul Humann

regulator. The tops of the walls – some just 20ft (6m) below the surface – are nearly as incredible as their depths. The snorkeling here can be fantastic. Coral and sponges of all types, colors and sizes cascade downward as you slowly descend along the wall.

Grand Cayman has plenty of shallow dives suitable for novices and snorkelers, including the legendary Stingray City, where stingrays can be approached on a sandy seafloor in less than 12ft (4m) of water. That said, these rays are fed using bait, and whether or not these artificial encounters are a good idea is open to debate.

Cuba

Despite the fact the diving facilities are not top-notch, Cuba is a great destination for divers and snorkelers. The best diving can be found at the Bay of Pigs, María la Gorda, the Península de Guanahacabibes and the Isla de la Juventud.

Curaçao

What once was a secret escape for savvy divers has recently spread to the point that Curaçao now ranks among the best diving destinations in the region, with a number of rewarding sites along its southern lee coast. Among the draws are a couple of wrecks in shallow water, including the *Tugboat*, to the southeast – even snorkelers can admire the swirl of life around the boat. One of the coolest dives on Curaçao, Mushroom Forest, is off the west end and peppered with coral mounds on a sandy plateau. Another atmospheric site is The Valley, an underwater groove between two reef systems.

Dominica

The strength of Dominica is its underwater topography. The island's rugged scenery continues below the surface, where it forms sheer drop-offs, volcanic arches, massive pinnacles, chasms, gullies and caves.

Many top dive sites are in the Soufriere Bay marine reserve. Scotts Head Drop-Off, the Pinnacle and the Soufriere Pinnacle are favorites and Champagne Reef, popular with beginners and snorkelers, is a subaquatic hot spring off Pointe Guignard where crystal bubbles rise from underwater vents.

The central west coast is another premier diving area. The topography is not as unique as in the southwest, making the dives less challenging. The focus is on the wealth of tropicals, midwater schooling fish and larger predators, such as amberjack and barracuda. It also has a few surprises, including the wrecks of a barge and tugboat off Canefield.

The northwest side of the island features a dozen sites suitable for snorkelers and divers alike. The reefs in the Cabrits area are the most scenic – think boulders encrusted with corals and other invertebrates, attracting many varieties of fish.

Dominican Republic

The Dominican Republic is mostly famous for its kitesurfing and windsurfing, but it shouldn't be sneezed at. There's a wide choice of easy dives lurking off the Península de Samaná on the northeastern coast. The main dive centers are Las Terrenas and Las Galeras. Facing the Atlantic, the water there is cooler and visibility is somewhat reduced but the terrain is varied and you'll find a few shipwrecks to keep you happy. All the main dive spots have shallow reefs where nondivers can snorkel.

Grenada

With extensive reefs and a wide variety of fish, turtles and other marine life, the waters around Grenada offer excellent diving.

GOOD TO KNOW

» Don't forget your C-card! If you are a certified diver, you'll be required to show proof before a reputable dive operator will rent you equipment or take you out on a dive. Your PADI, NAUI or other certification card will do the trick.

» While it's safe to dive soon after flying, your last dive should be completed at least 18 hours (some experts say 24 hours) before a flight to minimize the risk of decompression sickness caused by residual nitrogen in the blood.

» Some dive operators offer dedicated snorkeling trips, while others put snorkelers and divers on the same boat when the site is appropriate for both.

With warm, calm, crystalline waters, the Caribbean is an excellent place to get scuba certified or further your training with specialized courses, such as night, wreck, deep diving or digital underwater photography. Two reputable organizations are widely recognized as providing the best and most professional certification in the world: the Professional Association of Diving Instructors (PADI) and the National Association of Underwater Instructors (NAUI). Affiliation with either of these means the dive shop adheres to high standards of safety and professionalism. Avoid unaffiliated operators; the lower cost can be alluring but it often means dodgy service, old equipment and compromised safety.

If you want to experience diving for the first time, most operators offer a short beginner course for nondivers, commonly dubbed a 'resort course,' which includes brief instructions, followed by a shallow beach or boat dive. The cost generally ranges from US$75 to US$140, depending on the operation and whether a boat is used.

For those who want to jump into the sport wholeheartedly, a number of operators offer full open-water certification courses. The cost generally hovers around US$420, equipment included, and the course takes the better part of a week. If you plan to be certified but don't want to spend your vacation in a classroom, consider a 'warm-water referral' program, where you take the classes at home, then complete your open-water dives in the Caribbean.

The southwest coast has the majority of dive sites, with the wreck of the *Bianca C* ocean liner one of the most popular. Other good log entries for wreck buffs include the *King Mitch*, the *Rum Runner* and the *Hema 1*.

Molinière Point, north of St George's, has some of Grenada's best snorkeling. Land access is difficult, but most dive shops offer snorkel and dive excursions here.

Other top snorkeling spots include Sandy Island off the northeast coast of Grenada, and White Island and (another) Sandy Island off the coast of Carriacou.

Guadeloupe

Guadeloupe's top diving site is the Réserve Cousteau, at Pigeon Island off the west coast of Basse-Terre. This is a protected area, so you can expect myriad tropical fish, turtles and sponges, and a vibrant assemblage of hard- and soft-coral formations. There are also two superb wrecks in the vicinity: the *Gustavia* (for experienced divers) and the *Franjack* (suitable for novices). The Réserve Cousteau is also a magnet for snorkelers, with scenic spots in shallow, turquoise waters. One quibble: you won't have the sites to yourself – the reserve is always busy.

For those willing to venture away from the tourist areas, there's Les Saintes. This area is a true gem with numerous untouched sites, striking underwater scenery and a diverse fish population – not to mention the phenomenal Sec Pâté, which consists of two giant pitons in the channel between Basse-Terre and Les Saintes.

Jamaica

So, you want variety? Jamaica's your answer. Sure, nothing is really world-class, but Jamaica offers an assortment of diving experiences. Treasures here include shallow reefs, caverns and trenches, walls, drop-offs and wrecks just a few hundred meters offshore. This is especially true on the north coast from Negril to Ocho Rios, where diving and snorkeling conditions are exceptional. You're likely to encounter reef fish in great numbers, rays, turtles, barracuda and thriving coral formations. Tip: if you're after less-crowded dive sites, opt for Runaway Bay.

Martinique

Wrecks galore! St-Pierre is a must for wreck enthusiasts. Picture this: more than a dozen ships that were anchored in the harbor when the 1902 volcanic eruption hit now lie on the seabed, at depths ranging from around 30ft to 280ft (10m to 85m).

To the southwest, Grande Anse and Diamant also deserve attention. The area is a diver and snorkeler's treat, with a good balance of scenic seascapes, elaborate reef structures and dense marine life.

RESPONSIBLE DIVING

» Never use anchors on the reef and take care not to ground boats on coral.

» Avoid touching or standing on living marine organisms, or dragging equipment across the reef. Polyps can be damaged by even the gentlest contact. If you must hold on to the reef, only touch exposed rock or dead coral.

» Be conscious of your fins. Even without contact, the surge from fin strokes near the reef can damage delicate organisms. Take care not to kick up clouds of sand, which can smother organisms.

» Practice and maintain proper buoyancy control. Major damage can be done by divers descending too fast and colliding with the reef.

» Take great care in underwater caves. Spend as little time within them as possible as your air bubbles may be caught within the roof and thereby leave organisms high and dry. Take turns to inspect the interior of a small cave.

» Resist the temptation to collect or buy corals or shells or to loot marine archaeological sites (mainly shipwrecks).

» Ensure that you take home all your rubbish and any litter you may find. Plastics, in particular, are a serious threat to marine life.

» Do not feed fish.

» Minimize your disturbance of marine animals. Never ride on the backs of turtles.

Puerto Rico

You will find good snorkeling reefs off the coasts of Vieques, Culebra, Fajardo and the small cays east of Fajardo. The cays off the south and east coasts also have good shallow reefs. There's good diving off Rincón and Fajardo, as well as spectacular wall dives out of La Parguera on the south coast.

Saba

Saba is a diver's paradise. This stunning volcanic island might even be more scenic below the ocean's surface. Divers and snorkelers can find a bit of everything (except wrecks): steep wall dives just offshore, submerged pinnacles and prolific marine life, including nurse sharks, stingrays and turtles. The Saba Marine Park has protected the area since 1987 and offers many untouched, buoy-designated diving spots. Novice divers will feel comfortable, as dive conditions are less challenging than anywhere else (no current and shallow dives near the shore) but still offer electric fish action. Snorkeling is equally impressive.

Sint Eustatius

Hard-core divers will appreciate Sint Eustatius' focus on its underwater bounty, along with the sheer variety of its dive sites. The island's last volcanic eruption was 1600 years

ago but you can still see evidence of the lava flow on the seabed, in its deep trenches and fissures. Vestiges of 18th-century colonial Sint Eustatius are also found beneath the surface, such as portions of quay wall that have slipped into the sea. Old ballast stones, anchors, cannons and ship remains have become vibrant coral reefs, protected by the Statia Marine Park.

Sint Eustatius has gained a glowing reputation as one of the Caribbean's finest areas for wreck dives. A collection of ships has been purposefully sunk over the past 15 years, adding diving variety.

St Kitts & Nevis

Nevis' diving scene is a low-key affair, featuring undisturbed coral reefs that are seldom visited. Two highlights off Nevis are Monkey Shoals, a densely covered reef close to Oualie Beach, and Devil's Caves, on the western side of the island, with coral grottoes and underwater lava tubes in 40ft (12m) of water.

St Kitts has healthy, expansive reefs and varied marine life that includes rays, barracuda, nurse sharks, turtles, sea fans, giant barrel sponges and black coral. A popular dive spot is Sandy Point Bay, below Brimstone Hill, with an array of corals, sponges and reef fish as well as coral-encrusted anchors from the colonial era. Among a handful of wreck dives is the 148ft (45m) freighter *River Taw*.

St Lucia

If you think the above-ground scenery is spectacular in St Lucia, you should see it under the sea. Off the southwest coast, it's the dramatic underwater terrain that impresses more than anything. The area near Soufrière – Anse Cochon, Anse Chastanet and the Pitons – boasts spectacular, near-shore reefs, with a wide variety of corals, sponges, fans and reef fish. It's excellent for both diving and snorkeling. Wreck enthusiasts will enjoy *Lesleen*, a 165ft (50m) freighter that was deliberately sunk in 1986 to create an artificial reef near Anse Cochon.

To the northwest, Rodney Bay is the main jumping-off point to a variety of good dives, although the topography is less impressive than around Soufrière. Pigeon Point, at the tip of Pigeon Island National Landmark, offers relaxed diving and snorkeling.

St Vincent & the Grenadines

The cays and islands that compose the Grenadines stretch out in a bracelet of tropical jewels between St Vincent and Grenada. The sparsely inhabited islands and bays shelter thriving offshore reefs. You'll find steep walls decorated with black coral around St Vincent, giant schools of fish around Bequia, and a coral wonderland around Canouan. There's also pure bliss in the Tobago Cays – these five palm-studded, deserted islands surrounded by shallow reefs are part of a protected marine sanctuary and offer some of the most pristine reef diving in the Caribbean.

Snorkeling is also superlative. Most dive shops run snorkeling trips parallel to their dive excursions.

Trinidad & Tobago

Tobago is most definitely a diving destination. Situated on the South American Continental Shelf between the Caribbean and Atlantic, the island is massaged by the Guyana and North Equatorial Currents. Also injected with periodic pulses of nutrient-rich water from the Orinoco River, Tobago's waters teem with marine life, including pelagics (read: hammerhead sharks). The variety of corals, sponges and ancient sea fans make this a top destination. For experienced divers, a number of drift dives await. Most dive shops are in Crown Point, at the island's western end, but they will take divers all over the island. The other concentration is in Speyside, at the eastern tip of Tobago, where larger hotels sport their own shops. Speyside is the launching pad for Little Tobago island, which is famous for its large brain corals and is also a mecca for snorkelers. Little Tobago used to be a fantastic place to spot manta rays but sightings are now rare.

Turks & Caicos

Salt Cay is a diving highlight, where you can dive with humpback whales during their annual migration. Grand Turk has pristine reefs and spectacular wall diving, while the exceptional diving on rarely visited South Caicos is worth the hassle of getting there. There is also diving off Provo, where you can get the chance to see dolphins and numerous reef species.

US Virgin Islands

The sister islands of St Thomas and St John offer top-notch diving and snorkeling conditions, with a combination of fringing reefs and a contoured topography (arches, caves, pinnacles, tunnels and vertical walls). St Croix features a fascinating mix of wreck (Butler Bay shelters no fewer than five wrecks) and wall dives; advanced divers will make a beeline for the aptly named Vertigo dive site.

Outdoors

Top Activities

Boating & Sailing A top activity on almost every island, the purpose of many trips.

Diving & Snorkeling See our entire chapter on the Caribbean's top activity (p39).

Fishing Hemingway made it famous and fishing the blue waters continues to challenge many.

Golf Famous courses dot the larger islands

Hiking Myriad possibilities on almost every island.

Kayaking The best way to see hidden coves and beaches or wildlife-rich mangroves.

Surfing The Beach Boys sang about Rincón and pros rave about Barbados.

Windsurfing & Kitesurfing It blows a lot in the islands and there's plenty of ways to catch the wind.

For anyone tired of lazing around (imagine that!), the islands have plenty to offer and, with water everywhere, it's no wonder aquatic sports dominate the activity roster for most vacationers. But you'll also be seduced by fun on land, like hikes through rainforests and up volcanoes, or even a round of golf on a famous course.

Boating & Sailing

The Caribbean is a first-rate sailing destination – boats and rum-sipping, salty-skinned sailors are everywhere. On many public beaches and at resorts, water-sports huts rent out Hobie Cats or other small sailboats for near-shore exploring. Many sailboat charter companies run day trips to other islands and offer party trips aboard tall ships or sunset cruises on catamarans (usually complete with champagne or rum cocktails).

The region is one of the world's prime yachting locales, offering diversity, warm weather and fine scenery. The many small islands grouped closely together are not only fun to explore but also form a barrier, providing relatively calm sailing waters.

The major yachting base is Tortola on the British Virgin Islands (BVI); the Bahamas, Grenadines and BVI are the most popular island groups for exploring by yacht. Other yachting bases include Grenada, Guadeloupe and Martinique. See p52 for more info.

Highlights include the following:

Anguilla Prickly Pear is a super-secluded mini-Anguilla with 360 degrees of flaxen sand reachable only by boat.

Antigua & Barbuda Yachting base. Dickenson Bay is a popular anchorage with resorts ashore and a good beach, while English Harbour is a historic and premier yacht harbor.

The Bahamas Yachting base. The Abacos is the self-proclaimed 'Sailing Capital of the World' so take time to tool around the Loyalist Cays with a rental boat. The Berry Islands are a yachtie's heaven, untouched by tourism. Explore the 365 Exuma Cays at your leisure with a rental boat.

British Virgin Islands Sailing here is a top Caribbean activity thanks to steady trade winds, hundreds of protected bays and an abundance of charter boats. Tortola is the charter boat capital of the Caribbean.

Dominica Experience the watery side of the jungle on a silent glide by boat on the Indian River.

Dominican Republic Parque Nacional Los Haitises operates boat trips. Take a whale-watching tour around Bahía de Samaná to see 30-tonne humpbacks or visit Bahía de Las Águilas, best reached by boat.

Jamaica Montego Bay, Kingston, Ocho Rios and Port Antonio are all major ports for yachts.

St Lucia Yachting base. Popular ports and anchorages are Rodney Bay, Castries, Marigot Bay, Soufrière, Pigeon Island and Vieux Fort. Take a day trip by boat up the beautiful west coast of the island.

St-Martin/Sint Maarten Yachting base. Popular ports include Marigot, Anse Marcel and Philipsburg.

St Vincent & the Grenadines Yachting base. Sailing the Grenadines is a top Caribbean activity. Bequia is one of the Caribbean's best small islands and a lovely anchorage for yachts. Union Island is a popular anchorage with a busy harbor.

Trinidad & Tobago Chaguaramas, a Tobago peninsula, is lined with little yacht harbors that are popular refuges during hurricane season.

Turks & Caicos These little islands are popular stops between the Bahamas and the Eastern Caribbean.

US Virgin Islands Sailing here is a top Caribbean activity.

Fishing

There's good deep-sea fishing in the Caribbean, with marlin, tuna, wahoo and barracuda among the prime catches. Charter fishing-boat rentals are available on most islands. Expect a half-day of fishing for four to six people to run to about US$400. Boats are usually individually owned and, consequently, the list of available skippers tends to fluctuate.

Highlights include the following:

The Bahamas The Biminis were good enough for Hemingway!

Cayman Islands There are many charter boat operators on Grand Cayman; blue marlin is a big catch.

Cuba Cayo Guillermo boasts more Hemingway-standard fishing.

Dominican Republic Resorts on Bávaro and Punta Cana organize trips and cook the catch.

Jamaica Montego Bay and Negril resorts organize trips and cook the catch.

St Lucia Billfish, marlin and yellowfin tuna can be caught from November to January, and wahoo and dorado from February to May. Vigie is a good place to get on a boat.

Trinidad & Tobago Chaguaramas is a good place for fishing trips.

Turks & Caicos The country's biggest fishing competition, the Grand Turk Game Fishing Tournament, gets under way at the end of July. Providenciales is the center for sport-fishing.

US Virgin Islands Deep-sea fishing charters depart from the St Thomas port of Red Hook.

Golf

The Caribbean has some of the world's most beautiful and challenging golf courses, where both major and local tournaments are held throughout the year. Green fees vary greatly, from around US$30 at smaller courses to US$200 and more, plus caddy and cart, at the renowned courses. Club rentals are easy, but serious golfers tend to bring their own.

Most major islands have at least one course. Highlights include the following:

The Bahamas Grand Bahama has several top courses open to the public.

Barbados Several links, including Barbados Golf Club (p208) in Durants.

Cayman Islands Play famous courses near Seven Mile Beach.

Dominican Republic Bávaro and Punta Cana are noted for their courses.

Guadeloupe St-François has an excellent public course.

St Kitts & Nevis Four Seasons Golf Course on Nevis (p688).

St Lucia St Lucia Golf & Country Club (p705).

Hiking

Verdant peaks rise high above dramatic valleys, volcanoes simmer, waterfalls rumble in the distance and rainforests resonate to a chorus of birdsong. Most people come to the Caribbean for the beaches, but many islands draw hikers seeking rugged terrain and stunning mountain vistas. Of course some just hike the beautiful beaches.

Highlights include the following:

Antigua & Barbuda Hikes around Shirley Heights, including Carpenters Rock Trail, have beautiful views of English Harbour.

Aruba Roam around Arikok National Wildlife Park for gardens, old gold mines, and wild beaches.

The Bahamas Search for blue holes while avoiding the mythical chickcharnies on hikes in the pristine Androsian forests.

Barbados The Barbados National Trust (p214) leads guided hikes. Hike through botanic gardens in central Barbados.

Bonaire Washington-Slagbaai National Park has lush and desert-like trails, and pink flamingos.

British Virgin Islands Take watery hikes at aptly named the Baths, wading around boulders and through grottoes at sunrise.

Cayman Islands Hike the Lighthouse Footpath on Cayman Brac and see the National Trust Parrot Reserve. Along the Mastic Trail through the heart of Grand Cayman, you might see a blue iguana.

Cuba The best hikes are to be found at Parque Nacional Alejandro de Humboldt in Guantánamo province, Topes de Collantes near Trinidad, and Valle de Viñales near Viñales.

Dominica The hiking king of the Caribbean. Take an easy rainforest loop trail or hire a guide for an arduous trek. Morne Trois Pitons National Park has trails to Boiling Lake through ancient rainforest and Waitukubuli National Trail is a challenging long-distance hike.

Dominican Republic Cabarete has canyoning trips. At Jarabacoa, climb Pico Duarte and navigate its trek-filled parks or take canyoning trips at Rancho Baiguate.

Grenada Grand Etang National Park has a volcanic lake and plenty of hiking trails, or hike around the island microparadise of Petit Martinique.

Guadeloupe Hike well-marked rainforest trails to Chutes du Carbet. Rainforest hikes to Grand Étang offer views of a smoldering volcano, or hike to the misty summit of the active volcano, La Soufrière. Walk the tiny island Terre-de-Haut, full of low-key sophistication and history.

Haiti Parc National La Visite offers excellent hiking east of Port-au-Prince.

Jamaica Hike the many trails in the Blue Mountains, some amid coffee plantations.

Martinique Walk the foothills of the volcano Mont Pelée, exploring the soaring interior. Hike the dramatic and pristine 20km trail along the northern coast, from Grand-Rivière to Anse Couleuvre.

Montserrat Enjoy a glimpse of the island's surviving rainforest on the short Oriole Walkway.

Puerto Rico Hike the dry forest in Bosque Estatal de Guánica to experience one of the most unique climates in the Caribbean. At Culebra, there's a 2.5-mile hike from Dewey to idyllic Playa Flamenco, then explore the rainforest trails and misty waterfalls of El Yunque.

Saba Has a lightly trodden network of footpaths that once connected the villages. Walk the Sandy Cruz Trail at Mt Scenery.

Sint Eustatius Hike the Quill, climbing the extinct volcano, then winding your way down to the bottom through rainforest.

St-Barthélemy Explore the island's dramatic vertical peak and score killer views of the sea below.

St Kitts & Nevis Mt Liamuiga (St Kitts) has volcanic hikes. Mt Nevis (Nevis) has hikes to the top of the volcanic crater, plus less demanding walks through gorgeous foothills.

St Lucia Gros Piton is an amazing climb. Hike to see parrots around inland park Millet Bird Sanctuary. Don't miss the Tet Paul Nature Trail at Soufrière.

St Vincent & the Grenadines The Vermont Nature Trail (St Vincent) takes you through thick rainforest. There's also a cross-island route around volcanic La Soufrière.

Trinidad & Tobago Hike to waterfalls big and small at Brasso Seco.

US Virgin Islands Virgin Islands National Park on St John is a regional hiking highlight with 20 cool trails, including ones that lead to petroglyphs, sugar-mill ruins and isolated beaches rich with marine life.

Kayaking

You can rent kayaks across the Caribbean. Explore beach-dotted coasts, wildlife-filled mangroves and more. Many tour companies now offer kayak adventures, some at night in bioluminescent waters.

Highlights:

Antigua & Barbuda Kayak around the Robinson Crusoe islands off the east coast of Antigua.

Aruba Kayak through mangroves and old pirate sites with Aruba Kayak Adventure (p137).

The Bahamas The Exuma Cays offer endless exploration for kayakers. Lucayan National Park on Grand Bahama has mangrove swamps and blue holes; Grand Bahamas Nature Tours (p169) offers kayak tours with naturalist guides.

Bonaire The Mangrove Info & Kayak Center (p232) offers highly recommended tours through mangroves.

British Virgin Islands Cow Wreck Bay, on Anegada, has shallow waters for exploring.

Cayman Islands Grand Cayman has mangrove tours; from Little Cayman, take day trips by kayak to Owen Island.

Dominica The Soufriere/Scotts Head Marine Reserve is popular for excursions.

Grenada Spice Kayaking & Eco Tours (p471) explores Grenada's shores and mangroves.

Montserrat The only white-sand beach, at Rendezvous Bay, is best reached by kayak.

Puerto Rico Island Adventures (p618) on Vieques leads tours of the bay; Vieques Adventure Company (p617) has totally transparent kayaks that let you see the action.

US Virgin Islands Night tours through the bioluminescent Salt River Bay on St Croix.

Surfing

Except for Barbados, which is further out into the open Atlantic, the islands of the Eastern Caribbean aren't really great for surfing. Once you head north and west, however, you can find surfable swells.

In late summer swells made by tropical storms off the African coast begin to race toward Barbados, creating the Caribbean's highest waves and finest surfing conditions. The most reliable time for catching good, high breaks is September to November.

Among the highlights:

Barbados At Silver Sands there are good south coast breaks and a fine surf school. Soup Bowl is a legendary east coast break at Bathsheba.

British Virgin Islands Apple Bay has good surfing on Tortola's north coast.

Dominican Republic The best waves – up to 13ft (4m) – are to be found at Cabarete, breaking over reefs on Playa Encuentro.

Guadeloupe Le Moule has hosted the world surf championships.

Jamaica Boston Bay boasts the best surfing in Jamaica.

Puerto Rico Rincón is well known for perfect tubes and a Beach Boys song.

Trinidad & Tobago Head for Trinidad's Grande Riviere; Las Cuevas is another beautiful bay.

US Virgin Islands Hull Bay is St Thomas' most popular break.

Windsurfing & Kitesurfing

The favorable winds and good water conditions found throughout the Caribbean have boosted the popularity of windsurfing and kitesurfing. Activity outfits, resorts and vendors rent out equipment and offer lessons to first-timers at many islands in the region.

Highlights:

Antigua & Barbuda Antigua's Jabberwock Beach.

Aruba Hadicurari Beach, just north of the highrise resorts, is superb.

Barbados Set on one of the hemisphere's premier spots, deAction Beach Shop (p208) at Silver Sands is run by windsurfing legend Brian Talma.

Bonaire Lac Bay has fantastic windsurfing and kitesurfing for much of the year.

Cayman Islands Barkers National Park is an excellent spot on Grand Cayman.

Dominican Republic Cabarete and Las Terrenas are both excellent areas.

Martinique Pointe du Bout offers top conditions and a good school.

US Virgin Islands The North Shore beaches on St John.

Island Hopping

Best Ways to Island Hop

Airplane Airlines link every island with an airport to its neighbors.
Ferry Not comprehensive but, where they exist, the most scenic links.
Sailboat Aboard a rental yacht, you have the ultimate freedom to island hop.

What You Need

Time With two weeks you can see a lot of a region; with a month you'll live the fantasy.
Sense of Adventure Unexpected experiences will be the most memorable.
Money Perhaps not as much as you think as you'll be traveling like a local.

The Ultimate Itinerary

Check our itinerary on p52 to see how you can get from Aruba in the far south to The Bahamas in the north, stopping at every major island on the way.

It's quite easy to island hop really. Planes and/or boats link all the main Caribbean islands with their neighbors. Because tickets are priced for the local market, with advance planning, you can find airline tickets for about US$100 or less. Ferry tickets are almost always under US$50.

The list below shows links between neighboring islands. See the individual chapters for full details of these services and those further afield.

Anguilla Air: St-Martin/Sint Maarten; Sea: St-Martin/Sint Maarten

Antigua & Barbuda Air: Guadeloupe, Montserrat, Nevis, St Kitts, St-Martin/Sint Maarten

Aruba Air: Bonaire, Curaçao

The Bahamas Air: Cuba, Jamaica, Trinidad and Tobago, Turks and Caicos

Barbados Air: Grenada, St Lucia, St Vincent and the Grenadines, Trinidad and Tobago

Bonaire Air: Aruba, Curaçao

British Virgin Islands Air: Puerto Rico, St-Martin/Sint Maarten, US Virgin Islands; Sea: US Virgin Islands

Cayman Islands Air: Cuba, Jamaica

Cuba Air: The Bahamas, Cayman Islands, Dominican Republic, Haiti

Curaçao Air: Aruba, Bonaire, Trinidad

Dominica Air: Antigua, Guadeloupe; Sea: Guadeloupe, Martinique, St Lucia

Dominican Republic Air: Cuba, Puerto Rico, Turks and Caicos; Land: Haiti; Sea: Puerto Rico

You will hear the Caribbean islands referred to in numerous ways – the Leewards, the Windwards, the West Indies etc. It can get confusing, so here's a quick primer in Caribbean geography.

» **Caribbean islands** An archipelago of thousands of islands that stretch from the southeast coast of Florida in the USA to the northern coast of Venezuela. The largest island within the Caribbean Sea is Cuba, followed by the island of Hispaniola (shared by the nations of Haiti and the Dominican Republic), then Jamaica and Puerto Rico. The Bahamas, to the north, are technically outside of the Caribbean archipelago – although we have covered them in this book.

» **Greater Antilles** Consists of the large islands, such as Hispaniola, Cuba and Jamaica at the top of the Caribbean and extends east as far as Puerto Rico. It also includes the Cayman Islands, due to their western location.

» **Lesser Antilles** The archipelago that extends east and southeastward from the Virgin Islands down to Trinidad and Tobago, just off the northern coast of Venezuela. Also called the Eastern Caribbean Islands, the Lesser Antilles are further divided into the Leeward Islands and the Windward Islands.

» **Leeward Islands** From north to south: the US Virgin Islands (USVI), the British Virgin Islands (BVI), Anguilla, St-Martin/Sint Maarten, St-Barthélemy, Saba, Sint Eustatius (Statia), St Kitts and Nevis, Antigua and Barbuda, Montserrat, and Guadeloupe.

» **Windward Islands** From north to south: Dominica, Martinique, St Lucia, St Vincent and the Grenadines, and Grenada. Barbados, and Trinidad and Tobago are often geographically considered part of the Windwards, but do not belong to the Windward Islands geopolitical group.

Grenada Air: Barbados, St Vincent and the Grenadines, Trinidad and Tobago; Sea: St Vincent and the Grenadines

Guadeloupe Air: Antigua, Dominica, St Lucia; Sea: Dominica, Martinique, St Lucia

Haiti Air: The Bahamas, Cuba, Dominican Republic, Turks and Caicos; Land: Dominican Republic

Jamaica Air: The Bahamas, Cayman Islands, Turks and Caicos

Martinique Air: Guadeloupe, Puerto Rico, St Lucia; Sea: Dominica, Guadeloupe, St Lucia

Montserrat Air: Antigua

Puerto Rico Air: Anguilla, British Virgin Islands, Dominican Republic, US Virgin Islands

Saba Air: St-Martin/Sint Maarten; Sea: St-Martin/Sint Maarten

Sint Eustatius Air: St-Martin/Sint Maarten; Sea: St-Martin/Sint Maarten

St-Barthélemy Air: St-Martin/Sint Maarten; St-Martin/Sint Maarten

St Kitts & Nevis Air: Antigua, St-Martin/Sint Maarten

St Lucia Air: Barbados, Martinique, St Vincent; Sea: Dominica, Guadeloupe, Martinique

St-Martin/Sint Maarten Air: Anguilla, Antigua, Saba, Sint Eustatius, St-Barthélemy, St Kitts and Nevis, US Virgin Islands; Sea: Anguilla, Saba, St-Barthélemy

St Vincent & the Grenadines Air: Barbados, Grenada, St Lucia; Sea: Grenada

Trinidad & Tobago Air: Barbados, Curaçao (with Trinidad only), Grenada

Turks & Caicos Air: The Bahamas, Dominican Republic, Haiti, Jamaica

US Virgin Islands Air: British Virgin Islands, Puerto Rico, St-Martin/Sint Maarten; Sea: British Virgin Islands

Getting Around

Air

Regional airlines, large and small, travel around the Caribbean. A certain level of patience and understanding is required when you island hop. Schedules can change at a moment's notice or there may be delays without explanation. Your best bet is to embrace island time, relax and enjoy the ride.

Regional planes are sometimes like old buses, seemingly stopping at every possible corner to pick up passengers – a boon for island hoppers! You'll sometimes get stuck on what you could call the 'LIAT shuffle,' where your plane touches down and takes off again

This trip lets you see every chapter in this book, starting in the south. Ferries are used when possible, supplanted by planes. Don't have the time or cash for this mammoth adventure? Cut off a chunk and do just that part. A full tour could take from three weeks to one month.

Start in the resorts of **Aruba**, then fly to **Curaçao** for old Willemstad and then to **Bonaire** for diving. Now it's a flight to Port of Spain, **Trinidad**, followed by a ferry trip to the natural beauty of **Tobago**. From here fly to lovely beaches and even better surfing in **Barbados**, then take a flight to surprising **Grenada**. Here you can take boats (ferries and mail boats) island hopping up through **St Vincent and the Grenadines**. Don't miss Bequia.

A quick flight to **St Lucia** and you are again island hopping. Going north, make the ferry voyages to *très Française* **Martinique** and on to the waterfalls and wilds of **Dominica** and then the twin cones of **Guadeloupe**. You are back on a plane to **Antigua**, from where you can take a boat round-trip to beautiful **Barbuda** before making the 20-minute flights round-trip for plucky **Montserrat** and its active volcano.

Leave the Antigua hub by plane for **Nevis**, followed by a chance to get spray in your face on a ferry to the volcanic perfection of **St Kitts**. From here it's 30 minutes by air to the transport hub of **St-Martin/Sint Maarten**, with its awesome runway beach and bar.

Do round-trip ferry visits to upscale **Anguilla**, tiny **Saba**, very French **St-Barthélemy** and volcanic **Sint Eustatius** and its ruins. Now fly to St Thomas in the **US Virgin Islands** and escape by boat to lovely **St Croix**. Get a ferry to the **British Virgin Islands** and then a flight to **Puerto Rico** and beautiful Old San Juan. Fly to the **Dominican Republic** and then go for a bus adventure to **Haiti** (or fly). Another plane takes you to the **Turks and Caicos** where you can continue by air to reggae-licious **Jamaica**. Fly to the **Cayman Islands**, stroke a stingray, and continue on to amazing, intoxicating and confounding **Cuba**. From here it is a short flight from Havana across to Nassau in the **Bahamas**, where you can lose yourself amid hundreds of islands.

from several different airports. For example, if you're flying from St Thomas to Trinidad, you might stop in Antigua, St Lucia and St Vincent before arriving.

There are many airlines operating within the Caribbean. You'll find full details in the Getting There & Away sections of each destination. However, there are some large carriers with dozens of connections, which will give you ideas for itinerary building:

American Airlines/American Eagle (www.aa.com) Provides a huge network of service from its hubs in Miami and San Juan, Puerto Rico.

Caribbean Airlines (www.caribbean-airlines. com) Links to major islands from its hubs in Barbados and Trinidad; expanding local service in the region.

LIAT (www.liat.com) The major local carrier of the Eastern Caribbean: you're bound to fly it. Locals love to zing it with phrases like Leaves Island Any Time. Based in Antigua, it flies medium-sized prop planes and serves almost every island with an airport in the Leeward and Windward Islands. Note it changes schedules up until the last mo-

ment and people connecting to its flights from other airlines can be stranded when the day's only flight up and leaves hours earlier than expected.

Ferry

For a place surrounded by water, the Caribbean doesn't have as many ferries as you'd think. However, there are regional ferries, which travel between several island groups. These can be a nice change of pace after cramped airplanes, smelly buses and dodgy rental cars.

See the list of island-hopping connections earlier in the chapter, and the individual island chapters for more details. When available, ferries tend to be reasonably modern and a great travel option.

Yacht

The Caribbean is a prime locale for yachting. The many small islands grouped closely together are not only fun to explore but also provide calm sailing waters. See our chapter on outdoor activities (p46) for the best yachting destinations.

Information on specific ports and marinas can be found in the Getting There & Away sections of relevant chapters.

It's easiest to sail down-island, from north to south, as on the reverse trip boats must beat back into the wind. Because of this, several yacht-charter companies only allow sailors to take the boats in one direction, arranging for their own crews to bring the boats back to home base later.

For information about crewing on a boat to reach the Caribbean, or to island hop once there, see p874.

Yacht charters are the ultimate Caribbean fantasy, sailing in a large boat from idyllic island to idyllic island. And it's a surprisingly achievable – albeit not cheap – fantasy.

Start by choosing from two basic types of yacht charter: bareboat or crewed.

On a bareboat charter, you skipper a fully equipped sailboat after you've proved your qualifications; sail where you want, when you want. With a crewed charter, you sip a drink on deck while the rental boat's crew swabs the poop deck and does everything else (usually including cooking, and bringing you that drink). You can either make your own detailed itinerary or provide a vague idea of the kind of places you'd like to visit and let the captain decide where to anchor.

The cost of a bareboat charter for a week for four people begins at about US$3000 and goes up from there. Crewed options are much more and all prices vary hugely by season, type of boat, crew etc. The British Virgin Islands are the top destination for renters. See p263 for more details on yacht rental.

The following charter companies offer both bareboat and crewed yacht charters in the Caribbean: **Catamaran Company** (www.catamarans.com), **Horizon Yacht Charters** (www.horizonyachtcharters.com), **Moorings** (www.moorings.com), **Sunsail** (www.sunsail.com) and **TMM Yacht Charters** (www.sailtmm.com).

For those who don't want to be bothered shopping around, charter-yacht brokers work on commission, like travel agents, and they match you to a rental boat. Better-known charter-yacht brokers include **Ed Hamilton & Co** (www.ed-hamilton.com), **Lynn Jachney Charters** (www.lynnjachneycharters.com) and **Nicholson Yacht Charters** (www.yachtvacations.com).

Cruising the Caribbean

Best Ports of Call

Bridgetown, Barbados A vibrant, modern Caribbean capital with loads of shops popular with locals and cruisers alike. Plus you can walk to a great beach.

Road Town, Tortola, British Virgin Islands Port of fancy for yachties, this lovely spot handles visitors with aplomb, never hitting a false note.

Havana, Cuba Begin exploring the endlessly fascinating old parts of the city as soon as you step off the gangplank.

St George's, Grenada A beautiful old port town with interesting shops and top-notch strolling.

Old San Juan, Puerto Rico Cruisers blend right into this ever-surprising, vast and historic neighborhood of tiny bars, cafes, shops and ancient buildings.

More than two million cruise-ship passengers sail the Caribbean annually, making it the world's largest cruise-ship destination. While the ships get bigger (new ships carry over 5000 passengers) the amenities also grow, and today ships can have everything from climbing walls and an in-line skating rink to nightclubs and waterfalls. Ships sail at night and sit in ports by day, typically 8am to 4pm.

The typical cruise-ship holiday is the ultimate package tour. Other than the effort involved in selecting a cruise, it requires minimal planning – just pay and show up – and for many people this is a large part of the appeal.

For the most part, the smaller, 'nontraditional' ships put greater emphasis on the local aspects of their cruises, both in terms of the time spent on land and the degree of interaction with islanders.

Stops in ports of call are what you make of them. Excursions sold on ships tend to emphasize shopping and experiences geared for mass appeal. But you can make your own arrangements and see the island the way you'd like if this doesn't suit.

Because travel in the Caribbean can be expensive, and because cruises cover accommodations, meals, entertainment and transportation in one all-inclusive price, they can also be comparatively economical.

Main Routes

While there are variations, cruise itineraries tend to concentrate on three main areas.

Eastern Caribbean

Cruises can last three to seven days, with few days during which you're only at sea due to the profusion of port calls. Some itineraries may venture south to Barbados or even to Aruba, Bonaire and Curaçao; there is much overlap between the eastern and southern itineraries. Islands in the eastern area: Antigua, Bahamas, British Virgin Islands, Dominican Republic, Guadeloupe, Puerto Rico, St Kitts and Nevis, St-Martin/Sint Maarten, Turks and Caicos, US Virgin Islands.

Southern Caribbean

Itineraries are usually at least seven days due to the distance from the main departure ports. There is often some overlap with the Eastern Caribbean islands, with stops at the US Virgin Islands common. Islands in the southern area: Aruba, Barbados, Bonaire, Curaçao, Dominica, Grenada, Martinique, St Lucia, St Vincent and the Grenadines, Trinidad and Tobago.

Western Caribbean

Often only five days in length, the western itineraries usually also include Mexican ports, such as Cancun. There are often stops at Puerto Rico and other eastern ports and longer itineraries may include southern stops. Islands in the western area: Cayman Islands, Cuba (stops here are not common), Jamaica.

Ports of Departure

Main departure ports for Caribbean cruises are Fort Lauderdale and Miami, Florida; and San Juan, Puerto Rico. All three cities are well equipped to deal with vast numbers of departing and arriving cruise-ship passengers and are closest to the Caribbean.

Secondary departure ports are typically set up for local markets and won't see the line's biggest or flashiest ships (though some veteran cruisers like that). These include Galveston, Texas; New Orleans, Louisiana; Port Canaveral and Tampa, Florida. Cruises from these ports need more time at sea to travel to and from the Caribbean.

Ports of Call

There are many choices of where to visit on a cruise. You'll find a rundown of the most popular ports of call, with descriptions and typical excursions, on p56. For more details, also check the Port of Call boxed texts in the relevant chapters. Note that some cruise lines stop at 'private islands,' which are beaches that function as an extension of the shipboard experience. A prime example is 'Labadie', used by ships under the Royal Caribbean umbrella and which is really a walled-off beach on Haiti's north coast.

Costs

The cost of a cruise can vary widely, depending on the season and vacancies. While it will save you money to book early, keep in mind that cruise lines want to sail full, so many will offer excellent last-minute discounts – sometimes up to 50% off the full fare.

You'll pay less for an inside room deep within the ship, but beware that the really cheap rooms are often claustrophobic and poorly located (be sure to ask before booking). Some packages provide free or discounted airfares to and from the port of embarkation (or will provide a rebate if you make your own transportation arrangements).

Most cruises end up costing US$200 to US$500 per person, per day, including airfare from a major US gateway city. Port charges and government taxes typically add on another US$150 per cruise. Be sure to check the fine print about deposits, cancellation and refund policies, and travel insurance.

Extras on Board

Alcoholic drinks are usually not included in the price of the cruise and are a profit center for the lines. Meals, typically frequent and abundant, are no longer universally included in the cruise price. A new profitable trend is for ships to have several extra-cost restaurants where for, say, US$20 you can get a steak dinner in an exclusive setting. Meals in large dining rooms and buffets remain included in the price, although veteran cruisers complain that the quality of food has dropped on some cruise lines.

Tipping

Note that tipping is usually expected and can add 20% or more to your shipboard account. Many lines have gotten around the discretionary nature of tips (which are the primary wages for the crew) by automatically putting them on your bill in the form of 18% to 20% gratuity fees.

Shore Excursions

Numerous guided tours and activities are offered at each port of call, each generally costing US$40 to US$100 or more. These

POPULAR PORTS OF CALL

Unless otherwise noted, ships dock at ports located in or very near town.

PORT	DESCRIPTION	EXCURSIONS	PORT OF CALL BOX
Antigua: St John's	Busy, vibrant capital with lots of daily life and shopping at markets.	Rainforest canopy tours, Stingray City Antigua, English Harbour, beaches, market, kayaking	p112
Aruba: Oranjestad	Commercial hub divided between a zone of malls (some quite tired) serving cruisers, and a regular shopping area.	Natural sites on the east coast, beaches	p135
The Bahamas: Nassau	The country's busy, main cruise-ship port. Passengers can walk to the sights of downtown, which revolves around cruisers.	Aquaventure Waterpark, diving and snorkeling at Stuart Cove	p162
The Bahamas: Lucaya	Lucaya's port is a few miles from Lucaya and Freeport. Cruise-ship passengers have to take a bus or taxi to town.	Trips to Garden of the Groves, hanging out on Lucaya Beach	p169
Barbados: Bridgetown	Attractive capital with plenty of locally owned shops. It's big so absorbs crowds easily.	Beaches, rum distilleries, nature and wildlife	p202
Bonaire: Kralendijk	Tiny with only a few shops so large ships bring a tsunami of people; it's best to get a driver and leave.	Diving, windsurfing, sightseeing, flamingo spotting	p230
British Virgin Islands: Road Town	Vibrant place that accepts cruisers with aplomb, but gets crowded.	Taxi to Cane Garden Bay, ferry to Virgin Gorda	p242
Cayman Islands: George Town	Has a busy, compact centre with a mix of local- and tourist-oriented businesses. Ships don't dock; tenders are used.	Seven Mile Beach, Stingray City, turtle farm	p271
Cuba: Havana	This is one place you don't need an excursion. It's a fascinating city perfect for wandering, especially the old Habana Vieja area near the port	Exploring the old city, shopping, museums	p295
Curaçao: Willemstad	The harbor cleaves the city in two – it's a spectacular place to arrive by ship. Most central shops are geared towards cruisers.	Tours of historic Willemstad, museums, beaches, snorkeling	p355
Dominica: Roseau	Gets smaller cruise ships and is blissfully unaffected.	Boiling Lake, Morne Trois Piton National Park, Titou Gorge, snorkeling	p387
Dominican Republic: Samaná	Lovely old port town with waterside parks and cafes. Ships don't dock; tenders are used.	Beaches of Cayo Levantado, Cascada El Limón waterfall, whale-watching (in season)	p413
Dominican Republic: Santo Domingo	Has two ports: one basically in Zona Colonial, the other directly across the river.	Walking tour of the remarkable Zona Colonial to absorb its culture	p413
Grenada: St George's	One of the Caribbean's most beautiful old cities – a mini San Francisco. It has interesting local shops hidden about.	Touring the town, Grand Anse Beach, Grand Etang hikes	p456

PORT	DESCRIPTION	EXCURSIONS	PORT OF CALL BOX
Guadeloupe: Pointe-à-Pitre	Not a big stop for cruise ships. It's a steamy, chaotic city with charms away from the new cruise dock	Hiking in Parc National de la Guadeloupe is worth the effort	p480
Jamaica: Montego Bay	Bustling city that many cruisers miss. The trendy areas get packed when many ships arrive. Dock is 2.5 miles south of town.	Doctor's Cave Beach (walkable from town), exploring downtown Montego, shopping, diving	p540
Jamaica: Ocho Rios	Very sleepy place when cruise ships aren't in port; doesn't get crowded	Dunn's River Falls, Turtle Beach, Nine Mile	p540
Martinique: Fort-de-France	Appealing town that easily accommodates cruisers. Ships may use tenders if the port is busy.	Exploring the colorful spice market in Fort-de-France, experiencing French culture in St-Pierre	p572
Nevis: Charlestown	A small, historic and lovely capital. Tenders are used to bring passengers to the port in town.	Touring the plantation inns	p686
Puerto Rico: Old San Juan	Has the region's best combination of historic, cultural, drinking and shopping spots. Gets crowded with cruisers.	El Morro, El Yunque, beaches and casinos of Isla Verde	p605
St Kitts: Basseterre	Compact, working Caribbean port town interesting for about an hour's wander beyond the non-alluring port shops	Cockleshell Bay, Brimstone Hill Fortress, Mt Liamuiga volcano, St Kitts Scenic Railway	p680
St Lucia: Castries	Has two ports. Feel the modern French vibe while smelling bananas and spices in the market.	Reduit Beach (Rodney Bay), Pigeon Island National Landmark, zip-lining	p702
St-Martin/ Sint Maarten: Philipsburg	Has a vast area of malls by the dock, with prices reputed to be at least 20% cheaper than other islands. Gets crowded with cruisers.	Chartering a cab to remote beaches, Oyster Pond, shopping	p723
St Vincent: Kingstown	Seems little changed in 150 years. The streets teem with locals out shopping for staples while socializing.	Boat to the Falls of Baleine, ferry to beautiful Bequia	p743
Tobago: Scarborough	An interesting small town where you can browse stores and markets – most quite authentic.	Pigeon Point Beach, Tobago Forest Reserve, Argyle Falls	p773
Trinidad: Port of Spain	Pulsing city that moves to the beat of beloved local music; port is in a lively part of town.	Asa Wright Nature Centre, Caroni Bird Sanctuary, Maracas Bay	p773
Turks & Caicos: Grand Turk	Small Grand Turk has a cruise center with beaches and a range of facilities. Port is 3 miles south of town.	Snorkeling and diving trips, wandering charming Cockburn Town, whale-watching (in season)	p824
US Virgin Islands: Charlotte Amalie	An old town filled with new duty-free megashops and good local food. Port is 1 mile from town. It gets crowded with cruisers.	Magens Bay beach, strolling downtown Charlotte Amalie, ferry to St John's beaches	p836
US Virgin Islands: Frederiksted	A tiny, uncrowded place that seems empty with no cruise ships visiting.	Cruzan Rum Distillery, Estate Whim Plantation Museum, Christiansted	p836

» (above) Cruise ship anchored off the coast of the Bahamas
» (left) Sunbathing atop the waters of Barbados

tours are also a major profit earner for the cruise lines so there is great pressure for passengers to join – some reported heavy-handed tactics include cruise lines suggesting that people who booked tours with third parties have been left behind in port. But note that there is no need to book tours via the cruise lines. Besides saving on costs, by going outside of the cruise line's shore excursions, travelers can set their own itinerary and avoid the less-appealing mandatory stops.

Many cruisers find activities in advance and book over the internet. These can include set tours and customized ones. Many tours that can be booked by cruisers are reviewed in this book. Passengers will also often find local drivers waiting at cruise-ship ports offering their services as tour guides and convenient transport to the sights of your choice.

Booking a Cruise

There are several options for researching and booking a cruise. A cruise line's own website will offer deals or upgrades not found elsewhere and there are big discounts for booking with them up to a year in advance. Large travel-booking sites like Expedia, Orbitz and Travelocity also have oodles of options; Hotwire, Priceline and the like often have last-minute discounts.

Specialist Cruise Sites

Some specialist websites for cruising have spectacular deals as lines dump trips at the last moment that otherwise would go unsold. Some recommended sites:

Cruise411 (www.cruise411.com)

Cruise.com (www.cruise.com)

Cruise Outlet (www.thecruiseoutlet.com)

Vacations to Go (www.vacationstogo.com) Especially good last-minute deals

Travel Agents

Most cities have travel agents that specialize in cruises; these can be very helpful if you are new to cruising. Read weekend newspaper travel sections, check the Yellow Pages or try these industry websites for referrals:

American Society of Travel Agents (www.asta.org)

Cruise Lines International Association (www.cruising.org)

National Association Cruise Oriented Agencies (www.nacoaonline.com)

Useful Resources

Good sources of further cruise information before you book:

Cruise Critic (www.cruisecritic.com) An in-depth site for people who like to cruise. The message boards are excellent, with detailed critical opinions and information on ships, islands and more.

Cruise Junkie (www.cruisejunkie.com) An excellent site providing a well-rounded overview of the industry, including safety and environmental issues.

Flying Wheels Travel (www.flyingwheelstravel. com) Offers disabled-accessible Caribbean cruises.

Choosing a Cruise

So many options! So many decisions! Things to consider:

Budget How much can you spend? Can you trade a cabin with a balcony (the most common kind now) for a cheaper, windowless room on a nicer ship for a longer voyage?

Style A mass-market, upscale or specialist cruise? Consider your budget; whether you prefer numerous formal evenings, or to keep things casual; and any special interests you have.

Itinerary Where do you want to go and what ports of call appeal? Do you like the idea of days spent just at sea?

Size matters The megaships are geared for various budgets, so the important decision is how many people you want to sail with. On large ships, you can have 5000 potential new friends and also have the greatest range of shipboard diversions. Small ships, while sometimes exclusive and luxurious, are not always so, and usually lack the flashier amenities (like climbing walls). Smaller ships will also call at smaller ports on less-visited islands.

Season High season for Caribbean cruising is the same as at resorts in the islands: mid-December to April. The largest number of ships sail at this time and prices are at their highest. At other times there are much fewer voyages but prices drop. Storms are more likely to cause itineraries to suddenly change during hurricane season June to November.

Demographics Different cruise lines, and even ships within cruise lines, tend to appeal to different groups. Although cruisers in general tend to be slightly older, some ships have quite a party reputation; others are known for their art auctions and oldies rock in the lounges. Also consider if you're looking for a family- or singles-oriented cruise.

WHAT TO PACK

Clothes and personal items like toiletries and medications are the important things to pack. Sundries can be bought at high prices on board or at regular prices in ports of call. Most cruise lines offer good packing advice geared to the style of your cruise. Don't forget:

» Bathing suit

» Shorts or lightweight skirt

» Comfortable, casual cotton wear

» Comfortable, cool walking shoes for shore excursions

» Waterproof sandals for around the pool and active shore excursions

» Khakis, a dress and shirts with collars for evening dining

» Outfits for cruises with formal nights you intend to join (men can often rent tuxes in advance through the cruise line)

Cruise Lines

Cruising is huge business and the major players earn billions of dollars a year. Many lines are actually brands owned by one of the two big players: Carnival and Royal Caribbean control 90% of the market in the Caribbean.

There are also nontraditional cruises, where you can feel the wind at your back on large sailing ships equipped with modern technology.

Research the lines carefully before choosing. Ultimately the differences between middle-market behemoths Carnival, NCL and Royal Caribbean are not great.

Popular Cruise Lines

The following cruise lines sail large vessels on numerous itineraries in the Caribbean:

Carnival Cruise Lines (www.carnival.com) The largest cruise line in the world. Its enormous ships offer cruising on myriad Caribbean itineraries.

Celebrity Cruises (www.celebritycruises.com) An important brand of Royal Caribbean, it has huge ships that offer a more upscale experience than Carnival and RCI. It is a major Caribbean player.

Costa Cruises (www.costacruises.com) Owned by Carnival, Costa is aimed at European travelers – bigger spas, smaller cabins and better coffee. Ships are huge, similar to Carnival's megaships.

Crystal Cruises (www.crystalcruises.com) Luxury cruise line with ships carrying about 800 passengers – small by modern standards. Attracts affluent, older clients who enjoy a wide range of cultural activities and formal evenings.

Cunard Line (www.cunard.com) Owned by Carnival, Cunard Line operates the huge *Queen Mary II*

and *Queen Victoria*. The focus is on 'classic luxury' and the ships have limited Caribbean sailings.

Disney Cruise Line (www.disneycruise.com) Disney's large ships are like floating theme parks, with children's programs and large staterooms that appeal to families.

Holland America (www.hollandamerica.com) Owned by Carnival. Holland America offers a traditional cruising experience, generally to older passengers. It has limited sailings in the Caribbean during the Alaska winter (its summer market).

Norwegian Cruise Line (NCL; www.ncl.com) Offers 'freestyle cruising' on large cruise ships, which means that dress codes are relaxed and dining options more flexible than on other lines. There are lots of extra-fee dining choices.

Princess Cruises (www.princess.com) Owned by Carnival, Princess has large ships that ply the Caribbean and offer a slightly older crowd a range of activities and classes while aboard.

Regent Seven Seas Cruises (www.rssc.com) Smaller ships (maximum 700 passengers) with a focus on luxury cabins and excellent food.

Royal Caribbean International (RCI; www.royalcaribbean.com) The archrival to Carnival has a huge fleet of megaships (some carry over 5600 people), aimed right at the middle of the market. It has itineraries everywhere in the Caribbean all the time and offers lots of activities for kids.

Nontraditional Cruises

Sea Cloud Cruises (www.seacloud.com) The fleet includes a four-masted, 360ft (110m) ship dating from 1931 and a modern sibling. On both, the sails are set by hand. This German-American company operates luxury cruises in the Eastern Caribbean.

» (above) View from the beach at Great Bay, Philipsburg, Sint Maarten
» (left) Magens Bay, US Virgin Islands, as seen from on deck

» (below) Cruise ships in port, Philipsburg, Sint Maarten

Although all travel comes with an environmental cost, by their very size, cruise ships have an outsize effect. Among the main issues:

» **Air pollution** According to UK-based Climate Care, a carbon offsetting company, cruise ships emit more carbon per passenger than airplanes – nearly twice as much – and that's not including the flights that most passengers take to get to their point of departure. Most ships also burn low-grade bunker fuel, which contains more sulfur and particulates than higher-quality fuel.

The US and Canada have set new fuel quality regulations for ships calling on their coastlines, which take effect starting in 2012. In July 2011, the US Environmental Protection Agency (EPA) won approval from the International Maritime Organization to extend these standards to the waters surrounding Puerto Rico and the US Virgin Islands. These regulations will be phased in starting in 2014. Cruise lines had argued that this would add too much to their costs but the EPA contends that switching to cleaner fuel will cost about 60 cents per passenger per day on a typical cruise.

At publication time there was no word on whether other Caribbean countries or territories would press for similar measures, but with the US Virgin Islands and Puerto Rico combined receiving 2.8 million cruise passengers in 2010 – surpassed only by the Bahamas – these regulations have the potential to have a considerable effect

» **Water pollution** Cruise ships generate enormous amounts of sewage, solid waste and gray water. While some countries and states have imposed regulations on sewage treatment (with which the cruise lines comply), there's little regulation in the Caribbean. The United Nations instituted a ban on ships dumping solid waste in the water. However, as the Associated Press reported in a March 2008 article, few Caribbean islands have signed onto the ban as few have means to accept waste for treatment/disposal on shore; as a result, many ships still dump.

» **Cultural impact** Although cruise lines generate money for their ports of call, thousands of people arriving at once can change the character of a town and seem overwhelming to locals and noncruising travelers. In Bonaire, for example, 7000 cruisers can arrive in one day – half the country's population.

The cruise industry notes it complies with international regulations, and adapts as necessary to stricter laws in places like Alaska and the US west coast. It is equipping some ships with new wastewater treatment facilities, LED lighting and solar panels. Princess Cruises partnered with Juneau, Alaska, to develop 'cold-ironing,' whereby ships in port plug into electric power; this is also done in San Francisco, Vancouver and Seattle. But ports in the Caribbean don't have such facilities. Stricter government regulations are unlikely in most of this multicountry, tourism-dependent region, but public demand for greener cruising could hasten changes.

What You Can Do

If you're planning a cruise, it's worth doing some research. Email the cruise lines and ask them about their environmental policies – wastewater treatment, recycling initiatives, and whether they use alternative energy sources. Knowing that customers care about these things has an impact. There are also organizations that review lines and ships on their environmental records.These include the following:

» **Friends of the Earth** (www.foe.org/cruisereportcard) Letter grades given to cruise lines and ships for environmental and human health impacts.

» **US Centers for Disease Control & Prevention** (www.cdc.gov) Follow the travel links to the well-regarded sanitation ratings for ships calling in US ports.

» **World Travel Awards** (www.worldtravelawards.com) Annual awards for the 'World's Leading Green Cruise Line.'

Star Clippers (www.starclippers.com) These modern four-masted clipper ships have tall-ship designs and carry 180 passengers. Itineraries take in smaller islands of the Eastern Caribbean.

Windstar Cruises (www.windstarcruises.com) Windstar's luxury four-masted, 440ft (134m) vessels have high-tech, computer-operated sails and carry under 400 passengers. Note that the sails aren't the main means of propulsion most of the time. Trips travel throughout the Windward and Leeward Islands.

Theme Cruises
Special Interests

Old TV shows, science fiction, computers, musicians, (very) minor celebrities, soap operas, sports teams, authors... What these all have in common is that they're all themes for cruises.

Cruise lines sell group space to promoters of theme cruises but typically no theme is enough to fill an entire ship. Rather, a critical mass of people will occupy a block of cabins and have activities day and night just for them, including lectures, autograph sessions, costume balls and performances.

If you're keen to spend several days on a ship with others who are equally gaga over your special interest, consider the following:

» Do an online search for your interest and 'cruise' and see what happens – *Star Trek*, the Green Bay Packers and Lynnrd Skinnard all hit pay dirt.

» The cruise may not attract the very top names. You may find yourself at sea with an extra who had three lines in your favourite show, or the third-string quarterback in your beloved team. (With Skinnard however, you get the real musician and he performs.)

» No interest is too obscure or improbable. There are specialist cruises for *Titanic* geeks, cougars (not the cat; older women looking to 'date' younger men), and *Twilight* fans.

LBGT Cruises

One of the largest segments of special-interest cruises are those aimed at lesbian, bisexual, gay and transgender people. So popular are these cruises that often an entire ship will be devoted to catering for LBGT passengers. Start by checking out the following operators:

Gay Cruise Vacations (www.gaycruisevacations. com) These popular all-gay vacations on giant cruise ships travel throughout the Caribbean on mostly seven-day trips.

Olivia (www.olivia.com) Organizes cruises for lesbians with as many as 1800 passengers.

RSVP Vacations (www.rsvpvacations.com) Good for active travelers, RSVP has trips on both large cruise ships and smaller yachts.

Weddings & Honeymoons

Best Types of Caribbean Wedding

Big adventure Enjoy one of the Caribbean's off-the-beaten-path locations where you can hike, kayak or dive etc. These are good for couples who want a nontraditional ceremony.

Intimate luxe Live large in a small, exclusive resort. These can be expensive, so it could limit the number of guests. Luxury boutique resorts will usually handle all details and customize anything.

Resort ball Group rates at a large resort mean that you can send out invites far and wide for an event that is not out of reach. Resorts can usually organize a traditional ceremony and reception.

The Caribbean is a world-class destination for love. You can find virtually any kind of experience on one of the islands. If you're getting married, you'll join the numerous couples who've exchanged vows in one of these beautiful places.

The table on p66 lists the main islands where you might consider a wedding, honeymoon or just time alone with someone special. The 'Best for' column details the type of wedding as defined on the left.

Wedding Considerations

Some points to consider ahead of your Caribbean wedding:

Size

By their very nature Caribbean weddings tend to limit the number of guests who can attend. Costs and time off for the trip are issues, although some large resorts give very good rates for large wedding parties, so your nuptials could be an excuse for a holiday.

But if you want to gather together just a few friends, then it's easy to find gorgeous

---

ROMANCE NEEDS NO EXCUSE

You don't need to get hitched or rehitched to enjoy the romantic ideas in this chapter. We have oodles of places here that you and someone special won't want to leave.

ISLANDS	BEST FOR	DESCRIPTION	RECOMMENDATIONS
Anguilla	Intimate luxe, big adventure	Exclusive and expensive for something exquisite and exotic	Rent your own villa with a butler
Antigua & Barbuda	Intimate luxe, big adventure	A popular destination for Brits thanks to good air links and colonial history	Rendezvous Bay, Antigua (p118); Lighthouse Bay, Barbuda (p123)
Aruba	Resort ball	Plenty of resorts specializing in weddings	Any of the resorts at Palm Beach (p138)
The Bahamas	Big adventure, intimate luxe, resort ball	Private islands where you can indulge in almost anything	Kamalame Cay, Andros (p188); The Cove, Atlantis (p160); Harbour Island, Eleuthera (p179)
Barbados	Big adventure, intimate luxe, resort ball	A full array of services for any style of wedding; good UK connections make this popular with Brits	Coral Reef Club (p211); Crane Beach Hotel (p209) Sea-U! Guest House (p215)
Bonaire	Big adventure	Perfect for outdoor nuptials with a twist	Get married at a small waterfront resort, then go diving with the bridal party
British Virgin Islands	Big adventure	Tortola is the center of Caribbean yachting; great for boat-based weddings or for honeymoons	Get a few of your favorite couples and laze your way through the islands on a chartered yacht
Cayman Islands	Resort ball	Plenty of resorts that offer good group rates	Seven Mile Beach (p276)
Cuba	Big adventure	A great adventure; don't count on legally recognized marriage certificates	Post-nuptials drive in a classic convertible past clapping throngs on the streets of Havana
Dominica	Big adventure	With so much outdoors action you might be too pooped to... no, of course not	River Rush Eco Retreat (p398)
Dominican Republic	Big adventure, resort ball	Big resorts or more intimate options	Resorts at Punta Cana (p420) or secluded coves such as Playas Madama & Frontón (p427)
Grenada	Big adventure	Small, secluded lodges with warm hospitality	Anse la Roche (p464); Green Roof Inn (p464)
Jamaica	Big adventure, intimate luxe, resort ball	One of the top Caribbean wedding destinations. Some major resorts offer free ceremonies if you book enough rooms.	Treasure Beach (p554); Boston Bay (p538)
Puerto Rico	Big adventure, resort ball	Large resorts or hidden retreats; marriage legalities simple for Americans	Vieques (p617); Culebra (p620); Isla Culebrita (p621)
Saba	Big adventure	An island so small that a wedding party would almost take it over	No beaches but plenty of outdoorsy fun
St-Barthélemy	Intimate luxe	Excels at small, top-end weddings	Rent a villa with staff for your special day
St Kitts & Nevis	Intimate luxe, resort ball	Bliss-inducing pampering on Nevis and a resort vibe on St Kitts	Four Seasons, Nevis (p688); Ottley's Plantation Inn, St Kitts (p684)

ISLANDS	BEST FOR	DESCRIPTION	RECOMMENDATIONS
St Lucia	Big adventure, intimate luxe	Boutique options with a French accent	Fond Doux Holiday Plantation (p710); Ladera (p711); Inn on the Bay (p707)
St-Martin/Sint Maarten	Resort ball	Dutch and French resorts that host fabulous weddings	Get a group together and take over a resort
St Vincent & the Grenadines	Big adventure intimate luxe	Plenty of accommodation options for groups; also offers top-end luxury hidden away from the paparazzi	Palm Island Beach Club (p755); Petit St Vincent Resort (p755)
Trinidad & Tobago	Big adventure	Relaxed hideaways –a quirky, offbeat option	Acajou (p785); Kariwak Village Holistic Haven (p788)
Turks & Caicos	Intimate luxe	Small resorts and one of the longest and most beautiful beaches in the Caribbean	Parrot Cay (p819); the resorts at Grace Bay (p815)
US Virgin Islands	Big adventure, intimate luxe, resort ball	Everything from lavish resorts to secluded eco-escapes	Honeymoon Beach on Water Island (p843)

locations where you'll enjoy each other's company for days on end.

Style

Large resorts are good places for traditional wedding ceremonies as they can arrange for cakes, flowers, photographers and all the other accoutrements. Trying to organise all the trimmings at a secluded retreat or small lodge, especially while making the arrangements from your home country, may be very difficult. But that may also be the point if you want to shed traditional touches.

Costs

You can quickly go nuts adding treats and options to your sweetest day. Work with hotels and resorts to figure prices and make sure you allow for the licenses, service fees and other extras.

Papers

It is vital that you confirm in advance what you'll need for a marriage license. It varies greatly by country. Get info from the national tourism authority or a resort that specializes in weddings and then double-check it all.

Below are just some of the bureaucratic hoops you may need to bound through.

» Original birth certificates

» Legal proof of divorce or death of previous spouse

» Legal proof of the marriage officiant's status

» A local marriage license (up to US$300 or more some places)

» Blood tests

There can also be delays in processing – some islands need 48 hours or more to process a license request; others require that you be on the island 48 hours or more in advance of the ceremony

If the red tape proves too much, you can always have the unofficial ceremony of your dreams in the Caribbean while saving the legal ceremony for your home country.

Shopping

Best Shopping Advice

Understand duty-free It may not be the bargain you think.

Learn to bargain Take the fear and mystery out of the process and make it fun.

Buying rum Sample your way to greater knowledge.

Best Places to Shop

Harbour Island, Bahamas All the style you can afford.

Havana, Cuba Rum and cigars aplenty.

St George's, Grenada Beautiful port city for browsing.

St Lucia Great for artwork and crafts.

Kingstown, St Vincent Heaving local market.

Port of Spain, Trinidad CDs of the legendary local music.

Watches, jewelry, designer clothing, crystal, spirits (rum!), cosmetics, electronics and much, much more are part of the Caribbean shopping experience. Duty-free shops and upscale malls abound wherever cruise ships call, but prices may not be that much of a bargain. Places like the Bahamas, the British Virgin Islands, the Cayman Islands and the US Virgin Islands are hugely popular with shoppers for their duty-free jewelry and other luxury items, but there's nothing you can't find at home. St-Martin/Sint Maarten delivers the goods with prices at least 30% less than you'll find in your home country; Philipsburg is now the top discount shopping destination in the Caribbean. Curaçao also has truly discounted prices on timepieces and on jewelry.

But truly unique items such as exquisite local craft items and artworks are harder to find.

Where to Shop

Following are our tips for the most interesting places to shop in the Caribbean.

Antigua

For local color in St John's, skip Heritage Quay's duty-free shops and instead head over to Market St, Thames St and St Mary's St.

Aruba

The malls clustered around Lloyd G Smith Blvd in Oranjestad are surprisingly tired.

DOING YOUR DUTY

The entire concept of 'duty-free' is fraught with confusion, most of which can cost you money.

There are two kinds of duty:

» Duty you pay when you buy something in a foreign country; this can be national taxes, value-added taxes (VAT), alcohol taxes etc.

» Duty you pay when you return home, such as customs levies on alcohol beyond the allowed duty-free purchase.

Typically 'duty-free shops' spare you the local taxes and fees on the purchase. You may have to show a passport or otherwise show that you'll be leaving the country. Note that just because the store has 'duty-free' in the name doesn't mean it is. Some still charge local sales taxes etc.

And note these additional considerations:

» Duty-free prices are not necessarily cheaper than what you'd pay at home, even with taxes.

» Duty or VAT reimbursement schemes – where you save receipts and fill out forms on leaving the country – may be so burdensome that you'll wish you'd paid tax.

» Bottles of perfume, booze and other liquids won't be allowed in your carry-on/hand luggage when you fly home. You will have to put them in checked luggage. (A few schemes are trying to change this.)

» Cruise lines may well seize your purchased liquor when you reboard the ship and stow it until you disembark, thus foiling your plans for a cheap party in your cabin.

A much better option is strolling Caya GF Betico Croes, the main shopping street.

The Bahamas

Duty-free shopping may have been invented here. Choices are vast in Grand Bahama's Port Lucaya Marketplace and Nassau's Bay St, known for diamonds. The best bet is Festival Place, where everything is Bahamian-made. Harbour Island, with its chic boutiques, attracts celebrities and regularly makes lists of best places to shop.

Barbados

The rum distilleries here are the obvious choice. In Bridgetown, try Broad St and pedestrian-only Swan St, which buzzes with the rhythms of local culture. The Pelican Craft Village has good galleries and workshops selling actual art.

Cuba

Definitely not known as a consumer paradise but there are two items well worth buying at stores aimed at visitors with convertible currency: rum and cigars. In Havana, don't miss the Museo del Ron (rum) and Partagá's cigar factory.

Dominican Republic

Shop around for amber and larimar, stones that are considered national treasures and which are virtually ubiquitous in stores. Santo Domingo's Zona Colonial is also great for cigars.

Grenada

Nutmeg remains a top local item and sales support the hurricane-ravaged industry. Look for tours of the sweet-smelling factories. St George's Market Square is the largest public market; expect to find almost anything Friday and Saturday mornings. Wander appealing streets for off-beat little shops.

Jamaica

Everything is for sale, especially from ubiquitous beach vendors. Buy coffee beans and search out quality artworks. Browse the West Indian art galleries in Montego Bay.

Martinique

Shop for French perfumes and interesting handmade items. The main quality boutique area is along Rue Victor Hugo in Fort-de-France.

Puerto Rico

It's like the 51st state in terms of shopping, with no duty or limits for Americans returning home. The best arts and crafts shopping is on San Francisco and Fortaleza, the two main arteries in beautiful Old San Juan.

Saba

Saban lace uses a special stitching technique that has been passed down for a few generations. Windwardside's 'Lace Ladies' gather on Thursdays at the Eugenius Centre to do beautiful Saban stitching.

RUM *JOSH KRIST*

If you could taste them, what would sunsets and long days at the beach taste like? Most likely, rum. In a daiquiri, by itself, or with sugar and a slice of lime, rum is *the* drink of the Caribbean. Rum is the top purchase by people visiting the Caribbean and you will see it offered everywhere, usually at prices much cheaper than you'll find at home.

Rum Tours

More enjoyable than getting a good deal on rum of course is trying rum. At factories throughout the region you can see how it is made and learn some of its history. Many people find these tours to be trip highlights.

» **Bacardí Rum Factory, Puerto Rico** (p616) A good introduction to rum production – fermenting mashed sugarcane or molasses in huge vats, capturing the alcohol through distillation, aging it in wooden casks in big hot warehouses – and there are free tastings. The brand itself is a worldwide icon.

» **Cruzan Rum Distillery, US Virgin Islands** (p859) A pleasant 20-minute tour with tastings at the end.

» **Museo del Ron, Cuba** (p295) Some say that Cuban rum is the best (certainly the makers of best-selling Havana Club would agree). Do some investigation at this Havana institution where in addition to the usual tour and tasting there's a re-creation of a traditional distillery, complete with a model railway.

» **Musée du Rhum St James, Martinique** (p579) There are many distilleries on this French island, but English speakers will learn the most at this enjoyable stop. Martinique is the epicenter of high-quality, pure-cane rums, which are called *rhum agricole*.

» **Mount Gay Rum Visitors Centre, Barbados** (p203) The aged rums here are some of Barbados' best. This is a very traditional tour at a working distillery.

» **Malibu Beach Club & Visitor Centre, Barbados** (p203) Coconut-flavored Malibu is more of an export to Americans barely old enough to drink than a traditional rum, but the company has a popular tour at the beachfront distillery.

Tasting Rum

Top rums include Bermudez Anniversario from the Dominican Republic, Haiti's Barbancourt Five Star and Mount Gay Extra Old from Barbados. The color of rum ranges from clear to honey brown. The darker the drink, the older, usually. Unlike Scotch, however, older does not necessarily equal better, especially considering that some distilleries add coloring and fresh product to the casks for 'aged rum' because of the thirsty angels.

Distillers explain that because of the warm Caribbean climate up to 15% of the rum evaporates every year during aging. This evaporation is called 'the angel's share' at distilleries around the world and usually averages closer to 5%. The angels in the Caribbean are living it up, apparently.

Let taste be your guide; take a small sniff of straight rum with your mouth slightly open. This gives you an idea of the taste without being overwhelmed by the alcohol burn. In the better rums you might smell some vanilla, a hint of flowers, or even, oddly enough, cotton candy – it is just cooked sugar that soaked up the flavors of sun-warmed casks, after all.

St Lucia

Look for silk-screen paintings, woodcarvings, batik and handmade clothing at Castries Central Market or Bagshaws.

St Vincent

It often still feels like decades ago on this island that still relies on banana plantations for much of its wealth. Kingstown becomes a chaotic – and compelling – madhouse on Saturday, the main market day.

Trinidad & Tobago

On islands that pulses with music, local CDs are an excellent purchase. In Port of Spain, centrally located Independence Sq, Charlotte St and Frederick St are filled with malls and arcades selling everything from spices to fabric by the yard.

The Art of Bargaining

Whether it's the beach vendor with the necklace you just have to have, the market stall owner with the cutest stuffed iguana or the slick jewelry store sales clerk, you will likely have a chance to try out your bargaining skills at some point in the Caribbean.

Note however that fixed prices are also common, especially at large stores and duty-free malls. Know that 'no bargaining' can mean just that and isn't a ploy.

Also note that it isn't just that bauble in the window that you can bargain for. Especially in the low season, almost everything, including accommodations, can be negotiated. Ask for a better room or a discount if you are staying for a few days.

Although many people are put off at the prospect, bargaining can be an enjoyable part of shopping, so maintain your sense of humor and keep things in perspective. Try following these steps:

» Have some idea what the item is worth. Why pay more than you would at home.

» Establish a starting price – ask the seller for their price rather than make an initial offer.

» Your first price can be from one-third to two-thirds of the asking price – assuming that the asking price is not outrageous.

» With offer and counter-offer, move closer to an acceptable price.

» If you don't get to an acceptable price, you're entitled to walk – the vendor may call you back with a lower price.

» Note that when you name a price, you're committed – you must buy if your offer is accepted.

» Keep things in perspective. Is it worth aggravation to save one last dollar in dealing with a vendor who may only make a few dollars a week?

Budget Caribbean

Best Budget Tips

Shop online Always look for internet specials, flight + hotel combos, etc.

Travel in groups Bring your friends and other couples along with you and rent a villa.

Book far in advance For high season but low season may see last-minute deals.

Follow the divers They demand great value near beautiful waters.

Ride buses and ferries You meet folks and may have an adventure.

Live like a local Save money while having a more authentic visit.

Travel sustainably It's the right thing to do *and* it saves you money. See p75.

Travel in low season Prices can dip up to 50%.

Budget Rating Guide

The following rating system is used in the table in this chapter:

$ Great value!

$$ You'll have to look carefully for bargains

$$$ Only if cost is not an issue

The Caribbean is not cheap, but there are ways to get the most bang for your buck with a little forward planning and some savvy choices. In this chapter, our authors share strategies for saving money, plus we rate the islands for their budget-friendliness.

Quick Getaways

With competitive airfares from the US and Canada and resorts offering great deals online, several Caribbean islands are well suited to a quick, affordable getaway. Consider the following:

» **Montego Bay, Jamaica** Famous resort town with a huge range of beachside accommodations.

» **Old San Juan, Puerto Rico** Explore forts and beaches by day; wander lively streets by night.

» **St-Martin/Sint Maarten** The choice of a French frolic or Dutch treat.

Live Like a Local

Take time to meet the locals by doing what they do – you'll enjoy a more affordable and authentic experience. Some simple, common-sense tips:

» Eat at lunch wagons or stalls. The local fare is cheap and often incredibly good.

» Drop by a local bar – often the de facto community center. Besides a drink, you'll get all sorts of useful – or wonderfully frivolous – advice.

» Look for community fish fries or barbecues in the Eastern Caribbean, especially Barbados.

ISLANDS	RATING	OVERVIEW
Anguilla	$$$	One of the most exclusive and expensive islands in the Caribbean; not a budget option.
Antigua	$$	Expensive island: mostly higher-end resorts; few guesthouses and those are not appealing. Rent an apartment and self-cater. Vacation rentals have become more prevalent – try along the southwest coast near Cades Bay. Public transportation is OK in developed areas but rare to the remote east and southeast.
Aruba	$$	The beaches are lined with mostly top-end resorts but Eagle Beach – our favorite – does have some good midrange options. Stay 10 minutes' walk from the beach and you can get a good room with a kitchen for under US$100 a night. Public transportation is excellent.
The Bahamas	$$	Go in the hurricane season (late summer/early fall). The weather's generally pretty good, but prices nosedive. Eleuthera is becoming a more popular budget destination, in contrast to pricey Harbour Island. Grand Bahama is a good budget spot, as hotels are scrambling for guests.
Barbados	$$$	The west coast with its old-money resorts and mansions can be pricey, although there are good-value apartments 10 minutes from the beaches. The south is filled with budget and midrange choices close to the sand. Good public transportation.
Barbuda	$$$	At least one third more expensive than Antigua. Only way to save money is by staying in guesthouses but these are very basic. Getting around is ridiculously expensive.
Bonaire	$	Excellent budget choice. Small resorts on the water cater to divers who are value-conscious. Car rentals – almost a must – are well priced.
British Virgin Islands	$$	Tortola is the secret to budget travel in the BVI. It has a good range of guesthouses and moderate resorts.
Cayman Islands	$	Most of the accommodation is on beautiful Seven Mile Beach and is quite expensive. Consider other areas like Bodden Town on Grand Cayman or tiny, beautiful Little Cayman. Public transportation is excellent.
Cuba	$	Stay in casas particulares (private homes) – rooms cost CUC$20 to CUC$40, and there are thousands across the island (3000 in Havana alone!). All are government checked. Resorts can be overpriced and disappointing. Viñales and Baracoa are two affordable and engaging towns.
Curaçao	$$	Budget accommodation in beautiful Willemstad is often not worth the cheap prices, but some better midrange options are opening. Holiday apartments on north-coast beaches are good value. Public transportation is OK.
Dominica	$	One of the Caribbean's best bargains: everything is much cheaper than the region's averages, especially lodging and eating; public transportation is excellent and comprehensive.
Dominican Republic	$$	Travel outside of high season and find bargains online. The central highlands are better value than elsewhere because most tourists are only on day trips. Great off-the-beaten-path places to stay: Tubagua Village and Sonido del Yaque; Bahía de Las Águilas. Buses cover the country.
Grenada	$$	Generally affordable. There are some modest resorts in and around George Town plus excellent local restaurants. A car will be good for a couple days' exploration. On Carriacou Hillsborough has a few good budget accommodation options.
The Grenadines	$$$	Some islands quite expensive (eg Mustique, Canouan) but others like gorgeous Bequia have excellent good-value choices near town and beach. You can walk where you want to go.
Guadeloupe	$$	Good budget/midrange options are available throughout the country – think US$50 per night. Good buses; ferries to the tiny offshore islands are cheap and fun.

ISLANDS	RATING	OVERVIEW
Haiti	$$	Haiti is an infrastructure-poor country with services at a minimum; budget travel is difficult. Things are cheaper outside Port-au-Prince, however.
Jamaica	$$	Treasure Beach and the south (St Elizabeth parish), plus Port Antonio and the northeast are fantastic for getting a taste of the 'real' Jamaica outside of resorts. Public transportation is good albeit adventurous.
Martinique	$$	Budget/cheap midrange options are available throughout the country – think $50 per night. Ferries and buses provide good links.
Montserrat	$	Definitely a budget island: great value and high standards, even at guesthouses. Local eateries are cheap and excellent. Limited public transportation; taxis are not too expensive.
Nevis	$$$	Stay in Charlestown, which has some reasonably priced lodging options plus markets and simple eateries. The rest of the island is very expensive.
Puerto Rico	$$	In San Juan there's an abundance of hotels: internet deals for four-star resorts for US$100 are common. Save huge at state-operated facilities at beach *centros vacacionales*. Good public transportation.
Saba	$	A tiny island with few accommodation choices but some nice ones for under US$100.
Sint Eustatius	$	Although choices are few, limited tourism except for value-conscious divers means accommodation choices are good value, even January to March.
St-Barthélemy	$$$	Prohibitively expensive in high season; other times you might find an affordable villa rental online. Splurge at the luxury restaurants with their €29 'value' meals.
St Kitts	$$$	Expensive island. Avoid plantation inns; look for online specials at the resorts on the nice beaches in the south. Use the decent public transportation and get a room with a kitchen.
St Lucia	$$	Consider staying in midrange places such as inns, guesthouses that are not directly on the beach. Travel in low season.
St-Martin/Sint Maarten	$$	Consider staying in the island's towns – like Philipsburg or Marigot. Shop at local markets (ask the locals where they buy their groceries). Public transportation is just OK.
St Vincent	$$	There are some good modest resorts near Kingstown, which also has a good inn in town. Public transportation just OK.
Trinidad	$	Not particularly tourist oriented, so many good-value options. Inexpensive in comparison to other islands. Public transportation and street food are cheap and good.
Tobago	$	As in Trinidad, there are many good-value options. Crown Point has the majority of places to stay, and competition keeps prices low.
Turks & Caicos	$$	The best value is at cheap diving resorts in Providenciales and Grand Turk.
US Virgin Islands	$$	Rates are very seasonal, falling 40% or more in slack times. Resorts tend to be pricey but holiday apartments can be good value. For fun *and* low rates, try ecocamping: Maho Bay Camps and Concordia Eco-Tents on St John, Virgin Islands Campground on Water Island (off St Thomas), Mt Victory Campground on St Croix.

Traveling Sustainably

Sustainable Seafood

Many species in the Caribbean are at risk due to overfishing. Where you can, try to order dishes that use sustainable catches.

Good Seafood Choices

Barramundi (farm-raised)
Conch (farm-raised)
Maine lobster
Shrimp
Tilapia (farm-raised)
Yellowtail snapper

Seafood to Avoid

Atlantic salmon
Conch (wild-caught)
Florida pompano
Grouper
Spiny lobster
Wild turtle

Tourism pays the bills in most of the Caribbean, and the impact on the environment and the culture is huge. Most islands are still putting economic development ahead of the environment because poverty is so widespread, but there are some 'green' trailblazers worth supporting. Sustainable listings in this book have been selected by Lonely Planet authors because they demonstrate an active sustainable-tourism policy, are involved in conservation or environmental education, or are operated with a view to maintaining and preserving regional identity and culture.

Environmental Issues

The popularity of the Caribbean as a tourist destination means that many environmental problems have been created or aggravated by an influx of visitors.

There is a reliance on fossil fuels to power resorts, which is a problem in an area that is gas- and oil-poor (Trinidad excepted). But there are plenty of volcanoes, and work is under way on St Lucia to exploit geothermal power.

The reef around Tobago Cays off St Vincent and the Grenadines, a popular anchorage for sailors, and the reefs around the Virgin Islands, have been damaged by careless snorkelers and divers. Thankfully, this has spurred new protection efforts at both sites.

Waste is a big problem in the region. Mountains of garbage crowd Havana, acrid refuse burns from Vieques to Puerto

CHOOSING THE RIGHT FISH

Trying to set an environmentally conscious course through the seafood menus of the Caribbean can be tough.

The **Cayman Islands National Trust** offers a downloadable guide (see www.nationaltrust.org.ky/ seasense.html) to sensible seafood choices, as well as a list of member Cayman restaurants that only serve sustainable catches.

Plata, and sewage needs somewhere to go – too often it flows directly into the sea. St-Barthélemy is one island finding creative answers, such as converting burning trash into energy.

Overfishing is a major problem. The Bahamas outlawed long-line fishing in 1959, the first Caribbean island to do so, but the country now struggles with poachers. National marine reserves have been established in many countries to protect their shores.

Larger islands have had difficulty inculcating a culture of conservation. Despite deforestation laws, only 10% of the Dominican Republic is forested. Neighboring Haiti – the most impoverished country in the western hemisphere – features in university environmental-management courses as a case study in how massive deforestation (95%) can destroy a country.

Consume Less

You can do your part and make a difference. Here are a few pointers for minimizing your impact on the environment.

» **Turn off the tap** Fresh water is an extremely precious commodity on all of the islands, where desalination plants work overtime converting saltwater to fresh. Many islanders depend only on rainwater collected in cisterns. Keep in mind that winter – peak tourism time – is the driest time of year.

» **Skip bottled water** If the water is safe to drink (see the Health section in each chapter for details), use it to fill containers so you can skip bottled water and its transport and refuse costs.

» **Turn off the air-con** Rarely is it so hot in the Caribbean that you need air-con at night; turn it off and let the breezes in.

» **Ride the bus** Instead of renting a car, immerse yourself in local culture while you save gas. Islands such as Aruba, Barbados and Grand Cayman have excellent bus networks.

» **Return the car early** Decide if you need a rental car for your entire stay. You might only need it for a day or two of exploration.

» **Say no to plastic** On Barbados and some other islands, stores will ask you if you want a plastic bag rather than just giving you one. Straws are also best avoided because they float around for years.

Be Ecosmart

» **Go green** Look for hotels and resorts that carry an audited green certification. A good place to start your search is at **Eco-Index Sustainable Tourism** (www.eco-indextourism .org), which features businesses that have been recognized as environmentally and socially responsible.

» **Ask questions** Ask your hotel or tour operator about its green practices. Even if they have none, it'll tell them it matters to customers.

» **Travel globally, shop locally** Not only will buying local products infuse the local economy, it will also help to save you money. Local beer is always fresher than imported.

» **Avoid coral** Don't touch it in the wild and don't buy it in shops or from vendors. Also avoid any souvenirs made of seashell or turtle shell. Buying goods made with any of these only encourages environmental destruction and hunting.

» **Don't litter** Sure, you'll see many locals do it (especially with KFC boxes), but don't do it yourself. Almost everything discarded on land makes its way to the sea, where it can wreak havoc on marine life. Carry your trash off beaches, trails and campsites.

» **Consider the dolphins** Be aware that wild dolphins are often captured to be used in enclosed swim-with-dolphins tourist attractions, a practice that has been condemned by wildlife conservationists.

Recommended Businesses

Green awareness is growing in the Caribbean, especially as visitors make this a priority.

Aruba

Manchebo Beach Resort Despite being in a built-up tourist area, this resort wears its green credentials proudly (p138).

The Bahamas

On islands where golf carts are a popular mode of transport (Loyalist Cays, Harbour Island), choose an electric cart rather than a gas-powered one.

Higgins' Landing (p185) A luxurious boutique hotel powered by solar energy; uses only rainwater in the bathrooms.

Small Hope Bay Lodge (p188) This laid-back ecoresort takes a genuine interest in sustainability, composting food and making drinking glasses from old wine bottles.

Barbados

Sea-U! Guest House (p215) Excellent green cred not far from the most natural beach in Barbados.

Barbuda

The small population of Barbuda is quite environmentally aware.

Barbuda Cottages (p123) A new, solar-powered villa on stilts.

Bonaire

The entire coast of the island is a marine reserve and conservation is taken seriously.

Captain Don's Habitat (p227) Leads the way in local environmental causes.

Cuba

Staying in a casa particular (private home that lets rooms to foreigners) is more 'eco' as the food is always locally produced and you're putting money into the pockets of Cubans.

La Moka (p317) The sole place to stay in a Unesco Biosphere Reserve.

Dominica

Cocoa Cottages (p390) A cluster of ecocottages; serves organic meals around communal tables.

Zandoli Inn (p393) Set in a remote corner of the island is this quiet, arty ecolodge.

Jungle Bay Resort & Spa (p393) A fully serviced ecoresort with 35 luxurious cottages.

Manicou River Resort (p395) Octagonal cottages built from recycled materials.

Comfortel De Champ (p395) A small hotel with superb hilltop views and solar panels.

Dominican Republic

Explora Eco Tours (p419) Customized tours of national parks, nature preserves and rural communities.

Natura Park Eco-Resort & Spa (p422) A beach resort with abundant birdlife.

Tubagua Plantation Eco-Village (p435) Simple, low-impact wooden cabins on a mountaintop.

Sonido del Yaque (p439) Basic jungle cabins run by a collective of local women.

Grenada

Maca Bana (p459) Luxury ecovillas scattered along a hillside.

Guadeloupe

Ti Gli Gli (p492) Rustic bungalows set on a steep slope. The place to come if you want to engage with nature and local culture.

Puerto Rico

Hix Island House (p619) A groundbreaking designer ecolodge with minimalist architecture and a leafy setting.

St Lucia

Ladera (p711) A solid green ethos and one of the island's best-located resorts.

Hotel Chocolat It's not just a tasty name. Set in a cocoa planation, this resort prides itself on the contribution it makes to the local community (p711).

SAVE THE GROUPER (& CONCH)!

It graces many a menu but it may not for long. The big and slow grouper is also a slow breeder and overfishing may doom this dinner favorite to extinction. It's a similar situation with the conch, as numbers in the wild fall fast.

One solution that visitors can help with is to eat less of both species. If you've got the taste for conch, make sure you opt for farm-raised versions. There are many good alternatives to Caribbean ocean species that are endangered – see the list on p75.

GREEN DOMINICA

Dominica is the eco-isle par excellence. It generates some 40% of power from hydroelectric power and has huge areas designated as national parks, which enjoy a standard of protection and conservation rarely found in Caribbean. It was named in the 2011 'Developing World's Best Ethical Destinations' report by *Ethical Traveler*, a San Francisco–based watchdog group, based on its record of environmental protection, social welfare and human rights.

There are lots and lots of ecolodges (see p77 for some ideas), which use solar water heaters, collect rainwater, make use of solar panels for energy, employ locals to build and make furniture, and recycle. Food is mostly homegrown and organic.

Turks & Caicos

Green Bean (p817) A cafe in Providenciales setting a great example for the region. It uses organic produce, compostable packaging and, where possible, locally sourced ingredients.

US Virgin Islands

The USVI has several extra-green campgrounds.

Virgin Islands Campground (p843) Self-contained 'tent-cottages' on Water Island.

Maho Bay Camps (p850) Popular tent-cabins with adjoining ecofriendly condos. To conserve water, guests use low-flush toilets and solar-heated showers.

Mt Victory Campground (p859) Located on a small working farm, this campground uses no electricity; guests share the solar-heated bathhouse .

Northside Valley (p859) Eight villas with ocean views; green initiatives include the use of ecofriendly cleaning supplies.

Travel with Children

Children's Highlights

Here are some of the activities kids can look forward to on their best islands for families:

Exciting Critters

Stingrays you can pet on Antigua and Grand Cayman, and a lot more.

Fun Beaches

Build sand castles, learn to surf, frolic in the water or simply run around until you can't any longer – the region's beaches are an unlimited playground.

Amazing Adventures

Learn to sail, surf, dive and more at resorts before zip-lining through the rainforest.

Pirates!

Almost every island has pirate stories.

Taking the kids on their first-ever boat ride, building sand castles, wandering rainforest trails or meeting local children – it's simple adventures like these that make the Caribbean such a great region for families.

Caribbean Islands for Kids

The Caribbean isn't just a huge playground for adults, it's one for kids too. Like any playground some parts are more fun than others. Islands dedicated to adult pursuits, like diving or hiking, might leave little ones out of the action, but plenty more islands have myriad activities for children. Islands with large beach resorts may seem positively designed for kids – at least to the younger mind.

Planning
Where to Stay

Resorts offer scores of kid-friendly amenities, but some families prefer staying in simpler places closer to island life. Before booking any lodging, ask for details to assess its appropriateness. For example:

» Does it welcome kids or accept them grudgingly?

» If it's a resort, what sort of kids activities does it offer?

» Does the room have a DVD player and wi-fi?

» Is there a kitchen or at least a refrigerator, so you can avoid the expense of always eating out?

» Are there safe places where kids can play?

BEST ISLANDS FOR KIDS

The following islands all offer something for children. Kids will never want to leave islands rated ✓✓✓, while those rated ✓✓ have some interesting diversions. See individual chapters for full details and also look out for the 🌟symbol, indicating family-friendly facilities are available.

Antigua & Barbuda	✓✓	Good beaches for playing plus several fun activities: Antigua Rainforest Canopy Tour (p116), Stingray City Antigua (p120).
Aruba	✓✓✓	Large resorts with kids' activities, excellent beaches, mostly calm seas and lots of adventure activities, including water sports.
The Bahamas	✓✓✓	Grand Bahama is clean, easy to get around and affordable, Nassau has family attractions galore and Paradise Island has waterslides and walk-through shark tanks – it's tops!
Barbados	✓✓	Lots of family-friendly beaches in the south and west, and popular kids' surfing lessons, but few large resorts with kids programs.
Bonaire	✓✓	Good for older kids who want to learn how to dive and wind-surf, but limited beaches.
British Virgin Islands	✓✓	Many islands have no special kiddie allure but at the Bitter End Yacht Club & Resort (p252), on Virgin Gorda, youngsters learn to sail, windsurf, kayak and more.
Cayman Islands	✓✓✓	Seven Mile Beach is great for families. Large resorts have kids programs, the water is calm, businesses sell ice cream and other treats, and the turtle farm is a huge hit, as is Stingray City (p274).
Dominican Republic	✓✓	The resorts of Punta Cana and Bávaro cater to kids, who can make friends with other young holiday-makers from around the world.
Jamaica	✓✓	Montego Bay and Ocho Rios have resorts good for families, but some resorts are aimed at partying, adults-only – avoid proximity.
Puerto Rico	✓✓✓	Old San Juan has resorts nearby that are good for kids. Top attractions include the Museo del Niño (p605), amazing forts with pirate history and the Arecibo Observatory (p616). Playa Flamenco in Culebra is one of the world's best beaches and has lifeguards.
St Lucia	✓✓	Many resorts cater to families, plus there are lots of kid-friendly activities, such as zip-lining, hiking and horseback riding.
St-Martin/Sint Maarten	✓✓	Popular beaches and resorts, with lots of water sports for the kids.
US Virgin Islands	✓✓✓	One of the best destinations for kids. Highlights are abundant and include resort fun, tourist towns with child-friendly allure on all three islands, lifeguard-patrolled Magens Bay beach (p840), and Maho Bay's sea turtles (p850).

» Even if the beach is nearby, is it across a heavily trafficked street?

» Does it provide cribs, change tables and other baby supplies?

» Does they offer on-site babysitting?

Keeping Safe

To help kids acclimatize to the Caribbean heat, take it easy at first and make sure they drink plenty of water. Children should wear a high-protection sunscreen and cover up whenever they're outside to avoid sunburn and heatstroke.

Bring insect repellent formulated for children and whatever medication you normally use to treat insect bites.

What to Pack

Be prepared for lots of time in the sun and sea. Most lodgings provide beach towels, chairs and umbrellas. You can buy sand pails, snorkel masks and anything else you forget at beach shops in resort areas. Elsewhere you'll need to bring what you want in the diversions department.

☐ Sun protection (sunscreen, hats, sunglasses, long-sleeved shirts)

☐ Insect repellent

☐ Snorkel gear (especially masks) that you've tested for leaks and proper fit

☐ Water wings and other flotation devices

☐ Pails and shovels

☐ Sturdy reef shoes

☐ Flip-flops

☐ Underwater camera

☐ Car seat if driving a lot

islands at a glance

Part of the Caribbean's allure is its diversity. Sure, you'll find great climate and fab beaches across the region, but there are plenty of local characteristics that set each island apart from the next – you can zero in on the islands that best suit you. Whether your interests are history, music, food or diving, there are islands that will meet your travel needs. If your idea of pleasure is a night dancing to local rhythms, or simply taking time to smell the flowers, you can find that here too.

Anguilla

Beaches ✓✓✓
Food ✓
Water Sports ✓

This scrubby limestone bump may not be as visually striking as its neighbors, but Anguilla's ethereal beaches make up for it. Neon-blue waves crash against powder-white shores where you'll find locals barbecuing succulent local fare.
p90

Antigua & Barbuda

Beaches ✓✓✓
History ✓✓
Activities ✓✓

Antigua is the place to frolic on the beach, play golf, indulge in a fancy meal or explore Britain's naval history, whereas Barbuda, with its pearly-white beaches, is a remote, unspoiled place where winged creatures outnumber people.
p105

Aruba

Resorts ✓✓
Beaches ✓✓✓
Party ✓✓

Choose from beachside resorts great and small, from flashy to funky, from high-rise to low-rise. Hit the beaches by day, then hit bars, restaurants and clubs, as you would at home if it was warmer.
p130

The Bahamas

Diving ✓✓✓
Beaches ✓✓✓
Fishing ✓✓✓

This watery wonderland, with its 700 islands, hundreds of miles of white sand and innumerable hidden coves, is paradise for beach bums, history buffs, diving enthusiasts, sailors, anglers and, well, pretty much everybody else.
p146

Barbados

Water Sports ✓✓✓
Resorts ✓✓
Nature ✓✓

From surfing the waves to windsurfing the shallows to snorkeling the reefs, you may never dry off. But if you do, this genteel island's verdant interior might lure you for a tropical hike.
p196

Bonaire

Diving ✓✓✓
Nightlife ✓
History ✓✓

Take a look at Bonaire's easily explored history during the day and after dark join Kralendijk's small, but surprisingly fun, bar scene. Or visit some of the world's best dive spots – right off shore.
p224

British Virgin Islands

Sailing ✓✓✓
Islands ✓✓
Beaches ✓✓

Tortola lets its hair down with sailing, surfing and full-moon parties, while Virgin Gorda offers boulder-studded beaches and billionaire yacht havens. Jost Van Dyke is the 'barefoot island,' where Main St is a hammock-lined beach.
p236

Cayman Islands

Beach ✓✓✓
Water Sports ✓✓✓
Islands ✓

'Seven Mile Beach' says it all. People return year after year to this sandy, civilized strip. You don't party on Grand Cayman but you do see remarkable underwater sights. Escape everything at fab Little Cayman.
p265

Cuba

Music ✓✓✓
Architecture ✓✓
Beaches ✓✓

Cuba's musical prowess is no secret – the whole archipelago rocks to an eclectic pot of live sounds – and the nation's 50-year political time warp has unwittingly led to benefits such as well-preserved architecture and unblemished beaches.
p291

Curaçao

History ✓✓✓
Nightlife ✓✓
Beaches ✓

The Dutch colonial legacy is hundreds of beautiful old buildings in Willemstad neighborhoods dripping with character. Join the raucous music culture that practices for Carnival year-round or explore the coast and discover a hidden beach.
p351

Dominica

Nature ✓✓✓
Adventure ✓✓✓
Hiking ✓✓✓

With thundering waterfalls, a boiling lake, bushy jungle, hot sulfur springs, secret swimming holes, sprightly rivers, teeming reefs and dramatic coastline, this untamed and mass-tourism-free 'nature island' promises unusual experiences and adventures.
p381

Dominican Republic

History ✓✓✓
Beaches ✓✓✓
Outdoor Adventure ✓✓✓

The country's coastline – a mix of postcard-perfect beaches and isolated coves – offers windswept conditions for water sports. Roaring rivers and mountain peaks draw active travelers, while Santo Domingo's Zona Colonial transports you back in time.
p406

Grenada

Beaches ✓✓✓
Island Hopping ✓✓✓
Diving & Snorkeling ✓✓

White sand, turquoise sea, palm trees and no crowds make Grenada's beaches truly sublime. And if the mainland's too much fun, island hop to Carriacou and Petit Martinique, or dive into the underwater sculpture park.
p449

Guadeloupe

Hiking ✓✓✓
Islands ✓✓
Diving ✓

Guadeloupe offers world-class hiking in Basse-Terre, superb beaches with some of the Caribbean's best diving on Grande-Terre, and a selection of remote and virtually pristine islands perfect for the ultimate getaway.
p474

Haiti

History ✓✓
Art ✓✓
Resilience ✓✓✓

Home to the world's only successful slave revolution, Haiti continues to struggle with uncertainty, not least the aftermath of the January 12, 2010, earthquake. But reconstruction continues apace, and the country and its artistic culture are again ready to be experienced.
p507

Jamaica

Music ✓✓✓
Food ✓✓✓
Outdoors ✓✓

Jamaica and music are inseparable concepts, while the concept of finding a spice rub more delicious than true Jamaican Jerk is pure madness. Raft Black River and the Martha Brae to find Jamaica's jungly interior.
p526

Martinique

Beaches ✓✓
Hiking ✓✓
Flowers ✓

Southern Martinique has great beaches, friendly fishing villages and lots of activities to keep you busy, while the north, with its mountains and botanical gardens, is perfect for hikers and nature lovers.
p567

Montserrat

Novelty ✓✓✓
Nature ✓✓
Wildlife ✓

Stand in awe of nature's destructive power when surveying the damage done by the mean-but-majestic Soufrière Hills Volcano, the key attraction of this tranquil and charming island. Exhilarating diving, bird-watching and nature walks also beckon.
p593

Puerto Rico

Nightlife ✓✓✓
History ✓✓✓
Nature ✓✓

Atop the ramparts of El Morro, visitors look over the cobblestone labyrinth of Old San Juan and the Atlantic's endless sparkle. Soak up sunshine and hike the rainforest before grooving to libidinous late-night rhythms.
p601

Saba

Diving ✓✓✓
Hiking ✓✓✓
Crafts ✓

Dive deep to cavort with sharks in the colorful playground of reefs that encircles Saba's skyscraping volcano. On land, wander through six unique ecosystems that wind up the jagged granite spire.
p633

Sint Eustatius

Diving ✓✓
Hiking ✓✓
History ✓✓✓

Crowned by a lonely volcano, this forgotten islet was once a hub of activity as goods were passed between Old and New Worlds. Signs of former greatness dot the landscape amid quaint clapboard shacks.
p646

St-Barthélemy

Beaches ✓✓✓
Food ✓✓✓
Water Sports ✓✓

A brilliant tapestry of arid, cactus-clad cliffs and ebbing azure waters sets the scene on this idyllic isle, which lures celebrities and other discerning travelers with top-notch fusion cuisine and acres of silky sand.
p658

St Kitts & Nevis

History ✓✓
Party ✓✓
Beaches ✓✓

Wander in the footsteps of Nelson, Hamilton and African slaves while exploring these verdant twin islands, which are dotted with romantic sugar-plantation inns, ringed by beautiful beaches and lorded over by a cloud-fringed (dormant) volcano.
p672

St Lucia

Outdoors ✓✓✓
Village Life ✓✓
Beaches ✓

Take an enticing coastline, add rainforest and mountains, then sprinkle in attractive coastal towns. Next, pepper this island with history and culture, spike it with an array of outdoor activities, and there you have St Lucia.
p696

St-Martin/Sint Maarten

Beaches ✓✓
Food ✓✓
Nightlife ✓✓

A bit of everything yet nothing in moderation, St-Martin/Sint Maarten is a kaleidoscope of Caribbean clichés: postcard-worthy beaches, savory local restaurants and roaring bars that spill over every crevice – even right up to the airport's runway.
p718

St Vincent & the Grenadines

Islands ✓✓✓
Adventure ✓✓✓
Beauty ✓✓

Hike the impossibly green jungles of St Vincent and then set off by slow boat to the beautiful beach-ringed islands of the Grenadines, starting with perfect little Bequia. Take time to explore wonders underwater.
p736

Trinidad & Tobago

Music & Nightlife ✓✓✓
Bird-watching ✓✓
Hiking ✓✓

Trinidad and Tobago's party mentality leaks into every walk of life, and there's tip-top bird-watching, too. Trinidad's wild Northern Range and Tobago's ancient protected rainforest are laced with trails and swimmable waterfalls.
p761

Turks & Caicos

Diving ✓✓✓
Beaches ✓✓✓
Wildlife ✓✓

With some of the whitest beaches, the clearest waters and the most varied marine life in the Caribbean, Turks and Caicos will thrill anyone who likes to spend time in or by the water.
p808

US Virgin Islands

Food ✓✓
Parks ✓✓✓
Diving ✓✓

St Thomas sets the table with fungi, callaloo (spicy soup) and West Indian fare. St John goes green with hiking, snorkeling and ecocamping in VI National Park. St Croix offers divers the 'wall' and drinkers the rum factory.
p833

Look out for these icons:

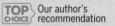 **TOP CHOICE** Our author's recommendation

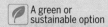 A green or sustainable option

FREE No payment required

See the Index for a full list of destinations covered in this book.

On the Road

Anguilla

Includes »

Best Beaches

» Shoal Bay East (p99)

» Meads Bay (p96)

» Junk's Hole (p100)

Best Places to Stay

» Lloyd's (p93)

» Ambia (p95)

» La Vue (p95)

Why Go?

Something old, something new, something borrowed, something blue – wedding bells immediately come to mind, but what about Anguilla? As rabid consumerism devours many Caribbean hot spots, this little limestone bump in the sea has, thus far, maintained its charming menagerie of clapboard shacks (something old) while quietly weaving stunning vacation properties (something new) into the mix. Visitors will discover a melting pot of cultures (something borrowed) set along mind-blowing beaches (something very, very blue).

Anguilla is, however, not the place for a vacation 'on a shoestring' – authenticity comes at a premium here. Although the island has garnered somewhat of a reputation as St-Barth's stunt-double, it really is anything but. Anguilla flaunts its down-to-earth charms to the jetset subset who crave a vacation off the radar.

When to Go

From late December to early January, Anguilla is a veritable star safari that gives St-Barth a run for its money. In March the holiday rush finally starts to die down – brilliant beaches are yours for the taking. From July to August prices drop to reasonable levels – capitalize on breezy weather before the humidity kicks in. The lightest rainfall is generally from February to April and the heaviest from October to December. Inflated high-season rates start around mid-December and go until mid-April. Many hotels shut down for the entire month of September and often October as well.

Itineraries

ONE DAY

After arriving either at the airport or the ferry pier, rent a car and head to the Valley for an early lunch at one of the local BBQ tents. Continue east and spend the afternoon basking in the turquoise waters at Shoal Bay East, and then, depending on your mood, finish the day with a romantic dinner along Meads Bay, or hit the quaint bar scene in Sandy Ground.

THREE DAYS

Grab a hotel room along Shoal Bay East or in the west end (penny-pinchers should try the Valley) and spend your days slowly making your way across the island while sampling finger-licking Anguillan cuisine and testing out some of the world's best beaches.

ONE WEEK

Try out a villa rental rather than a hotel room for the utmost in privacy. Divide your time between doing absolutely nothing and taste-testing the flavorful local cuisine. Spend a sun-soaked day at Prickly Pear, and do a day trip to St-Martin/Sint Maarten to remind yourself why quiet Anguilla is tops for relaxation.

GETTING TO NEIGHBORING ISLANDS

A short boat ride connects Anguilla to St-Martin/Sint Maarten from where you can take a flight to a handful of island destinations. Direct connections to a few islands – such as Antigua – are possible from Anguilla's airport.

Essential Food & Drink

» **Lobster & crayfish** Lobster (common spiny lobster sans claws, like the ones in New England) and crayfish are two of Anguilla's locally caught specialties. Crayfish, while smaller than lobsters, are reasonably sized creatures that have sweet, tender meat, and are commonly served three to an order.

» **BBQ tents** Popular weekend tents serving smoky ribs spring up on the side of the road.

» **Homegrown veggies** Keep an eye out on the side of the road for streetside vendors selling organic, locally grown produce.

AT A GLANCE

» **Currency** Eastern Caribbean dollar (EC$); US dollar commonly used

» **Language** English

» **Money** ATMs dispense local and US dollars

» **Visas** Not necessary for most nationalities; see p103

Fast Facts

» **Area** 35 sq miles
» **Population** 14,750
» **Capital** The Valley
» **Telephone country code** ☑264
» **Emergency** ☑911

Set Your Budget

» **Budget hotel room** US$130

» **Two-course evening meal** US$60

» **Rental of two beach chairs and an umbrella** US$10

» **Beer** US$4

» **Daily car rental** US$50

Resources

» **AHTA** (www.ahta.ai) Hotel and Tourism Association

» **Anguilla Guide** (www.anguillaguide.com) Accommodations, events, forums

» **Anguilla Vacation** (www.anguilla-vacation.com) Anguilla Tourist Board website

Anguilla Highlights

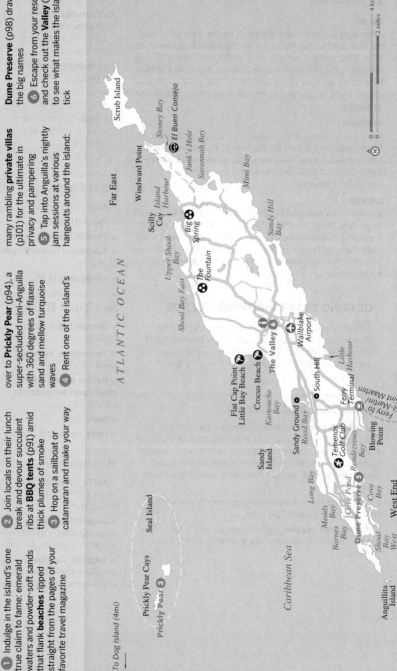

1 Indulge in the island's one true claim to fame: emerald waters and powder-soft sands that flank **beaches** ripped straight from the pages of your favorite travel magazine

2 Join locals on their lunch break and devour succulent ribs at **BBQ tents** (p91) amid thick plumes of smoke

over to **Prickly Pear** (p94), a super-secluded mini-Anguilla with 360 degrees of flaxen sand and mellow turquoise waves

4 Rent one of the island's

many rambling **private villas** (p101) for the ultimate in privacy and pampering

5 Tap into Anguilla's nightly jam sessions at various hangouts around the island:

6 Escape from your resort and check out the **Valley** (p93) to see what makes the island tick

Dune Preserve (p98) draws in the big names

CENTRAL ANGUILLA

Central Anguilla is devoted to function more than luxury. Here you will find the Valley (the island's capital) and Anguilla's airport.

The Valley

Although no part of Anguilla feels particularly urban, the Valley has the island's conglomeration of government buildings, which gives it a more conspicuous village vibe. The area was chosen as the colonial capital largely because of the abundance of arable soil; the island is mostly a limestone formation and thus there are only tiny pockets of viable land for farming. The main post office and most banks are located here, as are several large supermarkets.

◉ Sights

Wallblake House   HISTORIC BUILDING
(☑497-2944; ⊘tours 10am-2pm Mon, Wed & Fri) The Valley's most interesting building is Wallblake House. Built in 1787, it's the oldest structure on Anguilla and the only remaining plantation house on the island. Get a double dose of Caribbean history and check out the interior of the adjacent **St Gerard's church**, which has a unique design incorporating a decorative stone front, open-air side walls and a ceiling shaped like the hull of a ship.

National Trust of Anguilla   NOTABLE BUILDING
(☑497-5297; www.axanationaltrust.org; ⊘8am-4pm Mon-Fri) Swing by the National Trust of Anguilla and sign up for one of its heritage tours (free). There's not much in the way of preserved local history, but it's a good way to get under the skin of the island. It's best to book your tour 24 hours in advance and expect an 8am departure time.

⮡ Sleeping

All accommodations in the Valley are located in the northwest part of town toward Crocus Bay. Prices here are reasonable compared with the rest of the island because of its inland location.

TOP CHOICE Lloyd's   B&B $
(☑497-2351; www.lloyds.ai; Crocus Hill; s/d incl breakfast & tax US$99/135; ❊@☏) Freshly renovated Lloyd's is hands down the best bang for your buck on Anguilla. This lovely plantation-style B&B is slathered in bright yellows and accented by lime green clapboard shutters. Rooms are on the small side and have a palpable farmhouse quality, but that's all part of the charm. There are no ocean views, but the elevated terrain offers glimpses of the intriguing architectural jumble in the Valley.

✕ Eating

If you're thinking about picking up groceries, the Valley has the largest selection at the lowest prices. All groceries are priced in EC dollars but US dollars are accepted everywhere. Try **JW Proctor** (jwproctors@anguilla net.com; The Quarter; ⊘8am-8:30pm Mon-Fri, to 9:30pm Sat) or **Albert Lakes Marketplace** (Stoney Ground; ⊘8am-8pm Mon-Fri, to 9pm Sat), which also has a great little hut in the parking lot called **Fat Cat** (☑497-2307; mains US$5-10; ⊘lunch & dinner), specializing in takeaway meals of various shapes and sizes. Call ahead for a picnic lunch prepared in a handy hamper. Fresh produce imported from St Lucia and Dominica is also available at the People's Market, a small green stall opposite the Anglican Church.

Hungry's   FOOD TRUCK $$
(The Valley Rd; mains US$5-20; ⊘lunch & dinner Mon-Sat) Opposite the post office under a large almond tree, this popular operation serves up hearty island faves from a colorful truck covered in Caribbean stencil art. Irad and Papy, the owners/chefs, cater to long lines of working locals who stop through on their lunch break to grab a bowl of delectable conch soup or unique lobster quesadillas.

Ken's   BBQ $
(mains US$8; ⊘lunch & dinner Fri & Sat) Every weekend, Ken's clan of spit-wielding cooks set up shop beside English Rose, near the corner of Carter Rey Blvd and Landsome Rd. Great puffs of smoke and steam billow out from underneath the large white tent as hungry customers gingerly smack their lips with anticipation. The juicy ribs are turned out by the dozen, and the do-it-yourself sauce bucket allows you to drench your platter with an unlimited amount of sweet barbecue goodness. Grab a flaky johnnycake and browse the collection of DVDs of dubious authenticity.

English Rose   ANGUILLAN $
(Carter Rey Blvd; mains US$8-15; ⊘lunch & dinner Mon-Sat) Lunches are served cafeteria-style

PRICKLY PEAR

Lonely Prickly Pear sits off the coast of Anguilla just far enough to feel like a tiny colony in its own right. This windswept limestone bump above the waves features nothing but creamy beige sand ambushed by curls of rolling turquoise waves.

Prickly Pear has excellent snorkeling conditions. Tour boats leave Sandy Ground for Prickly Pear at around 10am, returning around 4pm; the cost averages US$80, including lunch, drinks and snorkeling gear.

The island is easily accessible by catamaran or sailboat on a day-trip tour from either Anguilla or St-Martin/Sint Maarten.

as locals line up to choose between savory goat stew, jerk chicken, and a selection of delectable side dishes such as garlic pasta and creamy mashed potatoes. Make sure to get here on the early side – only one round of food is made for the day, and once it's gone, it closes until dinnertime. In the evenings, this casual spot retains its local vibe; small groups hunker down to watch the cricket match as the background thrums with island gossip and belly laughter.

Da'Vida FUSION **$$$**
(☎498-5433; www.davidaanguilla.com; Crocus Bay; mains US$25-42; ⊙lunch & dinner Mon-Sat) A lofty enterprise engulfing the shores of Crocus Bay, Da'Vida is a shiny new establishment that feels noticeably out of place sitting next to slightly ramshackle cottages and a desalination plant. Nonetheless, the beachside restaurant and lounge offers a flash of class for those seeking a slice of jetsetterdom. It's more about the seaside location and setting sun than topnotch cuisine, and customers don't seem to mind. During the day, beach bums can snag lunch from the faux-shabby snack shack next door.

Koal Keel CREOLE **$$$**
(☎497-2930; Coronation Ave, Crocus Hill; mains US$24-30; ⊙hrs vary) Housed in the original warden's quarters (one of the oldest structures on the island), the Valley's most romantic spot serves fusion Caribbean fare on crisp white tablecloths. You'll have to place your order 24 hours in advance for Koal Keel's specialty: 'rock oven chicken.' The in-house patisserie adds a certain French twist to the otherwise upscale West Indian atmosphere. Stop by on weekend evenings for some local live music.

ℹ Information

Anguilla Tourist Board (☎497-2759, in USA 800-553-4939; www.anguilla-vacation.com; Coronation Ave, The Valley)

Caribbean Commercial Bank (CCB; www.ccb.ai)

First Caribbean International Bank (www.firstcaribbeanbank.com)

National Bank of Anguilla (NBA; www.nba.ai; The Valley)

Post office (www.gov.ai/angstamp; The Valley Rd; ⊙8am-3:30pm Mon-Thu, to 5pm Fri) Near Hungry's food truck.

Princess Alexandra Hospital (☎497-2551; The Valley Rd) In the north end of town.

Public library (Albert Lake Dr, The Valley; per 30min EC$5; ⊙9am-5pm Mon-Fri, to noon Sat) Has internet access and a book swap.

Scotiabank Anguilla (bns.anguilla@scotiabank.com; The Valley)

Sandy Ground

Although Sandy Ground isn't tops for ocean vistas, it's a worthy sleeping spot for those who only want to be a short stumble away from Anguilla's 'bar scene' (and we use that term loosely – true partiers should head one island over to St-Martin/Sint Maarten). The quaint cluster of bars and restaurants sits between the impossibly clear waters of Road Bay and a murky salt pond out back, which was commercially harvested until the 1970s, when it became economically unfeasible.

🏊 Activities

Special 'D' Diving DIVING
(☎235-8438; www.dougcarty.com) Friendly divemaster Dougie can practically call each fish, shark and turtle by name. And they'll come. He doesn't have an office, so it's best to book ahead by phone or email. Boat tours are also on offer.

🛏 Sleeping

Sandy Ground has a few options on the cheaper side of the spectrum; those searching for a true beach holiday should look elsewhere.

Ambia
B&B **$$**

(✆498-8686, in USA 203-699-8686; www.ambia
-anguilla.com; South Hill; r/ste US$350/450;
❄@🌐🏊) Perched on the side of a scrubby
hill, Ambia's unassuming facade opens onto
a large Zen space flanked by smooth wooden
balusters and bursts of bamboo. The rooms
incorporate Asian stylistic elements (namely
minimalism), and offer views of the distant
moorings on Road Bay.

La Vue
HOTEL **$$**

(✆497-6623; www.lavueanguilla.com; Back St,
South Hill; ste incl breakfast US$165-265; ❄@🌐🏊)
Finding its groove at the budget-friendly
side of Anguilla's overpriced accommodation spectrum, La Vue's two-dozen rooms
are a great place to call home during your
Caribbean foray. Rooms come with unmem-
orable catalog-ordered furnishings, but who
can complain when the staff is uberfriendly
and the price tag is a solid US$150 lower
than comparable options on the island. Try
for a room with a *vue* – the vistas of Sandy
Ground down below are dream-inducing.

Sea View Guest House
GUESTHOUSE **$**

(✆497-2427; www.inns.ai/seaview; Sandy Ground
Rd; 1-/2-bedroom apt US$65/130; ❄) Across
from the beach, these apartments are outfitted for a longer stay, with full kitchens
and maid service every other day. You'll be
downstairs from a local Anguillan family
who can help arrange diving and sightseeing adventures.

Syd-An's Apartments & Villas
GUESTHOUSE **$**

(✆497-3180; www.inns.ai/sydans; Sandy Ground
Rd; r US$75-95; ❄@) On Sandy Ground's main
strip, across from the beach, Syd-An's has 14
ramshackle apartments with separate bedrooms, full kitchens and cable TV, situated
around a convivial courtyard. Rooms with
air-con cost a tad more.

✖ Eating & Drinking

The undisputed top spot on Anguilla to get
your drink on, Sandy Ground is chockablock
with pub-style hangouts. On any given night
of the week at least one establishment offers
up an enticing deal, whether it's live music,
discount dinners, or two-for-one happy hours.

SANDY GROUND ROAD

SandBar
TAPAS **$$**

(sandbar.anguilla@gmail.com; tapas US$10; ☉din-
ner Tue-Sat) The newest hit in town, SandBar
serves up perfected cocktails and scrump-
tious tapas treats at affordable prices. The

owner, Denise, was the executive chef at the
glitzy CuisinArt resort, and she brings her
culinary savviness to the table at this ca-
sual seaside hangout. Her husband, Joash,
sets the mood as the charismatic host and
encourages patrons to loiter on the comfy
couches and chairs for hours while sampling
snacks from around the globe.

Bonjour Café
CAFE **$**

(mains US$5-17; ☉breakfast & lunch; 🌐🍴) A self-
titled 'cottage in the woods,' Bonjour is a
friendly spot cradled under a generous gath-
ering of shade-bearing trees. Grab a curling
paperback off the wall and tuck into your
home-cooked meal, be it islands fare (the
owner is from Trinidad) or French-inspired
nibbles. Service can be a bit slow, but pa-
trons rarely mind.

Pumphouse
INTERNATIONAL **$$**

(✆497-5154; mains US$13-37; ☉dinner; 🌐) At the
far end of Sandy Ground, this former salt-
works plant is now one of Anguilla's most
chilled-out spots. The food is traditional pub
grub with an international twist (such as Ko-
rean quesadillas). Everyone gathers around
on Thursday night for cheap drinks and live
music.

Johnno's
INTERNATIONAL **$$**

(meals US$7-16; ☉noon-midnight Tue-Sun) No
shirt and no shoes will still get you service at
this happening beach shack. Johnno's offers
casual fare and tropical drinks to a blend of
locals and travelers. Happy hours are from
5pm to 7pm, and there's live jazz on Sunday
afternoons. Try the second location out on
Prickly Pear island.

Veya
FUSION **$$$**

(✆498-8392; www.veya-axa.com; mains US$28-
48; ☉dinner Mon-Sat) 'Cuisine of the sun' is
the name of the game at this fusion favorite
nested within the inland trees near Sandy
Ground's stretch of beachside bars. Ingredients have been sourced from the earth's diverse equatorial regions to create a medley of
flavorful dishes. Although there are no ocean
views, Veya is nonetheless a smash hit –
especially for big-portion-seeking North
Americans. Downstairs during the day,
Veya's former sous-chef runs an informal
canteen, **Café at Veya**, that serves up tasty
panini and fresh salads for under US$12.

Ripples
INTERNATIONAL **$$**

(mains US$15-25; ☉lunch & dinner; 🌐) The hip
and happening spot for locals and travelers

alike, Ripples serves staples such as burgers and salads, but also Caribbean fusion dishes such as Cajun fish with pineapple and lime salsa. It's open till midnight.

Roy's Bayside Grill INTERNATIONAL $$$
(mains US$18-38; ☺lunch & dinner; 🐾) On the south end of Sandy Ground, Roy's feels a bit like a British pub along the beach. The conch chowder is a must, but the pièce de résistance is the battered fish and chips. Stop by for Friday-night happy hour (times vary) and take advantage of the discounted meals and drinks.

Elvis' Beach Bar BAR $
(drinks from US$3) Affable Elvis, with his PhD in mixology, stirs up some serious island ale that'll make your lips pucker. His clique of loyal local patrons sits along log benches and bar stools around the colorful bar – a beached wooden ship.

SOUTH HILL
The following restaurants are located up the hill from Sandy Ground, along the main road connecting the Valley to the western end of the island.

Geraud's FRENCH $
(www.anguillacakesandcatering.com; South Hill Plaza; mains US$5-12; ☺breakfast & lunch Tue-Sun) At the far west end of South Hill, just before entering the west end of the island, this quaint *boulangerie* bounces in the wee hours of the morning as the French chef hustles to bake the daily bread. Fun fact: he used to work for Castro! By 2pm everything's been devoured, including the tasty smoked-salmon sandwiches and quiche lorraine.

Tasty's ANGUILLAN $$$
(☎497-2737; mains US$18-33; ☺breakfast, lunch & dinner Fri-Wed) A tad less expensive than the other island favorites of the same caliber, Tasty's offers creatively fused dishes, such as grilled tuna steak with orange Creole sauce or coconut-crusted fish fillet with spicy banana rum sauce. The bright teal and purple walls are smothered in shells and kitschy tropical paraphernalia.

E's Oven ANGUILLAN $$
(☎498-8258; mains US$10-29; ☺lunch & dinner Wed-Mon) E's earns top marks across the board for great local food and competitive prices. Try the sweet-potato-and-lobster pancake, the chef's signature appetizer. Choosing the main course is a real nail-biter –

should it be the Creole conch or grilled crayfish? Either way you can't go wrong.

Blowing Point

If you're coming to Anguilla by ferry, Blowing Point will be the first community you encounter. Centered on the tiny pier, this little village consists of a small grocery, several parking lots full of rental cars and one quiet place to stay.

A quick walk from the ferry pier, the seven apartment-style suites at the **Ferryboat Inn** (☎497-6613; www.ferryboatinn.ai; ste from US$185; 🌀🐾) offer stellar views of the jagged volcanic peaks of St-Martin/Sint Maarten nearby. The in-house restaurant with the same name spins delicious island cuisine.

If you're in the neighborhood and looking for some beach reading fodder, follow the clearly marked signs out to the adorable **Coral Reef Bookstore** (Little Harbour; ☺8am-5pm Mon-Fri, 9am-4pm Sat), where you'll find a surprisingly diverse and up-to-date selection of reads, from children's books to sci-fi.

WESTERN ANGUILLA

As the island snakes in a westerly direction, lavish resorts unfurl along thick stretches of sand.

Meads Bay

Beautiful Meads Bay has a fat beach with thick dunelike sand. A row of resorts straddles the sea, although it feels significantly less crowded than Shoal Bay East.

The Dutch-run **Anguillian Divers** (☎235-7742, 497-4750; www.anguilliandivers.com; Meads Bay) center operates on the west end of the island.

🛏 Sleeping

Anacaona HOTEL $$
(☎497-6827; http://anacaonahotel.com; r from US$250; 🌀@🐾🏊) Everyone fumbles over the name – even the locals (Anaconda?) – all you need to know is this: it's pretty much as good as it gets on Anguilla for less than US$300. Fresh coats of paint and a smattering of new features have spruced up this inland treasure, and although you won't get ocean views, you have direct access to

the sand and two inviting pools at your disposal. During the summer months, prices are slashed in half depending on the type of room.

Frangipani
HOTEL $$

(☏497-6442, in USA 866-780-5165; www.frangipaniresort.com; r US$395-545, ste US$695-1675; ❋🕾) This rambling Italian villa sits along a splendid stretch of perfect powdery sand that is punctuated with charming thatched umbrellas. Although decidedly Mediterranean in style, Frangipani incorporates a dash of Caribbean flair noticeable in the vibrant floral-print bedspreads and hanging watercolors. Cheaper rooms face the gravel parking lot, while the large suites offer sweeping views of the sea and come with brand-spankin'-new kitchens. A small continental breakfast is included in the price.

Viceroy
LUXURY HOTEL $$$

(☏497-7000; www.viceroyhotelsandresorts.com/anguilla; ste from US$895; ❋@🕾🏊) The mega-resort mothership represents a new era in Anguillan accommodation with its sprawling campus of sleek, marble-studded apartment blocks and long, arcade-like paths that cut through the resort. There are moments of impressive beauty – such as the serene views from the restaurant and spa – but overall Viceroy is a victim of an inflated design budget and subsequently overworked decor.

Malliouhana
LUXURY HOTEL $$$

(☏497-6111, in USA 800-835-0796; www.malliouhana.com; r from US$860; ❋@🕾🏊) On a low cliff at the east end of Meads Bay, Malliouhana is one of the island's most fashionable luxury hotels. The rooms are gracefully appointed with Italian tile floors, marble baths, rattan furnishings, original artwork and large patios. Just strolling through the 25 acres of Mediterranean-style architecture and gardens will instill instant relaxation, and that's before you stroll to one of three adjacent beaches or get a massage at the top-notch spa.

Carimar Beach Club
HOTEL $$

(☏497-6881, in USA 800-235-8667; www.carimar.com; 1-/2-bedroom ste from US$425/565; ❋🕾) Each bougainvillea-draped Spanish-style apartment is equipped with a kitchen, living and dining rooms, and a balcony or patio. Ask the lovely staff about discounted low-season rates and special honeymoon packages.

✖ Eating

Almost every hotel along Meads Bay has a decent restaurant offering upscale fare and ocean views.

B & D's
BBQ $

(Long Bay; ribs US$7; ⊙lunch & dinner Fri & Sat) Just around the corner from the majestic Malliouhana, this tented BBQ shack gets rave reviews from locals and tourists alike; vacationing celebs have been known to stop here for some down-to-earth cookin'. Stock up on smoky barbecued perfection and don't forget to top off your ribs with the bread pudding and rum sauce. The hours tend to fluctuate – sometimes it's also open on Thursday evenings and Sunday afternoons.

Straw Hat
CARIBBEAN $$$

(☏497-8300; www.strawhat.com; mains US$28-33; ⊙breakfast, lunch & dinner) With its new seaside location at the Frangipani hotel, Straw Hat now offers a feet-in-the-sand atmosphere to accompany its gut-busting platters of honest-to-goodness Caribbean cooking. Listen to the tide roll in while dipping your hands into the straw hats full of yummy baked bread.

West End

Anguilla's rugged west end is largely the domain of wealthy vacationers who drop a thousand dollars per night on luxurious, butler-serviced suites.

◉ Sights & Activities

Temenos Golf Course
GOLF

(☏222-8200; www.temenosgolfclub.com; green fee US$400) Stop by the Temenos Golf Club, an 18-hole, 7100yd course designed by Greg Norman, to witness the fastest way in the world to drop a cool US$400 on a round of golf. The upside to playing at Temenos? You'll probably be the only one on the course.

Cheddie's Carving Studio
WOOD CARVINGS

(The Cove) Master wood-carver Cheddie displays his inspired pieces of art at his studio along the West End's main drag near the turnoff to Meads Bay. Stop by to witness the magical transformation as pieces of forgotten driftwood are turned into striking sculptures with uncanny precision.

🏖 Beaches

The pearly-white sand at **Rendezvous Bay** beckons one to stroll its full 1.5-mile length. **Cove Bay** is next to Rendezvous Bay, within easy walking distance. **Seaside Stables** (☎235-3667; www.seaside-stables.com) is located here, offering horseback rides along the beach. Further along, **Shoal Bay West** isn't as stunning as its eastern namesake, but it has fabulous snorkeling and a few nearby dive sites.

🛏 Sleeping

Most of Anguilla's celeb-seducing resorts are located along the milky sands of the island's secluded west end.

Cap Juluca   LUXURY HOTEL **$$$**
(☎497-6666, in USA 888-858-5822; www.capjuluca.com; Maunday's Bay; r from US$995, ste from US$1675; ✳@🛜🏊) One of Anguilla's sexiest resorts by far, Cap Juluca's long row of exclusive beachfront villas boasts idyllic views of the sea. If you're the type of traveler who likes to take home hotel mementos (soaps, slippers etc), you should consider bringing along an empty suitcase – each suite is loaded with designer fragrances, sandals, bathrobes. You name it, it has it.

CuisinArt   LUXURY HOTEL **$$$**
(☎498-2000, in USA 800-943-3210; www.cuisinartresort.com; Rendezvous Bay; ste from US$815; ✳@🛜🏊) Although the name sounds more like a food processor than a top-notch resort, this expansive whitewashed paradise has so many perks and quirks that you'll probably never want to leave the grounds. Tag along on a detailed tour of the hotel's 18,000-sq-ft hydroponic greenhouse, which provides almost all of the fresh produce served in the on-site restaurants.

Covecastles   LUXURY HOTEL **$$$**
(☎497-6801, in USA 800-223-1108; www.covecastles.com; Shoal Bay West; villas US$895-3700; ✳@🛜🏊) The curiously shaped villas at Covecastles look like the space-shuttle capsule that washes ashore during the opening credits of *I Dream of Jeannie*. While the exteriors are noticeably modern, the 20-year-old interiors are fairly sedate, sporting loads of sturdy wicker. The property was once owned by Chuck Norris, although fortunately (or unfortunately) only the dark mission-style terracotta tile harkens any flicker of a *Walker, Texas Ranger* theme.

Anguilla Great House   HOTEL **$$**
(☎497-6061, in USA 800-583-9247; www.anguillagreathouse.com; Rendezvous Bay; r from US$290; ✳@🛜) Although the name is a bit of a misnomer (it's more like the Anguilla Not-So-Great House), the rows of dated West Indian cottages offer ocean views at a smaller price tag than most of the other resorts on the island.

Paradise Cove Resort   HOTEL **$$**
(☎497-6603; www.paradise.ai; Cove Bay; ste from US$300; ✳@🛜🏊) A popular choice for those without a bottomless bank account, Paradise Cove is a comfy enclave featuring spacious rooms stocked with light Caribbean furnishings. The only downside is its inland location, although the ocean is only a 12-minute walk away.

🍴 Eating

Picante   MEXICAN **$$**
(☎498-1616; www.picantebwi.com; mains US$13-23; ◷dinner, closed Tue) A Caribbean taqueria? Why not. This unassuming roadside restaurant on the far west of the island's Albert Hughes Rd is a popular spot for a cheap nosh (by Anguilla's expensive standards). A Californian couple runs the open-air, tin-roofed casual Mexican space, which seats about 30 on wood benches. Try the home-baked tortillas, enchiladas and fish tacos, and wash it all down with a salty margarita.

Smokey's   INTERNATIONAL **$$**
(Cove Bay; mains from US$9; ◷lunch & dinner Tue-Sun) Occupying a great spot right on the beach and open until the last person stumbles home, Smokey's offers a selection of local creations and typical North American fare. Pizza and burgers are available for lunch, and dishes such as curried goat are the mainstay of the dinner menu.

Lucy's   ANGUILLAN **$$**
(Long Bay; mains US$15-25; ◷lunch & dinner Thu-Tue) Specializing in Anguillan home cookin', Lucy, the owner and chef, whips up scrumptious island faves such as curried seafood, steaming stews and Creole goat.

☆ Entertainment

Dune Preserve   BAR
(www.thedunepreserve.com; ◷whenever) Imagine if a reggae star was given a huge pile of driftwood and old boats, and got to build his very own tree house on the beach. The result would be this, one of the grooviest places on the island. Hometown star Bankie Banx has jammed and limed here for two-dozen years. Live music takes the stage on Wednesday, Friday and Saturday (plus Tues-

day and Sunday during high season), and if you're lucky, you'll hear Bankie himself. Even if you aren't into the jammin' music scene, it's still worth stopping by. Try the Dune shine: fresh ginger, pineapple juice, white rum and bitters. Take the road past the CuisinArt resort (a dirt road) and make the first left turn down a seemingly impossible rocky road. This is also the home of the Moonsplash festival.

EASTERN ANGUILLA

The quiet eastern end of Anguilla features loads of rambling villas set along some of the island's most stunning beaches.

Shoal Bay East

Close your eyes and imagine the quintessential Caribbean stretch of white-sand beach. You've just pictured Shoal Bay East, a 2-mile-long beach with pristine sand, thoughtfully placed reefs ideal for snorkeling, and glassy turquoise water.

Shoal Bay Scuba (☑497-4371, 235-1482; www.shoalbayscuba.com) is a professional diving operation with high-quality equipment, good boats and a staff of well-trained divemasters. Matthew, the owner, has been living on Anguilla for almost 25 years and knows all the ins and outs of every dive spot around (and can offer some great dining tips postdive). Half-day trips to Prickly Pear cost US$55 per person; a two-take boat dive will set you back US$90.

Sleeping

Shoal Bay Villas   APARTMENTS **$$**
(☑497-2051; www.sbvillas.ai; r from US$370, ste US$385-555; ✲@🛜🐾) A splendid beachfront location, this place has 15 large, comfortable units with prim, tropical decor. All have ceiling fans, a kitchen, and a patio or balcony. Some rooms literally step onto the sandy stretch of perfection that will be your front yard. Babysitting available.

Kú   HOTEL **$$**
(☑497-2011, in USA 800-869-5827; www.kuanguilla. com; ste US$315-420; ✲@🛜🐾) Kú's strongest suit is its prime slice of beachfront sand in the center of Shoal Bay East. The rooms are covered in coats of sterile white paint with nary a wall hanging in sight. It all feels a bit institutional and it doesn't help that the air-

COVER UP   **99**

British law requires all beach bums to wear appropriate bathing attire. Topless sun worshippers are subject to government fines.

con is borderline cryogenic. However, the outside hangout spots foster an excellent social vibe, and there's a cool fountain at the entrance, which, in the evenings, gushes with water while bursting with flames.

Elodia's   APARTMENTS **$**
(☑467-3363; www.elodias.ai; r US$160-196, ste US$230-300; ✲🛜) Little Elodia's occupies two cubes of apartment-style hotel rooms about 100yd from the beach along a clump of thick green grass. The suites could use a little sprucing up, but they get the job done, especially since there are sea views from every unit.

Eating & Drinking

Zara's   SEAFOOD **$$$**
(☑497-3229; mains US$20-29; ☉dinner) Located at the Allamanda Beach Club, Zara's serves up a hearty mix of seafood and 'Rasta pasta' created by Shamash, the iconic local chef who gleefully sings his heart out while preparing your meal. Catch him in the winter months because during the summer he closes up and heads to the Hamptons to spread his Caribbean joie de vivre to cynical New Yorkers.

Uncle Ernie's   FAST FOOD **$**
(mains US$6-16; ☉breakfast, lunch & dinner) The cheapest place on Anguilla to buy a Coke (US$1), this bright green and purple shack teems with beachaholics lounging on the wobbly plastic patio furniture while taking a break from the Caribbean sun. The food is far from tops, but hey, what do you really expect for US$6 on one of the most expensive islands in the world?

Gwen's   BBQ **$$**
(mains US$12-25; ☉breakfast & lunch) Some thin sheets of wood, a generous smattering of patio furniture, a few cotton hammocks and voilà – welcome to Gwen's. It may not look like much from the outside, but this beachside cook shack inspires great devotion from yearly returnees who come for an unhurried day of BBQ and sun.

ANGUILLA'S HERITAGE TRAIL

After perfecting your Caribbean tan, rent a car and grab a copy of the *Anguilla's Heritage Trail* brochure to learn about the island's colorful past. The pamphlet has heaps of information about Anguilla's evolution and details 10 interesting spots around the island from historical structures to important natural landmarks. The route starts in the far east and loops through the Valley before making its way west down to Rendezvous Bay. Allow for around 90 minutes to two hours depending on your pacing.

Limestone markers point to each of the 10 sights featured on the trail – they are erected from the local stone that flanks most of the island.

Far East

After Shoal Bay East, the quiet eastern seascape is a narrowing strip of breezy coves dotted by casbah-like villas and hidden eateries. **Island Harbour** is a working fishing village, not a resort area, and its beach is lined with brightly colored fishing boats rather than chaise longues. There are another half-dozen semisecluded beaches in the area, of which **Junk's Hole** is tops. This silent stretch of windswept sand gently forms a curving bay flanked by crooked palms – it's the perfect place to live out your castaway fantasies.

Here you'll find **Heritage Museum** (adult/child US$5/3; ⊙10am-5pm Mon-Sat), Anguilla's only museum. It's set within a small bungalow and details the island's history through an impressive assortment of artifacts. Amble through the different rooms while experiencing a cleverly curated time line of events, from the settling of the ancient Arawaks to a recent visit from Queen Elizabeth II.

🛏 Sleeping

Arawak Beach Inn   HOTEL **$$**
(☑497-4888; www.arawakbeach.com; Island Harbour; r from US$245; ❋🤍📺) Colorful Arawak Beach Inn sits on the far west side of picturesque Island Harbour. Stacks of hexagon-shaped rooms stretch across the

rock-strewn coast, and feature weathered wooden furnishings.

🍴 Eating

Hibernia Restaurant & Art Gallery   FUSION **$$$**
(☑497-4290; www.hiberniarestaurant.com; mains US$32-42; ⊙lunch Tue-Sat, dinner Tue-Sun, closed Jun & mid-Aug–Nov) The owners of Hibernia travel to Asia – from Myanmar to Bali – every year during low season and bring back an assortment of exotic spices and flavors, which they incorporate into their ever-growing repertoire of brilliant fusion recipes. The adjacent art gallery features purchasable paintings and trinkets from their unusual journeys. Hibernia is located about half a mile east of Island Harbour; follow the signs. Reservations advised.

Palm Grove   SEAFOOD **$$$**
(ethne24@hotmail.com; Junk's Hole; lobster salad US$25; ⊙lunch) As you careen down the treacherous dirt road to Junk's Hole, you'll feel like you've made a wrong turn; fear not, a tasty lunch is soon in store. No doubt the only beachside shack ever featured in *Bon Appetit* magazine, Palm Grove magically churns out tasty seafood despite having no electrical power. Put your order in with chef-owner Nat – be it lobster or crayfish – and head down to the beach for the hour (or two) wait.

Scilly Cay   SEAFOOD **$$$**
(☑497-5123; mains US$25-40; ⊙Wed & Sun, closed Sep-Oct & in rough weather) Pronounced 'silly key', this unique lunchtime experience occupies a teeny atoll all to itself. Wave at the island and staff will send a boat over to the Island Harbour pier to pick you up. Sunday afternoon's reggae band lures locals and tourists alike, and there's live music on Wednesday. Reputedly serves the best rum punch on the island.

UNDERSTAND ANGUILLA

History

First settled by the Arawaks from South America over 3500 years ago, Anguilla was called 'Malliouhana,' meaning arrow-shaped sea serpent. The Arawaks settled the island for millennia, evidenced by many cave sites with petroglyphs and artifacts still visible today and studied by archaeologists.

Columbus sailed by in 1493, but didn't land on the island (probably because he didn't notice it since it's extremely flat compared with St-Martin/Sint Maarten next door). Britain sent a colony in 1650 to take advantage of soil that was hospitable to growing corn and tobacco. However, it wasn't hospitable to much else, and the plantation colonies that bloomed on nearby Caribbean islands, such as St Kitts and Nevis, never defined Anguilla.

When the sugar plantations were abandoned due to a lack of viable soil and insufficient rain, small-scale industries, such as sailing, fishing and private farming, began to crop up on the island. In 1834 Britain abolished slavery in its colonies, and many Anguillan ex-slaves took up positions as farmers, sailors and fishermen.

Soon after, Anguilla formed a federation with St Kitts and Nevis, which was disliked by most of the ex-slave population. Anguilla was allowed only one freeholder representative to the House of Assembly on St Kitts and was largely ignored, eventually culminating in the Anguilla Revolution in 1967. Anguilla Day marks May 30, 1967, the day Anguillans forced the Royal St Kitts Police Force off the island for good.

As a result of its revolt against St Kitts, Anguilla returned to Britain and once again became an overseas territory. Under the Anguilla constitution, which came into effect in 1982, one queen-appointed representative acts as the British governor and presides over the Executive Council and an elected Anguilla House of Assembly.

Culture

Anguillan culture is a blend of West Indian, British and African influences. Anguilla's local population is almost entirely descended from African slaves brought to the Caribbean several centuries ago. Over the last three decades many US and British nationals have moved to the island and obtained Anguillan citizenship.

As hockey is to Canada, sailboat racing is to Anguilla – the national sport and a vital part of everyday life. Races are a common occurrence and are a great way to hang out with the community. Upscale tourism drives the economy, and today, almost three-quarters of the island's inhabitants work in hospitality or commerce. Anguillans take pride in maintaining the balance between tourist development and the preservation of a thriving local society.

For a small island, Anguilla has an impressive arts and crafts scene that mostly focuses on inventive local artists rather than a rich textile history. There are currently about two-dozen resident artists on the island and 10 galleries displaying their work. A brochure for a self-guided tour is available from the tourist office.

Landscape & Wildlife

Anguilla lies 5 miles north of St-Martin/Sint Maarten, an arid island shaped like an eel (its namesake). Almost 30 white-sand beaches have prompted countless imaginations to linger over whether one could subsist on a diet of coconuts to take an early retirement here.

Over 100 bird species can be spotted on the island, including the Antillean crested hummingbird, frigate, brown pelican, snow egret and black-necked stilt. Endangered sea turtles, like the hawksbill, can be spotted offshore in five protected marine parks: Prickly Pear and Seal Island Reef, Dog Island, Little Bay, Sandy Island and Shoal Bay Island Harbour Reef. The most commonplace creatures on the island are the many roaming goats and sheep. Hint: if you see a slightly fuzzier-looking goat with its tail down, not up, it's actually a Caribbean sheep.

Like many Caribbean islands, Anguilla desalinates much of its water. Be mindful of letting the water run needlessly.

SURVIVAL GUIDE

Directory A–Z
Accommodations

Anguilla has a reputation as an expensive destination because...well, it is. You'll be hard-pressed to find any semblance of a luxury vacation for under US$300 a night. Most hotel rooms and villas around the island have kitchens or kitchenettes. Consider picking up some groceries in the Valley to reduce the costs of your vacation.

High-season rates usually run December 15 to April 15, but it's around Christmas and New Year's when prices rise astronomically.

PRACTICALITIES

» **Electricity** 110V, 60 cycles; standard American three-pin plugs are used.

» **Newspapers & Magazines** The weekly *Anguillian* newspaper comes out on Friday.

» **Radio & TV** Radio Anguilla is at 1505AM and 95.5FM. Cable TV is available with local programming on Channel 3.

» **Weights & Measures** Imperial system.

Most hotels charge significantly less in the low season.

Hotels charge a 10% government tax and 10% service charge. This is not included in any of the published rates in this chapter unless otherwise noted.

$	budget	under US$200
$$	midrange	US$200 to US$400
$$$	top end	more than US$400

One of Anguilla's many charms is its plethora of villas. Prices range from around US$1000 per week for a studio during summer to US$75,000 per night for a seven-bedroom mansion at Christmas.

The following rental agencies can hook you up with a variety of properties fitting all different price ranges, or check out the agencies listed at http://villas.ai. Note: roosters don't pay heed to quiet-hour signs posted at hotels or villas, no matter the level of luxury – bring earplugs.

Anguilla Luxury Collection (☑497-6049; www.anguillaluxurycollection.com) Highly recommended for all of your Anguilla needs.

Island Dream Properties (☑498-3200; www.islanddreamproperties.com) Also recommended.

Keene Enterprises (☑497-2544; www.keenevillas.com)

My Caribbean (☑in USA 321-392-0828; www.mycaribbean.com)

Activities

Although it doesn't hold the allure of nearby dive havens, such as Sint Eustatius or Saba, Anguilla has clear water and good reef formations. In addition, a number of ships have been deliberately sunk to create new dive areas, bringing Anguilla's total to almost two-dozen diverse sites. Offshore sites popular for diving include Prickly Pear Cays, with caverns, ledges, barracudas and nurse sharks; several wrecks, including the 1772 Spanish galleon *El Buen Consejo* (which sunk naturally), 109yd off Stoney Bay; and Sandy Island, which has soft corals and sea fans.

There are three diving operations on the island, located in Sandy Ground, Meads Bay and Shoal Bay East. Shoal Bay East, Sandy Island and Little Bay are popular snorkeling spots.

Business Hours

Other than the standard opening hours given here, the rest of the establishments on the island pretty much run according to island time, meaning that they open and close as they please. Food service after 9pm is limited to a couple of beach bars in Sandy Ground and a smattering of Chinese grub huts and BBQ stands.

Government offices 8am-3pm Mon-Fri

Restaurants Breakfast 7-10am, lunch 11:30am-2:30pm, dinner 6-9pm

Supermarkets Around 8am-9pm Mon-Sat, shorter hours Sun

Embassies & Consulates

There are no official embassies on the island. However, those seeking consular services can get in touch with the **Anguilla Tourist Board** (☑497-2759, in USA 800-553-4939; www.anguilla-vacation.com; Coronation Ave, The Valley), which has a list of local contacts who represent foreign nations.

Festivals & Events

Moonsplash (www.thedunepreserve.com; ☉Mar) The hippest of Anguilla's festivals. Bankie Banx invites all his old reggae friends to the Dune Preserve in March for some late-night jamming. Guests have included Third World, the Wailers, and Toots and the Maytals.

Anguilla Summer Festival (www.festival.ai) Anguilla's Carnival is its main festival. It starts on the weekend preceding August Monday (first Monday in August) and continues until the following weekend. Events include traditional boat racing, Carnival costumed parades, a beauty pageant, and calypso competitions with continuous music and dancing.

Tranquility Jazz Festival (www.anguillajazz.org; ☺early Nov) This jazz festival attracts big names as well as talented local musicians, who play to an international audience of jazz aficionados in various hotels and other locations. The event culminates in a free beach jazz concert in Sandy Ground.

Food

A 15% service charge is added to most restaurant bills and no further tipping is necessary.

Eateries in this chapter have been categorized according to the following price brackets, which relate to the cost of a main meal:

$	budget	under US$10
$$	midrange	US$10 to US$20
$$$	top end	more than US$20

Health

The island's small **Princess Alexandra Hospital** (☎497-2551) is in the Valley.

Most of the island's water is collected in cisterns, so it's advisable to use bottled water for drinking.

Money

The Eastern Caribbean dollar (EC$) is the local currency but the US dollar is commonly used.

There are four international banks on Anguilla; all are located in the Valley, and have ATMs dispensing US and EC dollars.

Most restaurant bills include a 15% service charge; no further tipping is necessary.

Public Holidays

In addition to the holidays observed throughout the region (p872), Anguilla has the following public holidays:

Anguilla Day May 30

Queen's Birthday June 11

August Monday (Emancipation Day) First Monday in August

August Thursday First Thursday in August

Constitution Day August 6

Separation Day December 19

Telephone

Anguilla's country code is ☎264 and is followed by a seven-digit local number. If you are calling locally, simply dial the local number. To call the island from North America, dial ☎1 + 264 + the local number. From elsewhere, dial your country's international dialing code + 264 + the local number. We have included only the seven-digit local number in Anguilla listings in this chapter.

Visa

Citizens of many African, South American and former Soviet countries need to obtain visas.

Getting There & Away

Entering Anguilla

Visitors entering Anguilla must carry valid ID in the form of a passport and must declare the date on which they will be departing.

Air

Anguilla's **Wallblake Airport** (AXA; ☎497-2514) accepts mostly smaller aircraft and will require a transfer before arriving from most international destinations (unless you are coming on your private jet).

The following airlines fly to and from Anguilla from within the Caribbean:

Cape Air (www.flycapeair.com) Flights to/from San Juan.

Continental (www.continental.com) Services to/from San Juan.

LIAT (☎497-5002; www.liatairline.com) Flights to/from Antigua and St Thomas.

Sea

FERRY

Ferries make the 25-minute run from Marigot Bay in St-Martin/Sint Maarten to Blowing Point in Anguilla an average of once every 45 minutes from 8:15am to 7pm. From Anguilla to St-Martin/Sint Maarten the ferries run from 7am to 6:15pm. Boats also depart Blowing Point directly for Simpson Bay (Juliana Airport) on St-Martin/Sint Maarten. They leave in conjunction with the Marigot-bound boats and cost US$35 (roughly the same price as taking a boat to Marigot then a taxi to Juliana Airport). You can simply show up for the time you wish to take the boat across. The ferry terminal at Blowing Point is 4 miles southwest of the Valley.

The one-way fare per person is US$15 plus the US$20 departure tax when leaving (US$5 if you're doing a day trip away from the island). The fare for the passage is paid onboard the boat.

YACHT

The main ports of entry are at Sandy Ground in Road Bay or Blowing Point. The **immigration and customs office** (☏497-2451; ⊘8:30am-noon & 1-4pm Sun-Fri, 1-4pm Sat) can be contacted on VHF channel 16.

Getting Around

There is no official public transportation on Anguilla. Visitors will either need to rent a car or rely on pricey taxi drivers. You may see bus-stop signs in various spots – there is a private company on the island that drives a shuttle around; however, there is no set schedule.

Car

DRIVER'S LICENSE

Visitors must buy a temporary Anguillan driver's license for US$20 cash, which is a small pink paper issued on the spot by the car-rental companies. Make sure each person driving has a valid license, as hefty fines are imposed on unlicensed drivers.

RENTAL

Compact air-conditioned cars rent for about US$50 a day (usually US$10 cheaper in summer). Petrol prices are extremely high on the island: US$5 for 1 gallon of gas. Do not fill your tank up to the brim, especially if you are staying on the island for less than a week. The island is very flat and there is rarely traffic – it takes quite a while to go through a tank of gas. If you're arriving by ferry, there are car-rental operations right at the pier. From the airport, most rental services are just a short ride away. It's best to book in advance during high season.

Try the following rental agencies:

Apex/Avis (☏497-2642; avisaxa@anguillanet.com; The Valley)

Boo's Cars & Cycle Rentals (☏497-8523; oboo@anguillanet.com; Rock Farm)

Carib Rent A Car (☏497-6020; caribcarrental@anguillanet.com; Meads Bay)

Connor's Car Rental (☏497-6433; mauricec@caribserve.net; South Hill)

Island Car Rental (☏497-2723; www.islandcar.ai, islandcar@anguillanet.com; Airport Rd)

Romcan Car Rental (☏497-6265; www.romcancarrental.com; Airport Rd)

Triple K Car Rental (☏497-2934; hertz triplek@anguilla.net; Airport Rd)

ROAD RULES & CONDITIONS

Unlike the other islands in the region, on Anguilla you drive on the left-hand side of the road. Steering wheels can be either on the left or right. The main roads around the island are well paved but the streets in the Valley are bumpy and riddled with potholes.

The island has six gas stations, all well marked on the tourist maps. Most close on Sundays.

Taxi

Taxi fares have been standardized across the island, although don't be surprised when your driver magically doesn't have any change to give you when you pay. Taxis are readily available at the airport and ferry; there is a small taxi booth in both locations that can organize your transportation needs. Figure US$18 from the ferry terminal to Meads Bay. Rates are for one to two people, with an additional person paying US$4, and service between 6pm and midnight costs an extra US$2 (service between midnight and 6am is an additional US$5).

Antigua & Barbuda

Best Beaches

» Rendezvous Bay (p117)

» Half Moon Bay (p119)

» Valley Church Beach (p115)

» Any beach in Barbuda
(p120)

Best Places to Stay

» Ocean Inn (p118)

» Lighthouse Bay (p123)

» Sugar Ridge Resort (p115)

» Inn at English Harbour
(p118)

Why Go?

On Antigua, life is a beach. It may seem like a cliché, but this improbably shaped splotch of land is ringed with beaches of the finest white sand, made all the more dramatic by the azure waters, which are so clear they'll bring a tear to your eye or a giggle to your holiday-hungry throat.

If life on Antigua is a beach, its isolated neighbor Barbuda *is* a beach: one smooth, sandy low-rise amid the reef-filled waters. Birds, especially the huffing and puffing frigates, greatly outnumber people.

Back on Antigua, there are lots of people, many famous. Guitar-picker Eric Clapton, rag-trader Giorgio Armani and tastemaker for the masses Oprah all have winter homes here. Some of the Caribbean's most exclusive resorts shelter in the myriad bays and inlets. But don't worry, mere mortals thrive here as well. No matter your budget, you will find a beach with your name on it.

When to Go

In January and February, the coolest months, the daily high temperature averages 81°F (27°C), while the nightly low temperature averages 72°F (22°C). In July and August, the hottest months, the high averages 86°F (30°C) and the low 77°F (25°C). Antigua averages about 45in of rain annually. The wettest months are September to November, when measurable precipitation occurs, on average, eight days each month. February to April is the driest period, with an average of three rainy days each month.

Antigua hosts a couple of major annual events. Antigua Sailing Week in April is the largest regatta in the Caribbean, while Antigua's 10-day Carnival culminates in a parade on the first Tuesday in August.

Fast Facts

» **Area** 108 sq miles (Antigua), 62 sq miles (Barbuda)

» **Population** 86,500 (Antigua), 1250 (Barbuda)

» **Capital** St John's (Antigua), Codrington (Barbuda)

» **Telephone country code** ✆268

» **Emergency** ✆911 or 999

Set Your Budget

» **Budget hotel room** US$75

» **Two-course evening meal** EC$80

» **Museum entrance** EC$8 to EC$18

» **Beer** EC$5

» **City transport ticket** EC$1.50 to EC$5

Resources

» **Department of Tourism** (www.antigua-barbuda.org)

» **Antigua Nice** (www.antiguanice.com)

» **Barbudaful** (www.barbudaful.net)

» **Food & Drink Guide** (www.foodanddrink-caribbean.com)

Itineraries

THREE OR FOUR DAYS

Spend the morning wandering St John's, taking in the museum, cathedral and market, then take a couple of hours in the afternoon to relax on the beach and have sunset drinks in Dickenson Bay. The following day head south along the coast, sampling beaches and then cutting across Fig Tree Dr to English Harbour and Nelson's Dockyard. Spend the next day or two roaming the rugged east coast, stopping at Devil's Bridge, and taking a dip on the crisp-crumb beaches at Half Moon and Long Bays. Consider a kayak nature trip.

ONE WEEK

Do everything above and then force yourself to spend another day searching out your favorite beach. After that, make a two-day trip to Barbuda to relax on isolated sandy shores and for some incredible bird-watching.

GETTING TO NEIGHBORING ISLANDS

At the time of writing, flight operations to Barbuda had ceased, so the ferry is your only option. Montserrat is served by air and by ferry, although the latter does not operate on a reliable schedule. Antigua is the hub of regional airline LIAT, and has frequent flights to St Kitts, Nevis, St-Martin/Sint Maarten and other islands. Winair flies to Dominica.

Essential Food & Drink

» **Pepperpot** Antigua's national dish is a hearty stew blending meat and vegetables, such as okra, spinach, eggplant, squash and potatoes. It's often served with fungi, which are not mushrooms but cornmeal patties or dumplings.

» **Black pineapple** The local pineapple was first introduced by the Arawaks and is smaller than your garden variety. It's known as 'black' because it's at its sweetest when kind of dark green. It grows primarily on the southwest coast, near Cades Bay.

» **Rock lobster** This hulking crustacean has a succulent tail but no claws and is best served grilled. (And you'll be forgiven if after a few rum punches you're humming a tune by the B-52s while digging in.)

» **Wadadli** Antigua Brewery makes this local brew, a fresh pale lager, with desalinated seawater.

» **Cavalier** and **English Harbour** are the locally produced rums and best mixed with fruit juice for a refreshing – if potentially lethal – punch.

ANTIGUA

Unlike its smooth-edged neighbors, Antigua looks like something that went 'splat' on the pavement. But oh if everything that went splat were this good. Its myriad craggy inlets and corrugated coasts hug scores of perfect little beaches, while the sheltered bays have provided refuge for boats, from Admiral Nelson to pirates to sun-scorched yachties.

There's a distinct English accent to this classic Caribbean island with its narrow roads punctuated with candy-colored villages. You can explore most everything quickly, although the superb sites of historic English Harbour will steal hours from your day. Take the time to savor the sand and sea: the former bright white, the latter beguiling blue.

❶ Getting Around

BICYCLE Some hotels rent out bikes, or try one of these oufits:

Bike Plus (☑462-2453; bikeplus@candw.ag; Independence Dr, St John's; bikes per day from US$17.50)

Paradise Boat Sales (☑460-7125; www.paradiseboats.com; Jolly Harbour; mountain bikes per day from US$15)

BUS Antigua's buses are privately owned minivans that post their routes behind the windshield. Fares range from EC$1.50 to EC$5. The main bus station (West Bus Station) in St John's is opposite the Public Market. Buses don't leave until full and generally run from about 6am until 7pm; there are very few buses on Sunday. Buses to English Harbour may run as late as midnight, but do confirm this with the driver.

Buses to the east side of the island leave from the East Bus Station, near the corner of Independence Ave and High St. There's no practical bus service to the airport, Dickenson Bay or other resort areas in the island's north.

CAR International and local car-rental agencies split the business on Antigua. Daily rates start at about US$40 for a compact. For the best deals, shop online before arriving. Because of the poor road conditions, most vehicles have dents and scratches; ask the agent to record all existing damage before taking over the car. Most agencies will deliver cars to your hotel free of charge. Gas stations are scattered around the island, including one outside the airport. Gas sells for around EC$12 per gallon.

International car-rental companies include Avis, Dollar and Hertz, while **Big's Car Rental** (☑562-4901; www.bigscarrental.net) and **Titi Car Rental** (☑460-1452) are local companies based in English Harbour.

TAXI Fares are regulated by the government, but be sure to confirm the fare with the driver before riding away. Fares are for up to four persons; a fifth person costs an additional 25%. Private island tours are charged at about US$24 per hour for up to four people with a two-hour minimum. Waiting times cost US$5 per 30 minutes. See www.antigua-barbuda.org for a full list of official rates (link to 'Transportation').

Sample fares:

Airport to St John's US$13

Airport to Dickenson Bay US$16

Airport to Jolly Harbour US$24

Airport to English Harbour US$31

Cruise-ship pier to Dickenson Bay US$12

Cruise-ship pier to English Harbour US$24

In St John's there's a taxi stand opposite the Public Market, and taxi drivers also hang around Heritage Quay.

St John's

POP 36,000

Intriguingly shabby, St John's is worth a day's exploration. Good cafes, idiosyncratic shops, a grand cathedral, a cute little museum, a thriving market and more line the busy streets of the fairly compact center. There's a mélange of buildings ranging from 19th-century survivors to modern-day horrors.

Almost half of the island's residents live in and around St John's, which is busy during the day from Monday to Friday and on Saturday morning. It all but shuts down at night and on Sundays.

◉ Sights

St John's sights are all within walking distance of the cruise-ship pier. Shutterbugs should trek up to hilltop Mt St John's Medical Centre for dazzling bird's-eye views of the town.

Museum of Antigua & Barbuda   MUSEUM
(www.antiguamuseums.org; cnr Market & Long Sts; adult/child EC$8/free; ⊙8:30am-4pm Mon-Fri, 10am-2pm Sat) In the stately 1750 courthouse, this local history museum displays few objects (mostly pottery shards, tools, coins and cannonballs) but panels do a reasonably good job at interpreting facets of island history. All the key players are introduced, from the indigenous tribes to pirates and buccaneers, British plantation owners and the scores of slaves brought in to work the fields. It's well worth a half-hour spin.

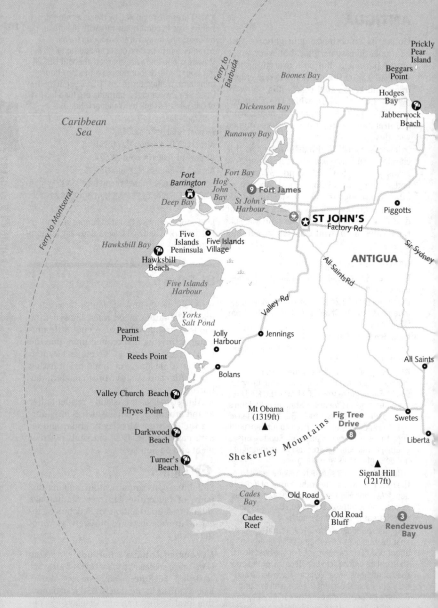

Antigua & Barbuda Highlights

1 Flash back to colonial times at **Nelson's Dockyard** (p117), a restored 18th-century naval base

2 Marvel at the magnificent winged denizens of Barbuda's **Frigate Bird Sanctuary** (p122)

3 Traipse through the thick rainforest to the shimmering sands of deserted **Rendezvous Bay** (p117)

4 Sway your hips to steel drum and reggae during the Sunday-afternoon party at **Shirley Heights Lookout** (p119)

Antigua & Barbuda

Frigate Bird Sanctuary
Codrington
Barbuda

Antigua

ATLANTIC OCEAN

Long Island
Dutchman's Bay
Winthorpes Bay
Maiden Island
North Sound National Park
Great Bird Island
VC Bird International Airport
Fitches Creek Bay
Parham Harbour
Guiana Island
Parham
Guiana Bay
Crump Island
Pelican Island
Mercers Creek Bay
Long Bay
Indian Town Point
Devil's Bridge
Sir Vivian Richards Cricket Ground Hwy
Pares
Seatons
Willikies
Betty's Hope
Nonsuch Bay
Green Island
Potworks Dam
Great Deep Bay
York Island
Bethesda
Willoughby Bay
Half Moon Bay
Hudson Point
Falmouth
English Harbour
Shirley Heights
Falmouth Harbour
Nelson's Dockyard
Mamora Bay
Pigeon Point Beach
Galleon Beach
English Harbour

N
0   4 km
0   2 miles

5 Commune with colorful fish while snorkeling off uninhabited **Great Bird Island** (p114)

6 Soak up the sun, then play in the waves of shimmering **Half Moon Bay** (p119)

7 Enjoy a cold Wadadli beer at a beach bar: any beach bar

8 Taste the sweetness of a black pineapple at a fruit stand along **Fig Tree Drive** (p116)

9 Watch the sun drop into the ocean from **Fort James** (p112)

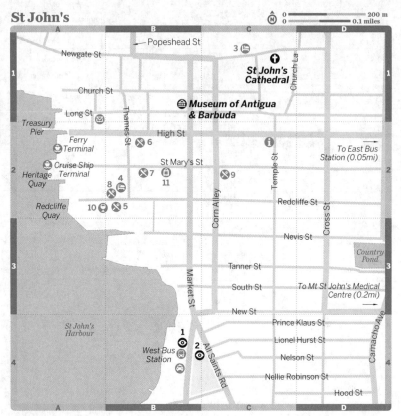

Upstairs are the offices of the **Environmental Awareness Group of Antigua & Barbuda** (www.eagantigua.org). Aside from raising awareness about issues of conservation and sustainability, staff also organize workshops and guided hikes. The website has details on upcoming events. It also publishes a trail guide available at the museum and at Nelson's Dockyard in English Harbour.

St John's Cathedral   CHURCH

(☑497-2235; btwn Newgate & Long Sts) This twin-spired cathedral is St John's most prominent landmark. After an 1843 earthquake leveled the original 1681 wooden church, it was quickly replaced with the current neobaroque stone structure. The unique pitch-pine interior creates a church-within-a-church effect and almost feels like you're inside an old sailing ship. Closed for renovation for some time to come, it can only be seen on special guided tours set up through the deanery.

Public Market   MARKET

(Market St; ☉6am-6pm Mon-Sat) Bananas, limes, mangos, eggplant – you'll find mountains of them at this covered market that is at its most vibrant on Friday and Saturday mornings. Keep an eye out for produce you're unlikely to find at the supermarket back home, including black pineapple, the reddish flowers of antioxidant-rich sorrel and black tamarind pods. It's a fun place for a browse, snack or people-watching. The amiably bombastic painted bust outside the market entrance depicts Sir Vere Cornwall Bird. Follow your nose to the **fish market** across the street, next to the bus station. Upon request, vendors will fillet your selection.

🛏 Sleeping

It's slim pickings for accommodations in St John's, but most visitors tend to favor beach resorts anyway.

St John's

Heritage Hotel
HOTEL $

(☏462-1247; www.heritagehotelantigua.com; Thames St; d US$60-80; ❋📶) If you must stay downtown, this well-established hotel near the cruise-ship pier is a decent option. A waterfront annex has 19 rooms with kitchens while the main building (with shops on the ground floor) has 25 standard rooms.

City View Hotel
HOTEL $$

(☏562-0259; www.cityviewantigua.com; Newgate St; s/d from US$139/170; ❋@📶) Close to the cathedral, this newly renovated 50-room hotel caters largely to the suit brigade. Rooms have private patios, cheery bedspreads and flat-screen cable TVs.

✖ Eating & Drinking

Self-caterers can stock up at local groceries, the Public Market, and the massive Epicurean and 1st Choice supermarkets.

[TOP CHOICE] Papa Zouk
SEAFOOD $$

(☏464-6044; Hilda Davis Dr, Gambles Terrace; most mains EC$55; ☺dinner Mon-Sat) This casual bistro turns out some of the most sophisticated seafood dishes on the island. The menu always reflects what's fresh and you can specify your preparation. The bar stocks 200 kinds of rum; insiders ask for a P'tit Punch, an addictive concoction with marinated

rum. If you have more than one, take a cab. Go north on Popeshead St, off Newgate St, then turn left on Hilda Davis Dr. The restaurant will be on your right.

Hemingways
INTERNATIONAL $$

(www.hemingwayantigua.com; St Mary's St; dinner mains EC$50-70; ☺breakfast, lunch & dinner Mon-Sat) Enjoy fine casual fare on the breezy 2nd-floor veranda at this popular restaurant-bar in an 1829 building. Start the day with cinnamon-scented banana pancakes, move on to salads and sandwiches at lunchtime and finish the day with conch fritters, rock lobster and other fine Creole cuisine. Service is cheery and the rum punch respectable.

Big Banana
PIZZA $

(www.bigbanana-antigua.com; Redcliffe Quay; pizzas EC$25-80; ☺lunch & dinner Mon-Sat) Both locals and visitors have been lusting after Banana's thin-crust pizzas for about a quarter century. Match your appetite to one of the four sizes and gobble up your pie in the patio or inside amid pictures of Che and Ghandi. For preflight cravings, there's another branch at the airport.

Cafe Bambula
FRENCH $$

(☏562-6289; Lower High St; mains EC$55-70; ☺lunch daily, dinner Fri) This flowery courtyard cafe is a lovely escape from St John's downtown hustle. Watch the staff buzz around the open kitchen behind a long bar as you anticipate mouthwatering bouillabaisse, homemade foie gras or juicy steak au poivre.

C&C
BAR & RESTAURANT $

(☏470-7025; Redcliffe Quay; nibbles EC$7-30; ☺lunch & dinner Tue-Sun) This cozy courtyard bar specializes in handpicked South African wines and tasty nibbles. It gets mobbed on Thursday nights, when owners Cutie and Claudine dish up their famous lasagne (EC$30) to a capacity crowd ranging from janitors to judges. Book ahead or forget about it.

Kalabashé
CAFE $

(Redcliffe St; mains EC$20-30; ☺lunch Mon-Sat; ✎) Vegan fare and fresh fruit juices served by a local Rasta.

Roti King
ROTI $

(St Mary's St; roti EC$15-23; ☺8:30am-midnight Mon-Sat) Delectable roti stuffed with curried chicken, shrimp, veggies or conch.

Epicurean
SUPERMARKET $

(Woods Centre, Friars Hill Rd; ☺8am-10pm) Upscale market caters to expats; it has fresh

PORT OF CALL – ST JOHN'S

The cruise-ship port is close to town. Stingray City Antigua (p120) and zip-lining on a rainforest canopy tour (p116) are both very popular shore excursions. If you are docked for a few hours, you can also do the following:

» Transport yourself back to colonial times at Nelson's Dockyard (p117), then enjoy the views over lunch on Shirley Heights (p119)

» Steer towards Dickenson Bay (p113) for all sorts of beach activities, plus beach bars galore

» Splash and snorkel in the aquamarine waters of remote Half Moon Bay (p119)

» Buy a black pineapple at the Public Market (p110), then have lunch at Cecilia's High Point Cafe (p114)

» Fancy yourself Robinson Crusoe while kayaking around the uninhabited islands off the east coast (p129)

local foods and imported international foods. It's in the Woods Centre shopping mall. Get there by going north on Cross St, which turns into Friars Hill Rd north of Newgate St. The mall and market will shortly appear on your right.

1st Choice SUPERMARKET **$**
(Anchorage Rd) Cheaper and more local products. It's about 2mi north of the town centre, via Popeshead St, which turns first into Fort Rd and then into Anchorage Rd.

 Shopping

Duty-free shops cluster in Heritage Quay just off the cruise-ship pier, but don't expect major bargains. The adjacent Redcliffe Quay has a few interesting boutiques, but for more local color, skip over a block or two to Market St, Thames St and St Mary's St. **Best of Books** (St Mary's St) is a well-stocked bookstore.

 Information

EMERGENCY Police (cnr Newgate & Market Sts) Main downtown police station.
INTERNET ACCESS Best of Books (562-3198; St Mary's St; per 30min EC$8; 8:30am-5:30pm Mon-Thu, to 8pm Fri, 10am-3pm Sun)
Public library (Market St; 9:30am-5pm Mon-Thu, to 3:30pm Fri) Free wi-fi.
Rituals Coffee House (Lower St Mary's St; 8am-7pm) Free wi-fi.
MEDICAL SERVICES Mt St John's Medical Centre (484-2700; Michael's Mountain) Brand new, state-of-the-art hospital. Get there by following New St east to Queen Elizabeth Hwy. It's the big building on the hill.
City Store & Pharmacy (562-4721; Thames St; 7am-9pm Mon-Fri, 7am-10pm Sat, 9am-5pm Sun)

MONEY Banks with ATMs, including the Royal Bank of Canada, cluster around the intersection of Market and High Sts.
POST Post office (Long St; 8:15am-4:30pm Mon-Thu, to 3pm Fri)
TELEPHONE There are public pay phones along Temple St, south of St John's Cathedral. Avoid the pricey credit-card phones in Heritage Quay.
Lime (cnr High St & Corn Alley; 8am-5pm Mon-Fri, 9am-noon Sat) Phone cards and local SIM cards.
Digicel (Redcliffe St; 8am-5pm Mon-Fri, 9am-noon Sat) Ditto.
TOURIST INFORMATION Tourist office (562-7600; www.antigua-barbuda.org; ACB Financial Centre, High St; 10am-4pm Mon-Fri) Also operates an information kiosk at Heritage Quay on cruise-ship days.

Fort James

Fort James, a small stronghold at the north side of St John's Harbour, dates back to 1706, but most of what you see today was built in 1739. It still has a few of its 36 cannons, a powder magazine and a fair portion of its walls intact. The site drips with atmosphere: it's moodily run-down and is rarely the scene of crowds.

Fort Bay, a narrow beach backed by trees that stretches north from the fort, is popular with islanders but has no facilities.

In the fort's reconstructed officers quarters, bluff-top **Russell's** (462-5479; mains EC$40-90; noon-10pm Mon-Sat, 4-11pm Sun) offers drinks and seafood with awesome eyefuls of the ocean and passing boats from its wide verandas. Sunsets can be achingly beautiful and live jazz on Sunday nights (sometimes also on Friday) really packs 'em in. The menu includes garlic shrimp, lobster and steaks.

Runaway Bay

Runaway Bay is a simple strip of sand just south of popular Dickenson Bay. It was battered by 1995's Hurricane Luis and has never fully recovered. Several of the modest beachfront hotels are in decline. On the plus side, the beach is seldom crowded.

Dickenson Bay

The middle market of Antigua's holidaymakers finds fun and refuge at this long but fairly narrow crescent of white sand on the northwest coast. The swimming is good and there's no shortage of aquatic activities to lure punters off their loungers. At nightfall, as you enjoy a vivid sunset, classic beach bars serve rum punches by the bucketful.

The beach can get crowded, what with the vendors peddling wares, women hoping to braid hair and the hordes of funseekers from the massive Sandals resort. Still, the pervasive strains of reggae set the mood for a quintessential Caribbean beach vacation.

🏃 Activities

Tony's Water Sports WATER SPORTS
(☑462-6326; next to Sandals) Run by the son of local calypso great King Short Shirt, well-established Tony's gets you waterborne with Hobie Cats, jet skis, banana boats and water skis (about US$50 each per session). Hooking a tuna on a deep-sea fishing expedition

will set you back about US$400 for the half-day trip.

🛏 Sleeping

Buccaneer Beach Club RESORT $$
(☑562-6785; www.buccaneerbeach.com; 1-/2-bedroom apt US$225/450; ❋@❄➤) This well-maintained beachfront getaway has modern, spacious and functionally furnished apartments that are perfect for families and self-caterers. After a day on the immaculate, sugary beach, whip up entire meals in the full kitchen, then spend a quiet evening lingering on the terrace before retiring to ultracomfy beds. Bonuses: mountain-bike rentals and free guest laundry.

Siboney Beach Resort RESORT $$
(☑462-0806; www.caribbean-resort-antigua-hotel-siboney-beach.com; d US$150-205; ❋@❄➤) Set in its own little jungle on the beach, Siboney has a variety of rooms and apartments in three-story blocks. It's not fancy, but it is awfully nice and cheery. Most units have small kitchenettes, nicely updated bathrooms and patios or balconies.

Dickenson Bay Cottages APARTMENTS $$
(☑462-4940; www.dickensonbaycottages.com; 1-/2-bedroom apt US$155/275; ❋@➤) A small, secluded complex of vibrantly decorated and nicely furnished units set around a pool. It's family friendly and a five-minute walk from the beach.

🍴 Eating

Chippy Antigua SEAFOOD $
(mains EC$25-35; ⊙4-9pm Wed & Fri) It doesn't look like much. In fact, it looks like what it

---

CRAZY FOR CRICKET

To Antiguans, cricket is not a sport but a religion. The tiny island state has produced some of the world's best cricketers, including Andy Roberts, Curtly Ambrose and, most famously, Sir Vivian Richards, aka King Viv or the 'Master-Blaster.' Known for his aggressive style of batting, he became captain of the West Indies team and captained 27 wins in 50 tests between 1980 and 1991.

Not surprisingly, when it came time to build a new stadium for the 2007 World Cup (with major financing courtesy of mainland China), it was named after Antigua's famous son. About 4 miles east of St John's, the 10,000-seat **Sir Vivian Richards Cricket Ground** (☑tickets 481-2490 or 460-9966, information 481-2450; www.windiescricket.com) ranks among the region's top cricket facilities yet has been dogged by difficulties from the start. The worst blow came in 2009 when the International Cricket Council imposed a one-year ban after a Test match between West Indies and England had to be called off for unhealthy playing conditions. Play resumed in February 2010 and these days the new-and-improved stadium again hosts regional and international matches. If you want to see local passion in action, check www.windiescricket.com or www.antigua-barbuda.org for the schedule.

is: a snack truck parked on gravel by the side of the road. But what snacks! Meals really, including flaky fish-and-chips, succulent scampi and homemade pies. There's a full bar and you can enjoy it all at plastic tables under the stars. The truck parks next to the Buccaneer Beach Club.

Coconut Grove
CREOLE **$$$**

(☎462-1538; www.coconutgroveantigua.net; mains EC$50-90; ⊙breakfast, lunch & dinner) Watch dive-bombing pelicans from your perch at this Creole restaurant next to the silvery sliver of sand at Siboney Beach Resort. The rock lobster is a winner, the rum punch deceitfully mellow and fresh-tasting (it kicks). Popular happy hours from 4pm to 7pm. Reservations necessary.

North Shore

Antigua's northern reaches between Dickenson Bay and the airport boast posh residential areas, a golf course, fancy restaurants and surf sports off Jabberwock Beach. Nearby, a catamaran shuttles anyone with villa or restaurant reservations to the private **Jumby Bay Resort** (www.jumbybayresort.com) on offshore Long Island. The newly revamped retreat regularly wins plaudits for being one of the Caribbean's top resorts.

In the distance beckons the unspoiled nature of **Great Bird Island**. Part of the **North Sound National Park**, this aptly named island is a bird-watcher's delight and teems with frigate birds, laughing gulls, purple martins, red-billed tropic birds and other winged creatures. Mangroves lure a bevy of marine life, making this a great snorkeling destination, as well. For guided tours to the island, see p129.

Windsurf Antigua
WINDSURFING

(☎461-9463; www.windsurfantigua.net; Jabberwock Beach) Local windsurfing guru Patrick Scales guarantees to get you up on the board and onto the water in one session (from US$55 for two hours). Boards can be rented for US$25 per hour or US$70 per day and can be delivered islandwide. Prebooking advised.

Kite Antigua
KITESURFING

(☎720-5483; www.kitesurfantigua.com; Jabberwock Beach) Offers a four-hour introductory course (US$260) and a 10-hour clinic (US$650) and also rents equipment to experienced riders (kite and board per hour US$30). Prebooking advised.

Cedar Valley Golf Club
GOLF

(☎462-0161; www.cedarvalleygolf.ag) This is an 18-hole, par 70 course with a 300yd driving range. The green fee is US$49 and clubs rent for US$30.

🛏 Sleeping & Eating

Wind Chimes Inn
B&B **$$**

(☎728-2917; www.windchimesinnantigua.com; s/d incl breakfast US$85/95; 🅿🅰🕸) Plane spotters will cherish the runway views from their private terrace at this modern seven-room inn just 2 miles from the airport. With earplugs, though, anyone can enjoy the spotless, spacious rooms with fridge and microwave. Turn off the main road at the Hertz rental-car sign.

TOP CHOICE Cecilia's High Point Cafe
ITALIAN **$$**

(☎562-4487; www.highpointantigua.com; Dutchman's Bay; mains EC$50-100; ⊙dinner Mon, lunch Thu-Mon, closed Jun & Jul; 🕸🍴) There are few places more conducive to a leisurely lunch than this cozy beachfront cottage presided over by the formidable Cecilia, a former Helmut Newton model (scan the walls for photographs). The blackboard menu is progressive Italian paired with a couple of Swedish dishes from Cecilia's homeland. Free wi-fi, beach chairs, a kiddie playground and swoonworthy desserts make it even harder to leave.

Le Bistro
FRENCH **$$$**

(☎462-3881; www.antigualebistro.com; Hodges Bay; mains EC$80-140; ⊙dinner Tue-Sun) This little beacon amid the scrubland not only draws the Hodges Bay swells but gourmets from across the island. Owner and top toque Patrick Gauducheau leads a talented team in orchestrating flavors into culinary symphonies that sound simple but are not. Case in point: linguini tossed with lobster. Presentations are exquisite, service immaculate, reservations essential.

Five Islands Peninsula

A single road connects the low-key villages of this peninsula west of St John's. The coast is a series of coves and beaches, dotted with resorts.

⊙ Sights & Activities

Deep Bay
ACTIVITIES, RESORT BEACH

This curvy little bay has a sandy beach and protected waters lorded over by the Grand Royal Antiguan Hotel. A salt pond separates Deep Bay from smaller Hog John Bay, where there's a beach, a couple of hotels and views of St John's.

There's a fair amount of resort activity, but it's a good-sized strand and a nice swimming spot. The coral-encrusted **Andes wreck** lies in the middle of Deep Bay with its mast poking out of the water. Approximately 100 years have passed since this bark caught fire and went down, complete with a load of pitch from Trinidad. It's popular with snorkelers but divers tend to bypass it because ooze still kicks up pretty easily from the bottom.

Fort Barrington   FORT
The remains of this fort, which once protected the southern entrance of St John's Harbour, are atop Goat Hill at the north end of Deep Bay. Originally built in the mid-17th century, most of the present fortifications date from 1779. To get to the fort walk north along the beach at Deep Bay for about 10 minutes.

Hawksbill Bay   RESORT, NUDIST BEACH
Named for a landmark rock formation, this bay has a string of four lovely beaches. The turnoff for the first one is before you get to Hawksbill by rex resort, but the other three must be accessed through the resort. The furthest one is Antigua's only official nudist beach.

🛏 Sleeping

Hawksbill by Rex Resort   RESORT $$$
(☏462-0301; www.hawksbill.com; Five Islands Village; r all-incl from US$450; 🗲🌊) Near the south end of the peninsula, on Hawksbill Bay, this well-established resort offers 111 rooms, cottages and apartments. It tends to attract more-mature guests as well as Brits who appreciate the 'no shorts' rules at night. Rooms are airy, some with pitched ceilings and traditional decor.

Jolly Harbour to Cades Bay

A short drive south of St John's, Jolly Harbour is a busy marina and dockside condominium village with an ATM, pharmacy, internet place, boat rentals and charters, and a few restaurants and bars. South of here, the coastal road skirts some of Antigua's best beaches. They're popular with locals on weekends but otherwise usually deserted unless there's a cruise ship in town. After Crab Hill, the road passes pineapple patches, swaying century palms and pastures with grazing cattle and donkeys. Hills hug the road, culminating at 1319ft, the island's

highest point. Traditionally known as Boggy Peak, it was renamed **Mt Obama** by the local government in 2009 in honor of the US president, a move eliciting mixed feelings on the island.

👁 Sights & Activities

Valley Church Beach   FAMILY BEACH
With its calm and shallow aquamarine waters and powdery white sand, this secluded palm-lined beach is great for families. Alas, it's a bit hard to find. Just past the Sugar Ridge Resort look for a dirt road and a tattered sign pointing to the **Nest** (🕙11am-sunset), a funky restaurant-bar that also rents beach chairs (US$5). This beach is particularly good for families.

Darkwood Beach   ACTIVITIES BEACH
Another half-mile south, this road-adjacent swath of beige sand makes for a convenient swimming and snorkeling spot. The beachside **cafe** (🕙10am-sunset) has a shower (US$1), changing rooms and also rents beach chairs.

Turner's Beach   FAMILY BEACH
Also known as Crab Hill Beach, this sandy strip is rarely packed and great for sunning and swimming. It's also home to OJ's, a fun beachfront eatery.

Jolly Dive   DIVING
(☏462-8305; www.jollydive.com; Jolly Harbour) This dive shop has a fine reputation and charges US$95 for a two-tank dive. Popular diving sites include the 2-mile-long Cades Reef, Sunken Rock off the south coast and the wreck of the *Jettias,* a 310ft steamer that sank in 1917.

🛏 Sleeping

TOP CHOICE Sugar Ridge Resort   RESORT $$$
(☏562-7700; www.sugarridgeantigua.com; Bolans; r incl breakfast from US$350; ❄🗲🌊) A short drive south of Jolly Harbour, this notable newcomer welcomes guests to 60 hillside rooms that beautifully blend contemporary and colonial touches. All have verandas, and the lower units come with private plunge pools. It's not on the beach but three pools and a posh Aveda spa provide ample diversion.

Cocobay Resort   RESORT $$$
(☏562-2400; www.cocobayresort.com; all-incl per person US$360-840; ❄@🗲🌊) This 49-unit development on a hillside south of Jolly

Harbour is a stylish retreat that eschews the usual resort paradigms. After a day by the infinity pool or on nearby Valley Church Beach, retire to Creole garden cottages sheathed in pale Mediterranean colors. The **Sheer Rocks restaurant** is a romantic dinner spot and also does lunch on weekends.

Reefview Apartments   APARTMENTS $$
(☑560-4354; www.reefviewapartments.com; Cades Bay; apt from US$139; ✸🤶) Energetic expat Karoll maintains three gorgeous apartments close to the beach and with views of Cades Bay. Rates include airport transfer and a welcome drink.

Ocean View Apartments   APARTMENTS $$
(☑560-4933; www.scova-antigua.com; Cades Bay; apt US$115-140; ⊙closed Jun & Jul; ✸🤶) A steep road deposits you at Rudi and Wilma's four spanking one-bedroom apartments with subdued tropical decor, tranquil vibe and breezy terraces.

✗ Eating

Carmichaels   FUSION $$$
(☑562-7700; mains EC$55-90; ⊙lunch & dinner) After some initial hiccups, Sugar Ridge's fine-dining outpost is now one of the island's star restaurants. It certainly has the most dramatic setting in its aerie high above the hotel. The Carib-Continental cuisine is a winning combination of substance and style. Bring a swim suit for a predinner dip in the infinity pool.

OJ's   SEAFOOD $$
(Crab Hill; sandwiches EC$20-27, mains EC$35-80; ⊙lunch & dinner) With its nautical decor, hammocks and waterfront tables, OJ's is your quintessential beach hangout. Regulars swear by the grilled snapper, lobster salad and wicked rum punch. There is live entertainment on Friday and Sunday nights.

Epicurean   SUPERMARKET $
(Jolly Harbour; ⊙8am-8pm) Big, high-end supermarket with local and international groceries, fresh sandwiches, liquor and British newspapers.

Fig Tree Drive

Old Road, a village that juxtaposes a fair amount of poverty with two swank lodges (Curtain Bluff and Carlisle Bay), marks the start of Fig Tree Dr. One of the most picturesque routes on the island, this narrow 5-mile-long road serpentines through patches of rainforest past bananas (called 'figs' in Antigua), coconut palms and big old mango trees. Roadside stands sell fruit and fresh juices. Fig Tree Dr ends at the village of Swetes. En route, pop into **Fig Tree Studio Art Gallery** (⊙9:30am-5:30pm Mon-Sat Nov-Jun) to see what the local art scene is up to.

✗ Activities

Antigua Rainforest Canopy Tour   ZIP-LINING
(☑562-6363; www.antiguarainforest.com; ⊙Mon-Sat) Channel your inner Tarzan or Jane while roaring through the treetops suspended on zip lines. Options include one-hour tours (over/under age 16 US$60/40) with five zips, including the aptly named 328ft 'Screamer'; and the 2½-hour Full Canopy Tour (US$105/65), which includes short hikes between suspension bridges and nine zips. Book ahead.

Footsteps Hiking   HIKING
(☑460-1234, 773-2345; www.footstepshiking.com; over/under 16yr US$30/15; ⊙Tue & Thu) For an in-depth immersion into the rainforest, join local Rasta Dassa for a fun two-hour ramble past the Wallings Reservoir, a beautiful Victorian-era dam, and up Signal Hill for 360-degree views of the island. Tours depart from the Fig Tree Studio Art Gallery.

English Harbour

At the far southern tip of Antigua, the village of English Harbour sits atop two bays: Falmouth Harbour and English Harbour. The two are separated by a peninsula that is the site of Nelson's Dockyard, considered the one must-see historical attraction on Antigua. A restored 18th-century British naval base, it was named for English captain Lord Horatio Nelson, who spent the early years of his career here.

Although there is the village of Falmouth on the north side of the eponymous bay, most businesses, bars and restaurants are located in English Harbour village, which, confusingly, sits near the Falmouth Harbour Marina. The marina caters specifically to giant luxury yachts up to 330ft long and also hosts such major boating events as Antigua Sailing Week in late April.

The main thoroughfare, English Harbour Rd, dead-ends in a huge parking lot at Nelson's Dockyard. The east side of English Harbour bay is accessed via Shirley Heights road.

⊙ Sights

TOP CHOICE Nelson's Dockyard   HISTORIC SITE
(www.nationalparksantigua.com; adult/child 12yr
& under EC$18/free; ⊙9am-5pm) This historic
dockyard is Antigua's most popular tourist
sight, as well as the island's main port of
entry for yachts. The dockyard, which dates
from 1745, was abandoned in 1889 following
a decline in Antigua's economic and strategic importance to the British Crown.

Restoration work began in the 1950s, and
this former royal naval base now has a new
life closely paralleling its old one – that of an
active dockyard. It's the only working Georgian marina in the western hemisphere.
Souvenir shops, restaurants and inns as well
as boating facilities occupy the handsome
old brick-and-stone naval buildings, whose
history is outlined on interpretive plaques.
It's easy to imagine a British frigate being
prepared to sail out and blast a few French
or pirate ships.

A must-stop is the two-floor **Dockyard
Museum** in a former officers residence. It
has exhibits on the history of the island, the
construction of the dockyard, and daily life
at the local forts. There is also the Nelson
Room, where displays examine the 'irritation, lust, piety and jealousy' he felt for the
(married) Lady Emma Hamilton.

TOP CHOICE Shirley Heights   HISTORIC SITE
With its scattered 18th-century fort ruins
and wonderful hilltop views, Shirley Heights
is a fun place to explore. For the best views
and main concentration of ruins, continue
past the museum; the road will fork after
half a mile. The left fork takes you to **Block-
house Hill**, where you'll find remains of officers quarters that date from 1787, and a clear
view of sheltered Mamora Bay to the east.

The right fork leads to **Fort Shirley**,
which has more ruins, including one that
has been turned into a casual restaurant
and bar. There's a sweeping view of English
Harbour from the rear of the restaurant. The
best view, extending all the way to Montserrat and Guadeloupe, is from the **Lookout**,
just a minute's walk from the parking lot.
Take your sweetie up here for a romantic
sunset.

Fort Berkley   FORT
For a fine harbor view, take the easy 10-min-
ute stroll to what's left of this small fort
above the western entrance of English Harbour. Dating from 1704, it served as the har-

bor's first line of defense. You'll find intact
walls, a powder magazine, a small guardhouse and a solitary cannon, the last of 25
cannons that once lined the fortress walls.
The trail starts behind the Copper & Lumber Store Hotel on the back side of the wall
paralleling the water-taxi jetty.

Dows Hill Interpretation Centre   MUSEUM
(admission EC$13, free with Nelson's Dockyard
ticket; ⊙9am-5pm) Along the road up Shirley
Heights, this multimedia presentation traces island history from the Amerindian era to
the present. A platform provides good views
of English Harbour.

St Paul's Anglican Church   CHURCH
On the main road in the village of Falmouth,
this is Antigua's oldest church (1676) and
once doubled as a courthouse. Soak up its
long history by poking around the overgrown churchyard, which has some interesting colonial-era gravestones. Charles Pitt,
the brother of the English prime minister
William Pitt, was buried here in 1780.

☔ Beaches

TOP CHOICE Rendezvous Bay   SECLUDED BEACH
One of Antigua's most attractive beaches
is also among its remotest, reachable only
by high-clearance 4WD, by boat or after
a 90-minute walk through the rainforest. Make the effort, though, and you'll be
rewarded with dreamy golden sand and
footprint-free solitude. Locals can help with
directions.

Galleon Beach   ACTIVITIES BEACH
Galleon has plenty of facilities, calm waters and a snorkeling reef close to shore. It
is wide and long but since it's attached to
a resort, it can be fairly crowded. If you're

FUN FACTS FROM THE DOCKYARD MUSEUM

» The museum's plank floor is painted
red, the same color as the decks of
warships to disguise the bloodshed
during battle.

» Antigua was first called Wadadli;
centuries later the name inspired that
of the local beer Wadadli.

» When Nelson left Antigua as a sick
man in 1787, he carried a barrel of rum
to preserve his body in case he died
en route.

driving, the turnoff is off the Shirley Heights road. Or hop on a **water taxi** (EC$10; ⏲9am-6pm) at the little jetty behind the Copper & Lumber Store Hotel.

Pigeon Point Beach FAMILY BEACH
This tree-shaded, easily accessible community beach has trees, facilities and a bar. Popular with families, it can get crowded, especially on Sunday afternoons. Snorkeling is so-so. The access road veers off to the right just before the Nelson's Dockyard parking lot. Avoid at night – this is where an American cruise-ship passenger was killed in 2010.

Activities

Well-established **Dockyard Divers** (☎460-1178; www.dockyard-divers.com) in Nelson's Dockyard, and relative newcomer **Soul Immersion Dive Centre** (☎728-5377), on the main road opposite the gas station, offer dive and snorkeling trips. Snorkeling gear can be rented for US$10 per day.

Carpenters Rock Trail HIKING
This moderate to strenuous 1½-mile long trail up Shirley Heights starts at the far end of Freeman's Bay, at the end of Galleon Beach. It takes you past a ruined fort and treats you to supreme views of the rugged coastline and rock formations. Do watch out for cactus thorns, which can pierce right through shoe soles; bring a pocketknife or pliers to remove them right away.

Sleeping

TOP CHOICE **Inn at English Harbour** HOTEL $$$
(☎460-1014; www.theinn.ag; r from US$500; ❄@📶🏊) With great views of the bay and Nelson's Dockyard, this colonial-style boutique beach resort recently catapulted into the 21st century thanks to extensive upgrades. The 28 refined and airy rooms and suites sport marble or mahogany floors, big balconies as well as flat-screen TVs and iPod docking stations.

TOP CHOICE **Ocean Inn** B&B $$
(☎463-7950; www.theoceaninn.com; r incl breakfast US$110-170; ❄📶🏊) This charming inn on flowery, terraced grounds above English Harbour delivers five-star views at three-star prices. The nicest rooms are the cottages with private veranda but we also like the two breezy 'ocean budget rooms,' even though they share a bathroom. Avoid the windowless room 5. Nice touch: the honor bar.

Copper & Lumber Store Hotel HOTEL $$
(☎460-1058; www.copperandlumberhotel.com; r US$195-325; @📶) This beautifully restored hotel was built in the 1780s to store the copper and lumber needed for ship repairs. It now has 14 studios and suites, all with kitchens and ceiling fans, and some with antique furnishings. Rooms surround a lush courtyard and there's a good, vintage-feeling bar.

Admiral's Inn HOTEL $$
(☎460-1027; r US$120-190; ❄@📶) Built as a warehouse in 1788, the inn has 14 rooms with open-beam ceilings above its restaurant. Rooms vary in size and decor, and some are quite small. Room 6 is larger and a good choice, while room 3 is a quiet corner room with a fine harbor view. Some rooms have air-con, none have tubs. Enjoy alfresco salads and seafood at the harborside restaurant (mains EC$60 to EC$100). Wi-fi works in the front rooms and restaurant area only.

Anchorage Rooms INN $
(☎561-0845, 785-1302; www.theanchoragerooms.com; d US$68; 📶) Antigua and budget usually don't mix, so this well-run crash pad near Nelson's Dockyard is a welcome exception. Rooms are basic and clean and come with fans and good-size private bathrooms. Potential downside: it's right above a popular burger joint with live music on weekends, so light sleepers beware.

Eating

Trappas INTERNATIONAL $$
(☎562-3534; mains EC$30-50; ⏲dinner Tue-Sat) It's often standing room only at Simon and Caroline's hipster joint. Locals, expats and visitors descend for the upscale comfort food such as fried calamari, grilled grouper and creative curries written up on a blackboard menu. The bar is a lively meet-and-greet zone.

Caribbean Taste CARIBBEAN $$
(☎562-3049; mains EC$20-55; ⏲lunch & dinner Mon-Sat) If you want authentic local food, steer your compass to Gretel's cheerily painted cottage just off the main road to Nelson's Dockyard. Be adventurous with conch stew, goat curry or octopus ceviche or stay safe with grilled snapper and garlic shrimp.

Grace Before Meals CARIBBEAN $
(mains EC$15-20; ⏲8am-4pm & 6-11pm Mon-Fri) A great budget bite, this bright orange bungalow dishes up divine local fare at blessedly low prices. The baked chicken is a specialty,

ALGUNA

DON'T MISS

HILLTOP LIMING

For nearly three decades, locals and clued-in visitors have made the pilgrimage to **Shirley Heights Lookout** ([📞]728-0636; www.shirleyheightslookout.com; ⊙9am-sunset Mon, to 10pm Tue-Sun) on Sunday afternoons. That's when this dazzlingly located hilltop restaurant and bar hosts wildly popular barbecues (admission EC$20, mains EC$20 to EC$30) that vibrate with a steel-drum band in the afternoon and live reggae and calypso after 7pm. Come for romantic sunsets and dancing under the stars, all fuelled by wicked rum punches. Views of English Harbour are truly breathtaking. On other days it's quieter but still worth the trek for lunch and sunset drinks. The other party night is Thursday from 4pm to 8pm, when a steel band plays its gentle rhythms (admission free). The cab ride from English Harbour is US$10.

but Grace also makes a mean lamb chop and pork stew. For a vitamin kick, order one of the freshly blended fruit smoothies.

Abracadabra　　　　　　　　ITALIAN **$$**
([📞]460-1732; www.theabracadabra.com; mains EC$35-90; ⊙dinner Mon-Sat) Fondly known as 'Abra,' Salvatore's outpost is all things to all people: a restaurant where you can devour homemade pastas or the signature suckling pig, a chilled-out bar and lounge, and an energetic open-air dance club that's buzzing on Saturday nights. Pure magic! Next to the Nelson's Dockyard parking lot.

Dockyard Bakery　　　　　　BAKERY **$**
(⊙breakfast & lunch Mon-Sat) Behind the museum at Nelson's Dockyard, the baked goods here will draw you in like a sailor to rum. Sandwiches are best enjoyed under the 300-year-old sandbox tree out front.

☆ Entertainment

For additional party spots, see Abracadabra, and the 'Hilltop Liming' boxed text.

Mad Mongoose　　　　　BAR, RESTAURANT
([📞]463-7900; http://madmongooseantigua.com; ⊙11am-late daily Nov-Apr, Fri-Mon May-Oct; 🛜) This Rasta-colored yachtie and expat favorite is the place to come for a rollicking good time. The long bar, pool and foosball tables are conducive to making new friends, as are the rum-fuelled live-music jams on Fridays. The full menu (mains EC$40 to EC$60) should help restore balance to the brain.

❶ Information

The following are just past the entrance to Nelson's Dockyard.
Bank of Antigua (⊙9am-1pm Mon-Thu, 9am-noon & 2-4pm Fri, 9am-noon Sat) Has an ATM.
Post office (⊙8:15am-3pm Mon-Thu, to 1pm Fri)

Half Moon Bay

Half Moon Bay, in the southeast of the island, is an undeveloped crescent-shaped bay with yet another beautiful white-sand beach lapped by water the color of Blue Curaçao. There's usually pretty good body-surfing along the northern end, while the calmer waters to the south offer decent snorkeling conditions. There's no shade, and facilities are limited to **Smiling Harry's**, a funky bar that's (in)famous for its 'Thirst Quencher.'

The drive from English Harbour to Half Moon Bay takes about 30 to 45 minutes and presents you with spectacular views of Willoughby Bay. Near the village of Bethesda, it passes by the **Antigua Donkey Sanctuary** (admission free; ⊙10am-4pm Mon-Sat; 🛝). Run by the Humane Society, it shelters some 80 rescued donkeys and welcomes visitors. Kids love it.

Nonsuch Bay & Harmony Hall

In a remote corner of Antigua, **Harmony Hall** ([📞]460-4120; www.harmonyhallantigua.com; s/d US$180/200; ❄🍴) commands stunning views of Nonsuch Bay from its hilltop perch. Set amid the sturdy stone structures of an old sugar mill, it's a quiet six-room hideaway where conches line the garden paths and local art is sprinkled throughout. A short trail leads down to a cozy sandy beach with a small dinghy dock, where boats to uninhabited Green Island depart daily at 11am and 1:30pm for a couple of hours of swimming and snorkeling. The trip is free for hotel guests, US$10 for restaurant guests and US$20 for walk-ins.

ANTIGUA & BARBUDA BARBUDA

The garden setting of the **restaurant** (☑460-4120; mains EC$50-100; ☺lunch daily, dinner Wed-Sat) is the perfect foil for the upscale Italian fare, including homemade pasta and osso bucco. Reservations are advised.

In recent years, Nonsuch Bay has seen some development, most notably the sprawling Nonsuch Bay Resort, a cluster of ritzy villas and condos built into the hillside.

Long Bay

On the east side of Antigua, Long Bay has clear-blue, kid-friendly waters and a gorgeous white-sand beach that's reef-protected and good for snorkeling. Two resorts bookend the beach, which is lined with souvenir shops, a water-sports concession and a couple of bars. If you have a car, Long Bay makes a good day trip.

Just before the bay, a spur road veers off to **Devil's Bridge**, a modest sea arch at Indian Town Point, an area thought to be the site of an early Arawak settlement. Dramatic waves add excitement as they sometimes break over the rocks and erupt through blowholes. It's about a minute's walk to the east of the roundabout where the road ends.

The road to Long Bay runs past the village of Seatons, which is the base not just of Antigua Paddles (p129) but also of **Stingray City Antigua** (☑562-7297; tours US$50; ☺9am, 11am & 1pm), where you can feed, pet and swim with several-dozen stingrays in calm waters encircled by a coral reef. Turn off at the church.

Betty's Hope

Just southeast of the village of Pares, **Betty's Hope** (www.antiguamuseums.org; admission EC$5; ☺9am-4pm Mon-Sat) was the island's first sugar plantation, founded in 1650 by Governor Christopher Keynall. In 1674 it was granted to the Codrington family and named in honor of one of their daughters, Betty. Ruins of two old stone windmills, a stillhouse (distillery) and a few other stone structures remain. One of the mills has been painstakingly restored and returned to working condition. Although operated only on special occasions, its sails remain up most of the year. Displays document Antigua's sugar industry.

BARBUDA

Desert island. The mere phrase conjures up images of isolation, white-silk beaches, palm trees and the ephemeral concept of 'getting away from it all.' Barbuda (pronounced 'bar-*byoo*-duh') may well be the model for the iconic desert isle.

A mere blip on the map some 25 miles north of Antigua, Barbuda remains one of the Eastern Caribbean's least-visited places. Other than its teeming frigate-bird colony and breathtaking beaches, there's just not much here. It's essentially a little island with a very big beach. And that's perhaps its greatest appeal.

In fact, all this isolated splendor spelled the death of such high-society resorts as the famous K Club, a favorite of Princess Diana in the last years of her life. There are whispers that it may reopen, but just when and how is anybody's guess.

The only village, Codrington, is home to most residents and the minuscule airport. Most of the 1250 islanders share half a dozen surnames and can trace their lineage to a small group of slaves brought to Barbuda by the Codrington brothers Christopher and John. They leased the island in 1685 from the British Crown and used it to grow food for the slaves working on Antigua's sugar plantations. The family also quietly salvaged untold riches from ships that had run afoul of the surrounding reef. Many of these shipwrecks are now popular diving sites. A dive shop attached to the Green Door Tavern rents equipment, although most people organize the logistics through a dive shop on Antigua.

During the 18th century, the Codrington family managed to keep their lease, which was negotiated at an annual rental payment of 'one fattened sheep,' for nearly two centuries. Their legacy remains well beyond the town's name – from the communal land-use policies that still govern Barbuda to the introduced goats, sheep and feral donkeys that range freely (to the detriment of the island flora). You can visit the ruins of their estate, the Highland House, about 2½ miles east of Codrington.

Besides having the Caribbean's largest colony of frigate birds, Barbuda hosts 170 other species, including tropical mockingbirds, warblers, pelicans, ibis, oystercatchers, herons and numerous kinds of ducks. It also has a decent population of wild boar

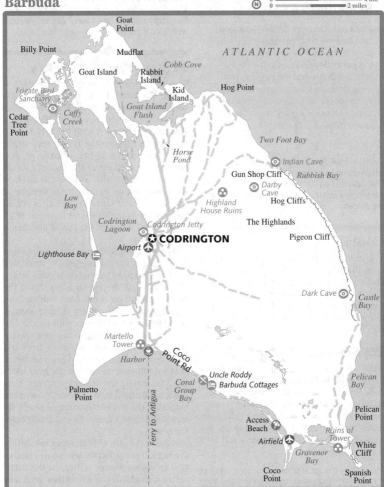

and white-tailed deer, both of which are legally hunted.

ℹ Getting There & Away

Many people visit Barbuda on a day trip from Antigua. At the time of writing, Winair (www.fly-winair.com) had stopped flying to tiny Codrington airport; check the website in case service has resumed.

For details on the ferry service between the two islands, see p128.

ℹ Getting Around

Barbuda has no public transportation and taxi rides are expensive. Prices are set by the government and posted at the ferry landing. The trip to Codrington, for instance, costs US$20 for up to four people. There are usually some taxis waiting at the dock or you can arrange a pick-up in advance through the tourist office. Unfortunately, Barbuda has a reputation for tours that fail to materialize, drivers who don't show up at the airport or some other missing link. Confirm all reservations.

Car rentals are available for about US$60 per day from **Andrea Rental** (☏560-2826, 775-0168) and **Junie Car Rentals** (☏771-9444). Both can issue a local driver's license for US$20. If you obtained one on Antigua, it's also good on Barbuda.

BARBUDA IN A DAY

Barbuda Express (📞560-7989; www. antiguaferries.com) operates a Barbuda Day Tour (US$159), which includes the ferry ride and visits to the Frigate Bird Sanctuary and the caves as well as lunch and a swim on a pretty beach. Alternatively, with advance notice the tourist office in Codrington can arrange island tours.

Alternatively, the tourist office can help you set up island tours with a local guide/driver. Rates depend on distance, time and number of passengers and must be negotiated directly with the guides.

Codrington

The quiet and modest town of Codrington is on the inland side of Codrington Lagoon, about 3.5 miles north of the ferry landing. This is where you'll find the post office, a bank with an ATM, tiny shops, modest restaurants and a spanking-new fisheries complex.

🛏 Sleeping & Eating

Ilene's Guest House   GUESTHOUSE $
(📞460-0419; 1-/2-bedroom cottages US$50/63) A Barbudan who used to live in the UK, Ilene keeps her two cottages – on a residential street in Codrington – very tidy. Amenities are minimalist and bathrooms are shared, but there's kitchen access and little porches for relaxing.

Palm Tree Guest House   GUESTHOUSE $$
(📞560-0517; s/d/ste US$65/80/130; ❄) This well-maintained guesthouse close to central Codrington has eight rooms, each with a fridge and satellite TV. The two-room suite also has a kitchen and living room.

Green Door Tavern   CARIBBEAN $$
(📞783-7243; mains EC$25-50; ⓢ7am-late) You can't make a joke about what's behind this Green Door as it's almost always open. Local fare is on offer, including crowd-pleasers such as ling, liver, tripe and on Saturdays, goat water. A popular drink is made from sea moss.

ℹ Information

Hanna Thomas Hospital (📞460-0076; River Rd) About a mile south of Codrington.

Tourist office (📞562-7066; ⓢ8am-4:30pm Mon-Thu, to 3pm Fri) Near the Codrington jetty; has maps and brochures and it can set you up with a local guide.

Frigate Bird Sanctuary

The expansive, shallow **Codrington Lagoon National Park** (http://nationalparks barbuda.com), which runs along Barbuda's west coast, supports one of the world's largest colonies of frigate birds (for more on these birds, see the boxed text, p125). Over 5000 of these black-feathered critters nest in sections of the lagoon's scrubby mangroves – with as many as a dozen birds roosting on a single bush. Because of this density, the birds' nesting sites are all abuzz with squawking, and the sight of all those blood-red inflating throat pouches is mesmerizing.

The most popular time to visit the rookery is during the mating season, from September to April (December is peak time). While the male frigate birds line up in the bushes, arch their heads back and puff out their pouches with an air of machismo as part of the elaborate courtship rituals, the females take to the sky. When one spots a suitor that impresses her, she'll land and initiate a mating ritual. After mating, a nest is built from twigs that the male gathers. The female lays a single egg that both birds incubate in turn. It takes about seven weeks for the chick to hatch, and nearly six months for it to learn to fly and finally leave the nest.

Among the other bird species inhabiting the lagoon are pelicans, terns and gulls, as well as such endemic critters as the tropical mockingbird, the Christmas bird and the endangered West Indian whistling tree duck.

The nesting site is in the upper lagoon and can only be reached by sea taxi from the Codrington jetty near the tourist office. A couple of authorized operators take visitors out to the rookery, but arrangements generally need to be made a day in advance. Check with the tourist office or contact **Foster Hopkins** (📞785-2742). The cost for the 90-minute trip is US$50 per boat for up to four people, with an additional US$12 for a drop-off at a beach. An EC$5.40 national park admission fee is payable at the office near the jetty.

West & South Coasts

Barbuda's west coast is lined with magnificent **beaches** and crystal-clear waters. From Palmetto Point northward there's a beautiful pinkish strand that extends 11 miles, most of it lining the narrow barrier of land separating Codrington Lagoon from the ocean. Because of its isolation, however, the beach remains the domain of a few lone boaters and a boutique hotel. More-accessible beaches are found along the coast south of the harbor.

The **harbor**, where the ferry landing is located, has a customs office and a sand-loading operation – Barbuda's sands are used to bolster some of Antigua's resort beaches. A short walk northwest of the landing is the 56ft-high **Martello Tower**, a former fortified lookout station that from a distance looks like an old sugar mill.

There's another string of magnificent beaches along the southern shore, including Coral Group Bay and Access Beach, about a half-mile north of Coco Point, which has near-shore coral formations that provide good snorkeling.

The pristine waters of **Gravenor Bay**, between Coco and Spanish Points, are a favored yacht anchorage and have reef formations and excellent snorkeling. Near the center of the bay is an old, deteriorating pier,

---

CAVES

Barbuda is riddled with caves, some of which are accessible, although, for safety reasons and even just to locate them, it's best to hire a local guide. Ask at the tourist office for a referral.

The most interesting and accessible is **Indian Cave** at Two Foot Bay, northeast of Codrington, which features Arawak petroglyphs and a bat chamber. The entrance is near roofless stone ruins near the shore. Not far from here, **Darby Cave** is a 300ft-wide sinkhole with palm trees growing out of it and 8ft-high stalagmites forming below the overhang. Three miles south, near Castle Hill, via a bumpy road and rocky trail, **Dark Cave** is an expansive underground cavern system with pools of deep water inhabited by blind shrimp and other crustaceans.

---

while the ruins of a small **tower** lie about a half-mile away to the east.

Archaeologists believe that the uninhabited peninsula leading to **Spanish Point** was once the site of a major Arawak settlement. A dirt track connects both ends of the bay, and another leads northward from the east side of the salt pond.

🛏 Sleeping & Eating

TOP CHOICE **Lighthouse Bay** BOUTIQUE HOTEL **$$$**
(☏562-1481; www.lighthousebayresort.com; d from US$1000; ❊@🐾🏊) Checking in at this nine-room, all-inclusive property, wedged between the sea and the lagoon, feels a bit like bunking with your billionaire uncle. The only property on a 19-mile-long stretch of pristine beach, it's so remote that it can only be reached by boat or helicopter.

Barbuda Cottages COTTAGES **$$$**
(☏722-3050; www.barbudacottages.com; r US$215-375, 4-night min) Fall asleep to the ocean breezes at this newly built, solar-powered wooden villa on stilts that is within a Frisbee toss of pearly Coral Group Bay beach and Uncle Roddy. It sleeps up to six in three bedrooms.

Uncle Roddy CARIBBEAN **$$**
(☏785-3268; Coral Group Bay beach; meals EC$30-75; ◷lunch) Roddy's remote solar-powered beachy outpost is the best place on the island for grilled lobster, although anything that makes it onto the barbecue makes a memorable meal. Bring bug spray: the sand flies are especially pesky here. Reservations are key.

UNDERSTAND ANTIGUA & BARBUDA

History

Early Times to the 17th Century

The first permanent residents in the area are thought to have been migrating Arawaks, who called today's Antigua 'Wadadli,' a name still commonly used today. They first established agricultural communities about 4000 years ago. Around AD 1200 the Arawaks were forced out by invading Caribs, who used the islands as bases for their forays in the region, but apparently didn't settle there.

Columbus sighted Antigua in 1493 and named it after a church in Seville, Spain. In 1632 the British colonized Antigua, establishing a settlement at Parham, on the east side of the island. The settlers started planting indigo and tobacco, but a glut in the supply of those crops soon drove down prices, leaving growers looking for something new.

In 1674 Sir Christopher Codrington arrived on Antigua and established the first sugar plantation, Betty's Hope. By the end of the century, a plantation economy had developed, huge numbers of slaves were imported, and the central valleys were deforested and planted with cane. To feed the slaves, Codrington leased Barbuda from the British Crown and planted it with food crops.

Nelson & Co

As Antigua prospered, the British built numerous fortifications around the island, turning it into one of their most secure bases in the Caribbean. What is today's Nelson's Dockyard was continually expanded and improved throughout the 18th century. Other forts included Fort James and Fort Barrington, both near St John's.

The military couldn't secure the economy, however, and in the early 1800s the sugar market began to bottom out. With the abolition of slavery in 1834, the plantations went into a steady decline. Unlike on some other Caribbean islands, the land was not turned over to former slaves when the plantations went under, but was instead consolidated under the ownership of a few landowners. Consequently, the lot of most people only worsened. Many former slaves moved off the plantations and into shantytowns, while others crowded onto properties held by the church.

A military-related construction boom during WWII, and the development of a tourist industry during the postwar period, helped spur economic growth (although the shantytowns that remain along the outskirts of St John's are ample evidence that not everyone has benefited).

On November 1, 1981, the islands became an independent state within the British Commonwealth.

Nest of Birds

Vere Cornwall (VC) Bird became the nation's first prime minister, and despite leading a government marred by political scandals, he held that position through four consecutive terms. He stepped down in 1994 to be succeeded by his son Lester.

Another son, Vere Bird Jr, received international attention in 1991 as the subject of a judicial inquiry that investigated his involvement in smuggling Israeli weapons to the Medellín drug cartel. As a consequence of the inquiry, Vere Bird Jr was pressured into resigning his cabinet post, but was allowed to keep his parliamentary position. A third son of VC Bird, Ivor, was convicted of cocaine smuggling in 1995.

Throughout the five terms that the family had a hold on government, controversy continued to surround the Birds. In 1997, Prime Minister Lester Bird announced that a group of ecosensitive islands, including Guiana Island, was being sold to Malaysian developers, who planned to build a 1000-room hotel, an 18-hole golf course and a casino. The highly controversial project stalled when the Malaysian developers failed to pay up. However, it was revived when Bird's old ally, and single biggest Antigua investor, Texas billionaire Allen Stanford, agreed to step in instead. A series of lawsuits brought by environmental activists further delayed the development.

In March 2004, the Birds' reign of the 'aviary' (as Antigua had become known) ended when the United Progressive Party won a landslide victory and Baldwin Spencer became prime minister.

In the years since, the government has struggled with the poverty found across much of the island. It has promoted tourism while at the same time edging politically closer to Cuba and Venezuela. It has also challenged the US ban on internet gambling sites and has had some success with the World Trade Organization. Many of these sites are based in Antigua.

Spencer was reelected in 2009, the same year the local economy was dealt a major blow when the FBI arrested Stanford for 'massive ongoing fraud' centered on US$8 billion managed by his Stanford International Bank. As of this writing, he's still awaiting trial in the US. The Guiana project seems on indefinite hold.

In addition, the global downturn, compounded by a decline in tourism, led to a major increase in Antigua and Barbuda's national debt, which soared to 130% in late 2010.

Culture

Away from the resorts, Antigua retains its traditional West Indian character, albeit with a strong British stamp. It's manifested in the gingerbread architecture found around the capital, the popularity of steelpan (steel-band), calypso and reggae music, and in festivities, such as Carnival. English traditions also play an important role, as is evident in the national sport of cricket.

Many Barbudans originally come from or have spent time living on their sister island, Antigua, and favor the quieter pace of life on the more isolated Barbuda. In fact, many Barbudans working in tourism are happy with the trickle of tourists that the remote island attracts, and have been reluctant to court the kind of development Antigua has seen.

Approximately 90% of the 86,500 people who live on Antigua are of African descent. There are also small minority populations of British, Portuguese and Lebanese ancestry. The population of Barbuda is approximately 1250, with most of African descent.

Besides the Anglican Church, Antiguans belong to a host of religious denominations, which include Roman Catholic, Moravian, Methodist, Seventh Day Adventist, Lutheran and Jehovah's Witness. On Sundays, services at the more fundamentalist churches draw such crowds that roads are blocked and drivers pray for divine intervention.

Sports

One of the best things Britain did for the West Indies was to introduce the local populace to cricket. It soon became the national passion of Antigua and is played everywhere – on beaches, in backyards or anywhere there's some flat, open ground. National and international matches, including the annual Digicel International Cricket Series, are played at the Sir Vivian Richards Cricket Ground. Cricket season runs from January to July.

Soccer (football) and basketball are increasing in popularity, and national and club soccer games can produce much the same atmosphere as cricket. Sailing is another passion, especially down south in English Harbour. Antigua Sailing Week and Antigua Classic Yacht Regatta, both held in April, are huge draws.

Arts

Reggae and zouk (the latter means 'party,' and is a rhythmic music that originated in Martinique and Guadeloupe in the 1980s) are both popular on Antigua. You'll also hear calypso, a style of singing rooted in slave culture that was developed as a means of communication when slaves weren't allowed to speak; and soca, a rhythmic, more soulful style of calypso. By far the most popular musical style on Antigua is steel pan (also known as steel band or steel drum), the melodic percussion music that comes from tapping oil drums topped with specially made tin pans. Originally from Trinidad, the form has been adapted in Antigua, and has become an integral part of the annual Carnival and Christmas festivities.

The soca-band Burning Flames is the best-known Antiguan music group and backed up late soca star Arrow from nearby Montserrat.

Landscape & Wildlife

Unlike Montserrat, its (at times) smoking neighbor to the southwest, Antigua is not dominated by a dramatic volcano. However, the southwest corner is volcanic in origin and quite hilly, rising to 1319ft at Mt Obama (known as Boggy Peak until 2009), the island's highest point. The rest of the island,

---

FRIGATE BIRDS

Frigate birds skim the water's surface for fish, but because their feathers lack the water-resistant oils common to other seabirds, they cannot dive into water. Also known as the man-of-war bird, the frigate bird has evolved into an aerial pirate that supplements its own fishing efforts by harassing other seabirds until they release their catch, which the frigate bird then swoops up in mid-flight.

While awkward on the ground, the frigate bird, with its distinctive forked tail and 6ft wingspan, is beautifully graceful in flight. It has the lightest weight-to-wingspan ratio of any bird and can soar at great heights for hours on end – making it possible for the bird to feed along the coast of distant islands and return home to roost at sunset without having landed anywhere other than its nesting site.

PRACTICALITIES

» **Electricity** 220V, 60 cycles. Some places provide 110V, 60 cycles, some provide both. American two-pin sockets dominate, UK sockets are rare.

» **Local Taxes** 8.5% government tax at hotels and restaurants.

» **Newspapers & Magazines** *Antigua Sun*, *Daily Observer*.

» **Radio** Gem Radio (93.9FM), Observer Radio (91.1FM).

» **Weights & Measures** Imperial system.

which is predominantly of limestone and coral formation, is given to a more gently undulating terrain of open plains and scrubland.

Antigua's land area is 108 sq miles. The island is vaguely rounded in shape, averaging about 11 miles across. The coastline is cut by numerous coves and bays, many lined with white-sand beaches.

Barbuda, 25 miles north of Antigua, is nearly as flat as the surrounding ocean. A low-lying coral island, Barbuda's highest point is a mere 145ft above sea level. The west side of Barbuda encompasses the expansive Codrington Lagoon, which is bound by a long, undeveloped barrier beach of blindingly white sand.

As a consequence of colonial-era deforestation for sugar production, most of Antigua's vegetation is dryland scrub. The island's marshes and salt ponds attract a fair number of stilts, egrets, ducks and pelicans, while hummingbirds are found in garden settings. Codrington Lagoon has the largest frigate-bird colony in the Lesser Antilles.

SURVIVAL GUIDE

Directory A–Z

Accommodations

Antigua is expensive and besides a few guesthouses and moderately priced properties, resort-type complexes (often all-inclusive) dominate the market. Overnighting on Barbuda means either more or less roughing it in a basic guesthouse in or around Codrington or forking over megabucks for a luxury abode.

In this chapter we list rates for the peak season (December to April), so expect significant discounts at other times. The price breakdown for a double room with private bathroom is as follows:

$	budget	under US$75
$$	midrange	US$75 to US$200
$$$	top end	more than US$200

In most cases, rates listed do not include the 8.5% government tax and a 10% to 15% service charge. Many hotels close for several weeks between August and October.

Business Hours

In this chapter we only list opening hours if they differ from the following standards:

Banks 8am-2pm Mon-Thu, to 4pm Fri

Bars noon-11pm or midnight

Businesses 8am-5pm Mon-Fri, to 2pm Sat

Restaurants breakfast 7:30-10am, lunch noon-2:30pm, dinner 6-9:30pm

Shops 9am-5pm Mon-Sat, later and on Sun for touristy places and supermarkets

Embassies & Consulates

Honorary consuls include the following:

Germany (☎462-3171)

UK (☎561-5046; robert.wilkinson-honcon@fconet.fco.gov.uk)

USA (☎463-631, 726-6531)

Food

Price ranges quoted in our Eating listings refer to a meal consisting of an appetizer and a main course. For Antigua and Barbuda, the breakdown is as follows:

$	budget	under EC$30
$$	midrange	EC$30 to EC$80
$$$	top end	more than EC$80

Gay & Lesbian Travelers

While there is no real gay scene on Antigua, there is no overt discrimination either. However, homosexual relationships are on the books as illegal in Antigua and Barbuda and theoretically punishable by up to 10 years in jail. Enforcement, however, is practically nonexistent. Just be discreet and avoid PDA (public displays of affection).

Health

The US Centers for Disease Control and Prevention recommends not drinking tap water in Antigua and Barbuda, but generally it's fine for people that are not overly sensitive. However, because of the high chlorination most prefer bottled water.

For details of medical facilities on Antigua, see p112; for Barbuda, see p122.

Money

Antigua and Barbuda use the Eastern Caribbean dollar (EC$).

US dollars are widely accepted. However, unless rates are posted in US dollars, as is the norm with accommodations, it usually works out better to use EC dollars. If you pay in US dollars you will likely get change in EC dollars.

A 10% service charge is added to most restaurant bills, in which case no tipping is necessary.

Public Holidays

In addition to holidays observed throughout the region (p872), Antigua and Barbuda observe the following public holidays:

Labour Day First Monday in May

Carnival Monday & Tuesday First Monday and Tuesday in August

Antigua & Barbuda Independence Day November 1

VC Bird Day December 9

Safe Travel

Overall crime rates are low, despite a disconcerting number of tourist murders in recent years (five since 2008; the most recent was the January 2011 shooting death of a British tourist in his holiday apartment). The vast majority of visits, though, are trouble-free and Antigua is by and large a safe and welcoming place. That doesn't mean you should let your guard down, hang out alone in isolated areas or stroll around unsavory-looking neighborhoods.

Though not deadly, mosquitoes and sand flies (mostly on Barbuda) can be a major pest, especially at sunrise and after sunset. Take the precautions outlined on p881. Stinging jellyfish do make an appearance at times in the Codrington Lagoon and along Antigua's west coast. Jellyfish Squish, sold locally in big supermarkets such as Epicurean, quickly takes out the sting.

Telephone

Antigua and Barbuda's country code is ☎268. To call from North America, dial ☎1-268, followed by the local number. From elsewhere, dial your country's international access code + ☎268 + the local phone number. When making a local call on the island, you only need to dial the seven-digit number.

Phone calling cards are widely available. Local cell phones use the GSM system.

Avoid credit-card phones, as they charge a rapacious US$2 per minute or more locally, US$4 to other Caribbean islands or the US, and up to US$8 elsewhere.

For directory assistance, dial ☎411.

Tourist Information

The only local tourist office is in St John's (p112).

Travelers with Disabilities

The big resorts can generally accommodate people with disabilities. Otherwise, much of Antigua is something of a challenge. The must-see sights at English Harbour are set on wide, flat grounds, although individual buildings may be inaccessible.

Women Travelers

Women traveling alone may attract a fair amount of attention from men, some of whome seem to regard themselves as God's gift to women tourists and see nothing wrong with making crude sexual come-ons. Ignore them and you'll likely be left in peace.

Getting There & Away

Entering Antigua & Barbuda

All visitors need a valid passport and a round-trip or onward ticket. On arrival, you'll be given an immigration form to complete.

Air

VC Bird International Airport (ANU) is about 5 miles east of St John's. It has an ATM, a currency exchange office, car-rental companies, a post office and a Big Banana restaurant branch. Once past security, there are a few small duty-free shops, a large souvenir shop, a bookstore and a snack bar.

Facilities are very crammed and long waits at immigration are not uncommon, especially when the big British Airways and

DEPARTURE TAX

The departure tax is US$28 or EC$70 for stays over 24 hours. You can pay (cash only) after check-in at the airport.

Virgin flights come in. Also expect long lines, as well as slow and officious service, when going through security upon departure.

AIRLINES

International airlines such as Air Canada, American/American Eagle, British Airways, Continental, Delta, US Airways and Virgin Atlantic all service Antigua, along with the following region-specific airlines.

Caribbean Airlines (www.caribbean-airlines. com) Flights to New York (JFK), Barbados, Kingston in Jamaica and Port of Spain in Trinidad.

Fly Montserrat (www.flymontserrat.com) Flights to Montserrat.

LIAT (www.fly-liat.com) Flights to Anguilla, Barbados, Dominica, Dominican Republic, Nevis, San Juan, St Kitts, St Lucia, St-Martin/Sint Maarten, St Thomas, St Vincent, Tortola and Trinidad.

Sea

CRUISE SHIP

Antigua is a major port of call for cruise ships. The cruise-ship pier, at Heritage Quay in St John's Harbour, segues into a duty-free shopping center, and is within easy walking distance of St John's main sights.

FERRY

There is a sometime ferry service between Antigua and Montserrat. Call ☑722-8188 to inquire if it's running. Montserrat's tourist office site (www.visitmontserrat.com) also posts the latest schedule. The fare for the one-hour trip is EC$150 each way.

YACHT

Antigua's many fine, protected ports make it one of the major yachting centers of the Caribbean. A favorite place to clear customs is at Nelson's Dockyard in English Harbour. Other ports of entry are Falmouth Harbour, Jolly Harbour, St John's Harbour, and Crabbs Marina in Parham Harbour. If you're going on to Barbuda, ask for a cruising permit, which will allow you to visit that island without further formalities.

Antigua has many protected harbors and bays, and fine anchorages are found all around the island. Full-service marinas are at English Harbour, Falmouth Harbour, Jolly Harbour and Parham Harbour. Boaters can make reservations at many restaurants around Falmouth Harbour and English Harbour via VHF channel 68.

Barbuda's reefs, which extend several miles from shore, are thought to have claimed a good 200 ships since colonial times – a rather impressive number, considering that Barbuda has never been a major port. Some reefs remain poorly charted, and the challenge of navigating through them is one reason Barbuda remains well off the beaten path. If you're sailing to the island, bring everything you'll need in advance, because there are no yachting facilities on Barbuda.

Getting Around

Air

At the time of writing, there was no air service between Antigua and Barbuda.

Bicycle

Check with your hotel, as many rent out a bike or two to guests. A couple of outfits on Antigua rent bikes (p107).

Boat

Barbuda Express (☑560-7989; www.antigua ferries.com; one-way adult/child EC$110/80) runs bumpy 1¾-hour rides aboard a catamaran from Heritage Quay in St John's. Call ahead to confirm departure times and to make reservations, and take precautions if you're prone to seasickness. For details about the company's day tour to Barbuda, see p123.

Bus

There is no public transportation on Barbuda, but Antigua has a decent system of private minivans and small buses. Fares cost from EC$1.50 to EC$5.

Car & Motorcycle

DRIVER'S LICENSE

A local driving permit, available from car-rental agencies, is required for driving on Antigua or Barbuda. It costs US$20 or EC$50 and is valid for three months.

RENTAL

Antigua has numerous car-rental agencies, including all the major international companies. On Barbuda, some locals rent out vehicles.

ROAD CONDITIONS

Antigua's roads range from smooth to rough to deadly. You'll be cruising along when suddenly a hubcap-popping pothole appears. If you plan to get off the beaten track (especially in the east), it's best to hire a 4WD.

Be aware of goats darting across the road and of narrow roads in built-up areas, which can also be crowded with children after school finishes.

Finding your way around Antigua can prove difficult at times. The island is randomly dotted with green road signs pointing you in the right direction, but they peter out the further away you get from the main centers. Private signs pointing the way to restaurants, hotels and a few other tourist spots are far more frequent. Beyond that, locals are always happy to offer advice – at times an adventure in itself.

ROAD RULES

Driving is on the left-hand side. The speed limit is generally 20mph in built-up areas and 40mph on highways.

Taxi

Taxis on Antigua have number plates beginning with 'TX.' On both Antigua and Barbuda, fares are regulated by the government, but it's best to confirm this with the driver before riding away.

Tours

Adventure Antigua (☎726-6355; www.adventureantigua.com) Run by Eli Fuller, a third-generation local. Many rave about his Eco-Tour (US$100), which takes in such unspoiled islands as Great Bird Island. The full day includes nature walks, snorkeling and a vast amount of information on the flora and fauna of the islands. A second tour, the Xtreme Circumnav (US$170) aboard a powerboat, includes a snorkel trip, a stop at Stingray City and a swim at remote Rendezvous Bay. Book online for a 10% discount.

Antigua Paddles (☎463-1944; www.antiguapaddles.com; Seatons; adult/child US$55/45) Gives a no-brainer hint of its tour type in its name. The half-day trips include a motorboat shuttle, kayaking around mangroves and shallows of the North Sound National Park off the island's east coast, snorkeling and the de rigueur time on a deserted beach.

Treasure Island Cruises (☎461-8675; www.treasureislandcruises.ag) Operates a variety of tours aboard a 70ft catamaran that combine sailing, snorkeling, entertainment and a barbecue. Options include the Circumnavigation tour (US$120), the Cades Reef tour (US$120) and the Bird Island tour (US$100).

Aruba

Best Beaches

» Eagle Beach (p135)

» Manchebo Beach (p135)

» Andicuri Beach (p141)

Best Places to Stay

» Bucuti Beach Resort
(p138)

» Manchebo Beach Resort
(p138)

» Beach House Aruba (p141)

Why Go?

Americans from the east coast fleeing winter make Aruba the most touristed island in the southern Caribbean.

And that's not really surprising given that it has miles of the best beaches, plenty of package resorts and a compact and cute main town, Oranjestad, which is ideally suited for the two-hour strolls favored by day-tripping cruise-ship passengers. It's all about sun, fun and spending money (lots of money – it's an expensive island).

But venture away from the resorts and you'll find that Aruba offers more. At the island's extreme ends are rugged, windswept vistas and uncrowded beaches. Arikok National Wildlife Park is an alien landscape of cactuses, twisted divi-divi trees and abandoned gold mines.

Mostly, however, Aruba is a place to do as little as possible. It wears its hospitality on its sleeve and in the national anthem, which includes the unlyrical line 'The greatness of our people is their great cordiality.'

When to Go

Average temperature for Aruba is a perfect 28°C (82°F). High noon is a bit warmer and at night it can get breezy, but mostly you'll be fine in shorts and T-shirt. The island is fairly dry, averaging a little over 2.5cm of rain per month. Much of this falls from September to early December. Aruba usually misses the Caribbean hurricane season; in recent years January rains have caused minor flooding. December to April is high season. High season for cruise ships runs October to April.

Itineraries

THREE DAYS

Find your hotel, head out to the beach and stay there. Maybe spend half a day exploring some other part of the island, but really just stay put on the lovely white sand of your choice. You may need to do a little sampling first, but that's part of the holiday.

ONE WEEK

Once you've reenergized after lying around a beach, spend a couple of days exploring Aruba. That's all you'll need to see it all, including the simple capital, Oranjestad, and the wilds of Arikok National Wildlife Park.

TWO WEEKS

All the above, but also consider a visit to the neighboring islands of Bonaire and Curaçao, each of which has a completely different personality to Aruba.

GETTING TO NEIGHBORING ISLANDS

Plans for ferries within the ABCs perpetually run aground. But flights between Aruba and Bonaire and Curaçao are frequent and last about 20 minutes.

Essential Food & Drink

Because of the arid conditions, food in Aruba has always been hearty. Thick stews made with meats such as goat and chicken, and with vegetables such as okra and squash, are predominant. Spices are used to give things variety.

» **Goat (cabrito) stew** A classic dish that most Arubans will say is made best by their own mother. Also appears in curries.

» **Cheese** An obvious Dutch legacy, usually eaten straight with a beer. When used in cooking it was traditionally a special treat.

» **Keshi yena** Comes in myriad variations: a cheese casserole with chicken, okra and a few raisins for seasoning. Much better than it sounds.

» **Seafood** Common and good, especially shellfish. Fish is popular in curries.

» **Funchi** Based on cornmeal, it is formed into cakes and fried, mixed with okra and fried, or used as a coating for chicken and fish.

» **Nasi goreng** Indonesian fried rice via the colonial Dutch.

» **Frikandel** Classic Dutch deep-fried, meaty snack.

» **Bitterballen** Another Dutch classic – little deep-fried meaty balls served at roadside stands.

» **Balashi** Aruba's lager is popular because it is *not* Dutch or American.

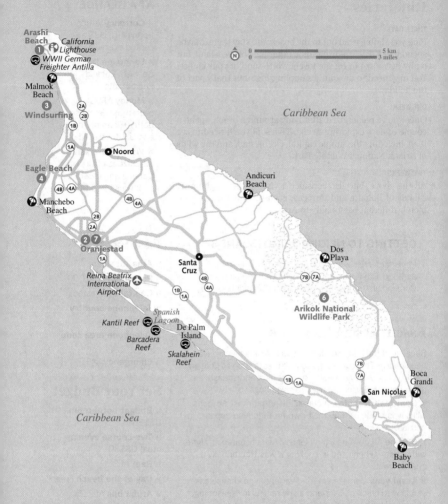

Aruba Highlights

1 Savor **Arashi Beach** (p141), the least-touristed of Aruba's many fine white beaches

2 Munch a lobster at one of Oranjestad's **traditional seafood restaurants** (p133)

3 Thar she blows! That's wind, not whale – the waters off the northwest coast

are famous for their ideal **windsurfing** (p137)

4 Frolic on a long ribbon of powdery sand at **Eagle Beach** (p135), the best beach on an island famous for them

5 It's bottoms up, literally, at one of Aruba's **rum shops** (p140), where the day's events

are dissected and you never know what will happen next

6 Walk, hike, drive and swim on the wild side at **Arikok National Wildlife Park** (p142)

7 Discover the island's newest sight, the compelling **Aruba Archaeological Museum** (p133) in Oranjestad

Oranjestad

POP 33,000

Aruba's capital is a large island town that combines a mix of local commerce with the breathless pursuit of visitor business. It's an interesting place to wander around, if for no other reason than the glimpse of daily Aruban life it provides. But when cruise ships are in port everything is jammed.

Oranjestad has an appealing mix of old and new structures intermingled with scads of shops, bars and restaurants. At night the town is quiet.

⊙ Sights

Oranjestad is good for walking; very little is more than a 10-minute walk from the Yacht Basin. It lacks any real must-see sight; rather, it's best to just stroll and enjoy the scores of small Dutch colonial buildings painted in a profusion of colors. All of the following sights are easily visited on foot.

TOP CHOICE Aruba Archaeological Museum   MUSEUM

(Schelpstraat; admission free; ◷10am-5pm Tue-Fri, 10am-2pm Sat & Sun) Grand 1920s colonial buildings house this brilliant new museum. The engaging exhibits range from stone tools found on Aruba dating from 4000 BC to displays detailing Arawak life and the colonial era.

Fort Zoutman   FORT

Not much to look at, but what's left dates from the 18th century. Best-preserved is the **Willem III Tower**, built to warn of approaching pirates. Fortunately, at that time Aruba was seen as having little in the booty department and pirates typically gave the island a pass.

In the base of the tower is the **Aruba Historical Museum** (☑582-6099; Fort Zoutman 4; ◷8:30am-4pm Mon-Fri). See how a mélange of cultures (African, European, Caribbean and indigenous) have combined to create the island's unique character.

Dr Eloy Ahrends House   HISTORIC SITE

(Oranjestraat) An elegant, thick-walled 1922 house, which is now part of the city-council complex. At night it's lit up like an emerald.

Wilhelmina Park   PARK

Across Lloyd G Smith Blvd by the Yacht Basin is this shady refuge, replete with lush tropical gardens.

⚜ Festivals & Events

TOP CHOICE Carnival   FESTIVAL

(Jan or Feb) This is a big deal on the islands, where a packed schedule of fun begins right after New Year's Day. Aruba's parades are an explosion of sound and color.

Aruba Music Festival   MUSIC FESTIVAL

(Oct) Aruba's annual two-day international concert attracts international and local talent.

Bon Bini Festival   FESTIVAL

(admission US$3; ◷6:30-8:30pm Tue) Staged at Fort Zoutman by the tourism association, the event attracts some top folkloric talent from around the island; local foods and handicrafts are sold.

⛏ Sleeping

Almost every hotel is north of Oranjestad but the one option here is worth considering.

Renaissance Aruba Resort   RESORT $$$

(☑583-6000; www.renaissancearuba.com; Lloyd G Smith Blvd 82; r US$200-450; ☒◉☎☀) The Renaissance Aruba Resort splits its 560 rooms between a large complex with a casino and shopping mall in the heart of town, and a lush tropical complex out by the water. The two are linked by little shuttle boats that leave from a watery atrium in the city complex, and both are linked by boat to a third facility: a small island offshore with a beach. The rooms are comfortable and span the gamut, but be sure to avoid the gloomy ones overlooking the indoor atrium.

✖ Eating

Snack trucks are an island institution. Look for these spotless trucks in the parking lots near the Yacht Basin serving up a range of ultrafresh food from sunset well into the wee hours. Locals debate who sells the best conch sandwich and you may want to conduct your own research. Other tasty options include ribs and anything with curry. Most snacks are under Afl10.

TOP CHOICE Old Fisherman   CONTINENTAL $$

(Havenstraat 36; mains US$8-25; ◷breakfast, lunch & dinner; ☒) It smells like garlic as you enter this compact and crowded local favorite. Breakfast omelets are fluffy, while lunch highlights include excellent salads. At night seafood shines: lobster and shrimp come in various forms. Service is quick yet gracious; there's a full bar.

Driftwood
SEAFOOD **$$$**

(☑583-2515; Klipstraat 12; mains US$18-50; ⊘dinner Wed-Mon) Toss back too many of the serious cocktails at this 1960s supper club and you'll expect Dean Martin to walk in. It's owned by a local fisherman, and the changing menu reflects what he and his pals have caught. Grilled lobster is simple and simply terrific. The US$25 three-course special is a bargain.

Yemanja
GRILL **$$$**

(☑588-4711; Wilhelminastraat 2; mains US$20-35; ⊘dinner) Two colonial buildings behind the Aruba Parliament have been transformed into one of Aruba's most stylish eateries. Cobalt-blue glassware provides accents to the sleek and airy dining areas. Most items on the menu are grilled over wood. Try the seared tuna, the marinated rock lobster or the tenderloin. There's a couple good veggie options as well.

Qué Pasa
INTERNATIONAL **$$**

(Wilhelminastraat 18; mains US$12-25; ⊘lunch Mon-Fri, dinner daily; ☎) The accent is Spanish but the language is global at this effusive cafe. A huge upstairs terrace is just the place to settle in for good drinks, conversation and dishes with myriad inspiration. Check out the art gallery and have a glass of chilled white.

Baby Back Grill
BBQ $

(Caya GF Betico Croes; meals from Afl14; ⊘11am-11pm; 🖘) Like a snack truck, but it doesn't go anywhere and there are shady picnic tables. This completely open-air restaurant grills up tender ribs, steaks, chicken and more for appreciative masses.

Happy Spot
ICE CREAM $

(Caya GF Betico Croes; ⊘11am-8pm) More than a dozen blenders are kept busy making milkshakes and fresh juice drinks at the open-air hut on the main shopping drag. Go on, have a triple cone.

🍸 Drinking & Entertainment

Aruba is not the place to come if you want the latest in techno – it caters to a post-disco crowd more prone to hitting a casino.

Cafe Chaos
BAR

(Lloyd G Smith Blvd 60; ⊘7pm-2am Sun-Fri, 7pm-4am Sat) Crooners warble from the jukebox at this smallish place popular with local professionals. On many nights there's live acoustic, jazz or blues.

Mambo Jambo
BAR-CLUB

(Royal Plaza Mall, Lloyd G Smith Blvd 94; ⊘11am-4am) Overlooking the street from the small mall, Mambo Jambo has drinks as colorful as the straws you use to suck them down. Pop music with a Latin-Euro beat plays till very late.

🔒 Shopping

Numerous shopping malls cluster around Lloyd G Smith Blvd and the cruise-ship port, and most are surprisingly tired. There are vendor huts selling 'crafts' along Lloyd G Smith Blvd, but note these knick-knacks are mostly made by Chinese artisans. Much better is strolling **Caya GF Betico Croes**, Oranjestad's main shopping street. Choices range from international luxury brands to dollar stores. It's a lively mix. Bargaining is not encouraged.

Renaissance Mall
MALL

(Lloyd G Smith Blvd) The retail annex to the luxury hotel is the best mall in Oranjestad. Lots of upscale chains and galleries.

De Wit Bookshop
BOOKSTORE

(Caya GF Betico Croes 94; ⊘8:30am-5pm Mon-Sat) Bestsellers, magazines and Barbie.

Resort Area

Almost all of Aruba's hotels and resorts are on a long strip along some of the Caribbean's best beaches. Beginning 3km northwest of Oranjestad, the resort area has wide roads, lush landscaping and excellent beaches. It's really a world unto itself, similar to beachside developments found the world over.

Both conveniently and accurately, the hotels and condos along Eagle Beach are known as the Low-Rise Resorts. A rapidly developing area leads north of here for about 1.5km to the High-Rise Resorts along Palm Beach. This is also where you'll find a fast-growing zone of upscale malls and nightlife.

🏖 Beaches

TOP CHOICE Eagle Beach
FAMILY, RESORT BEACH

Fronting a stretch of the Low-Rise Resorts just northwest of Oranjestad, Eagle is a long stretch of white sand that regularly makes lists of the best in the world. Portions have shade trees and you can obtain every service you need here, from a lounger to a cold drink. The best all-round choice for everyone, from singles to couples to families with kids.

Manchebo Beach
BEACH

Just south of Eagle, this large beach reaches out to a point. It is popular with topless sunbathers (an activity frowned on elsewhere)

ARUBA RESORT AREA

PORT OF CALL – ORANJESTAD

A long dock can handle several megaships at once, which is good given Aruba's popularity as a cruise-ship destination. Once off the boat, either head off to explore or press into Oranjestad proper. Don't be put off by the humdrum collection of shops closest to the pier. If you're docked for a few hours, don't miss the following:

» An excursion to the many sights on the wild Northeast Coast (p141)

» Time pounding the sand on Eagle Beach, Aruba's best

» Oranjestad's backstreets (p133), where old buildings hold shops and places for a local snack

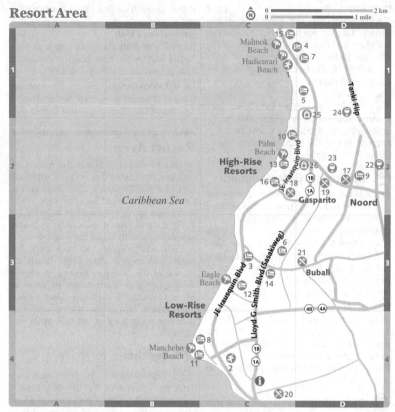

and offers the best chance on the strip to get away from others.

Palm Beach   FAMILY, RESORT BEACH
A classic white-sand beauty, but only for those who enjoy the company of lots of people, as it fronts the High-Rise Resorts. During high season the sands can get jammed, but for some that's part of the scene.

🏃 Activities

Much as people think they want to spend days on end by the beach or pool, the reality is that they soon get bored. Fortunately Aruba has scores of fun activities pegged to its wind and water. All are more energizing than the heavily promoted 4WD tours, ATV tours and numerous other acronym-related tours.

It always seems to be blowing on Aruba. That, coupled with the usually flat water on the west side of the island makes Aruba a premier place for windsurfing and kitesurf-

ing. Day spas are also popular on Aruba and are a feature of many resorts. Treatments usually start at about US$100 and go swiftly upward.

Most activities companies will provide transport to/from your hotel.

Diving & Snorkeling

Aruba has some world-class diving around its shores. One of the most popular spots is the wreck of the large WWII German freighter *Antilla,* which is close to shore and at times is visible above the surface. It lies between Arashi and Malmok Beaches.

Visibility is often upward of 30m, which makes for excellent fish spotting and photography. Reefs are plentiful, with many right off **De Palm Island**, the barrier island off the southwest coast. **Kantil Reef** here has a steep drop-off, and it's easy to spot perky parrotfish, bitchy barracudas and spiny lobsters. Noted nearby reefs include **Skalahein** and **Barcadera**.

Costs for diving and snorkeling are competitive. Daily snorkeling gear rental is about US$20, two-tank dives with all equipment about US$80 and week-long PADI open-water courses about US$400.

Most hotels have a close relationship with at least one dive operator. Conversely, many dive shops can set you up with cheap accommodation. Some recommended dive shops:

Mermaid Sport Divers   DIVING
(☑587-4103; www.scubadivers-aruba.com) Mermaid has a huge range of dive packages plus its own pool for training.

Native Divers Aruba   DIVING
(☑586-4763; www.nativedivers.com) Offers custom trips and certification training.

Roberto's   DIVING
(☑993-2850; www.robertoswatersports.com) Group snorkeling trips US$35; custom snorkeling trips US$125 for two.

Other Activities

TOP CHOICE **Aruba Active Vacations**   WINDSURFING
(☑741-2991; www.aruba-active-vacations.com; Hadicurari Beach) The island's main windsurfing operator is based on Hadicurari Beach at the Fisherman's Huts, a prime bit of windsurfing water south of Malmok Beach. Rentals start at US$55 per day and a variety of lessons are available. It also does kitesurfing for similar rates.

Aruba Kayak Adventure   KAYAKING
(☑582-5520; www.arubakayak.com; tours from US$72) Novices and pros alike enjoy a fascinating circuit of the mangroves and shoreline near Spanish Lagoon on the south coast. Some options include lunch and snorkeling. Although you're unlikely to encounter one now, this was one of the few spots on the island pirates were known to visit. What's a pirate's favorite island? Arrrrrrrrr-ruba.

Aruba Nature Sensitive Hiking & Jeep Tours   HIKING
(☑594-5017; www.naturesensitivetours.com; tours from US$80) Join the former top ranger at Arikok park who now leads hiking tours of the seldom explored parts of the island, mostly in the east. Hikes range from easy to strenuous, and longer itineraries include the use of jeeps to link areas. There's a strong environmental focus to the tours.

Rancho Daimari   HORSEBACK RIDING
(☑585-0290; tours from US$65) One of the better outfits for touring Aruba by horse. It offers rides to the Natural Pool and Andicuri Beach on the rugged northeast coast. Certainly, riding a fertilizer-producing critter to these attractions is better than tearing

across the landscape in a 4WD – as many operators promote.

Mandara Spa SPA
(☑520-6750; www.mandaraspa.com; Aruba Marriott Resort, Lloyd G Smith Blvd 101) A branch of the worldwide chain of luxe spas.

Intermezzo Day Spa SPA
(☑586-0613; www.arubaspa.com; Westin Aruba Resort, JE Irausquin Blvd 77) Has several locations in the ABCs.

Links at Divi Aruba GOLF
(www.divigolf.com; JE Irausquin Blvd; green fee US$85, club rental US$25) A nine-hole links amid the Divi resort empire in the Low-Rise Resorts area. Fees include the use of a cart.

☞ Tours

Scores of companies offer day trips on sailboats and yachts. Many are pegged to the sunset. Other outfits organize pub crawls aboard garishly decorated school buses replete with horns blaring what might be 'Babba-loo!'

Atlantis Submarine UNDERWATER TOURS
(☑588-6881; www.atlantisadventures.com; adult/child US$100/50) Popular with kids and kid-like adults, this is the Aruba edition of the attraction found at islands throughout the Caribbean and Hawaii. In an hour-long tour, you submerge over 30m and, as Tony Soprano might say, 'go swimming with the fishes.'

De Palm Tours SIGHTSEEING TOURS
(☑582-4400; www.depalm.com) De Palm's heavily promoted tours crisscross the island, taking vacationers on a dizzying variety of trips. Tour prices start at US$40 for a sightseeing tour and most include a stop on its outdoor activities island.

🛏 Sleeping

Accommodations on Aruba are ideally suited to the large-resort-seeking tourists the island targets. The two main clusters of resorts – the descriptively named Low-Rise Resorts and High-Rise Resorts – comprise fairly large three- and four-star properties. This is not the island for little boutique inns or posh five-star resorts. In fact the area between the two clusters is rapidly filling in with what could give it the name 'Time-Share Land.'

Lower-priced places to stay tend to be inland away from the beaches, although the drive or walk can be fairly short. Most have a certain utilitarian charm and are good choices for divers or others planning all-day activities where the joys of a beachfront hotel would be unappreciated.

LOW-RISE RESORTS AREA
The best area for families and fronted by Eagle Beach, Aruba's best.

TOP CHOICE **Bucuti Beach Resort** RESORT $$$
(☑583-1100; www.bucuti.com; Lloyd G Smith Blvd 55B; r US$300-500; ❋@🛜☒) One of the classiest choices among the Manchebo Beach low-rises, the 63-room Bucuti has a vaguely Spanish feel. Guest rooms are large, with kitchenettes and deep balconies, many with ocean views. The Tara wing is quite luxurious. There is a cafe in a concrete pirate ship. (What's a pirate's favorite movie? Booty and the Beast.) Rates include a breakfast buffet and many other extras.

BucutiCam (www.bucuticam.com) is a daily webcam picture shot at a designated time at the Bucuti Beach Resort. Vacationers pose for the folks back home, hold up signs and in some cases show off amazing tans.

Manchebo Beach Resort RESORT $$$
(☑582-3444; wwww.manchebo.com; JE Irausquin Blvd 55; r US$300-500; ❋@🛜☒) Right on the eponymous beach, this crescent of two-story blocks sits at a discreet distance from the surf. It's all understated luxury here, there's no flash – although the little row of wooden cottages near the waves comes close. Most of the rooms have had a stylish refit. The resort wears its green credentials proudly; all-inclusive packages are available.

Amsterdam Manor Beach Resort HOTEL $$$
(☑587-1492; www.amsterdammanor.com; JE Irausquin Blvd 252; r US$200-350; ❋@🛜☒) At the north end of blindingly white Eagle Beach, this 72-unit family-run resort mimics a Dutch village, without the frosty weather. Rooms and buildings come in a variety of shapes and sizes; all have kitchenettes. Some have sizable balconies or terraces with views.

MVC Eagle Beach Aruba HOTEL $$
(☑587-0110; www.mvceaglebeach.com; JE Irausquin Blvd 240; r US$90-150; ❋@☒) Thank Dutch taxpayers for this amazing deal right across from Eagle Beach. Owned by the Dutch Navy, it's a basic two-story block with 16 rooms facing a small pool. Although beefy seaman-types abound, it's open to the mass-

es, who enjoy the best deal in Aruba for the location. Don't expect any frills, but it does have a convivial bar-restaurant.

HIGH-RISE RESORTS AREA

The High-Rise Resorts area is the top-end holiday spot of Aruba, where almost all the hotels are affiliated with major chains. The properties accommodate thousands of guests, who compete for pool loungers, elbow each other on crowded Palm Beach and seek comfort in US$15 rum punches. It's not an area that will appeal to many independent travelers. Behind the resorts there is a plethora of development adding upscale malls and nightlife to the mix.

Radisson Aruba Resort
RESORT **$$$**

(📞586-6555; www.radisson.com/aruba; JE Irausquin Blvd 81; r US$275-600; ✳@🛜🏊) The pick of the litter. Extensive, lush grounds; 359 rooms.

Aruba Marriott Resort
RESORT **$$$**

(📞586-9000; www.marriottaruba.com; Lloyd G Smith Blvd 101; r US$300-500; ✳@🛜🏊) Over 400 rooms with large balconies but seems to function as a venue for sales of time-shares.

Hyatt Regency Aruba Resort
RESORT **$$$**

(📞586-1234; www.aruba.hyatt.com; JE Irausquin Blvd 85; r US$300-600; ✳@🛜🏊) Has an elegant Moorish motif, but the beach is crowded, as are the tropical birds displayed in small cages; 360 rooms.

Westin Aruba Resort
RESORT **$$$**

(📞586-4466; www.westin.com; JE Irausquin Blvd 77; r US$250-500; ✳@🛜🏊) A cramped site and at its roots a 1970s property with 480 rooms. Also has tropical birds in cages.

INLAND

This is where the budget lodgings are found. The beach is usually about a 10- to 15-minute walk. Bonuses include being away from the crowds and closer to authentic Aruban life.

Coconut Inn
HOTEL **$$**

(📞586-6288; www.coconutinn.com; Noord 31; r US$70-110; ✳@🏊) Near the collection of restaurants in Noord on a small road north of Noord Ave, the Coconut has a few of the eponymous trees in its simple grounds. The 40 rooms are motel-room basic but the pool is a large rectangle of aqua joy.

Arubiana Inn
HOTEL **$$**

(📞587-7700; www.arubianainn.com; Bubali 74; r US$80-110; ✳🛜🏊) About a 15-minute walk east from Eagle Beach and near some food outlets, this spartan hotel is popular with

Europeans on budget packages. The rooms have a dash of style and services include free coolers for taking drinks to the beach.

Sasaki Apartments
HOTEL **$$**

(📞587-7482; www.sasaki-apartments.com; Bubali 143, Noord; r US$80-110; ✳@🛜🏊) This simple complex is just a couple of busy roads away from Eagle Beach. The 24 studio apartments are spare in decor but have fully equipped kitchens. There's a pool, a barbecue grill and you're a short walk from a little village of bakeries and stores.

🍴 Eating

Close to the resorts are plenty of overpriced joints, franchises (Hooters!) and fast-food outlets but a short walk or drive inland to Noord and you'll find a nice range of locally owned places.

TOP CHOICE Carte Blanche
INTERNATIONAL **$$$**

(📞586-3339; www.carteblanchearuba.com; JE Irausquin Blvd 330; dinner US$70; ⏲dinner Tue-Sat) It's like being invited to a dinner party thrown by your impossibly talented friends, except this is probably better. Fourteen seats are arrayed in a sleek open kitchen where you interact with chef Dennis van Daatselaar while he prepares a five-course meal that changes nightly. Meanwhile Glen Bonset is preparing drinks and seeing to your comfort. In high season you have to book weeks in advance; no one aged under 18 is allowed.

Gasparito Restaurant
CARIBBEAN **$$$**

(📞586-7044; www.gasparito.com; Gasparito 3, Noord; mains US$20-35; ⏲dinner) Gasparito has fine Aruban dining inside a classic old country house or outside on the candlelit patio. Old family recipes prepared here include *keshi yena*, a meat-filled cheese wonder, and shrimp marinated in brandy and coconut milk. A vegetarian platter is the menu sleeper: plantains and more in a Creole sauce.

Bingo
BAR-GRILL **$$**

(Palm Beach 6D, Noord; meals US$10-20; ⏲dinner; 🛜) This popular Dutch-run cafe is both a genial bar and a good place for a casual meal. Enjoy pub fare such as burgers at tables inside and out or opt for more ambitious steak and seafood mains. The bar stays open until 2am.

Sunrise Bakery
BAKERY **$**

(Bubali 72; snacks Afl4; ⏲8am-5pm) This aromatic bakery with sweet and savory

RUM SHOPS

Throughout Aruba's hinterlands you will see rum shops. These island institutions are part bar, part cafe and part social center. Here's where you'll meet anyone from taxi drivers to accountants. Although there are dozens and they come in all sizes, it's not hard to identify them as they invariably are plastered with Balashi, Amstel and/or Heineken signs. The rum itself is often locally produced and may drive you to drink – beer.

The rules are simple: you stand, drink rum – or beer – have a snack and unburden yourself to whoever is nearby. On Friday after work, crowds spill out into the streets.

A good place to sample this culture is the easily accessible **Caribbean Store** (586-5544; Noord; 8am-11pm), which is east of the High-Rise Resorts; it has stand-up tables in a dirt parking lot and a cheery bar inside.

Another good choice for locals and visitors alike is the **JJ Snack** (Tanki Flip, Noord; 11am-7pm). You can't miss the Heineken banners on the outside. Inside enjoy Creole accented snacks.

Finally, for a rum shop with a strong Dutch accent try **Cafe 080** (Tanki Flip, Noord; 3pm-midnight), which has old furniture under a huge shade tree. It's at the turn for the road to the Chapel of Alto Vista.

ARUBA

treats is near budget hotels and close to other popularly priced takeaways, cafes and groceries.

Ling & Sons　　　　　　SUPERMARKET $
(Schotlandstraat 41; 8am-8pm Mon-Sat, 8am-1pm Sun) All those kitchenettes demand a good supermarket and this is it. It has a large deli, a salad bar and more.

🍷 Drinking

With resorts hogging so much of the waterfront, Aruba lacks the kind of bamboo beach shacks peddling rum punches that are basic to so many a Caribbean holiday. Instead, opt for a local spot where you can make friends and let the evening drift away. Bingo in Noord is a popular place for a drink. Nearby rum shops (see the 'Rum Shops' boxed text) are another amiable option.

Cafe Rembrandt　　　　　　BAR
(www.rembrandt-aruba.com; South Beach Centre; 8am-1am, to 3am Fri & Sat) A fine option for a drink with a cool crowd, this Dutch-accented cafe is in a large open space within a newish mall. But you'll forget that as you lounge about and let the trendy tunes work their magic.

☆ Entertainment

Nightlife in the Low-Rise Resorts area is blissfully sedate. In the High-Rise Resorts area it is focused in and around several high-concept malls with a plethora of mostly chain bars, lounges and cinemas.

Almost every high-rise resort has a casino, many of which are surprisingly small. Slot machines are by far the most common game, and facilities at even the flashiest places are not comparable to anything in Las Vegas. Slots are typically open 10am to 4am, tables 6pm to 4am.

Stellaris Casino　　　　　　CASINO
(Aruba Marriott Resort, Lloyd G Smith Blvd 101; 24hr) One of the largest casinos, always busy and a bit flashy.

Copa Cabana Casino　　　　　　CASINO
(Hyatt Regency Aruba Resort; JE Irausquin Blvd 85) Glitzy; cover bands offer distraction while you lose your shirt.

🛍 Shopping

Flashy new shopping centers are appearing in the midst of the High-Rise Resorts. They give the area another jolt of activity, especially at night when visitors wander, window-shop, people-watch, have a drink in the many cafes or go bowling. Note that a lack of overall planning means that you may end up walking in the mud between high-fashion malls.

Paseo Herrencia　　　　　　MALL
Glossiest of the new malls, it has brilliant illuminated water shows at night. There's a cinema, dinner theatre and a lot of chain restaurants and shops.

South Beach Centre　　　　　　MALL
Large mall that has some interesting shops and bars mixed in with predictable chains like Hard Rock.

Northwest Coast

The glitz of the resort area is quickly forgotten in this adjoining region of decent beaches, gracious homes and some significant Aruban landmarks.

◎ Sights & Activities

TOP CHOICE **California Lighthouse** LANDMARK
Near Arashi Beach, watch for a road leading to the island's northern tip. This tall sentinel is named for an old shipwreck named *California*, which is *not* the ship of the same name that stood by ineffectually while the *Titanic* sank (despite much local lore to the contrary). The views over the flat land from the lighthouse knoll extend in all directions, and when it's especially clear you can see all the way to Oranjestad. The surf is always pounding and dunes extend far inland.

Arashi Beach FAMILY BEACH
Near the island's northwest tip, this is a favorite with locals and popular with families. There is good bodysurfing, some shade and just a few rocks right offshore.

Malmok Beach WINDSURFING BEACH
Shallow waters extending far out from shore make this a popular spot for windsurfers. Not the best place for simple sunbathing, as it's rather rocky. Just south of here are the iconic old **Fisherman's Huts**.

🛏 Sleeping

Almost in the shadow of the generic international resorts just south on Palm Beach, the hotels of the north are a characterful bunch with sunset views and a 30-second walk to the admittedly thin beach.

TOP CHOICE **Beach House Aruba** HOTEL $$
(☎586-2384; www.beach-house-aruba.com; Lloyd G Smith Blvd 450; r US$75-320; ❋@🅟🏊) Funky doesn't begin to describe this sprawling collection of beach huts set in a dense garden across from the ocean.

Sunset Beach Studios HOTEL $$
(☎586-3940; www.aruba-sunsetblvds.com; Lloyd G Smith Blvd 486; r US$80-140; ❋@🅟🏊) Right across the coast road from rocky Malmok Beach, this 10-room property has a carefree funky charm. Units in front can take in the sunset, while those in back view the pool. All have kitchenettes. Some of the island's best windsurfing is right out front.

Aruba Beach Villas HOTEL $$
(☎586-1072; www.arubabeachvillas.com; Lloyd G Smith Blvd 462; r $100-250; ❋@🅟🏊) Nicely located across the coast road from Malmok Beach, the 31 units here are bright and have kitchenettes. Those facing the beach have large patios with sun chairs. Guests have free use of snorkeling and windsurfing gear, plus kayaks. The high-rise beach area is a five-minute walk south.

Northeast Coast

Aruba may be small but you'll feel like you've left the island behind on its remote and wild northeast coast, where wind and wave add atmosphere to the desolation.

◎ Sights & Activities

Chapel of Alto Vista CHURCH
This remote 1950s church is built on the site of one dating to 1750. The road to salvation here is lined with signs bearing prayers. Look for the divi-divi tree right out of central casting – it looks like a question mark caught in a hurricane.

Natural Bridge NATURAL FEATURE
One of several natural bridge rock formations on Aruba, this one has a decent road and a gift shop. Wave action hollowed out a limestone cave on the sea cliffs that later collapsed, leaving the 'bridge.' It's crowded when cruise ships are in port; otherwise it's a moody and windswept spot (unless some group on an ATV tour roars through...).

Ayo Rock NATURAL FEATURE
Just off the road to Natural Bridge, look for this smooth-sided geological wonder popular with rock climbers. It boasts ancient drawings. For postcard shots, you should also visit **Casibari Rock**, about 1.5km west of Ayo Rock. Steps lead to the top where there are good **views** across the island.

TOP CHOICE **Andicuri Beach** SECLUDED BEACH
A black-pebble beach on the isolated east coast, this hidden gem is often the scene of photo shoots. It's reached by a road that demands 4WD. Swimming can be treacherous; the winds make reading a challenge.

Donkey Sanctuary ANIMAL SHELTER
(☎584-1063; www.arubandonkey.org; donations appreciated) Make an ass out of yourself petting these winsome critters. Originally brought to Aruba by the Spaniards, many

WORTH A TRIP

TAKING A NATURAL DIP

The descriptively named **Natural Pool** is a depression behind a limestone ridge that often fills with seawater thanks to wave action. Given the rough swimming conditions on the east coast of Aruba, this is a good spot for a dip. It lies just inside the northern boundary of Arikok National Wildlife Park. You can reach it by 4WD or – better – a 1.5mi walk from the visitors center.

donkeys now live in the wild, where they fall prey to speeding tour buses. Injured ones are brought here to recuperate. The sanctuary is usually open during daylight hours; call ahead to check.

Arikok National Wildlife Park

Arid and rugged, Arikok National Wildlife Park comprises 20% of Aruba and is the top nonbeach natural attraction.

The park has an impressive new **Visitors Center** (☑585-1234; www.arubanationalpark.org; adult/child US$5/free; ☉ticket sales 8am-5pm, park gate 24hr) at the entrance. Here you'll find displays on the park and its natural features, which include some rather unhappy-looking boa constrictors and rattlesnakes. There's a small cafe and a wide veranda for soaking up the park while you enjoy your coffee.

Two gardens inside the park entrance are worth visiting. **Cunucu Arikok** and **Shon Shoco** have short trails with signs and labels describing the many native plants. More than 70% of the types of plant here are used in traditional medicine. The land is mostly pretty scruffy and there are remnants of **old gold mines** built long ago by Europeans and slaves.

The principal road is about 11km long and links the west entrance with the southern one near San Nicolas, allowing a circular tour. Although slow going, it's doable in a budget rental car. A 4WD vehicle will let you enjoy tracks off the main circuit that include sand dunes, rocky coves, caves and remote hiking trails. Watch out for the many iguanas as you drive and stop once and a while and listen for the bray of **wild donkeys**.

Numerous hiking trails lead across the hilly terrain. Bring water and ask for rec-

ommendations from the friendly rangers at the visitors center. Look for the park's three main types of **trees**: the iconic and bizarrely twisted divi-divi; the *kwihi*, with its tasty sweet-sour long yellow beans; and the *hubada*, which has sharp, tough thorns. Spiky aloe plants abound – see how many of the 70 varieties of cactus you can identify.

Near the coast you will see a small creek, which is the only natural supply of water on Aruba. It flows into a mangrove by the ocean. Here you can also see vast **sand dunes**. At **Boca Prins** on the coast there is a dramatic and dangerous beach in a narrow cove that forms explosive surf. Nearby, your table stays crumb-free at **Boca Prins Cafe** (☑584-5455; meals US$10-15; ☉10am-6pm) as it is buffeted by the constant winds.

For safer swimming, a rough road leads north to **Dos Playa**, which as the name implies is two beaches. Otherwise, from Boca Prins you can head south along the wave-tossed coast and end up in San Nicolas.

Guided hikes (US$25 per group) are lead by park rangers and cover a variety of themes. Book at least one day in advance with the visitor center.

San Nicolas

A small town near the island's ill-placed oil refinery, San Nicolas preserves Aruba's former rough-and-ready character long since banished from Oranjestad. Prostitution is legal here and a string of windowless bars in the 'Red Zone' open at night. It's all tightly regulated and the streets are pretty safe.

Beaches

Escape the crowds of the north at these two fine southern beaches.

Baby Beach   SECLUDED BEACH
Nice curve of sand in the uncrowded south. The waters are calm. Nearby Coco's Beach is almost as nice, except for the view of the refinery.

Boca Grandi   WINDSURFING BEACH
Reached by a rough road, this small cove is often deserted but for a few windsurfers. As is typical of windward beaches, conditions here are often hazardous, albeit dramatic.

Drinking

Charlie's Bar   BAR-GRILL **$$**
(Zeppenfeldstraat 56; meals US$8-25; ☉11am-late)
Charlie's Bar is the big draw here. Started in

1941, it is still run by the same family and is a community institution. The walls are lined with a hodgepodge of stuff collected over the decades: everything from beach flotsam to local sports trophies to artwork by customers. The food combines local dishes with plenty of fresh seafood.

UNDERSTAND ARUBA

History

Humans are first thought to have lived on Aruba some 4000 years ago. Spain claimed the island in 1499, but its inhospitable arid landscape provoked little colonial enthusiasm and the native Arawaks were largely left alone. The Dutch took claim in 1636 and, except for a British interlude in the early 19th century, have maintained control since.

Prosperity came to the island in the form of the huge oil refinery built to refine Venezuelan crude oil in the 1920s. This large complex occupies the southeastern end of Aruba and dominates the blue-collar town of San Nicolas. Jobs at the plant contributed to the development of a local middle class. Automation meant workers had to look elsewhere, and the island has successfully transferred its economy from dependence on refining oil to relaxing tourists.

The three islands of the ABCs have never been chums, and Aruba was able to leverage its affluence to break away from the rest of the Netherlands Antilles and become an autonomous entity within the Netherlands in 1986. Talk of achieving full independence has not become anything more than that: talk.

Aruba made an unwanted media splash in the US starting in 2005 when an Atlanta teenager, Natalie Holloway, disappeared while on holiday. The resulting controversy has left deep scars on the island and continues to have twists and turns that beggar belief. It remains a favorite subject for sensationalist American media and has ensnared people in the Netherlands and South America as well as Aruba and the US.

Culture

The main form of art on Aruba is music. No style is sacred and improvisation is the rule. At times you'll hear Creole, blues, jazz, rock, pop, rap and more. Making music is popular and many people on the island play in small groups with friends and relatives. No social gathering of any significance is complete without some live music. Aruba was not part of the slave trade and today the population is primarily mestizo, people who are a mixture of indigenous American and European heritage. About 20% of the population are Dutch and American expats.

Landscape & Wildlife

Aruba is primarily arid, with cactuses and other hardy plants that can make do with the minimal rainfall each year. Reptiles – especially huge iguanas – are the main creatures native to the land.

Aruba's most visible environmental woe is the puffing stacks of the oil refinery at the south end of the island, although smog also comes from the world's second-largest desalination plant, south of the airport, which roars away 24/7. The need to balance the island's healthy economy with its limited water and other resources has been a major point of discussion on the island, and a factor in elections, and locals have pressed for growth controls. This has slowed but by no means stopped the rampant development of hotels and condos on the long strip to the north.

SURVIVAL GUIDE

Directory A–Z

Accommodations

Aruba has a long strip of beach resorts great and small (well, not-so-big). More modest-priced places are found about a 10-minute walk inland. Camping is uncommon. High-season prices usually run mid-December to mid-April.

Hotel taxes and fees are 6% tax plus 10% to 15% service charge.

$	budget	less than US$75
$$	midrange	US$75 to $200
$$$	top end	more than US$200

Business Hours

The following are standard business hours across the island. Exceptions are noted in

PRACTICALITIES

» **Electricity** 110V, 60Hz; US-style two- and three-pin plugs are used.

» **Radio & TV** 89.9FM features the cheery touristy boosterisms of the Dick Miller Show between 7pm and 8pm.

» **Weights & Measures** Metric system.

specific listings. Outside of tourist areas, much is closed on Sunday.

Banks 9am-4pm Mon-Fri

Restaurants 11am-10pm

Shops 9am-6pm Mon-Fri, to 1pm Sat (in tourist areas to 8pm daily)

Children

Aruba is a good destination for families. Almost all resorts have activities for kids. In addition, the famous reefs protect the beaches from really nasty surf, although the windward sides of the island can get rough.

Food

The following price categories for the cost of a main course are used in the listings in this chapter:

$	budget	less than US$10
$$	midrange	US$10 to $25
$$$	top end	more than US$25

Health

There are excellent medical facilities in Aruba. Tap water is safe to drink.

Dr Horacio Oduber Hospital (587-4300; off Lloyd G Smith Blvd; 24hr) is a large and well-equipped hospital, near the Low-Rise Resorts.

Language

If you only speak English, you won't have a problem on Aruba. Arubans are multilingual: Dutch and Papiamento are the official languages; English is widespread.

Money

You can pay for just about everything in US dollars on Aruba. Sometimes you will get change back in US currency, other times you will receive it in Aruban florins (Afl).

In restaurants, a 20% overall tip is reasonable, though a 15% service charge is often added to the bill. In taxis a 10% tip is usual. Hotels usually add a 15% service charge to the bill.

Public Holidays

In addition to those observed throughout the region (p872), Aruba has the following public holidays:

GF (Betico) Croes Day January 25

Carnival Monday Monday before Ash Wednesday

National Day March 18

Queen's Birthday April 30

Labour Day May 1

Ascension Day Sixth Thursday after Easter

Telephone

Aruba's country code is 1; the area code is 297. To call any other country with a country code of 1 (most of North America and the Caribbean), just dial 1 and the 10-digit number. For other countries, dial the international access code 011 + country code + number.

GSM cell phones are compatible with local SIM cards. There is also 3G service. The main operators are **Digicel** (www.digicelaruba .com) and **Setar** (www.setar.aw).

Tourist Information

Aruba Tourism Authority (582-3777; www.aruba.com; Lloyd G Smith Blvd; 7:30am-noon & 1-4:30pm Mon-Fri) is a well-funded entity, with a comprehensive and useful website. It has an Oranjestad office, part of a trio of buildings that comprise the Aruban tourism-industrial complex, with helpful staff.

Getting There & Away
Entering Aruba

All visitors need a passport and a return or onward ticket to enter Aruba.

Air

Aruba's **Reina Beatrix International Airport** (www.airportaruba.com) is a busy, modern airport with services (some seasonal) from North America with Air Canada, American Airlines, Delta, JetBlue, United and US Airways. KLM flies from Amsterdam. Other airlines connecting Aruba with the region:

Avianca (www.avianca.com) Bogota, Colombia

DAE (www.flydae.com) Bonaire, Curaçao

Insel Air (www.fly-inselair.com) Bonaire, Curaçao

Tiara Air (www.tiara-air.com) Bonaire, Curaçao

Venezolona (www.ravsa.com.ve) Caracas

Sea

The ABCs are part of cruise-ship itineraries that cover the southern Caribbean, often on longer 10-day and two-week trips.

Cruise ships flock to Aruba; it's not unusual to have more than 10,000 passengers descend on the island in a day. Boats dock at the port in the middle of Oranjestad.

Getting Around

If you just want to stay at your hotel with only a few forays into Oranjestad and perhaps a hotel-arranged tour, then you won't need a car. Taxis and local buses will get the job done; however, buses don't travel to the more extreme parts of the island to the north, east or south, or into Arikok National Wildlife Park. For freedom to explore Aruba, a car or a bike – at least for a couple of days – is essential.

To/From the Airport

Hotels and resorts usually do not do airport pickups. The taxi fare to the main resort area is about US$25; to Oranjestad is US$20.

Public buses 1 and 8 link Oranjestad to the airport every 30 to 60 minutes. You can connect to the resort areas.

Bicycle

Although there are no bike lanes on Aruba, many people enjoy riding along the mostly flat roads. You can easily rent bikes at many resorts.

Bus

The main **bus depot** (Lloyd G Smith Blvd) is right in the center of Oranjestad. **Arubus** (☎588-0616; www.arubus.com) buses 10, 10A and 10B serve the hotel areas from Oranjestad. Buses run every 15 to 30 minutes from 6am to 11:30pm and cost one-way/round-trip Afl2.25/4.

Buses do not go to the rugged parts of the island to the north, east or south, or into Arikok National Wildlife Park.

Car & Motorcycle

RENTAL

You'll know the tourists not only by the V-registrations of their rental cars but also by their actual use of turn signals. All the major car-rental companies have offices at the airport. It's worth comparing prices with local outfits, including **Economy Car Rental** (☎583-0200; www.economyaruba.com) and **Optima Rent-A-Car** (☎582-4828; www.optimarentacar.com).

ROAD CONDITIONS

Main roads are generally in pretty good condition; however, roads in the national park and other remote spots can be quite rough. Consider renting a 4WD or other vehicle with high ground clearance if you want to go exploring. Gasoline is easily found; road signs are sporadic.

ROAD RULES

Driving is on the right-hand side, seat belts are required and motorcyclists must use helmets.

Taxi

Taxis are easy to come by at hotels and resorts. Fares are set for fixed distances. From the airport to the High-Rise Resorts costs US$25, for example. Extra passengers cost US$2 and you can charter a taxi for touring for US$45 per hour.

 DEPARTING ARUBA

Passengers flying to the US absolutely must check in three hours before flight time. Actually four hours might be better because all US-bound passengers clear customs and immigration *before* they leave Aruba. Most flights back to the US leave during a small timeslot in the afternoon and the US-staffed immigration facilities are often mobbed. If possible, try to avoid going home on a weekend, when things are worst. Once ensconced in the terminal, there are bookstores, places for internet access and fast-food places.

The Bahamas

Why Go?

Scattered like dabs of silver and green paint on an artist's palette, the Bahamas are ready-made for exploration. Just ask Christopher Columbus – he bumped against these limestone landscapes in 1492 and changed the course of history. But the adventure didn't end with the *Niña*, the *Pinta* and the *Santa Maria*. From pirates and blockade dodgers to rum smugglers, wily go-getters have converged and caroused on the country's 700 islands and 2400 cays for centuries.

So what's in it for travelers? There's sailing around the Abacos' history-filled Loyalist Cays. Partying til dawn at Paradise Island's over-the-top Atlantis resort. Diving the spooky blue holes of Andros. Kayaking the 365 Exuma Cays. Lounging on Eleuthera's pink-sand beaches. Pondering pirates in Nassau. There's a Bahamian island to match most every water-and-sand-based compulsion, each framed by a backdrop of gorgeous, mesmerizing blue.

So paint your own adventure – the palette awaits.

When to Go

The Bahamas enjoy around 320 sunny days a year. Daytime temperatures December to April average 70°F (21°C), and June to September a perfect 80°F (26°C). In general, the islands are balmy year-round, with cooling, near-constant trade winds blowing by day from the east. The so-called rainy season extends from late May to November; hurricane season is June to November.

High season typically runs from mid-December to mid-April, when hotel prices are at their most expensive. Some hotels are booked solid around Christmas and Easter, and college spring break in March means Nassau and Grand Bahama crawl with rum-fueled revelers. During low season, many hotels reduce their rates significantly. Some Out Island hotels close, but tourist accommodations are always available.

Best Beaches

» Cabbage Beach (p154)
» Cable Beach (p161)
» Pink Sands Beach (p179)
» Treasure Cay Beach (p174)
» Gold Rock Beach (p172)

Best Places to Stay

» Graycliff Hotel (p157)
» Hope Town Harbour Lodge (p177)
» Pink Sands Resort (p179)
» Kamalame Cay (p188)

Itineraries

THREE DAYS

Explore Pirates of Nassau, the National Art Gallery and Fort Fincastle in downtown Nassau, grab a *jitney* for beach-bar cocktails, hike over the Paradise Island bridge to gawk at Atlantis' shark tanks, and snooze on Cabbage Beach.

ONE WEEK

Add a Bahamas ferry ride to Harbour Island for pink-sand shores and boutique browsing, or to Andros for mind-blowing dives to the Tongue of the Ocean and hikes to hidden blue holes.

TWO WEEKS

Add a trip to the Abacos for cay hopping, or to the Exumas for kayaking, kitesurfing and adventuring.

GETTING TO NEIGHBORING ISLANDS

Lynden Pindling International Airport in Nassau is the Bahamas' number-one entry point. From here, island hoppers can make the jump to nearby island nations such as the Turks and Caicos, Jamaica, and Trinidad and Tobago. A variety of airlines service these routes, making interisland travel a snap. Though mail boats and ferries run between the various Bahamian islands, there is no regular sea service to other island nations. If you're dead set on seeing multiple Caribbean islands by sea, chartering a yacht or signing up for a cruise are your best bets.

Essential Food & Drink

» **Conch** Roasted, cracked (fried), chopped into salads or dipped in dough and fried into fritters, this chewy sea snail is the most ubiquitous food in the Bahamas. Think calamari. Starchy side dishes like peas 'n' rice (rice with beans), mac 'n' cheese and potato salad round out the menu.

» **Boil fish** A breakfast dish of grouper stewed with lime juice, onions and potatoes. Usually served with johnnycake, a type of flat cornbread.

» **Spiny Caribbean lobster** The Bahamas' native lobster, often served sauteed with onions and pepper.

» **Souse** A thick stew of lamb, sheep's head, pig's trotter or other 'leftover' meats.

» **Guava duff** Boiled pastry filled with sweet guava paste and topped off with rum or cream sauce.

» **Beer** Wash everything down with a cold Kalik or Sands beer.

» **Rum cocktails** Try Goombay Smash or a Bahama Mama.

AT A GLANCE

» **Currency** Bahamian (BS$) and US dollars are equal and interchangeable

» **Language** English

» **Money** ATMs widely available on Nassau and Grand Bahama, rarer in the Out Islands

» **Visas** Not necessary for Americans, Europeans and citizens of most Commonwealth countries

Fast Facts

» **Area** 5358 sq miles

» **Population** 354,000

» **Capital** Nassau

» **Telephone country code** ☑242

» **Emergency** ♪911 or 919

Set Your Budget

» **Budget hotel room** BS$100

» **Two-course evening meal** BS$40

» **Museum entrance** BS$10

» **Beer** BS$4

» **Bus ticket** BS$1

Resources

» **Lonely Planet Bahamas** (www.lonelyplanet.com/the-bahamas) Destination information, hotel bookings, traveler forum and more

» **Bahamas Ministry of Tourism** (www.bahamas.com) Useful hotel, dining, transportation, activity and events info

The Bahamas Highlights

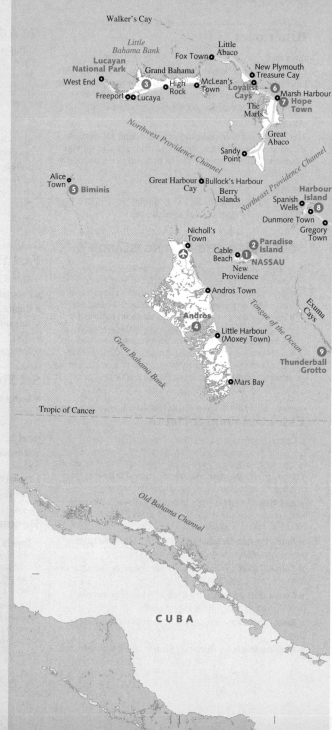

1 Munching cracked conch, sipping on sky juice, and dancing with the locals at Nassau's **Arawak Cay** (p162) fish fry

2 Hurtling down a 200ft waterslide at Atlantis' high-octane **Aquaventure Waterpark** (p154) on Paradise Island

3 Paddling a kayak through the mangrove swamps of Grand Bahama's **Lucayan National Park** (p172)

4 Hiking through vast, unspoilt forests, searching for blue holes and avoiding the mythical chickcharnies in **Andros** (p186)

5 Channeling the spirit of Hemingway by angling for marlin off the **Biminis** (p188)

6 Hanging out with yachties, locals and everyone at the Sunday pig roast at **Nipper's** (p178) on Great Guana Cay in the Loyalist Cays

7 Climbing the iconic red-and-white **lighthouse** (p176) at Hope Town, Elbow Cay

8 Strolling Harbour Island's ethereal **Pink Sands Beach** (p179)

9 Snorkeling or diving in the Exumas' exquisite **Thunderball Grotto** (p184)

10 Experience an exquisite Cat Island sunrise from Father Jerome's hilltop **Mt Alvernia Hermitage** (p187)

THE
BAHAMAS

ATLANTIC

OCEAN

Eleuthera

Governor's
Harbour

Tarpum Bay

Exuma Sound

Arthur's Town

Little San
Salvador

Cat Island

New Bight

Mt Alvernia
(206ft)

Winding
Bay

Staniel Cay

Cockburn
Town

San Salvador

Conception
Island

Rum
Cay

Great
Exuma

Seymours

Port
Nelson

Barreterre

Stocking
Island

Stella
Maris

Tropic of Cancer

George Town

Little
Exuma

William's
Town

Long Island

Guana
Key

Deadman's
Cay

Turtle Cove

Samana Cay

Clarence Town

Jumento
Cays

Gordons

Crooked Island Passage

Colonel
Hill

Crooked
Island

Plana
Cays

Ragged
Island
Range

Long Cay

Chesters

Albert Town

Spring Point

Acklins
Island

Mayaguana Passage

Mayaguana

Abraham
Bay

Caicos Passage

Duncan Town

Little
Ragged
Island

North
Caicos

Providenciales

Providenciales

Caicos
Bank

Little
Inagua

West
Caicos

TURKS
AND
CAICOS
(UK)

Bahamas National
Trust Park

Great
Inagua

Matthew
Town

0   100 km
0   60 miles

NEW PROVIDENCE

POP 249,000

What New Providence lacks in size, it more than makes up for in energy, attitude and devil-may-care spirit. In fact, this 21-mile-long powerhouse of an island is a perfect fit for the type A tourist with money to burn. Plummet down a 50ft waterslide, puff on a hand-rolled stogie, place your bets on a high-stakes hand and carouse like a pirate into the wee hours – it's all there for the grabbing. Even rejuvenation is high-energy, with Paradise Island and Cable Beach boasting some of the liveliest beaches around. But who'd expect less on an island 007 calls home?

But all is not lost for value-minded type Bs, who can escape the go-go party track with minimal effort. In Nassau, just a few blocks off Bay St, there are engaging museums, historic buildings and locally owned restaurants that are crowd-free and full of personality. Scenery hounds can head to the island's western shores and hilltops as well as a few spots on Paradise Island. Those really wanting to disappear should make a beeline for the ferry terminals, where sailing jaunts, fishing trips and snorkeling cruises are only an impulse away.

ℹ Getting There & Away

For information on international flights to and from the Bahamas, as well as travel information between the Bahamian islands, see p193 and p193.

There are ferries and mail boats from Nassau to other Bahamian islands; see p194 for details.

ℹ Getting Around

TO/FROM THE AIRPORT No buses travel to or from **Lynden Pindling International Airport**. A few hotels provide shuttles, and taxis line the forecourts of hotels and outside the airport arrivals lounge. For **taxi bookings** (☑242-323-5111/4555), call a day ahead. Rates are fixed by the government and displayed on the wall; all are for two people; each additional person costs BS$3. One-way rates: Cable Beach BS$18; downtown Nassau and Prince George Wharf BS$27; Paradise Island BS$32.

BOAT Ferries and water taxis run between Woodes Rogers Walk and the Paradise Island Ferry Terminal for BS$6, round-trip.

BUS Nassau and New Providence are well served by minibuses called *jitneys*, which run from 6am to 8pm, although there are no fixed schedules. No buses run to Paradise Island, only to the connecting bridges (the Paradise Island Exit Bridge and the New Paradise Island Bridge). Buses depart downtown from the corner of Frederick and Bay Sts, the corner of West Bay and Queen, and designated bus stops. Destinations are clearly marked on the buses, which can be waved down. To request a stop, simply ask the driver. Standard bus fare is BS$1 to BS$1.50. There are numerous buses and routes, but no central listing. Check with the Bahamas Ministry of Tourism Welcome Centre (p165) for specifics, look at the destinations marked on the front of the *jitney*, or try one of these common routes:

Buses 10 & 10A Cable Beach, Sandyport Bay and Lyford Cay

Buses 1, 7 & 7A Paradise Island bridges

CAR & SCOOTER You don't need a car to explore downtown Nassau or to get to the beaches. If you intend to explore New Providence, it's worth saving taxi fares to and from Nassau by hiring a car. The major car-rental companies have booths at the airport. Local companies may rent more cheaply. Ask your hotel to recommend a company or try **Orange Creek Rentals** (☑242-323-4967, 800-891-7655; W Bay St, Nassau).

Scooters are widely available and can be found outside most major hotels or at the Prince George Wharf. Try **Bowcar Scooter Rentals** (☑242-328-7300; www.bahamasscooterrentals.com; Welcome Centre, Festival Pl, Nassau), which charges about BS$50 per day.

TAXI Can be hailed along Woodes Rogers Walk.

Nassau

Who needs Red Bull when there's downtown Nassau? This cacophonous blur of bouncing *jitneys*, hustling cabbies, bargaining vendors, trash-talking pirates and elbow-knocking shoppers, is a guaranteed pick-me-up for even the sleepiest of cruise-ship day-trippers.

And it's been luring high-energy hustlers for centuries. From the 17th-century pirates who blew their doubloons on women and wine to the dashing blockade runners who smuggled cargo from the Confederacy during the American Civil War, the city has a history of accommodating the young and the reckless. The trend continues today, with bankers dodging between downtown's international banks as they manipulate millions on this offshore banking haven. But Nassau's not just for those wanting to earn or burn a quick buck. Banished royalty and camera-fleeing celebs have found refuge in Nassau too, with the disgraced Duke and Duchess of Windsor keeping tongues wagging in the 1940s and the ultimately tragic Anna Nicole Smith hiding out here in 2006.

Today, duty-free shops on Bay St jostle for attention with jewelry, coins, perfumes and rum cakes. Just east, historic Georgian-style government buildings glow like pink cotton candy confections. West of the wharf, the informative Pompey Museum describes the slaves' journey from Africa to the Caribbean, while faux buccaneers set a rowdier mood at the Pirates of Nassau museum, a few steps south.

Nassau has a grittier vibe than you might expect from a cruise-ship destination, but don't be put off by the initial hustle. Slow down, look around, then embrace its unabashed verve – it might be the perfect antidote to your lingering case of cabin fever.

⊙ Sights

DOWNTOWN NASSAU & BAY STREET

For those stepping off a quiet cruise ship, Bay St may seem to teeter on the verge of absolute chaos. Scooters, trucks and *jitneys* hurtle through the center of town on this narrow artery, dodging throngs of tourists looking for duty-free deals. But there's more to downtown than liquor stores and T-shirt shops.

TOP CHOICE **Pirates of Nassau** MUSEUM
(Map p158; www.pirates-of-nassau.com; King St; adult/child BS$12/6; ⊙9am-6pm Mon-Fri, to 12:30pm Sat) Don't even try to ignore the pirate pacing outside the museum. Like any seafaring ruffian worth his parrot and peg leg, he had you in his sights the moment you turned the corner. But that's OK – with its partial re-creation of a 130ft-long sailing ship, animatronic pirates and accessible exhibits on everything from marooning to pirate Hall of Famers, this museum provides the right mix of entertainment and history for kids, parents and students of piratology. There's a great gift shop, Plunder, next door.

It may be blasphemous to mention in this piratical context, but a dashing **statue** of pirate menace Woodes Rogers stands guard just across the street.

Rawson Square MONUMENT
(Map p158; Bay St) The heart of town for tourists is Rawson Sq, on the south side of Bay St. It's a natural place to begin a tour of downtown Nassau. Guided walking tours also begin here. Nearby is a life-sized bronze **Bahamian Woman statue**, which honors the role of women during 'years of adversity.' She holds a small child. In the center of the square is a **bust of Sir Milo Butler**, the first governor-general of the independent nation, and a fountain pool with leaping bronze dolphins.

Parliament Square MONUMENT
(Map p158; Bay St) The area immediately south of Rawson Sqe on Bay St is known as Parliament Sq. On three sides of the square nestle three pink-and-white Georgian neoclassical buildings (1805–1813) that house the offices of the leader of the opposition (on the left), the Assembly House (right), and the Senate (facing Bay St). In their midst sits the 1905 **Queen Victoria statue**, whose presence reflects still-held allegiances.

Prince George Wharf SHOPPING DISTRICT
(Map p158) The historic cruise-ship wharf, north of Rawson Sq and Bay St, is the gateway to Nassau for more than a million visitors a year. The wharf is fronted by bustling **Woodes Rogers Walk**; lined with souvenir stalls, fast-food outlets, the **Junkanoo Expo** (BS$2) with displays of masks and costumes, and a canopied stand where **horse-drawn surreys** await customers.

Fort Fincastle & the Queen's Staircase FORT
(Map p158; Elizabeth Ave; admission BS$1; ⊙8am-4pm) Shaped like a paddle-wheel steamer, this hilltop fort was built by Lord Dunmore in 1793 to guard the harbor against invaders. Never used, it was eventually converted into a lighthouse. The fort itself is not particularly fascinating, but it's worth the trip for the sweeping panoramic views from the top. Young 'tour guides' will try to offer their services – you won't need them. The Queen's Staircase leads the way up. Carved by slaves from solid limestone, it's one of the island's most enduring landmarks.

Nassau Public Library LIBRARY
(Map p158; Shirley St; admission free; ⊙10am-8pm Mon-Thu, to 5pm Fri, to 2pm Sat) For chills with your historical thrills, stop by this 1797 pink octagon, once a jail. Ask the librarian for the key to the tiny but creepy dungeon underneath the building. The dank walls bear scratches on their surfaces – somber markings of days by prisoners long dead?

Straw Market MARKET
(Map p158; Bay St; ⊙7am-7pm) Currently undergoing renovation, this frenetic market has long been the go-to place for knock-off purses, cheap souvenir T-shirts, and cheap, made-in-China straw goods. Tacky as can be, but fun for a browse. For Bahamian-made products and straw goods, stay in **Festival Place** at Prince George Wharf.

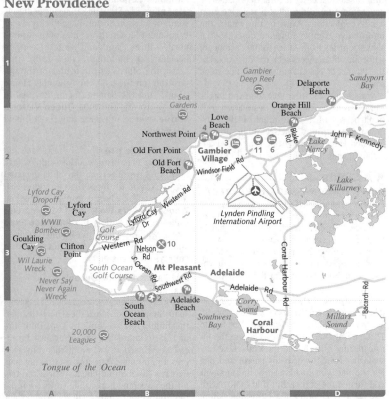

WEST & EAST HILL STREETS

TOP CHOICE National Art Gallery of the Bahamas   MUSEUM

(Map p158; www.nagb.org.bs; adult/child B$5/free; ◉10am-4pm Tue-Sat) Inside the stately 1860s-era Villa Doyle, this grand art museum is one of the gems in the Bahamas' crown. The permanent collection focuses on modern and contemporary Bahamian artists, from renowned sculptor Antonius Roberts to folk painter Wellington Bridgewater. Temporary exhibits cover hot topics like global warming and the Haitian earthquake. If you're jangled by the chaos of Bay St, the peaceful gallery is a welcome oasis.

TOP CHOICE Graycliff Cigar Co   CIGAR FACTORY

(Map p158; 8-12 West Hill St, Nassau; admission free; ◉9am-5pm Mon-Fri) Wandering into the back room of the **Humidor Churrascaria** steak house (p161), on the grounds of the **Graycliff Hotel** (p157), is like falling from 2010s

Bahamas into 1920s Cuba. In a narrow, smoke-yellowed room with old-fashioned mosaic floors, a dozen *torcedores* (cigar rollers) are busy at work, their fingers a blur as they roll hand-dried tobacco leaves into premium stogies. Until his recent death, the company's head *torcedor* was Avelino Lara, the former personal cigar roller for Fidel Castro. If you speak Spanish, the rollers will be happy to chat with you about their craft.

Government House   GOVERNMENT BUILDING

(Map p158) This splendid Georgian mansion, residence of the Bahamas' governor-general, sits atop Hill St like a pink candied topping. Below, the **statue of Christopher Columbus** has maintained a jaunty pose on the steps overlooking Duke St since 1830. The original home was built in 1737 by Governor Fitzwilliam but was destroyed by a hurricane in 1929. The current building was completed in 1932, and the lavish decorations

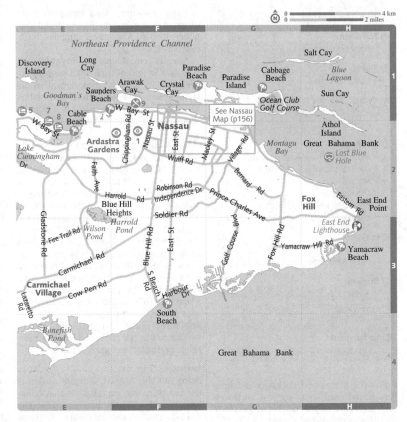

date from the Duke of Windsor's time as governor in the 1940s.

EAST & WEST OF DOWNTOWN

TOP CHOICE **Ardastra Gardens, Zoo & Conservation Center**   GARDEN, ZOO
(Map p152; www.ardastra.com; Chippingham Rd, Nassau; adult/child/under 4yr BS$15/7.50/free; ⊙9am-5pm, last admission 4:15pm) This sunny mini-zoo is home to nearly 300 species of animals. Crowd-pleasers include the Madagascan lemurs, a pair of jaguar siblings, and a small herd of African pygmy goats. The undisputed highlight, however, is the small regiment of marching West Indian flamingos, who strut their stuff at 10:30am, 2:10pm and 4:10pm daily. Pint-sized visitors will thrill at feeding the lory parrots by hand at 11am, 1:30pm and 3:30pm.

Fort Charlotte   FORT
(Map p152; Bay St; admission free; ⊙8am-4pm) Built between 1787 and 1790 to guard the west entrance to Nassau Harbour, this massive fort was the pet project of Lord Dunmore, who named it after King George III's wife. Ill-designed (the troop's barracks were built directly in the line of fire!) and over-budget, it quickly took on the name 'Dunmore's Folly'. What's more, it was never used. Today its moat, dungeon and underground tunnels make an intriguing excursion. Kids will especially enjoy the re-creation of a torture chamber. Tours are free, but guides expect a tip.

Potter's Cay Market   MARKET
(Map p156) The liveliest market in town sits beneath the Paradise Island Exit Bridge, where fishing boats from the Family Islands arrive daily, carrying the sea's harvest, as well as fruit, herbs, biting pepper sauces and vegetables. It's a great place to hang out and watch the pandemonium whenever a boat returns, or to grab a cheap meal of conch salad or souse at one of the wooden food

New Providence

stalls. The offices and docks for Bahamas Ferries and mail boats are just northwest and northeast of the market respectively. The area can be dodgy at night.

PARADISE ISLAND

Shimmering Paradise Island, linked to Nassau by two great arcing bridges, is built for one thing and one thing only – pleasure. Its landscape seems entirely man-made: glittering hotel towers, hangar-sized casinos, prefab shopping villages, impeccably manicured lawns. Paradise Island is a magical kingdom unto itself.

It wasn't always this way. Back in the day, Paradise was a muddy plot of farmland known by the far less melodious moniker of 'Hog Island.' All that changed with the 1959 arrival of A&P supermarket heir Huntington Hartford II, who renamed the place Paradise Island, with an eye toward turning it into the next Monte Carlo. In 1998 South African billionaire Sol Kerzner opened Atlantis, a vast and ever-expanding resort, shopping complex and waterpark, which now dominates the landscape.

Today, Paradise Island caters to every sector of fun-seeker: families with children, honeymooners, high-stakes gamblers, bachelor partiers.

Atlantis' central hotel, the **Royal Towers**, is a sight in and of itself, with shops, a casino, and faux archaeological excavation and giant aquarium windows in its lower lobby. The adjacent **Marina Village** is a popular shopping and eating destination.

TOP CHOICE **Aquaventure Waterpark**   WATERPARK
(Map p156; www.atlantis.com; adult/child/hotel guests BS$110/90/free) Kids and adults alike will hyperventilate at the sight of this astonishing 141-acre waterpark, an Indiana Jones–style vision of the ruins of the Lost City of Atlantis. The vast park – one of the largest in the hemisphere – is centered on a five-story Mayan temple, with multiple waterslides shooting guests into a variety of grottoes and caves. The most insane of them all, the Leap of Faith, sends brave vacationers through a Plexiglas tube that plummets down through a lagoon full of sharks. If you're not an adrenaline junkie, you can meander along the artificial rapids of a mile-long river ride, swim in various grotto-style pools, and kayak or snorkel in a peaceful man-made lagoon.

Versailles Gardens   GARDEN
(Map p156) This hushed, intimate garden is the last thing you expect to find on bling-lovin' Paradise Island, but here it is. The formal, multi-tiered landscape is lined with classical statues depicting great men throughout the ages: Hercules, Napoleon and Roosevelt, to name a few. The garden's big photo op is the **Cloisters**, a rectangular stone colonnade built by Augustinian monks in 12th-century France. Huntington Hartford purchased the cloisters from newspaper magnate William Randolph Hearst and had it shipped piece by piece to the Bahamas. Another don't-miss is the waterfront **gazebo**, a popular wedding spot.

Cabbage Beach   ACTIVITIES BEACH
This powder-sand stunner stretches 2 miles along the north shore, with plenty of activities and water sports. Look out for banana boats, jet-ski rental, parasailing and more. Several resorts have facilities at the west end.

Paradise Beach   RESORT BEACH
Another beauty, Paradise Beach curves gently along the northwest shore of the island; it is very lonesome to the west. The resorts

have their own facilities, but nonguests pay for privileges.

Snorkeler's Cove Beach SNORKELING BEACH
East of Cabbage Beach, this beach favored by day-trippers on picnicking and snorkeling excursions from Nassau.

🏊 Activities

Diving & Snorkeling
There's superb diving close to shore, including fantastic shallow-reef, wall and wreck dives. The most noted sites lie off the southwest coast between Coral Harbour and Lyford Cay.

Stuart Cove's Dive & Snorkel Bahamas (Map p152; ☑242-362-4171; www.stuartcove.com; Southwest Rd) is one of the Bahamas' best and largest dive operators. It offers a range of diving, PADI certification and snorkeling choices, including a bone-rattling shark wall and shark-feeding dive (BS$150); a two-tank dive trip (BS$109); and a three-dive 'Seafari' trip to the blue holes and plunging walls of Andros island (BS$225). Nondivers can snorkel (adult/child BS$65/30) or – better yet! – pilot their own SUB (Scenic Underwater Bubble), a scooter with air wheels and a giant plastic bubble that envelops your shoulders and head (BS$119). Equipment can also be rented.

Boat Trips
There's a jaunt for every type of adventurer in New Providence. Dozens of operators run snorkel trips, island trips, party boats and sunset and dinner cruises. Most vessels depart from the Woodes Rogers Walk area or the Paradise Island Ferry Terminal, between the Paradise Island bridges.

TOP CHOICE Seaworld Explorer SUBMARINE TOUR
(Map p156; ☑242-356-2548; www.seaworldtours.com; Paradise Island Ferry Terminal; adult/child BS$45/25) It's not every day you get to ride in a semisubmarine, is it? One of the island's more unique experiences, this window-lined 45-passenger semisubmarine takes an ultra-cool 90-minute excursion above the fish-filled coral reefs of the **Sea Gardens Marine Park**, off the north shore of Paradise Island.

Powerboat Adventures BOAT TRIP
(Map p156; ☑242-363-1466; www.powerboatadventures.com; Paradise Island Ferry Terminal; adult/child BS$199/140) A thrilling powerboat trip that zips you from Nassau to the Exuma Cays in an hour. Chock-full of snorkeling, shark feeding and iguana gawking, topped off with plenty of rum.

Bahamas Ferries BOAT TRIP
(Map p156; ☑242-323-2166; www.bahamasferries.com; adult/child BS$184/124) Hop on one of these sleek passenger ferries for an excursion to shimmering Harbour Island, just off the coast of northern Eleuthera.

Flying Cloud Catamaran Cruises & Snorkeling Tours SNORKELING, CRUISE
(Map p156; ☑242-363-4430; www.flyingcloud.info; Paradise Island Ferry Terminal) These fast-flying catamarans whisk you away for half-day snorkel adventures on a secluded beach (adult/child BS$70/35), or for romantic sunset cruises (BS$70/35).

Fishing
Nassau is a great base for sportfishing, with superb sites just 20 minutes away. Game species include blue marlin, sailfish, yellowfin tuna,

---

NASSAU FOR CHILDREN

From pirate-history museums and massive waterparks to dolphin-filled lagoons, Nassau is one big playground!

» Plunge down waterslides and float through shark tanks at the 141-acre **Aquaventure Waterpark** (p154) at the Atlantis resort. The littlest kids will love the Mayan-themed shallow water playground.

» Sit and wave at people from your **horse-drawn surrey** (p151).

» Salute a marching flamingo, yawn at a dozing iguana, cluck at a Bahama parrot and smile at a big cat at **Ardastra Gardens, Zoo & Conservation Center** (p153).

» Walk past a bunch of wicked and wanton buccaneers and their pirate ship at the brilliant interactive **Pirates of Nassau museum** (p151).

» Ride in a glass-hulled semisubmarine with **Seaworld Explorer** (p155).

» **Cable Beach** (p161) and **Cabbage Beach** (p154) are both lined with operators offering water-sports activities and equipment for hire. Beachside resorts usually have their own facilities, which are open to nonguests upon the purchase of a day ticket.

THE BAHAMAS NEW PROVIDENCE

Nassau

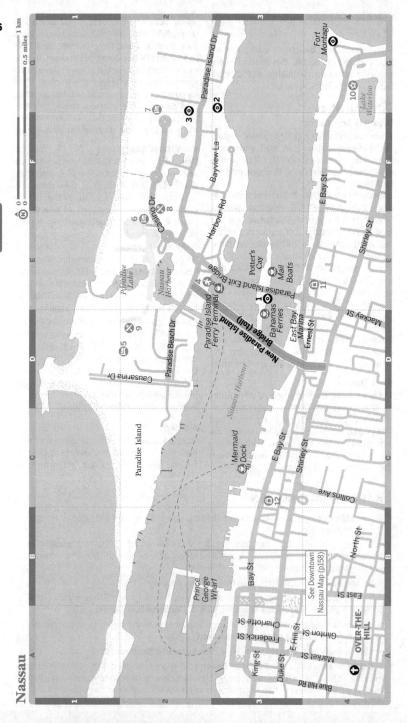

1 km
0.5 miles

Paradise Island

Paradise Lake

Nassau Harbour

Paradise Beach Dr

Casuarina Dr

Casino Dr

Bayview La

Harbour Rd

Paradise Island Dr

Fort Montagu

Lake Waterloo

Potter's Cay

Mail Boats

Paradise Island Exit Bridge

Paradise Island Ferry Terminal

Bahamas Ferries

East Bay Marina

New Paradise Island Bridge (toll)

Nassau Harbour

Mermaid Dock

Prince George Wharf

E Bay St

Shirley St

Collins Ave

North St

Ernest St

Mackey St

E Bay St

Shirley St

E Bay St

King St

Duke St

Market St

East St

Bay St

Charlotte St

Frederick St

E Hill St

Clinton St

Blue Hill Rd

See Downtown Nassau Map (p158)

OVER-THE-HILL

7

3

2

8

6

5

9

4

1

10

11

12

Nassau

mahimahi and wahoo. Charters can be arranged at most major hotels or by calling a charter company. The following companies mainly offer sportfishing, but will also happily take you exploring, diving and snorkeling: **Born Free Charter Service** (☑242-393-4144; www.bornfreefishing.com), **Chubasco Charters** (☑242-324-3474; www.chubascocharters.com), **Hunter Charters** (☑242-364-1546; www.huntercharters.com) and **Paradise Island Charters** (☑242-363-4458; www.paradise-island-charters.com). They charge two to six people from BS$500 to $700 per half day, and from BS$900 to $1400 per full day.

☞ Tours

Nearly all hotels have tour desks that will offer a number of choices and make all bookings on your behalf. Also refer to the recommended boat trips that are listed on p155.

Nassau's quaint horse-drawn surreys (p151) are a great way to explore downtown Nassau at an easy pace.

Bahamas Outdoors   NATURE TOUR
(☑242-457-0329;   www.bahamasoutdoors.com) Get down and dirty with these ecoadventures, including an all-terrain bike trip through woodlands, beach and mangrove swamps (BS$79), a summer-only kayak trip (BS$79), and an expert-led bird-watching tour of the area's wetlands and seashore (half/full day BS$69/109).

Discover Atlantis Tour   AQUARIUM
(Map p156; www.atlantis.com; Atlantis, Paradise Island; adult/child/hotel guest BS$35/25/free; ⊙9am-5pm) Strolling through a clear glass tunnel while sharks glide overhead is, simply put, awesome. This underwater thrill is found in the Predator's Lagoon, one of the exhibits on this popular walking tour of Atlantis' aquariums and faux archaeological sites. Look for manta rays, spiny lobsters, striped Nemos, translucent jellyfish and thousands of other sea creatures in the underground Great Hall of Waters, noting the fake hieroglyphics and ersatz artifacts along the way.

Bahamas Segway Tours   SEGWAY TOUR
(☑242-376-9016; www.bahamassegwaytours.com; tours BS$65) It's hard not to feel a little bit goofy zipping along on a Segway 'personal transporter,' but try to lose your inhibitions! After a quick bus tour of downtown, you'll be whisked to a private beachfront property for an all-terrain ride across sand and mud.

⊟ Sleeping

Nassau hotel rooms can be shockingly expensive, and quality varies widely. Guest charges can push daily rates up by 20% to 30%. Web rates are often dramatically lower than official listed prices – it pays to shop around.

DOWNTOWN NASSAU

The hotels listed here tend to be cheaper than those in Cable Beach and Paradise Island, but be aware that downtown gets awfully quiet after 5pm.

ᴛᴏᴘ CHOICE Graycliff Hotel   BOUTIQUE HOTEL $$$
(Map p158; ☑242-322-2796/97; www.graycliff.com; 8-12 W Hill St, Nassau; r/ste BS$325/450; ❋@🛜☀) Nassau's most discreet and character-laden hotel is this slightly spooky 260-year-old home built by a wealthy pirate. Hidden above town on West Hill St, the Georgian-style

THE BAHAMAS NEW PROVIDENCE

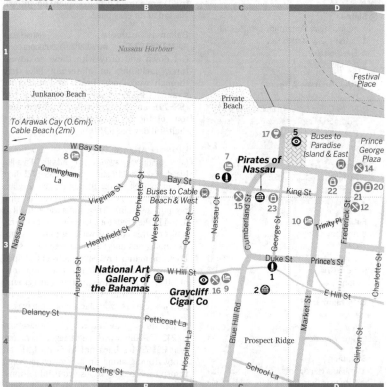

main house is filled with high-ceilinged rooms, musty antiques, mismatched oriental rugs, and intriguing nooks and corners begging further exploration. Huge gardenside cottages are equally alluring. An extraordinary Spanish-tiled pool, an astonishing wine cellar (250,000-plus bottles!) and a library resplendent with the rich aroma of Cuban cigars have kept guests like Winston Churchill and the Beatles happy. There are two main buildings on the grounds: one is the hotel itself, which includes the **Graycliff Restaurant** (p161), and the other contains the **Humidor Churrascaria** steak house (p161) and the **Graycliff Cigar Co** (p152).

British Colonial Hilton　HOTEL **$$$**
(Map p158; ☑242-322-9036; www.hiltoncaribbean. com/nassau; 1 Bay St; r BS$195-450; ❂❋❄⟰) Built in 1922, this seven-story grand dame is a downtown Nassau institution. The hotel was a location for two James Bond movies, and it's easy to see why – with its gleaming marble

lobby and sleek graphite-and-mahogany common spaces, it has the timeless international elegance of 007 himself. The 288 rooms and suites have tastefully muted contemporary decor, with marble-lined bathrooms and crisp white linens. Several on-site restaurants and bars offer excellent people-watching – this is where Bahamian big shots wheel and deal.

El Greco　HOTEL **$$**
(Map p158; ☑242-325-1121; www.hotels-nassau -bahamas.com; cnr W Bay & Augusta Sts; r BS$125- 275; ❂❋❄⟰) Choose your room wisely and this Spanish-style hotel can be a sweet deal. What to pick: a sunny end room with gracefully arched entranceways and a view over the bougainvillea-draped balconies. What to avoid: a dim, gloomy interior room with motel-style beds.

Mignon Guest House　GUESTHOUSE **$**
(Map p158; ☑242-322-4771; 12 Market St; s/d BS$55/60; ❂❋❄) Run by a very sweet

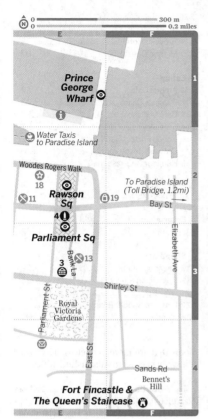

dominates the Cable Beach scene. Rooms are more tasteful than the exterior might suggest, with slick modern furniture and private balconies. Fun-lovers will revel in the **Crystal Palace Casino**, a cabaret nightclub, golf course, tennis and squash courts, shopping plaza and several bars and restaurants. The hotel also has a **kids club**, with supervised activities and theme days. The landscaped beachfront courtyard has a 100ft waterslide, Jacuzzi and swim-up bar – what else do you need?

Sheraton Nassau Beach
RESORT $$
(Map p152; ☑242-327-6000; www.starwoodho tels.com; W Bay St; r BS$179-249; ☉✻🛜🌊♨) The Wyndham's lower-key sister is slated to become a Baha Mar property, and its 694 rooms have already been upgraded accordingly. Style is crisp and nautical, with lots of white, khaki and navy blue. The property is chockablock with resort activities and amenities: three pools with flowing waterfalls, a swim-up bar, several restaurants, a fitness center, a **kids camp** (ages 4–12) and an interior walkway to the Wyndham's Crystal Palace Casino.

Marley Resort
BOUTIQUE HOTEL $$$
(Map p152; ☑242-702-2800; www.marleyresort. com; W Bay St; r BS$295-495, ste BS$495-900; ✻@🛜🌊) Bob Marley's old Bahamian getaway is now an intimate 16-room boutique hotel run by his wife and daughter (though they spend most of their time in Jamaica). Rooms, each named after a Marley song, are spare-no-expense luxurious – hand-carved mahogany furniture, rich linens and original Africana art.

WEST OF DOWNTOWN

A Stone's Throw Away
TOP CHOICE
B&B $$$
(Map p152; ☑242-327-7030; www.astonesthrow away.com; W Bay St, Nassau; r BS$175-290; ✻@🛜🌊) Talk about dramatic entrances: getting to this extraordinary B&B requires climbing steep stone stairs through a cliffside tunnel, to emerge into a tropical garden that's like something out of a Merchant Ivory film. Burnished wood, worn oriental rugs, a rock grotto swimming pool. Lovely.

Orange Hill Beach Inn
GUESTHOUSE $$
(Map p152; ☑242-327-7157; www.orangehill.com; W Bay St, Orange Hill Beach; r BS$120-170; ✻@🛜🌊) Divers and international backpackers adore this homey hillside guesthouse, with its Fawlty Towers sign and just-like-family staff.

(though slightly hard-of-hearing!) elderly Greek couple, this 2nd-floor guesthouse is a bargain in the heart of downtown. Six guest rooms are bare-bones but clean, with personal air-conditioning units and cable TVs. Shared bathrooms are in the hallway. Two locked iron gates will make you feel safe.

CABLE BEACH
West of downtown, Cable Beach is New Providence's most popular stretch of sand, lined with dozens of beachfront resorts and time-share complexes. Changes are afoot in the area, as the BS$2.6 billion Baha Mar megaresort, which hopes to rival Atlantis, inches further toward reality.

Wyndham Nassau Resort
RESORT $$
(Map p152; ☑242-327-6200; www.wyndhamnas sauresort.com; W Bay St; r BS$199; ☉✻🛜🌊♨) With its retro-futuristic peach and turquoise towers, this gaudy behemoth resort

The sprawling property has a wide range of rooms, from basic motel units (upper rooms are nicer) to full apartments. At night, everyone congregates in the funky main house, with its self-serve bar and shelves full of used books.

Compass Point Beach Resort HOTEL **$$$**
(Map p152; ☎242-327-4500; www.compasspoint beachresort.com; W Bay St, Gambier Village; r BS$150-400; ✳@☎☒) With a color scheme best described as jellybean Junkanoo, this jumble of crayon-bright luxury huts is an automatic mood enhancer. The huts are on the small side, but hip furniture, cute porches and astounding views make up for tight quarters. And who's staying inside when **Love Beach** and a sweet poolside **bar** are steps away? Monthly house parties draw local and international hipsters, as does the daily happy hour.

PARADISE ISLAND

Those who choose to stay within Paradise Island's magic bubble do so at a price – rooms are at least 50% more here than in downtown Nassau or Cable Beach. Atlantis dominates the scene, both literally and figuratively, but several other properties offer rooms that are more budget friendly, while still having access to Atlantis' amenities.

TOP CHOICE/ **Atlantis** RESORT **$$$**
(Map p156; ☎242-363-3000; www.atlantis.com; r BS$300-1100; ✳@☎☒❀) If Disneyland, Vegas and Sea World birthed a lovechild, this watery wonderland would be its overpriced but irresistible spawn. The Lost World of Atlantis–themed megaresort has a number of separate hotels, all within walking distance of one another. The **Royal Towers** (BS$350 to BS$700) is the signature property – it's the 23-story pink palace with the enormous central arch you see on all the brochures. It's the most heavily invested in the Atlantis mythology – aquarium windows in the lobby, faux hieroglyphics everywhere, and a replica of King Triton's throne – and is the nexus of all activity. There is a massive casino, an indoor shopping mall gleaming with Versace and Cartier, and celebrity-chef restaurants pumping loud electronica. Set at a tasteful distance, the **Cove** (BS$800 to BS$1100) is Atlantis's most adult property – all koi ponds and minimalist chandeliers, and an adults-only pool area with wandering masseuses. the **Reef** (BS$450 to BS$700) is a stylish condo-style hotel perfect for families.

Beach Towers (BS$300 to BS$450) and Coral Towers (BS$350 to BS$600) are, relatively speaking, less flashy, more affordable options.

One & Only Ocean Club RESORT $$$
(Map p156; ☑242-363-2501; oceanclub.oneandonly resorts.com; Casino Dr; BS$600-1300; ❋@☎☒) Paradise Island's most elite hotel, this is the kind of place where people with marquee names come to get away from it all (paparazzi and other hoi polloi are kept out by a guarded gate). Guests potter around in spa robes, drinking scotch or flipping through art books in the seaside sitting area. Rooms come with personal butlers, who will sprinkle rose petals on your bed or bring you your afternoon champagne.

Comfort Suites RESORT $$$
(Map p156; ☑242-363-3680; www.comfortsuitespi .com; Casino Dr; r incl breakfast BS$270-450; ❋@ ☎☒⛱) Though this above-average beach hotel is not part of Atlantis, guests here get full pool and waterpark privileges at the neighboring megaresort. The 200-plus rooms are newly renovated with bright tropical appeal, and several on-site restaurants and bars are good for lazy days.

✖ Eating

Dining in Nassau can be a demoralizing experience, with high prices, huge crowds and low-quality food. But don't despair – with a little extra patience and forethought, you can find anything from cheap and authentic Bahamian home cooking to the kind of haute cuisine that would feel at home in Paris or New York.

⟨TOP CHOICE⟩ Café Matisse ITALIAN, INTERNATIONAL $$
(Map p158; ☑242-356-7012; www.cafe-matisse. com; Bank Lane; mains BS$15-26; ⊙lunch & dinner Tue-Sat) Tucked in the shadows of historic buildings and leafy palms, this casually elegant bistro just off Parliament Sq is a delightful escape from the cruise-ship-and-Bay-St mob scene. Savor top-notch pastas, pizzas and seafood dishes on the inviting back patio, where you'll be served by crisp-shirted waiters to the sounds of cool world beats. If you don't opt for wine, try the refreshing ginger lemonade.

Graycliff Restaurant CONTINENTAL $$$
(Map p158; ☑242-322-2796; www.graycliff.com; Graycliff Hotel, 8-12 W Hill St; mains BS$35-68; ⊙lunch Mon-Fri, dinner daily) Make like a colonial-era dignitary at this hushed restaurant in the atmospherically creaky parlor of the 18th-century **Graycliff Hotel** (p157). French-style dishes take inspiration from the tropics – think crispy duck with Bahamian citrus sauce and lobster in puff pastry. The wine cellar is legendary, with precious vintages, such as an 1865 Château Lafite, among its 250,000 bottles.

Humidor
Churrascaria BRAZILIAN, STEAK HOUSE $$$
(Map p158; ☑242-322-2796, ext 301; www.gray-cliff.com; 8-12 W Hill St; mains BS$40; ⊙dinner Mon-Sat) Machismo hangs in the smoky air at this Brazilian steak house, in the building next to the Graycliff Hotel (p157), where hunks of dripping meat are delivered table-side on wicked-looking metal skewers. The prix-fixe menu includes a salad bar stuffed

---

DON'T MISS

NEW PROVIDENCE BEACHES

Cable Beach (Map p152) New Providence's biggest and most popular beach is three curving miles of white sand and sparkling turquoise sea, just west of downtown Nassau. Named for the undersea telegraphic cable that came ashore here in 1892, Cable Beach has for years been populated with nondescript beach resorts. Currently, these resorts and the casino are in the midst of a massive redevelopment project overseen by Baha Mar Resorts. Currently, the beach is vibrant with vacationing families, spring breakers, water-sports operators, hair braiders and roving souvenir vendors. If you want a beach chair, pay a day-use fee at one of the hotels for use of its facilities.

Delaporte Beach (Map p152) Adjoining Cable Beach on the west, this is a quiet spot with soft sand, gin-clear water and few crowds.

Junkanoo Beach (Map p158) The closest beach to downtown, this smallish stretch is crowded with locals and budget travelers from nearby hotels. It ain't fancy, but the water's just as clear and aqua as anywhere on the island.

PORT OF CALL – NASSAU

There are lots of options for even a short visit in port at Nassau:

» Go diving and snorkeling at Stuart Cove (p155)

» Shop for duty-free gems on Bay St

» Plunge down high-octane waterslides at Atlantis Aquaventure Waterpark (p154)

» Sip cocktails in the sun on Cable Beach (p161)

» Munch cracked conch and listen to Junkanoo beats at Arawak Cay (p162)

» Try your luck at the Crystal Palace Casino (p164) and the Atlantis Casino (p164)

» Puff a hand-rolled stogie at the Graycliff Cigar Co (p152)

» Stroll through the Cloisters at romantic Versailles Gardens (p154)

with seafood appetizers, veggies and pastas. Conclude with a fine stogie, hand-rolled at the on-site **Graycliff Cigar Co** (p152).

Brussels Bistro　　　　　　BELGIAN **$$**
(Map p158; www.brusselsbistro.biz; Frederick St; mains BS$15-29; ☺lunch & dinner) You'd swear you were in old-world Belgium at this intimate side-street cafe, with its dim interior of burnished wood and brass, and chalkboard menu of crepes, baguette sandwiches and *moules frites*.

Athena Cafe　　　　　　　　GREEK **$$**
(Map p158; cnr Bay & Charlotte Sts; mains BS$15-35; ☺breakfast & lunch 8:30am-6pm Mon-Fri, to 4pm Sun) Locals have a love–hate affair with this cozy second-story Greek cafe. The authentic Greek food may be scrumptious (try the grilled octopus), but BS$15 for a gyro? Enter through the jewelry store.

Café Skan's　　　　BAHAMIAN, AMERICAN **$$**
(Map p158; cnr Bay & Frederick Sts, Nassau; mains BS$7-23; ☺breakfast, lunch & dinner) Typically stretched to its deep-fried seams, this downhome diner bustles with office workers, vacationing families, and the occasional hungry cop. If the happy hordes and friendly service don't pull you in, the tiered dessert case by the door should close the deal.

Conch Fritters Bar & Grill　　BAHAMIAN **$**
(Map p158; Marlborough St; mains BS$9-16; ☺lunch & dinner) Clean, shiny fast-food-style place specializing in conch, barbecue ribs, wings and other local snacks.

WEST OF DOWNTOWN

TOP CHOICE **Arawak Cay**　　　　　BAHAMIAN **$**
(Map p152; mains BS$8-20; ☺breakfast, lunch & dinner) There's always a party on at this colorful village of seafood shacks, known to locals as 'the fish fry'. No trip to Nassau is complete

without a pilgrimage here – it's a mile or so west of downtown. Come for conch fritters, fried snapper, and 'sky juice' (a high-octane libation of coconut water and gin). Stay for rake 'n' scrape bands, Junkanoo dances and friendly chatter. Tourists tend to gravitate toward **Twin Brothers** and **Goldie's**, two of the bigger sit-down establishments, but we suggest following locals' leads and queuing up at whatever takeout stand has the longest line.

Goodfellow Farms　　　　　MARKET **$**
(Map p152; ☑242-377-5000; www.goodfellow farms.com; Nelson Rd, Mt Pleasant; mains BS$6-14; ☺lunch 11am-2pm Mon-Sat, 10am-3pm Sun, market 9am-4pm Mon-Sat, 10am-3pm Sun) As far off the beaten path as you can get in New Providence, this farmstand and cafe is a favourite of yachties, picnickers and Lyford Cayers who lunch. Grab a pork tenderloin wrap or a cranberry chicken salad sandwich and relax on the patio overlooking the fields. The greens and herbs are all homegrown; the owner's husband, a pilot, flies in regularly with fresh berries and meats from the US.

PARADISE ISLAND

Expect major bill-shock on Paradise Island, as most restaurants are contained within the Atlantis monopoly. That said, there's some truly fine dining on the island, mostly of the bigger-is-better celebrity-chef variety.

TOP CHOICE **Mesa Grill**　　　　SOUTHWESTERN **$$$**
(Map p156; ☑242-363-3000; The Cove, Atlantis; mains BS$32-49; ☺dinner) Southwestern style gets the Atlantis treatment at Bobby Flay's latest, in the ever-so-chic Cove. Think cow-print chairs, undulating stone walls, and a stadium-sized open kitchen with enough hammered copper to keep the Bahamas in pennies for a

decade. Clientele are moneyed and glam, dining on New Mexican spice-rubbed pork tenderloin and sipping top-drawer margaritas.

Nobu JAPANESE $$$
(Map p156; ☎242-363-3000; www.atlantis.com; Royal Towers, Atlantis; mains BS$18-48; ☺dinner) Dot-com bubble? Recession? What? The heady days of the go-go 1990s are still alive and sipping saketinis at Nobu Atlantis, one of celebrity chef Nobu Matsuhisa's many international outposts. Choose from a range of designer sushi rolls or noodle dishes, or go with Matsuhisa's signature black cod with miso. Decor might be described as 'Zen on steroids' – towering ceilings, avant-garde light fixtures, and a glowing stone sushi bar.

Dune FUSION $$$
(Map p156; ☎242-363-2501; oceanclub.oneandonlyresorts.com; One & Only Ocean Club; mains BS$22-60; ☺breakfast, lunch & dinner) International celebrity chef Jean-Georges Vongerichten created the menu at this ultrapopular (and ultrapricey) fusion restaurant, floating atop a dune in front of the genteel Ocean Club hotel. The menu globe hops with impunity: Asian fish dishes, French-inflected lamb, Caribbean-flavored calamari. Don't miss Jean-Georges' signature molten chocolate cake (he's said to have invented the now-ubiquitous dessert).

Carmine's ITALIAN $$$
(Map p156; www.atlantis.com; Marina Village; mains BS$34-46; ☺dinner) Waiting time for dinner at this theme-park-like Italian joint routinely tops an hour or more, which speaks to its popularity among vacationing families. All the classics are here – spaghetti with meatballs, chicken parmigiana, tiramisu – all big enough to feed a crowd.

Anthony's Grill AMERICAN $$
(Map p156; www.anthonysgrillparadiseisland.com; Paradise Island Shopping Center, Casino Dr; mains BS$14-32; ☺breakfast, lunch & dinner) One of

Paradise Island's few nonhotel restaurants, this Caribbean-bright diner is a favorite with families for its big menu of burgers, pizzas, pastas and big American-style breakfasts.

🍷 Drinking

Compass Point Bar BAR
(Map p152; www.compasspointbeachresort.com; Compass Point Beach Resort, W Bay St, Gambier Village) A stylish crowd sips potent cocktails on the pool deck with the deep blue sea as a backdrop. Monthly house parties are major events.

Arawak Cay BARS, MUSIC
(Map p152) Head to Arawak Cay on the weekends for 'fish fry' – a neighborhood party with food, and rockin' reggae and Junkanoo music, at the various seafood shacks and daiquiri bars.

Señor Frog's PUB
(Map p158; www.senorfrogs.com; Woodes Rogers Walk, Nassau; mains BS$11-18; ☺11am-1pm) Snubbed by locals, this raucous Mexican-themed tourist trap is actually kind of fun if your mood's right.

Travellers' Rest BAR, CAFE
(Map p152; www.bahamastravellersrest.com; W Bay St, Gambier Village; ☺11am-11pm Mon-Sat) For laid-back ocean views framed by palm trees, head west to this roadside bar and cafe, popular with locals and visitors alike.

☆ Entertainment

Aura NIGHTCLUB
(Map p156; www.atlantis.com; Atlantis, Paradise Island; ☺9:30pm-4am Thu-Sat) Designed to recreate the exclusive feel of a trendy New York nightclub, Atlantis' premier dance spot is one 'VIP' lounge after another.

Club Waterloo NIGHTCLUB
(Map p156; www.clubwaterloo.com; E Bay St, Nassau; ☺9pm-4am) In an old lakeside mansion

THE BAHAMAS NASSAU

JUST SAY OM

In the backyard of the Atlantis megaresort is something quite unexpected: a yoga ashram. On a heavily forested 5½-acre patch of Paradise Island, **Sivananda Yoga Ashram** (☎242-363-3783; www.sivananda.org) has been attracting both hard-core yoga devotees and spandex-clad chippers for 40 years. Staying at Sivananda means following the rules: eight daily hours of outdoor yoga and meditation, and no meat, alcohol or cigarettes. Accommodations range from tent camping (BS$60) to bare-bones dorms (BS$70) and nicely furnished private huts (BS$130). If that's not your idea of a vacation, you can drop in on yoga classes or meals for BS$10. The only way to get here is by boat, which leaves regularly from Mermaid Dock on East Bay St in Nassau.

JUMPING AT JUNKANOO

You feel the music before you see it – a frenzied barrage of whistles and horns overriding the *ka-LICK-ka-LICK* of cowbells, the rumble of drums and the joyful blasts of conch shells. Then the costumed revelers stream into view, whirling and gyrating like a kaleidoscope in rhythm with the cacophony. This is Junkanoo, the national festival of the Bahamas; a mass of energy and color that starts in the twilight hours of Boxing Day.

Junkanoo is fiercely competitive and many marchers belong to 'shacks': groups who vie to produce the best performance, costumes, dancing and music. The most elaborately costumed performers are one-person parade floats, whose costume can weigh over 200lb (90kg) and depict exotic scenes adorned with glittering beads, foils and rhinestones.

The name (junk-uh-noo) is thought to come from a West African term for 'deadly sorcerer.' Others say it's named for John Canoe, the tribal leader who demanded that his enslaved people be allowed to enjoy a festivity. Junkanoo, which had its origins in West African secret societies, evolved on the plantations of the British Caribbean among slaves who were forbidden to observe their sacred rites and hid their identity with masks.

In Nassau, the first 'rush,' as the parade is known, is on Boxing Day (December 26); the second occurs New Year's Day and the third in summer, when teams practice. Parades begin at about 3am. Elbow into a viewing spot along Shirley St or Bay St, where crowds can be thick and rowdy. For a less hectic bleacher seat, contact the **Ministry of Tourism** (☏242-302-2000; www.bahamas.com) for information on obtaining tickets.

east of downtown, the sprawling Waterloo has been getting spring breakers drunk and dancing for 30 years.

Bambu　　　　　　　　　NIGHTCLUB
(Map p158; www.bambunassau.com; Prince George Plaza, Prince George Wharf, Nassau; ◷9am-5pm Thu-Sat) This new rooftop dance club promises an Ibiza vibe: throbbing house music, skin-to-skin crowds, shoooooort skirts.

Atlantis Casino　　　　　　CASINO
(Map p156; www.atlantis.com; Royal Towers, Atlantis, Paradise Island; ◷10am-4am) The nerve center of the Atlantis complex, this seven-acre casino has 90 game tables and 850 slot machines tinkling away 24/7.

Crystal Palace Casino　　　CASINO
(Map p152; ☏242-327-6200; Wyndham Nassau Resort, W Bay St) Spend enough time in this vast, 24-hour black and gold casino and you'll forget whether it's night or day outside.

🛍 Shopping

The masses flock to Bay St or Atlantis' Crystal Court Shops for duty-free liquor, jewelry, perfume and cigars, but savings are not guaranteed; check prices at home before your trip. Most stores close at night and on Sunday, even when the cruise ships are in port. Bahamian-made products are sold at booths throughout Festival Place at Prince George Wharf.

Doongalik Studios　　　　　ART
(Map p156; www.doongalik.com; 18 Village Rd; second location in Marina Village, Paradise Island) The best gallery for modern Bahamian art.

Bahama Handprints　　　　CLOTHING
(Map p156;www.bahamahandprints.com; Island Trader's Bldg, Ernest St, Nassau) Handmade interior design fabric, in tropical seashell or fish prints.

Plunder　　　　　　　　PIRATE GEAR
(Map p158; www.pirates-of-nassau.com; cnr King & George Sts, Nassau) Eye patches, black flags, pirate tees and a good selection of pirate lit for buccaneering bookworms.

Bahamas Rum Cake Factory　　CAKES
(Map p156; 602 E Bay St, Nassau) Made from Grand Bahama's Don Lorenzo rum, these buttery little bundt cakes sell for about BS$16 in a decorative tin.

Bacardi Outlet　　　　　　LIQUOR
(Map p158; cnr Bay & East Sts, Nassau) Get your duty-free Bacardi rum (including the rare 16-year-old Reserva Limitada) and Bacardi-themed hats, towels, shot glasses and more at this two-story retail outlet.

Graycliff Cigar Co　　　　CIGARS
(Map p158; www.graycliff.com; 8-12 W Hill St, Nassau) A team of Cuban *torcedores* (cigar rollers) hunker down at antique desks to hand-roll these gorgeous stogies; see also p152.

Colombian Emeralds JEWELRY
(Map p158; www.colombianemeralds.com; Bay St, Nassau) Grass-green emeralds as big as your thumb, and much more, at this Caribbean-wide chain store.

John Bull DUTY-FREE GOODS
(Map p158; www.johnbull.com, Bay St, Nassau) This ubiquitous chain, with locations throughout New Providence, has a jaw-dropping variety of luxury goods.

Perfume Shop & Beauty Spot PERFUME, COSMETICS
(Map p158; cnr Bay & Frederick Sts, Nassau) A vast collection of designer sniffs and international cosmetics.

ℹ Information

EMERGENCY ☏911
Air Sea Rescue Association (☏242-325-8864)
Ambulance (☏242-323-2597)
Med-Evac (☏242-322-2881)
Police (☏242-322-3335; E Hill St)

INTERNET ACCESS There's free wi-fi along downtown Nassau's Woodes Rogers Walk, in Paradise Island's Marina Village, at the Wyndham Casino, and in all Starbucks stores. All hotels have wi-fi; sometimes free, sometimes not.
Bahamas Internet Café (Bay St; ⊙9am-5pm)

MEDICAL SERVICES Pharmacies exist in all shopping malls, but mainly keep standard shop hours.
Doctor's Hospital (☏242-322-8411, 242-302-4600; www.doctorshosp.com; cnr Shirley St & Collins Ave; ⊙emergencies 24hr) Privately owned full-service hospital, east of Princess Margaret Hospital; provides emergency services and acute care.
Princess Margaret Hospital (☏242-322-2861; cnr Elizabeth Ave & Sands Rd; ⊙emergencies 24hr) This government-run, full-service hospital is the island's main facility, providing emergency services and acute care.

MONEY Banks are clustered around Rawson Sq and Bay St; ATMs dispensing US and Bahamian dollars are found throughout Nassau and at banks like the **Royal Bank of Canada** and **Scotiabank**.
POST **FedEx** (www.fedex.com; EE McKay Plaza, Thompson Blvd)
Main post office (cnr E Hill & Parliament Sts; ⊙8:30am-5:30pm Mon-Fri, to 12:30pm Sat)
TOURIST INFORMATION **Bahamas Ministry of Tourism** (www.bahamas.com) Welcome Centre (☏242-323-3182, 242-322-7680; Prince George Wharf); Airport Arrivals Terminal (☏242-377-6806)

WEBSITES **Nassau and Paradise Island** (www.nassauparadiseisland.com) Run by the Ministry of Tourism.

GRAND BAHAMA

POP 51,800

After years of playing second banana to bigger, more glamorous Nassau, Grand Bahama is finally coming into its own. If you're looking for a laid-back, affordable getaway with a minimum of fuss, this is your place. The streets of Freeport, its main city, and Lucaya are clean and calm. Its golden beaches and aquamarine waters are rarely overcrowded, even in high season. All the amenities of a perfect vacation – dive shops, restaurants, pubs, boutiques – are at your fingertips within a few-block radius. No wonder Grand Bahama has become so popular with cruise-ship tourists and families on quick weekend breaks.

Outside the city, the 85-mile-long island is an unexplored playground of mangrove swamps, sea caves and sandy cays. There's world-class diving and snorkeling, great kayaking and bonefishing. All this just a hop, skip and 55-mile jump from the US.

ℹ Getting There & Away

For international and regional flight information, see p193 and p193. For information on mail boats to/from Nassau, see p194.

Pinder's Ferry runs a small boat – maximum 20 people – from McLean's Town, Grand Bahama, to Crown Haven, Little Abaco.

ℹ Getting Around

TO/FROM THE AIRPORT **Grand Bahama International Airport** (Map p166; ☏242-352-6020) lies 2 miles north of Freeport. There's no bus service to or from the airport, but car-rental booths are based in the arrivals hall and taxis

---

DANGERS & ANNOYANCES

Crime was a hot topic in 2010, with an increase in violence largely centered in Nassau's disadvantaged Over-the-Hill neighborhood. The vast majority of violence involves young men in the drug trade; tourists are rarely affected. Take care when visiting Over-the-Hill, and avoid the area at night. Watch your wallet in downtown Nassau – pickpocketing is a known problem.

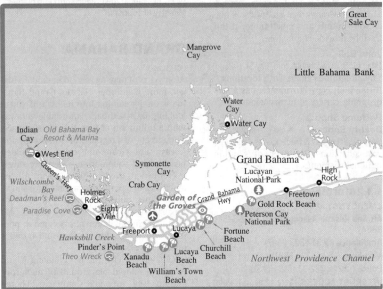

meet each flight. Displayed fares are set by the government. Taxi rides for two people to/from the airport are: BS$15 to/from Freeport and BS$22 to/from Lucaya. Each additional passenger costs BS$3.

BUS A handful of private minibuses operate as 'public buses' on assigned routes from the bus depot at Winn Dixie Plaza in Freeport, traveling as far afield as West End and McLean's Town. Buses are frequent and depart when the driver decides he has enough passengers. In Lucaya, the main bus stop is on Seahorse Dr, 400yd west of the Port Lucaya Marketplace.

Fares from Freetown include: Port Lucaya Marketplace (BS$1.25), East End (BS$8, twice daily) and West End (BS$4, twice daily). Though drivers are meant to stick to their circuit, they'll often function as impromptu taxis, taking you wherever you want for a fee. Just ask.

Free shuttles also run between most downtown hotels, the beach and town.

CAR & SCOOTER The following companies have car-rental agencies at the airport. The local companies are cheaper than the internationals, and daily car hire is from BS$50. Collision waiver insurance is about BS$15 a day.

Avis (242-352-7666; www.avis.com)

Brad's (242-352-7930; www.bradscarrental .com)

Dollar (242-352-9325; www.dollar.com)

KSR Rent A Car (242-351-5737; krsrentacar .biz)

Millie's (242-351-3486; www.millies-cars. com)

You can rent a scooter in the parking lot of the Port Lucaya Marketplace for about BS$40 a day, plus a hefty cash deposit.

TAXI You'll find taxis at the airport and major hotels. Fares are fixed by the government for short distances. Bonded taxis (with white license plates) can't go outside the tax-free zone. You can call for a radio-dispatched taxi from **Freeport Taxi** (242-352-6666) or **Grand Bahama Taxi Union** (242-352-7101).

Freeport & Lucaya

POP 27,000

Freeport, Grand Bahama's only urban settlement, was built seemingly overnight in the 1950s to serve as a duty-free tourist destination for Rat Pack–era pleasure-seekers. Half a century and several major hurricanes later, it's now an uninspiring grid of banks, strip malls and government buildings, with little appeal for travelers.

Lucaya, a modern coastal suburb of Freeport, is where most of the vacation action takes place. Its tidy – some might say antiseptic – strip of shops and restaurants appeals to a largely cruise-ship-based tourist contingent, who appreciate its safety and walkability. On warm nights, when the mu-

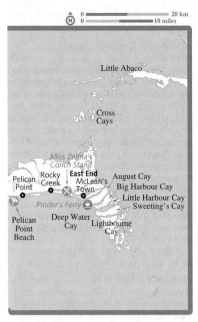

this pink-and-white mock-colonial mansion, labcoat-wearing technicians mix, strain and bottle perfumes and colognes for Fragrances of the Bahamas. Buy a bottle of the popular Pink Pearl – a frangipani-tinged scent with a pink conch pearl inside – or create your own blend.

Port Lucaya Marketplace   MARKET
(Map p170) At Lucaya's heart, this tidied-up pastel version of a traditional Bahamian marketplace has the majority of the area's shopping, dining and entertainment options. Haggle for tote bags and batik cloth at the **straw market**, peruse duty-free emeralds at one of the many jewelry shops, or have a cocktail overlooking the Bell Channel waterway. At the market's center is **Count Basie Square**, which hops with goombay bands, church choirs and karaoke parties on weekends.

International Bazaar   MARKET
(Map p168; Freeport; ⊙some shops daily, others only for cruise-ship tours) Back in the 1960s, this warren of international-themed shops and restaurants was a cutting-edge attraction, with faux European alleys, mock Chinese temples and simulated Middle Eastern souks. Today it's a half-abandoned curiosity, notable mostly for its decay. Despite the ghost-town vibe, a handful of interesting shops remains.

🏖 Beaches

Lucaya Beach   FAMILY, ACTIVITIES BEACH
(Map p170) At the doorstep of the Our Lucaya Beach & Golf Resort, this is far and away Grand Bahama's most crowded beach. You won't lack for something to keep you occupied here – go parasailing, snorkel, get your hair braided, or order a bowl of conch salad at **Billy Joe's** (p171).

Taino Beach   FAMILY BEACH
(Map p170) The island's second most popular beach, this postcard-perfect stretch of white sand has ample parking and a handful of **seafood shacks**. Drive or take the ferry behind Pelican Bay Hotel.

Xanadu Beach   SUNBATHING BEACH
(Map p166) Dominated by the decaying Xanadu Resort, where eccentric millionaire Howard Hughes spent the last years of his life holed up, Xanadu Beach is far enough from Port Lucaya to keep the crowds thin, but close enough for an easy afternoon trip.

sic is thumping at the Port Lucaya Marketplace bandstand, this is the place to be.

⊙ Sights

TOP CHOICE Garden of the Groves   GARDEN
(Map p166; 242-373-5668; www.thegardenofthegroves.com; cnr Midshipman Rd & Magellan Dr, Freeport; adult/child BS$15/10; ⊙9am-5pm) This 12-acre botanical garden is a lush tropical refuge on an island that's otherwise mostly scrub pine and asphalt. A walking trail meanders through groves of tamarind and java plum trees, past cascading (man-made) waterfalls, a placid lagoon, and a tiny 19th-century hilltop chapel. The spiritually minded will enjoy a meditative stroll through the limestone labyrinth, a replica of the one at Chartres Cathedral in France. And kids will definitely dig the raccoon habitat, where trapped specimens of the invasive critter come to retire. The gardens are several miles east of Freeport on Midshipman Rd; a minibus will take you there for about $5 if you ask.

TOP CHOICE Perfume Factory   FACTORY
(Map p168; 242-352-9391; behind the International Bazaar, Freeport; admission free; ⊙9am-5:30pm) Have you ever wanted a perfume named after you, à la J Lo? Now's your chance. Inside

Freeport

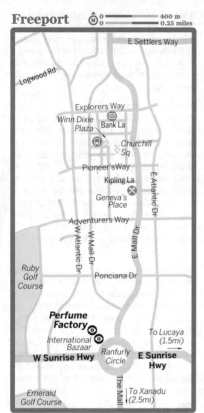

The area is also superb for both bonefishing and sportfishing.

Underwater Explorers Society (UNEXSO)
DIVING

(Map p170; ☑242-373-1244; www.unexso.com; Port Lucaya Marina, Lucaya; 2-tank dives BS$99, dolphin dive BS$219, equipment rental BS$40) One of the world's premiere diving centers, PADI five-star-certified UNEXSO offers the full range of scuba activities. Choose from multiple daily reef and wreck dives, or check out one of UNEXSO's specialty trips. For the less adventurous (or more prudent), the center's popular dolphin dive gives you the chance to socialize with Flipper and his open-sea friends.

Pat & Diane Fantasia Tours
SNORKELING

(Map p170; ☑242-373-8681; www.snorkelingbahamas.com; Port Lucaya Marketplace, Lucaya; adult/child BS$40/25) Offers two-hour snorkeling and fish-feeding trips to shallow coral reefs on its Snorkeling Sea Safari catamaran.

Junkanoo Beach Club
SNORKELING

(Map p170; ☑242-373-8018; www.junkanoobeachfreeport.com; Jolly Roger Dr, Lucaya; snorkeling trip BS$19; 🏇) Beach club with a restaurant, changing facilities and free use of beach chairs and paddleboats.

Phil & Mel's Bonefishing Guide Service
FISHING

(Map p166; ☑242-353-3023; www.bahamasbonefishing.net; McLean's Town; half-/full day BS$350/450) Runs charters out of McLean's Town, with free transport from Freeport.

Reef Tours
FISHING

(Map p170; ☑242-373-5880; www.bahamasvg.com/reeftours; Pt Lucaya Marketplace, Lucaya) Offers both bottom fishing and deep-sea trolling for tuna, wahoo, marlin and more.

Exotic Adventures
FISHING

(☑242-374-2278; www.exoticadventuresbahamas.com) Captain AJ runs rum-fueled deep-sea and bottom-fishing trips.

Our Lucaya Golf Course
GOLF

(Map p170; ☑242-373-2004; cnr Balao & Midshipman Rds, Lucaya) The island's first golf course features 6800yd of tight doglegs and elevated greens.

Reef Golf Course
GOLF

(Map p170; ☑242-373-2004; Seahorse Rd, Lucaya) The island's largest course (6920yd).

Ruby Golf Course
GOLF

(Map p168; ☑242-352-1851; West Sunrise Hwy, Freeport) Newly redesigned and considered relatively easy.

Churchill Beach & Fortune Beach
FAMILY, SUNBATHING BEACH

(Map p166) East of Taino Beach, Churchill and Fortune Beaches are equally glorious and even less crowded.

William's Town Beach
PARTY BEACH

(Map p166) Also known as Island Seas Beach, this narrow strip of sand just west of Lucaya Beach is known not for its beauty, but for its numerous beach bars.

🏃 Activities

Diving is excellent here. One prime site is the *Theo* wreck, a 230ft-long sunken freighter with safe swim-through areas; and East End Paradise, an underwater coral range. Another good spot is Deadman's Reef, off Paradise Cove; see p173 for details.

Golf is a popular pastime on the island, which is home to four championship courses. All clubs are open to the public and rent equipment and carts.

🔍 Tours

The following places need to be contacted by phone and they will arrange a hotel pick-up.

TOP CHOICE Grand Bahamas Nature Tours
NATURE TOURS

(☎242-373-2485; www.grandbahamanaturetours.com) One of the island's top operators has a number of high-quality trips. Top among them include the kayak and snorkel trip (BS$79) to uninhabited Peterson Cay, and a kayak journey through the jade-colored waterways of Lucayan National Park (BS$79). These trips display the natural quiet and splendor of the park and its many scaled, furry and feathered inhabitants. The certified and trainee guides really know their stuff.

Smiling Pat's Adventures
CULTURAL TOURS

(☎242-359-2921; www.smilingpat.com) The ever-cheerful Pat earns top ratings for her energetic bus tours, which include a culture-oriented West End tour (BS$40) that ends in a trip to her grandmother's bakery, and a beach tour (BS$40) that hits Lucayan National Park and the filming location of *Pirates of the Caribbean II* and *III*.

Superior Watersports
CRUISE

(☎242-373-7863; www.superiorwatersport.com; BS$39-59) Runs two very popular party tours on board the *Bahama Mama*.

Ocean Motion
WATER SPORTS

(Map p170; ☎242-374-2425; www.oceanmotion-bahamas.com; Lucaya) On the beach in front of Our Lucaya Beach & Golf Resort, the island's largest outfitter has virtually every water sport under the sun.

Bahamas EcoVentures
CRUISE

(☎242-352-9323; www.bahamasecoventures.com; ⊙Wed, Fri & Sun) A yellow airboat zips you through the shallows as a guide points out blue holes (underwater sea caves), turtles, sharks and bonefish.

Reef Tours
CRUISE

(Map p170; ☎242-373-5880; www.bahamasvg.com/reeftours; Port Lucaya Marketplace, Lucaya) Has a wine- and-cheese-fueled Enchanted Evening Sailing Cruise ($40), a glass-bottomed boat tour (adult/child BS$30/18), and a snorkel and fish-feeding trip (adult/child BS$40/20), among others.

🎊 Festivals & Events

New Year's Day Junkanoo Parade
PARADE

The flamboyant music, dancing and costumes of Junkanoo are publicly judged and awarded, with much crowd support and hollering.

Junkanoo Summer Festival
SUMMER FESTIVAL

Held in July at Taino Beach, where Junkanoo shacks compete for the Best Music title.

McClean's Town Conch Cracking Festival
CONCH FESTIVAL

In October, watch the conch shells fly at this don't-miss event, which includes a category for tourists.

Junkanoo Boxing Day Parade
PARADE

A highlight of the social calendar, the parade kicks off at 5am with costumed revelers and a cacophony of sounds.

🛏️ Sleeping

Grand Bahama has some of the best budget options in the country. Online deals are often the best. Look out for hidden fees. The majority of the appealing options are in Lucaya or its adjacent beaches; downtown Freeport has little to offer tourists.

TOP CHOICE Pelican Bay Hotel
BOUTIQUE HOTEL **$$$**

(Map p170; ☎242-373-9550; www.pelicanbayhotel.com; Port Lucaya Marina, Lucaya; r from BS$190; 🅿️❄️🌐) Lucaya's chicest property has an upscale British Colonial vibe, with a series of interconnected villas decked out with punchy tropical colors and white shutters. Rooms continue the theme, with lots of dark

---

PORT OF CALL – LUCAYA

The port is a few miles from Lucaya and Freeport – take a bus or taxi to town. With a few hours here, you can do the following:

» Kayak Lucayan National Park with Grand Bahamas Nature Tours (p169)

» Whip up your own blend at the Perfume Factory (p167)

» Dine, drink and shop duty-free at Port Lucaya Marketplace (p167)

» Snorkel at Junkanoo Beach Club (p168)

» Stroll and bird-watch at Garden of the Groves (p167)

» Swim and parasail at Lucaya Beach (p167)

» Splash with the dolphins at the UNEXSO Dolphin Experience (p168)

THE BAHAMAS GRAND BAHAMA

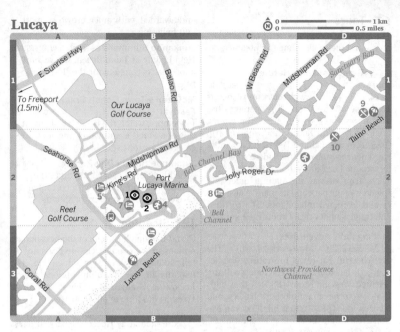

Lucaya

wood, canopy beds and private balconies. Though the hotel isn't oceanfront, the views of Bell Channel from the pool deck are lovely at sunset.

TOP CHOICE ⟩ **Our Lucaya Beach & Golf Resort**   RESORT **$$**

(Map p170; ☏242-373-1333; www.ourlucaya.com; Seahorse Rd, Port Lucaya Marina, Lucaya; Radisson r from BS$176, Reef Village r from BS$159; ❄@

🛜🏊🎣) Incorporating two hotels, the Radisson and the Reef Village, this perfectly coiffed beachfront complex hogs the best views of stunning Lucaya Beach. The resort sits on 7.5 acres and incorporates numerous restaurants, bars, spas, a casino, and multiple swimming pools of every style and variety, all directly across the street from the action of Port Lucaya Marketplace. The ambience at the pricier Radisson is a bit more sophisticated, while the Reef's playgrounds and wading pools are unabashedly family-friendly.

Bell Channel Inn
MOTEL $

(Map p170; ☑242-373-1053; www.bellchannelinn. com; King's Rd, Port Lucaya Marina, Lucaya; r from BS$85; P🖵❄🏊) On the far side of Bell Channel from the Port Lucaya Marketplace, this aging pink hotel is popular with divers, who can book package room-and-scuba deals with the on-site dive center.

Taino Beach Resort & Club
HOTEL $$

(Map p170; ☑242-373-4682; www.tainobeach. com; Jolly Roger Dr, Taino Beach; r from BS$150; ❄🛜🏊👨) On the far end of Taino Beach, this low-key complex encompasses three buildings: the upscale Marlin, the midrange Coral, and the dated but budget-friendly Ocean. The all-suite setup is good for families and longer-term visitors, with one-bedrooms, efficiencies and studios.

Viva Wyndham Fortuna Beach
RESORT $$

(Map p166; ☑242-373-4000; www.wyndham.com; Fortune Beach; r from BS$140; P🖵❄🍴@🛜🏊👨) The island's only all-inclusive resort bustles with groups of largely Spanish, Italian and German-speaking tourists, who come here to veg out on the white sand or snooze poolside, cocktail in hand. Rooms, while adequate, are older and motel basic.

🍴 Eating

As with accommodations, most of the eateries worth visiting are in Lucaya. Port Lucaya Marketplace draws crowds with dozens of restaurants and bars, as does the Our Lucaya resort complex. Head further afield for authentic fish fries and Bahamian cafes.

Sabor
FUSION $$

(Map p170; ☑242-373-5588; Port Lucaya Marina, Lucaya; mains BS$17-28; 🕒brunch, lunch, dinner) With a hip young Icelandic chef and a prime location on the pool deck of the Pelican Bay Hotel, Sabor is Lucaya's most talked-about new restaurant. Mojito-sipping beautiful people crowd the small outdoor tables, nibbling treats like ginger calamari, curry mussels and guava cheesecake. A long list of burgers keeps things casual. At night, salsa music and free-flowing cocktails lend a nightclub vibe.

Billy Joe's on the Beach
BAHAMIAN, SEAFOOD $

(Map p170; ☑305-735-8267; Lucaya Beach, Lucaya; mains BS$8-13; 🕒lunch & dinner Mon-Sat) Tucking into a bowl of Billy Joe's conch salad as you wiggle your bare feet in the sand is a quintessential Grand Bahama experience. **171** This venerable waterfront conch shack was here long before the Our Lucaya complex took over the beach, and it's still the place to go for cold Kalik and conch cooked any way you like it.

TOP CHOICE Smith's Point
Fish Fry
BAHAMIAN, SEAFOOD $

(Map p170; Taino Beach; mains BS$7-15; 🕒from 6pm Wed & Sat) Wednesday night at the Fish Fry is like a giant neighborhood party. Several beachfront shacks fire up oildrum cookers and fry turbot, lobster and conch fritters for crowds of locals, who gossip the night away eating and drinking cold Kaliks and rum punch. The scene heats up after 9pm, when the live music gets rolling. Saturday nights are lower key but still good fun.

Geneva's Place
BAHAMIAN $$

(Map p168; ☑242-352-5085; cnr E Mall Dr & Kipling La, Freeport; mains BS$5-26; 🕒breakfast, lunch & dinner) You'll hardly spot a non-Bahamian face in this huge, fluorescent-lit dining room, popular with locals for traditional breakfasts like pig's feet souse and sardines and grits. Lunch means cracked conch or fish sandwiches, while dinner features massive portions of fish, chicken or steak.

Tony Macaroni's Conch Experience
BAHAMIAN, SEAFOOD $$

(Map p170; ☑242-533-6766; www.tonybahamas. com; Taino Beach; mains BS$10-22; 🕒lunch & dinner Wed-Sun) Tony Macaroni, the self-proclaimed 'most unique man in the Bahamas' and proprietor of this famed Taino Beach conch shack, is a bit of an acquired taste. Get ready for nonstop teasing and (if you're female) flirting along with your roast conch or conch salad. It's all part of the 'experience'.

China Beach
ASIAN $$

(Map p170; ☑242-373-1333; Our Lucaya, Lucaya; mains BS$20-28; 🕒dinner Mon-Sat) One of Our Lucaya's more popular dinner spots, this mod Asian bistro is heavy on the atmosphere: pagoda-style bar, Buddha statues and stone lions. The menu leans toward old-school Chinese classics like sweet-and-sour chicken, though hand-rolled sushi adds a fresh touch. Killer views over the water.

Zorba's
GREEK $$

(Map p170; ☑242-373-6137; www.zorbasbahamas. com; Port Lucaya Marketplace, Lucaya; mains BS$7-26; 🕒breakfast, lunch & dinner; 👨) Savor souvlaki and spanakopitas beneath a canopy of grapevines and pink bougainvillea at this reasonably priced and commonly recommended Greek diner.

Churchill's Chophouse
STEAK HOUSE $$$

(Map p170; ☑242-373-1333; Our Lucaya, Lucaya; mains BS$25-68; ☺dinner) Swill martinis and slice into truly excellent dry-aged beef at this clubby, opulent steak house. For special occasions, you can't go wrong here.

Island Java
CAFE $

(Map p170; Port Lucaya Marketplace, Lucaya; items BS$3-12; ☺breakfast & lunch; ☜) Lucaya's go-to spot for your caffeine fix, this sweet little cafe has a range of pastries, salads and sandwiches, as well as free wi-fi.

Drinking & Entertainment

Port Lucaya Marketplace and the Our Lucaya complex have dozens of bars and cafes, from Irish pubs to cigar bars. On weekends, the marketplace's Count Basie Sq hops with live music. Other options include the following.

TOP CHOICE **Margaritaville Sandbar**
BAR

(Churchill Beach, Mather Town) It's tricky to find (ask a local), but this funky little beach shack is an under-the-radar classic.

Club XS
NIGHTCLUB

(Les Fountains Plaza, Sunrise Hwy, Freeport; ☺9pm-late Wed-Sat) Locals swear by this capacious new nightclub, where DJs spin techno and reggae beats inside while music videos flash on a big screen on the patio.

Treasure Bay Casino
CASINO

(Map p170; ☑242-373-2396; www.ourlucaya.com; Our Lucaya, Lucaya) This 35,000-sq-ft casino has 400 slot machines and 21 tables of baccarat, Caribbean stud poker, blackjack and roulette.

Shopping

The **Port Lucaya Marketplace** (Map p170; Lucaya) and, to a lesser degree, the **International Bazaar** (Map p168; Freeport) have tons of duty-free shops and boutiques selling everything from emeralds and cigars to local wood carvings. Both places have small **straw markets** where bargaining is accepted.

❶ Information

EMERGENCY ☑911
Ambulance (☑242-352-2689)

INTERNET ACCESS Many restaurants and nearly all hotels offer free wi-fi access for guests. There's free wi-fi at the Port Lucaya Marketplace, as evidenced by park benches full of people hunched over laptops.

MEDICAL SERVICES Health Enhancing Pharmacy (☑242-352-7327; 1 W Mall Dr, Freeport; ☺8am-9pm Mon-Sat)

Lucayan Medical Centre (☑242-373-7400; www.lucayanmedical.com; E Sunrise Hwy, Lucaya; ☺8:30am-5:30pm Mon-Fri, to 1pm Sat) Has six full-time doctors and two dentists on staff.

Rand Memorial Hospital (☑242-352-6735; www.phabahamas.org; E Atlantic Dr, Freeport; ☺24hr) This public hospital has the island's only emergency room.

MONEY There's no shortage of banks with ATMs in both towns. The ATM at the Treasure Bay Casino dispenses American dollars.

POST Post office (Explorers Way, Freeport)

FedEx (Seventeen Plaza, cnr Bank La & Explorers Way, Freeport)

TOURIST INFORMATION Grand Bahama Island Tourism Board (☑242-350-8600; www.grandbahama.com)

Grand Bahama Ministry of Tourism (☑242-352-2052; www.bahamas.com) Has a brochure kiosk at the airport.

East of Freeport & Lucaya

East of the Grand Lucayan Waterway (a 7.5-mile canal), the Grand Bahama Hwy runs parallel to the shore to the east end of the island. Side roads lead to the south shore's talcum-powder-soft beaches.

LUCAYAN NATIONAL PARK

This 40-acre **national park** (Map p170; www.bnt.bs/parks_lucayan.php; admission BS$3; ☺8:30am-4:30pm) is Grand Bahama's finest treasure. About 25 miles east of Ranfurly Circle, the park is known for its underwater cave system, which is one of the longest in the world. Visitors can easily check out two of the caves – **Ben's Cave** and **Burial Mound Cave** – via a short footpath. Bones of the island's earliest inhabitants, the Lucayans, were discovered in Burial Mound Cave in 1986. The park is also unique because it's home to all six of the Bahamas' vegetation zones.

Mangrove trails spill out onto the secluded and beautiful **Gold Rock Beach**, definitely worth a stop if you're out this way. You'll see more raccoons and seabirds than people, but watch your food at the picnic area near the beach - the raccoons are unabashed (but harmless) beggars.

MCLEAN'S TOWN

This East End village is a popular jumping-off point for bonefishing in the uninhabited cays. Anglers should call up **Captain Phil & Mel's Bonefishing Guide Service** (Map p166; 242-353-3960; www.bahamasbonefishing.net; half-/full day BS$350/450), which provides customers with transport to and from Freeport.

If you get hungry, stop by **Miss Zelma's Conch Stand** (Map p166) for some of Zelma's outstanding cracked conch or crab rice. It's the pink house on the right as you enter McLean's Town; cash only.

West of Freeport

West of Freeport, a slender, scrub-covered peninsula, separated from the 'mainland' by Freeport Harbour Channel, extends northwest to West End.

Down a sandy side road, **Paradise Cove** (242-349-2677; www.deadmansreef.com; Paradise Cove; 1-/2-bedroom cottages BS$175/225;) is one of the island's best day-trip destinations. This friendly beach club has clusters of psychedelic-colored reef just offshore, so rent snorkel gear (BS$15) and wade right in. Not a snorkeler? Lounging on the beach, kayaking, playing volleyball and enjoying a grouper sandwich and a Kalik at the resort's tiny **Red Bar** are also on tap. Overnighters can snag one of two modern, beachy cottages on stilts.

In the old rumrunners outpost of West End, the **Old Bahama Bay Resort & Marina** (242-346-6500; www.oldbahamabay.com; Bayshore Rd; r from BS$249;) has swank pink stucco cottages, attracting well-heeled yachties from Florida, just 55 miles west. Facilities include walking and snorkeling trails, a vast heated swimming pool with massage jets, a gym, spa, restaurant, bar and helipad.

OUT ISLANDS

Just when the glossy mags started touting the Out Islands as 'in,' the Ministry of Tourism slapped a new label on them and confused the issue. In order to highlight the slower pace and small-town values of the islands scattered beyond New Providence and Grand Bahama, they're now also marketed

as 'the Family Islands.' Whatever you call them, it's hard to deny the allure of the quiet rhythms and unspoiled views that make the Out Islands the best of the Bahamas for off-the-beaten-path exploring. For helpful info on beaches, landmarks and hotels, see the website of **Out Islands of the Bahamas** (www.myoutislands.com), run by the Out Islands Promotion Board.

Abacos

POP 16,700

Though the Out Islands might rightly be described as sleepy, the Abacos will be the first to shake off the snooze. Yachtsmen and divers flock to this glittering crescent of islands and cays – stretching south for 200 miles just east of Grand Bahama – for stellar sailing, spectacular reef diving and sunny ports of call.

The main island is 130-mile-long Great Abaco, with most Abaconians living in bustling Marsh Harbour. Home to the Out Islands' only stoplight – a lone beacon of either progress or doom depending on who's got your ear – this marina-crammed community is a prime launching pad for exploring the surrounding cays and reefs. The Loyalist Cays – Elbow, Great Guana, Man O' War and Green Turtle – beckon offshore just a short ferry ride away. Named after the 18th-century settlers who came here to avoid prosecution during the American Revolution, they're an inviting collection of clapboard homes, narrow streets and chock-ablock museums. The Great Abaco Barrier Reef, allegedly the third largest in the world, lures divers and snorkelers, with some of the best snorkeling just a short kick from shore.

Getting There & Away

TO/FROM THE AIRPORT The Abacos has two airports: **Marsh Harbour International Airport** and **Treasure Cay International Airport**. Taxis between Treasure Cay and Marsh Harbour can run over BS$60, so pick the right airport when making reservations. For information on air travel to and from the Abacos, see p193 and p193.

BOAT Bahamas Ferries (242-323-2166; www.bahamasferries.com) runs between Great Abaco (Sandy Point) and Nassau. At the time of writing there was no bus service between Marsh Harbour and Sandy Point, which is 60 miles south of the city. This means savings garnered from the ferry may be lost on cab fare, which is about BS$120.

Pinder's Ferry (242-365-2356) sets off twice daily from Grand Bahama (McLean's Town) for (Little Abaco) Crown Haven (one-way BS$40, one hour).

There's also a **mail boat** between Nassau and Abaco (see p194 for details).

ℹ Getting Around

BOAT Ferry schedules can be found on maps, in the *Abaconian*, the island's weekly newspaper, or on the websites for Albury's ferries. You can set your watch by the latter. Get to the departure dock on time.

Albury's Ferry Service (☎242-367-3147; www.alburysferry.com; one-way/round-trip BS$15/25, children half price) From Marsh Harbour, operates scheduled daily water taxis to Hope Town on Elbow Cay (20 minutes, seven times daily 7:15am to 5:45pm), Man O' War Cay (20 minutes, five times daily 10:30am to 5:45pm) and Guana Cay/Scotland Cay (30 minutes, five times daily 6:45am to 5:45pm). The dock for Elbow and Man O' War services is at the east end of Bay St; the dock for Guana Cay services is at the Conch Inn Hotel & Marina.

Green Turtle Ferry (☎242-365-4166; one-way/round-trip BS$15/7) Makes trips between the Treasure Cay dock, a few miles north of Treasure Cay town, and Green Turtle Cay (eight daily 8:30am to 5pm).

CAR, MOTORCYCLE & GOLF CART Golf carts can be hired on the cay docks for around BS$50 per day.

Rental Wheels (☎242-367-4643; www .rentalwheels.com; Bay St, Marsh Harbour; ⊙8am-5pm Mon-Fri, 9am-1pm Sat & Sun) Located in the tourist center of Marsh Harbour. It's the only outfit open on Sundays. Bicycles are BS$10/45 per day/week, motorbikes are BS$45/200 and cars are BS$65/300.

Sea Star Rentals (☎242-367-4887; Marsh Harbour International Airport; ⊙8:30am-5pm Mon-Sat) Rents cars from BS$65 per day.

A&P Auto Rentals (☎242-367-2655; Don McKay Blvd, Marsh Harbour) Rents older-model cars from BS$70 per day.

TAXI Fares are preestablished. A ride between Marsh Harbour International Airport and most hotels costs BS$15 for two people. Taxis run up and down Marsh Harbour and are easy to flag down. The fare from Marsh Harbour to Treasure Cay is upwards of BS$60 – you might as well rent a car.

MARSH HARBOUR

Believe it or not, this one-stoplight town is the third-largest city in the Bahamas. Situated on a peninsula, quiet Marsh Harbour has worked to establish itself as a small tourism and boating center for visitors to the Abacos. It's a pleasant enough place, with most of the hotels and restaurants lining a small strip of road alongside the marina. Most visitors stop here to refuel, shop for groceries, get cash (take advantage of the ATM) or rest

for a night or two before sailing on or hopping a ferry to the cays.

For Treasure Cay, follow the Bootle Hwy 17 miles north from Marsh Harbour.

◎ Sights & Activities

There are some tremendous and easy **snorkeling sites** to enjoy in the Abacos. **Sandy Cay Reef** in Pelican Cays Land & Sea Park is renowned for its population of spotted eagle rays and huge stingrays, **Fowl Cay Reef** in Fowl Cay Preserve for friendly groupers, and **Pelican Park** in Pelican Cays Land & Sea Park for eagle rays and sea turtles.

A huge variety of **dive sites** take in wrecks, walls, caverns and coral kingdoms, including **Bonita Wreck**, a WWII wreck populated by groupers that like to be handfed; **Cathedral**, a swim-through cavern with rays and parrotfish; and **Tarpon Cave**, a 50ft drop-off with smiling moray eels.

Sailboats and **motorboats** can be rented at most marinas. Demand often exceeds supply, so reserve early. See the Visitors' Guide in the weekly *Abaconian* newspaper for a full listing of rental companies.

Most outfitters in Marsh Harbour are clustered on Bay St, east of Don McKay Blvd. A few sights and tour companies are based in Treasure Cay.

Treasure Cay Beach   BEACH
The pin-up girl of the Abacos. Her white sand and turquoise shallows routinely land Top 10 Most Beautiful Beaches lists.

The Marls   MANGROVE FLATS, FISHING
This 400-sq-mile stretch of mangrove flats on the island's uninhabited southwest side, is a bonefisher's Valhalla. The average price for bonefishing commences at around BS$400/500 per half-/full-day excursion. Sportfishing is also excellent here; the warm seas are teeming with marlin, wahoo and blackfin tuna.

Above and Below Abaco   DIVING
(☎242-367-0350; www.scuba-diving-abaco-bahamas.com; Bay St) This operator has two-tank dives (BS$125), all-day island-hopping tours (BS$135, includes one dive) and full NAUI certification courses (from BS$550). Don't miss the **Mystical Blue Hole**, a stalactite-filled inland sinkhole where the water's as clear as air.

Dive Abaco   DIVING
(☎242-367-2787; www.diveabaco.com; Conch Inn Hotel & Marina, Bay St) Offers two-tank dives

(BS$115) in the vibrant reef of Fowl Cay, night dives (BS$115) and NAUI and PADI certification courses (BS$635). Specialties include a shark observation dive (BS$135), and inland blue hole dive (BS$135).

JR's Bonefish   FISHING
(☎242-366-3058; www.jrsbonefishabaco.com; Casuarina Point) JR and his guides know the best secluded flats for spotting the elusive 'gray ghosts.' They can also take you wild boar hunting.

Justin Sands Bonefishing   FISHING
(☎242-367-3526; www.bahamasvg.com/justfish. html; Marsh Harbour) Run by Captain Justin Sands, a past Abaco Bonefish Champion, which means he knows where to find the slippery critters you desire.

Blue Wave Boat Rentals   BOATING
(☎242-367-3910; www.bluewaverentals.com; Harbour View Marina) Charges BS$200/500/1000 per day/three days/week for a 21ft Dusky. Has larger boats on offer too.

Seahorse Boat Rentals   BOATING
(☎242-367-5460; www.seahorseboatrentals.com; Abaco Beach Resort, Bay St) Will rent a 17ft Boston Whaler for BS$165/735 per day/week or a 20-foot Albury Brothers for BS$210/1015 per day/week, among others.

🛏 Sleeping

Marsh Harbour is a good central base for day-tripping to the various cays.

TOP CHOICE Lofty Fig Villas   HOTEL $$
(☎242-367-2681; loftyfig.com; Bay St; r from BS$120; ☀❄🛜🏊🅿) This minivillage of canary-bright duplexes works well for budget-minded travelers wanting to be close to the harborside action. Each of the airy villas has a small kitchen, flat-screen TV and an open porch. Don't doubt any helpful tips provided by the Fig's friendly owner, Sid. The man knows the Abacos and if he says it's cheaper to rent a car than hire a taxi to get to Treasure Cay, believe him.

Conch Inn Hotel & Marina   HOTEL $$
(☎242-367-4000; www.conchinn.com; Bay St; r BS$120; ☀❄🛜🏊) Yachties, divers and cay hoppers inevitably buzz past this queen bee during extended Abacos vacations. Centrally located, it's a well-situated gateway for exploring. Midsized rooms have white tile floors, wicker-style furniture, a fridge and a coffeemaker.

(☎242-367-2158; www.abacobeachresort.com; Bay St; r from BS$290; ☀❄🛜🏊) Down a gated drive, Marsh Harbour's only resort sits on several fragrant acres of manicured hibiscus and casuarina palms, set against a fat wedge of private beach. Rooms, while beachy and pleasant, don't quite warrant the price tag (expect to spend an additional BS$100 or more per night on taxes and fees).

🍴 Eating & Drinking

Get your grub on while you're in town, as the options for dining in the cays can be... limited.

TOP CHOICE Conchy Joe's   SEAFOOD $
(Bay St; mains BS$5-10; ☺11am-3pm & 5pm-late Tue-Sat) Stand on the gangway of this floating conch shack and watch Conchy Joe (aka Brent) expertly flay live conch, tossing the shells into the water with a splash. If you're lucky, he'll let you sample the pissle (don't ask)! Sides vary. No seating.

Snappa's   PUB, SEAFOOD $$
(www.snappasbar.com; Bay St; mains BS$11-30; ☺11am-late) We love Snappa's for its awesome grilled seafood – which can be darn hard to find on the Out Islands. Live music is the evening draw at this marina-side mecca Wednesday through Saturday, with the biggest crowds descending on Friday.

Jamie's Place   BAHAMIAN, AMERICAN $$
(☎242-367-2880; Bay St; mains BS$7-18; ☺breakfast, lunch & dinner) It's T-shirts, ball caps and flip-flops at this sparely decorated diner, where locals greet each other by name and Bahamian and American dishes like fried chicken and mac 'n' cheese are served up piping hot.

Jib Room Restaurant & Bar   SEAFOOD $
(☎242-367-2700; www.jibroom.com; Pelican Shores Rd; lunch BS$10-15, dinner BS$25; ☺lunch Wed-Sat, dinner Wed & Sat) Order a salad or sandwich on the Jib's harborside deck and tell fish tales as the yachts pull in. On Saturday nights, everyone's here for steaks, live music and dancing.

Maxwell's Supermarket   SUPERMARKET $
(Nathan Key Dr; ☺8am-7pm Mon-Thu, to 8pm Fri & Sat, 9am-3pm Sun) Stock up on groceries at this shiny new supermarket, with a standout selection of produce and imported goods.

Bahamas Family Market BAHAMIAN, FAST FOOD **$**
(Queen Elizabeth Dr; mains BS$3-10; ⊙5:30am-8pm) This friendly convenience store is our pick for cheap breakfasts and lunches of coconut bread or meat patties.

Java COFFEE SHOP **$**
(Bay St; mains BS$4-6; ⊙8am-5pm Sun-Tue, to 9pm Wed-Sat) A morning must for java, pastries and local art.

❶ Information

There are plenty of **ATMs** in Marsh Harbour – hit one up before heading to the Loyalist Cays. Most hotels have **wireless** internet.

Abaco Island Pharmacy (☑242-367-2544; Don McKay Blvd; ⊙8:30am-6pm Mon-Sat, 9am-12pm Sun)

Abaco Tourist Office (☑242-367-3067; www.go-abacos.com; Memorial Plaza, Queen Elizabeth Dr; ⊙9am-5:30pm Mon-Fri)

Emergency (☑919)

Fire (☑242-367-2000)

Marsh Harbour Government Clinic (☑242-367-0633; Don McKay Blvd) Should have a doctor on call 24 hours.

Ministry of Tourism (destinationabaco.com) Very useful website for details on entertainment, special events and accommodations.

Police (☑242-367-2560; Dundas Town Rd)

Post office (Don McKay Blvd)

Elbow Cay

Postcard-pretty **Hope Town** welcomes your arrival on Elbow Cay, with its 120ft-high red-and-white lighthouse, set on the eastern slope of a splendid harbor. As you approach the docks, an entrancing collection of immaculate white-and-pastel cottages will come into view. Tiny gardens full of bougainvillea and flowering shrubs spill their blossoms over picket fences and walls, and pedestrians stroll along the two narrow lanes that encircle the village.

Lying 6 miles east of Marsh Harbour, this 5-mile-long island mostly relies on low-key tourism for its income. Hope Town's council is responsible for the conservative but charming community by maintaining strict building and business codes, and banning cars in the village. The hamlet was founded in 1785 by Loyalists from South Carolina, whose blond-haired, blue-eyed descendants still live here, interacting, but not intermarrying, with African-Abaconians.

◉ Sights & Activities

Elbow Cay Lighthouse LIGHTHOUSE
(⊙8am-4pm Mon-Fri, to noon Sat) The island's signature attraction, this candy-striped lighthouse was an object of community-wide loathing when built in 1863. Many here supplemented their incomes by salvaging loot off ships that crashed against the cay's treacherous reefs – usually one a month – and an 89ft lighthouse was the last thing these 'wreckers' needed. Today, you can check out views from the top, if you dare. To get here, ask the ferry operator to drop you at the lighthouse. Catch the next mainland ferry back by waving to the captain from the dock.

TOP CHOICE Wyannie Malone Museum MUSEUM
(www.hopetownmuseum.com; Back St; adult/family BS$3/5; ⊙10am-3pm Mon-Sat, closed Aug-Oct) Wyannie Malone, a South Carolina Loyalist whose husband was killed during the American Revolution, fled to Elbow Cay with her four children and helped found Hope Town. Today, the Malone name is spread across the Bahamas, and Wyannie is considered the spiritual matriarch of Hope Town. Her story, and that of Elbow Cay, is told at this small but engaging museum.

Tahiti Beach BEACH
South of Hope Town, follow the road through an upscale residential neighborhood to get to this somewhat hidden path of sand (there are 'private property' signs, but this is the only way to get to the beach and the path is regularly used by locals without issue). Though small, its waters are warm and exquisitely clear. For the best views, go round the peninsula on foot.

Froggies Out Island Adventures DIVING, SNORKELING
(☑242-366-0431; www.froggiesabaco.com) The reefs off the Atlantic side of the cay are excellent for diving and snorkeling. The waters near Hope Town and the northern tip of the cay are calmer and easily reached by swimming from shore. Staghorn, elkhorn, star and brain coral are abundant. Froggies offers one-/two-tank dives for BS$110/145 and snorkeling excursions (BS$70/55 per adult/child) in the coral wonderlands of Fowl Cay Preserve and Sandy Cay Reef, as well as day-trip excursions.

There are several good **surfing** breaks on the south Atlantic shore, especially in winter. Try **Rush Reef** or the reef off **Garbanzo Beach** for some of the Bahamas' best surfing. Rent boards for BS$30 per day at **Sun-dried T's** (☑242-366-0616), located beside the Government Dock.

🛏 Sleeping & Eating

TOP CHOICE **Hope Town Harbour Lodge**   BOUTIQUE HOTEL **$$**
(☑242-366-0095; www.hopeownlodge.com; Queen's Hwy; r & cottages BS$99-325; ❰P❱❰⊛❱❰❄❱❰❄❱❰❄❱) With her white-picket fence and frosting-blue balconies, this hilltop charm-cake will have you at hello, and palm-framed harbor views will keep you from saying goodbye. Rooms in the main house are smallish; bluff-top cottages more spacious. Everyone's invited to chill by the tiled freshwater pool (nonguests just need to buy some food at the outdoor **grill**) or dine at the adjacent white-tablecloth **restaurant**.

Abaco Inn   HOTEL **$$**
(☑242-366-0133; www.abacoinn.net; Queen's Hwy; r BS$160; ❰P❱❰⊛❱❰❄❱❰❄❱❰❄❱) Talk about location! Straddling the bluff that forms the island's narrowest point, the Abaco Inn has killer views of two gorgeous, but very different, beaches. The 20 rustic cottages have painted wood paneling, postage-stamp-sized bathrooms, and private hammocks. A lively tiki bar and dramatically situated oceanfront pool tie things together.

Cap'n Jack's   PUB **$$**
(Hope Town; mains BS$8-17; ⊙breakfast, lunch & dinner Mon-Sat) If *Cheers*' barflies Norm and Cliff drank beer in the Abacos, this wood-planked watering hole is where you'd likely find them. Locals linger over burgers, salads and fish sandwiches at tight booths inside, while tourists opt for marina views on the waterside deck. Everyone heads here for live music on Wednesday and Friday nights.

❶ Information

Public **restrooms**, the **post office**, and a slim-pickings **tourist information** board are across from the Government Dock.

Green Turtle Cay

If you've got time for only one cay, make it Green Turtle, by far the friendliest island in the Abacos, if not the Bahamas. The inhabitants are more than willing to point you in the right direction for hearty dining, primo diving and Loyalist-minded sightseeing. And being the birthplace of the goombay smash isn't such a shabby distinction either. The northernmost of the four Loyalist Cays, it takes a little more effort to get here, but only the most determined curmudgeons will leave unhappy.

The compact town of New Plymouth is easily explored on foot, though golf carts are available for rent near the ferry dock at **Kool Karts** (☑242-365-4176; per day BS$50). Note that many shops and businesses close for lunch.

◉ Sights

Take a left off the ferry dock, walk to Mission St and turn right. Miss Emily's Blue Bee is on your right. You'll be stopping here later. Just past the Blue Bee are the pink ruins of **Ye Olde Jail**. Diagonally across the intersection is a small, windswept **cemetery** where the headstones have spectacular views of Great Abaco. Head the other way down the main street to see the creepy, blank-eyed busts of notable Bahamian loyalists at the **Loyalist Memorial Sculpture Garden**.

TOP CHOICE **Albert Lowe Museum**   MUSEUM
(Parliament & King Sts, Loyalist Rd, New Plymouth; admission BS$5; ⊙9am-noon & 1-4pm Mon-Sat) Every small town needs a musty, knicknack-filled repository, and this 1825 house museum serves this purpose admirably. Once home to former British Prime Minister Neville Chamberlain, the museum now boasts a fine collection of locally crafted model ships and B&W photographs highlighting the cay's history. Museum director Ivy Roberts knows everything and more about the island, and loves to chat.

🐟 Beaches

On the island's northern tip, **Coco Bay** is a sugar-white wedge of sand with calm turquoise waters protected by a horseshoe-shaped bay. Half a mile east of town, handsome **Gillam Bay Beach** is heaven for shell collectors. On the island's west side, **White Sound** is a deep bay protected by a bluff-faced peninsula. Half an hour north of Green Turtle, uninhabited **Manjack Cay** is a desert island straight out of central casting. If you don't have your own boat, ask around at the docks about charters.

🏃 Activities

Brendal's Dive Center   DIVING, SNORKELING
(☑242-365-4411; www.brendal.com; White Sound) This well-established and highly regarded diving outfit offers two-tank dives (BS$112),

night dives (BS$95), open-water certification courses (BS$650) and snorkel trips (BS$70). Ask about meeting the divers' wild 'pets': groupers Junkanoo and Calypso, who cuddle up like dogs, and Goombay the grinning green moray eel. Specialty trips include diving and hand-feeding a family of wild stingrays (BS$105, including fresh seafood picnic).

🛏 Sleeping & Eating

TOP CHOICE Green Turtle Club & Marina
RESORT $$$

(☏242-365-4271; www.greenturtleclub.com; White Sound; r per day/week BS$149-469; P❄🏊🛜🐾) This colony of cottages exudes good taste: all sage green linens and British colonial–style dark wood furniture. The central lobby has a kind of tropical-ski-lodge feel, with a fireplace and charmingly dim pub. The Caribbean-flavored **restaurant** (dinners BS$22 to BS$35) is one of the island's top dining spots.

TOP CHOICE Miss Emily's Blue Bee Bar
BAR

(Victoria St, New Plymouth) From the walls layered with business cards, photographs and personal messages, to the convivial customers who return year after year, it's clear that this bar is truly loved. A portrait of the original owner, Miss Emily, perches high above the front counter; a perfect vantage point for watching over the happy hordes enjoying her signature drink, the goombay smash. Created for a thirsty customer decades ago, the potent concoction is poured straight from a plastic gallon jug into your cup – the exact ingredients are still a secret.

New Plymouth Club Inn
HOTEL $$

(☏242-365-4161; newplymouthinn.com; Parliament St, New Plymouth; s/d BS$100/130; P❄🛜🐾) There's something slightly spooky about this imposing pink colonial place, built in 1830. Creaky, old-fashioned rooms have period touches like quilts and pedestal sinks. Say hi to the friendly resident ghost.

McIntosh Restaurant & Bakery
BAHAMIAN, AMERICAN $

(Parliament St, New Plymouth; mains BS$5-15; ⏰breakfast, lunch & dinner) It could be 1955 inside this humble New Plymouth cafe, with plastic-covered tables, carpeted floors and gut-busting Bahamian and American dishes like cracked conch, cheesy omelets and key lime pie.

ℹ Information

The **police station** (☏242-365-4450, 911) and **post office** (☏242-365-4242) are located inside an old pink-and-white building on Parliament St.

Great Guana Cay

Everyone's here for one reason. Maybe two. But trust me, if you ask your ferry mates if they're heading to **Nipper's Beach Bar & Grill** (☏242-365-5143; www.nippersbar.com; mains BS$10-30; ⏰lunch & dinner), it's almost guaranteed they'll say yes. This candy-bright beachside Shangri-la is a forget-your-cares kind of place, where Kaliks taste better, your sweetie looks cuter and everyone in sight is your new best friend. The Sunday-afternoon pig roast is legendary, drawing locals and intrepid tourists from across the Abacos. There's 5.5 miles of stunning white sand for those itching to slip the crowds. Other distractions include tasty burgers, a gift shop, inviting pools and an Australian owner who looks like Russell Crowe.

The second big draw? Awesome **snorkeling** off the **Great Abaco Barrier Reef**. It's a short beach stroll and a few strong kicks from the bar. Forget your gear? No worries, Nipper's has some for the borrowing.

Man O' War Cay

This tiny ribbon of an island is home to a proud and insular Loyalist culture, the origins of which are audible in the archaic British-tinged accents of the people. Almost as powerful is the 200-year-old boatbuilding industry that still thrives today.

The island is undoubtedly one of the most conservative parts of the Bahamas. The village, with its tidy New England–style cottages, is clean and quiet, its residents polite but highly reserved – no bikinis, no booze. As there are no hotels, few restaurants and only a handful of shops, it's best visited on a day trip.

Chat up the seamstresses at **Albury's Sail Shop** (⏰7am-5pm Mon-Sat), where generations of Man O' War women stitch retro-cool duffle bags and toiletry kits from bright-colored cast-off sailcloth. To get here, turn left off the ferry and walk along the Queen's Hwy.

The **beach**, a short walk over the hill from the ferry dock, is empty and lovely, though sometimes rough.

Eleuthera

POP 7800

So what do you do in Eleuthera, a 100-mile-long wisp of land curving east like an archer's bow? According to literature, research and dependable local gossips, most people come here to do...absolutely nothing. That's right. The beach bum is the true king here, his every do-nothing need met by mile upon mile of obliging shores. These are the supermodels of the beach world: pink sand, sunlight dancing on cerulean waters, sheltered coves, dramatic cliffs.

For those looking for more than a suntan, Eleuthera offers a number of high-energy distractions. Wreck divers can explore the **Devil's Backbone**, fashionistas and foodies can salivate at the upscale boutiques and bistros of **Harbour Island**, and seasoned surfers can catch the waves of the eastern shore.

While Harbour Island, a celebrity favorite, is developed and pricey (though fabulous), 'mainland' Eleuthera is ripe for off-the-beaten-path exploration.

ℹ Getting There & Around

AIR Most flights arrive at **North Eleuthera International Airport** (☎242-335-1242), located in North Eleuthera, at the top end of the mainland, or at **Governor's Harbour Airport** (☎242-332-2321), halfway down the island. Some also fly to **Rock Sound Airport** (☎242-334-2177) down south. For air travel information, see p193 and p193.

BOAT **Ferries** and **mail boats** run to Harbour Island and Governor's Harbour from Nassau; see p194 for details. One-day vacation packages are also available; see p173. From Harbour Island, **water taxis** run between the Government Dock and North Eleuthera (BS$10).

HARBOUR ISLAND

It's hard to live up to the accolade of being the prettiest island in the Caribbean, but 'Briland', as it's known, doesn't disappoint. The three-mile speck is a winsome mix of rustic and chic – humble pastel cottages abut BS$800-a-night boutique hotels, wild chickens peck in the dust in front of sleek French bistros, and local fishermen wave to millionaire businessmen as they speed past each other in identical golf carts.

Quaint **Dunmore Town**, on the harbor side, harks back 300 years. The town was laid out in 1791 by Lord Dunmore, governor of the Bahamas (1787–96), who had a summer residence here. The clip-clop of hooves may have been replaced with the whir of golf carts, but the daily pace has not changed much.

Briland's laid-back glamour has attracted an international mix of celebrities – if you spot Mick Jagger or Diane Von Furstenberg wandering around, just say 'good afternoon' and wander along.

◉ Sights & Activities

The wide and stunning length of **Pink Sands Beach**, on the opposite side of the island to Dunmore Town, is Harbour Island's main attraction. The powdery sand shimmers with a pink glow – a result of finely pulverized coral – that's a faint blush by day and a rosy red when fired by the dawn or sunset. It's been called the world's most beautiful beach by a slew of glossies, and we won't argue. Follow Chapel St or Court St to public access paths to the Atlantic side shores.

One of the finest examples of Loyalist architecture is the **Loyalist Cottage** located on Bay St, west of Princess St, dating back to 1797.

The funky side of things is to be found at the corner of Dunmore and Clarence Sts, where a mishmash of signs, international license plates and driftwood relics are displayed, painted with humorous limericks and aphorisms.

Harbour Island is surrounded by superb **snorkeling** and **dive sites**, highlighted by the **Devil's Backbone**. The pristine reefs are littered with ancient wrecks. **Valentine's Dive Center** (☎242-333-2080; www.valentinesdive.com; Bay St), the island's biggest and best diving operation, offers two-tank dives (BS$105) and snorkeling (BS$60), among other options. You can charter a **bonefishing** trip for BS$800 per half day.

Michael's Cycles (☎242-333-2384; Colebrook St) rents bikes (BS$12) and scooters (BS$40).

🛏 Sleeping

Prices and quality are both high at Harbour Island's hotels. All of the below can be found in Dunmore Town.

TOP CHOICE **Pink Sands Resort** COTTAGE RESORT **$$$** (☎242-333-2030; www.pinksandsresort.com; Chapel St; cottages BS$495-2600; ❄@🛜🏊) Rock stars, supermodels and other rich and famous types have long adored this 20-acre hideaway. Walking into the intimate open-air lobby, with its koi pond, carved Moroccan swing and ancient fig trees, feels like entering an *Arabian Nights* fairy tale. The 25 sleek cottages are their own private small kingdoms, with sitting areas and porches, and minibars stocked with everything from champagne to popcorn snacks.

Runaway Hill   BOUTIQUE HOTEL **$$$**
(242-333-2150; www.runawayhill.com; cnr Colebrook St & Love Lane; r BS$325-475;) Built in the 1940s as the private estate of a wealthy American, this secluded hilltop hotel still has that WWII-era charm: black-and-white tiled lobby, dark wood library, flagpole in the front yard. Rooms in the main house and in several outbuildings, are done up in airy whites and vintage woods. There's a fabulous pool deck overlooking the slope down to the crashing sea. Children welcome.

Rock House   BOUTIQUE HOTEL **$$$**
(242-333-2053; www.rockhousebahamas.com; Chapel St; r incl breakfast BS$300-495, ste BS$575-950;) A seriously stylish crowd lounges on swinging daybeds by the pool at this intimate hilltop retreat. Nine rooms are smallish but luxe, with crisp white decor broken up by designer touches like vintage birdcages and live orchids. Each comes with its own private cabana.

Tingum Village   HOTEL **$$**
(242-333-2161; www.tingumvillage.com; Queen's Hwy; r BS$95-150, ste BS$160-250;) One of Briland's few midrange accommodations, friendly Tingum Village has a range of spick-and-span rooms and suites surrounding a hillside garden. The cheaper rooms are simple, tiled and dim, while the fancier suites have stylish touches like stone accent walls and in-room tubs.

Eating

Harbour Island's Dunmore Town probably has better fine dining than all the other Out Island options combined. The hotel dining rooms at the **Landing** (242-333-2707; www.harbourislandlanding.com; Bay St) and **Rock House** hotel are particularly fab.

Some of the island's best meals are served at the **shacks** lining Bay St, north of the harbor. There's always a line for Bahamian fare at **Harry O's** and people risk missing the ferry for a fresh, tart bowl of conch salad at **Queen Conch**.

TOP CHOICE **Arthur's Bakery & Café**   BAKERY **$**
(Dunmore St; mains BS$6-13; 8am-2pm Mon-Sat;) One of the friendliest spots in town, this cornerside nook is the place to catch up on gossip, gather travel advice and relax over coffee, banana pancakes and croissants. Lunch means salads, sandwiches and lazy people-watching. Owner Robert Arthur is a one-time screenwriter and well-known man-about-town; his baker wife Anna makes a mean key lime tart.

Ma Ruby's   BAHAMIAN, AMERICAN **$$**
(www.tingumvillage.com; Tingum Village, Queen's Hwy; mains BS$10-20; lunch & dinner;) The 'cheeseburger in paradise' at this family-run patio restaurant is worth a trip to Harbour Island in and of itself. Cooked to order and served smothered with gooey cheese on thick slices of toasted brioche, it has earned legions of fans from across the globe.

Sip Sip   FUSION **$$**
(242-333-3316; Court Rd; mains BS$15-25; lunch Wed-Mon) Treat yourself to a little taste of fabulous at this pop art-y lime box, which sits preening at the far end of Court Rd. Gourmet fusion lunches – lobster quesadillas, conch chili – are best nibbled on the crisp white deck. Here you can enjoy pink-sand views while indulging in a little 'sip sip' – the local term for gossip.

Angela's Starfish Restaurant   BAHAMIAN **$**
(Nesbit St; mains BS$6-13; lunch & dinner) Grandmotherly Angela will cook you a heaping plate of conch with peas and rice at this cozy local joint, decorated in beachy kitsch like old street signs and tiki dancer dolls. Never refuse a slice of her homemade pineapple cake.

Drinking

Vic-Hum Club   NIGHTCLUB
(cnr Barrack & Munnings Sts; 11am-late) For ramshackle good times, park your putter at this late-night party shack and abandon all reserve at the door. From kick-back natives to Aussie kiteboarders and yacht crews on shore leave, it's a funky, rum-fueled bazaar where a basketball court doubles as a dance floor. Miss it and forever rue the day. Pronunciation is key: Viccum.

Gusty's Bar   BAR
(Coconut Grove St; 10pm-late) Jimmy Buffet has been known to jam at this ramshackle north-end cottage.

Shopping

Harbour Island's not kidding around when it comes to boutiques, even earning kudos from *Travel + Leisure* as the best Caribbean island for shopping.

There's a waterfront **straw market** facing Sugar Mill Trading Company. Most stores are closed Sundays. All of the below are in Dunmore Town.

Sugar Mill Trading Company BOUTIQUE, GIFTS (Bay St) Owned by socialite designer and cousin to Prince Charles India Hicks, this upscale boutique has an impeccably edited selection of men's and women's clothes and island-inspired gifts.

Blue Rooster BOUTIQUE
(cnr King & Dunmore Sts) Try this blue-shuttered boutique for stylish sundresses, wraps and accessories.

Dilly Dally BOUTIQUE
(Dunmore St) Bold, bright, unfussy, un-abashedly jam-packed with flip-flops, bikinis, Briland tees and Bahamian books.

ℹ Information

Dunmore Town is the island's administrative center and dates back 300 years.

Bahamas Ministry of Tourism (☏242-333-2621; Dunmore St; ⊙9am-5:30pm Mon-Fri) Harbour Island (☏242-333-2621; Bay St)

Harbour Island Medical Clinic (☏242-333-2227; Church St; ⊙9am-5pm Mon-Fri, to noon Sat)

Harbourside Pharmacy (☏242-363-2514; Bay St)

Police (☏242-332-2111, 919; Gaol St)

Post office (☏242-332-2215; Gaol St)

Royal Bank of Canada (☏242-333-2250; Murray St; ⊙9am-1pm Mon-Fri) The only bank here.

ℹ Getting Around

Briland is a mini-LA – no one walks if they can help it. You can rent **carts** from taxi drivers and rental agencies who are based at the dock for BS$40 to BS$50 per day. Try **Johnson's Rentals** (☏242-332-2376; Bay St) or **Michael's Cycles** (☏242-333-2384; Colebrook St), which also rents **bikes**.

Taxis on Harbour Island are slightly pricier than elsewhere in Eleuthera. Try **Reggie Major** (☏242-333-2116).

GREGORY TOWN

Quiet six nights out of the week, this low-key village is 25 miles north of Governor's Harbour and five miles south of the **Glass Window Bridge**, where the island narrows dramatically to a thin span straddling the divide between pounding Atlantic waves and the tranquil green shoals of the **Bight of Eleuthera**. A hurricane destroyed the natural bridge that was once there, so a narrow man-made substitute is now the only thing

Lighthouse Beach The harrowing drive down the impossibly rutted 3-mile road will feel worth it when you emerge onto this dazzling stretch of South Eleuthera beach.

Tay Bay Beach Beyond Preacher's Cave, this utterly secluded strip has pinkish sands and calm waters.

Ben Bay Beach South of Palmetto Point; the waters are shallow and perfect for beachcombing.

connecting north and south Eleuthera. It's one of the island's premier photo ops.

Once famous for its thriving pineapple industry, Gregory Town sits above a steep cove on a sharp bend in the Queen's Hwy.

◎ Sights & Activities

Hatchet Bay Caves CAVES
Turn south onto the dirt road near the three old silos to find the mouth to this half-mile-long cave system. You'll find several chambers bearing charcoal signatures dating back to the mid 19th century. If exploring beyond the first few chambers, you'll need a flashlight, long pants and local guide. The caves are just north of James Cistern on the west side of the Queen's Hwy.

Gaulding Cay SNORKELING BEACH
This semisecluded central Eleuthera beach, 3.5 miles north of Gregory Town, has shallow, gin-clear water and great **snorkeling** around a small rocky island in the middle of the bay. The beach is just north of Gregory Town on the west side of the Queen's Hwy.

Surfer's Beach SURFING BEACH
Windswept bluffs at this beach, two miles south of Gregory Town, are a primo perch for watching surfers catch waves below. To get here, follow the signs up the rugged hill on the east side of the Queen's Hwy. Beware: this is a seriously axle-testing road.

Bahamas Out-Island Adventures SNORKELING, KAYAKING
(☏242-335-0349; www.bahamasadventures.com; Surfer's Beach; half/full day BS$59/99) Tom Glucksmann (also owner of Surfer's Haven guesthouse) runs ecominded kayaking, snorkeling and nature trips. The man knows his birds and is a passionate advocate for

preserving lonely **Lighthouse Point** at the southern tip of the island.

Rebecca's Beach Shop SURFING
(☑242-335-5436; Queen's Hwy) Stop in at Rebecca's, at the bottom of the hill, just before the bend in the highway, where groovy American expat Ponytail Pete gives surf lessons (BS$70) and hawks his wife's Pirate's Revenge hot sauce (it's damn good).

🛏 Sleeping & Eating

Elvina's Bar & Restaurant BAR, RESTAURANT
(☑242-335-5032; Queen's Hwy) On the one not-so-quiet night of the week (Friday), Elvina hosts Jam Night. By 9:30pm this old-school party shack, just south of the bend, is rumblin' with half-hour sets by natives and visiting musicians. Don't count on getting food at this hour, but you might just see local landowner Lenny Kravitz strolling through the upbeat crowd of low-key locals, red-faced yachties, sun-dried surfers and befuddled tourists, who can't figure out where all these people came from. Everyone's here or on the way.

Surfer's Haven GUESTHOUSE $
(☑242-333-3282; www.surfershavenbahamas.com; Surfer's Beach; r BS$55, camping BS$30) A laid-back, hostel-style guesthouse, five minutes' walk from Surfer's Beach. Rooms are inside or attached to the main house, with full use of the den, kitchen and large wooden deck with sea views. The owner, Tom, also runs the tour company Bahamas Out-Island Adventures.

Rainbow Inn ITALIAN, INTERNATIONAL $$
(☑242-335-0294; www.rainbowinn.com; Queen's Hwy; mains BS$18-39; ⊙lunch & dinner) This octagonal inn is legendary for its steaks and rollicking weekend fun. Just past the Hatchet Bay Caves.

GOVERNOR'S HARBOUR
The sleepy island 'capital' overlooks a broad harbor that runs west along a peninsula to **Cupid's Cay**, apparently the original settlement of the Eleutheran Adventurers in 1648. Just south of the town is **Club Med Beach**; its softly curving shore is one of the prettiest beaches in the Bahamas (though Club Med is long gone).

Governor's Harbour is a great home base for exploring the rest of the island.

🛏 Sleeping

TOP CHOICE Duck Inn B&B $$
(☑242-332-2608; www.theduckinn.com; Queen's Hwy; cottages BS$150-300; ⊙❋❢❢) In central Governor's Harbour, this 200-year-old colonial complex is clustered around the owner's carefully tended orchid garden. Three homey cottages are decked out in pale shades of pink and lavender, with an eclectic mix of vintage furniture and shelves full of dog-eared paperbacks.

Cocodimama Charming Resort HOTEL $$$
(☑242-332-3150; www.cocodimama.com; Queen's Hwy; r BS$210; P⊙❋) North of town, this is a little slice of the Riviera in the Bahamas. The main house feels like an Italian beach villa owned by an arty Milanese jet-setter – think whitewashed walls, mosaic floors, avant-garde driftwood chandeliers. Sunny guest rooms are set on a private beach lined with palm thatch umbrellas. Excellent on-site Italian **restaurant**.

✕ Eating
There's a Friday-night **fish fry** by the harbor, always a rollicking good time.

TOP CHOICE Tippy's Bar & Beach Restaurant INTERNATIONAL $$
(☑242-332-3331; Banks Rd, North Palmetto Point Beach; mains BS$18-30; ⊙lunch & dinner) Almost too cool for its own good, this upscale beach shack is the darling of visiting celebs, the *New York Times* and a host of fawning travel mags. Tippy's specializes in globally influenced seafood dishes – lobster wraps, shrimp pizzas and hogfish with Thai curry – presented on a giant chalkboard menu that's carried to your table with a flourish. Jam-packed even in low season, it gets totally wild on busy weekend nights, when the piano music starts up and the people at the next table start taking tequila shots.

Beach House TAPAS $$
(☑242-332-3387; Banks Rd; tapas BS$8-14, mains BS$20-28; ⊙lunch & dinner) The well-heeled expat clientele at this intimate tapas lounge, just south of Governor's Harbour, all seem to know each other, but you'll be welcomed too. Nosh on international tapas – spicy shrimp, Spanish chorizo and Indian-style chickpeas – on the patio overlooking Club Med Beach.

New Sunset Inn BAHAMIAN $
(Queen's Hwy; mains BS$10-18; ⊙lunch & dinner) The ample patio of this friendly seaside bar and grill is the place to down a cold Kalik at sunset while nibbling cracked conch and Christine's famous coconut pie.

❶ Information

Bahamas Tourist Office (☎242-332-2142; Queen's Hwy)

First Caribbean International Bank (Queen's Hwy; ☺9:30am-3pm Mon-Thu, to 4pm Fri) Has an ATM.

Government Medical Clinic (☎242-332-2774; Haynes Ave; ☺9am-5pm Mon-Fri)

Police station (☎242-332-2111; Queen's Hwy)

Post office (Haynes Ave; ☺9am-4pm Mon-Fri)

❶ Getting Around

To hire a taxi or rent a car, call **Cecil Cooper's Taxi Service** (☎242-332-1576) or **Clement Cooper** (☎242-332-1726).

Exumas

POP 3600

Life's a little snappier in the Exumas. Whether you're kayaking, kiteboarding or trimming a sail, a crisp palette of ocean blues sharpens every adventure. And with 365 cays unspooling over more than 100 miles, there's a lot of adventure to go around. Wannabe Robinson Crusoes can wander lonely isles in Exuma Cays Land & Sea Park. Lifetime-to-do-listers can paddle shimmering Moriah Cay. Determined bonefishers can track wily prey on glass-clear shallows. And that's without mentioning the gregarious yachtsmen who can mix their way to the perfect on-deck cocktail during the festive Family Island Regatta.

Landlubbers have distractions too, with the 62-mile Queen's Hwy winding past historic ruins, hidden beaches and convivial beach bars on Great Exuma and Little Exuma, the two largest islands in the chain. In fact, the biggest thrill in Exuma may be the hair-raising one-lane bridge that connects them.

The launch pad for exploring is George Town, the bustling administrative center of Great Exuma that sits on the western shore of the sail-dotted blue waters of Elizabeth Harbour. Bordering the harbor to the east is Stocking Island, a sliver of land best known for its soft white sand and the infamous Chat & Chill Sunday pig roast.

◉ Sights

GEORGE TOWN

The sugar-pink-and-white neoclassical **Government Administration Building** houses the post office and jail. Just south, the small **straw market** (☺9am-5pm) sells Bahamian-made straw goods. Stock up here instead of in Nassau. Just north of town is the se-rene white-stoned **St Andrew's Anglican Church**, which sits atop a bluff above Lake Victoria. For a great photo op, stop by the rainbow-colored **city mileage markers**, stacked high at the southern junction of the Queen's Hwy and the city loop.

SOUTH OF GEORGE TOWN

The first major settlement south of George Town is **Rolle Town**. Follow the main road, Queen's Hwy, to the town's hilltop crossroads. Here, turn north and drive along a short ridge for panoramic views – you might see a parasailer catching gusts off Man O' War Cay.

South of the crossroad, follow the signs a short distance to the **Rolle Town Tombs**. Here lie a few solitary 18th-century tombs, one dated 1792 and shaped like a stone double bed. The plaque notes that the young wife of a Scottish overseer, Captain Alexander McKay, slumbers there with an infant child. The captain died the following year, some said from a broken heart.

Next up is a keep-on-your-toes **one-lane bridge** linking Great and Little Exuma islands at the town of **Ferry**. Further on down the Queen's Hwy is the town of **Forbes Hill**. Beyond it, two stunning **beaches** await. After passing the 'Leaving Forbes Hill' sign, there's a dangerous curve, then a beach access sign on your left (sometimes the signs disappear). Park anywhere – all four wheels off the highway – then follow the dirt track past an old stone building and an overturned 4WD to the glimmering, usually shallow, turquoise water.

About 2.5 miles past the Leaving Forbes Hill sign is a series of dirt roads on the left. Take one of them – if you get to the 'Lonesome Conch' cottage on Queen's Hwy you've gone too far. These 'roads' lead to poorly marked Ocean Rd, running parallel to the **Tropic of Cancer Beach**. Turn right on Ocean Rd and follow it to a wooden beachside hut with a small parking area. Stand on the Tropic of Cancer – there's a faded blue line marking the spot. The *Pirates of the Caribbean II* and *III* crew loaded gear onto boats here before heading to southern cays.

Keep driving down the Queen's Hwy from Forbes Hill and you'll soon reach lonely **William's Town**. Just past **Santana's Grill** (see p185), follow the sign road to the overgrown ruins of the **Hermitage Estate**, a cotton plantation once run by a prominent Loyalist family. They also sold salt drawn from nearby salt ponds.

STOCKING ISLAND

This 600-acre (240-hectare) slip of an island beckons about a mile off the coast, separated from George Town by the turquoise beauty of Elizabeth Harbour. For a day trip appealing to adventurers and beach bums alike, grab one of the two daily ferries (10am and 1pm, BS$12) departing **Club Peace & Plenty** (see p186) to **Hamburger Beach** on the northern side of the island. Here you can snorkel, stroll over talcum-fine sand, or bushwack up a nature 'trail' to the island's highest point. Don't miss the short hike across the island to the Atlantic for more deep-blue views.

Order a hamburger or conch burger at **Peace and Plenty Beach Club** (242-336-2551; mains BS$8-15; lunch). This great beach club, on the aptly named Hamburger Beach, serves up delicious burgers that keep both locals and traveling yachties returning again and again.

There are no roads on the island and all access is by boat. For a cocktail or burger at the popular **Chat & Chill Bar & Grill** (242-336-2700; www.chatnchill.com; mains BS$15; 11am-7pm) on the other end of the island, call Elvis at **Exuma Water Taxi** (242-464-1558) for a shuttle (one-way/round-trip BS$10/12) that will pick you up at Club Peace & Plenty. You can also look for a water taxi on the government dock, or your taxi driver or hotel can call the bar. The Chat & Chill's **Sunday-afternoon pig roast** (BS$15) is a don't-miss affair.

EXUMA CAYS

The Exuma Cays are a world unto themselves and the stuff of Caribbean fantasy. Tantalisingly inaccessible (you'll need to have your own boat or pay someone with one to make it to most places), the cays begin at the barren Sail Rocks, 40 miles southeast of New Providence, and continue in a long line of some 360 islets to Great Exuma. Though they may seem alike, each has its own quirky character and many are privately owned.

If you're in your own boat, discovering new beaches, seeing wonderful **Thunderball Grotto** (appearing in the James Bond film, *Thunderball*), or dropping anchor to snorkel around pristine reefs makes for an unbeatable Bahamas experience. A visit to **Staniel Cay** is another must.

The first marine 'replenishment nursery' in the world, created in 1958, the **Exuma Cays Land & Sea Park** boasts 112,640 acres (175 sq miles) of protected islands and surrounding seas. All fishing and collecting is banned – this includes plants and shells.

Activities

The Exumas offer a plethora of activities, including diving, snorkeling, boat trips, fishing, kayaking and kitesurfing. Call or stop by Exuma's Ministry of Tourism Office (p186) for a list of bonefishing guides.

Dive Exuma   DIVING
(242-336-2893; www.dive-exuma.com; February Point, Queen's Hwy) The most highly recommended dive operation in town, Dive Exuma offers packages of six dives for BS$480, including all equipment. There's a 10% reduction for bookings made four days in advance.

Starfish   WATER SPORTS
(242-336-3033; www.starfishexuma.com; Queen's Hwy, George Town) Starfish presents a variety of activities, including renting kayaks by the day (BS$50) and week (BS$225), and guided trips to Moriah Cay and around Elizabeth Harbour and the nearby beaches.

Minn's Water Sports   BOATING
(242-336-3483; www.mwsboats.com; Queen's Hwy, George Town) Rents out boats from BS$45/90 per half-/full day, but rates are reduced for bookings over three days. The boats vary in size from 15ft to 22ft, and a BS$200 cash deposit is required.

Exuma Kitesurfing   KITESURFING
(242-524-0523; www.exumakitesurfing.com; George Town) Offers a dizzying array of packages, including a learn-to-kiteboard three-day package (BS$985) and a five-hour 'kiteventure' package from BS$295.

Off Island Adventures   TOURS
(242-524-0524; www.offislandadventures.com; George Town) A day of snorkeling? Blue hole exploration? Sunset cruising? Call to customize your own adventure.

Festivals & Events

For a full listing, check out the Ministry of Tourism's website (www.bahamas.com).

During the **Family Island Regatta**, held in the last week of April, hundreds of yachts from near and far congregate in Elizabeth Harbour for racing, socializing and general mayhem. The premier regatta in the Bahamas, it's an excuse for the hoi polloi and yachting elite to mingle.

Sleeping

TOP CHOICE **Higgins' Landing** BOUTIQUE HOTEL **$$$**
(☎242-357-0008, www.higginslanding.com; Stocking Island; r incl dinner BS$495; ❄️🛜🌊) On Stocking Island, this exquisite refuge from the world can almost justify its eye-wateringly high prices with its easy charm and genteel comfort. There are just four very private cottages (one of which accommodates two couples in separate rooms) and each boasts antique wooden furniture, white timber walls and private decks for sunbathing. The feel is much more private club than resort, with most things, from snorkeling equipment to use of the kayaks and the small gym, being free. Dinner is an elaborate affair, and the **restaurant** is considered to be one of the Exumas' best. The entire place is powered by solar energy and only rainwater is used in the bathrooms.

Coral Gardens B&B **$**
(www.coralgardensbahamas.com; Hooper's Bay; r from BS$99; ❄️🛜) Run by retired Brits Peter and Betty, this charming house is located a few hundred meters inland from lovely Hooper's Bay, and is one of the best deals on the island. The three bedrooms all have private bathrooms, and two small apartments make this a great and good-value option. Peter, who can help with arranging all activities as well as car rental, is a mine of local information after a decade in the Exumas. The owners also let out a range of **beachfront apartments** (www.bahamasbeachapartments.com) and a superb **beach house** (www.coralsandsbahamas.com) on Hooper's Bay.

Club Peace & Plenty HOTEL **$$$**
(☎242-336-2551; www.peaceandplenty.com; Elizabeth Harbour; r from BS$219; ❄️🛜🌊) Built on the location of an old slave market, this plucky hotel in the middle of George Town has 32 bright, Caribbean-style rooms set around a small pool, bar area and dock. The staff are very friendly and most rooms have great views toward Stocking Island. Snorkel gear and sailboards can be rented from Peace & Plenty Beach Club on Stocking Island, which guests can reach by using the complimentary twice-daily ferry.

Staniel Cay Yacht Club & Resort RESORT **$$**
(☎242-355-2024; www.stanielcay.com; Staniel Cay; r from BS$165, mains BS$15-28; ❄️🛜🌊) On Staniel Cay, a tiny island in the northern Exumas, this resort is truly a place for lovers of perfect seafront views. Spacious verandas overlook the sea and create a feeling of total relaxation. There are cool and comfortable cottages (with kitchenettes) or suites (with kitchens) and great weekly rates. Use one of the resort's free Boston Whalers or Sunfish sailboats, take along the free scuba gear, and go visit gorgeous Major Cay. Book ahead.

Regatta Point GUESTHOUSE **$$**
(☎242-336-2206; www.regattapointbahamas.com; Regatta Point; d BS$148; 🅿️➡️❄️) At the end of a promontory with great 360-degree sea views, this secluded spot is nevertheless just a couple of minutes' walk east from the amenities of George Town. All six rooms enjoy full kitchens, outdoor spaces and pointedly have no TV or wireless. Rooms are fan cooled, hot water is solar powered and the welcome is warm.

Eating & Drinking

TOP CHOICE **Café Alesha** MODERN BAHAMIAN **$$**
(☎242-336-2203; Queen's Hwy, Old Hooper's Bay; mains BS$14-25; ☺lunch & dinner Mon-Fri, dinner Sat & Sun) This highly regarded newcomer, north of George Town, has quickly sealed its local reputation with innovative takes on Bahamian cooking. Run by two sisters who clearly want to raise the bar of local cuisine, the restaurant is a spacious and relatively formal affair. The small menu includes novel spins on old favorites, such as mushroom-glazed pork chops with sweet potato or (more standard) grilled lobster tail and conch fritters.

TOP CHOICE **Santana's Grill** BAHAMIAN **$$**
(☎242-345-4102; Queen's Hwy, William's Town; mains BS$10-22; ☺lunch Tue-Sat, dinner by arrangement) Pull up a barstool at one of the Exumas' most relaxed and enjoyable eateries.

WORTH A TRIP

HAVE YOU SEEN THE LITTLE PIGGIES?

Only a short boat trip away from Staniel Cay, tiny **Major Cay** is a great place for a day of snorkeling and sunning. Don't forget a picnic for yourself and the friendly porcine population to enjoy! Yes, that's right, Major Cay has some famous swimming pigs that like nothing better than a splash, pat and a peanut-butter sandwich.

Run by the formidable Denise Rolle, this friendly grill offers the best-value fresh lobster in the Exumas and its many regulars often entertain diners with increasingly tall stories from the *Pirates of the Caribbean* shoot, part of which took place at nearby Sandy Point (ask to see their photo albums). There's also a great beach just a few feet from the bar.

Eddy's Edgewater Club CAFE $

(Queen's Hwy, George Town; mains BS$7-12; ☺7am-10pm, to midnight Fri & Sat, closed Sun) This very reliable, friendly and informal restaurant serves up three tasty Bahamian meals a day, including changing daily specials. There's a pleasant terrace, with views over Lake Victoria, a more formal dining room at the back, and a large bar that's always packed on Mondays for the island's most popular rake 'n' scrape music evening.

ⓘ Information

Bahamas Ministry of Tourism (☎242-336-2430; www.bahamas.com; Queen's Hwy, George Town)

Emergency (☎919)

Exuma Web Cafe (Queen's Hwy, George Town; per 30min BS$6; ☺8am-8pm)

Government Medical Clinic (☎242-336-2088; George Town)

Police (☎242-336-2666; George Town)

Post office (George Town)

Royal Bank of Canada (Queen's Hwy, George Town)

ⓘ Getting There & Away

For **air travel** information to the Exumas, see p193 and p193. For information on transport by **ferry** or **mail boat**, see p194.

ⓘ Getting Around

TO/FROM THE AIRPORT Taxis await the arrival of all flights to the **Exuma International Airport** and cost BS$30 to George Town. However, two good car-rental agencies are based at the airport.

BOAT There are two separate ferries to different parts of Stocking Island, departing from George Town. The main ferry is the water taxi from Government Wharf run by **Elvis Ferguson** (☎242-464-1558; return BS$12), who offers a roughly hourly service to the Chat & Chill Bar & Grill and the St Francis Resort, from 10am until 5pm daily.

A second service departs the dock at **Club Peace & Plenty** (☎242-336-2551; round-trip BS$12, free for guests) for Stocking Island's

Hamburger Beach at 10am and 1pm, returning at 1.10pm and 4pm.

CAR **Don's Rent A Car** (☎242-345-0112, donsrentacar@hotmail.com; Exuma International Airport) Rents vehicles from BS$70 per day.

Airport Car Rental (☎242-345-0090; taro@coralwave.com; Exuma International Airport) Rents cars from around BS$70 per day.

TAXI **Exuma Transit Services** (☎242-345-0232) and **Leslie Dames** (☎242-357-0015) both run taxi services around the island.

Andros

POP 7400

Known to Bahamians as 'the Big Yard,' Andros is the country's unexplored backcountry – a whopping 2300 sq miles of mangrove swamps, palm savannas and eerie primal forests full of wild boar and (as legend has it) an evil man-bird known as the chickcharnie. By far the biggest island in the Bahamas, it's the least densely populated – its eastern shores are dotted with ramshackle, blink-and-you'll-miss-'em hamlets, while the entire western side is an uninhabited patchwork of swampland known, appropriately, as 'The Mud.'

Diving and bonefishing are the two main draws for most visitors. A 140-mile-long coral reef, the world's third largest, lies a few hundred yards off the east shore. Beyond it, the continental shelf drops into the blackness of the 6000ft-deep Tongue of the Ocean. The island's bizarre blue holes – water-filled vertical caves occurring both inland and offshore – attract both advanced divers and National Geographic crews.

Travel in Andros is not easy. Public transportation is almost nil, roads rough, restaurants mostly nonexistent. Unless you're staying at one of the islands' all-inclusive resorts, plan on having a very DIY experience.

ⓘ Getting There & Around

AIR There are four airports.

San Andros Airport (☎242-329-4224) Ten miles south of Nicholl's Town; serves North Andros.

Andros Town Airport (☎242-368-2030) Three miles south of Fresh Creek; serves Central Andros.

Mangrove Cay Airport (☎242-369-0083) On Mangrove Cay.

Congo Town Airport (☎242-369-2640) Serves South Andros.

For information on air travel, see p193 and p193.

BOAT There are mail boats and ferries to Andros; for details, see p194.

TAXI Taxis meet arriving flights and ferries. Ask at your hotel about renting a car.

NORTH & CENTRAL ANDROS
Technically one island, North and Central Andros are two separate administrative districts. Sleepy **Nicholl's Town** (population 500) is the closest settlement to San Andros Airport and the center of activity for all of North Andros. It's got some extraordinary hidden beaches and coves – ask a local. Further south, the **Stafford Creek** area has a handful of accommodations. In Central Andros, the **Fresh Creek** area (made up of Andros Town and Coakley Town) is another population and tourism center.

◉ Sights & Activities
Bonefishing is huge here, especially around the Cargill Creek area of Central Andros. Ask at your hotel about a guide.

Uncle Charlie's Blue Hole   BLUE HOLE
Near Nicholl's Town, this bottomless blue hole, hidden deep in the pine forest, was made famous by Jacques Cousteau. Today, local kids use a dangling rope swing to splash their way into the hole's black waters. To get here, follow the signs from Queen's Hwy and drive down a short dirt road.

Morgan's Bluff   BEACH, CAVE
Morgan's Bluff is a few miles north of Nicholl's Town. There's a nice **beach** west of the bluff, and an eerie, shipwreck-filled harbor. If you believe local lore, Henry Morgan, the wily Welsh pirate, hid his treasure in a cave – **Henry Morgan's Cave** – about 30yd from the road (it's well signed). Bring a flashlight.

ANDROS LOGISTICS

Andros is divided into three discrete islands: North and Central Andros, Mangrove Cay, and South Andros. South Andros and Mangrove Cay are connected by a twice-daily government ferry, but that's it for interisland transport. To get from, say, North Andros to South Andros, you'll have to charter a plane or fly back to Nassau to catch a connecting flight.

Androsia Ltd   BATIK FACTORY
(www.androsia.com; Fresh Creek; ◷9am-4pm Mon-Fri, 8am-1pm Sat) This factory produces the gorgeous batiks sold throughout the Bahamas. Watch workers create fabric with age-old wax techniques, then buy some for yourself at the adjacent outlet. After you cross the bridge, turn east on the first road you see, then right on an unpaved dirt road.

Small Hope Bay Lodge   DIVING, SNORKELING
(☎242-368-2013/4; www.smallhope.com; Calabash Bay) This highly acclaimed dive resort offers one-/two-tank dives (BS$80/100), night dives (BS$80) and shark dives (BS$85), as well as snorkeling safaris (BS$35). Ask about specialty trips, including blue hole dives and wall dives to 185ft.

🛏 Sleeping & Eating
Nicholl's Town and Fresh Creek both have a handful of accommodations. Small Hope is about six miles north of Fresh Creek on the Queen's Hwy.

WORTH A TRIP

CAT ISLAND

The heart of traditional Bahamian culture still beats on Cat Island, one of the islands least touched by tourism. Obeah and bush medicine are still practiced. Cat has several interesting historic sites, including plantation ruins and the **Mt Alvernia Hermitage**.

The island's second-largest settlement is **Arthur's Town**, 30 miles (48km) north of New Bight, the governmental administrative center. The hamlet's main claim to fame is that it was the boyhood home of Sir Sidney Poitier, the Academy Award–winning actor. Sadly his childhood home is now derelict.

On top of **Mt Alvernia** (206ft; 62m), or Como Hill as it is called by locals, is a blanched-stone church, built by the hermit Father Jerome, with a bell tower that looks like something Merlin might have conjured up in the days of King Arthur. You can enter the small chapel, tiny cloister and a guest cell the size of a large kennel. It's reached by a rock staircase hewn into the side of the hill. From the top, there's a spiritually reviving 360-degree view. Try to make it at sunrise or sunset. Fly here from Nassau on Cat Island Air (www.flycatislandair.com).

WORTH A TRIP

LONG ISLAND & THE BIMINIS

Long Island is one of the most scenic Out Islands, stretching almost 80 miles south – only 4 miles at the widest – past stunning white and sky-blue churches, lush greenery, bougainvillea-draped villages and pastel-colored schoolyards. The lone highway leads to magnificent bays, blue holes and miles of empty beach. Fly here from Nassau on Bahamas Air.

For deep-sea fishing, you can't beat the teeny **Biminis**, Hemingway's old haunt on the edge of the Gulf Stream. It's also tops for diving and snorkeling – check out the mysterious Bimini Road, said to be the lost city of Atlantis.

Fly here from Nassau on Western Air (www.westernairbahamas.com).

TOP CHOICE **Small Hope Bay Lodge** RESORT $$$
(242-368-2014; www.smallhope.com; Calabash Bay; r per person BS$260;) This laid-back ecoresort is small and isolated enough that everyone gets to know each other – stay a week, and you're sure to come away with new friends. Guests wander around barefoot in the chalet-like main lodge, chatting with the owner or watching movies on a rec room TV. Most people are here on dive packages, though the lodge is also popular with anglers. Everything, from bikes to kayaks to dinners, is included in the daily rate. The lodge takes a genuine interest in sustainability, composting food and making drinking glasses from old wine bottles.

Taste & See BAHAMIAN $$
(Love Hill; mains BS$10-20; lunch & dinner) Expect to be embraced when you walk into this homey cafe – literally! Owner Cinderella Hinsey hugs all her guests, whether or not she's met them before. Her love overflows into the food – delectable cracked conch, sautéed lobster and BBQ turkey.

Kamalame Cay RESORT $$$
(242-368-6281; www.kamalame.com; villas BS$840-1500;) A barge whisks lucky guests across the water to a 97-acre private island, home to this exquisite luxury resort. Ultraprivate villas are tucked away down paths lined with kamalame trees, wild dilly, casuarina and love vine. Don't miss a massage at the spa, perched on stilts above the aqua ocean. Access near Stafford Creek.

Pineville Motel MOTEL $
(242-329-2788; www.pinevillemotel.com; Nicholl's Town; r from BS$70;) Independent travelers couldn't ask for a better base than this eclectic motel complex. Owner Eugene knows everything – everything! – about the island, and is happy to share. Motel-style rooms and suites surround a funky man-made forest garden and petting zoo.

ℹ Information

Bahamas Ministry of Tourism (242-368-2286; Andros Town)

Government Medical Clinic (242-368-2038) On the north side of the Fresh Creek Bridge.

Police (242-368-2626, 919; Coakley Town)

Post office (Coakley Town)

Royal Bank of Canada (Calabash Bay; 9:30am-3:30pm Wed) Has an ATM.

MANGROVE CAY & SOUTH ANDROS

The most rural and isolated chunk of the Andros, Mangrove Cay has forests, beaches and blue holes galore. If you're looking to drop off the grid for a while, this is the place.

Virtually bypassed by tourists, South Andros has superb bonefishing and some extraordinary silver-and-pink beaches.

Seascape Inn CABANA RESORT $
(242-369-0342; www.seascapeinn.com; Mangrove Cay; cabanas incl breakfast BS$159;) New Yorkers Mickey and Joan McGowan escaped city life to run this Swiss Family Robinson–like colony of beach cabanas, and their friendliness has earned them a loyal following. Snorkel, kayak, borrow a bike, pet the dogs, or shoot the breeze with other guests in the small on-site restaurant and pub.

Tiamo RESORT $$$
(242-369-2330; www.tiamoresorts.com; South Andros; per couple from BS$895;) Only accessible by boat from South Andros, this all-inclusive resort caters to couples seeking intimacy and exclusivity. Ten cottages have a luxe ecochic vibe; all pale wood, slate tile and textured linens. Guests lounge on their private porches, swim in the placid, protected beach or sip cocktails on the tiered terraces overlooking the infinity pool. The Michelin-trained chef at the open-air **restaurant** serves highly rated Caribbean-fusion

cuisine. Everything but liquor is included. No kids under 14 years.

UNDERSTAND THE BAHAMAS

History

The original inhabitants of the Bahamas were a tribe of Arawaks, the peaceful Lucayans, who arrived near the turn of the 9th century. Christopher Columbus arrived in 1492, and soon after the Spanish began shipping out the Lucayans as slaves.

Infamous pirates like Blackbeard and Calico Jack took over New Providence in the 1600s, establishing a pirates' paradise lined with brothels and taverns for 'common cheats, thieves and lewd persons.' With the aid of Woodes Rogers, the Bahamas' first Royal Governor and a former privateer, the British finally established order, and an administration answerable to the English Crown, in 1718. The Bahamas' new motto was *Expulsis Piratis – Restituta Commercia* (Pirates Expelled – Commerce Restored).

Following the American Revolution, Loyalist refugees – many quite rich or entrepreneurial – began arriving, giving new vigor to the city. These wealthy landowners lived well and kept slaves until the British Empire abolished the slave trade. During the American Civil War the islands were an exchange center for blockade runners transferring munitions and supplies for Southern cotton.

While Nassauvians illicitly supplied liquor to the US during Prohibition, Yankees flocked to Nassau and her new casinos. When Fidel Castro spun Cuba into Soviet orbit in 1961, the subsequent US embargo forced revelers to seek their pleasures elsewhere; Nassau became *the* new hot spot.

Tourism and finance bloomed together. The government promoted the nascent banking industry, encouraging British investors escaping onerous taxes.

This upturn in fortunes coincided with the evolution of party politics and festering ethnic tensions, as the white elite and a growing black middle class reaped profits from the boom. Middle-class blacks' aspirations for representation coalesced with the pent-up frustrations of their impoverished brothers, leading to the victory of the black-led Progressive Liberal party and leader Sir Lynden Pindling in 1967. On July 10, 1973, the Bahamas officially became a new nation – the Independent Commonwealth of the Bahamas – ending 325 years of British rule.

Devastating hurricanes ravaged various islands between 1999 and 2007, wreaking havoc on tourism. Despite these storms, the tourism juggernaut continues and massive resorts on New Providence, Grand Bahama and several Out Islands are chugging toward completion. Look out for the massive new Baha Mar resort complex, set to break ground on Nassau's Cable Beach any minute now.

Culture

People

Contemporary Bahamian culture still revolves around family, church and the sea, but the proximity of North America and the arrival of cable TV has had a profound influence on contemporary life and material values.

In Nassau and Freeport, most working people are employed in banking, tourism or government work and live a nine-to-five lifestyle.

The citizens inhabiting the islands outside of New Providence and Grand Bahama, called the Out Islands or Family Islands, are a bit more neighborly and traditional. Thus the practice of Obeah (a form of African-based ritual magic), bush medicine, and folkloric songs and tales still infuse their daily lives. Though tourism is bringing change to the Out Islands, many still live simple lives centered around fishing, catching conch and lobster, and raising corn, bananas and other crops.

The Arts

The Bahamas rock to the soul-riveting sounds of calypso, soca, reggae and its own distinctive music, which echoes African rhythms and synthesizes Caribbean calypso, soca and English folk songs into its own goombay beat.

Goombay – the name comes from an African word for 'rhythm' – derives its melody from a guitar, piano or horn instrument, accompanied by any combination of goatskin goombay drums, maracas, rhythm sticks, rattles, conch-shell horns, fifes, flutes and cowbells, to add a kalik-kalik-kalik sound.

Rake 'n' scrape is the Bahamas' down-home, working-class music, usually featuring a guitar, an accordion, shakers made from the pods of poinciana trees, and other makeshift instruments, such as a saw played with a screwdriver.

Landscape & Wildlife

The Land

The Bahamian islands are strewn in a linear fashion from northwest to southeast. Several of them – Great Abaco, Eleuthera, Long Island and Andros – are more than 100 miles (160km) in length. Few, however, are more than a few miles wide. All are low-lying, and the highest point in the Bahamas – Mt Alvernia on Cat Island – is only 206ft (62m) above sea level.

Virtually the entire length of these shores is lined by white- or pinkish-sand beaches – about 2200 miles (3540km) in all – shelving into turquoise shallows. The interiors are generally marked by scrub-filled forests and, on some of the more remote islands, the plants found here are still used in bush medicine remedies.

The islands are pocked by blue holes – water-filled circular pits that open to underground and submarine caves and descend as far as 600ft (182m).

Wildlife

The islands are a bird-watcher's paradise, with about 300 recorded species of birds. Only a few are endemic, including the Bahama swallow, the endangered Bahama parrot, and the Bahama woodstar hummingbird, a pugnacious bird weighing less than a US nickel. The West Indian (Caribbean) flamingo – the national bird – inhabits Crooked Island, Long Cay and the sanctuary of Great Inagua.

Iguanas inhabit some outlying isles and cays, and are protected. The archipelago's largest native land animal, they can reach 4ft (1.2m) in length.

The region's marine life is as varied as its islands and coral reefs. Depending on who you believe, the Bahamas have between 900 and 2700 sq miles (2330 and 6992 sq km) of coral reef, and countless species of fish, such as bonito, stingrays, sharks, kingfish, jewelfish and deep-blue Creole wrasse.

Humpback whales pass through the waters windward of the Bahamas and blue whales are also frequently sighted.

Environmental Issues

The Bahamas National Trust maintains 22 national parks and reserves, including large sections of the barrier reef, but outside of the national park system, inappropriate development, pollution and overexploitation increasingly threaten wildlife and marine resources. Although the Bahamas was the first Caribbean nation to outlaw long-line fishing, the islands' stocks of grouper, spiny lobster, and conch all face the consequences of overfishing.

Today, local groups are leading the eco-charge. The Abacos' Friends of the Environment (www.friendsoftheenvironment.org) organizes communitywide projects and passes the message along in schools. In Eleuthera, the Eleuthera School (www.islandschool.org) is earning kudos as an environmental learning center, drawing US high schoolers as well as adult 'students' looking to become environmentally engaged global citizens.

The Bahamas banned hunting and eating sea turtles, an endangered species, in 2009.

PRACTICALITIES

» **Electricity** Hotels operate on 120 volts/60 cycles, which is compatible with US appliances. Plug sockets are two- or three-pin US standard.

» **Newspapers & Magazines** Daily New Providence newspapers include the *Nassau Guardian*, the *Tribune* and the *Bahama Journal*. Grand Bahama offers the daily *Freeport News*, and Abaconians enjoy the weekly *Abaconian*.

» **Radio & TV** The government-owned Bahamas Broadcasting Corporation operates TV-channel 13 (ZNS) and the radio stations ZNS-1, ZNS-2, ZNS-FM and ZNS-3. Commercial radio stations include Love 97FM, More 94.9FM and Jam 100FM. Most hotels also offer American cable TV.

» **Weights & Measures** The imperial and metric systems are both in use.

SURVIVAL GUIDE

Directory A–Z

Accommodations

The Bahamian islands offer a range of lodging that includes cottages, inns, condos, hotels and resorts. Prices tend to be high, and taxes and imaginative surcharges can hike up your bill by around 20% to 30%. Check prior to booking that quoted rates are inclusive of all these additional costs.

Nearly all hotels change their rates at least twice a year between low and high season. While this guide quotes high-season rates, be aware that some hotels charge even higher prices from Christmas Eve through to New Year's Day. The good news? The low season (or summer) extends for most of the year from mid-April to mid-December. During this period accommodations prices drop between 20% and 60%, so although this region is pricey, it is possible to find value-for-money lodgings.

Weekly rentals and all-inclusive resorts are also options on many islands. Camping, however, is not: it's illegal on the beaches and there are no official campsites, even in wilderness areas.

$	budget	less than BS$100
$$	midrange	BS$100 to $200
$$$	top end	more than BS$200

Activities

Diving, snorkeling, fishing, kayaking, sailing and swimming are all on the menu in the Bahamas. Hiking's not bad for landlubbers, though trails are usually short. See individual destinations for details.

Business Hours

Exceptions to the following business hours are noted in specific listings. Banks on smaller Out Islands and cays may be open only once or twice a week.

Banks 9am-3pm Mon-Thu, 9am-5pm Fri

Businesses 9am-5pm Mon-Fri

Shops 9am-5pm Mon-Fri, 9 or 10am-5pm Sat

Post offices 9am-5pm Mon-Fri, 9am-noon Sat

Restaurants breakfast 7-10am, lunch noon-2pm, dinner 6-9pm

Tourist information 9am-5pm Mon-Fri

Children

The Bahamas pursue family travelers aggressively and the larger hotels provide good facilities and a full range of activities for children. Many have a babysitter or nanny service. Children under 12 years normally room with their parents for free.

See p155 for activities and sights for kids in Nassau.

Embassies & Consulates

Most countries are represented by honorary consuls. All listings below are located in Nassau, New Providence.

Australia (☑242-326-0083, ext 107; 2 Nassau Ct)

Canada (☑242-393-2123; Shirley St)

Germany (☑242-394-6161; Alliance House, E Bay St)

Netherlands (☑242-361-6398; Gladstone Rd)

UK (☑242-325-7471/3; East St)

USA (☑242-322-1181/2/3, emergencies 242-328-2206; 42 Queen St)

Food

The following price categories are used in restaurant reviews in this chapter, and are based on the price of a dinner meal or the equivalent.

$	budget	less than BS$12
$$	midrange	BS$12 to BS$25
$$$	top end	more than BS$25

Gay & Lesbian Travelers

The pink dollar isn't particularly welcome in the Bahamas and there's not much public support for Bahamian gay and lesbian populations across the islands. Discretion is the better part of affection here. Antigay protesters met a gay-family-values cruise with placards and protests in 2004 and many gay-themed cruises now avoid Nassau. For more information, contact the gay-rights group **Rainbow Alliance of the Bahamas** (http://bahamianglad.tripod.com).

Health

Many of the Out Islands are serviced by small government clinics, usually found off the Queen's Hwy in the major settlements. Clinics are usually open 9am to 5pm, though most have a doctor on call. In Nassau and on Grand Bahama, emergency rooms are open

24/7. See each destination for local hospital and medical clinic listings.

The tap water is fine to drink.

Internet Access

» Almost all hotels have wi-fi.

» Larger hotels may have a business center with computers.

» Downtown Nassau and Grand Bahama have a handful of internet cafes, as well as public wi-fi hot spots.

Money

The Bahamian dollar (BS$) is linked one-to-one with the US dollar, so you can use US currency everywhere. There are plenty of banks with ATMs in the major tourist centers, though they can be rare to nonexistent on the Out Islands. Many Out Island hotels and restaurants do not accept credit cards. You can use your credit card to get cash advances at most commercial banks.

A tip of 15% or so is the norm for restaurants, but it's often added to your bill automatically – check before you pay! About 15% is the norm for taxis, while a dollar per bag is routine for bellhops.

Public Holidays

Bahamian national holidays that fall on Saturday or Sunday are usually observed on the previous Friday or following Monday. In addition to those observed throughout the region (p872), the Bahamas have the following public holidays:

Labour Day First Friday in June

Independence Day July 10

Emancipation Day First Monday in August

Discovery Day October 12

Telephone

Cell phones Unlocked European or Australian phones can be used with Bahamian SIM cards. Most US phones are locked, and can only be used when roaming. Service is poor on many of the Out Islands.

Hotel phones Rates are expensive across the region and should be avoided when possible. Many hotels also charge for an unanswered call after the receiving phone has rung five times.

Phone codes The Bahamian country code is ☎242. You need to dial this when making interisland calls. To call the Bahamas from the US and Canada, dial ☎1-242.

From elsewhere, dial your country's international access code + ☎242 + the local number. Most US toll-free numbers can't be accessed from the Bahamas. Usually you must dial ☎1-880, plus the last seven digits of the number.

Public phones The government-owned **Bahamas Telecommunications Corporation** (☎242-302-7000; John F Kennedy Dr, Nassau, New Providence), or BaTelCo, has an office on most Bahamian islands. Even the smallest settlement usually has at least one public phone.

Travelers with Disabilities

Disabled travelers will need to plan their vacation carefully, as few allowances have been made for them in the Bahamas. Tourism boards can provide a list of hotels with wheelchair ramps, as can the **Bahamas Council for the Disabled** (☎242-353-7720; 11A Kipling Bldg, Freeport, Grand Bahama) and the **Bahamas Association for the Physically Disabled** (☎242-322-2393; Dolphin Dr, Nassau, New Providence). The latter can also hire out a van and portable ramps for those with wheelchairs.

Visas

Residents of the US, Europe and most Commonwealth countries do not need a visa to enter the Bahamas for a 90-day tourist stay. Everyone needs a passport.

Women Travelers

It is relatively unusual for women to travel alone in the Bahamas, so expect inquiries about your husband's whereabouts. These are meant to be friendly. The islands are largely safe for solo women, though take obvious precautions at night and dress appropriately; you'll rarely see a Bahamian woman in shorts, let alone a bikini top, around town.

Getting There & Away

Entering the Bahamas

All visitors must carry a valid passport and a return or onward ticket as well as sufficient funds to support their stay.

This section addresses transportation to the Bahamas from other countries. See Getting Around for information on travel between the islands.

Airports & Airlines

The Bahamas have seven international airports, including two major hubs at Nassau and Freeport.

Exuma International Airport (☎242-345-0095) George Town, the Exumas

Freeport International Airport (☎242-352-6020) Freeport, Grand Bahama

Lynden Pindling International Airport (☎242-377-7281; www.nassauairport.com) Nassau, New Providence

Marsh Harbour International Airport (☎242-367-3039) Marsh Harbour, Great Abaco

Moss Town Exuma International Airport (☎242-345-0030) Moss Town, the Exumas

North Eleuthera International Airport (☎242-335-1242) North Eleuthera

Treasure Cay International Airport Located 25 miles north of Marsh Harbour, Great Abaco

AIRLINES FLYING TO/FROM THE BAHAMAS

The Bahamas are well served by flights from North America and Europe. Their proximity to Florida means regular, relatively inexpensive flights from Miami, Fort Lauderdale and Orlando, as well as other east-coast gateways. A few airlines fly directly to airports on the larger Out Islands, but the majority of flights arrive in Nassau or Freeport where passengers will connect to another flight before continuing to the Out Islands. For a brief summary of airlines and flight schedules by island, check www.bahamas.com.

The national airline **Bahamasair** (www.bahamasair.com) has an unblemished safety record and its pilots have an excellent reputation (see www.airsafe.com for details). Delays, however, are regular occurrences and flights are canceled without warning. Bahamians say 'If you have time to spare, fly Bahamasair.'

The following major international airlines have offices at Nassau airport.

Air Canada (www.aircanada.ca)

Air Jamaica (www.airjamaica.com)

American Airlines/American Eagle (www.aa.com)

Bahamasair (www.bahamasair.com)

British Airways (www.british-airways.com)

Continental/Gulfstream International (www.continental.com)

Delta Air Lines/Comair (www.delta.com)

US Airways/US Air Express (www.usair.com)

Sea

CRUISE SHIP & YACHT

Numerous cruise ships dock in Nassau and Grand Bahama. Most originate in Florida.

The sheltered waters of the 750-mile-long archipelago attract thousands of yachters each year. Winds and currents favor the passage south. Sailing conditions are at their best in summer, though hurricanes can be a threat throughout the season.

FERRY

With both options below, you can stay overnight and cruise home later if you wish.

Discovery Cruise (☎1800-937-4477; www.discoverycruise.com) Runs a daily party and gambling cruise between Fort Lauderdale and Freeport, Grand Bahama (BS$129).

Bahamas Celebration (☎800-314-7735; www.bahamascelebration.com; from $99) Leaves Palm Beach in the afternoon, spends the night at sea, then docks in Grand Bahama the following morning before returning that evening.

Getting Around

Perusing a map, it's tempting to think that island hopping down the chain is easy. Unfortunately, it's not – that is, unless you have your own boat or plane. Interisland air is centered on Nassau. Getting between the islands without constantly backtracking is a bit of a feat. Even the mail boats are Nassau-centric.

Air

Interisland flights offer the only quick and convenient way to travel within the Bahamas and islanders ride airplanes like Londoners use buses. Private charter flights can be an economical option for those traveling in a group.

There are several airlines operating in the Bahamas.

Abaco Air (☎242-367-2266; www.abacoaviationcentre.com) Flies between Great Abaco (Marsh Harbour) and Nassau, North Eleuthera and Moore's Island.

Cat Island Air (☎242-377-3318; www.flycat islandair.com) Flies from Nassau to Cat Island, Rum Cay, San Salvador and the Berry Islands (Great Harbour Cay).

Flamingo Air (☎242-377-0354; www.flamingo airbah.com) Flies from Freeport to Moore's Island and the Berry Islands (Great Harbour Cay), and from Nassau to Staniel Cay, Black Point, Great Harbour Cay, the Exumas, and Andros (Mangrove Cay).

LeAir (☎242-377-2356; www.leaircharters.com) Has two daily flights from Nassau to Andros (Andros Town), and charter service to all the airports.

Pineapple Air (☎242-377-0140; www.pine appleair.com) Flies from Nassau to Eleuthera (Governor's Harbour, Rock Sound, North Eleuthera) as well as Crooked Island, Acklins Island, Deadman's Cay and Long Island (Stella Maris).

Regional Air (☎242-351-5614; www.goregional air.com) Based in Freeport, with services to the Biminis, the Abacos (Marsh Harbour, Treasure Cay, Walker's Cay), North Eleuthera and Andros (San Andros).

Sky Bahamas (☎242-377-8777; www.skyba hamas.net) A large carrier; flies between Nassau and Cat Island, the Biminis, Freeport, Great Abaco (Marsh Harbour) and the Exumas, as well as between Freeport and the Turks and Caicos.

Southern Air (☎242-377-2014; www.southern aircharter.com) Flies from Nassau to Eleuthera (Governor's Harbour, Rock Sound and North Eleuthera) and to Long Island (Stella Maris).

Western Air (☎242-329-4000; www.western airbahamas.com) The country's largest private airline flies from Nassau to Freeport, Great Abaco (Marsh Harbour), Andros (San Andros and Congo Town), the Biminis, the Exumas, and Kingston in Jamaica.

For connections to Nassau (prices are for one-way fares):

Abacos BS$85, 30 minutes, three daily

Andros BS$75, 15 minutes, two daily

Biminis BS$85, 20 minutes, two daily

Cat Island BS$75, one hour, two daily

Crooked Island BS$105, two hours, two weekly

Eleuthera BS$75, 15 minutes, two daily

Exumas BS$80, one hour 20 minutes, three daily

Grand Bahama BS$85, 45 minutes, six daily

Inagua BS$110, 1½ hours, three weekly

Long Island BS$85, 45 minutes, one daily

San Salvador BS$80, 1¾ hours, three weekly

Bicycle

Cycling is not huge in the Bahamas. It's not safe in traffic-clogged Nassau, though can be pleasant on Paradise Island, Grand Bahama and the Out Islands. Many hotels rent bikes for about BS$15 a day.

Boat

FERRY

The only major interisland ferry operator in the Bahamas is **Bahamas Ferries** (☎242-323-2166/8; www.bahamasferries.com), which runs a high-speed ferry linking Nassau, Andros, the Abacos, Eleuthera and the Exumas. Services from Nassau:

Current, Eleuthera BS$50, 4pm Friday and Sunday

Fresh Creek, Andros BS$50, 8am Friday and Sunday

George Town, the Exumas BS$60, 8:30pm Monday and Wednesday

Governor's Harbour BS$50, 7am Thursday and Friday, 4:15pm Sunday April to December; 7am Wednesday, 4:15pm Friday and Sunday February to March

Harbour Island BS$65, 8am daily

Morgan's Bluff, Andros BS$50, 8am Saturday April to December only

Sandy Point, Great Abaco BS$60, 11am Friday and Sunday April to December only

MAIL BOAT & WATER TAXI

Around 30 mail boats sail under government contract to most inhabited islands. They regularly depart Potter's Cay for Grand Bahama and all the Family Islands. Traditionally sailing overnight, boat journeys last between five and 24 hours. Always call the **Dockmaster's Office** (☎242-394-1237) and check with the **Bahamas Ministry of Tourism** (☎242-322-7500; www.bahamas.com) for the latest schedules and prices.

In New Providence, water taxis zip back and forth between Prince George Wharf, Nassau, and Paradise Island. Several other offshore islands and their neighboring cays are served by private water taxis.

Government-run water taxis link islands that are a short distance apart, such as North and South Bimini, Mangrove Cay and South Andros, and Crooked and Acklins Islands.

Bus

Nassau and Freeport Have dozens of *jitneys* (private minibuses) licensed to operate on preestablished routes.

Out Islands There's not much public transportation, as the taxi drivers' union is too powerful. Likewise, few hotels are permitted to operate their own transfer service for guests. A number of adventure outfitters and tours, however, will send courtesy shuttles to your hotel before and after reserved trips.

Car & Golf Cart

Road conditions Driving in traffic-clogged downtown Nassau can be a pain. On the Out Islands, expect potholes and poor lighting.

Rental Several major international car-rental companies have outlets in Nassau and Freeport, along with smaller local firms. In the Out Islands there are some very good local agencies. Ask your hotel or look for display boards at the airport. Renters must be 21 (some companies

rent only to those 25 or older). Collision damage waiver insurance is BS$15 per day. Local companies may not offer insurance. Rates start at around BS$70 per day. Golf carts are popular on the smaller islands and cays, and rent for about BS$40 per day.

Road rules In order to drive you must have a current license from your home country or state. A visitor can drive on his or her home license for three months. Drive on the left-hand side. At traffic circles (roundabouts), remember to circle in a clockwise direction, entering to the left. You must give way to traffic already in the circle. It's compulsory to wear a helmet when riding a motorcycle or scooter.

Taxi

There's no shortage of licensed taxis in Nassau and Freeport, where they can be hailed on the streets. Taxis are also the main local transportation in the Out Islands, where they meet all incoming planes and ferries in the larger settlements.

All taxi operators are licensed. Taxi fares are fixed by the government according to distance: rates are usually for two people. Each additional person is charged a flat rate of BS$3. Fixed rates have been established from airports and cruise terminals to specific hotels and major destinations. These rates should be displayed in the taxi.

Barbados

Best Beaches

» Crane Beach (p209)

» Paynes Bay (p210)

» Accra Beach (p204)

» Miami Beach (p207)

» Bath Beach (p216)

Best Places to Stay

» Little Arches Hotel (p208)

» Surfer's Point Guest House (p208)

» Sea-U! Guest House (p215)

» Coral Reef Club (p211)

Why Go?

Barbados is ringed by azure water and white-sand visions that fuel the fantasies of those stuck in chilly winter climes.

No matter your budget or style, you'll find a place to stay, especially on the popular south and west coasts. Elsewhere, however, is where you'll find what makes the island special. Barbados has lush scenery among rolling hills dotted with fascinating survivors of the colonial past. Vast plantation homes show the wealth of European settlers, while several botanical gardens exploit the beauty possible from the perfect growing conditions.

The wild Atlantic-battered east coast is a legend with surfers; those looking for action will also find windsurfing, hiking, diving and more. Away from the glitz, it's still a civilized place (with a 98% literacy rate) of classic calypso rhythms, an island-time vibe and world-famous rums.

When to Go

The climate in Barbados tends to be nice year-round: in January, the average daily high temperature is 28°C (83°F), while the low average is 21°C (70°F). In July, the average daily high is 30°C (86°F), while the average low is 23°C (74°F). April averages only seven days of rain, while July is the wettest month, with some 18 days of rain. The tourist high season runs from mid-December through mid-April. June through October is the hurricane season – although many years see none.

Itineraries

FOUR DAYS

Depending on your budget, stay on the mid-priced south coast or the fancier west coast, go diving or snorkeling (maybe surfing in the south) and spend an afternoon wandering the island's heart: Bridgetown.

ONE WEEK

As above, but spend a couple of days exploring the interior and the east coast. Or stay in the wet and wild east and make trips west. Or try it all and split your time between the south or west and east. This will give you time away from crowds plus time partying with crowds.

TWO WEEKS

The same as for one week but with more time to utterly chill out. Get lost! Head into the hills of central Barbados and take roads at random. It's green, beautiful and full of sights and surprises. Plus you're on an island, so you can't get lost for long.

GETTING TO NEIGHBORING ISLANDS

Short of sailing your own boat – or hitching a ride – the only way to and from Barbados is by air. Every so often there is talk of a ferry service to neighboring islands like St Lucia or St Vincent but it never materializes. Air links are comprehensive and frequent.

Essential Food & Drink

» **Flying fish** Served fried in delicious sandwiches all over the country. It's a mild white fish that is great sautéed or deep-fried.

» **Conkies** A mixture of cornmeal, coconut, pumpkin, sweet potato, raisins and spices, steamed in a plantain leaf.

» **Fish cakes** There are myriad Bajan recipes, made from salt cod and deep-fried.

» **Cou-cou** A creamy cornmeal and okra mash.

» **Cutters** Meat or fish sandwiches in a salt-bread roll.

» **Jug-jug** A mixture of cornmeal, green peas and salted meat.

» **Roti** A curry filling rolled inside flat bread.

» **Bananas** Local varieties are green even when ripe (look for them in markets).

» **Barbadian rum** Considered some of the finest in the Caribbean, with Mount Gay being the best-known label.

» **Banks** The island's crisp lager is refreshing after a day in the hot sun.

AT A GLANCE

» **Currency** Barbadian dollar (B$)

» **Language** English

» **Money** ATMs all over; some dispense Barbadian and US dollars

» **Visas** Not required for citizens of the US, Canada and most European and Commonwealth countries

Fast Facts

» **Area** 432 sq km

» **Population** 286,000

» **Capital** Bridgetown

» **Telephone country code** ☎1

» **Telephone area code** ☎246

» **Emergency** Fire ☎311, police ☎211, ambulance ☎511

Set Your Budget

» **Budget hotel room** B$100

» **Two-course evening meal** B$30

» **Beer** B$5

» **Flying-fish sandwich** B$10

» **Bus** B$1.50

Resources

» **Barbados Tourism Authority** (www.visitbarbados.org)

» **Barbados Hotel & Tourism Association** (www.bhta.org)

» **Barbados National Trust** (http://trust.funbarbados.com)

» **National News** (www.nationnews.com)

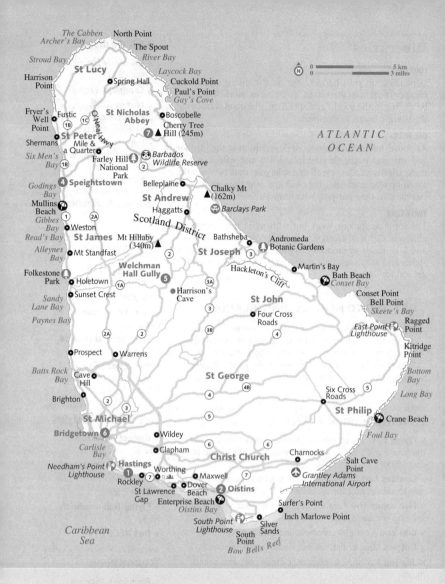

Barbados Highlights

1 Unwind on the blissful beaches fringing the island, such as the perfectly white **Accra Beach** (p204) in Hastings

2 Revel in one of the Caribbean's great parties, the weekly **Oistins Fish Fry** (p209)

3 Join the raucous crowds at a **cricket match** (p218), one of the island's sporting passions

4 Stroll through the beautiful Bajan past in the old port town of **Speightstown** (p212)

5 Enjoy the lush beauty of the island's rich floral wonders, such as **Welchman Hall Gully** (p214)

6 Sample Barbados' most popular meal, a **flying-fish dish** at a cafe in Bridgetown (p200)

7 Experience the beautiful present and ugly past at grand plantation homes such as **St Nicholas Abbey** (p213)

BRIDGETOWN

POP 101,000

Barbados' bustling capital, Bridgetown, is also the island's only city and is situated on its only natural harbor, attractive Carlisle Bay. Wandering around its many sights and old colonial buildings can easily occupy a day. Head along the side streets of the main drags to discover residential neighborhoods scattered with rum shops and chattel houses.

Many visitors enjoy taking a rest from sightseeing at one of the cafes or snack stands along the south banks of the Constitution River. There is good shopping, especially along Broad St and on pedestrian-only Swan St, which buzzes with the rhythms of local culture. Bay St, south of the center, has a nice beach and several bars, and further on are some important sights. The entire area is in St Michael Parish.

◉ Sights & Activities

All of the following sites can be reached on foot.

St Michael's Cathedral CATHEDRAL
(St Michael's Row; ⊗9am-4pm Sun-Fri, to 1pm Sat) The island's Anglican cathedral was originally completed in 1665 to accommodate 3000 worshippers, but came tumbling down in a hurricane a century later. The scaled-down but still substantial structure (it's also a hurricane shelter) that stands today dates from 1789 and seats 1600. At the time of construction it was said to have the widest arched ceiling of its type in the world. Among the island notables tightly packed into the rather shambolic adjacent churchyard are Sir Grantley Adams (Barbados' first premier and the head of the West Indies Federation from 1958 to 1962) and his son Tom (prime minister of Barbados from 1976 to 1985).

National Heroes Square MONUMENT
The triangular square (formerly known as Trafalgar Sq) marks the bustling center of the city. The square once celebrated Battle of Trafalgar hero Lord Horatio Nelson (whose statue still stands on the west side of the square), but was eventually changed to honor 10 Bajan heroes – from cricket greats to slave leaders.

Parliament Buildings NOTABLE BUILDINGS
On the north side of National Heroes Sq are two stone-block, neo-Gothic-style buildings constructed in 1871. The west-side building

with the clock tower contains public offices; the building on the east side houses the Senate and House of Assembly and is adorned with stained-glass windows depicting British monarchs. Parliament meets most Tuesdays and you can line up for a free spot in the gallery, but be sure to dress accordingly: long pants and skirts plus proper shoes.

At the **museum** (admission $5; ⊗9am-4pm Mon, Wed-Sat) learn about the island's proud democratic heritage (it regularly finishes in surveys of the top tier of countries with the least corruption, ahead of the UK and US); museum entry includes a tour of the parliament buildings.

Barbados Synagogue SYNAGOGUE
(Synagogue Lane; ⊗9am-4pm Mon-Fri) Built in 1833, this small synagogue between James St and Magazine Lane, near National Heroes Sq, was abandoned in 1929 and beautifully restored in 1986. The island's first synagogue was built on this site in the 1600s, when Barbados had a Jewish population of more than 800. Over the following years the population dwindled, owing to emigration and Christian conversion, leaving only one person by 1929. In 1931 the Jewish population of Barbados rebounded when a large group arrived after fleeing discrimination in Poland. In decline again, the community now numbers about 90.

Nidhe Israel Museum MUSEUM
(Synagogue Lane; adult/child B$25/12.50; ⊗9am-4pm Mon-Fri) Housed in a restored 1750 Jewish community center, this museum documents the fascinating story of the Barbados Jewish community. It's massively built from cut coral blocks that glow in the sun and is near the synagogue.

Carlisle Wharf PUBLIC SPACE
(Hincks St) A small commercial building has benches on the waterside which overlook the harbor; interesting plaques chart the local maritime heritage.

🛏 Sleeping

Few visitors stay in Bridgetown and there are few accommodations available. Aquatic Gap, just south of town, is the first spot with any hotels to speak of; however, it is recommended that you head the few minutes further to Hastings, Rockley, Worthing, St Lawrence Gap or beyond for a more relaxed beach atmosphere.

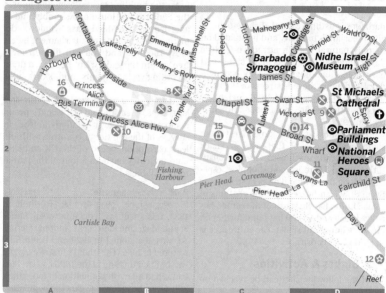

✗ Eating

TOP CHOICE **Mustor's Restaurant** CARIBBEAN $
(McGregor St; lunch from B$14; ☺lunch Mon-Sat) Climb the stairs past the small snack bar and bar to a large, plain dining room. Choose from staples such as beef and pork stew, flying fish and chicken in various forms. Then select the sides – we love the macaroni pie (like mac 'n' cheese but better) and the split peas and rice. If you're lucky you'll snag one of three balcony tables where you can gaze down on passers-by *not* enjoying what you're enjoying.

Lobster Alive SEAFOOD $$$
(☎435-0305; www.lobsteralive.net; Bay St; meals from B$40; ☺lunch & dinner) The name is only true until you order. Lobster bisque and grilled lobster are just some of the choices on the crustacean-heavy menu at this ramshackle joint on the beach. A huge tank holds hundreds of the namesake critters at any given time – all flown in, one-way, from the Grenadines. Smooth jazz (Tuesday, Thursday and Sunday nights) is also a trademark.

Balcony Restaurant CARIBBEAN $
(Broad St; lunch from B$12; ☺lunch Mon-Sat) The in-house restaurant at the landmark Cave Shepherd Department Store has a small daily buffet of island favorites like curries and salads. Ask a local where they go for lunch, and they'll point here. The fresh juices are excellent.

Waterfront Cafe CAFE $$
(Careenage; meals from B$25; ☺lunch & dinner) Always packed, especially the breezy tables on the river. Lunches include a fine version of a flying-fish sandwich; dinners are more elaborate and have Mediterranean color and flair. There's live music ranging from steel pan to jazz.

Cheapside Market MARKET $
(Cheapside; ☺7am-3pm Mon-Sat) Even if you're not intending to buy, this is a fascinating place to browse local produce in a grand old market hall recently restored by the thoughtful Chinese government. It has some nice snack stands on the 2nd floor. The best times to visit are Friday and Saturday mornings. Southwest across Princess Alice Hwy, the open-air **public market** has all things briny fresh from the boats.

Paris Bakery BAKERY $
(Cheapside; snacks from B$3; ☺breakfast & lunch Mon-Fri) Enjoy take-out banana bread, coconut bread and other treats at this delectable little bakery.

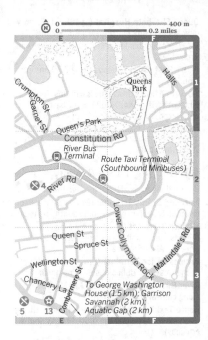

Parliament Market CARIBBEAN $

(Palmetto St; meals from B$10; ⊗lunch Mon-Sat) A series of small wooden huts behind the Parliament buildings has both produce and lunch items. Some of the region's finest chicken soup comes from a green hut without a sign but with a pile of sugar beets out front.

Fairchild St Market MARKET $

(Fairchild St; ⊗7am-3pm Mon-Sat) Have a meal or a cheery drink with amiable and voluble locals; has snack stands, cafes and rum shops in a long row along the river. The markets are usually open 7am to late afternoon Monday to Saturday.

Palmetto Market MARKET $

(Swan St; ⊗7am-3pm Mon-Sat) At the east end. A good place for fresh produce and snacks.

🍷 Drinking

Bridgetown's many rum shops are patronized by local regulars, though visitors are not unwelcome. Along Baxters Rd, just north of the center, you'll find a concentration of these bars, where alcohol flows and fish is fried up until late at night. Although women will not be turned away, be warned that rum shops are a macho haunt.

Boatyard BEACH BAR

(www.theboatyard.com; Bay St; ⊗11am-2am) An over-amped beach bar that pushes the sex-on-the-beach angle hard, the Boatyard gets visitors by the busload who come for the daytime drinking contests and beach activities. By day there's a cover charge to use the many beach facilities. Late night it's a club with DJs and live music (cover varies). There's free transportation to and from the cruise dock or it's a 30-minute walk through the heart of town.

Smith Corner Pub BAR

(Bay St; ⊗5pm-late) For an accessible rum-shop-style experience check out this old place, which is one of several on the stretch. Note how old cannons are now used as posts.

🔒 Shopping

Broad St in the center is the place for shops great and small.

PORT OF CALL – BRIDGETOWN

Traveling on foot from the cruise-ship dock you can spend an intriguing day exploring the buzzing town of Bridgetown. Check out the Broad St stores, traditional markets and cafes serving tasty Bajan favorites. A little further afield:

» Taste rum at the famous local distilleries (p203)

» See sea turtles on a west-coast snorkeling tour (p211)

» Lose yourself in ancient forests and gardens at Welchman Hall Gully (p214) and Flower Forest of Barbados (p214)

Pelican Craft Village CRAFTS
(Princess Alice Hwy) This ever-evolving complex of galleries and workshops, between downtown and the cruise-ship terminal, features the works of many local artists. The **Barbados Arts Council** (www.barbados artscouncil.com) has a shop here with the works of more than 100 of its members usually on show.

Cave Shepherd DEPARTMENT STORE
(Broad St) The island's grand old department store has well-priced rum and a quality souvenir section. There's camera supplies and a decent book department, with a wide selection of Caribbean and international literature plus the UK's *Sunday Times*. The Balcony Restaurant is a local lunch fave.

Cloister Bookstore BOOKSTORE
(☑426-2662; Hincks St) Carries local and international literature and bestsellers.

❶ Information

INTERNET ACCESS Connect (Shop 9, 27 Broad St; per 10min B$3; ☺9am-5pm Mon-Fri, 9:30am-4pm Sat) Upstairs in the Galleria Mall behind Nelson's Arms (enter from Lancaster Lane). Laptop connections and cheap calls.

LIBRARIES National Library (Coleridge St; ☺9am-5pm Mon-Sat) To check out books here you'll pay a refundable deposit of B$20. The deposit is valid also at Holetown, Speightstown and Oistins branches.

MEDICAL SERVICES Collins Pharmacy (28 Broad St) Prescriptions, sundries, shoe and watch repair. Fun to browse even if you're ailment-free.

Queen Elizabeth Hospital (☑436-6450; www. qehconnect.com; Martindale's Rd; ☺24hr)

MONEY Major banks for currency exchange line Broad St.

POST Post office (Cheapside; ☺7:30am-5pm Mon-Fri)

TOURIST INFORMATION Barbados Tourism Authority (☑427-2623; www.barbados. org; Harbour Rd; ☺8:15am-4:30pm Mon-Fri) Answers questions, offers brochures; a branch office at the cruise-ship terminal opens when ships are in port.

❶ Getting There & Away

Bus stations are scattered through town.

Fairchild St Bus Terminal (Bridge St) North of Fairchild St; public buses going south and east.

Minibus Terminal (Princess Alice Hwy) At the west end; minibuses going north. Adjoins Princess Alice Terminal.

Princess Alice Terminal (Princess Alice Hwy) At the west end; public buses going north.

River Bus Terminal (Nursery Rd) Minibuses along central and eastern routes.

Route Taxi Terminal (Nursery Rd) Along the river; minibuses along the tourist-heavy southern coast.

❶ Getting Around

Bridgetown is easily covered on foot, although **taxis** can be flagged on the street if necessary, or hailed from the waiting area. The set taxi fare from one end of town to the other is B$6.

Around Bridgetown

The following sights are within 5km of Bridgetown's center.

◉ Sights

Barbados Museum MUSEUM
(Garrison; adult/child B$15/7.50; ☺9am-5pm Mon-Sat, 2-6pm Sun) This excellent museum is housed in an early-19th-century military prison. It has engaging displays on all aspects of the island's history, beginning with its early indigenous residents. The most extensive collections cover the colonial era, with exhibits on slavery, emancipation, military history and plantation-house furniture, all accompanied by insightful narratives.

George Washington House MUSEUM
(Bush Hill, Garrison; adult/child B$20/5; ☺9am-4:30pm Mon-Fri) Just west of the Barbados Museum, they can truly claim that the great

man slept here. After decades of research and debate, it was finally shown that this 18th-century estate had been the home of the future US president and his brother Lawrence during their fateful stay in 1751. The beautifully restored home shows what it must have looked like during their stay. A large museum brings 1750s Barbados to life. Lush gardens include a herb patch and cafe.

Garrison Savannah Area   HISTORIC AREA
About 2km south of central Bridgetown, spreading inland from the south side of Carlisle Bay, was the home base of the British Windward and Leeward Islands Command in the 1800s. A focal point is the oval-shaped **Savannah**, which was once parade grounds and is now used for cricket games, jogging and Saturday horse races. Standing along the west side of the Savannah are some of the Garrison's more ornate colonial buildings, where you'll find the world's largest collection of 17th-century iron cannons.

Pebbles Beach   BEACH
(Hwy 7) A fine beach close to downtown Bridgetown (a 10-minute walk) that makes a good break before and after lunch and shopping. Lots of parking and shade trees plus shacks selling drinks.

☞ Tours

Rum has long been a critical part of local life and you can make it part of your life as well at two facilities run by famous local distilleries.

Malibu Beach Club & Visitor Centre   RUM TOUR
(☑425-9393; Brighton Beach; tours B$20; ☺9am-4pm Mon-Fri) Coconut-flavored Malibu is more of an export to Americans barely old enough to drink than a Bajan drink, but the company has a popular tour at the beachfront distillery. Spend time in a beach chair after the tour and samples. It's about 3km north of the center; call to arrange transportation.

Mount Gay Rum Visitors Centre   RUM TOUR
(www.mountgay.com; Spring Garden Hwy; tours B$14; ☺hourly tours 9:30am-3:30pm Mon-Fri, 10:30am-2:30pm Sat) The aged rums here are some of Barbados' best. The visitors centre is about a kilometer north of Bridgetown Harbour. Other tour options include transportation and cocktails, from B$70.

🛏 Sleeping & Eating

Island Inn Hotel   RESORT $$$
(☑436-6393; www.islandinnbarbados.com; Aquatic Gap; r from US$300; ❄@☎≋) This 24-room all-inclusive hotel is partially built in a restored 1804 garrison building that was originally a military rum store. It is near the beach off Bay St and close to town. It was given a complete renovation in 2009 and has muted island-chic motifs.

Brown Sugar   CARIBBEAN $$
(☑426-7684; lunch buffet B$55, dinner mains B$40-70; ☺lunch Sun-Fri, dinner daily) The much-loved Brown Sugar, next to the Island Inn Hotel at Aquatic Gap, is a lush paradise inside and out. The excellent West Indian buffet is popular; dinner is off a menu that includes shrimp Creole, lobster, flying fish and much more. The Bajan bread pudding is a rummy delight. Book for dinner.

☆ Entertainment

Cricket matches are played throughout the year at the **Kensington Oval** (☺9am-4pm) in Garrison near Bridgetown, which was the site of the final in the 2007 World Cup. The **Barbados Cricket Association** (www.bcacricket.org) is the source of all things cricket.

Horse races are held at the Garrison Savannah on Saturday afternoons throughout the year, except April and September. **Barbados Turf Club** (www.barbadosturfclub.com) offers seats in the grandstand starting at B$20, but for no charge you can also watch the races from benches under the trees around the outside of the track – you can also place a bet at booths on the south or west side.

GEORGE WASHINGTON SLEPT HERE

In 1751, at age 19 – some 38 years before he would become the first US president – George Washington visited Barbados as a companion to his half-brother Lawrence, who suffered from tuberculosis. It was hoped that the tropical climate would prove therapeutic.

The two rented a house in the Garrison area south of Bridgetown and stayed on the island for six weeks. The restored George Washington House (see p202) gives a fascinating glimpse of the trip and the time. As it was, Lawrence never recovered and died the next year.

SOUTH COAST

The south coast is the island's tourism epicenter, with most of the budget-to-midrange accommodations along its fine white-sand beaches. This virtually uninterrupted stretch of development runs from the outskirts of Bridgetown all the way to the airport.

Hastings, Rockley and Worthing are part of one long commercial strip. St Lawrence Gap and Dover Beach is a surprisingly appealing area off the main road. East of Oistins, development begins to thin. Starting with Silver Sands the coast is fairly sedate (except for the surf and wind). All are linked by the main road along the coast, which, while designated Hwy 7, is never called that. The entire area is in Christ Church Parish.

Frequent minibuses from the Route Taxi Terminal in Bridgetown run along Main Rd (Hwy 7) on the southern coast and link all the south-coast villages. Private taxis are relatively easy to find in the main tourist areas.

Hastings & Rockley

POP 24,000

Just a 15-minute bus ride from Bridgetown are the first major tourist areas of Hastings and Rockley. They are home to a lot of aging budget and midrange hotels plus some attractive, popular beaches. Commercialism rules, and the streetscape is a Babel of signs. About halfway between Bridgetown and Rockley is **Hastings Rock**, a nice spot to enjoy views of the ocean. On weekends, community groups set up flea markets and hold activities around the gazebo in the small park above the water.

🏃 Beaches

TOP CHOICE **Accra Beach**   BEACH

The largest beach in the area, it is a picture-perfect crescent of sand that you'll want to immediately photograph and post on Facebook to irritate those left at home. Backed by shade trees, there's surf to make things interesting but nothing too dramatic. Parking is copious, as are nearby cafes and snack shops. A new boardwalk allows you to walk west for more than 3km to Hastings.

Rockley Beach   BEACH

The center of activity here, this roadside white-sand public beach has shade trees, snack kiosks and clothing vendors.

🛏 Sleeping

Coconut Court Beach Resort   HOTEL $$

(📞427-1655; www.coconut-court.com; Main Rd, Hastings; r US$150-250; ❄@🏊) Coconut Court is a five-story beachfront 112-room hotel filled with package tourists – it's good for families. In the right light, the institutional green paint can take on a turquoise hue from the azure waters right out front. Rooms have balconies or terraces plus kitchen facilities.

Tree Haven Beach Apartments   APARTMENTS $$

(📞435-6673; kentolaya@caribsurf.com; Main Rd, Rockley; apt from US$90; ❄) This affordable, laid-back option has three OK units just across the road from the beach and right near Bubba's bar. This is one of the cheapest options here; try for the 2nd-floor unit.

🍴 Eating & Drinking

Just Grillin'   CARIBBEAN $

(Quayside Centre, Hwy 7, Rockley; meals from B$16; ☺11:30am-10pm) A welcome dash of style to the strip, this barbecue does exactly what the name implies. Grilled jerk chicken, burgers, fish and more. Except for the salad and rice (!), the sides are all grilled as well; the veggies will woo any carnivore.

Champers   SEAFOOD $$$

(📞435-6644; Rockley; mains B$50-80; ☺lunch & dinner Mon-Sat) This longtime favorite has a dreamy location off the main road right on the water overlooking Accra Beach. There's barely an obstruction between you and the view. Elegant meals are served on cream-colored tablecloths and include the usual range of grilled seafood plus fresh pasta. Brits will understand the name means 'Champagne' – drink some at the lower-level lounge.

Mojo   BAR, GRILL $$

(Hwy 7, Rockley; meals from B$20; ☺11am-late) A big old house by the side of the road, Mojo has a wide open-air veranda plus all sorts of nooks inside for nuzzling your companion or listening to the excellent music. Monday is open-mike night and some of the island's best acoustic players drop by. Food ranges from burgers to bar snacks.

ℹ Information

There are plenty of shops, banks and ATMs along the main road, Hwy 7.

Worthing

POP 8500

Worthing is between the popular tourist areas of Hastings and Rockley and St Lawrence Gap. It's a good base if you're on a tight budget but still want to be near all the action. It has relatively inexpensive places at which to eat and a handful of lower-priced guesthouses that are either on the beach or a short walk away. The walk at night on the narrow, busy road to nearby St Lawrence Gap can be perilous.

◉ Sights & Activities

Sandy Beach
BEACH

A nice strip of white powder without a clever name that's well off the main road down some tiny lanes. It's a nice little scene with some sand-floor bars such as the Carib Beach Bar. Several budget guesthouses are stashed away on the small nearby streets. Parking is elusive at best.

Graeme Hall Nature Sanctuary
NATURE RESERVE

(☑435-9727; www.graemehall.com; Main Rd; ⊗8am-5pm) Just east of Worthing, this preserve protects the last major mangroves on the island, but, at the time of our visit, the foundation that runs it had closed the grounds to protest decisions allowing development that may threaten the site. Meanwhile, the lush gardens spread over 14 hectares, boardwalks, trails and displays remain perfectly groomed for reopening. You can get a glimpse of the beauty from the outdoor tables at the excellent cafe. Check for sporadic opening days.

⌊▭⌉ Sleeping

TOP CHOICE Coral Mist Beach Hotel
HOTEL $$$

(☑435-7712; www.coralmistbarbados.com; Hwy 7, Worthing; US$125-250; ❋🛜🐾) This small and traditional beachfront hotel wins plaudits for its exceptionally warm and gracious staff. All rooms have kitchen facilities and most are either studios or one-bedrooms; some have no internet access. All have balconies and views of the blinding-white beach. There's plenty nearby in walking distance.

Maraval Guesthouse & Apartments
GUESTHOUSE $

(☑435-7437; www.maravalbarbados.com; 3rd Ave; r from US$40, apt US$60-130) On a tiny lane near

Sandy Beach, Maraval has six attractive, simple rooms with shared bathroom and in-room sinks in a vintage two-story house. There's access to a well-equipped kitchen and a pleasant living room with TV and stereo. Nearby are several apartments that are right on the beach, some with air-con. All are bargain-priced for Barbados.

House Cleverdale
GUESTHOUSE $

(☑428-3172; www.vrbo.com/11696; 3rd Ave; r from US$30-45, apt US$55-65; @🛜) Set back just a bit from Sandy Beach and away from the main road, this large wooden home is a popular budget spot. The three rooms and two apartments have mosquito nets, fans and wi-fi. Bathrooms and a large kitchen are shared. It's rustic but if you want to meet other travelers in the common rooms and never, ever wear shoes you'll love it. The owner has other cheap places nearby.

✖ Eating

Worthing has some good inexpensive dining choices and a few garish midrange themed restaurants. For a nice dinner you are better off heading down the road to St Lawrence Gap.

TOP CHOICE Carib Beach Bar & Restaurant
BEACH BAR $$

(2nd Ave; meals B$20-40; ⊗11am-midnight) This open-air eatery right on Sandy Beach is the hub of local holiday life. Seafood and burgers are the main items on the menu, enjoy 'em at picnic tables on the sand while you watch waves break on the reef offshore and hear the soft rustle of palm trees overhead. The bar boogies long after the kitchen closes.

Graeme Hall Nature Sanctuary Cafe
CAFE $

(www.graemehall.com; off Hwy 7, Worthing; ⊗8am-5pm) Until the nature preserve itself reopens, you can still get a view of the mangroves from the picnic tables here on a little knoll. But the food and fine coffees alone are reason enough to stop. Excellent sandwiches and baked goods are served all day.

ⓘ Information

Big B Supermarket (Hwy 7, Worthing; ⊗8am-6:30pm Mon-Thu, 8am-7:30pm Fri & Sat, 9am-2pm Sun) Literally offers one-stop shopping. It has a deli, bank, ATM, pharmacy and a decent bookstore. It's just north of the main road at the central intersection.

BOAT TRIPS

Day cruises are a popular way to explore the island from a pirate's vantage point. Many of the larger boats are floating parties, while the smaller operations tend to be more tranquil. For those who want the scuba experience without getting wet, there are submarine cruises. Boats take passengers from across the island; ask about transportation options when you book.

Atlantis (☎436-8929; www.atlantisadventures.com; adult/child US$104/52) With siblings in most of the Caribbean's major destinations, the *Atlantis* is a 28-seat submarine lined with portholes. Departs from Bridgetown and tours the coral reef off the island's west coast.

El Tigre (☎417-7245; www.eltigrecruises.com; cruises adult/child from US$70/35) Offers a three-hour cruise with snorkeling plus lunch voyages and more from B$120.

Tall Ships Cruises (☎430-0900; www.tallshipscruises.com; cruises adult/child from US$60/45) A range of cruises aboard vessels that include the *Harbour Master*, a four-deck party vessel with a waterslide attached. Options include turtle-viewing and pirate-themed party cruises. Arrrrr!

St Lawrence Gap & Dover Beach

POP 26,000

The town of St Lawrence is almost lost along the busy main road. Instead the real action lies along a mile-long road that runs close to the beach. Lined with hotels, bars, restaurants and shops, this street is actually more pleasurable than it sounds. It's not commercialized to the point of being gross and it's mostly free of traffic, allowing nighttime strolling. However, some huge new projects being built may give the Gap more of a Miami Beach vibe.

The west end is known as St Lawrence Gap; the east end carries the Dover Beach moniker.

Dover Beach itself has a nice, broad ribbon of white sand that attracts swimmers, bodysurfers and windsurfers. Breakwaters maintain a good strip of sand right in the center of the main strip. Catch the sunset and enjoy a drink from the many little stands back from the beach. It's a mellow and friendly scene.

🛏 Sleeping

Accommodation options in the Gap span the gamut from backpacker-oriented hostels to flash resorts. Most fall into the middle: smaller hotels on or near the water that have a mellow, pretense-free charm. Some have been enjoyed by the same regular guests each year for decades, all gracefully aging together.

TOP CHOICE Southern Palms
Beach Club   RESORT $$$
(☎428-7171; www.southernpalms.net; St Lawrence Gap; r from US$280; ✳@🛜🌊) A traditional beach resort that stays in the pink – literally. Most of the various three-story blocks are decked out in a cheery pink tone. Interiors are closer to motel standard but the balconies and patios are large. Off at one end there are Hollywood-style bungalows (from US$500) where you can indulge your inner celebrity.

Dover Beach Hotel   HOTEL $$
(☎428-8076; www.doverbeach.com; St Lawrence Gap; r $120-200; ✳@🛜🌊) You go down a tiny lane to reach this gracious, secluded and older beach hotel, tucked into a corner at the east end of the Gap. A three-story building surrounds a good-sized pool and large oceanfront terrace. A pocket of beach adjoins. All units have balconies with views varying from garden to ocean.

Yellow Bird Hotel   HOTEL $$
(☎418-8444; www.yellowbirdbarbados.com; St Lawrence Gap; r US$120-170; ✳🌊) This modern, four-story block sits rather modestly right at the west entrance to the Gap. Studios have kitchens, and sunset views from the balconies. It's across a narrow street from the water and there's a small pool in front. Larger apartments are also available.

Dover Woods Guest House   GUESTHOUSE $
(☎420-6599; www.doverwoodsguesthouse.com; Dover Beach; r US$45-75; 🛜) Huge trees keep this large house shaded and cool. Located on estate-sized grounds (which are home

to a family of monkeys) at the east end of the strip, it has four large rooms that share a kitchen, TV lounge and covered patio. Two rooms share a bathroom, one has air-con.

Rio Guest House HOSTEL **$**
(428-1546; www.rioguesthouse.hostel.com; St Lawrence Gap; r US$40-65;) This back-packer special has nine unpretentious fan-cooled rooms. Singles share a bathroom and some rooms have optional air-con and kitchens. It's in a tranquil location, off the main drag but about one minute from the beach and nightlife.

✖ Eating & Drinking

One of the pleasures of the Gap is wandering the street at night comparing the many res-taurants. Your hunger will be spurred on by the many street vendors who set up at night selling juicy burgers, grilled chicken and the ubiquitous macaroni pie. Bars range from humble to vaguely swank. Blues and show tunes at many of them keep the chatter mel-low until past midnight.

TOP CHOICE Sweet Potatoes CARIBBEAN **$$**
(420-7668; St Lawrence Gap; noon-10pm) A long terrace lit by tiny lights looks out over the water and sunset at this fabulous place for Bajan treats. Sure you can get a variety of fresh seafood, burgers and the like but, really now, eat local! *Bol jol* is a terrific starter that you spread on bread; it's made with marinated local codfish. Try one of the flying-fish dishes and be sure to get it with *cou-cou*, a form of polenta made with okra. Ask about the cooking classes.

Pisces SEAFOOD **$$$**
(435-6564; St Lawrence Gap; mains B$55-75; dinner) This ever-popular large restaurant stretches right along the waterfront; waves lap against the foundations below. The view at sunset followed by the twinkling lights of the coast and fishing boats is captivating. Little candles illuminate fine seafood dishes (as you'd expect from the name). The wine list favors the US, France and Australia. It's always busy – come at 9pm for a relaxing time after the rush.

David's Place CARIBBEAN **$$$**
(435-9755; St Lawrence Gap; mains B$60-95; dinner Tue-Sun) One of the most romantic choices in the Gap. You first encounter a proper bar as you enter; further in the lights dim and you're at tables overlooking the bay,

which laps gently below. Waiters glide about with seafood and steak dishes that feature accents of Creole and curry. It's all very gen-teel and there is a dress code.

Scotty's CONVENIENCE STORE **$**
(Dover Beach; meals from B$10; 7am-9pm) It looks like another convenience store but this one comes with a hot buffet. Enjoy trad fare like curries and stews at tables outside. Scotty's shines, however, when cricket is on the tube: TVs outside attract a jovial mob who serve themselves beer from the coolers and cheer on the Bajan players.

☆ Entertainment

Several popular venues in the Gap jam with live bands and DJs. Most have a cover charge, sometimes up to B$30 and sometimes par-tially redeemable for drinks. Several of the bars have live music one or more nights. Strolling the Gap, especially near the pub-lic access point for Dover Beach, you'll find many simple joints along the road where you can enjoy low-key drinks all night.

Reggae Lounge LIVE MUSIC
(435-6462; St Lawrence Gap; cover varies; 9pm-late) The Reggae Lounge not only plays classic reggae, but dancehall, hip-hop and more. Although the cover charge can hit B$30, everything's gonna be all right, espe-cially on Mondays, when the cover includes unlimited drinks.

Oistins

POP 17,000

This decidedly local yet modern town a few miles east of St Lawrence is best known as the center of the island's fishing industry. Oistins' heart is the large, bustling seaside fish market, which on Friday and Saturday hosts the island's best party.

🏖 Beaches

TOP CHOICE Miami Beach SECLUDED BEACH
A somewhat hidden gem that is the anti-thesis of its American namesake. Small, shady and intimate, it is well removed from the often frenetic south-coast pace. It gets crowded on weekends but is wide open dur-ing the week. Look for Mr Delicious, a ven-dor selling rum punch and fab fish cutters (sandwiches). Take the small road heading towards South Point Lighthouse from Ois-tins, then curl back west to the beach.

Enterprise Beach BEACH

Immediately east of the fish market, this long and shady public beach has full facilities, lively surf, shady trees and a good vibe from a mix of locals and tourists.

🛏 Sleeping & Eating

Some of the stalls at the fish-fry complex stay open during the week for lunch and dinner. The bars never close, and get a genial mix of fishing types, locals and visitors.

TOP CHOICE Little Arches Hotel BOUTIQUE HOTEL $$$

(📞420-4689; www.littlearches.com; Miami Beach; r US$220-500; 🏊@🛜🛉) Possibly the best boutique hotel on the south coast. Once a Mediterranean-style mansion, the hotel now has 10 rooms in a variety of shapes and sizes, some with private whirlpool baths. Privacy is at a maximum and there are lots of artful touches throughout. The decor combines bright Caribbean colors with restrained luxury such as deeply comfortable wicker chairs. It's on the quiet Miami Beach access road.

Lexie's BAR

(Fish Market, Oistins Beach; ⏲24hr) With ballroom dancing on a literally hot open-air dance floor, this combo of beach and fishing bar stands out from its nearby contemporaries.

Silver Sands

POP 12,000

At the southernmost tip of the island, between Oistins and the airport, is the breezy Silver Sands area, which includes Inch Marlow. Although you should avoid some characterless large resorts, there are good small choices popular with kitesurfers and windsurfers. In January and February, accommodations fill up when everything literally blows in the right direction.

🏃 Activities

Surfing, whether by board, kite or sail, is the huge draw here.

Surfing

Barbados has good windsurfing and kitesurfing, with the best winds from December to June. Silver Sands, at the southern tip of the island, has excellent conditions for advanced boarders, while Maxwell, just to the west, is better for intermediates.

TOP CHOICE deAction Beach Shop WINDSURFING

(📞428-2027; www.briantalma.com; Silver Sands) Run by board-legend Brian Talma, this shop is set on one of the hemisphere's premier spots for windsurfing and kitesurfing. Complete gear rentals average US$80 per day; lessons begin at US$60 per hour. Watch huge kites twirl about the sky while riders hop the waves below with a cold Banks at the cafe.

Zed's Surfing Adventures SURFING

(📞428-7873; www.barbadossurfholidays.com; Surfer's Point) Runs beginners' surf classes (US$80), rents boards (US$25 per day, US$40 for a stand-up paddleboard) and offers surf tours around the island. It's affiliated with Surfer's Point Guest House.

Horseback Riding

Wilcox Riding Stables (📞428-3610; rides from US$60) These stables near the airport offer one-hour rides. The trails are in Long Beach on the southeast coast, and prices include hotel pickup.

Golf

The well-heeled of Barbados support several golf courses. The oldest public course is the **Barbados Golf Club** (📞428-8463; www.barbadosgolfclub.com; Durants), where green fees begin at US$120; top-end hotels often offer discounts to guests. It was redesigned in 2000 by Ron Kirby and is 6km long.

🛏 Sleeping

In addition to the following listings, there are a number of private places in the Silver Sands area that can be rented by the week. Many windsurfers stay a night or two in a hotel and then, through word of mouth, find a shared house or apartment nearby (simple doubles for US$40 a night can be found in season – ask at the activity shops). The appeal of Surfer's Point at the east end speaks for itself.

TOP CHOICE Surfer's Point Guest House GUESTHOUSE $$

(📞428-7873; www.barbadossurfholidays.com; Surfer's Point; apt US$80-250; 🏊@🛜) The HQ of Zed's Surfing Adventures is on a little point amid a very good break. The seven units here come in various sizes; some have balconies with views, all have kitchens and wi-fi. There's a small protected pool out front for kids.

OISTINS FISH FRY

With soca, reggae, pop and country music, vendors selling barbecued fish and plenty of rum drinking, the legendary **Oistins Fish Fry** (☉food 6-10:30pm) is *the* weekly social event on the island. It's roughly 60% locals, 40% tourists and there's a joyous electricity in the air on Friday night, which is just a tad more fun than the fish fry's other night, Saturday. It's held in a complex of low-rise modern buildings right on the sand next to the fish market.

Here are some tips to have a great time:

» **Standard menu** Most of the stalls serve the same menu: grilled fish and shellfish, pork chops, ribs and chicken. Sides include macaroni pie, chips, plaintains, grilled breadfruit, garlic bread and more. Unless you specify, you'll get a bit of each side with your main. It costs about B$35 per person.

» **Standards vary** Just because there's more than 30 vendors serving the same menu doesn't mean all are created equal. Where one will have some fish slowly drying out on an electric frying pan, another (like hugely popular **Pat's Place**) will have a line of 100 people waiting to order and vast flaming grills.

» **It's chaotic but orderly** Order at the vendor's window. Despite the lines and ruckus, you almost always end up with the correct plate. And despite the crowds, space at a picnic table always seems to open up when you need it.

» **Park early** Roads to Oistins get jammed on Friday night; when you get sort of close, park. You'll walk past hundreds of cars trying to get 200m closer.

» **Party!** Buy a cheap and icy bottle of Banks (B$3) and wander the scene, enjoying the live music, ignoring the karaoke, possibly nabbing a snog in a shadowy corner of the beach and generally hooting it up. Some of the open-air bars among the stalls never close.

Peach and Quiet Hotel　　　HOTEL **$$**
(☎428-5682; www.peachandquiet.com; Inch Marlow; r from US$120; ⊠) Like mushrooms after the rain, organic shapes abound here. The 22 airy rooms come with sea-view patios set around a secluded pool. There's an ocean-side bar and a restaurant. The owners ban children, lead walks across the island that are booked years in advance and are generally as idiosyncratic as this charming inn.

Ocean Spray Beach Apartments　　　APARTMENTS **$$**
(☎428-5426; www.oceansprayapartments.com; Inch Marlow; r US$85-150; ☎) Salt spray from the pounding surf mists the air at this attractive and modern 25-unit apartment complex. Balconies on rooms with views offer a captivating spectacle of the famous local surf. Relax with a cranberry juice and vodka.

SOUTHEAST COAST

St Philip, the diamond-shaped parish east of the airport, is sparsely populated, with a scattering of small villages. Along the coast are a couple of resort hotels and fine beaches.

Some minibuses continue into the southeast after heading east from Oistins.

Crane Beach

Crane Beach, situated 7km northeast of the airport, is a hidden beach cove backed by cliffs and fronted by aqua-blue waters. It is generally regarded as one of the best beaches on the island.

An adventurous trail over rocks along the water accesses the beach from the end of a small road about 700m east of the Crane Beach Hotel. Parking is competitive but the sands are simply wonderful. Bring a picnic and make a day of it.

To really blaze a trail, follow the road east another 500m and you'll come to a cow pasture where a path leads down to a long, lovely and very much less-crowded strip of sand.

Crane Beach Hotel　　　RESORT **$$$**
(☎423-6220; www.thecrane.com; r from US$210; ✳@☎⊠) Dating to 1887, the roots of this gracious resort can still be found in the

lovely restaurants that overlook the beach and ocean (L'Azure, for example, has upscale Caribbean fare, with lunch and dinner from US$30; book in advance). Much of the complex is quite modern, with hundreds of condos and lavish resort facilities. If you like the kind of place that has an entire shop devoted to items bearing its logo, you'll love this sprawling, swank Shangri-la.

WEST COAST

Barbados' west coast has lovely tranquil beaches that are largely hidden by the majority of the island's luxury hotels and walled estates. Known to some as the Platinum Coast, it gets this moniker either from the color of the sand or the color of the credit cards.

In colonial times, the area was a popular holiday retreat for the upper crust of British society. These days, the villas that haven't been converted to resorts are owned by the wealthy and famous. That's on the water side of course. On the *other* side of Hwy 1 are modest huts and simple vacation retreats. Although the beaches are all public, the near constant development means that you only get a few coastal glimpses.

Hwy 1, the narrow, busy and at times perilous two-laner that runs north from Bridgetown to Speightstown, has a mad mix of roaring buses and the occasional Rolls Royce. It is bordered much of the way by a mix of tourist facilities and residential areas. If you don't have your own wheels, minibuses and public buses run frequently.

Paynes Bay

Fringed by a fine stretch of white sand, gently curving Paynes Bay in St James is endlessly popular and is the west coast's most popular spot for swimming and snorkeling (you will almost certainly see sea turtles). Beach access walkways are clearly marked by roadside signs.

The main **public beach** site at the southern end of the bay has chair rental, picnic tables, restrooms, laid-back bars and a Friday-night fish fry. Parking can be a hassle; take a bus.

🛏 Sleeping

TOP CHOICE **Tamarind Cove Hotel**   RESORT $$$
(📞432-1332; www.tamarindcovehotel.com; Paynes Bay; r from US$350; 🕸@🛜🏊) Right on the

beach at Paynes Bay, everything is discreet about this understated luxury resort, which has a hacienda motif. The 110 units are decked out in a restful palette of beachy pastels. All have balconies or patios and views of either one of the three pools or the ocean. The lushly landscaped grounds boast many fountains.

Angler Apartments   APARTMENTS $$
(📞432-0817; www.anglerapartments.com; Clarke's Rd 1, Derricks; r US$80-140; 🕸) An unpretentious place with 13 older, basic apartments. Studios in an adjacent old plantation house are similar but smaller. There's a little patio bar. It's at the south end of Paynes Bay, off a road east of the main road.

Holetown

POP 32,000
The first English settlers to Barbados landed at Holetown in 1627. An obelisk **monument** along the main road in the town center commemorates the event – although the date on the monument, which reads 'July 1605,' is clearly on island time.

Long a bastion of understated luxury, Holetown now boasts a flashy, upscale mall, Limegrove. Still, the cute little nightlife area squeezed into a wedge between the main road and the beach retains its charm.

👁 Sights & Activities

Barbados Marine Reserve   SNORKELING
(Folkstone Beach; museum adult/child B$1.50/0.50; ⏰9am-5pm Mon-Fri) At the north end of Holetown, the marine reserve's **visitor centre** (admission B$5; ⏰9:30am-5pm Mon-Fri, 10am-6pm Sat & Sun) includes a small museum with displays on the reserve, which extends for a few miles north and south. You can rent snorkeling gear (from B$20) and there are lockers. From here you can walk along the water to Holetown.

Hightide Watersports   DIVING
(📞432-0931; www.divehightide.com; Coral Reef Club) One of the better dive shops on the west coast.

🛏 Sleeping

The Holetown area can be a black hole for those on a budget, although you can find little apartments on the east side of Hwy 1. Many of the island's poshest resorts, such as the Fairmont Glitter Bay (the former home of the Cunard family), occupy vast swaths of beach while charging the moon.

The west coast of Barbados has reef dives with soft corals, gorgonians and colorful sponges. There are also about a dozen shipwrecks. The largest and most popular, the 111m freighter *Stavronikita*, sits upright off the central west coast in 42m of water, with the rigging reaching to within 6m of the surface. In Bridgetown's Carlisle Bay, the coral-encrusted tug *Berwyn* lies in only 7m of water and makes for good snorkeling as well as diving.

Not surprisingly, good dive shops are as common as flying fish along the west coast. Locations include Holetown, Mt Standfast and Speightstown.

One-tank dives with gear average B$120. For beginners, most dive companies offer a brief resort course and a shallow dive for B$120 to B$160. Rates often include free transportation from your hotel.

Snorkeling sets can be rented for about B$20 per day at west-coast beaches and dive shops. Snorkeling tours are common; many dive shops offer good ones. The Barbados Marine Reserve (p210) has good snorkeling and you can rent gear there.

TOP CHOICE **Coral Reef Club**   RESORT **$$$**
(☑422-2372; www.coralreefbarbados.com; Holetown; r US$420-900; ❈@☎⛱) This family-owned 88-unit luxury hotel has 12 acres of gorgeous landscaped grounds surrounding an elegant gingerbread fantasy of a main building. Unlike some other top-end places around Holetown, this place oozes with character. You may actually find yourself needing to be convinced to leave the grounds.

Discovery Bay   RESORT **$$**
(☑432-1301; www.rexresorts.com; Holetown; r US$150-300; ❈@☎⛱) On the north side of Holetown, if this resort could speak, it would have a middle-class English accent from Kent. This older property has a faded charm that wears like a beloved old cardigan. The grassy grounds back up a tiny sandy cove. Rooms are pretty basic but those with large terraces overlooking the gardens are the best pick. Skip all-inclusive options for the bounty of Holetown.

🍴 Eating & Drinking

Holetown's best attribute is its little enclave of bars and restaurants. Mostly off noxious Hwy 1, it mixes the grand with the pedestrian. At a couple of mellow rum shops, swells in pink shirts and loafers mix with locals.

Beach House   CONTINENTAL **$$$**
(☑432-1163; www.thebeachhousebarbados.com; lunch/dinner from B$30/100; ☺11am-10pm) Anchored by a vast terrace right on the water, the Beach House fulfills all your holiday dining fantasies. The drinks and wine list is encyclopedic. The menu segues from comfy lunch food (burgers, salads) to set menus of steaks and seafood at night.

Ragamuffins   CARIBBEAN **$$**
(1st St; mains from B$50; ☺dinner) Ragamuffins is in a 60-year-old chattel house painted a stylish olive and turquoise. Dishes are all Caribbean with some added attitude: the blackened fish with aioli is pure joy. On Sunday there's a drag show.

ⓘ Information

Holetown is the center for all services north of Bridgetown. Besides banks, ATMs and gourmet markets, a branch of **Cave Shepherd** (☺8:30am-6pm Mon-Fri, 8am-4pm Sat, 9am-2pm Sun) has sundries and a good book department.

Mt Standfast

Popular with hawksbill turtles that feed on sea grasses just off its shore and with the snorkelers that come to watch, Mt Standfast also has a good **beach**. Most snorkeling tours make a stop here for turtle feeding; without a tour, you can rent snorkeling gear at the beach and get advice for freelance turtle viewing. **Dive Barbados** (☑422-3133; www.divebarbados.net) is a well-known local dive shop.

Weston

This is the west coast in a nutshell: a fish market and fruit stand on the waterfront with a couple of church steeples as a backdrop. The nearby rum shop, **John Moore Bar**, offers a heady mix of genial local characters and their newfound visitor friends.

Mullins Beach

A popular and family-friendly beach along Hwy 1 between Holetown and Speightstown, the one off note at Mullins is the poor parking. But the waters are usually calm and good for swimming and snorkeling. Drinks from the boisterous cafe are delivered to your beach chair.

Escape it all just south at uncommercialized **Gibbes Beach**.

Speightstown

POP 46,000

Easily the most evocative small town on Barbados, Speightstown combines old colonial charms with a vibe that has more rough edges than the endlessly upscale precincts to the south. The town is a good place for a wander. Since the main road was moved east, traffic is modest, so take time to look up at the battered old wooden facades, many with overhanging galleries.

During the sugarcane boom, Speightstown was a thriving port and the main shipping line ran directly from here to Bristol, England.

Sights & Activities

A radiant vision in white stucco, **Arlington House** (Queen St; adult/child B$25/12.50; ⏰10am-5pm Mon-Fri, 10am-3pm Sat) is an 18th-century colonial house that now houses an engaging museum run by the National Trust. It covers the colonial period locally with exhibits over three floors.

A good local dive shop is **Reefers & Wreckers** (☑422-5450; www.scubadiving.bb).

WORTH A TRIP

ARCHERS BAY

Fierce waves pummel stone cliffs, eroding them into giant mushroom-shaped oddities at Archers Bay, a desolate and ruggedly gorgeous bit of the north coast. To get there, follow the signs off Hwys 1B and 1C to Grape Hall, then keep driving north 500m and follow the 'Public Beach Access' sign that directs you down a short dirt road and a grassy parking area near the cliff. The views are stunning; a short but steep trail leads down to a tiny pocket beach. Swimming is unsafe.

🛏 Sleeping

Speightstown has a number of modest holiday apartments along its historic main drag, which is bookended by tiny, cute beaches. Check with the Fisherman's Pub for leads.

Sunset Sands Apartments   APARTMENTS **$$**
(☑438-1096; www.sunsetsands.com; Sand St; apt from US$120; ▣) Just north of the town center across from the small beach, the Sunset Sands has four attractive units in a building with solid colonial charm. The upstairs apartments have stunning ocean views and there's a secluded garden.

🍴 Eating & Drinking

TOP CHOICE **Fisherman's Pub**   CARIBBEAN **$**
(☑422-2703; Queen St; meals from B$10; ⏰11am-late Mon-Sat, 6pm-late Sun) Worth the trip, this waterfront cafe is a local institution that serves up fish from the boats floating off the side deck. Like a seal with a new ball, it's always lively and unpredictable. On Wednesdays, there is steel-pan music and a buffet. As the evening wears on, the scene gets more Bajan. Line up for the ever-changing and excellent fare; try the national dish of *cou-cou* and flying fish here. Or if you're lucky it will have some of the super Creole banana and fish.

Cassareep Cafe   CAFE **$$**
(coffees B$5, meals from B$40; ⏰8am-4pm Mon-Sat, 6:30-10:30pm Wed-Sat; 🛜) A real find tucked down an alley in the heart of town, this joyous little cafe serves coffees, snacks and drinks at tables on a tiny beach out back. For dinner it offers Asian-accented fare.

Mango's by the Sea   SEAFOOD **$$$**
(Queen St; mains B$50-90; ⏰dinner Sun-Fri) Overlooking the water, the interior here mixes elegant (white tablecloths, candles, local art) with the casual (thatched decor). Dinners comprise the usual shellfish and steaks with nightly specials. The herb-and-garlic shrimp are an explosion of local flavors. Look for a mango-colored wooden building tucked down a little alley.

Heywoods Beach

The best strand on the west coast for daytrippers from elsewhere on the island, Heywoods Beach offers good parking, a location well off Hwy 1, and lots of powdery, uncrowded sand (especially on weekdays).

It's about 500m north of the road into Speightstown from the north.

Shermans

Just past the road that turns inland to St Lucy, Shermans is a narrow enclave of fine holiday homes and lovely local places; they seem to be competing to grow the most flowers. The narrow road runs through the tiny fishing village of **Fustic**, which has a couple of good rum shops.

The boutique hotel **Little Good Harbour** (☎439-3000; www.littlegoodharbourbarbados.com; Shermans; villas from US$300; ✻@☎✱) has 21 one- to three-bedroom villas in a little compound near the water. The decor combines wicker with linens in units that open completely to the outside and flowering trees. The **Fish Pot Restaurant** (mains B$30-70; ☺lunch & dinner) is renowned for its views and seafood.

CENTRAL BARBADOS

Several important roads cross the rolling hills of the island's interior. There's a wealth of historical and natural sights here and you can spend days winding around small roads far from the hustle and crowds of the west and south coasts. What follows are three main routes that take in major attractions and which can be combined in various ways to produce some delightful circle tours of Barbados.

Having your own transportation will give you total freedom on the routes listed here, but you can also cover most of them by public bus, as the main roads all have service. There will be some walking to access sites off the main road. One real hike, but a beautiful 6.5km one, is necessary to access the St Nicholas Abbey and Cherry Tree Hill off Hwy 2.

Speightstown to Bathsheba

The road going into the hills east of Speightstown steadily climbs through historic sugarcane fields. The ruins of mills dot the landscape. Including the jaunt to St Nicholas Abbey, this route covers about 26km.

Eventually after about six miles you'll come to a fork in the road – if you continue on Hwy 2 to the east, you'll encounter **Farley Hill National Park** (☎422-3555; Hwy 2; per car B$3.50; ☺8:30am-3:30pm), which has 7 hectares of lovely gardens surrounding the ruins of an old estate. Bajans love this park for its views to the Atlantic, and picnic here in droves on Sundays.

Barbados Wildlife Reserve (adult/child under 12yr B$24/12; ☺10am-4pm) is a walk-through zoo opposite Farley Hill, with short paths that meander through a mahogany forest. The main attraction here is a colony of green monkeys. From September to January, the monkeys go marauding across the countryside in search of food and monkey business. If they're out when you're there, you'll get a ticket so you can come back again. Note that if the monkeys seem on good behavior, it's because the reserve is run by the Barbados Primate Research Centre, whose activities are just what the name implies.

Just above the reserve, it is a five-minute hike to the 19th-century **Grenade Hall Signal Station**, which has been restored. It was used by British troops for communications using flags and semaphores and was part of the chain that included one at Gun Hill (p214).

Back at the fork in the road, if you turn to the left (north) you are on one of the best little scenic drives on Barbados, with a narrow road winding under a cathedral of huge mahogany trees arching overhead to **St Nicholas Abbey** (www.stnicholasabbey.com; adult/child B$35/20; ☺10am-3:30pm Sun-Fri), a Jacobean-style mansion that is one of the oldest plantation houses in the Caribbean and a must-see stop on any island itinerary. Owner and local architect Larry Warren has undertaken a massive improvement program. The grounds are now simply gorgeous, with guinea fowl wandering among the flowers. The interior re-creates the mansion's 17th-century look, right down to the furniture. An old steam engine has been restored and the plantation is again bottling its own rum and molasses; you can taste some and enjoy a snack at the serene cafe. Be sure to read the lurid history of the plantation's founders: murder, intrigue, sex!

About 700m southeast of the abbey, the road passes **Cherry Tree Hill**, which has grand views right across the Atlantic coast. From here the road heads downhill through fields of sugarcane that seem to envelop the car.

On the right you'll see the remains of the **Morgan Lewis Sugar Mill**, 2km southeast of Cherry Tree Hill, which claims to be the largest sugar windmill (barely) surviving in the Caribbean.

The road continues on a sinuous path downhill until it rejoins Hwy 2. Heading toward the coast, you pass through the little town of Belleplaine, where you veer east to the road to Bathsheba. Running along the rugged coast through low sand dunes, this is one of the great ocean roads. Look for **Barclays Park** (⊙8am-5pm), which has picnic tables under the trees, tidy bathrooms and constantly roiling waves pounding the seemingly endless beach. Many who try to swim here wash ashore in South Africa.

The coast road continues another 5km south to Bathsheba.

Bridgetown to Belleplaine

This route takes you past sites that show the beauty of the myriad plants that thrive on Barbados. It also goes near Harrison's Cave, a subterranean attraction that has been closed while new whiz-bang gewgaws are added. The road, Hwy 2, runs for about 16km to Belleplaine.

Tyrol Cot Heritage Village (Codrington Hill; adult/child B$12/6; ⊙9am-5pm Mon-Fri) is a somewhat contrived 1920s Bajan village centered on the former home of Sir Grantley Adams, first premier of Barbados. The site, on Hwy 2 just north of Bridgetown, is complete with chattel houses where artists work on their crafts.

About 8km northeast of the Everton Weeks Roundabout on the bypass, look for a road crossing Hwy 2. About 400m west, **Welchman Hall Gully** (Hwy 2, Welchman Hall; adult/child B$24/12; ⊙9am-4pm) is a thickly wooded ravine with a walking track that leads you through nearly 200 species of plant, including spices like nutmeg. Such gullies were too difficult for growing crops and as a result preserve some of the tropical forests that once covered the island. Look

for bearded fig trees, which gave their old Portuguese name *Los Barbados* (the bearded ones) to the island.

Worth a detour, **Flower Forest of Barbados** (☎433-8152; Hwy 2; adult/child B$20/10; ⊙8am-4pm) is another worthy natural sight. The 20-hectare botanic garden is on the site of a former sugar estate which has many stately mature citrus and breadfruit trees. Paths meander among examples of almost every plant growing on the island. It is reached by taking an access road some 700m off a meandering road that links Hwys 2 and 3A. Look for signs.

Hwy 2 curves down through more sugarcane before reaching Belleplaine. Here you have a decision: turn west for the beauty of St Nicholas Abbey (p213) or turn east for the wild beauty of the Atlantic coast.

Bridgetown to Bathsheba

Hwy 3 is a lovely road that goes up and over the middle of Barbados, on a 16km route that links the west and east coasts. Along the way there are some historic sights and some bucolic scenery.

Driving Hwy 3, 3km east of the Clyde Wolcott Roundabout on the bypass, look for signs for **Gun Hill** (☎429-1358; Fusilier Rd; adult/child B$10/5; ⊙9am-5pm Mon-Sat) on a small road turning south. There's a couple of twists and turns as you travel 1.5km to this 1818 hilltop signal tower with its impressive views of the surrounding valleys and the southwest coast. The island was once connected by six such signal towers that used flags and lanterns to relay messages. The official function of the towers was to keep watch for approaching enemy ships, but they also signaled colonial authorities in the event of a slave revolt. There is a cute cafe here.

About 8km after the Gun Hill turn on Hwy 3, you'll see squat little **St Joseph's**

HIKING BARBADOS

The **Barbados National Trust** (☎228-8027, 266-8027; www.hikebarbados.com) leads guided hikes in the countryside. Hike leaders share insights into local history, geology and wildlife. Locations vary, but all hikes end where they start, cover about 8km and are run on Sundays at 6am and 3:30pm. There is no fee. Route information can be found in the free tourist publications and is also available by calling the trust.

A nice hike to do on your own is along the old railroad bed that runs along the east coast from Belleplaine to Martin's Bay. The whole walk is about 20km, but it can be broken into shorter stretches.

BRIGHTON FARMERS MARKET

Early on Saturdays, foodies, chefs, artisans and more converge on the **Brighton Farmers Market** (☺6-10am Sat) in the heart of the fertile St George Valley on Hwy 4B. It's a festival of the finest produce, prepared foods and crafts. Grab a cup of coffee, enjoy some local gab and see what treasures you root out.

This entire farm-filled region is good for wandering by car any day of the week. For instance, Hwy 3B runs northeast of Gun Hill through gorgeous valleys and plains. It's worthwhile to literally lose yourself here amid the pretty farms punctuated with the odd colonial-era building. Turn north on one of the many small roads any time you want to rejoin Hwy 3.

Church on the left. Turn on the road that goes south to the right and after only 250m you'll see the unrestored 1819 **Cotton Tower**, another of the signal towers. From here it is a short drive downhill on Hwy 3 to Bathsheba.

EASTERN BARBADOS

The wild Atlantic waters of the east coast are far removed from the rest of the island. The population is small, the coast craggy and the waves incessant. It's a place of beautiful windblown vistas and is becoming internationally famous for surfing. For sights along the coast road north of Bathsheba, see p214.

Bathsheba

POP 5300

Bathsheba is the main destination on the east coast, although there's no real 'there' here as things are scattered along about 1.5km of sandy, wave-tossed shore and in the hills immediately behind. This is prime surfing country. It's also good for long beach walks as you contemplate feeling you've reached the end of the world. It's an idyllic image of sand, sea and palm trees.

At night, it's very quiet here. For excitement there are the lyrical croaks of whistling frogs and the flash of fireflies.

◉ Sights & Activities

Andromeda Botanic Gardens　　GARDEN
(☏433-9261; http://andromeda.cavehill.uwi.edu; Hwy 3; adult/child B$25/12.50; ☺9am-5pm, last admission 4:30pm) At the top of the southern entrance to Bathsheba, the splendid Andromeda Botanic Gardens cover 2.5 hectares and have a wide collection of introduced tropical plants, including orchids, ferns, water lilies, bougainvillea, cacti and palms.

Self-guided walks of various lengths enjoy the floral beauty and splendid views.

TOP CHOICE Soup Bowl　　SURF BREAK
The world-famous reef break known as the Soup Bowl is right off the beach in northern Bathsheba. It is one of the best waves in the Caribbean islands. Don't underestimate the break just because the region is not known for powerful surf – Soup Bowl gets big. Moreover, the reef is shallow and covered in parts by spiny sea urchins. This is not a spot for beginners.

It's a strong right-handed break which has three takeoff points that can be surfed point to point if you are fast and can read the wave. Overall, the best months are August to March. For good surfers, it's September to November during hurricane season and the start of cold fronts. Famed surfer Kelly Slater calls it a 9+ on a scale of one to 10. For beginners March to May is best.

Bathsheba Beach　　BEACH
If you're not an expert swimmer, this is not really the place to go into the water; rather, enjoy the wave-tossed scenery on long beach walks. Bifurcated by huge rocks, much of the modest action is at the south end, where reefs afford enough protection for very limited swimming. Note the iconic **Mushroom Rock**, one of several rocks carved into shapes that will cause mycologists to swoon.

⌑ Sleeping & Eating

Accommodation is limited in Bathsheba and that's good. Who wants crowds?

TOP CHOICE Sea-U! Guest House BOUTIQUE HOTEL **$$**
(☏433-9450; www.seaubarbados.com; Tent Bay, Bathsheba; r US$110-200; @☎) The pick of Bathsheba lodging, the Sea-U has a mannered main house with an addictive porch

looking out to sea from the hillside location. Cottages and a restaurant pavilion round out the verdant site. The nine units have kitchen facilities, and a nonclichéd island motif. There's no TV, kids under eight or smoking. Dinner is served daily. Has good green cred.

Atlantis Hotel   HOTEL **$$$**
(☑433-9445; www.atlantisbarbados.com; Tent Bay, Bathsheba; r from US$255; ✴@🛜🏊) One cove south of Bathsheba, Atlantis was the original hotel in the area. Now lavishly renovated, it has 10 units in a solid old wooden building facing the sea. The views are sweeping and you have a choice of one-bedroom suites in the original building or apartments in a new wing by the small pool. The restaurant is good through the day, although on some days it gets busy with tour groups.

Roundhouse Restaurant   CARIBBEAN **$$**
(☑433-9678; meals from B$40; ⊘breakfast, lunch & dinner) This popular touristy restaurant has customers throughout the day who sit around, sip cocktails and savor the views south over Soup Bowl. You can enjoy banana bread with your breakfast, sandwiches and salads at lunch, and specials such as bread-fruit soup at dinner.

Bathsheba Railway Bar   CARIBBEAN **$**
(meals from B$10; ⊘9am-6pm) Near the sand, this elevated hut serves classic local lunch fare plus burgers and various fruit juices.

Sea Side Bar   CARIBBEAN **$**
(meals from B$10; ⊘11am-late) More bar than cafe (although local stews and the like are served on the deck at lunch), this joint hums with energy through the day as lo-cals and surfers do their best to out-shout each other.

❶ Getting There & Away

A **taxi** can be negotiated for about B$70 from Bridgetown or the south coast, or catch one of the regular **buses** from Bridgetown that travel Hwys 2 and 3. The trip takes about 45 minutes.

Bathsheba South to Christ Church Parish

Few people take the time to follow the coast south of Bathsheba. They should. Look for signs on the road, which stays well up the hillside, for **Martin's Bay**, a little notch in the coast that features a sliver of a beach and a sweet little rum shop. Like elsewhere, this isn't swimming country, but the ceaseless surf is captivating.

After about two more miles look for another steep road, this one leading down to gorgeous **Bath Beach**. It's about 1.5km and has a long beach of golden sand. Unlike other parts of this coast, a reef makes swimming possible. Oodles of picnic tables are empty on weekdays, but are crowded with laughing families on weekends.

The road continues south before turning inland through cane fields. Look for an iconic Anglican pile of rocks, **St Philip Church**. Here you turn south, following signs to **Sunbury Plantation House** (☑423-6270; www.barbadosgreathouse.com; tours adult/child B$20/10; ⊘9am-4:30pm). Built in the mid-17th century, it was painstakingly restored after a fire in 1995. The house has 60cm-thick walls made from local coral blocks and ballast stones, the latter coming from the ships

---

SURFING BARBADOS

Barbados has gained international fame for its east-coast breaks. Ground Zero is the **Soup Bowl** (p215), off Bathsheba, and another spot called **Duppies**, up the coast. **South Point**, **Silver Sands** and **Rockley Beach** on the south coast are sometimes good, as is **Brandon's**, which is next to the Hilton Hotel at Needham's Point. There are some 30 other named breaks.

There are local guys renting out boards on the beach at most of the popular surf spots. Prices are negotiable depending on the quality of the board, but even the nicest board should never be over B$15 to B$20 per hour. Also nice are the locals, who are generally welcoming to outsiders.

There are two good surf schools of note: **Zed's Surfing Adventures** (p208), based at Silver Sands; and **Surf Barbados** (☑256-3906; www.surf-barbados.com), which transports clients to various spots depending on conditions. Surf Barbados' beginners class costs US$75 for two hours; it also rents boards and arranges custom trips for advanced surfers.

that set sail from England to pick up Bajan sugar. The interior retains its plantation-era ambience and is furnished with antiques. The grounds serve as mere backdrops to the busloads of tourists who come for the lunch buffets (B$50).

Continuing south from the plantation house, you reach the busy village of Six Cross Roads, where your route options live up to the promise of the name. You can head southeast to Crane Beach, southwest to Oistins or west to Bridgetown.

UNDERSTAND BARBADOS

History

The original inhabitants of Barbados were Arawaks, who were driven off the island around AD 1200 by Caribs from South America. The Caribs, in turn, abandoned (or fled) Barbados close to the arrival of the first Europeans. The Portuguese visited the island in 1536, but Barbados was uninhabited by the time Captain John Powell claimed it for England in 1625. Two years later, a group of settlers established the island's first European settlement, Jamestown, in present-day Holetown. Within a few years, the colonists had cleared much of the forest, planting tobacco and cotton fields. In the 1640s they switched to sugarcane. The new sugar plantations were labor-intensive, and the landowners began to import large numbers of African slaves. These large sugar plantations – some of the first in the Caribbean – proved immensely profitable, and gave rise to a wealthy colonial class. A visit to a plantation estate, like the one at St Nicholas Abbey, will give some idea of the money involved.

Sugar Boom

The sugar industry boomed during the next century, and continued to prosper after the abolition of slavery in 1834. As the planters owned all of the best land, there was little choice for the freed slaves other than to stay on at the cane fields for a pittance.

Social tensions flared during the 1930s, and Barbados' black majority gradually gained more access to the political process. The economy was diversified through the international tourism boom and gave more islanders the opportunity for economic success and self-determination. England granted Barbados internal self-government in 1961 and it became an independent nation on November 30, 1966, with Errol Barrow as its first prime minister. While not flawless, Barbados has remained a stable democracy.

Owen Arthur and the Barbados Labour Party were in power from 1993 to 2008. In a campaign that saw 'change' as the popular theme, David Thompson and the left-leaning Democratic Labour Party won the election. But in late 2010 he died suddenly, which was a traumatic event for a nation used to political stability. He was succeeded by Deputy Prime Minister Freundel Stewart. A general election must be held by January 2013.

Unlike other Caribbean islands, Barbados maintains its sugar industry, although the majority of the economy is now based on tourism and offshore banking. Condos are being built as fast as the concrete dries.

Culture

Bajan culture displays some trappings of English life: cricket, polo and horse racing are popular pastimes, business is performed in a highly organized fashion, gardens are lovingly tended, older women often wear prim little hats and special events are carried out with a great deal of pomp and ceremony.

However, on closer examination, Barbados is very deeply rooted in Afro-Caribbean tradition. Family life, art, food, music, architecture, religion and dress have more in common with the nearby Windward Islands than with London. The African and East Indian influences are especially apparent in the spicy cuisine, rhythmic music and pulsating festivals.

Like other Caribbean cultures, Bajans are relatively conservative and the men are macho, but the ongoing bond with a cosmopolitan center like London has made Barbados slightly more socially progressive than its neighbors.

Bajan youth are fully within the media orbit of North America. The NBA and New York hip-hop fashion are as popular in Bridgetown as in Brooklyn.

Another similarity to the US is the suburban sprawl around Bridgetown. Traffic is often a problem and you can join the masses at a growing number of air-conditioned malls.

BARBADOS BOOKS

Numerous books cover Bajan history and sights. *The History of Barbados* by Robert H Schomburg is a thorough study of the island's past. *To Hell or Barbados: the Ethnic Cleansing of Ireland* by Sean O'Callaghan traces the scores of Irish sent by Cromwell to work as slaves on sugar plantations.

Treasures of Barbados by Henry Fraser, a past president of the Barbados National Trust, surveys island architecture.

The Barbadian Rum Shop: the Other Watering Hole, by Peter Laurie, is an overview of the history of the rum shop and the role that it has played in Bajan life.

In the Castle of My Skin by George Lamming is a much-acclaimed 1953 novel about growing up black in colonial Barbados.

Sports

The national sport, if not national obsession, is cricket. Per capita, Bajans boast more world-class cricket players than any other nation. One of the world's top all-rounders, Bajan native Sir Garfield Sobers, was knighted by Queen Elizabeth II during her 1975 visit to Barbados, while another cricket hero, Sir Frank Worrell, appears on the face of the B$5 bill.

In Barbados you can catch an international test match, a heated local First Division match or even just a friendly game on the beach or grassy field. Thousands of Bajans and other West Indians pour into the world-class cricket matches at **Kensington Oval**, in Garrison near Bridgetown, which was the site of the final in the 2007 World Cup. For information, schedules and tickets, contact the **Barbados Cricket Association** (☎436-1397; www.bcacricket.org).

Horse races and polo (see www.barbados poloclub.com) are at their peak during the tourist season.

Music

Bajan contributions to West Indian music are renowned in the region, having produced such greats as the calypso artist the Mighty Gabby, whose songs on cultural identity and political protest speak for emerging black pride throughout the Caribbean. These days, Bajan music leans toward the faster beats of soca (an energetic offspring of calypso), *rapso* (a fusion of soca and hip-hop) and dancehall (a contemporary offshoot of reggae with faster, digital beats and an MC). Hugely popular Bajan soca artist Rupee brings the sound of the island to audiences worldwide.

The hugely popular singer Rihanna has achieved worldwide fame while being idolized at home. Her reggae-style rap has won many Grammy awards, including Best Rap Song and Best Dance Recording.

Landscape & Wildlife

Barbados lies 160km east of the Windward Islands. It is somewhat pear-shaped, measuring 34km from north to south and 22km at its widest. The island is composed largely of coral accumulations built on sedimentary rocks. Water permeates the soft coral cap, creating underground streams, springs and limestone caverns.

Most of the island's terrain is relatively flat, rising to low, gentle hills in the interior. However, the northeastern part of the island, known as the Scotland District, rises to a relatively lofty 340m at Barbados' highest point, Mt Hillaby. The west coast has white-sand beaches and calm turquoise waters, while the east side of the island has turbulent Atlantic waters and a coastline punctuated with cliffs. Coral reefs surround most of the island and contribute to the fine white sands on the western and southern beaches.

Two good places to enjoy the island's lush natural beauty are Andromeda Botanic Gardens, in a gorgeous setting above Bathsheba with a huge range of beautifully displayed local flora; and Welchman Hall Gully, off the main road from Bridgetown to Belleplaine, which has examples of the island's ancient forests.

Wildlife

The majority of Barbados' indigenous wildlife was overwhelmed by agriculture and competition with introduced species. Found only on Barbados is the harmless and elusive grass snake. The island also shelters a species of small, nonpoisonous, blind snake;

plus whistling frogs, lizards, red-footed tortoises and eight species of bat.

Hawksbill turtles regularly come ashore to lay their eggs, as does the occasional leatherback turtle. As elsewhere, the turtles face numerous threats from pollution and human interference. The **Barbados Sea Turtle Project** (www.barbadosseaturtles.org) is working to restore habitat and populations.

Most if not all mammals found in the wild on Barbados have been introduced. They include wild green monkeys, mongooses, European hares, mice and rats.

More than 180 species of bird have been sighted on Barbados. Most of them are migrating shorebirds and waders that breed in North America and stop over in Barbados en route to winter feeding grounds in South America.

Environmental Issues

The forests that once covered Barbados were long ago felled by the British planters. One of the knock-on effects is that the country now has a problem with soil erosion. This loose dirt, along with pollution from ships and illegally dumped solid wastes, threatens to contaminate the aquifers that supply the island's drinking water.

SURVIVAL GUIDE

Directory A–Z

Accommodations

You can find some place to stay at every price point on Barbados, although there are quite a few more places at the top end than at the budget end.

The west coast, or tellingly the 'Platinum Coast,' is home to most of the posh resorts and boutique hotels plus rental apartments and a smattering of more affordable places. The south coast aims for the masses and there are many places to stay, ranging from simple guesthouses to beachfront hotels. Your money will go further in the south; the west is where you go if money is no concern. Throughout the rest of the island you'll find a number of interesting places, including cool and funky places in and around Bathsheba.

In high season (December to April), expect to spend at least US$150 per night for a nice midrange double on, or more likely

near, a beach. But shop around online as there are deals to be had.

The **Barbados Tourism Authority** (www .visitbarbados.org) maintains a list of families who rent out bedrooms in their homes, from about US$30 per person per night. The staff at its **booth** (⊙8am-10pm or until the last flight arrives) in the airport can help you book a room. Camping is generally not allowed.

Most hotels add a 7.5% government tax plus a 10% service charge, and many have a minimum stay in high season. As elsewhere in the Caribbean, rates decline by as much as 40% outside of high season.

$	budget	less than US$75
$$	midrange	US$75 to US$200
$$$	top end	more than US$200

Business Hours

The following are standard business hours across the island. Exceptions are noted in specific listings. Some bars stay open 24 hours. Note that much is closed on Sunday. .

Banks 9am-3pm Mon-Fri

Restaurants noon-10pm

Shops 9am-5pm Mon-Fri, to 1pm Sat (in tourist areas to 8pm Mon-Sat)

Children

Barbados is generally a family-friendly destination. A number of resorts have organized children's activities or in-house daycare/babysitting.

Most beaches are safe for children to play on and many of the south- and west-coast beaches are calm enough for younger swimmers. The east-coast surf is too powerful for novice swimmers of any age.

Older kids enjoy surfing lessons.

Dangers & Annoyances

Crime, including assaults on tourists, is not unknown on Barbados. Most crimes, however, are simple tourist scams – normal precautions should suffice.

Beware of pickpockets in Bridgetown – keep your valuables secure around the bustling center on Swan and Broad Sts. There are some slick hustlers who hang out at the entrance to St Lawrence Gap and also around south-coast nightlife venues. Steer clear unless you want to invest in someone's habit.

Sidewalks are narrow or nonexistent and roads are curvy, so use caution even while walking along quiet streets.

Portuguese man-of-war jellyfish are occasionally encountered in Bajan waters (although they are large, slow and usually easy to spot), and poisonous manchineel trees grow along some beaches.

Truth be told, the greatest risk is a bad sunburn.

Embassies & Consulates

Canada (☑429-3780; www.canadainternational.gc.ca; Bishop's Court Hill, St Michael)

UK (☑430-7800; www.ukinbarbados.fco.gov.uk; Lower Collymore Rock, St Michael)

USA (☑227-4000; http://barbados.usembassy.gov; Wildey Business Park, Wildey, St Michael)

Festivals & Events

Barbados has visitor-friendly events through the year. The island's compact size means you can enjoy them no matter where you're staying. One worth a trip is the **Crop-Over Festival** (www.barbadoscropoverfestival.com). The island's top event, this festival originated in colonial times as a celebration to mark the end of the sugarcane harvest. Festivities stretch over a three-week period beginning in mid-July with spirited calypso competitions, fairs, and other activities. The festival culminates with a Carnival-like costume parade and fireworks on **Kadooment Day**, a national holiday, in August. Thousands cavort, dance and strut their stuff in a madcap procession where the air pulses with music and is alive with wafting feathers.

Other large festivals:

Jazz Festival (www.barbadosjazzfestival.com) In January. Celebrates Bajans' historic love of jazz; took a hiatus in 2011 but there is great hope it will resume.

Holetown Festival (www.holetownfestivalbarbados.com) This festival celebrates February 17, 1627 – the arrival of the first English settlers on Barbados. Holetown's week-long festivities include street fairs, a music festival at the historic parish church and a road race.

Oistins Fish Festival Commemorates the signing of the Charter of Barbados and celebrates the skills of local fishermen. It's a seaside festivity with events focusing on boat races, fish-filleting competitions, local foods, crafts and dancing. Held over the Easter weekend.

National Independence Festival of Creative Arts (www.ncf.bb) Held in November. Features talent contests in dance, drama, singing and the like. Performances by the finalists are held on Independence Day (November 30).

Food

The following price categories for the cost of a main course are used in Eating listings in this chapter.

$	budget	less than B$25
$$	midrange	B$25 to B$60
$$$	top end	more than B$60

Gay & Lesbian Travelers

Barbados is a conservative and religious place that is generally opposed to homosexuality. That said, there are a few openly homosexual Bajan couples (although they still tend to be discreet) and even the rare transvestite.

Homosexual visitors to Barbados will need to be judicious outside of international resorts and especially in smaller, more traditional towns.

Health

There are excellent medical facilities in Barbados. For minor illnesses, nearly all hotels will have a doctor on call or will be able to help you find assistance. Be sure to have travel insurance that covers medical care.

The country's main hospital is in Bridgetown (p202).

Tap water is safe to drink.

Internet Access

There are a few internet places in Bridgetown and most of the tourist centers. Wi-fi is common at hotels and many have a computer that guests can use. Public hot spots usually come with a fee.

Money

You'll certainly want some Barbadian dollars on hand, but larger payments can be made in US dollars, frequently with a major credit card. Hotels and guesthouses quote rates in US dollars (as do many dive shops and some restaurants), although you can use either US or Bajan currency to settle the account.

The common street exchange rate is B$2 to US$1 for traveler's checks or cash, although true rates can fluctuate a couple of cents either way.

A tip of 10% to 15% is the norm in restaurants (often added to the bill); 10% in hotels (usually added to the bill). A 10% tip is the norm in taxis.

Public Holidays

In addition to those observed throughout the region (p872), Barbados has the following public holidays:

Errol Barrow Day January 21

Heroes' Day April 28

Labour Day May 1

Emancipation Day August 1

Kadooment Day First Monday in August

UN Day First Monday in October

Independence Day November 30

Telephone

Barbados' country code is ☏1; the area code is ☏246. To call any other country with a country code of ☏1 (most of North America and the Caribbean), just dial 1 and the 10-digit number. For other countries, dial the international access code ☏011 + country code + number.

GSM cell phones are compatible with local SIM cards. There is also 3G service. The main operators are **Digicel** (www.digicelbarbados.com) and **Lime** (www.time4lime.com/bb).

Tourist Information

The free annual, *Ins & Outs of Barbados* (www.insandoutsofbarbados.com), is encyclopedic, filled with watch ads and so large that your holiday will be over if you drop it on your toe.

Barbados Hotel & Tourism Association (www.bhta.org; 4th Ave, Belleville, St Michael; ☺8am-5pm Mon-Sat)

Barbados Tourism Authority (www.visitbarbados.org) Bridgetown (Harbour Rd; ☺8:15am-4:30pm Mon-Fri); Grantley Adams International Airport (☺8am-10pm or until the last flight arrives); Cruise-ship terminal (☺when ships are in port)

Getting There & Away

Entering Barbados

Nearly all visitors will enter the country through Grantley Adams International Airport or Bridgetown's cruise-ship terminal. All foreigners entering Barbados should be in possession of a valid passport and a return or onward ticket. And although it's not often enforced, officers may ask for proof that you have a ticket back to your country of origin or residence. So if you are island hopping, show that you intend to eventually return home and if you live outside the country of your passport, have your residency permit.

Cruise-ship passengers who stay less than 24 hours are not required to carry a valid passport.

Air

Grantley Adams International Airport (www.gaiainc.bb) is on the island's southeast corner, about 16km from Bridgetown. It is the largest airport in the Eastern Caribbean and the major point of entry for the region.

Barbados is served by major airlines flying from North America, including Air Canada, American Airlines, Delta, JetBlue, US Airways and WestJet. British Airways and Virgin Atlantic fly from London.

Airlines connecting Barbados with the region:

LIAT (www.liat.com) The main locally based carrier, known for changing flight schedules at the last moment. Flights to Antigua, Dominica, Grenada, St Lucia, St Vincent, Tobago and Trinidad.

Caribbean Airlines (www.caribbean-airlines.com) Flights to Antigua, Sint Maarten and

Trinidad. Has announced plans to challenge LIAT on regional routes.

Sea

CRUISE SHIP

About 450,000 cruise-ship passengers arrive in Barbados each year as part of Eastern Caribbean itineraries. Ships dock at Bridgetown Harbour, about 1km west of the city center.

Ships dock in the port, which has the usual duty-free shops and a branch office of the **Barbados Tourism Authority** (⊘when ships are in port). The center of Bridgetown is about 1km away.

YACHT

Because of Barbados' easterly position and challenging sailing conditions, it is well off the main track for most sailors.

Getting Around

To/From the Airport

If you're traveling light, it's possible to walk out of the airport to the road and wait for a passing bus (B$1.50). Look for buses marked 'Sam Lord's Castle' (or just 'Castle') if you're going east, 'Bridgetown' if you're going to the south coast. For the west coast, occasional buses run to Speightstown, bypassing the capital; alternatively, take a bus to Bridgetown, where you'll have to change to the west-coast terminal. Make sure the bus driver knows your destination.

Taxis are plentiful. Some 'official' prices (subject to negotiation) from the airport to the island's main destinations:

Bathsheba B$73

Bridgetown Harbour B$46

Holetown B$58

Prospect B$53

Speightstown B$73

Many hotels offer pickup services for only somewhat more.

Bicycle

Barbados offers good riding for the adventurous. It's hilly but roads are not usually steep (excepting parts of the east). However most roads are quite narrow, so traffic is a constant bother in the west and south.

Most shops require a credit card or B$100 deposit for rentals. Your hotel can hook you

up with a rental; there are also usually bikes available at the cruise-ship port.

Bus

It's possible to get to virtually any place on the island by public bus. There are three kinds of bus:

Government-operated public buses Large and blue with a yellow stripe.

Privately operated minibuses Intermediate-sized buses painted yellow with a blue stripe.

Route taxis Individually owned minivans that have 'ZR' on their license plates and are painted white.

All types of bus charge the same fare: B$1.50 to any place on the island. You should have exact change when you board the government bus, but minibuses and route taxis will make change.

Most buses transit through Bridgetown, although a few north–south buses bypass the city. Buses to the southeast part of the island generally transit through Oistins.

Bus stops around the island are marked with red-and-white signs printed with the direction in which the bus is heading ('To City' or 'Out of City'). Buses usually have their destinations posted on or above the front windshield.

Buses along the main routes, such as Bridgetown to Oistins or Speightstown, are frequent, running from 6am to around midnight. You can get complete schedule information on any route from the **Transport Board** (☑436-6820; www.transportboard.com).

Car & Motorcycle

DRIVER'S LICENSE

Visitors must obtain a temporary driver's license from their car-rental agency (B$10); you'll need to show a valid driver's license from your home country.

RENTAL

Barbados doesn't have any car-rental agents affiliated with major international rental chains. There are, instead, scores of independent car-rental companies, some so small that they are based out of private homes.

Despite the number of companies, prices don't seem to vary much. The going rate for a small car is about B$150 a day including unlimited mileage and insurance.

Previously it was common for companies to rent out strange, small convertible cars called 'mokes' (they look like the odd car in *Fantasy Island*), which don't have doors. These are an acquired taste and small economy cars are more common now. Rental cars are marked with an 'H' on the license plate.

While most car-rental companies don't have booths at the airport, most will deliver your car there or to your hotel. Note that among the small agencies, some aren't especially professional and complaints are common.

Some of the larger, more established companies:

Courtesy Rent-A-Car (☎431-4160; www.courtesyrentacar.com)

Stoutes Car Rental (☎416-4456; www.stoutescar.com)

Top Class Car Rentals (☎228-7368; www.topclassrentals.com)

ROAD CONDITIONS

Highways are not very well marked, although landmarks are clearly labeled, as are some roundabouts (traffic circles) and major intersections. The most consistent highway markings are often the low yellow cement posts at the side of the road; they show the highway number and below that the number of kilometers from Bridgetown.

All primary and main secondary roads are paved, although some are a bit narrow. There are plenty of gas stations around the island except on the east coast. Some stations in the Bridgetown area are open 24 hours.

Expect rush-hour traffic on the roads around booming Bridgetown.

ROAD RULES

In Barbados, you drive on the left. At intersections and narrow passages, drivers may flash their lights to indicate that you should proceed.

Taxi

Taxis have a 'Z' on the license plate and usually a 'taxi' sign on the roof. They're easy to find and often wait at the side of the road in popular tourist areas.

Although fares are fixed by the government, taxis are not metered and you will have to haggle for a fair price. The rate per kilometer is about B$2 and the flat hourly rate B$50. 'Official' fares from Bridgetown include: Bathsheba (B$58), Oistins (B$31) and Speightstown (B$46).

Tours

Most tour companies offer a variety of half- and full-day options that either provide an overview with stops at key sights or emphasize special interests such as nature and gardens. There is a huge range of choices, as you'll see from the brochure racks. Most, however, follow very set routes and you may well feel part of a herd. The various 4WD options are for those with Hummer envy.

One delightful option is run by the **Barbados Transport Board** (☎436-6820; www.transportboard.com; adult/child B$20/12; ⊙tours 2-7pm Sun). These engaging tours of the island are popular with locals and the itinerary varies each week. Buses depart from Independence Sq, Bridgetown.

The going rate for custom tours by taxi drivers is B$50 an hour, but you can usually negotiate with individual drivers to work out your own deal. Hotels usually have drivers they work with.

See p206 for information on boat trips.

Bonaire

Best Beaches

» Turtle Beach (p227)
» Lac Bay Beach (p232)
» Pink Beach (p232)

Best Places to Stay

» Captain Don's Habitat (p227)
» Harbour Village Beach Club (p227)
» Buddy Dive Resort (p227)

Why Go?

Bonaire's appeal is its amazing reef-lined coast. Entirely designated a national park, the beautiful waters lure divers from across the globe. But while no diving (or snorkeling) initiate will be disappointed, Bonaire also has much to offer above the surface, including world-class windsurfing. Although the beaches are mostly slivers of rocky sand, several take on a pink hue from ground coral washed ashore. Also in the pink are the flamingos found throughout the salt flats and mangroves of the south.

Bonaire has a real community feel: your innkeeper may be your divemaster by day or your waiter at a friend's restaurant at night. Kralendijk has a modest but enjoyable nightlife. Even if you're not a diver, you'll find this small island a restful and intriguing destination.

When to Go

Average temperature for Bonaire is a perfect 28°C (82°F). High noon is a bit warmer and at night it can get breezy, but mostly you'll be fine in shorts and T-shirt. The island is fairly dry, averaging a little over 2.5cm of rain per month. Much of this falls from September to early December. Bonaire usually misses the Caribbean hurricane season; in recent years January rains have caused minor flooding and muddied the waters for divers. High season for cruise ships runs October to April.

Itineraries

THREE DAYS
Get a room at one of the waterfront diving resorts and take the plunge into the incredible shore diving. Think about a journey to one of the 90 named dive sites around the island.

ONE WEEK
Dry yourself off from time in the water and explore the island. Hike and drive the alternately lush and desertlike trails of Washington-Slagbaai National Park. Get to know the postcolonial town of Rincon. Spend time in the south amid the bold horizon-filling colors of the salt ponds and see how many flamingos you spot. Learn about Bonaire's slave past at sites across the island.

TWO WEEKS
All the above, but consider a visit to the neighboring islands of Aruba and Curaçao, each of which has a completely different personality to Bonaire.

GETTING TO NEIGHBORING ISLANDS

Plans for ferries within the ABCs perpetually run aground. But flights between Bonaire and Aruba and Curaçao are frequent and last about 20 minutes.

Essential Food & Drink

Because of the arid conditions, food in Bonaire has always been hearty – and salty. Thick stews made with meats such as goat and chicken, and with vegetables such as okra and squash, are predominant. Spices are used to give things variety.

» **Goat (kabritu) stew** Still a classic dish that most folk will say is made best by their own mother. Also appears in curries.

» **Pastechi** Dough pockets filled with meats and/or Dutch cheese, and deep-fried.

» **Keshi yena** Comes in myriad variations: a cheese casserole with chicken, okra and a few raisins for seasoning. Much better than it sounds.

» **Yambo** A Creole gumbo stew with plenty of okra.

» **Seafood** Common and good, especially shellfish. Fish is popular in curries.

» **Funchi** Based on cornmeal, it is formed in to cakes and fried, mixed with okra and fried, or used as a coating for chicken and fish.

» **Satay** Indonesian skewers of barbecued meat with a savory peanut sauce, via the colonial Dutch.

» **Frikandel** Classic Dutch deep-fried, meaty snack.

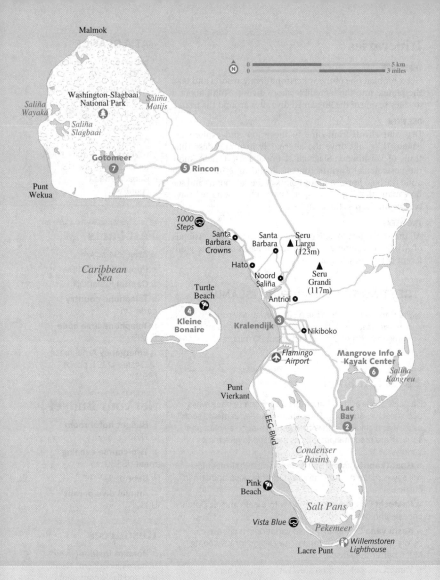

Bonaire Highlights

1 Dive **Bonaire National Marine Park** (p231), a Unesco-recognized world treasure of underwater beauty close to shore right around the island

2 Windsurf on breezy **Lac Bay** (p232), which is one of the world's premier destinations for beginners and pros alike – and it has a good beach

3 Step out at night in **Kralendijk** (p227), which makes up in character and quality of nightspots what it lacks in number

4 Take a short boat ride to **Kleine Bonaire** (p227), for fun on isolated Turtle Beach

5 Explore Bonaire's second town, **Rincon** (p230), which

was founded by Spaniards 500 years ago

6 Go kayaking and/or snorkeling at the **Mangrove Info & Kayak Center** (p232), where you'll see Bonaire's many wild creatures

7 Spot an iconic pink flamingo on placid **Gotomeer** (p230) in the north

Kralendijk

POP 3500

Bonaire's capital and main town has a long seafront that's good for strolling day or night. The smattering of low-rise colonial-era buildings in mustard and pastels add charm. The small but delightful selection of restaurants, cafes and bars mean that fun is never far. Shops are limited but you can get all the essentials – including pricey baubles.

⊙ Sights

Fort Oranje FORT

Follow the cannons south along the waterfront to a small bastion built in the 1700s by the Dutch and modified often through the years. It's now the courthouse. In an adjoining room, there is a small **museum** (admission free; ⊙8am-noon & 1:30-4:30pm Mon-Fri) that has a good display of vintage photos among other exhibits. Behind an unmarked door to the left of the museum are the cleanest public toilets in town.

Bonaire Museum MUSEUM

(☑717-8868; Kaya J Ree 7; adult/child US$1.50/1; ⊙8am-noon & 2-5pm Mon-Fri) Slightly out from the town center, this museum is in an 1885 house filled with folklore displays. Look for the detailed paintings of local mythology by Winifred Dania.

🏖 Beaches

Bonaire doesn't have many eye-popping beaches but its pint-sized sibling, **Kleine Bonaire**, does. Trips for a day of sandy frolicking on **Turtle Beach** and snorkeling are popular. Recommended operators:

Bonaire Nautico Marina BOATS

(⊙Mon-Sat) Boat owners offer shuttles to the island from this dock for a negotiable US$20.

Karel's BOAT TOURS

(☑790-8330) Runs daily boats (US$20 per person; up to four trips per day) to Turtle Beach.

🏃 Activities

Roads to the south end of the island with its windswept flat expanses and Lac Bay are ideal for cycling.

Cycle Bonaire CYCLING

(☑717-2229; www.bonairediveandadventure.com; Harbour Village Beach Club, Kaya Gobernador N Debrot 77A; ⊙8:30am-4:30pm) Rents high-end

bikes from US$20 per day, and organizes guided excursions.

De Freewielen CYCLING

(☑717-8545; www.bonairefreewieler.com; Kaya Grandi 61; ⊙8:30am-5:30pm Mon-Fri, 8:30am-1:30pm Sat) Run by a Dutch cyclist, with rentals per day from US$20.

☞ Tours

Outdoor Bonaire OUTDOOR ACTIVITIES

(☑791-6272; www.outdoorbonaire.com) Leads active tours that include rock climbing, kayaking, caving, biking and more; tours from US$40.

🛏 Sleeping

Bonaire has an interesting and varied selection of places to stay. Unlike other Caribbean islands it doesn't have much in the way of large resorts; instead hotels are smaller and often excellent value. Divers are catered for at many places; at some you can enjoy excellent shore diving right off your terrace.

See the tourist information websites for oodles of apartment and condo rentals.

TOP CHOICE **Captain Don's Habitat** RESORT $$

(☑717-8290; www.habitatbonaire.com; Kaya Gobernador N Debrot; r & apt US$130-300; ✳@🛜🌊) Belying that logo of a pirate flag bearing a skull impaled by a sword, the Captain runs a very comfortable resort. The 85 large units are set on spacious grounds, located 1km north of the town. Air tanks are available 24 hours a day. The resort is a leader in local environmental causes and the eponymous Captain Don is much honored for leading conservation efforts. He's in the lounge at least every Monday night.

Harbour Village Beach Club RESORT $$$

(☑717-7500; www.harbourvillage.com; Kaya Gobernador N Debrot 71; r US$275-450; ✳@🛜🌊) Bonaire's most lavish resort is still a relatively low-key affair. Set on a beach and a yacht harbor, it has sedately decorated rooms, studios and apartments set in widely spaced two-story blocks. The balconies/terraces are large. Amenities include iPod docks and luxury foam mattresses. Climb the rate card and you gain kitchenettes and more. Town is a 15-minute walk away.

Buddy Dive Resort RESORT $$

(☑717-5080; www.buddydive.com; Kaya Gobernador N Debrot 85; r/apt from US$125/200; ✳@🌊)

Kralendijk

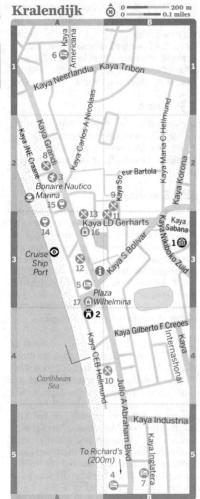

for easy dive-boat pickup. It's a short walk to the center.

Lizard Inn
GUESTHOUSE **$**

(☏717-6877; www.lizardinnbonaire.com; Kaya America 14; r from US$70; ❋🛜⛫) Proof that Bonaire offers good-value lodging. Only five minutes' walk from the shore and the center, this tidy compound has 12 basic but comfortable rooms. Nothing is fancy but it's well run and some larger units have cooking facilities.

Hotel Rochaline
HOTEL **$**

(☏717-8286; www.hotelrochalinebonaire.com; Kaya Grandi; s/d from US$60/70; ❋@🛜) Right in the center of town, the Rochaline's 17 rooms are basic but the location is excellent. No two are alike and there's a bewildering variety of bed, balcony, bathing and other options. Whether you love this place depends on how much you like to party: the ground-floor City Cafe is the most popular nightspot in town.

Coco Palm Garden
APARTMENTS **$**

(☏717-2108; www.cocopalmgarden.com; office Kaya van Eps 9; r & apt US$70-100; ❋@⛫) Coco

---

Divers never had it so good: the reef is right off the deck and there's a drive-through air-tank refill station out front. The more than 70 rooms and apartments are all large. All studios and apartments have kitchens and terraces or balconies.

Carib Inn
GUESTHOUSE **$$**

(☏717-8819; www.caribinn.com; Julio A Abraham Blvd; r & apt US$110-170; ❋🛜) There are 10 units here in a small compound right on the water; most have kitchens, some are studios and others have one or two bedrooms. You can get your tanks refilled and a dock allows

Palm rents a variety of rooms and apartments in various brightly painted houses in a little neighborhood just south of the airport. Bed sizes vary, as do amenities like sofas, patios, kitchens etc (although you can always count on a hammock). Wi-fi is best near the pool and office.

Lodge
B&B **$$**

(717-5410; www.thelodgebonaire.com; Kaya Inglatera 12; r from US$80; ✿@🛜) Balinese teak furniture and statues lend an exotic air to this otherwise simple B&B near the centre. Twelve rooms face a small courtyard. The decor is basic but the bathrooms are nicely tiled and there is a certain style. Town is a 10-minute walk away.

✖ Eating

The Kralendijk area has a splendid collection of places to eat. You can find everything from scrumptious local fare to beachside barbecues to fine (yet casual) dining.

The best supermarket is **Cultimara** (Kaya LD Gerharts 13; 7:30am-7pm Mon-Sat, 8am-2pm Sun).

TOP CHOICE Donna & Giorgio's
SEAFOOD **$$**

(717-3799; Kaya CEB Hellmund 25; mains US$15-30; dinner Thu-Tue) This inviting open-air restaurant is on a quiet corner near the center and across from the water. You won't miss the magenta color scheme adorning this 1912 house. The classic Italian menu has many treats: an *antipasti misto* for the indecisive, a *pasta gamberoni* for those wanting garlicky shrimp, and eggplant parmigiana for those wanting sensual comfort. Make sure you book. Live Caribbean tunes on weekends, jazz on Fridays.

Bistro de Paris
FRENCH **$$$**

(www.bistrodeparis.com; Kaya Gobernador N Debrot 46; mains US$15-30; lunch Mon-Fri, dinner Mon-Sat) If only the weather in Paris were this reliably nice. Proof you can't take Bonaire to France but you can bring France to Bonaire. Bistro classics, many made with fresh seafood, are prepared with skill. Choose from a table inside or out on the veranda. The wine list is *très bon!*

Richard's
SEAFOOD **$$$**

(717-5263; www.richardsofbonaire.com; Julio A Abraham Blvd 60; mains US$15-40; dinner Tue-Sun) The mood of casual elegance at the open-air tables on the water is set by the white tablecloths accented by blue napkins.

There's nothing between you and the ocean but the dock where the daily fresh fish specials are delivered. The best choice for a special waterfront meal; book.

Bobbejan's Take-Away
BBQ **$$**

(Kaya Albert Engelhardt 2; meals from US$12; dinner Fri-Sun) Don't let the name fool you; there are tables here out back under a nice tree. But getting one is a challenge as *everybody* comes here for the super-tender ribs and the velvety peanut sauce on the plate of Indonesian chicken satay.

Wil's Tropical Grill
CARIBBEAN **$$**

(Kaya LD Gerharts 9; mains US$18-25; dinner Mon-Sat) This much-loved top-end Caribbean bistro has dishes that seem to exude the bright colors of the region. Try the shrimp with Creole spices or the orange-glazed fresh fish. The sprightly flavors have influences from Jamaica to Brazil. Opt for a garden table at this converted house.

El Fogon Latino
SOUTH AMERICAN **$**

(Kaya Nikiboko Zuid; meals US$6-12; lunch & dinner Wed-Mon) Direct from Colombia, this little cafe has tables on a porch or in its breezy dining room. The light and crispy fried dorado fillet is superb, as are the many other meaty plate meals. Skip the potatoes for the succulent fried plantains. It's on the road to Lac Bay.

Mona Lisa
DUTCH **$$$**

(717-8718; Kaya Grandi 15; mains US$20-40; dinner Mon-Fri, bar to 2am) This local institution is a tropical version of a traditional Dutch brown cafe. Choose from excellent steaks and seafood displayed on a changing blackboard menu. Specials include a Dutch cheese salad and soup made with local fish. Book. The bar is the genteel alternative to City Cafe.

Exito Bakery
BAKERY **$**

(cnr Kaya LD Gerharts & Kaya Princes Marie; treats from US$2; 8am-5pm Mon-Sat) Upscale grocery and deli in front but the real treats are in the rear, where there's something new arriving from the bakery throughout the day. Get your picnic lunch for Kleine Bonaire here.

🍷 Drinking

Kralendijk does not party late – there are fish to spot at dawn.

TOP CHOICE City Cafe
BAR-CAFE

(Hotel Rochaline, Kaya Grandi; 7am-late; 🛜) *The* top place for carousing among locals, expats, divers and those who stumble past. Buzzes

PORT OF CALL – KRALENDIJK

The long dock can handle several megaships at once, which means that Kralendijk's population can triple or more on busy days. Options if you're docked for a few hours:

» Enjoy some of the world's best diving and snorkeling (p231)

» Windsurf on Lac Bay (p232)

» Explore historic Rincon (p230)

» Flamingo spotting, such as in Washington-Slagbaai National Park (p231)

with breakfasters in the morning but the real action is in the evening – happy hour starts at 5:30pm. And should someone say: 'Get a room,' you can, right upstairs.

Little Havana BAR
(Kaya Bonaire 4; ☺5pm-2:30am) A classic atmospheric bar in a historic whitewashed building. Walk through the open doors and you pass back many decades in time. Sit at the rich wooden bar and enjoy a fine Cuban cigar. The tunes lean towards classic rock. The tables out front get packed on weekend nights.

Karel's BAR
(Waterfront; ☺10am-2am) Two bars set on a concrete pier over the water. Many drink specials include free rum punch. Live Caribbean tunes or a DJ on weekends.

🛍 Shopping

The selection of shops on the short length of Kaya Grandi is not vast but it is good. Bonaire still has lots of interesting locally owned shops and boutiques that haven't been driven out by the duty-free emporiums. The **vendors and artisans market** (Plaza Wilhelmina), which operates on cruise-ship days, still has mostly local wares for sale. There's even locally made treats like *pastechi*.

Addo's Bookstore BOOKSTORE
(☑717-6618; Kaya Grandi 36; ☺9am-6pm Tue-Sat) Best sellers, regional fiction, guidebooks, maps and gifts.

ℹ Information

INTERNET ACCESS Most hotels have internet access points and wi-fi.

Chat 'n' Browse (Kaya Gobernador N Debrot 79; per hr US$8; ☺7:30am-7pm Mon-Fri,

7:30am-6pm Sat & Sun) Top choice. Stocks phonecards, Cuban cigars, ice cream and more. Wi-fi password US$5 per day.

MEDICAL SERVICES **St Franciscus Hospital** (☑717-8900; Kaya Soeur Bartola 2; ☺24hr) Has a well-staffed recompression chamber.

TOURIST INFORMATION **Bonaire Tourist Office** (☑717-8322; www.tourismbonaire.com; Kaya Grandi 2; ☺8am-noon, 1:30-5pm Mon-Fri) Answers questions and has a good selection of brochures.

North of Kralendijk

The road north along the coast is like a roller coaster, but in good shape. There are great vistas of the rocky seashore and frequent pullouts for the marked dive sites. About 5km north of Kralendijk the road becomes one-way, north, so you are committed at this point. After another 5km you reach a T-junction. To the right is the direct road to Rincon, Kaminda Karpata. Turn left (west), following the coast until the road turns sharply inland. Good views of the large inland lake, **Gotomeer**, are off on the left. **Flamingos** stalk about in search of bugs. The road passes through some lush growth and ends in Rincon.

RINCON

Bonaire's second town, Rincon, is rather sleepy and that may simply be because it's old. Over 500 years ago Spaniards established a settlement here because a) it was fertile and b) because it was hidden from passing pirates. Most of the residents are descended from slaves, who worked the farms and made the long trek to the salt flats in the south.

Bonaire's harvest festival, **Simadan**, is usually held here in early April, and celebrates traditional dance and food.

◎ Sights

The best sight is the town itself. Homes have a classic Caribbean look and are painted in myriad pastel shades. Look for a turn off Kaminda Karpata, about 500m before Rincon, which leads to a **lookout** with sweeping views across the north.

Cadushy of Bonaire DISTILLERY
(www.cadushy.com; Rincon; ☺9am-5pm Mon-Fri, plus any weekend day cruise ships are in port) See all the cactus growing on Bonaire? Here you can drink it. Eric and Jolande Gietman moved here to make their exotic liquor, Cadushy. The cloudy green stuff is rather allur-

ing and you can sit, sample and let them tell you all about Rincon's history.

TOP CHOICE **Mangazina di Rei** MUSEUM
(www.mangazinadirei.org; adult/child US$10/US$5; ⊙10am-5pm Tue-Sat) About 1.5km east of Rincon, look for the second-oldest stone building on Bonaire. It has been restored and includes exhibits about its use during the peak of slavery on Bonaire. Tours are fascinating and may include a glass of tasty sorghum juice. We like the lessons in building a cactus fence.

✖ Eating

Rincon has a popular **market** (⊙8am-2pm Sat) with oodles of the area's produce.

Rose Inn CARIBBEAN **$**
(meals from US$7; ⊙lunch Thu-Tue) A local institution run by Rose herself. A genial mix of folks enjoy plate lunches of local fare (fish stew, goat, fried chicken etc) at mismatched tables scattered under trees. You can get a

beer here be it day or night. Service can be erratic, but that's why you're here.

ℹ Information

Bonaire Heritage (www.bonaireheritage.com) Run by the Cadushy people, the website has extensive information on Rincon's heritage. It can also link you up with walking tours and more.

WASHINGTON-SLAGBAAI NATIONAL PARK

Covering the northwest portion of the island and comprising almost 20% of the land, Washington-Slagbaai National Park is a great place to explore. Roads are rough and all but impassable after rain, but it's well worth the effort. The terrain is mostly tropical desert, and there is a proliferation of cactuses and birds. Look for flamingos in the lowlands and parrots perched on shrubs. Large bright-green iguanas are just one of the many reptile species you might find. You'll also see lingering evidence of the aloe plantation and goat ranch that used to be

---

DON'T MISS

DIVING & SNORKELING IN BONAIRE

Bonaire's dive sites are strung along the west side of the island. The closeness of the reefs and the clarity of the waters make for unparalleled access for divers. You can reach more than half of the identified dive sites from shore (or your hotel!). The range of fish species is amazing, and diving goes on around the clock.

Bonaire National Marine Park

The Unesco World Heritage **Bonaire National Marine Park** (☑717-8444; www.bmp.org) covers the entire coast of the island to a depth of 200ft (60m). There are more than 90 named dive sites and they are numbered using a system adopted by all the dive operators on the island. Most maps show the sites and as you are driving along coastal roads you'll see painted yellow rocks identifying some of the sites.

Conservation is taken seriously. Divers new to Bonaire must receive an orientation from a dive operator. Anyone diving or snorkeling must purchase a tag from any dive operator, with the proceeds going to infrastructure maintenance – tags are either day passes (US$10 for diving, US$2 for snorkeling only) or annual passes (US$25 for diving, US$10 for snorkeling only).

The park website is an excellent resource. Additionally, the widely distributed and free *Bonaire Dive Guide* has basic descriptions and a map of all the sites.

Dive Operators

Every hotel and resort has a relationship with a dive operator or conversely – like Captain Don's Habitat (p227) – is a dive operator with a place to stay. Most offer myriad packages, including many options for snorkelers.

Well-regarded operators include **Bonaire Dive & Adventure** (☑717-2229; www.bonairediveandadventure.com; Kaya Gobernador N Debrot 77A; ⊙8:30am-4:30pm), a free-standing dive operation. Unlimited tanks of air or nitrox for six days cost US$165. **Rec Tek Scuba** (☑780-6537; www.rectekscuba.com) specializes in technical diving and offers training in using rebreathers (introductory dives US$110).

BONAIRE

GET YOUR GOAT

About midway to Lac Bay, watch on the east side of the dirt road for **Maiky Snack** (meals from US$10; ⊗lunch Fri-Wed), a much-loved outlet for traditional local fare. You'll already be familiar with the main ingredient: hint, you saw a lot of the playful guys unaware of the nearby peril on the small road in. Yes, goat is big here (you might call the many wild ones 'free range') and comes in many forms (people have asked for seconds of the 'stewed head and liver'). Sides include a long list of old favorites like funchi (cornmeal cakes), *yambo* (okra soup) and papaya.

here – don't run over any wild descendants of the latter.

An excellent **information center** (www. stinapa.org; adult/child US$10/5, free with diving/ snorkeling tag; ⊗8am-5pm, last entry at 2:45pm), small **museum** and **cafe** are at the entrance. From here you can take one of two drives: a 2½-hour, 34km route or a 1½-hour, 24km route. There are picnic, dive and swimming stops along the way.

Two hikes are best done well before the heat of noon: the 90-minute Lagadishi loop, which takes you past ancient stone walls, a blowhole and the rugged coast; and the two-hour Kasikunda climbing trail, which takes you up a challenging path to the top of a hill for sweeping views.

The park entrance is at the end of a good 4km concrete road from Rincon.

East of Kralendijk

The road from Kralendijk to Lac Bay is a highlight. Off the main road, a branch goes around the north side of the water. At first you drive through groves of cactus so thick that it's like driving through someone's crew cut. Close to the water there are dense mangroves and flocks of flamingos. It's a popular ride for cyclists.

Along this road, the **Mangrove Info & Kayak Center** (⊘790-5353; www.mangrovecen ter.com; ⊗Mon-Sat) is right on the mangroves and offers kayak and snorkeling tours (from US$25). It has displays with information about the protected Lac Bay mangroves, which are part of the marine park. About

5.5km from the turnoff the road ends at Lac Cai, a sandy point with a small beach, a snack stand, and mountains of huge pearly white and pink conch shells.

LAC BAY

Lac Bay is one of the world's premier **windsurfing** destinations. The windswept shallows are good year-round for beginners; peak conditions are November to July and pros descend in May and June. The powdery beach is good year-round.

At the end of the main road on the south side, **Bonaire Windsurf Place** (www. bonairewindsurfplace.com; ⊗10am-6pm) rents equipment (from US$40) and gives lessons (from US$45). It has a cafe and a good veranda for watching the action on the water.

Next door, **Jibe City** (www.jibecity.com; ⊗10am-6pm) has similar rates and a cafe open to the breeze.

South of Lac Bay, a good road follows the flat windward coast, which has pounding surf along a desolate shore littered with flotsam. You'll see nary another human.

South of Kralendijk

The south end of Bonaire is flat and arid, and you can see for many miles in all directions. Multihued salt pans where ocean water evaporates to produce salt dominate the landscape. Metal windmills are used to transfer water out of the ponds. As evaporation progresses, the water takes on a vibrant pink color from tiny sea organisms. The color complements the flamingos, which live in a sanctuary and feed in the ponds.

Along the coast you will see the legacy of a vile chapter in Bonaire's past: tiny restored slave huts. Living conditions in these minuscule shelters are hard to imagine now, but they were home to hundreds of slaves, who worked in the salt ponds through the 19th century. The four different-colored 10m pyramids along the coast are another legacy of the Dutch colonial era. Colored flags matching one of the pyramids were flown to tell ships where they should drop anchor to load salt.

Just north of the slave huts, **Pink Beach** is a long sliver of sand that takes its color from pink coral washed ashore. It's pretty rough and you'll want a thick pad for sunbathing, but the swimming (not to mention the diving and snorkeling) is good. The beach is even better to the south at the **Vista Blue** dive spot.

On the south side of the airport runway, 2.5km east of the coast road, the nonprofit **Donkey Sanctuary** (☑9560-7607; adult/child US$6/3; ☺10am-4pm) is home to offspring of donkeys left to wander the island when slave-era salt production ceased. About 400 are still wild; 300 others live here after they get sick, injured or, as the staff says, just get lonely.

UNDERSTAND BONAIRE

History & Culture

The Arawaks lived on Bonaire for thousands of years before Spain laid claim to it in 1499. A mere 20 years later there were none left as the Spanish sent all the natives to work in mines elsewhere in the empire. The only reminder that the Arawaks once lived on Bonaire are a few inscriptions in remote caves.

The depopulated Bonaire stayed pretty quiet until 1634, when the Dutch took control. Soon the Dutch looked to the flat land in the south and saw a future in salt production. Thousands of slaves were imported to work in horrific conditions. You can see a few surviving huts at the south end of the island. When slavery was abolished in the 19th century, the salt factories closed. The population, a mix of ex-slaves, Dutch and people from South America, lived pretty simple lives until after WWII, when the reopening of the salt ponds (this time with machines doing the hard work) coupled with the postwar booms in tourism and diving gave a real boost to the economy.

Meanwhile relations with Curaçao, capital of the Netherlands Antilles (NA), slowly turned frosty. Locals felt ignored by their wealthier neighbor and lobbied for change. In 2008 Bonaire returned to direct Dutch rule as a rather far-flung special municipality within the Netherlands, a designation it shares with Saba and Sint Eustatius. The NA was formally dissolved in 2010.

Landscape & Wildlife

Bonaire is primarily arid, as the vast salt flats in the south show. But it also has mangroves rich with birdlife, including iconic pink flamingos. In the water is where Bonaire is truly rich in life. Coral reefs grow in profusion along the lee coast, often just a few meters from the shore. Hundreds of species of fish and dozens of corals thrive in the clear, warm waters. Sharks, dolphins and rays are among the larger creatures swimming about.

Bonaire has few major environmental concerns. Protections of the marine park, which encompasses the coast, are strict and any environmental damage from the salt ponds is limited mostly to the ponds themselves.

SURVIVAL GUIDE

Directory A–Z
Accommodations

Bonaire has small inns and resorts geared toward divers. Most have in-house dive operations and some have rooms where you can don your diving gear and step from your terrace right into the water. Because winter brings rain that can muddy the waters, Bonaire does not have a massive high-season spike in visitors from December to April.

Hotel taxes and fees are US$6.50 per person plus 10% to 15% service charge.

$	budget	less than US$75
$$	midrange	US$75 to US$200
$$$	top end	more than US$200

Activities

Diving, snorkeling and windsurfing are major draws. See page p231 for more on diving.

Business Hours

The following are standard business hours across the island. Exceptions are noted in specific listings. Outside of tourist areas, much is closed on Sunday.

Banks 9am-4pm Mon-Fri

PRACTICALITIES

» **Electricity** 110V, 60Hz; US-style two- and three-pin plugs are used.

» **Media** Bonaire Reporter (www.bonairereporter.com) is a free newspaper that actually covers controversial issues on the island. Bonaire Affair and Bonaire Nights are good tourist freebies.

» **Weights & Measures** Metric system is used.

Restaurants 11am-9pm

Shops 9am-6pm Mon-Sat

Food

The following price categories for the cost of a main course are used in the Eating listings in this chapter.

$	budget	less than US$10
$$	midrange	US$10 to US$25
$$$	top end	more than US$25

Health

There are good medical facilities in Bonaire. Tap water is safe to drink.

Language

If you only speak English, you won't have a problem on Bonaire, where most locals are multilingual. Dutch is the official language but English and Papiamento are spoken widely.

Money

The US dollar (US$) is the official currency.

A 20% overall tip is the norm in restaurants; 15% is often added to the bill. A tip of 15% is usually added to the bill in hotels. A 10% tip is the norm in taxis.

Public Holidays

In addition to those observed throughout the region (p872), Bonaire has the following public holidays:

Ash Wednesday Usually in February, after Carnival

Queen's Birthday April 30

Labour Day May 1

Ascension Day Sixth Thursday after Easter

Bonaire Flag Day September 6

Telephone

Bonaire's country code is ☑1; the area code is ☑599. To call any other country with a country code of ☑1 (most of North America and the Caribbean), just dial 1 and the 10-digit number. For other countries, dial the international access code ☑011 + country code + number.

CELL PHONES

GSM cell phones are compatible with local SIM cards. There is also 3G service. The main operator is Digicel (www.digicelbonaire.com).

Getting There & Away

All visitors need a passport and a return or onward ticket to enter Bonaire.

Air

Bonaire's Flamingo Airport (www.flamingoairport.com) is immediately south of Kralendijk. Departure tax for international flights is US$35, for Aruba and Curaçao US$9 (confirm it is not included in the ticket price).

There are flights to Bonaire from North America with Delta and United, and from Amsterdam with KLM. The following airlines also serve Bonaire (some services are seasonal):

DAE (www.flydae.com) Aruba, Curaçao

Insel Air (www.fly-inselair.com) Aruba, Curaçao, Miami

Tiara Air (www.tiara-air.com) Aruba

Sea

Bonaire is on many cruise-ship itineraries that cover the southern Caribbean, often on longer 10-day and two-week trips.

Many cruise ships call at Bonaire; on days when more than one arrives, the thousands of visitors almost swamp the island. Boats dock directly at the port in the middle of Kralendijk.

Getting Around

There is no public bus service on Bonaire. However, dive operators will haul you wherever you need to go. You can see all of the island in one or two days of driving, so you might consider renting a car for just that period. Many places to stay offer packages with a car thrown in cheap.

To/From the Airport

Hotels and resorts usually do not do airport pickups. The taxi fare to hotels is about US$10 to US$20.

Bicycle

Although there are no bike lanes on Bonaire, people enjoy riding along the many flat roads, especially in the south. You can rent at hotels and bike shops in Kralendijk.

Car & Motorcycle

Most international car-rental firms are at the airport and rates are cheap for the Caribbean. Shop online for daily fees starting at US$25. The main operators:

AB Carrental (☎717-8980; www.abcarrental .com)

Budget (www.budget.com)

Hertz (www.hertz.com)

Total (☎717-7424; www.totalbonaire.com)

Main roads are generally in pretty good condition; however, roads in the national park and other remote spots can be quite rough. Gasoline can be found in Kralendijk; road signs are sporadic. Driving is on the right-hand side, seat belts are required and motorcyclists must use helmets.

Taxi

For a taxi, call ☎717-8100.

British Virgin Islands

Best Beaches

» White Bay (p254)
» Savannah Bay (p252)
» Josiah's Bay (p246)
» Cow Wreck Bay (p256)
» Cane Garden Bay (p244)

Best Places to Stay

» Guavaberry Spring Bay
Homes (p250)
» Sugar Mill Hotel (p244)
» Hummingbird House
(p240)
» White Bay Campground
(p254)
» Cow Wreck Villas (p256)

Why Go?

The British Virgin Islands (BVI) are territories of Her Majesty's land, but they mostly resemble their cousins, the US Virgin Islands (USVI), though they're quirkier and blissfully less developed. Take Jost Van Dyke, population 200, where a man named Foxy is king and time flies when you're doing very little, as the T-shirts proclaim (though in slightly different words). Main island Tortola is known for its full-moon parties, fungi bands and fire jugglers. Billionaires and yachties swoon over Virgin Gorda; you'll understand the ardor once you've seen its national parks. Anegada floats in a remote reef and has a hammock waiting for those serious about unplugging. Then there are the 40-plus out islands – some uninhabited, some with just a beach bar, some with shipwrecks to dive on. You'll need your own boat to reach them, but since the BVI are the Caribbean's charter-boat capital, you're in luck.

When to Go

Mid-December through April is the prime-weather high season, when visitors from northern climes descend and set sail in charter boats. Big bashes take place in spring and summer, including the BVI Spring Regatta (late March–early April), BVI Music Festival (late May) and the year's biggest bash: the Emancipation Festival (late July to early August). November through July is lobster season, so they're widely available and at their juiciest during these months. The full moon is a good time to visit, when parties rock Tortola.

Itineraries

ONE WEEK

Spend the first three days on Tortola. Drink and dine in Road Town, then fan out to explore Apple Bay, home to Bomba's world-famous surfers' bar, and Cane Garden Bay, the island's live-music hot spot. Day-trip to jovial Jost Van Dyke or sleepy Anegada; both have populations of fewer than 200 and are easy to reach by ferry. Spend the last four days on Virgin Gorda. Poke around the boulder-studded Baths and view-worthy Virgin Gorda Peak. Hail water taxis around North Sound to sail and drink with the yachtsfolk.

TWO WEEKS

Island hop: spend time on each of the four main islands, then ferry over to nearby St Thomas and St John in the US Virgin Islands. Better yet, get adventurous and charter a boat to explore the out islands and barely inhabited cays such as Norman, Peter and Cooper Islands. Here, life is reduced to the pleasures of snorkeling, diving and sleeping under a shade tree (after partying aboard a floating pirate-ship bar, of course).

GETTING TO NEIGHBORING ISLANDS

Tortola is the ferry hub, with vessels making quick jaunts to Virgin Gorda and Jost Van Dyke several times daily. Ferries also depart for the US Virgin Islands' St Thomas and St John often each day; trips take between 30 and 60 minutes. Ferries to farther-flung Anegada make the run on Monday, Wednesday and Friday; you can charter a flight at other times. Most of the out islands are reachable only by charter boat – of which there are many in the BVI! Nonstop flights go daily to island-neighbors Puerto Rico, St Thomas and Antigua.

Essential Food & Drink

» **Anegada lobster** Hulking crustaceans plucked from the water in front of your eyes and grilled on the beach in converted oil drums.

» **Roti** Fiery chutney sets off the curried chicken, beef, conch (a local shellfish) or vegetable fillings in these burrito-like flat-bread wraps.

» **Fungi** (*foon*-ghee) A polenta-like cornmeal cooked with okra, typically topped by fish and gravy.

» **Pate** (*paw*-tay) Flaky fried dough pockets stuffed with spiced chicken, fish or other meat.

» **Painkiller** Jost Van Dyke's Soggy Dollar Bar supposedly invented this sweet mix of rum, coconut, pineapple, orange juice and nutmeg.

AT A GLANCE

» **Currency** US dollar (US$)

» **Language** English

» **Money** ATMs on Tortola and Virgin Gorda (none on smaller islands); they dispense US dollars

» **Visas** Not required for citizens of USA, Canada and most EU countries

Fast Facts

» **Area** 59 sq miles

» **Population** 25,400

» **Capital** Road Town

» **Telephone country code** ☎1

» **Telephone area code** ☎284

» **Emergency** ☎911 or 999

Set Your Budget

» **Budget hotel room** US$90

» **Two-course evening meal** US$30

» **Botanic Gardens entrance** US$3

» **Bottle of beer** US$3

» **Round-trip Virgin Gorda ferry** US$30

Resources

» **BVI Tourist Board** (www.bvitourism.com) Official site with comprehensive lodging and activity info

» **BVI Welcome Guide** (www.bviwelcome.com)

» **BVI Music** (www.bvimusic.com)

» **Limin' Times** (www.limin-times.com)

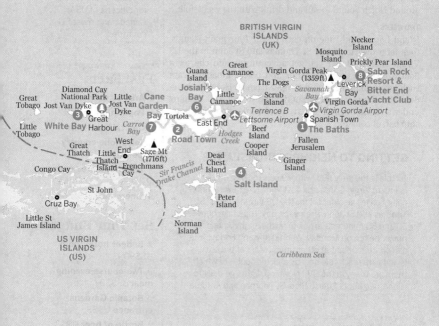

ATLANTIC OCEAN

Cow Wreck
Bay
Flamingo
Pond
Pomato Point
Captain Auguste
George Airport
Red
Pond
Anegada
Loblolly
Bay
Flash
of
Beauty
The
Settlement

BRITISH VIRGIN
ISLANDS
(UK)

Necker
Island
Mosquito
Island
Prickly Pear Island
Saba Rock
Resort &
Bitter End
Yacht Club
Leverick
Bay

Guana
Island
Great
Camanoe
Virgin Gorda Peak
(1359ft)
The Dogs
Josiah's
Bay
Little
Camanoe
Scrub
Island
Savannah
Bay
Virgin Gorda
Virgin Gorda Airport

Great
Tobago
Diamond Cay
National Park
Jost Van Dyke
Little
Jost Van
Dyke
Great
Harbour
Cane
Garden
Bay
Tortola
Carrot
Bay
Terrence B
Lettsome Airport
Spanish Town
The Baths

White Bay
West
End
Road Town
East End
Beef
Island
Fallen
Jerusalem

Little
Tobago

Great
Thatch
Little
Thatch
Island
Frenchmans
Cay
Sage Mt
(1716ft)
Hodges
Creek
Cooper
Island
Ginger
Island

Congo Cay
Sir Francis
Drake Channel
Dead
Chest
Island
Salt Island

St John

Cruz Bay
Peter
Island

Little St
James Island
US VIRGIN
ISLANDS
(US)
Norman
Island
Caribbean Sea

N
0   20 km
0   10 miles

British Virgin Islands Highlights

1 Wade around boulders and through grottoes at sunrise at **the Baths** (p249)

2 **Charter a boat** (p263) in Road Town and set sail around the islands

3 Drink a rum-soaked Painkiller on the dazzling sand at **White Bay** (p254)

4 Snorkel or dive at the 1867 *Rhone* shipwreck by **Salt Island** (p248)

5 Leave the world behind on remote **Anegada** (p255), home to hammocks and lobster dinners

6 Kick back on the dramatic strand of sand at **Josiah's Bay** (p246)

7 Dance to reggae at the beach bars at **Cane Garden Bay** (p245)

8 Join the yachties for happy hour at **Saba Rock Resort** (p252) or **Bitter End Yacht Club & Resort** (p252)

TORTOLA

POP 19,600

Among Tortola's sharp peaks and bougainvillea-clad hillsides you'll find a mash-up of play places. Guesthouses and mountain villas are interspersed with beachside resorts. Cooks for *Bon Appétit* magazine make island dishes next to elderly Mrs Scatliffe, who prepares meals using ingredients from her garden. You even get your choice of full-moon parties – artsy with Aragorn or mushroom-tea-fueled with Bomba.

About 80% of the BVI's 25,000 citizens live and work on Tortola, so it's not surprising there's a lot of choice here. It's also the BVI's governmental and commercial center, plus its air and ferry hub.

As for the name: in Spanish, *tortola* means 'turtledove,' which was the type of bird flying around with distinctive coos when Christopher Columbus came ashore. Most have since flown the coop.

ⓘ Getting There & Around

AIR Terrence B Lettsome Airport (☑494-3701) is on Beef Island, connected to Tortola by a bridge on the island's east end. It is a 25-minute drive between the airport and Road Town.

BOAT Tortola is the hub for ferries to the rest of the Virgins. The two main marine terminals are at **Road Town** (ferries to Virgin Gorda, Anegada and St Thomas' Charlotte Amalie) and **West End** (ferries to Jost Van Dyke, St John and St Thomas' Red Hook). A smaller dock at **Trellis Bay/Beef Island** has boats to Virgin Gorda's north-end resorts.

See p262 for more ferry details.

CAR Although everything looks close on the map, the ruggedness of Tortola's topography makes for slow travel. There are several local car-rental agencies on Tortola. High-season rates begin at about US$55 per day, and can run as high as US$90.

Dollar (☑494-6093; www.dollarcar.com; East End)

Hertz Airport (☑495-2763); Road Town (☑494-6228; Wickhams Cay 1); West End (☑495-4405; near the ferry terminal)

Itgo Car Rentals (☑494-5150; www.itgobvi .com; Road Town) Good indie agency; located at Wickhams Cay 1.

TAXI Taxis are widely available in the main tourist areas. Rates are government-set. The fare from Road Town to West End or the airport is the same (US$27).

Let's be honest: the BVI's capital is nothing special – no mega sights to see or scenery to drop your jaw. But there's nothing wrong with Road Town, either (unless it's all the traffic and exhaust fumes). It's a perfectly decent place to spend a day or night, and most visitors do exactly that when they charter their own boat or take the ferries to the outlying islands.

Most of the town's pubs and restaurants are along Waterfront Dr. Main St, Road Town's primary shopping venue, is a nice retreat for anyone seeking shade and quiet. The narrow street winds along the western edge of town and has a collection of wooden and stone buildings dating back about 200 years.

◉ Sights

JR O'Neal Botanic Gardens GARDEN
(cnr Botanic Rd & Main St; admission US$3; ☺8am-4pm) The gardens are a four-acre national park and a pleasant refuge from Road Town's traffic, noise and heat. Benches are set amid indigenous and exotic tropical plants and there is also an orchid house, lily pond, small rainforest, cactus grove and herb garden. It's about two blocks north of the town's main roundabout.

Government House MUSEUM
(Main St; admission US$3; ☺9am-3pm Mon-Fri, to 1pm Sat) Standing at the extreme south end of Main St like an imperial symbol, this whitewashed manor is a classic example of British colonial architecture. Once the home of England's appointed governor to the BVI, it is now a small museum with period furniture and artifacts.

Main Street HISTORICAL BUILDINGS
If you start at Government House and meander down Main St, here are some of the historic buildings you'll see (in order):

St George's Episcopal (Anglican) Church
This neat Anglican chapel is a survivor of the 18th century but was rebuilt in the early 19th century following a hurricane.

HMS Prison
Located at the heart of Main St, these stark, white rubble walls date back to the 18th century and mark the oldest building in Road Town. The prison sits empty these days.

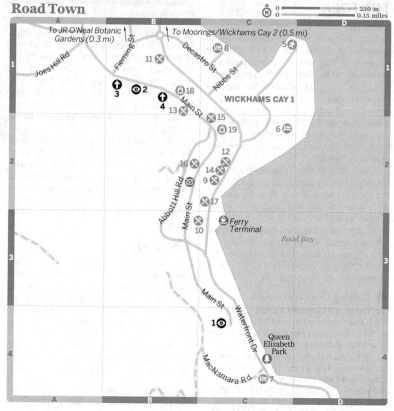

Methodist Church
Flanking the north side of the prison, this working Methodist house of worship dates from 1924. It's a fine example of classic West Indian timber-framed construction.

🏃 Activities

Boat charters are big, big business in the BVI, and Road Town is where it all happens (primarily from the Moorings at Wickhams Cay 2). For more information on bareboat or crewed-boat charters, see p263.

The following operators run day trips to the Baths, Cooper Island, Salt Island and Norman Island, among others. Expect to pay around US$110, which typically includes gear.

White Squall II   SNORKELING, BOAT TRIPS
(www.whitesquall2.com; Village Cay Marina) Feel the wind in a traditional, 80ft schooner.

Lionheart   SNORKELING, BOAT TRIPS
(www.aristocatcharters.com; Village Cay Marina) This one is a 48ft catamaran.

BVI Scuba Co   DIVING
(www.bviscubaco.com; Inner Harbor Marina) By the cruise-ship dock.

🎊 Festivals & Events

BVI Spring Regatta   SAILING
(www.bvispringregatta.org; ⊙late Mar–early Apr) One of the Caribbean's biggest parties, with seven days of bands, boats and beer.

BVI Emancipation Festival   CULTURAL
(www.bvitourism.com; ⊙late Jul–early Aug) This marks the 1834 Emancipation Act that abolished slavery in the BVI. Activities include everything from a beauty pageant to 'rise and shine tramps' (noisy parades led by reggae bands in the back of a truck that start at 3am).

🛏 Sleeping

Hummingbird House   B&B $$
TOP CHOICE
(📞494-0039; www.hummingbirdbvi.com; Pasea; r incl breakfast US$140-155; ❄@🖘🌊) This is a

real B&B (the BVI's only one), run by long-time UK transplant Yvonne. Tile floors, batik decor and thick towels fill the four breezy rooms; you'll feel like you're staying in a friend's big ol' guest room. Breakfast is a full cooked affair served poolside. There are surcharges to use the air-con (per night US$20) and internet (per 30 minutes US$5), though wi-fi access is free. Hummingbird is located in the leafy Pasea neighborhood (near Wickhams Cay 2), a 25-minute walk or US$5 cab ride from town.

Village Cay Hotel & Marina　　HOTEL **$$**
(☑494-2771; www.villagecayhotelandmarina.com; Wickhams Cay 1; r US$150-225; ❋@☎☒) Located smack in the middle of Road Town overlooking the bay's yacht slips, Village Cay is a sweet place to rest your head, especially if you want to schmooze with fellow boaters. The 23 rooms, suites and condos have first-class amenities for less than you'll find elsewhere in town. It books up fast. If nothing else, come for a drink at the pierside bar-restaurant.

Maria's by the Sea　　HOTEL **$$**
(☑494-2595; www.mariasbythesea.com; Wickhams Cay 1; r US$160-280; ❋☎☒) Maria's is on the harbor (no beach) at Wickhams Cay 1. If you like watching the coming and going of charter yachts from a seaside pool and sundeck, this expansive three-story operation with 40 units may be for you. All rooms have balconies, kitchenettes and tropical but plain-Jane decor. At the time of writing, the property was adding new rooms.

Sea View Hotel　　HOTEL **$**
(☑494-2483; seaviewhotel@surfbvi.com; cnr Waterfront Dr & MacNamara Rd; r/apt incl tax US$85/125; ❋☒) At the southern end of town, this budget property has about 20 small rooms and apartment with fridge and partial kitchen efficiency apartments. It's nothing fancy (and despite the name, there's no view), but the motel-like rooms are clean and well kept. Unfortunately, the hotel fronts a busy road, so noise can be a problem.

✗ Eating & Drinking

Tortolians love to eat out, and Road Town has restaurants to match every wallet. Pick up the free *Limin' Times* for entertainment listings.

TOP CHOICE Road Town Bakery　　BAKERY **$**
(Main St; sandwiches US$5-8; ☺7am-6:30pm Mon-Sat, to 2pm Sun) New England Culinary Institute students bake the goods here. The small counter mostly serves takeaway, though you can eat at the four outdoor tables along with the chickens pecking for scraps. The soups and sandwiches are dandy, but it's the pumpkin spice muffins, brownies and fat slices of cake that will set you free.

Roti Palace　　CARIBBEAN **$$**
(☑494-4196; Abbott Hill Rd; rotis US$10-14; ☺10am-5pm Mon-Fri) On a side street that leads up the hill off Main St (look for Samarkand Jewelers and go up the stairs beside it), this cramped little restaurant serves some of the island's best roti at its

PORT OF CALL – ROAD TOWN

Ships call at Road Town almost daily during peak season. The dock is downtown. With a few hours, you can do the following:

» Ferry over to Virgin Gorda to splash around the otherworldly Baths (p249)

» Hoist a drink at reggae-fueled beach bars in Cane Garden Bay (p245)

» Day sail to the out islands (p240) and snorkel or dive on fishy reefs and shipwrecks

open-air plastic tables. Fiery chutney sets off the chicken, beef, conch or vegetable fillings, which you can try to tame with a cold beer.

Dove FRENCH $$$
(☑494-0313; Main St; mains US$20-45; ☉dinner Tue-Sat) The cozy, French-flaired Dove, set in a historic house, is pretty much the top address in town. The menu changes but you might see pan-seared foie gras, dry aged steaks, charcuterie platters, even some sushi. For something lighter, head upstairs to the wine bar for tapas. Oh, did we mention the wine? The list at the Dove is supposedly the BVI's largest.

Capriccio di Mare ITALIAN $$
(☑494-5369; Waterfront Dr; mains US$10-17; ☉breakfast, lunch & dinner Mon-Sat) Set on the porch of a classic West Indian house across from the ferry dock, this Italian cafe draws both locals and travelers. Breakfast includes pastries and cappuccino. Lunch and dinner feature salads, pasta dishes and pizza, with plenty of wines to wash it all down.

Le Grand Cafe FRENCH $$
(☑494-8660; Waterfront Dr; mains US$24-32; ☉lunch & dinner; ☎) It concocts its *croque-monsieur*, foie gras and seafood dishes using provisions flown in from French St-Martin. The open-air terrace, carved from a classic West Indian house, becomes a happenin' scene at night with DJs and live music.

Midtown Restaurant CARIBBEAN $$
(☑494-2764; Main St; mains US$8-15; ☉breakfast, lunch & dinner) Midtown is a storefront operation right out of the 1950s. Johnnycakes,

pancakes, eggs, bacon, toast and coffee make a bountiful breakfast. Lunch and dinner feature curried conch and beef, baked chicken, oxtail stew, whelk and salt fish.

Pusser's Pub PIZZA, BURGERS $$
(☑494-3897; www.pussers.com; Waterfront Dr; mains US$12-24; ☉lunch & dinner) Pusser's English-style, nautical-themed pub gets lively with pizza, burger and sandwich eaters whooping it up at brass-ringed tables.

Three Sheets Sports Bar BURGERS, SEAFOOD $$
(☑494-8295; Waterfront Dr; mains US$13-22; ☉lunch & dinner; ☎) Free wi-fi and satellite TV make this a swell place to hang out if you're waiting for a ferry.

La Dolce Vita ICE-CREAM PARLOR $
(Waterfront Dr; ice cream US$3-5; ☉10am-8pm Mon-Thu, to 9pm Fri-Sun; ☑) Real-deal rich creamy gelato, plus soy flavors for vegans.

🔒 Shopping

Craft hawkers come out in droves around Wickhams Cay 1 when cruise ships sail into port, but the top shops are on Main St.

Pusser's Company Store SOUVENIRS
(www.pussers.com; Waterfront Dr) Adjoining Pusser's Pub, this shop sells logoed clothing and accessories, as well as bottles of Pusser's Rum – the blend served on Her Majesty's Royal Navy ships for 300 years.

Sunny Caribbee Spice Shop SOUVENIRS
(www.sunnycaribbee.com; Main St) It's a favorite for its colorful array of island-made seasonings such as 'rum peppers' and 'mango magic'. Spices are also packaged as hangover cures and bad-spirit repellents.

Serendipity Books BOOKSTORE
(Main St) It stocks an excellent selection of adult and children's books, including works by West Indian and BVI authors.

Riteway Food Market FOOD
(Pasea; ☉7:30am-10pm Mon-Sat, to 9pm Sun) This is the main supermarket, located east of downtown, just beyond Wickhams Cay 2.

ℹ Information

Branches of Scotiabank, FirstBank and First Caribbean are all found on Wickhams Cay 1 near Decastro and Nibbs Sts. All have ATMs.

Bits 'n' Pieces (Wickhams Cay 1; per 30min US$3; ☉closed Sun) Internet access: has four computer terminals and a printer.

Tourist office (www.bvitourism.com; ⊘8:30am-4:30pm Mon-Fri) Drop by the tiny office at the ferry terminal for a free, useful road map or *BVI Welcome Guide* book.

Peebles Hospital (✐494-3497; Main St; ⊘24hr) Has complete emergency services.

Around Road Town

Just west of Road Town the road hugs the shoreline around Sea Cow Bay. A couple of big resorts are here, and they offer a slew of wet and wild activities.

On the southwestern border of Road Town, a short distance beyond Fort Burt, sits **Prospect Reef Resort** (✐494-3311, 800-356-8937; www.prospectreefbvi.com; r US$155-480; ✻☒), Tortola's largest resort. The place has certainly seen better days, but as long as you're not expecting luxury there's decent value to be had here. While there's no beach, the Olympic lap pool can satisfy the swimming urge. Tennis, fishing and yacht charters are at your doorstep, as is diving instruction with **Blue Water Divers** (✐494-2847; www.bluewaterdiversbvi.com; 1-/2-tank dives US$80/110).

Dolphin Discovery (www.dolphindiscovery. com/tortola) – a 'swim with the dolphins' program – also operates at Prospect Reef, but remember: these are wild animals brought here forcibly, a practice that is widely condemned by environmental groups.

Nanny Cay Resort & Marina (✐494-2512; www.nannycay.com; d US$180-260; ✻@☒), 3 miles west of Road Town, describes itself as 'an island unto itself,' and the description fits. The 42-room resort has two pools, two restaurants, a marina, windsurfing school, dive shop, mountain-bike center, boutiques and a minimarket – in short, it's a self-contained pleasure dome on a 25-acre islet. Rooms have kitchenettes, private balconies and wooden cathedral ceilings.

Island Surf & Sail (✐494-0123; www.bvi watertoys.com) at Nanny Cay rents all kinds of boards and sail equipment, and provides surfing, windsurfing and stand-up paddleboarding lessons, as well as kayak tours.

West End

The small settlement of West End has a busy little ferry terminal for vessels going to and from Jost Van Dyke, as well as the US Virgin Islands' St Thomas and St John. For details, see p262.

Sopers Hole (www.sopershole.com), the former site of a 16th-century pirates' den, is a major anchorage, with a marina and shopping wharf that has some great restaurants and bars. Anyone needing transportation can call **West End Taxi Association** (✐495-4934).

On the north side of Sopers Hole next to the ferry dock, **Jolly Roger Inn** (✐495-4559; www.jollyrogerbvi.com; mains US$10-20; ⊘breakfast, lunch & dinner, closed Aug & Sep) is a hearty waterfront pub. Pizza is the popular beer chaser here, though the chefs serve up delicious grilled fish with Asian-tinged sauces, too. Locals and travelers flock to the Caribbean barbecue and live music on Friday and Saturday nights. Five very basic rooms (doubles US$85 to US$106), some with shared bathroom, sit above the restaurant.

Pusser's Landing (✐495-4603; www.puss ers.com; mains US$14-27; ⊘lunch & dinner; 🛜) offers outdoor harborside seating and a fun, Margaritaville ambience. The seafood-based dinners are a bit pricey for their quality. It's best to stick to snacks and booze (happy hour is from 5pm to 6:30pm).

Cane Garden Bay Area

A turquoise cove ringed by steep green hills, Cane Garden Bay is exactly the kind of place Jimmy Buffett would immortalize in song – which he did in 1978's 'Mañana.' The area's perfecto 1-mile beach and throngs of rum-serving bars and restaurants make it Tortola's most popular party zone.

Rid yourself of visions of a sprawling resort area, however; the sheer mountains dominate the landscape, so everything hugs the water along a small strip of road. South of Cane Garden Bay is a series of picturesque bays. Speckled amid clumps of shoreside holiday villas are small West Indian settlements. When you stay out here you're living among locals.

The north shore lies only a few miles as the crow flies from Road Town, but the winding, precipitous roads travel over the mountains, making it about a 25-minute drive.

◉ Sights & Activities

Sage Mountain National Park PARK
(Ridge Rd; admission US$3; ⊘sunrise-sunset) At 1716ft, Sage Mountain rises higher than any other peak in the Virgin Islands. Seven trails

crisscross the 92-acre surrounding park, including the main path that leaves from the car park and moseys up through the greenery. A sign showing all the routes is at the trailhead.

The park is not a rainforest in the true sense, because it receives less than 100in of rain per year, but the lush area possesses many rainforest characteristics. It's cool and damp, populated by bo-peep frogs and lizards. Hikers should keep an eye out for 20ft fern trees, mahogany trees, cocoplum shrubs and other flora that have not changed since the dinosaur days. You'll also see spectacular vistas of both the USVI and BVI. Allow two hours for your rambles.

Callwood Rum Distillery   RUM FACTORY
(Cane Garden Bay; admission US$2; ☉7:30am-5pm) Just off the North Coast Rd at the west end of Cane Garden Bay, this is the oldest continuously operated distillery in the Eastern Caribbean. The Callwood family has been producing Arundel rum here for more than 300 years, using copper vats and wooden aging casks. A small store sells the delicious local liquor and offers tours through the atmospheric structure (highly recommended).

North Shore Shell Museum   MUSEUM
(Carrot Bay; admission free but donation requested; ☉hrs vary) It's more of a folk art gallery/junk shop than museum, but it's funky by whatever name you call it. The hours vary depending on when the proprietor, Egbert Donovan, is around to show you through. He'll also encourage you to buy something or to eat in the upstairs restaurant.

Cane Garden Bay   ACTIVITIES BEACH
Cane Garden Bay is probably on the postcard that drew you to the BVI in the first place. The gently sloping crescent of sand hosts plenty of beachside bars and watersports vendors. It's a popular yacht anchorage, and becomes a full-on madhouse when cruise ships arrive in Road Town and shuttle passengers over for the day.

Brewers Bay   ACTIVITIES BEACH
Travelers like Brewers Bay, a palm-fringed bay on the north shore east of Cane Garden Bay. It has excellent snorkeling and a tranquil scene – possibly because getting here involves either an expensive cab ride or a brake-smoking, do-it-yourself drive down steep switchbacks. There are a couple of beach bars and a campground here.

Apple Bay   SURFING BEACH
Located southwest of Cane Garden Bay, this is known as the 'surfing beach,' especially from late December to March when the consistent swells roll in. On many maps, Apple Bay includes Cappoons Bay, home of the infamous Bomba's Surfside Shack.

Long Bay   WALKING BEACH
Another sweet beach as you move from Apple Bay toward West End. It's an attractive 1-mile stretch of white sand well used by joggers and walkers. A top-end resort sits on the eastern portion.

Smuggler's Cove   SECLUDED BEACH
At the island's northwestern tip, Smuggler's is a gorgeous cove with a bar, snack stand and good snorkeling off the beach.

★☆ Festivals & Events
The **BVI Music Festival** (www.bvimusicfestival.com) brings big-name acts such as Percy Sledge and Wyclef Jean to wail at Cane Garden Bay in late May.

🛏 Sleeping
You could feasibly stay at Cane Garden Bay's beachside digs without a car, but you'll need wheels to stay at any of the other lodgings.

[TOP CHOICE] Sugar Mill Hotel   BOUTIQUE HOTEL $$$
(☑495-4355, 800-462-8834; www.sugarmillhotel.com; Apple Bay; studios/ste from US$325/365; ✳🛜☒) In a league of its own for ambience, intimacy and customer service, this boutique hotel rises from the ruins of the Appleby Plantation that gave Apple Bay its name. Guests stay in the 21 studios and suites that hide on the steep hillside among mahogany trees, bougainvillea and palms. The property's centerpiece is its gourmet restaurant.

Heritage Inn   APARTMENTS $$$
(☑494-5842; www.heritageinnbvi.com; Windy Hill; 1-/2-bedroom apt US$200/315; ✳☒) High on Windy Hill between Cane Garden Bay and Carrot Bay, this property has nine spacious apartments that seem to hang out in thin air. If you like the feel of a self-contained oasis with a pool, sundeck, restaurant and bar, Heritage Inn could be for you. Minimum stay three nights.

Rhymer's Beach Hotel   HOTEL $$
(☑495-4639; www.canegardenbaybeachhotel.com; Cane Garden Bay; r US$100; ✳) Smack on the beach and right in the center of

the action, Rhymer's was one of the area's first inns. The big pink concrete building with its restaurant and laundry shows serious signs of hard use, but the price and energy of the place make up for it. Rooms are mostly studios with kitchenettes and patios.

Ole Works Inn
HOTEL $$

(☑495-4837; www.quitorymer.com; Cane Garden Bay; d with hill/beach view from US$110/145; ❋❀) Reggae master Quito Rymer built this bright-yellow, 18-room inn within the walls of a centuries-old rum factory. Rooms are fairly small and dated, though that may change as Quito has recently turned the property over to new managers.

Sebastian's on the Beach
HOTEL $$

(☑495-4212, 800-336-4870; www.sebastiansbvi. com; Little Apple Bay; r US$135-245; ❋☎) Well known for its friendly staff and its pretty stretch of beachfront, Sebastian's 26 motel-style rooms come in a wide range of sizes and locations (some on the beach, some not). Take a good look around before deciding: room decor and brightness vary even within the same price bracket. There's a good on-site restaurant.

Brewers Bay Campground
CAMPGROUND $

(☑494-3463; Brewers Bay; campsites/equipped tents US$20/40) Tortola's only commercial campground is around the bend from Cane Garden Bay, although it's a hell of a ride over zigzagging mountain roads. The sites sit under sea-grape trees and tall palms right on the beach. You can bring a tent or use the prepared sites (which include two cots, linens and a cook stove); the latter are a bit worn and gloomy, so you're better off with your own gear. Everyone shares the cold-water bathhouse and flush toilets. There's a beach bar for beer and other sustenance. Cash only.

✗ Eating & Drinking

Many Cane Garden Bay restaurants turn into bars at night, offering live music, dancing or just solid boozing time. Check the free weekly tabloid *Limin' Times* (www.limintimes.com) or the website **BVI Music** (www .bvimusic.com) to find out what's on.

⌁ TOP CHOICE Sugar Mill Restaurant
CARIBBEAN $$$

(☑495-4355; www.sugarmillhotel.com; Apple Bay; mains US$28-38; ❁dinner) Foodies salivate over the mod Caribbean concoctions such

as poached lobster and eggplant Creole. Owners Jeff and Jinx Morgan, contributing writers for *Bon Appétit* magazine, oversee the constantly changing menu that's served in the restored, candlelit boiling house of the plantation's rum distillery. Wines, cocktails and decadent desserts complete the sensory experience. Reservations are a must.

Mrs Scatliffe's Restaurant
CARIBBEAN $$

(☑495-4556; Carrot Bay; mains US$29-36; ❁dinner) Senior citizen Mrs Scatliffe serves West Indian dishes on her deck, using fruits and veggies she yanks straight from her garden. You must call for reservations before 5pm, since she'll be making the chicken-in-coconut or conch soup just for you. She's in the yellow building across from the primary school. Cash only.

Palm's Delight
CARIBBEAN $$

(☑495-4863; Carrot Bay; mains US$9-18; ❁dinner) Located right on the water's edge, this family-style West Indian restaurant serves up great *pates*, rotis, fish Creole and local ambience. Friday nights provide a lively scene, with families eating on the patio and a bar crowd watching cricket or baseball on the TV.

North Shore Shell Museum
CARIBBEAN $$

(☑495-4714; Carrot Bay; mains US$9-19; ❁breakfast, lunch & dinner) This zany mix of folk art gallery and eatery, owned by Egbert Donovan, specializes in delicious big breakfasts and grilled fish dinners. The staff often leads the patrons in making fungi music by blowing and banging on conch shells. Call before coming, as hours can be erratic.

Quito's Gazebo
SEAFOOD $$

(☑495-4837; Cane Garden Bay; mains US$16-33; ❁lunch & dinner, closed Mon) This beachside bar-restaurant takes its name from its owner, Quito Rymer, whose band has toured with Ziggy Marley. You can dance up a storm to Quito's reggae rhythms, and hundreds pack the restaurant on weekends to do just that. Rotis and fresh salads make for popular light luncheons. At night, grilled items such as snapper fill the menu.

Rhymer's
BURGERS, SEAFOOD $$

(☑495-4639; Cane Garden Bay; mains US$15-33; ❁breakfast, lunch & dinner) Beachside Rhymer's (attached to the eponymous hotel) serves a great breakfast. The dinner menu includes

BOMBA'S FOR FULL MOONS & MUSHROOMS

Bomba's Surfside Shack (☎495-4148; Cappoons Bay) near Apple Bay has achieved mythic status in the Caribbean for reasons including bras, booze, full moons and trippy mushrooms.

The place truly is a shack, built from a mishmash of license plates, surfboards and graffiti-covered signposts espousing carnal wisdom such as 'Wood is Good!'. Bras and panties are woven throughout, along with snapshots of topless women. Very often, sitting smack in the middle of these photos and wearing a wide grin along with his trademark sunglasses, is Bomba.

Bomba started his bar-restaurant more than 30 years ago to feed the surfers who still ride the waves curling out front. Today the shack is famous for its monthly full-moon parties, which feature an outdoor barbecue, live reggae and plenty of dancing and drinking. Bomba also serves free psychoactive mushroom tea (mushrooms grow wild on Tortola and are legal), and up to 500 people, both tourists and locals, show up for his bacchanals. Note to those who don't wish to end up topless in photos: mind your intake of tea and rum punch.

Even if you're not on the island during the full moon, the Bomba shack is a sight to behold. Stop by for a beer with the surfers.

fish, ribs and conch. The bar draws beachgoers seeking refreshment.

East End

Tortola's eastern end is a mix of steep mountains, remote bays and thickly settled West Indian communities. **Beef Island**, the large isle off the tip, is home to the BVI's only major airport, as well as an arts collective that ramps up during the full moon. A ferry dock lies within walking distance of the airport at **Trellis Bay**, where water taxis depart for Virgin Gorda and the out islands.

◉ Sights & Activities

Aragorn's Studio   ARTS CENTER
(www.aragornsstudio.com; Trellis Bay) Local metal sculptor Aragorn Dick-Read started his studio under the sea-grape trees fronting Trellis Bay, the broad beach just east of the airport. It grew to include space for potters, coconut carvers and batik makers, many of whom you can see at work in the now-sprawling arts center. Aragorn also hosts family-friendly full-moon parties.

Boardsailing BVI   WINDSURFING
(www.windsurfing.vi; Trellis Bay) It's the biggest windsurfing operator on the islands, with loads of gear for beginners to advanced sailors. Two-hour lessons take place out front in Trellis Bay; money-back guarantee if you aren't sailing by the end.

Josiah's Bay   SURFING BEACH
An undeveloped gem on the north shore near the East End, Josiah's Bay is a dramatic strand at the foot of a valley that has excellent surf with a point break in winter. Many say it offers Tortola's best surfing. Lifeguards patrol the water, and a couple of beach bars serve cold Red Stripes and snacks; they also rent boards. Several charming and inexpensive guesthouses lie inland on the valley slopes.

🛏 Sleeping

Serendipity House   APARTMENTS $$
(☎499-1999; www.serhouse.com; Josiah's Hill; apt US$90-205; ❄❋❖) For tropical seclusion about half a mile from Josiah's Bay, this is one of the best values on Tortola, with special deals for longer stays. Canadians Carol and Bill Campbell welcome travelers with the invitation to 'spend a vacation, not a fortune.' There are four units, ranging from an apartment to a two-bedroom villa, all with kitchens.

Tamarind Club Hotel   HOTEL $$
(☎495-2477; www.tamarindclub.com; Josiah's Hill; r incl breakfast US$139-199; ⊘closed Aug & Sep; ❄❋) Just 100yd down the hill from Serendipity House near Josiah's Bay, the eight rooms at this red-roofed, West Indian–style building surround a central garden and pool. The rooms have batik-print decor, but are a bit dark; each has a private veranda. The on-site restaurant serves

good local dishes, and the swim-up bar is a fine touch.

Beef Island Guest House   GUESTHOUSE $$
(495-2303; www.beefislandguesthouse.com; Trellis Bay; r incl breakfast & tax US$150) Located on Trellis Bay next to De Loose Mongoose restaurant, this place is a five-minute walk to the airport and therefore an excellent choice for anyone with a late arrival or early departure. The four rooms have unexpected character, with beam ceilings and carpeted floors; all come with a private bathroom and fan.

Near-D-Beach Limin' Bar & Hostel   HOSTEL $
(443-7833; www.josiahsbaybvi.com; Josiah's Bay; r with shared/private bathroom US$60/80) This no-frills spot caters mostly to surfers, since it's only a five-minute walk from the popular surfing beach. The three rooms each have a queen-size bed and simple furnishings; they all share gender-segregated, cold-water bathrooms and a game-filled common room. There's also a studio apartment with a private, hot-water bathroom and kitchenette. A funky bar (with snacks) is on-site. Cash only.

✖ Eating

Trellis Bay's cafes are good places to hang out if you're waiting for a flight or boat.

De Loose Mongoose   CAFE $$
(TOP CHOICE) (495-2303; www.beefislandguesthouse.com; Trellis Bay; mains US$15-25; ☺breakfast, lunch & dinner, closed Mon) Next to the Beef Island Guest House, this windsurfer hangout is a great place to have breakfast, eat lunch or watch the sunset over dinner. Try the conch fritters, arguably the BVI's best.

Secret Garden   CARIBBEAN $$
(495-1834; Josiah's Bay Plantation; mains US$19-33; ☺dinner, closed Tue) One of the most delightful places to eat on Tortola, Secret Garden sets its outdoor tables amid the distilling buildings of an old plantation. The imaginative menu ranges from grilled swordfish Creole to coconut chicken or Bajan flying-fish pie. Reservations required.

VIRGIN GORDA

POP 3500

It's certainly a testament to Virgin Gorda's awesomeness that a billionaire such as Richard Branson – who could live anywhere in the world – chooses this little patch of earth.

Of course, it should be noted he's not actually on Virgin Gorda, but has his very own personal island right offshore. But you get the point. And you should get to Virgin Gorda, an ideal blend of extraordinary sights, easy access, good restaurants and villas and, somehow, no rampant commercialism.

The giant granite rock formations of the Baths are the BVI's biggest tourist attraction, and guess what? They live up to the hype, especially when combined with the hike up, over, around and through them to Devil's Bay. Hikers can also summit Virgin Gorda Peak, relishing the cool breeze, and meander around wind-pounded Copper Mine National Park. Sea dogs can take ferries over to Bitter End Yacht Club and Saba Rock Resort to drink with the yachties.

❶ Getting There & Around

AIR **Virgin Gorda Airport** (495-5621) is on the Valley's east side, about 1 mile from Spanish Town. At the time of writing, only private charters were permitted to fly in. **Air Sunshine** (www.airsunshine.com), a commercial carrier with flights from St Thomas, is trying to change that. In the interim, it flies into Tortola's airport and provides a free ferry to Spanish Town.

BOAT Check the **BVI Welcome Guide** (www.bviwelcome.com) for schedules.

Ferries sail **between Spanish Town and Road Town**, Tortola almost every hour during the daytime (round-trip US$30, 30 minutes):
Smith's Ferry (494-4454; www.smithsferry.com)
Speedy's (495-5240; www.speedysbvi.com)

There's direct service **between Spanish Town and Charlotte Amalie**, St Thomas on Tuesday, Thursday and Saturday (round-trip US$70, 90 minutes):
Speedy's (495-5240; www.speedysbvi.com)

DON'T MISS

FIREBALL FULL-MOON PARTY

Aragorn's Studio and the Trellis Bay Kitchen combine to put on the **Trellis Bay Full Moon Party** (www.windsurfing.vi/fullmoon.htm), which is the artsy, family-friendly alternative to Bomba's raucous event. The party kicks off around 7pm with fungi music, stilt walkers and fire jugglers. At 9pm Aragorn sets his steel 'fireball sculptures' ablaze on the ocean – a must to see.

OUT ISLANDS

The BVI's 'out islands' (a Creole expression for remote or undeveloped cays) are a wonderful mix of uninhabited wildlife sanctuaries, luxurious hideaways for the rich and famous, and provisioning stops for sailors. Most are reachable only by charter or private boat. If you don't have your own vessel, hook up with a Tortola or Virgin Gorda day-sail tour (see destinations' Activities sections).

Norman Island

Since 1843, writers have alleged that treasure is buried on Norman Island, supposedly the prototype for Robert Louis Stevenson's book *Treasure Island*. It fits the bill: Norman is the BVI's largest uninhabited landmass.

Two fantastic beach bars lure boaters. The **William Thornton** (Willy T; ☎496-8603; www.williamthornton.com) is a schooner converted into a restaurant-bar and moored in the bight. On the beach, **Pirate's Bight** (☎496-7827; www.piratesbight.com) is an open-air pavilion. Both have good food and the owners often bring in live West Indian bands or just crank Bob Marley and Jimmy Buffett over high-voltage sound systems.

Weekends are always a huge party scene; as one local puts it, 'Everyone just gets [bleeping] mental.'

Peter Island

This lofty L-shaped island, about 4 miles south of Tortola, is the BVI's fifth-largest and home to the luxurious **Peter Island Resort** (☎495-2000, 800-346-4451; www.peter island.com; r from US$740; ✻@⑤⑤☒).

Anyone with reservations can come to the resort's **Tradewinds restaurant** (☎495-2000; mains US$25-55; ⊙dinner) for gourmet West Indian cuisine, or **Deadman's Bay Bar & Grill** (mains US$21-38; ⊙lunch & dinner) for wood-fired pizzas. The Peter Island ferry (round-trip US$20, free for restaurant customers) sails from Road Town; call for times and location.

Cooper Island

Lying about 4 miles south of Tortola, Cooper Island is a moderately hilly cay and is virtually undeveloped except for the **Cooper Island Beach Club** (☎495-9084; www.cooper -island.com), whose restaurant makes it a popular anchorage for cruising yachts. Divers also swarm to the island's surrounding wrecks and sites.

Salt Island

This T-shaped island is a forlorn place. The salt making (which gave the island its name) still goes on here, but the RMS *Rhone* is the big attraction. The *Rhone* crashed against the rocks off the southwest coast during a hurricane in 1867. Now a national park, the steamer's remains are extensive, making it one of the Caribbean's best wreck dives. See the boxed text, p251.

The Dogs

This clutch of six islands lies halfway between Tortola and Virgin Gorda. Protected by the BVI National Parks Trust, the Dogs are sanctuaries for birds and marine animals. The diving and snorkeling here are excellent.

Necker Island

Private **Necker Island** (www.neckerisland.virgin.com) belongs to Richard Branson, famous adventurer and scion of Virgin Atlantic Airways and Virgin Records. About 1 mile north of Virgin Gorda, Necker is one of the world's most luxurious retreats. If you've got US$53,000 you can rent it for the day (Branson not included, though submarine with driver is).

From **Trellis Bay/Beef Island**, Tortola. ferries sail to both **Spanish Town** (round-trip US$40) and **North Sound** (round-trip US$65) several times daily (except no service Sunday):

North Sound Express (☑495-2138) Reservations required.

CAR Virgin Gorda has several 4WD rental companies that will pick you up from the ferry and drop you off almost anywhere on the island. You'll pay US$55 to US$85 per day.

Mahogany Car Rentals (☑495-5469; www.mahoganycarrentalsbvi.com)

Speedy's Car Rental (☑495-5240; www.speedysbvi.com)

TAXI Taxi fares are set. The rate from the North Sound resorts or Gun Creek to Spanish Town is US$30 one-way; from the ferry dock to the Baths is US$8 round-trip. Reliable companies:

Andy's Taxis (☑495-5252/5160)

Mahogany Taxi Service (☑495-5469)

Spanish Town & the Valley

Spanish Town isn't a town so much as a long road with businesses strung along it. It's the commercial center of Virgin Gorda, and probably gets its name from a (severe) corruption of the English word 'penniston,' a blue woolen fabric used long ago for making slave clothing on the island, rather than from any Spanish connections. Islanders referred to their settlement as Penniston well into the 1850s.

The harbor dredged here in the 1960s is home to today's Yacht Harbour, the heart of Spanish Town. Overall the settlement is a sleepy place, but the mix of islanders, yachties and land travelers creates a festive vibe.

'The Valley' is the long rolling plain that covers the island's southern half, including Spanish Town.

◉ Sights & Activities

The Baths   PARK
(admission US$3; ☺sunrise-sunset) This collection of sky-high boulders, near the island's southwest corner, marks a national park and the BVI's most popular tourist attraction. The rocks – volcanic lava leftovers from up to 70 million years ago, according to some estimates – form a series of grottoes that flood with sea water. The area makes for unique swimming and snorkeling; the latter is distinctive as many boulders also lurk under water.

The Baths would easily live up to its reputation for greatness if it wasn't overshadowed by adjacent **Devil's Bay National Park** to the south, and the cool trail one must take to get there. Actually, there are two trails. The less exciting one takes off behind the taxis at the Baths' parking lot. But the trail you want leaves from the Baths' beach and goes through the 'Caves.' During the 20-minute trek, you'll clamber over boulders, slosh through tidal pools, squeeze into impossibly narrow passages and bash your feet against rocks. Then you'll drop out onto a sugar-sand beach.

While the Baths and environs stir the imagination, the places are often overrun with tourists. By 9am each morning fleets of yachts have moored off the coast, and visitors have been shuttled in from resorts and cruise ships. All you have to do, though, is come at sunrise or late in the afternoon, and you'll get a lot more elbow room.

The Baths' beach has bathrooms with showers, a snack shack and snorkel gear rental (US$10). Taxis run constantly between the park and ferry dock (round-trip US$8).

Spring Bay   SNORKELING BEACH
An excellent beach with national-park designation, Spring Bay abuts the Baths to the north. The beauty here is having a Baths-like setting but without the crowds. Hulking boulders dot the fine white sand. There's clear water and good snorkeling off the area called 'the Crawl' (a large pool enclosed by boulders and protected from the sea). Sea-grape trees shade a scattering of picnic tables, but that's the extent of the facilities.

To get here, watch for the Spring Bay sign just before Guavaberry Spring Bay Homes on the road to the Baths; turn off to reach a parking area.

Copper Mine National Park   PARK
(☺sunrise-sunset) You'll drive a heck of a winding road to reach this forlorn bluff at Virgin Gorda's southwest tip, but it's worth it to see the impressive stone ruins (including a chimney, cistern and mine-shaft house) that comprise the park. Cornish miners worked the area between 1838 and 1867 and extracted as much as 10,000 tons of copper, then abandoned the mine to the elements. A couple of trails meander through the ruins, and the hillside makes

an excellent place for a picnic as the blue sea pounds below.

Dive BVI
DIVING

(www.divebvi.com; 1-/2-tank dives US$85/110) This dive shop, with outlets at both Yacht Harbour and Leverick Bay, has several fast boats that take you diving at any of the BVI sites.

Boat Trips

Day-sail operators depart from Yacht Harbour and offer a variety of trips to Anegada and the out islands. The boats usually stop for snorkeling breaks and lunch somewhere (food is not included in the price, though beer and soda are).

Dive BVI
BOAT TRIPS

(www.divebvi.com; full-day trips from US$85) This dive operator also offers well-run snorkel trips aboard a catamaran.

Spirit of Anegada
BOAT TRIPS

(www.spiritofanegada.com; half-/full-day trips US$65/95) A red-sailed 44ft schooner.

Double 'D'
BOAT TRIPS

(www.doubledbvi.com; full-day trips from US$89) A 50ft sloop.

★ Festivals & Events

Spanish Town around the yacht harbor fills with *mocko jumbies* (costumed stilt walkers representing spirits of the dead), fungi bands, a food fair and parades for the **Virgin Gorda Easter Festival** (www.bvitourism.com), held Friday through Sunday during the Christian holiday (usually late March or April).

⊫ Sleeping

Lodging is pricey on Virgin Gorda, with no real budget options during high season.

TOP CHOICE Guavaberry Spring Bay
Homes
APARTMENTS **$$$**

(☑495-5227; www.guavaberryspringbay.com; apt US$235-300; @☂) A stone's throw from the Baths and plopped amid similar hulking boulders, Guavaberry's circular cottages come with one or two bedrooms, a kitchen, dining area and sun porch. The setting amazes. There's a common area with wi-fi (for a small fee), games, books and cable TV, and a commissary stocked with alcohol, snacks and meals to cook in your cottage. It's a short walk to both the Baths and Spring Bay beach.

Bayview Vacation
Apartments
APARTMENTS **$$**

(☑495-5329; www.bayviewbvi.com; apt US$140-165; ✳☂) Each of these apartments, behind Chez Bamboo restaurant, has two bedrooms, a full kitchen, dining facilities and an airy living room. It has a plain-Jane ambience, with faded rattan furnishings, but it can be a good deal, especially if you have three or four people. There is a roof deck for sunbathing and free shuttle pickup from the ferry docks.

Fischer's Cove Beach Hotel
HOTEL **$$**

(☑495-5252; www.fischerscove.com; d/cottage US$165/190) Surrounded by gardens and located just a few steps from the beach, Fischer's Cove has a collection of eight triangular-shaped cottages and a main hotel building with 20 no-frills studios. The cottages have full kitchens, but no phones, TVs or air-con (they're also located by a drainage ditch). The hotel units do have phones and TVs, and a few also have air-con. The popular open-air restaurant overlooks the property's beach. It's a 15-minute walk from the ferry dock.

Little Dix Bay
HOTEL **$$$**

(☑495-5555, 888-767-3966; www.littledixbay.com; r from US$750; ✳☂☀) This is the resort that rocketed Virgin Gorda to glory, and it remains the island's swankiest, celebrity-filled digs. An army of staff keeps the grounds and 98 rooms perfectly coiffed, and it wafts an overall South Seas vibe. Free use of water sports gear (Hobie Cats, kayaks, snorkel gear) is included. Wi-fi costs $20 per day.

✗ Eating & Drinking

Dinner reservations are a good idea. Some places charge an extra 5% to pay by credit card.

Mermaid's Dockside Bar &
Grill
SEAFOOD **$$**

(☑495-6663; mains US$16-27; ☉lunch & dinner) Mermaid's is indeed dockside, on a breezy pier over the true-blue water. It specializes in seafood with Spanish flair. Staff members grill your mahimahi, snapper or other fish right on the dock and plates it alongside rice and pigeon peas and lots of veggies. Sunset vistas compliment the casual, open-air vibe. It's located on the road leading west from the roundabout.

Thelma's Hideout
CARIBBEAN $$

(☑495-5646; mains US$17-25; ☺breakfast, lunch & dinner) Find this West Indian hangout on the side road leading to Little Dix Bay resort. Seating is in an open-air courtyard, and there is a stage where a band plays during high season. Thelma will serve you breakfast, but most travelers come here for her conch stew. You must make dinner reservations by 3pm.

Mad Dog
SANDWICH SHOP $

(☑495-5830; mains US$8-12; ☺10am-6pm; 🛜) Expatriates and tourists often gather at this airy little pavilion set among the rocks where the road ends at the Baths. They can't resist the fat sandwiches – turkey and bacon wins particular plaudits – to help take the edge off the killer, secret-recipe piña coladas.

Mine Shaft Cafe
SEAFOOD $$

(☑495-5260; www.mineshaftbvi.com; mains US$18-30; ☺lunch & dinner) You can't beat the location, high on a hill overlooking the Atlantic Ocean on Copper Mine Rd. The food is pretty good, too, including burgers, wraps and mains such as lobster in rum-lemon-cream sauce. If nothing else, come here for a view-tastic sunset cocktail.

Rock Cafe
ITALIAN $$

(☑495-5482; www.bvidining.com; mains US$20-38; ☺dinner) Nestled among the boulders at the traffic circle south of Spanish Town, this place has indoor and outdoor dining, plus a popular terrace bar that rocks with live music. The cuisine is mostly Italian, with pizzas, pastas and fish. Many locals think it bakes the best lobster on the island.

Bath & Turtle
PIZZA, BURGERS $$

(☑495-5239; mains US$14-21; ☺breakfast, lunch & dinner; 🛜) In a courtyard surrounded by the Yacht Harbour mall, this casual pub cooks up pizza, quesadillas and seared ahi tuna salad. At night it's a fun scene.

Buck's Food Market
SUPERMARKET

(☺7am-7pm) The island's main grocery store is located in Yacht Harbour's mall.

Information

The Yacht Harbour mall holds most of the island's services, including banks.

BVI'S BEST DIVING & SNORKELING

Top Five Dive Sites

» **Wreck of the RMS Rhone** This famous 310ft shipwreck sits in just 20ft to 80ft of water off Salt Island, making it an accessible wreck dive for all levels.

» **Blond Rock** A pinnacle between Dead Chest and Salt Islands, this coral ledge has many caves, crevices and deep holes.

» **Alice in Wonderland** This spot off Ginger Island has some of the best deep-water coral formations in the BVIs.

» **The Indians** Just off Pelican Island, three cone-shaped rock formations rise from 36ft underwater to 30ft above water.

» **Angel Reef** Off Norman Island, this site is a crossroads for species from different habitats, with shallow canyons rising to the surface.

Top Five Snorkel Sites

» **Dry Rocks East** Cooper Island's top-notch shallow spot offers lots of fish activity and, at times, challenging conditions.

» **The Caves** Three large caves on Norman Island feature shallow waters and many small fish, which in turn attract larger predators.

» **Loblolly Bay** Kick through a widespread area on remote Anegada with spotted eagle rays and barracudas.

» **The Baths** Huge boulders above and below the water create an otherworldly environment to explore on Virgin Gorda.

» **RMS Rhone – stern** Although most of the famed Salt Island shipwreck is in deep water, the stern section is shallow – you can see the bronze propeller, rudder, drive shaft and aft mast from the surface.

Chandlery Ship Store (Yacht Harbour mall; per 10min US$5; ⊙7am-5pm Mon-Fri, 8am-noon Sat) Has a couple of internet terminals.

Virgin Gorda Baths (www.virgingordabaths. com) Website for a tour operator, but it has good general information about the island, attractions and beaches.

North Sound & Around

Steep mountain slopes rise on Virgin Gorda's midsection, culminating at hike-worthy Virgin Gorda Peak. Beyond lies North Sound, a little settlement whose job is to serve the big resorts and myriad yachts anchored in the surrounding bays. A mini-armada of ferries tootle back and forth from the Sound's Gun Creek to Bitter End Yacht Club & Resort and Saba Rock Resort, both excellent for a happy-hour drink and sea views at their bars, even if you're not staying there.

◎ Sights & Activities

Savannah Bay   WALKING BEACH
A short distance north of the Valley, Savannah Bay features more than a mile of white sand. Except for the beaches of Anegada, no other shore provides such opportunities for long, solitary walks. Sunsets here can be fabulous. A small sign off North Sound Rd points the way to a little parking area.

Mahoe Bay, **Mountain Trunk Bay**, **Nail Bay** and **Long Bay** unfurl to the north of Savannah and are dotted with resorts.

Gorda Peak National Park   PARK
(⊙sunrise-sunset) At 1359ft, Gorda Peak is the island's highest point. Two well-marked trails lead to the summit off North Sound Rd, and make a sweet hike. If you are coming from the Valley, the first trailhead you see marks the start of the longer trail (about 1.5 miles). It's easier to begin at the higher-up trailhead, from where it's a 30-minute, half-mile walk to the crest. You'll see Christmas orchids, bromeliads (pineapple family members) and hummingbirds. The lookout tower at the top provides vistas of the entire archipelago.

⌂ Sleeping & Eating

For luxury villas, try **Virgin Gorda Villa Rentals** (☑495-7421, 800-848-7081; www.virgin gordabvi.com), which manages properties at Leverick Bay and Mahoe Bay.

Leverick Bay Resort   RESORT $$
(☑495-7421, 800-848-7081; www.leverickbay. com; r from US$149; ❋🛜❋) When you see the purple, green and turquoise buildings splashed up the hillside, you'll know you've arrived. The 14 rooms are dandy, each with two double beds, rattan furnishings, free wi-fi and a private balcony. Then there's the beach, marina, tennis court, dive shop, spa, market, internet cafe… Oh, and the popular restaurant, too; it's open for breakfast, lunch and dinner (mains US$30 to $45) for wood-fired pizzas, lobster ravioli and other Italian dishes. The Friday-night pig roast with stilt walkers and live music draws throngs of locals and visitors.

Saba Rock Resort   BOUTIQUE HOTEL $$
(☑495-9966/7711; www.sabarock.com; r incl breakfast from US$150; ❋🛜) On a fleck of island just offshore from Bitter End Yacht Club & Resort, Saba Rock is a charismatic boutique hotel with eight rooms, a restaurant and a bar. The latter is a very cool place for a drink, especially during happy hour from 4:30pm to 5:30pm. Check out all the shipwreck booty on-site, such as the cannon from the RMS *Rhone*. Also keep an eye out for big fish and turtles lurking in the water by your table. Come over on the free ferry from Gun Creek or Bitter End; call ☑495-7711 to arrange pickup.

Bitter End Yacht Club & Resort   RESORT $$$
(☑494-2746, 800-872-2392; www.beyc.com; d incl meals US$760-1100; @🛜❋🛝) This all-inclusive resort at the east end of North Sound has 85 hillside villas adorned with batik bedspreads and teak floors. Some villas have hammocks, wrap-around verandas and are open to the trade winds; others have air-con and decks; none have TVs. Rates include three meals a day and unlimited use of the resort's bountiful equipment for sailing, windsurfing, kayaking and much more.

The water-sports facilities and Yacht Club bar are open to the paying public. Many people also come to the Clubhouse Grille for the monumental buffet (brunch/dinner US$30/45). Whatever the pretense, you definitely should make the trip to Bitter End. A free ferry departs Gun Creek on the half hour.

Mango Bay Resort   RESORT $$
(☑495-5672; www.mangobayresort.com; apt from US$195; ❋) Located on the beach at

Mahoe Bay, this resort is a compound of 12 Italian-style duplex villas.

ⓘ Getting There & Away

North Sound Express (☏495-2138) runs ferries here from the airport at Trellis Bay/Beef Island, Tortola.

JOST VAN DYKE

POP 200

Jost (pronounced 'yoast') is a little island with a big personality. It may only take up 4 sq miles of teal-blue sea, but its good-time reputation has spread thousands of miles beyond. A lot of that is due to calypsonian and philosopher Foxy Callwood, the island's main man. But more on him later.

For over 400 years Jost has been an oasis for seafarers and adventurers. A Dutch pirate (the island's namesake) used the island as a base in the 17th century. In the 18th century it became a homestead for Quakers escaping religious tyranny in England. Quaker surnames, such as Lettsome and Callwood, survive among the islanders, mostly descendants of freed Quaker slaves.

In the late 1960s free-spirited boaters found Jost's unspoiled shores, and Foxy built a bar to greet them. The tide ebbed and flowed for a quarter century, and not much changed. Electricity arrived in 1991 and roads were cut a few years later.

Though locals may all have cell phones and websites, and Jost is no secret to yachters and glitterati (Jimmy Buffett and Keith Richards stop by), the island's green hills and blinding beaches remain untrammeled by development. As one local says, 'When Main Street is still a beach, you know life is good.' Hear, hear!

The island has no banks and relatively few accommodations. Many businesses shut down in September and early October.

ⓘ Getting There & Around

BOAT Most visitors arrive by yacht. Landlubbers can get here by ferry from Tortola or St John. Ferries land at the pier on the west side of Great Harbour. It's about a 10-minute walk from the pier to the town center.

New Horizon Ferry (☏495-9278; round-trip US$25) Sails five times daily to/from Tortola's West End (twice in the morning, three times in the afternoon); 25-minute trip; cash only.

Inter-Island (☏340-776-6597; www.interislandboatservices.vi; round-trip US$70) Sails twice daily to/from Red Hook, St Thomas and Cruz Bay, St John. It leaves Jost at 9:15am and 3pm. No service Wednesday or Thursday.

Dohm's Water Taxi (☏340-775-6501; www.watertaxi-vi.com) A customized, much pricier way to get between Jost and St John or St Thomas.

CAR A car is more of a luxury than necessity on Jost. Expect to pay US$60 to US$80 per day for a 4WD.

Abe & Eunicey (☏495-9329)
Paradise Jeep Rental (☏495-9477)

TAXI Taxis wait by the ferry dock. Fares are set. It costs US$10 per person to White Bay, US$12 to Little Harbour.

Great Harbour

In Jost's foremost settlement, Main St is a beach lined with hammocks and open-air bar-restaurants – which might give you a hint as to the vibe here. Kick off your shoes, then join Foxy and friends to let the good times roll.

Other than hanging out, there's not much to do besides stop by **JVD Scuba** (☏495-0271; www.jostvandykescuba.com), which can set you up with ecotours, kayak rentals and dives.

🛏 Sleeping & Eating

A list of favorite spots follows, but there are plenty more to choose from – wander down Main St to have a look.

Ali Baba's   GUESTHOUSE $$

(☏495-9280; www.alibabasheavenlyroomsbvi.com; r from US$160) This long-standing restaurant recently began offering rooms on its 2nd floor. The compact, whitewashed, wicker-furnished units face the beach and have a wind-cooled balcony from which to view the action. Given the location, noise can sometimes be an issue. The **restaurant** (mains US$22-35; ⊗breakfast, lunch & dinner) has a lazy, down-island atmosphere on its open-air patio. Patrons come for fresh fish and the Monday-night pig roast.

Sea Crest Inn   APARTMENTS $$

(☏495-9024, 340-775-6389; seacrestinn@hotmail.com; apt from US$145; ❄) The gracious Ivy Chinnery Moses has four large studio apartments, each with a kitchenette, TV, queen-size bed, private bathroom and balcony. It's just east of Foxy's.

DON'T MISS

SHIP AHOY

No, it's not the booze playing tricks with your eyes. If you walk 'round back of Foxy's complex, you really do see a 32ft wooden sloop rising from the yard. It's the handiwork of the **JVD Preservation Society** (www.jvdps.org) or, more accurately, the local teenagers employed by the society to construct the *Endeavor II*.

It's part of a nonprofit project to provide Jost's kids with traditional boat-building skills and to keep them from straying into off-island temptations. The society pays the boys and girls for their efforts, they stay on the island and learn a time-honored trade, and in the process Jost preserves its culture.

The group has been hammering away since 2004; the *Endeavor II* is scheduled for completion, er, sometime soon. The kids will then learn to sail the sloop, as well as study local marine science and conservation.

Check **Sloop News** (www.sloopnews .org) for reports of their progress.

TOP CHOICE Foxy's Tamarind Bar
BURGERS, SEAFOOD $$

(☑495-9258; www.foxysbar.com; mains US$22-42; ⊙lunch & dinner) You probably heard about him long before you arrived. So who is this Foxy? Well, he's Foxy (Philician) Callwood, born on Jost in 1938, and he single-handedly put the island on the map with his beach bar. Local bands play several nights a week (usually Thursday through Saturday) in season and draw a mix of islanders and party animals off the boats. The light fare is a mix of rotis and darn good burgers, while the dinner mains are mostly meat and seafood. Foxy has his own microbrewery onsite, so fresh tap beers accompany the food. The best time to catch Foxy hanging out and singing his improvisational calypso is around 10am.

Corsairs
PIZZA, SEAFOOD $$

(☑495-9294; www.corsairsbvi.com; mains US$25-40; ⊙breakfast, lunch & dinner) Corsairs provides a variation on the usual seafood theme with a menu of pizzas and pastas, along with eclectic Tex-Mex, Thai and other fusion dishes. Most incorporate seafood in some fashion, including fish tacos, shrimp fettuccine and coconut-pumpkin-sauced lobster. The bar hosts limbo contests and the BVI's only Jägermeister machine (you've been warned...).

Christine's Bakery
BAKERY $

(☑495-9281; mains US$3-10; ⊙breakfast & lunch) Christine has the settlement filled with the scent of banana bread, coconut and coffee by 8am. She also rents out a couple of simple rooms (from US$85) above the bakery.

White Bay

Wriggle your toes in the crazy-white sand, sip a Painkiller and watch people stumble in off yachts at Jost's most striking beach. It's a primo place to stay, thanks to its multibudget lodging options and highly entertaining bars. The long white crescent is a hilly, 1-mile, bun-burning walk from Great Harbour.

🛏 Sleeping & Eating

TOP CHOICE White Bay Campground
CAMPGROUND $

(☑495-9358, 340-513-1095; www.ivanscamp ground.com; campsites/equipped tents US$20/40, cabins US$65-75) It's one of the Virgin Islands' most popular stops for backpackers. Ivan, the owner, mixes it up by offering bare sites (the best of the bunch, right on the beach, where you can string your hammock between sea-grape trees), equipped platform tents (with beds and linens) and cabins (add electricity along with the beds and linens). Everyone shares the communal kitchen and cold-water bathhouse. The tents, cabins and facilities are very barebones, which may explain why Ivan added a couple of apartments with private bathrooms (from US$150).

Ivan's Stress-Free Bar is a Jost institution. If no one is around you simply grab your own drinks at the shell-strewn bar using the honor system. The Thursday-night cookouts (fish, chicken and ribs) draw a crowd.

TOP CHOICE Perfect Pineapple
GUESTHOUSE $$

(☑495-9401; www.perfectpineapple.com; ste from US$160; ❋) Foxy's son Greg owns this property set on a steep hill back from the beach. The three one-bedroom suites each have a full kitchen and private porch with ocean views. There are also a couple of larger cottages on-site. The family owns Gertrude's restaurant down on the beach if you don't want to cook your own meals.

Sandcastle Hotel
HOTEL **$$$**

(☑495-9888; www.soggydollar.com; d US$285-310) Situated smack on the beach, the Sandcastle offers four cottages and two hotel rooms, all sans phone and TV (and only the hotel rooms have air-con). The grounds hold the infamous **Soggy Dollar Bar**, which takes its name from the sailors swimming ashore to spend wet bills. It's also the bar that created the Painkiller, the BVI's delicious-yet-lethal cocktail of rum, coconut, pineapple, orange juice and nutmeg. The restaurant offers a four-course gourmet candlelit dinner for US$40 per person.

White Bay Villas & Seaside Cottages
APARTMENTS **$$$**

(☑410-571-6692, 800-778-8066; www.jostvandyke. com; cottages per week from US$2000; ✿@⌨) It rents out beachfront villas, some private and some with shared common areas. Rentals typically are for weekly stays, but you might snag a three- or five-night opening.

One Love Bar & Grill
BURGERS, SEAFOOD **$$**

(☑495-9829; www.onelovebar.com; mains US$14-22; ⊗lunch & dinner) Foxy's son Seddy owns this reggae-blasting beach bar. He'll wow you with his magic tricks, and certainly magic is how he gets the place to hold together – old buoys, life preservers and other beach junk form its 'walls.'

Little Harbour

This is Jost's quieter side, with just a few businesses. Little Harbour's east edge has a thin, steep strand of white sand perfect for sunbathing and swimming in water totally protected from wind and waves.

Bubbly Pool is a natural whirlpool formed by odd rock outcrops. When waves crash in, swimmers experience bubbling water like that of a Jacuzzi. Don't worry: it's enclosed and safe. Reach it via a goat trail from Foxy's Taboo restaurant (about a 20-minute walk).

✖ Eating & Drinking

A new bakery was slated to open behind Foxy's Taboo, which should be handy for picnic provisions en route to Bubbly Pool.

Foxy's Taboo
BURGERS, SEAFOOD **$$**

(☑495-0218; mains US$13-25; ⊗lunch & dinner) Foxy teams up with daughter Justine at Foxy's Taboo to serve easy, breezy dishes such as pizza and pepper-jack cheeseburgers for lunch, and more sophisticated fare (say lobster-stuffed tilapia) for dinner, all accompanied by Foxy's microbrews. Taboo sits in a scenic dockside building by Diamond Cay National Park.

Sidney's Peace and Love
BURGERS, SEAFOOD **$$**

(☑495-9271; mains US$20-45; ⊗lunch & dinner) The specialty here is lobster, but Sidney's serves up plenty of West Indian fish dishes, along with burgers and barbecue. Pour your own drinks to go with the goods at the honor bar. T-shirts left behind by visiting revelers decorate the rafters. Saturday night rocks particularly hard with charter-yacht crews.

Harris' Place
BURGERS, SEAFOOD **$$**

(☑495-9302; mains US$19-40; ⊗breakfast, lunch & dinner; ☎) Amiable Cynthia Jones runs this harborside pavilion known for homey comfort food. Burgers, pork, ribs, chicken and fruit smoothies make appearances. On Monday night, feast on all-you-can-eat lobster in garlic butter sauce.

ANEGADA

POP 200

Anegada is a killer island. Literally. It takes its name from the Spanish word for 'drowned' or 'flooded,' and that's what it did to more than 300 ships in the early years – it sunk them. The island is so low (28ft above sea level at its highest) that mariners couldn't see it to get their bearings until they were trapped in the surrounding coral maze known as Horseshoe Reef.

Today it's the salt ponds rife with flamingos, blooming cacti and giant rock iguanas that will slay you (figuratively, of course!). You can dive on many of the shipwrecks, or snorkel from ridiculously blue-watered beaches such as Loblolly Bay and Flash of Beauty.

The ferry takes only 1½ hours to reach this easternmost Virgin, about 12 miles from Virgin Gorda, but you'll think you've landed on another planet. Its desert landscape looks that different, and its wee clutch of restaurants and guesthouses are that baked-in-the-sun mellow. It's a mysterious, magical and lonesome place to hang your hammock for a stretch.

Anegada has no banks, so stock up before you get here.

ℹ Getting There & Around

AIR Tiny **Captain Auguste George Airport** lies in the island's center. There is no commercial service, only charter planes from Tortola and Virgin Gorda. **Fly BVI** (www.bviaircharters.com) and **Island Birds** (www.islandbirds.com) offer day-trip packages for around US$155.

BICYCLE & SCOOTER If you feel like you have the stamina to ride on rough, dusty roads in the hot sun (not an easy feat), you can rent a bike near the ferry dock at **Lil Bit** (☑495-9932; per day US$20), which also rents scooters (per day US$40 to US$50).

BOAT Road Town Fast Ferry (☑494-2323; www.roadtownfastferry.com; round-trip US$45) sails from Road Town, Tortola on Monday, Wednesday and Friday at 6:45am and 3:30pm; it departs Anegada at 8:30am and 5pm. The boat makes a quick stop at Spanish Town, Virgin Gorda, en route. Many travelers use this public ferry to do a day trip.

CAR 4WD rentals cost about US$75 per day at the **Anegada Reef Hotel** (☑495-8002; www. anegadareef.com) by the ferry dock. Roads are unpaved sand, other than a short stretch between the dock and the Settlement.

TAXI Taxis wait by the ferry dock. A three-hour island tour costs around US$55. Shuttles (per person round-trip US$8) run to the beaches from the Anegada Reef Hotel.

West End

If you take the ferry to Anegada, you'll arrive at Setting Point, by the Anegada Reef Hotel, which serves as the island's unofficial information center. If you're interested in **deep-sea fishing** inquire at the hotel's office, or contact **Danny's Bonefishing** (☑441-6334; www.dannysbonefishing.com; per half/full day US$300/500) to cast on the nearby flats.

The large salt pond at the island's west end is home to a flock of flamingos, which biologists reintroduced to Anegada in 1992. The BVI National Parks Trust designated **Flamingo Pond** and its surrounding wetlands as a bird sanctuary; you can also see egrets, terns and ospreys nesting and feeding in the area.

Secluded **Cow Wreck Bay** stretches along the island's northwest end and offers good **snorkeling** in its shallow waters; **kayaks** (per day US$50) are available, too.

🛏 Sleeping & Eating

TOP CHOICE Cow Wreck Villas APARTMENTS $$$
(☑495-8047; www.cowwreckbeach.com; 1-/2-bedroom apt US$250/375; ❋) You want peace and quiet? It'll just be you and the wandering bovines who share the grounds at Cow Wreck. Three sunny yellow-and-green cottages front the perfect, hammock-strewn beach. The open-air **restaurant** (mains US$24-53; ☺lunch & dinner) features lobster, conch and shellfish cooked on the outdoor grill.

Neptune's Treasure HOTEL $$
(☑495-9439; www.neptunestreasure.com; s/d from US$108/148; ❋🐾) The nine simple, color-washed rooms sit right on the sand and garner lots of loyal patrons. The rooms surround a **restaurant** (mains US$22-50; ☺breakfast, lunch & dinner) that has a meat-and-seafood menu similar to the island's other waterfront establishments, but with one difference: it's served in an air-conditioned dining room rather than the great outdoors. It's a 15-minute walk west from the ferry dock.

Anegada Beach Cottages APARTMENTS $$$
(☑495-9234; www.anegadabeachcottages.com; apt from US$250) Pomato Point is the site of these three concrete bungalows on stilts. They're the island standard – unfussy, clean, on the beach, with a kitchen. The difference here is a little extra peace and privacy. The on-site **Pomato Point Restaurant** (mains US$26-50; ☺lunch & dinner) has a cool 'museum' to explore (basically a side room that exhibits a bizarre mix of archaeological relics and shipwreck items owner Wilfred Creque collected from local waters).

Anegada Reef Hotel HOTEL $$
(☑495-8002; www.anegadareef.com; d with garden/ocean view US$175/200; ❋@) The island's first and largest hotel, this seaside lodge by the ferry dock has the feel of a classic out-island fishing camp. The property's 16 rooms and two-bedroom villas are nothing fancy, but the fishing dock, **restaurant** (mains US$22-50; ☺breakfast, lunch & dinner) and beach bar here are Anegada's social epicenter. A lot of yachts pull up to join the party, while fish and lobster sizzle on the grill. For those on budgets: if you ask nicely, the owners will let you pitch a tent (US$20) in the garden.

TOP CHOICE Potter's by the Sea SEAFOOD $$$
(☑495-9182; www.pottersbythesea.com; mains US$25-50; ☺dinner; 🐾) Potter's is the first

place you stumble into when departing the ferry dock. Potter lived in Queens, New York, and worked in the restaurant biz there for years, so he knows how to make customers feel at home while serving them ribs, fettuccine, curried shrimp and lobster. Graffiti and T-shirts cover the open-air walls; live bands occasionally play.

Pam's Kitchen & Bakery BAKERY $
(✆495-9237; mains US$7-12; ⊙8am-5pm) At her bakery next to Neptune's Treasure, Pam cranks out loaves of herb bread, key lime pies, cinnamon rolls and brownies. It's a terrific breakfast stop for an egg-stuffed sandwich, or for a lunchtime savory snack like a burger or fish *pate*. Her homemade hot sauce gives a jolt to local conch and fish.

East End

The **Settlement**, Anegada's only town, lies on the East End. It's a picture of dead cars (you can get them onto the island, but you can't get them off), laundry drying in the breeze and folks feeding goats and chickens. There are a couple of teensy shops where you can buy food and supplies.

The **Rock Iguana Nursery** (admission free; ⊙8am-4pm) sits behind the government administration building; just let yourself in. The Parks Trust started the facility because feral cats were eating the island's baby iguanas, endangering the rare species. So workers now bring the babes to the nursery's cages to grow safely. After two years, they're big enough to be released back into the wild, where they'll sprout to around 5ft from tip to tail.

Top beaches with thatched-umbrella shelters and bar-restaurants include **Loblolly Bay** on the northeast shore, about 2 miles from the Settlement. You can snorkel over a widespread area with spotted eagle rays and barracudas. **North Shore Divers** (www.diveanegada.com) has a shop on-site for snorkel gear rental (per hour $5); it can arrange local shipwreck dives, as well. Snorkeling at **Flash of Beauty**, just east of Loblolly, is across a more compact area but with bigger coral and lots of funny-looking fish.

Aubrey Levons' tiki-esque restaurant-bar **Big Bamboo** (✆495-2019; mains US$14-40; ⊙lunch & dinner) is on the beach at Loblolly Bay's west end and always packs a crowd. It specializes in island recipes for lobster, fish and chicken.

> **LOBSTER LOWDOWN**
>
> Cracking an Anegada lobster is a tourist rite of passage. Every restaurant serves the massive crustaceans, usually grilled on the beach in a converted oil drum and spiced with the chef's secret seasonings. Because the critters are plucked fresh from the surrounding waters, you must call ahead by 4pm to place your order so each restaurant knows how many to stock. Most places charge around US$50 to indulge. Note that lobster fishing is prohibited from August 1 through November 1 so stocks can replenish, thus they're not on menus (nor is conch) during that time.

After you finish snorkeling, climb up to shore to **Flash of Beauty Restaurant** (✆495-8014, 441-5815; mains US$10-40; ⊙lunch & dinner), where the staff awaits with sandwiches, burgers, conch stew and, yep, lobster (it's usually a bit lower-priced here than elsewhere on the island). The staff also makes a mean 'bushwhacker' – a milkshake-esque drink using seven liquors.

Locals come to small, tin-roofed **Dotsy's Bakery & Sandwich Shop** (✆495-9667; mains US$6-12; ⊙8:30am-7pm) in the Settlement for her fresh-baked breads, breakfasts, fish-and-chips, burgers and pizzas.

UNDERSTAND THE BRITISH VIRGIN ISLANDS

History
Columbus & the Pirates

On Christopher Columbus' second trip to the Caribbean in 1493, Caribs led him to an archipelago of pristine islands that he dubbed Santa Ursula y Las Once Mil Vírgenes (St Ursula and the 11,000 Virgins), in honor of a 4th-century princess raped and murdered, along with 11,000 maidens, in Cologne by marauding Huns.

By 1595 the famous English privateers Sir Francis Drake and Jack Hawkins were using the Virgin Islands as a staging ground for attacks on Spanish shipping. In the wake of Drake and Hawkins came French corsairs and Dutch freebooters. All knew that the Virgin Islands had some of the most secure and unattended harbors in the West Indies. Places like Sopers Hole at Tortola's West End and the Bight at Norman Island were legendary pirates' dens.

While the Danes settled on what is now the US Virgin Islands, the English had a firm hold on today's BVI. The middle island of St John remained disputed territory until 1717, when the Danish side claimed it for good. The Narrows between St John and Tortola has divided the eastern Virgins (BVI) from the western Virgins (USVI) for more than 250 years.

Queen Elizabeth & the Offshore Companies

Following WWII, British citizens in the islands clamored for more independence. In 1949 BVI citizens demonstrated for a representative government and got a so-called presidential legislature the next year. By 1967 the BVI had become an independent colony of Britain, with its own political parties, a legislative council and an elected premier (with elections every four years). Queen Elizabeth II also made her first royal visit to the BVIs in 1967, casting a glow of celebrity on the islands that they enjoy to this day. Royal family members still cruise through every few years.

In the mid-1980s the government had the shrewd idea of offering offshore registration to companies wishing to incorporate in the islands. Incorporation fees – along with tourism – now prop up the economy. According to a recent survey done by KPMG, around 41% of all the offshore companies in the world can be found in the BVI. Some locals laughingly call their financial services industry 'legal money laundering,' and while that's not quite the case (although odd, one must admit, that this population of 25,000 people hosts 450,000 active registered companies), it has created an unusual island population infused with foreign accountants, trust lawyers and investment brokers.

The offshore business fuels local politics, as well. In the territory's last elections in 2007, the VI Party won on promises to be more inward focused and to help the 'little man.' Its main competition is the National Democratic Party, which looks toward outside interests and development. The next election will be in fall 2011, and it is expected to be tight.

Culture

Despite the name, apart from little touches like Cadbury chocolate, the culture of the British Virgin Islands is West Indian to the core. The population is a mix of professional people working in financial services, folks working the tourist trade or raising livestock, and adventurers whose biochemistry is intricately tied to the seas. The official ethnic breakdown is 82% black, 7% white and the remainder mixed, East Indian or other.

The BVI have one of the Caribbean's most stable economies. The per-capita GDP is US$38,500 – higher than the UK, according to UN statistics. In general, most people live quite comfortably.

Some visitors complain that the locals (particularly on Tortola) are unfriendly. The demeanor is not rude so much as reserved.

FUNGI MUSIC

Fungi (*foon*-ghee, also an island food made of cornmeal) is the BVI's local folk music. It uses homemade percussion such as washboards, ribbed gourds and conch shells to accompany a singer. The full-moon festivals at Aragorn's Studio and Bomba's Surfside Shack are good places to hear it live. In addition, Road Town hosts the **VI Fungi Fest** (www.vifungifest.com; ☾mid-Nov), which brings musicians from around the islands for a weekend of nonstop concerts.

Landscape & Wildlife
The Land

The BVI consist of more than 40 islands and cays. On most, steep mountains dominate the island interiors. The one exception is easternmost Anegada, which is a flat coral atoll. Sage Mountain on Tortola is the highest point on the islands, at 1716ft.

Thousands of tropical plant varieties grow on the islands, and a short drive can transport a nature lover between entirely different ecosystems. Mangrove swamps, coconut groves and sea-grape trees dominate the coast, while mountain peaks support

» **Electricity** 110 volts; North American–style plugs have two (flat) or three (two flat, one round) pins.

» **Newspapers** The *BVI Beacon* and *StandPoint* are the BVI's main newspapers; they're published weekly. BVI News (www.bvinews.com) offers free daily content online. The free, weekly *Limin' Times* has entertainment listings.

» **Radio** ZBVI (780AM) airs talk and music from Tortola, including BBC broadcasts.

» **Smoking** Smoking is banned in all restaurants, bars and other public venues.

» **Weights & Measures** The islands use imperial measurements. Distances are in feet and miles; gasoline is measured in gallons.

wet forest with mahogany, lignum vitae, palmetto and more than 30 varieties of wild orchid.

Islanders also grow and collect hundreds of different roots and herbs as ingredients for 'bush medicine.' Psychoactive mushrooms grow wild (and are consumed) on the islands, particularly on Tortola.

Wildlife

Few land mammals are natives; most were accidentally or intentionally introduced. Virtually every island has a feral population of goats and donkeys, and some islands have wild pigs, horses, cats and dogs.

More than 200 species of bird inhabit the islands, adding bright colors and a symphony of sound to the tropical environment. A few snake species (none of which are poisonous) slither around, along with a host of small and not-so-small lizards, including the 5ft-long rock iguanas of Anegada and the common green iguana found throughout the islands. Anoles and gecko lizards are ubiquitous, and numerous species of toad and frog populate the islands.

Environmental Issues

Rapid urbanization, deforestation, soil erosion, mangrove destruction and a lack of freshwater keep environmentalists wringing their hands with worry. On Tortola, almost all of the flat land has been developed, and houses hang on mountain slopes like Christmas ornaments. High population growth and density have kept sewage treatment plants in a constant scramble to prevent the islands from soiling themselves.

Desalination plants make fresh water out of sea water and without them the islands would seriously lack water. When a storm strikes, islands lose power and diesel facilities shut down, forcing islanders to use rainwater cisterns.

Prior years of overfishing have put conch and lobster in a precarious situation. Currently, fishing for these creatures is not allowed from August 1 through November 1 so stocks can replenish.

Environmental concerns have resulted in the formation of the BVI National Parks Trust, which protects 15 parks and six islands, including the Dogs and Fallen Jerusalem, which are excellent dive sites. The entire southwest coast of Virgin Gorda is a collection of national parks that includes the giant boulder formations at the Baths.

SURVIVAL GUIDE

Directory A–Z

Accommodations

Accommodations in the BVI range from moderately priced guesthouses to swanky resorts. The **BVI Tourist Board** (www.bvitourism.com) publishes listings online.

Peak season is winter, from mid-December through April, when prices are highest. It's best to book ahead during this time, as rooms can be scarce. Some lodgings close in September, the heart of low season.

While air-conditioning is widely available, it is not a standard amenity, even at top-end places. If you want it, be sure to ask about it when you book.

Rental accommodations are widely available, ranging toward the top end for costs (though you might find a few one-bed places for US$250 per night). The following companies rent properties in the BVI:

Areana Villas (☑494-5864; www.areanavillas.com)

Caribbean Villas & Resorts (☎340-776-6152, 800-338-0987; www.caribbeanvilla.com)

McLaughlin Anderson Luxury Villas (☎340-776-0635, 800-537-6246; www.mclaughlin anderson.com)

Purple Pineapple (☎305-396-1586; www .purplepineapple.com)

Tropical Care Services (☎495-6493; www .tropicalcareservices.com)

Also check **Vacation Rental by Owner** (www.vrbo.com). Many BVI visitors say it provides the best results since you work out all the details with the property owners themselves.

Prices listed in this chapter are for peak-season travel and, unless stated otherwise, do not include taxes (which are typically 17%).

$	budget	less than US$100
$$	midrange	US$100 to US$300
$$$	top end	more than US$300

Activities

Sailing is the BVI's main claim to fame; see p263 to get on board. Clear water, secluded coves and shipwrecks make for primo diving and snorkeling (p251). Surfing and windsurfing are also popular at sites such as Josiah's Bay and Trellis Bay on Tortola's East End (p246).

BVI Scuba Organization (www.bviscuba.org) Links to dive sites and dive shops.

BVI Charter Yacht Society (www.bvicrewed yachts.com) Lists BVI companies and prices.

BVI Mountain Bike Club Organizes races and social events; look for the club on Facebook.

Business Hours

The list below provides 'normal' opening hours for businesses. Reviews throughout this chapter show specific hours only if they vary from these standards. Note, too, that hours can vary by season. Our listings depict peak season (December through April) operating times.

Many places close on Sunday.

Banks 9am-3pm Mon-Thu, to 5pm Fri

Bars & pubs noon-midnight

General office hours 8am-5pm Mon-Fri

Restaurants breakfast 7-11am, lunch 11am-2pm, dinner 5-9pm daily; some open for brunch 10am-2pm Sun

Shops 9am-5pm Mon-Sat

Children

Many resorts offer children's programs and babysitting services. Because the British Virgin Islands is such a big yachting and sailing destination, you'll see a lot of families around the marinas.

On Virgin Gorda, **Tropical Nannies** (www.tropicalnannies.com) provides babysitting services by trained, professional nannies. They'll come to your hotel or take the kids off your hands starting at US$20 per hour.

Embassies & Consulates

There are no foreign embassies or consulates in the BVI. The closest cache is in nearby San Juan, Puerto Rico.

Food

Price ranges in this chapter denote the cost of a main dish for dinner.

$	budget	less than US$12
$$	midrange	US$12 to US$30
$$$	top end	more than US$30

Gay & Lesbian Travelers

West Indian taboos on the gay and lesbian lifestyle are slow to crumble, so while there are gay islanders, you're not likely to meet many who are 'out,' nor are you likely to see public displays of affection among gay couples.

Health

Pesky mosquitoes and no see 'ums (tiny sand flies) bite throughout the islands, so slather on insect repellent. Tap water is safe to drink.

Internet Access

Internet cafes cluster in the main tourist areas, often near marinas and cruise-ship docks. Access generally costs US$5 per 30 minutes.

Wi-fi is widely available. Most lodgings have it for free in their public areas (though it is less common in rooms), as do many restaurants and bars in the main towns.

Legal Matters

The blood-alcohol limit in the BVI is 0.08%. Driving under the influence of alcohol is a serious offense, subject to stiff fines and even imprisonment.

Money

The US dollar (US$) is used throughout the islands.

Banks with ATMs hooked into worldwide networks (Plus, Cirrus, Exchange etc) are in the main towns on Tortola and Virgin Gorda. Jost Van Dyke, Anegada and the out islands do not have ATMs, so you'll need to cash up beforehand.

TIPPING

In restaurants, a 15% to 20% tip is the norm; 10% to 15% in taxis. Tip bellhops US$1 to US$2 per bag. A tip of 10% to 20% is reasonable for dive-boat operators and yacht crews.

Public Holidays

Islanders celebrate several local holidays, in addition to those observed throughout the region (p872). Banks, schools and government offices close on these days.

HL Stoutt's Birthday First Monday in March

Commonwealth Day Second Monday in March

Sovereign's Birthday Mid-June (date varies)

Territory Day July 1

BVI Festival Days First Monday to Wednesday in August

St Ursula's Day October 21

Telephone

The phone system works like the US system. Be prepared for whopping charges – the BVI is one of the most expensive places in the world for calls. Note that working pay phones are few and far between.

All BVI phone numbers consist of a three-digit area code (☎284), followed by a seven-digit local number.

If you are calling from abroad, dial all 10 digits preceded by ☎1. If you are calling locally, just dial the seven-digit number. For direct international calls, such as to Europe, dial ☎011 + country code + area code + local phone number.

CELL PHONES

You should be able to use your cell phone on the islands, but watch out for exorbitant roaming fees.

CCT Global (www.cctwireless.com), Lime (www.time4lime.com) and Digicel (www.digicel bvi.com) provide the local service.

If you have a European, Australian or other type of unlocked GSM phone, buy a local SIM card to reduce costs. They cost about US$20, which includes US$10 of air time (at roughly US$0.30 per minute calling time to the USA). SIM cards are easy to get at local shops.

Travelers with Disabilities

The BVI is not particularly accessible and does not have any specific services geared toward travelers with disabilities.

Visas

Visitors from most Western countries do not need a visa to enter the BVI for 30 days or less. If your home country does not qualify for visa exemption, contact your nearest British embassy (www.ukvisas.gov.uk) or the BVI Immigration Department (www.bviimmigration.gov.vg).

Women Travelers

It's safe for women to travel solo in the BVI. Just use the same degree of caution you would in a big city at home: be aware of your surroundings and don't walk alone at night in unfamiliar areas. Avoid isolated beaches at any time of day or night.

Getting There & Away

Entering the British Virgin Islands

Everyone needs a passport to enter the BVI by air. Citizens of the US who enter the BVI by ferry can also opt for using the less-expensive passport card; see the **Western Hemisphere Travel Initiative** (www.gety ouhome.gov) for more. All other nationalities need a passport to enter by ferry.

Whether arriving by air or sea, you'll go through BVI immigration and customs. Officials might ask to see a return ticket and proof of funds, though that's rare. It can take half an hour or so to clear customs. There's no reason why, other than it's just a slow-moving process. If you're arriving on a ferry,

BVI DEPARTURE TAX

You must pay a US$20 departure tax to leave the BVI by air. The tax is US$5 to leave by ferry. This is not included in the ticket price, and must be paid separately at the airport or ferry terminal (usually at a window by the departure lounge).

you'll clear through a **customs house** (www.bviports.org) near the dock.

Air

AIRPORTS

Tortola's **Terrence B Lettsome Airport** (☑494-3701) is the gateway. It's a modern facility with an ATM, car rental, internet cafe and food concessions. The tiny airports on Virgin Gorda and Anegada are for small charter planes only.

AIRLINES

There are no direct flights to the BVI from the US mainland, Canada or Europe. Flights usually connect via Puerto Rico, St Thomas or Antigua. The **BVI Tourism Board** (www.bvitourism.com, click 'Getting Here') provides handy information on the most direct routes to Tortola, depending on your point of origin.

The following airlines have flights to and from Tortola:

Air Sunshine (www.airsunshine.com) Serves San Juan, St Thomas, daily.

American Airlines (www.aa.com) Flies to San Juan daily.

BVI Airways (www.gobvi.com) St-Martin/Sint Maarten flights three times weekly.

Cape Air (www.flycapeair.com) Flies to San Juan daily.

LIAT (www.liatairline.com) Flies to Antigua and St-Martin/Sint Maarten daily.

Winair (www.fly-winair.com) Flies to Antigua and St-Martin/Sint Maarten daily.

Sea

CRUISE SHIP

Ships call at Road Town almost daily during peak season. The dock is downtown, so no tenders are needed (except in rare cases when the dock is particularly busy) – passengers disembark and they're in the heart of the action.

FERRY

There are excellent ferry connections linking Tortola, Virgin Gorda and Jost Van Dyke with the US Virgin Islands' St Thomas and St John. The free tourist magazines publish full schedules each month. Good online sources to check are the **BVI Welcome Guide** (www.bviwelcome.com) and **VI Now** (www.vinow.com).

For trips between the USVI and BVI, a passport (or passport card in some cases) is required.

Ferries between the USVI and BVI run until about 5pm only. Watch out for scheduling issues if you're trying to get between the two territories in the evening. The one exception is a 9pm ferry between Red Hook, St Thomas and Road Town, Tortola that operates Thursday through Sunday via Road Town Fast Ferry.

Ferry companies include the following:

Inter-Island (☑340-776-6597; www.interislandboatservices.vi)

Native Son (☑495-4617; www.nativesonferry.com)

Road Town Fast Ferry (☑494-2323; www.roadtownfastferry.com)

Smith's Ferry (☑494-4454; www.smithsferry.com)

Speedy's (☑495-5240; www.speedysbvi.com)

Ferries from Tortola (Road Town):

St Thomas (Charlotte Amalie) direct
US$30 one-way, 45 minutes, several daily

St Thomas (Charlotte Amalie) via West End US$25 to US$28 one-way, 60 minutes, several daily; Smith's and Native Son

Ferries from Tortola (West End):

St Thomas (Red Hook) US$25 to US$28 one-way, 35 minutes, four daily; Smith's and Native Son

St John US$30 one-way, 30 minutes, three daily; Inter-Island

Ferries from Virgin Gorda:

St Thomas (Charlotte Amalie) US$40 one-way, 90 minutes, three days weekly; Speedy's

St Thomas (Red Hook) via St John US$60 one-way, one hour and 15 minutes, two days weekly; Inter-Island

Ferries from Jost Van Dyke:

St Thomas (Red Hook) via St John
US$45 one-way, 45 minutes, two daily (except none Wednesday and Thursday); Inter-Island

YACHT
Lots of yachts drift into the BVI. The busiest marinas (and good places to inquire about becoming a crew member) include the following:

Tortola the Moorings, Road Town

Virgin Gorda Yacht Harbour, Spanish Town

Jost Van Dyke Great Harbour

Anegada Setting Point

BOAT-CHARTER BASICS

The British Virgin Islands provide it all: a year-round balmy climate, steady trade winds, little to worry about in the way of tides or currents, a protected thoroughfare in the 35-mile-long Sir Francis Drake Channel, and hundreds of anchorages, each within sight of one another. These factors make the islands one of the easiest places to sail, which explains why more than a third of all visitors come to do just that.

If you want to sail, there are three basic options: a crewed boat, with skipper and cook; a 'bareboat' sans staff that you operate on your own; or a sailing-school vessel.

A typical weeklong itinerary involves sampling the islands, while partially circumnavigating Tortola. The attraction of a sailing vacation is that you can sail or stay put as long as you want, look for quiet anchorages or head for the party spots and add on diving, hiking or shopping trips at will.

The cost of chartering a boat depends on the vessel's size and age and the time of year. It is a misconception that sailing is too expensive; once you do a little research you might be pleasantly surprised.

Choosing a Company

Charter companies depend on their reputations. Ask for references and spend time talking with the company's representatives. Most companies sail out of the Moorings at Wickhams Cay 2 in Road Town.

The following is a list of respected charter services based in the BVI. Each can arrange bareboat charters, as well as a variety of crew options.

Barecat Charters (www.barecat.com) Smaller company specializing in catamarans.

BVI Yacht Charters (www.bviyachtcharters.com) Long-standing company.

Catamaran Company (www.catamaranco.com) Another catamaran specialist.

Footloose Sailing Charters (www.footloosecharters.com) Billed as a 'budget' company. It works in conjunction with the Moorings.

Horizon Yacht Charters (www.horizonyachtcharters.com) Smaller company.

Moorings (www.moorings.com) It started the BVI bareboat business and remains the islands' largest yacht company.

Sunsail Yacht Charters (www.sunsail.com) The BVI's second-largest company.

Tortola Marine Management (www.sailtmm.com) Smaller company that provides free wi-fi aboard all its boats.

Sailing Schools

Offshore Sailing School (www.offshoresailing.com) Venerable company offering courses out of the Moorings in Road Town.

Rob Swain Sailing School (www.swainsailing.com) Well-rated, smaller school operating out of Nanny Cay, Tortola.

Sistership Sailing School (www.sailsistership.com) Specializes in instruction for women, couples and families; based at Nanny Cay, Tortola.

Getting Around

Air

You'll need to charter a plane to fly between islands. Good companies for the Tortola to Anegada jaunt (roughly US$155 round-trip) include **Fly BVI** (www.bviaircharters.com) and **Island Birds** (www.islandbirds.com).

Boat

Frequent ferries run between the islands. Tortola is the hub, and all boats route through its various docks. Main routes are listed here. The **BVI Welcome Guide** (www.bviwelcome.com) prints the full timetables. To get around on your own by chartering a boat, see the boxed text, p263.

Ferry companies include the following:

New Horizon Ferry (495-9278)

North Sound Express (495-2138)

Road Town Fast Ferry (494-2323; www.roadtownfastferry.com)

Smith's Ferry (494-4454; www.smithsferry.com)

Speedy's (495-5240; www.speedysbvi.com)

Ferries from Tortola:

Virgin Gorda (Spanish Town) US$30 round-trip, 30 minutes, roughly every hour, arrival/departure at Road Town; Speedy's and Smith's

Virgin Gorda (North Sound & Spanish Town) US$40 to US$65 round-trip, 15 to 35 minutes, several times daily (except none Sunday), arrival/departure at Trellis Bay/Beef Island; North Sound Express

Jost Van Dyke 25 minutes, US$25 round-trip, five daily, arrival/departure at West End; New Horizon

Anegada US$45 round-trip, 90 minutes, Monday, Wednesday and Friday, arrival/departure at Road Town (via Spanish Town); Road Town Fast Ferry

Car

Driving is undoubtedly the most convenient way to get around, as public transportation is limited and taxi fares add up in a hurry.

You can drive in the BVI using a valid license from your home country. A temporary license is required if you're staying longer than 30 days; any car-rental agency can provide the paperwork.

RENTAL

To rent a car in the BVI you generally need to be at least 25 years old, hold a valid driver's license and have a major credit card.

Cars cost between US$55 and US$90 per day. If you're traveling in peak season, it's wise to reserve a couple of months in advance, as supplies are limited. Major international car-rental companies have branches at the airports and sometimes at ferry terminals. See the Getting There & Around sections of each destination for local rental agencies.

ROAD CONDITIONS

Be prepared for challenging road conditions. Steep, winding roads are often the same width as your car, and the potholes can be outrageous.

Chickens, cows, goats and donkeys dart in and out of the roadway. Keep your eyes peeled for critters.

ROAD RULES

» Rule number one: drive on the left-hand side of the road!
» The steering wheel is on the left side.
» Seat-belt use is compulsory; children under five years must be in a car seat.
» Driving while using a handheld cell phone is illegal (but earpieces are permitted).
» Proceed clockwise at traffic roundabouts.

Taxi

All of the islands have taxis that are easily accessible in the main tourist areas. Most vehicles are vans that carry up to 12 passengers; sometimes they're open-air pickup trucks with bench seats and awnings. Rates are set, with prices listed in the free tourist guides. You can also access rate sheets from the **BVI Tourist Board** (www.bvitourism.com).

Reliable companies:

Beef Island Taxi Association (495-1982)

BVI Taxi Association (494-3942)

West End Taxi Association (495-4934)

Cayman Islands

Best Beaches

» Seven Mile Beach (p271)

» Governor's Beach (p271)

» Rum Point (p281)

» Sandy Point (p284)

» Owen Island (p284)

Best Places to Stay

» Grandview (p275)

» Turtle Nest Inn (p280)

» Walton's Mango Manor (p282)

» Southern Cross Club (p285)

» Pirates Point Resort (p285)

Why Go?

What's so surprising about the three Cayman Islands at first is how un-British they are for a British territory – Grand Cayman seems straight from the US, with ubiquitous SUVs jostling for space at upscale malls and US dollars changing hands as if they were the national currency. Think of it as a much more orderly version of South Florida.

But get away from the crowded commercialism of Grand Cayman's long western coastline and explore the low-key rest of the island. Or visit tiny Cayman Brac and Little Cayman. Here life runs at a slow pace and the natural delights that see people coming back again and again – from birdwatching and hiking to diving and snorkeling – are never far away.

While synonymous worldwide with tax havens and beach holidays, the Cayman Islands appeal to those who want to avoid gaudy diversions and stop worrying after applying their sunscreen.

When to Go

The best time to visit is from December to April, when the temperature averages a pleasant 75°F (24°C) and humidity is at its lowest. During the low season, temperatures average 83°F (28°C), with July and August usually being uncomfortably hot. During these times crowds dissipate, particularly on Cayman Brac and Little Cayman, lodging rates fall and beaches are vast expanses of open sand. Rainfall is highest from mid-May through to October, with frequent afternoon showers that clear as quickly as they arrive.

Itineraries

THREE DAYS

Join the crowds on wonderful Seven Mile Beach, shop yourself silly in George Town and experience the extraordinary Stingray City. Head east to the quiet end of the island on a day-long driving circle tour.

ONE WEEK

After several days in the west just beach-bumming, explore some of Grand Cayman's lesser-known attractions. Try the Botanic Park and Rum Point, and get some diving in. Take a day trip – or an overnight jaunt to either Cayman Brac or Little Cayman.

TWO WEEKS

Add on Cayman Brac and Little Cayman for some nature hikes, superb diving, secluded beaches and a wonderful taste of the traditional Caribbean. And relax: don't be in a rush to see or do anything – the islands are small.

GETTING TO NEIGHBORING ISLANDS

There is no ferry service within the Cayman Islands, nor is there a service to neighboring islands. To get any place you'll need to fly; air connections to Cuba and Jamaica are frequent and easy.

Essential Food & Drink

You'll eat superbly almost anywhere in the Cayman Islands – the combination of a large international community and plenty of cash sloshing about means that no effort is spared to import excellent fresh food and specialties from around the world. Local foods are limited to some seafood. (Check out www.nationaltrust.org.ky/seasense, which guides diners to sustainable seafood choices.) For casual meals, Jamaican-style jerk and barbecue are popular

» **Conch** A popular item on restaurant menus – look for farm-raised versions as conch in the wild are endangered. This large pink mollusk is cooked with onion and spices in a stew, fried up as fritters, or sliced raw and served with a lime marinade.

» **Mannish water** Stewy mixture of yams plus the head and foot of a goat; *may* cure impotency.

» **Tortuga rum cake** A heavy, moist cake available in a number of addictive flavors; makes a great gift to take home.

» **Jelly ice** Chilled coconut water sucked from the shell.

» **Mudslide** A creamy cocktail combining Kahlua, Baileys and vodka – invented at Rum Point.

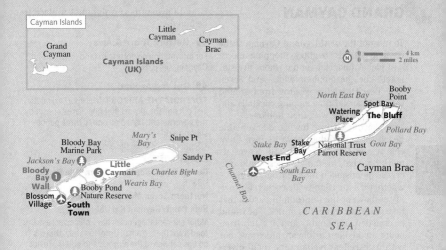

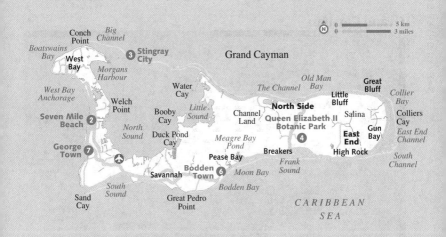

Cayman Islands Highlights

1 Explore some of the best diving in the Caribbean, with sites such as legendary **Bloody Bay Wall** (p285) on Little Cayman

2 Enjoy swimming, sunbathing and more on Grand Cayman's superb **Seven Mile Beach** (p271)

3 Have huge, fearless stingrays eating squid directly from your hands as you snorkel in **Stingray City** (p274)

4 Besides beautiful gardens and nature hikes, **Queen Elizabeth II Botanic Park** (p280) is the home to Cayman's huge blue iguanas

5 Take life at a slower pace on tiny **Little Cayman** (p283), which is packed with quiet charm and rad diving

6 Discover old Cayman exploring the historic highlights of **Bodden Town** (p279)

7 Taste trad Cayman fare in **George Town** (p276)

GRAND CAYMAN

POP 39,000

To most of the world, Grand Cayman *is* the Cayman Islands, a glitzy shopping mecca and global financial center where five-star hotels line the fabulous white-sand Seven Mile Beach and the wealthy from around the world spend time sipping cocktails and discreetly playing with their millions.

Yet beyond George Town and Seven Mile Beach the island does have its own quiet charm and Caribbean life still leaves its mark on what, in many places, could otherwise be mistaken for suburban Florida – whether it's the islandwide cockerels crowing at dawn or the impromptu parties that take place at a moment's notice. The island is crowded, no doubt, and it's far from being an idyllic Caribbean hideaway, but with its excellent restaurants, retail diversions, activities and things to see and do, Grand Cayman is certainly not a place to be bored.

❶ Getting There & Away

For information on getting to (and from) Grand Cayman, see p289.

❶ Getting Around

TO/FROM THE AIRPORT There's a taxi queue just outside the airport building. Fares are set by the government, based on one to three people sharing a ride.

Sample fares from the airport:

East End US$70

George Town, Southern Seven Mile Beach US$15

Northern Seven Mile Beach US$25

Rum Point/Cayman Kai US$80

Major car-rental agencies have offices across the road from the terminal. Unfortunately, there is no bus service to the airport, and hotels are not permitted to collect guests on arrival.

BICYCLE & SCOOTER With its flat terrain and always stunning views of the sea, Grand Cay-

Grand Cayman

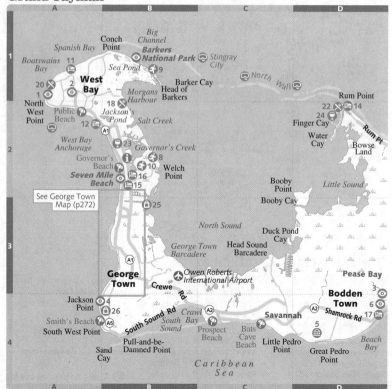

man is a pleasure for cyclists (many hotels make bikes available to guests). Renting a scooter will enable you to easily access the far reaches of the island. **Cayman Cycle Rentals** (☏945-4021; Coconut Place Shopping Center, West Bay Rd, Seven Mile Beach; per day mountain bike/scooter US$20/40) also supplies locks and maps.

BUS The public **bus terminal** (Edward St), located adjacent to the public library in downtown George Town, serves as the dispatch point for buses to all districts of Grand Cayman. The system uses color-coded logos to indicate routes on the **minibuses** (fares CI$2-3.50; ☺8am-11pm). Frequencies average 15 minutes in the west but can be much less often in the east. Ask drivers for information.

The main routes from George Town:
West Bay Routes 1 (yellow), 2 (lime green)
Bodden Town Routes 3 (blue), 4 (purple), 5 (red), 8 (orange), 9 (dark blue)
East End Routes 4 (purple), 5 (red), 9 (dark blue)

North Side via Frank Sound Dr Routes 3 (blue), 5 (red), 8 (orange)

CAR During the peak season, rates for a compact car start at around US$50 per day; rentals during the low season may be 25% less. The following are among the main agents. The airport offices are in a building that's across a road to the left as you exit the terminal.

Andy's Rent-a-Car (☏949-8111; www.andys. ky; Owen Roberts International Airport)

Avis (☏949-2468; www.aviscayman.com; Owen Roberts International Airport) Other branches are at the Ritz Carlton, Marriott Hotel and Westin.

Budget (☏949-5605; www.budgetcayman. com; Owen Roberts International Airport)

Cayman Auto Rentals (☏949-1013; www. caymanautorentals.net; West Bay Rd)

Coconut Car Rentals (☏949-4037; www. coconutcarrentals.com; Owen Roberts International Airport) Also at Coconut Place, Seven Mile Beach.

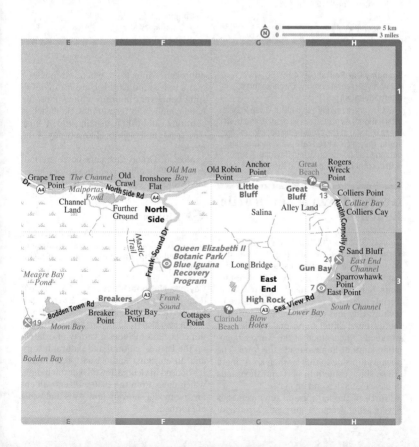

Grand Cayman

Economy Car Rental (✆949-9550; www.economycarrental.com.ky; Owen Roberts International Airport)

TAXI Taxis are readily available at Owen Roberts International Airport, from all resorts and from the taxi stand at the cruise-ship dock in George Town. They offer a fixed rate per vehicle or per person to all points on Grand Cayman. A sign with current rates is posted at the dock.

George Town & Seven Mile Beach

POP 23,000

George Town is the supremely wealthy but surprisingly modest capital of the Cayman Islands. While no doubt cosmopolitan, with more than its fair share of excellent restaurants, bars and shopping, there's something terribly unassuming about the place as well – it's tiny, tidy and easy to walk around, and there's often little going on, especially at weekends when much of the worker population stays at home outside the town. The obvious flip side to this is when six or more cruise ships come into port and thousands of passengers descend en masse.

North of the harbor and town center is Seven Mile Beach, a gorgeous stretch of unbroken white sand where Grand Cayman's tourist industry is concentrated. Despite being very built up with condos, big hotels, malls and restaurants, the beach is stunning, and you'll usually find it busy with locals and visitors alike any day of the week.

Most of Grand Cayman's hotels, restaurants and shopping complexes line the island's busiest thoroughfare, West Bay Rd, which travels alongside Seven Mile Beach.

◉ Sights

There is nothing you can't miss in George Town – it's pleasant enough to stroll around, eat and shop in, but the sights are of negligible interest.

Cayman National Museum   MUSEUM
(Map p272; www.museum.ky; cnr Harbour Dr & Shedden Rd, George Town; adult/child CI$4/2; ⊙9am-5pm Mon-Fri, 10am-2pm Sat) The museum collection includes a variety of exhibits on the islands' cultural and natural history and an engaging audiovisual presentation. It's housed in George Town's oldest building, which dates from the 1830s. Divers will enjoy the model showing how reefs and walls are formed.

FREE National Gallery of the Cayman
Islands   GALLERY
(Map p272; www.nationalgallery.org.ky; ground
fl, Harbour Pl, South Church St, George Town;
⊙9am-5pm Mon-Fri, 11am-2pm Sat) Located
somewhat incongruously in a mall devoted to duty-free shopping, the work of local artist Margaret Barwick sits alongside
other imports. Note: the gallery hopes to
move into a new building outside of downtown in 2012.

Ugland House   LANDMARK
(Map p272; South Church St) On the outside it
looks like a slightly gaudy, slightly dated
smallish office building, yet more than
18,000 corporate entities have registered
this place as their address. It led US President Barack Obama to say in 2009: 'Either
this is the largest building in the world or
the largest tax scam in the world.' While
obviously far from being the largest office
building in the world, Ugland House's role
in the world of international finance and
taxation is subject to much debate.

🏖 Beaches

TOP CHOICE Seven Mile Beach   BEACH
(Map p272) Although it's really only 5½
miles long, this gorgeous strand of flawless
white sand stretches north from George
Town and anchors Grand Cayman's tourist
industry. It's perfectly maintained, features
shady trees in parts and is untrod by vendors. Open sand can get scarce near large
resorts but the sheer size of this beach
means there's always a place to call your
own. Public access is common, although
one large area called 'Seven Mile Beach'
features plenty of parking, shops, beach
bars and more. It's the top destination for
day-trippers.

Governor's Beach   BEACH
(Map p268) A beach area within Seven Mile
Beach, this is the antidote to the carnival
atmosphere at the Seven Mile Beach public
access point. Hidden between resorts, the
tree-shaded parking lot opens onto a section
of beach that is rarely crowded. Locals in the
know come here; when it gets especially hot,
an ice-cream truck appears.

🏃 Activities

Diving & Snorkeling

Many people coming to Grand Cayman are
coming for one thing alone: the great diving.

While arguably better, more pristine sites
are available on Cayman Brac and Little
Cayman, the diving around Grand Cayman
should not be discounted. It boasts over 160
dive sites. One, Stingray City (see the boxed
text p274), is world famous.

USS Kittiwake   DIVING
(www.cita.ky) The furtive fish of Grand Cay-
man certainly owe a debt of thanks to the
US taxpayer. After 50 years of service with
the US Navy – and several more years of
wrangling – this 76m-long former submarine tender was sunk near West Bay in
2011 to form an artificial reef. If it attracts
diving tourists as well, so much the better.
Within weeks of the Kittiwake's sinking it
was home to all manner of small fish, happy
for the shelter from predators in its many
nooks and crannies. Most dive operators
can take you to the site.

Eden Rock Diving Center   DIVING
(Map p272; ☎949-7243; www.edenrockdive.com;
124 South Church St, George Town; 1-/2-tank dives
US$65/90) Overlooking the George Town har-
bor, this outfit combines dive sites and services you can enjoy, just three minutes from the
cruise-ship tender dock. It's an easy matter to
shore dive to the beautiful caves, tunnels and
grottoes of two of the Cayman Islands' most
celebrated dive sites: Eden Rocks and Devil's
Grotto. You can snorkel from here for free, although there's a locker fee.

DIVE OPERATORS

Grand Cayman has scores of good dive operators. Most offer Stingray City and snorkeling tours. Night dives and challenging

---

PORT OF CALL – GEORGE TOWN

With a few hours in port, you can avoid
'Hell' and do the following:

» Frolic on Grand Cayman's superb
Seven Mile Beach

» Pet stingrays while they eat squid
directly from your hands at Stingray
City (p274)

» Check out the green sea turtles at a
unique hatchery (p278)

» Escape the immediate port area
where the cruise-ship tenders dock
and stroll George Town, stopping at
one of the excellent eateries serving
island fare

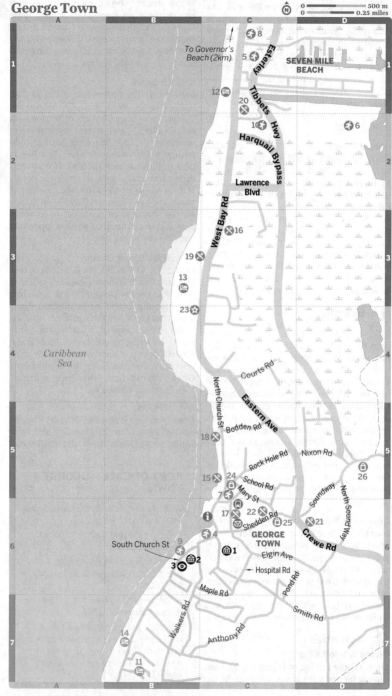

CAYMAN ISLANDS GRAND CAYMAN

0 ——— 500 m
0 ——— 0.25 miles

To Governor's
Beach (2km)

**SEVEN MILE
BEACH**

Esterley

Tibbets Hwy

Harquail Bypass

**Lawrence
Blvd**

West Bay Rd

*Caribbean
Sea*

Courts Rd

Eastern Ave

North Church St

Bodden Rd

Rock Hole Rd

Nixon Rd

School Rd

Mary St

Soundway

North Sound Way

Shedden Rd

**GEORGE
TOWN**

Crewe Rd

South Church St

Elgin Ave

Hospital Rd

Maple Rd

Pond Rd

Walkers Rd

Smith Rd

Anthony Rd

dives down the North Wall are just some of the advanced underwater options available for skilled divers. Basic one-/two-tank dives start at US$65/90.

Some well-established dive operations, many offering certifications:

Divers Down DIVING
(Map p272; ☑949-6796; www.diversdown.net; Coconut Pl, West Bay Rd, Seven Mile Beach) Offers many courses.

Divetech DIVING
(Map p268; ☑946-5658; www.divetech.com; Cobalt Coast Resort & Suites, West Bay) Located near the awesome North Wall.

Off the Wall Divers DIVING
(☑945-7525; www.otwdivers.com) Has off-the-beaten path mangrove tours.

Red Sail Sports DIVING
(Map p272; ☑949-8745; www.redsailcayman.com; Grand Cayman Beach Suites Resort, West Bay Rd, Seven Mile Beach) Largest and best known of the diving operators, offering excursions islandwide and numerous outlets across Grand Cayman, including at Rum Point for access to the North Wall.

Wall to Wall Diving DIVING
(☑916-6408; www.walltowalldiving.com; 1-/2-tank dives US$60/90)

Water Sports
Independent paddlers will find rental kayaks (from US$25 per hour) at the Seven Mile Beach public access. Windsurfing and kite-surfing are possible in Barkers National Park.

Action Watersports KAYAKING
(Map p268; ☑548-3147; www.ciactionmarine.com; Grand Caymanian Resort, Safe Haven) Rents kayaks and waverunners (US$75 per 30 minutes).

Blue Water Beach PARASAILING
(Map p272; ☑525-5400; www.bwbcayman.com; Royal Palms Beach Club; per ride US$70) Offers parasailing at Seven Mile Beach.

Cayman Kayaks KAYAKING TOURS
(☑945-5022; www.caymankayaks.com; tours from adult/child US$45/25) Mangrove tours and nighttime bioluminescent tours, which let you see eerie underwater lights.

Fishing
The clear, warm waters of the Cayman Islands are teeming with blue marlin, wahoo, tuna and mahimahi. Charter a boat (half-day charters about US$600, full-day charters US$900 to US$1200) with an experienced Caymanian captain and hook some real action.

Bayside Watersports FISHING TOURS
(☑949-3200; www.baysidewatersports.com; Batabano Rd, Morgan's Harbour) True Caymanian hospitality and fishing expertise.

Blue Water Excursions FISHING TOURS
(☑925-8738; www.bluewaterexcursions.ky; Morgan's Harbour) Local fisherman Capt Richard

CAYMAN ISLANDS GEORGE TOWN & SEVEN MILE BEACH

George Town

◉ Sights

DON'T MISS

STINGRAY CITY

This stretch of sandy seafloor in Grand Cayman's North Sound is the meeting place for southern stingrays hungry for a meal. As soon as you enter the water, several of the beautiful prehistoric-looking creatures will glide up to you to suck morsels of squid from your tentative fingers.

It began back in the 1980s when fishing boats would clean their catch here and a troupe of some 50 stingrays took up residence waiting for the daily bounty (evidently having the food ready to swallow beat the shells off the normal food: crabs). Dive operators soon took notice and today excursions here are a top Grand Cayman activity.

At the simplest, you catch a boat from somewhere along Seven Mile Beach, motor to Stingray City and hop out into the shallow, warm and protected waters. Armed with some chopped squid, you'll soon have plenty of stingray friends. It really is quite remarkable the first time you touch their velvety smooth skin and then watch them seem to effortlessly 'fly' through the water.

Tours generally include snorkeling gear and stops, which you don't need for the stingrays but which are useful for exploring deeper areas of North Sound and the North Wall. Some tours are geared to divers and make stops at scuba sites. Although stingrays got their name for the stinger in their tail, these guys seem to know who's doing the feeding and incidents are rare. Still, don't step on one in the shallows and don't – duh – grab the stinger.

On busy days there will be hundreds of people in the water but this just seems to add to the fun-filled frenzy, or in the stingrays' case, the feeding frenzy. Half-day trips start at US$45/35, longer trips and those that include diving cost more. Operators abound and the offerings are pretty standardized, especially at the 'feed, stroke and go home' level.

Orr is at the helm of his 32ft vessel *Trouble Maker*.

Captain Marvin's Watersports
FISHING TOURS

(Map p272; ☑949-3200; www.captainmarvins.com; Waterfront Centre, North Church St, George Town) In business since 1951; offers stingray trips and other boat excursions.

Golf

Plenty of great sunshine and world-class courses make the Cayman Islands a prime destination for golf nuts.

Britannia Golf Club
GOLF

(Map p272; ☑949-8020; www.britannia-golf.com; Grand Cayman Beach Suites Resort, West Bay Rd, Seven Mile Beach) Designed by Jack Nicklaus, this course is reminiscent of legendary Scottish courses with its traditional 'links' layout.

North Sound Club Golf Course
GOLF

(Map p268; ☑947-4653; www.northsoundclub.com; Safehaven Dr, Seven Mile Beach) A par-71 18-hole course in a stunning location, it is interwoven with the canals off the North Sound.

Horseback Riding

While Grand Cayman lacks the dramatic scenery of much of the Caribbean, horseback riding is still very popular here. The following places are recommended; expect to pay from US$75 per ride.

Honey Suckle Trail Rides
HORSEBACK RIDING

(☑916-5420; twoodenhorsepower@hotmail.com) Offers rides along the quiet beaches of Barkers National Park.

Pampered Ponies
HORSEBACK RIDING

(☑945-2262; www.ponies.ky) Offers dawn riding down deserted beaches for experienced riders, romantic sunset rides and awesome full-moon ones as well. The small groups are all led by professionals.

☞ Tours

Atlantis Adventures
SUBMARINE TOURS

(Map p272; ☑949-7700; www.atlantisadventures.com; 32 Goring Ave, George Town; adult/child US$84/59) It's possible to visit the underwater world without even mussing up your hair on a submarine expedition. The *Atlantis XI* submarine takes groups to a depth of 100ft, for which tours leave every hour Monday through Sunday.

Mangrove Eco-Tour
AQUATIC TOURS

(☑945-7525; www.caymanseaelements.com; tours from US$30) Offers boat and snorkeling tours of Grand Cayman's extensive mangroves around North Sound.

National Trust
CULTURE & NATURE TOURS

(Map p268; ☑749-1121; www.nationaltrust.org.ky; 558 South Church St; ⊙9am-5:30pm Mon-Fri, 9am-1pm Sat) Operates some of the most important historical and cultural sites around the island and offers guided tours and hikes.

🛏 Sleeping

Much of Seven Mile Beach is covered in luxury condos, guesthouses and sprawling hotel complexes. Grand Cayman caters to higher-end tourism and places to stay are all midrange and top end, with full services and plenty of family-friendly amenities.

Given the number of condos, it's a good idea to check with booking services that represent unit owners. Two good ones are **Cayman Villas** (www.caymanvillas.com), which represents properties across the Cayman Islands; and **Vacation Rentals by Owner** (www.vrbo.com), which has dozens of listings in all price ranges.

Grandview
CONDOS $$$

(Map p272; ☑945-4511; www.grandviewcondos.com; West Bay Rd, Seven Mile Beach; 2-bedroom condo US$350-550; ✳@🛜🏊) At the south end of the beach, this gracious condo complex is set back from the water on wide, grassy grounds. The three-story units have either balconies or terraces and all units either face the ocean or are right on the beach. Each condo has a full kitchen plus laundry facilities. You may not wish to leave.

Grand Cayman Beach Suites Resort
RESORT $$$

(Map p272; ☑949-1234; www.grand-cayman-beach-suites.com; West Bay Rd, Seven Mile Beach; 1-bedroom ste US$320-650; ✳@🛜🏊) This former Hyatt has 53 lavish suites set right on a fine stretch of the beach. Top-end travelers reserve the beachfront units months in advance. All rooms are large and beautifully fitted out, including kitchens, large bathrooms and balconies. The resort has a gym, three restaurants, a spa, two pools and an excellent diving center.

Discovery Point Club
CONDOS $$$

(Map p268; ☑945-4724; www.discoverypointclub.com; West Bay Rd, Seven Mile Beach; r US$210-240, 1-/2-bedroom ste from US$300/345; ✳@🛜🏊) This excellent condo complex is recom-

mended for a comfortable family beach holiday. At the far north end of Seven Mile Beach (in front of a good snorkeling area), all the suites have superb views, balconies or patios and kitchens. The smaller rooms don't have kitchens but share the excellent hotel facilities including the tennis courts, pool and spa.

Ritz-Carlton Grand Cayman
RESORT $$$

(Map p268; ☑943-9000; www.ritzcarlton.com; West Bay Rd, Seven Mile Beach; r US$300-1200; ✳@🛜🏊) The largest luxury resort in Grand Cayman is this vast 365-room property located on both sides of West Bay Rd, the two buildings connected by an enclosed pedestrian bridge. It's a bit on the gaudy side but despite this, it's undeniably a great place to stay, with two stunning pools, a beautiful stretch of beach, a spa, a private nine-hole golf course, tennis courts and numerous bars and restaurants.

Sunset House
HOTEL $$$

(Map p272; ☑949-7111; www.sunsethouse.com; 390 South Church St, George Town; r US$200-400; ✳@🛜🏊) Just south of George Town, this divers' haven is a great spot. As you'd expect, the whole operation revolves around diving, with a dive school boasting specialized guides as well as a famed underwater photography center. The rooms are clean and comfortable. The cheapest have courtyard views, others have balconies and ocean views. There's no beach, just large rocks.

Eldemire's Guest House Bed & Breakfast
B&B $$

(Map p272; ☑916-8369; www.eldemire.com; Glen Eden Rd, George Town; r US$110-160, 1-/2-bedroom ste from US$190/300; ✳@🛜) This guesthouse is the favorite of independent travelers and provides a large range of accommodations, from very basic rooms for seasonal workers to spacious suites. The suites have kitchens while guests in the main block share a well-equipped common kitchen. There are laundry facilities and bike rentals. Take South Church St from downtown and the turnoff is signposted.

Sunshine Suites
HOTEL $$

(Map p268; ☑949-3000; www.sunshinesuites.com; 1465 Esterley Tibbetts Hwy, Seven Mile Beach; r US$160-270; ✳@🛜🏊) This complex of 132 studios and apartments is like a condo with hotel services. Because it's a major road away from the beach (about a five-minute walk away), rates are lower than for waterfront places. Each unit is equipped with a full kitchen, making self-catering an easy option; a small pool lures you in for a dip.

Eating & Drinking

You'll eat well on Grand Cayman. From stylish restaurants catering to the leisurely rich to simpler cafes producing excellent fresh meals, it's hard to go wrong here. In George Town there's a range of places serving tasty Cayman faves to locals who demand value.

GEORGE TOWN

Day-trippers will want to move beyond the immediate zone of the cruise-ship tender dock, where humdrum restaurants hawk all-you-can-eat buffets to people who already get to eat 24/7. There's a range of simple places serving excellent local fare you can walk to as well as more traditionally raucous tourist joints.

TOP CHOICE **Corita's Copper Kettle** CARIBBEAN $
(Map p272; Edward St; meals CI$7-10; ⊙7am-3pm Mon-Sat) This old wooden house is home to an excellent Caribbean cafe that Corita has run for four decades. Breakfasts such as her signature sandwich, which combines eggs, bacon, cheese and grape jelly with a home-made fritter, are popular. Relax amid the hand-painted beach murals with comfort food like chicken and rice.

Casanova ITALIAN $$
(Map p272; www.casanova.ky; 65 North Church St; mains US$15-32; ⊙11am-11pm) This relatively affordable Italian restaurant overlooking the sea is a great spot for a quality dinner. Reserve a table with a view out on the veranda. The pizzas are good, as are the fresh fish and seafood dishes; the daily lobster specials attract splurgers.

Seymour's Jerk Centre CARIBBEAN $
(Map p272; Shedden Rd; meals CI$7-10; ⊙11:30am-midnight) A mere hut in a huge dirt parking lot near the center, Seymour's has spicy jerk chicken and pork, fried fish and other island treats. The air is redolent with barbecued meat and spices. A few picnic tables under cover provide seating. If your manhood is in doubt, order Mannish water (CI$4), an old Cayman stew of yams plus the head and foot of a goat. It's supposed to restore 'vibrancy.'

Hammerheads BURGERS $$
(Map p272; North Church St; mains US$10-20; ⊙lunch & dinner) This is a great spot to meet locals, who come in droves for sundowners and satisfying diner fare out on the large deck with great sea views. Burgers, fried chicken and some seriously good sandwiches are the main offerings – as well as killer cocktails. There's also tarpon feeding on the deck every evening at 9pm; the fish market is nearby.

Singh's Roti Shop & Bar CARIBBEAN $
(Map p272; cnr Doctor Roy's Dr & Shedden Rd; mains US$7-10; ⊙9am-midnight) This is one of George Town's best bargains. In a city where dinner often means a three-figure check, this cheerful hole-in-the-wall is a great place for some tongue-searing roti (curry filling, often potatoes and chicken, rolled inside flat bread).

SEVEN MILE BEACH

Hemingway's CONTINENTAL $$$
(Map p272; ☑945-5700; Grand Cayman Beach Suites Resort, West Bay Rd, Seven Mile Beach; mains US$20-40; ⊙breakfast, lunch & dinner) This exceptional restaurant is far from being just another hotel eatery and so, while it's the flagship restaurant of the Grand Cayman Beach Suites Resort, it's also a favorite with diners looking for a lavish experience. Fresh seafood, especially lobster, is the feature. You can enjoy the superb service inside or on the terrace. For a special occasion book the tiki-torch-lit table out on the sand.

Coconut Joe's BAR-GRILL $$
(Map p272; 362 West Bay Rd; meals US$8-16; ⊙noon-midnight) Dine and drink under a huge poinsettia tree at this casual joint on the east side of the road. Most tables are outside on the terrace and things get lively as the evening progresses. Fish tacos, burgers, salads and more go well with the many beers on tap, including the excellent local Ironshore Bock. On weekends DJs lend energy.

Ragazzi ITALIAN $$
(Map p272; Buckingham Sq, West Bay Rd; mains US$15-35; ⊙11:30am-11pm) This much-loved Italian place is far more than the pizzeria it bills itself as. Even though the pizzeria here is excellent (a nice crispy thin crust), there's plenty more of interest besides, with a rich list of antipasti, pasta and mains. Try *scaloppine limone* or Maryland crab ravioli for something different. The wine list is excel-

lent and the non-hotel/resort location a nice change.

Mezza
MEDITERRANEAN $$
(Map p272; West Bay Rd; mains US$18-36; ☺lunch & dinner Mon-Sat, brunch Sun) This buzzing bar-restaurant is a top Seven Mile Beach pick. The menu is made up of creative American-led standards at lunchtime, but becomes much more ambitious at night. Enjoy a broad range of tapas specials or full meals that take seafood and give it a Med flair. The dining room is upstairs from a small mall and has an open-air loft feel.

☆ Entertainment

People don't come to the Cayman Islands for the nightlife, although there's a few decent nightclubs around George Town and Seven Mile Beach – the only ones in the country.

The legal drinking age is 18. As a result of draconian laws, all clubs and bars close at midnight on Saturday, thus Thursday and Friday are the big nights to go out, although bars still close at 1am.

Outside the main tourist zone, consider cabbing it to Morgan's Harbour (raucous saloon highjinks) and Cracked Conch (best for sunsets) in West Bay.

OBar
CLUB
(Map p272; www.obar.ky; Queens Court Plaza, West Bay Rd, Seven Mile Beach; ☺10pm-3am Mon-Fri) Still the best club in town, this unpretentious mall-based nightclub and lounge has great resident DJs, alluring cocktails and occasional live performances.

Calico Jack's
BAR
(Map p268; West Bay Rd, Seven Mile Beach) A classic beach bar for locals, this is where you find your tour-bus driver drinking to forget another day of 'gone to Hell' jokes. It's high-energy fun and people party down in the sand while music echoes out of this entirely open-air shack. There's DJs on Saturday nights.

🔒 Shopping

At the malls clustered around the waterfront, you can buy the usual cruise-ship-port consumer goods such as watches, jewelry, sunglasses, designer clothing, crystal, spirits and cosmetics. You will also encounter a plethora of local treasures, including shell jewelry, thatch work, woodcarvings, crocheted items, pepper sauces, tropical fruit jams, honey and caymanite (Cayman's

semiprecious stone) figurines. Most of it is tat.

Tortuga Rum Co
FOOD
(Map p272; North Sound Way, George Town; ☺10am-5pm Mon-Fri) Some 10,000 addictive rum cakes are made here daily. Sure, you can buy them all over the island – and the region – but those at the factory are freshest and the samples the most generous.

Pure Art
CRAFTS
(Map p268; www.pureart.ky; cnr South Church St & Denham Thompson Way, George Town; ☺9am-5pm Mon-Sat) Head 1.5 miles south of the center for creative and interesting locally made arts and crafts.

Camana Bay
MALL
(Map p268; www.camanabay.com) A vast new upscale mall and development on the North Sound side of Seven Mile Beach. Features upscale chain stores, many condos and a free 75-foot observation tower.

BookNook
BOOKSTORE
(Map p272; Galleria Plaza, West Bay Rd, Seven Mile Beach) The island's largest bookstore has a vast selection.

Hobbies & Books
BOOKSTORE
(Map p272; Piccadilly Centre, Elgin Ave, George Town) Well placed for day-trippers who want reading material back on the boat. Large selection of magazines and newspapers.

ℹ Information

EMERGENCY Police (RCIP; ☎949-4222; Elgin Ave, George Town)

INTERNET ACCESS Cafe del Sol (☺7am-7pm Mon-Sat, 8am-7pm Sun) George Town (Aqua World Duty Free Mall, South Church St, George Town); Seven Mile Beach (cnr West Bay Rd & Lawrence Blvd, Seven Mile Beach) Stylish coffee bars with internet access.

Computer Geeks (Queen's Court, Seven Mile Beach; ☺9am-8pm Mon-Sat) Excellent source for printing and repairs.

MEDICAL SERVICES Cayman Islands Hospital (☎949-8600; www.hsa.ky; Hospital Rd, George Town) Houses a state-of-the-art recompression chamber: call ☎949-2989.

POST Main post office (cnr Edward St & Cardinal Ave, George Town; ☺8:15am-5pm Mon-Fri, 9am-12:30pm Sat)

TOURIST INFORMATION Cayman Islands Tourism Association (www.cita.ky; 1320 West Bay Rd; ☺9am-4pm Mon-Fri, 9am-2pm Sat) Operates a useful office near Seven Mile Beach.

ⓘ THAT'S CAYMAN, BUB

If there's one thing that gets the dander up of locals (in a polite way of course), it's hearing their nation referred to as 'the Caymans.' Don't ask why: they don't know any more than a resident of San Francisco shudders at hearing 'Frisco' – it's nails on a chalkboard. Preferred terms for the entire country are 'Cayman,' or 'Cayman Islands.' Individual islands are called by their correct names.

Department of Tourism (www.caymanislands.ky) The Cayman Islands' tourism department operates information booths that are located at the Owen Roberts International Airport and at the North Terminal cruise-ship dock at George Town harbor. The booth at the airport is open when flights arrive; the booth at the dock is only open when cruise ships are in port.

National Trust (Map p268; www.nationaltrust.org.ky; 558 S Church St; ◷9am-5:30pm Mon-Fri, 9am-1pm Sat) The main office has a wealth of information.

West Bay

North of George Town, West Bay is quietly suburban and home to an excellent turtle farm and the remotely alluring Barkers National Park – the first national park in Cayman.

◉ Sights

Boatswain's Beach   FARM, AMUSEMENT PARK
(Map p268; www.boatswainsbeach.ky; North West Point Rd; general admission adult/child US$45/25, turtle farm only adult/child US$30/20; ◷8am-4:30pm Mon-Sat) The closest thing Cayman has to Disneyland – and a firm favorite with kids.

The **turtle farm** is a unique hatchery where green sea turtles are raised from hatchlings to behemoths averaging over 300lb. While protecting wild populations by meeting market demand for turtle products, the farm has, over the years, also released more than 31,000 hatchlings into the waters surrounding the Cayman Islands. Visitors can peer into tanks filled with specimens ranging from babies to massive adults moshing about in their breeding pond.

Elsewhere in the complex for those paying the full price you have a huge swimming pool, complete with two waterfalls, a shark and predator tank (feeding time is always fun), a bird aviary, a butterfly grove and 'Caymanian Street,' a ye olde Caribbean street where fishermen and craftsmen magically flown in from 'yesteryear' tell stories to anyone unable to run away fast enough. If you have limited time, funds or patience, stick to the turtle farm.

Opposite Boatswain's Beach, **Dolphin Discovery** (www.dolphindiscovery.com) offers patrons the chance to swim with captive dolphins. Note that this is a practice condemned by many animal conservationist groups – including local group Keep Dolphins Free (http://dolphinfreecayman.org).

Hell   TOWN
(Map p268) Featured in thousands of cruise-ship tour brochures coyly promising to 'take you to Hell and back,' the hamlet of Hell is otherwise indistinguishable from the surrounding burbs of West Bay. But it does feature a bus-friendly parking lot complete with sign and gift shop so the masses can dutifully troop off, take a photo and yuck it up on the way to the next stop.

🛏 Sleeping & Eating

Cobalt Coast Resort & Suites   RESORT $$$
(Map p268; ☑946-5656; www.cobaltcoast.com; r US$250-280, ste US$450-550; ❋@☎☀) Most of the guests at this 18-unit resort, located on a pleasantly isolated strip beyond Boatswains Bay, are here to dive. The setting is dramatic, with crashing waves and a small, ever-growing white-sand beach that you have to clamber over rocks to get to. It's a friendly place with great rooms – very spacious and modern. Divetech is the in-house dive center.

Morgan's Harbour   SEAFOOD $$
(Map p268; www.morgansharbour.net; Morgan's Harbour; mains US$13-24; ◷11am-10pm) Right on the fishing dock, this seaman-filled place is popular with those who sail to sea to catch fish. The changing menu reflects the day's catch landed on the restaurant's docks. It's all very casual and the rollicking bar echoes with many a tall tale until, well, maybe midnight. Sunday barbecues (US$17) are popular.

Calypso Grill   SEAFOOD $$$
(Map p268; www.calypsogrillcayman.com; Morgan's Harbour, West Bay; mains US$20-40; ◷lunch & din-

ner Tue-Sun) Tucked away on Morgan's Harbour away from the crowds of Seven Mile Beach, Calypso Grill combines bentwood chairs, antiques and funky touches to produce a most appealing venue. Mains range from simple fresh fish cooked as you ask to more explorative and inventive dishes such as the signature crispy mango shrimp.

Cracked Conch
SEAFOOD, LOUNGE **$$$**

(Map p268; www.crackedconch.com.ky; Northwest Point Rd; mains US$18-48; ☻lunch & dinner) This oceanfront stunner of a restaurant and high-concept lounge has been open for nearly three decades, and despite sounding like a beach bar, it's all white tablecloths and sublime service. The lunch menu is simpler – including excellent salads, while dinner pulls out all the stops – expect elaborate preparations of Caribbean seafood. The vast wooden terrace is ideal at sunset.

Bodden Town
POP 5000

Historic Bodden Town (the surname Bodden will soon be a familiar one if you spend much time in Cayman) was the capital of the Cayman Islands until George Town scooped that honor in the mid-19th century. It's far removed from the bustle of the west in feel – if not distance – and is a worthy stop for a stroll on any round-island tour.

◎ Sights

Pedro St James
HISTORIC BUILDING

(Map p268; www.pedrostjames.ky; Pedro Rd, Savannah; adult/child US$10/free; ☻9am-5pm) An imposing waterfront Caribbean great house dating from 1780, 'Pedro's Castle' has served over the years as everything from jail to courthouse to parliament before making the transition to museum. Touted as the Cayman 'birthplace of democracy,' it was here in 1831 that the decision was made in favor of a public vote for elected representatives. Just as momentously, this is where the Slavery Abolition Act was read in 1835. The grounds showcase native flora, and there's a multimedia presentation evoking 18th-century Cayman. It's 4km west of Bodden Town proper.

Pirate Caves
CAVES

(Map p268; adult/child US$8/5; Bodden Town Rd; ☻9am-6pm) Right in Bodden Town, this is a big hit with kids, as you can explore caves where pirates apparently hid their treasures in the past, along with a mini-zoo, a petting pool for freshwater stingrays and displays of various pirate ephemera. Some of the caves are eerily beautiful even if the treasure hidden here remains elusive.

Mission House
HISTORIC BUILDING

(Map p268; www.nationaltrust.org.ky; 63 Gun Square Rd; adult/child US$6/3; ☻9am-5:30pm Tue-Sat) Two blocks west of Bodden Town's compact center is another of the island's oldest buildings. Battered by Hurricane Ivan in 2004, the mid-18th-century wood-frame house looks better than ever. Displays inside and out in the garden re-create life from 150 years ago.

⊨ Sleeping & Eating

Staying here you can feel you're on a quiet, traditional Caribbean island even as the bright lights of George Town shine 20 minutes west.

WORTH A TRIP

BARKERS NATIONAL PARK

Dedicated in 2004, Barkers National Park is the first land in Cayman to be designated as such. It combines low scrub, long sandy beaches and mangroves. Stingray City is 3km east offshore. A sandy road (OK for driving when not wet) winds through the park. Tracks veer off to the long and narrow beach along the reef-protected shore. Besides hanging out on the sand and swimming, the relatively few visitors also enjoy hikes on narrow trails.

It's windy here and kitesurfing is popular. **Kitesurf Cayman** (Map p268; ☎916-7742; www.kitesurfcayman.com; rental per day CI$100; ☻10am-4pm) has a sweet spot under a tree on the sand. One-on-one lessons cost CI$160 for two hours.

As yet the park has no facilities or visitors center, which is just as well – it's a peaceful place. Follow roads to Conch Point, then head east past the end of the pavement and a gate that's locked at night.

BLUE IGUANAS

At up to one meter in length and often with a brilliant azure hide, Grand Cayman's blue iguanas are a moving spectacle that never ceases to amaze. Yet as recently as 2002 there were fewer than a dozen left in the wild. Perfectly engineered for the dry, scrubby outback on Grand Cayman, the iguanas are poorly suited to modern life. Domestic dogs and cats eat the young and old. Iguanas in search of warmth take shelter under recently parked cars or take a snooze on hot asphalt – behaviors fraught with peril. Worse, the largest and toughest iguanas take the territories closest to food sources (human food scraps are a treat), which also happen to be the most dangerous. So the overall health of the species declines as the toughest animals are killed and are replaced by less-strong individuals from the outback.

But now, nearly 10 years after the blue iguana nadir, their numbers are resurgent thanks to the Blue Iguana Recovery Program at the Queen Elizabeth II Botanic Park. Besides breeding iguanas, the program has set up a vast protected habitat in the wilds of the East End. Today there are 500 iguanas and a population of 1000 is in sight.

Meanwhile on Little Cayman, the rock iguana, a close relative of the blue iguana, faces the same challenges. With the species still visible around the island, locals hope that early intervention will save the rock iguana from extinction as visitor and population numbers rise.

TOP CHOICE **Turtle Nest Inn** GUESTHOUSE **$$**
(Map p268; ☑947-8665; www.turtlenestinn.com; r US$120-200, apt US$160-300; ✳🐾🖥) Located in the town center and right on the water, this Spanish-style guesthouse has trouble keeping up with demands from repeat customers. Some apartments have balconies, others include oceanfront views. Larger units have kitchens and all rooms are spacious with light, tropical colors. Activity gear is included in rates.

TOP CHOICE **Chester's Fish Fry** CARIBBEAN **$**
(Map p268; 563 Bodden Town Rd; mains CI$8-12; ⊙10am-10pm) The nasal siren song of barbecue wafts out from this simple roadside house just east of the center. The smells of fresh fish grilling are irresistible. Picnic tables shelter from the road; a local vendor offers charming stories and hand-crafted artworks in equal proportion. As the sign says: buy one jerk, get one free.

North Side

North Side is geographically isolated from the rest of the island, and was the last district to be settled. Its earliest residents were freed slaves in search of unclaimed land. Today, the district is windswept and uncrowded, providing a direct link to Grand Cayman's past. Its botanic park is a must-see and the drive along the north coast a highlight.

TOP CHOICE **Queen Elizabeth II Botanic Park** GARDEN
(Map p268; www.botanic-park.ky; Frank Sound Dr; adult/child US$10/free; ⊙9am-5:30pm, to 6:30pm Apr-Sep) A veritable treasure trove for anyone wanting to experience the island's native species. The park is home to orchids (in bloom late May through June), parrots and other birds, and nature trails.

The real star here (or should we say stars?) is the **Blue Iguana Recovery Program** (www.blueiguana.ky). A resounding success in bringing the iconic local lizard back from the abyss, the program offers **tours** (adult/child incl garden admission US$30/20; ⊙11am Mon-Sat) of the breeding pens and other areas where the iguanas are encouraged to do what iguanas do.

Mastic Trail NATURE TRAIL
(www.nationaltrust.org.ky) This surprisingly lush 2-mile-long trail meanders through the old-growth forest that once supplied early settlers with timber. Hikers can explore deep into the old-growth forest of Grand Cayman's wild interior; new wooden walkways help you traverse marshy portions. Expect to see wild jasmine, wild coffee, myriad birds, land crabs and much more. Most people start the trail at a parking area on Mastic Rd west of the botanic gardens. The northern trailhead is off North Side Rd. The National Trust offers excellent guided hiking **tours** (☑949-0121; tours CI$20; ⊙most Wed, some Sat); call for details.

Rum Point

Swinging in hammocks and snorkeling are the main activities at this quiet **beach**, which draws fans from all over the island. Much of the time all you'll hear are the offshore breezes. Take some time to explore the trails along the reef-protected shore and mangroves.

🛏 Sleeping & Eating

Retreat at Rum Point   CONDO $$$
(Map p268; 947-9135; www.theretreat.com.ky; North Side/Rum Point; 1-bedroom condo US$250-350, 2-bedroom condo US$290-450; ❄@🛜⛱) The fantastic beach and an exclusive feel are the draw at this beachfront complex, which features screened-in porches for enjoying the night. Amenities include a tennis court, gym, sauna, racquetball court and laundry facilities.

TOP CHOICE Wreck Bar   BURGERS, BAR $
(Map p268; meals US$9-20; ⊙10am-5pm Mon-Sat, 10am-6pm Sun) Beach bars don't come much more friendly than this boozy refuge, which sets up chairs on the sand. Enjoy a famous mudslide cocktail with the sea views right on the beach. The burgers are worth the trip and best enjoyed at the tree-shaded picnic tables.

Rum Point Restaurant   SEAFOOD $$$
(Map p268; 947-9412; mains US$20-40; ⊙6-10pm Tue-Sun) Next door to the Wreck Bar but miles away in foodie aspirations, this long-running fave specializes in elaborate creations of seafood, flown in fresh from around the world. Book a table on the screened porch and call (both to book and to make sure it is open) before making the drive out.

East End

The East End is the place to head if you want a feel for traditional Caymanian life and don't have the time to visit the sister islands. Here, at the furthest point on the island from the commercial and tourism centers of George Town and Seven Mile Beach, open space, quiet hamlets and dramatic shoreline are the main features. To the east of the village itself is the **Wreck of the Ten Sails Park**, commemorating the spot where a legendary shipwreck occurred in 1794. Stroll to the monument and enjoy the sweeping views. West of here along Sea View Rd the reef ends, so there's often pounding surf.

🛏 Sleeping & Eating

Reef Resort   RESORT $$$
(Map p268; 947-0100; www.thereef.com; Collier's Bay; r US$200-400; ❄@🛜⛱) Could this be the next Seven Mile Beach? All 110 rooms in cheery yellow-hued three-story blocks face the sea along the very long, gorgeous beach. Standards are very high, with large, attractive rooms complete with all comforts. There's good snorkeling and diving nearby. Local musical hero Barefoot Man (think Jimmy Buffet without the family-friendly hokum) performs Tuesday and Thursday nights in the bar.

Miss Vivine's Kitchen   CARIBBEAN $
(Map p268; Austin Connolly Dr, Gun Bay; mains CI$5-15; ⊙11am-7pm) There really is a Miss Vivine and she really does live in this roadside home with stellar views of the ocean. Local treats such as red-bean soup, fish balls on rice, fish fritters and much more are served up home-style. Eat at a picnic table under a tree on the terrace and enjoy the scene.

CAYMAN BRAC

POP 1900

Named after the 'brac' or 'bluff' that makes up much of this cheese wedge of an island, the most easterly of the Cayman Islands is markedly different from both Grand and Little Cayman. The simple reason is that, unlike their cousins, the majority of locals do not work in the tourism industry and life here goes on much as it always has. With just one hotel of any size here, head to the Brac to escape the crowds and to engage with nature – the Brac boasts by far the most varied landscapes in the entire country.

The 14-sq-mile Brac is dominated by the Bluff, a dramatic limestone formation that rises gently from the flatlands of the west end to a height of 140ft, traveling the length of the island before plunging into the sea. The road to the top passes through the National Trust Parrot Reserve, a nesting ground for the islands' endangered emerald-green native species and a good place for hikes, and ends at a lighthouse at the blustery Northeast Point.

The island's four main settlements – West End, Stake Bay, Watering Place and Spot Bay – are on the western or northern ends. Resorts and beaches are clustered along the southern tip, including the peaceful expanses of the public beach.

◉ Sights

FREE **Cayman Brac Museum** MUSEUM
(Stake Bay; ☺9am-4pm Mon-Fri) Housed in a pretty white-and-blue-painted colonial house on the coastal road to Stake Bay. It's not very clear that it's a museum from the road, but it's just in front of the island administration buildings. The charming collection details life for early settlers on the island during a time when it was largely cut off from the rest of the world.

Bat Cave CAVE
You'll find oodles of the namesake residents here. Just off the road, the roof seems to drip down to the ground at this traditional hurricane shelter and geologic oddity.

🏃 Activities

Pick up the useful *Heritage Sites & Trails* leaflet, which includes a good map, from any hotel, the airport or the tourist office.

Hiking

TOP CHOICE **Bluff** NATURAL FEATURE
The best way to explore this literal high point of your visit is to walk along the **Lighthouse Footpath** that runs along the cliff's edge, giving incredible views and allowing you to see the varied birdlife such as brown boobies and frigate birds gliding in the updrafts. At 140ft, it is the highest point in Cayman. There's no circular trail, so you'll need to drive or cycle to the starting point at the **lighthouse** and then double back on yourself.

Another hiker-only trail, Bight Rd, crosses the Brac north and south through the National Trust Parrot Reserve, where you should have no trouble spotting one of the 400 remaining Cayman Brac parrots that are slowly reestablishing themselves. Start at the midpoint on Major Donald Dr or in the north at the staircase leading up the bluff from North East Bay Rd. It includes a 200m boardwalk through the dense forest that echoes with songbirds.

Westerly Ponds BIRD-WATCHING
Bird-watchers should head for the Westerly Ponds at the western tip of the island, where there are over 100 species of birds to be seen nesting around the wetlands and helpful viewing platforms have been built. Down the road beyond the airport runway there's also **Salt Water Pond**, where a large colony of least terns can be seen in residence from April to August.

Diving & Snorkeling

With crystal waters affording superb visibility and over 40 permanent dive moorings, Cayman Brac attracts its share of diving and snorkeling enthusiasts. Of particular interest is the wreck of a 315ft Russian frigate now named the *Captain Keith Tibbetts*. It was purchased from Cuba and intentionally sunk offshore off the northwest of the island to serve as a dive attraction.

Reef Divers (☎948-1642; www.bracreef.com; Brac Reef Resort, West End; 1-/2-tank dives US$65/95) is the longest-established dive operator on the island. Priority is given to resort guests, but nonguests are welcome too.

🛏 Sleeping

Accommodations range from casual Caymanian guest houses and private condos to the main resort, Brac Reef, which caters to diving enthusiasts. Lodging prices are cheaper here than elsewhere in the Cayman Islands.

TOP CHOICE **Walton's Mango Manor** B&B $$
(☎948-0518; www.waltonsmangomanor.com; Stake Bay; r US$120-140, villa US$185-210; ❄☎) This whimsical place is one of the more unusual guesthouses in Cayman. Guests are accommodated in the five-bedroom main house decorated with traditional antiques, including a banister made from the mast of an old sailing schooner. All rooms have private facilities and those upstairs (the best) have balconies. The lush garden runs down to the beach, where there's also a two-bedroom villa, as well as the only synagogue in Cayman.

Brac Reef Beach Resort RESORT $$
(☎948-1323; www.bracreef.com; West End; r US$145-200; ❄@☎☀) If this is as close to a resort as the Brac gets, then that's a great sign – Brac Reef is a relaxed and friendly diving hotel on a charming stretch of beach. The 40 rooms, each with either a small patio or balcony, are spread out around a pool and Jacuzzi. Bicycles and kayaks are available for guests and there

are nature trails, dotted with hammocks, through the grounds. Meal and diving packages are offered.

Carib Sands Beach Resort CONDO $$
(☎948-1121; www.caribsands.com; West End; 1-/2-/3-bedroom from US$150/250/310; ❄✿) This condo complex and the Brac Caribbean are next to each other and right on the beach. Both are managed by the same company. Both have great sea views and a pool, and offer a large choice of serviced, comfortably furnished apartments with balconies. The Carib Sands is a vision in three-story pink.

Brac Caribbean CONDO $$
(☎948-2265; www.866thebrac.com; West End; 1-/2-bedroom from US$165/220; ❄✿✿) Like its sibling, the Carib Sands, this condo complex offers well-run and understated luxury. The more demure of the duo, the three-story blocks are a stormy blue.

✕ Eating

TOP CHOICE **Aunt Sha's Kitchen** RESTAURANT $
(West End Rd; mains US$9-15; ◷8am-11pm) This Brac favorite (it seems that everybody on the island comes in for takeout lunch at least once a week) is in a tidy white and turquoise building fronted by a shady tree. Patrons wait on seats along the porch for the famously good Caymanian home cooking – fresh fish, goat curry, grilled tuna and chicken stew are all specialties.

Captain's Table RESTAURANT $$
(West End; mains US$12-35; ◷lunch & dinner) The restaurant of the Brac Caribbean condo resort, this is a good option, especially if you can get a table outside by the pool. The food is Caribbean and international, with burgers, seafood and salads served through the day. The bar is the perfect place to order a Rusty Nail cocktail.

Bucky's CAFE $
(West End Rd; mains US$8-20; ◷noon-9pm; 🛜) Cheap and cheerful food such as Jamaican jerk-flavored hot dogs and a very popular West Indian buffet are the food draws at this casual place. The slightly swank bar area is big with sports buffs.

ℹ Information

Cayman National Bank (West End Cross Rd; ◷9am-4pm Mon-Fri) Has a 24hr ATM and currency exchange.

Faith Hospital (☎948-2243; Stake Bay) This modern hospital serves both the Brac and Little Cayman.

Nature Cayman (www.naturecayman.com) Website that covers both the Brac and Little Cayman. Packed with information on everything from birds to marine life.

Post office (West End; ◷8:30am-5pm Mon-Fri) Internet access is available in the lobby (per 30 minutes/hour US$4/8).

Tourist office (☎948-1649; www.caymanislands.ky; North Bay Rd; ◷8:30am-5pm Mon-Fri) Hidden away just east of the airport adjacent to the West End Community Park, this is a good resource for information and maps. Ask about island tours.

ℹ Getting There & Around

AIR Flights from Grand Cayman and Little Cayman to Cayman Brac's **Gerrard Smith International Airport** are offered daily by **Cayman Airways Express** (www.caymanairways.com).

BICYCLE Bikes may be rented or borrowed from the resorts.

CAR Renting a car (about US$40 to US$60 per day) is the best way to enjoy the island.

B&S Motor Ventures Ltd (☎948-1646; www.bandsmv.com) Hires scooters, 4WDs and bikes as well as cars; free delivery.

CB Rent-A-Car (☎948-2329; www.cbrentacar.com; Gerrard Smith International Airport) Right across from the terminal.

HITCHHIKING There's no public transportation on Cayman Brac, but the negligible crime rate – and the amiability of the locals – makes hitch-hiking safe and easy. The mere sight of a visitor marching down the roadway often results in ride offers by passing motorists.

TAXIS There are few taxis; lodging providers will pick you up by prior arrangement.

Elo's Taxi (☎948-0220)

Hill's Taxi (☎948-0540)

LITTLE CAYMAN

POP 120

Tiny Little Cayman (the clue is indeed in the name) is a joy. With more resident iguanas than humans, this delightful island is the place to head for solitude, tranquility and the odd spot of extraordinary diving. Despite its small size (barely 30 sq km), Little Cayman is firmly established on the world map of great diving sites for its extraordinary Bloody Bay Marine Park, where you'll find some of the best wall diving anywhere in the world.

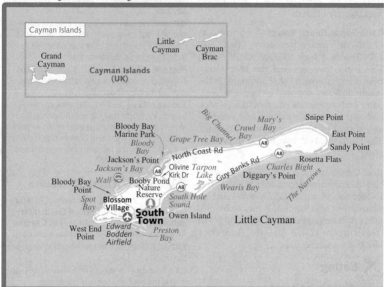

As your twin-prop plane swoops down over the vivid turquoise sea and onto the grass landing strip of the tiny airport, you'll know that you have arrived at one of the Caribbean's most unspoiled and untrammeled destinations (although the myriad 'for sale' signs on land hint at a more developed future, so don't delay, visit today). You can circle the island on the one main road in a couple of hours or bike your way around on a lazy day. Just watch for the endangered local rock iguanas: these close relatives of the equally huge blue iguana on Grand Cayman have the right of way.

◉ Sights

The sights of Little Cayman are almost entirely natural, whether they be the birds that nest in the wetlands, the iguanas that bask by the road or the marine life on the reef.

TOP CHOICE National Trust Visitors Centre   MUSEUM

(Guy Banks Rd; ◷9am-noon & 2-6pm Mon-Sat) This should be your first island stop. It's a combination of museum, cafe (the luscious homemade ice-cream is amazing), information center and gift shop (T-shirts read 'Little Boobies'). It backs onto the **Booby Pond Nature Reserve**, home to one of the hemisphere's largest breeding populations of red-footed boobies and a large colony of swooping frigate birds. The two-level veranda also has telescopes available for visitors.

FREE Little Cayman Museum   MUSEUM

(Guy Banks Rd, Blossom Village; ◷3-5pm Thu & Fri) A good place to start is the tiny old house containing local artifacts and beach treasures. A building next door has historical maritime flotsam. If you'd like to visit outside limited opening hours, call Nelvie Eldemire (✆948-2999) and she'll usually be happy to open it up for you. Nearby are old frame buildings that are decades old.

⚲ Beaches

Owen Island   ISLAND

Stroke your inner pirate at this deserted tiny island that's a short kayak ride or swim across a narrow channel from Southern Cross Club. The beach here is unspoiled and the vegetation thick and unexplored. Make a day of it with a picnic. The club rents **kayaks** to nonguests for US$45 per half day.

Sandy Point   BEACH

Little Cayman's best beach is a splotch of reef-protected powder that rarely has more

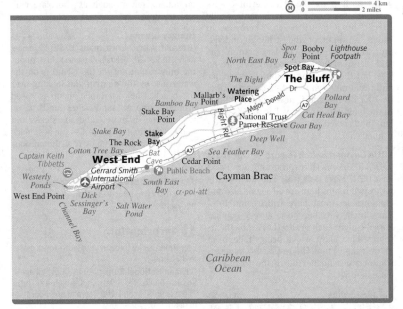

than half a dozen people visiting at any one time. There's a tiny pier, limited shade and breaking waves 200m out.

✦ Activities

Little Cayman has over 60 dive sites marked with moorings. Snorkelers and shore divers find plenty of satisfaction at many well-known sites.

The resorts have diving operations. Recommended diving outfitters (one-/two-tank dives average US$70/95) include **Pirates Point Resort** (☑949-1010; www.piratespoint resort.com; Guy Banks Rd) and **Southern Cross Club** (☑948-1099; www.southerncrossclub.com; Guy Banks Rd).

TOP CHOICE **Bloody Bay Marine Park**　　　DIVING
The main draw on the island is the excellent diving and snorkeling, which is legendary among divers, who come from all over the world for a truly exhilarating experience. Near the shore and at a depth of only 18ft, **Bloody Bay Wall** plummets vertically into aquamarine infinity as the divers hovering over the abyss wonder whether they are hallucinating. You can see an amazing image of it online at www .bloodybaywall.com.

Jackson's Point　　　SNORKELING
The perfect stop on a round-island bike ride is this series of underwater spots along a mini-wall just 50m from the narrow strip of rocky sand on the shore. Look for the 'Historic Anchorage' sign where Olivine Kirk Dr meets North Coast Rd.

⌂ Sleeping

For such a small island there's no shortage of low-key resorts here. Most offer favorable diving packages when booked in advance. Most prefer weeklong bookings.

TOP CHOICE **Southern Cross Club**　　　RESORT $$$
(☑948-1099; www.southerncrossclub.com; Guy Banks Rd; all-inclusive cottage five nights per person US$1390-1645; ✳@☂☀) Definitely the classiest place on the island, Southern Cross is a gorgeous, boutique creation smartly run by an expat couple. Most of the 12 bungalows are right on the beach, with outdoor showers and bright decor. Some have wi-fi. The management is ecoconscious. Free bikes and kayaks, excellent food, a top diving operator and friendly staff are other reasons to stay. Owen Island is just offshore.

Pirates Point Resort　　　RESORT $$$
(☑948-1010; www.piratespointresort.com; Guy Banks Rd; all-inclusive per person from US$235-300;

✽◉✇✉) Run by the characterful Gladys Howard, this rustic resort is fantastically located on a pretty beach. There are 10 rooms, all different and strikingly individual, with mosquito nets, large bathrooms and plenty of books to read. There are no TVs, but there's a busy clubhouse-style bar and restaurant (with an all-inclusive alcohol deal for divers) and it never closes. Wi-fi is in the main building only. The food is excellent (and served to nonguests) – Gladys is a trained chef.

Little Cayman Beach Resort   RESORT **$$$**
(⌨948-1033; www.littlecayman.com; Guy Banks Rd; r US$170-285; ✽◉✇✉) The 40 recently renovated rooms here are all a good size and comfortable; most have fridges and tubs. The Beach Nuts bar hosts a very popular karaoke night each Friday (hosted by the irrepressible Calay), which brings folks from all over the island. The resort also manages some condos further down the road. It is close to town.

Paradise Villas   VILLAS **$$**
(⌨948-0001; www.paradisevillas.com; Blossom Village; r US$175-210; ✽◉✇✉) You can practically step off the airplane and into your room here (it's a 100m walk) – but these 12 smart and comfortable cottages are right on the beach and are idyllic with verandas and hammocks coming as standard. Wi-fi doesn't reach all units.

Blue Lagoon   HOTEL **$$**
(⌨945-8096; Guy Banks Rd; r US$80-125; ✽◉✇) This is the cheapest hotel on the island, and it has 12 rooms in a couple of charming colonial-style buildings right on the beach. There's a screened-in cafe for meals which has a bar that can get loud. Larger apartments have kitchens. It's on an isolated bit of coast.

✗ Eating

Pirates Point Resort and Little Cayman Beach Resort have good restaurants and bars popular with nonguests.

TOP CHOICE **National Trust Visitors Centre**   CAFE **$**
(Guy Banks Rd; treats US$3; ⊙9am-noon & 2-6pm Mon-Sat) The cafe part of this excellent museum and visitors centre has excellent homemade food. The cakes, muffins and coffees are good but the real treat is the homemade ice cream. Luscious and creamy, it comes in

tantalizing flavors such as chocolate chili and key lime.

Hungry Iguana   RESTAURANT-BAR **$$**
(Blossom Village; lunch mains US$10-15, dinner mains US$24-38; ⊙lunch & dinner) Just about the only restaurant on the island is on the water just by the airstrip and looking over the beach. The vast lunch menu is based around burgers, sandwiches and pasta, while dinner is more elaborate: steaks and seafood dominate. This is also the best place to come for a drink; enjoy it at the outdoor tables.

Village Square Store   MARKET **$**
(Guy Banks Rd, Blossom Village; ⊙closed Sun) Has groceries, beer and other basic necessities.

❶ Information

Everything is clustered in tiny South Town, close to the airport.

Cayman National Bank (⌨948-0051; Village Sq, Guy Banks Rd; ⊙9am-2:30pm Mon & Thu) There is no ATM on Little Cayman and hours here are few.

Nature Cayman (www.naturecayman.com) Website that covers both the Brac and Little Cayman. Packed with information on everything from birds to marine life.

Post office (Village Office; ⊙9:30am-12:30pm, & 2-3:30pm Mon-Fri, 10:30am-1:30pm Sat) This tiny post office is located near the shore.

Village Square Store (Guy Banks Rd, Blossom Village; ⊙closed Sun) Phonecards can be purchased here. This is also the only shop for goods as diverse as sundries and fishing gear.

❶ Getting There & Around

AIR Flights from Grand Cayman and Cayman Brac to Little Cayman's tiny **Edward Bodden Airfield** are offered several times a day by Cayman Airways Express. It's security-free and you can walk to town and the beach. Talk of a new airport is just that, talk.

BICYCLE Cycling is the preferred mode of transportation on the island, and nearly every hotel makes bicycles available for guests. Next to the airport, **Paradise Villas** (www.paradise villas.com; per day US$10) rents bikes to daytrippers. Be sure to take plenty of water as your main source is the Village Square Store.

CAR & SCOOTER Rentals are available from **Scooten Scooters** (⌨916-4971; www.scooten scooters.com; half day from US$32), which delivers to you. For a vehicle, **McLaughlin Rentals** (⌨948-1000; littlecay@candw.ky; Guy Banks Rd; per day from US$80) provides small 4WDs from its office next door to the Village Square Store near the airport.

A basic looping tour of the island is eight miles long, some on packed gravel and dirt roads, and can be done either by car or bicycle.

UNDERSTAND CAYMAN ISLANDS

History

For the first century after Christopher Columbus happened upon the Cayman Islands in 1503, the islands remained un-inhabited by people – which may explain why multitudes of sea turtles were happy to call the place home, giving the islands their original Spanish name, Las Tortugas. The sun-bleached landscape languished in a near-pristine state, undisturbed but for the occasional intrusion of sailors stopping in to swipe some turtles and fill up on fresh water.

No permanent settlers set up house until well after the 1670 acquisition of the islands – and its turtles – by the British Crown, which has held dominion over the three islands ever since. Once settlers started trickling in from Jamaica in the early 18th century, Caymanians quickly established their reputation as world-class seafarers. From the 1780s the Caymanian shipbuilding industry produced schooners and other seacraft used for interisland trade and turtling.

By 1800 the population numbered fewer than 1000 – of whom half were slaves. After the Slavery Abolition Act was read at Pedro St James (near Bodden Town on Grand Cayman) in 1835, most freed slaves remained, and by 1900 the Cayman population had quintupled.

Tourists & Money Blow In

Until the mid-20th century, the economy remained tied to the sea with fishing, turtling and shipbuilding as the main industries. Divers put the Cayman Islands on the international tourist map as early as the 1950s; islanders were understandably protective of their little slice of paradise and were slow to relinquish their isolation. By the next decade, however, Caymanians had begun fashioning the tax structure that's made Grand Cayman an economic powerhouse – and

designing an infrastructure that's made it a capital of Caribbean tourism.

In September 2004, Hurricane Ivan gave Grand Cayman a body blow, causing such widespread destruction that tourism was halted and a curfew enforced for several months to prevent looting. Fortunately, Cayman Brac and Little Cayman did not receive a direct hit and damage to the smaller islands was limited. Reflecting the local can-do spirit, damage has been all but erased.

Culture

For centuries, the Cayman Islands had been left to simmer undisturbed in their own juices as the rest of the world rushed headlong into modernity. As recently as 50 years ago (aside from a few adventurers and fishing nuts) there were few tourists. Electric power was provided solely by noisy generators, and most islanders did without it. What has occurred between then and now constitutes a Caymanian cultural revolution. With the advent of large-scale tourism and big-business banking, life on the islands has changed so rapidly that cultural discourse has turned to measuring what's been gained and lost.

Historically, the population is an amalgamation with Jamaican, North American, European and African roots, but contemporary Cayman has become even more multifaceted. For better or worse, a large influx of expatriate workers – representing over 80 countries – has caused Caymanians to become a minority in their own country. The populous west end of Grand Cayman truly feels like a tidy corner of the US.

Landscape & Wildlife
Above & Below Water

Located approximately 150 miles south of Cuba and 180 miles west of Jamaica, the Cayman Islands consist of Grand Cayman and two smaller islands – Cayman Brac and Little Cayman – 75 miles to the northeast and 5 miles apart. All three islands are low-lying, flat-topped landmasses, although Cayman Brac does have a 140ft cliff, by far the most dramatic scenery in the country. In fact, the Cayman Islands are the tips of massive submarine mountains that just barely emerge from the awesome Cayman

PRACTICALITIES

» **Electricity** 110V, 60Hz; US-style three-pin plugs are used.

» **Newspapers & Magazines** Tourist publications abound; among the better is *Cayman Explore*. The *Caymanian Compass* is a daily with local stories, such as cows loose in George Town.

» **Radio** Radio Cayman – 89.9FM & 105.3FM; BBC News, local talk and music.

» **Weights & Measures** Imperial system.

Trench, an area with the deepest water in the Caribbean.

Encircling all three of the islands are shallow waters and a reef system harboring one of the world's richest accumulations of marine life. At Bloody Bay Wall, on the north shore of Little Cayman, the seafloor ends abruptly at a depth of only 18ft to 25ft, dropping off into a 6000ft vertical cliff. Along its sheer face grows an astonishing variety of corals, sponges and sea fans and thousands of mobile creatures going about their daily business as the occasional diver looks on, agog.

Wildlife

With nearly 200 native winged species, the islands offer outstanding bird-watching. Keep your eyes open and you'll spot parrots, boobies, yellow-bellied sapsuckers, herons and egrets. Reptiles include celebrities such as green sea turtles and blue and rock iguanas, and plenty of common geckos and lizards (the latter sometimes making an appearance in the baths of luxury hotels). The islands try to balance protecting the environment with development – driving on beaches is against the law due to the harm this can do to turtle habitats, iguanas have the right of way and there are plentiful marine replenishment zones where fishing is not permitted.

The islands aren't lush but rather dry and scrubby. Poisonous species include maiden plum (a weed with rash-causing sap), lady's hair or cowitch (a vine with fiberglass-like barbs) and the vicious manchineel tree, which produces a skin-blistering sap. Take care not to shelter under a manchineel in the rain! Other indigenous plants are cochineel, used as a shampoo as well as eaten, and pingwing, whose barbed branches were once fashioned into a natural fence.

SURVIVAL GUIDE

Directory A–Z

Accommodations

Accommodations aren't cheap in Cayman, but are usually of high standard. Condos and resorts cluster in the region of Seven Mile Beach.

Budget travelers should head for guesthouses where they exist, and try their best to travel outside of high season, when savings everywhere can be huge. A few resorts cater specifically to divers and include excursions and equipment rentals in their prices, as well as food. Always see if there's a self-catering and nondiving option to get a lower rate.

In high season your choices are very limited below US$150 a night; top resorts are well over US$350 a night.

Rates quoted are for walk-ins during the high season (mid-December through mid-April) and do not include the 10% government tax and 10% to 15% service tax. Many places will also expect a gratuity for staff. Low-season rates are as much as 40% cheaper.

$	budget	less than US$75
$$	midrange	US$75 to US$200
$$$	top end	more than US$200

Business Hours

The following are standard business hours across the islands. Exceptions are noted in specific listings. Note that much is closed on Sunday.

Banks 9am-3:30pm Mon-Fri

Bars 5pm-1am Mon-Fri, to midnight Sat & Sun

Restaurants noon-11pm

Shops 9am-6pm Mon-Sat

Children

Families with children couldn't hope for a better travel destination than the Cayman Islands. On Grand Cayman, kids of most ages will appreciate Boatswain's Beach turtle farm in West Bay and the Bodden Town Pirate Caves.

Most hotels have plenty of rooms that sleep four people or more, and many offer babysitting services and activity programs. The gentle sandy beaches provide a very safe playground for kids of all ages, and older kids can accompany the adults and enjoy the many water-sports activities. Most diving and water-sports operators offer programs for kids as well.

Embassies & Consulates

Citizens of the US should contact the embassy in Kingston, Jamaica.

UK (☑244-2401; Governor's Office, Ste 202, 154 Smith Rd, George Town)

Food

The following price categories for the cost of a main course are used in Eating listings in this chapter.

$	budget	less than US$10
$$	midrange	US$10 to US$25
$$$	top end	more than US$25

Gay & Lesbian Travelers

Homosexuality is legal in Cayman, but the islands remain very conservative so discretion is key. Most hotels accommodate same-sex couples but any kind of public display of affection is taboo. There are no gay bars or clubs in the Cayman Islands; most local gay contacts are made through the internet.

Public Holidays

In addition to those observed throughout the region (p872), Cayman has the following public holidays:

National Heroes' Day Fourth Monday in January

Ash Wednesday Late February

Discovery Day Third Monday in May

Queen's Birthday Second Monday in June

Constitution Day First Monday in July

Remembrance Day Second Monday in November

Health

There are excellent medical facilities in the Cayman Islands. For minor illnesses, nearly all hotels will have a doctor on call or will be able to help you find assistance. In more serious cases there is a good hospital on Grand Cayman (p277), and a smaller one on Cayman Brac (p283); anyone who falls ill on Little Cayman will usually be flown to the latter hospital.

All visitors to the Cayman Islands should have comprehensive medical insurance as no reciprocal health-care agreements exist with other countries.

Tap water is safe to drink.

Internet Access

Cayman has good web access. Most hotels and condos offer wi-fi. Public hot spots usually come with a fee.

Money

The official currency is the Cayman Islands dollar (CI$), permanently fixed at an exchange rate of CI$0.80 to US$1 (CI$1 equals US$1.25). Cayman dollars and US dollars are accepted throughout the islands, although you'll usually get change in CI$ even if you pay with US$.

A 10% to 15% tip is the norm in restaurants and taxis. In hotels, 10% is usually added to the bill.

Telephone

The Cayman Islands' country code is ☑1; the area code is ☑345. To call any other country with a country code of ☑1 (most of North America and the Caribbean), just dial 1 and the 10-digit number. For other countries, dial the international access code ☑011 + country code + number.

CELL PHONES

GSM cell phones are compatible with local SIM cards. There is also 3G service. The main operators are **Digicel** (www.digicelcayman.com) and **Lime** (www.time4lime.com/ky).

Getting There & Away

All visitors are required to have a valid passport and a return ticket.

Air

There are flights to Grand Cayman's Owen Roberts International Airport from the US with American Airlines, Delta, United and US Airways. Air Canada and British Airways also fly to Grand Cayman.

Cayman Airways (www.caymanairways. com) connects Grand Cayman with Havana, Cuba; Kingston and Montego Bay, Jamaica; and Chicago, Miami, New York and Tampa in the US. Cayman Airways also has a weekly service from Miami to Cayman Brac.

Sea

Scores of cruise ships drop anchor in George Town from Monday to Saturday. There are no deep-water port facilities so passengers shuttle ship to shore using frequent tenders.

Those entering Cayman waters by private yacht should display the red ensign version of the Cayman flag and report to the port authority in George Town to clear customs and immigration.

Getting Around

Air

Each island has an airport. See under each islands' Getting There & Away section for details.

Cayman Airways Express (www.cayman airways.com), a subsidiary of Cayman Airways, provides near-monopoly service between the three islands. All flights usually call at both sister islands on their way to and from Grand Cayman. With a little planning you can make quick visits to both smaller islands from Grand Cayman in one day.

Bicycle

Bikes are readily available on all three islands and are often included as part of an accommodations package. Flat terrain, relatively light traffic and near-constant sea access make cycling a pleasure, although the heavy traffic in and around George Town and Seven Mile Beach can be nettlesome on Grand Cayman.

Bus

Public minibuses operate on nine routes across Grand Cayman that radiate out from the bus depot on Edward St in George Town. Service is during daytime and frequency falls off the further east you go from George Town. Fares range from CI$2 to CI$3.50. Routes 1 and 2 cover George Town, West Bay and Seven Mile Beach. Ask at your accommodation for the nearest stop; bus drivers can advise on other details.

There is no bus service on Cayman Brac and Little Cayman.

Car & Motorcycle

DRIVER'S LICENSE

Visitors must obtain a temporary driver's license from their car-rental agency (US$7.50 to US$10 depending on who issues it); you'll need to show a valid driver's license from your home country.

RENTAL

Driving is an essential part of life on the islands, with limited public transportation and much of the island given over to parking. While traffic on the islands is light compared with big cities, it can still be surprisingly heavy in and around George Town and Seven Mile Beach, especially during rush hour. Driving on the sister islands is a joy as cars are very few and far between.

Most rentals are automatics, although 4WDs may have manual transmissions. A variety of models at competitive rates are available in Grand Cayman. On Cayman Brac, there are a limited number of cars, with fewer still on Little Cayman. Although you drive on the left, you will have a choice between left- and right-hand-drive cars.

You must be aged at least 21 to rent a car in the Cayman Islands, and some rental agencies' insurance will not cover renters under 25; check with your rental company in advance.

Scooter and motorcycle rentals are available on all three islands.

ROAD RULES

» Driving is on the left-hand side of the road.
» Seat-belt use is mandatory.
» Speed limits are very low; 25mph is common.
» Iguanas have right of way, which simply means don't hit the endangered critters.

Cuba

Best Beaches

Best Places to Stay

Why Go?

Cuba is a perennial learning curve. Just when you think you've sussed it out, it floors you with another unfathomable mystery. That's what makes it so compelling.

Cuba's intricacies are a result of its history, a tale of external interference and internal strife that has bred bloodshed, slavery, invasion, colonization and popular revolution. Sandwiched between the US to the north and Latin America to the south, the archipelago has long struggled to work out where it fits in. Even its ecology, as scientist Alexander von Humboldt once opined, is decidedly weird, a kind of 'Caribbean Galapagos' where contradictory phenomena coexist.

If you've arrived in search of sun, sea, sand and libidinous Caribbean rhythms, Cuba has them all in abundance. But in a land of few material possessions, it's the innumerable impossible-to-buy riches that leave the most lasting impressions. Escape from the resorts and seek them out.

When to Go

Peak times for travelers are Christmas, Easter, July and August. Overbooking and price hikes are the disadvantages at these times, especially during July and August, when it's also unpleasantly hot throughout much of the country. The ideal time to visit is January to May, when it's warm but uncrowded and there's no threat of hurricanes (which can be a problem on the coasts from June to November). Festivals happen all year round. Santiago de Cuba's July Carnaval and Havana's February jazz festival are highlights.

Fast Facts

» **Area** 110,860 sq km

» **Population** 11.2 million

» **Capital** Havana

» **Telephone country code** ☑53

» **Emergency** ☑106

Set Your Budget

» **Budget room** CUC$20 to CUC$35

» **Two-course evening meal** CUC$10 to CUC$15

» **Museum entrance** CUC$1 to CUC$5

» **Bottle of beer** CUC$1

» **City transport ticket** CUC$0.20

Resources

» **Cuba Absolutely** (www.cubaabsolutely.com) Magazine covering art, culture, business and travel

» **Center for Cuban Studies** (www.cubaupdate.org) Information on legal US travel to Cuba

» **Havana Journal** (www.havanajournal.com) Objective and up-to-date nexus for Cuban news stories

Itineraries

ONE WEEK

While seven days can easily be spent soaking up Havana's rich brew of culture, history and nightlife, an overnight trip to Viñales, Santa Clara or Trinidad is a great way to see some more of the country.

TWO WEEKS

After several days in Havana, either head west to Viñales and then go diving at María La Gorda, or east to Trinidad, Santa Clara and the beaches at Playa Ancón.

THREE WEEKS

Follow the two-week itinerary on the eastern route and then head east via Camagüey to Santiago de Cuba and Baracoa on Cuba's eastern tip.

GETTING TO NEIGHBORING ISLANDS

Connections between Cuba and other Caribbean islands aren't the piece of cake they should be, thanks largely to strict trading laws imposed by the US. Aside from organised cruises, there are no regular ferries to Cuba, although private boats may dock at any of seven international marinas, all of which have customs facilities.

Air connections are a better bet. There are flights to/from Havana to the Bahamas, Cayman Islands, Haiti, Dominican Republic and Guadeloupe.

Essential Food & Drink

Traditional Cuban food is called *comida criolla*, though after 50 years of on–off rationing, it is usually a leaner, pared-down version of what you might find on neighboring islands. Staples include rice, beans, pork and root vegetables.

» **Rice & beans** Known variously as *moros y cristianos* or *congrí*, these ingredients anchor nearly all Cuban dishes.

» **Ropa vieja** Shredded beef in a tomato-based sauce.

» **Tostones** Unripe green plantain, sliced and fried in a shallow pan.

» **Rum** Usually drunk neat by the locals, but also popular in cocktails such as mojitos, daiquiris and Cuba libres.

Tropic of Cancer

Long Island

Crooked Island

Acklins Island

Great Exuma

Cayo Jutías

Archipiélago de los Colorados

Cabo de San Antonio

Península de Guanahacabibes

María la Gorda

Punta Frances

Isla de la Juventud

NUEVA GERONA

Archipiélago de los Canarreos

Cayo Largo del Sur

Caribbean Sea

PINAR DEL RÍO

Las Terrazas

Soroa

Viñales ③

Autopista Havana

Autopista Pinar del Río

Playas del Este

HAVANA ①

Surgidero de Batabanó

Ciénaga de Zapata

Parque Nacional Zapata

Playa Larga

Bahía de Cochinos (Bay of Pigs)

Playa Girón

Autopista Nacional

Carretera Central

MATANZAS

Cárdenas

Varadero

Archipiélago de Sabana

Cienfuegos

Rancho Luna

Topes de Collantes

Meyer

Playa Ancón

Valle de los Ingenios

Trinidad ⑥

SANTA CLARA

Remedios

Cayo Santa María

Cayo Coco

Archipiélago de Camagüey

SANCTI SPÍRITUS

Morón

CIEGO DE ÁVILA

Cayo Guillermo ⑦

Cayo Coco

Archipiélago de los Jardines de la Reina

CAMAGÜEY ⑤

Carretera Central

Playa Santa Lucía

LAS TUNAS

Manzanillo

Marea del Portillo

Sierra Maestra

Pico Turquino (1972m)

BAYAMO

HOLGUÍN

Guardalavaca

Moa

SANTIAGO DE CUBA ②

Baconao

GUANTÁNAMO

Parque Nacional Alejandro de Humboldt

Baracoa ④

El Yunque (575m)

Archipiélago de Camagüey

Cayman Brac

Little Cayman

CAYMAN ISLANDS (UK)

Grand Cayman

GEORGE TOWN ✪

0   100 km
0   60 miles

N

Cuba Highlights

① Stay in a casa particular in **Havana** (p294), a city of grandeur and romance despite its decrepitude

② Discover **Santiago de Cuba** (p329), Cuba's second city, with a revolutionary history, legendary music and *mucho* charm

③ Escape urbanity in **Viñales** (p318), home to extraordinary landscapes

④ Visit oddball **Baracoa** (p337), a place that is different even by Cuban standards

⑤ Stop off in **Camagüey** (p327), a city of earthenware pots, winding lanes and half-forgotten churches

⑥ Take in the colonial plazas that emit long shadows at sunset in **Trinidad** (p324), Cuba's worst-kept secret

⑦ Follow in the footsteps of Hemingway at **Cayo Guillermo** (p329), a small north-coast key with deep-sea fishing and Cuba's best beach

HAVANA

🎵7 / POP 2.2 MILLION

Ah...Havana, city of jarring paradoxes and unfathomable contradictions, where seductive beauty sidles up to spectacular decay and revolutionary iconography is juxtaposed with sun, sea, sand, sex and a diluting slice of austere socialism. There's fascinating history here, wrapped up in erudite museums and foresighted restoration projects; and tremendous music too, from gritty street rumba to kitschy cabaret. But Havana's greatest allure is its street theater, the raw snippets of everyday life that go on all around you: the mother in rollers and the baseball-playing schoolkids, the wandering troubadours and the cigar-smoking doctor trying to jump-start his 1951 Plymouth. The attraction is in the authenticity. Habaneros (the people of Havana) don't just survive; they duck and dive, scheme and dream, create and debate, but, most of all, they *live* – with a rare passion.

◉ Sights

HABANA VIEJA

The core of the Cuban capital is the Unesco World Heritage site of Habana Vieja (Old Havana), a fantastic cluster of stunning buildings and churches, many of which have been beautifully restored from near ruins to their former glory over the past decade.

Plaza de la Catedral   HISTORIC SQUARE

(Map p296) Habana Vieja's most uniform square is a museum to Cuban baroque, with all the surrounding buildings, including the city's magnificent cathedral, dating from the 1700s. Despite this homogeneity, it is actually the newest of the four squares in the old town, with its present layout dating from the 18th century.

Catedral de San Cristóbal de
La Habana   CATHEDRAL

(Map p296; cnr San Ignacio & Empedrado; ⊘before noon) Dominated by two unequal towers and framed by a theatrical baroque facade designed by Italian architect Francesco Borromini, Havana's incredible cathedral was once described by novelist Alejo Carpentier as 'music set in stone.' The Jesuits began construction of the church in 1748 and work continued despite their expulsion in 1767. The remains of Columbus were interred here from 1795 until 1898, when they were moved to Seville.

Plaza de Armas   HISTORIC SQUARE

(Map p296) Havana's oldest square was laid out in the early 1520s, soon after the city's foundation, and was originally known as Plaza de Iglesia after a church – the Parroquial Mayor – that once stood on the site of the present-day Palacio de los Capitanes Generales. Today's plaza, along with most of the buildings around it, dates from the late 1700s.

In the center of the square, which is lined with royal palms and hosts a daily (except Sundays) secondhand book market, is a marble **statue of Carlos Manuel de Céspedes** (Map p296; 1955), the man who set Cuba on the road to independence in 1868.

Also of note on the square's eastern aspect is the late-18th-century **Palacio de los Condes de Santovenia** (Map p296), today the five-star, 27-room Hotel Santa Isabel.

Museo de la Ciudad   MUSEUM

(Map p296; Tacón No 1; admission CUC$3; ⊘9:30am-6pm) Filling the whole west side of Plaza de Armas, this museum is housed in the **Palacio de los Capitanes Generales**, dating from the 1770s. Built on the site of Havana's original church, it's a textbook example of Cuban baroque architecture hewn out of rock from the nearby San Lázaro quarries, and has served many purposes over the years. Since 1968 it has been home to the City Museum, one of Havana's most comprehensive and interesting collections. Artifacts include period furniture, military uniforms and old-fashioned 19th-century horse carriages, while old photos vividly recreate events from Havana's rollercoaster history, such as the 1898 sinking of US battleship *Maine* in the harbor.

Castillo de la Real Fuerza   MUSEUM, FORT

(Map p296) On the seaward side of Plaza de Armas is the oldest existing fort in the Americas, built between 1558 and 1577 on the site of an earlier fort destroyed by French privateers in 1555. Imposing and indomitable, the castle is ringed by an impressive moat and today shelters the **Museo de Navegación** (Map p296; admission CUC$2; ⊘9am-6pm), which opened in 2008 and displays interesting exposés on the history of the fort, the old town and its connections with the erstwhile Spanish empire. Look out for the huge scale model of the *Santíssima Trinidad* galleon.

TOP CHOICE **Calle Mercaderes** HISTORIC STREET
(Map p296) Cobbled, car-free Calle Mercaderes has been extensively restored by the City Historian's Office and offers an almost complete replication of its splendid 18th-century high-water mark. Interspersed with the museums, shops and restaurants are some real-life working social projects. Many of the myriad museums are free, including the **Maqueta de La Habana Vieja** (Map p296; Mercaderes No 114; admission unguided/guided CUC$1/2; ☺9am-6pm), a 1:500 scale model of Habana Vieja complete with an authentic soundtrack meant to replicate a day in the life of the city. There is also **Casa de la Obra Pía** (Map p296; Obrapía No 158; admission CUC$1; ☺9am-4:30pm Tue-Sat, 9:30am-12:30pm Sun), a typical aristocratic Havana residence originally built in 1665 that today also contains one of the City Historian's most commendable social projects, a sewing and needlecraft cooperative that has a workshop inside and a small shop selling clothes and textiles on Calle Mercaderes.

Plaza de San Francisco de Asís HISTORIC SQUARE
(Map p296) Facing Havana harbor, Plaza de San Francisco de Asís first grew up in the 16th century. It underwent a full restoration in the late 1990s and is most notable for its uneven cobbles and the white marble **Fuente de los Leones** (Map p296; Fountain of Lions), carved by the Italian sculptor Giuseppe Gaginni in 1836. On the eastern side of the plaza stands the **Terminal Sierra Maestra** (Map p296) cruise terminal, which dispatches shiploads of weekly tourists, while nearby the domed **Lonja del Comercio** (Map p296) is a former commodities market erected in 1909 and restored in 1996 to provide office space for foreign companies with joint ventures in Cuba.

Iglesia y Monasterio de San Francisco de Asís MUSEUM
(Map p296) The southern side of Plaza San Francisco de Asís is taken up by an erstwhile church-cum-monastery. Originally constructed in 1608 and rebuilt in the baroque style from 1719 to 1738, San Francisco de Asís was taken over by the Spanish state in 1841 when it ceased to be a church. Today

it's both a **concert hall** (Map p296) hosting classical music and the **Museo de Arte Religioso** (Map p296; admission unguided/guided CUC$2/3; ☺9am-6pm), replete with religious paintings, silverware, woodcarvings and ceramics.

Museo del Ron MUSEUM
(Map p296; San Pedro No 262; admission incl guide CUC$7; ☺9am-5pm Mon-Fri, 10am-4pm Sat & Sun) You don't have to be an Añejo Reserva quaffer to enjoy the Museo del Ron in the Fundación Havana Club, but it probably helps. The museum, with its bilingual guided tour, shows rum-making antiquities and the complex brewing process. A not overgenerous measure of rum is included in the price. There's a bar and shop on site, but the savvy reconvene to Bar Dos Hermanos next door.

TOP CHOICE **Plaza Vieja** HISTORIC SQUARE
(Map p296) Laid out in 1559, Plaza Vieja (Old Square) is Havana's most architecturally eclectic square, where Cuban baroque nestles seamlessly next to Gaudí-inspired art nouveau. Originally called Plaza Nueva (New Square), it was initially used for military exercises and later served as an open-air marketplace. During the Batista regime an ugly underground parking lot was constructed here, but the monstrosity was demolished in 1996 to make way for a massive renovation project. Sprinkled liberally with bars, restaurants and cafes, Plaza Vieja is home to, among other sights, a **Cámara Oscura** (Map p296; admission CUC$2; ☺9am-5pm Tue-Sat, 9am-1pm Sun) providing live, 360-degree

---

PORT OF CALL – HAVANA

You can take an organized tour (p302), but cruise-ship passengers will find that Havana is one place you don't need an excursion – just step off the dock and wander the city. Options if you're docked for a few hours:

» Wave goodbye to an organized schedule and wander at will through Habana Vieja (p294), taking in its four impressively renovated colonial squares

» Head over to Calle Mercaderes for traditional shops, small esoteric museums, and a drink inside the Museo del Chocolate (p313)

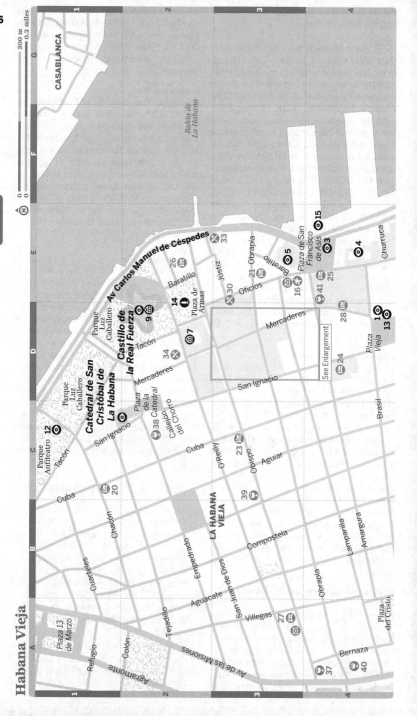

Habana Vieja

300 m
0.2 miles

CASABLANCA

Bahía de
La Habana

Av Carlos Manuel de Céspedes

Plaza 13
de Marzo

Parque
Anfiteatro **12**

Parque
Luz
Caballero

Catedral de San
Cristóbal de
La Habana

Parque
Luz
Caballero

Castillo de
la Real Fuerza

33

26

Baratillo

9

14

Plaza de
Armas

7

34

Mercaderes

30

Justiz

Oficios

Obrapía

Baratillo

21

5

16

Plaza de San
Francisco
de Asís

3

25

41

15

4

Churruca

Plaza
de la
Catedral

38

Callejón
del Chorro

San Ignacio

San Ignacio

Tacón

Mercaderes

Tacón

Cuba

Cuba

20

Chacón

Cuarteles

Refugio

Colón

Aramonte

Tejadillo

Empedrado

San Juan de Dios

Aguacate

LA HABANA
VIEJA

Compostela

Villegas

O'Reilly

Obispo

23

Aguiar

39

27

Bernaza

Av de las Misiones

See Enlargement

Mercaderes

San Ignacio

Brasil

24

28

Plaza
Vieja

1

13

Obrapía

Lamparilla

Amargura

Plaza
del Cristo

37

40

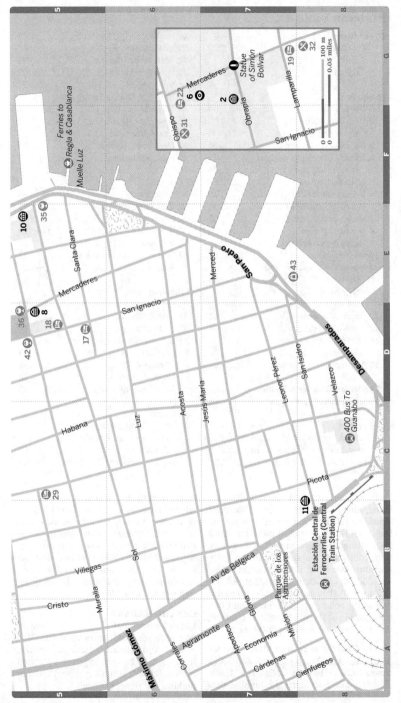

CUBA HAVANA

Ferries to
Regla & Casablanca

Muelle Luz

Santa Clara

Mercaderes

San Ignacio

San Pedro

Merced

Desamparados

Leonor Pérez

San Isidro

Velazco

Jesús María

Acosta

Luz

Habana

Picota

Estación Central de
Ferrocarriles (Central
Train Station)

400 Bus To
Guanabo

Av de Bélgica

Parque de los
Agrimensores

Gloria

Misión

Economía

Apodaca

Cárdenas

Cienfuegos

Agramonte

Corrales

Máximo Gómez

Cristo

Muralla

Villegas

Sol

Obispo

Mercaderes

Obrapía

Lamparilla

San Ignacio

Statue
of Simón
Bolívar

100 m
0.05 miles

views of the city from atop a 35m-tall tower; the **Museo de Naipes** (Map p296; Muralla No 101; admission free; ⊘9am-6pm Tue-Sun), a quirky playing-card museum with a 2000-strong collection including rock stars, rum drinks and round cards; and a **Planetarium** (Map p296; Calle Mercaderes; admission CUC$10; ⊘9:30am-5pm Wed-Sat, 9:30am-12:30pm Sun) showcasing a scale reproduction of the solar system inside a giant orb, a simulation of the Big Bang, and a theater that allows viewing of over 6000 stars.

Museo-Casa Natal de José Martí   MUSEUM
(Map p296; Leonor Pérez No 314; admission CUC$1, camera CUC$2; ⊘9am-5pm Tue-Sat) The Museo-Casa Natal de José Martí is a humble, two-story dwelling on the edge of Habana Vieja where Martí, the apostle of Cuban independence, was born on January 28, 1853. Today it's a small museum that displays letters, manuscripts, photos, books and other mementos of his life. While not as comprehensive as the Martí museum on Plaza de la Revolución, it's a charming little abode and well worth a small detour.

CENTRO HABANA
Capitolio Nacional   LANDMARK
(Map p300; admission unguided/guided CUC$3/4; ⊘9am-6:30pm) Havana's signature architectural sight is the very impressive Capitolio Nacional, which is similar to the US Capitol Building but richer in detail.

Initiated in 1929, the Capitolio took 5000 workers three years, two months and 20 days to build, at a cost of US$17 million. Everything is of a monumental scale, from the huge bronze doors to the 49-tonne, 17m statue of the republic, the third-largest indoor bronze statue in the world (only the Buddha in Nara, Japan, and the Lincoln Memorial in Washington, DC, are bigger). Below the Capitolio's 62m-high dome, a 24-carat diamond replica is set in the floor. Inside there is an internet club, a cafe and a selection of arts and crafts stalls.

Real Fábrica de Tabacos Partagás
CIGAR FACTORY
(Map p300; Industria No 520 btwn Barcelona & Dragones; admission CUC$10; ☺tours every 15min 9-10:15am & noon-1:30pm) Situated behind the Capitolio, this cigar factory built in 1845 is the only Havana cigar factory it's possible to visit with any ease. A tour here is a fascinating insight into both Cuba's most famous export and, perhaps even more so, into the lives of ordinary Cubans working in a factory. Few people leave unimpressed by the level of quality control that goes on here. Starting on the ground floor, where the leaves are unbundled and sorted, the tour moves to the upper floors to watch the tobacco being rolled, pressed, banded and boxed. The tours (in English, French or Spanish) culminate in a visit to the well-stocked cigar shop.

Gran Teatro de La Habana
THEATER
(Map p300; Paseo de Martí No 458; guided tours CUC$2; ☺9am-5pm) Just north of the Capitolio is this theater, constructed between 1907 and 1914 and an outrageously beautiful building inside and out. As well as visiting for a guided tour during the daytime, you can catch some of Havana's best performances here, most notably the Ballet Nacional de Cuba.

Parque Central & Around
PARK
(Map p300) Diminutive Parque Central is a scenic haven from the belching buses and roaring taxis that ply their way along the Prado. The park, long a microcosm of daily Havana life, was expanded to its present size in the late 19th century after the city walls were knocked down, and the 1905 marble **statue of José Martí** (Map p300) at its center was the first of thousands to be erected in Cuba. Hard to miss over to one side is the group of baseball fans who linger 24/7 at the famous **Esquina Caliente** (literally 'hot corner'), discussing form,

---

DON'T MISS

PARQUE HISTÓRICO MILITAR MORRO-CABAÑA

One of Havana's must-see sights is the impressive Parque Histórico Militar Morro-Cabaña, across the Bahía de la Habana from the city's port. The complex makes for a great half-day trip, and the views of Havana to be had from here are outstanding.

The **Castillo de los Tres Santos Reyes Magnos del Morro** (admission incl museum CUC$6; ☺8am-8pm) was erected between 1589 and 1630 on an abrupt limestone headland to protect the entrance to the harbor. In 1762 the British captured El Morro by attacking from the landward side and digging a tunnel under the walls. In 1845 the first lighthouse in Cuba was added to the castle (admission CUC$2). There is also a **maritime museum**.

The **Fortaleza de San Carlos de la Cabaña** (admission CUC$6; ☺8am-11pm) was built between 1763 and 1774 to deny attackers the long ridge overlooking Havana. It's one of the largest colonial fortresses in the Americas, replete with grassy moats, ancient chapel and cobblestone streets. Dictators Gerardo Machado y Morales and Batista used the fortress as a military prison, and Che Guevara established his revolutionary headquarters here. Be sure to visit the creative Havana skyline **mirador** (viewpoint) on the other side of the **Museo de Comandancia del Che**.

Nightly at 9pm a cannon is fired on the harbor side of La Cabaña by a squad attired in 19th-century uniforms, a hold-over from Spanish times when these shots signaled that the city gates were closing. The **cañonazo** begins at 8:30pm, and is usually followed by a music concert.

To get here, take the ferry from Muelle Luz (Map p296) to Casablanca (CUC$1, every 15 to 30 minutes dawn to dusk), from where it's an easy walk to the Parque Histórico Militar Morro-Cabaña.

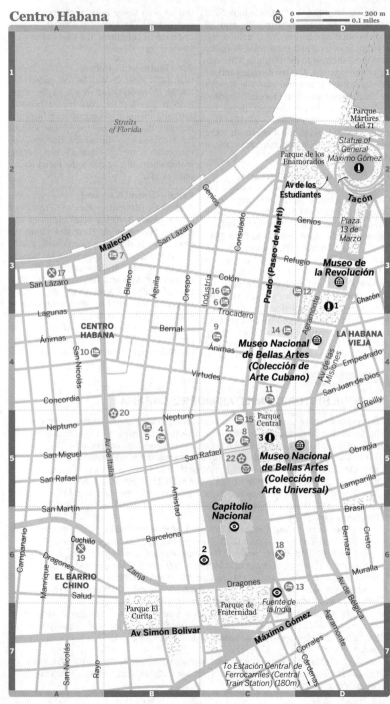

Centro Habana

Straits of Florida

Parque Mártires del 71

Statue of General Máximo Gómez

Parque de los Enamorados

Av de los Estudiantes

Tacón

Genios

Plaza 13 de Marzo

Refugio

Museo de la Revolución

Chacón

CENTRO HABANA

Colón

Trocadero

Ánimas

Museo Nacional de Bellas Artes (Colección de Arte Cubano)

LA HABANA VIEJA

Empedrado

San Juan de Dios

O'Reilly

Virtudes

Concordia

Neptuno

San Miguel

San Rafael

San Martín

Parque Central

Museo Nacional de Bellas Artes (Colección de Arte Universal)

Obrapía

Lamparilla

Brasil

Capitolio Nacional

EL BARRIO CHINO

Salud

Barcelona

Muralla

Parque El Curita

Parque de Fraternidad

Fuente de la India

Av Simón Bolívar

Máximo Gómez

To Estación Central de Ferrocarriles (Central Train Station) (180m)

tactics and the Havana teams' prospects in the play-offs.

Museo Nacional de Bellas Artes   MUSEUM
(admission 1/both buildings CUC$5/8; ⊙10am-6pm Tue-Sat, 10am-2pm Sun) Cuba's largest and most impressive art collection is housed in two striking buildings, collectively called the Museo Nacional de Bellas Artes. The main building, known as the **Colección de Arte Universal** (Map p300; cnr Agramonte & San Rafael), housed in the wonderful Centro Asturianas (a former Spanish social club), looks every bit the part of a national art collection and it doesn't disappoint, displaying a huge collection taking in world art from Greek sculpture and Roman mosaics to canvases by El Greco and Gainsborough.

The **Colección de Arte Cubano** (Map p300; Trocadero btwn Agramonte & Av de las Misiones) up the road is a showcase of purely Cuban art in a new, fully wheelchair-accessible and architecturally distinguished building. If you only visit one art gallery in Cuba, make sure that this is it. Look especially for works by Collazo, Blanco and Wilfredo Lam. Book in advance for the guided tours.

TOP CHOICE Museo de la Revolución   MUSEUM
(Map p300; Refugio No 1; admission CUC$6; ⊙10am-5pm) is one of Havana's most important sights and is well worth a few hours. Housed in the former Palacio Presidencial, site of the 1957 Batista assassination attempt and where Castro's cabinet convened until the '60s, the building alone is fascinating, with several offices preserved and the interiors decorated by Tiffany's. Everything you wanted to know about the Cuban Revolution is here, and a lot more. The exhibition boasts rare photographs, original documents and revolutionary ephemera. However, while individual events are documented in huge detail, there's no overall narrative linking them together, making it less than brilliant for newcomers to Cuban history. There are often good temporary exhibits in the downstairs **Hall of Mirrors**.

From the museum it's possible to walk out into the backyard and visit the glass-encased **Pavillón Granma** (Map p300), which since 1976 has been home to the 18m 'yacht' *Granma* that ushered Fidel Castro and 81 others into world history in 1956. Today this is one of the revolution's holiest shrines and has the eternal flame to prove it.

VEDADO

Vedado ('forest reserve') is a world away from Centro Habana and Habana Vieja, being developed only in the late 19th and early 20th centuries as a residential suburb for the wealthy. Despite that, it's in many senses the center of the city, with its most vibrant arts and cultural scenes, and the favored playground of both the business and political elite. The main streets of Vedado are Calle 23 and Línea – both full of shops, restaurants, bars, cinemas and theaters.

Necrópolis Cristóbal Colón   CEMETERY

(Map p304; entrance cnr Calzada de Zapata & Calle 12; admission CUC$5; 9am-5pm) Vedado's most obvious attraction to travelers is also Cuba's largest cemetery, famous for its elaborate mausoleums. It's very pleasant to stroll through, or you can take a free guided tour (tip expected) or just buy the map (CUC$1) at the ticket office and find your own way.

Universidad de la Habana   UNIVERSITY

(Map p304) Founded by Dominican monks in 1728 and secularized in 1842, Havana University began life in Habana Vieja before moving to its present site in 1902. The existing neoclassical complex dates from the second quarter of the 20th century, and is famous for its *escalinata* (stairway), **Alma Mater statue**, and two onsite museums: the **Museo de Historia Natural Felipe Poey** (Map p304; admission CUC$1; 9am-noon & 1-4pm Mon-Fri Sep-Jul), with stuffed specimens of Cuban flora and fauna dating from the 19th century, and the **Museo Antropológico Montané** (Map p304; admission CUC$1; 9am-noon & 1-4pm Mon-Fri Sep-Jul), with a rich collection of pre-Columbian Indian artifacts.

Plaza de la Revolución   HISTORIC SQUARE

(Map p304) Conceived by French urbanist Jean-Claude Forestier in the 1920s, the gigantic Plaza de la Revolución was part of Havana's 'new city' that grew up between 1920 and 1959.

Surrounded by gray, utilitarian buildings constructed in the late 1950s, the square today is the base of the Cuban government and a place where large-scale political rallies are held.

The ugly concrete block on the northern side of the Plaza is the **Ministerio del Interior** (Map p304), well known for its huge mural of Che Guevara (a copy of Alberto Korda's famous photograph taken in 1960) with the words *Hasta la Victoria Siempre* (always toward victory) emblazoned underneath. In 2009 a similarly designed image of Cuba's other heroic *guerrillero*, Camilo

Cienfuegos, was added on the adjacent telecommunications building.

Memorial a José Martí   MONUMENT, MUSEUM

(Map p304; admission CUC$5; 9:30am-5pm Mon-Sat) Center stage in Plaza de la Revolución is this craning monument which, at 138.5m, is Havana's tallest structure. Fronted by an impressive 17m marble statue of a seated Martí in pensive *Thinker* pose, the memorial houses a museum and a 129m lookout (reached via a small elevator, admission CUC$2) with fantastic city views.

TOP CHOICE Malecón   STREET

(Map p304) The Malecón, Havana's evocative 8km-long sea drive, is one of the city's most soulful and quintessentially Cuban thoroughfares.

Long a favored meeting place for assorted lovers, philosophers, poets, traveling minstrels, fishermen and wistful Floridagazers, Malecón's atmosphere is most potent at sunset when the weak yellow light from creamy Vedado filters like a dim torch onto the buildings of Centro Habana, lending their dilapidated facades a distinctly ethereal quality.

Hotel Nacional   NOTABLE HOTEL

(Map p304; cnr Calles O & 21) Built in 1930 as a copy of the Breakers Hotel in Palm Beach, Florida, the eclectic art-deco/neoclassical Hotel Nacional is a national monument and one of Havana's 'postcard' sights.

The hotel gained gained notoriety in 1946 when US mobsters Meyer Lansky and Lucky Luciano used it to host the largest ever get-together of the North American Mafia, who gathered here under the guise of a Frank Sinatra concert.

Nonguests are welcome to admire the Moorish lobby, stroll the breezy grounds and examine the photos of famous past guests on the walls inside.

Tours

Havana tours can be convenient if you've got little time or inclination to see the city alone, but they're definitely not necessary. General city tours start at aound CUC$18 for half a day and can be arranged through **Cubatur** (Map p304; 835-4155; www.cubatur .cu; Calle F No 157, Vedado). The best agency by far is **San Cristóbal Agencia de Viajes** (Map p296; 861-9171/2; www.viajessancristobal. cu; Calle de los Oficios No 110 bajos btwn Lamparilla & Amargura), connected to the City Historian's

Office, which offers intimate general and specialist tours. Recommended are its architectural, Art and Colour, and Social Projects excursions.

🛏 Sleeping

With nigh on 3000 private houses letting out rooms, you'll never struggle to find accommodation in Havana. Casas particulares go for anywhere between CUC$20 and CUC$40 per room, with Centro Habana offering the best bargains. Rock-bottom budget hotels can match casas for price, but not comfort. There's a dearth of decent midrange hotels, while Havana's top-end hotels are plentiful and offer oodles of atmosphere.

An excellent resource for prebooking casas is the website www.cubacasas.net.

HABANA VIEJA

TOP CHOICE Hostal Condes de Villanueva   HOTEL **$$**

(Map p296; ✆862-9293; Mercaderes No 202; s/d CUC$100/160; ❄) If you plan to splash out on one night of luxury in Havana, you'd do well to check out this highly lauded colonial gem. Restored under the watchful eye of City Historian Eusebio Leal Spengler in the late '90s, the Villanueva is a grandiose city mansion converted into an intimate and thoughtfully decorated hotel, with nine bedrooms spread spaciously around an attractive inner courtyard (complete with resident peacock).

Hotel San Felipe y Santiago de Bejúcal   HOTEL **$$$**

(Map p296; ✆864-9191; cnr Oficios & Amargura; s/d CUC$150/240; ❄@🛜) Cuban baroque meets modern minimalist in this newest offering from Habaguanex (the commercial arm of the City Historian's Office that runs over two dozen finely restored Havana hotels). The results are something to behold. Spreading 27 rooms over six floors in the blustery Plaza San Francisco de Asís, this place is living proof that Habaguanex's delicate restoration work is getting better and better.

Hotel Florida   HOTEL **$$**

(Map p296; ✆862-4127; Obispo No 252; s/d incl breakfast CUC$100/160; ❄@) They don't make them like this anymore. The Florida is an architectural extravaganza built in the purest colonial style, with arches and pillars clustered around an atmospheric central courtyard. Habaguanex has restored the building (constructed in 1836) with loving attention to detail, with the amply furnished rooms retaining their original high ceilings and wonderfully luxurious finishes.

Hotel Raquel   HOTEL **$$**

(Map p296; ✆860-8280; cnr Amargura & San Ignacio; s/d CUC$100/160; ❄@) Encased in a dazzling 1908 palace (once a bank), the Hotel Raquel takes your breath away with its grandiose columns, sleek marble statues and intricate stained-glass ceiling.

HAVANA FOR CHILDREN

Havana's exotic appeal will not be lost on your children. You can join in spontaneously with the locals, and/or investigate the following treats.

Fortaleza de San Carlos de la Cabaña (p299) Havana's huge fort has museums, battlements and a nightly cannon ceremony with soldiers in period costume.

Castillo de la Real Fuerza (p294) This centrally located Havana fort has a moat, lookouts and scale models of Spanish galleons.

Parque Maestranza (Map p296; Av Carlos Manuel de Céspedes, Habana Vieja; admission CUC$1; under 4yr only) Bouncy castles, fairground rides, and sweet snacks overlooking Havana harbor.

Circo Trompoloco (cnr Av 5 & Calle 112, Playa; admission CUC$10; ⏰7pm Thu-Sun) Havana's permanent 'Big Top' with a weekend matinee.

Isla de Coco Huge, newish Chinese-funded amusement park in Havana's Playa neighborhood.

Acuario Nacional (cnr Av 3 & Calle 62; adult/child CUC$5/3; ⏰10am-10pm Tue-Sun) Daily dolphin shows and a decent restaurant are the highlights of the nation's main aquarium, in Havana's Miramar district.

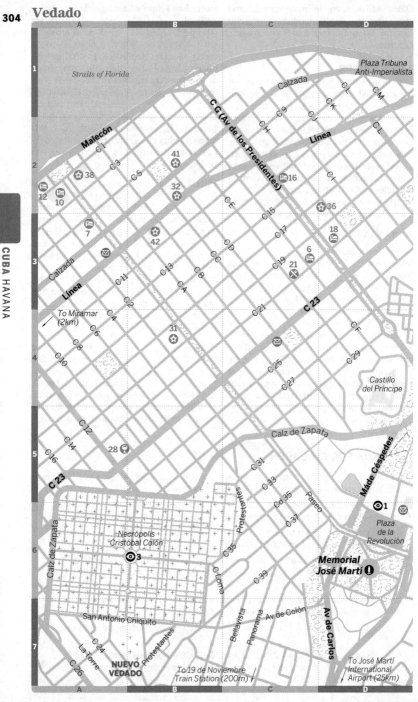

Straits of Florida

Plaza Tribuna
Anti-Imperialista

Calzada

C L
C K
C J
C M
C 9
C H
C G (Av de los Presidentes)

Malecón
Línea

C 1
C 3
C 5
C E
C 15
C I
C 17
C D
C 19
C C
C B
C A
C 21
C 23
C F
C 29

Línea
Calzada

C 11
C 2
C 4
C 6
C 8
C 10
C 13
C 25
C 27

To Miramar
(2km)

Castillo
del Príncipe

Calz de Zapata

C 12
C 14
C 16
C 23

28

C 31
C 33
Cd 35
C 37

Máde Céspedes

Protestantes

Calz de Zapata

Necrópolis
Cristóbal Colón

3

C 35
C Loma
C 39

Plaza
de la
Revolución

Memorial
José Martí

1

San Antonio Chiquito

Bellavista
Panorama
Av de Colón

Av de Carlos

NUEVO
VEDADO

C 24
C 26
La Torre
Protestantes

To 19 de Noviembre
Train Station (200m)

To José Martí
International
Airport (25km)

38 41 32 42 16 36 18 6 21 31
12 10 7

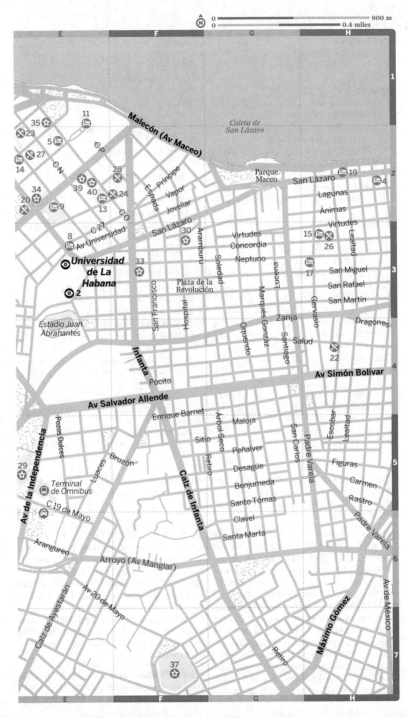

Behind its impressive architecture, the hotel offers well-presented if noisy rooms, a small gym/sauna, friendly staff and a great central location.

Hotel Santa Isabel HOTEL **$$$**
(Map p296; ☎860-8201; Baratillo No 9; s/d incl breakfast CUC$150/240; ❄@) Considered one of Havana's finest hotels, as well as one of its oldest (it first began operations in 1867), the Hotel Santa Isabel is housed in the Palacio de los Condes de Santovenia, the former crash pad of a decadent Spanish count. In 1998 this three-story baroque beauty was upgraded to five-star status but, unlike other posh Cuban hotels, the Santa Isabel actually comes close to justifying the billing. The 17 regular rooms have bundles of historic charm and are all kitted out with attractive Spanish colonial furniture as well as paintings by contemporary Cuban artists.

Hostal Valencia HOTEL **$$**
(Map p296; ☎867-1037; Oficios No 53; s/d incl breakfast CUC$80/130) The Valencia is decked out like a Spanish posada (inn) with hanging vines, doorways big enough to ride a horse through and a popular onsite paella restaurant. Slap-bang in the middle of the historical core of the city and with a price that makes it one of the cheapest offerings in the current Habaguanex stable, this hostel is an excellent old-world choice with good service and plenty of atmosphere.

Hostal Palacio O'Farrill HOTEL **$$**
(Map p296; ☎860-5080; Cuba No 102-108 btwn Chacón & Tejadillo; s/d CUC$100/160; ❄@)

Not an Irish joke, but one of Havana's most impressive period hotels, the Palacio O'Farrill is a staggeringly beautiful colonial palace that once belonged to Don Ricardo O'Farrill, a Cuban sugar entrepreneur who was descended from a family of Irish nobility.

Casa de Pepe & Rafaela   CASA PARTICULAR $

(Map p296; ☑862-9877; San Ignacio No 454 btwn Sol & Santa Clara; r CUC$30) One of Havana's best casas: antiques and Moorish tiles throughout, two rooms with balconies and gorgeous new baths, an excellent location and great hosts. The son also rents a charming colonial house at San Ignacio No 656 (same price).

Juan & Margarita   CASA PARTICULAR $

(Map p296; ☑867-9592; Obispo No 522 apt 8, btwn Bernaza & Villegas; r CUC$30, apt CUC$60) A two-bedroom apartment on Obispo, no less – Vieja's version of NYC's glamorous Fifth Ave. You can bag the whole place for CUC$60 – sitting room with TV and table, two clean bedrooms with bathrooms, and a balcony. A gentleman and a scholar, Juan speaks excellent English and has a lot of local knowledge.

Hostal Beltrán de la Santa Cruz   HOTEL $$

(Map p296; ☑860-8330; San Ignacio No 411 btwn Muralla & Sol; s/d incl breakfast CUC$80/130; ❄) Excellent location, friendly staff and plenty of old-world authenticity make this compact inn just off Plaza Vieja a winning combination. Housed in a sturdy 18th-century building and offering just 11 spacious rooms, intimacy is at a premium here and the standard of service has been regularly lauded by both travelers and reviewers.

Hotel Ambos Mundos   HOTEL $$

(Map p296; ☑860-9529; Obispo No 153; s/d CUC$100/160; ❄@) Hemingway's Havana hideout and the place where he is said to have penned his seminal guerrilla classic *For Whom the Bell Tolls*, the pastel-pink Ambos Mundos is an obligatory pit stop for anyone on a world tour of Hemingway-once-fell-over-in-here bars. Small, sometimes windowless rooms suggest overpricing, but the lobby bar is classic enough, and drinks at the rooftop restaurant one of the city's finest treats.

Mesón de la Flota   HOTEL $$

(Map p296; ☑863-3838; Mercaderes No 257 btwn Amargura & Brasil; s/d incl breakfast CUC$65/100)

Habana Vieja's smallest hotel is an old Spanish tavern decked out with maritime motifs and located within spitting distance of gracious Plaza Vieja. Five individually crafted rooms contain all of the modern comforts and amenities, while downstairs a busy restaurant serves up delicious tapas.

Pablo Rodríguez   CASA PARTICULAR $

(Map p296; ☑861-2111; pablo@sercomar.telemar.cu; Compostela No 532 btwn Brasil & Muralla; r CUC$30) Another lovely old colonial classic, this one with some original frescoes partially uncovered on the walls. It would be worth millions elsewhere, but here you can rent one of venerable Pablo's two rooms with bathrooms (one en-suite, one private but separate), fan and fridge for a giveaway CUC$30 per night.

CENTRO HABANA

TOP CHOICE Hotel NH Parque Central   HOTEL $$$

(Map p300; ☑860-6627; www.nh-hotels.com; Neptuno btwn Agramonte & Paseo de Martí; s/d CUC$200/300; ℗❄@❋❄) Outside Havana's two Meliás, the NH is, without a doubt, Havana's best international-standard hotel, with service and business facilities on a par with top-ranking five-star amenities elsewhere in the Caribbean. Facilities include a full-service business center, a rooftop swimming pool/fitness center/Jacuzzi, an elegant lobby bar, the celebrated El Paseo restaurant, plus excellent international telephone and internet links. In 2009 the Parque Central opened an even swankier new wing across Calle Virtudes connected to the rest of the hotel by means of an underground tunnel.

Hotel Saratoga   HOTEL $$$

(Map p300; ☑868-1000; Paseo de Martí No 603; s/d CUC$226/280; ℗❄@❋❄) One of Havana's newest, ritziest and most dramatic hotels, the glittering Saratoga is an architectural work of art that stands imposingly at the intersection of Prado and Dragones, with fantastic views over toward the Capitolio. Sharp, if officious, service is a feature here, as are the extra-comfortable beds, power showers and a truly decadent rooftop swimming pool.

Hotel Sevilla   HOTEL $$$

(Map p300; ☑860-8560; Trocadero No 55 btwn Paseo de Martí & Agramonte; s/d incl breakfast CUC$150/210; ℗❄@❋❄) Al Capone once hired out the whole 6th floor, Graham

Greene used it as a setting for his novel *Our Man in Havana* (room 501 to be exact) and the Mafia requisitioned it as its operations centre for its prerevolutionary North American drugs racket. Now run in partnership with the French Sofitel group, the Moorish Sevilla's rooms are spacious and equipped with comfortable beds. The ostentatious lobby could have been ripped straight out of the Alhambra.

Hotel Telégrafo HOTEL **$$**
(Map p300; ☎861-1010/4741; Paseo de Martí No 408; s/d CUC$100/160; 🌢@🌐) A bold royal-blue charmer on the northwest corner of Parque Central, this Habaguanex beauty juxtaposes old-style architectural features with futuristic design flourishes that include shiny silver sofas, a huge winding central staircase and an amazingly intricate tile mosaic emblazoned on the wall of the downstairs cafe. The rooms are equally spiffy.

Casa 1932 CASA PARTICULAR **$**
(Map p304; ☎863-6203, www.casahabana.net; Campanario 63 btwn San Lázaro & Lagunas; r CUC$20-35; 🌢) Prepare for an enchanting voyage back in time to art-deco Havana: everything you touch in this genteel house is nigh on an antique. But it's the owner who's the icing on the cake: an interior designer and local history expert who is a mine of information on everything from forgotten Cuban film to the history of pharmacy.

Hotel Lido HOTEL **$**
(Map p300; ☎867-1102; Consulado No 210 btwn Ánimas & Trocadero; s/d CUC$28/38; 🌢@) A travelers' institution, the lackluster Lido is Havana's unofficial backpacker nexus that has been popular for years for its central location, no-frills rooms with intermittent hot water and gritty neighborhood feel. It certainly ain't fancy (that's the point, isn't it?), but there's a handy internet terminal downstairs, breakfast on the roof and a helpful Cubanacán info desk.

Hotel Park View HOTEL **$$**
(Map p300; Colón No 101; s/d CUC$52/86; 🌢@) Built in 1928 with American money, the Park View has a reputation as the poor man's 'Sevilla' that isn't entirely justified. Its location alone (within baseball-pitching distance of the Museo de la Revolución) is enough to consider this mint-green city charmer a viable option. Chuck in friendly dooormen,

modern furnishings (it's Habaguanex-run) and a small but perfectly poised 7th-floor restaurant and you've got yourself a rare midrange bargain.

Hotel Inglaterra HOTEL **$$**
(Map p300; ☎860-8595; Paseo de Martí No 416; s/d/tr CUC$84/120/168; 🅿🌢@) It's José Martí's one-time Havana hotel of choice and it's still trading on the fact – which says something about the current state of affairs. The Inglaterra is a better place to hang out than actually to stay in, with its exquisite Moorish lobby and crusty colonial interior easily outshining the lackluster and often viewless rooms. The rooftop bar's a popular watering hole and the downstairs foyer is a hive of bustling activity where there's always live music blaring.

Esther Cardoso CASA PARTICULAR **$**
(Map p300; ☎862-0401; esthercv2551@cubarte. cult.cu; Águila No 367 btwn Neptuno & San Miguel; r CUC$25) Esther is an actress, meaning that this little palace shines like an oasis in Centro Habana's dilapidated desert, with tasteful decor, funky posters, spick-and-span bathrooms and a spectacular roof terrace. Book early – there are plenty in the know.

Villa Enano Rojo CASA PARTICULAR **$**
(Map p304; ☎863-5081; Malecón No 557 btwn Lealtad & Escobar; r CUC$25) The name translates as 'Red Dwarf House,' but you won't find any blushing little people here; just owners Lalo and Magda and a gracious upstairs apartment with two rooms, one of which has a front-row seat to that most romantic of evening cabarets – the Malecón.

Julio & Elsa Roque CASA PARTICULAR **$**
(Map p300; ☎861-8027; julioroq@yahoo.com; Consulado No 162 apt 2 btwn Colón & Trocadero; r CUC$25) Julio's a pediatrician who rents out two rooms in his friendly family house just a block from Prado. Taking advantage of the new liberalized rental laws, he has also recently opened **Hostal Peregrino**, with three more rooms and an independent apartment in a building nearby (book through number above). Services include airport pickup, internet, laundry, and cocktail bar. The accommodations are cozy and nicely furnished and both Julio and his wife Elsa are superhelpful and can tell you everything you need to know about Havana. English is spoken.

Hotel Deauville   HOTEL **$**
(Map p300; ☏866-8812; Av de Italia No 1 cnr
Malecón; s/d/tr CUC$36/72/108; P❄✲) The
Deauville is housed in a kitschy seafront
high-rise that sharp-eyed Havana-watchers
will recognize from picturesque Malecón-
at-sunset postcards. But while the location
might be postcard-perfect, the facilities inside this former Mafia gambling den don't
quite match up to the stellar views.

Hotel Lincoln   HOTEL **$**
(Map p300; ☏862-8061; Av de Italia btwn Virtudes
& Ánimas; s/d CUC$24/38; ✲) A peeling nine-
story giant on busy Galiano (Av de Italia),
the Hotel Lincoln was the second-tallest
building in Havana when it was built in
1926. Overshadowed by taller opposition
these days, the hotel still offers 135 air-con
rooms with bathroom and TV in an atmosphere that is more 1950s than 2010s. The
facilities are best described as timeworn.

Dulce Hostal – Dulce María
González   CASA PARTICULAR **$**
(Map p300; ☏863-2506; Amistad No 220 btwn
Neptuno & San Miguel; r CUC$20) The Dulce
(sweet) Hostal on Amistad (friendship)
street sounds like a good combination, and
sweet and friendly is what you get in this
beautiful colonial house with tile floors,
soaring ceilings and a quiet, helpful hostess.

Martha Obregón   CASA PARTICULAR **$**
(Map p304; ☏870-2095; marthaobregon@yahoo.
com; Gervasio No 308 Altos btwn Neptuno &
San Miguel; r CUC$20-25) A pleasant fam-
ily home with little balconies and street
views. You'll get a good sense of life in
the crowded central quarter here with its
whistling tradesmen and stickball-playing
kids.

La Casona Colonial –
José Díaz   CASA PARTICULAR **$**
(Map p304; ☏870-0489; Gervasio No 209 btwn
Concordia & Virtudes; r CUC$25) A colonial
house with a pleasant courtyard that has a
shared bathroom but plenty of bed space.
It's located in the thick of the Centro Ha-
bana action and has friendly owners.

VEDADO
Hotel Victoria   HOTEL **$$**
(Map p304; ☏833-3510; Calle 19 No 101; s/d incl
breakfast CUC$80/100; P❄@✲) A well-heeled
and oft-overlooked Vedado option, the Vic-
toria is a diminutive five-story hotel situated
within spitting distance of the larger and
more expensive Nacional. Deluxe and com-

pact, though (due to its size) invariably full,
this venerable establishment housed in an
attractive neoclassical building dating from
1928 contains a swimming pool, a bar and a
small shop.

Hotel Nacional   HOTEL **$$$**
(Map p304; ☏836-3564; cnr Calles O & 21; s/d/
tr CUC$120/170/238; P❄@✈✲) The Hotel
Nacional is as much a city monument as it
is an international accommodation option.
Even if you haven't got the money to stay
here, chances are you'll find yourself sipping at least one minty mojito in its exquisite oceanside bar. Steeped in history and
with rooms furnished with plaques advertising details of illustrious past occupants,
this towering Havana landmark sports two
swimming pools, a sweeping manicured
lawn, a couple of lavish restaurants and its
own top-class nighttime cabaret show, the
Parisién. While the rooms might lack some
of the fancy gadgets you'll find in the resorts
at Varadero, the ostentatious communal
areas and the erstwhile ghosts of Winston
Churchill and Lucky Luciano who haunt the
Moorish lobby make for an unforgettable
experience.

Hotel Meliá Cohiba   HOTEL **$$$**
(Map p304; ☏833-3636; Paseo btwn Calles 1 & 3;
r CUC$150/200; P❄@✈✲) Royally profes-
sional, this oceanside concrete giant built
in 1994 will satisfy the highest of interna-
tional expectations with its knowledgeable,
consistent staff and modern, well-polished
facilities. For workaholics there are special
'business-traveler rooms,' and 59 units have
Jacuzzis. On the lower levels gold-star facili-
ties include a shopping arcade, one of Ha-
vana's plushest gyms and the ever-popular
Habana Café.

Hotel Habana Libre   HOTEL **$$**
(Map p304; ☏834-6100; Calle L btwn Calles 23 &
25; d/ste incl breakfast CUC$120/160; P❄@✲)
Havana's biggest and boldest hotel opened
in March 1958 on the eve of Batista's last
waltz. Once part of the Hilton chain, in
January 1959 it was commandeered by
Castro's rebels, who put their boots over
all the plush furnishings and turned it into
their temporary HQ. Now managed by
Spain's Meliá chain, all 574 rooms in this
skyline-hogging giant are kitted out to international standard, though the lackluster
furnishings could do with an imaginative
makeover.

Hotel Riviera
HOTEL $$

(Map p304; ☎836-4051; cnr Paseo & Malecón; s/d incl breakfast CUC$63/106; P❄@☀) Meyer Lansky's magnificent Vegas-style palace has leapt back into fashion with its gloriously retro lobby, almost unchanged since 1957 (when it was the height of modernity). The trouble for modern-day visitors are the rooms (there are 354 of them), which, though luxurious 50 years ago, are now looking a little rough around the edges and struggle to justify their top-end price tag.

Marta Vitorte
CASA PARTICULAR $

(Map p304; ☎832-6475; martavitorte@hotmail.com; Calle G No 301 apt 14 btwn Calles 13 & 15; r CUC$35-40) Marta has lived in this sinuous apartment on Av de los Presidentes since 1960 – one look at the view and you'll see why – the glass-fronted wraparound terrace that soaks up 270 degrees of Havana's stunning panorama makes it seem as if you're standing atop the Martí monument. Not surprisingly, the two rooms are deluxe with lovely furnishings, minibars and safes. Then there are the breakfasts, the laundry, the parking space, the lift attendant...get the drift?

Eddy Gutiérrez Bouza
CASA PARTICULAR $

(Map p304; ☎832-5207; Calle 21 No 408 btwn Calles F & G; r CUC$30; P❄) Eddy is a fantastic host with a great knowledge of Havana, and his huge colonial house has hosted many visitors over the years. It's an inviting abode with a well-kept garden, grand exterior and Eddy's 1974 Argentinian-made Dodge parked in the driveway. Guests are accommodated out back in comfortable quarters, and one room comes equipped with a kitchenette.

Casa Particular Sandélis
CASA PARTICULAR $

(Map p304; ☎832-4422; Calle 21 No 4 apt 61 btwn Calles N & O; r CUC$30-35) Another casa in the art-deco block overlooking the Hotel Nacional, this house on the 6th floor combines a phenomenal location with the kindness and honesty of hosts Carolina and Lenin (who is a talented painter). There is a variety of rooms to choose from, all with en-suite bathrooms.

Mercedes González
CASA PARTICULAR $

(Map p304; ☎832-5840; mercylupe@hotmail.com; Calle 21 No 360 apt 2A btwn Calles G & H; r CUC$30-35) One of the most welcoming hosts in Havana, Mercedes comes highly recommended by readers, fellow travelers, other casa owners, you name it. Her lovely art-deco abode is a classic Vedado apartment with two fine rooms, an airy terrace and top-notch five-star service.

Manuel Martínez
CASA PARTICULAR $

(Map p304; ☎832-6713; Calle 21 No 4 apt 22 btwn Calles N & O; r CUC$30-35) There are 14 casas in this magnificent art-deco building constructed in 1945 opposite the Hotel Nacional, making it like a minihotel. This one overlooks the hotel gardens; about as close as you can get to Cuba's famous five-star without having to pay the five-star rates.

Hotel Vedado
HOTEL $$

(Map p304; ☎836-4072; Calle O No 244 btwn Calles 23 & 25; s/d CUC$65/80; ❄@☀) Ever popular with the tour-bus crowd, the Hotel Vedado is a tough sell. Granted, there's an OK pool (rare in Havana), along with a passable restaurant and not unpleasant rooms. But patchy service, perennially noisy lobby and almost total lack of character will leave you wondering if you wouldn't have been better off staying in a local casa particular – for half the price.

Guillermina & Roberto Abreu
CASA PARTICULAR $

(Map p304; ☎833-6401; Paseo No 126 apt 13A btwn Calle 5 & Calzada; r CUC$30; ❄) On the 13th floor of a Vedado apartment block built in 1958, this is another 'view' property with two rooms, private bathrooms and plush furnishings.

Hotel Colina
HOTEL $

(Map p304; ☎836-4071; cnr Calles L & 27; s/d CUC$34/42; ❄@) The friendliest and least fussy of Vedado's cheaper options, the 80-room Colina is situated directly outside the university and is a good choice if you're studying on a Spanish course.

✖ Eating

Havana's eating scene, while it has its moments, is on the whole a microcosm of that throughout the country – gems are out there, but they're extremely few and far between.

HABANA VIEJA

TOP CHOICE Restaurante El Templete
SEAFOOD $$$

(Map p296; Av del Puerto No 12; meals CUC$15-20; ⏰noon-11pm) Welcome to a rare Cuban breed: a restaurant that could compete with anything in Miami – and a government-run one at that! The Templete's specialty is fish, and special it is: fresh, succulent and cooked simply without any of the pretensions so rampant in celebrity-chef-obsessed America. Sure, it's a little *caro* (expensive), but worth every last *centivo*.

La Imprenta
INTERNATIONAL $$$

(Map p296; Mercaderes No 208; ⊘noon-midnight) This new Habaguanex restaurant has raised the bar for government-run places in the old town, with previously unheard-of Cuban innovations such as al dente pasta, creative seafood medleys and a stash of decent wines. Service is equally impressive, bucking the bored unmotivated waiters of yore, and the resplendent interior is filled with memorabilia from the building's previous incarnation as a printing works.

Restaurante La Dominica
ITALIAN $$

(Map p296; O'Reilly No 108; ⊘noon-midnight) Despite a tendency to be a little overgenerous with the olive oil, La Dominica – with its wood-fired pizza oven and al dente pasta – could quite legitimately stake its claim as Havana's finest Italian restaurant. Located in an elegantly restored dining room with alfresco seating on Calle O'Reilly, the menu offers Italy's 'usual suspects,' augmented by shrimp and lobster.

Restaurante La Paella
SPANISH $$

(Map p296; cnr Oficios & Obrapía; ⊘noon-11pm) Known for its paella (CUC$10), this place, attached to the Hostal Valencia, has an authentic ambience and tries hard to emulate its Spanish namesake (the birthplace of Spain's famous rice dish). Food can be variable, but on a good day you'll be scraping the rice off the bottom of your serving pan with relish.

Mesón de la Flota
TAPAS $$

(Map p296; Mercaderes No 257 btwn Amargura & Brasil) If Havana resembles any city it's Cádiz in Spain and this nautically themed tapas bar/restaurant might have been transported from Cádiz's Barrio de Santa María, so potent is the atmosphere. Old-world tapas include *garbanzos con chorizo* (chickpeas with sausage), calamari and tortilla. For music lovers, the real drawcard is the nightly *tablaos* (flamenco shows), the quality of which could rival anything in Andalusia.

Al Medina
MIDDLE EASTERN $$

(Map p296; Oficios No 12 btwn Obrapía & Obispo; ⊘noon-midnight; ▨) Havana takes on the Middle East in this exotic restaurant, appropriately situated in one of the city's 17th-century Mudejar-style buildings. Tucked into a beautiful patio off Calle Oficios, Al Medina is where you can dine like a Moroccan prince on lamb couscous and Lebanese sumac with a spicy twist. It's especially recommended for its voluminous vegetarian platter.

Café Santo Domingo
CAFE, BAKERY $

(Map p296; Obispo No 159 btwn San Ignacio & Mercaderes, Habana Vieja; ⊘9am-9pm) Tucked away upstairs above Habana Vieja's best bakery – and encased in one of its oldest buildings – this laid-back cafe is aromatic, tasty and light on the wallet. Check out the huge *sandwich especial,* or smuggle some cakes upstairs to enjoy over a steaming cup of *café con leche.*

CENTRO HABANA

TOP CHOICE Los Nardos
SPANISH, CARIBBEAN $$

(Map p300; Paseo de Martí No 563; ⊘noon-midnight) An open secret situated opposite the Capitolio but easy to miss (look out for the queue). Los Nardos is one of a handful of semiprivate Havana restaurants operated by the Spanish Asturianas society, and is touted in some quarters as one of the best eateries in the city. The dilapidated exterior promises little, but the leather/mahogany decor and astoundingly delicious dishes suggest otherwise. Portions are huge, service attentive, and the prices, which start at around CUC$4 for chicken and pork dishes, are mind-bogglingly cheap.

Paladar La Guarida
PALADAR $$$

(Map p304; ☑866-9047; Concordia No 418 btwn Gervasio & Escobar; ⊘noon-3pm & 7pm-midnight) Located on the top floor of a spectacularly dilapidated Havana tenement, La Guarida has a lofty reputation that rests on its movie-location setting (*Fresa y Chocolate* was filmed here). The food, as might be expected, is up there with Havana's best, shoehorning its captivating blend of Nueva Cocina Cubana into dishes such as sea bass in a coconut reduction, and chicken with honey and lemon sauce. Reservations required.

Flor de Loto
CHINESE $$

(Map p304; Salud No 303 btwn Gervasio & Escobar) Popularly considered to be Havana's – and, by definition, Cuba's – best Chinese restaurant, as the queues outside will testify.

Camouflaged beneath Centro Havana's decaying facades it serves up extra-large portions of lobster, fried rice and sweet-and-sour sauce in a frigidly air-conditioned interior.

Restaurante Tien-Tan
CHINESE $$

(Map p300; Cuchillo No 17 btwn Rayo & San Nicolás; ⊘11am-11pm) One of the Barrio Chino's best authentic Chinese restaurants, Tien-Tan (the 'Temple of Heaven') is run by a Chinese-Cuban couple and serves up an incredulous 130 different dishes. With such complexity you might have thought that you would be in for a long wait and that the food would, at best, be average. Thankfully, neither is the case. Try chop suey with vegetables or chicken with cashew nuts and sit outside in action-packed Cuchillo, one of Havana's most colorful and fastest-growing food streets.

Café Neruda
INTERNATIONAL $

(Map p300; Malecón No 203 btwn Manrique & San Nicolás, Centro Habana; ⊘11am-11pm) Barbecued Chilean ox, Nerudian skewer, Chilean turnover? Poor old Pablo Neruda would be turning in his grave if this weren't such an inviting place and a rare ray of light on the otherwise mildewed Malecón. Spend a poetic afternoon watching the waves splash over the sea wall.

VEDADO

TOP CHOICE La Torre
FRENCH, CARIBBEAN $$$

(Map p304; ☑838-3088; Edificio Focsa, cnr Calles 17 & M; mains CUC$30) One of Havana's tallest and most talked-about restaurants is perched high above downtown Vedado, atop the skyline-hogging Focsa building. A colossus of both modernist architecture and French/Cuban haute cuisine, this lofty fine-dining extravaganza combines sweeping city views with a progressive French-inspired menu that serves everything from artichokes to foie gras to *tart almandine*.

Paladar El Hurón Azul
PALADAR $$$

(Map p304; ☑879-1691; Humboldt No 153; meals CUC$15-20; ⊘noon-midnight Tue-Sun) This place is often touted as one of Havana's best private restaurants and is locally famous for its adventurous smoked pork served with a pineapple salsa. That said, it's not cheap. Reserve ahead.

Pain de París
CAFE, BAKERY $

(Map p304; Calle 25 No 164 btwn Infanta & Calle O; ⊘8am-midnight) With quite possibly the best cakes in Havana – including iced cinnamon buns – this small chain does box-up cakes, cappuccinos, croissants and the odd savory snack. If you've been ODing on paltry Cuban desserts, or have hit a sugar low after a superlight breakfast, get your 11 o'clock pick-me-up here.

El Gringo Viejo
PALADAR $$

(Map p304; ☑831-1946; Calle 21 No 454 btwn Calles E & F; ⊘noon-11pm) The Gringo offers a good atmosphere and large portions of invariably brilliant food. Locals and visitors love it for its speedy service, fine wine list and big portions of more adventurous plates, such as smoked salmon with olives and Gouda or crabmeat in red sauce (CUC$10 to CUC$12).

Paladar Los Amigos
PALADAR $$

(Map p304; Calle M No 253; meals CUC$10; ⊘noon-midnight) Paladar Los Amigos, situated in the back of a prerevolutionary house on the corner of Calles M and 19 near the Hotel Victoria, serves good Cuban meals. It's enthusiastically recommended by locals.

Café TV
FAST FOOD $

(Map p304; cnr Calles N & 19; ⊘10am-9pm) Hidden in the bowels of the Focsa building, this TV-themed cafe is a funky dinner/performance venue lauded by those in the know for its cheap food and hilarious comedy nights. If you're willing to brave the frigid air-con and rather foreboding underground entry tunnel, head here for fresh burgers, healthy salad, pasta and chicken cordon bleu.

Coppelia
ICE-CREAM $

(Map p304; Calles 23 & L; ⊘11am-10:30pm Tue-Sun) This classic Havana ice-cream mecca draws crowds from morning until closing time – look no further for your authentic experience of the capital than here, across the street from student favorite Cine Yara. Enter the *divisa* (CUC$) part on Calle 23 or wait in line for the real deal and pay peanuts in pesos.

🍺 Drinking

HABANA VIEJA & CENTRO HABANA

TOP CHOICE Taberna de la Muralla
BAR-RESTAURANT

(Map p296; cnr San Ignacio & Muralla; ⊘11am-midnight) Havana's only microbrewery is situated on a boisterous corner of Plaza Vieja.

Set up by an Austrian company in 2004, it sells smooth cold homemade beer at sturdy wooden benches set up outside on the cobbles or indoors in an atmospheric beer hall. Get a group together and you'll get the amber nectar in a tall plastic tube drawn from a tap at the bottom. There's also an outside grill.

Museo del Chocolate   CHOCOLATERY $
(Map p296; cnr Amargura & Mercaderes, Habana Vieja; ⊙9am-8pm) – with no irony intended – in Calle Amargura (literally: Bitterness Street), this sweet-toothed establishment is more a cafe than a museum, with a small cluster of marble tables set amid a sugary mélange of chocolate paraphernalia.

Café El Escorial   CAFE $
(Map p296; Mercaderes No 317 cnr Muralla, Habana Vieja; ⊙9am-9pm) Opening out onto Plaza Vieja and encased in a finely restored colonial mansion, there's something definitively European about El Escorial. It serves the best caffeine infusions in the city along with a sweet selection of delicate cakes.

La Bodeguita del Medio   BAR-RESTAURANT
(Map p296; Empedrado No 207; ⊙11am-midnight) A visit to Havana's most celebrated bar, made famous thanks to the rum-swilling exploits of Ernest Hemingway, has become de rigueur for tourists who haven't yet cottoned on to the fact that the mojitos are better and (far) cheaper elsewhere. Past visitors have included Salvador Allende, Fidel Castro, and Nat King Cole. These days the clientele is less luminous, with package tourists from Varadero outnumbering beatnik bohemians.

Bar Dos Hermanos   BAR
(Map p296; San Pedro No 304; ⊙24hr) Despite its erstwhile Hemingway connections, this bar has (so far) managed to remain off the standard Havana tourist itinerary. Out of the way and a little seedy, it was a favorite watering hole of Spanish poet Federico García Lorca during a three-month stopover in 1930. With its long wooden bar and salty seafaring atmosphere, it can't have changed much since.

El Floridita   BAR-RESTAURANT
(Map p296; Obispo No 557; ⊙11am-midnight) A bartender named Constante Ribalaigua invented the daiquiri here, but it was Hemingway who popularized it. His record – legend has it – was 13 doubles in one sitting. Any attempt to equal it at the current prices (CUC$7 and up for a shot) will cost you a small fortune – and a huge hangover.

La Lluvia de Oro   BAR
(Map p296; Obispo No 316; ⊙24hr) It's on Obispo and there's always live music belting through the doorway. But with a higher-than-average *jinetero/jinetera* (locals who attach themselves to foreigners for monetary or material gain) to tourist ratio, it's not the most intimate introduction to Havana.

Monserrate Bar   BAR
(Map p296; Obrapía No 410) A couple of doors down from El Floridita, Monserrate is a Hemingway-free zone, meaning the daiquiris are half the price.

VEDADO

Café Fresa y Chocolate   BAR
(Map p304; cnr Calles 23 & 12; ⊙10am-10pm Mon-Wed, noon-midnight Thu-Sun) An arty crowd patronizes this place, named after the cult '90s Cuban movie nominated for an Oscar. It adjoins the ICAIC film institute and attracts a solid crowd of actors, directors and theater folk.

☆ Entertainment

TOP CHOICE **Casa de la Música**   NIGHTCLUB, LIVE MUSIC
Centro Habana (Map p300; Av de Italia; 4pm matinee CUC$5, night CUC$15-25); Miramar (Calle 20 No 3308; admission CUC$15-20; ⊙8pm-2am Tue-Sat, shows 10pm) Of the two Casas de la Música in Havana, the outpost in distant Miramar is reckoned by locals to be the superior by far. It's probably worth swallowing the cab fare to get out here and enjoy a much more authentic program of music in a less touristy atmosphere, although the slightly divey Centro Habana club of the same name can be a lot of fun too.

Gran Teatro de La Habana   THEATER
(Map p300; ☎861-3077; cnr Paseo de Martí & San Rafael; per person CUC$20; ⊙box office 9am-6pm Mon-Sat, to 3pm Sun) The amazing neobaroque theater across from Parque Central is the seat of the acclaimed Ballet Nacional de Cuba, founded in 1948 by Alicia Alonso. It is also the home of the Cuban National Opera. A theater since 1838, the building contains the grandiose Teatro García Lorca along with two smaller concert halls, the Sala Alejo Carpentier and the Sala Ernesto

Lecuono – where art-house films are sometimes shown.

El Hurón Azul
TRADITIONAL MUSIC

(Map p304; cnr Calles 17 & H, Vedado) If you want to rub shoulders with some socialist celebrities, hang out at the social club of the Unión Nacional de Escritores y Artistas de Cuba (Uneac; Union of Cuban Writers and Artists), Cuba's leading cultural institution. Most performances take place outside in the garden. Wednesday is the Afro-Cuban rumba, Saturday is authentic Cuban boleros, and alternate Thursdays there's jazz and *trova* (traditional poetic singing).

Callejón de Hamel
RUMBA

(Map p304; ☺from noon Sun) Aside from its funky street murals and psychedelic art shops, the main reason to come to Havana's high temple of Afro-Cuban culture is for the frenetic rumba music that kicks off every Sunday at around noon.

Tropicana Nightclub
CABARET

(Calle 72 No 4504; ☺10pm) A city institution since it opened in 1939, the world-famous Tropicana was one of the few bastions of Havana's Las Vegas–style nightlife to survive the clampdowns of the puritanical Castro Revolution. The open-air cabaret show is little changed since its '50s heyday, featuring a bevy of scantily clad senoritas who climb nightly down from the palm trees to dance Latin salsa amid colorful flashing lights on stage. Tickets go for a slightly less than socialistic CUC$70. The Tropicana is way out in the Havana suburb of Marianao. The only practical way of getting there is by an organized tour (every travel agency offers it) or taxi. The ride should cost approximately CUC$10.

Jazz Café
JAZZ CLUB

(Map p304; top floor, Galerías de Paseo, cnr Calle 1 & Paseo, Vedado; drink minimum CUC$10; ☺noon-late) This upscale joint located in a shopping mall overlooking the Malecón is a kind of jazz supper club, with dinner tables and a decent menu. At night, the club swings into action with live jazz, *timba* and salsa.

Casa de la Amistad
TRADITIONAL MUSIC

(Map p304; Paseo No 416 btwn Calles 17 & 19, Vedado) Housed in a beautiful rose-colored mansion on leafy Paseo, the Casa de la Amistad mixes traditional *son* sounds with suave Benny Moré music in a classic Italian Re-

naissance–style garden. Other perks include a restaurant, bar, cigar shop and the house itself – an Italianite masterpiece.

El Gato Tuerto
TRADITIONAL MUSIC

(Map p304; Calle O No 14 btwn Calles 17 & 19, Vedado; drink minimum CUC$5; ☺noon-6am) Once the HQ of Havana's alternative artistic and sexual scene, the 'one-eyed cat' is now a nexus for karaoke-crazy baby boomers who come here to knock out rum-fuelled renditions of traditional Cuban boleros (ballads).

Café Cantante
NIGHTCLUB

(Map p304; cnr Paseo & Calle 39; admission CUC$10; ☺9pm-5am Tue-Sat) Below the Teatro Nacional de Cuba (side entrance), this place offers live salsa music and dancing, as well as bar snacks and food. The clientele is mainly 'yummies' (young urban Marxist managers) and aging male tourists with their youthful Cuban girlfriends.

Teatro Amadeo Roldán
CLASSICAL MUSIC

(Map p304; cnr Calzada & Calle D, Vedado; per person CUC$10) Named after the famous Cuban composer and the man responsible for bringing Afro-Cuban influences into modern classical music, this theater is one of Havana's grandest, with two different auditoriums. The Orquesta Sinfónica Nacional plays in the 886-seat Sala Amadeo Roldán.

Casa del Alba Cultural
TRADITIONAL MUSIC

(Map p304; Línea btwn Calles C & D, Vedado) This new venue was designed to strengthen cultural solidarity between the ALBA nations (Cuba, Venezuela, Bolivia, Ecuador, Nicaragua), but in reality it hosts a variety of artistic and music-based shows and expos. It was opened in December 2009 with Raúl Castro, Daniel Ortega and Hugo Chávez in attendance.

Jazz Club La Zorra y El Cuervo
JAZZ CLUB

(Map p304; cnr Calles 23 & O, Vedado; admission CUC$5-10; ☺10pm) Havana's most famous jazz club is on La Rampa, which opens its doors nightly at 10pm to long lines of committed music fiends. The freestyle jazz here is second to none and, in the past, the club has hosted such big names as Chucho Valdés and George Benson.

Pico Blanco
NIGHTCLUB

(Map p304; Calle O btwn Calles 23 & 25; admission CUC$5-10; ☺9pm) Situated on the 14th floor of Vedado's Hotel St John's, this insanely popular nightclub kicks off nightly at 9pm.

Some nights it's karaoke and cheesy boleros, another it's jamming with some rather famous Cuban musicians.

Piano Bar Delirio Habanero   NIGHTCLUB
(Map p304; cnr Paseo & Calle 39, Vedado; admission CUC$5; ⏰from 6pm Tue-Sun) This suave lounge upstairs in the Teatro Nacional de Cuba hosts everything from young *trovadores* to smooth, improvised jazz. The deep red couches abut a wall of glass overlooking the Plaza de la Revolución, and it's stunning at night with the Martí memorial alluringly backlit.

Habana Café   NIGHTCLUB, CABARET
(Map p304; Paseo btwn Calles 1 & 3, Vedado; admission CUC$10; ⏰from 9:30pm) A hip nightclub and cabaret show at the Hotel Meliá Cohiba laid out in 1950s American retro style. After 1am the tables are cleared and the place rocks to 'international music' until the cock crows.

Teatro Mella   THEATER
(Map p304; Línea No 657 btwn Calles A & B) Occupying the site of the old Rodi Cinema on Línea, the Teatro Mella offers one of Havana's most comprehensive programs, including an international ballet festival, comedy shows, theater, dance and intermittent performances from the famous Conjunto Folklórico Nacional. If you have kids, come to the children's show Sunday at 11am.

Estadio Latinoamericano   BASEBALL
(Map p304; Zequiera No 312, Vedado) From October to April, this 58,000-seat baseball stadium in Cerro is home to Los Industriales and Los Metropolitanos (they alternate home fixtures). Entry costs a few pesos (but they like to charge foreigners CUC$2). Games are 7:30pm Tuesday, Wednesday and Thursday, 1:30pm Saturday and Sunday.

Salón Chévere   NIGHTCLUB
(Parque Almendares, cnr Calles 49C & 28A; admission CUC$6-10; ⏰from 10pm) One of Havana's most popular discos, this alfresco place in a lush park setting hosts a good mix of locals and tourists.

Cine Infanta   CINEMA
(Map p304; Calzada de Infanta No 357, Centro Havana) Newly renovated Infanta is possibly Havana's plushest cinema. It's an important venue during the International Film Festival.

Cine Yara   CINEMA
(Map p304; cnr Calles 23 & L, Vedado) There's one big screen and two video *salas* (cinemas) here at Havana's most famous cinema and the venue for many a hot date.

Cinecito   CINEMA
(Map p300; San Rafael No 68, Centro Havana; 🎫) Films for kids behind the Hotel Inglaterra. There's another one next to Cine Chaplín on Calles 23 & 12.

🛍 Shopping

TOP CHOICE Centro Cultural Antiguos Almacenes de Deposito San José   ART, SOUVENIRS
(Map p296; Av del Puerto cnr San Pedro; ⏰10am-6pm Mon-Sat) In November 2009 Havana's open-air handicraft market moved under the cover of this old shipping warehouse in Av del Puerto. Check your socialist ideals at the door. Herein lies a hive of free enterprise and (unusually for Cuba) haggling. Possible souvenirs include paintings, *guayabera* shirts, woodwork, leather items, jewelry and numerous apparitions of El Che.

Fundación Havana Club Shop   RUM
(Map p296; 🎫861-1900; Av del Puerto; ⏰9am-9pm) Come to the Fundación Havana Club in the Museo del Ron for cool Havana Club gear, and the best selection of Cuban rum.

Promociones de ICAIC   SOUVENIRS
(Map p304; Calles 23 & L) A fabulous selection of original Cuban movie posters (CUC$10) is on offer here, in Cine Yara, making fantastic souvenirs. There are also film-themed T-shirts (CUC$7) and classic Cuban films on video and DVD. Another outlet is inside Café Fresa y Chocolate (corner Calles 23 and 12).

ℹ Information

EMERGENCY Call 🎫106 for ambulance and police.

INTERNET ACCESS Havana is the most internet-friendly place in the country, but access is still not cheap anywhere and computers can be slow. Those with their laptops can head to the NH Parque Central and use the wi-fi there (CUC$8 per hour). Another good option is to go into any Habaguanex-run hotel and buy a card to use its computer (CUC$6 for one hour).

Cibercafé Capitolio (Prado & Teniente Rey; per 30min/hr CUC$3/5; ⏰8am-8pm) Inside the main entrance of Capitolio Nacional, this is the cheapest access in town.

Etecsa (Habana 406 cnr Obispo; per hr CUC$6; ⏰8:30am-7:30pm)

MEDICAL SERVICES Clinica Central Cira García (☎204-2811; www.cirag.cu; Calle 20 No 4101, Playa)

Hospital Nacional Hermanos Ameijeiras (☎877-6053; www.hha.sld.cu; San Lázaro No 701) Enter below the parking lot off Padre Varela (ask for 'CEDA' in Section N).

Hotel Habana Libre Pharmacy (☎834-6100; Calle L btwn Calles 23 & 25, Vedado) A well-stocked pharmacy in Havana's largest hotel.

MONEY The only bank with a reliable ATM is the Cadeca in Havana Vieja on Obispo.

Banco de Crédito y Comercio Habana Vieja (Aguiar No 310, near Obispo; ☺8:30am-1:30pm Mon-Fri); Vedado (Airline Bldg, Calle 23 No 64)

Banco Financiero Internacional Centro Habana (Av Salvador Allende); Habana Vieja (cnr Oficios & Teniente Rey); Vedado (Tryp Habana Libre, Calle L btwn Calles 23 & 25)

Banco Metropolitano Calle M (Línea & Calle M); Paseo (Línea off Paseo); Vedado (Post office, Av de la Independencia)

Cadeca Habana Vieja (cnr Oficios & Lamparilla; ☺8am-7pm Mon-Sat, 8am-1pm Sun) Plaza de San Francisco); Habana Vieja (Obispo No 257 btwn Aguiar & Cuba; ☺8:30am-10pm); Vedado (Calle 23 btwn K & L; ☺7am-2:30pm, 3:30-10pm); Vedado (Línea btwn Paseo & Calle A) Cadeca gives cash advances and changes traveler's checks at higher commissions than banks. The Obispo, Habana Vieja branch has a reliable ATM.

POST DHL (Calzada No 818 btwn Calles 2 & 4; ☺8am-5pm Mon-Fri)

Post office Centro Habana (Paseo de Martí); Habana Vieja (Oficios No 102, Plaza de San Francisco); Vedado (Línea & Paseo; ☺8am-8pm Mon-Sat); Vedado (Av de la Independencia; ☺24hr)

TOURIST INFORMATION Infotur Airport (☎266-4094; Terminal 3 Aeropuerto Internacional José Martí; ☺8:30am-5:30pm); Habana Vieja (☎863-6884; www.infotur.cu; cnr Obispo & San Ignacio; ☺10am-1pm & 2-7pm) Infotur also has desks in the main hotels around Parque Central.

❶ Getting There & Away

AIR José Martí International Airport (☎649-5666) is at Av de la Independencia, 25km southwest of Havana. For information on flights to Havana, see p348.

BUS The **Víazul** (www.viazul.com; Calle 26 & Zoológico, Nuevo Vedado) terminal is located 3km southwest of Plaza de la Revolución. Infotur (p316) and **Cubatur** (Map p304; cnr Calles 23 & L) sell tickets. There's also a Víazul ticket office in the arrivals area of Terminal 3 at José Martí Airport, and several others scattered around town. See this page for bus services.

For Baracoa you have to change in Santiago de Cuba.

Víazul Departures from Havana (check www.viazul.com for updates):

Camagüey CUC$30, nine hours, 8:40am, 9:30am, 3:15pm, 6:15pm, 8:30pm, 10pm

Santa Clara CUC$18, 3¾ hours, 8:40am, 9:30am, 3:15pm, 10pm

Santiago de Cuba CUC$51, 15 hours, 9:30am, 3:15pm, 6:15pm, 10pm

Trinidad CUC$25, six hours, 8:15am, 1pm

Varadero CUC$10, three hours, 8am, 12pm, 5pm, 7pm

Viñales CUC$12, four hours, 9am, 4pm

CAR See p349 for information on car rental in Cuba.

TAXI Taxis at the **Víazul** (Calle 26 & Zoológico, Nuevo Vedado) bus terminal offer fares for up to four people to Varadero (CUC$65), Santa Clara (CUC$100), Cienfuegos (CUC$125) and Trinidad (CUC$140).

TRAIN Trains to most parts of Cuba depart from **Estación Central de Ferrocarriles** (Map p296; cnr Av de Bélgica & Arsenal), on the southwestern side of Habana Vieja. Foreigners must buy tickets in convertibles at **La Coubre station** (off Map p296; cnr Av del Puerto & Desamparados, Habana Vieja; ☺9am-3pm Mon-Fri).

Cuba's best train, the Tren Francés (an old French SNCF train), runs every third day between Havana and Santiago, stopping in Santa Clara (CUC$17) and Camagüey (CUC$32). It leaves Havana at 7pm and arrives in Santiago the following morning at 9am. There are no sleeper cars, but carriages are comfortable and air-conditioned and there's a snack service. Tickets cost CUC$62 for 1st class and CUC$50 for 2nd class.

❶ Getting Around

TO/FROM THE AIRPORT For all practical purposes, there is no public transportation from the airport to the city center, and taxi drivers work this to their full advantage. A taxi should cost CUC$20 (or CUC$15 from the city to the airport), but you'll be told CUC$25; bargain hard. You may also find yourself sharing a taxi with another traveler or two – this is perfectly normal, although make sure you're definitely not paying over CUC$20 in this case. A taxi between any of the terminals costs CUC$5 per person – bargaining doesn't seem to be an option on this one.

BUS The best bet for outsiders is the hop-on/hop-off **Havana Bus Tour**, which runs on three routes. The main stop is in Parque Central opposite the Hotel Inglaterra. This is the pickup point for bus T1 running from Habana Vieja to the Plaza de la Revolución, and bus T3, which runs from Centro Habana to Playas del Este (via

LAS TERRAZAS

The pioneering ecovillage of Las Terrazas in Artemisa, 55km west of Havana, dates back to a successful reforestation project in 1968: today it's a Unesco Biosphere Reserve, burgeoning activity center (with Cuba's only canopy tour), and site of the earliest surviving coffee plantations in Cuba. Not surprisingly, it attracts day-trippers from Havana by the busload.

La Moka (☑57-86-00; Las Terrazas; s/d CUC$80/110; Ⓟ❋≋) is the community's sole hotel. This mold-breaking, upmarket ecoresort was built between 1992 and 1994 by workers drawn from Las Terrazas with the aim of attracting foreign tourists. Close by, in the picturesque whitewashed village that overlooks a small lake, there's an active art community with open studios, woodwork and pottery workshops. But the region's biggest attraction is its verdant natural surroundings; ideal for hiking, relaxing and birdwatching.

Parque Histórico Militar Morro-Cabaña). Bus T2 runs from the Plaza de la Revolución (where it connects with T1) to Marina Hemingway (via Necrópolis Cristóbal Colón and Playa). All-day tickets are CUC$5. Services run from 9am to 9pm. At the time of writing the T2 service was suspended and the T1 bus was running all the way to Marina Hemingway.

TAXI Bici-taxis (two-seater taxis powered by a bicyclist) are available throughout Habana Vieja and Centro Habana and are great for short hops (CUC$1 to CUC$2). Agree on the price first. Coco-taxis are the yellow eggs-on-wheels you will see zipping all over town; they carry three people and cost CUC$0.50 per kilometer.

Panataxi (☑55-55-55) has the cheapest official taxis. Fancier taxis can be ordered from **TaxiOK** (☑877-6666) and **Transgaviota** (☑267-1626).

AROUND HAVANA

Playas del Este

Havana's pine-fringed Riviera, Playas del Este, begins at Bacuranao, 18km east of Havana, and continues east through **Santa María del Mar** (the nicest of the beaches here) to Guanabo, 27km from the capital. These beaches provide an effortless escape from Havana should you need it, and there are many casas particulares in Guanabo (look for the blue triangle).

The beach is lined with **rentals** including windsurfers (per hour CUC$6), catamarans (per hour CUC$12) and beach chairs (per three hours CUC$2). Several simple fish **restaurants** line the beach.

Bus 400 to Guanabo leaves hourly from the rotunda at Desamparados, near the train station in Habana Vieja. Bus 405 runs between Guanabacoa and Guanabo.

More comfortable is the new Havana Bus Tour (see p316).

PINAR DEL RÍO PROVINCE

The western flank of Cuba extends from Havana Province to the narrow Yucatán Channel separating Cuba from Mexico. This lush part of the island is home to endless tobacco plantations, pine trees, sugarcane and rice fields and is one of Cuba's most scenic. With rock climbing, caving, diving and birdwatching sprinkled throughout two Unesco Biosphere Reserves and one World Heritage site, this is Cuba's outdoor adventure hub. Beyond the uninteresting city of Pinar del Río, the countryside becomes breathtaking, as well as extremely rural.

Whether you go north to stunning Viñales, famous for its vast limestone hills, or continue heading west to the Península de Guanahacabibes, where superb diving, pristine beaches, and exciting hikes await you, you'll be guaranteed a rewarding trip.

Pinar del Río Province is also home to San Juan y Martínez and the Vuelta Abajo plantations, where the world's finest tobacco thrives in the sandy soil. The majority of export-quality tobacco comes from here. The best time to visit is at harvest time, from January to March.

Viñales

♪ 048 / POP 27,806

Embellished by soaring pine trees and scattered with bulbous limestone cliffs that teeter like giant haystacks above placid tobacco plantations, the village of Viñales and its surrounding national park is one of Cuba's most magnificent natural settings. Wedged spectacularly into the Sierra de los Órganos mountain range, this 11km-by-5km valley was declared a Unesco World Heritage site in 1999 for its dramatic *mogotes* (rocky limestone outcrops), copious caves and traditional tobacco farms.

Activity-wise, Viñales offers fine opportunities for hiking, rock climbing, horseback trekking and observing nature. On the accommodations front it has some first-class hotels and some of the best casas particulares in Cuba.

◉ Sights

The standout attractions of Viñales are its *mogotes* and the fascinating cave complex of Santo Tomás, a 20km drive from town. The town itself has a few mildly diverting sights, but it's really about kicking back and drinking in the scenery here.

Gran Caverna de Santo Tomás CAVES
(admission CUC$8; ⊙8:30am-4pm) A standout sight of the area is this humongous cave complex. Tours leave at half past the hour from 8:30am. With over 46km of galleries on eight levels, it's Cuba's largest cave system. Tours are given by friendly, if eccentric guides in both Spanish and English. Wear sturdy shoes, not sandals, as there's a fair bit of clambering to be done, often over slippery surfaces. Headlamps are provided for the 1km, 90-minute tour, which takes in surreal formations including giant stalagmites and stone percussive pipes that the guide will 'play'. The cavern is at El Moncada, off the road to Minas de Matahambre, 15km from Viñales. A cab there and back including waiting time will cost CUC$15.

 Cayo Jutías BEACH
Pinar del Río's most discovered 'undiscovered' beach is the 3km-long blanket of sand that adorns the northern coast of Cayo Jutías, a tiny mangrove-covered key situated approximately 65km northwest of Viñales and attached to the mainland by a short *pedraplén* (causeway).

The cayo's serenity is thanks to the lack of any permanent accommodations. The only facilities on the island are the airy oceanside **Restaurante Cayo Jutías** (⊙11am-5pm), specializing in local seafood, and a small beach hut that rents out kayaks for CUC$1 per hour and runs snorkeling trips to an offshore reef for CUC$12. The Cayo's access road starts about 4km west of Santa Lucía. Four kilometers further on you'll come to a control post at the beginning of the causeway where you'll need to pay a CUC$5 per person entry fee.

Tours from Viñales cost CUC$22 and will give you an adequate six hours' beach time. With your own wheels, the fastest and by far the prettiest route is Minas de Matahambre through rolling pine-clad hills.

Mural de la Prehistoria RUINS
(admission incl drink CUC$3) Four kilometers west of Viñales village on the side of Mogote dos Hermanas is a 120m-long painting designed in 1961 by Leovigildo González Morillo, a follower of Mexican artist Diego Rivera (the idea was hatched by Celia Sánchez, Alicia Alonso and Antonio Núñez Jiménez). On a cliff at the foot of the 617m-high Sierra de Viñales, the highest portion of the Sierra de los Órganos, this massive mural took 18 people four years to complete.

🏃 Activities

Hiking

The Parque Nacional has three official hikes. All of them can be arranged directly at the visitor center, the town's Museo Municipal, or at a tour agency. The cost is CUC$6 to CUC$8 per person.

Cocosolo Palmarito HIKING
This walk starts on a spur road just before La Ermita hotel and progresses for 8km past the Coco Solo and Palmarito *mogotes* and the **Mural de la Prehistoria**. There are good views here and plenty of opportunities to discover the local flora and fauna including a visit to a tobacco *finca* (farmhouse; ask about lunch with one of the families there). It returns you to the main road back to Viñales.

Maravillas de Viñales HIKING
A 5km loop beginning 1km before El Moncada and 13km from the Dos Hermanas turnoff, this hike takes in endemic plants, orchids and the biggest leafcutter ant hive in Cuba (so they say).

San Vicente/Ancón   HIKING

The trail around the more remote Valle Ancón enables you to check out still-functioning coffee communities in a valley surrounded by *mogotes*: it's an 8km loop.

Rock Climbing

You don't need to be Reinhold Messner to recognize the unique climbing potential of Viñales, Cuba's mini-Yosemite. It is sprinkled with steep-sided *mogotes* and bequeathed with whole photo-albums' worth of stunning natural vistas, and climbers from around the world have been coming here for over a decade to indulge in a sport that has yet to be officially sanctioned by the Cuban government.

Thanks to the numerous gray areas, Viñales climbing remains very much a word-of-mouth affair. If you are keen to get up onto the rock face, your first point of reference should be the comprehensive website of **Cuba Climbing** (www.cubaclimbing.com). Once on the ground, the best nexus for climbers is the Villa Cafetal.

Viñales has a handful of skillful Cuban guides, but there is no reliable equipment hire (bring your own) and no adequate safety procedures in place. Everything you do, you do at your own risk. Proceed with caution and care.

🛏 Sleeping

TOP CHOICE **Hotel Los Jazmines**   HOTEL $$
(☑79-64-11; s/d/ste incl breakfast CUC$66/72/90; P❋⛱) Prepare yourself: the vista from this pastel-pink colonial-style hotel is one of the best in Cuba. Open the shutters of your classic valley-facing room and drink in the shimmering sight of magnificent *mogotes*, red oxen-ploughed fields and palm-frond-covered tobacco drying houses.

'Villa Los Reyes' – Yoan & Yarelis Reyes   CASA PARTICULAR $
(☑69-52-25; joanmanuel2008@yahoo.es; Rafael Trejo No 134; r CUC$20-25; P❋) A great modern house with all amenities and a secluded patio for dining. The young owners can organize everything from salsa dancing to Spanish lessons. Yarelis is a biologist at the national park and Yoan has Viñales running through his veins.

La Ermita   HOTEL $
(☑79-62-50; Carretera de La Ermita 1.5; s/d incl breakfast CUC$46/54; P❋⛱) While Los Jazmines might edge the prize for best view, La Ermita takes top honors for architecture,

interior furnishings and all-round services and quality. Among a plethora of extracurricular attractions are an excellent pool, skillfully mixed cocktails, tennis courts, a shop, horseback riding and massage.

Hostal Doña Hilda   CASA PARTICULAR $
(☑79-60-53; Carretera a Pinar del Río Km 25 No 4; r CUC$20-25; ❋) One of the first houses in town on the road from Pinar del Río, Hilda's house is small, unpretentious, and classic Viñales – just like the perennially smiling hostess – with truly wonderful food.

Villa Pitín & Juana   CASA PARTICULAR $
(☑79-33-38; Carretera a Pinar del Río Km 25 No 2; r CUC$25; P❋) With two wonderful rooms on separate floors here (the top floor with the private double patio is the classic traveler retreat) and a fantastic family atmosphere, this place also benefits from delicious home cooking.

Villa Cafetal   CASA PARTICULAR $
(☑533-11752; Adela Ascuy Final; r CUC$15-20; ❋) The owners of this reader-recommended house are experts on climbing and have a shed stacked with equipment: appropriately, since the best climbs in Viñales are on their doorstep. Ensconced in a resplendent garden where the villa cultivates its own coffee, you can practically taste the mountain air here as you swing on the hammock.

Villa Purry & Isis   CASA PARTICULAR $
(☑69-69-21; Salvador Cisneros No 64; r CUC$20) This expansive colonial casa with one room on offer has a column-bedecked front terrace with rocking chairs to watch the world trundle by, and a rear patio too. It's a stone's throw from the plaza.

🍴 Eating

Viñales home-cooking is some of the best in Cuba; eating at your casa particular is a great option.

TOP CHOICE **El Ranchón**   CARIBBEAN $$
(Carretera a Esperanza Km 38; ⊙8am-5pm) You won't forget the experience of eating here. The set meal, which is a proverbial rite of passage on the tour-bus circuit, is melt-in-your-mouth delicious. You pay CUC$11 for a huge spread of roast pork and all the trimmings.

Restaurante La Casa de Don Tomás   CARIBBEAN, INTERNATIONAL $$
(Salvador Cisneros No 140) The oldest house in Viñales is also its best restaurant – by default

DIVING IN CUBA

You could write a book about diving in Cuba, so varied are the options. For those lacking time to venture south to the wondrous outlying islands (for the most pristine dives in the Caribbean) look no further than the following two locations.

María la Gorda (Pinar del Río Province)

Diving is María la Gorda's raison d'être and the prime reason most people trek out to Cuba's extreme western tip. The nerve center is the **Centro Internacional de Buceo** (☎048-77-13-06) next to the eponymous hotel, 14km south of La Bajada and the entrance to the Parque Nacional Península de Guanahacabibes. Good visibility and sheltered off-shore reefs are highlights, plus the proximity of over 50 marked dive sites to the shore. Couple this with the largest formation of black coral in the archipelago and you've got a recipe for arguably the best diving reefs on Cuba's main island. Food and accommodation are provided in the midrange **Hotel María la Gorda** (☎048-77-81-31; s/d incl breakfast CUC$54/76; P ✳) . For access, you'll need your own wheels or you can connect with one of the sporadic shuttle buses in Viñales.

Bay of Pigs (Matanzas Province)

Though it can't claim Cuba's best reefs, the Bay of Pigs can confidently trumpet the archipelago's most *accessible* dives. There's a huge drop-off running 30m to 40m off-shore for over 30km from Playa Larga down to Playa Girón, a fantastic natural feature that has created a 300m-high coral-encrusted wall with amazing swim-throughs, caves, gorgonians and marine life. Even better, the proximity of this wall to the coastline means that the region's 30-plus dive sites can be easily accessed without a boat – you just glide out from the shore.

The **International Scuba Center** (☎045-98-41-18), at Villa Playa Girón, is the main diving headquarters. The all-inclusive **Villa Playa Girón** (☎045-98-41-10; s/d all-inclusive high season CUC$46/65; P ✳ ≋) provides no-frills food and accommodation.

The Bay of Pigs is a two-hour drive from Havana. Alternatively you can get a Víazul bus to Jaguey Grande, followed by a taxi down to Guamá. From here a shuttle bus connects to Playa Girón.

(there's no real opposition). The casa, with its terracotta roof and exuberant flowering vines, is suitably salubrious and the house special, *las delicias de Don Tomás,* a mélange of rice, lobster, fish, pork, chicken and sausage with an egg on top (CUC$10), is divine.

Mural de la Prehistoria
Restaurant CARIBBEAN, INTERNATIONAL **$$**
(☺8am-7pm) Expensive but almost worth it, the Mural's humongous CUC$15 set lunch – tasty pork roasted and smoked over natural charcoal – ought to keep you going at least until tomorrow's breakfast.

☆ Entertainment

Centro Cultural Polo Montañez LIVE MUSIC
(cnr Salvador Cisneros & Joaquin Pérez; admission after 9pm CUC$2) Named for the late Pinar del Río resident turned *guajiro* (country folk) hero, Polo Montañez, this open-to-the-elements patio off the main plaza is a bar-

restaurant with a full-blown stage and lighting rig that comes alive after 9pm.

Patio del Decimista LIVE MUSIC
(Salvador Cisneros No 102; ☺music at 9pm) Smaller but equally ebullient is this long-standing place that serves live music, cold beers, snacks and great cocktails. Free admission.

❶ Information

Banco de Crédito y Comercio (Salvador Cisneros No 58; ☺8am-3pm Mon-Fri)
Cadeca (Salvador Cisneros & Adela Azcuy; ☺8:30am-6pm Mon-Sat) Gives cash advances and changes traveler's checks at higher commissions than banks.
Etecsa (Ceferino Fernández No 3) Internet access and international calls.
Post office (Ceferino Fernández No 14; ☺9am-6pm Mon-Sat)
Viñales Visitor Center (☺8am-6pm) On the main road into town from Pinar del Río before

Hotel Los Jazmines. Guided hikes (CUC$8, 2½ hours) can be booked.

Cubanacán (☑79-63-93; Salvador Cisneros No 63C; ☺9am-7pm Mon-Sat) Arranges tours, excursions and transfer buses.

ⓘ Getting There & Around

BUS Víazul (Salvador Cisneros No 63A; ☺8am-noon & 1-3pm) is opposite Viñales' main square. The daily Víazul bus for Havana via Pinar del Río departs at 8am and 2pm (CUC$12).

CAR Car hire can be arranged at **Cubacar** (Salvador Cisneros No 63C; ☺9am-7pm) in the Cubanacán office.

VIÑALES BUS TOUR The **Viñales Bus Tour** is a hop-on/hop-off minibus that runs nine times a day between the valley's spread-out sites. Starting and finishing in the town plaza, the whole circuit takes an hour and five minutes, with the first bus leaving at 9am and the last at 4:50pm.

CENTRAL CUBA

What central Cuba lacks in dramatic scenery it makes up for with a host of gorgeous colonial towns, including the single most-visited place on the island, the utterly lovely Trinidad. While the beauty of Trinidad remains incontestable, there's also a good choice of far-less-visited gems in central Cuba, such as cultural Santa Clara and gorgeous backwater Remedios.

Of course central Cuba is also home to the motherlode of Cuba's tourist industry, the megaresort town of Varadero, which, while not covered in this book, is still where approximately half the tourists arriving in Cuba are heading. There are excellent stretches of beaches across the north coast, as well as some good pockets in the south. You'll also find good hiking in Topes de Collantes and important historic monuments including Che Guevara's solemn last resting place in Santa Clara. So central Cuba shouldn't just be seen as a region to get through on the way to the Oriente – stop off as much as you can and you'll be amply rewarded.

By car or bicycle, you have the choice of the Autopista, a multilane highway that makes for fast driving, or the Carretera Central. While the latter is certainly more scenic, the driving can be laborious as you dodge horse carts, goats and tractors. From Havana there are daily Víazul (www.viazul.cu) buses to Trinidad, Santiago de Cuba (stopping in Santa Clara) and Camagüey.

There's also a service between Trinidad and Santiago de Cuba.

Santa Clara

☑42 / POP 239,091

Che city has long been hallowed turf for hero-worshipping, beret-wearing Guevara buffs, but away from the bombastic monuments the city pulsates with a youthful vitality that includes some of the country's most eclectic nighttime entertainment outside Havana. The celebrated cultural scene is thanks to the city hosting the country's second-most-prestigious university, a presence that has inspired impromptu concerts, drag shows and even a heavy metal festival.

Santa Clara is a great springboard, too, for almost anywhere else you want to get to in Cuba: no wonder that once Guevara had wrested this city from Batista's grasp the revolution was all but nailed.

⊙ Sights

The Ernesto Che Guevara and Tren Blindado monuments are within walking distance of the Parque Vidal if you have good legs; otherwise catch a taxi or horse carriage.

FREE **Monumento Ernesto**
Che Guevara   MONUMENT, MUSEUM
(Av de los Desfiles; ☺9am-5:30pm Tue-Sat, 9am-5pm Sun) Santa Clara's premier site is a semireligious monument, mausoleum and museum in honor of Ernesto 'Che' Guevara. The complex is just outside the town center and can be seen for miles around with its tall Che statue. The statue was erected in 1987 to mark the 20th anniversary of Guevara's murder in Bolivia, and the mausoleum below contains 38 stone-carved niches dedicated to the guerrillas killed in that failed revolutionary attempt. In 1997 the remains of 17 of them, including Guevara, were recovered from a secret mass grave in Bolivia and reburied here. Fidel Castro lit the eternal flame on October 17, 1997. The adjacent museum contains a large number of Che photographs – the great poser playing golf and eating what appears to be a hamburger are two of the less expected shots. Other ephemera include guns, letters, medical equipment and a rare late picture of Che shorn and looking uncannily like Brando in *The Godfather*.

Monumento a la Toma del Tren Blindado
MONUMENT, MUSEUM

(admission CUC$1; ⊙9am-5:30pm Mon-Sat) This rather eccentric train wreck (literally) is a reconstruction of Che's greatest military victory, when he led 18 men into a ridiculously brave ambush of a 22-car armored train containing 408 heavily armed Batista troops. Amazingly, this battle on December 29, 1958 only lasted 90 minutes. The museum, east on Independencia just over the Río Cubanicay, is contained within the very boxcars Che ambushed. Events are painstakingly documented, and it's a great spot simply to see how well everything has been reconstructed.

Parque Vidal
PARK

Parque Vidal is the charming central plaza of Santa Clara, around which the city is clustered. Any weekend evening you'll find live music here, whether impromptu or planned, small-scale or large.

Buildings of note include the 1885 **Teatro La Caridad** (Máximo Gómez; performances CUC$2), in the northwest corner of Parque Vidal, with frescoes by Camilo Zalaya. The **Museo de Artes Decorativas** (Parque Vidal No 27; admission CUC$3; ⊙9am-6pm Mon, Wed & Thu, 1-10pm Fri & Sat, 6-10pm Sun), just east of Teatro La Caridad, is an 18th-century building packed with period furniture and treasures. The inner patio is a treat.

Casa de la Ciudad
CULTURAL CENTER

(Independencia & JB Zayas; admission CUC$1; ⊙8am-5pm) West of Parque Vidal, this center shows the history of Santa Clara, hosts contemporary exhibitions and is a meeting place for the city's intellectuals. Check here for nighttime cultural activities.

Fábrica de Tabacos Constantino Pérez Carrodegua
CIGAR FACTORY

(Calle Maceo 181 btwn Julio Jover & Berenguer; admission CUC$4; ⊙9-11am & 1-3pm Mon-Sat) A glimpse inside the town's cigar factory is a fascinating experience, not least because it's relatively unvisited by tourists and as authentic a Cuban experience as can be had. Annoyingly you can't buy tickets there, but have to buy them from the **Cubanacán office** (Colon btwn 9 de Abril & Serafin García; ⊙8am-8pm Mon-Sat).

🛏 Sleeping

TOP CHOICE **Hostal Florida Center**
CASA PARTICULAR $

(☑20-81-61; Maestra Nicolasa Este No 56 btwn Colón & Maceo; r CUC$20-25; ❄) The Florida is a national treasure. It boasts more antiques than the local decorative-arts museum and serves better food than most Havana restaurants (in a jaw-dropping central patio replete with plants). Your main dilemma is which room to choose: the grandiose colonial suite, or the gloriously retro art-deco digs? Ángel, the owner, also runs a paladar.

Authentica Pérgola
CASA PARTICULAR $

(☑20-86-86; Luis Estévez No 61 btwn Independencia & Martí; r CUC$20-25; ❄) Delivering precisely what its name would suggest, the plant-packed Pérgola is celebrating four years in the business, although from the service you'll receive here you'd think the hosts had been catering far longer. A vast, leafy central *terraza* (terrace) with a fountain is the focal point: the rooms with their wonderfully hot showers lead off from that.

Hotel Santa Clara Libre
HOTEL $

(☑20-75-48; Parque Vidal No 6; s/d CUC$17/24; ❄) The only tourist hotel is accommodated in Santa Clara's tallest building, a minty-green 168-room eyesore that played a key role in the December 1958 battle for the city between Guevara and Batista's government troops. Inside, the pokey rooms appear worn, but there are cracking views from the 10th-floor restaurant.

Casa de Mercy
CASA PARTICULAR $

(☑21-69-41; Eduardo Machado No 4 btwn Cuba & Colón; r CUC$20-25; ❄) There are two rooms with private bathroom available in this beautiful family house with no fewer than two terraces, a dining room, a book exchange and a tempting cocktail menu.

Isidoro & Marta
CASA PARTICULAR $

(☑20-38-13; Maestra Nicolasa No 74 btwn Colón & Maceo; r CUC$20-25; ❄) This couple's more modern house is kept *muy limpia* (very clean). A long thin patio leads to two fine bedrooms sporting Santa Clara's best showers. Breakfast and dinner are served.

Mary & Raicort
CASA PARTICULAR $

(☑20-70-69; Placído No 54 btwn Independencia & Martí; r CUC$20-25; ❄) A charming 2nd-floor house with two rooms (one with a balcony) for rent and possibly Santa Clara's fruitiest *desayuno* (breakfast); steep stairs ascend to a roof terrace.

OUTSIDE TOWN

Villa la Granjita
HOTEL $

(☑21-81-90; Carretera de Maleza Km 21.5; s/d CUC$22/41; P❄@❄) Posing as a native Taíno village, La Granjita does well with its *bohío*-style (thatched) huts, equipped with all mod cons, but loses authenticity at night-time when a cheesy poolside show and blaring disco remind you you're still very much in 21st-century Cuba. Nevertheless the hotel is better than the usual out-of-town rustic affair, with a good on-site restaurant, a massage therapist and even horseback riding available.

Eating

Casas particulares trump the state-run joints.

TOP CHOICE El Alba PALADAR $
(R Pardo cnr Maceo; ☺noon-4pm & 6-9:30pm Tue-Sun) The town's best peso restaurant is a block east from Parque Vidal. It's a deservedly popular joint, and seating is limited, but comfy sofas and cozy decor ease the wait for a table and the food comes in copious quantities. Go for the fish if it has it.

La Concha CARIBBEAN, ITALIAN $
(cnr Carretera Central & Danielito; mains CUC$3-8) Easily top of the state-run eateries is this posh (well, relatively) spot on the outskirts of town. It does a good trade in capturing the coach parties on their way to and from the Che memorial. There are some classy lunchtime bands, and cheap but tasty pizza (from CUC$4).

Restaurante Colonial 1878 RESTAURANT $
(Máximo Gómez btwn Marta Abreu & Independencia; ☺noon-2pm & 7-10:30pm) Hold onto the table when you cut your steak here, or you might lose it on the floor. Tough meat aside, 1878 is amiable enough, though the food struggles to fit with the dusty colonial setting. Pop in for a cocktail or a light lunch.

La Toscana ITALIAN $
(Máximo Gómez cnr Marta Abreu; ☺10am-3:15pm & 6-11:15pm) Interior designers are, apparently, rarely recruited to lend Santa Clara's eateries any va-va-voom. Here the aspiration seems to have been to go for the American Midwest out-of-town retail-park look: soulless, in a word. The pizza's alright though.

☆ Entertainment

TOP CHOICE Club Mejunje LIVE MUSIC, NIGHTCLUB
(Marta Abreu No 107; ☺4pm-1am Tue-Sun) If you're here on Saturday night, come along to Cuba's only openly gay club, which is remarkably straight-friendly and attracts everyone from local stars of drag to young gangs of toughs. Set in the ruins of an old building, this is the heart of the city's alternative culture. There's usually dancing or theater every other night of the week, and there's nowhere else in Cuba quite like it.

Estadio Sandino BASEBALL
(Calle 9 de Abril Final) You can catch baseball games here from October to April. Villa Clara, nicknamed Las Naranjas (the Oranges) for its team strip is Cuba's third-biggest baseball team, after Havana and Santiago.

El Bar Club Boulevard NIGHTCLUB
(Independencia No 2 btwn Maceo & Pedro Estévez; admission CUC$2; ☺10pm-2am Tue-Sun) A fun cocktail lounge with comedy acts and live music.

🛍 Shopping

Stroll 'El Bulevar,' Independencia, between Maceo and Zayas for good secondhand clothes and consignment shops.

La Veguita CIGARS, RUM
(Calle Maceo No 176A btwn Julio Jover & Berenguer; ☺9am-6pm Mon-Sat) This excellent specialist shop opposite the cigar factory unsurprisingly sells cigars, and boasts an excellent humidor and smoking room, as well as offering coffee and a range of rums to take home. There's a friendly bar-cafe at the back where you'll get the best coffee in town.

ℹ Information

Banco Financiero Internacional (Cuba No 6 & Rafael Trista)

Cadeca (Rafael Tristá & Cuba on Parque Vidal; ☺8:30am-6pm Mon-Sat, 8:30am-12:30pm Sun) For cash advances and cashing traveler's checks.

Etecsa Telepunto (Marta Abreu No 55 btwn Máximo Gómez & Villuendas; per hr CUC$6; ☺8:30am-7:30pm) The most reliable internet access in town.

Post office (Colón No 10; ☺8am-6pm Mon-Sat, 8am-noon Sun)

Cubanacán (✆20-51-89; Colon btwn 9 de Abril & Serafin García; ☺8am-8pm Mon-Sat) Book tobacco factory tours here.

ℹ Getting There & Away

BUS The **Terminal de Ómnibus Nacionales** (✆20-34-70) is 2.5km out on the Carretera Central toward Matanzas, 500m north of the Che monument.

Tickets for air-conditioned **Víazul** (www.viazul.com) buses are sold at a special ticket window for foreigners at the station entrance.

Three buses leave for Havana (CUC$18, 3¾ hours). The Santiago de Cuba–bound bus departs four times daily.

The **intermunicipal bus station** (Carretera Central), west of the center via Calle Marta Abreu, has daily buses to Remedios (CUC$1.45).

TRAIN The **train station** (20-28-95) is straight up Luis Estévez from Parque Vidal on the north side of town. The **ticket office** (Luis Estévez Norte No 323) is across the park from the train station.

The comparatively luxurious Tren Francés passes through the city every third day heading for Santiago de Cuba (12¾ hours) via Camagüey (CUC$13, 4¼ hours).

In the opposite direction there are approximately five slower daily trains to Havana (CUC$14, five hours), most of which stop in Matanzas (CUC$8, 3½ hours).

ⓘ Getting Around

Horse carriages congregate outside the cathedral on Marta Abreu (two pesos per ride). Bici-taxis (from the northwest of the park) cost CUC$1 a ride.

CAR & MOPED Parque Vidal is thankfully closed to traffic.

Cubacar (Hotel Santa Clara Libre, Parque Vidal No 6) Rents wheels.

TAXI A state taxi to Remedios will cost approximately CUC$25. To get to Cayo Las Brujas, bank on CUC$50/$80 one-way/return including waiting time; drivers generally congregate in Parque Vidal outside Hotel Santa Clara Libre or you can call **Cubataxi** (20-25-55/03-63).

Trinidad

41 / POP 52,896

Trinidad is one of a kind, a perfectly preserved Spanish colonial settlement where the clocks stopped ticking in 1850 and – bar the odd gaggle of tourists – have yet to restart. Built on huge sugar fortunes amassed in the adjacent Valle de los Ingenios in the early 19th century, the riches of the town's pre War of Independence heyday are still very much in evidence in illustrious colonial-style mansions bedecked with Italian frescoes, Wedgewood china, Spanish furniture and French chandeliers.

Trinidad was declared a Unesco World Heritage site in 1988. It wasn't long before its secrets became public property and busloads of visitors started arriving to sample the beauty of Cuba's oldest and most enchanting 'outdoor museum.' Yet tourism has done little to deaden Trinidad's gentle southern sheen. The town retains a quiet, almost soporific air in its rambling cobbled streets replete with leather-faced *guajiros* (country folk), snorting donkeys and melodic guitar-wielding troubadours.

◉ Sights & Activities

In Trinidad, all roads lead to **Plaza Mayor**, the town's remarkably peaceful main square, located at the heart of the *casco histórico* (historic city center) and ringed by a quartet of impressive buildings.

Museo Histórico Municipal   MUSEUM
(Casa Cantero; Simón Bolívar No 423; admission CUC$2; 9am-5pm Sat-Thu) Near Plaza Mayor is the town's single most impressive museum, where the ill-gotten wealth of slave trader Justo Cantero is displayed in the stylish, neoclassical rooms. The view from the top of the tower alone is worth the admission price.

Museo Romántico   MUSEUM
(Echerri No 52; admission CUC$2; 9am-5pm Tue-Sat, 9am-1pm Sun) Near the church is this museum in the Palacio Brunet, built between 1740 and 1808. The mansion-turned-museum collects 19th-century furnishings, china and such. As with most old houses, the kitchen and bathroom are the most interesting rooms.

Museo Nacional de la Lucha Contra Bandidos   MUSEUM
(Echerri No 59; admission CUC$1; 9am-5pm Tue-Sat, 9am-1pm Sun) Housed in the former San Francisco de Asís convent, this photogenic museum is distinguished by its yellow campanile, the only part of the original building remaining. The collection relates to the struggle against counterrevolutionary bands in the Sierra del Escambray (1906–65). Climb the tower for good views.

Playa Ancón   BEACH
Playa Ancón, a precious ribbon of white beach on Sancti Spíritus' iridescent Caribbean shoreline, is usually touted – with good merit – to be the finest arc of sand on Cuba's south coast.

There are three all-inclusive hotels here and excellent snorkeling and diving just offshore or at the small reef islet of **Cayo Blanco**, 25km to the southeast. Diving with the **Cayo Blanco International Dive**

Center, located at Marina Trinidad, costs CUC$35 a dive and CUC$320 for an open-water course. The Marina also runs a seven-hour snorkeling-and-beach tour to Cayo Blanco for CUC$45 per person with lunch. Romantic types might want to check out the **Sunset Catamaran Cruise** (cruise with/without dinner CUC$35/20) enthusiastically recommended by readers.

Valle de los Ingenios
HERITAGE SITE

Dozens of crumbling 19th-century *ingenios* (sugar mills) dot this Unesco-listed valley. The royal palms, waving cane and rolling hills are timelessly beautiful, especially seen from the saddle (see Tours). The valley's main sight is the 1750 **Manaca Iznaga** (admission CUC$1), 16km east of Trinidad, a 44m-high tower with exquisite 360-degree views. The tourist train stops here; it's an hour's walk from the local train station at Meyer.

Topes de Collantes
PARK

The rugged 90km-long Sierra del Escambray mountain range, some 20km northwest of Trinidad, has some of Cuba's best unguided hiking. The **Carpeta Central information office** (⏰8am-5pm) sells a topographical map of the area (CUC$2.50), and offers campsites (CUC$10) and guides. The most popular hike is the 2.5km, 2½-hour round-trip trek to the **Salto del Caburní** (per person CUC$6.50), a 62m waterfall cascading into cool swimming holes. It's difficult to get here without a car.

Parque El Cubano
NATURE RESERVE

(admission CUC$6.50) This pleasant spot within a protected park consists of a *ranchón*-style restaurant that specializes in *pez gato* (catfish), a fish farm, and a 2km trail, known as **Huellas de la História**, to the refreshing **Javira waterfall**. There are also stables here and opportunities to partake in horseback riding. It's an 8km hike from Trinidad or you can organize a day tour (CUC$15) through Cubatur (p327).

☞ Tours

Cubatur (p327) and Paradiso (p327) sell similar excursions, including the popular Valle de los Ingenios **sugar train tour** (adult/child CUC$10/5), which starts at 9:30am, **horseback-riding** tours to the Cascada El Cubano (CUC$18 including transportation, park entrance fee, lunch and guide) and

day hikes (adult/child CUC$29/20) to Topes de Collantes.

Freelance guides lead **horseback-riding** (per person 3/6hr CUC$7/15) trips to the Valle de los Ingenios or Cascada El Cubano (add a CUC$6.50 park entry fee for the latter). A tour to the Guanajara National Park and its waterfall is also on offer (CUC$55 per person).

🛏 Sleeping

TOP CHOICE Casa Muñoz – Julio & Rosa
CASA PARTICULAR $

(☎99-36-73; www.trinidadphoto.com; José Martí No 401; r CUC$35; P ❋) Julio is an accomplished published photographer who runs workshops and courses out of his stunning colonial home (which has been featured in *National Geographic*). He also runs a local equestrian center. His house has three huge rooms, delicious food and highly professional service; book early – it's insanely popular.

Iberostar Grand Hotel
BOUTIQUE HOTEL $$

(☎99-60-70; cnr José Martí & General Lino Pérez; s/d CUC$118/148; ❋ @) One in a trio of Spanish-run Iberostar's Cuban hotels, the five-star Grand oozes luxury the moment you arrive in its fern-filled, tile-embellished lobby. Maintaining 36 classy rooms in a remodeled 19th-century building, the hotel shies away from the standard all-inclusive tourist tattle, preferring to press privacy, refinement and an appreciation of history.

'Hospedaje Yolanda' – Yolanda María Alvarez
CASA PARTICULAR $

(☎99-30-51; yolimar56@yahoo.com; Piro Guinart No 227; r CUC$25-30) This isn't a casa, it's a palace! Dating from the 1700s, its dazzling interior makes the Museo Romántico look like a jumble sale. Take the Italian tiles, the French frescoes, the rare Mexican spiral staircase, the fabulous terrace views; the list goes on...

Casa de Victor
CASA PARTICULAR $

(☎99-64-44; Maceo btwn Piro Guinart & P Pichs Girón; r CUC$20-25; ❋) If Casa Muñoz is full you can stay with other members of the family down at Victor's place, where two self-contained upstairs rooms share a couple of spacious *salas*, a balcony overlooking the street, and a fine *terraza* decorated with recycled ceramic pots.

Casa Gil Lemes
CASA PARTICULAR $

(☎99-31-42; José Martí No 263 btwn Colón & Zerquera; r CUC$25) More museum-standard digs on Calle Martí. Cast an eye over the noble arches in the front room, the religious statues, and save some breath (yes, you'll gasp) for the patio and fountain; a unique array of pots and sea serpents.

Casa de la Amistad HOTEL $
(Zerquera btwn José Martí & Francisco Pettersen; r CUC$25) This hostel, run by the Instituto Cubano de la Amistad, is popular among visitors politically sympathetic to Cuba. It has six clean and well-equipped rooms with brand-new showers and TVs, plus a small eating area and patio out the back.

Hostal Colina CASA PARTICULAR $
(✆99-23-19; Antonio Maceo No 374 btwn General Lino Pérez & Colón; r CUC$25-35; ✱) Two pastel-yellow rooms give out onto a patio where you can sit at the plush wooden bar and catch mangoes and avocados as they fall from the trees.

Mireya Medina Rodríguez CASA PARTICULAR $
(✆99-39-94; miretrini@yahoo.es; Antonio Maceo No 472 btwn Simón Bolívar & Zerquera; r CUC$20-25; ✱) Right in the center of things, Mireya is a popular dance teacher who rents out one room with private bathroom in her well-kept colonial house.

✗ Eating

Paladar Sol y Son PALADAR $$
(✆99-29-26; Simón Bolívar No 283 btwn Francisco Pettersen & José Martí; mains CUC$8-10; ⊘noon-2pm & 7:30-11pm) All the ingredients of a fine Trinidad evening – think antiques, an elegant patio and the dulcet strains of an eloquent *trovador* – plus good food thrown in. The house special is roast chicken and it's worth the wait.

Paladar Estela PALADAR $$
(✆99-43-29; Simón Bolívar No 557; ⊘2-11:30pm) You can choose the dining room or pretty rear garden in which to take your meals at this popular place located above the Plaza Mayor (the owner also rents rooms). *Cordero* (lamb) served shredded is the house specialty, and the portions are large.

Restaurante Plaza Mayor CARIBBEAN $$
(cnr Rubén Martínez Villena & Zerquera; dishes from CUC$4; ⊘11am-10pm) The best government-run bet, courtesy of its on-off lunchtime buffet, which, for around CUC$10, ought to fill you up until dinnertime. Nighttime offerings aren't bad either if you stick to the chicken and beef, though the atmosphere can be a little flat.

Mesón del Regidor CAFE $
(Simón Bolívar No 424; ⊘10am-10pm) A cafe-cum-restaurant with a friendly ambience and a revolving lineup of local musicians who'll drop by during the day to serenade you with a song over grilled cheese sandwiches and *café con leche*. Savor the surprise.

Cafetería Las Begonias CAFE $
(cnr Antonio Maceo & Simón Bolívar; ⊘9am-10pm; @) The daytime nexus for Trinidad's transient backpacker crowd, meaning it's a good font of local information and the best place in town to meet other travelers over sandwiches, espresso and ice cream.

☆ Entertainment

Get ready for the best nightlife outside of Havana.

TOP CHOICE ⟩**Palenque de los Congos Reales** RUMBA
(cnr Echerri & Av Jesús Menéndez; admission free) A must for rumba fans, this open patio on Trinidad's music alley has an eclectic menu. The highlight is the 10pm rumba drums with soulful African rhythms and energetic fire-eating dancers.

Casa de la Música NIGHTCLUB
(admission free) One of Trinidad's and Cuba's classic venues, this casa is an alfresco affair that congregates on the sweeping staircase beside the Iglesia Parroquial off Plaza Mayor. A good mix of tourists and locals take in the 10pm salsa/dance show here. Alternatively, full-on salsa concerts are held in the casa's rear courtyard

Casa Fischer CULTURAL CENTER
(General Lino Pérez No 312 btwn José Martí & Francisco Codania; admission CUC$1) This is the local ARTex patio, which cranks up at 10pm with a salsa orchestra (on Tuesday, Wednesday, Thursday, Saturday and Sunday) or a folklore show (Friday). If you're early, kill time at its art gallery (free) and chat to the staff at the on-site Paradiso office about salsa lessons and other courses.

Casa de la Trova TRADITIONAL MUSIC
(Echerri No 29; admission CUC$1; ⊘9pm-2am) Trinidad's spirited casa retains its earthy essence despite the high package-tourist-to-Cuban ratio. Local musicians to look out for here are Semillas del Son, Santa Palabra and the town's best *trovador,* Israel Moreno.

🛍 Shopping

Arts & Crafts Market   CRAFTS, SOUVENIRS
(Av Jesús Menéndez) This excellent open-air
market situated in front of the Casa de la
Trova is the place to buy souvenirs, especially textiles and crochet work.

**Fondo Cubano de Bienes
Culturales**   CRAFTS, SOUVENIRS
(Simón Bolívar No 418; ⊙9am-5pm Mon-Fri,
9am-3pm Sat & Sun) Just down from Plaza
Mayor, this store has a good selection of
Cuban handicrafts.

Casa del Habano   CIGARS
(Maceo cnr Zerquera; ⊙9am-7pm) Dodge the
street hustlers and satisfy your alcoholic
(rum) and tobacco vices here.

❶ Information

**INTERNET ACCESS Cafe Internet Las
Begonias** (Antonio Maceo No 473; per hr
CUC$6; ⊙7:30am-1am) Good place to meet
other travelers.

Etecsa (General Lino Pérez No 274; per hr
CUC$6; ⊙8:30am-7:30pm) On Parque
Céspedes.

**MEDICAL SERVICES Servimed Clínica In-
ternacional Cubanacán** (☑99-62-40; General
Lino Pérez No 103; ⊙24hr) Consultations
before/after 4pm CUC$25/30. Has an on-site
pharmacy.

MONEY Banco de Crédito y Comercio (José
Martí No 264)

Banco Financiero Internacional (cnr Camilo
Cienfuegos & José Martí; ⊙8am-3pm Mon-Fri)
Cash advances; ridiculously long lines.

Cadeca (Martí No 164 btwn Lino Pérez &
Camilo Cienfuegos)

POST Post office (Antonio Maceo No 420
btwn Colón & Zerquera)

TRAVEL AGENCIES Cubatur (Antonio Maceo
No 447; ⊙9am-8pm) Good for organizing
tours to Topes de Collantes and the Valle de los
Ingenios.

Infotur (Plaza Santa Ana, Camilo Cienfuegos)

Paradiso (General Lino Pérez No 306) Cultural
and general tours in English, Spanish and
French.

❶ Getting There & Away

BUS From the **bus station** (Piro Guinart No
224), regular **Viazul** (www.viazul.cu) buses
go to Havana (CUC$25, four daily), Varadero
(CUC$20, one daily), Santiago de Cuba
(CUC$33, one daily), Santa Clara (CUC$8, one
daily) and Cienfuegos (CUC$6, three daily).

CAR You can organize car hire at the offices of
Cubatur (Antonio Maceo No 447).

TRAIN Train transport out of Trinidad is awful even by Cuban standards. The town hasn't
been connected to the main rail network since a
hurricane in the early 1990s, meaning the only
functioning line runs up the Valle de Ingenios,
stopping in Iznaga (35 minutes) and terminating at Meyer (one hour 10 minutes). There are
supposedly four trains a day, the most reliable
leaving Trinidad at 9am and 1pm, but they often
don't run; always check ahead at the **terminal**
(Lino Pérez final) in a pink house across the train
tracks on the western side of the station.

❶ Getting Around

BICYCLE You can hire gear-less bikes at **Las
Ruinas del Teatro Brunet** (Antonio Maceo No
461 btwn Simón Bolívar & Zerquera; per day
CUC$3) or you can ask at your casa particular.
These are fine for getting to Playa Ancón, but
nowhere near adequate for the steep climbs up
to Topes de Collantes.

TRINIDAD TOUR BUS Trinidad now has a
handy hop-on/hop-off **minibus** (all-day ticket
CUC$5). It plies a route from outside the Cuba-
tur office in Calle Maceo to Playa Ancón via the
village of La Boca. It runs approximately five
times a day in either direction starting at 9am
and terminating at 6pm.

Camagüey

☑32 / POP 324,921

Welcome to the maze. Caught inadver-
tently in the tide of history, Camagüey is a
Latin American city without precedent. The
oddities lie in its unique urban layout. Two
centuries spent fighting off musket-toting
pirates such as Henry Morgan led the fledg-
ling settlement to develop a peculiar labyrinthine street pattern designed to confuse
pillaging invaders and provide cover for its
long-suffering residents (or so legend has it).
As a result, Camagüey's sinuous streets and
narrow winding alleys are more reminiscent
of a Moroccan medina than the geometric
grids of Lima or Mexico City.

In 2008, the well-preserved historical center of Cuba's third-largest city became the
nation's ninth Unesco World Heritage site.

◉ Sights

**TOP
CHOICE** **Plaza San Juan de Dios**   SQUARE
(cnr Hurtado & Paco Recio) Wide-open Plaza San
Juan de Dios is Camagüey's most picturesque
corner and the only town plaza to retain its
original layout and buildings. Its eastern
aspect is dominated by the **Museo de San
Juan de Dios** (admission CUC$1; ⊙9am-5pm

Tue-Sat, to 1pm Sun), housed in what was once a hospital. The hospital has a front cloister dating from 1728 and a unique triangular rear patio with Moorish touches, built in 1840. The museum inside chronicles Camagüey's history and exhibits some local paintings.

Museo Casa Natal de Ignacio Agramonte
MUSEUM

(Av Agramonte No 459; admission CUC$2; ⏰10am-5:45pm Tue-Thu, 8am-noon Sun) Opposite Iglesia de Nuestra Señora de la Merced, on the corner of Independencia, is the birthplace of the independence hero Ignacio Agramonte (1841–73), the cattle rancher who led the revolt against Spain in this area in 1868. In July 1869 rebel forces under Agramonte bombarded Camagüey, and four years later he was killed in action fighting bravely against the Spanish. This house – an elegant colonial building in its own right – tells the oft-overlooked role of Camagüey and Agramonte in the First War of Independence.

Churches
CHURCHES

If Cuba has a Catholic soul, it undoubtedly resides in Camagüey, a city of baroque churches and gilded altars, where haunting ecclesial spires rise like minarets above the narrow, labyrinthine streets.

Of the six notable churches within the colonial core, the most important is the **Catedral de Nuestra Señora de la Candelaria** (Cisneros No 168). This cathedral dating from the 1840s was fully restored with funds raised from the 1998 visit of Pope John Paul II and, while not Camagüey's most eye-catching church, it is noted for its noble Christ statue that sits atop a craning bell tower.

The **Iglesia de Nuestra Señora de la Merced** (Plaza de los Trabajadores), dating from 1748, is arguably Camagüey's most impressive colonial church, with a history imbued with local legend.

Another must-see is the **Iglesia de Nuestra Señora de la Soledad** (cnr República & Av Agramonte), a massive brick structure dating from 1779 whose picturesque cream-and-terracotta tower is a head-turning landmark on the city skyline.

🛏 Sleeping

TOP CHOICE **Gran Hotel**
HOTEL $

(☎29-20-93; Maceo No 67 btwn Av Agramonte & General Gómez; s/d incl breakfast CUC$44/70; P✴@✵) You'll swear you've been reincarnated as your father (or grandfather) in this time-warped city-center hotel dating from 1939. A potent prerevolutionary atmosphere stalks the 72 clean rooms reached by an ancient lift, replete with cap-doffing attendants and antique gate.

'Los Vitrales' – Emma Barreto & Rafael Requejo
CASA PARTICULAR $

(☎29-58-66; requejobarreto@gmail.com; Avellaneda No 3 btwn General Gómez & Martí; r CUC$20-25; P✴) This painstakingly restored colonial house was once a convent and sports broad arches, high ceilings and dozens of antiques. Three rooms are arranged around a shady patio embellished with 50 different types of plants and a fantastic tile mural.

Hotel Colón
HOTEL $

(☎28-11-85; República No 472 btwn J Ramón Silva & San Martín; s/d incl breakfast CUC$30/44; ✴) A classic long mahogany bar, colorful tile-flanked walls, and a stained-glass portrait of Christopher Columbus over the lobby door give this place a mixed colonial/fin-de-siècle feel. Located on busy Calle República, it's both a good base for exploring and a good place to relax.

🍴 Eating

TOP CHOICE **Café Ciudad**
CAFE $

(Martí cnr Cisneros; snacks CUC$2-5; ⏰10am-10pm) This lovely 'new' colonial cafe on Plaza Agramonte melds grandiosity with great service and comes out emulating anything in Habana Vieja. Try the Jamón Serrano or the ice cream and enjoy a *café con leche* under the louvers.

Restaurante La Isabella
ITALIAN $$

(cnr Av Agramonte & Independencia; pizzas CUC$5-8; ⏰11am-4pm & 6:30-10pm) Cool, cinematic and perennially crowded, Camagüey's funkiest restaurant blends Italian food with a maverick movie-themed decor; the 32 director-style seats are emblazoned with the names of Cuban 'film stars.'

Paladar La Terraza
PALADAR $$

(Santa Rosa No 8 btwn San Martín & El Soltario; dishes CUC$7-10; ⏰11am-11pm) This old Camagüey standby is popular for a reason: seriously good *comida criolla* and lots of it. Try the pull-off-the-bone lamb served in an upstairs terrace by polite waitstaff.

ℹ Getting There & Away

The comfortable Tren Francés heads east to Santiago de Cuba and west to Havana (stopping

CAYO GUILLERMO

Ah, Cayo Guillermo – haunt of pink flamingos, platinum-blond beaches and Cuba's second most famous Ernesto after Mr Guevara – Señor Hemingway. Long a prized deep-sea fishing spot, 13-sq-km Guillermo retains a more exotic feel than Cayo Coco, to which it is connected by a causeway. There are four all-inclusive hotels here, including the reasonably priced **Iberostar Daiquirí** (☑033-30-16-50; s/d CUC$105/150; P❄@▣).

Fishing trips (CUC$290 per half day for four people) can be organized at the **Marina Marlin Cayo Guillermo** on the right of the causeway as you arrive from Cayo Coco. Guillermo's highlight, however, is **Playa Pilar**, a sublime strip of sand regularly touted as being Cuba's – and the Caribbean's – greatest beach. Pilar's claim rests on two lofty pillars: its diamond-dust white powder, and its rugged 15m-high sand dunes crossed by rough trails that incite piratical exploration. There's an excellent bar-restaurant nestled in the dunes and a small islet, **Cayo Media Luna**, 1km offshore that's reachable by catamaran (CUC$11) and is great for snorkeling.

in Santa Clara) every third day from the **train station** (cnr Avellaneda & Finlay).

Long-distance **Víazul** (www.viazul.com) buses depart **Álvaro Barba Bus Station** (Carretera Central), 3km southeast of the center. Destinations include Havana (CUC$33, six daily), Holguín (CUC$11, five daily), Santiago de Cuba (CUC$18, six daily), Trinidad (CUC$15, one daily) and Varadero (CUC$24, one daily).

EASTERN CUBA

You can't claim to have really seen Cuba without a visit to 'El Oriente,' as the eastern half of the island is known. Here, things move slowly and a more simple yet exotic way of life prevails. This is Cuba's Caribbean heart – dramatic, steamy and moving to its very own unpredictable rhythm.

At the end of the island, of course, cultural heavyweight and second city Santiago de Cuba is the center of its own world, providing relief from Havana's domination of everything else in the country. The region also includes the infamous Guantánamo US Naval Base, as well as one of the country's most stunning roads – between Guantánamo and Baracoa, the charming town right on the eastern tip of the island, which is a great place to chill out off the beaten track.

❶ Getting There & Away

Santiago de Cuba's **Aeropuerto Antonio Maceo** receives a smattering of international flights, mainly from elsewhere in the Caribbean. Domestic flights connect Santiago to Havana. Baracoa also has an airport that connects it to Havana.

Train travel, though slow, is a possibility between Havana and Santiago de Cuba. However, most people either take the bus (12 hours) or drive the distance themselves, often stopping over in friendly Camagüey to break up the journey.

❶ Getting Around

Bus connections center on Santiago, and are limited, especially from Baracoa. The road network is fine, and it is possible to drive a loop from Santiago to Holguín via Baracoa, although the road is in bad repair for much of the journey beyond Baracoa. Despite that, it's easily doable in a normal car. The only local transportation up this way is by truck.

Santiago de Cuba

☑22 / POP 495,000

You can take Santiago de Cuba in one of two ways: a hot, aggravating city full of hustlers and hassle that'll have you gagging to get on the first bus back to Havana; or a glittering cultural capital that has played an instrumental part in the evolution of Cuban literature, music, architecture, politics and ethnology. Yes, Santiago divides opinion among Cubans and foreigners almost as much as one of its most famous former scholars, Fidel Castro. Some love it, others hate it; few are indifferent.

Caught dramatically between the indomitable Sierra Maestra and the azure Caribbean, Santiago's setting could rival any of the world's great cities and its timeworn, slightly neglected air is vaguely reminiscent of Salvador in Brazil, or New Orleans.

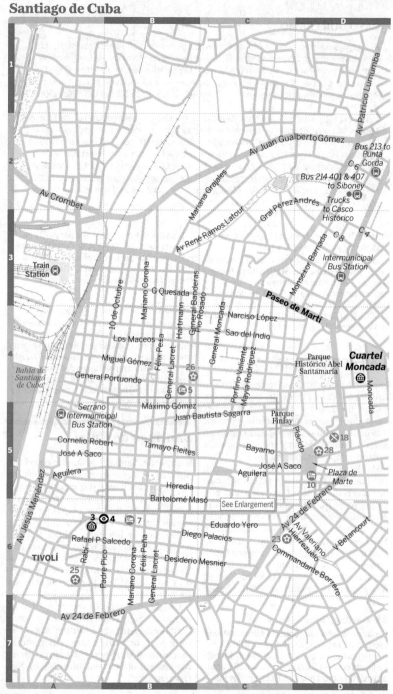

CUBA EASTERN CUBA

Av Patricio Lumumba

Av Juan Gualberto Gómez

Bus 213 to Punta Gorda
C 6

Bus 214 401 & 407 to Siboney

Gral Pérez Andrés

Trucks to Casco Histórico

C 8
C 4

Monseñor Barnada

Mariana Grajales

Av Crombet

Av René Ramos Latour

Train Station

Intermunicipal Bus Station

Paseo de Martí

10 de Octubre
Mariano Corona
G Quesada
Hartmann
General Banderas
Pío Rosado
General Moncada
Narciso López
Sao del Indio

Los Maceos
Félix Peña
General Lacret

Miguel Gómez

General Portuondo

Porfirio Valiente
Mayía Rodríguez

Parque Histórico Abel Santamaría

Cuartel Moncada

Moncada

26
5

Bahía de Santiago de Cuba

Serrano Intermunicipal Bus Station

Máximo Gómez

Juan Bautista Sagarra

Parque Finlay

Cornelio Robert
José A Saco

Tamayo Fleites

Bayamo

Plácido

18
28

Aguilera

José A Saco
Aguilera

10

Plaza de Marte

Av Jesús Menéndez

Heredia

Bartolomé Masó

See Enlargement

3
4
7

Eduardo Yero

Av 24 de Febrero

Rafael P Salcedo

Diego Palacios

23

Av Valeriano Hierrezuelo

V Betancourt

TIVOLÍ

Rabí
Padre Pico
Mariano Corona
Félix Peña
General Lacret

Desiderio Mesnier

Commandante Borrero

25

Av 24 de Febrero

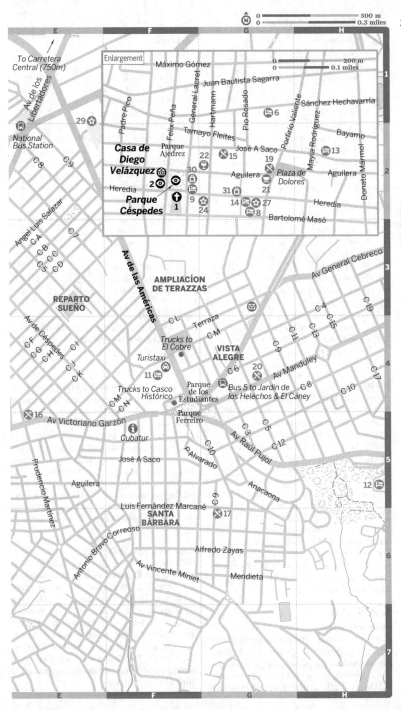

History

Founded in 1514, Santiago de Cuba was the first Cuban capital (1515–1607). After the capital shifted to Havana and Santiago's gold reserves and indigenous labor started giving out, the city lost prominence; despite being the 'cradle of the revolution,' it still nurses an inferiority complex.

On July 26, 1953, Fidel Castro and his companions stole away from the Granjita Siboney farm 20km southeast of Santiago and unsuccessfully attacked the Moncada Barracks, an embarrassingly badly planned attack now talked up as a key part of Castro's revolutionary myth. At his trial here Castro made his famous 'History Will Absolve Me' speech, which became the basic platform of the Cuban Revolution.

◎ Sights

Parque Céspedes SQUARE
If there's an archetype for romantic Cuban street life, Parque Céspedes is it. A throbbing kaleidoscope of walking, talking, hustling, flirting, guitar-strumming humanity, this most ebullient of city squares is a sight

to behold any time of day or night. Old ladies gossip on shady park benches, a guy in a panama hat drags his dilapidated double bass over toward the Casa de la Trova, while sultry senoritas in skin-tight lycra flutter their eyelashes at the male tourists on the terrace of the Hotel Casa Granda. Meanwhile, standing statuesque in the middle of all this activity, is a bronze **bust of Carlos Manuel de Céspedes**, the man who started it all when he issued the Grito de Yara declaring Cuban independence in 1868.

Casa de Diego Velázquez MUSEUM
(Felix Peña No 602) The oldest house still standing in Cuba dates fom 1522 and was the official residence of the island's first governor. Restored in the late 1960s, the Andalusian-style facade with fine, wooden lattice windows now houses the **Museo de Ambiente Histórico Cubano** (admission CUC$2; ◎9am-1pm & 2-4:45pm Mon-Thu, 2-4:45pm Fri, 9am-9pm Sat & Sun) displaying period furnishings and decoration from the 16th to 19th centuries.

Catedral de Nuestra Señora de la Asunción
CHURCH

(☉mass 6:30pm Mon & Wed-Fri, 5pm Sat, 9am & 6:30pm Sun) It might not be particularly old, but Santiago's most important church is stunning both inside and out. Meticulously restored, its interior is a magnificent mélange of intricate ceiling frescoes, hand-carved choir stalls and an altar honoring the venerated Virgen de la Caridad. The adjacent **Museo Arquidiocesano** (☉9am-5pm Mon-Fri, 9am-2pm Sat, 9am-noon Sun) houses a collection of furniture, liturgical objects and paintings including the *Ecce Homo,* believed to be Cuba's oldest painting.

Calle Heredia
STREET

The music never stops on Calle Heredia, Santiago's most sensuous street, and home to Cuba's original **Casa de la Trova** (Heredia No 208), a beautiful balconied town house redolent of New Orleans' French quarter that is dedicated to pioneering Cuban *trovador* José 'Pepe' Sánchez (1856–1928). It first opened in March 1968.

Tivolí
NEIGHBORHOOD

Santiago's old French quarter was first settled by colonists from Haiti in the late 18th and early 19th centuries. Set on a south-facing hillside overlooking the harbor, its red-tiled roofs and hidden patios are a tranquil haven these days, with old men pushing around dominoes and ebullient kids playing stickball amid pink splashes of bougainvillea. The century-old **Padre Pico steps**, cut into the steepest part of Calle Padre Pico, stand at the neighborhood's gateway. Prime sight here is the **Museo de la Lucha Clandestina** (admission CUC$1; General Jesús Rabí No 1; ☉9am-5pm Tue-Sun) a former police station attacked by M-26-7 (26th of July Movement) activists on November 30, 1956 that is now a museum detailing the underground struggle against Batista in the 1950s.

Cuartel Moncada
MUSEUM

(Moncada Barracks; admission CUC$2; ☉9am-5pm Mon-Sat, 9am-1pm Sun) Santiago's famous Cuartel Moncada is named after Guillermón Moncada, a War of Independence fighter who was held prisoner here in 1874, though these days the name is more synonymous with one of history's greatest failed putsches.

Moncada earned immortality on the morning of July 26, 1953, when more than 100 revolutionaries led by then little-known Fidel Castro stormed Batista's troops at what was then Cuba's second-most important military garrison.

After the revolution, the barracks was converted into a school, and in 1967 a museum was installed where the main attack took place. It contains a scale model of the barracks plus interesting and sometimes grisly artifacts of the attack, its planning and its aftermath.

Cementerio Santa Ifigenia
CEMETERY

(Av Crombet; admission CUC$1; ☉8am-6pm) Nestled peacefully on the western edge of the city, the Cementerio Santa Ifigenia is second only to Havana's Necrópolis Cristóbal Colón in its importance and grandiosity. Created in 1868 to accommodate the victims of the War of Independence and a simultaneous yellow-fever outbreak, the Santa Ifigenia includes many great historical figures among its 8000-plus tombs.

The highlight of the cemetery, for most, is the quasi-religious mausoleum to national hero, José Martí (1853–95). Erected in 1951 during the Batista era, the imposing hexagonal structure is positioned so that Martí's wooden casket (draped solemnly in a Cuban flag) receives daily shafts of sunlight. A round-the-clock guard of the mausoleum is changed, amid much pomp and ceremony, every 30 minutes.

TOP CHOICE **Castillo de San Pedro de la Roca del Morro**
FORT, MUSEUM

(admission CUC$4; ☉9am-5pm Mon-Fri, 8am-4pm Sat & Sun) A Unesco World Heritage site since 1997, the San Pedro fort sits like an impregnable citadel atop a 60m-high promontory at the entrance to Santiago harbor, 10km southwest of the city. The fort was designed in 1587 by famous Italian military engineer Giovanni Battista Antonelli to protect Santiago from pillaging pirates who had successfully sacked the city in 1554.

Today, the fort hosts the swashbuckling **Museo de Piratería**, with another room given over to the US–Spain naval battle that took place in the bay in 1898. The stupendous views from the upper terrace take in the wild western ribbon of Santiago's coastline backed by the velvety Sierra Maestra.

🛏 Sleeping

TOP CHOICE **Hostal San Basilio**
BOUTIQUE HOTEL $

(✆65-17-02; Bartolomé Masó No 403 btwn Pío Rosado & Porfirio Valiente; r CUC$60; ❈) The lovely eight-room San Basilio is another of Cubanacán's Encanto brand: think intimate, comfortable and refreshingly contemporary within a romantic colonial setting. Rooms come with clever little frills such as DVD players, umbrellas, bathroom scales and mini bottles of rum, and the communal patio is a riot of dripping ferns. There's a small restaurant serving breakfast and lunch.

Meliá Santiago de Cuba
HOTEL **$$**
(☑68-70-70; cnr Av de las Américas & Calle M; s/d CUC$110/140; P✶@🛜✱) A blue-mirrored monster (or marvel, depending on your taste) dreamt up by respected Cuban architect José A Choy in the early '90s, the Meliá is Santiago's only 'international' hotel. Raising its game for the business crowd, there are real bathtubs, three pools, four restaurants, various shopping facilities, a fancy bar on the 15th floor, and rooms for nonsmokers.

Hotel Casa Granda
HOTEL **$$**
(☑65-30-24; Heredia No 201; s/d CUC$78/112; ✶) This elegant hotel built in 1914, artfully described by Graham Greene in his book *Our Man in Havana,* has 58 rooms and a classic red-and-white-striped front awning. The hotel's 5th-floor **Roof Garden Bar** and the upstairs terrace is an obligatory photo stop for foreign tourists on the lookout for bird's-eye city views. There's music on the terrace most nights and an occasional buffet on the roof, where the views are spectacular. The downside is the service, which is like *Fawlty Towers* without the laughs.

Casa Colonial 'Maruchi'
CASA PARTICULAR **$**
(☑62-07-67; maruchib@yahoo.es; Hartmann No 357 btwn General Portuondo & Máximo Gómez; r CUC$25; ✶) Maruchi is quintessential Santiago and is the best advert the city could give. You'll meet all types here: *santeros* (priests of Santería), backpackers, foreign students studying for PhDs on the Regla de Ocha. The food's legendary and the fecund courtyard equally sublime. Book early, as it's no secret.

Hotel Libertad
HOTEL **$**
(☑62-77-10; Aguilera No 658; s/d CUC$24/36; ✶@) Cheap Cuban hotel chain Islazul breaks out of its ugly Soviet-themed concrete-block obsession and goes colonial in this venerable sky-blue beauty on Plaza de Marte. Eighteen clean high-ceilinged rooms

and a pleasant streetside restaurant are a bonus. The belting rooftop disco isn't.

Motel San Juan
HOTEL **$**
(☑68-72-00; San Juan Hill; s/d CUC$32/50; P✶✱🛜) Surrounded by beautiful grounds on historic Loma de San Juan, with lots of lawn and a children's pool, this place is great if you don't mind long walks (or taxi rides) into the city center. The rooms are laid out in small blocks and have good amenities with welcome little extras such as radios.

Casa Yisel
CASA PARTICULAR **$**
(☑62-05-22; martingisel78@yahoo.es; Diego Palacios No 177 btwn Padre Pico & Mariano Corona; r CUC$20-25; P✶) The young hosts run a surgically clean house three blocks from Céspedes and one from the Padre Pico steps. It's an apartment of sorts, with a living room, bedroom and superbig bath. There's a little patio and great coffee.

Nelson Aguilar Ferreiro & Deysi Ruíz Chaveco
CASA PARTICULAR **$**
(☑65-63-72; José A Saco No 513; r CUC$20-25) Slap-bang in the center but with a quieter more suburban feel, this is one of Santiago's best casas, with a secluded plant-filled patio off which lead two spick-and-span double rooms. The dinner menu is huge, with nearly 100 items.

Hotel Versalles
HOTEL **$**
(☑68-70-70; Alturas de Versalles; s/d incl breakfast CUC$43/62; P✶✱) Not to be confused with the resplendent home of Louis XIV of similar name, this modest hotel was once one of Cubanacán's tattier hotel choices, but a recent upgrade has injected some style into its inviting pool and comfortable rooms with small terraces.

Caridad Leyna Martínez
CASA PARTICULAR **$**
(☑64-29-55; Calle 14 No 352, Reparto Vista Alegre; r CUC$20-25) For a break from the motorbike noise you may want to consider this tranquil place out in once-posh Vista Alegre, where Caridad's pleasant house has one room with an en-suite bathroom up for grabs. It's located not far from Loma de San Juan.

Raimundo Ocana & Bertha Pena
CASA PARTICULAR **$**
(☑62-40-97; Heredia No 308 btwn Pío Rosado & Porfirio Valiente; r CUC$20-25; ✶) A classic 200-year-old house on Calle Heredia, meaning you can shimmy out of your

front door and be in the thick of the action within seconds.

Casa Nenita CASA PARTICULAR **$**
(☎65-41-10; Sánchez Hechavarría No 472 btwn Pío Rosado & Porfirio Valiente; r CUC$20-25) Dating from 1850, Nenita's house has soaring ceilings, original floor tiles and a truly amazing back patio. Sit back beneath the louvers and soak up the history.

✗ Eating

For a city of such fine cultural traditions, Santiago's restaurant scene is surprisingly lean. You'll find no hidden Havana-style experimentation here. Instead, the outlook is generally mediocre, with the odd get-out-of-jail card.

TOP CHOICE **El Barracón** CARIBBEAN **$**
(Av Victoriano Garzón; ☺noon-midnight) Santiago's finest food house – no contest! El Barracón aims to reignite the roots of Afro-Cuban culture with an interior that is a cross between an atmospheric *santería* shrine and a *cimarrón* (runaway slave village). Try the delicious *tostones* (fried plantain patties) filled with chorizo and cheese, or opt for the lamb special.

Paladar Salón Tropical PALADAR **$$$**
(☎64-11-61; Fernández Marcané No 310, Reparto Santa Barbara; ☺5pm-midnight Mon-Sat, noon-midnight Sun) The city's best paladar is on a pleasant rooftop terrace with fairy lights and city views. The food is plentiful and tasty, with a varying menu of succulent smoked pork, chicken and sometimes lamb, served with *congrí* (rice flecked with black beans), salad and plantains (green bananas) and delicious *yuca con mojo* (starchy root vegetable with garlic-lime sauce). Reservations are a good idea.

Ristorante Italiano La Fontana ITALIAN **$$**
(Meliá Santiago de Cuba, cnr Av de las Américas & Calle M; meals CUC$5-8; ☺11am-11pm) Pizza *deliciosa* and lasagna *formidable*, ravioli and garlic bread; *mamma mía,* this has to be the number-one option for breaking away from all that chicken and pork!

Hotel Casa Granda CAFE **$$**
(Heredia No 201; ☺9am-midnight) Positioned like a whitewashed theater box overlooking the colorful cabaret of Parque Céspedes, the Casa Granda's Parisian-style terrace cafe has to be one of the best people-watching locations in Cuba. Food-wise, you're talking snacks (burgers, hot dogs, sandwiches etc) and service-wise you're talking impassive, verging on the grumpy.

Restaurante Zunzún CARIBBEAN **$$$**
(Av Manduley No 159; ☺noon-10pm Mon-Sat, noon-3pm Sun) Dine in bygone bourgeois style in this urban mansion turned restaurant in the Vista Alegre neighborhood. Dishes include chicken curry, paella or a formidable cheese plate and cognac. Expect professional, attentive service and entertaining troubadours.

Restaurante España SEAFOOD **$**
(Victoriano Garzón) Santiago peso restaurant in decent-food shock! Readjust your Cuban food preconceptions before digging into seafood cooked with panache and – on occasion – fresh herbs. Try the lobster or tangy prawns, but bypass the Cuban wine, which is almost undrinkable.

Restaurante Matamoros CARIBBEAN **$$**
(cnr Aguilera & Porfirio Valiente) Some interesting wall art, a couple of bolero-singing muchachas, and a chicken- and pork-heavy menu have breathed new life into this once dingy joint on Plaza de Dolores.

Café Ven CAFE **$**
(José A Saco btwn Hartmann & Pío Rosado; ☺9am-9pm) Rare new cafe tucked into busy Enramadas (Saco) with lung-enriching air-con, interesting cafetal (coffee plantation) paraphernalia and lifesaving sandwiches and cakes.

♟ Drinking

El Baturro BAR
(Aguilera cnr Hartmann) A slavishly local downtown joint that looks like a leftover from the city's pirate days. Slightly seedy and very Santiago.

Café La Isabelica CAFE
(cnr Aguilera & Porfirio Valiente; ☺9am-9pm) Stronger, smokier, darker cantina-type equivalent of Café Ven, with the prices in pesos.

☆ Entertainment

'Spoilt for choice' would be an understatement in Santiago's entertainment scene. For what's happening, look for the bi-weekly *Cartelera Cultural.* Calle Heredia is Santiago's Bourbon Street, a musical cacophony of stabbing trumpets, multilayered bongos and lilting guitars.

TOP CHOICE Casa de las Tradiciones TRADITIONAL MUSIC
(Rabí No 154; admission CUC$1; ⊙from 8:30pm) The most discovered 'undiscovered' spot in Santiago still retains its smoke-filled, foot-stomping, front-room feel. Hidden in the genteel Tivolí district, some of Santiago de Cuba's most exciting ensembles, singers and soloists take turns improvising.

Casa de la Trova TRADITIONAL MUSIC
(Heredia No 208; admission from CUC$2; ⊙11am-3pm & 8:30-11pm Tue-Sun) Nearly 40 years after its initial incarnation, Santiago's shrine to the power of traditional music is still going strong and continuing to attract big names such as Buena Vista Social Club singer Eliades Ochoa. Warming up on the ground floor in the late afternoon, the action slowly gravitates upstairs where, come 10pm, everything starts to get a shade more *caliente*.

Patio ARTex TRADITIONAL MUSIC
(Heredia No 304 btwn Pío Rosado & Porfirio Valiente; admission free; ⊙11am-11pm) Art lines the walls of this shop-and-club combo that hosts live music both day and night in a quaint inner courtyard; a good bet if the Casa de la Trova is full, or too frenetic.

Ballet Folklórico Cutumba FOLKLÓRICO DANCE
(Teatro Galaxia, cnr Avs 24 de Febrero & Valeriano Hierrezuelo; admission CUC$2) This internationally known 56-strong Afro-Cuban-Franco-Haitian *folklórico* dance group was founded in 1960 and currently appears at Teatro Galaxia. You can pop in to see the group practice between 9am and 1pm Tuesday to Friday, or attend an electrifying *café teatro* at 10pm every Saturday.

Patio Los Dos Abuelos TRADITIONAL MUSIC
(Francisco Pérez Carbo No 5; admission CUC$2; ⊙10pm-1am Mon-Sat) The old-timers label carries a certain amount of truth. This relaxed live-music house is a bastion for traditional *son* sung the old-fashioned way. The musicians are seasoned pros and most of the patrons are perfect ladies and gentlemen.

Teatro José María Heredia THEATER
(☏64-31-90; cnr Avs de las Américas & de los Desfiles; ⊙box office 9am-noon & 1-4:30pm) Santiago's huge, modern theater and convention center was constructed during the city refurbishment in the early 1990s. Rock and folk concerts often take place in the 2459-seat Sala Principal, while the 120-seat

Café Cantante Niagara hosts more-esoteric events.

Foco Cultural Tumba Francesa FOLKLÓRICO DANCE
(Pío Rosado No 268) Another of Santiago's *folklórico* troupes, this colorful group of French-Haitian drumming masters can be seen in their rehearsal rooms on Tuesdays and Thursdays at 8pm.

🛍 Shopping

La Escalera BOOKSTORE
(Heredia No 265 btwn Pío Rosado & Hartmann; ⊙9am-9pm) Eddy Tamayo's wonderful antique bookshop shouldn't be missed. The fascinating collection includes some very rare gems, and Eddy is a mine of information on what he sells.

ARTex SOUVENIRS
(Heredia No 304 btwn Pío Rosado & Porfirio Valiente) The standard range of handicrafts, music, books, novelty gifts and a superior selection of postcards are available here. There's a small cafe out the back as well.

Galería de Arte de Oriente ART
(General Lacret No 656) This is probably the best gallery in Santiago de Cuba; the art here is consistently good.

ℹ Information

EMERGENCY Police (☏106; cnr Mariano Corona & Sánchez Hechevarría)

INTERNET ACCESS Etecsa (per hr CUC$6; ⊙8:30am-7:30pm) Heredia (cnr Heredia & Félix Peña); Tamayo Fleites (cnr Tamayo Fleites & Hartmann)

MEDICAL SERVICES Clínica Internacional Cubanacán Servimed (☏64-25-89; cnr Av Raúl Pujol & Calle 8, Vista Alegre; consultations CUC$30; ⊙24hr) Some English-speaking staff, plus a dentist.

Farmacia Cubanacán (cnr Av Raúl Pujol & Calle 8; ⊙24hr) Best pharmacy. Another is in the Meliá Santiago de Cuba, open from 8am to 6pm.

Farmacia Las Américas (Av Victoriano Garzón No 422; ⊙24hr)

Hospital Provincial Saturnino Lora (☏64-56-51; Av de los Libertadores; ⊙24hr)

MONEY Banco de Crédito y Comercio (Felix Peña No 614) ATM on Heredia.

Banco Financiero Internacional (Felix Peña No 565; ⊙8am-4pm Mon-Fri)

Cadeca (Aguilera No 508; ⊙8:30am-6pm Mon-Sat, 8:30am-noon Sun) Others are in the Meliá Santiago de Cuba and Hotel Las Américas.

POST **Post office** (Aguilera No 519)

TRAVEL AGENCIES **Cubatur** Heredia (Heredia No 701 cnr General Lacret); Garzón (Av Garzón No 364 btwn Calles 3 & 4) Also has desks in the main hotels.

Cubanacán (Heredia No 201) This very helpful desk is in the Hotel Casa Granda.

❶ Getting There & Away

AIR **Antonio Maceo International Airport** is 7km south of Santiago de Cuba, off the Carretera del Morro. It is served by flights from Havana, Holguín, Port-au-Prince (Haiti), Toronto (Canada) and Miami (US; charter only).

Cubana airlines (Saco & General Lacret; ⊗8:15am-4pm Mon, Wed & Fri, 8:15am-6:30pm Tue & Thu, 8:15am-11pm Sat)

BUS **Terminal Nacional** (National Bus Station; cnr Av de los Libertadores & Calle 9) is 3km northeast of Parque Céspedes. **Víazul** (www. viazul.com) buses serve Havana (CUC$51, four daily), Trinidad (CUC$34, one daily), Varadero (CUC$49, one daily) and Baracoa (CUC$15, one daily).

TRAIN The modern French-style **train station** (Av Jesús Menéndez cnr Martí) is situated near the rum factory northwest of the center. The Tren Francés leaves at 9pm every third day for Havana (CUC$62, 16 hours) stopping at Camagüey (CUC$11) and Santa Clara (CUC$20) en route.

Another slower *coche motor* (cross-island) train also plies the route to Havana every third day when a Tren Francés isn't running

❶ Getting Around

TO/FROM THE AIRPORT A taxi to the airport costs CUC$5. Taxis congregate in front of the Meliá Santiago de Cuba and around Parque Céspedes. Elsewhere call **Cubataxi** (☎65-10-38/39).

Buses 212 and 213 (40 centavos) travel to the airport; 212 is faster for going to the airport, while 213 is faster coming from the airport.

CAR Santiago de Cuba suffers from a chronic shortage of rental cars (especially in peak season) and you might find there are none available; though the locals have an indefatigable Cuban ability to *conseguir* (to manage, to get) and *resolver* (to resolve, work out). The airport offices usually have better availability than those in town.

Cubacar Airport (Antonio Maceo International Airport); Hotel Las Américas (cnr Avs de las Américas & General Cebreco; ⊗8am-10pm) The Hotel Las Américas office rents out mopeds for CUC$24 per day.

Baracoa   337

☎021 / POP 42,285

Take a pinch of Tolkien, a dash of Gabriel García Márquez, mix in a large cup of 1960s psychedelia and temper with a tranquilizing dose of Cold War–era socialism. Leave to stand for 400 years in a geographically isolated tropical wilderness with little or no contact with the outside world. The result: Baracoa – Cuba's weirdest, wildest, zaniest and most unique settlement, which materializes like a surreal apparition after the long dry plod along Guantánamo's southern coast.

Baracoa developed in relative isolation from the rest of Cuba until the opening in 1964 of La Farola (a steep 55km road across Guantánamo Province's rugged mountains), a factor that has strongly influenced its singular culture and traditions. Today its premier attractions include trekking up mysterious El Yunque, the region's signature flat-topped mountain, or indulging in some inspired local cooking using ingredients and flavors found nowhere else in Cuba.

❂ Sights & Activities

Founded in December 1511 by Diego Velázquez, Baracoa was the first Spanish settlement in Cuba. It served as the capital until 1515, when Velázquez moved the seat of government to Santiago de Cuba.

TOP CHOICE **Museo Arqueológico 'La Cueva del Paraíso'**   MUSEUM
(Moncada; admission CUC$3; ⊗8am-5pm) Baracoa's newest and most impressive museum is situated in Las Cuevas del Paraíso, 800m southeast of Hotel El Castillo. The exhibits, showcased in caves that once acted as Taíno burial chambers, include unearthed skeletons, ceramics, 3000-year-old petroglyphs and a replica of the *Ídolo de Tabaco,* a sculpture found in Maisí in 1903 that is considered to be one of the most important Taíno finds in the Caribbean.

Fuerte Matachín   FORT, MUSEUM
(cnr José Martí & Malecón) Baracoa is protected by a trio of muscular Spanish forts. This one, built in 1802 at the southern entrance to town, now houses the **Museo Municipal** (admission CUC$1; ⊗8am-noon & 2-6pm) showcasing an engaging chronology of Cuba's oldest settlement, including *polymita* snail shells, the story of Che Guevara and the

chocolate factory, and exhibits relating to pouty Magdalena Menasse (née Rovieskuya, 'La Rusa') after whom Alejo Carpentier based his famous book, *La Consagración de la Primavera* (The Rite of Spring).

Catedral de Nuestra Señora de la Asunción
CHURCH

(Antonio Maceo No 152) Crying out for a major renovation, this rapidly disintegrating church was constructed in 1833 on the site of a much older ecclesial building. Its most famous artifact is the priceless **Cruz de La Parra**, a wooden cross said to have been erected by Columbus near Baracoa in 1492. The church was closed at the time of writing and the cross was being displayed in the last house on Calle Antonio Maceo, behind the church to the right.

Facing the cathedral is the **Bust of Hatuey**, a rebellious Indian *cacique* (chief) who fell out with the Spanish and was burned at the stake near Baracoa in 1512 after refusing to convert to Catholicism.

Río Toa
RIVER, FARM

Ten kilometers northwest of Baracoa is the third-longest river on the north coast of Cuba and the country's most voluminous. The Toa is also an important bird and plant habitat. Cocoa trees and the ubiquitous coconut palm are grown in the Valle de Toa. **Rancho Toa** is a Palmares restaurant reached via a right-hand turnoff just before the Toa Bridge. You can organize boat or kayak trips here for CUC$3 to CUC$10 and watch acrobatic Baracoans scale *cocotero* (coconut palm) – contact Cubatur (p339). A traditional Cuban feast of whole roast pig is available if you can rustle up enough people (eight usually).

El Yunque
NATURE RESERVE

Baracoa's rite of passage is the 8km (up and down) hike to the top of this moody, mysterious mountain. At 575m, El Yunque (the anvil) isn't Kilimanjaro, but the views from the summit and the flora and birdlife along the way are stupendous. Cubatur (p340) offers this tour almost daily (CUC$18 per person, minimum two people). The fee covers admission, guide, transport and a sandwich. The hike is hot (bring at least 2L of water) and usually muddy. Bank on seeing *tocororo* (Cuba's national bird), *zunzún* (the world's smallest bird), butterflies and *polymitas*.

Playa Maguana
BEACH

Not quite the tranquil getaway it once was, Maguana is still nonetheless magical, a relatively undone Caribbean beach with a rustic food shack that is populated primarily by fun-seeking Cubans who roll up in their vintage American cars and haul their prized music boxes out of the boot. Aside from the fenced-off Villa Maguana and a couple of basic food concessions, there's no infrastructure here – all part of the attraction. Watch your valuables! To get here, drive 20km northwest out of Baracoa on the road to Moa.

🛏 Sleeping

Hotel El Castillo
HOTEL $

(☏64-51-64; Loma del Paraíso; s/d CUC$44/60; 🌢🏊) You could recline like a colonial-era conquistador in this historic place housed in the hilltop Castillo de Seboruco, except that conquistadors didn't have access to swimming pools, satellite TV or a maid who folds towels into ships, swans and other advanced forms of origami. This fine Gaviota-run hotel has just added 28 rooms in a new cleverly integrated block to add to the jaw-dropping El Yunque views and Baracoan friendliness.

Hostal La Habanera
HOTEL $

(☏64-52-73; Antonio Maceo No 126; s/d CUC$35/40; 🌢) Atmospheric and inviting in a way only Baracoa can muster, La Habanera sits in a restored pastel-pink colonial mansion where the cries of passing street hawkers compete with an effusive mix of hip-gyrating music emanating from the Casa de la Cultura next door. Bedrooms have tiled floors and rocking chairs, while the downstairs lobby boasts a bar/restaurant.

Nilson Abad Guilaré
CASA PARTICULAR $

(☏64-31-23; abadcub@gmail.com; Flor Crombet No 143 btwn Ciro Frías & Pelayo Cuervo; r CUC$25; 🌢) Nilson's a real gent who keeps what must be one of the cleanest houses in Cuba. This fantastic self-contained apartment has a huge bathroom, kitchen access and roof terrace with sea views. Nilson has also recently opened his house as a paladar called **La Terrazza**. The fish dinners with coconut sauce are to die for.

Casa Colonial – Gustavo & Yalina
CASA PARTICULAR $

(☏64-25-36; Flor Crombet No 125 btwn Frank País & Pelayo Cuervo; r CUC$15- 20; 🌢) This grand house was built in 1898 by a French sugar baron from Marseille, an esteemed ancestor of the current residents. The big rooms lack natural light but have antique furnishings, and culinary treats include local freshwater prawns and hot (Baracoan) chocolate for breakfast.

Casa Colonial Ykira Mahiquez
CASA PARTICULAR $
(☎64-38-81; Antonio Maceo No 168A btwn Ciro Frías & Céspedes; r CUC$20; ❄) Welcoming and hospitable, Ykira is Baracoa's hostess with the mostess and seasons her delicious cooking with homegrown herbs. Her central house has a full terrace and mirador with sea views.

Andrés Abella Fernánadez
CASA PARTICULAR $
(☎64-32-98; Maceo No 56; r CUC$20-25; ❄) Comfort reigns in Andrés' proud home, with two large clean-as-a-whistle rooms and a lovely intimate patio (unusual in Baracoa) with relaxing rockers.

✗ Eating

After the dull monotony of just about everywhere else, eating in Baracoa is a full-on sensory experience. Cooking here is creative, tasty and – above all – different. To experience the real deal, eat in your casa particular.

TOP CHOICE Restaurante La Punta
CARIBBEAN $$
(Fuerte la Punta; ⊙10am-11pm) At last! The La Punta fort gets a facelift and Baracoa gets a decent government-run restaurant befitting of a city that broadcasts its own distinctive cuisine. Cooled by Atlantic breezes, the Gaviota-run La Punta aims to impress with well-prepared, garnished food in lovely historical surroundings. Try the chicken and go on a Saturday night when there's accompanying music.

Paladar El Colonial
PALADAR $$
(José Martí No 123; mains CUC$10; ⊙lunch & dinner) This paladar is run out of a handsome wooden clapboard house on Calle José Martí. The menu has become a bit limited in recent times (less octopus and more chicken), though you still get the down-to-earth service and the delicious coconut sauce.

Casa del Chocolate
CHOCOLATERY $
(Antonio Maceo No 123; ⊙7:30am-11pm) It's enough to make even Willy Wonka wonder. You're sitting next to a chocolate factory but,

more often than not, there's none to be had in this bizarre little casa just off the main square. The quickest way to check out Baracoa's on-off supply situation is to stick your head around the door and question one of the bored-looking waitresses. *No hay* equals 'no,' a faint nod equals 'yes.' On a good day it sells chocolate ice cream and the hot stuff in mugs. For all its foibles, it's a Baracoa rite of passage.

Cafetería El Parque
FAST FOOD $
(Antonio Maceo No 142; ⊙24hr) This open terrace gets regularly drenched in Baracoa rain showers, but that doesn't seem to detract from its popularity. The favored meeting place of just about everyone in town, you're bound to end up here at some point tucking into spaghetti and pizza as you watch the world go by.

☆ Entertainment

TOP CHOICE Casa de la Trova Victorino Rodríguez
TRADITIONAL MUSIC
(Antonio Maceo No 149A) Cuba's smallest, zaniest, wildest and most atmospheric *casa de la trova* rocks nightly to the voodoo-like rhythms of *changüí-son*. Order a mojito in a jam jar and sit back and enjoy the show.

El Ranchón
NIGHTCLUB
(admission CUC$1; ⊙from 9pm) Atop a long flight of stairs at the western end of Coroneles Galano, El Ranchón mixes an exhilarating hilltop setting with taped disco and salsa music and legions of resident *jineteras*. Maybe that's why it's so insanely popular. Watch your step on the way down – it's a scary 146-step drunken tumble.

Casa de la Cultura
CULTURAL CENTER
(Antonio Maceo No 124 btwn Frank País & Maraví) This venue does a wide variety of shows including some good rumba. Go prepared for *mucho* audience participation.

La Terraza
CABARET
(Antonio Maceo btwn Maraví & Frank País; admission CUC$1; ⊙9pm-2am Mon-Thu, 9pm-4am Fri-Sun) A casual rooftop cabaret/variety show that kicks off most nights at 11pm; expect rumba, Benny Moré, and the local hairdresser singing Omara Portuondo.

❶ Information

Banco de Crédito y Comercio (Antonio Maceo No 99; ⊙8am-3pm Mon-Fri, 8-11am Sat)

Cadeca (José Martí No 241) Gives cash advances and changes traveler's checks.

Clínica Internacional Baracoa (☑64-10-38; Calle Martí 237 btwn Reyes &Sánchez; ⊙24hr) This excellent new clinic has English-speaking doctors on call and the best pharmacy in town.

Cubatur (Calle Martí No 181) Tours in English, Italian and German.

Ecotur (☑64-36-65; Coronel Cardoso No 24; ⊙9am-5pm) Organizes more-specialized nature tours to Duaba, Toa and Yumurí rivers.

Etecsa (cnr Antonio Maceo & Rafael Trejo, Parque Central; internet access per hr CUC$6; ⊙8:30am-7:30pm)

❶ Getting There & Away

AIR Gustavo Rizo Airport is 4km northwest of the town. **Cubana** (José Martí No 181; ⊙8am-noon & 2-4pm Mon-Fri) has two weekly flights from Havana to Baracoa (CUC$135 one-way, Thursday and Sunday).

BUS The **national bus station** (cnr Av Los Mártires & José Martí) has **Víazul** (www.viazul.com) buses to Guantánamo (CUC$10, three hours), continuing to Santiago de Cuba (CUC$16, five hours) daily at 2:15pm. Bus tickets can be reserved in advance through **Cubatur** (Antonio Maceo No 181), or you can usually stick your name on a waiting list a day or so beforehand.

TRUCK The **intermunicipal bus station** (cnr Coroneles Galano & Calixto García) has two or three trucks a day to Moa (90 minutes, departures from 6am) along an awful road passing Parque Nacional Alejandro de Humboldt. Prices are a few Cuban pesos.

❶ Getting Around

There's a helpful **Havanautos** (☑64-53-44) car-rental office at the airport. **Cubacar** (☑64-51-55) is at the Hotel Porto Santo. If you're driving, beware the northern route through Moa, a collection of holes held together by asphalt.

Most casas particulares will be able to procure you a bicycle for CUC$3 per day. The ultimate bike ride is the 20km ramble down to Playa Maguana.

Parque Nacional Alejandro de Humboldt

A Unesco World Heritage site 40km northwest of Baracoa, this beautiful **national park** perched above the Bahía de Taco should serve as a paradigm for Cuba's protection efforts. The 60,000 hectares of preserved land includes pristine forest, 1000 flowering plant species and 145 ferns, making it the Caribbean's most diverse plant habitat. As for fauna, it's the home to the world's smallest frog and the endangered

manatee, both of which you can see while hiking here.

Hikes are arranged at the **visitors center** (hikes per person CUC$5-10; ⊙9am-6pm). The three hikes currently offered are the challenging 7km Balcón de Iberia loop, with a 7m waterfall; El Recrea, a 3km bayside stroll; and the Bahía de Taco boat tour (with a manatee-friendly motor developed here); December to February is the best time to see the elusive manatee.

You can arrange a tour through Cubatur in Baracoa or get here independently on the Moa-bound truck or by rental car.

UNDERSTAND CUBA

History

European Arrivals

When Christopher Columbus neared Cuba on October 27, 1492, he described it as 'the most beautiful land human eyes have ever seen.' Spanish conquistadors, led by Diego Velázquez de Cuéllar, agreed: they came, they saw, they conquered and enslaved – despite resistance by indigenous chiefs Hatuey and Guamá. The native population was decimated, and by 1550 only about 5000 survivors remained from a population of around 120,000. The Spanish then began using Africans as slaves.

By the 1820s Cuba was the world's largest sugar producer and the US was sweet on it. So important was Cuban sugar that the US offered – twice – to buy Cuba from Spain. The slave trade continued furiously and by the 1840s there were some 400,000 Africans in Cuba, forever altering the country's makeup.

The Road to Independence

Fed up with the Spanish power structure, landowners plotted rebellion. On October 10, 1868, sugar baron Carlos Manuel de Céspedes launched the uprising by releasing his slaves and asking them to join his independence struggle. This began the First War of Independence, which extended into the Ten Years' War, costing some 200,000 lives before a pact improving conditions in Cuba – but not granting independence – was signed with the Spanish in February 1878. Around this time, some Cuban landowners began advocating annexation by the US.

Enter José Martí. Poet, patriot and independence leader, Martí organized feverishly for independence and, having convinced Antonio Maceo and Máximo Gómez to lead the revolution, landed in eastern Cuba in April 1895 from the United States: on May 19 Martí was shot and killed.

Gómez and Maceo stormed west in a scorched-earth policy that left the country in flames. Cuba was a mess: thousands were dead, including Antonio Maceo, killed south of Havana in December 1896. On February 15, 1898, the US battleship *Maine,* sent to Havana to 'protect US citizens,' exploded unexpectedly in Havana Harbor, killing 266 US sailors.

After the *Maine* debacle, the US scrambled for control, even trying to buy Cuba again (for US$300 million). The only important land battle of the war was on July 1, when the US Army, led by future US president Theodore Roosevelt, attacked Spanish positions on San Juan Hill in Santiago de Cuba. The Spaniards surrendered on July 17, 1898.

The US, Dictators & Revolutionaries

In November 1900, a Cuban constitution was drafted. Connecticut senator Orville Platt attached a rider giving the US the right to intervene militarily in Cuba whenever it saw fit. Given the choice of accepting this Platt Amendment or remaining under US military occupation indefinitely, the Cubans begrudgingly accepted the amendment; in 1903, the US used the amendment to grab the naval base at Guantánamo.

On May 20, 1902, Cuba became an independent republic, led by a series of corrupt governments, starting with the first president, Tomás Estrada Palma, right up to dictator Fulgencio Batista, who first took power in a 1933 coup.

Batista was duly elected president in 1940, when he drafted a democratic constitution guaranteeing many rights. He was succeeded by two corrupt and inefficient governments, and on March 10, 1952, he staged another coup.

A revolutionary circle formed in Havana, with Fidel Castro and many others at its core. On July 26, 1953, Castro led 119 rebels in an attack on the Moncada army barracks in Santiago de Cuba. The assault failed when a patrol 4WD encountered Castro's motor-

cade, costing the attackers the element of surprise.

Castro and a few others escaped into the nearby mountains, where they planned their guerrilla campaign. Soon after, Castro was captured and stood trial; he received a 15-year sentence on Isla de Pinos (now Isla de la Juventud).

In February 1955 Batista won the presidency and freed all political prisoners, including Castro, who went to Mexico and trained a revolutionary force called the 26th of July Movement ('M-26-7'). On December 2, 1956, Castro and 81 companions alighted from the *Granma* at Playa Las Coloradas in the Oriente. The group was quickly routed by Batista's army, but Castro and 11 others (including Argentine doctor Ernesto 'Che' Guevara, Fidel's brother Raúl, and Camilo Cienfuegos) escaped into the Sierra Maestra.

In May of the next year, Batista sent 10,000 troops into the mountains to liquidate Castro's 300 guerrillas. By August, the rebels had defeated this advance and captured a great quantity of arms. Che Guevara and Camilo Cienfuegos opened additional fronts in Las Villas Province, with Che capturing Santa Clara. Batista's troops finally surrendered on December 31, 1958.

The Revolution Triumphs

On January 1, 1959 Batista fled, taking with him US$40 million in government funds. Castro's column entered Santiago de Cuba that night and Guevara and Cienfuegos arrived in Havana on January 2.

The revolutionary government immediately enacted rent and electricity reductions, abolished racial discrimination and nationalized all holdings over 400 hectares, infuriating Cuba's largest landholders (mostly US companies). Many Cubans also protested at the new policies: between 1959 and 1970, 500,000 Cubans said *adios*. While clearly left-wing, Castro was no communist when he came to power. However, with US political and business will against him, he found himself driven into the arms of Nikita Khrushchev. The Soviet Union massively invested in Cuba and helped the regime through its early years with both military and technical know-how.

In January 1961 the US broke off diplomatic relations and banned US citizens from traveling to Cuba. On April 17, 1961, some 1400 CIA-trained émigrés attacked Cuba, landing at Playa Girón and Playa Larga in the Bahía de Cochinos (Bay of Pigs). The US took a drubbing.

After this defeat the US declared a full trade embargo (known as the *bloqueo*). In April 1962, amid rising Cold War tensions, Khrushchev secretly installed missiles in Cuba, sparking the Cuban Missile Crisis and bringing the world to the brink of nuclear war. Six days later, after receiving a secret assurance from US President Kennedy that Cuba would not be invaded, Khrushchev ordered the missiles to be dismantled. Castro was excluded from the deal-making.

The Wall Falls & the Special Period

When the Eastern bloc collapsed in 1989, the equivalent of US$5 billion in annual trade and credits to Cuba vanished, forcing Castro to declare a five-year *período especial* (special period) austerity program, technically ongoing. Rationing and rolling blackouts were instituted and food was scarce. Cubans share their survivor stories of this time willingly.

In August 1993 the US dollar was legalized to provide much-needed liquidity. Class differences reemerged as people with dollars gained access to goods and services not available in CUP (Cuban pesos); touts (known as *jinteros*, or jockeys) and prostitutes (*jineteras*) reappeared.

When it comes to sore subjects, US immigration policy runs a close second to the embargo. The Cuban Adjustment Act (1966) grants residency to any Cuban arriving on US shores. This has sparked immigration crises, including the *Mariel* boatlift in 1980, when 125,000 people left, and the 1994 *balsero* crisis, when some 35,000 people on makeshift rafts struggled across the Florida Straits; many died.

Although the US stance against Cuba hardened under the George W Bush administration, the Obama administration reversed the trend, allowing Cuban-Americans to visit without restrictions and issuing more legal licenses for educational, religious and cultural trips.

Life After Fidel

On February 18, 2008 in a letter to daily Communist newspaper *Granma,* Fidel Castro announced to the world that he would not 'aspire or accept' a further term as president and commander in chief. The announcement may have been a surprise (most observers were expecting Fidel to die in office) but there was no revelation about Castro's fitness; his brother and closest ally Raúl Castro had been running the country since Fidel was struck down by serious illness in 2006.

Raúl Castro was officially elected president in February 2008 and made some early, largely symbolic, reforms. A recovered Fidel still wields influence and it seems unlikely that the younger Castro will do anything earth-shattering as long as his older sibling is alive.

New Economic Realities

The 2008–09 recession played havoc with Cuba's already weak economy, exacerbating change. It finally arrived in late 2010 when Raúl Castro made the surprisingly nonsocialisitic move of laying off over half a million 'unproductive' government workers and loosening the laws that governed private enterprise. The plan initially left many ordinary Cubans flummoxed. For well over a generation, people in this tightly controlled socialist economy had lived under a paternalistic state apparatus that infiltrated every aspect of their daily lives. The standard of living wasn't high, but citizens didn't have to worry about mortgages, start-up costs, or hefty taxes. The new laws removed many of these assurances, and, while most have welcomed the opportunity to open up long-dreamt-about businesses ventures, many have found it difficult without the ability to advertise, arrange credit, or get access online.

As 2011 dawned, many new small businesses (everything from hairdressers to equestrian centers) were taking their first tentative steps in a newer, freer economy. It was a promising start. However, considering the many obstacles that remain – both internally and externally – it's unlikely that the road to economic growth will be smooth.

Culture

Take a dose of WWII rationing, and a pinch of Soviet-era austerity; add in the family values of South America, the educational virtues of the US, and the loquaciousness of the Irish. Mix with the tropical pace of Jamaica and innate musicality of pastoral Africa before dispersing liberally around the sultry streets of Havana, Santiago de Cuba, Camagüey and Pinar del Río.

Life in Cuba is an open and interactive brew. Spend time in a local home and you'll quickly start to piece together an archetype. There's the pot of coffee brewing on the stove, and the rusty Chinese bike leant languidly against the wall of the front room, the faded photo of José Martí above the TV, and the statue of the venerated Virgin of El Cobre lurking in the shadows. Aside from the house-owner and their mother, brother, sister and niece, every Cuban home has a seemingly endless queue of 'visitors' traipsing through. Then there are the sounds. A cock crowing, a saxophonist practicing his scales, dogs barking, car engines exploding, a salsa beat far off, and those all-too-familiar shouts from the street. *Dime, hermano! ¿Que pasa, mi amor? Ah, mi vida – no es fácil!*

Yes. *No es fácil* – it ain't easy. Life in Cuba is anything but easy; but, defying all logic, it's perennially colorful and rarely dull.

Music

Rich, vibrant, layered and soulful, Cuban music has long acted as a standard-bearer for the sounds and rhythms emanating out of Latin America. This is the land where salsa was born, where elegant white dances adopted edgy black rhythms, and where the African drum first fell in love with the Spanish guitar. From the down-at-heel docks of Matanzas to the bucolic villages of the Sierra Maestra, the amorous musical fusion went on to fuel everything from *son,* rumba, mambo*, chachachá, charanga changüí, danzón,* and more.

Aside from the obvious Spanish and African roots, Cuban music has drawn upon a number of other influences in the process of its embryonic development. Mixed into an already exotic melting pot are genres from France, the US, Haiti and Jamaica.

Landscape & Wildlife

Landscape

Cuba is the largest island in the Caribbean, a long, thin country with 5746km of coastline. Though more prone to winter cold fronts, the north shore has the Caribbean standard powdery sands and turquoise sea. The southern coast is more rocky, bedeviled by *diente de perro* (jagged rocks that line the

shore), but has good fishing and unexplored pockets with some lovely beaches too.

Over millions of years, Cuba's limestone bedrock has been eroded by underground rivers, creating interesting geological features like the 'haystack' hills of Viñales. Cuba has several important mountain ranges providing good hiking opportunities, including the Sierra del Escambray in the center of the country and the Sierra Maestra in the Oriente, featuring Pico Turquino (1972m), Cuba's highest peak.

At present, more than 14% of the country is protected in some way, and there are six national parks.

Wildlife

Cuba is home to 350 varieties of bird, including the toothpick-sized *zunzuncito* (bee hummingbird), the world's smallest bird. Cuba also boasts the world's smallest toad, the *ranita de Cuba* (Cuban tree toad, 1cm).

Land mammals have been hunted almost to extinction, except for the indigenous *jutía* (tree rat), a 4kg edible rodent. Marine fauna is more inspiring: manatees frequent Punta Frances on the Isla de la Juventud and the coastline around the Parque Nacional Alejandro de Humboldt in Guantánamo, and whale sharks swim around María la Gorda (August to November). Leatherback, loggerhead, green and hawksbill turtles also frequent Cuban seas. Iguanas are a common sight in the Parque Nacional Península de Guanahacabibes in Pinar del Río Province.

There are 90 types of palm, including the *palma real* (royal palm); the national tree, it figures prominently in Cuba's coat of arms and the Cristal beer logo (you'll see plenty of those!). Reforestation programs have been a priority for the Cuban government, which has planted over three million trees since 1959.

SURVIVAL GUIDE

Directory A–Z

Accommodations

Cuba has a huge range of accommodations, mostly substandard due to being state-run. By far the best accommodations in the country are in casas particulares (rooms in private homes), a '90s innovation that

PRACTICALITIES

» **Electricity** 110 volts, 60 cycles most common; you'll also find 220 volts. Sockets are a mix of North American–style flat two-prongs, North American-style flat three-prongs, and European-style rounded two-prongs.

» **Newspapers** *Granma, Juventud Rebelde* and *Trabajadores* are the three national papers.

» **Radio & TV** There are over 60 local radio stations and five TV channels; most midrange and top-end hotels have some cable.

» **Weights & Measures** The metric system is used, except in some fruit and vegetable markets.

allowed Cubans to rent out rooms in their homes to independent travelers. Casas particulares are cheaper, cleaner and friendlier than hotels, and in general they offer a better standard, although this of course varies tremendously. Accommodations are rented by the room (CUC$20 to CUC$40). An excellent resource for prebooking casas is **Cuba Casas** (www.cubacasas.net).

Hotels, with the exception of some four- and five-star foreign-managed joint ventures in the resorts, are generally disappointing by comparison. In Habana Vieja there are some excellent historic hotels, though.

Prices quoted in this chapter are for the high season; low-season prices are 10% to 25% cheaper.

$	budget	less than CUC$75
$$	midrange	CUC$75 to CUC$200
$$$	top end	more than CUC$200

Activities

If Cuba has a blue-ribbon activity, it is scuba diving (see also p320). There are over 30 dive centers throughout Cuba. Most equipment is older than that you'll be used to and safety standards are much lower than elsewhere in the Caribbean. Dives cost around CUC$35, while certification courses are CUC$300 to CUC$350, and introductory courses cost CUC$35 to CUC$50.

It's possible to hire reasonable outdoor gear in Cuba. But, if you do bring your own

supplies, any gear you can donate at the end of your trip will be greatly appreciated.

Naturalists and ornithologists in the various national parks and flora and fauna reserves are conscientious and well qualified. Hiking has traditionally been limited, but opportunities have expanded in recent years with companies such as Ecotur offering a wider variety of hikes. Cycling is refreshingly DIY, and all the better for it. Canyoning and climbing are new sports in Cuba that have a lot of local support but little official backing – as yet.

Ecotur (www.ecoturcuba.co.cu) Runs organized hiking, trekking, fishing and birdwatching trips to some of the country's otherwise inaccessible corners. It has offices in every province and a main HQ in Havana.

Cubamar Viajes (www.cubamarviajes.tur.cu) Runs Cuba's 80-plus campismos (rural chalets). It has Reservaciones de Campismo offices in every provincial capital and a helpful head office in Havana.

Business Hours

The following are the standard business hours used in this chapter; exceptions are noted in individual reviews. All businesses shut at noon on the last working day of each month.

Banks 9am-3pm Mon-Fri

Restaurants 10:30am-11pm Mon-Sun

Shops 9am-5pm Mon-Sat, 9am-noon Sun

Customs Regulations

Travelers are allowed to bring in personal belongings (including photography equipment, binoculars, musical instrument, tape recorder, radio, personal computer, tent, fishing rod, bicycle, canoe and other sporting gear), and gifts up to CUC$50.

You are allowed to export 50 boxed cigars duty-free (or 23 singles), US$5000 (or equivalent) in cash and only CUC$200.

For the full scoop see www.aduana.co.cu.

Dangers & Annoyances

'You wanna buy cigar, my fren?' – this refrain will follow you throughout the country. Welcome to the land of the *jintero* (tout), a profession raised to an art form by the Cubans, who, in their defense, have very few other ways to make money. Learn quickly to ignore them, don't make eye contact, say 'no thank you' clearly but firmly, never stop walking, and when you're asked where you're from, choose somewhere obscure (this avoids a rehearsed and interminably cutesy patter about your *jintero*'s sister working as a nurse in Liverpool or studying in Toronto). Harsh? Yes, but *jintero*ism is any traveler in Cuba's single biggest annoyance, so getting to grips with it will improve your holiday vastly.

Cuba is not a dangerous destination, although Centro Habana is the spot you're most likely to get mugged (a rarity, but just be aware at night). Apart from this and other small opportunistic crimes such as pickpocketing, you have almost nothing to be afraid of. Never leave valuables in any room; use the safe if there's one provided.

Embassies & Consulates

Canada Embassy (☏204-2516; www.havana .gc.ca; Calle 30 No 518, Miramar); Consulate (☏45-61-20-78; Calle 13 No 422, Varadero) Also represents Australia.

France (☏201-3131; www.ambafrance-cu.com; Calle 14 No 312 btwn Avs 3 & 5, Miramar)

Germany (☏833-2460; Calle 13 No 652, Vedado)

Italy (☏204-5615; Av 5 No 402, Miramar)

Netherlands (☏204-2511; http://cuba. nlambassade.org; Calle 8 No 307 btwn Avs 3 & 5, Miramar)

Spain (☏866-8025; Cárcel No 51, Centro Habana)

UK (☏204-1771; www.britishembassy.gov.uk/ cuba; Calle 34 No 702, Miramar) Also represents New Zealand.

US Interests Section (☏833-3551/52/53, out of hr 834-4400; http://havana.usinterest sec-tion.gov; Calzada btwn Calles L & M, Vedado)

Food

In this chapter, restaurant prices are categorized as follows, based on the cost of a meal:

$	budget	less than CUC$7
$$	midrange	CUC$7 to CUC$15
$$$	top end	more than CUC$15

Gay & Lesbian Travelers

These days Cuba is a surprisingly gay-friendly place (by pitiful Caribbean standards at least). The two main factors for this are the hit 1994 movie *Fresa y Chocolate*, which sparked a national dialogue about homosexuality, something that had previously been taboo, and, in more recent times, the campaigning efforts of Mariela Castro, daughter of President Raúl Castro and director of the National Center for Sex Education.

Despite this, gay life remains hidden from public view. With the exception of one progressive club in Santa Clara (Club Mejunje, p323) there are no openly gay clubs and gay life revolves heavily around internet contacts, cruising and private *fiestas de diez pesos* (private parties charging CUC$2 cover). These mostly gay parties are moving shindigs held on Friday and Saturday nights in Havana from around midnight; head to gay meeting spot Cine Yara (p315) and chat up the crowds of partygoers to find out where that night's party is happening.

For your own safety it's good to remain discreet at street level by avoiding public displays of affection.

Health

Cuban citizens famously enjoy far better free health care than their wealthier US neighbors, and continue to set high standards for developing nations, with excellent hospitals and doctors found throughout the country. Most medication is available in Cuba, although you should bring anything you know you'll need. It is a condition of entering Cuba that you have travel medical insurance covering you during your stay.

In large cities and places where many tourists visit there are usually clinics designed for foreigners, with English-speaking doctors and better supplies than elsewhere. Charges are made for treatment, but are tiny compared with treatment in Western private hospitals. The free health care in normal Cuban hospitals should only be used when there are no private clinics available.

It is best to err on the side of caution and avoid Cuban tap water.

Internet Access

Access to the internet is provided in all sizable towns by Etecsa (per hour CUC$6), from small and often slow internet cafes. You may be asked to show your passport or give your passport number when purchasing access cards. There's a smattering of wi-fi places in Havana, although none are free even for guests, with the exception of the Saratoga (p307). Despite not officially being allowed, some casas particulares have internet access, which you will usually be charged to use by your host family.

Money

CURRENCY & EXCHANGE

Two currencies circulate throughout Cuba – Cuban convertible pesos (CUC) and Cuban pesos (CUP), also called *moneda nacional* (MN). Most prices in this chapter are quoted in convertible pesos (CUC$) and nearly everything tourists buy is in this currency, although you can often buy street food and drinks in CUP, making it a good idea to change CUC$10 to CUC$20 for such sundries at a Cadeca.

Convertible pesos can only be bought and sold in Cuba with euros, British pounds, Canadian dollars and Swiss francs; these currencies are exchanged at the global exchange rate for the dollar, plus an 8% tax tacked on by the Cuban government. US dollars are also convertible, but with a huge 18% tax.

Convertible pesos are useless outside Cuba; you can reverse-exchange currency at the airport before you pass through immigration. Do not change money on the street as scams are rampant.

ATMS

ATMs have become much more reliable in recent years, but outside Havana and Santiago don't count on them working.

CREDIT CARDS

Credit cards are charged at an 8% commission. Generally, using them in better hotels and resorts is trouble-free, but again, never rely on them. Visa is the most widely accepted credit card. Due to embargo laws, no credit card issued by a US bank or subsidiary is accepted in Cuba.

TRAVELER'S CHECKS

Traveler's checks are a hassle in Cuba. Cashing them takes time, and smaller hotels don't accept them. They're virtually useless in the provinces. If you insist on carrying them, get Thomas Cook checks.

TIPPING

Washroom attendants expect CUC$0.05 to CUC$0.10, while *parqueadores* (parking attendants) should get CUC$0.25 for a short watch and CUC$1 per 12 hours. For a day tour, CUC$2 per person is appropriate for a tour guide. Taxi drivers will appreciate 10% of the meter fare, but if you've negotiated a ride without the meter, don't tip. Tipping can quickly *resolver las cosas* (fix things up). If you want to stay beyond the hotel checkout time or enter a site after hours, for instance, small tips (CUC$1 to CUC$5) bend rules.

Public Holidays

There are only a few holidays that might affect your travel plans, when shops close and local transportation is erratic.

January 1 Triumph of the Revolution; New Year's Day

May 1 International Worker's Day; no inner-city transportation

July 26 Celebrates start of the revolution on July 26, 1953

October 10 Start of the First War of Independence

December 25 Declared an official holiday after the Pope's 1998 visit

Telephone

Cuba's country code is ☎53. To call Cuba from North America, dial ☎1-53 + the local number. From elsewhere, dial your country's international access code, then Cuba's country code ☎53 + city or area code + local number. In this chapter, the city or area code is given in the statistics at the start of each section and only the local number is given in the listings.

To call internationally from a Cuban pay phone, dial ☎119 + country code + area code and the number. To the US, just dial ☎119-1 + area code and the number.

To place a collect call (reverse charges, *cobro revertido*) through an international operator, dial ☎012. This service is not available to all countries. You cannot call collect from public phones.

To call between provinces, dial ☎0 + area code + number. To call Havana from any other province, you just dial ☎7 + number.

CELL PHONES

Cuba's mobile-phone company is called **Cubacel** (www.cubacel.com). While you may be able to use your own phone, you have to have Cubacel activate it and pre-buy its services. Cubacel has more than 15 offices around the country (including the

In 1961 the US government imposed an order limiting the freedom of its citizens to visit Cuba, and airline offices and travel agencies in the US are forbidden to book tourist travel to Cuba via third countries.

Americans who do visit Cuba traditionally go via Canada, Mexico, the Bahamas, or any other third country, making travel arrangements through foreign travel agencies. Travel agents in those countries routinely arrange Cuban tourist cards, flight reservations and accommodations packages.

At the time of writing there were two types of licenses issued by the US government to visit Cuba: general licenses (typically for government officials, journalists and professional researchers) and specific licenses (for visiting family members, humanitarian projects, public performances, religious activities and educational activities).

In January 2011 the Obama administration revoked the George W Bush administration's clampdown on the issuing of legal licenses. This will pave the way for more educational, cultural and religious groups to apply for permission to visit the country through study-abroad programs, people-to-people exchanges and research trips.

For the latest information, check with the **US Department of the Treasury** (http://www.treasury.gov/resource-center/sanctions/Programs/pages/cuba.aspx). Travel arrangements for those eligible for a license can be made by specialized US companies such as **Marazul Charters Inc** (www.marazulcharters.com)

It is estimated that close to 100,000 US citizens a year travel to Cuba illegally with no consequences, but be aware that the maximum penalty for Americans making 'unauthorized' visits is US$250,000 and 10 years in prison. In practice, people are usually fined US$7500.

Havana airport) where you can do this. Its plan costs approximately CUC$3 per day, or CUC$6 per day if you use its equipment. Local calls cost from CUC$0.10 (reduced) to CUC$0.45 (normal) per minute. Calls abroad are between CUC$1.40 and CUC$1.80 per minute.

PHONECARDS

Etecsa is where you buy phonecards, use the internet and make international calls. Blue public Etecsa phones (most broken) are everywhere. Phonecards (magnetic or chip) are sold in convertible-peso denominations of CUC$5, CUC$10 and CUC$20, and *moneda nacional* denominations of CUP$3, CUP$5 and CUP$7. You can call nationally with either, but you can only call internationally with convertible-peso cards. International calls made with a card cost CUC$2 per minute to North America and CUC$5 per minute to Europe/Oceania.

Tourist Information

Cuba's official tourist information bureau is called **Infotur** (www.infotur.cu). It has offices in all the main provincial towns and desks in most of the bigger hotels and airports. Travel agencies, such as Cubanacán, Cubatur and Ecotur, can usually supply some general information.

Visas

Visitors initially get four weeks in Cuba with a *tarjeta de turista* (tourist card) issued by their airline or travel agency (the exception is Canadians, who get 90 days). Unlicensed US visitors buy their tourist card at the airline desk in the country through which they're traveling to Cuba (US$25); they are welcomed in the country like any other tourist. You cannot leave Cuba without presenting your tourist card (replacements cost CUC$25).

The 'address in Cuba' line should be filled in with a hotel or legal casa particular, if only to avoid unnecessary questioning.

Business travelers and journalists need visas. Applications should be made through a consulate at least three weeks in advance, preferably longer.

Obtaining an extension is easy: go to an immigration office and present your documents and CUC$25 in stamps (obtainable at local banks). You'll receive an additional four weeks, after which you'll need to leave Cuba and reenter anew if you need to stay longer. Attend to extensions at least a few business days before your visa is due to

DEPARTURE TAX

Everyone must pay a CUC$25 departure tax at the airport. It's payable in cash only.

expire. The following cities covered in this book all have immigration offices:

Baracoa (Martí No 177; ⊗8am-noon & 2-4pm Mon-Fri)

Havana (Desamparados No 110 btwn Habana & Compostela; ⊗8:30am-4pm Mon-Wed & Fri, 8:30-11am Thu & Sat)

Santa Clara (cnr Av Sandino & Sexta; ⊗8am-noon & 1-3pm Mon-Thu)

Santiago de Cuba (Calle 13 near Av General Cebreco, Vista Alegre; ⊗8am-5pm Mon, Tue, Thu & Fri)

Trinidad (Julio Cueva Díaz off Paseo Agramonte; ⊗8am-5pm Tue-Thu)

Viñales (cnr Salvador Cisneros & Ceferino Fernández; ⊗8am-5pm Mon-Fri)

Getting There & Away
Entering Cuba

For a country with such a fearsome reputation as a communist prison, Cuba's a very straightforward place to enter. The key thing is to have your passport, onward ticket and tourist card (usually included in your flight ticket), and know where you're staying (at least for your first night). Ensure you've filled out your tourist card before you arrive at the immigration counter, and if you don't know where you'll be staying make something up.

Since May 2010 it has been compulsory for all foreigners visiting Cuba to have proof of medical travel insurance.

Air

Over 99% of travelers arrive by air. The busiest passage is from Canada, followed by Europe, Mexico, the Caribbean, and South America. There are no direct flights from Asia and Australia and very few from Africa.

AIRPORTS

Cuba has 10 international airports. The largest by far is José Martí in Havana. The only other sizable airport is Juan Gualberto Gómez in Varadero. Cuba's other eight international airports receive mainly charter flights from Canada, Italy and the UK.

AIRLINES

Cuba's national airline is **Cubana de Aviación** (www.cubana.cu). Its modern fleet flies major routes and its fares are usually the cheapest. Still, overbooking and delays are nagging problems and it charges stiffly for every kilo above the 20kg luggage allowance.

Cubana operates regular flights to: Bogotá, Buenos Aires, Mexico City, Cancún, Caracas, Guatemala City, London, Madrid, Paris, Toronto, Montreal, San José (Costa Rica) and Santo Domingo (Dominican Republic).

There are flights to Cuba from Europe with Aeroflot, Air France, Air Italy, Iberia and Virgin Atlantic. Air Canada and Air Transat fly from Canada.

Other airlines serving Cuba:

Aerocaribbean (www.cubajet.com)

Aeroméxico (www.aeromexico.com) Cancún and Mexico City

Air Caraibes (www.aircaraibes.com) Pointe-a-Pitre, Guadeloupe

Bahamasair (www.bahamasair.com) Nassau

Cayman Airways (www.caymanairways.com) Grand Cayman

Copa Airlines (www.copaair.com) Panama City

TACA (www.taca.com) San Salvador

Sea

If you have your own private yacht or cruiser, Cuba has seven international entry ports equipped with customs facilities: Marina Hemingway (Havana), Marina Dásena (Varadero), Marina Cienfuegos, Marina Cayo Guillermo, Marina Santiago de Cuba, Puerto de Vita (near Guardalavaca in Holguín Province), Cayo Largo del Sur, and Cabo de San Antonio (far western tip of Pinar del Río Province).

Getting Around
Air

Internal flights – to Camagüey, Santiago de Cuba, Cayo Coco – are well provided for by national carrier **Cubana de Aviación** (www.cubana.cu) and **Aerocaribbean** (www.cubajet.com) but their safety records aren't good. Some embassies recommend against internal flights in Cuba.

To book or change a Cubana flight, take a number at the **Airline Bldg** (Calle 23 No 64, Vedado, Havana; ☺8:30am-4pm Mon-Fri, 8:30am-noon Sat). Most other airlines that have offices in Havana are located on this strip.

Bicycle

Cuba is legendary among cyclists and you'll see more bicycle enthusiasts here than divers, climbers and hikers put together. Cuba's status with cyclists dates from the mid-'90s when it first opened up to tourism, when cars were still few and far between.

Spare parts are difficult to find; *poncheras* fix flat tires and provide air. Bring your own strong locks as bicycle theft is rampant. Try to leave your bike at a *parqueo* – bicycle parking lots costing CUP$1, located wherever crowds congregate (markets, bus terminals etc). Riding after dark is not recommended. Trains with baggage carriages *(coches de equipaje* or *bagones)* take bikes for CUC$20. These compartments are guarded, but take your panniers with you and check over the bike when you arrive. Víazul buses also take bikes.

Bus

Bus travel is a dependable option with **Víazul** (www.viazul.cu; Calle 26 & Zoológico, Nuevo Vedado, Havana), which has punctual, air-conditioned coaches to destinations of interest to travelers. Sadly it's not possible for foreigners to travel on Astro buses, which cover the country far more comprehensively, meaning that if you want to get off the beaten path you're pretty much forced to hire a car or ride a bike. Bus reservations are advisable during peak travel periods (June to August, Christmas and Easter) and on popular routes (Havana–Trinidad, Trinidad–Santa Clara and Santiago de Cuba–Baracoa). See individual Getting There & Away sections for information about bus connections to and from other towns in Cuba.

Car

Renting a car in Cuba follows the predictable pattern of so much of Cuban life. It's pretty straightforward, but resign yourself to paying over the odds for a badly maintained and usually pretty crappy machine.

To rent a car, you'll need your passport, your home driver's license and a refundable CUC$200 deposit (in cash or with a non-US credit card). You can rent a car in one city

and drop it off in another for a reasonable fee. The cheapest cars start at CUC$50 per day for a Hyundai Atos and climb steeply to around CUC$70 per day minimum during the high season.

The following rental-car agencies are in Havana. You're often better off going directly to hotel representatives than calling the operators.

Cubacar (www.cubacar.info) Has representation at the airport and at Hotels Sevilla, NH Parque Central, Nacional and Ambos Mundos.

Rex (Línea cnr Malecón) Also has an office at the airport.

Vía Rent a Car (www.gaviota-grupo.com) At the Hotel Sevilla and the Hotel Habana Libre.

FUEL & SPARE PARTS
Cupet and Oro Negro *servicentros* (gas stations) selling hard-currency gas are nearly everywhere. Gas is sold by the liter and is either regular (per liter CUC$1.10) or *especial* (per liter CUC$1.30). Either works equally well, although car-hire companies ask you to put *especial* in your car.

ROAD CONDITIONS
The Autopista and Carretera Central are generally in good repair. While motorized traffic is refreshingly light, bicycles, pedestrians, tractors and livestock can test your driving skills. Driving at night is not recommended due to variable roads, crossing cows, poor lighting and drunk drivers (an ongoing problem despite a government educational campaign). Signage, though improving, is still appalling. Allow plenty of extra time and ask repeatedly to check you're going the right way.

Taxi, Bici-taxi & Coco-taxi

Car taxis are metered and cost CUC$1 to start, CUC$0.50 to CUC$0.65 per km thereafter. Cabbies usually offer foreigners a flat, off-meter rate that works out close to what you'll pay with the meter.

Bici-taxis are big tricycles with two seats behind the driver. Tourists pay CUC$1 to CUC$2 for a short hop; agree on the price beforehand. You'll be mobbed all over the country in tourist spots by the ubiquitous cry of 'taxi' from these guys.

So-called coco-taxis are egg-shaped motorbike taxis that hold two to three people and are mainly seen in Havana. Locals often refer to them as *huevitos* (literally 'little eggs'). Agree on a price before getting in.

Train

Public railways operated by Ferrocarriles de Cuba serve all the provincial capitals and are a great way to experience Cuba if you have time and patience, but a nightmare if you're keen to make progress and move about efficiently! Departure information provided in this chapter is purely theoretical. Getting a ticket is usually no problem – tourists will be charged in CUC$, though Spanish-speaking travelers frequently travel on trains for the local peso price. The most useful routes for travelers are Havana–Santiago de Cuba and Havana–Santa Clara. The bathrooms are foul. Watch your luggage and bring food.

Curaçao

Best Beaches
» Kleine St Michiel (p360)
» Kas Abou (p360)
» Playa Lagún (p361)
» Knip Beaches (p361)

Best Places to Stay
» Avila Beach Hotel (p355)
» Hotel Kura Hulanda (p355)
» Hotel Scharloo (p356)

Why Go?
Go-go Curaçao balances commerce with Unesco-recognized old Willemstad and an accessible beauty, thanks to hidden beaches along a lush coast. It's a wild mix of urban madness, remote vistas and a lust for life.

It has a rich history dating back to the 16th century. Central Willemstad boasts fascinating old buildings and excellent museums. Remnants of plantations dot the countryside – some are now parks. The west coast has oodles of beautiful little beaches, good for diving, snorkeling or just lazing.

Curaçao has a surging economy beyond tourism, which means that Willemstad, apart from its historical core, has factories, many humdrum neighborhoods and at times bad traffic. Catering to visitors is not the primary aim here, but if you're looking for a Caribbean island that is busy setting its own pace, Curaçao is for you.

When to Go
Average temperature for Curaçao is a perfect 28°C (82°F). High noon is a bit warmer and at night it can get breezy, but mostly you'll be fine in shorts and T-shirt. The island is fairly dry, averaging a little over 25mm of rain per month. Much of this falls from September to early December. Curaçao usually misses the Caribbean hurricane season, though in recent years January rains have caused minor flooding. December to April is high season. High season for cruise ships runs October to April.

» **Currency** Netherlands Antillean guilder (NAf); see p363

» **Languages** Dutch, Spanish, English, Papiamento

» **Money** ATMs all over; most dispense Netherlands Antillean guilders and US dollars

» **Visas** Not required for citizens of the US, Canada, Australia, New Zealand and most EU countries

Fast Facts

» **Area** 471 sq km

» **Population** 143,000

» **Capital** Willemstad

» **Telephone country code** ☑599

» **Telephone area code** ☑9

» **Emergency** Ambulance ☑912; fire and police ☑911

Set Your Budget

» **Budget hotel room** US$80

» **Two-course evening meal** US$30

» **Beer** US$4

» **Tour of harbor** NAf15

» **Sint Annabaai ferry** Free

Resources

» **Curaçao Tourist Board** (www.curacao.com)

» **Gay Curaçao** (www.gaycuracao.com)

» **National Parks** (www.carmabi.org) Fascinating info on Curaçao's treasures on land and sea

» **Webcam Curaçao** (www.webcamcuracao.com) Live images of huge ships passing through Willemstad

Itineraries

THREE DAYS

Set yourself up in a place to stay in or near Willemstad. Explore this fascinating and at times confounding old town. Shop the markets and admire the ongoing restorations of old neighborhoods. Take a day to drive the northern coast loop up and around through Westpunt, stopping at beaches and Christoffel National Park on the way.

ONE WEEK

Spend more time exploring. Do Kleine St Michiel and the road to Kas Abou on separate days. Spend time in the twists and turns of Spaanse Water. Compare as many of Curaçao's 38 named beaches as you can, go for a dive, decide on your favorite old Willemstad street.

TWO WEEKS

All the above, and consider a visit to the neighboring islands of Aruba and Bonaire, each of which has a completely different personality to Curaçao.

GETTING TO NEIGHBORING ISLANDS

Plans for ferries within the ABCs perpetually sink before they can be launched. But flights between Curaçao and Aruba and Bonaire are frequent and last about 20 minutes.

Essential Food & Drink

Reflecting the crops and animals that thrive in the semiarid climate, food in Curaçao is basic and filling. Thick stews made with meats such as goat and chicken, and with vegetables such as okra and squash, are predominant. Spices are used to give things variety.

» **Goat (cabrito) stew** A classic dish that most Curaçaoans will say is made best by their own mother. Also appears in curries.

» **Cheese** An obvious Dutch legacy, usually eaten straight with a beer; when used in cooking it was traditionally a special treat.

» **Keshi yena** Comes in many variations: a cheese casserole with chicken, okra and a few raisins for seasoning. Much better than it sounds.

» **Seafood** Common and good, especially shellfish. Fish is popular in curries.

» **Funchi** Based on cornmeal, it is formed into cakes and fried, mixed with okra and fried, used as a coating for chicken and fish etc.

» **Frikandel** Classic Dutch deep-fried, meaty snack.

» **Bitterballen** Another Dutch classic, little deep-fried meaty balls served at roadside stands.

» **Curaçao** Yes, there really is a liquor by the name. It's a startling blue, especially given its orange flavor.

Curaçao Highlights

① Immerse yourself in **Willemstad** (p354), with its Dutch colonial heritage and the grit of a busy port town

② Explore **hidden beaches** (p360) on the jagged west coast

③ Bear witness to Curaçao's horrible legacy of slavery at the **Museum Kura Hulanda**

(p354) in Willemstad's historic Otrobanda neighborhood

④ Feel the power of the windblown and wave-tossed east coast at **Christoffel National Park** (p362)

⑤ Thrill to the picture-perfect cove at **Playa Lagún** (p361), where you can snorkel right off the beach

⑥ Enjoy the relaxed **Plein Cafe** (p357), a classic bit of gregarious Dutch charm in the heart of Willemstad

⑦ Count all 60 species of coral as you **dive and snorkel** (p361) Curaçao's uncrowded waters, especially in the National Underwater Park

Willemstad

POP 75,000

Willemstad is both a big city and a small town. Residents live in the hills surrounding Schottegat, and much of the city is sprawling and rather mundane. But this all changes radically in the old town. Here the island's colonial Dutch heritage sets a genteel tone amid markets, museums and even a nascent cafe culture. Wandering the Unesco World Heritage–recognized old town and absorbing its rhythms can occupy a couple of days. The Queen Emma Bridge regularly swings open to let huge ships pass through the channel, a sight in itself, and these interruptions 'force' you to take one of the enjoyable ferries.

Once the capital of the dissolving Netherlands Antilles, central Willemstad seems content to remake itself as the favored destination for a growing number of cruise-ship passengers and visitors.

Dangers & Annoyances

Curaçao's urban mix includes some real poverty. Although street crime is not a huge concern, in some of the deeper recesses of Otrobanda drug-related crime is an everyday problem.

◉ Sights

To fully explore Willemstad you'll need at least a very full day, but probably two.

The old town of Curaçao is split by Sint Annabaai, which is really a channel to Schottegat. On the west side is Otrobanda, an old workers' neighborhood, which still has shops popular with the masses, and a mixture of beautifully restored buildings and areas rough around the edges. East of the channel – and linked by the swinging Queen Emma Bridge – is Punda, the old commercial center of town, and home to stores, offices and markets. North across Queen Wilhelmina Bridge is the old port and warehouse neighborhood of Scharloo.

Arching over all is the 56m-high Queen Juliana Bridge, which allows even the largest ships to pass underneath. (If more bridges are needed, the Netherlands will need more queens.)

PUNDA

TOP CHOICE **Queen Emma Bridge**   LANDMARK
(Map p356) One of Punda's sedate pleasures is sitting on the wall along the channel and watching huge ships pass while the Queen

Emma Bridge shuttles back and forth to make way. There's always someone leaping onto the end as it swings away from Punda. If the bridge is open, look for flags by the pilot's cabin: orange means it has been open less than 30 minutes, blue means it has been open longer and *may* soon close. When the bridge is open, two old free **public ferries** nearby cruise into action. The four-minute ride on these is a treat in itself.

Fort Amsterdam   FORT
(Map p356) The much modified fort is now home to government and official offices. Inside the large courtyard you can soak up the rich colors of the Dutch colonial architecture dating from the 1760s. Parts of the old battlements weave through the complex, and there is a small **museum** in the church.

Jewish Cultural-Historical Museum   MUSEUM
(Map p356; Hanchi Snoa 29; admission US$10; ⊙9-4:30pm Mon-Fri) Since 1651 the oldest continuously operating Jewish congregation in the western hemisphere is the Mikvé Israel Emanuel Synagogue, which houses a museum with items from the history of the congregation; the building dates to 1732.

OTROBANDA

Follow Wan Lennepstraat uphill into a safe and historic neighborhood for great views of the city and harbor.

TOP CHOICE **Museum Kura Hulanda**   MUSEUM
(Map p356; Klipstraat 9; adult/child NAfl15/9; ⊙10am-5pm) One of the best museums in the Caribbean, this is part of the boutique hotel of the same name and is housed in 19th-century slave quarters. The brutal history of slavery in the Caribbean is documented here in superb and extensive exhibits. Look for the unflinching account by John Gabriel Stedman of slavery in 1700s Suriname.

Curaçao Museum   MUSEUM
(Map p358; Van Leeuwenhoekstraat; adult/child US$3/1.75; ⊙8:30am-4:30pm Tue-Fri, 10am-4pm Sat & Sun) About 800m north of the bus station in a residential neighborhood, housed in an 1853 hospital for yellow-fever victims. Inside the beautiful verandas is lots of historical stuff, sort of like you'd find in a huge attic.

SCHARLOO

The docks in the neighborhood are mostly closed, but wander around and you'll see building restorations in progress, including the art-deco **Miami Building** (Map p356; Bitterstraat 3-9). Another amazing colonial survivor is the rambling **green building** (Map p356) on the south side of Bargestraat, just east of Van Raderstraat. Note the arched veranda with a profusion of neoclassical details. Throughout Scharloo, old mansions are being saved from a unique form of rot caused when the salt trapped in the original coral building blocks escapes and literally dissolves the structure.

Curaçao Maritime Museum   MUSEUM
(Map p356; www.curacaomaritime.com; Van Den Brandhofstraat 7; adult/child NAf10/6; ☺9am-4pm Tue-Sat) The other superb museum in Willemstad. Engaging displays trace the island's history, detailing how the Dutch West India Company kicked Spain's butt to gain control of the ABCs through to the commercial boom of the 20th century, when the port was where commerce from the US, Europe, the Caribbean and Latin America met. Well worth the 90-minute time investment are the museum's **harbor tours** (adult/child NAf15/7.50; ☺2pm Wed & Sat), which take in the industrial specter of Schottegat.

PIETERMAAI
Just east of Punda, this equally historic colonial area is under massive renovation. In the meantime it's a funky mix of decaying mansions, spiffy rehabs, oddball shops and quixotic cafes. The spine, **Nieuwestraat**, is a necessary stroll.

Tours

Several local historians offer **walking tours** (www.otrobanda-pundatour.com) of the Unesco World Heritage–listed old town. Booking is essential.

Old City Tours   WALKING TOUR
(☑461-3554; NAf15; ☺5:15pm Thu) Architect Anko van der Woude focuses on the buildings of Otrobanda during a weekly walk.

🛏 Sleeping

With the very notable exceptions of Avila Beach Hotel and Hotel Kura Hulanda, accommodations in Willemstad place function over form...when they function.

PUNDA & EAST
TOP
CHOICE Avila Beach Hotel   BOUTIQUE HOTEL **$$$**
(Map p358; ☑461-4377; www.avilahotel.com; Penstraat 130; r US$200-500; ✳@🛜🏊) The Avila Beach combines rooms in the 18th-century

home of a Dutch governor with modern wings of luxurious accommodation. The grounds are elegant and the beach is a fine crescent of sand. The **Octagon Museum** (☺by appointment) in the hotel is dedicated to revolutionary Simón Bolívar, who stayed here plotting his assault on the Spanish. This hotel perfectly combines Curaçao's rich heritage with its beachy charms.

Plaza Hotel Curaçao   HOTEL **$$**
(Map p356; ☑461-2500; www.plazahotelcuracao.com; Plasa Pier, Punda; r US$120-250; ✳@🛜🏊) This prominent hotel at the entrance to Sint Annabaai has many pluses: location, location, location. The views of ship traffic from the mezzanine-level pool are superb. But it does have some rough edges and most of the average rooms in the 14-story tower lack balconies. Part of the hotel is built into old battlements and the pool bar is a fine place for sunset views of huge ships leaving port.

OTROBANDA
TOP
CHOICE Hotel Kura
Hulanda   BOUTIQUE HOTEL **$$$**
(Map p356; ☑434-7700; www.kurahulanda.com; Langestraat 3,; r US$140-300; ✳@🛜🏊) One of Willemstad's best hotels is also a sight in itself. Architect Jacob Gelt Dekker took a run-down neighborhood in Otrobanda and created an amazing hotel that is really a village of restaurants, cafes and rooms. The 80 rooms, with their hand-carved mahogany furniture and old-time luxuries, may make you feel like a plantation pasha.

Howard Johnson Plaza Hotel   HOTEL **$**
(Map p356; ☑462-7800; www.howardjohnson.com; Bionplein; r from US$70; ✳@🏊) Willemstad is lacking in decent inexpensive hotels

---

PORT OF CALL – WILLEMSTAD

Historic, picturesque and compact, Willemstad is a very popular stop for cruise ships. With a few hours in port, you can do the following:

» Wander Willemstad's Unesco-recognized streets and neighborhoods

» Learn of Curaçao's slave heritage at the Museum Kura Hulanda (p354)

» Visit beaches for sunning and snorkeling

CURAÇAO

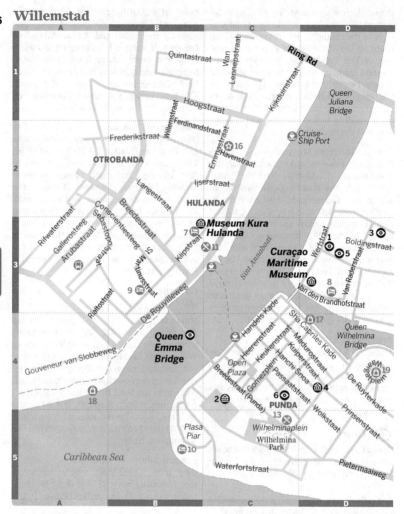

that aren't dumps. When this budget hotel opened it was a spiffy option but since then it seems to have become determined to go the route of other modest hotels locally. It could be cleaner and maintenance is long overdue. But the location and price may trump those considerations for you.

SCHARLOO

TOP CHOICE **Hotel Scharloo** HOTEL **$$**
(Map p356; ☎465-1012; www.hotelscharloo.com; Van den Brandhofstraat 12; r from US$70, ste from US$130; ❊☎) What a find! A 200-year-old trader's mansion in a historic neighborhood

has been converted into a 20-room inn. Suites on the top floor of the original building have views to the Floating Market and harbor. More-modest rooms are in a more modern wing in the rear. Some have air-con, others not; some have balconies, others not.

PISCADERA BAY

Floris Suite Hotel BOUTIQUE HOTEL **$$$**
(Map p358; ☎462-6111; www.florissuitehotel.com; John F Kennedy Blvd, Piscadera Bay; ste US$165-300; ❊@☎☎) The Floris' striking and minimalist design makes up for it not being right on the beach. The 71 rooms – more

CURAÇAO WILLEMSTAD

✖ Eating

The cafes on Wilhelminaplein are splendid for letting a pleasant hour drift past. Keep your eyes open for humble backstreet eateries serving good traditional fare. But keep your wallet closed for most of the touristy places lining the Punda side of Sint Annabaai and the Waterfront Terrace in the old walls south of the Plaza Hotel.

TOP CHOICE Plein Cafe CAFE $$
(Map p356; Wilhelminaplein 19-23, Punda; meals from NAf10; ☉7:30am-11pm; ☎) This Dutch cafe and its neighboring twin are so authentic that if it were -1°C (30°F) and raining, you'd think you were in Amsterdam. Waiters scamper among the outdoor tables with trays of drinks and dishes of simple food

like suites – are large and look out onto lush grounds with Piscadera Bay beyond. If you read *Wallpaper**, you'll feel right at home. Service wins raves from repeat guests.

Curaçao Marriott Beach Resort RESORT $$$
(Map p358; ☎736-8800; www.marriott.com; John F Kennedy Blvd, Piscadera Bay; r US$200-300; ❄@☎⊛) With its own beach on Piscadera Bay, this 247-room resort has a lush tropical feel. Rooms have decent-size balconies, and most have views of the large pool and ocean. This is the choice among the large chains on Curaçao and it has a good kids' program.

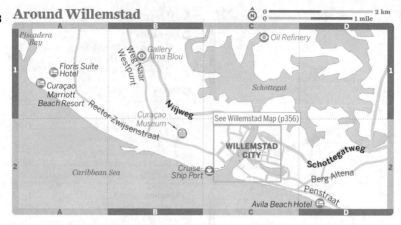

such as sandwiches (try the *frikandel*, a meaty Dutch classic).

Mundo Bizzarro
CAFE $$
(Map p356; Nieuwestraat, Pietermaai; meals US$8-16) The Addams Family goes to Havana at this eclectic cafe in the fast-gentrifying neighborhood of Pietermaai. The ground floor is open to the street and there are metal chairs outside with vivid purple cushions. Inside it's got a faux look of urban Cuban decay. Upstairs there's a bar. Food has a Creole-Cuban vibe. Latin music many nights. Good for just hanging on a sofa with a drink.

Gouverneur De Rouville
DUTCH $$
(Map p356; De Rouvilleweg 9, Otrobanda; mains US$15-25; ☺lunch & dinner, bar to 1am) The Dutch and Caribbean food served in this restored colonial building is good, but the views of Sint Annabaai are magic, especially when a huge freighter passes at night amid a carnival of colored lights. Avoid the cute but viewless courtyard; the bar is classy and has a terrace.

Museum Restaurant
FUSION $$
(Map p356; Hotel Kura Hulanda, Langestraat 8, Otrobanda; mains US$12-25; ☺lunch & dinner) An excellent casual restaurant in the grounds of the Kura Hulanda; dine under a canopy of lush tropical trees amid historic buildings. The menu is eclectic – from salads to sandwiches to pasta – with regional touches, like Cuban banana cream soup.

Sombrero
FOOD STAND $
(Map p356; Westersteeg, Scharloo; snacks under NAf6; ☺7am-11pm) Ask the name of this unsigned stand and people will point at the shape of the roof. But a sign isn't needed to find the long list of simple local street fare on offer. Sit on a plastic chair on the sidewalk, enjoy the passing parade and delight in empanadas, sandwiches and beer.

Centrum Supermarket
SUPERMARKET $
(cnr Weg Naar Westpunt & Weg Naar Bullenbaai; ☺8am-7:30pm Mon-Sat, 8am-1pm Sun) A popular large supermarket with a bakery and a deli.

🍷 Drinking

Yes, you can drink curaçao here, but note that the namesake booze of the island is now a generic term for liquor flavored with bitter oranges. For obscure reasons the concoction is often dyed a shocking shade of blue.

The Plein Cafe, Mundo Bizarro and Gouverneur De Rouville listed under Eating are good for cocktails.

Blues
BAR
(Map p358; Avila Beach Hotel, Penstraat 130; ☺5pm-11pm Tue-Sun) On a pier over the water, this swanky bar is the coolest venue in town. It has live jazz Thursday and Saturday and happy hours nightly, plus a good tapas menu.

Miles
JAZZ BAR
(Map p356; Nieuwestraat, Pietermaai; ☺5pm-2am Mon-Sat) That's Miles as in Davis, one of the inspirations for this too-funky-to-be-this-new divey nightspot in Pietermaai. Monday is open-mike night.

☆ Entertainment

Willemstad has several clubs catering to the local passion for music and dancing. Places come and go: check out the free weekly *K-Pasa*, which lists entertainment around the island. The beach-party place Wet & Wild (p360) lives up to its name on weekend nights.

Asia de Cuba
NIGHTCLUB

(Zuikertuin Mall; ☺5pm-late) Set in an open-air building at an upscale mall off Santa Rosa Weg, this hip and stylish venue morphs between being a gregarious spot for drinks and snacks with friends early in the evening to a dance venue later on. DJs and live bands play cutting-edge dance tracks.

Teatro Luna Blou
THEATER

(Map p356; ☑462-2209; www.lunablou.org; Havenstraat 2-4, Otrobanda) Offers a varying schedule of offbeat films, dance and live theater. There's a shady open-air cafe before performances.

🛍 Shopping

Real shops favored by locals are fleeing Punda for strip malls in the suburbs, leaving a lot of watch and gem vendors in their wake. Watch for huge sales on timepieces, jewelry and other luxury items. You can find some interesting items by wandering the backstreets and waterfront.

TOP CHOICE Market
MARKET

(Map p356; Waaigatplein; ☺7am-2pm Mon-Sat) Near the Floating Market, this large UFO-shaped market sells cheap household goods, snacks, produce, herbal remedies and more. Still a focus of Willemstad life.

Floating Market
MARKET

(Map p356; Sha Capriles Kade) A colorful place to see piles of papayas, melons, tomatoes and much more. The vendors sail their boats the 70km from Venezuela every morning.

Fort Riffart
MALL

(Map p356) A shadow of its former solid self, this old fort's walls have been punched out for gift shops aimed at day-trippers plowing through from the nearby cruise-ship port.

Zuikertuin Mall
MALL

This upscale suburban mall off Santa Rosa Weg has a good upscale market.

Bruna Bookstore
BOOKSTORE

(Zuikertuin Mall; ☺9am-8pm Mon-Sat) An excellent selection of books and magazines.

❶ Information

On Sundays when cruise ships are in port, many places open that are normally closed for business that day.

Botica Popular (Columbusstraat 15, Punda; ☺8am-8pm) Full-service pharmacy.

St Elisabeth Hospital (☑462-5100; www.stelisabethhospital.com; Breedestraat 193, Otrobanda; ☺24hr) Large and well equipped.

Tourist Information kiosk (☺8am-4:30pm Mon-Sat, Sun when cruise ship is in port) This kiosk by the Queen Emma Bridge on the Punda side has a wealth of information.

❶ Getting There & Around

BUS The bus network is designed to transport the local commuter; trying to cover the island north of Willemstad by bus will be an all-day affair, with a lot of waiting by the side of the road.

Two routes useful for visitors:

No 4B Links the airport to Otrobanda (20 minutes, departs hourly)

No 9A Follows the coastal road to Westpunt (one hour, every two hours)

The **bus stations** (Punda ☑465-0201, Otrobanda ☑462-8359) are near the post office in Punda and near the base of Arubastraat in Otrobanda.

Fares are NAf1.50 to NAf2 depending on distance, and services run from 7am to 9pm.

TAXI Taxis wait at large hotels; otherwise order one from **central dispatch** (☑869-0747).

WILLEMSTAD GALLERIES

Willemstad has a healthy art scene.

D'Art Gallery (Map p356; Werfstraat 6, Scharloo; ☺9am-5pm Mon-Fri) In Scharloo behind the restored mansion, Villa Maria. Specializes in contemporary styles.

Nena Sanchez Gallery (Map p356; Windstraat 15, Punda; ☺10am-6pm Mon-Sat) Displays the vibrant and colorful works of the longtime local artist.

Gallery Alma Blou (Map p358; Frater Radulphusweg 4; ☺9am-12:30pm & 2-5:30pm Mon-Sat) Located about 3km northwest of Otrobanda; has the largest collection of works by local artists. It's housed in the restored Landhuis Habaai, a Dutch plantation house from the 17th century.

Southeast of Willemstad

Residential neighborhoods make up much of the land immediately south of the center of Willemstad and there is a long beach parallel to the coast road. **Spaanse Water**, a large enclosed bay to rival Schottegat, is becoming an upscale residential area as people are drawn to its beaches and sheltered waters. There's little further south to the tip of Curaçao except arid scrub.

Curaçao Sea Aquarium   AQUARIUM
(www.curacao-sea-aquarium.com; Bapor Kibra; adult/child US$18.50/9.50; ☺8am-5pm) On a man-made island, this heavily hyped attraction anchors an entire development that includes hotels, bars and artificial beaches. The Seaquarium, as it's known, is home to over 600 marine species including sea lions, stingrays and sharks. Rather controversial is the 'Dolphin Academy' attraction, in which visitors can get in the water with mammals (from US$89). The hype encourages you to pet the porpoise. We'd rather not.

Mambo Beach   BEACH BAR $$
(Bapor Kibra; meals US$6-20; ☺9am-late) By day this ribbon of white sand is a family-friendly beach cafe and bar with a full range of beach activities (adult/child NAf6/3; not charged if you just eat and drink). By night the name takes on new and at times literal meanings as it transforms into a beach club and disco branded **Wet & Wild**. Music is provided by

---

WORTH A TRIP

CARACAS BAY ISLAND

Amid the upscale homes dotting the curving and gnarled coast and hills around Spaanse Water is Caracas Bay Island, a little isthmus dividing the inland water from the ocean. The beach may be rocky but it attracts a huge crowd at weekends. One draw is **Windsurfing Curaçao** (www.windsurfing caracao.com; rental per hr NAf30; ☺10am-5:30pm), which is right on the smooth yet breezy waters of Spaanse Water.

Another draw is **Pop's Place** (meals from NAf12; ☺10am-late), a wooden shack on the sand where you can get people-pleasers like goat stew, a burger and cold drinks. On many weekends Pop's has live music at night that inspires a beach party.

DJs and the in-house radio station (Dolphin Radio 97.3FM). The action gets frenetic after midnight from Thursdays onward, when the shadowy recesses of the beach provide cover for no end of lurid activity.

North of Willemstad

Looping around the northern part of Curaçao from Willemstad is central to any visitor's itinerary. Parks, villages and beaches all await discovery. You can do the loop in a day but if you want to spend time on any of the fine beaches you'll need two days. (Nonstop, the drive would take a little over two hours.)

Buses travel along both coasts to/from Willemstad and Westpunt about once every two hours.

KLEINE ST MICHIEL

About 6km north from Otrobanda, Kleine St Michiel is a traditional fishing village on a tiny bay. The small ruins of a 17th-century Dutch fort are on the cliffs above the water. There are a few beachfront cafes and bars. On weekends there is usually a live band playing a heady mix of Curaçaoan Creole. The place jams.

WEST COAST

There are scores of beautiful **beaches** hidden in coves along the west coast.

To head to the north end of the island via the northwest coast, take the main road, Weg Naar Westpunt (literally, 'road to Westpunt'), 8km from Willemstad to Kunuku Abao, where you turn west onto Weg Naar St Willibrordus. For 18km you drive through some of the most lush countryside in the southern Caribbean. At some points huge trees form canopies over the road. Follow signs for Soto and Lagun.

Shortly after the turn west, the road runs past old farms with thatched roofs, and salt flats with pink flamingos. The village of **St Willibrordus** is dominated by an 1880s church.

About 4km past the village, look for signs to the beautiful beach **Kas Abou**. It's another 4km down a narrow toll road (NAf10 to NAf12.50 per car), but the reward is worth it, with turquoise waters, good snorkeling and an excellent cafe-bar.

Passing through the hamlet of **Soto**, there are a couple of stores where you can stop for a cold drink. **Landhuis Groot Santa Martha** (admission NAf5; ☺8am-4pm Mon-Fri) is one of the best preserved of the

DIVING & SNORKELING IN CURAÇAO

Curaçao's reefs are home to almost 60 species of coral, much of it the hard variety. That, coupled with the 98ft (30m) visibility and the warm water, makes the island very popular with divers, especially locals. The main areas for diving are from Westpunt south to St Marie; central Curaçao up and down the coast from St Michiel; and the south, beginning at the Curaçao Sea Aquarium. The latter coast and reefs have been protected as part of the **National Underwater Park**. There are hundreds of species of fish, including reef octopus, trumpetfish, bridled burrfish and yellow goatfish.

Most resorts have relationships with dive operations. Among the better-known operators are **Discover Diving** (p361) and **Lions Dive & Beach Resort** (☑434-8888; www .lionsdive.com; Bapor Kibra).

dozens of Dutch colonial houses that dot the islands. A sugarcane plantation was started here in the 17th century to supply the rum and molasses trade. The main house dates from 1700 and is part of a large complex of relics from the era. Recent restorations have worked wonders, and the complex is now a vocational school for mentally and physically challenged people. Some produce beautiful handicrafts which are for sale.

PLAYA LAGÚN

At Lagún the coast road nears the coast and the first of many fabulous beaches. Playa Lagún is a narrow and secluded beach situated on a picture-perfect narrow cove sided with sheer rock faces. There's shade and a snack bar. Just back from the sand, **Discover Diving** (☑864-1652; www.discoverdiving.nl) rents diving and snorkeling equipment (US$9), leads tours and gives lessons. Its introductory dive for novices is a bargain at US$60.

On the north cliffs overlooking the cove, **Bahia Apartments** (☑864-1000; www.bahia -apartments.com; apt from €90; ❄@) is a modest holiday apartment complex with good views down to the beach.

About 2km on from Lagún is **Landhuis Kenepa**, the main house of another 17th-century plantation. The hilltop site is stunning, but the real importance here is that this was where a slave rebellion started in 1795. Several dozen torched their miserable huts and joined up with hundreds of others who were refusing to work. Eventually the plantation owners regained control and killed the leaders, but the event set in motion protests that continued for decades. A museum here, the **Museo Tula** (☑888-6396; adult/child US$3/1; ☉9am-4:30pm Tue-Sun), tells this story and explores the African roots of Curaçao. Call in advance to check on fascinating walking tours.

KNIP BEACHES

Playa Knip is really two beaches: **Groot Knip** (aka Kenepa Grande) is the size of a football field, while **Klein Knip** (aka Kenepa Chiki) is, well, small. Both have brilliant white sand, shady shelters, azure waters, places to rent snorkeling gear, and snack bars. Avoid weekends, when half the island shows up for a dip. Knip is just down the hill from Landhuis Kenepa.

WESTPUNT

Your journey's goal whether from the west or east; the small village of Westpunt has a beach, **Playa Kalki**, as a worthy reward. It has parking, lockers and kayak rental.

🛏 Sleeping & Eating

Kura Hulanda Lodge RESORT $$$
(☑839-3600; www.kurahulanda.com; Westpunt; r US$150-400; ❄@🛜🏊) Willemstad's excellent Hotel Kura Hulanda is behind this boutique beach resort. The grounds are a tropical garden, there's a private white-sand beach and the common areas are in thatched huts around a pool. The 74 units are in more-substantial villas and come with various view and size options. There is a dive shop on-site.

TOP CHOICE **Jaanchie's** CURAÇAOAN $
(mains US$6-15; ☉noon-8pm) Unmissable at the side of the main road. Here you can sample a full menu of island delicacies such as okra soup and goat stew. Some of the meats are rather exotic, but fear not: it all tastes like chicken. Don't worry about choosing – the waitresses will sort you out.

Playa Forti CARIBBEAN
(Westpunt; mains NAf16-35; ☉11am-9pm) Faded wedding photos of European royalty surround the cash register of this seaside restaurant with commanding views of the eponymous beach. Lots of whole-fish

dishes served in agreeably disheveled surrounds.

EAST COAST

The windward side of the island is rugged and little developed. To take this route from Willemstad, stay on Weg Naar Westpunt past the junction at Kunuku Abao as you head north. Much of the route follows the underpopulated, windswept coast

◉ Sights & Activities

TOP CHOICE **Christoffel National Park** PARK
(☎864-0363; www.christoffelpark.org; adult/child US$10/4.50; ⊙7:30am-4pm Mon-Sat, 6am-3pm Sun, last entrance 90min before closing) This 1800-hectare preserve is formed from three old plantations. The main house for one of the plantations, **Landhuis Savonet**, is at the entrance to the park. It was built in 1662 by a director of the Dutch West India Company. It's now an excellent **museum** (www.savonetmuseum.org; admission NAfl2.50) on the colonial era.

The park has two driving routes over 32km of dirt roads, and sights include cacti, orchids, iguanas, deer, wave-battered limestone cliffs and caves with ancient drawings. You can also make arrangements to **tour** (adult/child US$30/20) the park by 4WD. Christoffel is about 25km north of Willemstad.

Shete Boka National Park PARK
(admission NAf3; ⊙9am-5pm) A geologic and oceanic festival. Trails lead from a parking area right off the coast road to natural limestone bridges on the shore, sea-turtle sanctuaries, a big blowhole and isolated little beaches in narrow coves. **Boka Tabla**, a cave in the cliffs facing the water, is the most popular – and closest – walk.

🛏 Sleeping & Eating

Landhuis Daniel GUESTHOUSE **$**
(☎864-8400; www.landhuisdaniel.com; r US$50-70; ❄@🛜🏊) A lodge and restaurant run by a Dutch family. The eight rooms are basic

---

PRACTICALITIES

» **Electricity** 110V, 60Hz; US-style two- and three-pin plugs are used; a few resorts catering to Europeans have 220V EU-style sockets.

» **Media** Of the many free tourist publications, two are essential: *Cityguide Willemstad* and *Curacao Traveler*.

» **Weights & Measures** Metric system.

(some fan only), but the pool and gardens have country charm. The all-day restaurant (mains US$8 to US$20) has a menu of local, Creole and French dishes prepared with ingredients from the organic garden. Kids love all 25 types of pancake. Just beyond the turn for the west coast, look east for the orchid- and bougainvillea-lined entrance.

UNDERSTAND CURAÇAO

History

Curaçao was home to the Arawaks until the Spanish laid claim in 1499. Origins of the island's name are lost: one story links it to the name of an Arawak tribe, while another (more improbably) says that it derives from the Spanish *curación* (cure), as several sailors were cured of illness on the island.

Either way, the arrival of the Spanish proved the opposite of a cure for the locals, who were soon carted off to work elsewhere in the empire or killed. The Dutch West India Company arrived in 1634, and so did slavery, commerce and trade. Half the slaves destined for the Caribbean passed through the markets of Curaçao. Many of the plantation houses have been restored and can be visited, including Landhuis Kenepa, which has displays on Curaçao's African heritage.

Slavery Ends

The end of slavery and colonialism sent Curaçao into a 19th-century economic decline. Subsistence aloe and orange farming provided a meager living for most. Oil refineries to process Venezuelan oil were built in the early 20th century and this fuelled the economy. Relative affluence and Dutch political stability have made Curaçao a regional center for commerce and banking. Tourism and a growing expat population provide additional income. In 2010, with the dissolution of the Netherlands Antilles, Curaçao became an independent entity within the Netherlands.

Culture

Curaçao was populated by African slaves, but the cultural roots today are a mix of Afro-Caribbean, Latin American and European. Willemstad is, at different times, relaxed, frenetic and buttoned-down. The population is growing and there's money to be made. In the country, increasingly the home of commuters, traditional ways of life are fading.

Landscape & Wildlife

Curaçao is a mix of lush areas near the coasts and more arid regions inland. Human development has meant that wildlife is mostly limited to birds, although the reefs offshore are rich with marine life.

The main environmental issue is air and water pollution from the Venezuelan-run oil refinery and other industry on the inner harbor (Schottegat) of Willemstad. Given the importance of these installations to the local economy, efforts to control their negative effects are modest at best. The growing traffic problem and exhaust-spewing diesels mean that getting stuck in a traffic jam is both a possibility and very unpleasant.

SURVIVAL GUIDE

Directory A–Z

Accommodations

Curaçao has the most varied range of places to stay, with some interesting nonbeach choices in Willemstad. Camping is uncommon. High-season prices usually run mid-December to mid-April.

Hotel taxes and fees are 7% room tax plus 12% service charge.

$	budget	less than US$75
$$	midrange	US$75 to US$200
$$$	top end	more than $200

Business Hours

The following are standard business hours across the island. Exceptions are noted in specific listings. Outside of tourist areas, much is closed on Sunday.

Banks 9am-4pm Mon-Fri

Restaurants 11am-9pm

Shops 9am-6pm Mon-Sat

Festivals & Events

Two events to plan your trip around:

Carnival (January or February) This is a big deal on the islands, especially Curaçao,

where a packed schedule of fun begins right after New Year's Day.

Séu Parade (Easter Monday) Curaçao's 'Feast of the Harvest' features parades replete with lots of folk music and dancing. People in rural areas go a little nuts.

Food

The following price categories for the cost of a main course are used in the Eating listings in this chapter.

$	budget	less than US$10
$$	midrange	US$10 to US$25
$$$	top end	more than US$25

Gay & Lesbian Travelers

Curaçao is tolerant of homosexuality; gays and lesbians should expect little trouble.

Health

There are good medical facilities in Curaçao. Tap water is safe to drink.

Language

If you only speak English, you won't have a problem on Curaçao. While Dutch and Papiamento are the official languages, many people speak English.

Money

You can pay for just about everything in US dollars in touristed areas of Curaçao. At the time of writing, the Netherlands Antillean guilder (NAf) was official currency, but plans were being debated to switch to either US dollars, or use a new currency, the Caribbean guilder (CMg). A decision could be made by 2012, later or not at all. Check on the latest currency news before you travel; prices in this chapter are given in NAf where applicable.

A 15% tip, often added to the bill, is customary in restaurants; in taxis 10% is the norm.

Public Holidays

In addition to those observed throughout the region (p872), Curaçao has the following public holidays:

Carnival Monday Monday before Ash Wednesday

Queen's Birthday April 30

Labour Day May 1

Ascension Day Sixth Thursday after Easter

Flag Day July 2

Telephone

Curaçao's country code is ☏599; the area code is ☏9.

To call out from Curaçao to any country with a country code of ☏1, just dial 1 and the local number. To reach other countries, dial the international access code ☏00 + country code + the number.

To dial Curaçao from another country, dial the country's international access code + ☏599 + 9 + the local number. Within Curaçao there is no need to dial the area code.

CELL PHONES

GSM cell phones are compatible with local SIM cards. There is also 3G service. The main operator is **Digicel** (www.digicelcuracao.com).

Getting There & Away

Entering Curaçao

All visitors need a passport and a return or onward ticket to enter Curaçao.

Air

Hato International Airport (www.curacao-airport.com) receives international flights. It has a modern terminal with a few cafes and shops after security.

Departure tax (international US$35, Aruba and Bonaire US$9) is included in some tickets but not others.

The following airlines serve Curaçao from these cities (some services are seasonal):

American Airlines (www.aa.com) Miami

Avianca (www.avianca.com) Bogota

DAE (www.flydae.com) Aruba, Bonaire

Delta (www.delta.com) Atlanta

Insel Air (www.fly-inselair.com) Aruba, Bonaire

KLM (www.klm.com) Amsterdam

LIAT (www.liat.com) Trinidad

Tiara Air (www.tiara-air.com) Aruba

United (www.united.com) Newark

Sea

CRUISE SHIPS

Curaçao is part of cruise-ship itineraries that cover the southern Caribbean, often on longer 10-day and two-week trips.

Many cruise ships call in Curaçao. Boats dock directly at the cruise-ship port, which is just outside the stunning natural harbor in Willemstad.

Getting Around

The best part of a Curaçao visit is exploring the island. You'll want to have your own transport.

To/From the Airport

Hotels and resorts usually do not do airport pickups. The taxi fare to Willemstad is about US$25.

Bicycle

Although there are no bike lanes on Curaçao, many people enjoy riding along the beautiful coast roads. You can rent bikes at many resorts. Note that traffic around Willemstad can be perilous.

Bus

Travelling to far-flung parts of the island will require careful planning. See p359 for details on Curaçao's public bus network.

Car & Motorcycle

Driving is on the right-hand side, seat belts are required and motorcyclists must use helmets.

Main roads are generally in pretty good condition; there's nowhere you're likely to go that would require a 4WD. Gasoline is easily found; road signs are sporadic.

RENTAL

All of the major international rental firms have affiliates at the airport.

For whatever reasons, we see more problems with car rentals on Curaçao than most other places. Not on the roads either but at the start and end of rentals. No company seems immune from frequent delays and inexplicable slowness that endlessly frustrate the traveler hoping to get to their hotel or the person needing to catch a flight. For whatever the reason, assume that your counter time will take 20 minutes or more, coming and going.

Taxi

Taxis wait at the airport and large hotels. Most now have meters. For a taxi, call ☏869-0747.

Caribbean Rhythms

Beaches »
Caribbean Cuisine »
Diving & Snorkeling »
Sounds of the Caribbean »
Wildlife »
Pirates, Forts & Ruins »
Festivals »
Hidden Caribbean »

Palm-dotted beach at Punta Cana (p420), Dominican Republic

Beaches

Like Paris and art or Arizona and canyons, when you think of the Caribbean, you think beaches. Alluring beaches in Jamaica, perfect beaches in Grand Cayman, lost beaches in the Bahamas and unspoiled beaches in the Grenadines all await.

Grace Bay Beach, Caicos

1 This stretch of snow-white sand is perfect for relaxing, swimming and forgetting about home. Though it's dotted with resorts, its sheer size means that finding your own square of paradise is a snap (p812).

Marigot Bay, St Lucia

2 Marigot Bay is a stunning example of natural architecture. Sheltered by towering palms and surrounding hills, the narrow inlet hid the British fleet from French pursuers. Today it hides a fabulous beach (p706).

Seven Mile Beach, Grand Cayman

3 Walk the length of this beach, straight out of central casting, and see if it measures up – literally. Enjoy swimming, sunbathing and water sports galore on Grand Cayman's superb stretch of white sand (p276).

Shoal Bay East, Anguilla

4 Got a fantasy of an idyllic white-sand beach? You've just pictured Shoal Bay East, a 2-mile-long beach with pristine sand, reefs ideal for snorkeling, and glassy turquoise water (p99).

Les Salines, Martinique

5 Les Salines is probably Martinique's finest beach. The gorgeous long stretch of golden sand lures French tourists and local families alike, but it never seems crowded (p586).

Clockwise from top left
1. Grace Bay Beach 2. Marigot Bay 3. Seven Mile Beach 4. Shoal Bay

Caribbean Cuisine

Caribbean cuisine blends fruits and rice, seafood and spice, to create flavours as vibrant as the colors of the islands.

A fish still dripping with saltwater, thrown on the grill and spritzed with lime, has made many a Caribbean travel memory. So too has a tasty lobster, grilled over coals and then drenched in garlic butter.

As for meat, chicken rules the roost. Mixed with rice, it's called *arroz con pollo* in the Spanish-speaking islands and *pelau* in Trinidad and St Kitts. Other favorites are roast pork *(lechón asado)*, which features in Cuban and Puerto Rican sandwiches; and goat *(cabrito)*, a southern staple.

Tropical fruits are Caribbean icons. There are the usual suspects, like papaya, but be sure to sample sugar apple – a custardy fruit shot through with black pits – in the Bahamas *(anon* in Cuba); or *guinep*, a small lychee-like fruit, in Jamaica.

Minty mojitos and lemony daiquiris in Cuba, sugary ti-punch in Martinique and the smooth and fruity goombay smash in the Bahamas are just some of the drinks on offer. It's no surprise that all of these contain rum: the Caribbean makes the world's best, and while some venture no further than a regular old Cuba libre (rum and cola) or piña colada, a highball of exquisite seven-year-old *añejo* over ice, sipped as the sun sets, is liquid heaven.

FOODIE FAVORITES

» **Pepperpot** Antigua's national dish is a hearty stew of meat and vegetables and is found in many variations across the region

» **Roti** A tasty and ubiquitous south-Asian-derived flat bread filled with curried meats, vegetables and more

» **Mofongo** A plantain crust encases seafood or steak in this Puerto Rican classic

» **Callaloo** Spicy soup with okra, meats, greens and hot peppers

Clockwise from top
1. Preparing mojitos, Havana 2. Tropical fruit, Martinique
3. Grilled lobster on the beach, Jamaica

HOLGER LEUE/LONELY PLANET IMAGES ©

RODERICK CHEN/CORBIS

Diving & Snorkeling

Few places in the world offer such perfect conditions for underwater exploration, with a wonderfully diverse range of dive sites. You'll find shallow fringing reefs, coral-covered pinnacles and remnants of ancient shipwrecks.

British Virgin Islands

1 Fleeing a hurricane in 1867, the British steamship RMS *Rhone* was driven ashore. Preserved since the 1970s, it is one of the Caribbean's best wreck dives (p248).

Cayman Islands

2 Bloody Bay Marine Park on Little Cayman is the pick of the dive spots in the Cayman Islands, although both Grand Cayman and Cayman Brac also have fantastic dives and plenty of exciting wrecks to explore (p285).

Saba

3 A hidden marine jungle of fluorescent coral lurks deep beneath Saba's offshore moorings. Protected by strict environmental laws, this pristine habitat teems with sharks, sea turtles, rays and barracuda (p637).

Bonaire

4 Almost the entire coast of Bonaire is ringed by some of the healthiest coral reefs in the region. The Unesco-recognized shore reefs are part of the national marine park and most can be reached in simple shore dives (p231).

Guadeloupe

5 It's said that divers will have good dives for the rest of their lives if they pat the head of the Jacques Cousteau statue in the namesake underwater reserve in Guadeloupe (p491). True or not, the diving is incredible.

GREG JOHNSTON/LONELY PLANET IMAGES ©

ERNEST MANEWAL/LONELY PLANET IMAGES ©

Clockwise from top left
1. Diver swimming through a cave, British Virgin Islands
2. Wreck diving, Cayman Islands 3. Turtle encounter, Saba 4. Orange cup coral, Bonaire

Sounds of the Caribbean

From the brassy swagger of a salsa band to the lolling gait of reggae, the music of the Caribbean draws influences from both plantation fields and colonial parlors, and is as elemental to the islands as the sound of crashing surf.

Steel Pan & Calypso

1 Hammered from oil barrels, the ringing drums of steel-pan bands are a testament to the adaptive ingenuity of Caribbean muse. The drums play buoyant calypso, often punched up with braggadocio lyrics or laced with social commentary.

Reggae

2 Born in the late '60s, reggae is the musical descendant of uniquely Jamaican genres ska and rocksteady. With a languid off-beat shuffle and an ambassador in Bob Marley, it's a cornerstone of island culture.

Cuban Music

3 Though every destination has its own musical language, no place speaks as fluently as Cuba, where music seems to pour out of every alleyway.

Salsa

4 Like trade winds circling Puerto Rico, the Dominican Republic, Cuba and Nueva York, salsa's hip-grinding groove is a prized multi-island export. The sound has roots in African rhythms and indigenous islander instruments.

Merengue

5 The blistering rhythms of this Dominican genre of music are inseparable from the highly stylized, passionate dance bearing the same name.

Clockwise from top left
1. Steel drum **2.** Statue at the Bob Marley Museum, Jamaica **3.** Maracas for sale at market, Cuba.

MARLEY ROAD

2

Wildlife

If you're anxious to behold the Caribbean's richest fauna, you're going to get wet and you're going to see coral. Fish pecking away at nutritious tidbits or hiding out in coral reefs include the iridescent Creole wrasse, groupers, kingfish, sergeant majors and angelfish. Hang – or float – around and you might see inflatable porcupine fish, barracuda, nurse sharks, octopus, moray eels and manta rays.

Other species to seek out include pilot, sperm, blue and humpback whales, famous for their acrobatic breaching from January to March. Spinner, spotted and bottlenosed dolphins, and loggerhead, green, hawksbill and leatherback turtles are common sights for divers. Manatees or sea cows – herbivorous marine mammals so ugly they're cute – are found in waters around Cuba, the Dominican Republic, Haiti, Jamaica and Puerto Rico.

Apart from iguanas – especially Grand Cayman's spectacular blue variety – native land animals have largely vanished from Caribbean islands. Responsibility is shared between humans and other introduced species, including goats, cats, dogs and monkeys. Trinidad, home to 100 types of mammal, is the big exception.

Hundreds of bird species, both endemic and migratory, frequent scores of islands. Look for iconic pink flamingos in the Bahamas and Bonaire. Rainforests on islands like Dominica and St Vincent are home to all manner of colorful native birds.

Parrots in a profusion of colors are found on almost any island with forests. From jade green to iridescent yellow, they are always crowd-pleasers and the focus of many a daytime jungle hike. Spotting Dominica's two indigenous species is popular. While exploring Dominica's dense rainforests you'll likely see many other species in what is the region's best island for watching wildlife.

Clockwise from top
1. Green iguana, Bonaire 2. Dolphin in the Caribbean Sea
3. Flamingo, Curaçao

Pirates, Forts & Ruins

The Caribbean has a bounty of booty for pirate fans. Old forts and other crumbling ruins recall the days when sailing-ship dramas played out on the high seas.

Port Royal, Jamaica

1 A dilapidated, ramshackle place of tropical lassitude, today's funky fishing hamlet was once the pirate capital of the Caribbean. Later, it was the hub of British naval power in the West Indies. There are fascinating historic sites here, including old Fort Charles (p533).

Old San Juan

2 Two Unesco World Heritage forts are a commanding presence in Old San Juan. Secrets and surprises wait around every ancient corner, all in the huge shadow of 16th-century Fuertes San Felipe del Morro (El Morro) (p604) and San Cristóbal (p605).

Brimstone Hill Fortress, St Kitts

3 More than 8000 French troops fought with 1000 British troops for a month in order to seize Brimstone Hill Fortress. This amazing Unesco World Heritage fort has views north, west and south across the Caribbean (p683).

St Vincent

4 You can walk the very beaches and bay where much of the first *Pirates of the Caribbean* was filmed. Although the sets are fading away like old buccaneers, the small village and bay of Wallilabou is still recognizable (p745).

Île-à-Vache, Haiti

5 About 15km off the coast of Les Cayes, Île-à-Vache was the hideout in 1668 of Captain Morgan, the Welsh pirate who looted every Spanish galleon he saw. Today it's home to some good resorts (p516).

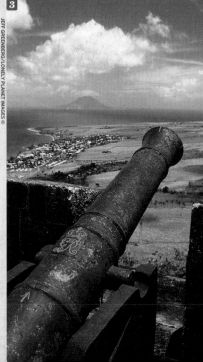

Clockwise from top
1. Courtyard of Fort Charles, Port Royal 2. Walls at Fuerte San Cristóbal, Old San Juan 3. View from a cannon at Brimstone Hill Fortress, St Kitts

ANTHONY PIDGEON/LONELY PLANET IMAGES ©

JEFF GREENBERG/LONELY PLANET IMAGES ©

Festivals

No matter which Caribbean island you land on, you'll quickly discover one thing: everybody loves to party. Any time of year, come rain or shine, you'll find plenty of live music, dancing in the streets and countless reasons to celebrate.

Carnival, Trinidad

1 Preparing for the Caribbean's biggest street party is a year-long affair in Trinidad. Steel-pan and calypso competitions, elaborate costumes, mud-covered revelers, and blasting soca music are all part of the wild and spirited Carnival scene (p770).

Junkanoo, the Bahamas

2 A frenzied party of dance, music and colorful costumes rolls into Nassau on Boxing Day (December 26). This is the Bahamas' high-energy national festival, where many marchers compete fiercely to put on the best performance (p164).

Crop-Over Festival, Barbados

3 This big festival marks the end of the sugarcane harvest. Over three weeks, beginning in mid-July, there are calypso competitions, fairs and more, finishing with a costume parade and fireworks on Kadooment Day in August (p220).

Pirates Week, Grand Cayman

4 What with the pirate craze that's swept the US, this extravaganza on Grand Cayman inspires many a trip south. Mock battles, planks that get walked and a booty of bad pirate jokes are among the pleasures (p31).

Reggae Sumfest, Jamaica

5 Rastas and Marley followers gather in Montego Bay for Jamaica's top reggae festival, held in July. Highlights include 50 world-class reggae artists, a beach party and four theme nights (p546).

Clockwise from top
1. Celebrating Carnival in Trinidad **2.** Color and music at Junkanoo, the Bahamas **3.** Costumed reveler at the Crop-Over Festival, Barbados

Hidden Caribbean

While more than 90% of the Caribbean's 7000 islands are minute and uninhabited, these are largely inaccessible to the average traveler. But there is a small club of islands well off the tourist track that are *almost* uninhabited, offering the adventurous traveler the kind of escape many dream about.

Little Cayman

1 Little Cayman (p283) has a population that barely cracks three figures – and that's the iguanas. Come here for some of the world's best wall diving.

Mayreau

2 A double crescent of perfect beaches awaits on Mayreau (p752), an island near the southern end of the Grenadines. The killer diving at Tobago Cays is nearby and it's possible to rent a room in a home.

Anegada

3 The nicknames of Anegada (p255) say it all: 'Mysterious Virgin' and 'Ghost Cay.' Hang your hammock in this magical, remote bit of sand in the British Virgin Islands.

Barbuda

4 Frigate birds outnumber humans on Barbuda (p120), an island that's happy to remain in the shadow of Antigua. Some beach cottages can only be reached by boat.

Petit Martinique

5 Grenada itself isn't exactly on the beaten path, and its island of Petit Martinique (p466) is almost unknown. The little beach here is just 10 minutes by foot from the guesthouses serving the island.

Right
1. Yellow tube sponges at Bloody Bay wall (p285), Little Cayman **2.** Afloat on the waters of Saltwhistle Bay (p752), Mayreau

MICHAEL LAWRENCE/LONELY PLANET IMAGES ©

KARL WEATHERLY/CORBIS

Dominica

Best Beaches

» Batibou Bay (p396)

» Champagne Beach (p392)

» Point Baptiste Beach (p397)

» Mero Beach (p393)

Best Places to Stay

» Jacoway Inn (p397)

» Pagua Bay House (p398)

» Silks Hotel (p398)

» River Rush Eco Retreat (p398)

» Cocoa Cottages (p390)

Why Go?

On Dominica, nature has been as creative and prolific as Picasso in his prime. Much of this volcanic island is blanketed by untamed rainforest that embraces you with the loft and grandeur of a Gothic cathedral. Experiences await that will forever etch themselves into your memory: an intense trek to a bubbling lake, soothing your muscles in hot sulfur springs, getting pummeled by a waterfall, snorkeling in a glass of 'champagne', swimming up a narrow gorge – the list of possible ecoadventures goes on.

In many ways, Dominica is the 'anti-Caribbean' island. It has been spared the mass tourism, in large part because there are very few sandy beaches, no flashy resorts and no direct international flights. The locals are so friendly that they often stop visitors just to wish them a good visit. Just as uniquely, Dominica is also home to about 2200 Caribs, the only pre-Columbian population remaining in the eastern Caribbean.

When to Go

Temperatures average between 75°F (24°C) and 86°F (30°C) year-round, with cooler temperatures in the mountains. There are short bursts of rainfall all year long. February to June, the island's driest months, are the most popular. The rainy season lasts from July to late October, almost coinciding with the Caribbean's hurricane season (peaks in August and September).

Dominica's Carnival celebrations run for two weeks prior to Ash Wednesday. In October, Roseau hosts the World Creole Music Festival. The week leading up to Independence Day (November 3), or Creole Day, is a vibrant celebration of local heritage.

» **Currency** Eastern Caribbean dollar (EC$); US dollars widely accepted

» **Language** English

» **Money** Outside of Roseau and Portsmouth, ATMs are thin on the ground. Currency dispensed is EC dollars.

» **Visas** Not required for citizens of the US, EU and Commonwealth for stays of under 21 days

Fast Facts

» **Area** 290 sq miles

» **Population** 70,400

» **Capital** Roseau

» **Telephone country code** ☑767

» **Emergency** ☑999

Set Your Budget

» **Budget hotel room** US$40

» **Two-course evening meal** EC$50

» **Museum entrance** EC$5 to EC$12

» **Beer** EC$5

» **Bus ticket** EC$1.50 to EC$12

Resources

» **Discover Dominica** (www.dominica.dm)

» **Visit Dominica** (www.visit-dominica.com)

» **Lennox Honychurch** (www.lennoxhonychurch.com) Cultural resources and history

» **A Virtual Dominica** (www.avirtualdominica.com)

Itineraries

THREE DAYS

Dominica in a nutshell: on day one drive south from Melville Airport via spectacular Pagua Bay through the Carib Territory to Roseau, briefly stopping for a dip in the grotto of shimmering Emerald Pool. Spend the next day's morning exploring Roseau, then head east to marvel at Trafalgar Falls, swim in Titou Gorge and soak in a hot sulfur spring at a Wotten Waven spa. Spend your final day driving north along the West Coast, stopping for a short rainforest hike to see endangered parrots in the Syndicate Parrot Reserve. In Portsmouth, follow in the footsteps of Caribs and Johnny Depp while rowing through the messy jungle of the Indian River. Head east and spend your final night in Calibishie.

ONE WEEK

Stretch the three-day itinerary into a saner five days. Use the extra time for the spectacular hike to Boiling Lake, soaking up Roseau's vibrant culture in more depth, snorkeling or diving in Champagne Reef and exploring Cabrits National Park near Portsmouth.

GETTING TO NEIGHBORING ISLANDS

There are regular ferries from Dominica to Guadeloupe, Martinique and St Lucia. LIAT flies to Antigua, Barbados and Guadeloupe.

Essential Food & Drink

» **Callaloo** A creamy thick soup or stew blending a variety of vegetables (eg dasheen, spinach, kale, onions, carrots, eggplant, garlic, okra) with coconut milk and sometimes crab or ham.

» **Fresh fruit** Dominica grows all sorts of fruit, including bananas, coconuts, papayas, guavas and pineapples, and mangoes so plentiful they litter the roadside in places.

» **Sea moss** Nonalcoholic beverage made from seaweed mixed with sugar and spices and sometimes with evaporated milk. It's sold in supermarkets and at snackettes.

» **Kubuli** Dominica uses the island's natural spring water for its home-grown beer label; you'll see red-and-white signs all over the island with Kubuli's concise slogan – 'The Beer We Drink.'

» **Macoucherie** Rum connoisseurs crave this local concoction. Don't be fooled by the plastic bottles or cheap-looking label, it's an undiscovered gem.

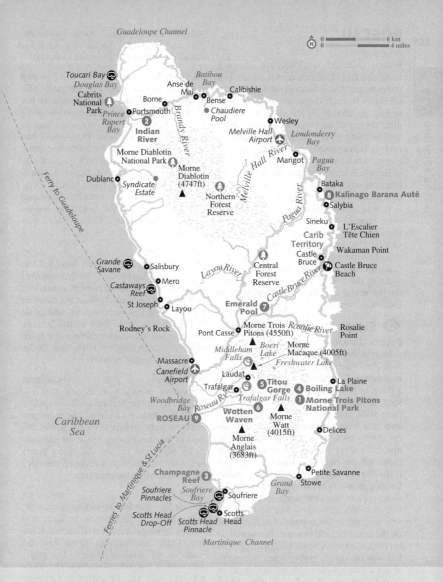

Dominica Highlights

1 Count the shades of green amid the breathtaking scenery of **Morne Trois Pitons National Park** (p390)

2 Experience the watery side of the jungle on a silent glide down the **Indian River** (p394)

3 Play in the bubbles of **Champagne Reef** (p392),

Dominica's star underwater attraction

4 Take an unforgettable hike to **Boiling Lake** (p390)

5 Swim to a waterfall in the canyon of **Titou Gorge** (p391)

6 Relax in the natural hot sulfur springs at **Wotten Waven** (p389)

7 Take a refreshing dip into crystal-clear **Emerald Pool** (p399)

8 Find out about native Caribs at the **Kalinago Barana Autê** heritage village (p399)

9 Soak up the baffling bustle, beauty and history of **Roseau** (p384)

ROSEAU

POP 15,000

Roseau (*rose*-oh) is Dominica's compact, noisy, chaotic but vibrant capital, situated on the coast and the Roseau River. Reggae music blares through the narrow streets while people zip around in the daytime, but at night the city all but empties. Roseau's streets are lined with historic stone-and-wood buildings in states ranging from ramshackle to elegant. Look closely and you'll spot a blend of French, English and Spanish architectural elements, such as porticoes, louvers, hurricane shutters and overhanging verandas.

Roseau is best explored on foot, especially since many sights are clustered around the cruise-ship dock along Dame Eugenia Charles Blvd (also known as Bayfront). The most historic section is the French Quarter, south of bustling King George V St. Just south of the center, along the coastal road, are the 'suburbs' of Newtown, Citronier and Castle Comfort.

◉ Sights

Botanic Gardens   GARDEN

(www.da-academy.org/dagardens.html; ☺6am-7pm) The beautiful 40-acre botanic gardens in northern Roseau were created in 1889 as a place to propagate crop seedlings for the local farmers. Today, the sprawling grounds teem with mature banyan, century palms and ficus trees along with flowering tropical shrubs such as orchids and African tulips. It's a great place for a wander and a picnic on the expansive lawns. A must-see is the **Parrot Conservation and Research Centre**, an aviary housing rare Jaco and Sisserou parrots, the two parrot species found in Dominica's rainforests. The most bizarre site, however, is the **memorial** to Hurricane David: a rusting yellow school bus squashed beneath a giant African baobab tree. The bus was thankfully empty when the hurricane's 150mph winds ravaged the island in 1979. It's adjacent to the Forest Office, which has brochures describing the island's parks and trails. **'Jack's Walk'**, the short but steep and winding half-mile trail to the top of Morne Bruce starts behind the aviary.

Old Market   SQUARE

This cobblestone plaza has been the center of action in Roseau for the last 300 years. It's been the site of political meetings, farmers markets and, more ominously, public executions and a slave market. Nowadays it's a big souvenir stall hawking T-shirts, handicrafts, rum and everything Rasta. JB's Juice Bar across the way makes awesome smoothies.

Dominica Museum   MUSEUM

(Bayfront near King George V St; admission US$2; ☺9am-4pm Mon-Fri, to noon Sat) This small but interesting museum gives an overview of the history of Dominica and its people. Besides pictures of a young Jean Rhys, you'll find Native American artifacts, including stone axes and other tools, *adornos* (Arawak clay figurines) and a gommier dugout. Informative displays delve into Carib lifestyles, Creole culture and the slave trade. Old photos and drawings trace the history of Roseau from a swampy marsh to the island's biggest city.

Public Market   MARKET

(☺6am-6pm Mon, Wed & Fri, 6am-5pm Tue & Thu, 4am-6pm Sat) This bustling riverfront market is a good place to have a bowl of goat water, pick up a bottle of sea moss or put together a picnic from the loads of fruit, vegetables and spices brought in fresh by the farmers. A conch shell sounds every time a new batch of fresh fish arrives. It's busiest on Friday night and Saturday morning.

Morne Bruce   NEIGHBORHOOD

Dominica's president is among the residents of this rather exclusive hillside enclave above the Botanic Gardens. The main reason to venture up here is for the panoramic vista of Roseau. Pick up either the half-mile Jack's Walk trail behind the parrot aviary in the Botanic Garden or drive up the steep road just south of the cemetery.

Public Library   HISTORIC SITE

(Victoria St; ☺8am-6pm Mon-Fri, to noon Sat; ☎) This handsome 1906 stone building was funded by US philanthropist Andrew Carnegie. Enjoy sweeping sea views from the wrap-around porch or relax in the grassy area with a few stone benches. The white mansion with the expansive lawn across the street is the **State House**, used by the government for official receptions. The government meets in the adjacent **Assembly Building**.

St George's Anglican Church   CHURCH

(cnr Victoria St & Turkey Lane) Opposite Fort Young, this gray 19th-century stone church was left with only its shell standing in 1979 after Hurricane David ripped off the original roof. The new roof is now made of tin.

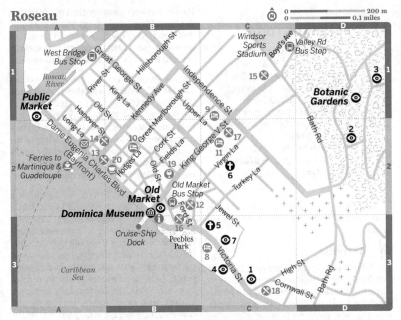

Roseau

St Patrick's Catholic Cathedral   CHURCH
(Virgin Lane) Gothic meets Caribbean at this 19th-century landmark cathedral. The upper windows are stained glass, but much like a typical Creole home, the lower windows are wooden shutters that open for natural ventilation.

Old Mill Cultural Center   VENUE
(☏449-1804; Canefield) A short drive north of Roseau, this old sugar mill has taken on new

ROSEAU ON FOOT

For an in-depth tour, pick up the handy *Walking Tour of Historic Roseau* illustrated leaflet put together by the **Society for Heritage, Architecture, Preservation & Enhancement** (SHAPE; www.shape.dm). It costs US$5 (EC$12.50) and is available at the tourist office and such places as the Talipot Cafe & Gallery (p387) and the Cocorico Café (p387). The website has a free 30-minute podcast.

life as Dominica's main centre for cultural events and also displays the work of local artists.

Activities

The following dive shops are both in Castle Comfort, 1 mile south of central Roseau along the coastal road. Both also run whale-watching tours for US$50. Cetacean sightings are most common between November and March.

Anchorage Dive Center   DIVING
(☎448-2638; www.anchoragehotel.dm; Anchorage Hotel; 1-/2-tank dive US$55/75)

Dive Dominica   DIVING
(☎448-2188; www.divedominica.com; Castle Comfort Lodge; 1-/2-tank dive US$55/90) The island's oldest dive shop.

Tours

Ken's Hinterland Adventure Tours   TOURS
(☎448-4850; www.khattstours.com; Fort Young Hotel, Victoria St) Ken has shown the sights to Mick Jagger and the likes. He offers a wide variety of tours, including a snorkeling tour (US$65), hikes to Boiling Lake (US$50) and other destinations, birdwatching in the Syndicate rainforest (US$60) and waterfalls tours (from US$35). Ken also rents snorkeling gear (US$10) and runs dive trips (one-/two-tank dives US$62/103).

Sleeping

CENTRAL ROSEAU

Fort Young Hotel   HOTEL $$
(☎448-5000; www.fortyounghotel.com; Victoria St; r US$115-250; ❃@🛜🏊) The old cannons that decorate this full-service 71-room hotel are a testament to its origin as an 18th-century fort. Now, it's the swankiest option in town –

the oceanfront rooms are the best, with stylish furnishings, dark wood floors, big baths and balconies. Cheaper ones have no or limited ocean views. There are wheelchair-accessible rooms and a spa for chill-seekers.

Sutton Place Hotel   HOTEL $$
(☎449-8700; www.suttonplacehoteldominica.com; 25 Old St; s/d US$75/95, ste s/d US$105/135, all incl breakfast; ❃@🛜) Roseau's answer to a boutique hotel, this place strikes a good balance between style and comfort. Many of the rooms have four-poster beds and the suites have kitchenettes. The bar in the stone cellar recalls the building's 19th-century pedigree.

Narakiel's Inn   GUESTHOUSE $
(☎276-3652, in the US ☎877-281-4529; http://narakielsinn.com; r US$68-88; ❃🛜) This new five-room property in a converted apartment on the Roseau River offers great value for money. Quality furnishings and decor characterize the rooms, which, despite being petite, pack in more amenities than most four-star hotels, including a fully furnished kitchen with oven, fridge, microwave and coffeemaker. Smoking is only allowed on the shared riverfacing balcony. To get here, follow Independence St north across the river and make an immediate right.

Ma Bass Central Guest House   GUESTHOUSE $
(☎448-2999; 44 Fields Lane; s/d US$55/60; ❃) One of the best deals in Roseau. The friendly owner, Theresa Emanuel (better known as Ma Bass), earned her name from the medical students who stayed with her before she converted her home into a proper guesthouse. She keeps the place clean and goes out of her way to make guests feel at home.

Syme-Zee's Hotel   GUESTHOUSE $
(☎448-2494; symeszee@aol.com; 34 King George V St; r without/with air-con US$48/62; ❃) Above a popular restaurant-bar, this barebones abode has eight rooms, three of which have air-conditioning. The street-facing lounge has a balcony and TV.

CASTLE COMFORT

About 1 mile south of Roseau along the coastal road, Castle Comfort has a row of somewhat worn oceanfront hotels (no beach) catering primarily to divers.

Anchorage Hotel   HOTEL $$
(☎448-2638; www.anchoragehotel.dm; d incl breakfast US$110-145; ❃🛜🏊) With an on-site restaurant, dive school and whale-watching

trips, this place has it all – including the skeleton of a giant sperm whale in the bar. Rooms are simple but well appointed and have either sea-facing windows or a balcony. The Ocean Terrace is a casual seaside dining room and lounge with Thursday night BBQ, pizza night on Wednesday and happy-hour sunset drinks every day.

Evergreen Hotel
HOTEL **$$**

(☎448-3288; www.evergreenhoteldominica.com; d incl breakfast US$117-156; ❉🌐❄) This family-run hotel has spacious grounds, a nice pool, a pretty restaurant and a cool barman. Alas, the smallish rooms are getting a bit long on the tooth. The nicest are in the detached lodge (called the Honeymoon Hut).

Castle Comfort Lodge
INN **$$**

(☎448-2188; www.castlecomfortdivelodge.com; 4-/7-night package US$735/1210; ❉🌐) This dedicated dive lodge rents its 14 rooms as part of dive packages only. Rates include breakfast, two-tank boat dives, airport transfers and free sea kayaks and unlimited offshore diving. Dive Dominica is the onsite dive shop. Nondivers can stay at reduced rates (four/seven nights US$556/850).

 ## Eating

 Talipot Cafe & Gallery
INTERNATIONAL **$$**

(☎276-3747; www.talipotgallery.com; 11 Victoria St; mains US$10-30; ⊙lunch Mon-Fri, dinner Wed-Sat; 🌐) Art, wine and food form a happy blend at this Canadian-run eatery in historic Palm Cottage that doubles as a gallery. The kitch-

en gives the gourmet treatment to such local dishes as goat curry, coconut shrimp, pumpkin soup or panfried kingfish. Gobble it up while sitting on the veranda with glorious views of the sea.

Pearl's
TAKEAWAY, RESTAURANT **$**

(50 King George V St; snacks EC$8-20, lunch buffet EC$40; ⊙9am-6pm Mon-Sat) It's old-school, beloved for over two decades and one of the best places in town for authentic local fare like callaloo soup and salted codfish. The takeaway has sandwiches, chicken and fish, while the upstairs restaurant is famous for its coma-inducing lunch buffet. Grab a seat on the balcony overlooking the King George V St bustle.

Cocorico Café
FRENCH-CREOLE **$$**

(☎449-8686; www.natureisle.com/cocorico; cnr Dame Eugenia Charles Blvd & Kennedy Ave; sandwiches EC$12-20, mains EC$23-46; ⊙8:30am-4:30pm Mon-Fri, to 2pm Sat; @🌐) Cocorico is the French word for the call of the rooster and the French-Creole food at this breezy cafe and art gallery is indeed something to crow about. Tousled tourists, gabby girlfriends and bronzed expats – everybody's here for the tasty crêpes, crisp salads and yummy hot dishes such as the coconut curry chicken. The rum punches are some of the spiciest around.

Ancient Capital
PAN-ASIAN **$$**

(☎448-6628; 10 Church St; mains EC$30-60; ⊙lunch Mon-Sat, dinner daily) At this upstairs restaurant with indoor and balcony seating the menu is long enough to confuse

---

PORTS OF CALL

There are lots of options for even a short visit in port:

Roseau

» Hike to the gurgling Boiling Lake (p390)

» Rappel down rainforest waterfalls (p391) in Morne Trois Pitons National Park

» Swim up Titou Gorge (p391)

» Soak sore muscles in a Wotten Waven spa (p389)

» Swim, snorkel or dive amid crystal bubbles at Champagne Reef (p392)

Portsmouth

» Look for parrots on an easy hike through the Syndicate Parrot Reserve (p394)

» Mingle with seahorses, sand eels, flying gunards and batfish on a dive in Douglas Bay (p395)

» Wander the remains of a colonial fort at Cabrits National Park (p394)

» Glide through the dense rainforest along the romantic Indian River (p394)

Confucius. Although it features sushi and curries, it does not sacrifice a lick to the Chinese food gods with nicely executed classics such as kung pao chicken and beef fried rice.

La Robe Creole CARIBBEAN $$
(☎448-2896; 3 Victoria St; mains EC$25-80; ☺lunch & dinner Mon-Sat) Serves top-notch Creole dishes and seafood all day in a friendly environment that you don't need to dress up for. The bar has an extensive wine and spirits selection and the home-made rum punch is quite the treat. Anything seafood is highly recommended and the daily specials are indeed special.

Sutton Grille INTERNATIONAL $$
(☎449-8700; 25 Old St; mains EC$50-120; ☺breakfast, lunch & dinner, closed dinner Sat; ☎) At the Sutton Place Hotel, this courtyard restaurant has a slightly Gothic, sumptuous feel with its thick stone walls and wrought-iron gates. Fancy sandwiches or a buffet lunch are available by day with a more elaborate fish and steak menu later on.

Garage Bar & Grill CARIBBEAN $$
(☎448-5433; 15 Hanover St; mains EC$14-25; ☺lunch & dinner Tue-Sat) In an old stone house, this happening place feels more like an old castle than a garage – except for the bar stools that use old tires as a base. The food, especially the barbecue, is excellent. Lots of locals wet their whistles after dark and it's often the last place to shut down in Roseau.

J Astaphan & Co SUPERMARKET $
(☎448-3221; 65 King George V St; ☺8am-7pm Mon-Sat) The place to go for snacks, dinner fixings or rum at local prices. Department store upstairs.

🍷 Drinking & Entertainment

TOP CHOICE Zam Zam BAR-RESTAURANT
(Castle Comfort, next to Anchorage Hotel; ☺4pm-10:30pm Sun, Wed & Thu, to midnight Fri & Sat; ☎☎) With its waterfront deck, mellow world music, laid-back staff and potent cocktails, this little hangout exudes a distinctive Margaritaville vibe. Quite appropriately, the all-veg, organic menu (mains EC$20 to EC$35) features such Mexican classics as quesadillas and burritos, all expertly prepared by the Mexican co-owner.

Cove BAR, CLUB
(Canefield; ☺8am-5pm Mon-Wed on cruise-ship days, 6pm-10pm Wed-Sat, 10am-10pm Sun) Try

to stop your hips from moving when DJs or live local bands crank up the volume at this indoor/outdoor dance club, sports bar and restaurant (great burgers). It's a bit north of Roseau, near the Canefield airport.

Rituals Coffee House CAFE
(Dame Eugenia Charles Blvd; ☺6am-6pm; ☎) This Caribbean spin on Starbucks has coffees, teas, baked goods, sandwiches and free wi-fi.

JR's Bar & Grill BAR-RESTAURANT
(☎245-8389; cnr King George V St & Cross Lane; ☺7am-late Mon-Sat, noon-late Sun) There's always something going on at JR's, like poetry night, Caribbean night or karaoke, along with good-sized portions of Creole food to sop up the rum.

Bala's Bar BAR
(Fort Young Hotel, Victoria St) Friday happy hour is the place to ring in the weekend at this Fort Young Hotel bar. On Mondays, it does a BBQ buffet with a live band from 7pm.

Harlem Plaza BAR, LIVE MUSIC
(Newtown) Just south of central Roseau, this joint in a restored historic building is the place for live reggae on Friday.

Syme-Zee's BAR-RESTAURANT
(Syme-Zee's Hotel, 34 King George V St) Live jazz on Thursdays.

ℹ Information

Cyberland Internet Café (☎440-2605; cnr Cork & Great George Sts; 30-min access code valid for 24 hrs EC$3.50; ☺8am-10pm Mon-Fri, 10am-7pm Sat) Fast connections in air-conditioned comfort.

LIME Dominica (Hanover St; ☺8am-7pm Mon-Fri) For phone card, fax and email services.

First Caribbean International Bank (Old St) Has an ATM.

New Charles Pharmacy (☎448-3198; cnr Fields St & Cross Lane)

Post office (Dame Eugenia Charles Blvd; ☺8am-5pm Mon, to 4pm Tue-Fri) Check out the mural detailing the history of Dominica's postal service – Anthony Trollope came here in 1856 to set up the system, and policemen were the first mail carriers.

Princess Margaret Hospital (☎448-2231) In the Goodwill area on the north side of Roseau, off Federation Dr.

Royal Bank of Canada (Dame Eugenia Charles Blvd)

Tourist office (☎448-2045; www.dominica.dm; Dame Eugenia Charles Blvd; ☺8am-5pm

Mon, to 4pm Tue-Fri) On the ground floor beneath the Dominica Museum.

ℹ Getting There & Away

AIR See p404 for information on flights to/from Dominica.

BOAT For information on the ferry services between Roseau, Guadeloupe, Martinique and St Lucia, see p404.

BUS The bus service is operated by private minivans, recognizable by number plates that begin with the letter 'H.' You can hail a passing van from the street. There are three bus stops: buses going south congregate at the Old Market, while those going north stop at West Bridge. Buses to Laudat and the Roseau Valley leave from Valley Rd, corner of Bath Rd. Bus service stops soon after the working day is over.

CAR For information on car-rental agencies, see p404.

ℹ Getting Around

TO/FROM THE AIRPORT Avis and Budget are at Canefield Airport and other agencies provide customers with free airport pick-up. Taxis are readily available and charge EC$25 into town. Melville Hall has a wider selection of car-rental companies and the hour-plus taxi ride between Roseau is set at EC$100.

TAXI Pick up a taxi on the street or call **Dominica Taxi Association** (☏449-8553).

ROSEAU VALLEY

East of Roseau, the Roseau Valley is a ribbon of rural villages giving access to some of Dominica's most dramatic terrain and top wilderness sites. In the north, Laudat is the gateway to the Unesco-protected Morne Trois Pitons National Park, a stunning pastiche of lakes, fumaroles, volcanoes, hot springs and dense forest. The village of Trafalgar is famous for its twin waterfalls, while Wotten Waven's hot sulfur springs are said to have medicinal benefits. You can visit the area on a day trip but staying overnight definitely has its rewards.

Trafalgar Falls

Your camera will have a love affair with these misty twin **waterfalls** (admission US$5), whose easy access puts them on the must-see list of just about every visitor to Dominica. If you don't like crowds, come before 10am or after 4pm.

The visitor center is about 1 mile east of the village of Trafalgar at the top of a paved road flanked by a hydro-electric plant and the Papillote Wilderness Retreat. An easy 0.4-mile trail (lots of steps, though) leads to a viewing platform. Water from the upper falls crosses the Titou Gorge before plunging down the sheer 200ft rock face and feeding the hydro-electric plant downhill. The lower falls flow from the Trois Pitons River in the Boiling Lake area. This waterfall, gentler and broader than the upper falls, has a deep and wide pool at its base made for swimming.

Following the narrow, rocky trail beyond the platform means negotiating slippery moss-covered boulders, so wear sturdy shoes and watch your step. As a reward, you can cool off in shallow river pools or loll in the warm sulfur springs below the taller fall. Look for yellow streaks on the rocks.

Flash floods from heavy rains in the mountains pose serious danger, so stick to the platform if there's any risk.

🛏 Sleeping & Eating

Papillote Wilderness Retreat   HOTEL **$$**
(☏448-2287; www.papillote.dm; s/d US$121/139, with breakfast & dinner per person extra US$57; @ 🛜) Lovely gardens with nearly 100 types of tropical flowers and trees, a location within walking distance of Trafalgar Falls and four hot mineral pools right on the premises are among the assets of this popular inn. Alas, it's been around for over 30 years and the rooms are showing their age. And if you're in one next to the adjacent hydro-electric plant, staying here won't feel either like wilderness or a retreat. Garden tours cost US$10.

Wotten Waven

Across the valley from Trafalgar, and linked to it by a road across the River Blanc, Wotten Waven is famous for its natural hot sulfur springs and, thanks to some enterprising locals, has become a low-key 'spa' destination.

🏃 Activities

There are three spas, each with a different set-up and vibe.

Screw's Sulfur Spa   SPA
(per hour US$10; ⊙10am-10pm) Owned by a charismatic Rasta, the biggest spa has six stonewalled pools of varying temperatures.

Sulfur mud wraps and lava scrubs (US$75) are available. It gets busy when cruise ships are in port.

Tia's Bamboo Lodge
SPA

(private hut per person per 30min EC$10; ⊙9am-11pm Mon-Sat, 3pm-11pm Sun) Right in the village and set amid beautiful tropical gardens, Tia's has three open-air pools and two private ones inside bamboo huts, one of them wheelchair accessible. There's also a restaurant and four cozy **cottages** (per night EC$170) with handcrafted bamboo walls, wooden floors and private sitting areas.

Ti Kwen Glo Cho
SPA

(admission US$10; ⊙8am-11pm) Above the village, this one has lovely gardens inhabited by birds and turtles. Get pummeled by a waterfall or dip into a hot mud sulfur pool.

🛏 Sleeping & Eating

🍴 Cocoa Cottages
INN $$

(📋448-0412; www.cocoacottages.com; r US$100-125, breakfast US$15, dinner US$35; 🛜) Exuding a 'hostel for grown-ups' vibe, this charmer consists of five immaculate cottages uniquely decorated with art, painted fans, louvered walls or swinging beds. Guests returning from the trail or sightseeing gather in the open kitchen for a cup of tea while Iris and her staff are busy preparing dinner using ingredients grown on the grounds. Meals are organic, light and eaten at round communal tables. The living room has a drum kit, acoustic guitar, couches, books and games.

Le Petit Paradis
GUESTHOUSE, RESTAURANT $

(📋448-5946; lepetitparadis200@hotmail.com; r US$20-45, breakfast/lunch/dinner US$6/10/20; @🛜) Beg, steal and lie to snag one of the three handsome rooms with private bathroom, fridge and porch. The cheaper ones are not nearly as comfortable and may share facilities but at these rates you know you're not getting the Ritz. The biggest asset here, though, is the big-hearted owner, Joan, who's also a killer cook. Even if you're not staying, do come for a memorable meal in the lovely restaurant.

ℹ Getting There & Away

Buses to the Roseau Valley make the trip from the Valley Rd stop in Roseau to Wotten Waven in about 20 minutes and to Trafalgar in about 30 minutes (check with the driver to make sure you're on the right bus). If you're driving yourself, follow Valley Rd to the hamlet of Fond Cani where the road forks, with the right turn going to

Wotten Waven and the left turn to Trafalgar and Laudat. Valley Rd can get clogged when there's a cruise ship in town, but recent upgrades should make travel a little more tolerable.

Morne Trois Pitons National Park

This national park stretches across 17,000 acres of Dominica's mountainous volcanic interior. Most of it is primordial rainforest, varying from jungles thick with tall, pillar-like *gommier* trees to the stunted cloud-forest cover on the upper slopes of Morne Trois Pitons (4550ft), Dominica's second-highest mountain. The park embraces such top wilderness sites as Boiling Lake, Boeri Lake, Freshwater Lake and Middleham Falls. Hikes to all four start in the mountain village of Laudat (elevation 1970ft), which has a lodge and a cafe that sell the ecotourism site pass (see the boxed text, p403).

See p399 for a description of Emerald Pool, located at the northernmost tip of the national park.

🏃 Activities

Boiling Lake
HIKE

Dominica's pre-eminent trek, and one of the hardest, is the six-hour roundtrip to the world's second-largest actively boiling lake (the largest is in New Zealand). Geologists believe the 207ft-wide lake is a flooded fumarole – a crack in the earth that allows hot gases to vent from the molten lava below. The fizzing, eerie-looking lake sits inside a deep cauldron, its grayish waters veiled in steam, its center emitting bubbly burps. It's a spectacular sight.

The hike traverses the aptly named Valley of Desolation, whose sulfur rivers, belching steam vents and geysers evoke post-atomic grace. It then follows narrow ridges, snakes up and down mountains and runs along hot streams. Wear sturdy walking shoes and expect to get wet and muddy; better yet, bring a change of clothes.

The strenuous 6-mile hike to the lake begins at Titou Gorge and requires a guide. Ask for a referral at your hotel or check with the tourist office in Roseau. The cost should be about US$40 per person.

To get to the trailhead, drive to Laudat and turn left at the bizarre socialist-style statue. The trailhead is a short walk from the parking lot next to the Rainforest Aerial Tram.

Titou Gorge
SWIMMING HOLE, WATERFALL

A swimming hole gives way to this narrow gorge ending at a torrential waterfall. The eerily quiet, short swim through the crystal-clear water is a spooky experience. It's dark down there, with steep vine-clad lava walls no more than 5ft or 7ft apart, hence the name which is Creole for 'small throat'. If you're not a swimmer, you can just take a refreshing dip in the swimming hole which is fed by a hot mineral spring. Don't swim the gorge after heavy rains when dangerous flash floods may occur. The gorge is at the Boiling Lake trailhead; see that entry for directions.

Middleham Falls
HIKE

The trail to Middleham Falls, one of Dominica's highest waterfalls (200ft), takes you on an interesting rainforest walk. More than 60 tree species, including the tall buttressed chataignier, form a leafy canopy that inhibits undergrowth and keeps the forest floor relatively clear. The main trailhead is along the Roseau–Laudat road, about 5 miles east of Roseau. The hike starts at 1600ft, climbs to 2200ft and then drops down to the falls. The trail is steep in places but well defined and can usually be done without a guide. Allow about two to three hours roundtrip.

Freshwater Lake
HIKE

Shimmering softly in various shades of blue and green, Freshwater is the largest of Dominica's four lakes, and the source of the Roseau River. It is easily reached via a paved road that veers uphill (left) off the main road just before Laudat. As it climbs, sweeping views of the valley, Morne Anglais and the sea open up. When you get to a T-junction, turn right for the lake parking lot and pick up the easy, 2.5-mile loop trail around the lake to the right of the visitor center, past a hydro-electric station. Vegetation at this elevation (2500ft) is very different from the rainforest; trees are short and thin and shrubs, ferns and herbs blanket the forest floor. Birders love it here: keep an eye out for the mountain whistler, hummingbirds and egrets. Bring a sweater or light jacket; it gets chilly up here.

Boeri Lake Trail
HIKE

At an elevation of 2800ft, deep and cold Boeri Lake is the highest in Dominica and fills a volcanic crater wedged between soaring Morne Trois Pitons and Morne Macaque. To get to the trailhead, follow the road to Freshwater Lake but turn left at the T-junction and continue to the parking lot.

From here, it's a scenic 45-minute jaunt past mountain streams, hot and cold springs and elfin woodland to the lake.

Extreme Dominica
CANYONING

(295-7272 or 295-6828; www.extremedominica.com; US$150) Based near Cocoa Cottages in Wotton Waven, this pro outfit runs exhilarating half-day adventures that have you rappelling down waterfalls like Spiderman and floating in crystal-clear pools at the bottom of deep canyon walls. As owner Richard puts it, 'A lot of people come to Dominica to look at waterfalls, but with canyoning you get to taste them, feel them, be in them.' No experience is necessary and there's no need to be super fit.

Morne Trois Pitons
HIKE

You need to hire a guide to tackle the park's tallest peak – ask at your hotel or the tourist office (rates need to be negotiated and generally depend on group size and pick-up point). It's a rough trail that cuts through patches of sharp saw grass and requires scrambling over steep rocks. The trail begins at Pont Casse, at the north end of the park, and takes about five hours round-trip.

Rain Forest Aerial Tram
AERIAL TRAM

(448-8775 in Roseau or 440-3266 in Laudat; www.rainforestadventure.com; Laudat; adult/child US$64/46; closed May-Oct) This attraction offers a quick and easy introduction to the diverse flora and fauna of the rainforest. The experience starts with a slow aerial gondola ride through the canopy, followed by a short downhill hike and a walk across a dizzyingly high suspension bridge from where you can spot five waterfalls. Note that the park is only open whenever organized tours are booked in advance, so definitely call ahead. The entrance is near the trailhead for Boiling Lake; see that entry for directions.

🛏 Sleeping & Eating

Roxy's Mountain Lodge
INN $$

(448-4845; www.avirtualdominica.com/eiroxys.htm; Laudat; r US$53-102; @) The only lodging option in the national park, Roxy's has appealing Swiss chalet looks and is naturally popular with hikers. Not all rooms are created equal, though, so inspect a few before committing. The food is filling, but quality can be uneven.

Cafe Mon Plezi
CAFE $

The only other place in Laudat to obtain drink and food (well, a sandwich anyway) is this teensy cafe-bar en route to the park-

HIKE THE WAITUKUBULI NATIONAL TRAIL

If all goes according to plan, a new long-distance hiking trail, the Waitukubuli National Trail, will have opened by the time you read this. The 115-mile trail links the far south with the far north of the island, hitting all the key beauty spots along the way, from Scotts Head to Boiling Lake and Emerald Pool. It's divided into 14 segments of various length and difficulty but each one is designed to be completed in one day. Some sections of the trail are already done. Stay tuned via www.trail.agriculture.gov.dm.

ing lot for Boiling Lake, Titou Gorge and the Rainforest Aerial Tram.

❶ Getting There & Away

Buses to Laudat (40 minutes) leave from the Valley Rd bus stop in Roseau. A **taxi** ride to Laudat costs EC$80. To get to Laudat by **car**, follow Valley Rd to Fond Cani and turn left at the fork marked 'Laudat.' The trail to Middleham Falls begins on the left 2.5 miles up.

SOUTH OF ROSEAU

The coastal road south of Roseau takes you through a handful of seaside villages clinging to Mediterranean-flavored Soufriere Bay, dead-ending at Scotts Head in about 30 minutes. Some of the island's best dives, including Scotts Head Drop-Off, the Soufriere Pinnacle and Champagne Reef, are here in the Soufriere/Scotts Head Marine Reserve.

The hot sulfur spring at Soufriere is another key attraction and further evidence of the island's volcanic origins. Numerous hiking trails lead into the rainforest.

Champagne Beach & Reef

This is one of Dominica's most unusual underwater playgrounds. Volcanic bubbles emerge from vents beneath the sea floor, rising up as drops of liquid crystal and making it feel like you're swimming in a giant glass of champagne. Best of all, you can snorkel right off the (rocky) beach. Technicolor fish and coral abound.

Irie Safari (☑440-5085; www.iriesafaridominica.com) rents snorkeling gear for US$12

per day, which includes the US$2 user fee for the marine reserve. It also sells snacks and refreshments. Keep an eye out for the resident iguanas (some 5ft long) scampering about the hillside. For dive trips, enquire at Nature Island Dive in Soufriere, the next village down.

Between the town and Champagne Reef, **Melvina's** (☑440-5480) may look like just another oceanfront bar and seafood restaurant, but on Friday nights it's a scene and a half when locals swing by for steamed fish, barbecued chicken and rum punches starting about 9pm.

Soufriere

POP 950

At the heart of Soufriere Bay, which is the rim of a sunken volcanic crater, Soufriere is a sleepy fishing village whose undisputed 'hot spot' is the **Soufriere Sulfur Springs** (site fee US$5). It's the source of a steaming hot stream in the hills above town whose water is captured in a series of stone pools. It may look a bit murky but is actually clean and said to have healing properties. The recently improved grounds include facilities, a picnic area and a snackette. To get there, take the first left as you enter the village and continue for about one mile. A trail leading up the ridge and over to Tete Morne also starts at the springs.

Another place to take a dip is back in town right in front of the old and photogenic **stone church**. You can often see locals splashing about in a small basin that catches water heated by subterranean volcanic vents and bubbling up through the sand.

Nature Island Dive (☑449-8181; www.natureislanddive.com; 1-/2-tank dive US$50/80) takes divers to top dive spots just minutes away in the Soufriere/Scotts Head Marine Reserve. Bikes rent for US$25 per day and combined kayak-snorkeling tours are US$60.

Scotts Head

POP 800

On Dominica's southernmost tip, the fishing village of Scotts Head has a gem of a setting along the gently curving shoreline of Soufriere Bay. Activity centers on the waterfront where old men hang out on the porches of pastel-painted houses, and barbecues and dancing in the local bars enliven the picture. At the southern end, a narrow isthmus separating the Atlantic and the Caribbean leads to the eponymous 'Scotts Head', the rocky outcrop named for an 18th-century British governor. Only a few small ruins remain of the fort he erected in defense of the bay.

The hilltop **Ocean View Apartments** (☑449-8266; oceanview_apts@hotmail.com; s/d US$50/60; 🛜) has three handsome apartments facing a garden where guests can help themselves to cherries, limes and coconuts.

Grand Bay

This sweeping bay is on Dominica's south coast. Turn inland at Loubiere onto a wide and largely pothole-free curving road skirting the base of Morne Anglais and crossing a few rivers before reaching the coast.

This remote, quiet corner of the island is a perfect setting for **Zandoli Inn** (☑446-3161; www.zandoli.com; Roche Cassée, Stowe; s/d US$135/145, breakfast & dinner per person US$50; @☒), an artistic retreat designed to induce a state of Zen, Caribbean-style. There aren't any TVs or radios and guests are asked to use headphones when listening to music. The five sun-drenched rooms have private balconies, dreamy views of scalloped Grand Bay, beautiful artwork and solar hot-water showers. Work up an appetite for the gourmet dinners strolling the grounds and looking out for scampering zandoli lizards (a sign of good luck).

Further east, the 35 cottages of **Jungle Bay Resort & Spa** (☑446-1789; www.junglebaydominica.com; Pointe Mulatre; r incl breakfast US$219; @☒) blend beautifully into the jungle. The resort captures the ecozeitgeist with showers that use water from a spring-fed stream, locally made furniture and organic meals. Full packages include boarding, spa treatments, yoga classes, meals and such daily activities as rum-shop tours, snorkeling trips or Caribbean cooking classes (s/d US$377/566 with three-night minimum).

❶ Getting There & Away

Buses leaving from the Old Market in Roseau travel south to Soufriere and Scotts Head (EC$3.25). There is no bus to Grand Bay.

WEST COAST

The drive along the west coast takes you past Canefield Airport and through several villages, including the charmingly named Massacre. The west coast's nicest beach is at Mero, there's good diving at Salisbury and a unique parrot reserve further north in the Morne Diablotin National Park. The only sizeable town is Portsmouth.

Mero & Salisbury

About halfway up the coast, grayish-black Mero Beach is the west coast's most popular sandy strand. It's accessed via a narrow one-way road off the main highway – keep an eye out for the sign. A few bars serve refreshments and rent beach chairs.

⊙ Sights & Activities

East Carib Dive　　　　　　　　DIVING
(☑449-6575; www.east-carib-dive.com; Salisbury; 1-/2-tank dives US$50/80) This outfit has run boat dives, night dives and snorkeling trips for over 20 years. There are some beautiful dive sites just a 10-minute boat ride away, including Coral Gardens, Rena's Reef and Whale Shark Reef.

Macoucherie Distillery　　　　DISTILLERY
(☑449-6409; www.shillingfordestateltd.com) Shillingford Estate in the village of Macoucherie (between Layou and Salisbury) has been distilling premium rum from pure sugar cane juice for over half a century. It grows its own sugar and then uses a water mill to crush the cane, the way it's been done for 200 years. The spicy Macoucherie Bois Bandé is supposed to have aphrodisiacal benefits. Call ahead to arrange a tour.

🛏 Sleeping & Eating

Tamarind Tree Hotel　　　　HOTEL $$
(☑449-7395; www.tamarindtreedominica.com; Salisbury; r US$113-153; closed Sep; ✳@🛜☒) This 12-room property run by a Swiss-German couple sits on a seaside cliff amid nicely landscaped grounds. All rooms have a fridge, fans and solar-heated water; the upper units feature air-con. There are lounge chairs on the shared porch for relaxing and a rooftop sitting area with a telescope for stargazing. Dive packages with East Carib Dive are available. The restaurant serves Kubuli on tap.

Sunset Bay Club　　　　　　RESORT $$$
(☑446-6522; www.sunsetbayclub.com; s/d with breakfast from US$100/147, all-inclusive from US$150/250; @🛜☒) About 1 mile north of Salisbury, this beachside hotel is set on lush

grounds where lizards scamper. There's an on-site dive center, a small pool, a sauna and a nice open-air restaurant (mains EC$30 to EC$50; open lunch and dinner).

Connie's Mero Beach Bar   BAR-RESTAURANT $
(Mero Beach; snacks EC$4-10, meals EC$12-20; ⊙8am-late, dinner by reservation) A Mero Beach institution, Connie serves snacks, drinks and friendly advice on local attractions. The menu changes daily, but goat curry, steamed fish and fried chicken are typical mains.

Morne Diablotin National Park

Established in 2000 to protect the habitat of the national bird, the Sisserou parrot, and its pretty red-necked cousin, the Jaco parrot, this national park is part of the Northern Forest Reserve and covers some 8242 acres. It's named for Dominica's tallest peak (4747ft) and is cloaked in rainforest, montane forest and, at higher elevations, elfin woodland. Various palm species, gommier trees, heliconia, anthuriums and moss-covered bromeliads thrive here.

Syndicate Parrot Reserve   HIKE
(site fee US$5) This easy one-hour loop trail through the Syndicate Rainforest on the western slopes of Morne Diablotin is your best chance to see Dominica's endemic (and endangered) parrots, the Jaco and the much larger Imperial, the national bird also known as Sisserou, in their natural habitat. The best time to spot them is in the early morning and late afternoon. There are plenty of other bird species as well, including all four local varieties of hummingbird.

A short detour takes you to the pretty **Milton Falls**, but the trail is not signposted and is poorly marked.

To get to the reserve, turn onto the signposted road just north of the village of Dublanc and continue to Syndicate Estate, about 4.5 miles inland.

Morne Diablotin Trail   HIKE
(site fee US$5) The parrot reserve is also the starting point of the grueling trek up Morne Diablotin. Budget at least two to 2½ hours for the 1.25 miles to the top. Parrots, a huge white mangrove and glorious mountain views are among the rewards. A guide is recommended – contact the tourist office in Roseau for a referral.

Portsmouth

POP 3600

Dominica's second-largest town, set on attractive Prince Rupert Bay, is popular with the sail-boat set but otherwise not particularly attractive. The bay is littered with rusting wrecks; the legacy of Hurricane Dean that lashed through here in 2007. The cargo vessel blocking the mouth of the Indian River is especially unsightly.

Much nicer and livelier is the southern suburb of Picard, home to Ross University School of Medicine, which plays a major factor in the local economy. In recent years, candy-colored apartment buildings and a few bars and cafes have cropped up across from the campus along what has been dubbed the 'Banana Trail'.

The main area attractions are Cabrits National Park, north of town and the Indian River, to the south. There's also some good diving and snorkeling to be done around here.

◉ Sights & Activities

TOP
CHOICE **Indian River**   NATURE SITE
(site fee US$5) The slow and silent **boat trip** along this shady mangrove-lined river is a memorable experience as you glide past buttressed bwa mang trees whose trunks rise out of the shallows, their roots stretching out laterally along the riverbanks. Enjoy close-up views of egrets, crabs, iguanas, hummingbirds and other creatures that live in the air and in the jungle. Ask your guide to point out where scenes from *Pirates of the Caribbean* were filmed.

Rowers are waiting at the mouth of the river and charge EC$40 to EC$50 per person for the 1½-hour trip, including a stop at the **Indian River Bush Bar**, run by the affable 'Cobra' (aka Andrew O'Brian). The 'Dynamite' rum punch is the bar's signature drink, a mixture of fruits, herbs and 'local atmosphere,' as Cobra puts it. Although the bar looks like it's only accessible via the river, locals can point you to a walking path that takes 10 minutes or so from town.

Cabrits National Park   NATIONAL PARK
(admission US$5; ⊙8am-6pm) Located on a scenic peninsula 1.25 miles north of Portsmouth, this is the site of **Fort Shirley**, an impressive, though ruined, 18th-century British garrison. In addition to the peninsula, the park encompasses the surrounding

coastal area, as well as the island's largest swamp. The Cabrits Peninsula, formed by two extinct volcanoes, separates Prince Rupert Bay from Douglas Bay. The coral reefs and waters of the latter are also part of the park, and good for diving and snorkeling.

Cabrits is a fun place to explore. Some of the fort's stone ruins have been cleared and partially reconstructed, while others remain half-hidden in the jungle. The powder magazine to the right of the fort entrance has been turned into a small museum with restoration exhibits and a display of unearthed artifacts.

The fort is home to scores of hermit crabs, harmless snakes and ground lizards that scurry about the ruins and along the hiking trails that lead up to the two volcanic peaks. The trail up the 560ft West Cabrit begins at the back side of Fort Shirley and the hike takes about 30 minutes. Most of the walk passes through a wooded area, but there's a panoramic view at the top.

Cabrits Dive Center
DIVING

(☑445-3010; www.cabritsdive.com; 1-/2-tank dives US$60/80) This five-star PADI operator is the only dive shop in northern Dominica where some of the island's most spectacular sites, including Toucari Caves and Douglas Bay Point, are located. Most sites are only a short boat ride away. Snorkeling gear rents for US$22 per day, snorkeling trips are US$33.

🛏 Sleeping

Some excellent lodging options have recently opened, though not in Portsmouth proper but a short drive north or south.

📷 Manicou River Resort
RESORT $$

(☑616-8903; www.manicouriverresort.com; Everton Hall Estate, Tanetane; cottage US$125) About 10 minutes north of Portsmouth, this new eco-retreat sits about 400ft above the Caribbean and affords picture-perfect views over the water and the Cabrits. Stay in individual octagonal cottages built from red and white cedar and brimming with unique design details such as handblown glass sinks in the bathrooms. Soak up the site's serenity while swinging in a hammock on your balcony or taking a dip in a pool fed by volcanic spring-water. Kitchens and beds are both king size.

Heaven's Best Guest House
GUESTHOUSE $$

(☑445-6677; www.heavensbestguesthouse.com; r US$95; ✹@✿) A short drive north of central Portsmouth, in the village of Savanne Paille,

this friendly newcomer has nine rooms, some with forest-view balconies and/or full kitchens. Cell phone and laptop rentals are available. The **restaurant** (mains EC$45 to EC$80; closed Sunday) serves inspired American-Caribbean fusion fare that has quickly garnered plaudits from locals and visitors. Bring your own wine or beer.

📷 Comfortel De Champ
INN $$

(☑445-4452 or 275-3660; www.godominica .com; Picard; d incl breakfast US$110-150; ✹@✿) This small hotel clings to a steep hill above Picard, meaning superb views are guaranteed. There are two rooms at garden level and three upstairs, all with small fridge, widescreen TV, water cooker and a porch with lounge chairs. Eco-efforts include solar panels and rain water purification. The **sunset bar** (☺5-9pm) is a perfect for sipping Spanish cava and munching on snacks made by host Lise.

📷 Picard Beach Eco-Cottages
RESORT $$$

(☑445-5131; www.picardbeachcottages.dm; Picard; r US$160-220; ✹✿) Kudos for the beautiful setting and the eco-efforts, but the 18 cottages are definitely snug and could use a spruce-up. The nicest border a small beach. Ask for discounts.

🍴 Eating & Drinking

Tomato
CAFE $$

(☑445-3334; www.thetomatocafe.com; Picard; dishes EC$13-40; ☺11am-9pm Mon-Sat; ✿) Right on the 'Banana Trail', Canadians Whitney and Rob feed hungry tummies with crisp salads, bulging sandwiches and satisfying pasta in their delightfully funky upstairs cafe. There's Kubuli on tap and, according to an autographed picture of Orlando Bloom, the 'best chocolate cake in the Caribbean.'

Big Papa's Bar & Restaurant
CARIBBEAN $$

(☑445-6444; Michael Douglas Blvd; mains EC$35-55; ☺9am-11pm; ✿) On a decent beach north of town, this Jamaican joint is presided over by Aldrin and Gloria. Yachties and locals crowd around the rustic tables knocking back the Kubuli and clamoring for the delicious seafood, super spicy jerk chicken and goat curry. Reggae fiends invade for the live band on Wednesday night. Happy hour is from 4pm to 6pm.

Blue Bay Restaurant
SEAFOOD $$

(☑445-4985; www.bluebayrestaurant.multiply. com; Lagon; mains EC$33-70; ☺dinner Mon-Sat; ✿)

CHAUDIERE POOL

Nicknamed the 'Emerald Pool' of the north, Chaudiere Pool is a refreshing swimming hole at the end of a moderately difficult 45-minute hike through an old plantation. It's deep enough for daredevils to leap off the surrounding rocks into the water.

The trailhead is in the village of Bense. There's a sign at the turn-off to the trailhead but the access road is in pretty bad shape, especially after heavy rains, so unless you have a 4WD, you may have to walk. The trail is well marked and takes you to the confluence of two rivers. Cross the river to get to the pool. The round-trip trek takes about 90 minutes and the scenery and deep swimming hole are well worth it. Look out for parrots!

It looks just like any other funky beach restaurant, but Blue Bay's cuisine is a step from the run-of-the mill local fare. The seafood platters never fail to impress, but the goat and pork dishes are also respectable. Reservations required.

Shacks   TAKEAWAY **$**
(Michael Douglas Blvd, Picard; meals EC$20; ☺8am-10pm) This row of food stalls caters primarily to the local student population but anyone is welcome to fill up on the cheap with pizza, burgers, barbecued meats, nachos, crepes and other comfort foods. Not all stalls are open all the time.

Purple Turtle Beach Club Bar & Restaurant   BAR-RESTAURANT **$$**
(Michael Douglas Blvd; Lagon; mains EC$30-50; ☺lunch & dinner) This Portsmouth institution sits on a strip of black sand and is a favorite end-of-day drinking spot for locals and boaters alike.

❶ Information

Computer Resource Center (Bay Rd; per 30min EC$5; ☺9am-10pm Mon-Sat) Fast internet connections; also sells computer accessories.

National Bank of Dominica Just south of the town square parking lot (where you pick up the bus to Roseau).

Police (Bay Rd)

❶ Getting There & Away

Buses up the west coast leave from the West Bridge bus stop in Roseau. In Portsmouth, buses leave from the town square on Bay Rd.

NORTHEASTERN COAST

The road cutting to the east coast from Portsmouth across Dominica's remote and sparsely populated north is a stunning drive past massive ferns, towering palms and thick banana groves. The road itself is in decent condition but very narrow and has intestine-like bends, so keep your wits about you. There are plenty of blind corners, stray dogs and goats coming out of nowhere and locals balancing sacks of mangos and coconuts ambling along the side of the road. Budget about two hours for the drive.

The road skirts several rustic villages. The Waitukubuli National Trail (p392) passes through **Borne**, where you'll also find the trailhead to Brandy Falls. The village of **Anse de Mai** has a gas station, while the turnoff for Chaudiere Pool is near **Bense**.

As you approach **Calibishie**, the first sizeable town along here, several beautiful views of the rocky coastline open up. Numerous scenes from *Pirates of the Caribbean* were filmed in this area and there isn't a local without his or her own personal Johnny Depp story (see 'Hollywood's Treasure Island' boxed text).

Calibishie

Calibishie is an attractive fishing village with the best beaches on the island, some excellent inns and restaurants, grocery stores, an ATM and a car-rental agency. It makes a good pitstop for lunch or an overnight stay, particularly if you're catching a morning flight from nearby Melville Hall Airport.

◉ Sights & Activities

If you plan to snorkel, it's best to have your own gear, because the closest rental is Cabrits Dive Shop in Portsmouth.

TOP CHOICE **Batibou Bay**   SECLUDED BEACH
Dominica's best beach sits at the end of a bumpy dirt road that after heavy rains is often only accessible by 4WD. Ask the locals about conditions and be prepared to walk. Trust us, it's worth it. This coconut palm-fringed crescent has good swimming and snorkeling with

a coral reef just offshore. The turnoff is not marked, so ask locally for directions or take the bus and ask to be dropped off.

Point Baptiste
Beach
SWIMMING & SNORKELING BEACH

Accessed via the Red Rock Haven B&B, this beautiful and quiet strand at the foot of a massive rock face has reddish sand, shallow waters and lots of shady coconut palms. You can snorkel right off the beach.

🛌 Sleeping & Eating

Unless noted, all establishments are located along the main road.

TOP CHOICE Jacoway Inn
B&B $$

(📞445-8872; www.calibishie.net; r incl breakfast US$80-85; 🛜) Thumbs up, way up, for this darling two-room B&B run by the irrepressible Carol Ann: gourmet cook, comedian, bon vivant and hostess with the mostest. Enjoy plenty of elbow room amid artsy decor, quality furnishings, a kitchenette and fresh fruit and flowers. The upstairs unit has a big balcony with dreamy views out to sea. The home-cooked breakfasts easily tide you over till the afternoon, while dinners (from US$15) are practically gourmet affairs. Jacoway is high above the village, up a steep road opposite the Calibishie Lodge. Look for the sign.

Veranda View
B&B $$

(📞613-9493; www.lodgingdominica.com; r incl breakfast US$95-105; 🛜) You'll realize just how aptly named this brightly decorated two-room beachfront inn is when watching the waves, cold Kubuli in hand, from its eponymous beachfront veranda. The owner, Hermien, is a consummate host and excellent cook who can whip up delicious dinners for an extra EC$30.

Red Rock Haven
B&B $$$

(📞445-797; www.redrockhaven.com; r US$200, villa US$650; 🛜) This discreet retreat sits amid tropical gardens overlooking Point Baptiste Beach. Breezes filter in through wooden louvers into just two rooms, each appointed in rich woods, beautiful furniture and a deck for relaxing. The upstairs has an open floor plan with no toilet door. The superluxe villa has a private infinity pool.

TOP CHOICE Escape Bar & Grill
INTERNATIONAL $$

(📞275-7997; Point Baptiste Beach at Red Rock Haven inn; mains lunch EC$25-35, dinner EC$60-95; ⏱lunch & dinner Wed-Sun) Fine dining in a beach-adjacent coconut grove, toes tucked into the cool sand and romantic twinkle lights all around you – does it get any better? The menu looks familiar: burgers and salads for lunch, steak, lobster and mahi mahi for dinner (by reservation only), but the execution and presentation are first rate.

Other places worth considering:

Sea View Apartments
APARTMENTS $$

(📞445-8537; www.dominicaseaviewapartments.com; apt US$85-95; 🛜) Well-stocked self-catering apartments. Check in at Calibishie Lodges.

Calibishie Lodges
HOTEL $$

(📞445-8537; www.calibishie-lodges.com; ste US$125-215; 🛜🏊) Popular and well established.

Bamboo Restaurant
INTERNATIONAL $$

(mains EC$25-75; ⏱breakfast, lunch & dinner) Local dinners, seafood specialties like crayfish and lobster, plus pasta and pork dishes. At Calibishie Lodges.

ℹ Information

ATM (Low Price Centre grocery store)

Tourist office (📞445-8344; www.calibishiecoast.com; ⏱9am-5pm Mon-Fri) Smart staff, free maps and mags, internet access (EC$5 per hour) and free wi-fi.

Wesley

This pretty village is dominated by a huge hilltop church but the main reason to stop is the wonderful Creole fare at **Randi's** (📞315-7474; meals EC$25-40; ⏱9am-10pm). A former Chippendale dancer with a big infectious

---

HOLLYWOOD'S TREASURE ISLAND

With its wild coast, thick jungle and hidden coves, Dominica has always been a popular haunt of pirates between pillages, so it was only natural that Hollywood came calling when location scouting for the *Pirates of the Caribbean* films. In 2005, hundreds of cast and crew, led by Johnny, Orlando and Keira, invaded the island to shoot scenes of films two and three in locations such as Titou Gorge, Soufriere, the Indian River and Batibou Beach. And if that wasn't enough, two years later, CBS filmed the reality show *Pirate Master* all around Dominica. Arrgh, mateys!

JAZZ IN THE JUNGLE

Picture this: a thatched-roof restaurant-bar tucked deep into the rainforest; two streams twisting through a dense profusion of tropical trees and flowering plants; a plate of scrambled eggs and fresh papaya on your table; and a four-piece band playing Marvin Gaye and Sam Cooke. That's 'Jazz in the Jungle,' the brainchild of Mo Melina from Calgary, herself a seasoned sax player. Every Sunday, clued-in locals descend upon Mo's personal little piece of paradise for brunch (EC$50), music and perhaps a dip in the river. Called **River Rush Eco Retreat** (☑295-7266; www.river-rush.com; Stonefield; r incl breakfast US$100-150), and a 15-minute drive south of Melville Airport, the grounds also cradle five wooden guest cottages on stilts. Fall asleep to the sound of a river in four-poster beds, separated from nature only by a mosquito net and hurricane shutters. There's no phone, no TV, no internet. Just you and the jungle.

smile, Randi does triple duty as owner, cook and waiter. Meals (try the chicken curry) are best enjoyed in the shade of the mango tree.

Marigot & Pagua Bay

Sprawling **Marigot** encompasses Melville Hall Airport, a huge fisheries complex and several neighborhoods strung along the highway. Aside from the gas station (the last before Roseau!), there's little to make you want to stop. Instead, push on to gorgeous **Pagua Bay**, which has a rocky beach suitable for bodysurfing. Beyond here the road forks, with one route traversing the Central Forest Reserve, the other passing through the Carib Territory. Both end up in Roseau; the route through the reserve is faster.

🛏 Sleeping & Eating

Pagua Bay House   BOUTIQUE INN **$$$**
(☑445-8888; www.paguabayhouse.com; r US$150-200; ✻🕸🗲) The brainchild of Rich and Alicia Davison, these four stylish oceanfront cabanas (more are planned for 2011) could easily feature on the pages of *Architectural Digest*. The industrial-flavored galvanized steel facade beautifully contrasts with the warm wooden interiors that lack no modern comforts. Rates include use of kayaks and boogie boards.

Silks Hotel   BOUTIQUE HOTEL **$$$**
(☑445-8846; www.silkshotel.com; r incl breakfast US$165; 🗲🏊) A 17th-century rum distillery has taken on a new life as a gorgeous five-room boutique hotel. A stay comes with swims in the river and the sparkling pool, leisurely lunches at the restaurant, strolls through the tropical garden and relaxing nights in richly furnished rooms. 'Pirates' Keira Knightley and Geoffrey Rush loved it.

🏖 Hibiscus Valley Inn   GUESTHOUSE **$$**
(☑445-8195,   225-3965;   www.hisbiscusvalley.com; r US$33-121, breakfast/lunch/dinner US$7/10/15; 🗲) This convivial rainforest lodge 15 minutes from Melville Airport brings together a United Nations of folks who, at the end of the day, retreat to whatever room their money can buy: a 'simple room' with shared facilities down by the river; a 'nature bungalow' with a veranda for lounging in a hammock; or a hotel standard room with air-con, TV and fridge. The chef prepares delicious local fare and can take you on a crayfish safari (US$25), while the Adventure Center runs various tours, including a popular tubing trip (with/without lunch US$35/25) down the Pagua River.

TOP CHOICE Pagua Bar & Grill   MODERN AMERICAN **$$**
(☑445-8888; www.paguabayhouse.com; mains lunch EC$15-30, dinner EC$60-130; ⊙lunch & dinner Tue-Sun; 🗲) Atop Pagua Bay, Rick and Alicia's restaurant has arguably the most breathtaking view of any eatery on Dominica. The look is urban hip and the food is modern American. Ceviche, Caesar salad and fish tacos are the menu stars at lunchtime, while dinners shine the spotlight on Angus steaks and mahi mahi. Many of the vegetables are home-grown.

CARIB TERRITORY

The 3700-acre Carib Territory, which begins around the village of Bataka and continues south for 7.5 miles, is home to most of Dominica's 2200 Caribs – properly known as Kalinago. It's a rural area with cultivated bananas, breadfruit trees and wild heliconia growing along the roadside. Many of the houses are traditional wooden structures on log stilts, but there are also simple cement homes and, in the poorer areas, shanties made of corrugated tin and tar paper. Stalls and small shops selling baskets and other handicraft line the main road. The roadside Cassava Bakery in Salybia sells traditional Carib bread.

◉ Sights

⬛ Kalinago Barana Autê HERITAGE VILLAGE
(☑445-7979; www.kalinagobaranaaaute.com; Old Coast Rd; guided tour EC$26; ◷10am-5pm, closed Mon mid-Oct–mid-Apr & Wed & Thu mid-Apr–mid-Oct) This recreated traditional village is a good spot to learn about Kalinago history and culture. The 30- to 45-minute tour includes stops at a 'karbet', or 'men's house', a 10ft-long dugout canoe carved from a single tree, and a waterfall. Tours conclude at a snack bar and gift shop where Kalinago women weave their ornate baskets.

🛏 Sleeping & Eating

⬛ Beau Rive Hotel HOTEL $$
(☑445-8992; www.beaurive.com; s/d incl breakfast US$137/180, 2-night minimum, closed Aug & Sep; @🖳) Set in tropical gardens with a pool overlooking Wakaman Point, this hushed and elegant hotel welcomes guests to 10 spacious rooms with shiny wooden floors, ultra-comfortable beds and ocean views. The only TV, along with a DVD library, is in the communal lounge with its overstuffed sofas. The restaurant serves a three-course dinner (US$35) for guests only.

Domcan's Guest House APARTMENTS $
(☑445-7794; www.domcansguesthouse.com; Castle Bruce; apt US$60; 🛜) The name is short for Dominican and Canadian, which are the home-lands of owners Harry and Grace. Together they've built this great-value pit stop with six spotless, functionally furnished apartments with kitchenette, sitting area and balcony. The restaurant gets high marks for its international and local fare.

Islet View Restaurant & Bar BAR-RESTAURANT $
(New Rd, Castle Bruce; mains EC$10-25; ◷breakfast, lunch & dinner) The big outdoor porch overlooks Castle Bruce Beach and is the perfect spot for taking a break from the road. The thatched walls and big selection of hand-labeled bush rums behind the bar make the restaurant, with only one or two meals on the menu, look more like a friendly witch doctor's house than a roadside eatery.

UNDERSTAND DOMINICA

History

Dominica was the last of the Caribbean islands to be colonized by Europeans due chiefly to the fierce resistance of the native Caribs. The Caribs, who settled here in the 14th century, called the island Waitikubuli, which means 'Tall is her Body.' Christopher Columbus, with less poetic flair, named the island after the day of the week on which he spotted it – a Sunday ('Doménica' in Italian) – on November 3, 1493.

Daunted by the Caribs and discouraged by the absence of gold, the Spanish took little interest in Dominica. France laid claim to the island in 1635 and wrestled with the British over it through the 18th century.

In 1805 the French burned much of Roseau to the ground and from then on the island remained firmly in the possession of the British, who established sugar

---

WORTH A TRIP

EMERALD POOL

Easily accessible Emerald Pool (site fee US$5) takes its name from its lush green setting and clear water. At the base of a 40ft waterfall, the pool is deep enough for a refreshing dip. The 0.3-mile path to get here winds through a rainforest of massive ferns and tall trees. On the way back there are two viewpoints – one is a panorama of the Atlantic Coast and the other is a great view of Morne Trois Pitons, Dominica's second-highest mountain. The path can get a bit slippery in places so it's best to wear sturdy shoes rather than sandals, especially after rain. Come before 10am or after 3pm to avoid crowds.

The pool is on the well-maintained road linking Canefield and Castle Bruce. The drive is about 30 minutes from either.

plantations on Dominica's more accessible slopes.

Independence

In 1967 Dominica gained autonomy in internal affairs as a West Indies Associated State, and on November 3, 1978 (the 485th anniversary of Columbus' 'discovery'), Dominica became an independent republic within the Commonwealth.

The initial year of independence was a turbulent one. In June 1979 the island's first prime minister, Patrick John, was forced to resign after a series of corrupt schemes surfaced, including one clandestine land deal to transfer 15% of the island to US developers. In August 1979 Hurricane David, packing winds of 150mph, struck the island with devastating force. Forty-two people were killed and 75% of the islanders' homes were destroyed or severely damaged.

In July 1980 Dame Mary Eugenia Charles was elected prime minister, the first woman in the Caribbean to hold the office. She survived two unsuccessful coups right after her inauguration and subsequently managed to stay in office for 15 years.

21st-Century Dominica

Dominica's more recent political history has also been somewhat of a rollercoaster ride. After the sudden death of popular prime minister Roosevelt Douglas ('Rosie') in 2000, after only eight months in office, his successor – the radical Pierre Charles – also died on the job, four years later. In 2004 the then 31-year-old Roosevelt Skerrit stepped into the breach. A popular choice with young people, Skerrit comes from a Rastafarian farming family in the north of the island; he was reelected in 2009.

Skerrit moved quickly to sever long-standing diplomatic relations with Taiwan in favor of ties with mainland China in exchange for US$100 million in aid. The filming of the second and third *Pirates of the Caribbean* movies in 2005 was another major boost to the island's economy.

In August 2007 Hurricane Dean beat up Dominica and the nearby islands, causing at least two deaths and wiping out 99% of Dominica's banana crop, putting huge economic pressure on the small island nation.

In January 2008 Dominica joined the Bolivarian Alternative for the Americas (ALBA) – a trade group that includes Venezuela, Cuba, Bolivia and Nicaragua, designed to counterbalance American trade power. Following a special ALBA meeting in February 2009, Skerrit announced that he had secured at least part of a US$49 million fund to boost food security in the Caribbean.

In November 2010, the Office of the Carib Council petitioned the Dominican government to officially replace the term 'Carib', which is rooted in colonial times, to the indigenous community's original name, the Kalinago people. At the time of writing, this request had not been granted.

Culture

Dominica draws on a mix of cultures: French place names feature as often as English; African language, foods and customs mingle with European traditions as part of the island's Creole culture; and the Caribs still carve dugouts (canoes), build houses on stilts and weave distinctive basketwork. Rastafarian influences are strong here.

About a third of Dominica's 70,400 people live in and around Roseau. Some 87% are of African descent and about 2200 are indigenous Kalinago (aka Caribs).

With a 61.5% Roman Catholic population and religious observance commonplace, conservative values are strong and family holds an important place in Dominican society.

Much ado has been made of the number of centenarians who live here – Ma Pampo is the most famous, dying at 128 years of

---

DOMINICA & CHINA

March 1, 2011 saw the beginning of the Roseau to Portsmouth Road Rehabilitation project, which is entirely funded by the Chinese government. It is the third of the so-called 'Four Pillar Projects,' a series of gifts promised by mainland China in exchange for cutting diplomatic relations with Taiwan in 2004. A grammar school and the snazzy Windsor Sports Stadium in Roseau have already been completed; the rehabilitation of Princess Margaret Hospital will be the fourth pillar of this dollar diplomacy.

age in 2003. There are currently about two dozen centenarians and even the average life expectancy at birth is 75.7 years, making Dominica 76th in terms of life expectancy out of 222 countries.

Arts

Dominica's most celebrated author, Jean Rhys, was born in Roseau in 1890. Although she moved to England at age 16 and made only one brief return visit to Dominica, much of her work draws upon her childhood experiences in the West Indies. Rhys touches lightly upon her life in Dominica in *Voyage in the Dark* (1934) and in her autobiography, *Smile Please* (1979). Her most famous work, *Wide Sargasso Sea* (1966), a novel set mostly in Jamaica and an unmentioned Dominica, was made into a film in 1993.

Landscape & Wildlife

Dominica is an island of dramatic mountains that seem to drop straight down to the sea, and what few beaches there are have been very lightly developed. For the most part the nature here is untouched, save for the rusted cars that dot the roadsides like so many memorials to bad driving.

The Land

Dominica is 29 miles long and 16 miles wide and embraces the highest mountains in the Eastern Caribbean; the loftiest peak, Morne Diablotin, is 4747ft high. The mountains, which act as a magnet for rain, serve as a water source for the island's purported 365 rivers. En route to the coast, many of the rivers cascade over steep cliffs, giving the island an abundance of waterfalls – about 40% of local power is generated by hydroelectricity.

Wildlife

Whales and dolphins patrol the deep waters off Dominica's sheltered west coast. Sperm whales, which grow to a length of 70ft, are the most commonly sighted cetacean; the main season is October to March.

For near-shore divers, the marine life tends to be of the smaller variety – sea horses included – but there are spotted eagle rays, barracuda and sea turtles as well.

More than 160 bird species have been sighted on Dominica, giving it some of the most diverse birdlife in the Eastern Carib-

bean. Of these, 59 species nest on the island, including two endemic and endangered parrot species: Dominica's national bird, the Sisserou parrot, and the smaller Jaco parrot.

The island has small tree frogs, many lizards, 13 bat species, 55 butterfly species, boa constrictors that grow nearly 10ft in length and four other types of snake (none poisonous).

Dominica also used to have an abundance of large frogs known as 'mountain chicken', which live only here and on Montserrat. Its numbers have been dwindling significantly, first because of overconsumption (it's considered a culinary delicacy) and second because of a virulent fungus. The frogs now enjoy protected status and may no longer be eaten.

The most abundant tree on the island is the gommier, a huge gum tree used by the Kalinago to make dugouts.

Environmental Issues

In 2010, Dominica was named among the top ten Developing World's Best Ethical Destinations by *Ethical Traveler*, a San Francisco-based watchdog group, based on its record of environmental protection, social welfare and human rights. Contributing to the distinction was that, since 2008, Dominica no longer allows the Japanese to engage in commercial whaling in its waters. Nevertheless, environmentalists are worried about the impact of the massive cruise ships that dock here to refill water supplies and dump waste. The government's plan to allow Venezuela to build an oil refinery in Dominica also met with major objections from environmentalists but the plan has stalled for now.

SURVIVAL GUIDE

Directory A–Z

Accommodations

Dominica has no big resorts but it does have all sorts of wonderful places to hang your hat, from cottages tucked into the jungle, artsy boutique inns, guesthouses dripping with local color and remote ecohideaways. Prices are very reasonable compared to other Caribbean islands. However, off-property dining options may be elusive at some of the more far-flung places, and on-site meal

PRACTICALITIES

» **Electricity** 220/240V, 50/60 cycles; North American two-pin sockets.

» **Local taxes** 15% VAT for food and goods, 10% VAT for hotel bills.

» **Newspapers** The weekly *Chronicle* is the national newspaper.

» **Radio** State broadcaster DBS on 88.1FM and 595AM.

» **Weights & Measures** Imperial system.

plans can easily add US$50 per person to your daily tally.

In this book we list rates for the peak season (December to April), so expect significant discounts at other times. The price breakdown is as follows:

$	budget	under US$75
$$	midrange	US$75 to US$200
$$$	top end	over US$200

In most cases, room rates listed do not include the 10% value-added tax (VAT) and a 10% to 15% service charge. Always enquire what's included when making a reservation.

Activities

There is a free pdf hiking guide on www.dominica.dm. In addition, trail maps published by the Dominica's Forestry Division are available for a small fee at the forestry office in Roseau's botanic gardens. The division can also refer you to guides who are expert in the flora and fauna of the island. Certified guides are also recommended for some of the hikes, most notably the one to Boiling Lake. The tourist office (☑448-2045) can also make referrals.

Business Hours

In this book we only list opening hours if they differ from these standards.

Banks 8am-2pm Mon-Thu, to 5pm Fri

Bars noon-11pm

Businesses 8am-4pm Mon-Fri, lunch break 1-2pm

Restaurants breakfast 7:30-10am, lunch noon-2:30pm, dinner 6-9:30pm

Shops 8am-4pm Mon-Fri, to 1pm Sat (lunch break 1-2pm)

Embassies & Consulates

The nearest US embassy is in Barbados.

UK (☑440-2340; http://ukinbarbados.fco.gov.uk/en/) Honorary consul.

Food

Price ranges quoted with our restaurant listings refer to a meal consisting of an appetizer and a main course. For Dominica, the breakdown is as follows:

$	budget	less than EC$30
$$	midrange	US$30 to US$50
$$$	top end	more than EC$50

Gay & Lesbian Travelers

Same-sex sexual activity is still on the books as being illegal and punishable by up to 10 years in prison. Even though the law is not enforced, it's worth remembering that Dominica is a socially conservative and deeply religious country. Discretion is advised, so no PDA (public displays of affection). In hotels, to be on the safe side, get a room with two beds and don't advertise that you'll be sharing one.

Health

The Princess Margaret Hospital (with a hyperbaric chamber for decompression sickness) in Roseau, Marigot Hospital and the Portsmouth Hospital are the three main medical facilities. Intensive care units are available at Princess Margaret and Portsmouth hospitals.

According to the US Center for Disease Control, drinking tap water on Dominica is not recommended, although many people do it without any problems. Most, however, prefer the taste of bottled water, which is cheap and widely available.

Internet Access

Dominica is extremely well wired and even the most basic guesthouse in the rainforest will likely have an internet hookup or wi-fi. Public libraries and an increasing number of cafes offer free wi-fi. Dedicated internet cafes are only found in Roseau and Portsmouth. Charges range from EC$3 to EC$8 per half-hour.

Money

The Eastern Caribbean dollar (EC$) is used and US dollars are widely accepted. Unless rates are posted in US dollars, as is the norm with accommodations, it usually works out better to use EC dollars.

There aren't many ATMs outside of Roseau and Portsmouth.

Some restaurant bills already include a 10% service charge, in which case additional tipping is optional. For exceptional service, a small extra amount will be much appreciated. If service is not included, tip 10% to 15%. Housekeeping staff get about US$2 or US$3 per day, while for porters and bellhops a tip of US$1 per bag is appropriate.

Post

The main post office is in Roseau; there are small post offices in larger villages.

If you're sending anything to Dominica, it's important to include 'Commonwealth of Dominica' in the address to prevent it being accidentally sent to the Dominican Republic.

Public Holidays

In addition to the holidays observed throughout the region (p872), Dominica has the following public holidays:

Carnival Monday & Tuesday Two days preceding Ash Wednesday (the beginning of Lent, 46 days before Easter)

May Day May 1

August Monday First Monday in August

Independence Day/Creole Day November 3

Community Service Day November 4

Telephone

Dominica's country code is ⏎767. To call from North America, dial ⏎1-767 + the seven-digit local number. Elsewhere, dial your country's international access code, + ⏎767 + the local number. Within Dominica you just need to dial the seven-digit local number. For directory information dial ⏎118; for international calls dial ⏎0.

Dominica has coin and (more commonly) card phones. You can buy phonecards at telecommunications offices and convenience stores. Prepaid SIM cards for unlocked cell phones are available at Digicel stores and some convenience stores throughout Dominica. Rates are between EC$0.25 and EC$0.85 for outgoing calls. Incoming calls are free. Some hotels and rental-car companies also provide cell phones for free or a small fee.

Tourist Information

There are local tourist offices in Roseau and Calibishie.

Travelers with Disabilities

Because of the mountainous landscape, most inland accommodations have steep stairs that tend to be hard to navigate. Some of the bigger hotels in Roseau, Castle Comfort and Portsmouth can make arrangements for disabled travelers.

Getting There & Away

Entering Dominica

Visitors to Dominica must have a valid passport and – in principle – a round-trip or onward ticket. French nationals may visit for up to two weeks with an official Carte d'Identité.

ECOTOURISM SITES PASSES

Dominica's ecotourism sites are its biggest attraction. In order to help maintain them, a site fee of US$5 is levied on all foreign visitors for each of the following sites: Boeri Lake, Boiling Lake, Indian River, Morne Trois Pitons, Middleham Falls, Freshwater Lake, Morne Diablotin Trail, Cabrits National Park, Emerald Pool, Trafalgar Falls, Soufriere Sulfur Springs and the Syndicate Parrot Preserve. Permits for the latter five can be purchased at the entrance to the site; for the others, there are vendors in the vicinity. A weekly pass for US$12 grants unlimited access to all sites except Soufriere Sulfur Springs. There is also a US$2 user fee per dive, snorkel or kayak excursion in the Soufriere/Scotts Head Marine Park. Proceeds go to conservation efforts and park maintenance.

Air

There are no direct flights from Europe or the US, so overseas visitors must travel via a gateway island such as Antigua, Barbados or Sint Maarten.

Dominica has two airports; the small **Canefield Airport** about 15 minutes north of Roseau handles only regional flights on small aircraft. Most flights arrive at **Melville Hall Airport**, on the northeast side of the island about a 90-minute drive away from Roseau. Both airports have ATMs, a snack bar and free wi-fi.

There is an EC$59 (US$23) departure tax for anyone over age 12 when leaving Dominica. Bring cash.

The following airlines serve Dominica from these destinations:

American Eagle (www.aa.com) San Juan

LIAT (www.fly-liat.com) Antigua, Barbados, Guadeloupe

Sea

CRUISE SHIP

Cruise ships docks at Bayfront in central Roseau, Woodbridge Bay, north of Roseau and Cabrits, north of Portsmouth. Bayfront is by far the busiest port.

FERRY

L'Express des Îles (☑448-2181; www.express-des-iles.com) connects Dominica several times weekly on 300-seater catamarans with the following nearby islands. (There are discounts of 60% for children under two; 25% for students and children ages two to 12; and 10% for passengers younger than 26 or older than 60.)

Pointe-à-Pitre (Guadeloupe) one-way/return €67/100, 1¾ hours

Fort-de-France (Martinique) one-way/return €67/100, 1½ hours

Castries (St Lucia) one-way/return €67/100, 4½ hours

Getting Around

Bus

Bus travel is the most economical way of getting around Dominica. Private minibuses run between major cities from 6am to 7pm Monday to Saturday, stopping as needed along the way. Fares are set by the government and range from EC$1.75 to EC$11.

Car & Motorcycle

DRIVER'S LICENSE

Drivers need a local license issued by a car-rental agency. It costs US$12 or EC$30 and is valid for one month. You must be aged between 25 and 65 and have at least two years' of driving experience.

RENTAL

Rates start at US$40 per day for sedans and US$45 for 4WD; many of the local agencies give discounts for rentals over two days. A 4WD is recommended for exploring in the mountains – even some of the main roads at the higher altitudes are in bad condition. Basic liability is included but taking out collision damage waiver (CDW) costs an extra US$10 to US$15 per day with a deductible of around US$800. A 15% VAT charge is added to the total bill. All companies offer free pick-ups and drop-offs, unlimited mileage and cell phone rentals.

Budget Rent-a-Car (☑449-2080; www.budget.com)

Courtesy Car Rental (☑448-7763; www.dominicacarrentals.com)

Island Car Rentals (☑255-6844; www.islandcar.dm)

Road Runner Car Rental (☑440-2952; www.roadrunnercarrental.com)

Valley Rent-A-Car (☑448-3233; www.valleyrentacar.com).

ROAD CONDITIONS

Dominican roads are narrow, have no dividing lines and are often hemmed in by deep, axle-killing rain gutters: three inches too far to the left and your wheels will enter a yawning concrete ditch; three inches too far to the right and you risk swapping rearview mirrors with oncoming cars. Or worse. Other dangers: potholes big enough to swallow small goats, blindingly blind curves, visitors not accustomed to driving on the left and locals getting impatient with them. Road upgrades are in the works, hopefully soon, making driving a little less of a suicidal proposition.

ROAD RULES

Dominicans drive on the left-hand side of the road. Outside of Roseau, gas stations are few and far between. You'll find some in larger towns, including Canefield, Portsmouth and Marigot. The speed limit in towns is 20mph.

Honk the horn often around the blind curves. If causing a backup, the polite thing to do is pull over to the side of the road whenever it's safe to let traffic pass.

Hitchhiking

Hitchhiking, alone or in a group, is always a risky proposition and is not advised. However, picking up hitchhikers, especially if there is only one of them and two or more of you, is a great way to meet locals and pick up good insider tips. Locals of either sex and of all ages hitchhike here.

Taxi

Taxi fares are regulated by the government, but be sure to confirm the fare with the driver. To order a cab, call the **Dominica Taxi Association** (☎449-8553). Sample fares from Melville Hall Airport to the following:

Roseau or Portsmouth US$26

Calibishie or Carib Territory US$15

Scott's Head US$34

Castle Comfort US$28

Dominican Republic

Best Beaches

» Playa Rincón (p427)
» Bahía de las Águilas (p419)
» Bávaro (p420)
» Playa Limón (p420)
» Playa Encuentro (p433)

Best Places to Stay

» Sofitel Nicolás de Ovando (p415)
» Lomita Maravilla (p431)
» Natura Cabañas (p435)
» Peninsula House (p432)
» Rancho Baiguate (p439)

Why Go?

The Dominican Republic is defined by its hundreds of miles of coastline – some with picturesque white-sand beaches shaded by rows of palm trees, other parts lined dramatically with rocky cliffs. Symbolizing both limits and escapes, the sea is the common denominator across fishing villages, where the shoreline is used for mooring boats, indulgent tourist playgrounds, small towns, and cities like Santo Domingo – the Caribbean's largest and the site of New World firsts.

Beyond the capital, much of the DR is distinctly rural. Further inland are vistas reminiscent of the European alps: four of the Caribbean's five highest peaks rise above the fertile lowlands surrounding Santiago. Remote deserts extend through the southwest, giving the DR a complexity not found on other islands. The country's roller-coaster past is writ large in the diversity of its ethnicities, not to mention the physical design of its towns and cities.

When to Go

Except in the central mountains, temperatures don't vary much, averaging a summery 28°C (81°F) to 31°C (87°F). The rainy season is May to October, though in Samaná and on the north coast it can last until December. August and September constitute hurricane season. The main tourist seasons are December to February, July to August, and Semana Santa (the week before Easter). Expect higher prices and more-crowded beaches at these times. February has great weather and you can enjoy Carnaval and the whales in Samaná. November is good, too – you'll miss the whales but catch baseball season.

Itineraries

ONE WEEK

Spend a full day exploring Santo Domingo's old colonial center, then make your base at the deservedly popular beaches of Bávaro and Punta Cana. Not far south of here is Bayahibe, with the DR's best scuba diving and a number of excursion options. Allow for some relaxing beach time – for more privacy head to deserted Playa Limón further up the coast.

TWO WEEKS

With two weeks, spend a couple of days in Santo Domingo. Visit the waterfalls of Jarabacoa on day three, with whitewater rafting or canyoning the next day. Then go north to Cabarete, which has world-class water sports and mountain biking. There's great diving and beaches in nearby Sosúa and Río San Juan – enough to keep you happy for two or three days.

Next you're off to the Península de Samaná. If it's mid-January to mid-March, go whale-watching. Otherwise, visit the waterfall near El Limón. Spend another two days hiking or boating around Las Galeras. For a bit more nightlife, base yourself in Las Terrenas instead.

GETTING TO NEIGHBORING ISLANDS

There is a ferry from Santo Domingo to Puerto Rico. Airlines connect the DR to Cuba, Puerto Rico, and Turks and Caicos.

Essential Food & Drink

» **La Bandera (the flag)** The most typically Dominican meal. Consists of white rice, *habichuela* (red beans), stewed meat, salad and fried green plantains.

» **Bananas (guineos)** A staple served stewed, candied or boiled and mashed. With plantains, the dish is called *mangú*; with pork rinds mixed in it is called *mofongo*.

» **Fish** Central to the Dominican diet – usually served in one of four ways: *al ajillo* (with garlic), *al coco* (in coconut sauce), *al criolla* (with a mild tomato sauce) or *a la diabla* (with a spicy tomato sauce).

» **Pastelitos** By far the most common snack in the DR – fried dough containing beef or chicken, which has been stewed with onions, olives, tomatoes and then chopped and mixed with peas, nuts and raisins.

» **Dominican ron (rum)** Known for its smoothness and hearty taste. Dozens of local brands are available, but the big three are Brugal, Barceló and Bermudez.

AT A GLANCE

» **Currency** Dominican Republic peso (RD$); US dollars (US$) also accepted some places

» **Language** Spanish

» **Money** ATMs widely available; only dispense Dominican Republic pesos

» **Visas** Generally not required for stays up to 30 days; see p446

Fast Facts

» **Area** 48,717 sq km
» **Population** 9 million
» **Capital** Santo Domingo
» **Telephone country code** ☑809
» **Emergency** ☑911

Set Your Budget

» **Budget hotel room** RD$800
» **Two-course evening meal** RD$600
» **Museum entrance** RD$60
» **Beer** RD$60
» **City bus ticket** RD$12

Resources

» **Dominican Republic One** (www.dr1.com) Daily news, travel information and a busy forum

» **Dominican Today** (www.dominicantoday.com) News from the DR in English

» **Go Dominican Republic** (www.godominicanrepublic.com) Official site of DR tourism authority; good overview of destinations and practical information

Dominican Republic Highlights

1 Wander the cobblestone backstreets of Santo Domingo's **Zona Colonial** (p409)

2 Enjoy miles of beautiful beach and fun at **Bávaro and Punta Cana** (p420)

3 Feel very small after witnessing 30-ton humpbacks breaching and diving on a **whale-watching trip** (p425)

4 Strap yourself to the board and get swept up in the thrill

of skimming across the waves while **kitesurfing** (p433)

5 Snorkel undisturbed around some of the best reefs the country has to offer at **Playa Frontón** (p427)

6 Down a cocktail at an oceanside restaurant in cosmopolitan **Las Terrenas** (p429)

7 Go white-water rafting on the Caribbean's only raftable

river, the turbulent **Río Yaque del Norte** (p438)

8 Linger at the top of **Pico Duarte** (p437), taking in views of the Atlantic and the Caribbean

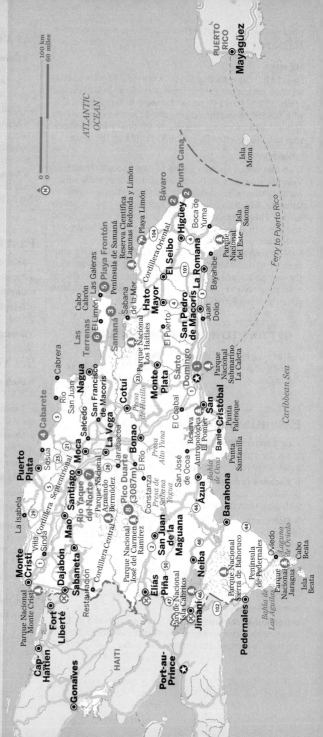

SANTO DOMINGO

POP 2.9 MILLION

Santo Domingo, or 'La Capital' as it's typically called, is a collage of cultures and neighborhoods. It's where the sounds of life – domino pieces slapped on tables, backfiring mufflers and horns from chaotic traffic, merengue and *bachata* (Dominican music) blasting from *colmados* (corner stores) – are most intense. At the heart of the city is the Zona Colonial, where you'll find one of the oldest churches and the oldest surviving European fortress, among other New World firsts. Amid the cobblestone streets, it would be easy to forget Santo Domingo is in the Caribbean. But this is an intensely urban city, home not only to colonial-era architecture but also to hot clubs, vibrant cultural institutions and elegant restaurants. Santo Domingo somehow manages to embody the contradictions central to the Dominican experience: a living museum, a metropolis crossed with a seaside resort, and a business, political and media center with a laid-back, casual spirit.

◎ Sights & Activities

Most of Santo Domingo's historical and interesting sites are in the Zona Colonial and are easily explored on foot. Sites further afield, like the Faro a Colón and Jardín Botánico, are best reached by taxi.

ZONA COLONIAL

For those fascinated by the origin of the 'New World,' by the dramatic and complicated story of the first encounter between native people of the Americas and Europeans, the Zona Colonial, listed as a Unesco World Heritage site, is a fascinating place to explore. It is 11 square blocks, a mix of cobblestone and paved streets on the west bank of the Río Ozama, where the deep river meets the Caribbean Sea.

Catedral Primada de América   CHURCH
(Primate Cathedral of America; Parque Colón; ◎9am-4pm) The oldest cathedral in operation in the Américas. Diego Columbus set the first stone in 1514, but construction didn't begin in earnest until the arrival of the first bishop in 1521. Numerous architects worked on the cathedral until 1540, which is why its vault is Gothic, its arches are Romanesque and its ornamentation is baroque. Signs in English and Spanish beside each of the 14 interior chapels and other features describe their rich histories. Shorts and tank tops are strictly prohibited.

TOP CHOICE Museo Alcázar de Colón   MUSEUM
(Museum Citadel of Columbus; ☏809-682-4750; Plaza España; admission RD$60; ◎9am-5pm Tue-Sat, to 4pm Sun) Designed in the Gothic-Mudejar transitional style, this was once the residence of Columbus' son, Diego, and his wife, Doña María de Toledo, during the early 16th century. The magnificent building we see today is the result of three restorations, the last in 1992. Today it houses many household pieces said to have belonged to the Columbus family. The building itself – if not the objects inside – is definitely worth a look.

Museo de las Casas Reales   MUSEUM
(Museum of the Royal Houses; ☏809-682-4202; Las Damas; admission RD$50; ◎9am-5pm, closed Mon) Built in the Renaissance style during the 16th century, this building was the longtime seat of Spanish authority for the entire Caribbean region, housing the governor's office and the powerful Audiencia Real (Royal Court), among others. It showcases colonial-period objects, including many treasures recovered from Spanish galleons that foundered in nearby waters. Each room has been restored according to its original style, and displays range from Taíno artifacts to dozens of hand-blown wine bottles and period furnishings.

FREE Museo Mundo de Ambar   MUSEUM
(World of Amber Museum; ☏809-682-3309; www.amberworldmuseum.com; 2nd fl, Arzobispo Meriño 452; ◎9am-6pm Mon-Sat, to 2pm Sun) An impressive collection of amber samples from around the world, and excellent exhibits explaining in Spanish and English its prehistoric origins, its use throughout the ages, Dominican mining processes, and its present-day value to the science and art worlds. The 1st-floor shop sells jewelry made from amber, larimar and more ordinary stones.

FREE Larimar Museum   MUSEUM
(☏809-689-6605; www.larimarmuseum.com; 2nd fl, Isabel la Católica 54; ◎8am-6pm Mon-Sat, to 2pm Sun) This museum is the best place to learn about larimar, though of course it's meant to inspire you to make a purchase from the 1st-floor jewelry store. Signage is in Spanish and English.

FREE Convento de la Orden de los Predicadores   CHURCH
(cnr Hostos & Padre Billini; ◎hrs vary) Built in 1510, this was the first convent of the Dominican order in the Americas. It is also the

SANTO DOMINGO

DOMINICAN REPUBLIC SANTO DOMINGO

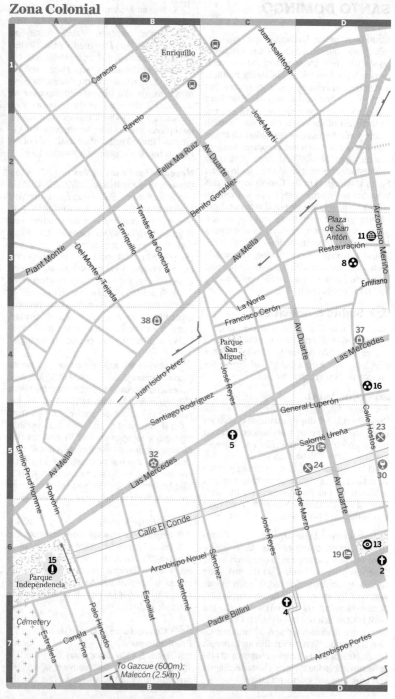

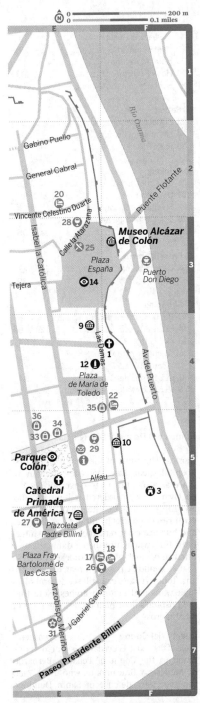

place where Father Bartolomé de las Casas – the famous chronicler of Spanish atrocities committed against indigenous peoples – did most of his writing. Be sure to take a look at the vault of the chapel; it is remarkable for its stone zodiac wheel, which is carved with mythological and astrological representations.

Iglesia de Nuestra Señora de las Mercedes
CHURCH

(Church of Our Lady of Mercy; cnr Las Mercedes & José Reyes; ⊘varies) Constructed during the first half of the 16th century, the church was reconstructed on numerous occasions following pirate attacks, earthquakes and hurricanes. It is remarkable for its pulpit, which is sustained by a support in the shape of a serpent demon.

Parque Colón
PARK

(cnr El Conde & Isabel la Católica) Beside the Catedral Primada de América, this historic park contains several shade trees and a large statue of Admiral Columbus himself. It's the meeting place for local residents and is alive with tourists, townsfolk, hawkers, guides, taxi drivers, shoeshine boys, tourist police and thousands of pigeons all day long.

Plaza España
PARK

This large, open area in front of the Museo Alcázar de Colón has been made over many times. Numerous restaurants run along its northwest side in buildings that served as warehouses through most of the 16th and 17th centuries. This is a popular place for a meal or a drink at an outdoor table around sunset.

Fortaleza Ozama
HISTORIC SITE

(☑809-686-0222; Las Damas; admission RD$70; ⊘9am-6:30pm Mon-Sat, to 4pm Sun) This is the oldest colonial military edifice in the New World. Construction began in 1502, and it served as a military garrison and prison until the 1970s, when it was opened to the public for touring. **Torre del Homenaje** (Tower of Homage) is the main structure, with 1.8m-(6ft-)thick walls containing dozens of riflemen's embrasures and offering great rooftop views. Near the door there are several guides whose knowledge of the fort is generally quite impressive. A 20-minute tour should cost around US$3.50 per person.

FREE Panteón Nacional
MONUMENT

(National Pantheon; Las Damas; ⊘9am-5pm, closed Mon) Originally constructed in 1747 as a Jesuit

Zona Colonial

church, this was also a tobacco warehouse and a theater before dictator Trujillo restored the building in 1958 as the final resting place of the country's most illustrious persons. Shorts and tank tops are discouraged.

Monasterio de San Francisco HISTORIC SITE
(Hostos) The first monastery in the New World belonged to the first order of Franciscan friars who arrived to evangelize the island. Dating from 1508, the monastery was set ablaze by Sir Francis Drake in 1586, rebuilt, devastated by an earthquake in 1673, rebuilt, ruined by another earthquake in 1751 and rebuilt again. From 1881 until the 1930s it was used as an insane asylum – portions of the chains used to secure inmates can still be seen – until a powerful hurricane shut it down for good. Today the site is a dramatic set of ruins that is occasionally used to stage concerts and artistic performances.

Ruinas del Hospital San Nicolás de Barí HISTORIC SITE
(Hostos) The ruins of the New World's first hospital, near Las Mercedes, remain in place as a monument to Governor Nicolás de Ovando, who ordered it built in 1503. So sturdy was the edifice that it survived centuries of attacks by pirates, earthquakes and hurricanes. It remained virtually intact until 1911, when, after being damaged by a hurricane, much of it was knocked down so that it wouldn't pose a threat to pedestrians. Today visitors can still see several of its high walls and Moorish arches. Note that the hospital's floor plan follows the form of a Latin cross.

Puerta del Conde MONUMENT
(Gate of the Count; El Conde) This gate owes its name to the Count of Peñalba, Bernardo de Meneses y Bracamonte, who in 1655 led the successful defense of Santo Domingo

against an invading force of 13,000 British troops. The gate is the supreme symbol of Dominican patriotism because right beside it, in February 1844, a handful of brave Dominicans executed a bloodless coup against occupying Haitian forces; their actions resulted in the creation of a wholly independent Dominican Republic. It also was atop this gate that the very first Dominican flag was raised. Just west of the gate inside **Parque Independencia** look for the **Altar de la Patria**, a mausoleum that holds the remains of three national heroes: Juan Pablo Duarte, Francisco del Rosario Sánchez and Ramón Matías Mella. The park itself has a few benches but little shade.

Other notable churches in the Zona Colonial include **Capilla de Nuestra Señora de los Remedios** (cnr de las Damas & Las Mercedes), **Iglesia de Santa Clara** (cnr Padre Billini & Isabel la Católica) and **Iglesia de la Regina Angelorum** (cnr Padre Billini & José Reyes).

OTHER NEIGHBORHOODS

Faro a Colón   MONUMENT
(Columbus Lighthouse; Parque Mirador del Este; admission RD$65; ☺9am-5:15pm Tue-Sun) Resembling a cross between a Soviet-era apartment block and a Las Vegas version of an ancient Mayan ruin, this massive monument is worth visiting for its controversial and complicated history. East of the Río Ozama, the Faro's massive cement flanks stretch nearly a block and stand some 10 stories high, forming the shape of a cross. High-powered lights on the roof can project a blinding white cross into the sky but are rarely turned on because doing so causes blackouts in surrounding neighborhoods. At the intersection of the cross's arms is a guarded tomb that purportedly contains Columbus' remains. However, Spain and Italy dispute that claim, both saying that *they* have the admiral's bones. Inside the monument a long series of exhibition halls displays documents (mostly reproductions) relating to Columbus' voyages and the exploration and conquest of the Americas.

Jardín Botánico Nacional   GARDEN
(National Botanic Garden; www.jbn-sdq.org; Av República de Colombia; adult/child RD$50/40; ☺9am-6pm, ticket booth to 5pm) The lush grounds here cover 2 sq km and include vast areas devoted to aquatic plants, orchids, bromeliads, ferns, endemic plants, palm

trees, a Japanese garden and much more. The on-site **Ecological Museum** (☺9am-4pm, ticket booth to 5pm) exhibits and explains the major ecosystems found in the DR, including mangroves and cloud forests, plus a special display on Parque Nacional Los Haitises. Once inside you can stay until 6pm. An **open-air trolley** (☺every 30min to 4:30pm) takes passengers on a pleasant half-hour turn about the park and is especially enjoyable for children.

The garden is located in a neighborhood in the northwest corner of the city, and is a bit hard to find. A taxi from the Zona Colonial costs around RD$250; be sure to arrange a return trip with the driver, as you won't find many taxis out here.

Museo del Hombre Dominicano   MUSEUM
(Museum of the Dominican Man; Plaza de la Cultura; admission RD$75; ☺10am-5pm Tue-Sun) The most extensive of the museums clustered around the Plaza de la Cultura in Gazcue; highlights here are an impressive collection of Taíno artifacts, including stone axes and intriguing urns. Other displays focus on slavery, the colonial period and Carnaval. The explanations are all in Spanish and the displays are very old-fashioned. English-speaking guides can be requested at the entry – the service is free, but small tips are customary.

PORTS OF CALL

There are a number of options even for a short visit in these ports.

Santo Domingo

The city's most interesting sights are all located in the cobblestone blocks of the Zona Colonial only steps from the port.

» Take a walking tour of Zona Colonial (p414), eat in a restaurant in Plaza España (p411) and walk part of the Malecón

Samaná

» Take a boat out to the island of Cayo Levantado (p424)

» Hang out at a cafe at Las Terrenas (p429)

» Ride a horse to Cascada El Limón (p424)

» Sunbathe at Playa Rincón (p427)

SANTO DOMINGO FOR CHILDREN

Santo Domingo isn't particularly kid-friendly. Outside of the Zona Colonial, it doesn't cater for pedestrians, and there are no beaches and few parks, or at least few that are well maintained and shady. **Parque Colón** (cnr El Conde & Isabel la Católica) and **Parque Duarte** (cnr Padre Billini & Av Duarte) in the Zona Colonial are basically flagstone plazas where you can sit on a bench and feed pigeons.

Museo Infantil Trampolín (☑809-685-5551; www.trampolin.org.do, in Spanish; Las Damas; adult/child RD$100/60; ☺9am-5pm Tue-Fri, 10am-6pm Sat & Sun) is a high-tech, hands-on natural-history, biology, science, ecology and social museum all wrapped into one. Enthusiastic guides (most are Spanish-speaking) lead kids through the exhibits: the earthquake machines and volcano simulations are big hits, less so the exhibit on children's legal rights.

If the kids won't have a chance to snorkel and see underwater creatures in their natural habitat, the **Acuario Nacional** (National Aquarium; ☑809-766-1709; Av España; adult/child RD$50/20; ☺9am-5:30pm Tue-Sun) can substitute. Though run-down in parts, it has an exciting underwater walkway where you can watch sea turtles, stingrays and huge fish pass overhead. Signs are in Spanish only. Across the street is **Agua Splash Caribe** (☑809-591-5927; adult/child RD$200/150; ☺11am-7pm Tue-Sun), a not-very-well-tended water park. It's a lot of concrete, and safety probably isn't the best but... The easiest way to reach both these attractions east of the Río Ozama and on the way to the airport is taxi.

Adrian Tropical (p417) is an especially good place to eat with unruly youngsters. Hotels with pools – all those along the Malecón (p416) – are especially recommended and will allow you and the kids to take a break from sightseeing for several relaxing hours.

Museo de Arte Moderno   MUSEUM
(Plaza de la Cultura; admission RD$50; ☺10am-6pm Tue-Sun) The permanent collection here includes paintings and a few sculptures by the DR's best-known modern artists, including Luís Desangles, Adriana Billini and Martín Santos, but the temporary exhibitions tend to be fresher and more inventive. Also in Gazcue.

☞ Tours

Zona Colonial Walking Tours   WALKING TOUR
Interesting and informative walking tours of the Zona Colonial are offered daily by a number of official guides – look for men dressed in khakis and light-blue dress shirts, but always ask to see their official state-tourism license. Tours cover the most important buildings in the zone and can be tailored to your specific interests. Walks typically last 2½ hours and cost between US$20 and US$30 depending on the language that the tour is given in (ie Spanish and English are less expensive). To find a guide, head to Parque Colón – you'll find a number of them hanging out under the trees. Also be sure to agree upon a fee before setting out.

Horse-drawn Carriages   CARRIAGE TOUR
(with/without guide US$50/30) A more leisurely option is a horse-drawn carriage tour. Look

for them pulled to the side of the road near the corner of Calle Las Damas and El Conde.

★☆ Festivals & Events

Carnaval   CARNIVAL
Celebrated throughout the country every Sunday in February, culminating in a huge blowout in Santo Domingo the last weekend of the month or first weekend of March. Av George Washington (the Malecón) becomes an enormous party scene all day and night. Central to the celebration are the competitions of floats, costumes and masks representing traditional Carnaval characters.

Latin Music Festival   MUSIC
Held at the Olympic Stadium at the end of August (dates can change – inquire ahead), this huge three-day event attracts the top names in Latin music – jazz, salsa, merengue and *bachata*. Jennifer Lopez and Marc Anthony have performed in the past.

Merengue Festival   DANCE
The largest in the country, a two-week celebration of the DR's favorite music held every year at the end of July and beginning of August. Most of the activity is on the Malecón, but there are related events across the city.

🛌 Sleeping

The Zona Colonial is the most distinctive part of the city and therefore where most travelers prefer to stay. All of the sights and restaurants are within walking distance and there's an excellent choice of midrange and top-end hotels, some in attractive restored colonial-era buildings. Gazcue, a quiet residential area southwest of Parque Independencia, has several hotels in the midrange category, though there are far fewer eating options. The high-rise hotels on the Malecón are best if you're looking for resort-style amenities.

ZONA COLONIAL

Sofitel Nicolás de
Ovando   HISTORIC HOTEL $$$
(☎809-685-9955; www.sofitel.com; Las Damas; s US$220-336, d US$238-354; P❋⊛⊚) Even heads of state must thrill when they learn they're sleeping in the former home of the first governor of the Americas. Oozing character, old-world charm and a historic pedigree tough to beat, the Nicolás de Ovando is as far from a chain hotel as you can get. Indisputably one of the nicest hotels in the city, if not the nicest, it has 107 rooms that are definitely 21st-century – flat-screen TV, recessed Jacuzzi, luxurious boutique-style fixtures and linens. However, all this modernity is offset by beautifully crafted wood and stone interiors, cobblestone walkways, lushly shaded courtyards and a commanding view of the Río Ozama – the fabulous pool probably didn't exist during the governor's time. An excellent buffet breakfast is included in the rate; **La Residence** (mains US$17-35; ⊙lunch & dinner), the hotel's superb and elegant restaurant, has a separate entrance down the street.

TOP CHOICE Coco Boutique Hotel   BOUTIQUE HOTEL $
(☎809-685-8467;   www.cocoboutiquehotel.com; Arzobispo Portes 7; s/d US$70/90; ❋⊚) There's little traffic on this block in the southeastern corner of the Zona Colonial, which makes this hotel, four rooms in a renovated home, a particularly peaceful refuge. It doesn't have the character of some of the other renovated hotels, but the owners have designed each room individually with particular color schemes and themes; the black-vanilla room is probably the nicest. All have beautifully polished wood floors and access to the rooftop lounge with a Balinese-style bed and waterfront vistas. The meticulously maintained Plaza de Castro is right out the front door.

Hotel Atarazana   BOUTIQUE HOTEL $$
(☎809-688-3693;   www.hotel-atarazana.com; Vicente Celestino Duarte 19; s/d incl breakfast US$80/100; ❋⊚) A boutique hotel for the design conscious only a few meters away from Plaza España. Housed in a beautifully renovated building from the 1860s, all six rooms sport custom-made furniture from native materials along with high-concept fixtures and textiles you'd find in a magazine. Each of the light and airy rooms has a balcony, and breakfast is served in a secret garden-like patio shaded by lush vegetation; there's even a small Jacuzzi to relax in. Another option is the rooftop, which has fabulous views of the Zona Colonial and river.

El Beaterío
Guest House   HISTORIC GUESTHOUSE $
(☎809-687-8657; www.elbeaterio.com; Av Duarte 8; s/d incl breakfast with fan US$50/60, with air-con US$60/70; ❋⊚) Take thee to this nunnery – if you're looking for austere elegance. It's easy to imagine the former function of this 16th-century building with its heavy stone facade. The dark and vaulted front room is now a beautiful reading room and dining area, and there's a lush and sunny inner courtyard inspiring peace and tranquillity. Each of the 11 large rooms is sparsely furnished, but the wood-beamed ceilings and stone floors are truly special; the bathrooms are modern and well maintained.

Casa Naemie Hotel   HOTEL $$
(☎809-689-2215; www.casanaemie.com; Av Isabel la Católica 11; s/d incl breakfast RD$2000/3000; ❋⊚) This charming oasis only a few blocks from the oldest cathedral in the Americas feels like a European pension. Surrounding a narrow central courtyard are three floors of cozy, clean rooms with large modern bathrooms. An elegant lobby with a vaulted entranceway and brick flooring does double duty in the morning when the excellent breakfast is served.

Hotel Palacio   HOTEL $
(☎809-682-4730; www.hotel-palacio.com; Av Duarte 106; s/d incl breakfast from US$70/90; P❋⊚) Cross colonial with a little touch of medieval and you have the Palacio, a maze-like hotel occupying a 17th-century mansion only a block north of the Calle El Conde pedestrian mall. Service is exceptional and you'll need it to find your way past the charming nooks and crannies, which include reading areas, a gym, a small bar, a lush interior courtyard and stone-walled walkways. First-floor

rooms are German conquistador minimalist, while the larger 2nd-floor rooms are more modern and generic. The small rooftop pool is a big plus, as is the gym for the physically fit.

Hostal Nómadas
HOTEL $

(☎809-689-0057; www.hostalnomadas.com; Hostos 209; s/d incl breakfast US$30/50; ✳🛜) Good value for its central location on a quiet block only a few blocks from Parque Colón. The eight rooms here are rather nondescript with small TVs as well as bathrooms, but the rooftop terrace and restaurant is a big plus.

GAZCUE

Hotel La Danae
HOTEL $

(☎809-238-5609; www.ladanaehotel.com; Danae 18; s/d US$29/40; ✳) Dominican-owned La Danae is the best of a number of similar small hotels located on this quiet residential street. Choose from the older, cheaper rooms in the front building or the more modern ones in the back annex. The former have higher ceilings but are subject to street noise. All have cable TV, and there's a kitchen area for common use.

Hostal Duque de Wellington
HOTEL $

(☎809-682-4525; www.hotelduque.com; Av Independencia 304; s/d RD$1500/2000; P✳@🛜) With such an old-fashioned name, it's not surprising this hotel isn't fashionably modern. In fact, it's downright conservative, with room furnishings and decor that try terribly to be tasteful but are in the end fairly dowdy. Rooms on the 2nd floor have higher ceilings, and more expensive ones have balconies that provide more light. There's a restaurant and travel agency on the 1st floor.

MALECÓN

Hilton Hotel
HOTEL $$

(☎809-685-0000; www.hiltoncaribbean.com/santodomingo; Av George Washington 500; r from US$130; P✳@🛜) Easily the nicest of the luxury hotels on the Malecón, the Hilton is part of a huge complex including a casino, movie theaters and several restaurants, but much of it still remains vacant. As it's the highest of the high-rises, there's a long elevator ride to the top. Rooms are nicer and newer than its nearby competitors', and there's a bar and restaurant with stunning ocean views.

Hotel InterContinental
RESORT $$

(☎809-221-0000; www.intercontinental.com/santodomingo; Av George Washington 218; r from US$120; P✳@🛜) Other than the Hilton, the InterContinental has the plushest lobby of the hotels on the Malecón and an even more hip bar-lounge area. Like all the big hotels on the waterfront, the hotel also has pool, spa, tennis courts and casino, popular with tourists, and Dominicans on weekends.

✖ Eating

Santo Domingo has a good selection of restaurants in various price ranges. The ones in the Zona Colonial are usually the most convenient.

ZONA COLONIAL

Pat'e Palo
SPANISH, MEDITERRANEAN $$$

(☎809-687-8089; la Atarazana 25; mains RD$550; ⏰4:30pm-late Mon-Thu, 1:30pm-late Fri-Sun) Part of Plaza España's restaurant row, Pat'e Palo is for gourmands and anyone tired of the same old bland pasta and chicken. Everything here is special, but a personal recommendation is the Chilean sea bass served over Spanish-sausage risotto in a creamy beer sauce.

El Meson de Luis
DOMINICAN $$

(Hostos; mains RD$250; ⏰lunch & dinner) This simple and unpretentious restaurant is a downscale version of Mesón D'Bari across the street. It's mostly loyal locals who line up at the small bar or in the open-air dining room for filling plates of seafood and meat. Even though service isn't with a smile, it's a good choice, especially at dinnertime when it's not uncommon for a trio of musicians to serenade your table.

La Cafetera Colonial
DINER $

(El Conde; RD$60; ⏰breakfast, lunch & dinner) Everyone knows everyone else's name here. That can seem intimidating at first, especially because the narrow entranceway means new customers can't pull up a stool at the long lunch counter unnoticed. It's a classic greasy-spoon menu: eggs and toast, simple sandwiches and strong espresso (RD$30).

GAZCUE & MALECÓN

Hermanos Villar
DOMINICAN $$

(cnr Avs Independencia & Pasteur; RD$175; ⏰breakfast, lunch & dinner) Occupying almost an entire city block, Hermanos Villar has two parts: the bustling Dominican-style diner serving cafeteria food and hot, grilled deli sandwiches and the large outdoor garden restaurant slightly more upscale in terms of menu. The chicken *mofongo* (mashed plantains; RD$175) is delicious.

Adrian Tropical
DOMINICAN **$$**

(Av George Washington; mains RD$200; 8am-11pm Mon-Fri, 24hr Sat & Sun;) This popular family-friendly chain occupies a spectacular location overlooking the Caribbean. Waiters scurry throughout the two floors and outdoor dining area doling out Dominican specialties like *mofongo* and standard meat dishes.

Drinking

Los Tres Mosqueteros
BAR-CAFE

(El Conde 56; lunch-late;) This bar-cafe is one of several lining a cobblestone alleyway a few steps from Parque Colón. In addition to outdoor seating, it has an elegant indoor space with high ceilings and overhead fans. For those looking to make an afternoon of it, there's free wi-fi and a full menu.

Double's Bar
BAR

(Arzobispo Meriño; 6pm-late) Good-looking 20-somethings grind away to loud pop and Latin music at Double's. Others lounge around in groups downing bottles of Presidente, while the classic long wood bar is better for conversation.

Blue Limon Bar & Lounge
BAR

(cnr Isabel la Católica & Arzobispo Portes; 4pm-midnight Tue-Sun) A small, sophisticated spot with a table or two on a quiet plaza in the Zona Colonial.

El Patio del Canario
COCKTAIL BAR

(la Atarazana 1) Owned by a Dominican salsa star, this bar is for grown-ups; if the music gets too loud step out into the beautiful courtyard.

Onno's Bar
BAR

(Hostos btwn El Conde & Arzobispo Nouel; 5pm-1am Sun-Thu, to 3am Fri & Sat) There's always something going on at this fashionable hot spot just off El Conde: several flat-screen TVs, lasers, illuminated bar, DJs and smoke machine...

☆ Entertainment

Estadio Quisqueya
BASEBALL STADIUM

(www.estadioquisqueya.com.do; cnr Avs Tiradentes & San Cristóbal; tickets RD$250-1000; games 5pm Sun, 8pm Tue, Wed, Fri & Sat) The boys of summer play in the winter here, in this *béisbol*-mad city. Soon after the US major-league season ends in October, the 48-game Dominican season kicks off. From mid-November until early February, the top players from the DR with a handful of major and minor leaguers from the US compete all over the country. Esadio Quisqueya, the home field for two of the DR's six professional teams, Licey (www.licey.com) and Escogido (www.escogido), is one of the better places to see a game and experience the madness. Asking for the best seats available at the box office will likely run you RD$1000 and put you within several feet of either the ballplayers or the between-innings dancers.

The stadium is northwest of the Zona Colonial next to the neighborhood of Ensanche La Fe.

Guácara Taína
NIGHTCLUB

(www.guacarataina.net; Av Mirador del Sur 655; admission RD$300; 9pm-3am Thu-Sun) A somewhat legendary nightclub, now maybe at least as popular with cruise-ship passengers as Dominicans, Guácara Taína is still an interesting place to party. Located inside a huge underground cave in the Parque Mirador del Sur, this club hosts everything from raves to live merengue and hip-hop acts. The park is just northwest of the Centro de los Héroes in the western part of the city.

Centro Cultural Español
CULTURAL CENTER

(Spanish Cultural Center; www.ccesd.org, in Spanish; cnr Arzobispo Meriño & Arzobispo Portes; 10am-9pm Tue-Sun) Run by the Spanish embassy. Regularly hosts art exhibits, film festivals and concerts, all with a Spanish bent. It also has 15,000 items in its lending library. For a listing of events, stop by for a brochure. Admission is generally free but depends on the event.

CHA
NIGHTCLUB

(Av George Washington 165; 6pm-3am Fri-Sun, to 1am Sun) A fun gay club with a Miami-beach vibe. West of the Zona Colonial along the Malecón.

Esedeku
BAR

(Las Mercedes 341; 8pm-late Tue-Sun) Only a block from Calle El Conde, Esedeku is an intimate lesbian bar, popular with local professionals and with a huge selection of cocktails; not for hustlers.

Jubilee
NIGHTCLUB

(Renaissance Jaragua Hotel, Av George Washington 367; 9pm-late Tue-Sat) Still one of the hottest Malecón discos; admission is up to RD$250 when there's a DJ (most nights),

RD$350 when there's a band. Dress to impress.

Hotel Santo Domingo CASINO
(cnr Avs Independencia & Abraham Lincoln; ⏲4pm-late) West from the Zona Colonial along the Malecón; near the Francisco Alberto Caamaño Deño metro stop.

 Shopping

If you are considering buying something in amber or larimar, it's good to shop around, since these stones, considered national treasures, are virtually ubiquitous in Santo Domingo. Typically they're presented as jewelry items, but occasionally you'll find figurines, rosaries and other small objects. Quality and price vary greatly and fakes aren't uncommon.

In Zona Colonial, the most recommended places are the Museo Mundo de Ambar (p409) and Larimar Museum (p409). **Flor Ambar** (Las Damas 44; ⏲9am-6pm) is another recommended shop.

Mercado Modelo MARKET
(Av Mella; ⏲9am-5pm) Bargain hard at this local market, which sells everything from love potions to woodcarvings and jewelry. The more you look like a tourist, the higher the asking price.

Galería de Arte María del Carmen ART
(Arzobispo Meriño 207; ⏲9am-7pm Mon-Sat, 10am-1pm Sun) This place has been selling art long enough to attract a wide range of talented Dominican painters.

Boutique del Fumador CIGARS
(El Conde 109; ⏲9am-7pm Mon-Sat, 10am-3:30pm Sun) Boutique shop selling Cohibas (boxes of hand-rolled cigars from RD$430) and other brands; also organic Dominican chocolate (RD$200), coffee (RD$160) and rum (RD$140). Can explain the process from start to finish. See *tabacos* being rolled in the upstairs workshop.

Felipe & Co HANDICRAFTS
(El Conde 105; ⏲9am-8pm Mon-Sat, 10am-6pm Sun) This shop on Parque Colón is stocked with charming high-quality handicrafts, like ceramics, jewelry and handbags, with also a good selection of paintings. Some of the best finds are stocked way in the back of this deep shop, easily one of the best in the Zona Colonial.

La Leyenda del Cigarro CIGARS
(Hostos 402) This small shop has a good selection of premium cigars. Equally importantly, the helpful staff members are more than willing to answer the naive questions of cigar novices.

Librería Cuesta BOOKS
(cnr Avs 27 de Febrero & Abraham Lincoln; ⏲9am-9pm Mon-Sat, 10am-8pm Sun) This modern, two-story Dominican version of Barnes & Noble is easily the nicest and largest bookstore in the city; the upstairs cafe has wi-fi. The store is attached to the Supermercado Nacional, west of the Zona Colonial and north of the Zona Universitaría, on one of the busiest intersections in the city.

 Information

EMERGENCY Politur (Tourist Police; ☏809-682-2151; cnr El Conde & José Reyes; ⏲24hr) Can handle most situations; for general police, ambulance and fire dial ☏911.

INTERNET & TELEPHONE Most places charge around RD$35 per hour for internet use.

Abel Brawn's Internet World (Plaza Lomba, 2nd fl; ⏲9am-9pm Mon-Sat, 10am-4pm Sat) Fast internet access, as well as international phone service.

Centro de Internet (Av Independencia 201; ⏲8:30am-9pm Mon-Sat, to 3pm Sun) Internet and call center in Gazcue.

Codetel Centro de Comunicaciones (El Conde 202; ⏲8am-9:30pm) Large call center with internet access.

Cyber Red (Sánchez 201; ⏲9am-9pm Mon-Sat) Just off Calle El Conde; you can also make international calls here.

MEDICAL SERVICES Clínica Abreu (☏809-687-4922; cnr Avs Independencia & Beller; ⏲24hr) Widely regarded as the best hospital in the city, this is where members of many of the embassies go.

Farmacia San Judas (☏809-685-8165; cnr Avs Independencia & Pichardo; ⏲24hr) Free delivery.

Hospital Padre Billini (☏809-221-8272; Av Sánchez; ⏲24hr) The closest public hospital to the Zona Colonial; service is free, but expect long waiting lines.

MONEY Ban Reservas (cnr Isabel la Católica & Las Mercedes)

Banco Popular (cnr Avs Abraham Lincoln & Gustavo Mejia Ricart)

Banco Progreso (cnr Avs Independencia & Socorro Sánchez)

Scotiabank (cnr Isabel la Católica & Las Mercedes)

POST Post office (Isabel la Católica; ⊘8am-5pm Mon-Fri, 9am-noon Sat) Facing Parque Colón.

TOURIST INFORMATION Tourist office (Isabel la Católica 103; ⊘9am-3pm Mon-Fri) Located beside Parque Colón, this office has a handful of brochures and maps. Some English and French spoken.

TRAVEL AGENCIES Colonial Tour & Travel (www.colonialtours.com.do; Arzobispo Meriño 209) A few meters north of Calle El Conde; long-running professional outfit good for booking flights, hotel rooms and all excursions. English, Italian and French spoken.

Explora Eco Tours (www.exploraecotours. com; Gustavo Mejia Ricart 43) Specializes in customized day- to weeklong tours of national parks, nature preserves and rural communities. Website announces regularly scheduled trips.

ⓘ Getting There & Away

AIR Aeropuerto Internacional Las Américas (☏809-947-2220) is 22km east of the city. The smaller Aeropuerto Internacional La Isabela-Dr Joaquin Balaguer (Higuero; ☏809-826-4003), north of the city, handles mostly domestic carriers and air-taxi companies.

AeroDomca, Air Century, Caribbean Air Sign, DominicanShuttles and Volair connect Santo Domingo, primarily Aeropuerto La Isabela, to Punta Cana (US$99), Las Terrenas (US$80), Santiago and La Romana.

For details on international air travel to and from the Santo Domingo area, see p446.

BOAT Cruise ships dock at Puerto Don Diego on Av del Puerto opposite Fortaleza Ozama in the Zona Colonial or **Puerto Sans Souci** (www .sanssouci.com.do) on the eastern bank of the Río Ozama, directly across from the Zona Colonial. Both are modern and well equipped to facilitate short sightseeing trips of the Zona Colonial.

BUS For info on 1st-class services, see p447.

There are four 2nd-class depots near Parque Enriquillo in the Zona Colonial. All buses make numerous stops en route. Because the buses tend to be small, there can be a scrum for seats, especially for destinations with one to a few daily departures.

CAR Numerous car-rental companies have offices in Santo Domingo and at Las Américas airport – the majority have a booth in a small building just across the street from the arrivals exit.

ⓘ Getting Around

TO/FROM THE AIRPORT There are no buses to or from the airports. From Las Américas, a taxi into town costs US$30 to US$35, with little room for negotiation. The fare from La Isabela is US$10 to US$15. There's no permanent taxi stand, but a couple of cabs meet every flight.

BUS City buses (RD$10) tend to follow major thoroughfares, including Av Independencia (eastbound) and Av Bolivar (westbound), both of which intersect with Parque Independencia.

CAR Driving can be difficult in Santo Domingo due to traffic and aggressive drivers, especially those of taxis and buses. Many midrange and top-end hotels have parking with 24-hour

---

WORTH A TRIP

BAHÍA DE LAS ÁGUILAS

If you believe in fairy-tale utopian beaches, pristine Bahía de Las Águilas fits the bill. Located in the extremely remote southwestern corner of the DR, it's not on the way to anything else, but those who do make it are rewarded with 10km of nearly deserted beach forming a slow arc between two prominent capes.

To get there, take the paved (and signed!) road to Cabo Rojo, about 12km east of Pedernales. From here you can get to the beach by (really good) 4WD, but the far more spectacular alternative is to go by boat, where the ride is every bit as jaw-dropping as the destination.

Gorgeously located restaurant **Rancho Tipico** (☏809-753-8058; rodriguezsantiago3@ hotmail.com; mains RD$250-700; ⊘breakfast, lunch & dinner), in Las Cuevas, offers tours. The price for groups of one to five is RD$1800 per boat; for six to eight, RD$325 per person; for nine to 10, RD$300 per person.

The **Pedernales guide association** (Aguinape; ☏809-214-1575; ⊘8am-6pm), which gathers around the national-park ranger station just off the parking lot in Las Cuevas, takes groups of one to five for RD$1800 per boat. The local **Las Cuevas guide association** (Asotur; ☏809-507-2294) will take up to five people for RD$1500. You can find them milling about the small pier a few meters past Rancho Tipico. Bring your own snorkeling equipment.

You'll also need to pay the national-park entrance fee (Dominicans/foreigners RD$50/100). Grouping up with others is also a possibility, especially on weekends.

PLAYA LIMÓN

The drive alone justifies the trip. Hwy 104 passes through rolling mountain scenery and past bucolic ranches, where any unrecognized vehicle is sure to turn the heads of locals walking with friends or on horseback; it practically qualifies as an event in the sleepy villages along the way. Playa Limón itself, about 20km east of Miches and just outside the hamlet of El Cedro, is a 3km-long, isolated beach lined with coconut trees leaning into the ocean. It's coveted property that you're likely to have to yourself for much of the day.

guards. Otherwise you'll probably have to leave your rental on the street. Do not leave any valuables inside in either case.

METRO At the time of writing, only line 1 from La Feria (Centro de los Héroes) near the Malecón to the far northern suburb of Villa Mella was in operation, running 6:30am to 11:30pm weekdays and to 10pm Saturday. The route primarily runs north–south above and below ground along Av Máximo Gómez. Each ride costs RD$20, but it's best to purchase an RD$50 card at one of the ticket booths; the card can be refilled when needed.

PÚBLICO More numerous than buses are *públicos* (RD$12 per ride) – mostly beat-up minivans and private cars that follow the same main routes but stop anywhere that someone flags them down. Be prepared for a tight squeeze – drivers will cram seven or even eight passengers into an ordinary four-door car.

TAXI Taxis in Santo Domingo don't have meters, so you should always agree on the price before climbing in. The standard fare is RD$150, less within the Zona Colonial. Taxi drivers don't typically cruise the streets, but you can always find cabs at Parque Colón and Parque Independencia, or call **Apolo Taxi** (☎809-537-7771) or **Super Taxi** (☎809-536-7014).

THE SOUTHEAST

This iconic region, synonymous with sun, sand and binge eating, is rightly popular with the hundreds of thousands of visitors who make it the economic engine of DR tourism. Sprawling resorts, some like city-states, line much of the beachfront from Punta Cana to Bávaro.

The fishing village of Bayahibe is the departure point for trips to the nearby islands in the Parque Nacional del Este. North of Bávaro is Playa Limón, an isolated stretch of beach backed by palm trees and, more unusually, a lagoon and several mountain peaks. Those who carry on west to Sabana de la Mar are rewarded with the Parque Nacional Los Haitises, a protected maze of caves and mangroves.

Bávaro & Punta Cana

This is the epicenter of all-inclusive tourism. If you were to tell a Dominican anywhere in the world that you visited their country, this is where they would assume you came. It's deservedly popular because its beaches rival those anywhere else in the Caribbean, both for their soft, white texture and for their warm aquamarine waters.

Beaches

Playa Arena Gorda   RESORT BEACH
North of El Cortecito; lined with all-inclusive resorts and their guests.

Playa El Cortecito   ACTIVITIES BEACH
Tends to be crowded with vendors, but you can stroll to nicer spots in front of resorts. Good place to parasail (12 to 15 minutes for US$40) or to find a boat operator to take you fishing or snorkeling.

Playa del Macao   BEACH
A further 9km north of Playa Arena Gorda is this gorgeous stretch of beach best reached by car. It's also a stop-off for a slew of ATV (All-Terrain Vehicle) tours that tear up and down the beach every day.

Playa Cabo Engaño   SECLUDED BEACH
Isolated beach south of Bávaro and El Cortecito. You'll need a car, preferably an SUV, to reach it.

Activities

Virtually every water activity is available but involves a long commute to the actual site. Every hotel has a tour desk offering snorkeling, diving and boat trips to destinations such as Isla Saona, a large island with picturesque beaches off the southeastern tip of the DR. Parasailing is done from the beach all over Punta Cana and Bávaro.

Parque Ecológico Puntacana   NATURE RESERVE
(Puntacana Ecological Park; ☎809-959-9221; www .puntacana.org; ☺8am-4pm) Half a kilometer

south of Puntacana Resort & Club, this park covers 6 sq km of protected coastal and inland habitat and is home to some 100 bird species, 160 insect species and 500 plant species. Visitors can take very worthwhile 90-minute **guided tours** (adult/child US$15/10) through a lush 30-hectare portion of the reserve known as Parque Ojos Indígenas (Indigenous Eyes Park), so named for its 11 freshwater lagoons, all fed by an underground river that flows into the ocean. One- or two-hour **horseback-riding tours** (US$45/65) through the park and along the coast can also be arranged with advance notice. Unfortunately, there is no hotel pickup service; a cab here will cost around US$35 each way from Bávaro or El Cortecito.

La Cana Golf Course   GOLF
(☑809-959-4653; www.puntacana.com; Puntacana Resort & Club, Punta Cana; ⊗7:30am-6pm) This is one of Punta Cana's best golf courses and is located at the area's top resort. Green fees are guest/nonguest US$135/175 for 18 holes or US$80 for nine (guests only), including a golf cart. The new Tom Fazio–designed Corales Golf Course, inaugurated in April 2010, features six oceanfront holes but is limited to Corales residents and Puntacana and Tortuga Bay hotel guests. A third course called Hacienda, designed by Pete Dye, should be open by the time you read this.

Catalonia Bávaro Resort   GOLF
(☑809-412-0000; Cabeza de Toro; ⊗7am-6:30pm) Has a decent nine-hole par-three course that costs US$90 for one round and US$110 (carts included) for two. Club rental is just US$25.

👉 Tours

Every resort has a tour desk that can arrange all variety of trips, from snorkeling and deep-sea fishing to the popular Isla Saona trip. A handful of locals set up on El Cortecito beach offer one-hour **snorkeling trips** (US$20 per person) and **glass-bottom boat rides** (US$35 per person) to a nearby reef. Most also offer **deep-sea fishing trips** (minimum 4 people; US$60 per person).

If you're looking to explore the region, **RH Tours and Excursions** (☑809-552-1425; www .rhtours.com; El Cortecito; ⊗9am-7pm) offers a number of decent day trips. Popular excursions include exploring Parque Nacional Los Haitises (US$115), boat trips to Isla Saona (US$79) and tours of Santo Domingo's Zona Colonial (US$69).

🛏 Sleeping

For resorts in the area, walk-in guests are about as common as snowstorms; if you can convince the suspicious security guards that your intentions are innocent and make it to the front desk, you'll be quoted rates that absolutely nobody staying at the resort is paying. Instead, book all-inclusive vacations online or through a travel agent, as they can offer discounts of up to 50% off rack rates. Bear in mind that most resorts cater to a particular niche, whether it's families, honeymooners, golfers or the spring-break crowd.

BÁVARO

Barceló Bávaro Palace Deluxe   RESORT $$$
(☑809-686-5797; www.barcelobavarobeach.com; Playa Bávaro; all-incl d from US$338; 🅿❄@ 🛜🏊🏋) Made over to the tune of US$250 million, this brand-new resort is an over-the-top behemoth but manages to come off as a boutique hotel with its beautiful public spaces and sleek rooms. The highlight: 897 new junior suites, each with an outdoor Jacuzzi patio, motion-sensor lighting and no shortage of Danish-like design touches. The main pool area (there are five) is gorgeous and you can choose from 16 restaurants, 13 bars and a disco to entertain yourself – leave the kids at the water park. Did we mention the 18-hole golf course redesigned by Pete Dye?

TOP CHOICE **Hard Rock Hotel Punta Cana**   RESORT $$$
(☑809-731-0099; www.hardrockhotelpuntacana .com; Playa Macao; all-incl d from US$492; 🅿❄🛜🏊) Imagine Las Vegas by the Caribbean. The old Moon Palace Resort was transformed into a den of decadence and cool in late 2010, catapulting it to the top of Punta Cana's bold and beautiful resorts. With memorabilia galore, the lobby now feels like a Rock and Roll Hall of Fame. It caters to a diverse crowd of hipsters who, with its 18-bars-to-nine-restaurants ratio, aren't here to linger at the buffet. The 13 pools (seven oceanfront) and sprawling grounds are mostly unchanged, with the rooms bridging the gap between old and new – they feature party-size Jacuzzis at the foot of the beds. There's nothing slicker in Punta Cana, and the gorgeous casino is the DR's largest.

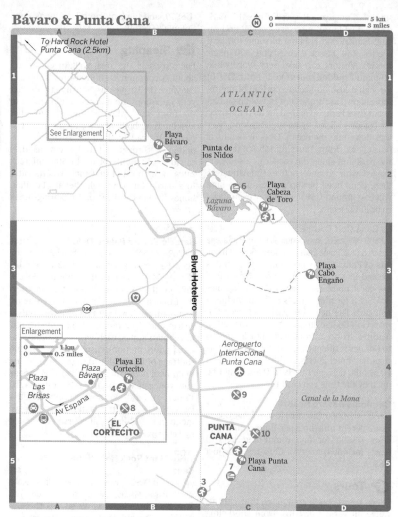

Natura Park Eco-Resort & Spa
HOTEL $$$

(☎809-221-2626; www.blau-hotels.com; Cabeza de Toro; d from US$218; P ❀ @ ☞ ☎) Natura Park has a narrow beach outside the village of Cabeza de Toro, halfway between Bávaro and Punta Cana. It's extra popular with Canadians and those who care more about reducing their carbon footprint than hopping in and out of bars and clubs at night. The pool is a bit small, but the beach is quite nice. Free-range swans, geese and flamingos and the Laguna Bávaro creeping on its doorstep mean nature is never too far away.

PUNTA CANA

Puntacana Resort & Club
RESORT $$

(☎809-959-2262; www.puntacana.com; Punta Cana; d incl breakfast US$120; P ❀ @ ☞ ☎) Famous for part-time residents like Julio Iglesias, Oscar de la Renta and Mikhail Baryshnikov, this discerning and quiet resort is also notable for its environmental efforts, especially the associated ecological park across the street from the resort entrance. Three-story buildings with newly modernized rooms line an average beach, which sees seaweed mucking up the sands but offers miraculous water, and there are

Bávaro & Punta Cana

six restaurants to choose from within the 60-sq-km complex, as well as a Six Senses Spa. It's a low-key resort for people happy to read a book by the pool, though service is hit-or-miss. The newer Tortuga Bay (designed by de la Renta), an enclave of 15 one-, two- and three-bedroom luxury villas, is part of the main resort property and sets the bar for luxury in Punta Cana.

✗ Eating

Most visitors are hardly hungry after gorging themselves at their resort's buffets, but there are enough condos, villas and locals to support a handful of eateries. Most are in various shopping centers in the area.

TOP CHOICE Chez Mon Ami FRENCH $$
(☑809-552-6714; Plaza Nautica, Bávaro; mains RD$350-780; ☺lunch & dinner Mon-Sat) This sexy French bistro, walking distance from El Cortecito, offers a lovely terrace on which to enjoy a mean filet of beef (RD$580), duck confit (RD$650) and the occasional curveball like fish carpaccio with spicy coconut sauce (RD$380). The chef and owner are French, so you're getting the real deal. Reservations are a good idea in high season.

Restaurante Playa Blanca FUSION $$$
(Puntacana Resort & Club, Punta Cana; mains US$11-29; ☺lunch & dinner) Flanked by an army of palms, this atmospheric, open-air restaurant is within the Puntacana resort but open to the public and worth the trip. The hip, white-on-white space reeks of cool, but the innovative surf-and-turf menu, highlighted by some wild cards like spicy Dominican

goat (UD$12) and *criolla*-style guinea fowl, (US$15) steals the show.

El Burrito Taqueria MEXICAN $$
(Punta Cana Village, Punta Cana; mains RD$160-550; ☺lunch & dinner, closed dinner Sun) The first sign of a great Mexican place is fresh chips and salsa, and our instincts proved correct at this small and festive taqueria. An excellent burrito the size of a shoebox followed (RD$360); and the tacos (RD$160 to RD$360) and enchiladas (RD$240 to RD$320) should quell your cravings when you're tired of ubiquitous fish and pasta choices.

ℹ Information

EMERGENCY Politur (☑809-552-0848) There are 24-hour stations next to the bus terminal in Bávaro, in Cabeza de Toro and at the Punta Cana airport.

INTERNET ACCESS & TELEPHONE Cone Xion.com (Plaza Punta Cana, Bávaro; per hr RD$60; ☺9am-10pm Mon-Sat, to 11pm Sun) A small internet place and call center.

Sea and Surf (El Cortecito; per hr RD$60; ☺9am-7pm) Along the main beach road in Cortecito proper.

MEDICAL SERVICES All-inclusive hotels have small on-site clinics and medical staff, who can provide first aid and basic care. Head to one of several good private hospitals in the area for more serious issues.

Hospitén Bávaro (www.hospiten.es) Best private hospital in Punta Cana, with English-, French- and German-speaking doctors and a 24-hour emergency room. The hospital is located on the road to Punta Cana, 500m from the turnoff to Bávaro.

Pharmacana (Punta Cana Village, Punta Cana; ☺9am-10pm Mon-Sat, 8am-11pm Sun) Punta Cana's main pharmacy.

MONEY Almost every major Dominican bank has at least one branch in the Bávaro area. All of the following have ATMs.

Banco León (Plaza Progresso, Bávaro)

BanReservas (Plaza Progresso, Bávaro)

Scotiabank Bávaro (Plaza Las Brisas); Punta Cana (Punta Cana Village)

ℹ Getting There & Away

AIR Aeropuerto Internacional Punta Cana is on the road to Punta Cana about 9km east of the turnoff to Bávaro.

Several airlines have offices here, including **American Airlines** (☑809-959-2420), **British Airways** (☑800-247-9297), **Continental** (☑809-959-2039), **Air France** (☑809-959-3002) and

LAN (☎809-959-0144), but they are tucked away behind the scenes and hard to find.

For domestic air connections, **Dominican-Shuttles** (☎in Santo Domingo 809-738-3014; www.dominicanshuttles.com) has direct flights between Punta Cana and Santo Domingo's La Isabela airport (US$99 one-way, 9:15am weekdays, 6:15pm Sunday to Friday and 4:30pm Saturday) and daily to Samaná/El Portillo (US$159 one-way, 3:30pm). It also serves Puerto Plata (US$149 one-way, 3:30pm Friday and 7am Monday).

Several car agencies have small booths near baggage claim.

Resort minivans transport the majority of tourists to nearby resorts, but taxis are plentiful. Fares between the airport and area resorts and hotels range from US$30 to US$80.

BUS The bus terminal is at Bávaro's main intersection, near the Texaco gas station, almost 2km inland from El Cortecito.

Expreso Santo Domingo Bávaro Bávaro (☎809-552-1678); Santo Domingo (☎809-682-9670) has direct 1st-class service between Bávaro and the capital (RD$350, four hours), with a stop in La Romana. Departure times in both directions are 7am, 10am, 2pm and 4pm.

Sitrabapu (☎809-552-0617) has departures to La Romana (RD$225) at 8:30am and 4:30pm from the same terminal. To all other destinations, take a local bus (marked Sitrabapu) to Higüey and transfer there. *Caliente* (literally 'hot'; without air-con) buses to Higüey (RD$110, 1½ hours, every 30 minutes from 1:30am to 10:30pm) leave Bávaro's main terminal, as does the express service (RD$120, 1¼ hours, every 30 minutes from 6am to 7:30pm).

❶ Getting Around

Local buses pass all the outdoor malls on the way to El Cortecito. Buses have the drivers' union acronym – Sitrabapu – printed in front; fares are RD$40. They are supposed to pass every 15 to 30 minutes but can sometimes take up to an hour.

Daytime traffic is sometimes gridlocked between the resorts clustered just north of Bávaro and El Cortecito. Despite the stop-and-go pace of driving, renting a car for a day or two is recommended if you prefer to see the surrounding area independently. Rental agencies include **Avis** (☎809-535-7191), **Europcar** (☎809-688-2121) and **National/Alamo** (☎809-466-1082).

Otherwise, there are numerous taxis in the area – look for stands at El Cortecito, Plaza Bávaro and at most all-inclusives. You can also call a cab – try **Arena Gorda taxi** (☎809-552-0711). Fares are typically US$6 to US$30.

PENÍNSULA DE SAMANÁ

This sliver of land is the antithesis of the Dominican Caribbean dream in the southeast, where resorts rule and patches of sand come at a first-class premium. Far more laid-back and, in a sense, more cosmopolitan, Samaná offers a European vibe as strong as espresso. Here, escape is the operative word, and French and Italian are at least as useful as Spanish. Most visitors come to gasp at migrating humpback whales, but the peninsula is no one-trick pony. Sophisticated Las Terrenas is the place to base yourself if you crave a lively social scene, and sleepy Las Galeras boasts several of the best beaches in the DR, their beauty enhanced by the effort it takes to get there.

Samaná

POP 50,000

For much of the year, Samaná follows the slow daily rhythms of an ordinary Dominican town – it's a compact place built on a series of bluffs overlooking Bahía de Samaná. In fact, it remained an isolated fishing village until 1985, when the first whale-watching expedition set out. Because North Atlantic humpbacks find the bay water particularly suitable for their annual version of speed dating, Samaná is transformed in whale-watching season by tens of thousands of tourists who flock here for this unparalleled natural spectacle.

◉ Sights

Cascada El Limón   WATERFALL

Travel agencies in Samaná offer trips to this 52m-high waterfall for around US$45, including transport, horses, guide and lunch. However, it's perfectly easy and much cheaper to do the trip yourself by taking a *guagua* to El Limón. See p429 for more details.

Cayo Levantado   ISLAND

Only the western third of this lush island 7km from Samaná is open to the public; the eastern two-thirds is occupied by a five-star hotel. The public beach here is gorgeous, with white sand and turquoise waters, but don't expect much peace and quiet. Large cruise ships dock here regularly and the facilities include a restaurant and bar – and 2000 lounge chairs. Boats at the pier go for RD$250 per person round-trip; if you have a group of up to 15 you can negotiate the boat round-trip for RD$1300.

BEST OF THE REST

Bayahibe, originally founded by fishermen from Puerto Rico in the 19th century, is like an actor playing many roles in the same performance. In the morning busloads of guests from resorts further east hop into boats bound for Isla Saona, but once this morning rush hour is over Bayahibe turns back into a drowsy village. There's another buzz of activity when the tourist groups return and then after sunset a further transformation. What sets Bayahibe apart is that it manages to maintain its character despite the continued encroachment of big tourism.

Meaning 'Land of the Mountains,' **Parque Nacional Los Haitises** (admission RD$100; ☺7am-8pm) is a 1375-sq-km park at the southwestern end of the Bahía de Samaná containing scores of lush hills jutting some 30m to 50m from the water and coastal wetlands. The knolls were formed one to two million years ago, when tectonic drift buckled the thick limestone shelf that had formed underwater. The area receives a tremendous amount of rainfall, creating perfect conditions for subtropical humid forest plants. In fact, Los Haitises contains over 700 species of flora, including four types of mangrove, making it one of the most highly biodiverse regions in the Caribbean. Los Haitises is also home to 110 species of bird, 13 of which are endemic to the island. Some of the park's series of limestone caves contain intriguing Taíno pictographs.

Tour outfits in Samaná offer trips here for around US$50 per person, including guide and transportation to, and inside, the park.

The area around the park has one of the DR's most special places to stay. **Paraíso Caño Hondo** (☎809-248-5995; www.paraisocanohondo.com; s/d/tr incl breakfast RD$2000/3150/4350; ☎P☎) couldn't be further from the typical beach-resort experience. The Jivales River, which runs through the property, has been channeled into 10 magical waterfall-fed pools, perfect for a soak any time of the day. Rooms are large and rustic, though extremely comfortable.

🏃 Activities

For sheer awe-inspiring impact, a whale-watching trip is hard to beat. Around 45,000 people travel to Samaná every year from January 15 to March 15 to see the majestic acrobatics of these massive creatures. Try to avoid coming during Carnaval, the busiest day of the year. There are around 43 vessels in total, eight companies, all owned or at least partly owned by Dominicans from Samaná, and around 12 independent operators.

Whale Samaná　　　　WHALE-WATCHING
(☎809-538-2494; www.whalesamana.com; cnr Mella & Av Malecón; adult/under 5yr/5-10yr US$55/free/30; ☺9am-1pm & 3-6pm) Samaná's most recommended outfit.

Luna Tours/Samaná Runners　　　　WHALE-WATCHING
(☎809-538-3109; www.bavarorunners.com; Av Circunvalación 41; ☺8:30am-6:30pm) Next to Hotel Bahía View.

Moto Marina　　　　WHALE-WATCHING
(☎809-538-2304; motomarina@yahoo.com; Av la Marina 3; ☺8am-noon & 2-6pm Mon-Sat, 8am-noon & 4-7pm Sun)

🛏 Sleeping

TOP CHOICE **Gran Bahía Principe Cayo Levantado**　　　　HOTEL $$$
(☎809-538-3232; www.bahia-principe.com; Cayo Levantado; all-incl r from US$208; ☎@☎☎) This romantic five-star hotel has a lot going for it, namely its 'private' beach on the supremely idyllic sands of Cayo Levantado. The hotel sits on extra-lush grounds and offers classic, though slightly stuffy, luxury. Rooms have hardwood floors and some have patio ocean views and vaulted ceilings. There are two excellent pools, the best of which is accessed via an outdoor elevator. The downside is you're on an island and need to take a boat (provided by the hotel) to get there.

Hotel Bahía View　　　　HOTEL $
(☎809-251-4000; wendydlsr@hotmail.com; Av Circunvalación 31; r with/without air-con RD$1600/1200; ☎☎) An enduringly popular hotel with independent travelers, the Bahía View unfortunately doesn't have great views of Bahía. Definitely ask for a room with a balcony anyway. Each of the 10 rooms is arranged differently, with multiple beds, but all have high ceilings and clean, modern

bathrooms, and there's a good Dominican **restaurant** (mains RD$90-425; ☺breakfast, lunch & dinner).

Gran Principe Cayacoa HOTEL $$$
(☎809-538-3131; www.bahiaprincipe.com; all-incl d per person US$280; P✳@☎☎) Samaná town's fanciest hotel is perched on a cliff above the city with spectacular views of the bay (and maybe even of humpbacks during whale season). Food and rooms, however, are less attractive than those at the sister property on Cayo Levantado, which trumps the Cayacoa in every way.

🍴 Eating & Drinking

The majority of restaurants are along Av Malecón.

Beginning around 6pm and lasting until the early hours of the morning, you can also get cheap eats at a series of food stands that line Av Malecón near Calle Maria Trinidad Sánchez.

TOP CHOICE **El Rancho Du' Vagabond'** ITALIAN $$
(Cristobal Colón 4A; pasta RD$275-375, pizza RD$265-395; ☺lunch & dinner, closed Tue) This pizzeria stands out as the real deal. Past the nondescript entrance is a charming back dining room, where you'll find no views whatsoever – this spot is all about the food. There's an extensive list of fresh pasta, concentrating on specialty gnocchi, and an even better pizza menu.

Restaurant Mate Rosada CARIBBEAN, SEAFOOD $$
(Av Malecón; mains RD$230-750; ☺lunch & dinner, closed dinner Wed)

L'Hacienda Restaurant STEAK HOUSE, SEAFOOD $$
(Santa Barbara; mains RD$390-680; ☺dinner, closed Wed)

Bambú Restaurant CARIBBEAN, SEAFOOD $$
(Av Malecón; mains RD$220-530; ☺lunch & dinner)

ℹ Information

Banco Popular (Av Malecón; ☺8:15am-4pm Mon-Fri, 9am-1pm Sat) Located on the Malecón across from the ferry dock.

BanReservas (Santa Barbara; ☺8am-5pm Mon-Fri, 9am-1pm Sat) One block north of the Malecón.

Farmacia Giselle (cnr Santa Barbara & Julio Labandier; ☺8am-9pm Mon-Sat, to 1pm Sun) Good selection of meds and toiletries.

Hospital Municipal (Trinidad Sanchez; ☺24hr) A very basic hospital near the Palacio de Justicia.

Internet Cafe & Snack Bar (Av Circunvalación; per hr RD$20; ☺8am-11pm) Cheapest and best internet in town, with private cabins.

ℹ Getting There & Away

AIR Aeropuerto Internacional El Portillo is just outside Las Terrenas. Aeropuerto El Catey is another option and receives international flights. See p446 and p447 for information on domestic and international flights.

BOAT Transporte Maritimo provides the only ferry service – passengers only, no vehicles – across the Bahía de Samaná to Sabana de la Mar (RD$200, one hour plus, 7am, 9am, 11am and 3pm). Buy tickets on board. From there, it's possible to catch *gua-guas* to several destinations in the southeast and on to Santo Domingo, though the road network in this part of the country is rough and public transportation is not so comfortable.

BUS Facing the pier, **Caribe Tours** (☎809-538-2229; Av Malecón) offers services to Santo Domingo (RD$310, 2½ hours, 8am, 10am, 2pm and 4pm). The same bus stops along the way at Sánchez (RD$60, 30 minutes).

For Puerto Plata, 210km west, **El Canario** (☎809-291-5594) direct buses leave at 11am from beside the Banco Popular. **Papagayo** (☎809-802-3534) – ask for Salvador – also has a direct service at 1:30pm from under the mango tree on the eastern side of the little park next to Banco Popular on the Malecón. Both charge RD$250 and the trip takes about 3½ to four hours. Call ahead to double-check the day's departures. Locals say the latter is a safer though slightly slower ride. Arrive 30 to 45 minutes early to reserve a seat.

For service to towns nearby, head to the **gua-gua terminal** (Av Malecón) at the *mercado municipal*, 200m west of the Politur station, near Angel Mesina. From here, trucks and minivans head to Las Galeras (RD$80, 45 minutes to one hour, every 15 minutes from 6:40am to 6pm), El Limón (RD$60, 30 minutes, every 15 minutes from 6:30am to 6:30pm), Las Terrenas (RD$100, 1¼ hours, hourly from 6:30am to 4:45pm), Sánchez (RD$70, 45 minutes, every 15 minutes from 6:30am to 8pm). Destinations farther afield also leave from the same block: Santo Domingo (RD$275, three hours, every 30 minutes from 4am to 4:30pm) and Santiago (RD$275, four hours, hourly from 4:30pm to 2:30pm).

ℹ Getting Around

Samaná is walkable, but if you're carrying luggage, catch a *motoconcho* (motorcycle taxi) –

they're everywhere. 4WD vehicles are your only option in terms of car rental – roads on the peninsula are bad enough to warrant the extra expense. Rates average around RD$2500 per day and discounts are typically given for rentals of a week or longer. Try **Xamaná Rent Motors** (☏809-435-6828; Av Malecón; ⊘8am-6pm Mon-Sat, to noon Sun).

Las Galeras

The road to this small fishing community 28km northeast of Samaná ends at a fish shack on the beach. So does everything else, metaphorically speaking. Las Galeras, as much as anywhere else on the peninsula, offers terrestrial and subaquatic adventures for those with wills strong enough to ignore the pull of inertia. Or you can do nothing more than lie around your bungalow or while away the day at a restaurant watching others do the same.

👁 Sights

Boca Del Diablo   BLOWHOLE
'Mouth of the Devil' is an impressive vent or blowhole, where waves rush up a natural channel and blast out of a hole in the rocks. Car or motorcycle is the best way to get there – look for an unmarked dirt road 7km south of town and about 100m beyond the well-marked turnoff to Playa Rincón. Follow the road eastward for about 8km, then walk the last 100m or so.

🏖 Beaches

Playa Rincón   SWIMMING BEACH
Playa Rincón is a pitch-perfect beach. Stretching uninterrupted for almost 3km of nearly white, soft sand and multihued water good for swimming, the beach even has a small stream at its far western end, great for a quick freshwater dip at the end of a long, sunny day. Rincón is large enough for every day-tripper to claim their own piece of real estate. A thick palm forest provides the backdrop. Several small restaurants serve mostly seafood dishes and rent beach chairs, making this a great place to spend the entire day. Most people arrive by boat. The standard option is to leave around 9am; boats return to pick you up at 4pm – it's around 20 minutes each way. If you join up with other beachgoers, it costs RD$500 to RD$1000 per person round-trip. You can also drive there, though the last kilometer or so is too rough for small or midsize cars. A round-trip taxi

to Rincón, including waiting time, should cost RD$1800.

Playas Madama & Frontón   SNORKELING & SWIMMING BEACHES
Preferred by some locals over Playa Rincón, 750m-long **Playa Frontón** boasts some of the best snorkeling in the area. **Playa Madama** is a small beach framed by high bluffs; keep in mind there's not much sunlight in the afternoon.

The trail to both begins at the far east end of the Grand Paradise Samaná beach, about 200m past the resort's entrance, near a private house which most people know as 'La Casa de los Ingleses' (House of the English) after its original owners. Coming from town, the house and trail will be on your right. There are several turnoffs that are easy to miss; it's much simpler to take a boat to either of these beaches for around RD$500 to RD$1000 per person round-trip, with a pickup in the afternoon.

Playita   SWIMMING BEACH
Better than the beach in town, Playita (Little Beach) is easy to get to on foot or by *motoconcho*. It's a swath of tannish sand, with mellow surf, backed by tall palm trees. There are two informal outdoor restaurants, basically thatched-roof shelters, where you can get grilled fish or chicken. On the main road just south of Las Galeras, look for signs for Hotel La Playita pointing down a dirt road headed west.

🏃 Activities

Cabo Cabrón   DIVING
For experienced divers, Bastard Point is one of the north coast's best sites. After an easy boat ride from Las Galeras, you're dropped into a churning channel with a giant coral formation that you can swim around; you may see dolphins here.

Las Galeras Divers   DIVING
(www.las-galeras-divers.com; Plaza Lusitania; ⊘8:30am-7pm) A well-respected, French-run dive shop at the main intersection. One-/two-tank dives including all equipment cost US$50/85 (US$10 less if you have your own gear). A 10-dive package brings the rate down to US$44 per dive, including gear.

Scuba Libre Diving Center   DIVING
(www.lacompagniadeicaraibi.com; ⊘8:30am-5pm) Located at the far end of Grand Paradise Samaná' resort's beach. Also offers snorkeling trips (US$15) and windsurfer and catamaran

rental and instruction (US$15 to US$20 per hour), all available to guests and nonguests alike.

La Hacienda   HORSEBACK RIDING

(http://www.larancheta.com) The Belgian owner of this guesthouse leads highly recommended tours to various spots around Las Galeras, including El Punto lookout, Playas Madama, Frontón and Rincón, as well as the surrounding hills. Her trips cater to all skill levels and range from two-hour excursions (US$35 per person) to full-day (US$70) and overnight (US$200) trips.

Piedra Bonita   DIVING

A 50m stone tower good for spotting jacks, barracuda and sea turtles.

Cathedral   DIVING

Enormous underwater cave opening to sunlight.

Container ship   DIVING

A 55m ship haunted by big morays.

Los Carriles   DIVING

A series of coral hills; one of several large, shallow coral patches good for beginner divers.

☞ Tours

You can hire a *motoconcho* driver to act as your chauffeur and guide. Tour operators include **Razor Tours** (☏809-729-5867; www.razortours-excursionsamana.com; Principal), **Dario Perez Excursiones** (☏809-924-6081; Plaza Lusitania) and Scuba Libre Diving Center. Numerous day trips include whale-watching in Bahía de Samaná (US$60 to US$72 per person with lunch), land and boat excursions through Parque Nacional Los Haitises (US$72 per person) and boat tours to the area's isolated beaches (US$30 to US$40 per person).

🛏 Sleeping

TOP CHOICE Casa Por Qué No?   B&B $

(☏809-712-5631; s/d incl breakfast US$50/60; ⊘closed May-Oct; P❄) Pierre and Monick, the charming French-Canadian owners of this B&B, are consummate hosts and rent out two rooms on either side of their cozy home – each room has a separate entrance and hammock. Only 25m or so north of the main intersection on your right as you're walking toward the beach, the house is fronted by a long, well-groomed garden where great breakfasts (deliciously crunchy homemade bread!) are served (RD$300 for nonguests).

TOP CHOICE Todo Blanco   BOUTIQUE HOTEL $$

(☏809-538-0201; www.hoteltodoblanco.com; r US$86; P❄@🛜) Whitewashed in colonial sophistication, this well-established inn run by a cheerful Dominican-Italian couple sits atop a small hillock a short walk from the end of the main drag. The multilevel grounds are nicely appointed with gardens and a gazebo, all with views of the ocean below. The rooms are large and airy, with high ceilings, private terraces overlooking the sea and pastel headboards. Rooms aren't fancy – in fact, rather sparse save the mosquito nets – but the homey living area has TV and DVD player.

El Cabito   CAMPGROUND, GUESTHOUSE $

(☏829-697-9506; www.elcabito.net; campsites/hammocks per person RD$250, tree houses RD$750, cabins RD$1400) For those looking to rough it, this property in lush farmland 4km east of the main intersection has one of the few campgrounds in the entire DR. If you like the out-of-the-way location but want a little more comfort, there's a tree house and two cabins. Stunning views are to be had all around, including from the dramatic restaurant perched over crashing waves below – the real coup here.

Sol Azul   BUNGALOWS $

(☏829-882-8790; www.elsolazul.com; bungalows incl breakfast US$50-70; P🛜🏊) A fun Swiss couple runs these four earthy, natural-hued and spacious bungalows, all set around a manicured garden and pleasant pool area just 50m or so from the main intersection. Two of the bungalows feature mezzanine levels – good for children – and the breakfast buffet gets high marks from travelers.

✕ Eating

TOP CHOICE Restaurant Rubi   CARIBBEAN, SEAFOOD $$

(Playa Rincón; mains RD$300-700; ⊘lunch) This dressed-up beach shack perhaps justifies the trip to Playa Rincón, regardless of the long and beautiful beach on whose eastern end it sits. Picnic-table-style seating is juiced up with bright tablecloths, and a single chalkboard relays the offerings: fresh fish, *langosta*, grilled chicken etc, all done up on a massive open-air grill.

Le Taínos
FUSION $$

(Principal; mains RD$270-410; ⊘dinner) The focal point of the town center, this atmospheric eatery is Las Galeras' most cosmopolitan, with all sorts of scrumptious dishes you don't see elsewhere, beautifully presented. The honey-oregano pork mignon (RD$330) is a real treat, as is the key lime chicken (RD$270) and seafood tabbouleh (RD$170), all served in a candlelit alfresco space with a designer thatched roof.

Restaurant El Cabito
DOMINICAN, SEAFOOD $$

(🖉829-697-9506; mains RD$180-750; ⊘breakfast, lunch & dinner) Clinging spectacularly onto the edge of the DR, this rustic, postcard-perfect restaurant has amazing cliff-hugging views. The best time is sunset, when a kaleidoscopic flurry of hues melts into the sea as you sip on Belgian beers. Go for the excellent grilled calamari (RD$550) or dorado (RD$650). Reservations are essential and there's a pickup/drop-off service to anywhere in Las Galeras.

❶ Information

Most of the relevant services are located on or around the main intersection, a short walk from the beach.

BanReservas (Principal) The most convenient ATM. There's another at Grand Paradise Samaná resort.

Las Galeras Tourist Service (Principal; internet per hr RD$180; ⊘9am-1pm & 2:30-7pm Mon-Sat) Internet and money exchange. Free wi-fi if you have a laptop.

❶ Getting There & Around

Gua-guas head to Samaná (RD$80, 45 minutes, every 15 minutes from 6:40am to 6:45pm) from the beach end of Principal and also cruise slowly out of town picking up passengers. There are also three daily buses to Santo Domingo (RD$325, three hours, 5:30am, 1pm and 3:05pm).

You can walk everywhere in Las Galeras proper. **Taxis** (🖉829-559-8217) are available at a stand just in front of the main town beach. Some sample one-way fares are Aeropuerto Catey (RD$1500), Las Terrenas (RD$1800) and Samaná (RD$700).

Renting a car is an excellent way to explore the peninsula on your own. Prices are generally US$65 to US$85 per day. Try **RP Rent-A-Car** (🖉809-538-0249; Principal; ⊘8am-7pm Mon-Sat, to 1pm Sun), on the way out of town, or **Caribe Fun Rentals** (🖉809-912-2440; ⊘9am-1pm & 3-6:30pm Mon-Sat). The latter is 50m west

of the intersection and offers quads (US$50 per day) and motorcycles (US$33) as well.

Las Terrenas

POP 15,000

No longer a rustic fishing village, Las Terrenas is a cosmopolitan town, seemingly as much French and Italian as Dominican. It's a balancing act between locals and expats, one that has produced a lively mix of styles and a social scene more vibrant than that anywhere else on the peninsula. A walk along the beach road in either direction leads to beachfront scattered with hotels, high palm trees and calm aquamarine waters.

◉ Sights

Cascada El Limón
WATERFALL

Tucked away in surprisingly rough landscape, and surrounded by peaks covered in lush greenery, this waterfall has a beautiful swimming hole at the bottom. The departure point for the falls is the small town of El Limón, only a half-hour from Las Terrenas.

Just about everyone who visits does so on horseback, and almost a dozen *paradas* (horseback-riding operations) in town and on the highway toward Samaná offer tours. (It is not recommended that you hire someone off the street, as there's little saving and the service is consistently substandard.) All outfits offer essentially the same thing: a 30- to 60-minute ride up the hill to the waterfalls, 30 to 60 minutes to take a dip and enjoy the scene and a 30- to 60-minute return trip, with lunch at the end. Your guide – whom you should tip, by the way – will be walking, not riding, which can feel a little weird but is the custom.

Otherwise it's a minimum 40-minute walk, sometimes up a very steep trail over rough terrain with even a river or two to ford. It's not especially difficult to follow the path once you find it, especially if there are groups out on the trail.

Spanish-owned **Santí** (🖉809-342-9776; www.cascadalimonsamana.com; rides per person with/without lunch RD$900/650; ⊘8am-6pm), at the main intersection in El Limón, is a good choice but also the most expensive. The lunch is excellent and the guides and staff (all adults) are better paid than elsewhere. If you book with a tour company in Las Terrenas, transportation to/from El Limón is often not included (*gua-guas* are US$50). Typically the tour (horse, guide and lunch)

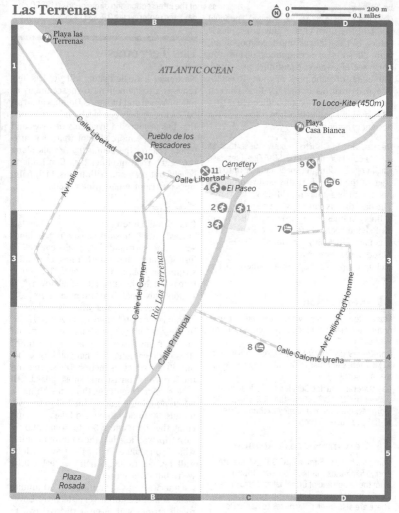

costs per person from US$35 to US$50. Most other operators charge around RD$750/375 with/without lunch.

🏃 Activities

Las Terrenas has reasonably good **diving** and **snorkeling**. Favorite dive spots include a wreck in 28m of water, and Isla Las Ballenas, visible from shore, with a large underwater cave. Most shops also offer special trips to Cabo Cabrón near Las Galeras and Dudu Cave near Río San Juan. Standard one-tank dives average US$55 with or without equipment. Four-, 10- and 12-dive pack-

ages don't save you more than about US$5 to US$15 per dive. Two-tank diving day trips to Cabo Cabrón are US$165, including gear, lunch and transport.

A popular full-day snorkel trip is to Playa Jackson, several kilometers west of town, reached by boat (US$120 per person including a lobster lunch).

Second to Cabarete, Las Terrenas is nevertheless a good place to try out a wind sport. The beach at Punta Popy, only a kilometer or so east of the main intersection, is a popular place for **kitesurfers** and **windsurfers**.

Las Terrenas

Loco-Kite　　　　　　　　　KITESURFING
(www.lasterrenas-kitesurf.com; Calle 27 de Febrero) Rents surfboards and kitesurfing equipment and provides lessons. Six hours of kitesurfing lessons (really the minimum needed to have a sporting chance of making it work) cost US$300; a two-hour surfing lesson is US$40.

Las Terrenas Divers　　　　　　　DIVING
(www.lt-divers.com; Hotel Bahía las Ballenas, Playa Bonita; ⊙9am-noon & 3-5pm) Well-respected German-run operation; also see p432.

Turtle Dive Center　　　　　　　DIVING
(www.turtledivecenter.com; El Paseo shopping center; ⊙8am-12:30pm & 2-7pm) SSI-affiliated shop run by a safety-first Frenchman.

🧭 Tours

Bahia Tours　　　　　　　　DAY TRIPS
(www.bahia-tours.com; Principal 237; ⊙8am-7pm Mon-Fri, 9:30am-1pm & 4:30-6:30pm Sat) Popular day trips include whale-watching in Bahía de Samaná (from US$55 per person), excursions to Parque Nacional Los Haitises (US$65 per person), visits to Playa El Rincón (US$90 per person) and horseback riding to Cascada El Limón (from US$30 per person).

Casa de las Terrenas　　　　OUTDOOR TOURS
(☎809-240-6251; www.lasterrenas-excursions .com; Principal 280) Small, friendly, French-run operation run out of a little kiosk in front of Plaza Taína.

Flora Tours　　　　　　　OUTDOOR TOURS
(☎809-360-2793; www.flora-tours.net; Principal 262) Specializes in Los Haitises, hard-to-access beaches and trekking.

🛏 Sleeping

TOP CHOICE **Lomita Maravilla**　　BOUTIQUE HOTEL **$$**
(☎809-240-6345; www.lomitamaravilla.com; Salome Ureña; villas US$120, with private Jacuzzi US$210; 🅿✴🛜🏊) A short walk down a dirt road – often muddy – off Av Duarte is one of the gems of Las Terrenas. This European-inspired, Swiss-run boutique hotel consists entirely of thatched-roof private bungalows set along palmed paths around a central swimming pool. Rooms are like boutique apartments, with TVs, DVD players, and fully loaded kitchens.

El Rincon de Abi　　　　　HOTEL **$**
(☎809-240-6639; www.el-rincon-de-abi.com; Av Emilio Prud'Homme; d/tr incl breakfast RD$1500/1800; 🅿🛜🏊) This French-owned hotel is well maintained and full of cute colors and character. There's a nice communal outdoor kitchen, a Jacuzzi that holds three, and a small pool. Rooms are in a white-washed two-story building topped with a thatched roof; roomy bungalows have more vibrant colors, wicker furniture and a nouveau-hippie vibe – for the same price.

Casa Robinson　　　　　HOTEL **$**
(☎809-240-6496; www.casarobinson.it; Av Emilio Prud'Homme; r/studios RD$1100/1400, apt RD$1500-1600; 🅿🛜) Set in leafy grounds down a side street a block from the beach, this family-run hotel offers privacy on the cheap. Fan-cooled rooms in the all-wood buildings are simple and clean and the little balconies have rocking chairs. Bathrooms, however, are more modern and some rooms have kitchenettes.

Casa del Mar Neptunia　　　　HOTEL **$**
(☎809-240-6617; www.casas-del-mar-neptunia.com; Av Emilio Prud'Homme; r incl breakfast RD$1500, apt RD$2000; 🅿🛜) An acceptable budget alternative to Abi and Casa Robinson and on the same street, this whitewashed hotel with 12 large, airy rooms is also homey and quiet.

🍴 Eating & Drinking

Most of the restaurants along Pueblo de los Pescadores are fairly interchangeable – a mix of pizza, pasta, fish, grilled meats and a sprinkling of Dominican specials. Most have bars and stay open well after the kitchen has closed.

TOP CHOICE **La Terrasse**　　　　FRENCH **$$**
(Pueblo de los Pescadores; mains RD$280-680; ⊙lunch & dinner) The Dominican chef at this

sophisticated bistro deserves a few Michelin stars for his steak au poivre (RD$480). The menu carries on with lovely seafood like calamari Provençal (RD$430) and a French cheese plate (RD$300).

Big Dan's Café Americano CAFE, AMERICAN $$
(Calle 27 de Febrero; mains RD$85-325; ☺break-fast, lunch & dinner Mon-Sat, dinner Sun; 🛜) Big Dan does American specialties like chilli, BBQ chicken and a cheeseburger and fries (RD$165) that can go toe-to-toe with any in the Caribbean. Daily lunch specials for RD$100 mean it's all extremely affordable as well.

La Yuca Caliente SPANISH, ITALIAN $$
(Libertad 6; mains RD$290-850, pizzas RD$120-350; ☺breakfast, lunch & dinner; 🛜) Unlike some of its trendier neighbors, La Yuca Caliente is casual in menu and appearance but a step above in food and service. Huge portions of Spanish, Italian, fish dishes and excellent pizzas are served by a professional and courteous staff.

Brasserie Bárrio Latíno CAFE $$
(El Paseo shopping center, Principal; breakfast RD$50-230, mains RD$150-420; ☺breakfast, lunch & dinner; 🛜) Occupying the busiest corner in town, this open-sided tropical brasserie has a large menu of international standards like sandwiches, burgers, pastas and meat dishes. It's a popular breakfast place as well.

ℹ️ Information

Banco Leon (Av Duarte) Has a 24-hour ATM.

Casa de Denis (Plaza Taína, Principal; internet per hr RD$50; ☺8:30am-8pm)

Centro de Especialidades Medicas (Principal; ☺24hr) Small private hospital.

ℹ️ Getting There & Away

AIR Domestic airlines service the mostly private **Aeropuerto Internacional El Portillo**, a one-strip airport 4km east of Las Terrenas along the coastal road. International flights arrive at **Aeropuerto Internacional El Catey**, 8km west of Sánchez and a 35-minute taxi ride (US$70) to Las Terrenas. **Air Canada** (✆888-760-0020) and **Westjet** (✆in Puerto Plata 809-586-0217) offer direct flights from El Catey to Montreal and Toronto respectively. There's also a handful of charter flights.

DominicanShuttles (www.dominicanshuttles.com) and **Aerodomca** (www.aerodomca.com) operate propeller planes between El Portillo and Santo Domingo.

BUS Las Terrenas has two *gua-gua* stops at opposite ends of Calle Principal. *Gua-guas* headed to Sánchez (RD$60, 30 minutes, every 20 minutes 7am to 6pm) take on passengers at a stop 100m north of the Esso gas station on the edge of town. From Sánchez you can connect to an El Caribe bus to Santo Domingo.

Those going to El Limón, 14km away (RD$50, 20 minutes, every 15 minutes, 7am to 5pm), leave from the corner of Calle Principal and the coastal road.

ℹ️ Getting Around

You can walk to and from most places in Las Terrenas, though getting from one end to the other can take a half-hour or more. Taxis charge US$15 each way to Playa Bonita and US$25 to El Limón. *Motoconchos* are cheaper – RD$100 to Playa Bonita – but less comfortable.

Fun Rental (✆809-240-6784; www.funrental.fr; Plaza Creole, Principal) rents quads (US$55 per day) and scooters (US$25).

Playa Bonita

A getaway from a getaway, this appropriately named beach only a few kilometers west of Las Terrenas is a better alternative for those seeking a more peaceful, reclusive vacation. The half-moon-shaped beach is fairly steep and narrow, and parts are strewn with palm-tree detritus. However, backed by a handful of tastefully landscaped hotels, this is an enticing spot.

Las Terrenas Divers (✆809-889-2422; www.lt-divers.com; Hotel Bahía las Ballenas; ☺9am-noon & 3-5pm) offers diving trips and courses (one tank US$50, equipment US$10, open-water certificates US$395) as well as snorkeling trips (US$15, one hour). You can also rent kayaks, bodyboards and surfboards by the hour or day.

🛏️ Sleeping & Eating

TOP CHOICE **Peninsula House** BOUTIQUE GUESTHOUSE $$$
(✆809-962-7447; www.thepeninsulahouse.com; Playa Cosón; r US$580; 🅿🛜) One of the Caribbean's most exquisite and luxurious hotels, this discerning Victorian B&B perched high on a hill overlooking Playa Cosón is the choice for those seeking the utmost exclusivity and service. Only six rooms grace this mansion, each different and dressed up French-chateau style. The three-course dinner is US$70; for lunch, open to the public, mains run RD$500 to RD$650.

Hotel Bahía las Ballenas

HOTEL $$

(☎809-240-6066; www.bahiaballenas.net; José Antonio Martínez; d incl breakfast UD$125-160; P 🛜 ❄ 🌊) Occupying a large swath of Playa Bonita property, this hotel combines the virtues of a luxurious resort and private retreat. Each one of the 32 huge airy villas scattered over the manicured lawn and garden is inspired by a Mexico–south-of-France aesthetic. Large wooden decks look out to an especially nice pool area, and an open-air restaurant serves international fusion food.

Hotel Atlantis

HOTEL $$

(☎809-240-6111; www.atlantis-hotel.com.do; F Peña Gomez; s/d incl breakfast from US$85/95; P ❄ @ 🛜) This charming hotel is straight out of a children's fairy tale – all twisting staircases, covered walkways and odd-shaped rooms. The furnishings are comfortable, not luxurious, and each of the 18 rooms is different. There's a palm-tree-covered patio and fine French restaurant on the premises.

❶ Getting There & Away

By car, Playa Bonita is reachable by a single dirt road that turns off from the Sánchez–Las Terrenas highway. A taxi ride here is US$10, a *motoconcho* around US$1.75.

NORTH COAST

Within two hours' drive of Puerto Plata airport you'll find all the best the north coast has to offer – water sports and beach nightlife in Cabarete, mountain biking in the coastal hills, the celebrated 27 waterfalls of Damajagua, sleepy little Dominican towns where it's still possible to escape the tourist hordes, and mile after mile of that famous Caribbean sand.

Cabarete

POP 15,000

This one-time farming hamlet is now the adventure-sports capital of the country, booming with condos and new development. You'll find a sophisticated, grown-up beach town, with top-notch hotels, and a beach-dining experience second to none (not to mention the best wind and waves on the island). Cabarete is an ideal spot to base yourself for exploring the area.

 Beaches

Cabarete's beaches are its main attractions, and not just for sun and sand. They're each home to a different water sport, and are great places to watch beginner and advanced athletes alike.

Playa Cabarete

BEACH

Main beach in front of town. Ideal for watching windsurfing, though the very best windsurfers are well offshore at the reef line. Look for them performing huge high-speed jumps and even end-over-end flips.

Bozo Beach

BEACH

On the western downwind side of Playa Cabarete, and so named because of all the beginner windsurfers and kitesurfers who don't yet know how to tack upwind and so wash up on Bozo's shore.

Kite Beach

BEACH

Two kilometers west of town. A sight to behold on windy days, when scores of kiters of all skill levels negotiate huge sails and 30m lines amid the waves and traffic. On those days there's no swimming here, as you're liable to get run over.

Playa Encuentro

SURFING BEACH

Four kilometers west of town. The place to go for surfing, though top windsurfers and kitesurfers sometimes come to take advantage of the larger waves. The beach itself is a long, narrow stretch of sand backed by lush tropical vegetation; strong tides and rocky shallows make swimming here difficult.

La Boca

WAKEBOARDING BEACH

At the mouth of the Río Yásica, 7km east of town. Ideal for wakeboarding – more than 2km of straight, flat river water to practise your latest trick.

🏃 Activities

Kitesurfing

Cabarete is one of the top places in the world to kitesurf; it has eclipsed windsurfing as the town's sport du jour. Kite Beach has ideal conditions for the sport, which entails strapping yourself to a modified surfboard and a huge inflatable wind foil, then skimming and soaring across the water. A number of kitesurfing schools offer multiday courses for those who want to learn – just to go out by yourself you'll need at least three to four days of instruction (two to three hours' instruction per day).

DON'T MISS

TWENTY-SEVEN WATERFALLS OF DAMAJAGUA

Travelers routinely describe the tour of the waterfalls at Damajagua as the coolest thing they did in the DR. We agree. Guides lead you up, swimming and climbing through the waterfalls. To get down you jump – as much as 8m – into the sparkling pools below.

It's mandatory to go with a guide and wear a helmet and life jacket, but there's no minimum group size, so you can go by yourself if you wish. You'll need around four hours to make it to the 27th waterfall and back. The falls are open 8:30am to 4pm, but go early, before the crowds arrive, and you might just have the whole place to yourself.

You can go up to the seventh, 12th or 27th waterfall. Most '4WD safari' package tours only go to the seventh. Iguana Mama (p435) runs trips to the 27th for US$85. You should be in good shape and over the age of 12. If you visit on your own, the entrance fee varies depending on your nationality and how far you go. Foreigners pay RD$460 to the highest waterfall, less to reach the lower ones; US$1 of every entrance fee goes to a community-development fund.

The big Texaco station at Imbert serves as a crossroads for the entire area. There is frequent *gua-gua* service to Santiago (RD$80, 1¼ hours) and Puerto Plata (RD$40, 30 minutes).

Expect to pay US$150 to US$180 for a three-hour beginner lesson, US$300 to US$500 for a three- to four-day course (around eight hours in total).

About half of the schools are on Kite Beach.

Kite Club   KITESURFING
(www.kiteclubcabarete.com; Kite Beach) Well run.

Kitexcite   KITESURFING
(www.kitexcite.com; Kite Beach) Award-winning school using radio helmets and optional offshore sessions to maximize instruction.

Laurel Eastman Kiteboarding   KITESURFING
(www.laureleastman.com; Bozo Beach) Friendly, safety-conscious shop run by one of the world's top kitesurfers.

Windsurfing

The combination of strong, steady winds, relatively shallow water and a rockless shore creates perfect conditions for windsurfing here.

Board and sail rentals average US$30 to US$35 per hour, US$60 to US$65 per day and US$280 to US$300 per week. For a bit more, shops offer 'nonconsecutive rentals,' so you get multiday prices but you don't have to go out every day. Renters are usually required to purchase damage insurance for an additional US$50 per week. Private lessons cost around US$50 for an hour, US$200 for a four-session course, with discounts for groups.

Vela Windsurf Center   WINDSURFING
(velacabarete.com) On the main beach. Uses excellent gear and works in conjunction with kitesurfing school Dare2Fly. Also rents sea kayaks (US$10 to US$15 per hour).

Surfing

Some of the best waves for surfing on the entire island – reaching up to 4m – break over reefs 4km west of Cabarete on Playa Encuentro. Several outfits in town and on Playa Encuentro rent surfboards and offer instruction.

Surfboard rental for a day is around US$25 to US$30; a three-hour course costs US$45 to US$50 per person, and five-day surf camps cost US$200 to US$225 per person.

Ali's Surf Camp   SURFING
(☏809-571-0733; alissurfcamp.com) Part of the hotel of the same name. Frequent shuttle service from Cabarete to Encuentro for surfers.

Cabarete Buena Onda   SURFING
(www.cabaretebuenaonda.com; Playa Encuentro)

Pau Hana Surf Center   SURFING
(☏809-975-3494; Playa Encuentro)

Take Off   SURFING
(www.321takeoff.com; Playa Encuentro) The German owner also organizes the Master of the Ocean competition (p435).

Diving

The well-respected Sosúa-based dive shop **Northern Coast Diving** (☑809-571-1028; www.northerncoastdiving.com) has a representative in the offices of Iguana Mama and can organize excursions from Río San Juan in the east to Monte Cristi in the west. You can also pop over to Sosúa to compare prices and services.

🎋 Tours

TOP CHOICE Iguana Mama OUTDOOR ADVENTURES
(☑809-571-0908; www.iguanamama.com) The leading adventure-sports tour operator on the north coast, Iguana Mama is in a class of its own. Its specialties are mountain biking (easy to insanely difficult, US$65) and cascading, and it's one of the few operators that take you to the 27th waterfall at Damajagua (US$85). There's also a variety of hiking trips; its Pico Duarte trek is expensive, but handy if you want transportation to and from Cabarete (per person US$450). Iguana Mama can also arrange a number of half- and full-day canyoning opportunities in the area (US$90 to US$125). Action and adventure junkies should ask about the one-week 'Mama Knows Best' tour – seven days of non-stop adrenaline.

🎆 Festivals & Events

Master of the Ocean WATER SPORTS
(☑809-963-7873; www.masteroftheocean.com) A triathlon of surfing, windsurfing and kitesurfing held in the final week of February.

International Sand Castle Competition SAND SCULPTURE
Also in the last week of February, sand-sculpture enthusiasts convene in Cabarete.

Dominican Jazz Festival MUSIC
(www.drjazzfestival.com) Held in Santiago and Cabarete in early November, this festival attracts top musical talent from around the country and even abroad.

🛏 Sleeping

Velero Beach Resort HOTEL, RESORT **$$**
(☑809-571-9727; www.velerobeach.com; La Punta 1; r from US$170; ⓟ❄@🐾) Distinguished by boutique-style rooms, the nicest in Cabarete, and its location down a small lane at the relatively lightly trafficked eastern end of town, Velero is an excellent choice. True to its four-star rating in service, professionalism and maintenance of the property, the Velero's only downside is it's on a small spit of a beach, but the pool and lounge area more than make up for this.

TOP CHOICE Natura Cabañas RESORT **$$**
(☑809-571-1507; www.naturacabana.com; s/d incl breakfast US$130/180; ⓟ@🐾) Think rustic-chic at this collection of marvelously designed thatched-roof bungalows about halfway between Cabarete and Sosuá. True to its name, everything is constructed from natural materials – mahogany, bamboo and stone – and a gravel path leads to a secluded beach. The two open-air restaurants serve exquisitely created and plated dishes (US$15 to US$30).

TOP CHOICE Ali's Surf Camp HOSTEL **$**
(☑809-571-0733; www.alissurfcamp.com; s US$29-44, d US$33-66, apt US$75-120; ⓟ❄🛜🐾) The closest thing Cabarete has to a backpackers, Ali's is ideal for groups of friends or couples looking to learn how to surf or kitesurf, or who already know the drill. Most of the accommodations are in small but colorfully painted rustic cabins; a two-story Victorian-style building has somewhat nicer rooms with kitchenettes.

WORTH A TRIP

TUBAGUA VILLAGE

Ideal for the ecoconscious traveler, this rustic mountaintop retreat is about as far from an all-inclusive resort as you can get. Set high on a ridge near Puerto Plata with breathtaking views of the valley below, **Tubagua Plantation Eco-Village** (☑809-696-6932; www.tubagua.com; r with shared bathroom incl breakfast US25; 🛜) is the vision of longtime DR resident and Canadian consul Tim Hall. By his own description, accommodation here is 'Robinson Crusoe style,' which shouldn't discourage anyone. There are several wooden cabins with *palapa* roofs (made from palm leaves) and basic bedding – simple but comfortable. Tim, an enthusiastic advocate of low-impact sustainable tourism, can arrange day, overnight and week-long itineraries for travel anywhere in the country. Don't try driving here at night – 20km from Puerto Plata (taxi US$30) and around 40km from Santiago – since the road is rough and there are no lights.

The property, a five-minute walk inland, is lush and shaded and includes a nice pool.

Hotel Villa Taína   HOTEL $$
(☑809-571-0722; www.villataina.com; incl breakfast s US$109-142, d US$119-142; P❋@❀☲) This appealing boutique-y hotel at the western end of town has 55 tastefully decorated rooms, each with balcony or terrace, air-con, comfortable beds and modern bathroom. There is a small, clean pool and a nice beach area fringed by palm trees.

Swell Surf Camp   HOTEL $$
(☑809-571-0672; www.swellsurfcamp.com; per week incl breakfast & 4 dinners dm/s/d US$425/635/1000; P❋❀☲) Purpose-built and designed with the discerning surfer in mind. The spare clean lines, plush bedding, modern photographs and funky furniture say 'boutique,' but the pool, ping-pong table and social vibe suggest otherwise.

✖ Eating

Dining out on Cabarete's beach is the quintessential Caribbean experience – paper lanterns hanging from palm trees, a gentle ocean breeze and excellent food. You can also find good, cheap Dominican set meals on the main street.

TOP CHOICE Otra Cosa   FRENCH $$$
(☑809-571-0607; La Punta; mains RD$500; ☺dinner, closed Tue; ☎) Simply a must, this romantic French-Caribbean restaurant occupies a secluded spot with marvelous sea breezes. Feast on *très délicieux* expertly prepared dishes like seared tuna in ginger flambéed in rum (RD$650).

Casanova   INTERNATIONAL $$
(mains RD$350; ☺breakfast, lunch & dinner) Lavishly decorated with Buddha statues and other Asian-inspired trinkets, Casanova will make you think you're on a beach in southern Thailand. The usual suspects like surf and turf make an appearance, as do fresh salads, pizza and inventive surprises.

Pomodoro   ITALIAN $$
(mains RD$300; ☺lunch & dinner) Run by an Italian jazz fiend, this pizza joint makes the best crispy-crust pizza on the beach. It uses only quality toppings – including pungent, imported Italian cheese – and there's live jazz on Thursday night.

Blue Cabarete Restaurant   INTERNATIONAL $$
(mains RD$250) Comfy, thick couches on the beach. Dinner prices are double those at lunchtime, when the menu includes good, healthy wraps.

☕ Drinking

Nikki Beach   BAR, NIGHTCLUB
(☺9am-late) St Tropez comes to the DR in this swish club with its own sommelier; DJs get the party started late.

Lax   RESTAURANT, NIGHTCLUB
(lax-cabarete.com; ☺9am-1am) This mellow bar and restaurant serves food until 10:30pm, when the DJ starts to spin.

Onno's   RESTAURANT, NIGHTCLUB
(☺9am-late) This edgy, Dutch-owned restaurant and nightclub is a European and hipster hangout and serves good-value food on the beach. At night a DJ spins a decent set.

Bambú   BAR, DISCO
(☺6pm-late) Just 100m west of Onno's, this bar and disco plays loud house music and reggaeton, and the crowd spills out onto the beach.

❶ Information

All City (per hr RD$35; ☺9am-9pm Mon-Sat, 10am-6pm Sun) Fast connection and headphones. There's also a small bank of phones for domestic and international calls.

Scotiabank (Av Principal)

Servi-Med (☑809-571-0964; ☺24hr) Highly recommended. English, German and Spanish spoken; house calls. Travel medical insurance and credit cards accepted.

❶ Getting There & Around

BUS None of the main companies services Cabarete. The closest depots are in Sosúa.

CAR The best place to arrange rental is at Puerto Plata airport when you arrive.

GUA-GUA Heaps of *gua-guas* ply this coastal road, including east to Río San Juan (RD$80, one hour) and west to Sosúa (RD$20, 20 minutes) and Puerto Plata (RD$50, 45 minutes).

MOTOCONCHO Transportation in town is dominated by *motoconchos*. A ride out to Encuentro should cost RD$100.

SCOOTERS A popular option for the many visitors who stay a week or longer is to rent a scooter or a motorcycle. Expect to pay around US$20 per day.

TAXI The motorcycle-shy can call a **taxi** (☑809-571-3819), which will cost RD$250 to Encuentro, US$25 to the airport, and US$35 to Puerto Plata. There's also a taxi stand in the middle of town.

CLIMBING PICO DUARTE

Pico Duarte (3087m) was first climbed in 1944 to commemorate the 100th anniversary of Dominican independence.

For all the effort involved to summit the mountain, there isn't a great deal to see. Up to around 2000m you travel through rainforest, passing foliage thick with ferns and some good birdlife. You quickly pass above this limit, however, and spend most of the trip in a wasteland; numerous forest fires have left the landscape barren and the only animals you're likely to see are marauding bands of cawing crows.

There are **ranger stations** (park admission RD$200; ☺8am-5pm) near the start of the major trails into the parks – at La Ciénaga, Sabaneta, Mata Grande, Las Lagunas and Constanza. As a safety precaution, everyone entering the park, even for a short hike, must be accompanied by a guide.

While the average temperature ranges between 12°C and 20°C most of the year, lows of -5°C are not uncommon, especially in December and January. Rainstorms can happen at any time during the year. While the soil is sandy and drains well, you'll still want a good raincoat plus sturdy shoes or boots.

Routes to the Top

The shortest and easiest route (and by far the most utilized) is from **La Ciénaga**, reached via Jarabacoa. It is 23km in each direction and involves approximately 2275m of vertical ascent. It's recommended to do this route in three days – one long day to arrive at the La Compartición campground, one easy day to summit and enjoy the views and one long day back out again. Consider adding a fourth day to do a side trip to the beautiful **Valle de Tetero** at the mountain's base.

The second most popular route is from **Mata Grande**. It's 45km to the summit and involves approximately 3800m of vertical ascent, including going over La Pelona, a peak only slightly lower than Pico Duarte itself. You'll spend the first night at the Río La Guácara campground and the second at the Valle de Bao campground. You can walk this route return in five days, but far more interesting is to walk out via the Valle de Tetero and La Ciénega (also five days).

Tours & Guides

The easiest way to summit Pico Duarte is to take a tour. Expect to pay roughly US$80 to US$100 per person per day. Be sure to book as far in advance as possible.

Rancho Baiguate (p438) is the best overall choice for non-Spanish speakers. Iguana Mama (p435) in Cabarete is good if you're in a hurry and want transportation to and from the north coast.

Your other option – assuming you speak good Spanish and you're not in a hurry – is to go to the trailhead in person and organize mules, food and a guide on your own. Mules and muleteers go for around US$15 per day each, the lead guide around US$30 per day (minimum one guide for every five hikers). Guides can organize basic provisions for you.

Attempting to summit Pico Duarte without mules is neither possible nor desirable – you can't enter the park without a guide and a guide won't go without mules. Mules are also essential in case someone gets injured.

Sleeping

There are approximately 14 campgrounds in the parks, each with a first-come, first-served cabin that hikers can use for free. Each cabin holds 20 or more people and consists of wood floors, wood walls and a wood ceiling (and rats), but no beds, mats or lockers – if you have a tent, consider bringing it along so you can avoid using the cabins altogether. Most of the cabins also have a stand-alone 'kitchen': an open-sided structure with concrete wood-burning stoves.

CENTRAL HIGHLANDS

Even diehard beach fanatics will eventually overdose on sun and sand. When you do, the cool mountainous playground of the central highlands is the place to come; where else can you sit at dusk, huddled in a sweater, watching the mist descend into the valley as the sun sets behind the mountains? Popular retreats, roaring rivers, soaring peaks and the only white-water rafting in the Caribbean, beckon. Economic life revolves around Santiago, the DR's second-largest city and the capital of a vast tobacco- and sugarcane-growing region.

Jarabacoa

POP 57,000 / ELEV 500M

Nestled in the low foothills of the Cordillera Central, Jarabacoa maintains an under-the-radar allure as the antithesis to the clichéd Caribbean vacation. Nighttime temperatures call for light sweaters, a roiling river winds past forested slopes that climb into the clouds, and local outdoor adventurers share their exploits over a beer in one of a handful of bars and clubs near the town's Parque Central. With a number of good hotels in the countryside outside town, this is the place to base yourself if you want to raft, hike, bike, horseback ride, go canyoning or simply explore rural life.

👁 Sights

The three nearby waterfalls are easy to visit if you've got your own transportation. If not, a *motoconcho* tour to all three will set you back around RD$700, a taxi US$60 to US$80.

Salto Jimenoa Uno   WATERFALL
(admission RD$100) This 60m waterfall – definitely the prettiest of the three – pours from a gaping hole in an otherwise solid rock cliff. There's a sandy beach and nice swimming hole, but the water is icy cold and potentially dangerous. The trailhead to the waterfall is 7km from the Shell station in Jarabacoa along the road to Constanza – admission comes with a bottle of water. The steep path down can be slippery after rain and sweat-inducing all other times (expect each way to take 15 to 30 minutes).

Salto de Baiguate   WATERFALL
In a lush canyon, Baiguate is not as visually impressive as the others, though it's the most accessible for swimming. To get there,

take Calle El Carmen east out of Jarabacoa for 3km until you see a sign for the waterfalls on the right-hand side of the road. From there, a badly rutted dirt road leads 3km to a parking lot and then a lovely 300m trail cut out of the canyon wall leads to the Salto.

Salto de Jimenoa Dos   WATERFALL
(admission RD$50) Generally just referred to as Salto Jimenoa, this 40m cascade is for the views only since access to bathing pools at its foot is fenced off. The turnoff is 4km northwest of Jarabacoa on the road to Hwy Duarte. From there, a paved road leads 6km past the golf course to a parking lot. The waterfall is a 500m walk from there, over a series of narrow suspension bridges and trails flanked by densely forested canyon walls.

🏃 Activities

The Río Yaque del Norte is the longest river in the country and **rafting** a portion of it can be a fun day trip. The rapids are rated two and three (including sections nicknamed 'Mike Tyson' and 'The Cemetery'), and part of the thrill is the risk your raft may turn over, dumping you into a rock-infested river.

There's a number of half-day and full-day **walks** you can take in the area. The best day hike is to **El Mogote**, a short peak just 2km west of town. To get there, hop a taxi (RD$400). Just past the entrance you'll encounter a Salesian monastery; from here it's a stiff five-hour slog to the summit. It's a slippery walk, nay, slide, down from the top.

👉 Tours

Rancho Baiguate   ADVENTURE TOURS
(📞809-574-6890; www.ranchobaiguate.com; Carretera a Constanza) Jarabacoa's biggest and best tour operator dominates the stage. Independent travelers are more than welcome to join any of the group trips, usually by calling a day or two in advance (except for Pico Duarte, which should be arranged with more notice).

Activities have the following prices, all including breakfast and lunch: **rafting** (US$50), **canyoning** at Salto de Baiguate (US$50), **mountain biking** (US$18 to US$50 depending on trail). Rancho Baiguate also offers **horseback/4WD tours** to the waterfalls (US$16 to US$21 with lunch, US$9 to US$11 without lunch). Its **Pico Duarte trips** range in price depending on the number of people and the side trips you take; a group of four people for three days with no side trips costs US$300 per person.

🛏 Sleeping

🖋 Rancho Baiguate
RESORT $$
(☎809-574-6890; www.ranchobaiguate.com; Carretera a Constanza; all-incl s US$77-107, d US$126-163, tr US$170-220, q US$252; P🛜🖥) A wonderful base from which to explore the mountains, Baiguate is an enormous 72-sq-km leafy compound/all-inclusive resort with solid green credentials (including worm farm and gray-water treatment plant). Ask for a room in the low-slung building along the river. The friendly staff speaks English, and the best adventure-tour company in the area is here. The hosts can pick you up from town around 4km away.

Jarabacoa River Club
HOTEL $$
(☎809-574-2456; www.jarabacoariverclub.com; s/d incl breakfast RD$2035/3670; P❄@🖥) This rambling multilevel fun-for-all-ages complex is on both sides of the Río Yaque del Norte around 26km north of town on the way to Manabao. A low-lying two-story building has spacious, modern rooms, but it's the views from the riverside restaurant and cafe that are special.

Hotel Gran Jimenoa
HOTEL $$
(☎809-574-6304; Av La Confluencia; www.gran jimenoa.com; s/d/tr incl breakfast RD$1650/2425/3150; P❄@🛜🖥) Set several kilometers north of town directly on the Río Ji-menoa, this is the Cordillera Central's most upscale hotel. It may be neither on the beach nor all-inclusive, but you could easily spend a week here without leaving the extensive grounds, which include a footbridge to a bar on the far bank of the river.

Hotel Brisas del Yaque II
HOTEL $
(☎809-574-2100; hotelbrisasdelyaque@hotmail .com; Independencia 13; r from RD$1500; P❄) The best place to stay in town, the Yaque II has large rooms and a front-desk staff able to answer travel-related questions.

🍴 Eating

Restaurant Del Parque Galería
DOMINICAN $$
(cnr Duarte & Mirabal; mains RD$300; ⊘break-fast, lunch & dinner) Built directly around a tree and miniature children's playground overlooking Parque Central, this is the nic-est place to eat in town. The large menu includes Dominican specialties as well as international favorites.

Pizza & Pepperoni
PIZZA $$
(☎809-574-4348; Paseo de los Maestros; pizzas RD$210) Excellent pepperoni pizzas are on the menu along with more than a dozen other varieties, but so are calzones, burgers, pasta and grilled meat and fish dishes.

ℹ Information

Banco Popular (cnr Avs Independencia & Colón)

Banco Progreso (Uribe near Av Independencia)

Clínica Dr Terrero (☎809-574-4597; Av Independencia 2-A)

New York Net Café (Plaza Ramirez; per hr RD$30; ⊘8am-midnight)

Politur (☎809-754-3216; cnr José Duran & Mario Galán) Behind the Caribe Tours terminal.

ℹ Getting There & Away

Caribe Tours (☎809-574-4796) has the only 1st-class bus service to Jarabacoa. Daily depar-tures to Santo Domingo (RD$250, 2½ hours, 7am, 10am, 1:30pm and 4:30pm) include a stop in La Vega (RD$75, 45 minutes). The terminal is on José Duran near Av Independencia.

A **gua-gua terminal** (cnr Avs Independencia & Duran) provides frequent service to La Vega (RD$70, 30 minutes, every 10 to 30 minutes 7am to 6pm).

Públicos to Constanza leave from the corner of Deligne and El Carmen (diagonally opposite

---

WORTH A TRIP

SONIDO DEL YAQUE

A short walk down a very steep hill brings you to **Sonido del Yaque** (☎809-846-7275; per person RD$400), a community-tourism project initiated by the women of the village of Los Calabazos, around halfway between Jarabacoa and Manabao. A handful of wood and concrete cabins with bunk beds are set amid lush jungle above the roaring Yaque del Norte river. Each cabin has electricity, mosquito nets and a porch with chairs. Showers are cold, but there'll be hot water in the future. Meals can be made upon request, with notice. A two-story lodge-restaurant with views of the surrounding mountains was being built at the time of writing. Groups of young Dominicans studying environmental sciences visit.

the Shell gas station) at 9am and 1pm daily (RD$150, 40 minutes).

Públicos to La Ciénaga (RD$85, 1½ hours) leave roughly every two hours from Calle Jiménez near Calle 16 de Agosto.

ⓘ Getting Around

The town of Jarabacoa is easily managed on foot, but to get to outlying hotels and sights you can easily flag down a *motoconcho* on any street corner during the day. If you prefer a cab, try **Jaroba Taxi** (☏809-574-4640), next to the Caribe Tours terminal.

UNDERSTAND THE DOMINICAN REPUBLIC

History
First Arrivals

Before Christopher Columbus arrived, the indigenous Taínos (meaning 'Friendly People') lived on the island now known as Hispaniola. Taínos gave the world sweet potatoes, peanuts, guava, pineapple and tobacco – even the word 'tobacco' is Taíno in origin. Yet the Taínos themselves were wiped out by Spanish diseases and slavery. Of the 400,000 Taínos who lived on Hispaniola at the time of European arrival, fewer than 1000 were still alive 30 years later. None exist today.

Independence & Occupation

Two colonies grew on Hispaniola, one Spanish and the other French. Both brought thousands of African slaves to work the land. In 1804, after a 70-year struggle, the French colony gained independence. Haiti, the Taíno name for the island, was the first majority-black republic in the New World.

In 1821 colonists in Santo Domingo declared their independence from Spain. Haiti, which had long aspired to unify the island, promptly invaded its neighbor and occupied it for more than two decades. But Dominicans never accepted Haitian rule and on February 27, 1844, Juan Pablo Duarte – considered the father of the country – led a bloodless coup and reclaimed Dominican autonomy. The country resubmitted to Spanish rule shortly thereafter but became independent for good in 1864.

The young country endured one disreputable *caudillo* (military leader) after the other. In 1916 US President Woodrow

Wilson sent the marines to the Dominican Republic, ostensibly to quell a coup attempt, but they ended up occupying the country for eight years. Though imperialistic, this occupation succeeded in stabilizing the DR.

The Rise of the Caudillo

Rafael Leonidas Trujillo, the then chief of the Dominican national police, maneuvered his way into the presidency in February 1930 and dominated the country until his assassination in 1961. He implemented a brutal system of repression, killing and imprisoning political opponents. Trujillo was also known to be deeply racist and xenophobic. In October 1937, after hearing reports that Haitian peasants were crossing into the DR, perhaps to steal cattle, he ordered the execution of all Haitians along the border and in a matter of days some 20,000 were killed. Trujillo never openly admitted a massacre had taken place, but in 1938, under international pressure, he and Haitian president Sténio Vicente agreed the DR would pay US$750,000 (US$50 per person) as reparation.

During these years Trujillo and his wife established monopolies and by 1934 he was the richest man on the island. Many Dominicans remember Trujillo's rule with a certain amount of fondness and nostalgia, in part because he did develop the economy. Factories were opened, a number of grandiose infrastructure and public-works projects were carried out, bridges and highways were built and peasants were given state land to cultivate.

Caudillo Redux

Joaquín Balaguer was Trujillo's president at the time of Trujillo's assassination. Civil unrest and another US occupation followed Trujillo's death, but Balaguer eventually regained the presidency, to which he clung fiercely for the next 12 years. And like his mentor, Balaguer remained a major political force long after he gave up official control. In 1986 he became president again, despite frail health and blindness. Repressive economic policies sent the peso tumbling.

Dominicans whose savings had evaporated protested and were met with violence from the national police. Many fled to the USA. By the end of 1990, 12% of the Dominican population – 900,000 people – had moved to New York.

After the 1990 and 1994 elections, widely accepted as being rigged by Balaguer, the military had grown weary of Balaguer's rule. He agreed to cut his last term short, hold elections and, most importantly, not run as a candidate. But it wouldn't be his last campaign – he would run once more at the age of 92, winning 23% of the vote in the 2000 presidential election. Thousands would mourn his death two years later, despite that he had prolonged the Trujillo-style dictatorship for decades. His most lasting legacy may be the Faro a Colón, an enormously expensive monument to the discovery of the Americas that drained Santo Domingo of electricity whenever the lighthouse was turned on.

Breaking with the Past

The Dominican people signaled their desire for change in electing Leonel Fernández, a 42-year-old lawyer who grew up in New York City, as president in the 1996 presidential election; he edged out three-time candidate José Francisco Peña Gómez in a runoff. But would too much change come too quickly? Shocking the nation, Fernández forcibly retired two dozen generals, encouraged his defense minister to submit to questioning by the civilian attorney general and fired the defense minister for insubordination – all in a single week. In the four years of his presidency, he oversaw strong economic growth, privatization, and lowered inflation, unemployment and illiteracy – although corruption remained pervasive.

Hipólito Mejía, a former tobacco farmer, succeeded Fernández in 2000 and immediately cut spending and increased fuel prices – not exactly the platform he ran on. The faltering US economy and World Trade Center attacks ate into Dominican exports as well as cash remittances and foreign tourism. Corruption scandals involving the civil service, unchecked spending, electricity shortages and several bank failures, which cost the government in the form of huge bailouts for depositors, all spelled doom for Mejía's reelection chances.

More of the Same

Familiar faces appear again and again in Dominican politics, and Fernández returned to the national stage by handily defeating Mejía in the 2004 presidential elections. Though he's widely considered competent and even forward thinking, it's not uncommon to hear people talk about him rather unenthusiastically as a typical politician beholden to special interests. In May 2008, with the US and world economies faltering and continued tensions with Haiti, Fernández was reelected for another presidential term. He avoided a runoff despite mounting questions about the spending US$700 million on Santo Domingo's subway system, rising gas prices, income inequality and criticisms over the government's response to Tropical Storm Noel in late October 2007.

DR Today

Young and old groan equally about corruption and lack of opportunities. While the government cuts spending on education, health care and other social programs, money goes towards large infrastructure projects like road building, loan payments and, according to many journalists in the DR, to line the pockets of politicians.

After the devastating earthquake that struck Haiti in January 2010, the Dominican government provided medical and humanitarian assistance, and much of the aid from other countries was shipped overland through the DR. However, the thaw in relations only lasted so long. Haiti's cholera epidemic of the following year led to the temporary closure of some border crossings; several Haitians were killed and scores injured in protests.

Incidents at the end of 2010 and beginning of 2011 left dozens more Haitians dead and hundreds injured in clashes in poor barrios around the DR. Some Dominicans claiming they were trying to evict illegal Haitians say they were justified by the threat of cholera and crime. In February 2011 the Dominican government initiated a widespread crackdown, deporting 'illegal' Haitians back over the border.

Culture

History is alive and well in the DR. With a past filled with strong-arm dictators and corrupt politicians, the average Dominican approaches the present with a healthy skepticism – why should things change now? What is extraordinary to the traveler is that despite this there's a general equanimity, or at the very least an ability to look on the bright side of things. It's not a cliché to say that Dominicans are willing to hope for the best and expect the worst – with a fortitude and patience that isn't common.

In general, it's an accepting and welcoming culture, though Dominicans' negative attitudes toward Haitian immigration has not subsided. 'If the country could just solve the "Haiti problem" things would work out' is not an unusual sentiment to hear.

Almost a quarter of Dominicans live in Santo Domingo, which is without question the country's political, economic and social center. But a large percentage of Dominicans still live by agriculture (or by fishing, along the coast).

Dominican families are large and very close-knit. Children are expected to stay close to home and help care for their parents as they grow older. That so many young Dominicans go to the United States creates a unique stress in their families – it's no surprise that Dominicans living abroad send so much money home.

The DR is a Catholic country, though not to the degree practiced in other Latin American countries – the churches are well maintained but often empty – and Dominicans have a liberal attitude toward premarital and recreational sex. This does not extend to homosexuality, though, which is still fairly taboo. Machismo is strong here and the physical, mainly in the way a woman looks or dances, is appreciated unashamedly by both sexes.

Baseball

Not just the USA's game, *beísbol* is part of the Dominican social and cultural landscape – so much so that ball players who have made good in the US major leagues are without doubt the most popular and revered figures in the country. Over 400 Dominicans have played in the major leagues, including stars like David Ortiz, Moises Alou, Julio Franco, Pedro Martinez, Albert Pujols and maybe most famously Sammy Sosa. Two dozen major-league teams have training facilities here.

The Dominican professional baseball league's season runs from October to January and is known as the Liga de Invierno (winter league; the winner of the DR league competes in the Caribbean World Series against other Latin American countries). The country has six professional teams. Because the US and Dominican seasons don't overlap, many Dominican players in the US major leagues and quite a few non-Dominicans play in the winter league in the DR as well.

Needless to say, the quality of play is high, but even if you're not a fan of the sport it's worth checking out a game or two. Fans decked out in their respective team's colors wave pennants and flags, and dancers in hot pants perform to loud merengue beats on top of the dugouts between innings.

Literature

Only a few Dominican novels have been translated into English. Viriato Sención's *They Forged the Signature of God* follows three seminary students in the DR suffering oppression at the hands of both the state and the church. Ten years after publishing the short story collection *Drown,* Junot Diaz received critical acclaim for his 2007 novel *The Wondrous Life of Oscar Wao,* a stylistically inventive story of a self-professed Dominican nerd in New Jersey and the tragic history of his family in the DR. Less well known than Diaz' novel, but maybe a more devastating picture of the Dominican diaspora's rejection of the conventional American dream, is Maritza Pérez' *Geographies of Home. In the Time of the Butterflies* is an award-winning novel by Julia Álvarez about three sisters slain for their part in a plot to overthrow Rafael Trujillo. Also by Álvarez is *How the García Girls Lost Their Accents,* describing an emigrant Dominican family in New York. Other well-known contemporary Dominican writers include José Goudy Pratt, Jeannette Miller and Ivan García Guerra.

Music

Merengue is truly the national music and from the moment you arrive you'll hear it on the bus, at the beach, in the taxi, everywhere – and usually at high volume. The nation's favorite merengue bands include Johnny Ventura, Coco Band, Wilfredo Vargas, Milly y Los Vecinos, Fernando Villalona, Joseito Mateo, Rubby Perez, Miriam Cruz, Milly Quezada and, perhaps the biggest name of all, Juan Luis Guerra.

If merengue is the DR's urban sound, *bachata* is definitely its 'country.' This is the music of breaking up and losing out, working hard and playing even harder. But widespread interest in and acceptance of the style grew largely due to the efforts of musician and composer Juan Luis Guerra, who introduced international audiences to this rich and sentimental form. Among the big names of *bachata* are Raulín Rodríguez, Antony Santos, Joe Veras, Luis Vargas, Quico Rodríguez and Leo Valdez.

Santiago

Held in February, Carnaval is big all over the country but is especially so in Santiago. The city is famous for its incredibly artistic and fantastical *caretas* (masks) and hosts an annual international *careta* competition leading up to Carnaval.

The Carnaval parade here is made up of rival neighborhoods: La Joya and Los Pepines. Onlookers watch from overpasses, apartment buildings, even the tops of lampposts. Costumes focus on two images: the *lechón* (piglet), which represents the devil, and the *pepín*, a fantastical animal that appears to be a cross between a cow and a duck. The most obvious difference between the two is that *lechón* masks have two smooth horns and those of the *pepínes* have horns with dozens of tiny papier-mâché spikes. All participants swing *vejigas* (inflated cow bladders) and hit each other – and onlookers – on the behind.

If you decide to come to Santiago for Carnaval, be sure to make reservations – rooms fill up fast this time of the year.

La Vega

This otherwise unremarkable city south of Santiago hosts the largest and most organized Carnaval in the country. Townspeople belong to one of numerous Carnaval groups, which range from 10 to 200 members and have unique names and costumes. The costumes (which can cost up to US$1000) are the best part of Carnaval here – a colorful baggy outfit (it looks like a clown but is supposed to represent a prince), a cape and a fantastic diabolic mask with bulging eyes and gruesome pointed teeth.

Groups march along a long loop through town, and spectators either watch from bleachers set up alongside or march right along with them. The latter do so at their own risk – the costume also includes a small whip with an inflated rubber bladder at the end, used to whack passersby on the backside.

Landscape & Wildlife

If a nation's wealth could be measured by its landscape, the DR would be the richest country in the Caribbean. Here you can reach the Caribbean's highest point (Pico Duarte, at 3087m) and its lowest (Lago Enriquillo, at 40m below sea level). Bisecting the country is the mighty Cordillera Central mountain range, which makes up one-third of Hispaniola's landmass. In the lowlands is a series of valleys filled with plantations of coffee, bananas, cacao, rice, tobacco and many other crops. Almost 1000 miles of coastline includes bountiful coral reefs and multitudes of tiny islands.

Over 250 species of birds have been found in the DR, including numerous endemics, and the country is known for its humpback whales, manatees and other marine mammals. Among a rich variety of reptiles, the most interesting of all has to be the Jaragua lizard, found in 1998, which is the world's smallest terrestrial vertebrate – adults measure only 25mm.

Environmental Issues

The DR has set aside large areas of forest as national parks and scientific reserves, but illegal logging remains a problem.

Large-scale tourist development along the coast is another potential environmental problem. While a few resorts have adopted ecofriendly practices, they are the exception, not the rule. Heavy boat traffic – not to mention the construction of piers suitable for large ships – can damage fragile coral reefs.

SURVIVAL GUIDE

Directory A–Z

Accommodations

Compared with other destinations in the Caribbean, lodging in the DR is relatively affordable, but there is a dearth of options for independent travelers wishing to make decisions on the fly and for whom cost is a concern. Much of the prime beachfront property throughout the country is occupied by all-inclusive resorts. The largest concentrations are at Bávaro and Punta Cana in the east and Playa Dorada in the north, though their numbers are growing in areas around Bayahibe, Río San Juan, Sosúa and Luperón.

Room rates are for the high season (generally from December to March and July to August). Sometimes price range is indicated where the low- or medium-season rates are significantly reduced (otherwise assume that low-season rates are from 20% to 50% less than high-season rates).

Rooms booked a minimum of three days in advance on the internet are shockingly cheaper (especially so at the all-inclusive resorts) than if you book via phone or, worst-case scenario, simply show up without a reservation.

Be sure the rate you are quoted already includes the 23% room tax. We've experienced sticker shock when paying the bill after making reservations and booking online.

Rates in accommodations reviews in this chapter are given in US$ or RD$, depending on which is most commonly quoted.

$	budget	less than US$40/RD$1500
$$	midrange	US$40 to US$80/RD$1500 to RD$3000
$$$	top end	more than US$80/ RD$3000

Business Hours

Banks 9am-4:30pm Mon-Fri, to 1pm Sat

Bars 6pm-late, to 2am in Santo Domingo

Government offices 7:30am-2:30pm Mon-Fri

Restaurants 8am-10pm Mon-Sat (some closed between lunch & dinner)

Shops 9am-7:30pm Mon-Sat; some open half-day Sun

Supermarkets 8am-10pm Mon-Sat

Embassies & Consulates

The following are located in Santo Domingo:

Canada (☏809-685-1136; Av Eugenio de Marchena 39)

Cuba (☏809-537-0139; Hatuey 808)

France (☏809-695-4300; Las Damas 42)

Germany (☏809-542-8949; Torre Piantini, 16th fl, Av Gustavo A Mejía Ricart 196)

Haiti (☏809-412-7112; Juan Sánchez Ramírez 33)

Netherlands (☏809-262-0320; Max Henriquez Ureña 50)

UK (☏809-472-7671; Hotel Santo Domingo, Suite 1108, cnr Avs Independencia & Abraham Lincoln)

USA (☏809-221-2171; cnr Avs César Nicolás Penson & Máximo Gómez)

Festivals & Events

For information on Carnaval, see p443.

Independence Day (February 27) On this day in 1844 the Dominican Republic gained independence from Haiti. The day is marked by street celebrations and military parades.

Semana Santa (Holy Week; week before Easter in March) The biggest travel holiday in the country and much of Latin America. Everyone heads to the water – expect crowded beaches, innumerable temporary food stands and music day and night.

Food

For travelers hoping to eat out on their own, food can be surprisingly expensive. Of course, prices tend to be much higher in heavily touristed areas, such as the Zona Colonial in Santo Domingo (comparable with US and European prices), and cheaper in small towns and isolated areas.

The following price categories, used in Eating listings in this chapter, refer to the cost of a meal with tax:

$	budget	less than RD$180/US$5
$$	midrange	RD$180 to RD$540/US$5 to US$15
$$$	top end	more than RD$540/US$15

Health

The DR is generally safe as long as you're reasonably careful about what you eat and drink. Mosquito-borne illnesses are not a significant concern, although there is a small but significant malaria risk in the western provinces and in La Altagracia (including Punta Cana).

Haiti's cholera epidemic of late 2010 spread across the border to the DR. As of April 2011, 650 people in the Dominican Republic have been diagnosed with cholera and seven people have died from the disease.

Many antibiotics are available at pharmacies without a prescription. Use caution when purchasing.

» **Electricity** 110 to 125 volts AC, 60 Hz, flat-pronged plugs; same system as USA and Canada.

» **Newspapers** *El Listín Diario* (www.listin.com.do), *Hoy* (www.hoy.com.do), *Diario Libre* (www.diariolibre.com) and *El Nacional* (www.elnacional.com.do), plus *International Herald Tribune*, the *New York Times* and the *Miami Herald* can be found in many tourist areas.

» **TV & Radio** About 150 radio stations, most playing merengue and *bachata*; seven local TV networks, though cable and satellite programming is very popular for baseball, movies and American soap operas.

» **Weights & Measures** Metric system used, except for gasoline (measured in gallons).

Drinking purified bottle water is recommended over drinking tap water in the DR.

Maps

Located in an aging office building, **Mapas Gaar** (3rd fl, cnr El Conde & Espaillat; ⊙8am-5:30pm Mon-Fri, to 2:30pm Sat) has the best variety and the largest number of maps in the DR. Road atlases are also sold here.

Money

There are one- and five-peso coins; notes are in denominations of 10, 20, 50, 100, 500 and 1000 pesos. Many tourist-related businesses, including most midrange and top-end hotels, list prices in US dollars but accept Dominican Republic pesos (RD$) at the going exchange rate. We've listed prices in the currency in which they're most commonly quoted on the ground.

ATMS

ATMs are common and are the best way to obtain Dominican Republic pesos and manage your money on the road. Most banks charge ATM fees of around RD$115; it's worth checking with your domestic bank before you travel. Most ATMs are in a small booth accessible from the street (and thus available 24 hours).

CREDIT CARDS

Visa and MasterCard are more common than Amex, but most cards are accepted in tourist areas. Some businesses add a credit-card surcharge (typically 16%) – the federal policy of withdrawing sales tax from credit-card transactions means merchants will add the cost directly to the bill.

MONEYCHANGERS

Moneychangers will approach you in a number of tourist centers. They are unlikely to be aggressive. You will get equally favorable rates, however, and much securer transactions, at ATMs, banks or exchange offices.

TAXES & TIPPING

There are two taxes on food and drink sales: a 16% sales tax (ITBIS) and a 10% service charge. The latter is supposed to be divided among the wait- and kitchen staff; some people choose to leave an additional 10% tip for exceptional service. There's a 23% tax on hotel rooms – ask whether the listed rates include taxes. It's customary to tip bellhops for carrying your bags and to leave US$1 to US$2 per night for the housecleaner at resorts. You should also tip tour guides, some of whom earn no other salary.

Public Holidays

New Year's Day January 1

Epiphany/Three Kings Day January 6

Our Lady of Altagracia January 21

Duarte Day January 26

Independence Day February 27

Holy Thursday, Holy Friday, Easter Sunday March or April

Pan-American Day April 14

Labor Day May 1

Foundation of Sociedad la Trinitaria July 16

Restoration Day August 16

Our Lady of Mercedes September 24

Columbus Day October 12

UN Day October 24

All Saints' Day November 1

Christmas Day December 25

Telephone

Remember that you must dial ☑1 + 809 or 829 for all calls within the DR, even local ones. There are no regional codes. Local calls cost US$0.14 per minute, national calls US$0.21 per minute. Toll-free numbers have 200 for their prefix (not the area code).

The easiest way to make a phone call in the DR is to pay per minute (average rates to USA US$0.20, to Europe US$0.50, to Haiti US$0.50) at a Codetel Centro de Comunicaciones (Codetel) call center or an internet cafe.

Local SIM cards can be used or cell phones can be set for roaming. There are GSM-suitable networks.

Phonecards can be used at public phones and are available in denominations of RD$50, RD$100, RD$150, RD$200 and RD$250.

Visas

The majority of foreign travelers do not need a visa. A tourist card (you don't need to retain it for your return flight), valid for up to 30 days, is issued for US$10 upon arrival to visitors from Argentina, Australia, Austria, Belgium, Brazil, Canada, Chile, Denmark, France, Germany, Greece, Ireland, Israel, Italy, Japan, Mexico, the Netherlands, Portugal, Russia, South Africa, Spain, Sweden, Switzerland, the UK and the USA, among many others.

Getting There & Away

Entering the Dominican Republic

All foreign visitors must have a valid passport. A tourist card is purchased on arrival.

Air

AIRPORTS

The main international airports:

Aeropuerto Internacional Las Américas (☑809-947-2220) The main international airport, 20km east of Santo Domingo. Modern facilities, including a strong wi-fi signal once past security.

Aeropuerto Internacional Punta Cana (☑809-959-2473) Serves Bávaro and Punta Cana; the DR's busiest airport.

Aeropuerto Internacional Gregorio Luperón (☑809-586-1992) Serves Playa Dorada and Puerto Plata.

Aeropuerto Internacional El Catey (☑809-338-0094) Located 40km west of Samaná; handles flights from various European cities and San Juan, Puerto Rico.

Other airports:

Aeropuerto Internacional Cibao (☑809-581-8072) Serves Santiago and the interior.

Aeropuerto Internacional El Portillo Domestic-flights airstrip a few kilometers from Las Terrenas; busiest during whale-watching season.

Aeropuerto Internacional La Isabela-Dr Joaquin Balaguer (☑809-826-4003) In Higuero, 16km north of Santo Domingo; services domestic airlines.

AIRLINES

Airlines flying to/from the DR:

Aeropostal (www.aeropostal.com)

Air Berlin (www.airberlin.com) Charter flights from Germany.

Air Canada (www.aircanada.ca)

Air Europa (www.aireuropa.com)

Air France (www.airfrance.com)

Air Jamaica (www.airjamaica.com)

Air Tran (www.airtran.com) Direct flights to Punta Cana.

Air Turks & Caicos (www.flyairtc.com)

American Airlines (www.aa.com) Flies to Samaná via San Juan (Puerto Rico); also flies to Santo Domingo, Santiago and Puerto Plata.

Blue Panorama (www.blue-panorama.com) Charter flights from Italy.

Condor (www.condor.com)

Continental Airlines (www.continental.com)

Copa Airlines (www.copaair.com) Several flights a week from Santo Domingo to Havana and Port of Spain (Trinidad).

Cubana Air (www.cubana.cu) Twice-weekly direct flights between Santo Domingo and Havana.

Delta (www.delta.com)

Iberia (www.iberia.com)

JetBlue (www.jetblue.com) Nonstop service between JFK and Puerto Plata, Santiago and Santo Domingo. Also nonstop service from Orlando to Santo Domingo.

Lan Chile (www.lan.com)

LTU (www.ltu.com) Flights from Germany and Austria to Samaná.

Lufthansa (www.lufthansa.com)

Martinair Holland (www.martinair.com) Flights from Amsterdam and Frankfurt to Puerto Plata and Punta Cana.

Mexicana (www.mexicana.com)

Spirit Airlines (www.spiritair.com) Nonstop flights from Fort Lauderdale to Santo Domingo and Punta Cana.

Thomson Airways (www.flights.thomson.co.uk) Charter flights from the UK.

US Airways (www.usair.com)

USA 3000 (www.usa3000.com) Nonstop flights between Punta Cana and Baltimore, Chicago, Cleveland, Pittsburgh, Philadelphia and St Louis.

Varig (www.varig.com)

Westjet (www.westjet.com) Flights from a number of Canadian cities to Punta Cana, Samaná and Puerto Plata.

Land

BORDER CROSSINGS

Listed following are the crossings between Haiti and the DR. Caribe Tours and Capital Coach Line service the Santo Domingo–Port-au-Prince route daily; Caribe Tours also has daily departures at noon from Santiago for Cap-Haïtien (see p447). From the north coast it's easy enough to reach Dajabón, but then you have to transfer to a Haitian vehicle on the other side.

Jimaní/Malpasse The most trafficked and organized crossing; on the road linking Santo Domingo and Port-au-Prince. Open to 7pm.

Dajabón/Ouanaminthe Busy crossing on the road between Santiago and Cap-Haïtien (only a six-hour drive); avoid crossing on market days (Monday and Friday) – crowds, and theft risk.

Pedernales/Ainse-a-Pietre Foot and motorcycle traffic use a small bridge; cars use a paved road through a generally shallow river. Relatively easy and calm crossing.

Comendador (Elías Piña)/Belladère Least trafficked and certainly the dodgiest. Your presence will draw attention. On the Haiti side, the immigration building is several hundred meters from the actual border. Transport further into Haiti is difficult to access.

Sea

Caribbean Fantasy (www.acferries.com) Santo Domingo (☎809-688-4400); Mayagüez (☎787-832-4800); San Juan (☎787-622-4800) offers a passenger and car ferry service between Santo Domingo and San Juan and Mayagüez, Puerto Rico (12 hours, three times weekly).

Getting Around

Air

The DR's inadequate road network means those with limited time should consider flying. Most one-way flights cost US$35 to US$170. The main domestic carriers and air-taxi companies include the following:

AeroDomca (☎809-826-4141; www.aerodomca.com) Flights between La Isabela and El Portillo (US$80); one daily flight to Aeropuerto Las Américas. Charter flights to almost any airport.

Air Century (☎809-826-4222; www.aircentury.com) Twice-daily flights from La Isabela to Punta Cana (US$99).

Caribbean Air Sign (☎809-696-7460; www.caribbeanairsigns.com) Daily evening flights between Aeropuerto Las Américas and Punta Cana.

DominicanShuttles (☎809-738-3014; www.dominicanshuttles.com) Flights between La Isabela and Punta Cana (US$99); two daily flights (US$99) between La Isabela and El Portillo.

Volair (☎809-826-4068; www.govolair.com) Daily flights from La Isabela to Punta Cana, Puerto Plata, Santiago and Arroyo Barril in Samaná.

Bicycle

The DR's under-maintained highways are not well suited for cycling, though mountain biking on back roads can be rewarding. A number of recommended tours are available from Jarabacoa and Cabarete.

Bus

FIRST-CLASS SERVICE

First-class buses have air-con and often TVs and a movie. Fares are low – the most expensive is less than US$10. Reservations aren't usually necessary.

The following are based in Santo Domingo; the Caribe Tours and Metro depots are west of the Zona Colonial – a taxi is the most convenient way to reach either station.

Caribe Tours (☎809-221-4422; www.caribe tours.com.do; cnr Avs 27 de Febrero & Leopoldo Navarro) The most extensive, with service everywhere but the southeast. Daily service to Port-au-Prince.

Metro (☎809-566-7126; www.metrotours.com.do; Francisco Prats Ramírez) Behind Plaza Central Shopping Mall; serves nine cities, mostly along the Santo Domingo–Puerto Plata corridor. Fares tend to be slightly more expensive than Caribe Tours'.

Capital Coach Line (☎809-531-0383; www.capitalcoachline.com; Plaza Lama, cnr Avs 27 de Febrero & Winston Churchill) Daily service to Port-au-Prince.

Expreso Bávaro Punta Cana (cnr Juan Sánchez Ruiz & Av Máximo Gómez) Direct service to Bávaro with a stop in La Romana. Departure times in both directions are 7am, 10am, 2pm and 4pm (RD$350, four hours).

GUA-GUAS

Gua-guas, with no toilets and rarely with air-con, range from minivans to midsize buses with room for around 30 passengers. They stop all along the route to pick up and drop off passengers – wave to be picked up. Most pass every 15 to 30 minutes and cost RD$35 to RD$70. They rarely have signs, so ask a local if you're unsure which one to take.

LOCAL BUS

Large cities like Santo Domingo have public bus systems that operate as they do in most places around the world. *Públicos* pass much more frequently.

Car

RENTAL

Multinational agencies have offices at Aeropuerto Internacional Las Américas (and pickup service at airports like Punta Cana), as well as in Santo Domingo and other cities. Their rates are usually much less than those of local or national agencies, their vehicles are of much better quality, and they provide reliable and comprehensive service and insurance. If you plan to do any driving outside major cities, a 4WD is recommended. Daily rates are US$40 to US$120, but if you make an internet reservation the discounts are substantial.

ROAD HAZARDS

Roads range from excellent to awful, sometimes along the same highway over a very short distance. Be alert for potholes, speed bumps and people walking along the roadside, especially near populated areas. On all roads, large or small, watch for slow-moving cars and especially motorcycles. Be particularly careful when driving at night, better yet, *never drive at night*.

ROAD RULES

In theory, road rules are the same as for most countries in the Americas and the lights and signs are the same shape and color you find in the US or Canada. Seat belts are required at all times. That said, driving in the DR is pretty much a free-for-all, a test of one's nerves and will, a continuous game of chicken where the loser is the one who decides to give way just before the moment of impact.

MOTOCONCHOS

Cheaper and easier to find than taxis, *motoconchos* (motorcycle taxis) are the best and sometimes only way to get around in many towns. An average ride should set you back no more than RD$30, but you might have to negotiate to get a fair price and we've even heard of travelers being unknowingly dropped off far short of their intended location. Accidents resulting in injuries and even deaths are not uncommon; ask the driver to slow down *(¡Más despacio por favor!)* if you think they're driving dangerously.

PÚBLICOS

These are banged-up cars, minivans or small pickup trucks that pick up passengers along set routes in towns. *Públicos* (also called *conchos* or *carros*) don't have signs, but the drivers hold their hands out the window to solicit fares. They are also identifiable by the crush of people inside them – up to seven in a midsize car! To flag one down, hold out your hand – the fare is around RD$12. If there is no one else in the car, be sure to tell the driver you want *servicio público* (public service) to avoid paying private taxi rates.

TAXIS

Dominican taxis rarely cruise for passengers – instead they wait at designated *sitios* (stops), which are located at hotels, bus terminals, tourist areas and main public parks. You also can phone a taxi service (or ask your hotel receptionist to call for you). Taxis do not have meters – agree on a price beforehand.

Grenada

Best Beaches

» Paradise Beach (p466)
» Levera Beach (p462)
» Sandy Island (p462)
» Morne Rouge Bay (p458)
» Grand Anse (p456)

Best Places to Stay

» Petite Anse (p462)
» La Sagesse Nature Centre (p460)
» Flamboyant Hotel (p457)
» Sunset Beach (p466)

Why Go?

The most southerly islands in the Windward chain, Grenada and Carriacou (plus little Petit Martinique) are best known for having been invaded by the US in the '80s and pummeled by Hurricane Ivan in the '90s. But the storm damage is long gone and the American occupation a distant memory, and today the islands are some of the Caribbean's most appealing. From palm-backed white sand and translucent water to gray-black dunes and rolling breakers, the beaches are gorgeous. Grenada's corrugated coastline rises up to mist-swathed rainforest laced with hiking trails and swimmable waterfalls; while St George's, with its market, forts and postcard-perfect Carenage harbor, makes for a picturesque and friendly capital, and is the departure point for ferries to the laid-back sister isles of Carriacou and Petit Martinique. And though cruise ships inject a regular flow of short-stay visitors to Grenada, you'll find all three islands refreshingly quiet and uncrowded.

When to Go

The steamy tropical climate is tempered by northeast trade winds, and in January the average daily high temperature is 84°F (29°C) and the average low is 75°F (24°C), rising to a high of 86°F (30°C) and a low of 77°F (25°C) in July. Rainy season (June to November) sees an average 22 days of rainfall per month in St George's. The driest months, January to April, see measurable rainfall for 12 days a month; this is the best time to visit, though if you like to party, the raucous August Carnival is also a brilliant time to be in Grenada.

Currency Eastern Caribbean dollar (EC$); US dollar (US$) accepted at most hotels, shops and restaurants

Language English

Money ATMs in all sizable towns, dispensing EC dollars

Visas Not required for citizens of the US, Canada and most European and Commonwealth countries

Fast Facts

» **Area** 132 sq miles

» **Population** 100,000

» **Capital** St George's

» **Telephone country code** ✆473

» **Emergency** ✆911

Set Your Budget

» **Budget hotel room** EC$145

» **Two-course evening meal** EC$80

» **Museum entrance** EC$10

» **Beer** EC$6

» **City transport ticket** EC$3

Resources

» **Grenada Board of Tourism** (www.grenada grenadines.com)

» **Carriacou and Petit Martinique Travel and Tourism Association** (www.carriacoupetitmarti nique.com) The lowdown on the smaller isles

» **Grenada Explorer** (www .grenadaexplorer.com) Online tourist guide with masses of helpful info

Itineraries

THREE DAYS

Stay on Grenada Island. Sample the beach at Grand Anse, then spend an afternoon in St George's, having lunch and strolling around the Carenage and checking out the fort, the market and the churches. Take a day relaxing on the sands of Morne Rouge, and another doing a round-the-island drive, stopping at the River Antoine rum factory and Levera or Bathway Beach on the east coast and Gouyave nutmeg plant or Concord Falls on the west.

ONE WEEK

After completing the three-day itinerary, take a day to head into Grenada's hills and check out the Grand Etang volcanic lake, then hike some of the misty trails through the rainforest. Cruise over to Carriacou and settle into a few days of exploration and relaxation. Be sure to head over to Windward, up to the hospital hill and down to Paradise Beach, and take a coastal walk along to stunning Anse la Roche.

10 DAYS

Go where few are bold enough to attempt and split your time between all three islands in the country. Start on Grenada Island, checking out the highlights from the three-day itinerary, then cruise over to Carriacou to see how the beaches measure up. Reboard the *Osprey* and head over to Petit Martinique to complete the triple play.

GETTING TO NEIGHBORING ISLANDS

From the Carenage in St George's, daily fast ferries and slower mail boats leave Grenada bound for Carriacou and Petit Martinique; there are also less-frequent mail boats to Union Island in St Vincent and the Grenadines; you can also hire a local pirogue to take you from Carriacou to Union Island. Daily flights to Carriacou and Petit Martinique offer a quicker way to island hop, and there are also direct flights to Trinidad, Tobago, Barbados, St Vincent and Canouan.

Essential Food &Drink

» **Roti** A tasty flat bread wrapped around curried meat and vegetables.

» **Oil down** Beef and salt pork stewed with coconut milk.

» **Saltfish and bake** Seasoned saltfish with onion and veg, and a side of baked or fried bread.

» **Lambi** The local name for conch.

» **Carib beer** Brewed in Grenada, and always served ice-cold.

» **Jack Iron rum** Ice sinks in this lethal local bellywash.

GRENADA ISLAND

POP 90,000

The island of Grenada is an almond-shaped, beach-rimmed gem of a place with 75 miles of coastline surrounding a lush interior, which is filled with tropical rainforest. Most of the tourist infrastructure is located on the southwest corner of the island, which – conveniently – is also where you'll find the airport and some of the nicest beaches.

🅘 Getting Around

Bus

Buses are a great way to get around Grenada. All services depart from the central terminal in St George's, also the place to find more information on specific routes. Fares in the greater St George's area and to Grand Anse are EC$1.50. From St George's, fares are EC$5 to La Sagesse or Grand Etang, EC$6 to Gouyave, EC$8 to Grenville, and EC$10 to Sauteurs. Depending on passengers, it takes about 45 minutes from St George's to Grenville and 1½ hours to Sauteurs.

Car

Grenada Island has numerous rental agencies. Most offer 4WDs/SUVs (from around US$65/US$80 per day), and some have regular cars (from US$55).

Grenadian agencies:

Archie Rentals (☑444-2535; www.archie rentals.com)

Indigo Car Rentals (☑439-3300; www.indigo carsgrenada.com)

Sanvics 4x4 (☑444-4753; www.sanvics.com)

Taxi

Taxi fares on Grenada are regulated by the government, although you can sometimes negotiate a bit with the drivers. From the airport to Grand Anse costs EC$40; to Lance aux Épines EC$45; to St George's EC$50. From central St George's it costs EC$40 to Grand Anse or Morne Rouge and EC$50 to Lance aux Épines. A taxi from the Lagoon to the Esplanade will set you back a hefty EC$25.

Otherwise, taxis charge a standard rate of EC$65 per hour, whether driving or waiting.

GRENADA

Grenada Highlights

1 Enjoy peace, quiet and beautiful beaches on **Carriacou** (p463)

2 Explore **St George's** (p452), one of the Caribbean's prettiest capitals

3 Revel in the isolation of **Levera** (p462), the ultimate deserted beach

4 Hike around the island microparadise of **Petit Martinique** (p466)

5 Sink your toes into the soft white sand and super-blue water of **Morne Rouge Bay** (p458)

6 Hike the trails and check out the volcanic lake at **Grand Etang National Park** (p461)

7 See unforgettably surreal coral-encrusted sculptures at the **Underwater Sculpture Park** (p457)

St George's

POP 30,500

St George's ticks all the boxes for a small island capital: overlooked by the requisite quota of handsome old buildings, the Carenage harbor is one of the prettiest in the Caribbean. Above the water, a jumble of streets cling to the hill that splits the city in two, lined by a picturesque mishmash of colorful post-hurricane rooftops, crumbling warehouses, grand old stone churches and an imposing fort. The main commercial centre is on the other side of the hill, with the modern Esplanade shopping mall at the water's edge along the main road, Bruce St. South of the Carenage, on its way to the resorts at Grand Anse, the road sweeps around the Lagoon, where a forest of masts and megayacht hulls mark the upmarket Port Louis marina.

◉ Sights

Fort George
FORT

(Church St; admission EC$5; ⊙6am-5pm) Grenada's oldest fort was established by the French in 1705 and is the centerpiece of the St George's skyline. The police headquarters now occupies the interior, but you can wander freely among the stone structure, explore the dank tunnels and climb to the top to see the cannons and a bird's-eye view over the town and the hills of the Grand Etang Forest Reserve. A plaque in the parade ground marks the spot where revolutionary leader Maurice Bishop was executed. Well worth the steep uphill walk via the new Sally Port entrance from the Esplanade.

Cathedral of the Immaculate Conception
CHURCH

(Church St) Sitting pretty at the top of the capital's hill, St George's Roman Catholic cathedral provides a great vantage point over the town. Though Ivan all but gutted the structure, it's since been painstakingly restored.

Carenage
HARBOR

The Carenage is a great place for a stroll along the water's edge, taking in the gift shops, indulging in some people-watching and smelling the fresh seafood wafting from the dockside restaurants. Colorful fishing boats bob around in the clear, fish-filled waters, and the wharfside is busy with cargo ships bringing supplies to and from Carriacou. At the northern end, the sturdy Georgian buildings overlooking the water – including the red-brick Grenada Public Library – have been beautifully restored.

Overlooking the water from the pavement (roughly in the middle of the Carenage), the bronze *Christ of the Deep* statue was donated by the owners of the *Bianca C* luxury liner as a gesture of thanks to the Grenadians who assisted in a rescue effort following an explosion in 1961, when the ship was anchored just off Grand Anse. Three crew members died in the blast, but thanks to the efforts of a flotilla of local fishing boats and pleasure yachts, all remaining passengers and crew were saved. The 600-foot ship is now one of the island's premier dive sites.

Grenada National Museum
MUSEUM

(cnr Young & Monckton Sts; adult/child EC$5/2.50; ⊙9am-4:30pm Mon-Fri, 10:30am-2pm Sat) This museum is in need of some love, but there is some decent information on the history of Grenada and colonial times, plus a lovely shell collection, though precious little on Maurice Bishop's revolution or the US invasion.

Sendall Tunnel
ROAD TUNNEL

Past the museum, Monckton St leads to the Sendall Tunnel, a narrow 340-foot passageway that burrows through the hill to reach Bruce St and the rest of St George's. It was built by former governor Sir Walter Sendall as an alternative to the steep, slippery (and then unpaved) Young St, which had been the principal route between the Carenage and St George's proper. Cars and pedestrians use it today; when walking, stick to the west side of the tunnel.

St Andrew's Presbyterian Church
CHURCH

(Church St) Immediately north of Fort George, the roofless St Andrew's fared worst of all the town's churches in the hurricane. There isn't much left of the interior, and, until fundraising for restoration is complete, the shell is all that remains intact.

St George's Anglican Church
CHURCH

(Church St) Erected in 1825, St George's is topped by a squat four-sided clock tower that serves as the town timepiece – still in working order despite the roofless state of the actual church building, whose interior and stained-glass windows are open to the elements. Repairs are under way to restore it to its former glory.

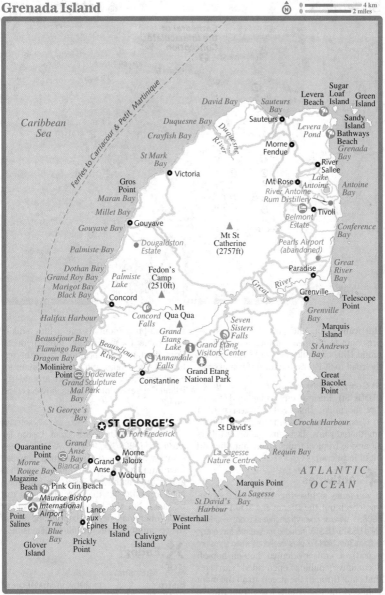

Fort Frederick FORT

(Richmond Heights; admission EC$5; ⊙8am-5pm)
Constructed by the French in 1779, Fort
Frederick was soon used – paradoxically –
by the British to defend against the French.
It's the island's best-preserved fort, and offers a striking panoramic view that includes
Quarantine Point, Point Salines, Glover Island and the adjacent Fort Matthew. On the
hill immediately below is Grenada's prison
complex, built around a colonial-era stone
structure that was partially destroyed by

St George's

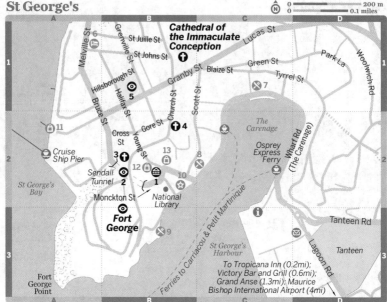

0 — 200 m
0 — 0.1 miles

Hurricane Ivan, allowing the majority of prisoners to escape. The fort is atop Richmond Hill, 1.25 miles east of St George's on the road to St Paul's; the turnoff is marked.

St George's Market Square　　MARKET
(Halifax St) Busiest on Friday and Saturday mornings, this is the largest market in Grenada, with stalls heaped with earth-smothered yams, dasheens and other tubers alongside tropical fruits, spices and the odd bit of local craft.

🏃 Activities

If you fancy sightseeing without the sweating, check out the **Discovery Train** (📞405-6608; www.discoverytraingrenada.com; adult/child US$15/US$10, includes museum & fort entry; ⏰8am-3pm Mon-Fri, plus weekends when ships are in port), a cruiser-oriented hop-on/hop-off 'locomotive' pulling open-sided carriages that chug through the streets to all the main points of interest. Trains leave from the Esplanade every hour.

🛏 Sleeping

Deyna's City Inn　　GUESTHOUSE **$$**
(📞435-7007; cityinn@spiceisle.com; Melville St; s/d US$78/90; ❄@) Right in the town centre, this is a brilliant little place, with a range of

well-equipped rooms (some a little small), with cable TV and bright, modern decor. Friendly staff, great local food from the restaurant downstairs, and very convenient for city sightseeing and transport around the island. There are lots of stairs, however, and no lifts.

Tropicana Inn　　HOTEL **$$**
(📞440-1586; www.tropicanainn.com; Lagoon Rd; s/d/tr US$77/103/124; P❄@📶) A St George's stalwart, right on the main road between town and the lagoon. Rooms are smallish and a little dated but are clean and have good amenities for the price. The road can be noisy, but the balconies on the upper floors offer good views of bobbing boats and the restaurant serves reliable local cuisine.

🍴 Eating

🏆 **Museum**

Bistro　　CARIBBEAN, MEDITERRANEAN **$$**
(📞416-7266; Monckton St; mains from EC$30; ⏰Mon-Sat noon-3pm, dinner by arrangement) Upstairs from the museum, and making the most of its shabby-chic antique setting, this Spanish-run restaurant offers a taste of something different: kingfish with olives, capers and peppers, for example, as well as lasagna, grilled chicken and breaded fish.

St George's

◉ Top Sights

◉ Sights

🛏 Sleeping

✴ Eating

✪ Entertainment

🛍 Shopping

Excellent natural juices, too – try the golden apple.

Deyna's Tasty Foods CARIBBEAN $
(Melville St; mains from EC$18; ⊙breakfast, lunch & dinner Mon-Sat) The perfect place to sample Grenadian food, with daily breakfasts of saltfish and bakes or local-style porridge. Lunchtime sees scrummy rotis and the likes of curried *lambi*, Creole fish or baked chicken served with callaloo, macaroni pie, salad and rice.

Native Food and Fruits CARIBBEAN $
(Esplanade Mall; soups EC$8/10, juices EC$7-8; ⊙lunch Mon-Sat) This spot is located in the international-style Esplanade Mall, but come lunchtime the counter is lined wide and deep with hungry Grenadians. They come from all over town for the soup: thick and fortifying beef, or a veggie version with pumpkin and split peas. Freshly blended juices range from passion or golden apple to peanut punch.

Ocean Grill RESTAURANT $$$
(The Carenage; mains from EC$30, dinner EC$50; ⊙8am-11pm Mon-Sat) On a deck over the waters of the Carenage, this is a shady spot for a bit of lunch – burgers, pasta and salads – or a more ambitious (and expensive) seafood dinner, from lobster to grilled fish.

Carenage Café CARIBBEAN $
(The Carenage; roti EC$15-20, pizzas EC$35; ⊙breakfast, lunch & dinner) Right in the hub of the harbor action and often packed out with cruise shippers, don't let its popularity put you off. It's a good spot for a roti, and the shady patio is a great spot for people-watching and consumption of cold Carib beers.

Nutmeg CARIBBEAN $$
(The Carenage; roti EC$15-21, mains EC$23-58; ⊙lunch & dinner) Those wanting to get above the hustle and bustle of the waterfront need look no further than Nutmeg. Its balcony dining room is a pleasant place for a roti or a nice plate of seafood or callaloo lasagne. The Wednesday lunch buffet (noon to 3pm; EC$25) is a good deal, too.

Victory Bar & Grill RESTAURANT $$
(Port Louis Marina; mains EC$20-60; ⊙lunch & dinner; 🖥) Located in the upmarket Port Louis marina, with tables overlooking boats and the occasional megayacht. It's busy with happy yachties eating fresh salads, burgers and seafood brochettes. The atmosphere is fun, and the food is great.

Foodland SUPERMARKET
(Lagoon Rd; ⊙7:30am-8pm Mon-Thu, to 10pm Fri & Sat) A well-stocked and well-maintained grocery store; has an ample selection of local favorites and imported goodies.

☆ Entertainment

Karma NIGHTCLUB
(www.karmavip.com; The Carenage; ⊙10pm-late Wed-Sat) Set in one of the Carenage's historic old buildings, yet with an ubermodern interior, this is a buzzing spot packed to the rafters with locals (and some travelers, too) dancing the night away to reggae, soca, hip-hop and R&B.

🛍 Shopping

Yellow Poui Art Gallery ART
(Young St) This decent commercial gallery features work from over 80 local artists. Beautiful watercolors, oils and mixed media line the walls and beg to be taken home.

On even a short visit in port, you can do the following:

» Head to St George's (p452) to explore the Carenage, the labyrinthine streets and the precipitous fort

» Visit Grand Etang National Park (p461) for its misty rainforest with monkeys, hiking trails and a volcanic crater lake

» Sun yourself on Grand Anse Beach (p456), with its white sand, blue waters and plenty of places to eat and drink

» Go on a trip to Annandale Falls (p461), an idyllic waterfall set in lush gardens, with a lovely pool to swim in at the base

» Check out the ancient rum factory at River Antoine (p461), then get the lowdown on cocoa production at Belmont Estate (p462)

Tikal SOUVENIRS
(Young St) With a large and varied selection of crafts, prints, fabrics and ceramics, Tikal is a good one-stop shop when it comes to quality gifts, though many are made in other Caribbean islands.

Sea Change Bookshop BOOKSTORE
(The Carenage) A fair selection of popular titles, local authors and pulp, with a gift shop too.

Esplanade Mall SOUVENIRS
(Bruce St; 🕾) An icily air-conditioned spot to pick up souvenirs, from calypso CDs to nutmeg and local chocolate.

❶ Information

There are free wireless hot spots in the centre of the Esplanade mall.

Astral Travel (📷440-5127; The Carenage; ⊙8am-5pm Mon-Fri, to noon Sat) Astral's a switched-on travel agency with info on and affiliation to all the relevant airlines and travel services.

Cable & Wireless (📷440-2200; www.candw .gd; Bruce St; ⊙7:30am-6pm Mon-Fri, 7:30am-1pm Sat) For telephone and fax services.

Compu-Data (📷443-0505; St John's St; per hr EC$7; ⊙8am-7pm) Internet cafe with the best price in town.

Grenada Tourist Board (📷440-6637; www .grenadagrenadines.com; ⊙8am-4pm Mon-Fri) At the southern end of the Carenage.

Main post office (📷440-2526; Lagoon Rd; ⊙8am-3:30pm Mon-Fri)

RBTT (📷440-3521; cnr Cross & Halifax Sts; ⊙8am-3pm Mon-Thu, 8am-5pm Fri) Has a 24-hour ATM.

Scotiabank (📷440-3274; cnr Halifax & Granby Sts; ⊙8am-3pm Mon-Thu, to 5pm Fri) Has a 24-hour ATM.

St George's General Hospital (📷440-2051; Fort George Point) The island's main medical facility.

❶ Getting Around

St George's is best (and most efficiently) explored on foot: the streets are narrow, the one-way systems are confusing and parking is limited. You can flag down any **bus** along Lagoon Rd to get you to the far end of town (EC$2.50), or hop aboard the **Discovery Train** (see p454).

A **taxi** to/from the airport costs EC$50 (EC$60 at night) and takes around 20 minutes.

Grand Anse

POP 22,000

A flowing strip of white-sand beach lined with hotels, craft markets and restaurants, the 'town' of Grand Anse is the closest Grenada gets to a resort. The beach is one of the island's best and is justifiably popular, though it never gets too busy, even on cruise-ship days when busloads of passengers spend the day on the sand. One of the best spots to swim is from Camerhogne Park, adjacent to the Spice Island Mall roundabout, where there are changing facilities (EC$1), sun loungers for rent and plenty of shade.

Several banks and ATMs are spread out along the beach road through town.

🏃 Activities

Aquanauts Grenada DIVING
(📷444-1126; www.aquanautsgrenada.com) This place offers all the usual dive-shop services, from boats to gear to training. Open-water courses cost US$520. There's also a branch at True Blue Bay.

Trailblazers CYCLING

(📞403-1379; rental per day US$20, tours US$15 per hour) Rents out mountain bikes (delivered to your hotel), and offers guided bike tours.

🛏 Sleeping

Jenny's Place GUESTHOUSE $$

(📞439-5186; www.jennysplacegrenada.com; ste from US$110; ❊ 🛜) Set in gardens just off the beach, with just four suites and two apartments. All are brightly decorated and comfortable, and the suites are very spacious, with full kitchen or kitchenette and patio. The staff is friendly, there's a good restaurant and it's a great alternative to the more anonymous large hotels.

Flamboyant Hotel HOTEL $$

(📞444-4247; www.flamboyant.com; r US$170-515; ❊@❊) Up on the hill above Grand Anse Beach, this sprawling property spans both sides of the road. There are great sea views and the rates are reasonable for the location; the rooms (and self-contained suites) are pleasant if a bit uninspiring. There's a lively restaurant and bar on-site to keep you fueled up, and complimentary snorkel gear is a nice touch.

Coyaba Beach Resort RESORT $$$

(📞444-4129; www.coyaba.com; r US$360; ❊@ 🛜❊) Set upon a great stretch of beach and priding itself on exceptional service; the luxurious rooms nearly justify the price. The grounds are beautifully landscaped and facilities are excellent, including a spa, plus the obligatory bar and restaurant, and legions of sun loungers on the beach.

Grenada Grand Beach Resort HOTEL $$$

(📞444-4371; www.grenadagrand.com; r from US$202; ❊@❊) Don't let the big exterior put you off; this enormous complex has a fairly intimate feel. The rooms are nothing special,

but the facilities are impressive. The river-like pool is a hit with little ones. The staff is friendly and there seems to be every amenity you'd need on-site. There are often good deals to be had, as the number of rooms is huge.

🍴 Eating

Grand Anse is more of a strip of hotels along the beach than it is a town. A whole host of eating options can be found along the strip. Most hotels have restaurants and happily accept nonguests dropping in for a meal. If you're craving a quick bite, there is decent budget eating at the Spiceland Mall food court; and weekends evenings see vendors set up sizzling barbecues opposite the banks near the Spiceland roundabout (known as Wall St) – music plays and it's a popular locals' limin' spot.

 Oasis RESTAURANT $$

(📞439-5186; mains from EC$35; ⊙lunch & dinner, closed Wed; 🚶) The best option for eating on Grand Anse itself, with tables on an open-air deck right at the water's edge. Under the same management as the renowned Bogles in Carriacou, and offering the same high standard of cooking, from salads to quiche and calamari, steaks to seafood or lamb shanks. English-style roast dinner on Sundays, live music on Thursday evenings, and a Friday happy hour (5:30pm to 8:30pm).

Southside Restaurant and Bar CARIBBEAN $

(rotis from EC$13; ⊙8am-8pm) Recognizable by the large Carlsberg beer logos on the roof and front, and the place to get some of the best rotis on the island; fillings include boneless chicken, veg and *lambi*.

La Boulangerie ITALIAN $$

(Le Marquis Centre; pizzas from EC$35; ⊙lunch & dinner) Italian food sold under a French name mixed in with Caribbean flavors. Gorgeous

---

SCULPTURES OF THE SEA

Think art galleries are all the same – white walls, wood floors, pretentious patrons? Well, not Grenada's **Underwater Sculpture Park**. For a start, it's almost 7ft beneath the surface of the sea, just north of St George's in Molinière Bay. The life-size sculptures include a circle of women clasping hands, a man at a desk and a solitary mountain biker, all slowly becoming encrusted with coral growth. The 65 original pieces, by Jason deCaires Taylor, were joined in 2010 by 14 new sculptures by local sculptor Troy Lewis, including a depiction of an Amerindian zemi idol. To see them, you'll have to get in the water – and it's well worth the effort. Local scuba companies (see p471) offer diving or snorkel excursions to the sculpture park, and some coastal cruises stop there, too. For a visual tour of the original works, visit deCaires Taylor's website, www.underwatersculpture.com.

pizzas and pastas that will bring you back for seconds – check out the daily specials, too. Very popular with expats, American medical students, travelers and the odd local.

Carib Sushi
JAPANESE $$

(Le Marquis Centre; mains from EC$30; ⏱lunch & dinner Mon-Sat) Local seafood is rolled into the mix at this casual sushi bar. Mix and mingle on the outdoor picnic tables (or cool off inside) before diving into tempura, sushi, sashimi and noodles.

Umbrellas
BURGERS $$

(burgers EC$19-24; ⏱noon-9pm Mon-Thu, noon-10pm Fri & Sat, noon-8pm Sun; ⏺) A stylish two-floor wooden building just back from the sand, with tables on the upper deck and inside. A happening new place for a frosty cocktail, cold beer or a light lunch or dinner, with a huge range of burgers and some interesting salads.

Real Value
SUPERMARKET

(Spiceland Mall; ⏱8am-9pm Mon-Thu, 8am-9pm Fri & Sat, 10am-7pm Sun) The biggest grocery store on the island; has everything you'd ever need to self-cater.

☆ Entertainment

Owl
BEACH BAR

(Flamboyant Hotel; ⏱daily to 3am) There's cricket on the TV, a sea breeze filtering in and a pool table to keep you busy. The staff keeps the party going into the wee hours with drink specials and other debaucherous means. It's a popular hangout for a whole range of locals, visitors and students.

Movie Palace
CINEMA

(⏱444-6688; www.moviepalace.gd; Excel Plaza; tickets EC$18) For a quiet evening, check out Hollywood films screened at this small theatre.

Morne Rouge Bay

POP 12,000

Though just down the way from Grand Anse Beach, the succulent sands of Morne Rouge are in a whole different league. This far superior stretch of beach is a shining example of the snow-white sand and crystal-clear blue water that the Caribbean is known for. It's mercifully quiet and pristine, there are only a handful of buildings housing hotels and restaurants, and lots of shade toward the far end.

🛏 Sleeping

LaLuna
HOTEL $$$

(⏱439-0001; www.laluna.com; cottages from US$545; @🛜🏊) There's a simple elegance to these 16 Balinese-inspired cottages with four-poster beds, private plunge pools and open-air bathrooms. A secluded beach and a delightfully delicious restaurant are provided to keep you occupied, as is yoga at the beachside pavilion or treatments in the spa. It's a little hard to find – just like paradise should be.

Gem Holiday Beach Resort
HOTEL $$

(⏱444-4224; www.gembeachreort.com; s/d US$103/126; ❄@) Just up from the beach, this place is a real gem. Nothing too fancy, and perhaps a bit dated, but all the basics you'd need. Tidy, friendly and a great budget option on one of the best beaches on the island.

Kalinago
HOTEL $$

(⏱444-5254; www.kalinagobeachresort.com; s/d US$150/160; ❄🛜🏊) Next door to Gem, and something of a step up, with spacious rooms overlooking the water (and just steps from the beach), plus a nice oceanside pool and great service from the friendly staff.

🍴 Eating

Sur La Mer
CARIBBEAN $$

(mains from EC$35; ⏱breakfast, lunch & dinner) There's no need to stray too far from the sand. This beachside restaurant will sort you out with a simple lunch or dinner. Sur La Mer serves up West Indian fare with a flair for seafood, and it has an enticing bar with views of the lapping waves.

☆ Entertainment

Fantasia 2001
NIGHTCLUB

(⏱10pm-late Wed, Fri & Sat) Fantasia has a dance floor that resembles a roller rink or maybe a bull-fighting ring, depending on your perspective. Fun, safe and lively, this is a great spot to groove with the locals and mix with other travelers into the wee hours.

Point Salines & True Blue

POP 16,000

The area around Point Salines is dominated by the oceanside airport, named Maurice Bishop International in honor of the island's revolutionary leader. It's also notable for the string of lovely beaches to the north of the runway, just off the airport road.

South of the airport, True Blue is a relaxed corner of the island with some nice top-end hotels, good eateries and multiple yacht marinas. Crowning the peninsula enclosing True Blue Bay, St George's Medical School (SGU) is a sprawling and pleasant campus inhabited almost exclusively by young Americans. It feels like you could be on a campus anywhere in the States – but perhaps that's the point – and the students do inject a bit of life into this otherwise sleepy corner of Grenada.

Sights & Activities

TOP CHOICE Pink Gin Beach
FAMILY BEACH

Accessed via the turnoff for the Beach House restaurant, Pink Gin (on some maps as Pingouin beach) is a lovely swath of powdery white sand with warm blue waters, good snorkeling and wonderful views over to St George's. There's an upmarket restaurant and a hotel overlooking the beach, but it still manages to feel very secluded.

Magazine Beach
FAMILY BEACH

The final port of call for travelers getting a last-minute dose of sea and sand before hopping on a plane, Magazine Beach is nicknamed by locals as the Caribbean's prettiest departure lounge. Its white sands and invigorating waters are bordered by a picturesque tumble of boulders at its southern end, and there's a great beach bar to get drinks and food, or rent snorkel gear.

Aquanauts Grenada
DIVING

(📞444-1126; www.aquanautsgrenada.com; True Blue Bay Resort) The dive-shop juggernaut on the island. It has it all, from the boats to the gear to an army of staff. Open-water courses cost US$520. There's also a branch at Grand Anse.

Sleeping

True Blue Bay Resort & Marina
HOTEL $$$

(📞433-8783; www.truebluebay.com; True Blue Bay; r US$292-444; ❋@🛜🏊) Built at the edge of a yacht-filled bay, this family-owned resort is an island favorite, with multicolored huts that pop off the green grass like a carpet of children's jellybeans lining the hill. Apartments feature full kitchens and a striking adobe decorative scheme, and the luxurious tower rooms have great views and neat touches like telescopes to scan the horizon.

Maca Bana
HOTEL $$$ 459

(📞439-5355; www.macabana.com; Point Salines; r US$515-610; ❋@🛜🏊) Maca Bana has gorgeous villas spreading down a hillside, with fabulous views down the coast to St George's and every possible detail attended to, from iPod docks and flat-screen TVs to espresso machines and private hot tubs out on the deck. Solar panels provide all the power and everything is done with sustainability in mind.

Eating & Drinking

Aquarium
RESTAURANT-BAR $$

(📞444-1410; www.aquariumgrenada.com; Point Salines; mains EC$40-100; ⏰10am-10pm Tues-Sun; 🅿🍴) Built right on the sands of Magazine Beach, this ever-popular place offers drinks and simple salad or burger lunches, plus more sophisticated choices at dinner, with plenty of seafood and a wealth of choices for meat lovers. The Sunday barbecue with live music is always oversubscribed – book ahead.

D Big Fish
RESTAURANT $$

(📞439-4401; True Blue; mains from EC$35 ⏰lunch & dinner) Popular with yachties, and with great views over the marina, this cool oceanside restaurant serves up great pizzas and quesadillas, plus fish dishes and burgers. There's live music on Tuesdays and Saturdays, and a happy hour (5pm to 7pm) on Tuesday, Friday and Saturday.

Bananas
RESTAURANT, NIGHTCLUB $$

(http://bananas.gd; True Blue Rd; mains from EC$36; ⏰9am-late) Popular with expat students from the nearby medical school, Bananas is a good place to come and check out the medics of tomorrow getting smashed and playing doctor with each other. The dance club out back is fun and the massive open-air patio is a good place to mingle. The food is a bit overpriced, but the drinks are cold and the atmosphere is hot.

Lance aux Épines

POP 9100

Lance aux Épines (lance-a-peen) is the peninsula that forms the southernmost point of Grenada. It's home to a pretty beach and some of the island's more upmarket establishments. The marina is a pleasant place to explore, with members of the sailing set and the student body spicing up the atmosphere. Glowering over the water adjacent to the marina is the striking Prickly Bay waterside development, whose multistory luxury apartments make a rather incongruous addition to the otherwise green and pleasant bayside.

With calm, shallow water lined with palms, and with yachts bobbing in the distance, it's a quiet and relaxed place to swim and sun. A couple of hotels border the sand but it's rarely busy, and is a great spot for young children. A beach bar serves up food and drink.

If you're here for diving, **ScubaTech** (☎439-4346; www.scubatech-grenada.com; Calabash Hotel) is well organized and delivers good wreck dives as well as snorkeling expeditions.

🛏 Sleeping

Lance aux Épines Cottages　　HOTEL **$$**
(☎444-4565; www.laecottages.com; r US$165-205; ❄@) You can't argue with the location. It's right on the beach, so your biggest worry is tracking sand into your cottage. Beautiful views are augmented by attractive rooms that come complete with kitchens and large living areas. Well set up for families, the games room is a big hit with children.

Calabash Hotel　　HOTEL **$$$**
(☎444-4334, www.calabashhotel.com; r incl breakfast from US$570; ❄@🛜🏊) Easily the area's nicest place to bed down for the night. The beautifully manicured grounds sit hand in hand with a standard of service that is second to none. Lovely touches include having breakfast delivered to your room, and the sweeping lawns and swaying palms on the beach make the setting ripe for relaxation. Rates include breakfast and afternoon tea.

🍴 Eating

Prickly Bay Marina Pizzeria　　ITALIAN **$$**
(pizzas from EC$30; ☺lunch & dinner) Pizzas that are renowned as the best in Grenada are baked, sliced and munched dockside. Picnic tables, a pool table and a cozy seaside bar all add up to a very chilled mix of food and fun. Quiz night on Tuesdays, live music on Fridays and a daily happy hour (5pm to 6pm).

Red Crab　　CARIBBEAN **$$**
(mains from EC$32; ☺11am-2pm & 6-11pm Mon-Sat) The roadside patio isn't the most aesthetic place to dine on the island, but the outstanding food more than makes up for it. This is a great place to sample some Grenadian cooking. There's a wide selection of seafood, and the service is impeccable, if a little slow at times.

ⓘ Information

There's a customs and immigration office at the full marina of **Spice Island Marine Services** (☎444-4257; www.spiceislandmarine.com; Prickly Bay).

La Sagesse Nature Centre

Sitting along a palm-lined bay with protected swimming and a network of hiking trails, **La Sagesse Nature Centre** (walks US$8, package incl lunch & transport US$52) occupies the former estate of the late Lord Brownlow, a cousin of Queen Elizabeth II. His beachside **manor house** (☎444-6458; www.lasagesse.com; r US$210), built in 1968, has been turned into a small inn. The stylish rooms in the new block are simple and alluring, with screened windows, while those in the manor house and the more secluded cottage have ocean views and verandas. The beachside **restaurant** (mains EC$28-80; ☺breakfast, lunch & dinner) has fish sandwiches, salads and plenty of seafood, all cooked with fresh local ingredients; it's also a great spot for a sunset cocktail or fresh fruit punch. Patrons are welcome to use the hotel's sun loungers and make a day of it on the beach, which is a lovely place to swim, with calm, shallow waters, sand tinted brown by volcanic deposits, and a very private feel – the hotel's access road is the only way in by land.

La Sagesse is about a 25-minute drive from St George's on the Eastern Main Rd. The entrance is opposite an old abandoned rum distillery. Buses bound for the province of St David can also drop you here (EC$5).

Grand Etang Road

Overhung with rainforest and snaking uphill in a series of switchback turns, the Grand Etang Rd is the antithesis of the sand and surf on the coast. The mountainous center of the island is often awash with misty clouds, and looks like a lost primordial world, its tangle of rainforest brimming with life – including monkeys that often get a bit too friendly. A series of hiking trails through the protected Grand Etang National Park provide access into the fertile forest.

To get to the area, take River Rd or Sans Souci Rd out of St George's, and when you reach the Mt Gay traffic circle, take the road north. Alternatively, take bus 9 (EC$5) from the main bus station in town and enjoy the views as the van winds its way along the twisting road.

ANNANDALE FALLS
An idyllic waterfall with a 30ft drop, Annandale Falls is surrounded by a grotto of lush vegetation, and has a large pool where you can take a refreshing swim. Try not to go when cruise ships are in port, as it can get a bit overcrowded.

In the village of Constantine, located 3.5 miles northeast of St George's, turn left on the road that leads downhill immediately past the ruined roofless church. After three-quarters of a mile you'll reach the **Annandale Falls visitor center** (admission EC$5; ⊙8am-4pm). The falls are just a two-minute walk downhill.

GRAND ETANG NATIONAL PARK
Two and a half miles northeast of Constantine, after the road winds steeply up to an elevation of 1900ft, a roadside sign welcomes visitors to **Grand Etang National Park** (admission EC$5). Half a mile past the road sign, the **Grand Etang visitor center** (⊘440-6160; ⊙8am-4pm) sits to the side of the road and has a few displays explaining the local foliage, fauna and history. Outside the center, a series of booths sell hot meals, drinks and souvenirs.

The following are some of the hiking trails in the park:

Concord Falls Serious hikers branch off shortly before the end of the Mt Qua Qua Trail to pick up this five-hour trek (one way from the visitor center) to Concord Falls. From the falls, you can walk another 1.5 miles to the village of Concord on the west coast and take a bus back to St George's.

Fedon's Camp A long, arduous hike that leads deep into the forested interior, to the site where Julien Fedon, a rebel French plantation owner, hid out after his 1795 rebellion.

Grand Etang Shoreline This 1½-hour loop walk around Grand Etang Lake is gentle, but it can get muddy and doesn't offer the same sort of views as the higher trails.

Morne La Baye This easy 15-minute walk starts behind the visitors center and takes in a few viewpoints, passing native vegetation along the way.

Mt Qua Qua This is a moderately difficult three-hour round-trip hike that leads to the top of a ridge, offering some of the best views of the interior forest.

Seven Sisters Falls The hike to this series of seven waterfalls in the rainforest east of the Grand Etang Rd is considered the best hike in Grenada. The main track starts from the tin shed used by the banana association, 1.25 miles north of the visitors center on the right side of the Grand Etang Rd. The hike takes only about two hours round-trip; a small fee is sometimes charged.

Grenville
POP 15,600

A trip along Grenada's east coast is the perfect antidote to the gloss and prefabricated tourism of Grand Anse. Halfway up the coast, bustling Grenville is the area's agricultural hub, and its busy streets offer a good insight into the daily lives of the average Grenadian, as well as some picturesque stone buildings to admire. Two miles north of town is the disused Pearls airport, which once served as the main landing strip for the island. It's derelict now, but a couple of rusting Cuban planes serve as poignant reminders of the American invasion.

Grenville is fairly easy to get to by bus 9 (EC$8, about 40 minutes) from St George's, along scenic Grand Etang Rd.

✖️ Eating

There are several small-scale eateries along Grenville's parallel main streets, including the hole-in-the-wall **My Place**, selling luscious rotis and other delectable snacks, which make an ideal takeaway picnic.

Melting Pot   CARIBBEAN $
(⊙lunch & dinner) Upstairs overlooking the waterfront, you're sure to meet up with the local crew here. Grenadian stalwarts such as callaloo, peas and rice and stewed fish are served up deli style; it's great food for an even better price.

North of Grenville

TOP CHOICE **River Antoine Rum Distillery**   DISTILLERY
(⊘442-7109; tours EC$5; ⊙8am-4pm Mon-Fri) River Antoine has produced rum since 1785 and claims to have the oldest working water wheel in the Caribbean. Tours cover all

aspects of the smoky, pungent production process, from the crushing of cane to fermentation and distillation. At the end of the tour, you can buy cut-price bottles of the finished product alongside a killer sorrel rum punch – try before you buy. It's about four miles north of Pearl's airport; carry straight on where the road divides by the Catholic church in Tivoli.

Lake Antoine   LAKE

A shallow crater lake in an extinct volcano, Lake Antoine hosts a large variety of wildlife. The perimeter trail makes for a beautiful walk, and it's excellent for bird-watchers. It's accessed via a signposted road about a mile north of River Antoine.

Belmont Estate   COCOA FACTORY, GARDEN

(☑442-9524; tours EC$10; ⊙9am-4pm, closed Sat) Hurricane Ivan decimated most of Grenada's nutmeg trees, and since then cocoa has taken over as the island's main crop. Visit Belmont on a Wednesday and you'll see farmers arriving to sell on their buckets of fermenting raw cocoa pods; guided tours also explain cocoa production, and you can walk the landscaped gardens and have lunch. The estate is a couple of miles northwest of River Antoine; turn inland at Tivoli.

Bathway Beach & Around

From River Sallee, a road leads to Bathway Beach, a lovely stretch of coral sands. At the north end, a rock shelf parallels the shoreline, creating a very long, 30ft-wide sheltered pool that's great for swimming. Booths sell food and drinks.

Sandy Island is one of three small islands that sit off the coast of Bathway. It's uninhabited and home to a beautiful beach on the leeward side that offers fine swimming and snorkeling in crystal-clear waters. Boats from Sauteurs to Sandy Island cost about EC$200 per boat, round-trip; make inquiries with the fishermen on Sauteurs beach.

Levera Beach

Backed by eroding sea cliffs, Levera Beach is a wild, beautiful sweep of sand. Just offshore is the high, pointed Sugar Loaf Island, while the Grenadine islands dot the horizon to the north. The beach, the mangrove swamp and the nearby pond have been incorporated into Grenada's national-park system and are an important waterfowl habitat and sea-turtle nesting site.

The road north from Bathway to Levera is rough and unpaved, but shouldn't pose a problem to most vehicles; walking it will take about 30 minutes.

Sauteurs
POP 15,000

On the northern tip of the island, the town of Sauteurs (whose French name translates as 'Jumpers') is best known for its grim history. In 1651, local Carib families elected to throw themselves off the 130ft-high cliffs that line the coast rather than surrender to the advancing French army. The **Carib's Leap exhibition** (admission EC$5; ⊙10am-5pm), adjacent to the Catholic church cemetery, consists of a few Amerindian artifacts and a marvelous viewing point over the cliffs.

🛏 Sleeping & Eating

TOP CHOICE Petite Anse   HOTEL, RESTAURANT **$$$**

(☑442-5252; www.petiteanse.com; r US$260-315; ✱❄🐾) By far the most upmarket of the two places to stay in this stretch, and with more in the way of facilities, including a slip of beach. Rooms are beautifully decorated, with four-poster beds and patios, and the restaurant (mains EC$35 to EC$85) has everything from salads and pasta to seafood.

Almost Paradise   HOTEL, RESTAURANT **$$**

(☑442-0608; www.almost-paradise-grenada.com; r US$88-121; @🐾) A little way around the coast from Petite Anse, and with even better views of the Grenadine islands. Rooms are simple and bright, with netted beds, kitchenette, and hammocks on the balcony. The restaurant is a great spot for lunch (Friday, Saturday and Sunday only), with a wide range of excellent Mediterranean-influenced food and delicious cocktails.

Gouyave
POP 14,700

Gouyave, roughly halfway up the west coast from St George's, is a supremely attractive fishing village with a warm small-town feel. It is well worth spending a couple of hours just walking around, having a drink and taking in the ambience.

On the town's main road is a large **nutmeg processing station** (admission US$1; ⊙8am-4pm Mon-Fri), where you can tour through fragrant vats of curing nuts and various sorting operations. On the south side of Gouyave, a road leads inland half a mile along the river to the **Dougaldston Estate**, where cocoa and spices are processed.

On Friday evenings from around 7pm, the town comes alive for the **fish fry**, with vendors selling fresh fish, lobster and all the trimmings from street stalls, and music echoing through the streets.

Concord Falls

There are a couple of scenic waterfalls along the Concord River. The lowest, a picturesque 100ft cascade, can be viewed by driving to the end of Concord Mountain Rd, a side road leading 1.5 miles inland from the village of Concord. These falls are on private property and the owner charges US$1 to visit them.

The half-mile trail to the upper falls begins at the end of the road. There have been some muggings in this area, so it is recommended that you don't hike alone, and leave valuables at your hotel.

CARRIACOU

POP 9000

The fact that most people don't realize that there are in fact *three* islands in the nation of Grenada is a fitting introduction to Carriacou (carry-a-cou). Like its minor island sibling Petit Martinique, this humble isle is often forgotten.

Where the island of Grenada can feel touristy and busy, you'll struggle to ever feel that way here. You won't find cruise ships, big resorts or souvenir shops – this is Caribbean life the way it was 50 years ago: quiet, laid-back and relaxed. Carriacou is off the radar of most travelers, with green hills that offer some tremendous hiking and beaches that are destined to make your all-time best-of list.

❶ Getting There & Away

To check on flights between Grenada Island and Carriacou, contact **SVG Air** (☑444-3549; www.svgair.com). See p472 for details of transport to/from Carriacou by boat.

❶ Getting Around

TO/FROM THE AIRPORT It is best to get to and from the airport by taxi. A ride into Hillsborough is EC$20, while Tyrrel Bay or Bogles is

EC$25. Taxi prices to all points are posted outside the tourist office in Hillsborough.

BUS Buses (privately owned minivans) charge EC$3.50 to go anywhere on the island, or EC$1 if the distance is less than a mile. The two main routes run from Hillsborough – one south to Tyrrel Bay, the other north to Windward. Minibuses start at around 7am and stop around sunset.

CAR There are a few places to rent vehicles on Carriacou, with rates typically around US$50 per day. **Wayne's Jeep Rental** (☑443-6120), in Hillsborough just up from Ade's Dream hotel, has good prices. There is a gas station on Patterson St in Hillsborough.

TAXI Most taxis are actually minibuses, and usually you can count on a couple of them swinging by the airport to meet flights or by the pier when the ferry arrives.

You can hire a taxi for a 2½-hour island tour, costing EC$200 for up to five people; the northern half alone, which takes half as long, costs EC$100. **Linky** (☑406-2457) is a reliable and knowledgeable driver.

Hillsborough

POP 5000

Carriacou's gentle pace is reflected in the sedate nature of its largest town, Hillsborough. With only a couple of streets lined with a mixture of modern blocks and classic Caribbean wooden structures, there is little to actually see or do here. Having said that, the quiet streets and welcoming locals leave an endearing impression, and it's a nice place for simply hanging out, or taking in the action at the lively pier area where the *Osprey* ferry and mail boats dock.

◉ Sights & Activities

Beausejour Bay FAMILY BEACH

Also known as Silver Bay, Hillsborough's beach isn't the island's best, but it's decent nonetheless. Fishing boats pull in along the Esplanade, where there are a couple of shady gazebos, and there's some nice shell collecting beyond this toward the northern headland. South of Hillsborough, it's a wilder affair, with crashing waves and pelicans roosting on the spines of long-gone piers.

Carriacou Museum MUSEUM

(☑443-8288; Patterson St; admission EC$5; ☺9:30am-3:45pm Mon-Fri) This small, community-run museum has an interesting array of Carib artifacts, including documentation of a skeleton recently found at Grand Bay, the

ANSE LA ROCHE

Anse la Roche, on Carriacou, is most definitely something special. This idyllic stretch of the softest sand you may ever get the pleasure of sinking your toes into is a hidden prize for those willing to make the effort to seek it out. Protected by dense bush and cliffs on its flanks, this secluded beauty – rarely visited, except by the adventurous, those in the know and the sea turtles that nest among the sand – is a private paradise.

The treasure trail goes a little like this. From the town of Bogles take a left at the (white) sign for the High North Park. Follow that road, which quickly turns to dirt, for 20 minutes on foot. Look for a red-painted rock on the left-hand side of the road and follow the rough path through the forest for 15 minutes. All going well, you should be spat out onto a beach that you'll be bragging about for years.

so called Harvey Vale Man, plus displays on African heritage and the colonial era, and paintings by local artists.

Carriacou Silver Diving DIVING
(✆443-7882; www.scubamax.com) The first and still the best dive shop on Carriacou. Has two-tank dives for US$95, PADI open-water courses US$500.

🛏 Sleeping

With so few choices in terms of dining, many travelers plump for self-contained villas rather than hotels in Carriacou. **Down Island** (✆443-8182; www.islandvillas.com) has some of the best options.

Ade's Dream GUESTHOUSE $
(✆443-7317; www.adesdream.com; Main St; r US$32-60; ❄🛜) Popular with interisland travelers, those on a budget and people wanting to be right among the action, Ade's is in the dead center of town, above a bustling grocery/hardware/liquor/everything-else store. There are basic rooms with shared facilities and self-contained units with kitchens, and it's often booked to the hilt when the rest of the island is a ghost town.

Green Roof Inn HOTEL $$
(✆443-6399; www.greenroofinn.com; s/d incl breakfast US$40/80; @❄👙) Half a mile up the road from Hillsborough, and set on the cliff overlooking the sea with sweeping views back toward Hillsborough, this is a quiet and beautiful play to stay. The simple rooms have mosquito-netted beds, and some have sea views. Breakfast is included.

John's Unique Resort HOTEL $
(✆443-8345; www.johnsuniqueresort.com; Main St; r US$32-70; ❄) Just on the outskirts of town toward Bogles, you'd be hard-pressed to name what is truly unique about John's –

but it is, nonetheless, a winner. Rooms are large and clean, with sunny balconies. The restaurant can put together a great plate of local food for a good price and the staff is friendly and helpful.

Grand View Hotel HOTEL $
(✆443-8659; www.carriacougrandview.com; r US$70-121; ❄@👙) With a bird's-eye view over the harbor and the surrounding hills, this is a quiet but friendly place, best if you've rented a car (as it's a bit isolated from the action in town). Rooms range in size, and the most expensive have the best views, but each has a private balcony, plus there's a bar and restaurant on-site.

Hotel Laurena HOTEL $$
(✆443-8759; www.hotellaurena.com; s/d US$85/95; ❄@👙) The largest accommodation option on the island, Laurena has spacious rooms with a good selection of amenities, from fridges and DVD players to kitchenettes and balconies. The staff is friendly and deluxe rooms have Jacuzzi tubs to soak your troubles away.

🍴 Eating & Drinking

Laurena II CARIBBEAN $
(mains from EC$15; ⏱lunch & dinner) Overlooking the Esplanade, this is often the liveliest spot in town. The Jamaican chef cooks up piles of jerk, fried or barbecue chicken, curried *lambi* or oxtail served up with rice and peas and salad to queues of hungry locals. The bar is also a nice option for a rum, beer or local juice.

Sandisland Café CARIBBEAN $
(breakfasts from EC$16; ⏱breakfast & lunch) A basic little place, with a wonderful location on a deck over the beach. Sandisland is best for a down-home breakfast of saltfish and eggs with still-warm roasted bake; regular eggs

and bacon are also available. Sandwiches, roti and local dishes are served up for lunch.

TOP CHOICE **Green Roof Inn** FUSION **$$$**
(443-6399; www.greenroofinn.com; mains from EC$60; ☺dinner; ♣) The most sophisticated option in the Hillsborough area, with tables on a veranda overlooking the sea. The menu changes according to what's fresh and available, but will be sure to feature fresh fish, steak and lobster if you're lucky. Though the cooking is refined, it's a laid-back place; the owners have children and are happy to accommodate kids. Be sure to reserve a spot as the tiny dining area fills fast.

Shopping

Simply Carriacou SOUVENIRS
(443-2029; Main St; ☺10am-5pm Mon-Sat; ♣) Lovely little gift shop selling quality craft from Grenada and the wider Caribbean; also operates a toy rental service.

Patty's Deli DELICATESSEN
(443-6258; Main St; ☺9am-4:30pm Mon, Wed & Fri, 9am-2pm Tues & Thurs, 9am-12.30pm Sat) Upmarket groceries, from deli meats and cheeses to fresh quiches and cakes, plus wines and all kinds of exotic ingredients.

ℹ Information

Ade's Dream guesthouse (443-7317; Main St; per hr EC$10) Reasonably fast internet connection, friendly folks and a nice spot.

Cable & Wireless (443-7000; Patterson St; ☺7:30am-6pm Mon-Fri, to 1pm Sat) Free wi-fi if you have your own laptop and are happy to pull up a chair in the waiting area.

National Commercial Bank (443-7289; Main St) Has a 24-hour ATM.

Post office (443-6014; Main St; ☺8am-3pm Mon-Fri) Located at the pier.

Princess Royal Hospital (443-7400) In Belair, outside of Hillsborough.

Tourist office (443-7948; Main St; ☺8am-noon & 1-4pm Mon-Fri) Located across from the pier.

North of Hillsborough

The northern part of Carriacou is a delightful place to explore, with some wonderfully unique towns and stunning scenery. The central road cuts across the spine of the island, making the journey as pleasant as the destination.

You can easily see the area by bus, car or taxi, but as a hike it's a fantastic – if grueling – afternoon out. From Hillsborough head north, taking Belair Rd, about a third of a mile north of town, and follow it uphill for half a mile, then bear right on the side road that leads to the hospital. The hospital sits atop the hill and has a magnificent view of the bay and offshore islands.

Continuing north from the hospital, the road traverses the crest of **Belvedere Hill**, providing sweeping views of the east coast and the islands of Petit St Vincent and Petit Martinique. There are also the remains of an **old stone sugar mill** just before the Belvedere Crossroads.

From here, the route northeast (called the High Rd) leads down to **Windward**, a charming small village with a shop, school and little else. It's the home of boatbuilding on the island, and if you're lucky the local men will be out building a traditional Carriacou sloop the same way they've done it for a century.

The road from Windward leads another mile to **Petit Carenage Bay**, at Carriacou's northeastern tip. There's a great beach, and fabulous views of the northern Grenadines from here.

The cottages at **Bayaleau Point** (443-7984; www.carriacoucottages.com; Windward; US$85-115; ☎) are a great choice if you're after some peace and quiet. There are blue, green, red and yellow varieties to choose from – all basic but with everything you need for a relaxed holiday, with balconies, hammocks and mosquito-netted beds. Meals are available, as are excursions aboard the owner's boat.

Reservation for Mr Frodo Baggins? **Bogles Round House** (443-7841; Bogles; mains from EC$55; ☺12:30-2pm Mon, Thurs, Fri & Sat, 12:30-4pm Sun) is, you guessed it, a round house, perhaps designed with Middle Earth in mind. It's run by an award-winning chef, so the food – European dishes infused with Caribbean classics all served up fresh – more than meets your expectations. There are also three rustic **cottages** (US$97 to US$109) scattered around the grounds, and a small beach at the bottom of the garden.

South of Hillsborough

The small village of **L'Esterre**, just southwest of the airport, is a quiet little place with precious little going on. The biggest reason to venture to this portion of the island is the aptly named **Paradise Beach**. The closest beach to Hillsborough, Paradise is a superb stretch of sand bordered by palms and sea-grape trees, with calm, warm waters and fantastic views over to Sandy Island and the distant conical peaks of Union Island. There are also a couple of great places to sleep, eat and drink, and buses to and from Hillsborough run right past regularly.

🛏 Sleeping & Eating

Sunset Beach HOTEL $
(☑443-8406; www.sunset-beach-hotel.com; r US$55-65) Charming sandside living, right on Paradise Beach. Eight simple rooms look onto a grassy courtyard and are only steps from the sea. There's a great little restaurant and bar, tucked under a tree even closer to the waves, that serves up a good meal.

Hard Wood Bar & Snacket CARIBBEAN $
(Paradise Beach; dinner from EC$35; ⊘breakfast, lunch & dinner) Near the center of Paradise Beach, this green, yellow and red shack dishes out cold beers and fresh fish meals oozing with local flavor. A serene, quintessentially Caribbean setting: locals, lifers, expats and the odd traveler pony up to the bar and settle in for a cold one on a hot day.

Cow Foot CARIBBEAN $
(Belview South; mains from EC$10; ⊘lunch & dinner) Sometimes the best restaurants have the worst names: take Cow Foot, a uniquely local establishment near the microtown of Belview South, just off the south coast. There's nothing flash here, just tables, chairs and hands-down the best roti on the island. The owner is a real character who makes it a memorable dining experience, not just for the delicious food.

🔒 Shopping

Fidel Productions SOUVENIRS
(☑404-8866; Paradise Beach; ⊘9am-5pm Mon-Sat) This charming little shop, built into an old shipping container, is a creative cave of niceties featuring locally made T-shirts, original artworks, jewelry, ceramics and some great photographs. Everything is well made and reasonably priced.

Tyrrel Bay

Tyrrel Bay (population 750) is a deep, protected bay with a sandy (although somewhat dirty) beach. It's a popular anchorage for visiting yachts and hosts a number of regattas throughout the year, as well as being home to a busy commercial dock. Buses run with some frequency to and from Hillsborough (15 minutes).

There are a few eating options in town, most selling local food such as *lambi*. The **Lazy Turtle** (pizzas EC$30-50, mains from EC$43; ⊘lunch & dinner; 🛜) has excellent thin-crust pizzas and authentic Italian pasta. It's well worth the drive from Hillsborough. Next door, **Lumbadive** (☑443-8566; www.lumbadive.com) is a professionally run outfit with PADI open-water courses at US$500.

Sandy & White Islands

Sandy Island, off the west side of Hillsborough Bay, is a favorite daytime destination for snorkelers and sailors. It's a tiny postcard-perfect reef island of glistening sands surrounded by turquoise waters. Snorkelers take to the shallow waters fronting Sandy Island, while the deeper waters on the far side are popular for diving. Water taxis (US$25) run from Hillsborough (15 minutes). Be clear about when you want to be picked up – as the island takes only a couple of minutes to walk around, and has little shade, a whole afternoon can tick by very slowly.

White Island makes for a nice day trip, with a good, sandy beach and a pristine reef for snorkeling. It's about one mile off the southern tip of Carriacou. Water taxis run from Tyrrel Bay (about US$45 round-trip, 30 minutes).

PETIT MARTINIQUE

POP 1000

They don't call it Petit for nothing – this little island is a scant 1 mile in diameter. Small, charismatic and infrequently visited, Petit Martinique is an ideal spot to get away from everything.

With a steep volcanic core rising a stout 740ft at its center, there is little room on the island for much else. The solitary road runs up the west coast, but it is rarely used – locals prefer to walk. Nothing is very far and what's the hurry? The population subsists on the fruits of the sea, either as fishermen or boat-taxi operators.

With barely a thousand inhabitants, most of whom are related to each other, this is a place to find peace, quiet – and precious little else.

Sleeping & Eating

Melodies GUESTHOUSE **$**
(☑443-9052; www.spiceisle.com/melodies; r
US$30-50) Melodies has simple rooms, some
with balconies facing the impossibly blue
ocean. It is worth the couple of extra dollars for an ocean-view room. The downstairs
restaurant and bar serves good local food
and stiff cocktails – sometimes followed by
a round of drunken karaoke.

Palm Beach GUESTHOUSE **$**
(☑443-9103; www.petitemartinique.com/palm
beachguesthouse; s/d US$39/60) Connected
to the **Palm Beach Restaurant**, this basic
guesthouse has two simple rooms with cable
TV and kitchenette. The location is great
and the atmosphere is endearing. It's a short
10-minute walk to the beach, and the apartments overlook the bay, providing wonderful views.

❶ Getting There & Away

The *Osprey* **catamaran** ferries passengers between Grenada, Carriacou and Petit Martinique daily (see p472 for the schedule).

A **water taxi** from Hillsborough to Petit Martinique costs US$60.

UNDERSTAND GRENADA

History

Colonial Competition

In 1498 Christopher Columbus became the
first European to sight the island of Grenada, during his third voyage to the New
World. It wasn't until 1609, however, that
English tobacco planters attempted to
settle; within a year, most were killed by
Caribs, who had first established communities on Grenada in around 1100, having
displaced the more peaceful Arawaks, the
island's first inhabitants. Some 40 years
later, the French 'purchased' the island
from the Caribs for a few hatchets, some
glass beads and two bottles of brandy.
But not all Caribs were pleased with the
land deal and skirmishes continued until
French troops chased the last of them to
Sauteurs Bay at the northern end of the
island. Rather than submitting to the colonists, the remaining Caribs – men, women
and children – jumped to their deaths from
the cliffs.

French planters established crops that
provided indigo, tobacco, coffee, cocoa
and sugar, and imported thousands of African slaves to tend to the fields. Grenada
remained under French control until 1762,
when Britain first recaptured the island.
Over the next two decades, colonial control
of the land shifted back and forth between
Britain and France – until 1783, when the
French ceded Grenada to the British under
the Treaty of Paris.

Animosity between the new British colonists and the remaining French settlers
persisted after the Treaty of Paris. In 1795,
a group of French Catholics, encouraged
by the French Revolution and supported
by comrades in Martinique, armed themselves for rebellion. Led by Julien Fedon,
an African-French planter from Grenada's
central mountains, they attacked the British at Grenville, capturing and executing the
British governor and other hostages. Fedon's
guerrillas controlled much of the island for
more than a year, but were finally overcome
by the British navy. Fedon was never captured. It's likely he escaped to Martinique,
or drowned attempting to get there, though
it's sometimes said that he lived out his days
hiding in Grenada's mountainous jungles.

In 1877 Grenada became a Crown colony,
and in 1967 it converted to an associated
state within the British Commonwealth.
Grenada, Carriacou and Petit Martinique
adopted a constitution in 1973 and gained
collective independence on February 7, 1974.

Independence

One-time trade unionist Eric Gairy rose
to prominence after organizing a successful labor strike in 1950, and was a leading
voice in Grenada's independence and labor
movements. He established ties with the
British government and monarchy and was
groomed to become the island's first prime
minister when Britain relinquished some
of its Caribbean colonies. After independence, Gairy's Grenada United Labour Party
(GULP) swept to power.

Gairy made early political missteps, such
as using his first opportunity to speak in
front of the UN to plead for more research
into UFOs and the Bermuda Triangle. There
were rumors of corruption, of ties with General Augusto Pinochet of Chile and of the
use of a group called the Mongoose Gang to
intimidate and eliminate adversaries. Power
went to Gairy's head and this former labor

A PHOENIX RISES

On September 7, 2004, Hurricane Ivan made landfall on Grenada. The first major storm to hit the island in 50 years, Ivan struck with huge force, leaving a wave of destruction that saw 90% of buildings damaged or destroyed, towns decimated and staple crops like nutmeg obliterated.

The following months and years were a dark chapter for this small Caribbean nation, whose economy was left in ruins. Nonetheless, new crops were sown (with fast-growing cocoa replacing nutmeg as the nation's main agricultural export), and homes, shops and offices rebuilt, with Caribbean neighbors lending support to help restore the damage. But within this period of rebirth, instead of simply rebuilding what was once there, opportunity was found.

Hotels, schools, churches and restaurants have been rebuilt bigger and better, incorporating sustainable practices and larger floor plans. Structures that were long overdue to be upgraded were leveled and the new buildings are a massive improvement to what was once there. Today, the only real evidence of Ivan's path is the odd roofless building – and a certain wariness among locals come hurricane season.

leader was soon referring to his political opposition as 'sweaty men in the streets.'

Revolutions, Coups & Invasions

Before dawn on March 13, 1979, while Gairy was overseas, a band of armed rebels supported by the opposition New Jewel Movement (NJM) party led a bloodless coup. Maurice Bishop, a young, charismatic, London-trained lawyer and head of the NJM, became prime minister of the new People's Revolutionary Government (PRG) regime.

As the head of a communist movement in the backyard of the US, Bishop tried to walk a very fine line. He had ties with Cuba and the USSR, but attempted to preserve private enterprise in Grenada. A schism developed between Bishop and hard-liners in the government who felt that he was incompetent and was stonewalling the advance of true communism. The ministers voted that Bishop should share power with the hard-line mastermind (and Bishop's childhood friend) Bernard Coard. Bishop refused and was placed under house arrest. While Coard had the support of the majority of the government and the military, Bishop had support of the vast majority of the public.

On October 19, 1983, thousands of supporters spontaneously freed Bishop from house arrest and marched with him and other sympathetic government ministers to Fort George. The army was unmoved by the display and Bishop, his pregnant girlfriend (Minister of Education Jacqueline Creft) and several of his followers were taken prisoner

and executed by a firing squad in the courtyard. To this day, it is unclear if the order came directly from Coard – although most believe that it did.

Meanwhile, America became ever more nervous of another potentially destabilizing communist nation in the Caribbean, and six days later 12,000 US marines (along with soldiers from half a dozen Caribbean countries) were on Grenadian shores. US President Ronald Reagan cited the risk to the safety of students at the US-run St George's University as a justification for the invasion; 70 Cubans, 42 Americans and 170 Grenadians were killed in the fighting that ensued. Most of the US forces withdrew in December 1983, although a joint Caribbean force and 300 US support troops remained on the island for two more years. The US sunk millions of dollars into establishing a new court system to try Coard and 16 of his closest collaborators.

Fourteen people, including Coard, were sentenced to death for the murder of Bishop. His death sentence was repealed in 2007 by Britain's Privy Council, and he was released from prison in September 2009.

The New Era

After the US invasion, elections were reinstituted in December 1985, and Herbert Blaize, with his New National Party, won handily. Many PRG members reinvented themselves politically and found jobs in the new administration. From 1989 to 1995, different political parties jockeyed for control and a few short-term leaders came and went, but all within the democratic process.

In 1995 Dr Keith Mitchell became prime minister, and remained in power for 13 years. Though he had some success building the tourism economy, his government was plagued by accusations of corruption and financial misdealing, and was sharply criticized for a weak initial response to the devastation of 2004's Hurricane Ivan. The 2008 election saw the centre-left National Democratic Congress (NDC) take over the reins under Tillman Thomas.

Culture

Grenadian culture is an eclectic mix of British, French, African and East and West Indian influences. A growing number of expats from the UK, Canada and, to a lesser extent, the United States are making Grenada home, bringing with them new attitudes and ways of life, while wider Caribbean influences also hold sway: as well as local calypso and soca, you'll hear Jamaican dancehall music blaring from speeding buses and nightclub dance floors.

Almost 60% of all Grenadians are Roman Catholic. There are also Anglicans, Seventh Day Adventists, Methodists, Christian Scientists, Presbyterians, Baptists, Baha'is and an increasing number of Jehovah's Witnesses. Because of the pervasive influence of Christian ideals, Sunday is a pretty quiet day around the islands, when many shops and services close.

The largely religious population makes for a fairly conservative culture, though once you scratch beneath the squeaky-clean veneer, you can see a population that enjoys having a few drinks and kicking up its heels, especially during the annual Carnival.

Education is on the rise and the population is quite learned. Political awareness is high, thanks in part to Grenada's brush with international infamy in the '80s. The shake-up of Hurricane Ivan in 2004 forced a deep cultural reexamination, something that many feel has led to a more mature and forward-thinking nation.

Grenadians themselves are friendly and welcoming. They are proud of their tiny nation and take care of it – there is less rubbish in the ditches and a sense of civic responsibility is palpable.

Though football is making inroads, cricket is followed with near fanaticism here, and remains the unofficial national sport.

The Land

Grenada Island, Carriacou and Petit Martinique comprise a total land area of 133 sq miles. Grenada Island, at 121 sq miles, measures 12 miles wide by 21 miles long. The island is volcanic, though part of the northern end is coral limestone. Grenada's rainy interior is rugged, thickly forested and dissected by valleys and streams. The island rises to 2757ft at Mt St Catherine in the northern interior. Grenada's indented southern coastline has jutting peninsulas, deep bays and small nearshore islands.

Carriacou, at just under 5 sq miles, is the largest of the Grenadine islands that lie between Grenada and St Vincent. Most of the others are uninhabited pinnacles or sandbars in the ocean.

Wildlife

Grenada has a wide range of distinct ecosystems. The lush rainforests that cover the hilly interior are home to armadillo, opossum and mongoose, while Mona monkeys were introduced from Africa a century ago.

The islands also support a rich array of birdlife, both migratory and resident. The interior of the islands is home to tiny hummingbirds; osprey and endangered hook-billed kites cruise the thermals; and pelicans, brown boobies and frigate birds patrol the coasts.

In the ocean, sea turtles cruise the grassy shoals and come ashore to nest and lay their eggs. Despite protected status, they are still sometimes slaughtered for their meat and shells; be sure to avoid buying anything made from turtle shell, or eating turtle meat.

Many different types of reef fish populate the surrounding waters. Snorkelers and divers have the pleasure of swimming among barracuda, butterfly fish and the odd nurse shark, as well as browsing forests of brightly colored hard and soft corals.

SURVIVAL GUIDE

Directory A–Z

Accommodations

Most of Grenada's accommodation is in the Grand Anse area, from big beach hotels to smaller guesthouses with cheaper rates but fewer facilities.

PRACTICALITIES

» **Electricity** The electrical current is 220V, 50 cycles. British-style three-pin plugs are most common, but you'll sometimes see US-style two-pin plugs.

» **Newspapers & Magazines** *Grenada Today* and *Grenadian Voice* are the island's two main weekly papers. International newspapers can be found in large grocery stores. The tourist office issues *Discover Grenada*, a glossy magazine with general information on Grenada, Carriacou and Petit Martinique; the similar *Lime & Dine* focuses on restaurants and entertainment.

» **Radio & TV** Grenada has three local TV stations and four radio stations.

» **Weights & Measures** Imperial system.

Though it's not in walking distance of a beach, St George's makes a lively base for exploring the island by public transportation, and has an excellent choice of places to eat and drink.

There are several top-class hotels along the beaches close to the airport and in True Blue, alongside good places to eat and drink, while Lance aux Épines is quieter, with an exclusive and secluded feel.

Carriacou has a string of accommodations in the capital and on Paradise Beach, often the liveliest places to be on this super-quiet island. There are great options further afield, though they can feel a bit isolated.

Petit Martinique is so small that you'll be sure to mix with the locals – they'll be your neighbors.

$	budget	less than US$75
$$	midrange	US$75 to US$200
$$$	top end	more than US$200

Business Hours

Banks 8am-3pm Mon-Thu, 8am-5pm Fri

Restaurants 8am-10pm or 12-10pm

Shops 9am-5pm Mon-Sat

Children

Grenada has many calm, gently shelving beaches perfectly suited to children, such as La Sagesse, Lance aux Épines and Morne Rouge; in Carriacou, Paradise Beach is a good bet. Keep your eye on small children around the roads in St George's as the traffic can be on the wild side; and bear in mind that some of the forts are without sufficient railings or barriers.

Dangers & Annoyances

For the most part, Grenada is very safe, with a relatively low crime rate. Taking common-sense measures in St George's at night, and hiring a guide or going in a group for remote hikes minimizes the possibility of opportunistic robberies.

On Grand Anse, you will be asked if you want to buy jewelry, T-shirts and spices; if you're not interested, a simple 'No, thank you' is adequate to dissuade most vendors.

Embassies & Consulates

USA (☑444-1173; usemb_gd@caribsurf.com; Lance aux Épines)

Food

Eating places in this chapter have been categorized according to the following price brackets, which relate to the cost of a main meal:

$	budget	less than US$25
$$	midrange	US$26 to US$75
$$$	top end	more than US$75

Gay & Lesbian Travelers

Attitudes to same-sex couples in Grenada (and the Caribbean generally) are not modern or tolerant. Gay and lesbian couples should be discreet in public to avoid hassles.

Health

There is a hospital in St George's and another on the hill above Hillsborough on Carriacou. The emergency number for an ambulance is ☑911.

Grenada's tap water is chlorinated and theoretically safe to drink, but to avoid a dodgy tummy it's best to stick to bottled water.

Internet Access

St George's has a growing number of internet cafes, and there are a couple in Hillsborough, Carriacou. Rates run from EC$7 to EC$10 per hour. Most hotels provide internet access and/or wi-fi, and many yacht marinas and restaurants offer free wi-fi to patrons.

Money

The official currency is the Eastern Caribbean dollar (EC$). There are 24-hour ATMs dispensing EC$ all over Grenada; in Hillsborough, Carriacou; and close to the boat dock in Petit Martinique.

Most hotels, shops and restaurants accept US dollars, but you'll get a better exchange rate by changing to Eastern Caribbean dollars at a bank and using local currency. Accommodation is usually priced in US dollars, as are tours and meals in more upmarket hotels; otherwise, EC is used. We've followed suit when quoting prices in this chapter.

Major credit cards are accepted by most hotels, top-end restaurants, dive shops and car-rental agencies. Be clear about whether prices are being quoted in Eastern Caribbean or US dollars, particularly with taxi drivers.

An 10% tax and 10% service charge is added to many hotel and restaurant bills. If no service charge is added at restaurants, a 10% tip is generally expected. Prices quoted in this chapter do not include the tax and charge.

Public Holidays

In addition to those observed throughout the region (p872), Aruba has the following public holidays:

Independence Day February 7

Labour Day May 1

Corpus Christi Ninth Thursday after Easter

Emancipation Days First Monday & Tuesday in August

Thanksgiving Day October 25

Telephone

Grenada's country code is ☑473. When calling from within Grenada, you only need to dial the seven-digit local phone number.

When calling from North America, dial ☑1-473 + the local number. From elsewhere, dial your country's international access code + ☑473 + the local number. We have included only the seven-digit local number for Grenada listings in this chapter.

Grenada has coin-operated and card phones. Coin phones take 25-cent coins (either EC or US) or EC$1 coins. Card phones accept the same Caribbean phonecard used on other Eastern Caribbean islands; cards are sold at the airport and numerous shops. Americans can also use US-based calling cards or credit cards to make long-distance calls – but it's best to check the rate before talking for too long.

Local SIM cards are available from LIME and Digicel outlets throughout Grenada and Carriacou.

Tourist Information

The **Grenada Board of Tourism** (www.grenadagrenadines.com; Grenada Island ☑440-2279; The Carenage, St George's; Carriacou ☑443-7948; Main St, Hillsborough) has offices on Grenada and Carriacou. There's also an information booth at Maurice Bishop International Airport, just before immigration, where you can pick up maps and brochures; staff can also help you book a room.

Tours

The following tours are for Grenada Island; for information on taxi tours of Carriacou, see p463. If you're interested in hiking and/or running, an excellent alternative to booking a hike with a tour operator is to hook up with the **Grenada Hash House Harriers** (http://grenadahash.com), a local group who take to the countryside to run or walk along a set trail, ending the day with food and plenty of drinks. You pay a small fee to participate, and you'll also need transport to the trailhead – though if you get in touch in advance, a fellow hasher may be able to offer a lift.

Adventure Jeep Tours (☑444-5337; www.adventuregrenada.com) This reputable operator has full-day tours that take in all of the major sights, plus river tubing and bike tours.

Grenada Seafaris (☑405-7800; www.grenadaseafaris.com) Powerboat coastal tours, with stops for snorkeling (including the Underwater Sculpture Park) and informed commentary on local fauna and flora.

Henry's Safari Tours (☑444-5313; www.henrysafari.com) Various treks into the interior are offered by this company, which specializes in hiking tours. Lunch and drinks are included. Try the five-hour tour that includes a hike to the Seven Sisters Falls.

Mandoo Tours (☑440-1428; www.grenadatours.com) Offers full- and half-day tours of the island and can be tailored for historical or photographic interests. It has quality vehicles with air-conditioning.

Spice Kayaking & Eco Tours (☑439-4942; www.spicekayaking.com) Go for a paddle among the beaches, mangroves and bays. The tours will have you on the water for half the day, or from dawn till dusk if you prefer.

Sunsation (☏444-1594; www.grenadasunsation.com) One of the larger companies, with island tours, hiking and sailing.

Women Travelers

Regular propositioning from local men is the main source of hassle for lone female travelers. Taking care if you're out after dark is prudent for both sexes. Otherwise, women needn't expect too many hassles.

Getting There & Away
Entering Grenada

All visitors must present a valid passport and an onward ticket, or sufficient funds to support your stay. You must also provide the local address of where you are staying.

Air

Maurice Bishop International Airport (☏444-4555; www.mbiagrenada.com) has car-rental offices, an ATM, wi-fi, pay phones and a restaurant. There's a tourist office booth in the arrivals section before immigration.

American Airlines and Delta fly to Grenada from Miami and New York; there are flights from London with British Airways, Monarch and Virgin Atlantic. Airlines serving destinations within the region:

Air Caribbean (www.caribbean-airlines.com) New York, Trinidad

American Eagle (www.aa.com) San Juan

LIAT (www.liatairline.com) Trinidad, Tobago, Barbados, St Vincent

Lauriston airport in Carriacou is a very modest affair with a single ticket counter for all flights. **Prime Travel** (☏443-7362) has a desk at the airport and can help with ticket sales, car rentals and other travel essentials.

SVG Air (☏444-3549; www.svgair.com) serves Carriacou and has flights to/from Grenada; plus charter flights to St Vincent, Bequia, Canouan, Mustique, Union Island, Palm Island, Mayreau, Petit St Vincent, Martinique, St Lucia and Barbados.

Sea

CRUISE SHIP

Grenada is a port of call for numerous cruise ships. They dock at the purpose-built pier just north of the harbor in St George's, Grenada Island. If more than two ships are in port, the old dock on the Carenage is also used; again, you can walk from the dock onto the Carenage.

FERRY

The **MV Jasper** mail boat runs between Carriacou and Union Island (EC$20, one hour) in St Vincent and the Grenadines. It departs from Union Island every Monday and Thursday at 7:30am for Carriacou, and returns at 12:30pm on the same days. For information on entry requirements, see p758.

The commercial ships that haul goods back and forth between Grenada, Carriacou, Petit Martinique and Union Island sometimes accept foot passengers; for more information, see p473.

WATER TAXI

Water taxis between Union Island and Carriacou cost US$75; it's a bumpy (and often wet) 40-minute ride. Boats can be chartered in Hillsborough or Windward in Carriacou, and Clifton in Union Island.

YACHT

Immigration (open 8am to 3:45pm Monday to Friday) can be cleared on Grenada Island at the following locations:

Prickly Bay Marina (☏444-4509) Prickly Bay

Grenada Yacht Club (☏440-3270) St George's

La Phare Bleu Marina (☏444-2400) Calivigny

Grenada Marine (☏443-1065) St David

Grenville (☏438-7678) St Andrew

On Carriacou, clearance can be made in **Hillsborough** (☏443-8399).

The most frequented anchorages are Prickly Bay, Mt Hartman Bay, Hog Island and True Blue Bay along the southwest side of Grenada; and Hillsborough and Tyrrel Bay in Carriacou.

Getting Around
Air

SVG Air (☏444-3549; www.svgair.com) has flights between Grenada and Carriacou.

Sea

CATAMARAN

The **Osprey** (☏440-8126; www.ospreylines.com) is a 144-seat motorized catamaran connecting Grenada, Carriacou and Petit Martinique in less than two hours (per person one-way/round-trip Grenada to Carriacou EC$80/160, Carriacou to Petit Martinique EC$30/60); it's a much cheaper and more environmentally friendly way of getting to the island than a flight. Reservations are rarely required, except on holidays. Tickets from Grenada are purchased on board, and from Carriacou at the office on Main St, Hillsborough. The *Osprey* arrives and departs at the east side of the Carenage opposite the fire station in Grenada; and from the Hillsborough pier in Carriacou.

The *Osprey* schedule:

Carriacou to Grenada Island Departs 6am and 3:30pm Monday to Saturday, and 3:30pm Sunday.

Carriacou to Petit Martinique Departs 10:30am Monday to Saturday, 7pm Monday to Thursday, 9:30am Sunday.

Grenada Island to Carriacou and Petit Martinique Departs 9am and 5:30pm Monday to Friday, 9am Saturday, and 8am and 5:30pm Sunday.

Petit Martinique to Carriacou and Grenada Island Departs 5:30am Tuesday to Friday, 3pm daily.

CARGO BOAT

Island hopping on the cargo boats that sail between Grenada, Carriacou and Petit Martinique is an adventurous and inexpensive way to travel. Departure times and dates are unscheduled and the best way to find out what's available is to ask around at the docks. On Grenada, head for the large boats that moor up on the north side of the Carenage in St George's; on Carriacou, they dock at Tyrrel Bay or Hillsborough pier. The fare is about EC$20 one-way; buy your ticket on board.

YACHT

Horizon Yacht Charters (439-1000; www .horizonyachtcharters.com; True Blue Bay Marina) is one of Grenada's largest yacht charter operators. You can arrange to have a crewed yacht, where all you have to do is sit back and enjoy the ride; or if you have sailing experience and are traveling with suitable crew, you can get a 'bareboat' charter where you get sole charge of the vessel.

Bus

Buses are a great way to get around Grenada and Carriacou. These privately run minivans run a series of set, numbered routes crisscrossing the islands, and are inexpensive and fun – though often reaching madcap speeds, with drivers maniacally tooting their horn at friends and potential passengers as they go.

Although main destinations are posted on the front of buses, alongside the route number, you may need to ask the conductor or driver which bus is best to get to smaller places outside St George's and Hillsborough. There are stops along all the major routes, and you can also flag down a bus pretty much anywhere.

Buses run frequently from around 7am to 7pm, but services start to thin out after 6pm, so start your return journey early enough to avoid getting stuck. Buses on all routes run infrequently on Sundays.

Car & Motorcycle

DRIVER'S LICENSE

To drive a vehicle you need to purchase a Grenadian driving license (US$12), which all car-rental companies can issue on the government's behalf. Grenada's larger towns, including Grenville, Gouyave and Victoria, have gas stations. On Carriacou, there's just one gas station, in Hillsborough.

RENTAL

There are many rental agencies on Grenada Island, and a few on Carriacou; see p451 and p463 for details.

ROAD RULES

Driving is technically on the left-hand side of the road, but you can expect buses in particular to be going full bore wherever the hell they want to, with full-beam lights on permanently after dark. The roads are very narrow and curvy and local drivers attack them with great speed. For safety, slow down when approaching blind curves and use your horn liberally. There are few road signs on the island, so a road map and a measure of caution are useful when driving.

Taxi

You'll find taxis on Grenada and Carriacou; see p451 and p463 for more information and sample fares.

Guadeloupe

Best Beaches

» Grande Anse (p487)

» Anse à la Gourde (p484)

» Plage de Clugny (p488)

» Plage des Raisins Clairs (p483)

Best Places to Stay

» Hostellerie des Châteaux (p484)

» La Métisse (p483)

» Auberge Les Petits Saints (p495)

» Ti Gli Gli (p492)

Why Go?

Guadeloupe is a fascinating archipelago of islands, with each island offering travelers something different while retaining its rich Franco-Caribbean culture and identity. Guadeloupe's two main islands look like the wings of a butterfly and are joined together by a mangrove swamp. Grande-Terre, the eastern of the two islands, has a string of beach towns that offer visitors marvelous stretches of sand to laze on and plenty of activities, while mountainous Basse-Terre, the western of the two, is home to the wonderful Guadeloupe National Park, which is crowned by the spectacular La Soufrière volcano.

South of the 'mainland' of Guadeloupe are a number of small islands that give a taste of Guadeloupe's yesteryear. Ranging from sheer relaxation on La Désirade to the charmingly village-like atmosphere of Les Saintes, the smaller islands each have their own character and round out the long list of ingredients that make up Guadeloupe.

When to Go

It's no accident that December to May is when most people visit Guadeloupe: the weather is warm and dry at this time. Measurable rain falls an average of seven days a month and the average humidity is around 77%. The wettest months are July to November, when rain falls about 14 days a month and the average humidity reaches 85%. Try to avoid Christmas, the French February holidays and July and August, as prices are sky-high and rooms scarce at this time.

Itineraries

THREE DAYS

If you only have a few days in Guadeloupe, prioritize beautiful Basse-Terre – drive the northern coast road and stop at the sublime beaches at Grande Anse and enjoy the relaxed atmosphere and good eating in Deshaies. Go diving at Pigeon Island and then return to Pointe-à-Pitre via the dramatic Route de la Traversée.

ONE WEEK

Having explored Basse-Terre at a more relaxed pace, including a visit to La Soufrière, catch a boat from Trois-Rivières to Les Saintes, and explore a truly remote slice of the French Caribbean. From Les Saintes take a ferry to St-François, and enjoy some beach hopping around Pointe des Châteaux before returning to Pointe-à-Pitre.

GETTING TO NEIGHBORING ISLANDS

There's a regular fast ferry service connecting Guadeloupe to Dominica, Martinique and St Lucia three days a week. See www.express-des-iles.com for more information. There are also direct flights from Pointe-à-Pitre to Fort-de-France, St-Martin, St-Barthélemy, San Juan, Havana, Antigua and St Lucia.

Essential Food & Drink

» **Acras** A universally popular hors d'oeuvre in Guadeloupe, *acras* are fried fish, seafood or vegetables fritters in tempura. *Acras de morue* (cod) and *crevettes* (shrimp) are the most common and are both delicious.

» **Ti-punch** Short for *petit punch*, this ubiquitous and strong cocktail is the normal *apéro* (aperitif) in Guadeloupe: a mix of rum, lime and cane syrup, but mainly rum.

» **Crabes farcis** Stuffed crabs are a typical local dish. Normally they're stuffed with a spicy mixture of crabmeat, garlic, shallots and parsley that is then cooked in the shell.

» **Blaff** This is the local term for white fish marinated in lime juice, garlic and peppers and then poached. It's a favorite dish in many of Guadeloupe's restaurants.

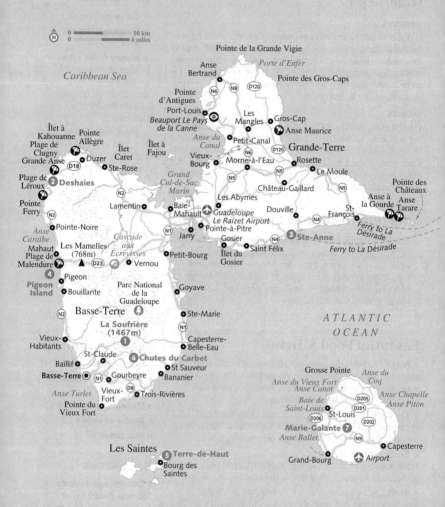

Guadeloupe Highlights

1 Hike through the rainforest to the misty summit of the brooding active volcano **La Soufrière** (p490)

2 Nourish your inner gourmet and encounter boaties from around the world in charming **Deshaies** (p487)

3 Soak up sun on the beautiful beach or the

happening scene at a seaside cafe in **Ste-Anne** (p481)

4 Touch the underwater Jacques Cousteau statue at the reserve that bears his name around pristine **Pigeon Island** (p491)

5 Walk across **Terre-de-Haut** (p492), a tiny island full

of low-key sophistication and history

6 Hike through the rainforest on well-marked trails to the **Chutes du Carbet** or **Grand Étang** (p489)

7 Find your own slice of beach heaven on the unspoilt sands of **Marie-Galante** (p496)

GRANDE-TERRE

The southern coast of Grande-Terre, with its reef-protected waters, is Guadeloupe's main resort area. The eastern side of the island is largely open to the Atlantic, with crashing surf, and in comparison with the southern coast is barely touched by tourism. Northern Grande-Terre doesn't have much in the way of accommodations but it's probably the best place to spend a day driving around – sea cliffs on one side and swaying fields of sugarcane on the other. Pointe-à-Pitre, the island's biggest city, is in the southeastern corner of Grande-Terre.

Pointe-à-Pitre

POP 17,300

In 1654 a merchant named Peter, a Dutch Jew who settled in Guadeloupe after being exiled from Brazil, began a fish market on an undeveloped harborside jut of land. The area became known as Peter's Point and eventually grew into the settlement of Pointe-à-Pitre.

From the outskirts, Pointe-à-Pitre looks pretty uninviting – a concrete jungle of highrises and sprawling traffic. Venture into the center, though, and you'll find a much more attractive old town with peeling colonial architecture and palm-fringed streets.

The town hub is Place de la Victoire, an open space punctuated with tall royal palms that extends north a few blocks from the inner harbor. There are sidewalk cafes opposite its west side, a line of big old mango trees to the north, and a relaxed air abounds. While Pointe-à-Pitre has little to attract most visitors, it's a hub of transportation for the entire island and beyond. If you do find yourself here, there are a few sights to keep you occupied for an hour or two.

Dangers & Annoyances

Locals report that drug abuse, especially crack cocaine, is a problem here. The Place de la Victoire area has enough people until late at night to feel safe, but other parts of the city are downright spooky, and prostitutes and drug dealers are not uncommon sights.

The area around the Centre Hospitalier is especially dangerous and visitors should take a cab there at night if need be. Whereas the rest of the island is friendly, at times there's an aggressive mood here.

◉ Sights & Activities

Musée St-John Perse MUSEUM
(9 Rue de Nozières; adult/child €2.50/1.50; ⊙9am-5pm Mon-Fri, 8:30am-12:30pm Sat) This three-level municipal museum occupies an attractive 19th-century colonial building. The museum is dedicated to the renowned poet and Nobel laureate Alexis Leger (1887–1975), better known as St-John Perse. The house offers a glimpse of a period Creole home and displays on Perse's life and work. Almost all of the exhibits are in French, but there are some newspaper illustrations and photographs from the city's past that make the admission price worth it.

Musée Schoelcher MUSEUM
(24 Rue Peynier; adult/under 18yr €2/1; ⊙9am-5pm Mon-Fri) Occupying an interesting period building, this museum is dedicated to abolitionist Victor Schoelcher. The main exhibits in the museum are art pieces that belonged to Schoelcher, and artifacts relating to slavery. Some of the editorial cartoons on display show how much the French establishment hated Schoelcher for his abolitionist actions. Displays are in French, but there are brochures in English. Schoelcher's original reasoning behind the seemingly random art and sculpture displays was to give the people of Guadeloupe a chance to appreciate the fine arts.

Cathédrale de St-Pierre et St-Paul CATHEDRAL
(Rue de l'Eglise) Rather than the traditional arches, this weathered sand-colored church, nicknamed the 'Iron Cathedral,' is supported by iron girders intended to brace it against earthquakes and hurricanes. The church, which is a couple of minutes' walk northwest of Place de la Victoire, is worth a look, particularly on Sunday. Check out the Ali Tur–designed art-deco **Palais du Justice** next door. There's a fun, colorful **open-air market** (⊙5am-2pm Mon-Sat) running along La Darse, the inner harbor. There are souvenir stalls on the little streets right next to the market, as well. The **Marché Couvert** (cnr Rues Peynier & Schoelcher; ⊙6am-4pm), another large public market, is just a few blocks to the west and has a good collection of handicrafts and spices.

✳ Festivals & Events

Carnival CARNIVAL
Starts warming up in January with roving groups of steel-band musicians and dancers,

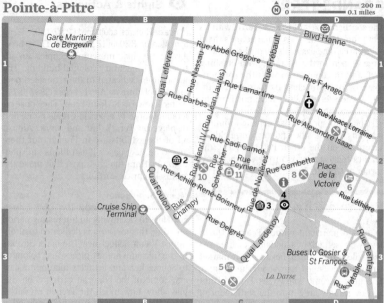

Map: Pointe-à-Pitre

but officially runs between the traditional weeklong Mardi Gras period, which ends on Ash Wednesday (46 days before Easter).

Fête des Cuisinières   FESTIVAL
(Festival of Women Cooks) A colorful event held in early August. Women in Creole dress, carrying baskets of traditional foods, parade through the streets to the cathedral, where they are blessed by the bishop.

🛏 Sleeping

Pointe-à-Pitre has few places to stay and even fewer reasons to spend the night. If you're looking for island culture or a cozy beachside getaway, keep moving. The only reason to stay here is if you're catching an international ferry the next morning.

Hôtel Saint-John Perse   HOTEL **$$**
(☏05-90-82-51-57; www.saint-john-perse.com; s/d/tr incl breakfast €75/90/115; 🕸🛜) In the Centre St-John Perse, this comfortable if unexciting midrange option is centrally located and extremely convenient if you're catching an early-morning boat. It has 44 rooms with shared balconies overlooking the harbor and is a reliable and safe (if rather pricey) option. There is free luggage storage for guests who want to travel light to the outlying islands.

Hôtel Victoria Palace   HOTEL **$**
(☏05-90-83-12-15, 06-90-53-94-20; 9 bis Place de la Victoire; r with/without air-con €40/35; 🕸) The only other secure option in town is this budget 12-room place above a cafe right on the Place de le Victoire. You can't miss its brightly painted orange exterior and while the rooms are simple (some share bathrooms, while others have private facilities), if you're lucky you might even get one with a balcony overlooking the square.

🍴 Eating & Drinking
DOWNTOWN

TOP
CHOICE **La Canne à Sucre**   INTERNATIONAL **$$**
(☏05-90-90-38-83; 1 Quai Foulon; mains €17-25; ⏱lunch Mon-Sat, dinner Fri) This stylish and rather glamorous restaurant gives you the best views over Pointe-à-Pitre's busy harbor from its terraced seating. The excellent food blends international and French cuisine with Creole flavors, and there's also friendly service and a sumptuous dessert list. It's usually worth reserving for dinner on Friday.

Restaurant Fairouz   LEBANESE **$**
(cnr Rue Jean Jaurès & Rue Peynier; mains €7-15; ⏱lunch & dinner) Housed in a charming old colonial house painted in white and red, this restaurant brings a dash of welcome Levan-

Pointe-à-Pitre

tine relief to the ubiquitous Creole menus elsewhere in town. The excellent *mezze* plate for two (€24) is the obvious choice for any first-time guest here, and orders for collection are also possible.

Bella Vita　　　　　　　　　　ITALIAN $
(Place de la Victoire; mains €9-16; ⊙7am-11pm) The decor is very basic – it looks like it used to be a sub sandwich shop, in fact, but the people who work here are warm and welcoming. The pizzas are solid and range from tuna to the delicious *mafioso*. One of the best bets for a later evening meal.

Café Caraïbe　　　　　　　　　　CAFE $$
(Place de la Victoire; mains €12-18; ⊙7am-10pm Mon-Sat) With shaded outdoor seating to one side of Place de la Victoire and a wide range of dishes available, from sandwiches to salads and full-on main courses, this is a popular place to socialize. There's also passable coffee and a good selection of cocktails.

New Shalimar　　　　　　　　　　INDIAN $
(Centre St-John Perse, Quai Foulon; mains from €10; ⊙7am-10pm Mon-Sat) This place certainly doesn't look like much from the outside – but don't be fooled by the lackluster outdoor dining: the Indian food here is good and the location at the base of the Hôtel Saint-John Perse is central, if rather 1970s.

MARINA DE BAS DU FORT
Pointe-à-Pitre's middle class seems to spontaneously vanish from the city at dusk – they're all usually to be found at the Marina de Bas du Fort, a mile or so to the west of town. Here a number of lively restaurants and drinking holes surround a harbor full of sailboats and yachts.

La Côte de Boeuf　　INTERNATIONAL $$
(mains €12-25; ⊙noon-11pm) This is a sophisticated place for a meal at any time of day, and popular with a wealthy yachtie crowd who are lured ashore for fine pizzas, grills and steaks accompanied by a good wine and followed by sublime desserts.

La Frégate　　　　　　　　　　SEAFOOD $$
(mains from €15; ⊙11am-midnight) It's the restaurant here with the best balance between price and quality, and the crowds to prove it. After you order the lobster dinner (€30) a server brings out the unlucky crustacean in a bucket, alive, and shows it like a bottle of wine.

🛍 Shopping

Marché Couvert　　　　　　CRAFT MARKET
(cnr Rues Peynier & Schoelcher; ⊙6am-4pm) A good place to buy island handicrafts, including straw dolls, straw hats and primitive African-style woodcarvings. It's also a good spot to pick up locally grown coffee and a wide array of fragrant spices.

ℹ️ Information

Cyber Ka (Place de la Victoire; internet per 30min €2; ⊙8am-8pm Mon-Fri, 8am-6pm Sat) A central and friendly place to check emails.

Centre Hospitalier Universitaire (CHU; ☎05-90-89-10-10; www.chu-guadeloupe.fr; Rte de Chauvel) The main hospital is north of the post office in a run-down neighborhood; take a cab at night.

Change Caraïbes (21 Rue Frebault; ⊙8am-4:45pm Mon-Fri) A money exchange.

Post office (Blvd Hanne; ⊙8am-6pm Mon-Fri, to noon Sat) A block north of the cathedral.

Tourist office (☎05-90-90-70-02; www.lesilesdeguadeloupe.com; 5 Sq de la Banque; ⊙8am-5pm Mon-Fri, to noon Sat) Near Place de la Victoire; the friendly staff speaks good English and there's a lot of information about activities, walking and hotels to be had here.

ℹ️ Getting There & Away

AIR For information on air travel to and from Grande-Terre, see p503.

PORT OF CALL – POINTE-À-PITRE

Cruise ships calling in Guadeloupe usually dock at Pointe-à-Pitre. Despite not looking like much from the sea, it's a perfectly pleasant and safe place to wander around during the daytime. It's a 15-minute walk from the cruise terminal into town. With a few hours in port you can do the following:

» Visit the Musée St-John Perse (p477) and the Musée Schoelcher (p477)

» Try some innovative cooking at La Canne à Sucre restaurant (p478)

» Take a trip to the Parc National de la Guadeloupe (p486) for spectacular scenery

BOAT For information on ferry travel to other Caribbean islands, see p504.

In Pointe-à-Pitre, all ferries leave from the Gare Maritime de Bergevin, 1km northwest of Hôtel Saint-John Perse.

BUS Buses to places in Basse-Terre leave from the northwest side of town near the Gare Maritime de Bergevin. It costs €5.60 to travel from Pointe-à-Pitre to the administrative capital of Basse-Terre, and €3.90 to Pointe-Noire (via Route de la Traversée).

① Getting Around

TO/FROM THE AIRPORT Taxis are easy to find at the airport; it costs about €30 into Pointe-à-Pitre center or you could rent a car on arrival. Thanks to the taxi union, there's no bus shuttle to town from the airport.

BUS Buses to Gosier, Ste-Anne and St-François leave from Rue Dubouchage at the east side of the harbor in Pointe-à-Pitre.

The bus from Pointe-à-Pitre to Gosier costs €1.80 (pay the driver) and takes about 15 minutes. If you're going to the Bas du Fort marina, you can take this bus and get off just past the university. Other fares from Pointe-à-Pitre are €2.30 to Ste-Anne, €2.40 to Moule and €3 to St-François.

CAR On weekdays, traffic in the center of Pointe-à-Pitre is congested and parking can be tight. There are parking meters (€1 per hour) along the east side of Place de la Victoire and on many of the side streets throughout the city. See p505 for car-rental information.

TAXI Dial ②05-90-82-00-00 or ②05-90-83-99-99 in the Pointe-à-Pitre area.

Gosier
POP 27,400

Set 8km southeast of Pointe-à-Pitre, Gosier is really two towns: a cluster of high-rise hotels full of French families on one side and a growing Caribbean village next door.

It's the biggest tourist spot in Guadeloupe, and it's not a particularly charming place. The hotels are packed one after the other and the lobbies can be madhouses in high season. But the series of scalloped coves gives almost every property a good beachside location.

The village center, about a 15-minute walk away from hotel central, feels a little run-down and lacks the fine beaches found in the main hotel area, but it is more local in character. It also has a small but swimmable beach and a good view across the water to Îlet du Gosier.

Many of Guadeloupe's most popular nightspots, attracting a young and fashionable French crowd until early morning, are clustered together on the outskirts of Gosier on the road to Pointe-à-Pitre.

Just 600m off Gosier village is a lovely little undeveloped island, **Îlet du Gosier**, surrounded by calm turquoise waters that have some nice snorkeling areas. Motorboats (one-way €5) shuttle beachgoers between Gosier and the island, departing from the little dock at the end of Rue Félix Éboué.

Beach huts in front of the resort hotels rent out snorkeling gear (€12 a day), windsurfing equipment, Sunfish sailboats and larger Hobie Cat boats. Also available are fun boards, pedal boats and other gear.

🛏 Sleeping

TOP CHOICE Hôtel Les Bananiers   HOTEL **$$**
(☑05-90-84-10-91; www.les-bananiers.com; Rue des Phares et Basils, Perinet; r/studio incl breakfast €65/75; ❄) It's a 15-minute walk to the beach from this pretty little complex, but if you don't fancy that there's a small pool around which the four rooms and four studios with kitchenettes are arranged, surrounded by a charming garden. The welcome is very warm here and breakfast on the terrace is lovely.

Auberge de la Vieille Tour   RESORT **$$$**
(☑05-90-84-23-23; www.accorhotels.com; Montauban; r from €280; ❄ ⊕ ⟲ 🏊) This gorgeous 103-room beach hotel incorporates an 18th-century windmill in the lobby and has a stunning location with its own beach. The

rooms are very comfortable with all comforts. This is also a great place for kids, as it's secure and set in its own grounds.

Karaïbes Hotel
HOTEL **$$**

(☎05-90-84-51-51; www.karaibeshotel.com; Route des Hôtels; s/d €70/80; ❄⃞🛜⃞🏊⃞) A two-star, brightly colored budget place in the main cluster of hotels, it has an ATM-like machine outside that takes a credit card and spits out keys for people with a reservation. Small but bright rooms and direct beach access make this the best bargain on the hotel strip, though wi-fi is not free.

La Formule Économique
HOTEL **$$**

(☎05-90-84-54-91; www.laformuleeconomique .com; 112 & 120 Lot Gisors; d/studio from €48/68; ❄⃞) Offering *hotellerie à la carte,* it calculates rates based on the amenities you select. It's not exactly a charming place with its makeshift furniture and cobbled-together feel, but it's cheap and clean. Follow the signs in the village to find this place at the end of a dilapidated alley.

Eating

The center of Gosier has a number of inexpensive and unremarkable eating options, and in the main beach hotel area, the Créole Village shopping center has half a dozen places to eat.

[TOP CHOICE] Les Quatre Épices
CREOLE **$$**

(☎05-90-84-76-01; 25 Blvd Charles de Gaulle; mains €16-30; ⊗lunch & dinner) A brightly decorated old house converted into a restaurant with eclectic decorations throughout – including a lawn jockey and funky lamps. The food at this village restaurant is divine; start with *le tour d'île,* a sampler plate with stuffed crab curry, fish pâté, *accra* and *boudin* (blood sausage). There's also a good selection of aged rums (€5 to €8) to choose from as a digestif. Evening reservations are worthwhile in the high season.

Restaurant de l'Auberge
FRENCH-CREOLE **$$$**

(☎05-90-84-23-23; Montauban; dinner mains €20-35; ⊗lunch & dinner) The Auberge de la Vieille Tour has Gosier's most upmarket fine-dining restaurant, serving traditional French and Creole cuisine. It's a good idea to reserve a table if you're not staying at the hotel.

Le Bord de Mer
SEAFOOD **$**

(Blvd Amédée Clara; mains €8-14; ☎lunch & dinner) Right on the water in the center of the village, this popular spot has wonderful views towards Îlet du Gosier and is popular day

and night. There's a broad choice of seafood and freshly landed fish specials as well.

Drinking

Gosier is easily the most hopping nightlife spot on the island. Most of the fancy hotels have live music and poolside barbecues on a regular basis.

La Route de la Bière
BEER BAR

(6 Rue Simon Radegonde; ⊙6pm-1am Tue-Sat) In the village near the Ecomax hypermarket, this is the place to go if you like good times of the sudsy variety. There are 60 different beers here, nine of them on draft. It also has pizza, Friday-night karaoke, Saturday-night dancing and a pool table.

La Cheyenne
NIGHTCLUB

(122 Ave de Montauban; ⊙Fri & Sat) If bachelor-or beach-themed nights are your thing, you'll enjoy this massive disco, with big screens and thumping beats. It's just outside of town; look for the big wooden head of a Native American.

Ste-Anne

POP 23,800

The busy town of Ste-Anne sees a lot of tourists but the big resorts are well hidden and there's a good balance of amenities for tourists and authentic modern village life. It has a seaside promenade along the west side of town, a lively market and a fine white-sand beach stretching along the east side. The beach, which offers good swimming and is shaded by sea-grape trees, is particularly popular with islanders.

Ste-Anne is a good base for those who want to visit the islands of Les Saintes and, if you've got the time, Marie-Galante and La Désirade (in high season).

In addition to the beach on the east side of town, white-sand **Caravelle Beach** stretches along the east side of the Caravelle Peninsula, about 2km west of the town center. Its main tenant is Club Med, but the entire beach is public. There is a guarded gate to get to the beach, but anyone is free to walk right in. The unmarked road to Caravelle Beach is off N4, opposite Motel l'Accra Ste-Anne.

🛏 Sleeping

[TOP CHOICE] Hôtel le Diwali
BEACH HOTEL **$$$**

(☎05-90-85-39-70; www.lediwali.com; Plage de Ste-Anne; r €220-320; ❄⃞🛜⃞) This airy oasis at the end of Ste-Anne Beach is a class act with its colonial flair and generous use of dark wood and rattan. The eight rooms are bright and comfortable, each with its own outdoor area. Guests can use the kayaks and snorkeling equipment for free, and the on-site restaurant is open to all visitors and serves dinner every evening (mains €15 to €35).

Ti Village Creole   STUDIOS **$$**
(☑05-90-85-45-68; www.tivillagecreole.fr; Dupré; studios/bungalows from €64/84; ❋🛜⛵) This is a little slice of paradise: you're in a 10-minute walk from the hustle and bustle of central Ste-Anne in a tranquil hillside setting run by the well-traveled and informative Vincent. The modern bungalows all have big porches outside, plus spacious living rooms and comfortable bedrooms within. Annoyingly, wi-fi is only accessible by the pool.

Casa Boubou   COTTAGES **$$**
(☑05-90-85-10-13; www.casaboubou.fr; 2-person cottages per night/week €85/595; ❋🛜) The 10 cottages here all have satellite TV, a DVD player that accepts memory cards, a hammock and a BBQ grill. Guests enjoy free use of snorkeling equipment and three canoes just a few minutes (150m) away on Caravelle Beach. Book far in advance.

Auberge le Grand Large   BUNGALOWS **$$**
(☑05-90-85-48-28; www.aubergelegrandlarge.com; Chemin de la Plage; r from €85; ❋🛜) There are eight one-bedroom bungalows with kitchenettes and two deluxe bungalows with spacious kitchens and two bedrooms. The property completed a renovation a few years ago, giving the rooms a fresh and bright feel. Just a few steps from the beach and a row of restaurants and bars, the location is prime and rooms fill up far in advance (most visitors are on the more economical weekly room rate), so book ahead.

Hôtel La Toubana   LUXURY HOTEL **$$$**
(☑05-90-88-25-78; www.toubana.com; 97180 Ste-Anne; bungalows from €300; ❋⛵) About 2km west of central Ste-Anne, on a quiet coastal cliff overlooking the Caravelle Peninsula, this place doesn't look like much from the road but from the moment you step inside on wooden walkways that skirt small, almost Japanese-looking ponds, you know this is something special. The 32 bungalows are all stylishly decorated and there's a small private beach and an excellent on-site restaurant.

 Eating

Opposite Ste-Anne Beach is a row of simple open-air restaurants with tables in the sand and barbecue grills at the side.

Koté Sud   CREOLE **$$$**
(☑05-90-88-17-31; Route de Rotabas; set meals €25-40; ⊘lunch, dinner Sun) This very well-loved restaurant is outside Ste-Anne itself, on the Route de Rotabas in the direction of Gosier – look for signs around the Esso station. This is where to come for the most impressive local cuisine, which combines Creole favorites such as conch with traditional European dishes such as lasagna and ravioli. It's worth reserving ahead.

Koté Mer Resto   CREOLE **$**
(Blvd Ibéné; mains €8-17; ⊘breakfast, lunch & dinner) A friendly welcome awaits you at this hugely popular beach restaurant. Its name means 'Restaurant Near the Sea,' and a strong wave will tickle toes; a rogue wave may just drink your ti-punch. The menu includes all the Creole favorites such as salads, chicken, fish and meat grills, as well as more-expensive lobster.

Kouleur Kreole   SEAFOOD **$**
(Chemin de la Plage; mains €10-20; ⊘11am-10pm Tue-Sun) A popular spot that serves big tasty seafood grills and a variety of fresh salads accompanied by lovely sea views and a jazz soundtrack. There's also a live band on Friday evenings.

Shopping

Village Artisanal   SOUVENIRS
(⊘8am-8pm) A bit west of the beach at the end of the promenade, it may look tacky at first glance but it's a good place to go for the bigger souvenirs (hammocks, sculptures) that are hard to find at the souvenir market in town.

Géograines   CRAFTS
(Durivage) Just west of the Village Artisanal, this quirky place specializes in making things out of seeds – and it all looks good. It has seed wall hangings and even a coffee table where black and white seeds are arranged to make a chess board set under glass. The shop only uses Guadeloupean artisans and materials.

St-François

POP 14,300

St-François is a town with two distinct identities. The west side of town is a sleepy provincial backwater that's quite spread out, while the east side feels a lot like the small upscale marina that it is. The center of the action is the deep U-shaped harbor, which is lined with a handful of restaurants, hotels, car-rental offices, boutiques and marina facilities. Parts of it are pretty and other parts are torn up as there are plans for a massive renovation to make the area a huge pedestrian mall. Just north of the marina there's a golf course.

An undistinguished strand runs along the south side of the town center, but the best beaches in the area are just a 10-minute drive east of town in the direction of Pointe des Châteaux. The **Plage des Raisins Clairs** is another very good stretch of sand just west of the town that is popular with families.

St-François is a major jumping-off point for trips to Guadeloupe's smaller islands; see p504 for details. The dock for boats to La Désirade, Marie-Galante, and Terre-de-Haut on Les Saintes is at the south side of the marina, as is free parking.

🏃 Activities

Arawak Surf Action
SURFING
(☑06-90-31-88-28; www.surfantilles.com; Base Nautique de St-François) The place to come for surfing, windsurfing or stand-up paddleboarding.

Awak
BOAT TRIPS
(☑05-90-85-00-55; Gare Maritime St-François; adult/under 12yr €65/40) Runs day trips to the small islands of Petite Terre for a spot of iguana-watching, beach lounging, lunch and snorkeling. Boats leave at 8.15am and return to St-François at 5pm.

Golf Municipal de St-François
GOLF
(☑05-90-88-41-87; Ave de l'Europe) St-François has Guadeloupe's only golf course, this 18-hole, par-71 course designed by Robert Trent Jones. It's opposite the marina.

Noa Plongée
DIVING
(☑05-90-89-57-78; www.anchorage-plongee .com; Marina St-François, 6 Ave de l'Europe; 1-tank dive €50) At the marina, this small and friendly outfit takes divers to the nearby and plenty of other sites in the area twice a day.

🛏 Sleeping

Near the harbor and fishing port are a load of residences that advertise solely by small signs and a phone number; rooms are somewhere in the €50 per night range, depending on the length of stay.

La Métisse
BOUTIQUE HOTEL $$
(☑05-90-88-70-00; www.hotel-lametisse.com; 66 Les Hauts de Saint François; r from €120; ❄ 🍽 🛜) Tucked away in a complex of hotels above St-François, this pretty place sports a pool in the abstracted shape of Guadeloupe and seven beautifully refitted rooms that combine Creole notes with minimalism. This is a sublime place to escape to and you'll feel miles away from the town, which is in fact just a short walk away.

Hôtel Amaudo
HOTEL $$
(☑05-90-88-87-00; www.amaudo.fr; Anse à la Barque; r from €130; ❄ 🍽 🛜) This special little place is in the hamlet of Anse à la Barque, a short distance to the west of St-François itself. It's a beautiful spot, with all of the communal areas attractively done in a colonial style and all 10 rooms having fantastic sea views, dark-wood beds, and private outdoor areas or balconies.

Le Bwa Chik Hôtel et Golf
HOTEL $$
(☑05-90-88-60-60; www.bwachik.com; Ave de L'Europe; r incl breakfast from €75; ❄ 🍽 🛜 🏌) Across from the 18-hole municipal golf course, this is the place for keen golfers. It's also right on the marina and has plenty of restaurants and activities on its doorsteps, making it a good base in St-François. There are 38 standard rooms and 23 renovated duplexes, which are far more modern and stylish, with further renovations on the way.

🍴 Eating

Grand Voile
FRENCH-CREOLE $$
(☑05-90-88-41-48; Rue de la République; mains €14-30; ⊙lunch & dinner) It's no surprise that this smart seafront bar and restaurant is very busy during the high season. Its location is excellent, right in the center of town, and with a fantastic terrace for alfresco dining. But the food is also very inventive – and while it's possible to eat cheaply at lunchtime (with a €12.50 set meal), the evening, for which reservations are a good idea in season, is for fine dining and prices rise accordingly.

TOP CHOICE **Café Iguana**   GOURMET **$$$**

(☑05-90-88-61-37; www.iguane-cafe.com Chemin rural La Coulée; mains €20-33; ☺lunch Sun, dinner Wed-Mon) On the road out of St-François toward Pointe des Châteaux you'll find what is probably Guadeloupe's finest restaurant. It's definitely a treat, but also unmissable for any gourmet. The food ranges from complicated seafood dishes (brick of conch in saffron sauce) to delectable meats (mango duck). Go ahead and blow the budget and order the €78 sampling menu for a true culinary experience. Reservations are advised.

Le Restaurant du Lagon   CREOLE **$$**

(Route du Lagon; mains €12-18; ☺lunch) At this jetty restaurant, south of the marina that shelters a big lagoon, the setting is ideal for a plate of freshly caught fish, and there's a gently buzzing ambience. It's also a great place to grab a ti-punch or juice and drink in the view.

❶ Information

Cyber Creation (internet per 30min €2; ☺9am-7pm Mon-Sat) Located near the fishing port in the Galerie Comerciale.

L@robas Café (internet per 30min €3; ☺7am-2am Mon-Sat, 4pm-2am Sun) At the marina.

Post office (☺8am-1pm Mon-Sat) A block west of the harbor.

Pointe des Châteaux

Just a 20-minute drive from St-François is windswept Pointe des Châteaux, the easternmost point of Grande-Terre. This dramatic coastal area has white-sand beaches, limestone cliffs and fine views of the jagged nearshore islets and the island of La Désirade.

Sometimes surfers set up on the small beach here to catch the rough, short-lived waves. A walk up a sandy path to the large cross takes about 10 minutes and is a good place to look back at Guadeloupe.

For fun away from the beach, **La Maison de la Noix de Coco** (☑05-90-85-00-92; www.maison-de-la-noix-de-coco.com; admission free; ☺9am-6.30pm) is a souvenir shop dedicated to all things coconut. There's the usual kitschy Caribbean mementos here (see the Rasta-man ashtray, fake hair and all) but many of the items, like polished coconut-husk lamps (from €70) are surprisingly classy. Visitors get a free sample of coconut milk on arrival.

There are some more-protected white-sand beaches further to the northwest of Pointe des Châteaux. **Anse Tarare** is a popular nudist beach situated in a sheltered cove 2km west of the road's end. The dirt road north of the main road is marked by a sign reading 'Plage Tarare.'

A few minutes' drive to the west, a side road (follow the 'Chez Honoré' signs) leads about 1km north to **Anse à la Gourde**, a gorgeous sweep of white coral sands. The waters are good for swimming and snorkeling, but be careful of nearshore coral shelves.

🛏 Sleeping & Eating

TOP CHOICE **Hostellerie des Châteaux**   HOTEL **$$**

(☑05-90-85-54-08; www.hostellerie-des-chateaux .com; r incl breakfast €95-110; ❋ ❒ ❒) Set on a spacious lawn inland from the road to Pointe des Châteaux, there are four bungalows and four rooms here, all named after local islands, with daily housekeeping included with both types of accommodations. The friendly owner is a mine of local information and this is a great place to escape with easy local beach access. The restaurant (mains €11 to €22; closed Sunday evening and all day Monday) is open to the public too and is a great place for a meal with great views towards the other islands of Guadeloupe.

Le Moule

POP 21,600

The town of Le Moule served as an early French capital of Guadeloupe, and was an important Native American settlement in precolonial times. Consequently, major archaeological excavations have taken place in the area, and Guadeloupe's archaeological museum – under renovation at the time of writing – is on the outskirts of town. That said, unless you're a surfer or a pre-Columbian history nut, Le Moule is unlikely to be on your itinerary.

Those passing through will enjoy the wide town square with a few historic buildings, including the town hall and a neoclassical Catholic church. Along the river are some discernible waterfront ruins from an old customs building and a fortress dating back to the original French settlement.

Baie du Moule, on the west side of town, is popular with kayakers and surfers, and has its own surf school. The world surf championships have taken place in Le Moule. Just outside the town is the Damoiseau Distillery – one of Guadeloupe's most popular.

◉ Sights

FREE **Edgar Clerc Archeological Museum** MUSEUM

(☺9am-5pm Mon-Tue & Thu, 9am-1pm Wed & Fri) On a coastal cliff in the Rosette area, this museum has a small display of Native American petroglyphs, pottery shards, and tools made of shells and stone that is open to the public while long-running renovations are completed. The museum is about 1km north on La Rosette road (D123), on the western outskirts of Le Moule. The exhibits open at present are only marked in French, although a small recompense is that the museum remains free to visitors until renovations are finally complete.

FREE **Damoiseau Distillery** DISTILLERY

(www.damoiseau.com; ☺self-guided tours 8am-2pm Mon-Sat, gift shop 8am-5:30pm Mon-Sat) For those who don't speak French but know how distilleries work, this is a nice chance to wander around at will. For those who don't know their fermentation from their distillation, the Musée du Rhum (p489) on Basse-Terre is a more educational option. The gift shop has a good selection of rums made on the premises and offers free tastings. To get to the distillery, look for the sign for Hotel Caraïbe after heading east out of town and take the first right. At the crossroads, take another right and look for the signs.

⏹ Sleeping & Eating

The tourist office can provide a list of vacation rentals, including gîtes (small family-run cottages) and apartments in the area. There are a few small grocery stores in downtown Le Moule.

Cottage Hotel STUDIOS $$

(☎05-90-23-78-38; www.cottage-residence.net; Rte de la Plage des Alizés; r per night/week €61/329; ✳) The two-floor studios here are a great deal, equipped as they are with outdoor kitchens, a fridge and balconies that face the water. The beach here is not stellar, but close, and you definitely feel a bit out of the action, which can be a good thing.

Le Spot CAFE $

(Blvd Maritime Damencourt; mains €11-21; ☺lunch & dinner Tue-Sun) The cafe for the surf school in the same place, this is *the* surfer hangout in Le Moule, and a great place to meet others or just watch the waves crash on the shore. There are pizzas, salads and fresh fish dishes.

ⓘ Information

Cyber Box Call Shop (44 Rue Duschassing; internet per hr €4; ☺8am-10pm)

Tourist office (☎05-96-23-89-03; www.ot-lemoule.com; Blvd Maritime Damencourt; ☺8:30am-noon & 2-5pm Mon-Fri, 8:30am-noon Sat) Lots of maps and free booklets (in French) on the area.

Northern Grande-Terre

A good place for a leisurely day of exploring, with plenty of sunbathing on quiet beaches included. The northern half of Grande-Terre is a rural area of grazing cattle and cane fields; the roads are gently winding but easy to drive.

From Le Moule, drive up past the archaeological museum in Rosette, then turn right on the D120 and follow that road north. As you get closer to Porte d'Enfer the route will be signposted.

ANSE MAURICE

The first sight on the D120 coming from Le Moule, the nearly empty beach of Anse Maurice is accessed via a small road with concrete tracks and grazing goats. The water is clear and very shallow until you walk out a bit, partly why it's a favorite with families with small children. There's a bar-restaurant here if you want to take a break from the sun.

PORTE D'ENFER

After soaking up Anse Maurice go north on the D120 and follow the signs to Vigier. On your right, keep your eyes peeled for the Chez Coco restaurant; at the time of research this was the only way to find Porte

---

WHAT'S IN A NAME?

At first glance, the names given to the twin islands that make up Guadeloupe proper are perplexing. The eastern island, which is smaller and flatter, is named Grande-Terre, which means 'big land,' while the larger, more mountainous western island is named Basse-Terre, meaning 'flat land.'

The names were not meant to describe the terrain, however, but the winds that blow over them. The trade winds, which come from the northeast, blow *grande* (big) over the flat plains of Grande-Terre but are stopped by the mountains to the west, ending up *basse* (flat) on Basse-Terre.

d'Enfer. The 'Port of Hell,' as it's called, is actually a long and narrow lagoon that could be mistaken for a river from the viewpoint further down the road. It's a great place to picnic, swim, or snorkel, but bring your own gear. The water crashing at the mouth of the lagoon would be the gates of hell for anyone foolish enough to venture beyond the calm waters.

POINTE DE LA GRANDE VIGIE

The island's northernmost point, Pointe de la Grande Vigie offers scenic views from its high sea cliffs. A rocky path – walkable in flip-flops but better in tennis shoes – makes a loop from the parking lot to the cliffs and has some fantastic views. Mind the cliffs – signs in French warn that there are sometimes rock slides and that people can fall off and die.

On a clear day you can see Antigua to the north and Montserrat to the northwest, both about 75km away.

ANSE BERTRAND

Anse Bertrand, where the D120 starts to loop back south, has more of a rocky, crashing coast than a beach, but a few restaurants facing the local church, and friendly locals, make it worth a pit stop.

South of Anse Bertrand, near Port-Louis, is **Beauport Le Pays de La Canne** (☑05-90-22-44-70; adult/child €9/6; ☉9am-5pm Mon-Sat), a shut-down sugarcane factory that's been turned into a learning center. Taking the 50-minute train ride through the old sugar plantation is great fun.

PETIT-CANAL

Petit-Canal was a major landing point for slaves kidnapped from Africa to work on the nearby sugar plantations. Near the church in the center of town are steps that lead to a stele that reads 'liberty.' The steps were built by slaves themselves and have the names of African tribes carved into them. South of Le Pays de La Canne, this is the place to go for a trip into the nearby mangroves.

Lesteflo (☑05-90-22-76-94; 7 lotissement Débarcadère; tours €25; ☉departures 9am & 2pm) offers a short sunset tour or a full-day outing with lunch and snorkeling included.

SOUTH TO MORNE-À-L'EAU

Besides a **crab festival** every April, what brings tourists is the city-within-a-city at the **cemetery**, where N6 meets the N5. There's parking near the police station (gendarmerie) but be careful crossing the road. Terraced with raised vaults and tombs, many decorated in checkered black-and-white tiles, this is Guadeloupe's most elaborate burial ground.

BASSE-TERRE

Basse-Terre is Guadeloupe's trump card. The bigger of the two main islands (and yes, they are separate entities despite being joined by a road), it's also by far the more dramatic, boasting soaring peaks and thick rainforest within the huge Parc National de la Guadeloupe as well as some excellent beaches and one of the best dive sites in the Caribbean around Pigeon Island and the fabulous Réserve Cousteau. Whatever you do in Guadeloupe, do not miss Basse-Terre.

Route de la Traversée

The road that heads across the center of the island, the Route de la Traversée (D23), slices through the **Parc National de la Guadeloupe**, a 17,300-hectare forest reserve that occupies the interior of Basse-Terre. It's a lovely mountain drive that passes fern-covered hillsides, thick bamboo stands and enormous mahogany and gum trees. Other rainforest vegetation en route includes orchids, heliconia and ginger.

The road begins off the N1 about 15 minutes west of Pointe-à-Pitre and is well signposted. There are a few switchbacks, but driving is not tricky if you don't rush, and it's a good two-lane road all the way. Although the road could easily be driven in an hour, give yourself double that to stop and enjoy the scenery – more if you want to do any hiking or to break for lunch.

There are 200km of **hiking trails** here, and the many signs with pull-offs on the side of the road are the beginning of trails. Start before 3pm or so, as night falls quickly here.

The trails are well marked and the longer the hike, the better your chances of seeing very few people. Trails can be very muddy and rocky with lots of slippery tree roots; at least wear tennis shoes, if not hiking boots.

Don't miss the **Cascade aux Écrevisses**, an idyllic little jungle waterfall that drops into a broad pool. From the parking area the waterfall is just a three-minute walk on a paved trail. The roadside pull-off is clearly marked on the D23, 2km after you enter the park's eastern boundary. Try to go early, as busloads of tourists arrive in the late afternoon. On the other side of the road from the parking lot is a trail to a picnic area with covered tables right near the river.

At **Maison de la Forêt**, 2km further west, there's a staffed **exhibit center** (☎05-90-80-86-00; www.guadeloupe-parcnational.com; ☺9:30am-4:30pm) with a few simple displays on the forest in French and pamphlets in English, including a basic map that shows the parking areas for trailheads and picnic areas. A map board and the beginning of an enjoyable 20-minute **loop trail** are at the back of the center. The trail crosses a bridge over the Bras David river and then proceeds through a jungle of *gommier* trees, tall ferns and squawking tropical birds. The **Bras David trail** (go left instead of right at the first fork) takes an hour, and is an enjoyable if muddy way to get deeper into the jungle.

Northern Basse-Terre

The northern half of Basse-Terre offers interesting contrasts. Starting from the west side of Route de la Traversée, most of the west coast is rocky and many of the drives snake along the tops of towering sea cliffs. There are a couple of attractive swimming beaches – Grande Anse is the most popular.

Once you reach the northern tip of the island the terrain becomes gentler and the vegetation dry and scrubby. Continuing down the east coast, the countryside turns into sugarcane fields and the towns become larger and more suburban as you approach Pointe-à-Pitre.

POINTE-NOIRE

Pointe-Noire, between Plage de Malendure and Deshaies, is the epicenter of places that each specialize in one thing – chocolate, coffee etc. Most of these establishments are just north of the D23 (Route de la Traversée) on the N2, and signs abound for all of them.

At **Maison du Cacao** (☎05-90-98-25-23; adult/child €5/2.50; ☺10am-5pm Mon-Sat year-round & Sun Dec-Feb), treat yourself to a cup of hot chocolate (€3) that's closer to the Mayan's sacrament of divinity than any powdered drink.

Set high on a hill off the D16, **Caféière Beauséjour** (☎05-90-98-10-09; www.cafeiere beausejour.com; adult/child €7.50/4; ☺10am-5pm Tue-Sat) is an old colonial house and working plantation that tells the history of coffee (in French), explains the traditional processing

of the bean, and lets people sample its product at tour's end. This fascinating place also offers full meals and accommodation.

With an outdoor park to show off different species of trees and indoor exhibits showing all the different ways to work with wood and products made out of wood, **Maison du Bois** (☎05-90-98-16-90; Rte des Plaines; adult/child €9/4.50; ☺9:30am-5pm Tue-Sat) is a tree-lover's dream located in beautiful grounds just south of Pointe-Noire.

Visitors must make accommodation or spa reservations to be allowed entry to **Le Parc aux Orchidées** (☎05-90-38-56-77; www .parcauxorchidees.com; cottages €595 per week; ✿🖘🌊), a private orchid garden located 3.5km north of Pointe-Terre, but it's well worth it. There are apparently more than 3000 orchids of 400 species in the spacious grounds here, making this the largest outdoor collection in the Caribbean. It's a wonderful place for escape – there are just three houses on the grounds, giving total privacy in sublime surroundings.

DESHAIES
POP 4400

This charmingly sleepy spot has just the right blend of traditional fishing village and good selection of eating and drinking options to keep visitors happy. There's a sweet little beach framed by green hills all around, but as Deshaies is a working fishing port, the best beach for swimming and sunbathing is at nearby Grande Anse.

◎ Sights & Activities

Thanks to its sheltered bay, the village is a popular stop with yachters and sailors and has an international feeling. The local seafaring traditions have carried on into the tourist trade, with several dive shops and deep-sea fishing boats operating from the pier.

Grande Anse   BEACH
This superb white-sand beach with no hotel development in sight is just 2km north of Deshaies. The waves break right near the shore and aren't terribly large, but are perfect for young bodysurfers. The entire place is no secret though, and you won't be alone, but it's easy to escape the crowds by walking down the bay. While there are no accommodations here, there are a number of beachside restaurants, some of which have their ocean views obstructed by the parking lot that's jam-packed during high season. Two that don't suffer from this problem are

Les Hibiscus (mains €4-11; ⏲lunch), which is right on the beach and has some of the best food and prices, and **Chez Edmond** (mains €6-8; ⏲lunch), a colorful shack overlooking a picturesque stream that flows into the sea here.

Plage de Clugny BEACH

Between Grande Anse and Ste-Rose, at the very tip of Basse-Terre, is the superb Plage de Clugny, a dazzling stretch of sand with views toward a dramatic islet in the bay, and beyond that, to Montserrat. The beach is totally undeveloped, so bring anything you'll need, and be careful as the water can be rough. This is also a nesting ground for three different types of turtle, so follow the rules and don't disturb their nests.

Sleeping

Au Ti Sucrier BUNGALOWS $$

(☎05-90-28-91-29; www.autisucrier.com; Pointe Ferry; r per week from €735; ❄📶🏊) Au Ti Sucrier is just 40m from Plage de Léroux. It has 14 modern bungalows that are typically rented out for a week at a time, each with outdoor kitchens and ocean views. The bungalows sleep four people in an open-plan arrangement (although some have two separate bedrooms) and one room also has disabled access. Wi-fi is a €5 flat rate for the duration of your stay.

Rayon Vert HOTEL $$

(☎05-90-28-43-23; http://hotel.lerayonvert.free.fr; La Coque Ferry; r/bungalows incl breakfast from €129/144; ❄📶🏊👪) Under new management that was doing a good job of refitting and modernizing this pleasant place when we visited, Rayon Vert is named after the band of green sometimes visible on the horizon right at sunset. The 22 rooms all have a porch that opens up to sea views, a minibar and big bathrooms. It has one wheelchair-accessible room, an on-site restaurant and an extremely friendly atmosphere.

Fort Royal RESORT $$

(☎05-90-68-76-70; www.fortroyal.eu; Petit Bas Vent; r from €142; ❄📶🏊👪) This impressive upmarket resort enjoys almost exclusive access to two fabulous stretches of beach either side of it, as well as having a large pool, full water-sports center, tennis courts and a diving school. Rooms, which come in a wide range of categories, are all stylishly furnished and enjoy sea views. Nonguests can use the beach, but chairs are €10 per day.

Domaine de la Pointe Batterie LUXURY HOTEL $$$

(☎05-90-28-57-03; www.pointe-batterie.com; Chemin de la Batterie; studios/villas €131/220; ❄📶🏊) A terraced property just outside of Deshaies, every luxurious room here has a sea view and the villas each have a small private pool. The entire complex is set in beautiful gardens, and the on-site spa, one of the main attractions of the hotel, means that you can spend days here being pampered.

Eating & Drinking

You'll find some of the best food around in the village and its hinterland.

TOP CHOICE **La Savane** INTERNATIONAL $$

(☎05-90-91-39-58; Blvd de Poissonniers; mains €19-25; ⏲lunch Sun, dinner Thu-Tue) Right in the heart of the town is this popular green-painted restaurant with a divine location right on the seafront and a terrace from which to drink it all in. It is owned by a Portuguese lady whose influence on the menu is clear, and the dishes, from *bacalhau com natas* (cod in cream) to foie gras with mangos, is some of the best on the island. Reservations are a good idea in season.

L'Amer FRENCH-CREOLE $$

(☎05-90-28-50-43; mains €16-35; ⏲dinner Mon-Sat) Unmissably orange on the outside, refined and stylish inside, this is a Deshaies favorite. The interesting menu takes in seafood and swordfish and combines French tradition with an eye to local flavors. Downstairs there's a simple **cafe** (⏲breakfast & lunch Tue-Sun) open during the day where you can eat a good sandwich or sweet crepe on the sunny terrace.

Le Coin des Pécheurs SEAFOOD $

(Rue de la Vague Bleue; mains €10-37; ⏲lunch & dinner) Just along from L'Amer, this similarly colorful one-story beach restaurant has a great position overlooking the bay. Its name – a spelling mistake or an intentional joke depending on whom you ask – means the Sinners' Corner, rather than the more obvious Fishermen's Corner *(Le Coin des Pêcheurs)*. Either way, it's a great place for a relaxed meal of fresh seafood or fish.

La Kaz CREOLE $$

(Blvd de Poissonniers; mains €14-20; ⏲lunch & dinner Tue-Sun) La Kaz is Creole for 'house,' and this red-painted wooden shack is certainly homely. A wide range of Creole cookery awaits and there's live music here on Saturday evening, when it becomes one of the jumpiest joints in town.

Hemingway
INTERNATIONAL $$

(☏05-90-28-57-17; Domaine de la Pointe Batterie; mains €18-25; ⊘lunch Fri-Sun, dinner daily) Down the road from the Domaine de la Pointe Batterie hotel, this new place has unbeatably good views of the bay and a terrace that's a treat to dine on as long as the wind isn't too strong. The whole place exudes style and the dishes, heavy on seafood and fish, are surprisingly affordable.

ℹ Information
Le Pélican Cyber Café (internet per hr €5, all-day wi-fi €5; ⊘8:30am-12:30pm & 4-7pm Mon-Sat) An unusually lively place for an internet cafe, it also sells a variety of colorful hammocks and hanging chairs.

STE-ROSE
POP 19,800

In days of yore, Ste-Rose was a major agricultural town. While sugar production has declined on Guadeloupe and a number of mills have closed, sugarcane is still an important crop on this northeastern tip of Basse-Terre, and there are a few rum-related tourist sights on the outskirts of town.

Visitors who follow the signs from the N2 to 'Bord de Mer' will find a row of restaurants, souvenir stalls, and places to take excursions to the nearby Îlet Caret, which one can see from the Bord de Mer. Reserve in advance.

BleuBlancVert (☏05-90-28-38-49; bleublancvert.web.ool.fr; adult/child €33/16.50) runs half-day trips to the island on a motorized raft. The trip includes a waterproof container, snorkeling gear and *planteurs* punch (a libation with rum, fruit juice and a little spice to make everything nice).

Nico Excursions (☏05-90-28-72-47; www.nicoexcursions.com; half-/full day €35/60) runs very popular trips to nearby islands and reefs with a maximum of 12 people and snorkeling gear provided.

Those who want to understand how the ambrosia called rum starts in the sugarcane fields and ends on their palates should really head to the excellent **Musée du Rhum** (Rum Museum; ☏05-90-28-70-04; http://musee-du-rhum.fr; adult/teenager/child €6/4/3; ⊘9am-5pm Mon-Sat), which has thorough explanations in English. It's at the site of the Reimonenq Distillery, about 500m inland from the N2 in the village of Bellevue, just southeast of Ste-Rose. Exhibits include an old distillery, cane-

extraction gears and a vapor machine dating from 1707. Also check out the 15-minute film in English about the distillation process, the collection of butterflies, model boats (including Noah's Ark) and *coiffes* (madras head wraps).

Guadeloupeans say **Chez Franko** (Blvd St Charles, Bord de Mer; mains €14-32; ⊘lunch Tue-Sun) is the best eating choice. It's a simple place, with novelties such as shark fritter (€9) and lobster fricassée on the otherwise totally standard Creole menu.

South to Capesterre-Belle-Eau

The N1, the road that runs along the east coast of Basse-Terre, travels through cattle pastures and sugarcane fields. For the most part it's pleasantly rural, but unless you're driving it may not be an area in which to spend much precious vacation time.

Valombreuse Floral Park (☏05-90-95-50-50; www.valombreuse.com; adult/child €6/3; ⊘8am-6pm), nestled in the hills west of Petit-Bourg, is a pleasant 14-hectare botanical garden with lots of activities for kids. There's also a path to a waterfall that spills into a swimming hole. The road leading off the N1 to the park, 5km inland, is well signposted.

In the center of the village of **Ste-Marie**, a bust of Columbus and two huge anchors comprise a modest roadside monument honoring the explorer who landed on this shore in 1493.

The road is lined with flamboyant trees on the north side of **Capesterre-Belle-Eau**, a good-sized town that has a supermarket, some local eateries and a gas station.

Chutes du Carbet

Unless it's overcast, the drive up to the Chutes du Carbet lookout gives a view of two magnificent waterfalls plunging down a sheer mountain face.

Starting from St-Sauveur on the N1, the road runs 8.5km inland, making for a nice 15-minute drive up through a rainforest. It's a good hard-surfaced road all the way, although it's a bit narrow and twisting. Nearly 3km before the end of the road is a marked stop at the trailhead to **Grand Étang**, a placid lake circled by a loop trail. It's just a five-minute walk from the roadside parking area down to the edge of the lake, and it takes about an hour more to stroll the lake's perimeter. Due to the danger of bilharzia (schistosomiasis) infection, this is not a place for a swim.

The road ends at the **Chutes du Carbet lookout** (adult/child/family €1.20/0.70/3). From here you can see the two highest waterfalls from the upper parking lot, where a signboard marks the trailhead to the base of the falls. The well-trodden walk to the second-highest waterfall (110m) takes 30 minutes; it's about a two-hour hike to the highest waterfall (115m). It's also possible to hike from the lookout to the summit of La Soufrière, a hardy three-hour walk with some wonderfully varied scenery.

There are picnic facilities at the lookout, along with a few food stalls selling plate lunches of simple barbecue fare. This is a very popular spot for outings and can get quite crowded on weekends and holidays.

Trois-Rivières

POP 9050

Most often visited as a jumping-off point to Les Saintes, this sleepy town has sharply curving streets, is surrounded by lush vegetation and has fine views of Les Saintes, just 10km offshore to the south.

For those who get seasick easily, Trois-Rivières has the shortest ferry ride and reputedly the calmest waters to Terre-de-Haut in Les Saintes. See p504 for details.

Don't miss the **Parc Archéologique des Roches Gravées** (☎05-90-92-91-88; admission €2; ⊙9am-5pm), featuring rocks carved with petroglyphs of human, animal and abstract forms. Some of the rocks were found on the site; others were brought from around Basse-Terre. The visitor center at the entrance has informative displays and pamphlets on island history and there's an adventurous boulder-filled trail through the park. The park is on the road to the ferry dock 200m north of the waterfront.

There are a number of places to stay scattered in and around town and a few places to eat; very few stay open once the working day ends.

The best place to stay in town is one of the four spacious bungalows at **Gîte Coco et Zabrico** (☎05-90-92-83-50; http://cocoetzabrico.monsite.wanadoo.fr; Route de Gaigneron; r from €65; ❋❄❄❄), a short distance from the center of town down a well-signposted dirt road. The houses are set in beautiful gardens and it's perfect for kids as there's a children's play area and plenty of enclosed space. There are also great views towards Les Saintes, and a resident excitable dog.

The pizzas at **Pizzeria Total Végétal** (pizzas €8-15; ⊙lunch & dinner) are available in the evenings only and you should be prepared to wait – this build-your-own-pie place is very popular. During the day hungry visitors have a choice of a few simple dishes like couscous and chicken or beef stew and rice. Order at the counter.

Signs at the west side of the town center point the way from the main road to the dock, 1km away, where the ferry leaves for Terre-de-Haut. There's a large parking lot just a few minutes' walk from the dock.

La Soufrière

From Trois-Rivières there are a couple of ways to get to La Soufrière, the active 1467m volcano that looms above the southern half of the island.

The most direct route to La Soufrière is to follow the D8 northwest from Trois-Rivières, turn west on the N1 for a few kilometers and then follow the signs north to St-Claude. This is a nice jungle drive into the mountains; you'll cross some small streams and pass banana plantations before reaching the village of St-Claude, just south of the national-park boundaries. There's no food available in the park, but St-Claude has a few local restaurants and small grocers.

From St-Claude, signs point to La Soufrière, 6km to the northeast on the D11. The steep road up into the park has a few beep-as-you-go hairpin turns, and it narrows in places to almost one lane, but it's a good solid road all the way. If it's fogged in, proceed slowly, as visibility can drop to just a few meters.

The closed Maison du Volcan is the trailhead for a couple of hour-long **walks**, including one to Chute de Galleon, a scenic 40m waterfall on the Galion River.

There are a couple of **viewpoints** and picnic areas as the road continues up the mountain for the 15-minute drive to La Savane à Mulet, a parking area at an elevation of 1142m. From here, there's a clear view straight up La Soufrière (when it's not covered in clouds or mist), and you can see and smell vapors rising from nearby fumaroles.

For an adventurous 1½-hour **hike** to La Soufrière's sulfurous, moonscapelike summit, a well-beaten trail starts at the end of the parking lot. It travels along a gravel bed and continues steeply up the mountain through a cover of low shrubs and thick ferns. In addition to a close-up view of the steaming volcano, the hike offers some fine vistas of the island. It's also possible to make a four-hour trek from La Savane à Mulet to the Chutes du Carbet lookout.

The road continues further east another 1.75km, taking in a lookout and views of sulfur vents before it dead-ends at a relay station.

Basse-Terre

POP 12,400

The rather grim administrative capital of Guadeloupe, Basse-Terre is somewhat active on weekdays during work hours, but almost deserted after dark and on weekends, with most shops and restaurants closed. The traffic getting in or out of the city moves at a snail's pace during daylight hours.

As an old colonial port town, there is some local character, but not much. The south side of town, along Blvd Gouverneur Général Félix Éboué, has a couple of rather imposing government buildings, including the Palais de Justice and the sprawling Conseil Général, the latter flanked by fountains. **Fort Louis Delgrès**, which dates from 1643, is on this side of town as well, as is the Rivière Sens Marina.

At the north side of town, opposite the commercial dock, is the old town square. It's bordered by the aging Hôtel de Ville (Town Hall), the tourist office, customs and some older two- and three-story buildings that are, overall, more run-down than quaint. There's an unadorned **cathedral** near the river, about five minutes' walk south of the square.

The **bus station** is on the shoreline at the western end of Blvd Gouverneur Général Félix Éboué. Opposite the north end of the station is the **public market**.

Plage de Malendure & Pigeon Island

This long stretch of beachside towns and villages is a mecca for divers who come to dive and snorkel at the superb Réserve Cousteau around little Pigeon Island and to relax on Plage de Malendure's dark-sand beaches. The entire area is backed by steep hills and this is a great starting point for hiking into the Parc National de la Guadeloupe.

☉ Sights & Activities

Réserve Cousteau   MARINE PARK
Jacques Cousteau brought Pigeon Island to international attention by declaring it to be one of the world's top dive sites. The waters surrounding the island are now protected as an underwater park. There's even a sub-aquatic statue of Mr Cousteau near the Jardins de Corail (Coral Gardens) dive site. Divers who touch the statue's head are supposed to have good luck, and good diving, for the rest of their underwater lives.

The majority of the dive sites around Pigeon Island are very scenic, with big schools of fish, coral walls and coral reefs that are shallow enough for good snorkeling. It's only a 10- to 15-minute boat ride to the dive sites, and almost all the shops have morning, noon and mid-afternoon outings.

There is a tourist information booth and a number of dive shops on Plage de Malendure; single-tank dives hover around €40. These shops are also the place to go to arrange snorkeling trips.

Archipel Plongée   DIVING
(☑05-90-98-93-93; www.archipel-plongee.fr; Plage de Malendure, Bouillante) Dive prices start at €35 here; a two-dive day out including a wreck dive and lunch on the boat is €85. There are daily departures at 10.15am, 12.45pm and 3.15pm – just show up 20 minutes beforehand.

Centre International de Plongée   DIVING
(☑05-90-98-81-72; www.cip-guadeloupe.com; Plage de Malendure, Bouillante) This diving outfit offers one-tank dives for €31, as well as competitive package prices for divers who plan to get a lot of underwater time in.

Les Heures Saines   DIVING
(☑05-90-98-86-63; www.heures-saines.gp; Le Rocher de Malendure, Bouillante) This extremely versatile operation is based under Le Rocher de Malendure restaurant. In addition to the standard dive offerings, it rents underwater cameras and offers Soufrière hikes, canyoning, dolphin-watching trips and deep-sea fishing.

Centre de Plongée des Îlets   DIVING
(☑05-90-41-09-61; www.plongee-guadeloupe. fr; Plage de Malendure, Bouillant) Diving here starts at an incredibly good-value €29 for divers with their own equipment. With two boats, this operation tends to have larger groups and offers all kinds of instruction for beginners.

Canopée

HIKING

(☑05-90-26-95-59; www.canopeeguadeloupe.
com; Plage de Malendure, Bouillante) This is the
area's best **canyoning** and **hiking** operation, offering a huge number of trips into
the nearby mountains from day trips to
two day bivouacs in the rain forest.

🛏 Sleeping

In the center of the village of Pigeon, just
south of Plage de Malendure, there is a huge
range of private accommodation from gîtes
and studios to more elaborate guesthouses.

TOP CHOICE Ti Gli Gli

ECOLODGE $$

(☑05-90-98-73-49; www.tigligli.com; Rue de Po-
irier; d/tr from €50/60; ☎) This rustic and
rather magical place soars above Pigeon
and just getting here up the steep slope feels
like a mini adventure. Run by an exception-
ally enthusiastic and engaged family, this is
the place to come if you want to commune
more with nature and local culture than
with creature comforts. André Exartier, the
owner, invites his musician friends to come
by for music nights a few times per month,
while his wife is a licensed mountain guide
who offers trips into the interior of Basse-
Terre suitable for all levels. The accommo-
dation is simple, in five naturally ventilated
bungalows each sleeping up to four people.

Le Jardin Tropical

HOTEL $$

(☑05-90-98-77-23; www.au-jardin-tropical.com;
Rue de Poirier; r from €70; ❄☎☒♿) Le Jardin
Tropical stands out because of its friendly
owners (when they're around), a pool that
feels nearly private and a little bar that
opens up every night serving wicked ti-
punch. The bungalow rooms are sparkling
clean, simply furnished and good value, and
all have outdoor patios, kitchens and sea
views, while the bigger apartments down
the hill are luxuriously kitted out and feel
like a private home, making them perfect for
families.

🍴 Eating

There are huts on Plage de Malendure selling cheap sandwiches and snacks, and a
couple of simple open-air beachside restaurants with more substantial meals as well as
a few larger-scale restaurants.

La Touna

SEAFOOD $$

(☑05-90-98-70-10; www.la-touna.com; Pigeon;
mains €16-24 ☺lunch & dinner Tue-Sat, dinner
Sun) This superfriendly, stylish place on the
seafront has a sumptuous Creole menu and
specializes in fresh seafood (there's a lobster
tank here where you can choose your din-
ner). The terrace has great views toward
Pigeon Island and is a lovely cool place to
round off your meal with a digestif to the
sound of the waves. Dinner reservations in
season are a good idea.

Le Rocher de Malendure

INTERNATIONAL $$

(☑05-90-98-70-84; Bouillante; mains €15-26
☺lunch & dinner Thu-Tue) The best-established
restaurant in Bouillante, this sprawling
complex is actually built on the eponymous
rock, and has incredible views on all sides.
The restaurant offers everything from sushi
plates to the fresh lobsters it keeps in a small
pool. The restaurant also rents simple studios from €65.

For supermarkets, you'll find a **Leader Price**
and a **Match** on the southern outskirts of
Plage de Malendure.

LES SAINTES

These tiny islands to the south of Basse-Terre
are many people's highlight of Guadeloupe,
as they allow visitors to enjoy a slice of the
old Caribbean, far from the development
and urban sprawl that has affected much of
the region. These tiny charmers are a real
secret – many day-trippers come over from
Basse-Terre, but very few people spend any
real time here exploring these gems. Don't
miss your chance.

Terre-de-Haut

POP 1800

Lying 10km off Guadeloupe is Terre-de-
Haut, the largest of the eight small islands
that make up Les Saintes. Since the island
was too hilly and dry for sugar plantations,
slavery never took hold here. Consequently,
the older islanders still trace their roots to
the early seafaring Norman and Breton colonists and many of the locals have light skin
and blond or red hair.

Terre-de-Haut is unhurried and feels like
a small slice of southern France transported
to the Caribbean. Lots of English is spoken
here thanks to a big international sailing
scene, and it's definitely the most cosmopolitan of Guadeloupe's outlying islands.

Terre-de-Haut is only 5km long and about
half as wide. Ferries dock right in the center

Terre-de-Haut & Terre-de-Bas

GUADELOUPE TERRE-DE-HAUT

2 km
1 mile
0
0

Pointe Zozio
Pointe du Vent
Roches Percées
Baie de Pont Pierre
Pointe Morel
Baie du Marigot
Trace des Crêtes
UCPA
Grande Anse
Pointe Rodrigue
Airfield
Bourg des Saintes
Kanaoa
Anse Rodrigue
Fort Napoléon
Pointe à l'Eau
Anse Du Figuier
Passe de la Baleine
Terre-de-Haut
Fond du Curé
Ferries to Pointe-à-Pitre, Ste-Anne & St-François
Fort Joséphine
Anse du Bourg
Anse Sable
(D412)
Pointe à Cabrit
Îlet à Cabrit
Anse du Petit Etang
Anse Galet
Pointe Sable
Anse sous le Vent
Bois Joli
Le Chameau (309m)
La Redonde
Passe du Pain de Sucre
Pain de Sucre
Anse Galet
Ferries to Trois-Rivières
Petite Anse
Anse à Cointe
Anse Crawen
Pointe Bois Joli
Passe Bois du Sud
Pointe des Colibris
Grande Îlet
▲ (165m)
Passe du Grand Îlet
Pointe Basse
Passe des Dames
La Coche
Les Augustins
La Vierge

AT LANTIC OCEAN

Le Pâté
Pointe Noire
Grande Anse
Embarcadère
Grande Baie
Anse du Petit Etang
Airfield
Pointe du Havre
Passe du Sud-Ouest
Grande Anse
Terre-de-Bas
Morne Sec (288m) ▲
Morne Paquette (209m) ▲
(D413)
Pointe Sud
Pointe à Vache
Anse à Chaux
Morne Abymes (293m) ▲
(D213)
Pointe du Cap
Anse Pujot
Pointe du Gouvernail
Anse Galet
Anse Petit Sable
Anse à Dos
Pointe Miquelon
Gros-Cap
Petites-Anses

Caribbean Sea

of Bourg des Saintes, the island's only village. The airstrip is to the east, a 10-minute walk from the village center.

❶ Getting There & Away

This is the easiest island to visit in terms of choice of transportation. By sea you can get here from four cities on the southern coast of mainland Guadeloupe and by air from Pointe-à-Pitre.

AIR The small airport in Terre-de-Haut was closed for much-needed renovations at the time of writing, but flights from Pointe-à-Pitre should resume once work is completed.

BOAT There are multiple daily ferries to Terre-de-Haut from Trois-Rivières (on Basse-Terre) and Pointe-à-Pitre, and less frequently from Ste-Anne and St-François (on Grande-Terre). Locally there's a small ferry running several times daily between Terre-de-Haut and Terre-de-Bas. See p504 for details.

❶ Getting Around

If you just want to eat and make the steep walk to Fort Napoléon there's no need to rent a motorbike.

MINIBUS Air-conditioned minibuses provide two-hour tours of the island for €15 per person, if there are enough people. Drivers canvass arriving ferry passengers, or you can look for vans parked along the street between the pier and the town hall.

MOTORCYCLE Motorbikes are a great way to tour the island. Although roads are narrow, there are only a few dozen cars on Terre-de-Haut, so you won't encounter much traffic. With a motorbike you can zip up to the top of Le Chameau and Fort Napoléon, get out to the beaches and explore the island pretty thoroughly in a day. The motorbikes are capable of carrying two people, but because the roads are so windy, it's not advisable to carry a passenger unless you're an experienced rider.

There are lots of rental locations on the main road leading south from the pier, but the ones that set up dockside seem as good as any. Try **Localizé** (✆05-90-99-51-99) or **Archipel Les Saintes** (✆05-90-99-50-97) if you want to book in advance. If you arrive on a busy day, it's wise to grab a bike as soon as possible, as they sometimes sell out. Most charge €20 to €25 for day visitors and require a €200 deposit or an imprint of a major credit card. Motorbikes come with gas but not damage insurance, so if you get in an accident or spill the bike, the repairs will be charged to your credit card.

Motorbike riding is prohibited in the center of Bourg des Saintes and helmets are obligatory. You'll see people ignoring the law, but if you're not wearing a helmet and you run into police, you can expect to be stopped.

BOURG DES SAINTES

Home to most of the island's residents, Bourg des Saintes is a picturesque village with a decidedly Norman accent. Its narrow streets are lined with whitewashed, red-roofed houses with shuttered windows and yards of flowering hibiscus.

At the end of the pier is a small courtyard with a gilded column commemorating the French Revolution. Turn right and in a minute you'll be at the central town square, flanked by the *mairie* (town hall) and an old stone church.

It's a fun town in which to kick around. There are restaurants, ice-cream shops, scooter rentals, galleries and gift shops clustered along the main road, which is pedestrian-only during the day. Most shops close around 1pm; some reopen in the evening, but in the low season many places stay closed.

◉ Sights

Fort Napoléon   FORT
(adult/child €4/2; ◔9am-12:30pm) The closest thing Terre-de-Haut has to a traditional tourist site. You can walk through on your own or join an informative 30-minute guided tour conducted in French. There's a cactus garden where iguanas often frolic, but the naval museum inside is only of interest to hard-core naval historians – the battle of Les Saintes is documented in exacting detail.

Built in the mid-19th century but never used in battle, the fort affords a fine view of Bourg des Saintes, and you can look across the channel to Fort Josephine, a small fortification on Îlet à Cabrit. On a clear day you can also see Marie-Galante and La Désirade.

The fort is 1.6km north of the center of Bourg des Saintes; simply turn left as you come off the pier and follow the road uphill.

Baie du Marigot   BEACH
Baie du Marigot is a pleasant little bay with a calm protected beach about 1km north of Bourg des Saintes. It's fairly close to Fort Napoléon, so you could combine a visit to the two; after visiting the fort, turn left at the bottom of the winding fort road and bear left again a few minutes later as you near the bay.

Baie de Pont Pierre   BEACH
The horseshoe-shaped Baie de Pont Pierre is a lovely reef-protected beach with light brown sand and a splendid setting; there are even tame goats that mosey onto the beach and lie down next to sunbathers. The beach is an easy 1.6km walk northeast of Bourg des Saintes.

East-Coast Beaches
BEACHES

The long, sandy **Grande Anse**, immediately east of the airport runway, has rough seas and water conditions, and swimming is not allowed. The north side of this windy beach is backed by clay cliffs.

South of Grande Anse and about 2km from town is **Anse Rodrigue**, a nice beach on a protected cove that usually has good swimming conditions.

Southwest Beaches
BEACHES

Two kilometres southwest of Bourg des Saintes is **Anse à Cointe**, a good beach for combining swimming and **snorkeling**. The snorkeling is best on the north side. You'll also find good snorkeling and a sandy beach at **Pain de Sucre** (Sugarloaf), the basalt peninsula that's about 700m to the north.

Anse Crawen, 500m south of Bois Joli, is a secluded, clothing-optional beach just a couple of minutes' walk down a dirt path that starts where the coastal road ends. It's a perfect spot for **nude snorkeling**; bring plenty of water and sunscreen.

Le Chameau
TOWER, LOOKOUT

A winding cement road leads to the summit of Le Chameau, which at 309m is the island's highest point.

To get to Le Chameau, turn south from the Bourg des Saintes pier and continue 1km on the coastal road. At Restaurant Plongée turn inland on the D214; 500m later, turn left on the cement road and follow it up 1.75km to where it ends at the tower.

From town it's a moderately difficult hour-long walk to the top. A more fun alternative is to ride a motorbike, which takes five minutes.

🏃 Activities

Aquatic Park
SWIMMING

Set behind the Ti Saintois restaurant and sandwich shop. The four swimming lanes in the harbor are a tad shorter than an Olympic-sized pool. Just show up and jump in.

Pisquettes Diving
DIVING

(☎05-90-99-88-80; www.pisquettes.com) Does morning and afternoon dives. Its name refers to the little silver fish you'll see in great numbers in the water here.

La Dive Bouteille
DIVING

(☎05-90-99-54-25; www.dive-bouteille.com) Offers certification courses, night dives, and kid-friendly dives in addition to the usual underwater outings. One-tank dives start at €58.

🛏 Sleeping

There are room-for-rent signs around the island. During high season the competition for rooms can be stiff, so book ahead.

Kanaoa
HOTEL **$$**

(☎05-90-99-51-36; www.hotelkanaoa.com; Anse Mire; s/d incl breakfast from €75/100, bungalows from €120; ❄❄) A five-minute walk from the village in the direction of Fort Napoléon, this two-star hotel sits on the beach and has a private pier and restaurant. The hotel runs a shuttle bus around the island during daylight hours for guests to visit the island sights and beaches. In addition to the 19 hotel rooms, there are four duplex bungalows with kitchenettes.

TOP CHOICE Auberge Les Petits Saints
GUESTHOUSE **$$**

(☎05-90-99-50-99; www.petitssaints.com; La Savane; studios €110, r €110-240; ❄❄) This former mayor's residence is set in an opulent villa and has quite a wonderful location. Each room is decorated with objets d'art, well-chosen antiques and big canopy beds, and it manages to have a refined feel without being stuffy. As well as the 12 rooms in the main building, there is a six-person apartment (€260) and two studios 100m away from the main building; they don't have the satellite TV and phones that the other rooms do. The decked swimming pool has fabulous views over the bay and there's even a small gym tucked behind the massive 200-year-old intricately carved wooden wall in the restaurant.

LoBleu Hôtel
HOTEL **$$**

(☎05-90-92-40-00; www.lobleuhotel.com; Fond de Curé; s/d incl breakfast €112/120; ❄❄) Right in the center of town, each of the 10 rooms in this brightly decorated hotel is accorded a different motif, and beware, the choices are a little on the gawdy side. The ground-level **Restaurant aux Saintes** (mains €13-20; ☉dinner) has a number of Lebanese dishes to compliment the Creole standards. With solar lamps that soak up the sun by day and glow at night, this is definitely the coolest place to be in the evenings.

🍴 Eating

There are many casual restaurants around town that cater to day-trippers and offer a meal of the day in the €10 to €16 range.

Auberge Les Petits Saints
SEAFOOD $$$

(☎05-90-99-50-99; La Savane; mains €20-30; ☻dinner Tue-Sun) The open-air terraced restaurant at this hotel specializes in fresh fish and seafood finely teamed with local produce. It's a sublime place to eat – order the lobster in advance. Reservations are a good idea in the high season.

Sole Mio
SEAFOOD $

(☎05-90-09-56-46; http://solemio.monsite.wana doo.fr; mains €10-20; ☻lunch & dinner Mon-Sat) A restaurant and small art gallery overlooking the water, Sole Mio has nice views both inside and out. Try the *espadon* (swordfish) tartare and the traditional Santoise dessert *tourment d'amour* (love's torment), a cake-like concoction with melted chocolate in the middle, historically made by local women to provide solace while their sailor husbands were at sea.

La Saladerie
CAFE $

(Anse Mirre; mains €8-17; ☻lunch & dinner Wed-Sun) A popular spot hidden down some steps, it has a make-your-own salad menu and serves a fish dishes. It's a few minutes' walk north of the pier on the main road.

❶ Information

There are card phones at the pier. Most of the following points of interest are marked on blue and white signs in town. Hotels here usually don't have signs on the street. There's an **ATM** on Rue de la Grande Anse, next to the tourist office. The **post office** is on the main road a few minutes' walk south of the town hall.

L'Etage Cybercafé (Upstairs Cybercafé; internet per hr €5; ☻9am-noon & 3-8pm) It also sells memory cards and small computer accessories. On the main street near the pier.

Tourist office (☎05-90-99-58-60; www .omtlessaintes.fr, in French; Rue Jean Calot; ☻9am-noon & 1-3pm Mon-Sat, 8am-2pm Sun) Has a website full of information that's sadly in French only. There's an out-of-hours number on the door to call for information or assistance.

Terre-de-Bas

POP 1100

Lying just 1km to the west of Terre-de-Haut, Terre-de-Bas is the only other inhabited island in Les Saintes. Terre-de-Bas once had small sugar and coffee plantations and is populated largely by the descendants of African slaves. It's a quiet rural island, and tourism has yet to take root, but there is a regular ferry service between the islands,

making it possible for visitors to poke around on a day excursion.

The main village, **Petites-Anses**, is on the west coast. It has hilly streets lined with trim houses, a small fishing harbor, and a quaint church with a graveyard of tombs decorated with conch shells and plastic flowers. **Grande Anse**, diagonally across the island on the east coast, is a small village with a little 17th-century church and a nice beach.

One-lane roads link the island's two villages; one of the roads cuts across the center of the island, passing between two peaks – Morne Abymes and Morne Paquette – and the other goes along the south coast. If you enjoy long country walks, it's possible to make a loop walk between the two villages (about 9km round-trip) by going out on one road and returning on the other. Otherwise, there's sometimes an inexpensive *jitney* (private minibus) that runs between the villages.

Petites-Anses has a good bakery and pastry shop, and both Petites-Anses and Grande Anse have a couple of reasonably priced local restaurants.

A ferry travels between Terre-de-Haut and Terre-de-Bas; see p504 for details.

MARIE-GALANTE

POP 16,500

Marie-Galante, the largest of Guadeloupe's outer islands, is a rural and agricultural island beloved by those who enjoy the quieter pleasures in life and particularly by beach lovers who want to escape the crowds.

Compared with the archipelago's other islands, Marie-Galante is relatively flat, its dual limestone plateaus rising only 150m. It is roughly round in shape, with a total land area of 158 sq km. Because of its shape, the island is often referred to as 'La Grande Galette,' which means 'the Big Crepe.'

❶ Getting There & Away

AIR Air Caraïbes (☎05-90-82-47-47; www. aircaraibes.com) has three to four weekly flights to Marie-Galante from Pointe-à-Pitre (20 minutes) for €150, round-trip. The airport is midway between Grand-Bourg and Capesterre, 5km from either.

BOAT The interisland crossing to Marie-Galante can be a bit rough, so if you're not used to bouncy seas it's best to travel on a light stomach and sit in the middle of the boat. One saving grace is that the boats leaving from Pointe-à-Pitre are very big (and more stable) and quite comfortable. Other boats travel here from St-François

(Grande-Terre). See p504 for details of ferry services.

ℹ️ Getting Around

BUS During the day, except for Sunday, inexpensive minibuses make regular runs between the three villages.

CAR & MOTORBIKE There are car- and motorbike-rental places facing the ferry pier. Cars generally start at €25 per day and motorbikes at €15 to €20.

Be sure to inspect your vehicle closely as some of them, especially scooters, are haggard. The stiff competition has kept the quality and prices about equal, but **Auto Moto Location** (📞05-90-97-19-42; www.automoto-location.com) rents mountain bikes for €12 per day. **Hertz** (📞05-90-97-59-80; www.hertz.com; 3 Rue de La République) only rents out cars but is an international, Anglophone-friendly chain.

MINIBUS Minibus tour drivers are usually waiting for arriving ferry passengers at the ferry port. A four-hour guided tour that makes a nearly complete circle around the island costs between €12 and €15. Stops on the tour usually include a distillery, the Ste-Marie Hospital parking lot (best view on the island), a shop where people make manioc flour, and an abandoned slave plantation.

The buses will sometimes leave you on the beach in St-Louis for a few hours and pick you up in time to make the boat back to the mainland. Some of the tour guides don't speak much standard French, let alone English, so be sure to converse a bit beforehand to make sure they can explain everything clearly.

Grand-Bourg

Grand-Bourg is the commercial and administrative center of the island. The town was leveled by fire in 1901, and its architecture is a mix of early-20th-century buildings and more recent, drab concrete structures.

The ferry dock is at the center of town. The post office, customs office and town hall are all within a few blocks of the waterfront.

The **tourist office** (📞05-90-97-56-54; www.ot-mariegalante.com; Rue du Fort) can provide you with information on local rental houses, gîtes and guesthouses. Its website has a comprehensive English-language section.

A pharmacy and a couple of banks with ATMs are on the square in front of the **Eglise Ste-Marie**, which is worth a peek inside for its stained-glassed windows.

The **market** (⏰7am-2pm), near the church, sells island trinkets and the usual assortment of flavored rums. There's a little

snack shop, **Tizong La** (mains €6-11), open whenever the market is.

Habitation Murat, about 2km from Grand-Bourg on the north side of the road to Capesterre, is a partially restored 18th-century sugar estate built stone by stone by more than 300 slaves. Check out the walled garden in the back corner of the sprawling estate – there's a gate but it's hard to find.

🛏️ Sleeping & Eating

Village de Canada　　　　　　HOTEL **$$**
(📞05-90-97-86-11; www.villagedecanada.com; Section Canada, Grand Bourg; r €70-90; ❄️🏊) Halfway between Grand-Bourg and St Louis, this charming Creole-style place offers eight bungalows and an apartment that sleeps four (€130). There are a few signs on the main road between the two towns that point the way.

L'Oasis　　　　　　　　　　　HOTEL **$$**
(📞05-90-97-59-55; oasis.mg@wanadoo.fr; Rue Sony Rupaire, Grande-Savane; r €70-90; ❄️) Each one of the three apartments here has something special to recommend it – a small tropical garden, a Jacuzzi or a terrace with views to Dominica. It's located in the center of the village, 1km from the beach; to find this friendly and clean place, head toward the Grande-Savane area and follow the signs.

Footy　　　　　　　　　　　CREOLE **$$**
(Blvd de la Marine; mains from €8; ⏰lunch & dinner) Owned by a former soccer player, this place has a great sea-view terrace and a local reputation for the best pork chops on the island (and if you notice all the giant black pigs on the island you'll understand that there's some stiff competition). It has live music in the club area in the back most Friday and Saturday nights. Make a right from the ferry dock on the main pier and head down the main road for a few minutes.

L'Ornata　　　　　　　　　　GRILL **$**
(Place Félix Éboué; snacks from €8-14; ⏰breakfast, lunch & dinner) Don't expect anything fancy, but it's is a popular choice for ending a day trip while waiting for your return ferry. It's in a pleasant old Creole house; most tables are on the front porch.

St-Louis

This fishing village is the island's main anchorage for yachters as well as a secondary port for ferries from mainland Guadeloupe. There's a little market at the end of the dock, and a couple of restaurants and the post office are just east of that.

Although there are beaches along the outskirts of St-Louis, some of the island's most beautiful strands lie a few kilometers to the north. There's a great photo opportunity at the north tip of the island at Gueule Grande Grouffre, a dramatic stone maw that lets out into electric-blue waters.

Village de Ménard   BUNGALOWS **$**
(✆05-90-97-09-45; www.villagedemenard.com; Section Vieux Fort; bungalows from €75, villas €90-125; ✳☒) This small complex of 11 comfortable bungalows and villas is on a cliff next to an old mill overlooking the bay. It's 2km from the beach in a quiet country setting. The poolside restaurant **Océanite** will prepare picnic baskets for day-trippers.

Location Bellevue   COTTAGES **$**
(✆05-90-97-00-57; www.location-bellevue.com; Section Romain; r from €50; ✳) This collection of free-standing cottages and guest rooms is scattered around the top of a very lovely hillside, giving guests the wonderful views from which this friendly and relaxed colonial-style place takes its name. This is also a good place to try local cooking – the farmer owners offer *table d'hôte*, the option of paying to dine in their homes.

Chez Henri   GRILL **$**
(www.chezhenri.net; 8 Ave des Caraïbes; mains from €11; ☉lunch & dinner Mon-Sat) This is an unexpected gem for such a tiny backwater: a lively jazz bar and a great beachside restaurant perfect for whiling away Caribbean evenings. Local art is on display, handmade local crafts are for sale, the live music is good and the simple Creole food is delicious (try the excellent Creole omelet).

Capesterre

Capesterre, on the southeast coast, is a seaside town with a little fish market on the main road near **Feuillère beach**, one of the nicest strands on an island full of them. From the village you can explore sea cliffs and hiking trails to the north.

Another attractive beach, **Petite Anse**, is about 1km to the southwest. There are a couple of attractive sleeping options here, both of which also have restaurants.

Le Touloulou (✆05-90-97-32-63; www.letouloulou.com; Plage de Petite Anse; r from €50; ✳☎) is set right on the sand on Petite Anse. The white timber bungalows at this wonderful spot all have spacious terraces for watching the waves roll in. Some also have kitchenettes, and for those without, there's an on-site **restaurant** (mains €15-30; ☉lunch & dinner Tue-Sat) and, somewhat bizarrely in such a tranquil spot, a nightclub that opens up on Fridays and Saturdays.

Le Soleil Levant (✆05-90-97-31-55; 42 Rue de la Marine; d from €45; ✳☒) actually has three locations; the main building is perched above the center of Capesterre and the two smaller buildings are in town. The main structure has a nice big sundeck with great sea view, and a downstairs bar-restaurant where locals gather.

LA DÉSIRADE

POP 1650

If a refuge from the troubles of the world is what you seek, look no further: La Désirade is Guadeloupe's least-developed and least-visited island. Even the nicest beaches are nearly deserted; for the ultimate do-nothing vacation it's a place that's hard to beat.

Looking somewhat like an overturned boat when viewed from Guadeloupe, La Désirade is only 11km long and 2km wide, with a central plateau that rises 273m at its highest point, Grand Montagne.

The uninhabited north side of the island has a rocky coastline with rough open seas, while the south side has sandy beaches and reef-protected waters. There are no diving

---

CANE JUICE

Rum distilleries are among the island's main sights. The **Distillerie Poisson** (✆05-90-97-03-79; Habitation Edouard, Rameau, Grand-Bourg; ☉7am-1pm Mon-Sat), midway between St-Louis and Grand-Bourg, bottles the island's best-known rum under the Père Labat label. **Distillerie Bielle** (✆05-90-97-93-62; Section Bielle, Grand-Bourg), between Grand-Bourg and Capesterre, offers tours of its age-old distillery operation. Worth a visit for its historic setting, as well as its rum, is **Domaine de Bellevue** (✆05-90-97-26-50; Section Bellevue, Capesterre; ☉9:30am-1pm). All of the distilleries have gift shops and rum is definitely one of the best gifts to bring back from Guadeloupe.

operations or places to rent snorkeling equipment on the island, so those who want to get underwater should bring their own gear.

La Désirade's harbor and airport are on the southwest side of the island in **Beauséjour**, the main village. The island's town hall, post office and library are also in Beauséjour. There are smaller settlements at **Le Souffleur** and **Baie Mahault**.

In 1725 Guadeloupe established a leper colony on La Désirade, and for more than two centuries victims of the disease were forced to make a one-way trip to the island. The **leprosarium**, which was run by the Catholic Sisters of Charity, closed in the mid-1950s. Its remains, a chapel and a cemetery, are just to the east of Baie Mahault.

La Désirade's main road runs along the southern coast and ends at an art-deco-style **weather station** on the eastern tip of the island. Nearby is a **lighthouse**. The trip is worthwhile for the scenery, if nothing else. Gangs of goats that apparently don't see many cars wander the windswept fields here – it's an area of desolate beauty.

🛏 Sleeping & Eating

TOP CHOICE **Oualiri Beach Hotel**   BEACH HOTEL **$$**
(📞05-90-20-20-08; www.rendezvouskarukera.com; Beauséjour; s/d/tr/q €80/98/108/118; ❋🛜♨) This fantastic place was designed to give people with children the possibility to combine a family holiday with total relaxation. There are six hotel rooms and two spacious bungalows set on a private beach, the on-site restaurant **Oulari Breeze** (mains €14-20; ☉breakfast, lunch & dinner) and a small kids' club with a playground in plain sight so kids can wear themselves out. There's also a free 4pm snack time and an outdoor shower for the wee ones. It has music nights every few weeks, and a brunch party every Sunday.

Hôtel Oasis   HOTEL **$$**
(📞05-90-20-01-00; www.oasisladesirade.com; s/d €42/47, q studios €60; ❋) About 250m from the beach, this very simple but pleasant hotel is set in a white two-level Creole-style building. Nearby it has a brightly colored restaurant, **Lagranlag** (mains €8-15; ☉lunch & dinner Tue-Sun), which specializes in gratins and seafood stews. Meal plans are available for an additional €12 to €22 per day.

La Payotte   CREOLE **$$**
(📞05-90-20-01-29; Grande Anse, Beauséjour; mains from €12-20; ☉breakfast, lunch & dinner, closed breakfast & lunch Sun) Right on Grande Anse, La Payotte serves a tasty variety of Creole dishes as well as a small breakfast menu on its charming beachside terrace. Reservations in the evenings during the high season is a good idea. It also rents six rooms (doubles/quads €50/90) in a nearby old house shrouded by bougainvilleas.

La Roulotte   CREOLE **$**
(Plage du Souffler; mains from €10; ☉breakfast, lunch & dinner Mon-Sat) With plastic tables in the sand, the food is nothing special but we love the sign that asks diners to order before swimming so that your meal is ready when you emerge from the water. It's 2.5km east of Beauséjour on the main road.

❶ Getting There & Away

There are ferries to St-François and Ste-Anne, both on Grande-Terre; see p504 for details.

❶ Getting Around

Scooter rentals are available at the ferry dock for €15 to €20 a day. The coastal road is a lot hillier than it appears from the boat, making cycling a sweaty workout. Most locals and visitors prefer the scooters. Just be sure to double-check your scooter – some of them barely roll straight.

UNDERSTAND GUADELOUPE

History

When sighted by Columbus on November 14, 1493, Guadeloupe was inhabited by Caribs, who called it Karukera (Island of Beautiful Waters). The Spanish made two attempts to settle Guadeloupe in the early 1500s but were repelled both times by fierce Carib resistance, and finally in 1604 they abandoned their claim to the island.

Three decades later, French colonists sponsored by the Compagnie des Îles d'Amérique, an association of French entrepreneurs, set sail to establish the first European settlement on Guadeloupe. On June 28, 1635, the party, led by Charles Liénard de l'Olive and Jean Duplessis d'Ossonville, landed on the southeastern shore of Basse-Terre and claimed Guadeloupe for France. They drove the Caribs off the island, planted crops and within a decade had built the first sugar mill. By the time France officially annexed the island in 1674, a slavery-based plantation system had been well established.

The English invaded Guadeloupe several times and occupied it from 1759 to 1763. During this time, they developed Pointe-à-Pitre into a major harbor, opened profitable English and North American markets to Guadeloupean sugar and allowed the planters to import cheap American lumber and food. Many French colonists actually grew wealthier under the British occupation, and the economy expanded rapidly. In 1763 British occupation ended with the signing of the Treaty of Paris, which relinquished French claims in Canada in exchange for the return of Guadeloupe.

Amid the chaos of the French Revolution, the British invaded Guadeloupe again in 1794. In response, the French sent a contingent of soldiers led by Victor Hugues, a black nationalist. Hugues freed and armed Guadeloupean slaves. On the day the British withdrew from Guadeloupe, Hugues went on a rampage and killed 300 royalists, many of them plantation owners. It marked the start of a reign of terror. In all, Hugues was responsible for the deaths of more than 1000 colonists, and as a consequence of his attacks on US ships, the USA declared war on France.

In 1802 Napoléon Bonaparte, anxious to get the situation under control, sent General Antoine Richepance to Guadeloupe. Richepance put down the uprising, restored the prerevolutionary government and reinstituted slavery.

Guadeloupe was the most prosperous island in the French West Indies, and the British continued to covet it, invading and occupying the island for most of the period between 1810 and 1816. The Treaty of Vienna restored the island to France, which has maintained sovereignty over it continuously since 1816.

Slavery was abolished in 1848, following a campaign led by French politician Victor Schoelcher (see p477). In the years that followed, planters brought laborers from Pondicherry, a French colony in India, to work in the cane fields. Since 1871 Guadeloupe has had representation in the French parliament, and since 1946 it has been an overseas department of France.

Guadeloupe's economy is heavily dependent upon subsidies from the French government and upon its economic ties with mainland France, which absorbs the majority of Guadeloupe's exports and provides 75% of its imports. Agriculture remains a cornerstone of the economy. The leading export crop is bananas, the bulk of which grow along the southern flanks of La Soufrière.

In August 2007 Hurricane Dean barreled through the Caribbean, destroying an estimated 80% of Guadeloupe's banana plantations with 160km/h winds that lifted the roofs right off buildings.

Just as Guadeloupe began a quick recovery from the hurricane, it was rocked by a series of general strikes in 2009. For a whole month during the tourism high season thousands of people protested about the cost of living and high unemployment rate by blockading the island's gas stations and bringing much of the public sector to a standstill. Millions of dollars of tourist revenue was lost due to cancelled holidays, and while the threat of future strikes is relatively low, the effect on the Guadeloupean economy can still be felt in many smaller resort towns, where many businesses have gone under as travelers have stayed away.

Culture

Guadeloupean culture draws from a pool of French, African, East Indian and West Indian influences. The mix is visible in the architecture, which ranges from French colonial buildings to traditional Creole homes; in the food, which merges influences from all the cultures into a unique Creole cuisine; and in the widely spoken local Creole language, the local dialect that is a heavily accented and very colloquial form of French. Guadeloupe is also one place in the Caribbean where you're likely to see women wearing traditional Creole dress, especially at festivals and cultural events.

There's much emphasis on the French rules of politeness; *bonjour* and *au revoir* are almost always heard when entering or leaving an establishment, and older Guadeloupeans usually give a collective *bonjour* to everyone in general when entering a crowded restaurant or bar. To start a conversation or ask a question without a greeting is rude.

The total population of Guadeloupe is about 405,000, with a third of the population aged under 20. About three-quarters of the population is of mixed ethnicity, a combination of African, European and East Indian descent. There's also a sizable population of white islanders who trace their ancestry to the early French settlers, as well as a number of more recently arrived French from the mainland.

The predominant religion is Roman Catholicism. There are also Methodist, Seventh Day Adventist, Jehovah's Witness and evangelical denominations, and a sizable Hindu community.

The island is fertile ground for the literary imagination, apparently. Guadeloupe's most renowned native son is St-John Perse, the pseudonym of Alexis Leger, who was born in Guadeloupe in 1887. Perse won the Nobel Prize for literature in 1960 for the evocative imagery of his poetry. One of his many noted works is *Anabase* (1925), which was translated into English by TS Eliot.

The leading contemporary novelist in the French West Indies is Guadeloupe native Maryse Condé. Many of her bestselling novels have been translated into English. The epic *Tree of Life* (1992) centers on the life of a Guadeloupean family, their roots and the identity of Guadeloupean society itself. *Crossing the Mangrove* (1995) is a perfect beach read. Set in Rivière au Sel near the Rivière Salée, it unravels the life, and untimely death, of a controversial villager.

Landscape & Wildlife

Beaches line nearly every shore in Guadeloupe, explaining its enduring attraction to generations of French holidaymakers. Outside of the mountainous Parc National de la Guadeloupe, the interior is made for the most part of gently rolling fields of sugarcane. The beaches, hiking trails and picnic areas here are almost always completely litter-free.

Underwater life includes small sea horses, lobsters, lots of parrot fish, and crabs. Divers may occasionally spot a ray or barracuda, but for the most part the waters here support large schools of smaller fish.

Birds found on Guadeloupe include various members of the heron family, pelicans, hummingbirds and the endangered Guadeloupe wren. A common sighting is the bright yellow-bellied banana quit, a small nectar-feeding bird that's a frequent visitor at open-air restaurants, where it raids unattended sugar bowls.

You'll probably see drawings of raccoons on park brochures and in Guadeloupean advertising; it is the official symbol of Parc National de la Guadeloupe and its main habitat is in the forests of Basse-Terre.

Guadeloupe has mongooses aplenty, introduced long ago in a futile attempt to control rats in the sugarcane fields. Agoutis (short-haired, short-eared rabbitlike rodents that look a bit like guinea pigs) are found on La Désirade. There are iguanas on Les Saintes and La Désirade.

SURVIVAL GUIDE

Directory A–Z
Accommodations

Hotel accommodations on Guadeloupe is generally of good standard. Resorts here are generally small by the standards of the Caribbean and large resorts are rare. Most hotels are midsized and midrange, and prices are reasonable by the standards of the region.

Room rates are for the high season (generally from December to April and July to August). Low-season rates can be much cheaper than those quoted in this chapter. Generally, you can expect a reduction of between 20% and 40% between May and July and from September to November.

Many of Guadeloupe's most charming accommodations are private guesthouses (*chambres d'hôte*) or freestanding houses and cottages to rent (gîtes), but they generally require booking by the week. See www.gitesdefrance.fr for more details.

Most hotels don't include breakfast in the room price, but the majority do serve it for an extra charge.

$	budget	less than €50
$$	midrange	€50 to €150
$$$	top end	more than €150

Business Hours

The following are normal business hours. Reviews don't include hours unless they differ from these standards.

Banks 9am-4pm Mon-Fri

Bars 6pm-midnight

Restaurants 11.30am-10pm Mon-Sat, some closed between lunch & dinner

PRACTICALITIES

» **Electricity** 220 volts, 50 cycles; European-style, two-round-pin plugs.

» **Newspapers** *France-Antilles* (www .martinique.franceantilles.fr) is the main daily newspaper for the French West Indies. French newspapers and magazines are commonly found everywhere; print editions in English are far rarer.

» **Radio & TV** Tune into Réseau Outre-Mer 1ère (www.la1ere.fr) or catch up on local TV on Guadeloupe 1ère (www .guadeloupe.la1ere.fr)

» **Weights & Measures** Guadeloupe uses the metric system for everything, and the 24-hour clock.

Shops 9am-7pm Mon-Sat

Sights 9am-6pm, many closed Sun or Mon

Supermarkets 8am-8pm Mon-Sat

Children

Because of all the French families that come here, there are a number of child-friendly hotels and activities. Many hotels have play areas and activities just for kids and a special children's menu. All restaurants will allow children to dine, and they'll often have a simple and good-value 'menu enfant' (children's set meal) to offer them.

Practically all hotels will provide cots, and some hotels provide babysitting services. European brands of baby formula, foods and diapers can be bought at pharmacies.

Dangers & Annoyances

Occasional islandwide strikes can grind tourism services to a screeching halt.

For the lowdown on the shady side of Pointe-à-Pitre, see p477.

Embassies & Consulates

There are no consulates or embassies on the island – you'll need to head to Dominica (p402) or Martinique (p588) – although there are a number of consular agents who may be able to help. These agents are listed under Practical Information on the website of the **Guadeloupe Islands Tourism Board** (www .lesilesdeguadeloupe.com).

Food

The following price categories for the cost of a main course are used in the Eating listings in this chapter.

$	budget	less than €12
$$	midrange	€12 to €20
$$$	top end	more than €20

Gay & Lesbian Travelers

Guadeloupe usually earns OK marks from gay travel organizations, as gay and lesbian rights are protected under French law. However, attitudes on the ground tend to be far less tolerant and prejudice against gay people is very common. Gay couples usually do not publicly express affection or advertise their sexual orientation, although hoteliers don't seem to care who shares a bed. There is little or no gay scene here – most introductions happen via the internet.

Health

Medical care is equivalent to mainland France: very good. The biggest hospital is the Centre Hospitalier in Pointe-à-Pitre, though there are smaller hospitals in almost every region. There are plenty of pharmacies everywhere; look for the green cross, often flashing in neon.

As in much of the Caribbean, dengue fever has made an unwelcome reappearance in Guadeloupe recently and it can be fatal. Dengue outbreaks tend to occur wherever there's standing water – more frequent in cities than in the countryside.

Bilharzia (schistosomiasis) is found throughout Grande-Terre and in much of Basse-Terre, including Grand Étang lake. The main method of prevention is to avoid swimming or wading in fresh water.

It's safe to drink the tap water in Gaudeloupe.

Internet Access

Internet cafes have been almost entirely replaced by wi-fi (sometimes called WLAN locally) in Guadeloupe. If you don't have a laptop or other wireless device with you, you'll have to ask around for a web cafe or expect to take a break from email for a week or two. Some hotels have terminals that can be used by guests, but these are exceptions rather than rules. Wireless access is nearly always provided for free in Guadeloupe.

Language

In the tourist towns near the capital (Gosier, Ste-Anne) and anyplace there's a large sailing community (Deshaies, St-François) a visitor can get by with just some basic French expressions. For exploration further afield a good command of basic French is very helpful. A phrase book is a great idea.

Money

Guadeloupe, as a department of France, uses the euro. Hotels, larger restaurants and car-rental agencies accept Visa, MasterCard and less commonly, American Express. ATMs are common across the island.

Avoid changing money at hotel lobbies, where the rates are worse than at exchange offices or banks. Currency-exchange offices, called *bureaux de change,* are scattered around Pointe-à-Pitre, and ATMs (called ABMs, *distributeurs de billets* or *distributeurs automatiques*) accept most international cards.

The standard tipping rate when dining out is 10%.

Post

There are post offices in all major towns. You can also buy postage stamps at some *tabacs* (tobacco shops), hotels and souvenir shops.

Mailing addresses given in this chapter should be followed by 'Guadeloupe, French West Indies.'

Public Holidays

In addition to those observed throughout the region (p872), Guadeloupe has the following public holidays:

Labor Day May 1

Victory Day May 8

Ascension Thursday 40th day after Easter

Slavery Abolition Day May 27

Bastille Day July 14

Schoelcher Day July 21

Assumption Day August 15

All Saints Day November 1

Armistice Day November 11

Telephone

The country code for Guadeloupe is ☎590. Confusingly, all local numbers begin with 05-90 as well. These numbers are separate, however, and therefore must be dialed twice

when calling from abroad. Local mobile numbers begin with 06-90.

To call Guadeloupe from North America, dial ☎001 + 590 + the local number (dropping the initial zero). When calling from within the French West Indies, simply dial the local 10-digit number. From elsewhere, dial your country's international access code, followed by the ☎590 country code and the local number (dropping the initial zero).

For directory assistance, dial ☎12.

SIM cards (starting at €10) are available for unlocked cell phones and usually include some talk time before recharging. Digicel and Orange are the two main SIM-card vendors.

Visas

Citizens of the US, Canada, Australia and New Zealand can stay for up to 90 days without a visa.

Citizens of the EU can stay in Guadeloupe indefinitely and need an official identity card or a valid passport to enter the country.

Getting There & Away
Entering Guadeloupe

All visitors to Guadeloupe must have a valid passport (or a valid national identity card if you're an EU citizen). A round-trip or onward ticket is officially required of visitors. This may be checked at customs upon arrival, though it's unlikely.

Air

Guadeloupe's only international airport is **Guadeloupe Le Raizet Airport** (Pole Caribes; www.guadeloupe.aeroport.fr; ☎05-90-21-14-72/98), which is north of Pointe-à-Pitre, 6km from the city center on the N5.

The following airlines serve Guadeloupe:

Air Antilles Express (www.airantilles.com) Flies from St-Barthélemy, St-Martin/Sint Maarten, Fort-de-France, Santo Domingo, Port-au-Prince, Havana

Air Canada (www.aircanada.com) Montreal

Air Caraïbes (www.aircaraibes.com) Cayenne, Fort-de-France, Paris, Santo Domingo, St-Barthélemy, St-Martin/Sint Maarten

Air France (www.airfrance.com) Cayenne, Fort-de-France, Miami, Paris

American Airlines (www.aa.com) San Juan

Corsairfly (www.corsairfly.com) Lyon, Nantes, Paris

LIAT (www.liat.com) Antigua, Dominica

Sea

FERRY

L'Express des Îles (☎05-90-91-11-05; www .express-des-iles.com; Gare Maritime, Bergevin) operates large, modern catamarans that have air-conditioned cabins with TVs and a snack bar.

There are usually crossings on Sunday, Wednesday and Friday from Pointe-à-Pitre to Roseau, Dominica (one-way/round-trip €67/100, 1½ hours), continuing to Fort-de-France, Martinique (one-way/round-trip €67/100, three hours) and then sometimes continuing to Castries, St Lucia (one-way/ round-trip €67/100, 4½ hours)

In the other direction there are departures from Castries in St Lucia on Monday, Thursday and Saturday calling at Fort-de-France and Roseau before arriving in Pointe-à-Pitre.

Note that it is possible to travel from Guadeloupe to Dominica, break your journey for a few days, and then continue to Guadeloupe or St Lucia for a single €67 ticket.

Departure days and times for these services change frequently and, due to weather conditions, often bear no relation to the printed schedule. The only way to be sure is to call L'Express des Îles or check with a local travel agent.

You can buy tickets in person at the Gare Maritime Bergevin in Pointe-à-Pitre, but you'll need your ID and the ID of all travelers wanting to travel. It's not currently possible to book online. There are discounts of 50% for children aged under two, 10% for students and passengers under 12 years old, and 5% for passengers younger than 26 or older than 60.

CRUISE SHIP

Cruise ships don't always call at Pointe-à-Pitre, as neither the port area nor the city itself is particularly attractive. However, when cruise ships do call, they normally dock right in the city at Centre St-John Perse, Pointe-à-Pitre's old port complex, and at the spiffy new cruise-ship terminal.

YACHT

Popular with yachties and sailors, Guadeloupe has three marinas:

Marina de Bas du Fort (☎05-90-90-66-20; www.caribbean-marinas.com/basdufort)

Between Pointe-à-Pitre and Gosier; has 1000 berths, 100 of which are available for visiting boats. There's a large number of restaurants, bars, cafes and excellent facilities here.

Marina de St-François (☎05-90-88-47-28) In the center of St-François. Has about 250 moorings, as well as fuel, water, ice and electricity.

Marina de Rivière-Sens (☎05-90-81-77-61) On the southern outskirts of the town of Basse-Terre. Has 220 moorings, fuel, water and ice.

Customs and immigration offices are located in Pointe-à-Pitre, Basse-Terre and Deshaies.

The yacht charter companies Antilles Sail (☎05-90-90-16-81; www.antilles-sail.com) and Dream Yacht Charter (☎05-90-22-19-30; www.dreamyachtcharter.com) are based at Marina de Bas du Fort near Pointe-à-Pitre.

Getting Around

For travelers visiting more than one place, a rental car is almost a necessity. The main tourist spots on the southern coast of Grande-Terre are navigable without a car, but for the most part a vehicle comes in handy. Many hotels can arrange airport pickup and car rental.

Air

Air Caraïbes (☎05-90-82-47-47; www.aircara ibes.com) has several flights per week between Pointe-à-Pitre and Marie-Galante. Normally there is also a daily service to Terre-de-Haut as well, but this was suspended at the time of writing due to the refurbishment of the Terre-de-Haut Airport.

Bicycle

Bicycles are an adventurous, somewhat strenuous way to see Terre-de-Haut and Marie-Galante. Rentals start at €10 per day.

Boat

Ferries are the principal way to get around between the islands of Guadeloupe. Multiple ferry operators run services between Grande-Terre and Terre-de-Haut, Marie-Galante and La Désirade. There are also ferries from Trois-Rivières on Basse-Terre to Terre-de-Haut in Les Saintes, and a ferry between Terre-de-Haut and Terre-de-Bas.

The main ferry operators are listed below. Prices tend to be similar, though shop around on the ground for the best deal. Many operators offer big discounts to people who book a day or more in advance.

Caribbean Spirit (☑05-90-91-45-15; www. caribbean-spirit.fr; Pointe-à-Pitre)

L'Express des Îles (☑05-90-91-11-05; www. express-des-iles.com; Pointe-à-Pitre)

Les Bateliers de l'Archipel (☑05-90-22-26-31 St-François, 05-90-30-86-07 Ste-Anne)

Arawak Maritime (☑05-90-85-00-55 St-François)

Société Maritime des Îles du Sud (☑05-90-85-00-55, Trois-Rivières)

Le Colibri (☑05-90-21-23-73; St-François)

CTM Deher (☑05-90-92-06-39; www.ctmdeher.com; Trois-Rivières)

Val'Ferry (☑05-90-91-45-15; Pointe-à-Pitre)

The ferry routes from mainland Guadeloupe to the islands:

Pointe-à-Pitre to Les Saintes 8am Tuesday and Thursday, return 4pm (Caribbean Spirit); 8:15am Thursday, return 4:30pm (L'Express des Îles)

Pointe-à-Pitre to Marie-Galante 7.45am Monday, Wednesday, Friday, Saturday, Sunday (Caribbean Spirit); 8.15am, 12.45pm, 5.15pm daily (L'Express des Îles)

Trois-Rivières to Les Saintes Multiple departures daily between 8am and 9am

Ste-Anne to Les Saintes or La Désirade Seasonal services: inquire locally

St-François to Les Saintes, Marie-Galante or La Désirade Multiple departures with multiple companies between 7am and 8am

Ferries from the islands to mainland Guadeloupe:

Les Saintes to Pointe-à-Pitre 4pm Tuesday and Thursday (Caribbean Spirit); 4.30pm Thursday (L'Express des Îles)

Les Saintes to Trois-Rivières Multiple departures with multiple companies daily between 4pm and 5pm

Les Saintes to Ste-Anne Seasonal services: inquire locally

Les Saintes to St-François Multiple departures with multiple companies between 4pm and 5pm

Marie-Galante to Pointe-à-Pitre 5pm Monday, Wednesday, Friday, Saturday, Sunday (Caribbean Spirit); 6am, 9.15pm, 4pm daily (L'Express des Îles)

Marie-Galante to St-François Multiple departures with multiple companies between 4pm and 5pm

La Désirade to Ste-Anne Seasonal services: inquire locally

La Désirade to St-François Multiple departures with multiple companies between 3pm and 4pm

Bus

Guadeloupe has a good public bus system that operates from about 5:30am to 6:30pm, with fairly frequent service on main routes. On Saturday afternoon service is much lighter, and there are almost no buses on Sunday.

Many bus routes start and end in Pointe-à-Pitre; see p480 for details.

Destinations are written on the buses. Bus stops have blue signs picturing a bus; in less developed areas you can wave buses down along their routes.

Car

A driver's license from your home country is necessary to drive here.

RENTAL

Several car-rental companies have offices at the airport and in major resort areas. Some agents will let you rent a car near your hotel and drop it off free of charge at the airport, which can save a hefty taxi fare.

Companies generally drop their rates the longer you keep the car, with the weekly rate working out to be about 15% cheaper, overall, than the daily rate. Nearly all companies use an unlimited-kilometers rate.

Rates for small cars are advertised from around €35 per day, although the rates offered on a walk-in basis and availability of cars can vary greatly with the season. It's a good idea to reserve ahead from December to May.

ROAD CONDITIONS

Roads are excellent by Caribbean standards and almost invariably hard-surfaced, although secondary and mountain roads are often narrow.

Around Pointe-à-Pitre there are multi-lane highways, with cars zipping along at 110km/h. Outside the Pointe-à-Pitre area, most highways have a single lane in each direction and an 80km/h speed limit.

ROAD RULES

In Guadeloupe, drive on the right. Traffic regulations and road signs are of European standards. Exits and intersections are clearly marked, and speed limits are posted.

Hitchhiking

Hitchhiking is fairly common on Guadeloupe, particularly when the bus drivers decide to go on strike. The proper stance is to hold out an open palm at a slightly downward angle. All the usual safety precautions apply.

Taxi

Taxis are plentiful but expensive. There are taxi stands at the airport in Pointe-à-Pitre.

Fares are 40% higher from 9pm to 7am nightly, as well as all day on Sunday and holidays. You can call for a taxi by dialing **Radio Taxis** (☏05-90-82-00-00) or **Taxi Leader** (☏05-90-82-26-26) in the Pointe-à-Pitre area.

Haiti

Best Beaches

» Port Salut (p516)

» Île-à-Vache (p516)

» Cormier Plage (p517)

Best Places to Stay

» St Joseph's Home for Boys, Port-au-Prince (p510)

» Hôtel Florita, Jacmel (p514)

» Hôtel Oloffson, Port-au-Prince (p511)

» Tamarin Place Charmant, Jeremie (p516)

Why Go?

Haiti continues to struggle with the aftermath of the devastating January 12, 2010, earthquake. But this is a proud country born of revolution, and its people are determined to rebuild for a better future.

With a modicum of stability, Haiti could yet become the Caribbean's alternative travel destination *par excellence*. It has palm-fringed beaches and rum punches aplenty, but its richness lies in its history and its culture, closer to its African roots more than any other Caribbean nation and ever present in its vibrant art and music scenes.

Haiti isn't the simplest country to travel in. You frequently need to keep an ear to the news, and it can be more expensive than you'd expect. But once you're there, travel is not only possible but also incredibly rewarding. It's truly an addictive country to visit.

When to Go

There's no particular season for visiting Haiti.

April to November are generally the wetter months, and hurricane season (August and September) can cause transport problems due to mudslides. From November to March it's hot and dry, and frequently rainy in the north.

The countrywide Vodou festival of Fet Gede is in November, and Carnival is celebrated in Port-au-Prince and Jacmel, usually in February. If you plan to visit during Carnival, book well in advance as a good hotel may be hard to find. Otherwise, hotel prices generally don't fluctuate through the year.

Fast Facts

» **Area** 27,750 sq km

» **Population** nine million

» **Capital** Port-au-Prince

» **Telephone country code** ☑509

» **Emergency** Police ☑122

Set Your Budget

» **Budget hotel room** US$40

» **Two-course evening meal** US$25

» **Beer** US$1.40

» **Motorbike taxi ride** US$0.50

» **Internal flight** US$90

Resources

» **Haitian Footsteps** (www .haitianfootsteps.com) Coverage of Haitian travel, culture and history

» **Haiti News** (www .haitinews.net) Useful news aggregator

» **Haitian Magazine** (www .haitiantoday.com) Haitian news and entertainment

Itineraries

ONE WEEK

Spend a couple of days taking in Port-au-Prince, with a side trip to the artists' village of Croix des Bouquets. Take a flight to Cap-Haïtien and overnight before making a day trip to the Citadelle and Sans Souci palace as well as checking out the beach at either Labadie or Cormier Plage.

Fly back to Port-au-Prince, and travel over the mountains to the town of Jacmel on the south coast, for its historic quarter and to stock up on its famous handicrafts, before returning to the capital.

GETTING TO NEIGHBORING ISLANDS

There are no ferries to neighboring islands. There are flights from Port-au-Prince to Cuba, Curaçao, St Martin/ Sint Maarten, Nassau and Guadeloupe, and from Cap-Haïtien to Providenciales. There are direct flights and overland coaches from Port-au-Prince to Santo Domingo in the Dominican Republic (DR).

Essential Food & Drink

The main types of meat eaten are chicken, pork, goat and beef; conch is also popular. Fresh fruit abounds – mangoes and avocados are particularly good.

» **Bannan** Fried plantain

» **Barbancourt** The best locally produced brand of rum.

» **Diri** Rice

» **Fritay** Street snack of fried meat, fish or plantain.

» **Griyo** Pork

» **Kabrit** Goat

» **Lambi** Conch

» **Pate** Savoury pastries; a good street snack.

» **Plat complet** A dish with the key elements of Haitian food – rice, beans and fried plantain – and meat, accompanied with a sauce.

» **Poule** Chicken

» **Prestige** The best locally produced brand of beer.

» **Pwa** Beans

» **Tasso** Beef

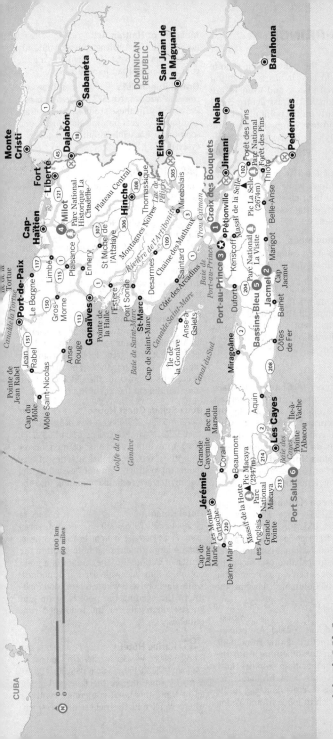

Haiti Highlights

1 See beautifully styled metal artworks, from high-concept art to pocket-sized souvenirs, at the unique artists' village of **Croix des Bouquets** (p513)

2 Pick up bright arts and crafts – huge carnival masks are a specialty – in handicrafts capital **Jacmel** (p514)

3 Groove to the band **RAM** (p513), who serve up Vodou-

styled roots and rhythm at Port-au-Prince's Oloffson hotel

4 Marvel at the mountaintop **Citadelle** (p518), one of the most dramatic historic sites in the Americas, with ruined

palace **Sans Souci** (p518) at its foot

5 Swim at **Bassins-Bleu** (p514), a series of grottos and waterfalls in the wooded hills above Jacmel

6 Feast your eyes on the miles-long palm-fringed beach of **Port Salut** (p516), proof that Haiti can do picture-postcard Caribbean as well as anywhere

PORT-AU-PRINCE

POP 3 MILLION

Port-au-Prince is the picture of a chaotic developing-world city. It has a reputation for impoverished chaos, and even before the 2010 earthquake, infrastructure could seem permanently on the point of collapse. Now, rubble and tent camps have become as much the city's signatures as its famous arts scene, live music and irrepressible spirit.

The center of the city is compact and manageable on foot, while on the hillsides above you'll find the rich suburb of Pétionville, where many of the best hotels and restaurants are based.

Dangers & Annoyances

Port-au-Prince is a lot calmer than preconceptions would have you believe. But street crime isn't unknown, so don't be ostentatious with your possessions. It's very unwise to walk around after dark, even around areas such as Champs de Mars. Avoid visiting the slum areas and tent camps, unless you have a specific invitation from a resident or local organization.

◉ Sights

The once-neat order of **Champs de Mars** (pronounced *'chanmas'*) is the starkest reminder of the damage wrought by the earthquake. A series of parks split by wide boulevards that collectively make up the **Place des Héros de l'Independence**, with the destroyed **Palais National** at its centre, this broken heart of Port-au-Prince is now a series of sprawling tent cities.

Musée du Panthéon National　　MUSEUM
(Mupanah; ☑2222-8337; Place du Champs de Mars; adult/student US$1.40/0.70; ◷8am-4pm Mon-Thu, to 5pm Fri, noon-5pm Sat, 10am-4pm Sun) The Panthéon National contains various items of historical interest, including King Christophe's suicide pistol and the rusting anchor of Columbus' flagship, the *Santa María*.

Marché de Fer　　HISTORIC MARKET
(Iron Market; Grand Rue; ◷daily) An exuberant red-metal structure dating from 1889, which looks akin to something from the *Arabian Nights* rather than tropical Haiti, the Iron Market has been brilliantly restored since being severely damaged in the earthquake. It's rich in food, art and Vodou paraphernalia.

Museum of Haitian Art　　MUSEUM
(☑2222-2510; Rue Légitime; admission US$1.40; ◷10am-5pm Mon-Sat, to 4pm Sun) Has a large collection of Haitian naïve art.

Grand Rue artists　　ART COOPERATIVE
(www.atis-rezistans.com; 622 Blvd Jean-Jacques Dessalines) Visit these studios, where scrap and found objects become startling Vodou sculpture – a Caribbean junkyard gone cyber-punk.

🛏 Sleeping

The main choice is heading downtown, or up to Pétionville.

TOP
CHOICE　**St Joseph's Home for Boys**
Guest House　　GUESTHOUSE $
(☑2257-4237/3449-9942; www.sjfamly.org; Delmas 91; shared r per person incl full board US$40; 🖚) Rebuilt with great fortitude after the original house collapsed in the earthquake, this home for ex-street boys still offers a fantastic Haitian experience. The new building will evolve during the life of this guide, but expect either twin rooms or sharing with bunks; buckets for showering and toilet flushing; and great food and company (meals are taken together). The turning for St Joseph's is opposite the old Radio Haiti Inter building at the top of Rte de Delmas.

Doux Sejour Guest House　　HOTEL $$
(☑2257-1533, 2257-1560; www.douxsejourhaiti.com; 32 Rue Magny, Pétionville; s/d from US$65/74; ✳🖚) A fun little guesthouse painted lobster pink, the Doux Sejour has a series of airy rooms interestingly laid out (ascending the balcony terrace feels like climbing into the trees).

Hotel Kinam　　HOTEL $$
(☑2944-6000/2955-6000; www.hotelkinam.com; Pl St-Pierre; s/d from US$92/103; 🅿✳@≋) A large gingerbread hotel right in the center of Pétionville, the Kinam is a good option. Rooms are well sized and modern, while the hotel as a whole offers good quality. In the evening the pool is lit up and guests congregate for the renowned rum punches.

TOP
CHOICE　**Karibe Hôtel**　　HOTEL $$$
(☑2256-9808; www.karibehotel.com; Juvenat 7; s/d from US$130/150, ste from US$230; 🅿✳@ 🖚≋) By some degree the fanciest big hotel in Haiti, this hotel–conference centre is where you'll find the richest businessmen,

On January 12, 2010, Haiti was shaken to its core by a 7.0-magnitude earthquake, its epicenter just outside the southern town of Léogâne, close to the densely crowded capital Port-au-Prince. It took just 35 seconds for the earthquake to do its terrible work, and although the tremors subsided relatively quickly, the social, political and economic aftershocks will be with Haiti for years to come.

Haitians quickly dubbed the earthquake *godou-godou*, named for the sound it made as the buildings collapsed. It's thought that 230,000 people were killed, 2.3 million people initially displaced and over 180,000 buildings damaged or destroyed, including 80% of the schools in the earthquake zone, and over half the hospitals. Nearly a fifth of all federal employees lost their lives. The Palais National was destroyed, along with 27 of the 28 government ministries, the National Assembly, the Supreme Court, Port-au-Prince's two cathedrals and the UN headquarters. Léogâne and Petit-Goâve were leveled, and Jacmel was badly damaged. Striking at the heart of what was already the poorest country in the Americas, *godou-godou* is the largest natural disaster on record.

A Haitian proverb sums up the rebuilding process: *Deye mon gen mon* (beyond the mountains there are more mountains). The mountains of rubble – around 10 million cu meters of it, equivalent to 10 World Trade Center sites – are just the start. By the first anniversary just under 10% of this had been cleared. (The World Trade Center site was cleared in around nine months.) Around 800,000 people were still recorded as living in tents, down from a peak of 1.5 million.

After a year, of the $4.46 billion of international aid pledged for both 2010 and 2011 combined, just 28.7% had been disbursed. Nearly 3000 temporary schools and 32,000 shelters had been built, with much of the progress outside the capital in towns like Léogâne. Major reconstruction had yet to start, however, and further delays were caused by the political limbo following the disputed presidential election in November.

While many in the humanitarian community judged that the immediate disaster-response phase had proceeded relatively well, the road to reconstruction has been more open to criticism. Even before the earthquake, Haiti had more aid organizations per capita than any other nation. With no governmental requirement to register, it's impossible to know how many NGOs operate in the country – the most common number cited is 10,000. (For more on Haitian aid organizations, see p523.)

Media coverage of the earthquake and the difficulties faced during the response effort prompted a healthy debate on the limits of aid in a disaster situation. Certainly, aid is just one strand – the Haitian government has been much criticized for failing to take the lead in directing rebuilding. Yet the scope of the disaster has simply proved overwhelming for many: a destructive force equivalent to that of the 2004 tsunami was unleashed on a densely populated area smaller than the US state of Connecticut. Ultimately, it is only Haitians who can rebuild their country, much as they did after the 13 years of revolutionary war that led to their independence. Recovering from January 12 is a challenge of equal magnitude.

HAITI PORT-AU-PRINCE

international consultants and even ex-presidents putting their bills on expenses. The Karibe Hotel is off Ave Lamartiniere in Juvenat, down the hill from Pétionville.

Coconut Villa Hôtel　　　HOTEL $$$
(☑2510-4901/2246-0234; www.coconutvillahotel.com; 3 Rue Berthold, Delmas 19; s/d US$100/150; P☀🛜☄) Set in large and leafy grounds, the Coconut Villa has quick and easy access to Rte de Delmas. Rooms in the main block are comfy, with the green calm of the surroundings (and the cool blue of the pool) making this a welcome retreat. The hotel is just off Delmas 19, from Rte de Delmas.

Hôtel Oloffson　　　HOTEL $$
(☑2223-4000; ww.hoteloloffson.com; 60 Ave Christophe; s/d from US$85/100; P☀@🛜☄) Immortalized as the Hotel Trianon in Graham Greene's *The Comedians,* this elegant gingerbread building is one of the city's loveliest, further tricked out with paintings and Vodou flags. There's a sociable bar and every Thursday the house band RAM plays up a storm until the small hours. Sadly, the

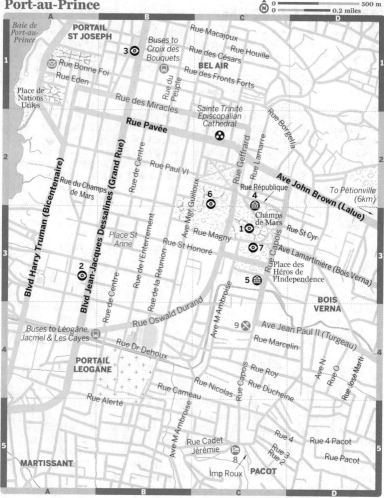

rooms, fixtures and service don't quite live up to the tariff, but it remains a lively scene.

✗ Eating

The sleeping listings all provide good eating options. For quick Creole food, 'bar-restos' are plentiful, although most stop serving food early in the evening.

Arc-en-Ciel CARIBBEAN, FAST FOOD **$**
(24 Rue Capois; mains around US$5; ⊙9am-2am) This is a decent no-frills sort of a place, serving up healthily large portions of Creole standards. Along with platters of *griyo*

(pork), plantain and the like, there's good jerked chicken and a dash of American fast food. Later in the evening, diners compete with dancers as the music and atmosphere crank up a pitch.

Épi d'Or FAST FOOD **$**
(☐2246-8560; Rte de Delmas, Delmas 56; sandwiches around US$2.50; ⊙6am-9pm) Always busy. As well as great sandwiches, it also serves crepes, pizza and 'MacEpi' burgers, and there's an in-house patisserie, all in bright surroundings and with cool air-con. Pay first, then present your ticket to com-

Port-au-Prince

plete the order. Épi d'Or is halfway up Rte de Delmas.

Quartier Latin　　　CONTINENTAL **$$**
(📞3455-3325; 10 Place Boyer, Pétionville; mains US$5-22; ⊙10:30am-11pm) Quartier Latin throws French, Italian and Spanish dishes into the mix, and serves up generous and tasty dishes as a result. There are a few tables outside in the garden, and regular live jazz.

TOP CHOICE **Assiette Creole**　　　CARIBBEAN **$**
(6 Rue Ogé, Pétionville; meals around US$3-4; ⊙noon-9pm, closed Sun) Tremendously popular with local office workers, this place serves up very generous portions of excellent-quality Creole cuisine. You can take away or sit at the tables with umbrellas.

Café Terrasse　　　CONTINENTAL **$$**
(81 Rue Grégoire, Pétionville; sandwiches US$7, mains US$12-24; ⊙11am-11pm; 📶) Formerly located downtown, Café Terrasse is a regular haunt for the NGO and embassy set. Its open layout and art-covered yellow walls give a chilled atmosphere; service is prompt and the food is good.

☆ Entertainment

Many bar-restaurants host live music, and serve booze well after the food runs out. Look out for billboards posted on major junctions advertising forthcoming concerts.

Several bands play regular concerts; they generally start between 11pm and midnight. Foremost is RAM at the **Hôtel Oloffson** (📞2223-4000/02; oloffsonram@aol.com; 60 Ave Christophe) every Thursday. Also worth check-

ing out is **Xtreme** (📞2257-0841; 64 Rue Grégoire, Pétionville) with plenty of *compas* (Haitian merengue), rapkreyol and R&B sounds.

❶ Information

All supermarkets have counters where you can change US dollars cash.

DNS Computer (Rue Capois; per hr US$0.80; ⊙8am-9pm)

Hôpital du Canapé Vert (📞2245-0984/85; 83 Rte de Canapé Vert) Has a 24-hour emergency department; 1.5km east of the center.

Post office (⊙8am-4pm Mon-Sat); Pétionville (Pl St Pierre); Port-au-Prince (Rue Bonne Foi, Bicentenaire)

Scotiabank (cnr Rues Geffrard & Louverture, Pétionville) ATM.

Sogebank Pétionville (Rue Lamarre); Port-au-Prince (Delmas 30) Both branches have ATMs.

❶ Getting There & Around

For more information on international and domestic air travel to and from Port-au-Prince, see p524. A taxi to the airport costs US$20 to US$40.

Buses for southwest Haiti, including Jacmel (US$23, three hours) and Les Cayes (US$8, four hours), depart from the junction of Rue Oswald Durand and Blvd Jean-Jacques Dessalines (Grand Rue). For Cap-Haïtien (US$12, seven hours) and points north, go to Estation O'Cap, at the corner of Grand Rue and Blvd La Saline, 1.5km north of the center.

To get around, taptaps (minibuses) run set routes along the major roads, including Grand Rue, Delmas, Ave John Brown (Lalue) and Canape Vert. The last three all go to Pétionville. Fares are HTG5 (US$0.15). *Publiques* (collective taxis) cost HTG25 (US$0.40).

AROUND PORT-AU-PRINCE

The clamor of Port-au-Prince can tire even the most die-hard traveler after a while – luckily there are several worthwhile sights within striking distance of the capital.

East of Port-Au-Prince

The market town of **Croix des Bouquets** (taptaps US$1, 30 minutes from Carrefour Trois Mains near Port-au-Prince airport) is famous for its iron workers, who hammer out incredible decorative art from flattened oil drums and vehicle bodies. It's great fun to wander around the Noailles districts watching the artisans and looking for souvenirs. There's a complete absence of hard sell.

East of Croix des Bouquets, the main road reaches **Lac Azueï**, Haiti's largest saltwater lake, which supports over 100 species. If you have time, it's worth making a detour to visit **Trou Caïman**, an excellent place for spotting waterfowl.

Kenscoff, above Pétionville, is the entry point for **Parc National La Visite**. A **hike** from here across the western section of Massif de la Selle to Seguin, overlooking the Caribbean, takes six to eight hours and is one of the most spectacular walks in Haiti. Start your trek at Carrefour Badyo, just beyond Kenscoff, and be prepared for sudden rain and chill as well as strong sun. Once you reach Seguin, you can stay at the cozy **Auberge de la Visite** (2246-0166; tiroyd@yahoo.com; r incl full board US$50) before descending to Marigot and catching transport to Jacmel.

North of Port-Au-Prince

Rte Nationale 1 is the main highway to Cap-Haïtien via Gonaïves. It skirts the coast, called the Côte des Arcadins, for most of the first 80km between Cabaret (the former Duvalierville satirized in Greene's *The Comedians*) and St-Marc. It is here that most of the country's beach resorts, packed at weekends, are situated. **Kaliko Beach Club** (3513-7548; www.kalikobeachclub.com; Km 61, Rte National 1; s/d incl full board US$110/150, day passes US$35; P ✳ @ ☎) is an attractive resort and home to dive operator **Pegasus** (3624-9486/9411/4775; nicolemarce_linroy@yahoo.com), which can arrange charters for qualified divers.

If you wish to take public transportation, catch a bus or taptap in Port-au-Prince from Estation O'Cap, beside the Shell gas station at the confluence of Blvd Jean-Jacques Dessalines (Grand Rue) and Blvd La Saline. Return transport is a lot more hit and miss, as you're reliant on flagging down passing buses – don't leave it too late in the afternoon.

SOUTHERN HAITI

Haiti's south is all about taking it easy. Pulling out of Port-au-Prince, the urban hustle is soon replaced by a much more relaxed air and rightly so – you're heading towards the Caribbean Sea.

Jacmel

POP 40,000

Jacmel is a 120km drive southwest of Port-au-Prince, via one of the best roads in the country. A busy coffee port at the turn of the 20th century, it retains much of its late-Victorian grace with wide streets lined by elegant town houses. It's an easy town to be charmed by. Famed as Haiti's handicrafts capital, much of its creativity can be seen in the fantastic papier-mâché masks made for the Carnival festivities.

⊙ Sights & Activities

Close to the seafront, **Rue du Commerce** has numerous fine examples of 19th-century warehouses, although many were damaged in the 2010 earthquake; at the eastern end of the street are the **customs house**, an old 18th-century **prison** and the **wharf**. There are **merchants' mansions** strewn all over town in varying states of decay, including the **Manoir Alexandre**, a rickety old hotel, and **Salubria Gallery**.

East of Pl d'Armes, the town square, is the red-and-green baroque **Marché de Fer**, built in 1895, resembling a scaled-down version of the grand Iron Market in Port-au-Prince. The pretty 19th-century **Cathédrale de St Phillippe et St Jacques** (Rue de l'Eglise) is close to the market.

The closest beach to town is **La Saline**, a 30-minute walk from the center past the cemetery (US$0.40 by moto-taxi), a small cove with crystal-clear water. The best beach is at **Cyvadier Plage**, 10km east of town.

Around 12km inland from Jacmel, reached on horseback or by vehicle, is **Bassins-Bleu**, a spectacular grotto of cascades and cobalt-blue pools (entrance fee US$2.50). Many guides in Jacmel will take you on the journey by horse, which takes about two hours each way. It is advisable to negotiate the full price before you set off to avoid endless squabbling en route. Consider paying about US$20 per person, but you may have to pay more. A broad hat and sunblock are recommended.

🛏 Sleeping & Eating

Hôtel Florita　　　　　　　HOTEL $$
(2288-2805; www.hotelflorita.com; 29 Rue du Commerce; s/d US$80/100; ✳ @) Damaged in the earthquake but rebuilt, this converted mansion from 1888 oozes charm. There are

polished floorboards and period furniture, while rooms are whitewashed and airy, with mosquito net and balcony. The bar is great, and chock-full of art.

Cyvadier Plage Hôtel
HOTEL $$
(☎2288-3323; www.hotelcyvadier.com; Rte de Cyvadier; s US$65-75, d US$82-104, tr US$158; P✳@🏊) Off the main highway, this is the furthest of the beach hotels from the center of Jacmel, but it's one of the best. Rooms in a cluster of buildings face the terrace restaurant and out to the private cove of Cyvadier Plage (nonresidents are welcome). The cheaper rooms have fans rather than air-con.

La Cascade Auberge
GUESTHOUSE $
(☎3695-0453; cascadauberge@yahoo.fr; 63 Ave Barranquilla; r US$40; ✳) This guesthouse is a great deal: the large and spotless rooms have gleaming private bathrooms. Management speaks some English; the only drawback here is that some rooms don't have external windows, making them a bit gloomy.

Guy's Guesthouse
HOTEL $
(☎2288-2569, 2288-9646; Ave de la Liberté; with shared bathroom s US$30-40, d US$50-60, tr US$65) There are invariably a few NGO workers staying at Guy's and it's easy to see why it remains popular. Everything is kept very clean, the rooms are comfy, and the staff is friendly and helpful. Breakfasts are huge, and the restaurant is good for lunch or dinner.

Congo Beach
CARIBBEAN $
(Jacmel beach; mains around US$5; ◷noon-midnight) Right on the beach, this is a collection of two dozen beach shacks, each serving up plenty of beer and cheap food, with accompanying sound systems. Fish, chicken and plantains are all filling staples, with plenty of lime-chilli dressing.

Petit Coin Restaurant
CARIBBEAN $
(☎2288-3067; Rue Bourbon; mains around US$7; ◷noon-11pm) A cozy little restaurant with a hint of French bistro. Three tables on a tiny terrace allow you to catch the last of the day's sun and people-spot before retiring to the interior. The menu is Creole, with a couple of French dishes, all of it tasty.

🛍 Shopping

Jacmel is a souvenir-buyer's paradise. Handicrafts include hand-painted placemats and boxes, wooden flowers, and models of tap-taps, jungle animals and boats. Prices are cheap, starting at a couple of dollars for the smallest items, and the atmosphere is very relaxed. Most of the shops can be found on Rue St-Anne near the old Hôtel la Jacmelienne sur Plage.

ℹ Information

Associations des Micro-Enterprises Touristiques du Sud'Est (AMETS; ☎2288-2840; amets_service@yahoo.fr; 40 Rue d'Orléans; ◷8am-4pm Mon-Fri, to 2pm Sat) It supplies maps of Jacmel, and can arrange car and horse hire.

CC Net (Ave Baranquilla; per hr HTG50; ◷9am-10pm)

Hôpital St Michel (☎2288-2151; Rue St-Philippe) For emergencies, but not brilliant.

Philippe Agent de Change (Ave Baranquilla) Changes euros and Canadian dollars.

Post office (Rue du Commerce; ◷8am-4pm Mon-Sat)

ℹ Getting There & Around

Buses to Port-au-Prince (US$2.70, three hours) leave from the Bassin Caïman station just outside of town. Some taptaps (US$3, 2½ hours) also leave from Marché Geffrard closer to the center. If you want to travel west, get off at Carrefour Duffourt and flag down passing buses; there are no direct buses west from Jacmel.

Les Cayes
POP 46,000

You'd be hard pressed to find a sense of urgency in this old rum port, as it's lulled into torpor by the gentle Caribbean breeze. More popularly known as Aux Cayes, it's sheltered by a series of reefs that have sent many ships to their graves. Though there's little here for visitors, it's the jumping-off point for nearby Île-à-Vache.

The **Concorde Hôtel** (☎2286-0079; Rue Gabions des Indigenes; s/d with fan US$42/46, with air-con US$70/80; P✳@🏊) is the best option, set in large, pleasant gardens. **La Cayenne Restaurant** (☎2286-1114; cnr Rue Geffrard & Mgr Maurice; mains US$6-9; ◷10am-10pm) serves big platters of chicken, *griyo* or *kabrit*, fries, plantains and rice plus fast-food options.

Buses, including to Port-au-Prince (US$8, four hours), leave from near Carrefour des Quatre Chemins. **Transport Chic** (☎3630-2576; 227 Ave des Quatre Chemins) has luxury air-con minibuses running daily to

Port-au-Prince (US$10, four hours). For travel to and from Jacmel, take a bus for Port-au-Prince and change at Léogâne. Taptaps to Port Salut (US$1, 45 minutes) are plentiful.

Île-à-Vache

About 15km off the coast of Les Cayes, Île-à-Vache makes a good tropical getaway, complete with rural houses, mangroves, the odd Arawak burial ground and some great beaches. Its history is tied closely to that of Captain Morgan, the famous buccaneer who was based here for a while.

Two equally excellent upmarket resorts make up the accommodation options: **Abaka Bay Resort** (☑3721-3691; www.abakabay.com; Anse Dufour; s/d incl ful board US$125/200; ✳@) and **Port Morgan** (☑3921-0000; www.port-morgan.com; Cayes Coq; s/d incl full board from US$225/420; P✳@✳). The former has the best beach, the latter the better food (and a two-night minimum stay). Both offer transfers for guests, otherwise boats leave from Les Cayes wharf several times a day (US$2, 30 minutes).

Port Salut

An excellent road leads west from Les Cayes to Port Salut, a one-street town strung for several miles along the coast. The main reason to come here is the beach: miles of palm-fringed white sand with barely a person on it, and the gorgeously warm Caribbean to splash around in.

The series of chalets that is **Hôtel du Village** (☑3779-1728; portsaluthotelduvillage@yahoo.fr; s/d US$75/95; P✳) has airy rooms, although you're not likely to spend much time inside since your front door opens straight onto the beach.

Attractive gingerbread-style rooms are the order of the day at **Dan's Creek** (☑3664-0404; www.danscreekhotel.com; r US$120; P✳@✳), with the beach seconds away. The restaurant-bar is the best in Port Salut.

A decent bar-resto, **Chez Guito** (mains US$4-9; ⊙lunch & dinner), opposite Hôtel du Village, is the place to head for fish, a cold Prestige and a sweet *compas* soundtrack. There are more candy-coloured beach bars 300m further up the road.

There are regular taptaps to Les Cayes (US$1, 45 minutes).

Parc National Macaya & Jérémie

The cloud forest–covered mountains of Parc National Macaya contain rough **trails** through some beautiful terrain. The most challenging trek, taking four days round-trip, is to the top of Pic Macaya.

A good guide based in Camp Perrin is **Jean-Denis Chéry** (☑3766-4331). Tents are necessary, as are food, water-purification paraphernalia and wet-weather gear.

Over the mountains (the road is terrible but spectacular) is the isolated port of Jérémie. It has a sleepy charm about it, and the beaches of Anse d'Azur nearby. The lovely **Tamarin Place Charmant** (☑3722-5222; tamarin_jeremie@hotmail.com; 2 Calasse; r incl half board $US65; P@✳) is more home than guesthouse.

Buses leave every afternoon for Port-au-Prince (US$14, 11 hours). There's also a ferry every Friday, but it's very creaky and often dangerously overloaded. The quickest way out is the heavily subscribed daily **Tortugair** (☑3610-0520) flight to Port-au-Prince (US$95, 35 minutes).

NORTHERN HAITI

If you're interested in how Haiti came to be how it is today, head for the north coast: it all happened here, and there are still many monuments to mark out the path of history.

Cap-Haïtien

POP 150,000

Known simply as 'Cap', Haiti's second city is a laid-back base for exploring the north. Its streets are in a grid, so it's difficult to get lost, and the architecture of high shop fronts and balconies makes it a pleasant place to wander. Under the French this was the richest port in the Caribbean.

◉ Sights

Cap-Haïtien has few sights, although it's fun exploring the streets between the central **Place d'Armes** with the Notre Dame Cathedral, and the busy **Marché de Fer** (Iron Market; ⊙Mon-Sat). There are a few interesting gingerbread houses tucked away on Rues 15 and 16.

If you follow Boulevard north past the suburb of Carenage, you'll come across three

French fort sites. The foundations of **Fort Etienne Magny** are marked by a group of cannon, followed by **Fort St Joseph**, on the edge of the cliff. If you continue north until the road peters out at Plage Rival, then continue along the sand for 500m, you'll reach **Fort Picolet**. The fort is ruined, but some quite large walls and staircases still stand, along with an array of cannon. It's a peaceful place to watch the sunset, although it's a dark walk home.

🛏 Sleeping & Eating

All hotels listed also have good restaurants.

Beau Rivage Hôtel HOTEL **$$**
(☑2262-3113; beaurivage@yahoo.com; 25 Blvd de Mer; s/d US$60/80; P✻🛜) Facing the seafront, the Beau Rivage is a good choice, though it lacks a sign to help find it: look for the big redbrick and cream balustrades next to Kokijaj. If some rooms are a little on the small and boxy side, they're all well appointed with modern fixtures and fittings.

TOP
CHOICE **Hostellerie du Roi Christophe** HOTEL **$$**
(☑2262-0414; Rue 24B; s/d US$86/120; P✻🛜🏊) Cap-Haïtien's most charming hotel, this French colonial building has something of the Spanish hacienda about it. There's an elegant, leafy central courtyard with plenty of rocking chairs, and a terrace restaurant. The rooms are large with plenty of period furniture and art; many have balconies.

Universal Hotel HOTEL **$**
(☑2262-0254; Rue 17B; r US$25-30, with shared bathroom US$20; ✻) Definitely one of the better budget options. A large hotel with several terraces, its rooms are simple and clean. Bible passages remind guests that the meek shall inherit the earth, but less-than-godly guests often check in for just an hour with a 'friend'.

Hôtel Les Jardins de l'Ocean HOTEL **$$**
(☑2262-2277; 90 Carenage; r US$65-95; P🛜✻) This French-run hotel seems to ramble up the side of the hill it sits on, so there's no shortage of terraces offering views to the sea (the rooms themselves have none). Rooms come in a variety of shapes and sizes, all individually decorated to the owner's taste.

TOP
CHOICE **Lakay** CARIBBEAN **$**
(☑2262-1442; Blvd de Mer; mains from US$8; ☺5-10pm) One of the busiest restaurants in Cap-Haïtien, and it's not hard to see why. There are tables facing the seafront where you can enjoy a drink, otherwise you step inside to eat under bamboo thatch and load up on generous plates of Creole food, plus a few pizzas. The atmosphere is lively, and at weekends there are often bands (an admission charge of US$4 applies).

Kokiyaj CARIBBEAN **$$**
(Blvd de Mer; mains US$8-15; ☺10.30am-11pm) A self-styled sports bar above a supermarket sounds unimpressive, but this restaurant is actually a cut above. As well as Creole classics there are some good continental and American mains, good service and a well-stocked bar.

ℹ Information

Streets parallel to the sea are lettered A through Q, while those perpendicular are numbered 1 through 24. The wide avenue running the length of the seafront is simply called Boulevard.

There's a useful cluster of banks along Rue 10-11A. When the banks are closed, you can change money on the street outside the Universal Hotel.

BEACHES NEAR CAP-HAÏTIEN

The road west out of Cap-Haïtien winds through the hills to the northwest of the cape. Here you'll find some of the most beautiful coastal scenery in Haiti, with lush forested hills tumbling into the Atlantic Ocean.

The road hits the north coast of the cape near the lovely beach of **Cormier Plage** and ends on the western edge of **Plage Labadie**, a small walled-off peninsula and the only place in Haiti where cruise ships visit.

Cormier Plage Resort (☑3702-0210; cormier@hughes.net; Rte de Labadie; s/d incl half board US$110/180; P✻@) is one of Haiti's better resorts, with a renowned seafood restaurant. A short boat-taxi hop from Labadie is **Norm's Place** (☑3810-5988, 3780-5680; normsplacelabadee@yahoo.com.com; Labadie; per person US$30; P✻@🏊), a restored fort.

Taptaps from Cap-Haïtien (US$0.60, 30 minutes) travel through Cormier Plage and terminate at Labadie.

Discount Cybercafé (Rue 14H; per hr US$1.15;
⊙8am-9pm)
Hôpital Justinien (☏2262-0512, 2262-0513;
Rue 17Q) Cap-Haïtien's main hospital.
Post office (Rue 16-17A)

ℹ Getting There & Away

For more information on international and
domestic flights to and from Cap-Haïtien, see
p524.

The bus station for destinations south including all points on the way to Port-au-Prince
(US$12, seven hours) is at Barriére Bouteille on
Rue L. If you're heading to Port-au-Prince, leave
early as it's not advisable to arrive in the area
of La Saline, where buses terminate, after dark.
Taptaps to Milot leave from Rue Lapont, those
for Cormier Plage from Rue 21Q.

The Citadelle & Sans Souci

Henri Christophe's twin triumphs, the
Citadelle and Sans Souci (Sans Souci/Sans
Souci & Citadelle US$12.50/25, horse rental US$50;
⊙8am-5pm), are a short taptap ride from
Cap-Haïtien, on the edge of the town of Mi-
lot (US$0.45, one hour).

Built in 1813 as a rival to the splendors
of Versailles in France, Christophe's elegant
palace of Sans Souci has lain abandoned
since an earthquake ruined it in 1842. The
years of neglect have left it partly reclaimed
by the tropical environment, creating a wonderfully bizarre and evocative monument.

From Sans Souci it's a 5km walk to the
Citadelle, situated in the Parc National His-
torique La Citadelle. If you have a vehicle,
you can drive another 3.5km to a parking
area at the fortress's base.

It took Christophe 15 years to build the
World Heritage–listed Citadelle, a vast
mountaintop fortress, constructed to com-
bat another invasion by the French. It is one
of the most inspiring sights in the Caribbean. The astounding structure was completed in 1820, having employed up to 20,000
people, many of whom died during the arduous task. With 4m-thick walls that reach
heights of 40m, the fortress was impenetra-
ble. The views are breathtaking.

The sight of a foreigner invariably attracts
a throng of would-be guides and horse-
wranglers eager for your custom, so be prepared for some hassle.

In Milot, the **Lakou Lakay** (☏2262-5189,
3667-6070; per person US$30, meals US$10) cultural center has accommodation, and wel-

comes lunch guests (call ahead) with drumming, dancing and a huge Creole feast.

UNDERSTAND HAITI

History

Hispaniola's earliest inhabitants arrived
around 2600 BC in huge dugout canoes,
coming from what is now eastern Venezuela.
They were called the Taínos, and by the time
Christopher Columbus landed on the island
in 1492, they numbered some 400,000. However, within 30 years of Columbus' landing,
the Taínos were gone, wiped out by disease
and abuse.

The Spanish neglected their colony of
Santo Domingo, and through the 17th century it became a haven for pirates and, later,
ambitious French colonists. In 1697 the
island was formally divided, and the French
colony of St-Domingue followed soon after.
The French turned St-Domingue over to sugar production on a huge scale. By the end of
the 18th century it was the richest colony in
the world, with 40,000 colonists lording it
over half a million black slaves.

Following the French Revolution in 1789,
free mulattos (offspring of colonists and female slaves) demanded equal rights, while
the slaves themselves launched a huge rebellion. Led by the inspiring slave leader
Toussaint Louverture, the slaves freed themselves by arms and forced France to abolish
slavery.

World's First Black Republic

French treachery dispatched Toussaint to a
prison death, but in May 1803 his general,
Jean-Jacques Dessalines, took the French
tricolor flag, and ripping the white out of
it, declared he was ripping the white man
out of the country. The red and blue were
stitched together with the motto *Liberté ou
la Mort* (Liberty or Death), creating Haiti's
flag.

Dessalines won a decisive victory against
the French at the Battle Vertières, near Cap-
Haïtien, and on January 1, 1804, at Gonaïves,
Dessalines proclaimed independence for
St-Domingue and restored its Taíno name,
Haiti, meaning 'Mountainous Land.'

Dessalines crowned himself Emperor of
Haiti and ratified a new constitution that
granted him absolute power. However,
his tyrannical approach to the throne in-

flamed large sections of society to revolt – his death in an ambush at Pont Rouge in 1806 marked the first of many violent overthrows that would plague Haiti for the next 200 years.

Dessalines' death sparked a civil war between the black north, led by Henri Christophe, and the mulatto south, led by Alexandre Pétion. Christophe crowned himself king, while Pétion became president of the southern republic. It took both their deaths (Christophe by suicide) to reunite the country, which happened in 1820 under new southern leader Jean-Pierre Boyer, who established a tenuous peace.

During his reign Boyer paid a crippling indemnity to France in return for diplomatic recognition. The debt took the rest of the century to pay off and turned Haiti into the first third-world debtor nation. Boyer also sought to unify Hispaniola by invading Santo Domingo. The whole of the island remained under Haitian control until 1849, when the eastern part proclaimed independence as the Dominican Republic.

The next half-century was characterized by continued rivalry between the ruling classes of wealthy mulattos and blacks. Of the 22 heads of state between 1843 and 1915, only one served his full term in office; the others were assassinated or forced into exile.

US Intervention

By the beginning of the 20th century, Haiti's strategic proximity to the new Panama Canal and increased German interests in the country reignited American interest. When Haitian President Vilbrun Guillaume Sam was killed by a mob in 1915, the US sent in the marines, with the stated aim of stabilizing the country.

During its nearly 20-year occupation of the country, the US replaced the Haitian constitution and built up the country's infrastructure by instituting the hated corvée, labor gangs of conscripted peasants. The occupation brought predictable resistance, with the Caco peasant rebellion led by Charlemagne Péralte from 1918 to 1920, in which thousands of Haitians were killed before the assassination of Péralte effectively put an end to the uprising – an episode of Haitian history still bitterly remembered in the country today. The occupation proved costly and the US pulled out in 1934.

The Duvaliers & Aristide

Haiti's string of tyrannical rulers reached its zenith in 1956 with the election of François 'Papa Doc' Duvalier, whose support came from the burgeoning black middle class and the politically isolated rural poor.

Duvalier consolidated his power by creating the notorious Tontons Macoutes. The name refers to a character in a Haitian folk story who carries off small children in his bag at night. The Tontons Macoutes were a private militia who used force with impunity in order to extort cash and crops from a cowed population.

'Papa Doc' died on April 21, 1971, and was succeeded by his son Jean-Claude 'Baby Doc' Duvalier. Periodic bouts of repression continued until major civil unrest forced Baby Doc to flee to France in February 1986.

Control changed hands between junta leaders until finally the Supreme Court ordered elections for December 1990. A young priest named Father Jean-Bertrand Aristide, standing as a surprise last-minute candidate with the slogan 'Lavalas' (Flood), won a landslide victory.

Aristide promised radical reforms to aid the poor, but after just seven months he was pushed out of office. An alliance of rich mulatto families and army generals staged a bloody coup. Despite international condemnation, an embargo against the junta was barely enforced, and thousands of Haitians fled political repression in boats to the USA. Many had seen Aristide as a radical socialist, so when a joint US-UN plan was finally brokered for his return, it was on the condition that he sign up to an economic restructuring plan that eviscerated his original ideas for reform.

Haiti Today

After a period in opposition, Aristide returned as president in 2001. His opponents boycotted the elections and disputed the results, leading to several years of political instability. Things came to a head in early 2004, soon after Haiti marked the 200th anniversary of independence. With violence rife from all sides, an armed revolt forced Aristide back into exile in February 2004. His supporters claim that US agents effectively kidnapped him (a claim the US denies).

The accession of pro-US Gerard Latortue did little to quell the violence, and the devastation of Tropical Storm Jeanne, which killed 3000, did little to improve matters. A UN peacekeeping mission, Minustah, was sent to the island, but it took until 2006 before the country appeared to have turned the corner. On the political front, René Préval returned as president, while a controversial military campaign by Minustah tackled the gang problem head-on, drastically reducing the violence and kidnappings that had become endemic.

Any progress was shattered by the earthquake of January 12, 2010. Rebuilding was hampered by a lethal cholera epidemic eight months later. In March 2011, disputed elections saw Michel Martelly elected as president. He faces a mountain of challenges to bring Haiti back to an even keel.

Culture

Haiti is predominantly made up of peasants who live a subsistence lifestyle in rural areas. Traditionally, the men plant and harvest the crops, while the women care for the children, prepare meals and sell surplus crops at the market.

As the growing population's demands exhaust the land, many peasants have sought a better life in the capital. But the mass rural exodus has created teeming slums such as Cité Soleil. Here much of the countryside's traditional communal spirit is lost in the everyday grind as about 200,000 people occupy 5 sq km of land, mainly reclaimed sea swamp, in some of the harshest conditions imaginable. Despite this move from the land, 80% of the population is still found in the country.

Another life altogether prevails in the cool hills above Port-au-Prince. The country's elite, the 1% of society that has nearly half the wealth, lives in mansions surrounded by high walls in and above Pétionville.

People of African origin make up about 95% of Haiti's population. The other 5% is made up of mulattos, Middle Easterners and people of other races. Members of the mulatto class, which constitutes half of the country's elite and controls most of the economy and political life, are the descendants of African slaves and French plantation owners.

A popular maxim has it that Haiti is 80% Catholic, 20% Protestant, but 100% Vodou. This uniquely Haitian religion, blending many traditional African religions with Catholic elements, permeates the country.

Arts

For its size and population, Haiti has an abundance of artists. Much of Haitian art has been classified as 'naïve' or 'primitive,' partly due to its simple style and avoidance of classical perspective.

The major factor contributing to the singular vision of Haiti's artists is their inextricable link with Vodou. Artists serve the lwa (Vodou spirits) by painting murals to decorate the walls of temples and making elaborate sequined flags for use in ceremonies.

Hector Hyppolite, now considered Haiti's greatest painter, was a Vodou priest. Other great naïves include Rigaud Benoît and Philomé Obin. The murals of Ste Trinité Episcopalian Cathedral in Port-au-Prince best showcase this classic period of Haitian art.

Musical expression in Haiti reflects both the fusion of cultural influences and, more recently, popular resistance and struggle in Haitian politics. Vodou ceremonies have always been accompanied by music, song and dance.

Racines (roots) music grew out of the Vodou jazz movement of the late 1970s, itself a fusion of American jazz with Vodou rhythms and melodies. Two of the best *racines* bands are RAM and Boukman Eksperyans.

Haiti's most important cultural flowering was in response to the 1915–34 US occupation. The Noirisme movement, and its artistic counterpart, Indigénisme, positively embraced Haiti's unique identity and African heritage. The leading Noiriste writers were Jean Price-Mars and Jacques Roumain, author of *Les gouverneurs de la rosée* (Masters of the Dew), considered to be Haiti's finest work of literature. Some of the best current Haitian writers are those of the diaspora, including novelist Edwidge Danticat, author of *Breath, Eyes, Memory* and *The Farming of Bones*.

Haiti's gingerbread houses and mansions are characterized by their graceful balconies, detailed wooden latticework and neo-Gothic designs. Many fine examples can still be seen in Port-au-Prince and Jacmel.

Landscape & Wildlife
The Land

Haiti occupies the mountainous western third of Hispaniola, sharing a 388km border with the DR. About the size of the US state of Maryland, the country is cut by hundreds of rivers and streams, many of which bring torrential flood waters and eroded soil during the hurricane season. Rising above these river valleys are four mountain chains; Haiti's tallest mountain is 2674m Pic La Selle, located in the southeast of the country. Haiti's largest drainage system, the Artibonite river, extends 400km through the center of the country. The river was dammed in its upper reaches in 1956, forming the Lac de Péligre behind Haiti's major hydroelectric facility. Its delta, south of Gonaïves, is a key rice-producing area.

Wildlife

Haiti is rich in birdlife, with 220 species, including the palmchat and the La Selle thrush. The gray-crowned palm tanager is a species unique to Haiti. Waterbirds include American flamingos and the black-capped petrel, a seabird that nests in the high cliffs of Massif de la Selle and the Massif de la Hotte.

Despite major habitat destruction, some endemic animals remain, including a small population of manatees in the coastal waters. Of the four types of sea turtle here, the largest is the leatherback, which can weigh up to 600kg. Reptiles include iguanas and American crocodiles, which can be seen at Étang Saumâtre.

Environmental Issues

Haiti is a popular university case study in environmental degradation and disaster, its situation perhaps equaled only by Madagascar and the more devastated parts of the Amazon rainforest. Unchecked clearing of the land for food production and fuel wood has depleted massive tracts of broadleaf forest. Only a small portion of virgin forest survives, including on the Massif de la Selle and the cloud forests of Massif de le Hotte.

The destruction of the forests for firewood and farmland has caused an untenable amount of soil erosion, as well as trapping Haiti's peasants in a cycle of subsistence farming with ever-diminishing returns. The bare hillsides can prove lethal during hurricane season, when rainfall easily causes terrible mudslides and floods. Neighboring DR, with its intact forest cover, comes out of the same storm systems in much better shape.

Directory A–Z

Accommodations

Accommodations aren't fantastic value in Haiti. There are few budget hotels aimed at foreigners, and those at the cheapest end frequently double as brothels. A decent budget hotel weighs in at around US$40; a midrange hotel should cost about US$70, for which you should get hot water, air-con and a decent electricity supply. Room standards can be highly variable. Port-au-Prince has the best choice, from good international standard hotels to cheap Christian-run guesthouses that can be excellent value.

Many hotels add a US$5 to US$10 electricity surcharge, included in the prices listed here. Midrange and top-end rates also include the 10% government tax added to the bill.

$	budget	less than US$40
$$	midrange	US$40 to US$80
$$$	top end	more than US$80

Activities

While not as developed as in other parts of the Caribbean, Haiti still has some great opportunities for snorkeling and scuba diving. The Côte des Arcadins has the best sites, including Amani, near St-Marc, where a wall descends to the home of the Elephant's Ear, believed to be the world's largest sea sponge. On the north coast, sites near the beach resort of Cormier Plage also offer rich diving possibilities.

Haiti's mountainous terrain lends itself well to hiking. A short drive from Port-au-Prince, the Parc National La Visite offers good hiking country, with superb views and cool pine forests to explore, along with many high-altitude bird species. Birders will also be amply rewarded by a visit to Trou Caïman, and the wild Parc National Macaya.

Business Hours

Banks 8:30am-1pm Mon-Fri, larger branches plus 2-5pm Mon-Fri

Offices 7am-4pm Mon-Fri, close earlier Fri

Restaurants 8am-9pm Mon-Sat

Shops 7am-4pm Mon-Sat, close earlier Fri

PRACTICALITIES

» **Electricity** Haiti uses the same electrical system as the USA and Canada (110V to 125V AC, 60Hz, flat-pronged plugs). Power cuts are ubiquitous, along with the sound of generators.

» **Newspapers** *Le Matin, Le Nouvelliste, Haiti Progrés* (has an English section), *Haiti en Marche* and *Libète* (Creole). International press available in Port-au-Prince.

» **Radio & TV** Stations include Radio One (90.1FM), Radio Soleil (107.5FM), Radio Lumiere 97.9FM, Radio Ibo (98.5FM). French and US TV available on satellite/cable.

» **Weights & Measures** Metric system used, although gasoline is sold in gallons.

Dangers & Annoyances

Haiti has rarely enjoyed a good media image abroad. Poverty and regular political turmoil play their part, and many governments currently advise against travel to the country.

The presence of UN soldiers has done much to bring stability, especially in dealing with the gang and kidnapping problems. But always keep your ear to the ground for current developments before traveling – trouble generally occurs around elections, although it's incredibly rare for foreigners to get caught up in it. Avoid demonstrations, and if you come across one, turn in the opposite direction.

A weak state and high poverty levels can foster street crime. Take advantage of hotel safes and don't carry anything you're not willing to lose (or money in your back pocket).

For all this, the main annoyance travelers are likely to face are the poor electricity supply and crazy traffic. Beggars can be persistent in some places, and at tourist spots such as the Citadelle expect persistent attention from faux guides. Try to discourage them before you set off – their only function seems to be to tell you how much tip you're going to have to pay at the end – as it's very hard to not pay them after they've run up a mountain alongside you.

Finally, while taking care to be sensible, it's important not to get too hung up on Haiti's bad name. Many travelers fear the worst and avoid the country; those who do make it here are more likely to come away with positive impressions rather than horror stories.

Embassies & Consulates

All of the embassies and consulates listed following are in Port-au-Prince or Pétionville. Australia, New Zealand and Ireland do not have diplomatic representation in Haiti.

Brazil (☑2256-7556; ppinto@mr.gov.br; 168 Rue Darguin, Pl Boyer, Pétionville)

Canada (☑2249-9000; www.port-au-prince.gc.ca; btwn Delmas 71-75, Rte de Delmas, Port-au-Prince)

Cuba (☑2256-3811; ecuhaiti@hainet.net; 3 Rue Marion, Pétionville)

Dominican Republic (☑2257-9215; embrep domhai@yahoo.com; 121 Ave Pan Américaine, Pétionville)

France (☑2222-0951; www.ambfrance.ht; 51 Rue Capois, Port-au-Prince)

Germany (☑2257-6131; fax 2257-4131; 2 Impasse Claudinette, Bois Moquette, Pétionville)

Mexico (☑2257-8100; embmxhai@yahoo.com; 2 Musseau, Delmas 60, Port-au-Prince)

UK (☑3744-6371; florence.boucard-hon@fconet. fco.gov.uk; 367 Rte de Delmas, Face ERF, Port-au-Prince) Honorary consulate only.

USA (☑2229-8000; http://haiti.usembassy.gov; 41 Rte de Tabarre, Tabarre, Port-au-Prince)

Venezuela (☑2222-0971; embavenzhaiti@ hainet; 2 Blvd Harry Truman, Port-au-Prince)

Food

Price ranges given for eateries in this chapter are based on the cost of a main course.

$	budget	less than US$7
$$	midrange	US$7 to $US20
$$$	top end	more than US$20

Gay & Lesbian Travelers

Haiti isn't as homophobic as some other places in the Caribbean. There are no dedicated gay venues, however; these were clamped down on in the 1980s following negative publicity about HIV/AIDS in Haiti. While you may commonly see friends of the same sex holding hands and being openly affectionate with each other throughout the country, any tourists doing this will attract attention. Same-sex couples sharing a room should have no problem, although some discretion, especially in the more religious establishments, is advisable.

Health

Port-au-Prince has the best medical facilities and a few international-standard hospitals. There are decent pharmacies across the country. A foreign-aid program means that there are many Cuban doctors in Haiti, along with the many medics around Port-au-Prince working in the aftermath of the earthquake.

Tap water is not safe to drink; lack of access to safe water is a major contributor to the spread of post-earthquake cholera. Treated drinking water is automatically provided by every hotel and restaurant. Pay particular attention to hand-washing and related matters of personal hygiene; hand sanitizer is worth bringing.

A trip to Haiti carries a small but real risk of malaria: take action to avoid being bitten by mosquitos and check with your medical practitioner before traveling for advice about prophylaxis.

Internet Access

Getting online isn't a problem, and internet cafes open and close with reckless abandon. Prices are around US$1.25 per hour. If you're bringing a laptop, top-end (and many midrange) hotels provide wi-fi access.

Money

The official currency is the gourde, and there are 100 centimes to one gourde. US dollars are also widely accepted for large purchases. The gourde used to be tied to the US dollar at a rate of one to five, with the result that HTG5 is universally known as one Haitian dollar. When buying something, always check whether people are quoting the price in gourdes or Haitian dollars.

Don't bother bringing traveler's checks as they're near impossible to change. There are ATMs in Port-au-Prince, but they can be unreliable (those in Pétionville tend to be better), so always make sure you have some US dollars as backup. Large businesses, and most midrange and all top-end hotels will accept credit cards.

TIPPING

Tipping is discretionary, but 10% to 15% in restaurants is usually fine.

Public Holidays

In addition to the holidays observed throughout the region (p872), Haiti has the following public holidays:

Independence Day January 1

Ancestors' Day January 2

Carnival January/February (three days before Ash Wednesday)

Agriculture and Labor Day May 1

Flag and University Day May 18

Anniversary of Jean-Jacques Dessalines' Death October 17

Anniversary of Toussaint Louverture's Death November 1

Anniversary of the Battle of Vertières November 18

Telephone

Landlines in Haiti can be very unreliable, and everyone uses cell (mobile) phones; a GSM SIM card for networks like Digicel and Voila will cost around US$20. You can make calls from Teleco offices, or the ubiquitous phone 'stands' – usually a youth on the street with a cell phone that looks like a regular desk phone.

Volunteering

The following aid groups have demonstrated they are in Haiti for the long haul; all welcome support from individuals interested in volunteering.

Fonkoze (www.fonkoze.org) A microcredit organization spread across the country, working in economic empowerment.

Lambi Fund (www.lambifund.org) A grassroots civil society NGO, working on sustainable development, environment and civic-empowerment programs in rural areas.

Gheskio (www.gheskio.org) A Haitian HIV/AIDS NGO, working since 1982 and providing free health care for HIV patients.

Partners In Health (www.pih.org) Set up by Dr Paul Farmer, providing health care across rural Haiti.

Konbit Pou Ayiti/KONPAY (www.konpay.org) Coalition of grassroots peasant groups, primarily with an environmental focus.

Fondam Haiti (www.fondam-haiti.org) Working on reforestation in the southwest.

Getting There & Away

All foreign visitors must have a valid passport to enter Haiti. Be sure you have room for both entry and exit stamps, and retain the green entry card you're given on arrival, as you must give this up on departure.

Air

Haiti has just two international airports.

Aéroport International Toussaint Louverture (☑2250-1120) The main international airport, in Port-au-Prince.

Aéroport International Cap-Haïtien (☑2262-8539) Limited international flights but scheduled for expansion.

International carriers with services to Haiti:

Aerocaribbean (www.cubajet.com) Flights from Havana, Santiago, Punta Cana (DR) and Port-au-Prince.

Air Canada (www.aircanada.com) Direct flights from Montreal.

Air France (www.airfrance.com) Flights from Paris via Pointe-á-Pitre, Guadeloupe or Miami.

Air Santo Domingo (http://airsantodomingo.com.do)

Air Turks & Caicos (www.airturksandcaicos.com)

American Airlines (www.aa.com) Direct flights from Miami, Fort Lauderdale and New York.

IBC Travel (www.ibcairways.com) Scheduled and charter flights from Cap-Haïtien to Miami and Fort Lauderdale.

Insel Air (www.fly-inselair.com) Flights to Curaçao, St-Martin/Sint Maarten and Miami.

Lynx Air (www.lynxair.com)

Spirit Airlines (www.spiritair.com)

Tortug'Air (www.tortugair.com) Flights to Santo Domingo, Nassau and Providenciales.

Land

There are four points where you can cross from Haiti into the Dominican Republic. The busiest, near Malpasse/Jimaní is on the road linking Port-au-Prince and Santo Domingo. Also in the south is the quieter crossing from Ainse-a-Pietre to Pedernales. In the north, the crossing at Ouanaminthe/Dajabón is on the road connecting Cap-Haïtien and Santiago. A less-used border is at Belladère/Elías Piña. These crossings close at 7pm.

There are coaches to Santo Domingo (DR): **Caribe Tours** (☑2257-9379; cnr Rues Clerveaux & Gabart, Pétionville), **Terra Bus** (☑2257-2153; Ave Pan Américaine, Pétionville) and **Capital Coach Line** (☑2512-5989; www.capitalcoachline.com; 8 Rue Borno, Pétionville). All have daily departures at around 8am, arriving in Santo Domingo nine hours later, with tickets costing around US$40 plus border taxes. **CaribeTours** (☑3444-5585; Rue 29A) runs a coach service from Cap-Haïtien to Santiago (DR) twice weekly.

Getting Around

Air

Haiti's small size means that flights are short (no flight is longer than 40 minutes), saving hours on bad roads. One-way tickets usually cost around US$100.

Domestic flights operate from **Aérogare Guy Malary** (☑2250-1127), near the international terminal. The following airlines have their offices there:

Salsa d'Haiti (www.flysalsa.com) Four daily flights to Cap-Haïtien.

Tortug'Air (www.tortugair.com) Twice-daily flights to Cap-Haïtien, daily to Jérémie and Port-de-Paix.

Missionary Flights International (www.missionaryflights.org) Flights to all major cities, plus many smaller towns with airstrips. Flights are for affiliated organizations only, although this is often flexibly interpreted on the ground.

Boat

There are quite a few islands and remote areas around Haiti accessible only by ferry. Routes include Port-au-Prince to Jérémie and Côte des Arcadins to Île de la Gonâve. Boats are rarely comfortable and often dangerously overcrowded. In some areas, such as Labidie and Île-à-Vache, small boats operate as water taxis. Fix the price before you board, as the owner may try to charge for the whole boat.

Bus & Taptap

Haiti's buses are big and seemingly indestructible affairs, and they need to be. They're cheap too – even the longest 12-hour trip gives change from US$15. There are no timetables; buses leave when full. A taptap is more likely to be a minibus or pickup truck, used for travel within cities, or hopping between towns. Bus and taptap stations are sprawling conglomerations of vehicles, people and market stalls: Haiti in microcosm.

Car & Motorcycle

Driving in Haiti is an adventure sport. Roads can be terrible, traffic signs are rare, and 'might is right' is the main rule. You'll need an International Driving Permit or a current license from your home country.

There are rental companies in Port-au-Prince, mostly near the airport. Fees are around US$70 per day for a saloon, and US$150 per day for a 4WD, the latter being better able to cope with the road conditions.

Taxi

Port-au-Prince and Cap-Haïtien have collective taxis called *publiques,* which run along set routes and charge around HTG25 (US$0.75) per trip. You can spot them by the red ribbon on the mirror – if the driver takes it off he's treating you as a private commission, and you'll have to negotiate the fee.

There are moto-taxis (motorcycle taxis) everywhere, with a trip rarely costing more than about HTG30 (US$0.70).

Tours

Haiti has three local tour operators, all offering excellent packages and services. These are a good option if you don't want to strike out on your own.

DOA/BN (☎3510-2223; www.haititravels.org)

Tour Haiti (☎2510-2223, 3711-1650; info@tourhaiti.net, www.tourhaiti.net; 31 Rue Casseus, Pacot, Port-au-Prince)

Voyages Lumière (☎3607-1321, 3557-0753; voyageslumierehaiti@gmail.com; www.voyageslumiere.com)

Jamaica

Best Beaches

» Frenchman's Beach (p554)

» Long Bay, Portland (p538)

» Doctor's Cave (p545)

» Long Bay, Negril (p551)

» Frenchman's Cove (p537)

Best Places to Stay

» Nuestra Casa Guest House (p554)

» Kanopi House (p538)

» Time N' Place (p551)

» Idler's Rest (p556)

» Blue House (p540)

Why Go?

Jamaica, at first blush, is the Caribbean island many know best thanks to its relentless exposure – is there a soul who's never listened to Bob Marley? – and dreadlocks, dancehall and beaches.

But did you know there are Chinese Jamaicans and Jewish Jamaicans and white Jamaicans who speak patois as fluently as downtown Kingston yardies? Jamaica, perhaps more than any other Caribbean nation, also keeps one foot (and much of its cultural heart) rooted in Africa.

Understand the above and you can better appreciate the good, red Jamaican soil; the respect Jamaicans have for life and nature; and the meaning 'One Love' has in a place like the Kingston ghettoes. To know Jamaica, experience it. As locals say, 'Rock-stone a river naah know sun hot'. That's patois for 'experience brings knowledge,' and so much more so on an island that can express such simple proverbs so beautifully.

When to Go

Jamaica has a pleasant tropical climate year-round – 26°C (79°F) to 30°C (86°F) – but there are definite dry and wet seasons. From December to April-ish, you can expect sun and clear skies. From June to September, there are frequent short bursts of heavy rain, but far fewer crowds. The exceptions are the northeast, like Port Antonio, where it's rainy year-round; and the southwest coast, where it's almost always dry. The island is crazy crowded during Christmas and the weeks surrounding it, as well as during the US Spring Break (late March to early April).

Itineraries

THREE DAYS

Hit the sand in Montego Bay for a day, then take a raft trip down the Martha Brae, a swim in the Glistening Waters and a walk around historic Falmouth.

ONE WEEK

Head straight to Treasure Beach and explore around the South Coast in areas like Black River and YS Falls, interspersed with relaxing on the beach.

TWO WEEKS

After the one-week itinerary, head to Portland parish for some rafting on the Rio Grande and surfing in Boston Bay.

THREE WEEKS

Follow the two-week itinerary, then visit cosmopolitan Kingston (the heartbeat of Jamaica), followed by a jaunt into the high Blue Mountains.

GETTING TO NEIGHBORING ISLANDS

There is no ferry service to other islands from Jamaica. Montego Bay and Kingston have international airports and daily flights to Nassau, Grand Cayman, Antigua, Puerto Rico, Trinidad, Guadeloupe, Grenada, Haiti and other islands. Flights are usually a little more expensive from Kingston, but check online, as deals are occasionally offered.

Essential Food & Drink

» **Jerk** Jamaica's most well-known dish, jerk is actually a cooking method: smother food in a tongue-searing marinade, then smoke over a wood fire.

» **Seafood** Snapper and parrotfish are popular. A favorite dish is escoveitched fish – pickled in vinegar then fried and simmered with peppers and onions.

» **Breadkinds** A catchall term for starchy sides, from plantains and yam to pancake-shaped cassava bread (bammy) and johnnycakes (fried dumplings).

» **Saltfish & Ackee** Jamaica's national dish, and a delicious breakfast besides. Ackee is a fleshy, somewhat bland fruit; saltfish is, well, salted fish. When mixed together they're delicious, somewhat resembling scrambled eggs.

» **Brown stew** Not a soup, brown stew is another popular method of cooking that involves simmering meat, fish or vegetables in savory-sweet sauce.

» **Patties** Baked shells filled with spicy beef, vegetables and whatever else folks desire. Cheap and filling.

» **Rum** Clear and light white rums, flavored rums, brain-bashing overproof rums (rum over 151 proof), deep dark rums, and the rare amber nectar of the finest premium rums.

AT A GLANCE

» **Currency** Jamaican dollar (J$); US dollars (US$) widely accepted

» **Language** English, patois

» **Money** ATMs in Montego Bay, Kingston, Mandeville and Port Antonio; some in Negril; thin on the ground elsewhere

» **Visas** See p564

Fast Facts

» **Area** 11,391 sq km

» **Population** 2.7 million

» **Capital** Kingston

» **Telephone country code** ☎876

» **Emergency** Ambulance/fire/police ☎011/110/119

Set Your Budget

» **Budget hotel room** US$75

» **Two-course evening meal** J$800 (local places), US$25 (tourist places)

» **Museum entrance** J$500

» **Beer** J$250

» **City transport ticket** J$80

Resources

» **Dancehall Reggae** (www.dancehallreggae.com) The latest on the music scene

» **Jamaica Gleaner** (www.jamaica-gleaner.com) Reliable newspaper

» **Visit Jamaica** (www.visitjamaica.com) The tourist board's attractions and lodging information

Jamaica Highlights

1 Find relaxation and community-tourism sensibility in **Treasure Beach** (p554)

2 Experience jerk at its most delicious and original in **Boston Bay** (p538)

3 See sunrise over **Blue Mountain Peak** (p535)

4 Delve into the life of Bob Marley at **Nine Mile** (p543)

5 Head to Jamaica's world-class midsummer festival,

Red Stripe Reggae Sumfest (p546), and dance all night

6 Travel by boat deep into river country teeming with crocodiles on the **Great Morass** (p556)

7 Take a plunge down the chutes at **Reach Falls** (p538)

8 Feel like you're swimming among the stars at **Glistening Waters** (p551)

9 Join the festivities and dance until your hips freeze up at Kingston's **Carnival** (p531)

10 Wander the historic streets of **Falmouth** (p550)

KINGSTON

POP 780,000

Jamaica's one true city, Kingston is something of an island within the island. It is Jamaica undiluted and unadulterated, its brisk business pace and chaotic traffic contrasting sharply with the timeless languor of resorts and villages elsewhere on the island. Justly proud for having been the launching pad for some of the world's most electrifying music, the city by no means trades on its past reputation; its spirited clubs and riotous street-system parties attest to the fact that the beat is still alive and bumping. The capital's cosmopolitan makeup has given rise to fine international dining but its dynamic galleries and museums remain unapologetically Jamaican.

Whether you approach it by air or by land, Kingston impresses you with its setting and overwhelms you with its sheer size, noise and traffic. This is the island's cultural and economic heart, where political deals are made, musicians come to follow in the footsteps of the greats, and you can be exposed to miserable squalor and great luxury within footsteps of each other.

You wanted 'real' Jamaica? This is it.

◉ Sights

DOWNTOWN
Parade SQUARE
William Grant Park, more commonly known as Parade, is the heart of downtown. Originally dubbed Victoria Park, the area was renamed in 1977 to honor Black Nationalist and labor leader Sir William Grant (1894–1977), who preached his Garveyite message of African redemption here. At the centre of the park is a whimsical four-tiered fountain.

At North Parade, the distinguished **Ward Theatre** (Map p530) is undergoing renovation; tours of its interior are expected once it is restored. For now, you can admire the cracked, sky-blue facade with white trim. The gleaming white edifice facing the park's southeast corner is **Kingston Parish Church** (Map p530), today serving a much-reduced congregation of true Kingstonians – those 'born under the clock' (within earshot of its bell). Marble plaques commemorate soldiers of the West Indian regiments who died of fever or other hardships during colonial wars.

South Parade, packed with street vendors' stalls, is known as 'Ben Dung Plaza' because passersby have to bend down to buy from hawkers whose goods are displayed on the ground. The place is clamorous, and stores blast reggae music loud enough to drive away even the most determined visitor (locals seem inured).

TOP CHOICE **National Gallery of Jamaica** ART GALLERY
(Map p530; www.natgalja.org.jm; 12 Ocean Blvd; admission J$250; ☺10am-4:30pm Tue-Thu, to 4pm Fri, to 3pm Sat) The superlative collection of Jamaican art housed by the National Gallery is the finest on the island. The core of the permanent collection is presented on the 1st floor in 10 galleries representing the Jamaican School, while temporary exhibitions focus on the African diaspora and contemporary art. **Guided tours** (☏reservations 922-1561; 45min tour J$1800) are available; advance reservations suggested.

Institute of Jamaica MUSEUM
(Map p530; ☏922-0620; www.instituteofjamaica.org.jm; 10-16 East St; adult/child J$200/100; ☺9:30am-4:30pm Mon-Thu, to 3:30pm Fri) Toward the south end of East St, the Institute of Jamaica is the nation's small-scale equivalent of the British Museum or Smithsonian. The upstairs area hosts excellent temporary historical exhibitions like 'Jamaican Servicemen During World War II'. The central building features the **National Library** (www.nlj.gov.jm), which incorporates the Caribbean's largest repository of books, maps, charts, paintings and documents on West Indian history. The small but informative **Museum of Music** on the top floor traces the history and development of Jamaica's music, from kumina, mento and ska to reggae and dancehall.

Trench Town Culture Yard & Around COMMUNITY PROJECT
Widely credited as the birthplace of ska, rocksteady and reggae music, this neighborhood has been immortalized in the gritty narratives of numerous reggae songs, including Bob Marley's *No Woman No Cry*, penned in a tiny bedroom of what is now the **Trench Town Museum** (☏572-4085; 6-10 Lower First St; entrance to the yard & museum J$1000, with a guided neighborhood tour J$1500; ☺8am-6pm).

Also on site is the **Trench Town Development Association** (TTDA; ☏757-6739,

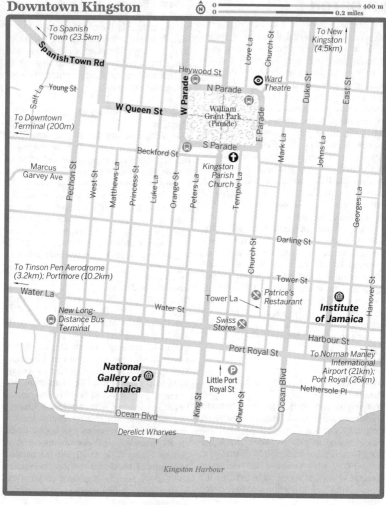

922-8462), responsible for transforming Bob Marley's former home into a community-based heritage site. The **Culture Yard**, which features a large mural of Marley, is one block off Marcus Garvey Dr. It is safe to visit, but don't go wandering elsewhere on your own. To visit, contact the TTDA.

Another successful community project is the nearby **Trench Town Reading Centre** (www.trenchtownreadingcentre.com; First St), established in 1994 in an effort to arm the neighborhood youth with knowledge rather than guns. Book donations are very welcome; see the website for suggestions.

UPTOWN

TOP CHOICE **Bob Marley Museum**   MUSEUM
(off Map p531; www.bobmarley-foundation.com/museum.html; 56 Hope Rd; adult/child J$1000/500; 9:30am-4pm Mon-Sat) For many, Jamaica means reggae, and reggae means Bob Marley. The large, creaky colonial-era wooden house, where Marley lived and recorded from 1975 until his death in 1981, is the city's most-visited site.

The house is shielded by a wall painted in Rasta colors and adorned with photos and Rastafarian murals, including those of his seven sons (though not his daughters). Marley's

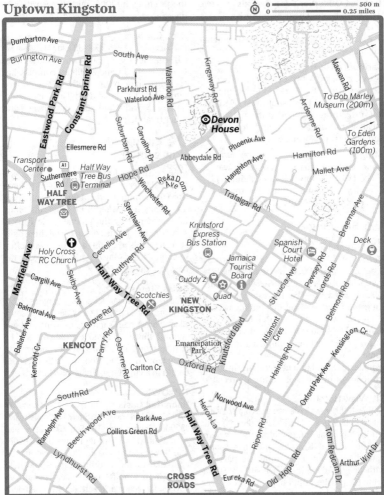

0   500 m
0   0.25 miles

gold and platinum records (*Exodus,* 1977; *Uprising,* 1980; and *Legend,* 1984) are on the walls, alongside Rastafarian religious cloaks.

Devon House   MUSEUM

(Map p531; 929-6602; www.devonhousejamaica. com; 26 Hope Rd; admission J$700; 9am-4:30pm Tue-Sat) This restored colonial home nestles in landscaped grounds on the northwest side of Hope Rd, at its junction with Waterloo Rd. A beautiful ochre-and-white house, it was built in 1881 by George Stiebel, a Jamaican wheelwright who rose to become the first black millionaire in Jamaica. The tree-shaded lawns attract Kingstonians who come here to canoodle and read.

🎊 Festivals & Events

Carnival   PARTY

(www.jamaicacarnival.com, www.bacchanaljamaica .com) Kingston's week-long Easter Carnival brings costumed revelers into the streets in droves. There's reggae and calypso, of course, but soca is king. Carnival climaxes in an enormous parade, when seemingly all of Kingston emerges in brilliantly colored costumes for a day-long throw-down.

Jamaica Observer Food Awards FOOD
'The Caribbean's Oscar Night of Food', with numerous booths presenting the best of the island's food offerings. Held in late July at Devon House.

Caribbean Heritagefest CULTURE
(www.jcdc.gov.jm) A two-day event in mid-October at the Jamworld Entertainment Complex at Portmore, southwest of Kingston. It features food and craft fairs, folk theatre, traditional dance and drumming, and musical performances.

Sting DANCEHALL
(www.stingjamaica.com.jm) New Year's Eve concert at the Jamworld Entertainment Complex in Portmore, featuring the best dancehall artists. Gritty atmosphere.

🛏 Sleeping

TOP CHOICE Spanish Court Hotel BOUTIQUE HOTEL $$$
(Map p531; ☑926-0000; www.spanishcourthotel.com; 1 St Lucia Ave; r US$189-289, ste US$379-1499; P❋@🐾🖂) The newest addition to Kingston's high-end set has rapidly become a favorite with discerning business elite. Thoroughly modern rooms, decorated in warm tones, exude minimalist chic and come equipped with plasma-screen TVs and iPod docks. Small touches, such as the single fresh flower by the bedside, are appreciated.

City View Hotel BOUTIQUE HOTEL $
(☑969-4009; www.cityviewjamaica.com; Mannings Hill Rd; r J$2781, ste J$3217-3894; P❋🛜) This family-run spot offers an incredible panoramic view of Kingston plus five rooms, named after Jamaica's different parishes, with delightful antique furnishings. St Andrew, the plushest option, particularly popular with newlyweds, boasts a Jacuzzi. The genial hosts treat guests like family and the staff are always on hand to let you in after a 3am clubbing session, or to help you plan a local excursion.

Mikuzi Guest House GUESTHOUSE $$
(☑978-4859, 813-0098; www.mikuzijamaica.com; 5 Upper Montrose Rd; r/ste J$7819/11,851; P❋🛜) Friendly, yellow, colonial-era guesthouse with comfortable rooms – all bright colors and funky furnishings, most with kitchenettes. All but the 'backpacker rooms' (J$3386) have air-con. There's a cushion-strewn gazebo in the lush garden for relaxing in. There was an armed robbery on the premises in 2009, putting security into question.

Eden Gardens HOTEL $$
(off Map p531; ☑946-9981; 39 Lady Musgrave Rd; r US$140; P❋🐾🖂) Set amid lush vegetation, this condo and wellness complex has spacious, light rooms with fully equipped kitchenette and large desk. The Therapeutic Spa comes with a full range of massages and other treatments.

🍴 Eating

DOWNTOWN

TOP CHOICE Patrice's Restaurant JAMAICAN $
(Map p530; Temple Lane; meals J$400; ☉lunch Mon-Fri) An unmarked hole-in-the-wall down an equally unmarked little lane, this dimly lit eatery, run by the indefatigable Patrice, serves superb home cooking. The three daily specials, chalked up on the little board, often include Patrice's stew pork, supposedly the best in Jamaica.

Swiss Stores CAFE $
(Map p530; cnr Church & Harbour Sts; meals J$450; ☉lunch) Jerk sausage, hearty pepperpot soup, Black Forest ham sandwiches, wine and air-conditioning – what more could you ask of a jewelry store! The stools aren't conducive to sitting, but the Blue Mountain coffee (J$125) comes in a cup the size of a soup tureen.

UPTOWN

Boon Hall Oasis JAMAICAN $$
(☑942-3064; 4 River Rd, Stony Hill; buffet lunch J$2000; ☉noon-5pm Thu-Sat, 10am-3pm Sun) A footpath leads through curtains of vines and flowers to this oasis. Take a seat among churchgoers and wedding parties and help yourself to a buffet of mackerel rundown, curry goat, ackee and saltfish, stew fish, jerk chicken and other Jamaican favorites.

Guilt Trip FUSION $$
(☑977-5130; 20 Barbican Rd; meals J$1600-2500; ☉dinner) The name alludes to imaginative, decadent desserts, such as white chocolate Guinness madness. That's not all: the chef constantly experiments with Caribbean-French fusion cuisine, producing concoctions like coconut curry sea bass with mango and chestnut salsa. Dress up.

Red Bones Blues Cafe FUSION $$$
(☑978-8262; 1 Argyle Rd; mains J$1693-3386; ☉noon-1am Mon-Fri, from 6pm Sat) This former colonial house has long been a beehive of cultural and culinary activity. Stellar dishes

include callaloo strudel, smoked marlin salad, and the pasta with seafood trio of shrimp, mussels and salmon sautéed in a spicy coconut sauce. In the evenings call ahead to snag a table overlooking the garden stage – they're in high demand.

Drinking & Entertainment

The Deck
BAR

(Map p531; 14 Trafalgar Rd; ⊙4:30pm-last customer leaves) This cavernous open-air bar, festooned with fishing nets, is a long-standing favorite with the older crowd for its easygoing atmosphere and good bar food. On Friday things get particularly lively during the ever-popular oldies After-Work Jam.

Cuddy'z
SPORTS BAR

(Map p531; 25 Dominica Dr) Perhaps the best sports bar in Jamaica, this hip establishment is the creation of the 'Big Man Inna Cricket,' Courtney Walsh. TVs in each booth and a lively bleachers section with an oversized screen make it a great place to catch the latest football, cricket and baseball games.

Quad
MUSIC MIX

(Map p531; 20-22 Trinidad Tce; admission US$15) You can easily spend all night moving between four different levels of this upmarket superclub. There's a tasteful jazz bar on the main floor, and every Wednesday, Friday and Saturday two clubs open up: the top-floor Voodoo Lounge, which draws a more urbane crowd with an oldies mix; and below that, Oxygen, which attracts a 20-something set ready to sweat to rocking dance beats until 4am.

ⓘ Information

DANGERS & ANNOYANCES Avoid Kingston during periods of political tension, when localized violence can spontaneously erupt. Most murders are drug-related or politically inspired and occur in the shantytowns of West Kingston. Parts of Spanish Town are heavily affected by gang violence. Beware of pickpocketing, especially at the market. Stick to the main streets – if in doubt ask your hotel concierge or manager to point out the trouble areas.

EMERGENCY Police headquarters (☎922-9321; 11 East Queen St); Half Way Tree (142 Maxfield Ave); Cross Roads (Brentford Rd)

INTERNET ACCESS Kingston & St Andrew Parish Library (2 Tom Redcam Ave; per 30 min J$100; ⊙9am-6pm Mon-Fri, 9am-5pm Sat) The cheapest option, though not the quietest.

MEDICAL SERVICES University Hospital (☎927-1620; University of the West Indies campus, Mona) The best, most up-to-date public hospital, with 24-hour emergency department.

Andrews Memorial Hospital (☎926-7401; 27 Hope Rd) Well-equipped private hospital with well-stocked pharmacy.

MONEY Scotiabank Main foreign-exchange centre (corner Duke and Port Royal Sts) and ATM (corner King and Tower Sts).

Western Union (7 Hillcrest Ave)

POST Main post office (13 King St; ⊙8am-5pm Mon-Thu, 9am-4pm Fri, 8am-1pm Sat) Gets crowded. There's a speedier option, with the same opening hours, in the **Liguanea Post Mall** (115 Hope Rd).

TOURIST INFORMATION Jamaica Tourist Board Uptown (☎929-9200; www.visitjamaica.com; 64 Knutsford Blvd); Norman Manley International Airport (arrivals hall) The uptown office offers maps, brochures and limited travel advice. Island maps featuring Jamaica's heritage sites for sale (J$250).

ⓘ Getting There & Around

AIR Norman Manley International Airport (☎924-8452/6; www.nmia.aero), 27km south-

PORT ROYAL

A dilapidated, ramshackle sprawl of tropical lassitude, Port Royal is replete with important historical buildings collapsing into dust. Today's fishing hamlet was once the pirate capital of the Caribbean. Later it was the hub of British naval power in the West Indies, but the remains give little hint of the town's former glory. The English settled the isolated cay in 1656, called it 'Cagway' or 'the Point' and built Fort Cromwell (renamed Fort Charles after the Restoration in 1660). Within two years General William Brayne was able to report that 'there is the faire beginning of a town upon the poynt of this harbor.' A massive earthquake in 1692 put an end to Port Royal's ascension, as survivors crossed the harbor to settle on the firmer ground of what would become Kingston.

The town has plenty of historic sites, including old **Fort Charles** (☎967-8438; adult/child US$5/2; ⊙9am-5pm, closed Good Friday, Christmas Day & New Year's Day) itself, the fully restored **Old Gaol House** (Gaol Alley) and the 1725 **St Peter's Church**.

CLIMBING BLUE MOUNTAIN PEAK

From Penlyne Castle to the summit of Blue Mountain Peak (2256m) is a 950m ascent and a three- or four-hour hike one-way. It's not a serious challenge, but you need to be reasonably fit.

Most hikers set off from Penlyne Castle, the base for hikes to and from the peak. It's about 12km away and you need to depart around 2am to reach the peak for sunrise. The first part of the trail – a series of steep, scree-covered switchbacks named **Jacob's Ladder** – is the toughest; following this painful bit of hiking it's basically a long, grinding ascent. You should arrive at the peak around 5:30am, while it is still dark. As the sun rises (and if the weather's clear) Cuba, 144km away, can be seen from the peak, which casts a distinct shadow over the land below.

Don't hike without a guide at night. Numerous spur trails lead off and it's easy to get lost. Although hiking boots or tough walking shoes are best, sneakers will suffice, though your feet will likely get wet. At the top, temperatures can approach freezing before sunrise, so wear plenty of layers. Rain gear is essential, as the weather can change rapidly.

east of downtown, handles international flights. Domestic flights depart and land at **Tinson Pen Aerodrome** (Marcus Garvey Dr) in west Kingston. There's daily service to and from Montego Bay and Ocho Rios from Norman Manley International Airport with **Air Jamaica** (☑888-359-2475; 4 St Lucia Ave).

Jamaica Air Shuttle (☑906-9026/30; www.jamaicaairshuttle.com) provides air-taxi services connecting Kingston with Montego Bay and Ocho Rios from Tinson Pen Airstrip. Charter flights to Port Antonio available.

Bus 98 operates between the international airport and Parade downtown (J$80, 35 minutes, every 30 minutes). The bus stop is opposite the arrivals hall. For Tinson Pen airstrip, take bus 22 or 22A from Parade (J$80, 15 minutes, hourly).

BUS Buses, coasters and route taxis run between Kingston and every point on the island. They arrive and depart from the **bus station** (cnr Beckford & Pechon Sts), five blocks west of the Parade.

Comfortable **Knutsford Express** (☑971-1822; www.knutsfordexpress.com) buses run from its own bus terminal in New Kingston to Ocho Rios (J$1250, two hours) and Montego Bay (J$2000, four hours). Book the Montego Bay ticket more than 24 hours in advance and get a discount of J$250. Be at the bus station 30 minutes before departure to register your ticket. Buses depart at 6am, 9:30am, 2pm and 5pm Monday to Friday, 6am, 9:30am and 4:30pm Saturday and 8:30am and 4:30pm Sunday.

CAR Most car-hire companies offer free airport shuttles. Reputable companies with offices at Normal Manley International airport:

Avis (☑924-8293; www.avis.com)

Budget (☑759-1793; www.budget.com)

Hertz (☑924-8028; www.hertz.com)

Island Car Rentals (☑924-8075; www.islandcarrentals.com)

PUBLIC TRANSPORTATION Buses, minibuses and route taxis arrive and depart from **North Parade** and **South Parade** in downtown, **Half Way Tree** bus station in uptown, **Cross Roads** (between uptown and downtown) and **Papine**, at the eastern edge of town off Old Hope Rd.

Kingston's **JUTC bus system** (www.jutc.com; fares J$80-170) operates a fleet of white and yellow Mercedes-Benz and Volvo buses. Most buses are air-conditioned. JUTC buses stop only at official stops.

THE BLUE MOUNTAINS

Looming over Kingston the majestic, forest-covered Blue Mountains throw the rest of the island into sharp relief. Their slopes, crags and fern forests seem light years from the capital's gritty streetscape, allowing you to hike old Maroon trails, go in search of the elusive streamertail hummingbird (Jamaica's national bird) or simply perch on a mountaintop, watching the valleys unfold out of the mist below.

◉ Sights & Activities

The Blue Mountains are a hiker's dream, and 30 recognized trails lace the hills. Many are overgrown due to lack of funding and ecological protection programs, but others remain the mainstay of communication for locals. These trails (called 'tracks' locally) are rarely marked. Get up-to-date information on trail conditions from the main ranger station at Holywell. When asking for directions from locals, remember that 'jus a likkle way' may in fact be a few hours of hiking.

By far the most popular route is the steep, well-maintained trail to 'The Peak,' which in Jamaica always means **Blue Mountain Peak** (p535).

If you're hiking alone, normal precautions apply: wear sturdy hiking shoes, bring snacks, plenty of water and a torch and let people know where you're headed. Buy the 1:50,000 or 1:12,500 Ordnance Survey topographic map series, available from the **Survey Department** (☎750-5263; www.nla.gov.jm; 23½ Charles St, Kingston).

It's highly recommended you hire a guide if you're looking to hike in the Blue Mountains; they can be hired at Hagley Gap or Penlyne Castle, or through most local accommodations, for US$55/70 per half/full day.

Forres Park Guest House & Farm　　　　　GUIDED HIKES
(☎927-8275; www.forrespark.com) Treks and walks in the Blue Mountains and surrounds.

Jamaica Conservation & Development Trust　　　　HIKING RESOURCE
(☎960-2848; www.jcdt.org.jm; 29 Dumbarton Ave, Kingston) Manages trails in the national park and can recommend hiking guides.

Sun Venture　　　　　　　　　TOURS
(☎960-6685; www.sunventuretours.com) Specializes in ecotours of areas like the Blue Mountains, Cockpit Country and other parts of the Jamaican hinterland.

Blue Mountain Bicycle Tours CYCLING TOURS
(☎974-7075; www.bmtoursja.com; 121 Main St, Ocho Rios; adult/child US$98/70) Offers pick up from Kingston or Ocho Rios, transfer to the Hardwar Gap (1700m) and an exhilarating downhill cycling tour.

🛏 Sleeping

Jamaica Conservation & Development Trust Cabin　　　CAMPING GROUND $
(☎960-2848/9; www.jcdt.org.jm; 29 Dumbarton Ave, Kingston; campsite/bed US$2/5) The Jamaica Conservation & Development Trust maintains two basic wooden cabins halfway up the Blue Mountain Peak trail at Portland Gap (4km above Abbey Green). You can camp outside, where there's a cooking area and water from a pipe. Bring your own tent, sleep on a bunk bed (bring own sleeping bag) or on the floor (foam mats available for rent; J$150). Reserve in advance.

Jah B's Guest House　　　　GUESTHOUSE $
(☎377-5206; bobotamo@yahoo.com; dm/r US$15/35; ℗🐕) In Penlyne Castle this friendly place, run by a family of Bobo Rastas, is popular with shoestring travelers. It has a basic but cozy wooden guesthouse with bunks and simple rooms. Jah B's son Alex cooks I-tal meals (about US$10) amid a cloud of ganja smoke and a nonstop volley of friendly banter; he can help arrange transfers from Kingston and will guide you up Blue Mountain Peak for US$55.

❶ Information

There are ranger stations at Holywell Recreation Area and Portland Gap, and at Millbank in the Upper Rio Grande Valley. Entry to the park is free, except for Holywell Recreation Area.

Jamaica Conservation & Development Trust (☎920-8278; www.jcdt.org.jm; 29 Dumbarton Ave, Kingston) provides management and supervision of the national park.

❶ Getting There & Away

BUS Minibuses and route taxis arrive from and depart to the mountains at the Park View Supermarket on the square in Papine. The frequency of service depends on demand. There is at least one morning and one afternoon run for the two main routes. Destinations include Mavis Bank (J$250, 1½ hours, 15km) and Newcastle (J$270, 1¼ hours, 23km).

CAR Travelling by your own vehicle is the best way to enjoy the Blue Mountains. There are no gas stations; fill up on gas in Papine.

From Kingston, Hope Rd leads to Papine, from where Gordon Town Rd (B1) leads into the mountains. At The Cooperage, the B1 (Mammee River Rd) forks left steeply uphill for Strawberry Hill resort (near Irish Town) and Newcastle. Gordon Town Rd continues straight from The Cooperage and winds east up the Hope River Valley to Gordon Town, then steeply to Mavis Bank and Hagley Gap. Penlyne Castle is reached via a 5km dirt road that ascends precipitously from Hagley Gap. Only 4WD vehicles with lowgear option can handle the dauntingly narrow and rugged road.

From the north coast, the B1 heads into the mountains from Buff Bay (closed at time of writing due to a landslide). There is no regular bus service from Buff Bay up the B1.

NORTHERN JAMAICA

The northeast coast of Jamaica trades tourists for heavy rains, lush jungle, prettily moldering colonial edifices and pocket-sized beaches that lay within scent of some of the

JAMAICA THE BLUE MOUNTAINS

best jerk on the island. Life goes slow in local fishing villages, where the travelers are almost as laid-back as local guesthouse owners.

Beautiful Portland parish, presided over by the sleepy town of Port Antonio, is the least-developed resort area in Jamaica – a fact that endears it to many. Further west the bustling port of Ocho Rios provides a convenient staging ground for excursions to some of Jamaica's most popular attractions, including the incomparable Dunn's River Falls.

Port Antonio

POP 13,250

Cupping an unruffled bay and backing into the sleepy Rio Grande valley, Port Antonio is the perfect capital for Portland. The parish's only sizable town is largely untarnished by the duty-free, tourist-over-friendliness of Ocho Rios or Montego Bay. Its streets, squares, quayside and market invite leisurely strolls – invitations that are freely accepted by the town's dog and goat populaces. Port Antonio makes an ideal base from which to explore Portland's hidden treasures.

⊙ Sights

Port Antonio's heart is the main square at the junction of West and Harbour Sts. It's centered on a **clock tower** and backed by a handsome red-brick Georgian **courthouse**, topped by a cupola. From here walk 45m down West St to the junction of William St, where the smaller Port Antonio Sq has a cenotaph honoring Jamaicans who gave their lives in the two world wars.

On the west side of the square is the clamorous and colorful **Musgrave Market**. To the north is the imposing facade of the **Village of St George**, a beautiful three-story complex with an exquisitely frescoed exterior in Dutch style; inside, you'll find an assortment of high-end shops.

Fort George St leads to the Titchfield Peninsula, where you'll find several dozen Victorian-style gingerbread houses, notably **DeMontevin Lodge** (21 Fort George St), an ornate rust-red mansion. Continue north to the remains of **Fort George** at the tip of the peninsula, dating from 1729. Several George III–era cannons can still be seen mounted in their embrasures in 3m-thick walls.

★☆ Festivals & Events

Portland Jerk Festival   FOOD
A food festival held in July for folks in love with the hot and spicy; sadly, a dispute between local and federal political parties may threaten the event's viability.

Portland Jamboree   CULTURAL
Floats, parades, costumes and lots of live music, held in mid-August.

🛏 Sleeping

Ivanhoe's   HOTEL $
(☎993-3043; 9 Queen St; r US$50-65; ❄🛜) Fantastic views across the whole of Port Antonio from breezy verandas, spotless white rooms and bargain rates are the hallmarks of the oldest guesthouse on historic Tichfield Hill. Lovely meals are cooked to order. Be sure to ask for a room with a view out over the harbor.

DeMontevin Lodge   HOTEL $$
(☎993-2604; demontevin@cwjamaica.com; 21 Fort George St; r US$50-160; ❄) This venerable Victorian guesthouse has a homey ambience that blends modern kitsch and antiques reminiscent of granny's parlor. The place could be the setting of a Sherlock Holmes novel were it not for the Disney-character bedsheets in some rooms (the effect is actually quite cute). The simple bedrooms (six with private bathrooms) are timeworn, but clean as a whistle.

Holiday Home   HOTEL $
(☎816-7258, 993-2425; holidayhomesilverabuckley@yahoo.com.sg; 5 Everleigh Park Rd; s/d/tr US$38/45/60; ❄) Some rooms in this creaky old house are little more than Victorian cupboards; others are wood-paneled antique pockets of charm. It's hardly a place that embraces modernity, but we love it for its relentless nostalgia.

🍴 Eating & Entertainment

TOP
CHOICE **Dickie's Best Kept Secret**   FUSION $$
(☎809-6276; dinner US$20-40; ⊙dinner) Almost too well kept a secret for its own good, Dickie's – an unsigned seaside hut on the A4, less than 1km west of Port Antonio – offers enormous five-course meals in rooms that look like they were decorated by Bob Marley after reading *Alice in Wonderland* too many times. Dickie and his wife promise to cook anything you want (provided they have the ingredients); believe us, anything will be delicious. Invariably the meal begins with a palate-cleansing fruit plate followed

by soup and a callaloo omelet. Reservations essential.

Anna Bananas Restaurant & Sports Bar
JAMAICAN $$

(☑715-6533; 7 Folly Rd; breakfast J$300, seafood dinners J$800-1500; ☺breakfast, lunch & dinner) Need seafood? Jerk? An open-air bar? Great; head to this breezy restaurant-bar, overlooking a small beach on the southern lip of the harbor. It specializes in jerk or barbecued chicken and pork and groaning plates of conch and lobster. Hit up the pool table or toss some darts afterwards.

Club La Best
NIGHTCLUB

(5 West St; ☺9:30-last person leaves) The newest, liveliest spot in Port Antonio, La Best assumes a different identity depending on the evening. Dancehall throbs into the wee hours on Friday; Sunday grooves to a mellow blend of reggae and old-school R&B; ladies' nights are Friday; and periodic live shows occur on Saturday.

❶ Information

The website www.portantoniojamaica.com is a good starting point for tourist information.

D-Tech (☑993-4184; upstairs, 3 West St; internet per 30min J$100; ☺9am-7pm Mon-Sat)

Port Antonio Hospital (☑993-2646; Nuttall Rd) On Naylor's Hill, south of West Harbour.

Portland Parish Library (☑993-2793; 1 Harbour St; internet per 30min US$1; ☺9am-6pm Mon-Fri, 9am-1pm Sat) Near the entrance to the marina.

Post office (☑993-2651) On the east side of the town square.

RBTT Bank (☑993-9755; 28 Harbour St)

Scotiabank (☑993-2523; 3 Harbour St)

❶ Getting There & Around

A **transportation center** (Gideon Ave) extends along the waterfront. Buses, coasters and route taxis leave regularly for Port Maria (where you change for Ocho Rios) and Kingston.

Eastern Rent-a-Car (☑993-3624; 16 West St) offers car rentals, while **JUTA** (☑993-2684) has taxi transfers from Montego Bay (US$300) and Kingston (US$160) airports.

Around Port Antonio

RIO GRANDE VALLEY

The Rio Grande rushes down from the Blue Mountains through a deeply cut gorge to the sea. The region is popular for **hiking**, but

trails are confusing and demanding and should not be attempted without a guide.

Rafting is also a big draw. Passengers make the three-hour, 9.5km journey on poled bamboo rafts from Grant's Level or Rafter's Village, just east of Berridale, all the way to St Margaret's Bay. En route you'll pass through Lovers Lane, a moss-covered narrow stream where you're supposed to kiss and make a wish. Try **Rio Grande Experience** (☑993-5778; Berridale; per raft US$65; ☺9am-5pm). This is a one-way trip, so if you're driving you need to hire a driver to bring your car from Berridale to St Margaret's Bay (Rio Grande Experience will help) or take a taxi from Port Antonio (US$20).

To enter the valley, take Red Hassell Rd south from Port Antonio to Fellowship.

FRENCHMAN'S COVE

This small cove, near the town of Drapers, 8km east of Port Antonio, boasts one of the prettiest beaches on the north coast of Jamaica, though most tourists won't have ever heard of it. A stream winds lazily to a white-sand **beach** (admission US$5; ☺closed Tue) that shelves steeply into the water; the road that comes here passes through misty, green jungle cliffs that could be a tropical version of the wild northern Scottish coast. The feeling is emphasized by the lurking white-stone grandeur of **Trident Castle**, a monument to the hubris of owners who have never ceased adding to the doomed structure. While closed to the public, the castle, facing the ocean and often seen wrapped in mist, makes for one hell of a landmark.

Drapers San Guest House (☑993-7118; www.go-jam.com/drapersan-e.html; Hwy A4, Drapers; s US$27, d US$48-52, all incl breakfast; ☒) is an agreeable guesthouse above Frenchman's Cove consisting of two pretty cottages and a series of double rooms, all artfully decorated and oozing idiosyncratic charm.

A route taxi from Port Antonio costs J$100.

BLUE LAGOON

The waters that launched Brooke Shields' movie career (and the site of a less-famous Jacques Cousteau dive), the Blue Lagoon, 11km east of Port Antonio, is by any measure one of the most beautiful spots in Jamaica. The 55m-deep 'Blue Hole' (as it is known locally) opens to the sea through a narrow funnel, but is fed by freshwater springs that come in at a depth of about 40m. Its color changes through every shade of jade and emerald during the day.

The lagoon is public property and accessible from the road. Blue Hole is an easy half-day trip from Port Antonio, but if you can afford it there's a grand reason to stay here.

TOP CHOICE **Kanopi House** (☎632-3213, 305-677-3525 from North America, 0203-318-1191 from UK; www.kanopihouse.com; Hwy A4, Drapers; r from US$300; ❄️🛜) is one of the few eco-resorts in Jamaica that deserves the title, as well as many well-deserved accolades in honor of its considerable luxury and comfort. Staying in these dark wood chalets, which seemingly grow from the jungle, feels like staying in a laid-back five-star hotel carved into a Banyan tree. The property makes great efforts to leave a low ecological footprint (gray-water system, local sustainable hardwoods used in construction, none of which were cut) and is stuffed with elegant Caribbean art. Fresh organic dinners are prepared on site, and the Jamaican owners are a dream to chat with.

BOSTON BAY

The pocket-sized beach of Boston Bay, 14.5km east of Port Antonio, shelves into jewel-like turquoise waters. There's not a lot of sand thanks to hurricane damage, but this is perhaps the best **surfing** spot in Jamaica. Surfboards in various states of decay are available for rent on the beach (US$15).

Besides surfing, Boston Bay is mainly known as the birthplace, and exemplar, of the art of jerk. Heavenly smelling chicken and pork sizzle away on smoky barbecue pits along the roadside. Lots of vendors will vie for your attention; we say go for **Mikey's**, right off the roadside, which produces a complexity of heat and sweet that has us shuddering at the memory.

One of the most unusual accommodations in Jamaica, **Great Huts** (☎353-3388; www.greathuts.com; Boston Beach Lane; African-style tent per person US$60-160, huts US$160-250; 🛜) perches on a scenic crag overlooking Boston Bay. There are four luxury tents and eight elegant 'huts' (including three tree houses), all lavishly designed with Afrocentric flair. These two-story, open-air structures have verandas, bamboo-walled bedrooms, Jacuzzis and are romantic as hell.

A route taxi from Port Antonio will cost you J$150.

LONG BAY

Guess what – there is a beach in Jamaica where there are barely any hustlers, and free spirits congregate out of sight of big-shot resorts. And it ain't Negril. Instead, come to Long Bay, a rugged 1.5km-wide harbor and hamlet of freaks, geeks, backpackers, bohemians and surfers. A number of expats have put down roots and opened guesthouses here, and it's not hard to see why. There's not much to do but chill, surf, chill more, maybe read, eat, chill. Wash (or not), rinse and repeat.

Likkle Paradise (☎913-7702, 528-8007; www.likkleparadise.com; r from US$40; ❄️🛜) is the home of lovely Herlett Kennedy. She rents out two lovingly furnished rooms and provides guests with loads of charm, advice and hospitality. A similar deal can be found at **Blue Heaven Resort** (☎715-4336, 448-9605; www.blueheavenjamaica.com; r from US$30-60; ❄️🛜), which consists of three funky cottages offered at an absolute steal. The digs may be a little basic but, c'mon, you get privacy and an oceanfront.

The fare to Long Bay from Port Antonio by route taxi is about J$250.

REACH FALLS

All of Jamaica's tumbling cascades are refreshing, but this waterfall is downright rejuvenating. This peaceful spot is surrounded by virgin rainforest and features a series of cascades tumbling over limestone tiers from one hollowed, jade-colored pool to another.

Once you enter the **falls** (adult/child US$10/5; ⏰8:30am-4:30pm Wed-Sun) a guide will offer his services. This is actually pretty crucial if you want to climb to the top pools, which we highly recommend (there's a little underground, underwater tunnel a bit up the falls; plunging through is a treat). Tip generously!

To get here, you can catch any of the minibuses and route taxis that run between Kingston and Port Antonio via Morant Bay. Ask to get off at Reach Falls, then walk or hitchhike 3km uphill to Reach Falls (the turnoff is signed, 1km south of Manchioneal). Taxis will pass by and offer to take you up for around US$10. A charter taxi from Port Antonio costs about US$60 round trip.

Ocho Rios

POP 17,000

In spite of Ocho Rios sometimes feeling like a theme park, with cruise ships disgorging hordes of passengers, all-inclusive hotels and appropriately tourist-friendly nightlife, the area around the third-largest town in Jamaica features some of the most beautiful (and popular) natural attractions on the island. Along the north coast you will find pleasant white-sand beaches, clear waters, spectacular waterfalls and lush mountainous terrain.

◉ Sights

Dunn's River Falls WATERFALL
(www.dunnsriverfallsja.com; adult/child J$1270/1016; ⊘8:30am-4pm Sat-Tue, 7am-4pm Wed-Fri) As long as you're not expecting a peaceful communion with nature, a morning at Dunn's River Falls, the nation's top tourist attraction, can be enjoyable. Join hands in a daisy chain at the bottom and clamber up the tiers of limestone that step 180m down to the beach in a series of cascades and pools. The water is refreshingly cool and the falls are shaded by tall rainforest and a number of magnificent tree specimens.

You must buy a ticket at the roadside ticket booth, then follow stairs down to the beach. Guides congregate at the bottom of the falls and can assist you with the climb (a tip is expected) and carry your camera, but their services are not necessary. The powerful current can sweep your feet from the slippery rocks, but as long as you stick to the left side of the falls the ascent is easily achieved by most able-bodied people. You can always exit to the side at a convenient point if your nerves give out.

It's a 30-minute climb, and swimwear is essential. There are changing rooms and you can rent lockers (J$500) and rubber booties (J$500). It's best to leave any valuables in your hotel safe, as the lockers are reputed to be unsecure.

Plan to arrive before 10am, when the tour buses arrive, or around 4pm after they depart. Also try to visit when the cruise ships aren't in town (usually Saturday to Tuesday). Route taxis (J$80) head west to Dunn's River Falls from Ocho Rios from Main St; it's a simple matter to flag one down.

Mystic Mountain THEME PARK
(www.rainforestbobsledjamaica.com; ⊘9am-4pm) One of Ochi's biggest attractions, featuring a series of zip lines crisscrossing the forest in what is possibly the best canopy tour in Jamaica, as well as the signature attraction: a thrilling 'bobsled' ride through the dense foliage.

To get to the park, you take the obligatory Sky Explorer chairlift through the forest canopy to the top of the mountain (J$3555), with superb views of the coastline along the way. You can either go in an individual 'bobsled' or link yours to your friends'; you

also control the speed of the ride, which can thus range from mild to exhilarating. A Sky Explorer and Bobsled combo is US$68.20; a Sky Explorer and Zipline combo is US$114.40, whereas a combination of all three is US$136.40. You can add on more rides once in the park. Avoid the park on cruise-ship days.

Mystic Mountain lies 3km west of Ocho Rios; to get here, catch a route taxi heading towards St Ann's Bay (J$100).

🏖 Beaches

The main beach of Ocho Rios, popular with tourists, is the long crescent known variously as **Turtle Beach** and **Ocho Rios Bay** (admission J$200; ⊘8am-5pm), stretching east from the Turtle Towers condominiums to the Renaissance Jamaica Grande Resort, fenced off and topped with barbed wire. There are changing rooms and palms for shade.

Island Village Beach (admission J$254; ⊘6am-6pm), located at the west end of Main St, is a peaceful, smaller beach that offers lockers (J$423), towels (J$423) and beach chairs and umbrellas (J$423 apiece).

Immediately west of Island Village Beach is tiny **Fishermen's Beach** (admission free), with colorful pirogues (fishing boats) and several eateries serving fresh fish and more.

Mahogany Beach (admission free), 1km east of the town centre, is a small and charming beach that's particularly popular with locals; it comes to life on weekends with loud music, smells of jerk cooking and impromptu football matches.

🏃 Activities

Virtually the entire shoreline east of Ocho Rios to Galina Point is fringed by a reef, and it's great for **snorkeling** and **diving**. One of the best sections is Devil's Reef, a pinnacle that drops more than 60m. Nurse sharks are abundant at Caverns, a shallow reef about 1km east of the White River estuary; it has many tunnels plus an ex-minesweeper, the *Kathryn*. Most resorts have their own diving facilities.

Garfield Diving Station DIVING
(✆395-7023; www.garfielddiving.com; Turtle Beach) Ocho Rios' longest-running watersports operator, with 29 years' experience. Dive packages include one-tank dives (US$60), a wreck dive (US$70) and PADI certification course (US$420). Other watersports are offered, such as snorkeling excursions (US$70),

PORTS OF CALL

There is plenty to see and do even on a short visit at these ports.

Montego Bay

» Achieving tanning Zen at Doctor's Cave (p545)

» Exploring Sam Sharpe Sq (p545)

» Scarfing the best in fusion Jamaican cuisine at the Native Restaurant (p547)

» Wincing at the overproof rum in the Reggae Bar (p548)

» Shopping around Montego Bay's art galleries and crafts markets (p548)

» Diving some serious sea walls at the Point (p546)

» Feeling the i-ray-tions at the Indigenous Rastafarian Village (p546)

Ocho Rios

» Funk up the scene at friendly Turtle Beach (p539)

» Pay tribute to Brother Bob at his birthplace in Nine Mile (p543)

» Climb with dozens more to the legendary cascades of Dunn's River Falls (p539)

» Take the bobsled down the old Mystic Mountain (p539)

» Enjoy fresh pasta at Toscanini (p541)

---

glass-bottom-boat trips (US$25) and jet-ski rental (30 minutes US$70). Boat charter is available for deep-sea fishing (half-day for up to four people US$500).

Resort Divers   DIVING
(☑881-5760; www.resortdivers.com; Royal DeCameron Club Caribbean, Runaway Bay) Dive packages available with pick up from Ocho Rios.

☞ Tours

Chukka Caribbean Adventure Tours   ADVENTURE TOURS
(☑972-2506; www.chukkacaribbean.com; tours US$42-90) Established multi-adventure specialist offering horseback-riding tours, river tubing, zip-line canopy tours, ATV safaris, adventure 4WD trips to Bob Marley's birthplace and even dog-sled tours.

Hooves   HORSEBACK RIDING
(☑972-0905; www.hoovesjamaica.com; 61 Windsor Rd, St Ann's Bay; US$65-115) Offers guided horseback tours from the Maima Seville Great House to the beach, with a bareback ride into the sea (beginners welcome) and the 'rainforest honeymoon ride,' for experienced riders. Reservations required.

Blue Mountain Bicycle Tours   CYCLING
(☑974-7075; www.bmtoursja.com; 121 Main St; Blue Mountain downhill tour adult/child US$95/75) Exhilarating downhill cycling tour of the

Blue Mountains, week-long eco-adventures in Portland and tours of Kingston.

🛏 Sleeping

TOP CHOICE **Blue House**   BOUTIQUE B&B $
(☑994-1367; www.thebluehousejamaica.com; White River; s/d US$50/70; [P][✷][@][🛜][❄]) This wonderful gem offers tiled, luxurious bedrooms decorated, as the name suggests, in cool blue hues. The separate two-bedroom Cozy Cottage provides even greater seclusion, with its private patio and hammock hidden behind a curtain of flowers. Darryl the Barefoot Chef cooks up some of the best fusion cuisine on the island, drawing on Chinese and Indian influences and the lavish three-course dinners are worth every penny. A share of the B&B's profits goes to support the area's destitute elderly, women and children.

Cottage at Te Moana   COTTAGES $$
(☑974-2870; www.harmonyhall.com; cottage US$130-150; [P][✷]) With its small clifftop garden overhanging a reef, this exquisite reclusive property with two delightful cottages offers a wonderful alternative to Ochi's resorts. At the Seaside Cottage the bedroom is reached via an external staircase and has a king-size bed, ceiling fan and a magnificent artist's aesthetic.

Jamaica Inn   GUESTHOUSE $$$
(☑974-2514; www.jamaicainn.com; ste US$479-746, cottage US$1164-1570; [P][✷][🛜][❄]) Winston

Churchill's favorite hotel, this exquisite family-run 'inn', tucked in a private cove, exudes patrician refinement. The suites are a soothing combination of whites and Wedgwood blues, with mahogany beds, Edwardian furnishings and colonial-theme prints. The West Wing veranda suites hang over the sea (East Wing rooms nudge up to the pristine, white sand beach). There's a library and a bar with a warm, clubby feel.

Hibiscus Lodge   HOTEL **$$**
(📞974-2676; www.hibiscusjamaica.com; 83 Main St; r US$140-152; P❄@⚓) A stairway descends alongside a cliff overhang, past flowering gardens overflowing with bougainvillea and down to a private sunning deck, perfect for a spontaneous jump in the sea. A small gallery of contemporary Jamaican art complements the main building.

Mahoe Villa & Guesthouse   GUESTHOUSE **$**
(📞974-6613; 11 Shaw Park Rd; r without bathroom US$25-35, r with bathroom US$45, r with bathroom & Jacuzzi US$85; P) One of the few decent budget digs in town, this large guesthouse, run by the effusive Michael and replete with original works of art, is great value for money. The spic-and-span, fan-cooled rooms share a communal kitchen and a chilled vibe prevails; you'll usually find fellow travelers lazing in the hammocks in the backyard.

✕ Eating

TOP CHOICE **Toscanini**   ITALIAN **$$$**
(📞975-4785; Harmony Hall; meals US$40-60; ⊘lunch & dinner Tue-Sun; 🖊) One of the finest restaurants on the island, this roadside spot is run by two gracious Italians who mix the freshest local ingredients into recipes from the motherland. Daily menu ranges widely, encompassing such appetizers as prosciutto with papaya or marinated marlin and mains like garlic lobster pasta or shrimp sautéed with garlic and Appleton rum.

Passage to India   INDIAN **$$$**
(📞795-3182; Soni's Plaza, 50 Main St; mains US$18-27; ⊘lunch daily, dinner Tue-Sun; 🖊) On the rooftop of a duty-free shopping center, Passage to India offers respite from the crowds below, in addition to very good northern Indian fare. The naan is crisp, the lassis flavorful, the curries sharp and the menu divided into extensive chicken, mutton, seafood and vegetarian sections. Try the 'vegetable bullets' ($8) and the curried conch ($18).

Ocho Rios Jerk Centre   JERK **$**
(📞974-2549; 16 DaCosta Dr; ⊘lunch & dinner) Its existing popularity further boosted by being the official Knutsford Express bus stop, the liveliest jerk joint in town serves excellent jerk pork (J$325), chicken (J$295) and conch (J$795), as well as BBQ ribs. There are daily specials, the best being curry goat (J$450) and goat head soup (J$100).

Scotchies   JERK **$**
(📞794-9457; Jack's Hall Fair Ground; quarter pound chicken J$300; ⊘lunch & dinner) This consistently excellent roadside offshoot of the famous jerk centre in Montego Bay lies adjacent to an Epping gas station just west of Dunn's River Falls.

Lion's Den   JAMAICAN **$**
(A3; meals J$650-1000; ⊘breakfast, lunch & dinner) West of town, between Dolphin Cove and Dunn's River Falls, this place looks like a tourist trap but it's worth a stop for the excellent, well-priced Jamaican fare and unique, artistic decor. The dining room resembles a Rastafarian chapel, with hand-carved columns and wicker 'tree limbs' reaching to the ceiling. The menu boasts local specialties such as curry goat, stew pork and dumpling and fried chicken.

🍷 Drinking & Entertainment

Amnesia   DANCEHALL
(70 Main St; admission J$350-550; ⊘Wed-Sun) A classic Jamaican dancehall, this remains the happening scene. Theme nights include an oldies jam on Sunday, ladies' night on Thursday and an after-work party on Friday. This all leads up to Saturday's dress-to-impress all-night dance marathon.

Jimmy Buffett's Margaritaville   BAR
(Island Village; admission charged for special events; ⊘9am-4am Mon, Wed & Sat, to 10pm other days) As with its counterparts in Montego Bay and Negril, the music is too loud and the signature margaritas are too expensive, but many tourists and locals find the orchestrated good-time vibe to be irresistible. The Wet'n'Wild Pool Party (J$1692) on Wednesday night is particularly debauched, with free drinks until 1am and half-price entry for guests in swimwear.

Ocean's 11 Watering Hole   BAR
(Fisherman's Point) Exceedingly popular with cruise-ship passengers who knock back Red Stripes and potent cocktails and cheer each other on during Tuesday night karaoke. The

upstairs space doubles as a small art gallery/coffee shop and serves excellent Blue Mountain coffee (J$339), which you can purchase by the pound.

H₂O
BAR

(Shop 22, Coconut Grove Shopping Centre; ⊙noon-4am) This inviting restobar fills up by night when locals and visitors alike stream in for the music events. Live band karaoke takes place on Friday night, the H₂O Flow event on Saturday features appearances from local and international artists, while Sunday revisits the glory days of reggae, ska and mento.

Shopping

Olde Craft Market
CRAFTS

(Main St) A better (and less expensive) choice than the rows and rows of identical crafts at Ocho Rios Craft Park and Dunn's River Craft Park, this market features quality ceramics and art, as well as the usual T-shirts with chirpy Jamaican slogans and Rasta tams with fake dreadlocks attached.

Harmony Hall
ART

(www.harmonyhall.com; ⊙10am-5:30pm Tue-Sun) An art gallery featuring the best of local art, Harmony Hall is renowned for its Christmas, Easter and mid-November craft fairs and regular exhibitions.

Ocho Rios Craft Park
SOUVENIRS

(Main St) For all your tacky T-shirt, batik, wooden sculpture and crafts-made-of-coconut-shells needs. Some of the traders also sell quality music-mix CDs.

ℹ Information

DANGERS & ANNOYANCES Ocho Rios' biggest annoyance is persistent hustlers, who are especially thick around the clock tower and DaCosta Dr. Avoid the area immediately behind the market south of the clock tower. Use caution at night anywhere, but particularly on James St, a poorly lit street with a rough reputation.

EMERGENCY **Police station** (☑974-2533) Off DaCosta Dr, just east of the clock tower.

INTERNET ACCESS **Computer Whizz** (shop 11, Island Plaza; per 30min/hr J$150/250; ⊙8:30am-7:30pm Mon-Sat) Has 10 computers as well as wi-fi access for those with laptops.

MEDICAL SERVICES **Kulkarni Medical Clinic** (☑974-3357; 16 Rennie Rd) Private practise used by upmarket hotels in the area; between RBTT and Jamaica National Bank.

St Ann's Bay Hospital (Seville Rd; ☑972-2272) The nearest hospital.

MONEY There are numerous banks along Main St, including Scotiabank. All have foreign-exchange facilities and ATMs.

POST **FedEx** (17 Main St; ⊙9am-5pm Mon-Sat)

Post office (Main St; ⊙8am-5pm Mon-Sat) Opposite the Ocho Rios Craft Park.

TELEPHONE **Call Direct Centre** (74 Main St) Economical calls overseas.

Digicell (70 Main St) East of the clock tower, sells SIM cards, cell phones and phone cards.

TOURIST INFORMATION **Tourist office** (☑974-7705; shop 3, Ocean Village, Main St; ⊙9am-5pm Mon-Thu, to 4pm Fri)

ℹ Getting There & Away

AIR The former Boscobel Airport had just reopened as the **Ian Fleming International Airport** (☑975-3101) at the time of writing, expanded primarily to accommodate private jets, as well as chartered flights. It is located at Boscobel, about 16km east of town. Most flight schedules were to be confirmed, though **Jamaica Air Shuttle** (☑906-9026/30; www.jamaicaairshuttle.com) offers regular flights to Kingston.

BUS Buses, minibuses and route taxis arrive and depart Ocho Rios at the **transportation centre** (Evelyn St). During daylight hours there are frequent departures for Kingston and destinations along the north coast; there are fewer departures on Sunday. There is no set schedule and they depart when full. If you are heading to Port Antonio, you will have to change buses at Port Maria (J$140) and possibly Annotto Bay. Sample destinations include:

Discovery Bay J$150, 35 minutes

Kingston J$320, two hours

Montego Bay J$330, two hours

Port Maria J$140, 50 minutes

Runaway Bay J$140, 30 minutes

St Ann's Bay J$80, 15 minutes

Knutsford Express (www.knutsfordexpress.com) has scheduled departures to Kingston (J$1200, two hours) and Montego Bay (J$1200, two hours) from its office in the car park of the Ocho Rios Jerk Centre. You have to arrive half an hour prior to departure to register your ticket. Departures are as follows:

Kingston 6:20am, 10:25am, 2:30pm, 6:30pm Monday to Friday; 7:20am, 5:55pm Saturday; 9:45am, 6pm Sunday

Montego Bay 7:45am, 11:20am, 3:45pm, 6:40pm Monday to Friday; 7:45am, 11:20am, 6pm Saturday; 10am, 6pm Sunday

TAXI **JUTA** (☑974-2292) is the main taxi agency catering to tourists. A licensed taxi will cost about US$110 between Ocho Rios and Montego Bay, and about US$100 between Ocho Rios and Kingston (US$110 to the international airport at Kingston).

Getting Around

TO/FROM THE AIRPORT There is no shuttle service from the airport to downtown. Local buses (J$100) and minibuses and route taxis (J$150) pass by. A tourist taxi will cost about US$25.

CAR & MOTORCYCLE Shopping malls along Main St have car parks, though not secure ones. Most hotels offer parking; all upmarket hotels offer secure parking. Main St during rush hour is one long traffic jam.

Car-rental outlets in Ocho Rios include **Budget** (☑974-1288; 15 Milford Rd), and **Bargain Rent-a-Car** (☑974-8047; shop 1A Pineapple Place Shopping Center, Main St).

PUBLIC TRANSPORTATION Minibuses and route taxis ply Main St and the coast road (J$80 for short hauls, J$150 to Boscobel or Mammee Bay).

TAXI Chartered taxis are in great abundance along Main St. Negotiate the fare before setting off, as drivers will quote any figure that comes to mind. If you want the driver to wait for you, don't hand over the full fare in advance.

Around Ocho Rios

NINE MILE

Despite its out-of-the-way location, 65km southwest of Ocho Rios, the village of Nine Mile is firmly on the tourist map for pilgrimages to Bob Marley's birth site and resting place. At the **Nine Mile Museum** (☑999-7003; www.ninemilejamaica.com; admission J$1600; ☺9am-5pm), after showing the room displaying various gold discs awarded for Bob Marley's albums, Rastafarian guides given to impromptu singing of Marley songs lead pilgrims uphill to the plainly furnished two-room house on Mt Zion – now festooned with devotional graffiti. Marley's body lies buried with his favorite Gibson Les Paul guitar, his football, the Bible and some marijuana in a 2.5m-tall oblong marble mausoleum inside a tiny church of traditional Ethiopian design. The stained-glass windows are tinged red, green and yellow, and a single window depicts three flowers, the 'three little birds' from the song of the same name.

Bob's widow, Rita, periodically expresses disdain at how her husband's legacy has been turned into a tourism 'product,' and she has spoken of exhuming him for burial in Africa, though there are rumors his remains have already been secretly spirited away to Ghana.

Note that the expensive entry fee does not include a tip for the guide.

FIREFLY

Set amid wide lawns high atop a hill 5km east of Oracabessa and 5km west of Port Maria, **Firefly** (admission J$847; ☺9am-5pm Mon-Thu & Sat) was the home of Sir Noel Coward, the English playwright, songwriter, actor and wit, preceded at this site by the notorious pirate Sir Henry Morgan. When he died in 1973, Coward left the estate to his partner Graham Payn, who gifted it to the nation.

Your guide will lead you to Coward's art studio, where he was schooled in oil painting by Winston Churchill. The studio displays Coward's original paintings and photographs of himself and a coterie of famous friends. The upper lounge features a glassless window that offers one of the most stunning coastal vistas in Jamaica. The view takes in Port Maria Bay and the coastline further west. Contrary to popular opinion Coward didn't write his famous song *A Room with a View* here (it was written in Hawaii in 1928). Coward lies buried beneath a plain white marble slab on the wide lawns where he entertained stars of stage and screen; a pensive statue of the man graces the lawn.

MONTEGO BAY & AROUND

Montego Bay is gateway to Jamaica for countless travelers and a backdrop of some of the island's most obvious contrasts, from the geographic to the cultural to the socioeconomic. Some people love it here – there are some beautiful beaches – and some can't leave soon enough. Nearby are stretches of groomed coastline studded with enormous resorts and crumbling Georgian architecture. To the south are mountains, crossroads, jungle and Cockpit Country, as wild and free of visitors as Montego is domesticated and crowded with them.

Montego Bay

POP 136,100

There's a good chance MoBay (as everyone calls it) will be your introduction to Jamaica – some 80% of travelers choose the country's second-largest city as their port of entry. Montego has made an interesting progression from local port to tourist-packaged commodity to an intriguing, if not terribly attractive, blend of both. As a result, while the 'Hip Strip,' a long stretch of

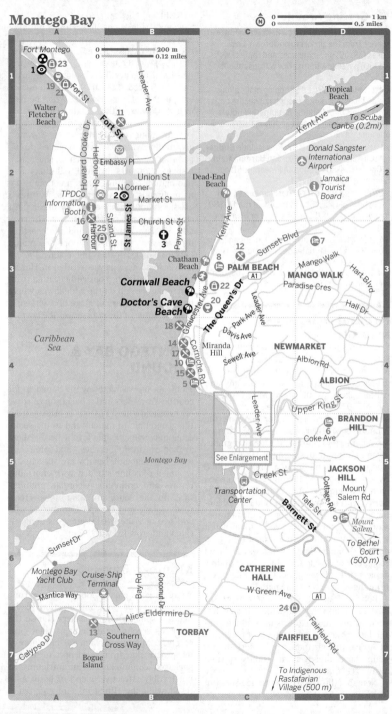

commercialized cheesiness, is initially off-putting in its crassness, it has also become a place to sample genuinely creative cuisine and a nightlife scene where surprising numbers of locals rub shoulders with day-shippers (ie cruise-liner passengers).

◉ Sights

HIP STRIP & THE BEACHES

Doctor's Cave Beach   ACTIVITIES BEACH
(www.doctorscavebathingclub.com; adult/child J$500/250; ⊘8:30am-sunset) It may sound like a rocky hole inhabited by lab-coated troglodytes, but this is actually Montego Bay's most famous beach. A pretty arc of sugary sand fronts a deep-blue gem studded with floating dive platforms and tourists sighing happily. Er, *lots* of tourists. And a fair few Jamaicans as well; if you're coming in winter you may have trouble finding a beach under all the sun tanners. The upside is that an admission charge keeps out most of the beach hustlers.

Cornwall Beach   ACTIVITIES BEACH
(www.cornwallbeachja.com; entry $J350; ⊘8am-6pm) If you're looking for a beach that feels like the place where the cool locals hang out (well, the cool locals willing to shell out $J350), this is your spot. There's a nice shallow shelf for snorkeling, clear water for swimming and white sand for you to look good on. Every Wednesday a (open bar!) beach party goes down here from 9pm till *ohgodisthatthesun*?

Walter Fletcher Beach & Aquasol Theme Park   FAMILY BEACH
(adult/child US$5/3; ⊘10am-10pm) Locals still call it Fletcher Beach, but officially this is the Aquasol Theme Park: a complex full of go-karts, boat rides, snorkeling excursions and swimming. There's a good deck bar on hand for sundowner drinks and more locals than you'll find at Doctor's Cave, but this unfortunately includes hustlers. As the sun sets this place evolves from kids' park to adult playground.

DOWNTOWN

Sam Sharpe Square   PLAZA
(Fort St) This bustling cobbled square, formerly called the Parade, is named for the Right Excellent Samuel Sharpe (1801–32), national hero and leader of the 1831 Christmas Rebellion. At the square's northwest corner is the **National Heroes Monument**, a bronze statue of Paul Bogle and Sam Sharpe, Bible in hand, speaking to three

Montego Bay

admirers. Also on the northwest corner is the **Cage**, a tiny cut-stone and brick building constructed in 1806 as a lockup, now a small souvenir shop.

Church Street HISTORIC STREET

Many of the most interesting buildings in town are clustered along Church St, the most picturesque street in MoBay, although you shouldn't expect a quiet historic district – this thoroughfare is as alive and chaotic as anywhere else downtown.

The highlight is **St James Parish Church** (📞952-2775; Church St), regarded as the finest church on the island. The current church was built between 1775 and 1782 in the shape of a Greek cross, but was so damaged by the earthquake of March 1, 1957, that it had to be rebuilt. With luck, the tall church doors will be open (if they're not, call the rector at the above number) and you can view the interior, one of the most beautiful rooms in Jamaica.

AROUND MONTEGO BAY

Indigenous Rastafarian Village VILLAGE (📞285-4750; Fairfield Rd; 2-hour/1-day tour US$25/100; ☉tours by appointment) If you want to learn about the Rastafari movement past the effort it takes to pop in an old Bob CD, come out to this...hmmm, 'living interpretive exhibit'. You'll be taken through a pretty, jungly settlement, village medicinal plants (not what you're thinking) and given a coherent breakdown of what the Rasta faith traditionally believed in. The all-day tour includes some lovely treks into the surrounding countryside, complete with swimming in natural pools. Located about 3km inland from MoBay, you'll need either your own wheels (it's a lovely drive) or to pre-arrange a visit with the village or your hotel.

✦ Activities

Diving

MoBay offers a few good dive sites. For advanced divers, the **Point** north of the airport has a good wall dive due to the dense corals and fish, sharks and rays that are fed by crystal-clear waters scoured by currents. The wall here starts at 20m and drops to at least 90m. **Airport Reef**, off the southwestern edge of the airport, is considered by some to be the best site on the island, with masses of coral canyons, caves and tunnels and a DC-3 wreck that's become a multi-colored fish mansion.

Besides boasting the sort of name you'd expect in a *Pirates of the Caribbean* movie, **Widowmakers Cave** is an incredible tunnel filled with sponges, barracuda and clouds of smaller fish that are as colorful as candy wrappers. **Chub Reef**, a 12m dive site located far to the east of the city, is named for the Bermuda Chub, rather than any physical squatness. **Rose Hall Reef**, a few kilometers east of the city, is a shallow reef suitable for less-experienced divers.

Most dive centers also offer snorkeling trips. All of the following provide multiple levels of PADI certification.

Resort Divers DIVE CENTER

(📞973-6131; www.resortdivers.com; 2 Gloucester Ave) On the Hip Strip.

Dive Seaworld DIVE CENTER

(📞953-2180; www.diveseaworld.com; Ironshore) Northeast of Montego Bay.

Scuba Caribe DIVE CENTER

(📞1-888-748-4990; www.scubacaribe.com) Operates out of the Riu Hotel, Montego Bay.

★ Festivals & Events

Montego Bay's most celebrated events are its two high-profile music festivals.

Jamaica Jazz & Blues Festival MUSIC

(www.jamaicajazzandblues.com) Brings internationally acclaimed acts to Cinnamon Hill, near Rose Hall, in late January for three nights of music under the stars.

Red Stripe Reggae Sumfest MUSIC

(www.reggaesumfest.com) Jamaica's premier reggae festival typically includes over 50 world-class reggae artists. Held in July, it starts with a beach party on Walter Fletcher Beach, followed by a week of nonstop partying.

⌖ Sleeping

TOP CHOICE Richmond Hill Inn HOTEL $$

(📞952-3859; www.richmond-hill-inn.com; Union St; s/d/ste US$85/115/189; P✷☎✹) It's hard to understand why anyone who can afford a night at the Richmond three times over (and that's *a lot* of tourists in Jamaica) would sleep elsewhere. This charming property is built of limestone, molasses and character. It's chock-full of antiques, some dating back to the early 1800s, and between its wooden furnishings, plush sitting rooms and elegant verandas, feels like that rarest of things: a modern hotel that successfully captures the elegance and opulence of the colonial era without descending into cheap imitation.

Toby Resorts
HOTEL $$

(☏952-4370, 1-888-790-5264; http://tobysresorts.com; cnr Gloucester Ave & Sunset Blvd; r from US$100; ❄☎➱) Located just off the 'top' of the Hip Strip, Toby's provides admirable local vibe with amenities geared for discerning international travelers. There are large grounds, comfy (although not luxurious) rooms, a big pool, a good bar and restaurant, easy access to the beaches and very friendly staff.

Altamont West
HOTEL $$

(☏620-4540, 979-9378; www.altamontwesthotel.com; 33 Gloucester Ave; r US$110-180; ❄☎➱) A brightly colored, vaguely deco option well placed near Walter Fletcher Beach, the Altamont has an airy common area offset with mustard-yellow and rust-red interior accents that add to the warm yet breezy conviviality of the place. Rooms are fine – well decked out and a match for most all-inclusives.

Wexford
HOTEL $$

(☏952-2854; www.thewexfordhotel.com; 39 Gloucester Ave; r/ste from US$120/200; ℗❄@➱) This hotel has undergone quite a few sprucings, and they've all been for the better. Rooms in the older wings are efficient but comfortable, while the newer wing offers elegant digs decked out in minimalist, boutique-style elegance – they're a better option but a bit more expensive.

Ridgeway Guest House
GUESTHOUSE $

(☏952-2709; www.ridgewayguesthouse.com; 34 Queens Dr; r $45-80; ❄☎) This homey guesthouse makes you feel just like that: a guest in a friendly house. The rooms surround a pretty garden and feature cozy beds, tiled floors and nice furnishings, all kept quite clean and presentable. The cheapest ones are fan-cooled, which isn't really a problem, especially in winter. Located away from the beaches, near the airport, but a free shuttle gets you to the sea and sand.

View Guest House
GUESTHOUSE $

(☏952-3175; 56 Jarrett Tce; r $50; ❄➱) On the southeast edge of town, on the road that leads to Mt Salem, is this family-run option. Rooms are basic but clean and come with a lot of love – the return guests at the View (and there are many) are fanatical in their loyalty to the place. Home-cooked meals are served, and it has a communal kitchen and bar, plus a view overlooking the city.

Bethel Court
HOSTEL $

(☏476-7239, 971-0134; http://bethelcourt.wordpress.com; Federal Ave; dm/r from US$20/40; ℗❄☎) Located in the outer neighborhood of Mt Salem, Bethel Court is one of the few dedicated hostels in Jamaica. Dorms are communal and clean, but remember, backpackers in Jamaica tend to love their reggae, so don't expect peace and quiet. The private rooms are fine, but you'll get more bang for your buck at similarly priced guesthouses, although those aren't as conducive to meeting other travelers.

✵ Eating

Houseboat Grill
GOURMET JAMAICAN $$$

(☏979-8845; Southern Cross Blvd; mains US$15-32; ☉dinner Tue-Sun; ✐) Moored in Bogue Bay at Montego Bay Freeport, this converted houseboat is one of the best restaurants in the country. The changing menu offers eclectic Caribbean fusion cuisine: tiger shrimp in a fiery red curry, or beef medallions with goat's cheese and plantain mashed potatoes. You can dine inside, or reclusively out on the moondeck. Reservations are strongly recommended, especially on weekends. Dress up, but not too much (smart casual).

Native Restaurant & Bar
JAMAICAN $$

(☏979-2769; 29 Gloucester Ave; mains US$8-25; ☉breakfast, lunch & dinner) The Native is one of Montego Bay's best practitioners of the haute Jamaican cuisine trope; the chicken cooked in a citrusy ginger sauce is a delicious example. If you're really hungry, consider the 'Boonoonoonoos' sampler (composed of ackee and saltfish, jerk chicken, curried goat, escoveitched fish, plantains and pineapple) – it's like taking a crash course in Jamaican food.

Dolly's Café
JAMAICAN $$

(Hotel Gloriana Plaza, 1 Sunset Blvd; mains US$6-20; ☉breakfast, lunch & dinner) This cozy pub-style dining room is the place for *real* Jamaican cooking. The menu features time-honored favorites like pepperpot soup, roast pumpkin and a unique, delectable snack that you'll want to take along for the ride: baked coconut chips.

Pelican
JAMAICAN $$

(Gloucester Ave; mains J$400-1000; ☉7am-11:30pm) The Pelican perches just over the Hip Strip, both in terms of location and quality of fare. This is one of many places in MoBay that does Jamaican food with a sit-down, refined twist: red snapper in parchment paper, cooked in a wine and béchamel sauce, is a rich, delicate evolution of peasant fare. The rest of the menu is a study in this sort of upgraded traditionalism.

Adwa
VEGETARIAN $

(City Centre Mall, Fort St; mains J$180-400; ☺breakfast & lunch; ✐) As is often the case in Jamaica, the diamonds are in the rough, or in this case, on the 2nd floor of a shopping mall. By 'diamond' we mean to say fantastic cheap vegetarian fare and fruit juice so fresh it tastes like liquid sunlight.

Nyam 'n' Jam
JAMAICAN $

(17 Harbour St; mains J$300-700; ☺breakfast, lunch & dinner) This is where Jamaicans who crave something a little different head. Sure there's jerked meat, callaloo and saltfish, but we've also seen cow mouth, soups that use hooves as a base and a frankly bewildering array of goat dishes, all of them lovely. The name is patois for 'eat and relax.'

Ma Lou's
JAMAICAN $$

(Coral Cliff Casino, Gloucester Ave; mains US$14-31; ☺dinner) You expect African-themed corniness in the Coral Cliff Casino; what comes as a surprise is an exciting nouvelle-Jamaican restaurant. Ma Lou is either humble or marketing-savvy enough to refer to her restaurant as a 'gourmet food shack.' A hole in the wall this ain't, but enough with the setting: how about the food? Roasted Peking chicken, curry with coconut and fried plantain, and specialty jerks grace this menu.

Pork Pit
JERK $

(27 Gloucester Ave; mains J$300-800; ☺11am-11pm) For many visitors the Pork Pit is their first jerk in Jamaica experience. So we want to make something clear: while quite good, this is not the best jerk in Jamaica, or even Montego Bay. It's a solid seven out of 10, and the festival (fried sweet cornbread) is like a nine out of 10, so enjoy. Just don't limit your jerk quest to the Pork Pit, which many people seem to do.

🍷 Drinking

MoBay Proper
BAR

(Fort St) Proper is often packed with friendly locals and expats returned to the motherland. It's a friendly, occasionally raucous spot and probably the easiest bar for tourists to access off the Hip Strip. Beneath a 'chandelier' of Heineken bottles, the pool table generates considerable heat, while dominoes are the rage with an older crowd out on the patio.

Reggae Bar
BAR

(Gloucester Ave) While it may not win the award for the most imaginatively named bar in Jamaica, this two-story shack, done up in (surprise, surprise) lots of reggae flags and Marleyesque art, does serve some of the cheapest drinks on the Hip Strip. J$80 for some overproof rum? Yes, please. Besides playing pool, listening to reggae and getting drunk, there's not much atmosphere.

Brewery
BAR

(Miranda Ridge Plaza) This is a popular sports bar with young and well-to-do Jamaicans, which makes it a good place for getting a bit of local vibe without leaving the confines of the Hip Strip. As the night gets later, the crowd gets more local-heavy; by 2am this bar is straight-up Jamaican.

Twisted Kilt
PUB

(Gloucester Ave; ☺11am-2am) Every town needs a faux-Irish pub and this is Montego Bay's contribution to the genre. The Kilt is a decent enough place for a beer (although we recommend sitting outside; they keep the interior frigid); the best draw is an extensive martini menu that makes for a nice break from Red Stripe.

🔒 Shopping

Gallery of West Indian Art
GALLERY

(✆952-4547; www.galleryofwestindianart.com; 11 Fairfield Rd) In the suburb of Catherine Hall, this is the best-quality gallery in town. It sells genuinely original arts and crafts from around the Caribbean, including Cuban canvases, hand-painted wooden animals, masks and handmade jewelry. Most of the work here is for sale.

Ambiente Gallery
GALLERY

(✆952-7747; 10 Fort St) Has a fine selection of fine-art prints by regional artists.

Craft Markets
MARKETS

For the largest selection head to the **Harbour Street Craft Market** (Harbour St; ☺7am-7pm), which extends for three blocks between Barnett and Market Sts. **Fort Montego Craft Market** (☺8am-7pm), behind the fort, and **Fantasy Craft Market** (☺8am-7pm), at the southern end of Gloucester Ave, offer less variety and quality. You can expect a hard sell at all of these places, so bring your haggling skills and don't be afraid to walk away from something you don't like.

ⓘ Information

DANGERS & ANNOYANCES Visitors can expect to be approached in none-too-subtle terms by locals offering their services (drugs and sex), which gets a bit wearying. Uniformed members of the Montego Bay Resort Patrol police the Hip Strip, so ironically you may deal with more hustlers off the strip. Downtown is not patrolled; it's safe to walk in the historic center during daylight hours but stick to the main streets and stay alert.

Cornwall Regional Hospital (☑952-5100; Mt Salem Rd) Has a 24-hour emergency ward.

Exchange bureau (◷24hr) In the arrival hall at Sangster International Airport. Better rates can be found on the main strip at **FX Trader** (☑952-3171; 37 Gloucester Ave; ◷9am-5pm Mon-Sat), upstairs at the Pelican restaurant; and **Cambio King** (☑971-5260; Gloucester Ave), at the northern end. Downtown – several bureaus can be found on St James and Fort Sts; look for 'cambio' signs.

Jamaica Tourist Board airport (☑952-3009); Cornwall Beach (◷8:30am-4:30pm Mon-Fri, 9am-1pm Sat); Gloucester Ave (☑952-4425; fax 952-3587) Opening hours are variable.

Official visitors guide (www.montego-bay-jamaica.com) Online resource for info on MoBay and environs; spotty updates.

Police station (☑952-2333/1557; 14 Barnett St)

Police Tourism Liaison Unit (☑952-1540; Summit Police Station, Sunset Blvd)

Post office (☑952-7016; Fort St)

ⓘ Getting There & Around

AIR Air Jamaica (☑922-4661, 888-359-2475, in the USA 800-523-5585; www.airjamaica.com; 9 Queen's Dr; ◷8:30am-4:30pm Mon-Fri) operates jet and prop-plane services between MoBay's Donald Sangster International Airport and Kingston's Norman Manley International Airport.

TimAir (☑952-2516, 979-1114; www.timair.net; domestic terminal, Donald Sangster International Airport), an air-taxi service, offers charter flights to Negril (US$179), Ocho Rios (US$362), Port Antonio (US$599) and Kingston (US$483).

You'll find taxis waiting outside the arrivals lounge at the airport. There is an official taxi booth immediately outside customs. Your taxi driver will probably call for a porter...who'll expect a tip for taking your luggage the 10m to your car! A tourist taxi to Gloucester Ave costs US$10. Alternatively you can catch a minibus or route taxi from the gas station at the entrance to the airport (J$80).

BOAT Cruise ships berth at the Montego Freeport, about 3km south of town. Taxis to downtown MoBay cost US$20.

Montego Bay Yacht Club (☑979-8038; fax 979-8262; Sunset Dr) has hookups, gasoline and diesel and will handle immigration and customs procedures.

BUS & MINIBUS Comfortable **Knutsford Express** (☑971-1822; www.knutsfordexpress.com) buses run from its own bus terminal near the Courts furniture store in downtown MoBay to Ocho Rios (J$1200, two hours) and Kingston (J$2000, four hours). Book a Kingston ticket more than 24 hours in advance and get a discount for J$250. Buses depart at 5am, 9am, 1pm and 5pm Monday to Friday; 6am and 4:30pm Saturday; and 8:30am, 1:30pm and 4:30pm Sunday.

Minibuses (ie vans) run directly to Ocho Rios (J$250 to J$300; onward transfers to Port Antonio and Kingston) and Lucea (J$200; onward transfers to Negril – some minibuses will continue on to Negril, thus eliminating the need for a transfer).

CAR Bargain (☑952-0762), **Budget** (☑952-3838), **Hertz** (☑979-0438) and **Island Rental Car** (☑952-5771) all have offices at Donald Sangster International Airport.

PUBLIC TRANSPORTATION There is no in-town bus service. Route taxis, recognizable by their red license plates, charge J$80 for trips between neighborhoods; you can see where a driver goes based on what's written on the side of his car. All depart from and arrive at the transportation station near the junction of St James and Barnett Sts.

TAXI Licensed JUTA taxis cruise Gloucester Ave; they charge a steep US$10 minimum. Published fares from Gloucester Ave are US$10 to the airport, US$23 to Greenwood, US$15 to Ironshore, US$15 to Montego Freeport and US$15 to Rose Hall.

Rose Hall to Greenwood

Rose Hall Great House   HISTORIC HOUSE
(☑953-2323; rosehall@cwjamaica.com; adult/child under 12 US$20/10; ◷9am-6pm, last tour at 5:15pm) This mansion, with its commanding hilltop position 3.2km east of Ironshore, is the most famous great house in Jamaica. Most of the attraction is the legend of Annie Palmer, the 'White Witch of Rose Hall,' a multiple murderer said to haunt the house. Her bedroom upstairs is decorated in crimson silk brocade, which is actually a new addition to the home. The cellars now house

an old-English-style pub and a well-stocked gift shop.

Minibuses and route taxis ply the A1 road. You'll pay about J$150 to J$200 to travel from MoBay to Rose Hall.

Greenwood Great House HISTORIC HOUSE
(☑953-1077; www.greenwoodgreathouse.com; admission US$15; ⊙9am-6pm) While the main attraction in these parts is Rose Hall Great House, visiting this estate is a far more intimate and, frankly, interesting experience. The furnishings are more authentic, the tour less breakneck and there are none of the silly ghost stories, although the exterior edifice is admittedly not as impressive.

Unique among local plantation houses, Greenwood survived unscathed during the slave rebellion of Christmas 1831. The original library is still intact, as are paintings, Dresden china, a court jester's chair and plentiful antiques, including a mantrap used for catching runaway slaves. The view from the front balcony down to the sea is stunning.

Buses traveling between Montego Bay and Falmouth will drop you anywhere along the A1; ask to be let off across from the Total gas station on the sea side of the road and walk up the road up the hill. It's a good 20-minute slog to the top.

Falmouth

Few other towns in Jamaica have retained their original architecture to the same degree as Falmouth, which has a faded Georgian splendor. The city, 37km east of Montego Bay, has been the capital of Trelawny parish since 1790. An enormous new cruise-ship dock was being built on the eastern edge of Falmouth at the time of this research. Locals are divided over its impact. Some eagerly await the hordes of foreign visitors and their wallets, while others bemoan environmental and cultural impacts to sleepy Falmouth.

◉ Sights & Activities

Town Center NOTABLE BUILDINGS
The best place to orient yourself is **Water Sq**, at the east end of Duke St. Named for an old circular stone reservoir dating to 1798, the square (actually a triangle) has a fountain topped by an old waterwheel. Today it forms a traffic roundabout, but back in the day this fountain pumped freshwater before New York City had any such luxury. Many

of the wooden shop fronts in this area are attractively disheveled relics.

The market structure on the east side of Water Sq, which dominates central Falmouth, was once the site of slave auctions. The current structure was built in 1894 and named the **Albert George Shopping & Historical Centre**, in honor of two of Queen Victoria's grandsons.

One block east of Water Sq is Seaboard St and the grandiose Georgian **courthouse** in Palladian style, fronted by a double curling staircase and Doric columns, with cannons to the side. The current building, dating from 1926, is a replica of the original 1815 structure that was destroyed by fire. The town council presides here.

On Cornwall St one of the most stately edifices is the restored **Baptist Manse** (cnr Market & Cornwall Sts), formerly the residence of nonconformist Baptist preacher William Knibb, who was instrumental in lobbying for passage of the Abolition Bill that ended slavery.

On July 31, 1838, slaves gathered outside **William Knibb Memorial Church** (cnr King & George Sts) for an all-night vigil, awaiting midnight and then the dawn of full freedom (to quote Knibbs: 'The monster is dead'), when slave shackles, a whip and an iron collar were symbolically buried in a coffin. In the grounds of the churchyard you can find Knibb's grave, as well as that of his wife. To get inside the church, ask at the Leaf of Life Hardware store on King St.

The oldest extant building in town is **St Peter's Anglican Church**, built in 1785 and enlarged in 1842. It lies four blocks west along Duke St. The graveyard tombstones are spookily sun-bleached, like bones.

Route taxis leave for Falmouth from the Barnett St Transportation Station in Montego Bay (J$150) several times each day.

Martha Brae

Most visitors come to this small village, 3km due south of Falmouth, for the exhilarating 1½-hour **rafting** trip on the Martha Brae River. Long bamboo rafts poled by a skilled guide cruise down the river and stop at Tarzan's Corner for a swing and swim in a calm pool. Trips begin from **Rafter's Village** (☑952-0889, 940-6398; www.jamaicarafting. com; 66 Claude Clarke Ave, Montego Bay; per raft 1-2 people US$75) about 1.5km south of Martha Brae. Remember to tip your raft guide.

Route taxis make the 10-minute ride from Falmouth to Martha Brae (J$80) during daylight hours on a continuous basis. There are also regular buses.

Glistening Waters

Located in an estuary near Rock, about 1.6km east of Falmouth, the waters of Glistening Waters, also known as the Luminous Lagoon, glow an eerie green when disturbed at night. The green glow is due to the presence of microorganisms that produce photochemical reactions when disturbed; the concentrations are so thick that fish swimming by look like green lanterns.

Needless to say, swimming through the luminous lagoon is just awesome, especially on starry nights, when it's hard to tell where the water ends and the sky begins. Half-hour **boat trips** are offered from **Glistening Waters Marina** (✆954-3229; per person US$25; ⊙7-9pm). Any hotel from Ocho Rios to Negril should be able to organize a trip out here.

The amazing **Time N' Place** (✆843-3625; www.mytimenplace.com; cottages US$80; P✷) has four quaint all-hardwood cottages (each housing up to three people) for rent right on World Beach; a tree house–like 'Bird's Nest' is also in the works. The cottages, for all their rustic charm, are quite modern and well-presented on the inside. The beach bar and restaurant is a great place to hang out – it was a setting in the movie *How Stella Got Her Groove Back* and has been the backdrop for many a photo shoot.

NEGRIL & THE WEST

If the popular tourist image of Jamaica is sun, beach life, rum, sun, sea, sun, diving and sunsets, chances are the popular tourist is thinking of Negril – or thinking in particular of Jamaica's longest swath of sugary white-sand beach at Long Bay (also known as Seven Mile Beach).

Negril

POP 4200

In the 1970s Negril lured hippies with its offbeat beach life to a countercultural Shangri-la where anything went. To some extent anything still goes here, except the innocent – they left long ago.

The gorgeous, 11km-long swath of sand that is Long Bay is still kissed by serene waters into which the sun melts evening after evening in a riot of color. And the easily accessible coral reefs offer some of the best diving in the Caribbean. Yet these undeniable attractions have done just that: attract. In the last three decades Negril has exploded as a tourist venue. With tourism comes the hustle – you're very likely to watch the sunset in the cloying company of a ganja dealer or an aspiring tour guide–cum–escort.

⊙ Sights & Activities

Long Bay   BEACH
This blindingly white, world-famous, 11km-long beach is Negril's claim to fame, and no matter how cynical you are, you gotta admit: this is one beautiful beach. It's a hell of a show: naked Europeans, tattooed Americans, gigolos and hustlers offering everything from sex to aloe massages and (always) drugs. Tourist police occasionally patrol but, by law, all Jamaican beaches must permit public access, so the hustlers are free to roam. Watersports concessions line the beach. By night, music pumps from reggae bars and discos.

Negril Lighthouse   LIGHTHOUSE
(West End Rd; admission free; ⊙9am-sunset)
Five kilometers south of Negril village, the gleaming-white, 20m-tall lighthouse illuminates the westernmost point of Jamaica. Wilson Johnson, the superintendent, will gladly lead the way up the 103 stairs for a bird's-eye view of the coast.

The waters off Negril are usually mirror-calm – ideal for all kinds of **watersports**. Numerous concessions along the beach rent out Jet Skis (about US$50 for 30 minutes), kayaks, sailboards and Sunfish (about US$20 per hour). They also offer water skiing (US$40 for 30 minutes) and banana-boat rides (using an inflatable banana-shaped raft towed by a speedboat; US$15).

Negril offers extensive offshore reefs and cliffs with grottoes. The shallow reefs are perfect for **diving** and **snorkeling**. Visibility often exceeds 30m and seas are dependably calm. Most dives are in 10.5m to 22.5m of water. Expect to pay about US$10 an hour for masks and fins from concession stands on the beach. The **Negril Scuba Centre** (✆877-7517; www.negrilscuba.com; 1-/2-tank dive US$40/80) is one of the oldest, most-established diving outfits in town.

🛏 Sleeping

LONG BAY

Rondel Village
HOTEL $$

(☑957-4413; www.rondelvillage.com; d US$100-185, 1-/2-bedroom villa US$245/345; ❄️🔌🏊) A highly affable and efficient hotel graced by walkways lined with an array of indigenous fruit trees, the family-owned Village offers well-appointed studios and beachfront rooms clustered around a small pool and Jacuzzi. Rooms are like lovely furnished apartments, and staff are very friendly.

Negril Yoga Centre
RESORT $

(☑957-4397; www.negrilyoga.com; Norman Manley Blvd; d US$50-84; ❄️🔌) These rustic yet atmospheric rooms and cottages – most with refrigerators and fans – surround an open-air, thatched, wood-floored yoga center set in a garden. Options range from a two-story, Thai-style wooden cabin to an adobe farmer's cottage; all are pleasingly if modestly furnished. Yoga classes are offered (guests/nonguests US$10/15). Air-conditioning in rooms runs an extra $11.50 per night.

Negril Tree House
HOTEL $$

(☑957-4287; www.negril-treehouse.com; r US$150-170, ste US$280-350; ❄️🔌🏊) This unpretentious resort is a favorite among low-key travelers. The vibe is chilled but the service and amenities are modern and efficient. Rooms are spacious and clean, while the elegant one- and two-bedroom suites feature kitchenette, king-size beds and a Murphy bed in the lounge, which opens onto a wide veranda.

Firefly Cottages
HOTEL $$

(☑957-4358; www.jamaicalink.com; cabins from US$50, ste & apt US$130-250; ❄️🔌) One of the more diverse accommodation options in Negril, the Firefly gives you a range of lodgings, starting from a crisp, single-occupancy studio apartment, to luxurious penthouse suites atop a small apartment complex, to beachside cottages. The 'Secrets Cabins' are a collection of (very) tiny chalets that can sleep two people and are priced for backpackers. Staff are professional and courteous. The nearby beach is nude-approved.

WEST END

TOP CHOICE Rockhouse
HOTEL $$

(☑957-4373; www.rockhousehotel.com; r/studio/villa US$160/185/355; ❄️🔌🏊) One of the West End's most beautiful and well-run hotels, with gorgeous thatched rondavels (round

huts; two are 'premium villas') of pine and stone, plus studios dramatically clinging to the cliffside above a small cove. Catwalks lead over the rocks to an open-sided, multilevel dining pavilion (with one of the best restaurants around) overhanging the ocean. A dramatically designed pool sits atop the cliffs.

TOP CHOICE Blue Cave Castle
HOTEL $$

(☑957-4845; www.bluecavecastle.com; s/d US$60/125; ❄️) Providing perhaps the best view of Long Bay from the West End, this atmospheric, all-stone concoction attracts nudists, travel junkies and freethinkers. The property really does resemble a castle, albeit one built by a mad genius who wanted to create a pastel lighthouse and didn't skimp on the quirkiness. Or comfort: bedrooms are equipped with a CD player, ceiling fan and refrigerator and tower rooms open to the stars and the ocean. Stairs from the castle lead down to a blue sea cave.

Catcha Falling Star
RESORT $$

(☑957-0390; www.catchajamaica.com; cottage US$95-350) In the inimitable West End style, these pleasant, fan-cooled cottages – including several with two bedrooms – sit on the cliffs. Each is named for an astrological sign and comes with microwave oven, fridge, bar, double beds draped in mosquito netting and lots of arty accents. A tiered cliff affords easy access to the sea, where clothing-optional bathing can be enjoyed in a private cove.

🍴 Eating & Drinking

LONG BAY

Cosmo's
SEAFOOD $

(Norman Manley Blvd; mains J$300-1000; ⏲10am-11pm) Our favorite spot for seafood in seaside Negril, Cosmo's eschews fine-dining flash for a few rough-hewn tables, a beachside location and plates of melt-in-your mouth, amazing seafood. The curry conch is deliciously spicy – enough kick to wake your mouth up, not so much to be unbearable.

Angela's
ITALIAN $$

(Bar-b-barn Hotel; mains US$6-20; ⏲breakfast, lunch & dinner) We don't know why pizza goes so well with the beach, but it does and the pizza at Angela's is some of the best in Negril. As are the pasta plates and a host of other Italian dishes, all of a quality we frankly weren't expecting on a Jamaican beach.

Selina's   CAFE **$**
(Norman Manley Blvd; mains J$150-400; ⊘break-fast & lunch) Selina's is the spot for premium fresh-roasted honest-to-God Blue Mountain coffee and lovely breakfasts served all day – we can never decide between the Jamaican ackee and saltfish or the equally fabulous Western options like pancakes and om-elets. And so we read a book off the book-exchange shelf, let our food digest and order another brekkie a little bit later...

Norma's on the Beach at
Sea Splash   JAMAICAN **$$$**
(Sea Splash Resort; mains US$15-32; ⊘breakfast, lunch & dinner) This Negril branch of Norma Shirley's celebrated Jamaican culinary em-pire seems to have escaped the hype sur-rounding her Kingston flagship, but the 'new world Caribbean' food at this stylish beach restaurant is just as adventurous. Expect to find the likes of lobster, Cornish game hen, jerk chicken and pasta as well as tricolored 'rasta pasta.'

WEST END

TOP CHOICE Rockhouse Restaurant
& Bar   FUSION **$$$**
(✆957-4373; Rockhouse Hotel; mains US$15-30; ⊘breakfast, lunch & dinner) Lamplit at night this pricey yet relaxed cliffside spot leads the pack when it comes to nouvelle Jamai-can cuisine in the western parishes. Dine and gush over dishes such as vegetable tem-pura with lime and ginger, specialty pastas and daily specials like watermelon spare ribs and blackened mahimahi with mango chutney. At the very least stop by for a sinful bananas Foster.

3 Dives Jerk Centre   JERK **$**
(West End Rd; quarter/half chicken J$350/600; ⊘noon-midnight) It's no small tribute to 3 Dives that its jerk overshadows its reputa-tion for lengthy waits (sometimes over an hour). Fortunately the chefs are more than happy to let you peek into the kitchen, where there's bound to be a pile of super-hot Scotch bonnet peppers threatening to spon-taneously combust.

Royal Kitchen Vegetarian Café   I-TAL **$**
(West End Rd; mains J$280-600; ⊘breakfast, lunch & dinner; ✐) The best I-tal (natural foods) eatery in Negril is popular with legit local Rastafarians and those who come to collect their pearls of wisdom. The fare – strictly vegetarian – is served on simple tables where

you are sure to make friends with inquisitive passersby. Juices are especially good.

☆ Entertainment

Negril's reggae concerts are legendary, with performances every night in peak season, when there's sure to be big talent in town. A handful of venues offer weekly jams, and they have a rotation system so they all get a piece of the action. Big-name acts usually perform at **MXIII** (West End Rd) in the West End, and at **Roots Bamboo** (✆957-4479; ⊘Wed & Sun) on Long Bay. You'll see shows advertised on billboards and hear about them from megaphone-equipped cars.

The **Jungle** (✆957-4005; ⊘4pm-late) is a classic nightclub on Long Bay Beach, with a thronged and sweaty dance floor down-stairs and a pleasant deck with pool tables. You will be told by everyone you meet that you cannot miss the sunset at **Rick's Cafe** (West End Rd); we find the experience overrat-ed and overcrowded, considering the same damn sun sets in the ocean minus the too-expensive beers when you watch from the beach, but hey.

ℹ Information

DANGERS & ANNOYANCES Negril has argu-ably the worst hustlers in Jamaica. On your first day on the beach they will mark you and approach with a sales pitch for tours, drugs, sex etc. Most back off after a polite but firm 'no', but some are worryingly aggressive. They'd never attack a tourist, but they know newcomers can be intimidated by a tough front, which manifests itself in accusing you of racism if you ignore them, bragging about their upbringing in hard parts of Jamaica etc. Try a firm 'No. Respect' and look them in the eye – this seems to work most of the time. Don't lose your temper.

While police patrol the beach, and resort owners watch out for tourists, robberies occur in Negril. Don't walk between Long Bay and the West End at night. Try to avoid unlit stretches of beach after dark.

Easy Rock Internet Café (✆957-0671; West End Rd; per hr US$5) The most pleasant and personable internet cafe.

Jamaica Tourist Board/TPDCo (✆957-4803/9314; Times Sq Plaza; ⊘9am-5pm Mon-Fri)

Negril Beach Medical Center (✆957-4888; fax 957-4347; Norman Manley Blvd; ⊘9am-5pm, doctors on call 24hr)

Police station (✆957-4268; Sheffield Rd)

Post office (✆957-9654; West End Rd) Be-tween A Fi Wi Plaza and King's Plaza.

Scotiabank (⟲957-4236) Between the West End and Long Beach, near other banks; has foreign exchange service and an ATM.

❶ Getting There & Away

Dozens of coasters and route taxis run between Negril and Montego Bay. The two-hour journey costs about J$400, especially if you factor in changing vehicles in Lucea. Be prepared for a hair-raising ride. Minibuses and route taxis also leave for Negril from Donald Sangster International Airport in Montego Bay (the price is negotiable, but expect to pay about US$10).

A licensed taxi between Montego Bay and Negril will cost at least US$65, but expect drivers to quote ridiculous rates and a lot of arguing.

❶ Getting Around

Negril stretches along more than 16km of shoreline, and it can be a withering walk. Coasters and route taxis cruise Norman Manley Blvd and West End Rd. You can flag them down anywhere. The fare between any two points should never be more than about J$150.

Car-rental options:

Jus Jeep (⟲957-0094/5; West End Rd)
Vernon's Car Rentals (⟲957-4354/522) At Fun Holiday Beach Resort and shop 22, Negril Plaza.

SOUTHERN JAMAICA

The South Coast and Central Highlands contain everything that makes Jamaica lovely – soft beaches, wild mountains, delicious food, kickin' music – with very few megaresorts to speak of and laid-back, low-impact tourism. Even the locals seem a little friendlier. Trust us. You'll come to St Elizabeth parish, see the way the gold light attaches to the red soil and realize what magic remains on this island.

Treasure Beach

The sun-kissed land southeast of Black River is sheltered from rain for most of the year by the Santa Cruz Mountains, so there is none of the lush greenery of the north coast. Instead, you'll find a thorny, surreally beautiful semi-desert, a landscape almost East African in it's scorched beauty. Acacia trees and cacti tower over fields of scallions guarded by fence rows of aloe vera. The region remains unsullied by resort-style tourism; here you can slip into a lazy, no-frills tropical lifestyle almost impossible to achieve elsewhere on the island's coast.

You'll be hard-pressed to find a more authentically charming and relaxing place in Jamaica. The sense of remoteness, the easy pace and the graciousness of the local farmers and fisherfolk attract travelers seeking an away-from-it-all, cares-to-the-wind lifestyle. Many have settled here – much to local pride.

A bicycle is a good means of getting around quiet Treasure Beach; most hotels and guesthouses rent them out for a small fee. There is one main road connecting all of the beaches, plus many smaller cow paths and dirt trails.

🏖 Beaches

Several fishing beaches, all sparsely sprinkled with tourists, beckon within easy walking distance of the accommodations we mention in this chapter. Watersports haven't yet caught on, but the waves are good for bodysurfing. Beware, as sometimes a vicious undertow tugs at area beaches.

At the eastern 'bottom' of Treasure Beach you'll find **Great Bay**, a pretty, rural patchwork of fields and beach; this is the least-developed portion of Treasure Beach, where the main business remains a Fishermen's Co-op building.

Jack Spratt Beach, at the western edge of Jake's Place, is next along as you head north and west; here brightly painted wooden fishing boats are pulled up on the sand and there is invariably a fisherman or two on hand tending the nets. This is the safest beach for swimming.

The next beach to the west is **Frenchman's Beach**, watched over by a landmark 'buttonwood' tree that has long attracted the attention of poets, painters and woodcarvers who ply their wares. Local boat captains congregate here, as does everyone else in the area once the sun starts to set. It's is a great place to arrange trips to the Pelican Bar or Black River.

In the opposite direction from Jake's there's **Calabash Bay Beach**, with a few cook and rum shops and a sandy beach, and **Old Wharf Beach**, the most private of the bunch, although still accessible by anyone who makes the effort to totter down to the sand.

🛏 Sleeping

[TOP CHOICE] **Nuestra Casa Guest House**   GUESTHOUSE $

(⟲965-0152; www.billysbay.com; d US$50; ❄️🛜)
This laid-back property consists of a pretty arid garden built into porous rocks, a wide veranda peppered with rockers and highly

personalized rooms kitted out in quirky, individual (and intellectual; the books on hand are amazing) decor. It's a tremendous deal at these rates, which decrease for longer stays. Meals are prepared by arrangement.

Jake's Place　　　　　　　　HOTEL **$$**
(☑965-3000, in the USA 800-688-7678, in the UK 020-7440-4360; www.jakeshotel.com; r from US$150, cottages US$225-450; ☎☒) If there is a quirky, bohemian-chic center to Treasure Beach's laid-back, community-tourism-oriented vibe, it's Jake's Place. There's a fantastical mix of rooms, suites, cottages and huts decked out like a fairy-tale illustration book with references to Greece and North Africa: mini-Moroccan *ksars,* terra-cotta tile floors, tile and glass-brick walk-in showers, exquisite handmade beds, onion-dome curves, blood-red walls and rough-hewn doors inset with colored bottles and glass beads.

Waikiki Guest House　　　GUESTHOUSE **$**
(☑965-3660, 345-9669; s/d US$25/50) Location, location, location: this excellent budget option literally abuts Frenchman's Beach. The rooms are clean and simple, nothing special and nothing to complain about either. The 2nd-floor double in Waikiki's odd concrete tower (prettier than it sounds) is awesome; you can step out onto a little veranda and watch the sun set right into the ocean.

Ital Rest　　　　　　　GUESTHOUSE **$**
(☑421-8909, 473-6145; www.italrest.com; r US$50) In the right setting a lack of electricity rockets a property right into the super-romantic category. Two exquisite all-wood thatched cabins are the sort of setting we're talking about. Hanging here with the Rasta owners as the sun sets, then retiring to a candlelit room with a loved one for a cool-water shower – good times. All rooms have toilets, and the upstairs room has a great sundeck.

✗ Eating

TOP CHOICE **Strikey's**　　　　　JAMAICAN **$**
(Billy's Bay; mains J$400-800; ⊙dinner, closed summer) The energetic, ever-friendly Chris Strikey has worked as a professional chef in the USA and at Jake's Place, but when the tourist season rolls around (roughly December to April), Strikey operates his own food shack, anchored by secret recipes and a hand-built jerk smoker. The man's food is sublime: Jamaican favorites, home-cooked and mouthwatering, especially the jerk.

Jack Sprat Café　　　　　　FUSION **$$**
(mains US$7-20; ⊙10am-11pm) An excellent barefoot beachside eatery affiliated with Jake's, this appealing joint features a diverse menu of Jamaican and Western standards: salads, crab cakes, smoked marlin, conch curry and lobster as well as excellent jerk or garlic shrimp. But for our money, it's all about the pizza, quite possibly the best on the island. The jerk-sausage topping in particular elicits audible moans of pleasure from satisfied customers. Takes credit cards.

Pelican Bar　　　　　　JAMAICAN **$$**
(mains US$5-15; ⊙morning-sunset) The Pelican Bar may be Jamaica's most famous spot for a drink: a thatched hut on stilts on a submerged sandbar 1km out to sea, where you can chill with a Red Stripe while watching dolphins flip in the surf a few meters away. It provides Jamaica's – and perhaps the planet's – most enjoyable spot for a drink. Getting there is half the fun: hire a local boat captain (most charge around US$35), who will call ahead to arrange things if you want to eat.

❶ Information

On the internet, a good starting point is www. treasurebeach.net. There are no banks serving international travelers here, but there is a 24-hour Scotiabank ATM in Crossroads, 5km north of Treasure Beach.

BREDS (☑965-9748; Kingfisher Plaza; per 30 min J$2003; ⊙9am-5pm) Internet access.

Dr Valerie M Elliott (☑607-9074; ⊙7am-10pm Mon, Tue & Fri) Available on call.

Police station (☑965-0163) Between Calabash Bay and Pedro Cross.

❶ Getting There & Around

There is no direct service to Treasure Beach from Montego Bay, Negril or Kingston. From Black River you can connect to Treasure Beach via route taxi or minibus (J$200). From Mandeville you'll need to get a route taxi to Junction or Santa Cruz (J$150) and another taxi to Treasure Beach (J$200). Most hotels arrange transfers from MoBay for US$80 to US$100.

Black River

Though capital of St Elizabeth and the parish's largest town, Black River has a transient feel. Most visitors are less interested in the town than in exploring what is beyond. Its namesake river, on whose western banks it rests, spirits day-trippers off to the southern half of the **Great Morass** to see crocodiles and eat at waterside jerk shacks.

The waters, stained by tannins and dark as molasses, are a complex ecosystem and a vital preserve for more than 100 bird species. The morass also forms Jamaica's most significant refuge for crocodiles; about 300 live in the swamps. Locals take to the waters in dugout canoes, tending funnel-shaped shrimp pots made of bamboo in the traditional manner of their West African forebears.

Black River Safaris (☎965-2513/086; ⊙tours 9am, 11am, 12:30pm, 2pm & 3:30pm), which offers 60- to 75-minute journeys aboard the *Safari Queen*, is a typical operator. Similar tours are offered by **St Elizabeth River Safari** (☎965-2374/229; ⊙tours 9am, 11am, 2pm & 3:30pm), behind the Hendricks Building; and **Irie Safaris** (☎965-2211; 12 High St; ⊙tours every 90min 9am-4:30pm), wharfside from a jetty just east of the bus station (Irie can also arrange **kayaking** trips in the area, which we highly recommend). At the time of research tours ran around US$20 to US$30; thanks to the price of petrol these rates can swing up and down at short notice.

A little ways out of town, **Idler's Rest** (☎965-9000; http://idlersrest.com; r from US$100; P❀🔊) hotel redefines 'irie,' which is to say, being utterly at peace with your surroundings and infused with good vibes. Owned by a friendly lawyer, this tasteful place is decorated in a comfy mix of modern chic, Caribbean color and pan-African art. Rooms are cooled by gentle sea breezes and you can wander the local beach while gazing at dolphins sparkling on the waves – sheesh, sometimes Jamaica really *is* paradise.

YS Falls

Among Jamaica's most spectacular falls, this series of eight **cascades** (☎997-6360; www. ysfalls.com; adult/child US$15/7.50; ⊙9:30am-3:30pm Tue-Sun, closed public holidays) fall 36.5m and are separated by cool pools that are perfect for swimming. The falls are hemmed in by limestone cliffs and are surrounded by towering forest.

The falls are on the YS Estate, 5.5km north of the A2 (the turn-off is 1.5km east of Middle Quarters). The entrance is just north of the junction of the B6 towards Maggotty.

Buses travel via YS Falls from the Shakespeare Plaza in Maggotty. On the A2, buses, coasters and route taxis will drop you at the junction to YS Falls, from where you can walk (it's about 3.2km) or catch an Ipswich-bound route taxi.

UNDERSTAND JAMAICA

History
Columbus & the Spanish Wave

Jamaica's first tourist was none other than Christopher Columbus, who landed on the island in 1494. At the time there were perhaps 100,000 peaceful Arawaks, who had settled Jamaica around AD 700. Spanish settlers arrived from 1510 and quickly introduced two things that would profoundly shape the island's future: sugarcane production and slavery. By the end of the 16th century the Arawak population had been entirely wiped out, worn down by hard labor, ill-treatment and European diseases.

The English Invasion

In 1654 an ill-equipped and badly organized English contingent sailed to the Caribbean. After failing to take Hispaniola, they turned to weakly defended Jamaica. Despite the ongoing efforts of Spanish loyalists and the guerilla-style campaigns of freed Spanish slaves (*cimarrones* – 'wild ones' – or Maroons), England took control of the island.

Slavery

New slaves kept on arriving; bloody insurrections kept occurring. The last and largest was the 1831 Christmas Rebellion, inspired by Sam Sharpe, an educated slave who incited passive resistance. The rebellion turned violent as up to 20,000 slaves razed plantations and murdered planters. When the slaves were tricked into laying down arms with a false promise of abolition – and 400 were hanged and hundreds more whipped – there was a wave of revulsion in England, causing the British parliament to finally abolish slavery.

The transition from a slave to wage-labor economy caused chaos, with most slaves rejecting the starvation wages offered on the estates and choosing to fend for themselves.

The Road to Independence

A banana-led economic recovery was halted by the Great Depression of the 1930s, and then kick-started again by WWII, when the Caribbean islands supplied food and raw materials to Britain. Adult suffrage for all Jamaicans was introduced in 1944, and virtual autonomy from Britain was granted in 1947. Jamaica seceded from the short-lived West Indies Federation in 1962 after a referendum called for the island's full independence.

Post-independence politics have been dominated by the legacy of two cousins: Alexander Bustamante, who formed the first trade union in the Caribbean just prior to WWII and later formed the Jamaican Labor Party (JLP); and Norman Manley, whose People's National Party (PNP) was the first political party on the island when it was convened in 1938. Manley's son, Michael, led the PNP towards democratic socialism in the mid-1970s, causing capital flight at a time when Jamaica could ill afford it. Bitterly opposed factions engaged in open urban warfare preceding the 1976 election, but the PNP won the election by a wide margin and Manley continued with his socialist agenda.

Coming to Terms

The US government was hostile to the socialist path Jamaica was taking and when Manley began to develop close ties with Cuba, the CIA purportedly planned to topple the government. Businesses pulled out, the economy went into sharp decline and the country lived virtually under siege. Almost 700 people were killed in the lead-up to the 1980 elections, which were won by the JLP's Edward Seaga. Seaga restored Jamaica's economic fortunes somewhat, severed ties with Cuba and courted Ronald Reagan's USA. Seaga was ousted in 1989 and replaced by Manley, who took a short, second crack at the prime ministerial office. He retired in 1992, handing the reins to his deputy, Percival James Patterson, Jamaica's first black prime minister.

Present & Future

In 2007 Bruce Golding of the JLP was elected prime minister, ending 18 years of PNP rule. In 2009 the United States called for the extradition of Christopher 'Dudus' Coke, the don of Tivoli Gardens ghetto and one of the most powerful men in Jamaica. The demand for extradition was originally refused by Golding, who claimed that the evidence against Dudus was gathered illegally, but after pressure from the US a warrant was issued for Dudus' arrest on May 18,

2010. Between May 24 and 27, heavy fighting broke out between Dudus' gunmen and the joint police-military force, leaving 67 dead. Dudus himself remained on the run for a month, before being apprehended at a road block, disguised as a woman and en route to the US embassy to negotiate his surrender. His absence left a power vacuum, with new blood fighting over the position of Jamaica's most influential don.

Modern Jamaica faces several battles, and most Jamaicans will tell you the greatest is crime and the brain drain to the USA, Canada and the UK. Illiteracy is also a major concern, as are threats to the environment through deforestation and overdevelopment. In the meantime the Jamaican people face the future with resolve and a measure of good humor – they've endured worse in the past.

Culture

Many Jamaicans will tell you their island is not part of the Caribbean, but Africa. While the vestiges of the slave era weigh heavily on the national psyche, over the last century the rise of Jamaican nationalism and an explosion in homegrown culture have engendered a proud and vibrant contemporary culture.

VISITOR DOS & DON'TS

» Don't ignore beggars, hustlers or higglers, as it will be taken as an insult. Offer a firm but polite 'sorry' or 'no, thank you.'

» Do relax. 'Soon come' is a favorite expression that means 'it'll happen when it happens.'

» Do try to understand the hardships that the majority of Jamaicans face and that most are simply trying to make a living in the face of great competition.

» Do be formal with strangers. Address people you meet with 'Mr' or 'Miss,' or even 'Sir' or 'Ma'am.' Using a first name can be taken as treating someone as inferior.

» Do ask before snapping a photo. Many Jamaicans enjoy being photographed, sometimes for a small fee, but others prefer not to pose for tourists and can respond angrily.

The Jamaican character has an intriguing contrast – both hard-working and happy-go-lucky. They are also generally helpful, courteous, genteel and full of humility. However, charged memories of slavery and racism continue to bring out the spirit of anarchy latent in a former slave society divided into rich and poor. Jamaicans struggling hard against poverty are disdainful of talk about a 'tropical paradise.'

Jamaicans love to debate, or 'reason.' They tend to express themselves forcefully, turning differences of opinion into voluble arguments with some confounding elliptical twists and stream-of-consciousness associations.

Jamaicans' sarcasm and sardonic wit is legendary. The deprecating humor has evolved as an escape valve that hides their true feelings. The saying that 'everyt'ing irie' is black humor, because life is a problem. Often Jamaican wit is laced with sexual undertones. Jamaicans like to make fun of others, but they accept being the source of similar jokes in good grace.

Living in Jamaica

Many Jamaicans live in the countryside, eking out a marginal existence in ramshackle villages and rural shacks, fishing, working the cane and banana fields and farming, sometimes in pockets of extreme poverty, as in Kingston's ghettoes and shanties. Job opportunities are difficult to come by without a proper education, which doesn't come cheap, so many low-income Jamaicans hustle, waiting in the street for an opportunity to present itself. The average per-capita income is only US$4390 and many Jamaicans are reliant on remittances sent by family members living abroad.

Jamaica has a significant middle class – well-educated, entrepreneurial and with a preference for shopping trips to Miami or New York. But many of the middle class live with a surprising lack of contact with the harsh reality in which the majority of Jamaicans live, and they seem to be able to muster little empathy. At the same time, others will employ a part-time gardener or maid not out of necessity, but to share their own good fortune.

'Out Of Many, One People'

The nation's motto reflects the diverse heritage of Jamaica. Tens of thousands of West Africans, plus large numbers of Irish, Scottish, Germans and Welsh, arrived through-out the colonial period, along with Hispanic and Portuguese Jews and those whom Jamaicans call 'Syrians' (a term for all those of Levantine extraction). In 1838, following emancipation, Chinese and Indian indentured laborers ('coolies') arrived from Hong Kong and India.

Jamaica proclaims itself a melting pot of racial harmony. Still, insecurities of identity have been carried down from the plantation era. Class lines drawn during the colonial era are still related to color; lighter-skinned Jamaicans are far more likely to hold better-paid jobs and it is still desirable to 'marry light.' Solidarity among all people of African descent never existed in Jamaica, while there is lingering resentment – as well as prejudice – against whites and disillusionment with post-independence Jamaica.

Religion & Spirituality

Jamaica professes to have the greatest number of churches per square kilometer in the world. Although most foreigners associate the island with Rastafarianism, more than 80% of Jamaicans identify themselves as Christian.

Literature

Through the years Jamaican literature has been haunted by the ghosts of slave history and the ambiguities of the country's relationship to Mother England. The classic novels tend to focus on survival in a grim colonial landscape and escape to Africa, which often proves to be even grimmer. Best known, perhaps, is Herbert de Lisser's classic gothic horror, *White Witch of Rose Hall*, which tells of Annie Palmer, the wicked mistress of Rose Hall who supposedly murdered three husbands and several slave lovers.

Perry Henzell's *Power Game* is a tale of power politics based on real events in the 1970s, told by the director of the movie *The Harder They Come*. The poignant novel of that name, written by Michael Thewell, recounts the story of a country boy who comes to Kingston, turns into a 'rude boy' (armed thug) and becomes fatally enmeshed in the savage drug culture. The mean streets of Kingston are also the setting for the gritty novels of Roger Mais, notably *The Hills Were Joyful Together* and *Brother Man*. Orlando Patterson's *The Children of Sisyphus* mines the same bleak terrain from a Rastafarian perspective.

In recent years a number of Jamaican female writers have gained notice: they

A faith rather than a church, Rastafarianism has no official doctrine and is composed of a core of social and spiritual tenets, developed by charismatic Rastafarian leader Leonard Percival Howell, whose 'Twenty-One Points' say the African race was one of God's chosen races, one of the Twelve Tribes of Israel descended from the Hebrews and displaced. Jamaica is Babylon (named after the place where the Israelites were enslaved) and their lot is in exile in a land that cannot be reformed.

Another tenet states that God (Jah) will one day lead Africans from Babylon – any place that 'downpresses' the masses – to Zion (the 'Promised Land,' or Ethiopia). A third states that historical Ethiopian monarch Haile Selassie (1892–1975) is the promised redeemer of Africa and the African diaspora.

Not all Rastafarians wear dreads, and others do not smoke ganja. All adherents, however, accept that Africa is the black race's spiritual home, to which they are destined to return. Rastafarianism evolved as an expression of poor, black Jamaicans seeking fulfillment in the 1930s, a period of growing nationalism and economic and political upheaval.

Many Rastafarians believe that ganja provides a line of communication with God. Through it they claim to gain wisdom and inner divinity through the ability to 'reason' more clearly. The search for truth – 'reasoning' – is integral to the faith and is meant to see through the corrupting influences of 'Babylon.'

The religion preaches love and nonviolence (unless you're homosexual; Rastafarians are some of the most vocally anti-gay voices in an already-loud Jamaican chorus), and adherents live by strict biblical codes that advocate living in harmony with Old Testament traditions. Strict Rastas eat vegetarian I-tal food, prepared without salt, and they are teetotalers who shun tobacco and the trappings of Western consumption.

include Christine Craig *(Mint Tea)*, Patricia Powell *(Me Dying Trial)*, Michelle Cliff *(Abeng, Land of Look Behind)* and Vanessa Spence *(Roads Are Down)*. *Lionheart Gal*, a lively collection of stories mostly in patois by the Sistren Collective, sheds light on the lives of women in Jamaica, while *Anancy and Miss Lou* by Louise Bennett continues the art of classic storytelling in patois.

Film

Jamaica has produced some excellent films, most notably cult classic *The Harder They Come* (1973), starring Jimmy Cliff as a 'rude boy' in Kingston's ghettoes. *Smile Orange* (1974) tells the story of Ringo, a hustling waiter at a resort – a theme not irrelevant today. *Rockers* (1978), another music-propelled, socially poignant fable, is a Jamaican reworking of the *Bicycle Thief*, featuring a cast of reggae all-stars.

The Lunatic, based on the Anthony Winkler novel, is a humorous exploration of the island's sexual taboos.

Jamaica's highest-grossing film of all time is Chris Browne's 2000 crime drama *Third World Cop*, in which old friends straddling both sides of the law must come to terms with each other; the gangster film *Shottas* (2002) follows in its footsteps. *One Love*

(2005) explores Jamaica's social divides against the backdrop of a controversial romance between a Rasta musician and a pastor's daughter.

Music

Music is everywhere – and it's loud! The sheer creativity and productivity of Jamaican music has produced a profound effect around the world. As reggae continues to attract and influence a massive international audience, Jamaica's sound-system-based dancehall culture continues to inform contemporary rap, rave and hip-hop cultures.

Reggae is the heartbeat of Jamaica, and it is as strongly identified with the island as R&B is with Detroit or jazz with New Orleans. But reggae is actually only one of several distinctly Jamaican sounds, and the nation's musical heritage runs much deeper. Inspired by the country's rich African folk heritage, music spans mento (a folk calypso), ska, rock-steady, 'roots' music and contemporary dancehall and ragga. Kingston is the 'Nashville of the Third World,' with recording studios pumping out as many as 500 new titles each month.

The term dancehall, although used to mean a sound-system venue, is also used specifically to refer to a kind of Caribbean rap music that focuses on earthly themes dear to the heart of young male Jamaicans, principally 'gal business,' gunplay and ganja. This is hardcore music, named for the loosely defined outdoor venues at which outlandishly named 'toasters' (rapper DJs) set up mobile discos with enormous speakers, and singers and DJs pumped-up with braggadocio perform live over instrumental rhythm tracks.

Landscape & Wildlife

The Land

At 11,425 sq km (about equal to the US state of Connecticut, or 5% of the size of Great Britain) Jamaica is the third-largest island in the Caribbean and the largest of the English-speaking islands. It is one of the Greater Antilles, which make up the westernmost part of the Caribbean islands.

Jamaica is rimmed by a narrow coastal plain except in the south, where broad flatlands cover extensive areas. Mountains form the island's spine, rising gradually from the west and culminating in the Blue Mountains in the east, which are capped by Blue Mountain Peak at 2256m. The island is cut by about 120 rivers, many of which are bone dry for much of the year but spring to life after heavy rains, causing great flooding.

Two-thirds of the island's surface is composed of soft, porous limestone (the compressed skeletons of coral, clams and other sea life), in places several kilometers thick and covered by thick red-clay soils rich in bauxite (the principal source of aluminum). Coastal mangrove and wetland preserves, montane cloud forests and other wild places are strewn across Jamaica.

Some of the most dramatic caves in the world can be found in Jamaica; contact the **Jamaican Caves Organisation** (www.jamaicancaves.org) for more information.

Wildlife

The island has more than 255 bird species. Stilt-legged, snowy-white cattle egrets are ubiquitous, as are 'John crows' (turkey vultures), which are the subject of several folk songs and proverbs. *Patoo* (a West African word) is the Jamaican name for the owl, which many islanders superstitiously regard as a harbinger of death. Jamaica has four of the 16 Caribbean species of hummingbird. The crown jewel of West Indian hummingbirds is the streamertail, the national bird, indigenous to Jamaica.

Coral reefs lie along the north shore, where the reef is almost continuous and much of it is within a few hundred meters of shore. Over 700 species of fish zip in and out of the exquisite reefs and swarm through the coral canyons. Last but not least, three species of endangered marine turtles – the green, hawksbill and loggerhead – lay eggs on Jamaica's beaches.

SURVIVAL GUIDE

Directory A–Z

Accommodations

If you're traveling on a shoestring, head to simple guesthouses. In the midrange category there's a wide range of choice in appealing small hotels, many with splendid gardens, sea views or both. If traveling with your family or a group, consider one of the hundreds of villas available to rent across the island. And if you've decided to splurge, Jamaica's luxury hotels rank among the finest in the world.

For better or worse Jamaica was the spawning ground for the all-inclusive resort. At chains like **Sandals** (www.sandals.com), **Couples** (www.couples.com) and **SuperClubs** (www.superclubs.com), guests pay a set price and (theoretically) pay nothing more once setting foot inside the resort.

Jamaica boasts hundreds of private houses for rent, from modest cottages to lavish beachfront estates. These arrangements are very cost-effective if you're traveling with family or a group of friends. Many include a cook and maid. Rates start as low as US$500 per week for budget units with minimal facilities and can run to US$10,000 or more for a multibedroom estate. **Jamaica Villas** (www.jamaicavillas.com) lists scores of economical short-term accommodations, or try **Jamaican Association of Villas & Apartments** (JAVA; ☎974-2508; www.villasinjamaica.com).

Rates quoted in this chapter are for the high season (mid-December to April), unless otherwise noted. At other times rates can be 20% to 60% lower. Accommodations are categorized as follows:

$	budget	less than US$75
$$	midrange	US$75 to US$200
$$$	top end	more than US$200

Activities

DIVING & SNORKELING

Jamaica's shores are as beautiful below the surface as they are above. The waters offer good visibility and temperatures of around 27°C year-round.

Most diving occurs in and around the Montego Bay and Negril Marine Parks, in proximity to a wide range of licensed dive operators offering rental equipment and group dives. See p546 and p551 for operators. Visitors to the north coast will find excellent diving along the reef that is aligned with the shoreline between Ocho Rios and Galina Point; see p539 for more.

By law all dives in Jamaican waters must be guided, and dives are restricted to a depth of 30m. If you spend enough time in the water, you're practically guaranteed to see parrotfish, angelfish, turtles, eels and the odd barracuda.

Dives cost around US$50/80 for one-/two-tank dives. A snorkeling excursion, which generally includes equipment and a boat trip, costs US$25 to US$50. 'Resort courses' for beginners (also called 'Discover Scuba') are offered at most major resorts (about US$80), which also offer Professional Association of Diving Instructors (PADI) certification courses (US$350 to US$500).

FISHING

Jamaica's waters are a pelagic playpen for schools of blue and white marlin, dolphin fish, wahoo, tuna and dozens of other species. Deepwater game fish run year-round through the Cayman Trench that begins just 3.2km from shore.

Charters can be arranged for around US$400/800 per half/full day through hotels or directly through operators in Montego Bay, Negril, Ocho Rios and Port Antonio. A charter includes captain, tackle, bait and crew. Most charter boats require a 50% deposit.

SURFING

Although Jamaica is little known as a surfing destination and board rentals on the island can be difficult to come by, the east coast is starting to attract surfers for its respectable waves coming in from the Atlantic. Boston Bay, 14.5km east of Port Antonio, is a well-known spot, as is Long Bay, 16km further south. The southeast coast, including the Palisadoes Peninsula, also gets good surf.

Jamnesia Surf Club (☑750-0103; www.jamnesia.20megsfree.com; PO Box 167, Kingston 2) provides general information about surfing

» **Electricity** The voltage used is 110V, 50Hz. Sockets are usually two- or three-pin – the US standard.

» **Newspapers & Magazines** The *Jamaica Gleaner* is the most respected newspaper; its rival is the *Jamaica Observer*.

» **Radio & TV** There are 30 radio stations and seven TV channels; most hotels have satellite.

» **Weights & Measures** Still transitioning from imperial to metric. Distances are measured in kilometers, and gas (petrol) in liters, but coffee is strictly by the pound.

in Jamaica, and operates a surf camp at Bull Bay, 13km east of Kingston.

Business Hours

The following are standard hours for Jamaica; exceptions are noted in reviews.

Bars around 6pm until the last guest leaves

Businesses 8:30am-4:30pm Mon-Fri

Restaurants breakfast dawn-11am, lunch noon-2pm, dinner 5:30-11pm

Shops 8am or 9am-5pm Mon-Fri, to noon Sat

Children

Some all-inclusive resorts cater specifically to families and have an impressive range of amenities for children. Most hotels also offer free accommodations or reduced rates for children staying in their parents' room. Many hotels provide a babysitter or nanny by advance request.

Dangers & Annoyances

If you don't like reggae music, can't cope with poverty or power outages and hate being hustled, Jamaica is definitely not for you. Moreover, if you prize efficient service, this place is liable to drive you nuts. It pays to take things in stride and keep a sense of perspective

Jamaica has an atrocious murder rate. Although the vast majority of violent crimes occur in ghettoes far from tourist centers, visitors are sometimes the victims of

JAMAICAN CUISINE

Jamaica's homegrown cuisine is a fusion of many ethnic traditions and influences. The Arawaks brought callaloo (a spinachlike green), cassava (a root vegetable), corn, sweet potatoes and several tropical fruits to the island. The Spanish adopted native spices, which were later enhanced by spices brought by slaves from their African homelands. Immigrants from India brought hot and flavorful curries, often served with locally made mango chutney. Middle Eastern dishes and Chinese influences have also become part of the national menu. And basic roasts and stews followed the flag during three centuries of British rule, as did Yorkshire pudding, meat pies and hot cross buns.

robbery and scams. Still, the overwhelming majority of visitors enjoy their vacations without incident.

Drugs – particularly ganja (marijuana) – are readily available in Jamaica, and you're almost certain to be approached by hustlers selling them. Possession and use are strictly illegal and penalties are severe. Roadblocks and random searches of cars are common. If you get caught in possession, you will *not* be getting on your plane home, however small the amount. A night (or a lengthy sentence) in a crowded-to-bursting Jamaican lockup is dangerous to your health!

The traveler's biggest problem in Jamaica is the vast army of hustlers who harass visitors, notably in and around major tourist centers. If you as much as glance in their direction, they'll attempt to reel you in like a flounder.

Embassies & Consulates

More than 40 countries have official diplomatic representation in Jamaica. Except for a couple of Montego Bay consulates, all are located in Kingston. If your country isn't represented in this list, check 'Embassies & High Commissions' in the Yellow Pages of the Greater Kingston telephone directory. The closest Australian High Commission is in Trinidad.

Canada High Commission (☑926-1500; 3 West Kings House Rd, Kingston); consulate (☑952-6198; 29 Gloucester Ave, Montego Bay)

France (☑946-4000; 13 Hillcrest Ave, Kingston 6)

Germany (☑631-7935, emergency 819-4351; www.kingston.diplo.de; 10 Waterloo Rd, Kingston 10)

UK (☑936-0700; http://ukinjamaica.fco.gov.uk/en; 28 Trafalgar Rd, Kingston)

US embassy (☑702-6000, after hr 702-6055; kingston.usembassy.gov; 142 Old Hope Rd, Kingston); consulate (☑953-0602, 952-5050; Unit EU-1, Whitter Village, Ironshore)

Food

The following price categories, used in reviews for eateries in this chapter, are based on the cost of an average meal.

$	budget	less than US$15 (J$1275)
$$	midrange	US$15 to US$25 (J$1275 to J$2125)
$$$	top end	more than US$25 (J$2125)

Festivals & Events

Throughout the year you'll find festivals in various towns around Jamaica, celebrating anything from jazz to jerk. Kingston is the place for New Year's Eve fireworks. See the Festivals & Events sections for each destination in this chapter for details. Other notable events include the following:

Trelawny Yam Festival (Albert Town) Yam-balancing races, the crowning of the Yam King and Queen – how can you resist? Held in late March.

Carnival (www.jamaicacarnival.com; Kingston & Ocho Rios) Street parties and soca music all night long in March/April.

Calabash International Literary Festival (☑922-4200; www.calabashfestival.org; Treasure Beach) This highly innovative literary festival in late May draws voices from near and far.

Gay & Lesbian Travelers

Jamaica is adamantly homophobic. Sexual acts between men are prohibited by law and punishable by up to 10 years in prison and hard labor. Many reggae dancehall lyrics by big-name stars seem intent on instigating violence against gays. Law enforcement in most cases looks the other way, and gay-bashing incidents are almost never prosecuted.

Most Jamaican gays are still in the closet. There is a gay scene in Kingston, but it is an underground affair, and to openly search it out is the height of folly. Nonetheless many hoteliers are tolerant of gay visitors, and you should not be put off from visiting the island. Just realize that displaying your sexuality openly could have life-threatening consequences. Check these websites for gay-friendly businesses and general information on the Jamaican LGBT scene.

Gay Jamaica Watch (www.gayjamaicawatch .blogspot.com)

Gay Journey (www.gayjourney.com/hotels/ jamaica.htm)

J-FLAG (www.jflag.org)

Purple Roofs (www.purpleroofs.com/carib bean/jamaica.html)

Health

Acceptable health care is available in most major cities and larger towns throughout Jamaica, but may be hard to locate in rural areas. To find a good local doctor, your best bet is to ask the management of the hotel where you are staying or to contact your embassy in Kingston or Montego Bay.

Many doctors expect payment in cash, regardless of whether or not you have travel health insurance. If you do develop a life-threatening medical problem, you'll probably want to be evacuated to a country with state-of-the-art medical care. Since this may cost tens of thousands of dollars, be sure you have insurance to cover this before you depart.

Many pharmacies are well supplied, but important medications may not be consistently available. Be sure to bring adequate supplies of all prescriptions.

In general, tap water is safe to drink in Jamaica, but it's best to be cautious in rural areas.

Internet Access

Wi-fi is appearing in more and more Jamaican hotels, but internet access is still almost nonexistent in rural areas. Most town libraries now offer internet access (US$1 for 30 minutes), though you may find there's only one or two terminals and the wait can be long. Most towns have at least one commercial entity where you can get online. Jamaican businesses aren't very good at maintaining (or even creating) a web presence, so don't rely too heavily on online research before your trip.

Language

Officially English is the spoken language. In reality, Jamaica is a bilingual country, and English is far more widely understood than spoken. The unofficial lingo is patois (*pa*-twah), a musical dialect with a staccato rhythm and cadence, laced with salty idioms and wonderfully witty compressed proverbs.

Patois evolved from Creole English peppered with African, Portuguese and Spanish terms and, in the last century, Rastafarian slang. Linguists agree that it is more than simplified pidgin English, and has its own identifiable syntax.

Patois is deepest in rural areas, where many people do not know much standard English. Although it is mostly the lingua franca of the poor, all sectors of Jamaica understand patois, and even polite, educated Jamaicans lapse into patois at unguarded moments.

Money

The unit of currency is the Jamaican dollar ($), the 'jay.' Jamaican currency is issued in bank notes of J$50, J$100, J$500, J$1000 and (rarely) J$5000. Prices for hotels and valuable items are usually quoted in US dollars, which are widely accepted.

Commercial banks have branches throughout the island. Those in major towns maintain a foreign exchange booth. Traveler's checks are widely accepted in Jamaica, although some hotels, restaurants and exchange bureaus charge a hefty fee for cashing them. Most city bank branches have 24-hour ATMs linked to international networks such as Cirrus or Plus. In more remote areas look for ATMs at gas stations.

A 10% tip is normal in hotels and restaurants. Some restaurants automatically add a 10% to 15% service charge to your bill. Check your bill carefully, as the charge is often hidden. Some all-inclusive resorts have a strictly enforced no-tipping policy. Outside Kingston, tourist taxi drivers often ask for tips but it is not necessary; JUTA (Jamaica Union of Travelers Association) route taxis do not expect tips.

Public Holidays

In addition to holidays observed throughout the region (p872), Jamaica also has the following public holidays:

Bob Marley Day February 6

Ash Wednesday Six weeks before Easter

Labor Day May 23

Emancipation Day August 1

Independence Day August 6

National Heroes' Day October 19

Telephone

Jamaica's country code is 📞876. To call Jamaica from the US, dial 📞1-876 plus the seven-digit local number. From elsewhere dial your country's international dialing code, then 📞876 and the local number.

For calls within the same parish in Jamaica, just dial the local number. Between parishes, dial 📞1 plus the local number. We have included only the seven-digit local number in listings in this chapter.

CELL PHONES

You can bring your own cellular phone into Jamaica (GSM or CDMA), but if your phone is locked by a specific carrier, don't bother. Another option is to purchase an inexpensive cellular phone (from US$35) at a **Digicel** (📞888-344-4235; www.digiceljamaica.com), **Claro** (📞621-1000; www.claro.com.jm) or **Lime** (📞888-225-5295; www.time4lime.com/jm) outlet and purchase a prepaid SIM card. These are sold in denominations of up to J$1000, and you'll find them at many gas stations and stationery shops.

Visas

For stays of six months or less, no visas are required for citizens of the EU, the US, Commonwealth countries, Mexico, Japan and Israel. Nationals of Argentina, Brazil, Chile, Costa Rica, Ecuador, Greece and Japan don't need a visa for stays of up to 30 days.

All other nationals require visas (nationals of most countries can obtain a visa on arrival, provided they are holding valid onward or return tickets and evidence of sufficient funds).

Getting There & Away

Entering Jamaica

All visitors must arrive with a valid passport. US citizens must show a valid US passport when traveling from the Caribbean in order to re-enter the US (see p875).

Immigration formalities require every person to show a return or onward airline ticket when arriving in Jamaica.

Air

The majority of international visitors to Jamaica arrive at Montego Bay's **Donald Sangster International Airport** (MBJ; 📞952-3124; www.mbjairport.com). In Kingston **Norman Manley International Airport** (KIN; 📞924-8452; www.nmia.aero), around 11km southeast of downtown, handles international flights. The national carrier, **Air Jamaica** (📞922-3460; www.airjamaica.com), doesn't have the best reputation for efficiency or service; major American, British, Canadian and Caribbean carriers all fly into MBJ and KIN.

Sea

Jamaica is a popular destination on the cruising roster, mainly for passenger liners but also for private yachters.

If all you're after is a one-day taste of Jamaica, then consider arriving by cruise ship. Port visits usually take the form of one-day stopovers at either Ocho Rios or Montego Bay. See p55 for more information on cruises.

Many yachters make the trip to Jamaica from North America. Upon arrival in Jamaica you *must* clear customs and immigration at Montego Bay, Kingston, Ocho Rios or Port Antonio. In addition you'll need to clear customs at *each* port of call. Yachts frequently call at the following places:

Errol Flynn Marina, Port Antonio (📞715-6044; www.errolflynnmarina.com) GPS 18.168984, -76.450556

Montego Bay Yacht Club (📞979-8038; www.mobayyachtclub.com; Sunset Dr) GPS 18.462452, -77.943267

Royal Jamaican Yacht Club, Kingston (📞924-8685; www.rjyc.org.jm; Norman Manley Dr, Kingston) GPS 17.940939, -76.764939

Getting Around

Air

There are four domestic airports: Tinson Pen Aerodrome in Kingston, Ian Fleming International Airport (formerly Boscobel Airport) near Ocho Rios, Negril Aerodrome and Ken Jones Aerodrome at Port Antonio. Montego Bay's Donald Sangster International Airport has a domestic terminal adjacent to the international terminal. **Air Jamaica Express** (📞922-3460; www.airjamaica.com) operates scheduled services between Kingston and Montego Bay. **TimAir** (☎952-2516; www. timair.net) air-taxi service covers all of the domestic airports.

Bicycle

Mountain bikes and 'beach cruisers' can be rented at most major resorts (US$10 to US$30 per day). Road conditions are hazardous and Jamaican drivers aren't considerate to cyclists. For serious touring bring your own mountain or hybrid bike; you'll need sturdy wheels to handle the potholed roads.

Bus

The island's extensive transportation network links virtually every village and comprises several options, ranging from standard public buses to 'coasters' and 'route taxis.' These depart from and arrive at each town's transportation station, which is usually near the main market. Locals can direct you to the appropriate vehicle, which should have its destination marked above the front window (for buses) or on its side.

COASTER

'Coasters' (private minibuses) have traditionally been the workhorses of Jamaica's regional public transportation system. All major towns and virtually every village in the country is served.

Licensed minibuses display red license plates with the initials PPV (public passenger vehicle) or have a Jamaican Union of Travelers Association (JUTA) insignia. JUTA buses are exclusively for tourists. They usually depart their point of origin when they're full, often overflowing, with people hanging from the open doors. Minibuses fill fastest in the morning and around 5pm (ie when people are going to work and coming home). Short 30-minute hops between towns cost around J$150 to J$250; a ride from Kingston to Sav-la-Mar (ie across the country) cost J$700 at the time of research.

PUBLIC BUS

Kingston and Montego Bay have modern municipal bus systems. Throughout the island bus stops are located at most road intersections along the routes, but you can usually flag down a bus anywhere (except in major cities, where they only pause at designated stops). When you want to get off, shout 'One stop!' or 'Driver!' The conductor will usually echo your request with, 'Let off!'

You'll be pressed to pay more than J$100 for a fare.

ROUTE TAXI

These communal taxis are the most universal mode of public transportation, reaching every part of the country. They operate like coasters (and cost about the same), picking up as many people as they can squeeze in along their specified routes.

Most are white Toyota Corolla station wagons marked by red license plates. They should have 'Route Taxi' marked on the front door, and they are not to be confused with identical licensed taxis, which charge more.

Car

Exploring by rental car can be a truly liberating experience, but make no mistake: driving in Jamaica can be a nightmare. Taxis and minibuses are a serious menace and health risk. Don't be surprised if police stop you and ask for a little bribe or search your car extensively for even a trace of ganja; if they find any you'll be lucky to get away with a payoff.

A paved coastal highway circles the entire island; in the southern parishes it runs about 32km inland. Main roads cross the central mountain chains, north to south, linking all of the main towns. A web of minor roads, country lanes and dirt tracks provides access to more-remote areas.

DRIVER'S LICENSE

To drive in Jamaica, you must have a valid International Driver's License (IDL) or a current license for your home country or state, valid for up to six months. You can obtain an IDL by applying with your current license to any automobile association office.

FUEL & SPARE PARTS

Many gas stations close after 7pm or so. In rural areas stations usually close on Sunday.

RENTAL

Several major international car-rental companies operate in Jamaica, along with dozens of local firms. Rates begin at about US$45 per day and can run as high as US$150, depending on the vehicle. Some companies include unlimited mileage, while others set a limit and charge a fee for excess kilometers driven. Most firms require a deposit of at least US$500, but will accept a credit card imprint. Renters must be at least

21 years of age (some companies will rent only to those 25 years of age or older).

There are rental companies in large towns, including Kingston (p534), Montego Bay (p549), Ocho Rios (p543) and Negril (p554).

ROAD CONDITIONS

Main roads are usually in reasonable condition, despite numerous potholes. Many secondary roads (B-roads) are in appalling condition and are best tackled with a 4WD. Most roads are narrow, with frequent bends.

ROAD HAZARDS

Driving in Jamaica is dangerous. Licenses can be bought without taking a driving test, and the roads are governed by an infatua-tion with speed completely incongruous with the rest of Jamaican life. Look out for people along the roads or animals that might dash in front of you, and pay extra attention at roundabouts, where driving on the left is not always adhered to. Pedestrians should beware of the many drivers who would as soon hit you as slow down.

ROAD RULES

Always drive on the left. Remember: 'De left side is de right side; de right side is suicide!' The speed limit is 30mph (about 50km/h) in towns and 50mph (around 80km/h) on highways. Typing that made us laugh considering the speeds Jamaicans actually drive at, but police will pull you over for speeding.

Martinique

Includes »

Best Beaches

» Les Salines (p586)

» Anse d'Arlet (p583)

» Trois-Îlets (p580)

» Plage de Tartane (p579)

Best Places to Stay

» Le Domaine Saint Aubin (p579)

» L'Anse Bleue (p584)

» Localizé (p582)

» Hotel Bakoua (p582)

Why Go?

A slice of Gallic culture in the Caribbean, Martinique is an overseas département of France. While it's noticeably more tropical than the mainland, there's no denying the very French rhythm of life here. This is great for Francophiles, although it can also give rise to Martinique's – at times – distinctly un-Caribbean air.

Volcanic in origin, the island is a mountainous stunner crowned by the still-smoldering Mont Pelée, which wiped out Martinique's former capital of St-Pierre in 1902. Long luscious beaches, great diving and giant mountains covered in tropical forests are the main attractions here.

Far more developed than much of the Caribbean, Martinique suffers from uncontrolled urban sprawl in some places, particularly in and around the busy capital, Fort-de-France. Those wanting to avoid the modern world's encroachment should head to the beautiful beaches of the south or to the mountains of the island's remote north.

When to Go

Martinique enjoys a year-round tropical climate, but it is most popular during the dry season, from December to May. This high season can see the island crowded with French holiday makers, and hotel costs are at a premium. The rainy season begins in June and continues until the end of November, with heavy showers most days. September is the rainiest month and, along with August, is most prone to hurricanes – these are, perhaps, the better times to avoid Martinique.

Fast Facts

» **Area** 1080 sq km

» **Population** 400,000

» **Capital** Fort-de-France

» **Telephone country code** ☏596

» **Emergency** Ambulance ☏15, police ☏17, fire ☏18

Set Your Budget

» **Budget hotel room** €50

» **Two-course evening meal** €30

» **Museum entrance** €5

» **Bottle of beer** €3

» **Bus ticket** €4

Resources

» **Martinique** (www.martinique.org) Official tourism website

» **Martinique Scoop** (www.martinique.no-scoop.com, in French) Cultural guide to Martinique

» **France-Antilles** (www.martinique.franceantilles.fr, in French) Main newspaper of Martinique

» **Fort-de-France** (www.fortdefrance.fr, in French) Website of the capital

Itineraries

THREE DAYS

If it's beaches you like, concentrate on the south for a few days: base yourself somewhere along the coast around Grande Anse or Diamant. Don't miss the beautiful beach at Les Salines, the stunning views of Rocher du Diamant from the coastal road, or the eating and activity options around Trois-Îlets.

ONE WEEK

After enjoying a couple of days on the beach in the south, drive up the east coast of the island and explore the Presqu'île de Caravelle and enjoy the beach at Tartane before continuing to Grand-Rivière for remote hiking and superb scenery. Head back via stunning Mont Pelée and fascinating St-Pierre to the bustling capital, Fort-de-France.

GETTING TO NEIGHBORING ISLANDS

There's a fast ferry service connecting Martinique to St Lucia in the south, and to Dominica and Guadeloupe in the north, that runs most days. See www.express-des-iles.com for more information. There are also flights from Fort-de-France to Pointe-à-Pitre (Guadeloupe), St Lucia, Antigua, Barbados, Havana (Cuba), San Juan (Puerto Rico), St-Martin and Santo Domingo (Dominican Republic).

Essential Food & Drink

» **Acras** A universally popular hors d'oeuvre in Martinique, *acras* are fish, seafood or vegetables tempura. *Acras de morue* (cod) and *crevettes* (shrimp) are the most common and are both delicious.

» **Ti-punch** Short for *petit punch*; this ubiquitous and strong cocktail is the normal *apéro* (aperitif) in Martinique. It's a mix of rum, lime and cane syrup – but mainly rum.

» **Crabes farcis** Stuffed crabs are a common local dish. Normally they're stuffed with a spicy mixture of crabmeat, garlic, shallots and parsley, and cooked in their shells.

» **Blaff** This is the local term for white fish marinated in lime juice, garlic and peppers and then poached. While it's popular across the Caribbean, its true home is Martinique.

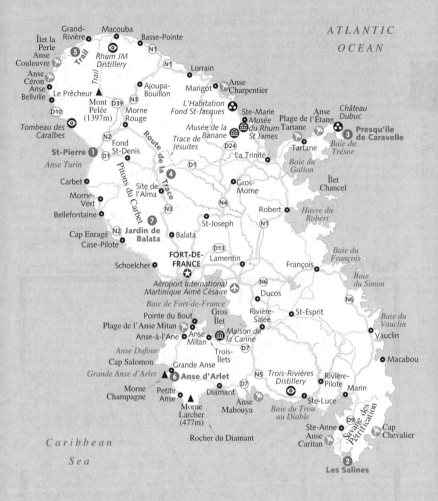

Martinique Highlights

1 See the devastation of Mont Pelée firsthand in the former capital of **St-Pierre** (p575), as the volcano broods in the distance

2 Wander one of the island's most beautiful beaches, **Les Salines** (p586)

3 Soak up the sun and sand by day – and the gourmet flavors by night – on the lovely **Presqu'île de Caravelle** (p579)

4 Drive the superb **Route de la Trace** (p576) and walk in the foothills of Mont Pelée

5 Hike the dramatic 20km **trail** (p578) from Grand-Rivière to Anse Couleuvre along Martinique's pristine northern coast

6 Enjoy a day on the beach overlooked by an 18th-century church and the surrounding hillside in village-like **Anse d'Arlet** (p583)

7 Put your botanist's hat on and explore the amazing variety of local plants at the excellent **Jardin de Balata** (p577)

FORT-DE-FRANCE

POP 90,500

Fort-de-France is the mercantile and political capital of Martinique, and the largest city in the French West Indies. While it's a busy commercial center and has some decent shopping and an attractive historic fort, most people simply pass through.

The narrow, busy streets are lined with a mixture of ordinary offices, bargain-basement shops and crumbling early 20th-century buildings with wrought-iron balconies that wouldn't look out of place in New Orleans.

If you do pass through, it is worth dedicating a few hours to wandering around the handful of historic sites, markets and museums the city has to offer. La Savane, the city park, lines the eastern end of the harbor. From here, look northwest to spot the distinctive spire of Cathédrale St-Louis.

⊙ Sights

Bibliothèque Schoelcher NOTABLE BUILDING
(Rue de la Liberté; admission free; ⊙1-5:30pm Mon, 8:30am-5:30pm Tue-Fri, 8:30am-noon Sat)
Fort-de-France's most visible landmark, the Bibliothèque Schoelcher, is an elaborate, colorful building with a Byzantine dome and an interesting ornate interior. The work of architect Henri Pick, a contemporary of Gustave Eiffel, the library was built in Paris and displayed at the 1889 World Exposition. It was then dismantled, shipped in pieces to Fort-de-France and reassembled in its current location. The front section contains antique books, a series of changing exhibits on local architecture and history, and period furnishing, while the back is a functioning lending library.

La Savane PARK
Normally, this large central park sports grassy lawns, tall trees, clumps of bamboo, lots of benches and souvenir stalls, but it

Fort-de-France

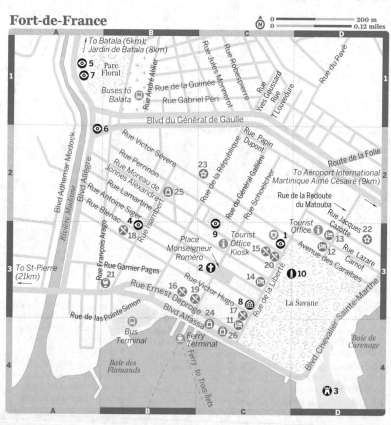

was undergoing a massive renovation at the time of writing. The plan is to turn the area into a cool, modern nexus of city life, with shopping and entertainment along a pedestrian-only mall.

Hopefully city planners will keep the **statue of Empress Josephine** holding a locket with a portrait of Napoleon. Years ago, the head was lopped off and red paint splashed over the body. The empress is not highly regarded by islanders, who believe she was directly responsible for convincing Napoleon to continue slavery in the French West Indies so that her family plantation in Trois-Îlets would not suffer.

Fort St-Louis   NOTABLE BUILDING
Opposite the south side of La Savane is Fort St-Louis. The original fort, built in the Marshal Vauban style, dates from 1640, although most of the extensive fort that stands today is the result of subsequent additions. It is still an active military base (no public tours).

Cathédrale St-Louis   CHURCH
(Rue Schoelcher; ⊙dawn-dusk) With its neo-Byzantine style and 57m steeple, the Cathédrale St-Louis is one of the city's most distinguished landmarks. Built in 1895 by Henri Pick, a block northwest of La Savane, the church fronts a small square and is picturesquely framed by two royal palms. The spacious, elaborate interior is well worth a look.

Musée Départemental d'Archéologie   MUSEUM
(9 Rue de la Liberté; ⊙1-5pm Mon, 8am-5pm Tue-Fri, 9am-noon Sat) For displays of Native American artifacts, including stone tools, ritual objects and pottery, head to this archaeological museum. The entire building was being renovated at the time of writing.

Palais de Justice   NOTABLE BUILDING
(Rue Schoelcher) The Palais de Justice, a neo-classical courthouse built in 1906, is two blocks northeast of the cathedral and can only be viewed from the outside. The design resembles a French railroad station, as the plaque out front explains. The square fronting the courthouse has a statue of French abolitionist Victor Schoelcher.

Parc Floral   PARK
This pleasant public park on the north side of the city is worth a stroll if you're nearby.

Grand Marché   MARKET
The best of the lot, this market can be found on the north side of Rue Isambert. It runs from 5am to sundown, but get there before noon for the best pickings.

Marché aux Épices   SPICE MARKET
Fort-de-France's late-19th-century, Henri Pick-designed spice market with its colorful stalls piled high with herbs, spices and local flowers is worth a visit, even if only

Fort-de-France

to grab a few snaps of the local stallholders (it's best to ask permission first), many in traditional garb. The spice market is located 100m north of the farmers market along the west side of Parc Floral.

Marché des Fermiers FARMERS MARKET
This bustling local market runs along the west side of Parc Floral and spills over into the street along the Rivière Madame.

Marché aux Poissons FISH MARKET
At the far end of Blvd du Général de Gaulle, this colorful and atmospheric place is best visited in the morning for the day's fresh catch.

Tours

A variety of tours can be arranged through the island's **tourist office** (☎05-96-60-27-73; www.tourismefdf.com; 76 Rue Lazare Carnot; tours €12-25; ☉8am-5pm Mon, Tue & Thu, to 12:30pm Wed & Fri). The offerings include a walk through the history of Fort-de-France, a tour of the area's chruches and a bus trip to nearby waterfalls and tropical gardens. The tourist office can also help to arrange English-speaking guides for hikes around the island.

Festivals & Events

Mardi Gras Carnival CARNIVAL
A spirited festival during the five-day period leading up to Ash Wednesday.

Semi-marathon MARATHON
(www.sport-up.fr/semifortdefrance) A 22km half-marathon around the city is held in November.

Guitar Festival MUSIC FESTIVAL
(www.cmac.asso.fr) A biennial festival held in December in even-numbered years.

Martinique Jazz Festival MUSIC FESTIVAL
This biennial, weeklong festival is held in December in odd-numbered years.

Sleeping

All of these hotels are centrally located near La Savane, unless noted otherwise. Parking can be near impossible, but this area of the city is so compact that the furthest point of interest is within a 10-minute walk.

TOP CHOICE l'Impératrice HOTEL $$
(☎05-96-63-06-82; www.limperatricehotel.fr; 15 Rue de la Liberté; s/d from €95/110; ❉☎) This newly refurbished hotel is by far the best in town, right in the middle of things and with a sleek art deco feel to its facade. All

PORT OF CALL – FORT-DE-FRANCE

All cruise ships calling in Martinique land at Pointe Simon in Fort-de-France. This is on the western side of the harbor and within easy walking distance of the city center and main sights. If the port is busy, ships may use tenders to bring passengers ashore.

For a detailed walking tour of the town, book with the tourist office. With a few hours in port:

» In Fort-de-France, visit the spice market and the beautiful Bibliothèque Schoelcher, and make sure to wander past La Savane to the Fort St Louis (p570)

» Hire a car or take a taxi (negotiate hard) for the impressive trip up the coast to the former capital St-Pierre (p575), where you can see the Volcano Museum and the remains of the town that was wiped out in 1902

23 rooms are excellent, with interesting antique furniture in a variety of styles and all modern comforts.

Le Beauséjour Hotel HOTEL $$
(☎05-96-75-53-57; www.lebeausejour-hotel.com; 44 La Jambette; s/d €68/80; ❉☎) A 10-minute drive east of town, this place is a great option if you need to be near Fort-de-France but don't mind not being in town itself. The charming villa set in exotic gardens has its own restaurant, and 12 rooms with TVs and private bathrooms. There are two disabled-access rooms.

Bayfront Hotel HOTEL $$
(☎05-96-55-55-55; bayfronthotel@yahoo.fr; 3 Rue de la Liberté; s/d €65/75; ❉☎) This modern business hotel above a small cafe boasts useful little touches such as kitchens in most rooms. The 12 rooms here all have a Creole flair, and some have views over the sea and La Savane.

Hotel Carib HOTEL $$
(☎05-96-60-19-85; www.caribhotel.new.fr; 9 Rue de Redoute du Matouba; r €60; ❉☎) Handily located in the center of town, this simple but perfectly fine hotel has rooms with a rather cobbled-together feel; some even have access to the large balcony wrapped around the building. The overall feel is rather down-at-heel, however.

Hotel Hortensia
HOTEL **$**

(☑05-96-60-29-59; 11 Rue de Redoute du Matouba; r with shared/private bathroom €36/40; ❄) This very simple hotel is the cheapest place to lay your head in town. The six rooms with private facilities are only marginally more than the six rooms that share bathrooms. Don't expect an overwhelmingly friendly welcome, but otherwise this place is fine for a night.

Eating & Drinking

The culinary options in town aren't always obvious, but there are a few gems. Plan ahead on Sundays, when nearly everything is closed.

Crew
FRENCH, CREOLE **$$**

(44 Rue Ernest Deproge; mains €16-25; ⊘breakfast, lunch & dinner Mon-Fri, lunch Sat) You might expect little from the uninspiring exterior, but inside this dark, nautical-themed place is the charm of a traditional harborside diner. A long list of French favorites and a rainbow of Creole standards are on offer here and there's a bar that's lively in the early evening.

La Cave à Vins
FRENCH **$$**

(☑05-96-70-33-02; 118 Rue Victor Hugo; mains €18-27; ⊘dinner) Calling itself a boutique restaurant, this charming little place is favored by the cognoscenti of the town, who come here for the elaborate main dishes (like scallops fried in parsley butter with vegetable spaghetti, or sea snail cooked in spices and chili peppers), a superb wine list (for which the restaurant is rightly named) and a warm and convivial atmosphere. Book ahead.

La Baie
CREOLE, BRETON **$$**

(☑05-96-42-20-38; Rue de la Liberté; mains €18-25; ⊘lunch & dinner Mon-Sat) This friendly and charming place is run by a native from Brittany. The classy, intimate 1st-floor dining room is a great place to sample an inventive menu, stretching from seafood and fish to delicious galettes (savory crepes made with buckwheat flour). There's a great terrace for alfresco dining with sea and park views. Book ahead for the evening.

Bistrot Savane
FRENCH **$$**

(☑05-96-68-58-49; 1 Bis Rue Perrinon; mains €12-24; ⊘lunch & dinner Tue-Fri, dinner Sat) A recent addition to the city's eating scene is this imaginatively run bar and restaurant, where live-music evenings and local art exhibits complement a large menu of French cooking. The team here is extremely friendly and the small downstairs bar is a great place to meet locals.

Le Foyaal
BRASSERIE **$**

(☑05-96-63-08-38; Rue Ernest Deproge; mains €9-20; ⊘7am-1.30am) A focal point of life in Fort-de-France, this smart complex includes a buzzing brasserie serving everything from sandwiches to beef carpaccio, a very smart upstairs restaurant serving gourmet food (book ahead), and a next-door takeaway (L'Ygloo) making crepes and wraps to go. When everything else is closed, this and McDonald's are usually your only options – choose Le Foyaal!

Terminal Café
BAR **$**

(Rue Ernest Deproge; drinks €3-10; ⊘7pm-midnight; ☎) This fun bar has a big range of European beers and a good selection of spirits and specialty drinks. The 'punch découverte' is a sampler of rum punches in four flavors (€8) and a good introduction to rum punches on the island.

Délifrance
SANDWICH SHOP **$**

(Rue de la Liberté; sandwiches €4-7)

Super Maxinis
SANDWICH SHOP **$**

(Rue de la Liberté; sandwiches €4-7)

☆ Entertainment

Fort-de-France's nightlife is fairly tame, but warms up surprisingly late in the evening in the Pointe Simon area. A handful of piano bars offer live zouk, jazz and French music; you can pick up fliers at the tourist office or in hotel foyers, or check out the listings site **Martinique Scoop** (www.martinique.no -scoop.com, in French).

Centre Martiniquais d'Action Culturelle
CULTURAL CENTER

(CMAC; ☑05-96-70-79-39; www.cmac.asso.fr; 6 Rue Jacques Cazotte; ⊘9am-7pm Tue-Fri, 10am-1pm Sat) This cultural center runs an interesting program of indie films and documentaries, and hosts theatrical shows in its state-of-the-art auditoriums.

Théâtre Aimé Césaire
THEATER

(☑05-96-59-43-29; Rue Victor Sévere) Offers a program of traditional French drama, dance and mime for adults and children.

Croisière Bar
LIVE MUSIC

(cnr Rues Ernest Deproge & Isambert; ⊘noon-10pm) This spacious restaurant and bar has a live band in the evenings. It's easy enough to hear from street level what's playing at the top of the stairs.

Shopping

The busy streets of downtown Fort-de-France are crammed with shops selling all manner of trinkets, clothing, jewelry and perfumes. The main boutique area is along Rue Victor Hugo, particularly from Rue de la République to Rue de la Liberté.

The large **Cour Perrinon** (Rue Perrinon) shopping mall has some of the best shops in town, with the extra attraction of air-con.

There's an artisan market at **Centre des Métiers d'Art** (Rue Ernest Deproge) that has a decent selection of regional handicrafts. Nearby is the **Marché Touristique** (Rue Ernest Deproge), a big indoor space packed with every type of souvenir, including madras dresses, T-shirts, wood carvings and beach towels adorned with Bob Marley's face.

Information

INTERNET ACCESS Internet cafes are thin on the ground in Fort-de-France. Most hotels offer wireless though, as do several restaurants and bars, including Terminal Café.

MEDICAL SERVICES Hôpital Pierre Zobda Quitman (☎ 05-96-55-20-00) Located on the D13 on the northeast side of Fort-de-France near Lamentin.

Pharmacie Glaudon (cnr Rues de la Liberté & Antoine Siger)

MONEY Full-service banks can be found next door to Money Change Caraïbes on Rue Ernest Deproge, and along Rue de la Liberté opposite La Savane. Expect to pay a slightly higher commission at money changers due to later opening hours.

Change Point (Rue Victor Hugo; ⊙8am-5:30pm Mon-Fri, to 12:30pm Sat)

POST Main post office (cnr Rues Antoine Siger & de la Liberté; ⊙7am-6pm Mon-Fri, to noon Sat)

TOURIST INFORMATION Tourist office (☎ 05-96-60-27-73; www.tourismefdf.com; 76 Rue Lazare Carnot; ⊙8am-5pm Mon, Tue & Thu, to 12:30pm Wed & Fri) Has some useful brochures in English on activities and accommodations, and can arrange English-language walking or hiking tours. In peak season a tourist office kiosk is open on Rue Lamartine, near Cathédrale St-Louis.

Getting There & Around

TO/FROM THE AIRPORT The Martinique Aimé Césaire International Airport is just a 15-minute drive from Fort-de-France. The traffic crawls during peak times (from 7am to 10am, and 4pm to 7pm), so leave yourself an extra couple of hours if catching a flight. If you need to refuel a rental car, head for one of the 24-hour gas stations on the N5 near the airport.

Taxis are readily available at the airport (about €30 to Fort-de-France). Because of the taxi union, there's no direct bus service from the airport.

BOAT There are boats from Fort-de-France to Trois-Îlets and Pointe du Bout; see p591 for details. The ferries dock at the quay fronting the minibus parking lot. Be sure to check you're on the right boat before it leaves as they are not clearly marked.

BUS The spiffy new Bus Mozaïk company transports passengers around the city and to the suburbs in air-conditioned comfort. Fares start at €1.10, and there are well-marked bus stops around town. The main bus terminal is on Rue de la Pointe Simon and buses to Balata leave from Parc Floral.

CAR Parking in the city is not a problem on weekends and holidays, but is quite a challenge on weekdays. There's a parking lot along the north side of La Savane that can be entered from the intersection of Ave des Caraïbes and Rue de la Liberté. Streetside parking is free in the evenings, on Sunday and on holidays.

TAXI There are often taxis prowling Rue Ernest Deproge looking for customers. There are also taxi stands at Pointe Simon and on Rue de la Liberte. Fares are normally metered, but if you don't see a meter then make sure you agree on a price before getting in.

NORTHERN MARTINIQUE

Several roads head north from Fort-de-France. The most interesting sightseeing routes are the coastal road (N2) to St-Pierre and the Route de la Trace (N3), a truly scenic road that crosses the mountainous interior before hitting Morne Rouge and veering toward the northeast coast. The two routes can be combined to make a fine loop drive; if doing the whole loop, give yourself a full day.

Fort-de-France to St-Pierre

The mountainous and in parts spectacular coastal road from Fort-de-France to the old capital of St-Pierre runs through a succession of small towns, fishing villages and the odd bit of urban sprawl. The 21km trip takes around 45 minutes.

It's worth swinging off the highway at **Case-Pilote** to take a peek at the old village center. Turn west off the N2 at the Total gas station and you'll come to a quaint stone church, one of Martinique's oldest. Just 75m south of that is a charming town square with a water fountain, historic town hall, tourist office and moderately priced cafe. There's also good diving nearby.

Back on the N2 and further north, you'll come to **Carbet**, where Columbus briefly came ashore in 1502. This pretty town fronts a long sandy beach and has a few tourist amenities, including several restaurants, and the excellent **Jardin Botanique du Carbet** (☑05-96-52-76-08; www.jardinbotaniquedu carbet.com; adult/child €7/3.50; ☺9.30am-5pm), which was built by Jean-Philippe Thoze, the designer of the bigger Jardin de Balata (see p577). The best of the restaurants, **L'Imprévu** (mains €12-15, set meals €15; ☺lunch & dinner), is right on the beach, serving up fresh seafood on an attractive shaded terrace.

Further along the highway, 1.5km north of Carbet, is **Anse Turin**, a long gray-sand beach that attracts a crowd on weekends. Here you'll find **Le Jardin des Papillons** (☑05-96-78-33-39; adult/child €5/2.50; ☺9am-1pm Mon-Sat year-round, to 5pm Dec-Apr & Jul-Aug), where the scattered stone ruins of one of the island's earliest plantations have been enhanced with gardens and a butterfly farm.

St-Pierre

POP 4500

It's hard to believe that St-Pierre was once the most cosmopolitan city in the Caribbean. The one-time thriving capital of Martinique was however wiped out in just 10 minutes at the beginning of the 20th century by the towering and still-active Mont Pelée 7km away.

Though a shadow of its former self, St-Pierre is an attractive and interesting place to wander. There are many blackened ruins throughout the city, some of which are little more than foundations, while others remain partially intact. Many of the surviving stone walls have been incorporated into the town's reconstruction. Even 'newer' buildings have a period character, with shuttered doors and wrought-iron balconies.

The center of St-Pierre is long and narrow, with two parallel one-way streets running its length. All of the major sights have signs in French and English, and you can explore the area thoroughly in a few hours.

The central gathering spot is the waterfront town park, next to the covered market. A beach of soft, dark gray sand fronts the town here and extends to the south. There are sailboats and fishing boats in the harbor, and the sunsets here are postcard-perfect. If

you want to escape the crowds and enjoy the quiet pace of life in a traditional Caribbean town, this is a great place to base yourself.

The helpful **tourist office** (☑05-96-78-10-39) offers guided tours of St-Pierre in French (though most guides speak some English) at 9.30am and 2pm Monday to Friday. You can buy tickets (adult/child €5/3) at the tourist office or the Maison de la Bourse on Pl Bertin, from where the tours leave.

◎ Sights & Activities

Musée Volcanologique   MUSEUM
(Musée Frank Perret; Rue Victor Hugo; adult/child €3/1; ☺9am-5pm) This small but very interesting museum, founded in 1932 by American adventurer and volcanologist Frank Perret, gives a glimpse of the devastating 1902 eruption of Mont Pelée. On display are items plucked from the rubble and historic photos of the town before and immediately after the eruption. The displays are in English and French. Maps of the city are handed out on request.

There's free parking adjacent to the museum, which occupies the site of an old hillside gun battery. The view from the old stone walls along the parking lot provides a good perspective of the harbor and city; look straight down and to the left to see a line of ruins on the street below.

Centre de Découverte des Sciences de la Terre   MUSEUM
(☑05-96-52-82-42; www.cdst.e-monsite.com; adult/child €5/3; ☺9am-4pm Tue-Sun) Just 1.5km north of town, the earth-science museum looks like a big white box set on top of some columns, and the parking lot is made entirely of grass. It hosts a permanent exhibit on Mont Pelée, in French, and there's a neat contraption that shows stereoscopic black-and-white period photos of the volcano's aftermath. Documentaries are screened all day long, but the one to watch is *Volcans des Antilles*, which recounts Pelée's eruption and the dire consequences. It's subtitled in English and shown at 9:30am, 1:30pm and 4pm.

Ruins   RUINS
St-Pierre's most impressive ruins are those of the old 18th-century **theater**, just 100m north of the museum. While most of the theater was destroyed, enough remains to give a sense of the former grandeur of this building, which once seated 800 and hosted theater troupes from mainland France. A

double set of stairs still leads up to the partial walls of the lower story.

On the northeast side of the theater you can enter the tiny, thick-walled **jail cell** that housed Cyparis, one of the town's only survivors.

Another area rich in ruins is the **Quartier du Figuier**, along Rue Bouillé and directly below the volcanology museum. Two sets of steps, one just north of the theater and the other just south of the museum, connect Rue Victor Hugo with the bay-front Rue Bouillé.

Tropicasub　　　　　　　　　DIVING
(☑05-96-78-38-03; www.tropicasub.com) This company offers a vast range of wreck dives (a number of ships sank in the 1902 eruption), canyon dives and trips to Îlet la Perle.

Surcouf Dive　　　　　　　　DIVING
(☑06-96-24-39-45; surcouf-dive@wanadoo.fr) Another dive outfit in St-Pierre, Surcouf Dive sends out groups in a new open-air dive boat daily, with a maximum of 12 people per group.

🛏 Sleeping & Eating

TOP CHOICE **Hôtel Villa Saint-Pierre**　　HOTEL **$$**
(☑05-96-78-68-45;　www.hotel-villastpierre.com; r incl breakfast €120; ❋ 🛜) The best place in town is right on the waterfront and has a small beach just meters from the front door. The eight modern and comfortable rooms have an almost boutique feel to them, and the welcome is very friendly. Add €20 for a sea view – it's well worth it.

Les Maisonnettes du Volcan　BUNGALOWS **$$**
(☑05-96-78-21-66;　roland.de-reynal@wanadoo.fr; bungalows per night/week €120/650; ❋ 🛜) These two bungalows, set 2km north of downtown St-Pierre in the middle of a wooded field, are made to sleep five people. This is a good place for people who want to spend time exploring the nearby volcano. Each bungalow has a washing machine, TV and kitchen.

Le Tamaya　　　　　FRENCH, CREOLE **$$**
(☑05-96-78-29-09; mains €14-25, set meals €14; ⏰dinner) Near the imposing Maison de la Bourse on the seafront road, this is the best restaurant in town. Every evening, dishes such as conch cooked in Breton cider and sea perch poached in a butter sauce, make their way to the cozy tables, which are scattered about under nautical paraphernalia and giant model boats.

Chez-Marie Claire　　　　　　CAFE **$**
(set meals €12-15; ⏰6am-5pm Mon-Sat) This restaurant sits at the top of some steps inside the covered market. Diners can look down on the bustle below while eating Creole dishes such as stewed beef and freshwater crayfish. It's a friendly place, and the cook often comes by to make sure that guests enjoyed their meal.

Le Guérin　　　　　　　　　　CAFE **$**
(set meals €12; ⏰lunch Mon-Sat) Also inside the covered market. There can be a wait during the lunch rush, but with some of the best *acras* (deep-fried balls of dough filled with fish or shrimp) on the island, the wait is worth it.

St-Pierre to Anse Céron

From St-Pierre, the N2 turns inland but the D10 continues north for 13km along the coast and makes a scenic side drive, ending in 20 minutes at a remote beach. The shoreline is rocky for much of the way and the landscape is lush, with roadside clumps of bamboo.

The limestone cliffs 4km north of St-Pierre, **Tombeau des Caraïbes**, are said to be the place where the last Caribs jumped to their deaths rather than succumb to capture by the French.

The road ends at **Anse Céron**, a nice black-sand beach backed by the thick jungle rolling off the base of Mont Pelée. Anse Céron faces **Îlet la Perle**, a rounded rock off the northwest coast. It's a popular **dive site** famous for its colorful, coral-covered walls, and it's a good place to see groupers, eels and lobsters when water conditions aren't too rough. The Anse Céron beach can get crowded, but it does have a shower, toilets, picnic tables and a snack shop.

A very steep one-lane route continues for 1.6km beyond the beach. This is the start of a six-hour, 20km **hike** around the undeveloped northern tip of the island to Grand-Rivière; see p578 for details.

Route de la Trace

The Route de la Trace (N3) winds up into the mountains north from Fort-de-France. It's a beautiful drive through a lush rainforest of tall tree ferns, anthurium-covered hillsides and thick clumps of roadside bamboo. The road passes along the eastern flanks of the volcanic mountain peaks of the Pitons du Carbet. Several well-marked hiking trails

THE ERUPTION OF MONT PELÉE

At the end of the 19th century, St-Pierre – then the capital of Martinique – was a flourishing port city. It was so cosmopolitan that it was dubbed the 'Little Paris of the West Indies.' Mont Pelée, the island's highest mountain at 1397m, was just a scenic backdrop to the city.

In the spring of 1902, sulfurous steam vents on Mont Pelée began emitting gases, and a crater lake started to fill with boiling water. Authorities dismissed it all as the normal cycle of the volcano, which had experienced harmless periods of activity in the past.

But on April 25 the volcano spewed a shower of ash onto St-Pierre. Some anxious residents sent their children to stay with relatives on other parts of the island. The governor of Martinique, hoping to allay fears, brought his family to St-Pierre.

At 8am on Sunday May 8, 1902, Mont Pelée exploded into a glowing burst of superheated gas and burning ash, with a force 40 times stronger than the later nuclear blast over Hiroshima. Between the suffocating gases and the fiery inferno, St-Pierre was laid to waste within minutes.

Of the city's 30,000 inhabitants, there were just three survivors. One of them, a prisoner named Cyparis, escaped with only minor burns – ironically, he owed his life to having been locked in a tomblike solitary-confinement cell at the local jail. Following the commutation of his prison sentence by the new governor, Cyparis joined the PT Barnum circus where he toured as a sideshow act.

Pelée continued to smolder for months, but by 1904 people began to resettle the town, building among the crumbled ruins.

lead from the Route de la Trace into the rainforest and up to the peaks.

The road follows a route cut by the Jesuits in the 17th century: the Trace de Jésuites. Islanders like to say that the Jesuits' fondness for rum accounts for the twisting nature of the road.

Less than a 10-minute drive north of Fort-de-France, in the village of Balata, is **Sacré-Coeur de Balata**, a scaled-down replica of the Sacré-Coeur Basilica in Paris. This domed church, in the Roman-Byzantine style, has a stunning hilltop setting – the Pitons du Carbet rise up as a backdrop, and there's a view across Fort-de-France to Pointe du Bout below.

On the west side of the N3, 10 minutes' drive north of the Balata church, is the **Jardin de Balata** (05-96-64-48-73; www.jardinde balata.fr; adult/child €12.50/7; 9am-6pm), a mature botanical garden in a rainforest setting. Despite its meteoric price rises in recent years, this remains one of Martinique's best attractions and will please anyone with even a passing interest in botany. The hour-long walk around the garden is clearly marked, and a series of tree walks will keep kids interested. There are some fantastic views from here down to the coast.

After the garden, the N3 winds up into the mountains and reaches an elevation of 600m before dropping down to **Site de l'Alma**, where a river runs through a lush gorge. There are riverside picnic tables, trinket sellers and a couple of short trails into the rainforest.

Some 4km later, the N3 is intersected by the D1, which used to be a very scenic drive and the gateway to a popular hike, but at the time of research was closed. Locals give differing stories as to why (one amusing tale has a road worker accidentally bringing down the whole side of a mountain onto the road).

Continuing north on the N3, the Route de la Trace passes banana plantations and flower nurseries before reaching a T-junction at **Morne Rouge**, which was partially destroyed by an eruption from Mont Pelée in August 1902, several months after the eruption that wiped out St-Pierre. At 450m it has the highest elevation of any town on Martinique, and it enjoys some nice mountain scenery.

About 2km north of the T-junction, a road (D39) signposted to Aileron leads 3km up the slopes of Mont Pelée, from where there's a rugged trail (four hours round-trip) up the volcano's south face to the summit.

Basse-Pointe & Around

As the N3 nears the Atlantic it meets the N1, which runs along the coast in both directions. The northern segment of the road edges the eastern slopes of Mont Pelée and passes through banana and pineapple

HIKING MONT PELÉE

There are strenuous trails leading up both the northern and southern flanks of Mont Pelée. The shortest and steepest is up the southern flank, beginning in Morne Rouge (p577), and takes about four hours round-trip. The hike up the northern flank is 8km long and takes about 4½ hours one-way; there are two trails, which begin just east of Grand-Rivière. Visit the Syndicat d'Initiative in Grand Rivière for detailed maps.

Walking maps and advice (in French) can be found in *La Martinique à Pied*, available at many bookstores in Martinique. Or pick up the latest copy of *Martinique: Terre de Randonnée*, published annually by the Office National des Forêts and available for free from tourist offices throughout the country – it has good maps and details several Mont Pelée walking trails.

plantations before reaching the uninspiring coastal town of Basse-Pointe, birthplace of négritude poet and early Black Power founder Aimé Césaire.

Grand-Rivière

POP 840

From Basse-Pointe there's an enjoyable 35-minute drive to Grand-Rivière along a winding, but good, paved road. En route you will go through the coastal village of Macouba (where there is the well-signposted **Rhum JM Distillery**), pass two trails leading up the northern flank of Mont Pelée, cross a couple of one-lane bridges and finally wind down into the town. Be sure to watch out for red lights and road signs, as there are a few one-way-only stretches of rural road regulated by traffic signals.

Grand-Rivière is an unspoiled fishing village scenically tucked beneath coastal cliffs at the northern tip of Martinique. Mont Pelée forms a rugged backdrop to the south, while there's a fine view of neighboring Dominica to the north. People are very warm for the most part, and the old men hanging out their windows seem to appreciate a friendly wave from visitors. Things happen very slowly here in this corner of the world, so don't be in a hurry.

The road dead-ends at the sea, where there's a fish market and rows of brightly coloured fishing boats lined up on a little black-sand beach. The waters on the west side of town are sometimes good for surfing. The **Syndicat d'Initiative** (☎05-96-55-72-74; www.grand-riviere.com) in the town center has local tourist information. Besides organizing hikes that range from 10km to 18km and take at least four hours, it also offers sea, canyoning and culinary excursions.

While there's no road around the tip of the island, there is a 20km **hiking** trail leading to Anse Couleuvre on the northwest coast. The trailhead begins on the road opposite the quaint two-story *mairie* (town hall), just up from the beach. It's a moderately difficult walk, so you might want to join one of the guided hikes organized by the Syndicat d'Initiative. Hikers arrive in Anse Couleuvre about five hours after losing sight of the town hall, then return to Grand-Rivière by boat. The Syndicat d'Initiative is also a great source of information on the two trails that climb the north face of Mont Pelée, just outside the town.

The name of **Le Bout du Bout** (mains €8-12), a humble cafe, means 'the end of the end,' and they're not lying because the N1 really does stop a few meters from here. If you drive past Le Bout du Bout you'll have to back out, as the road just ends. Don't be too embarrassed; it happens a few times every hour.

On the outskirts of town, near the river, people travel far and wide to **Yva Chez Vava** (☎05-96-55-72-72; meals €14-30; ⏲lunch) for large helpings of seafood and Antillaise specials; it's best to book ahead.

On a side street just north of the Syndicat d'Initiative, the Creole restaurant **Chez Tante Arlette** (☎05-96-55-75-75; carinetantearlette@wanadoo.fr; 3 Rue Lucy de Fossarieu; mains €12-20; ⏲lunch Tue-Sun, dinner available for hotel guests; ❄) is renowned for its seafood and lobster. There are three sleeping rooms available upstairs (room including breakfast €60). Various packages are also on offer, starting at €75 per person, for a weekend of hiking, romance or fine dining.

Basse-Pointe to Presqu'île de Caravelle

The highway (N1) from Basse-Pointe to Lamentin runs along relatively tame terrain and is not one of the island's most interesting drives, although there are a few worthwhile sights. The communities along the way are largely modern towns that become increasingly more suburban as you continue south.

Some 2km from Ste-Marie is l'Habitation Fond St-Jacques (☎05-96-69-10-12; admission €4; ☺9am-4pm), the site of an old Dominican monastery and sugar plantation dating from 1660. One of the early plantation managers, Father Jean-Baptiste Labat, created a type of boiler (the *père labat*) that modernized the distilling of rum. It's an impressive site, and wandering the ruins feels like wandering the heart of an old European village. The site is 150m inland from the N1. Look for road signs to 'Fond St-Jacques.' Parking is on the street.

The **Musée du Rhum St James** (☎05-96-69-30-02; admission free, train tours €3; ☺9am-5pm Mon-Fri, to 1pm Sat & Sun) is set in a beautiful colonial home on the site of St James plantation's working distillery. Some of the signs are in English, and the numbered photos on the ground level give a nice overview of how sugar cane becomes rum. In the tasting room you can sample different rums. There's an occasional train tour of the distillery and the cane-laden estate but it only runs if there are enough interested visitors, so the hours are sporadic. The plantation is on the D24, 200m west of the N1, on the southern outskirts of Ste-Marie.

The D24 road continues to twist, in a general southwesterly direction to the **Musée de la Banane** (☎05-96-76-27-09; admission €8; ☺9am-5pm Mon-Sat, to 1pm Sun) which is dedicated to all things banana. Set on a terraced plantation, it's a pretty place where you'll see each stage of banana production from planting to packaging. There's a banana cake and banana juice tasting at tour's end.

The N1 continues on south through cane fields and passes the Presqu'île de Caravelle.

Presqu'île de Caravelle

This charming peninsula has some gorgeous stretches of beach and a wild and untamed feel in parts. A gently twisting road with spectacular views runs through sugarcane fields to the peninsula's main village, Tartane, and then on to Baie du Galion. On the north side of the peninsula are a couple of protected beaches: the long, sandy **Plage de Tartane** fronts the village, and the gently shelving, palm-fringed beach of **Anse l'Étang** is one of the isalnd's nicest and is a good, uncrowded place to surf.

Tartane beach, the larger of the two strands, has lots of fishing shacks, a fish market and colorful *gommier* (gum tree) boats; both places have plenty of beachside restaurants.

◎ Sights & Activities

Château Dubuc   RUINS
(adult/child €3/1; ☺8am-6pm) Set on the tip of the peninsula are the deteriorated ruins of a 17th-century estate. These sprawling grounds have some of the most extensive plantation ruins in Martinique, and there's a very small museum. The master of the estate gained notoriety by using a lantern to lure ships into wrecking off the coast, and then gathering the loot. Several hiking trails start at the parking lot, including a 30-minute walk to the site of a historic lighthouse and stellar views.

Ecole de Surf Bliss   SURFING
(☎05-96-58-00-96; www.surfmartinique.com; btwn Anse l'Étang & Château Dubuc; private lessons per hr €40; ☺9am-5:30pm Fri-Wed) Offers group or private surf lessons for people of all ages and experience levels on the nearby beach; also rents surfboards and body boards. English is spoken.

🛏 Sleeping

TOP CHOICE Hotel Le Manguier   HOTEL $$
(☎05-96-58-48-95; www.hotellemanguier.com; r incl breakfast from €78; 🅿❄🛇) This charming collection of whitewashed units is perched high above the athletic grounds in the center of Tartane. The simple but comfortable

DON'T MISS

LE DOMAINE SAINT AUBIN

Between Ste-Marie and La Trinité lies the small village of Petite Rivière Salée, where you'll find what is perhaps Martinique's most atmospheric accommodation. **Le Domaine Saint Aubin** (☎05-96-69-34-77; www.ledomainesaint aubin.com; r €189; 🅿❄🛇) is a beautiful boutique hotel housed in a former plantation house, surrounded by acres of forested land. Rooms are decorated with antique furniture, but are very comfortable and well maintained. The owners, whose family have lived in Martinique since 1715, take very good care of their guests. Even if you're not one of the lucky ones, there's an excellent restaurant that's open to the public (reservations are advised).

rooms have small outdoor hot-plate kitchens and great balconies, many of which face the Atlantic Ocean. There's a small pool, and breakfast is served with a sea view.

Hotel Restaurant Caravelle HOTEL $$
(☑05-96-58-07-32; www.hotel-la-caravelle-martinique.com; Route du Château Dubuc; r from €81; ▣)
On the eastern outskirts of Tartane is this small, friendly, family-run hotel. There is a hibiscus-covered terrace with glorious views of the Atlantic, and the public areas are all beautifully furnished and well looked after. Rooms are very pleasant and come in several different sizes, including studios that have well-equipped kitchenettes on a spacious front porch with great views.

Residence Oceane Hotel HOTEL $$
(☑05-96-58-73-73; www.residenceoceane.com; Route du Château Dubuc, Anse l'Etang; r €99-125; ▣🔊▣) On the way to Château Dubuc, this friendly hotel is a beauty with stunning ocean views. It's within walking distance of Ecole de Surf Bliss and the beach. Some of the rooms have large terraces with kitchenettes, making self-catering an option.

🍴 Eating

TOP CHOICE **Dubuc Café** FRENCH $$$
(☑05-96-65-42-91; Route du Château Dubuc; set meals €25-34; ⊙lunch & dinner Tue-Sun) This high-end addition to Tartane's fairly middle-of-the-road eating scene is the place for a blow out, with their three-course set meals. Served up on the terrace, the food here is traditional French – think osso buco with pâté gratin, or entrecôte with Roquefort. There's also a curious cave-like bar if you just fancy a good glass of wine.

Le Kalicoucou PIZZA $
(☑05-96-58-02-38; Route du Château Dubuc; pizza €8-18; ⊙lunch Wed-Fri, dinner Tue-Sun) On the eastern end of the main strip in Tartane, this is the place for pizza and beer – or, if you needed a reminder of the French influence, crepes and wine. Choose from delivery, takeout and eat-in options.

Restaurant La Tartanaise CREOLE $$
(Route du Château Dubuc; set menu €16; ⊙breakfast, lunch & dinner) This ramshackle place in the middle of the seafront serves up popular fish, seafood and grilled meat dishes, including excellent *acra*. This is where many of the locals go for a *ti-punch* at day's end.

La Table de Mamy Nounou FRENCH, CREOLE $$
(mains €14-25; ⊙lunch & dinner) In the Hotel Restaurant Caravelle, this excellent restaurant features seafood, grills and wonderful desserts. You order, take your appetizers in the lounge, and you'll be shown to your table when the meal is ready – you never feel like you're waiting.

SOUTHERN MARTINIQUE

Martinique's south has by far the best beaches on the island and is definitely the center of gravity for tourism. Those looking for a straightforward beach holiday should head to Ste-Anne's beaches, which are probably the best on the island. But those who have their own transportation should consider basing themselves in Diamant, which has several good beaches within easy driving distance.

The largest concentration of places to stay is in the greater Trois-Îlets area, which encompasses the busy resort town of Pointe du Bout and the smaller, less visibly touristy villages of Grande Anse and Anse d'Arlet.

The interior of the island's southern half is largely a mix of agricultural land and residential areas. Lamentin, the site of the international airport, is Martinique's second-largest city but, like other interior cities and towns, has little to interest tourists.

Trois-Îlets

POP 3100

This small working town has a central square bordered by a little market, a quaint town hall and the church where local gal, the future Empress Josephine, was baptized in 1763. Despite its proximity to the island's busiest resort area, the town has so far avoided developers' attention, though its charm has been tarnished by a constant flow of traffic through its main street. Be aware that Trois-Îlets is also the name of the local commune, so some hotels and attractions supposedly located in Trois-Îlets may actually be in nearby towns or villages.

A former sugar estate outside Trois-Îlets was the birthplace of the Empress Josephine. A picturesque stone building, formerly the family kitchen, has been turned into the **Musée de la Pagerie** (☑05-96-68-33-06; adult/child €6/2.50; ⊙9am-5:30pm Tue-Sun), containing the empress' childhood bed and other memorabilia. Multilingual tour guides relate anecdotal tidbits about Josephine's life, such as the doctoring of the marriage certificate to make the bride, Napoleon's elder by six years, appear to be the same age as her spouse.

The worthwhile **Maison de la Canne** (Sugarcane Museum; ☏05-96-68-32-04; adult/child €3/1; ☺8:30am-5:30pm Tue-Sun) occupies the site of an old sugar refinery and distillery. Inside the main museum building are period photos and items such as the Code Noir (Black Code) outlining appropriate conduct between slaves and their owners. Displays are in French and English. The museum is on the D7, 3.5km east of Trois-Îlets' center.

There's a ferry between Fort-de-France and Trois-Îlets; see p591 for details.

Pointe du Bout

POP 7500

At the southern end of the Baie de Fort-de-France is Pointe du Bout, Martinique's most developed resort. Home to the island's most-frequented yachting marina and some of its largest resorts, though these are actually small by Caribbean standards. At the tip is a Y-shaped peninsula, with hotels fringing the coast and the marina in the middle. The concrete carcass of the derelict Hotel Kalenda gives the peninsula an air of decay, but there are still some very pleasant, if busy, beaches here.

Plage de l'Anse Mitan, the small public beach that runs along the western side of the neck of the peninsula, is a good swimming beach and many people bring masks and fins. There's also a swim park for the little ones, fenced by buoys.

The lodging in this area gets more expensive the closer it is to the water. There are plenty of restaurants, upscale shops and bars, and it's a lively place at night.

🏃 Activities

Attitude Plongée   DIVING, SNORKELING
(☏05-96-66-28-27; www.attitudeplongee.com; Pointe du Bout; snorkeling trip €25, 1-tank dive €50) Right in the heart of Pointe du Bout, this diving and snorkeling outfit goes out daily and offers very reasonably priced 'baptisms' to first-time divers with a one-day PADI Discover Scuba course (adult/child €55/45).

Schéhérazade   BOAT TOURS
(☏06-96-39-45-55; www.scheherazade.com; Pointe du Bout) This company runs €42 boat tours to the superb Rocher du Diamant (see p583), allowing you to swim on the reef, see a cave of bats and just get up close to this

amazing place. It also runs daily €72 boat trips to Fort-de-France. Both tours include food and drinks.

Espace Plongée   DIVING
(☏05-96-66-01-79; www.espace-plongee-martinique.com; Pointe du Bout; 1-tank dive €50) This outfit offers morning and afternoon dives every day and, if enough people want to go, night dives. It's located right beside the water in the marina and English is spoken.

Windsurf Club Martinique   WINDSURFING
(☏05-96-66-19-06; www.windsurf-martinique.com; Pointe du Bout; windsurfing per hr €20) This professionally run operation, based at the Hôtel Carayou, is the best established windsurfing club in Martinique.

Héliblue   HELICOPTER TOURS
(☏05-96-66-10-80; www.heliblue.com; Domaine Château Gaillard, Trois-Îlets) This helicopter tour operator offers a range of aerial journeys around Martinique from the Domaine Château Gaillard heliport near Trois-Îlets. Prices range from €34 per person for a six-minute flight to €175 per person for a tour around Mont Pelée.

🛏 Sleeping

Hotel de la Pagerie   HOTEL $$
(☏05-96-66-05-30; www.hotel-lapagerie.com; Pointe du Bout; s/d incl breakfast from €99/120; ✱🛜🏊) Tucked between a busy intersection and the inner harbor, this 94-bedroom hotel is housed in a Louisiana-style white timber building surrounded by tropical flowers and facing the sea. Its rooms are unexciting, but they're comfortable and some of the best value around the marina.

Le Panoramic Hotel   HOTEL $$
(☏05-96-68-34-34; www.lepanoramic.fr; Anse-à-l'Ane; s/d/tr €121/132//171; ✱🛜🏊) This hillside hotel in Anse-à-l'Ane, a short distance from Trois-Îlets, has a stunning location with views over the bay and down the coast. The 36 rooms are all the same, sharing a simple but comfortable style. The small village below is friendly and has a good beach.

Hotel Carayou   RESORT $$$
(☏05-96-66-04-04; www.hotel-carayou.com; Pointe du Bout; r incl breakfast from €160; ✱🛜🏊) The 207-room family-friendly Carayou sits on the peninsula that forms the northeast side of the marina. The modern rooms have brightly painted tropical-style furniture but no kitchenettes, though there

are two restaurants on the grounds. There's also a small beach for guests.

Hotel Bakoua
RESORT $$$

(☎05-96-66-02-02; www.accorhotels.com; Pointe du Bout; r €410, ste €650-850; ❋ 🛜 ❄ 🅿) The area's most exclusive resort has 132 rooms and suites that are very comfortably furnished (the best of the lot are right on the beach). Guests have access to one of the area's best beaches and the hotel's water toys, as well as an infinity pool with great views.

✗ Eating

The dining in Trois-Îlets is a mixed bag, and you'll find few authentic or particularly charming restaurants in and around Pointe du Bout. For something a bit more local consider driving down the coast to Grande Anse or Anse d'Arlet.

Le Corsaire
PIZZA, GRILL $

(Village Créole, Pointe du Bout; mains €10-18; ⏱lunch & dinner Fri-Tue) Inside the little Village Créole shopping area, this charming and friendly place offers outdoor tables set around a small fountain, as well as more formal indoor eating. The large menu runs from traditional Creole dishes to meat grills and pizza.

La Grange
GRILL, BAR $$

(Rue Cha-Cha, Pointe du Bout; mains €15-25; ⏱lunch & dinner; 🛜) The food, including fish tartar and grilled tuna, is good at this outdoor restaurant and indoor cigar bar: even better is the free wi-fi, quality cigars and a kicking bar with some very serious cocktails.

For a quick sandwich or snack, try the following two places.

Baguet Shop
SANDWICHES $

(Rue Cha-Cha, Pointe du Bout; sandwiches from €3) Does decent sandwiches, and mouthwatering pastries; has seating available, including tables outside.

Boule de Neige
CREPES $

(Rue Cha-Cha, Pointe du Bout; crepes from €4) Next door to the Baguet Shop, this friendly creperie has delicious galettes and crepes of all varieties.

ℹ️ Information

You'll find a **moneychanging office**, the port bureau and marine-supply shops at the Pointe du Bout marina. The Village Créole complex has shops and an **ATM**. There's also an **Otitour** (L'Office du Tourisme des Trois Ilets; ☎05-96-

68-47-63; www.trois-ilets.com; Rue Cha-Cha) tourism kiosk by the marina.

ℹ️ Getting There & Around

Ferries to and from Fort-de-France leave from the west side of Pointe du Bout's marina. Here you'll also find a number of **car-rental** firms.

Grande Anse
POP 600

The pleasant little village of Grande Anse is located on Grande Anse d'Arlet. It's set along a beachfront road lined with brightly painted boats and a string of restaurants. The main street is for pedestrians only, making it more enjoyable to stroll along the beach, which is nice to look at, but not so nice to tan on (due to fishing boats and no privacy).

🏃 Activities

Plongée Passion
DIVING

(☎05-96-68-71-78; www.plongeepassion.pag espro-orange.fr; 1 Allée des Raisiniers; 1-tank dive €50) On the beach next to Ti Plage, this friendly and well-known dive outfit offers morning and afternoon outings daily.

Alpha Plongée
DIVING

(☎05-96-48-30-34; www.alpha-plongee.com; 138 Rue Robert Deloy; 1-tank dive €50) It's on the main road, tucked behind a private home; follow the signs. Runs morning and early-afternoon dive trips.

🛏️ Sleeping & Eating

TOP CHOICE Localizé
HOTEL $$

(☎05-96-68-64-78; www.localize.fr; studios per week from €490; @) The 10 studios in this expansive single-level Creole place are set right on the beach. It's a pleasant place to stay, with a small library, a gardened exterior and all of the naturally ventilated rooms are decorated in exotic woods from around the world. Two of the studios can sleep four people with a main bedroom that's air-conditioned. Localizé also rents two fully equipped homes in the area.

Ti Payot
CREOLE $$

(1 Allée des Raisiniers; mains €12-18; ⏱lunch Tue-Sun) At this beautiful spot overlooking the water you can enjoy the waves running up under its wooden terrace as you eat. It's a lovely place for dinner and there are always new chef's suggestions determined by what's been landed fresh each morning.

The Carib name for Martinique was Madinina, meaning 'island of flowers,' and it's not difficult to see why – even if Columbus would barely recognize the little corner of paradise he visited five centuries ago. Martinique has lots of colorful flowering plants, with the vegetation varying with altitude and rainfall. Rainforests cover the slopes of the mountains in the northern interior: luxuriant with tree ferns, bamboo groves, climbing vines and hardwood trees like mahogany, rosewood, locust and *gommier*.

The drier southern part of the island has brushy savanna vegetation such as cacti, frangipani trees, balsam, logwood and acacia shrubs. Common landscape plantings include splashy bougainvillea, the ubiquitous red hibiscus, and yellow-flowered allamanda trees. To truly appreciate the range and magnificence of the island's varied flora, head to the unbeatable Jardin de Balata (p576) on the mountainous Route de la Trace and see the many flowers that gave Martinique its name.

Ti Sable   FRENCH, CREOLE **$$**
(☑05-96-68-62-44; www.tisablemartinique.com; mains €18-24; ☉lunch daily, dinner Fri-Sun; ☜) Ti Sable is a surprisingly large complex right on the beach that oozes class and has an imaginative menu to match. As well as a host of fish and seafood dishes, barbecued meats and exotic salads are also on the cards. There's live music on weekends and a superb Sunday lunch buffet (€28).

Bidjoul   CREOLE **$**
(mains €8-16, set meals €13-18) This charming wooden house on the beach has a very reasonably priced menu, and serves up all the Creole favorites, as well as pizza. Best of all, it has tables on the sand.

Anse d'Arlet

POP 3200

Anse d'Arlet is perhaps the most charming fishing village in southern Martinique; it retains an undiscovered feel, as there's just one small guesthouse here and (for the moment) very little else. There's a handsome coastal road crowned by an 18th-century Roman Catholic church whose doors open almost directly onto the beautiful beach, and the entire scene is framed with steep, verdant hills. Even if you're not staying here, make a trip to enjoy the sleepy village atmosphere and stellar beach.

There's a Crédit Mutuel with an ATM in the center of town and a small produce and fish market along the boardwalk.

The only accommodations in the village, **Résidence Madinakay** (☑05-96-68-70-76; madinakay.wifeo.com; 3 Allée des Arlésiens; r €58; ❋) is on the main street across from the beach. Run by the helpful Raymond de Laval, the eight simple, colorful studios all have kitchenettes, mosquito nets and balconies or terraces. Simple meals are also available for guests.

Restaurant de la Plage (Rue Eugène Larcher; mains from €14-17; ☉lunch & dinner) is the best place to eat in the village. Just beyond the post office, the restaurant has tables scattered about on the beach where it serves up fish, seafood, meat grills and large salad plates.

In the nearby village of **Petite Anse**, **Au Dessous du Volcan** (☑05-96-68-69-52; Rue des Pecheurs; mains €10-20; ☉lunch & dinner Fri-Wed) is a gorgeous place serving up Creole food in a beautiful tropical garden. Order in advance for the signature dish: roast lobster flambéed in rum.

Diamant

POP 3400

Diamant is a seaside town on the southern coast that's slightly more developed than its neighbors. The main road runs near, but not right on, the beach. The beaches here stretch for 2km beside town, but because of a bad current and violent waves, it's important to ask at your hotel for a safe place to swim.

For visitors, the best Diamant has to offer are some nice hotels, a row of pizzerias and snack places, an internet cafe and a few banks along the main drag. It's a good base to explore the western horn of the island – which, oddly enough, is shaped a little bit like France. The town also affords a nice view of **Rocher du Diamant**, a 176m-high volcanic islet that's a popular dive site, with interesting cave formations but tricky water conditions. To explore this underwater jewel, visit the dive operators at nearby Grande Anse.

Just north of town on the D7 is **Le Musée des Coquillages et de la Mer** (☑05-96-76-41-92; Hotel l'Ecrin Bleue; admission €5; ☺9am-6pm). Seeing hard-to-find shells found in Japan in the 1760s, or off the coast of South Africa in the 1880s, is actually fun.

🛏 Sleeping & Eating

TOP CHOICE **L'Anse Bleue** STUDIOS **$$**

(☑05-96-76-21-91; www.hotel-anse-bleue.com; r €49, studios for 2/4 €70/90; ❉❄✈⋔) This place is very simple, but somehow manages to get things just right – there are 25 delightful little bungalows spread out across spacious grounds, a decent-sized pool, a superb on-site restaurant (La Paillotte Bleue) and a peaceful location – all adding up to make this one of our favorite hotels in Martinique. Prices are remarkably low for the quality of the accommodation, and the studios all have kitchenettes and fridges, allowing plenty of opportunity to self-cater.

Diamant les Bains HOTEL **$$**

(☑05-96-76-40-14; diamantlesbains@wannadoo.fr; s/d incl breakfast €75/100, s/d bungalows incl breakfast €95/118; ❉❄✈⋔) While it appears small from the road outside, this charming, family-run hotel is actually set in a large plot of land that runs all the way down to the sea (although there's no beach). There's a great pool, and you're right in the center of things. Two bungalows have wheelchair access.

TOP CHOICE **La Paillotte Bleue** FRENCH **$$**

(☑05-96-58-33-21; mains €18-27; ☺dinner Thu-Tue, lunch Sun) Sublime poolside dining at Guy Uldry's superb restaurant is a real treat. Located at L'Anse Bleue (but run separately to the hotel) La Paillotte Bleue serves up classic French dishes with a dash of Caribbean influence, such as a veal ragout cooked with vanilla, or curried roast lamb. There's a good wine list and service is excellent, making this one of the best restaurants on the island.

In Diamant itself there are several simple, local restaurants that are good for an evening meal or a midday snack.

La Case Créole CREOLE **$**

(Rue Hilarion Giscon; mains €10-19; ☺lunch & dinner Fri-Wed) Just by the church, this place serves up standard Creole fare in a fan-cooled room with a small street terrace.

Planète Diamant CREOLE **$**

(Rue Justin Roc; mains €10-18; ☺11am-2am, closed Wed) Features menus shaped like Saturn and salads named after bodies in our solar system. The salads include the Venus, with crab, salmon and shrimp and the Mars, with grilled *lardon* (halfway between ham and bacon) and goat's cheese.

La Marée INTERNATIONAL **$$**

(9 Rue Hilarion Giscon; mains €12-18; ☺lunch & dinner) Hidden away behind a pizzeria on the main drag, this place serves up an inventive list of dishes, including kangaroo steaks and sashimi, as well as more typical Creole fare. There's also a pleasant airy terrace.

Ste-Luce

POP 9600

This busy town is, in itself, not really worth visiting, but the stretch of hotels along the coast in the suburbs of Gros Raisin and Trois-Rivières keeps visitors coming. The hotels are far enough away from the N5 highway for you not to feel like you're living on a freeway, but close enough to make this a great base to explore the southern half of the island. There's a Crédit Mutuel bank with two ATMs on Rue Schoelcher.

For divers, there are two operators and numerous sites to choose from. The beaches – **Anse Mabouya**, 4km to the west of the center of town, and **Anses Gros Raisin**, which is really two beaches side by side 2km west of the town center – aren't worth a special trip, but for those staying in the area they provide a pleasant break and are rarely crowded.

◉ Sights & Activities

Trois-Rivières Distillery RUM DISTILLERY

(☑05-96-62-51-78; www.plantationtroisrivieres.com; Quartier Trois-Rivières; admission €2.50; ☺9am-5:30pm Mon-Fri, to 1pm Sat) One of Martinique's oldest rum distilleries, this interesting place offers self-guided tours, with signs in English, starting from near the parking lot. However, many of the 'exhibits' are actually on-site souvenir and snack shops. The self-guided tour ends with a tasting at the rum boutique; it sells hard-to-find aged rums, but if you're just after normal rums you'll find them cheaper at most supermarkets.

Ste-Luce Plongée DIVING

(☑05-96-62-40-06; www.sainteluceplongee.fr; 43 Blvd Kennedy; 1-tank dive €55) Conducts two daily dives to either nearby sites or further out at Rocher du Diamant.

Okeanos Club   DIVING

(📞05-96-62-52-36; www.okeanos-club.com;
1-tank dive €45) Offers two, sometimes three,
daily dive outings. It's set in the Village
Pierres & Vacances. English is spoken.

🛏 Sleeping & Eating

Motorists should take the Trois-Rivière exit
on the eastbound N5 right before the Ste-
Luce exit. The hotels listed here are in the
rolling hills near the exit, and the town is
5km southeast of the exit on the D36 (make
a left toward the sea). On the D7, where
many of the hotels are located, is the 8 à
Huit supermarket.

[TOP CHOICE] Le Verger de Ste-Luce   STUDIOS **$$**

(📞05-96-62-20-72; www.vergerdesainteluce.com;
d/q €81/70; ❋🛜🏊) For a warm welcome,
look no further than to this charming place.
Bungalows surround a small pool with sun
chairs and there's a stand-alone Jacuzzi –
and the friendly owner loves to practice
her English. The simple bungalows all have
their own porch with a kitchenette and a
good amount of greenery keeps the small
place feeling private. Turn right after the
Trois-Rivières exit and keep looking on the
left – it's only 100m down the road.

Hotel Le Panoramique   HOTEL **$$**

(📞05-96-62-31-32; www.panoramiquehotel.fr; r
with/without kitchenette €60/70; ❋❋) Just a
little north of Le Verger de Ste-Luce on the
same road, this place is handy for access to
the beach. Five of the 15 rooms have kitchenettes, not to mention the best views, though
they also suffer from having a road right below them. There's a bar and restaurant on
the property, too.

Hotel Corail Résidence   HOTEL **$$**

(📞05-96-62-11-01; www.karibea.com; d from €98;
❋🛜🏊) All of the 26 rooms have kitchenettes
and little porches with mechanical blinds
that either shut out the morning light or
open up to great views of the bay. There's a
great pool area here and a relaxed vibe. The
only shame is that despite being right at the
water's edge, there's no direct access to the
sea – it's a 10-minute walk to Anse Mabouya.

[TOP CHOICE] Côté Sud   FRENCH, CREOLE **$$**

(📞05-96-62-59-63; Trois-Rivières; mains €16-25,
set lunch €20; ⊙lunch & dinner Tue-Sun) Right
on the water's edge in Trois-Rivières is this
gourmet restaurant offering a sublime menu
of local and French dishes such as cassolette

of sea snail or sea bass cooked in vanilla and
lime sauce. It's best to reserve ahead for evening meals.

L'Epi Soleil   CREOLE **$**

(📞05-96-62-36-12; 51 Blvd Kennedy; mains €9-14;
⊙closed Sun Apr-Jun, Sep & Oct) A local favorite,
the covered outdoor bar on the waterfront
across from the restaurant is a popular place
that stays open into the night. The restaurant serves sandwiches, salads and pizza as
well as more elaborate dishes such as grilled
lobster (€35), which you should order two
days in advance.

Ste-Anne

POP 3300

The southernmost village on Martinique,
Ste-Anne has a sleepy air and an attractive
seaside setting with painted wooden houses and numerous trinket shops. Its most
popular swimming beach is the long, lovely
strand that stretches along the peninsula
800m north of the town center. Despite the
large number of visitors that flock to the
town on weekends and during the winter
season, Ste-Anne remains a casual, low-key
place, with abundant near-shore reef formations that make for good snorkeling.

If the beach here is too crowded for you
Cap Chevalier is 6km east as the crow flies
and beautiful Macabou is 12km northeast.

There's a small **office of tourism** (www.
sainte-anne.to) kiosk in the town center, near
the pier, that has maps of the town and can
help with car or hotel arrangements.

🛏 Sleeping

There are a number of *gîtes* (cottages for
rent) scattered around the edge of the town's
center.

La Dunette   HOTEL **$$**

(📞05-96-76-73-90; www.ladunette.com; d/tr incl
breakfast €90/110; ❋🛜) In the center of town
and overlooking the water, this hotel has 13
rooms and a restaurant (mains €12 to €24).
The interior of the hotel is rather worn, but
rooms are spacious and clean. Get a room
on the 2nd level for the best sea views, or
alternatively enjoy a 10% discount for rooms
overlooking the street.

**Résidence Plage de l'Anse
Caritan**   RESORT **$$**

(📞05-96-76-92-00; www.anse-caritan.com; Rte
des Caraïbes; studios/ste from €82/135; ❋🛜🏊🍴)

This large, family-friendly hotel is at the end of a wooded lane just over 800m south of the village center. Rooms are divided into simple studios with kitchenettes, as well as more elaborate suites. There's a pleasant sandy beach complete with a water activities and dive center, and overall a very relaxed atmosphere.

✕ Eating

TOP CHOICE **Les Tamariniers** CREOLE $$
(☎05-96-76-75-62; 30 Rue Abbé Saffache; mains €12-22; ⊙lunch & dinner Thu-Tue) Definitely the best in town, this friendly place has a varied menu of Creole food, including excellent octopus fricassee and delicious rum flambé shrimp on a kebab. It's situated to one side of the church in the middle of town; reserve ahead for dinner.

Le Coco Neg' CREOLE $$
(☎05-96-76-94-82; 4 Rue Abbé-Hurard; mains €13-25; ⊙dinner) A block on from Les Tamariniers, this friendly spot serves up wonderful traditional Creole cuisine in a brightly painted dining room. Reservations are usually a good idea.

Paille Coco CREOLE $
(Rue J-M Tjibaou; mains €10-22; ⊙10am-4pm) Right on the water, this terrace restaurant is a good place for lunch in the sun, as you drink a cold beer and enjoy the great-value Creole cooking coming from the kitchen. Enter through the L'Epi Soleil bakery.

Les Salines

At the undeveloped southern tip of the island, Les Salines is probably Martinique's finest beach. The gorgeous long stretch of golden sand attracts scantily clad French tourists and local families alike on weekends and holidays. While it's big enough to accommodate everyone without feeling crowded, it might be necessary to pick a direction and keep walking along the beach until the crowds thin.

Les Salines gets its name from Étang des Salines, the large salt pond that backs it; it's about 5km south of Ste-Anne at the end of the D9. There are showers and food vans near the center of the beach, and about 500m further south you'll find snack shops selling reasonably priced sandwiches, burgers and chicken.

When we visited, the road that used to run along the beach was under construction, which meant that the parking lot was a big dirt field that got muddy and slippery after rain. While this situation continues, parking during peak times can be a messy hassle.

On a brighter note, this is one of the few beaches where camping is legal, but only during school holidays. Camp on the west side of the beach; signs depicting tents guide the way.

Beware of poisonous manchineel trees (most are marked with red paint) on the beach, particularly at the southeast end; rainwater dripping off them can cause rashes and blistering. There's some good snorkeling at the west end of the beach.

UNDERSTAND MARTINIQUE

History

French & British Occupation

When Christopher Columbus first sighted Martinique it was inhabited by Caribs, who called the island Madinina meaning 'island of flowers.' Three decades passed before the first party of French settlers, led by Pierre Belain d'Esnambuc, landed on the northwest side of the island. There they built a small fort and established a settlement that would become the capital city, St-Pierre. The next year, on October 31, 1636, King Louis XIII signed a decree authorizing the use of African slaves in the French West Indies.

The settlers quickly went about colonizing the land with the help of slave labor and by 1640 they had extended their grip south to Fort-de-France, where they constructed a fort on the rise above the harbor. As forests were cleared to make room for sugar plantations, conflicts with the native Caribs escalated into warfare, and in 1660 those Caribs who had survived the fighting were finally forced off the island.

The British also took a keen interest in Martinique, invading and holding the island for most of the period from 1794 to 1815. The island prospered under British occupation; the planters simply sold their sugar in British markets rather than French ones. Perhaps more importantly, the occupation allowed Martinique to avoid the turmoil of the French Revolution. By the time the British returned the island to France in 1815, the Napoleonic Wars had ended and the French empire was again entering a period of stability.

Not long after the French administration was re-established on Martinique did the golden era of sugarcane began to wane, as glutted markets and the introduction of sugar beets on mainland France eroded prices. With their wealth diminished, the aristocratic plantation owners lost much of their political influence, and the abolitionist movement, led by Victor Schoelcher, gained momentum.

It was Schoelcher, the French cabinet minister responsible for overseas possessions, who convinced the provisional government to sign the 1848 Emancipation Proclamation, which brought an end to slavery in the French West Indies. Widely reviled by the white aristocracy of the time, Schoelcher is now regarded as one of Martinique's heroes.

In 1946 Martinique went from being a colony to an overseas département of France, with a status similar to those of metropolitan départements. In 1974 it was further assimilated into the political fold as a Department of France.

Natural Disasters & After-effects

On May 8, 1902, in the most devastating natural disaster in Caribbean history, the eruption of the Mont Pelée volcano destroyed the city of St-Pierre and claimed the lives of its 30,000 inhabitants. Shortly thereafter, the capital was moved permanently to Fort-de-France. St-Pierre, which had been regarded as the most cultured city in the French West Indies, was eventually rebuilt, but it has never been more than a shadow of its former self.

In August 2007 Hurricane Dean pounded Martinique and entirely wiped out its banana crop. The hurricane caused damage estimated at $240 million and killed two people. Just as the island began to recover in February 2009, a general strike that originated in nearby Guadeloupe spread to Martinique. For a whole month during the tourism high season, thousands of people protested about the cost of living and the high unemployment rate by blockading the island's gas stations and bringing much of the public sector to a standstill. Racial tensions also increased, and Martinique lost millions in tourist revenue as thousands of holidays were cancelled. The effect of the 2009 strikes is still felt in many smaller resort towns, where restaurants and hotels have gone under as travelers have stayed away.

Culture

The earliest settlers on Martinique were from Normandy, Brittany, Paris and other parts of France; shortly afterward, African slaves were brought to the island. Later, smaller numbers of immigrants came from India, Syria and Lebanon. These days, Martinique is home to thousands of immigrants, some of them here illegally, from poorer Caribbean islands such as Dominica, St Lucia and Haiti. Martinique's population today hovers around 400,000 – more than a quarter of whom live in the Fort-de-France area.

Due to its colonial past, Martinique's society combines French traditions with Caribbean Creole culture. Politeness is highly valued on Martinique, so brush up on your manners. In general, always address people with the formal 'vous' rather than 'tu,' but know that if someone uses the more casual form of address first (which happens more often here than in France) it's fine to use 'tu' in response.

Only the high-end restaurants and clubs enforce a dress code; look for signs that read tenue correcte exigée (correct dress expected). Elsewhere, dress is casual but generally stylish – save beachwear for the beach. Topless bathing is very common on the island, particularly at resort beaches.

The majority of residents are of mixed ethnic origin. The Black Pride movement known as négritude emerged as a philosophical and literary movement in the 1930s, largely through the writings of Martinique native Aimé Césaire, a négritude poet who was eventually elected mayor of Fort-de-France. The movement advanced black social and cultural values and reestablished bonds with African traditions, which had been suppressed by French colonialism.

The beguine, an Afro-French style of dance music with a bolero rhythm, originated in Martinique in the 1930s. Zouk is a more contemporary French West Indies creation, drawing on the beguine and other French-Caribbean folk forms. Retaining the electronic influences of its '80s origins with its Carnival-like rhythm and hot dance beat, zouk has become as popular in Europe as it is in the French Caribbean.

Landscape & Wildlife

At 1080 sq km, Martinique is the second-largest island in the French West Indies. Roughly 65km long and 20km wide, it has a terrain punctuated by hills, plateaus and mountains.

The highest point is the 1397m Mont Pelée, an active volcano at the northern end of the island. The center of the island is dominated by the Pitons du Carbet, a scenic mountain range reaching 1207m. Martinique's irregular coastline is cut by deep bays and coves, while the mountainous rainforest in the interior feeds numerous rivers.

See also Island of Flowers (p583).

Wildlife

The underwater life tends to be of the smaller variety; lots of schools of tiny fish that swim by in a cloud of silver or red. There are a decent amount of lobsters hiding under rocks, and occasionally a ray will glide by.

Martinique is home to Anolis lizards, manicous (opossums), mongooses and venomous fer-de-lance snakes. The mongoose, which was introduced from India in the late 19th century, preys on eggs and has been responsible for the demise of many bird species. Some native birds, such as parrots, are no longer found on the island at all, while others have significantly declined in numbers. Endangered birds include the Martinique trembler, white-breasted trembler and white-breasted thrasher.

SURVIVAL GUIDE

Directory A–Z

Accommodations

Hotel accommodation in Martinique isn't, as a rule, particularly charming. That said, hotels here are generally small by Carribean standards and large resorts are rare. Most hotels are mid-sized and midrange, and prices are reasonable by the standards of the region. Many of Martinique's most charming accommodations are private guesthouses (chambres d'hôte) or freestanding houses and cottages to rent (gîtes), but they gener-ally require booking by the week. See www.gitesdefrance.fr for more details.

Room rates given in this chapter are for the high season (generally from December to April and July to August). Low season rates can be much cheaper than those quoted here. Generally, you can expect a reduction of between 20% and 40% between May and July and from September to November.

Price cateogries in this chapter are based on the cost of a double room.

$	budget	less than €50
$$	midrange	€50 to €150
$$$	top end	more than €150

Business Hours

The following are normal business hours. Reviews don't include hours unless they differ from these standards.

Banks 9am-4pm Mon-Fri

Bars 9pm-midnight

Restaurants 11.30am-10pm Mon-Sat (some closed between lunch & dinner)

Shops 9am-7pm Mon-Sat

Supermarkets 8am-8pm Mon-Sat

Children

Children will be welcome on vacation in Martinique. Many hotels are family oriented and the island is a very safe place overall. Practically all hotels will provide cots, and some hotels provide babysitting services.

All restaurants will allow children to dine, and they'll often have a simple and good-value menu enfant (children's set meal) to offer them. European brands of baby formula, foods and diapers can be bought at pharmacies.

Embassies & Consulates

The following are all honorary consuls who should be contacted only in an emergency.

Germany (☑05-96-42-79-21; Acajou, 97232 Lamentin)

Netherlands (☑05-96-63-30-04; 44-46 Ave Maurice Bishop, 97200 Fort-de-France)

UK (☑05-96-61-88-92; Route du Phare, 97200 Fort-de-France)

US (☑05-96-75-69-54; usconsulaireagence martinique@wanadoo.fr; Hotel Valmeniere 615, Ave des Arawaks, 97200 Fort-de-France)

Festivals & Events

Mardi Gras Carnival Martinique has a spirited Carnival during the five-day period leading up to Ash Wednesday, though most of the action centers on Fort-de-France.

St-Pierre The island commemorates the 8 May 1902 eruption of Mont Pelée with live jazz performances and a candlelight procession from the cathedral. On a smaller scale, every village in Martinique has its own festivities to celebrate the day of its patron saint (dates vary).

Tour de la Martinique Weeklong bicycle race in mid-July.

Tour des Yoles Rondes Weeklong race of traditional sailboats in early August.

Food

This chapter uses the following price categories for eateries (based on the cost of a main meal):

$	budget	less than €12
$$	midrange	€12 to €20
$$$	top end	more than €20

Gay & Lesbian Travelers

Gay rights are legally protected in Martinique, as a part of France. However overall homophobia is still very prevalent and there is little or no gay scene on the island. Gay and lesbian travelers have nothing to worry about though – in general, those working in the hotel industry are perfectly used to gay travelers and booking a double room will cause no raised eyebrows.

Health

As in much of the Caribbean, dengue fever has made an unwelcome reappearance in Martinique. Dengue is transmitted by mosquito bites, so wear long sleeves and cover your legs in the evenings, and sleep under a mosquito net. Consult a doctor immediately if you experience fever, exhaustion or extreme fatigue.

There is also a risk of bilharzia (schistosomiasis) infection throughout the island; the main precaution is to avoid wading or swimming in fresh water.

The fer-de-lance, an aggressive pit viper, resides on Martinique. The snake's bite is highly toxic and sometimes fatal so it's essential for victims to get an antivenin injection as soon as possible. They favor overgrown

and brushy fields, so hikers should be alert for the snakes and stick to established trails. Beware of manchineel trees found on some beaches, particularly on the south coast, as rainwater dripping off them can cause skin rashes and blistering. They're usually marked with a band of red paint.

Tap water is safe to drink in Martinique.

Internet Access

Internet cafes have been almost entirely replaced by wireless (sometimes called WLAN locally) in Martinique. This wireless access is nearly always provided for free.

If you don't have a laptop or other wireless device with you, you'll have to find an internet cafe or expect to take a break from email for the duration of your stay. Some hotels have terminals that can be used by guests, but these are the exception to the rule.

Money

Martinique, as a département of France, uses the euro; it's a bad idea to bring anything else, as exchange rates aren't great. Hotels, larger restaurants and car-rental agencies accept Visa, MasterCard and, less commonly, American Express. ATMs are common across the island. 10% is the standard tipping rate when dining out.

Public Holidays

In addition to the holidays observed throughout the region (except Whit Monday and Boxing Day; p872), Martinique has the following public holidays:

Easter Sunday Late March/early April

Ascension Thursday Fortieth day after Easter

Pentecost Monday Eighth Monday after Easter

Labor Day May 1

Victory Day May 8

Slavery Abolition Day May 22

Bastille Day July 14

Schoelcher Day July 21

Assumption Day August 15

All Saints Day November 1

Fête des Morts November 2

Armistice Day November 11

Safe Travel

Occasional islandwide strikes can bring tourism services to a screeching halt. And it's not advisable to wander around the backstreets of Fort-de-France after dark; mugging is the main concern.

Telephone

The country code for Martinique is ☏596. Confusingly, all eight-digit local numbers begin with ☏0596 as well. These numbers are separate, however, and therefore must be dialed twice when calling from abroad.

When calling from within the French West Indies, simply dial the local eight-digit number. From elsewhere, dial your country's international access code, followed by the ☏596 country code and the local number (omit the first zero). For directory assistance, dial ☏12.

To see whether you can use your phone on the island's GSM networks, check whther your cell service provider has a roaming agreement with any of the service operators. SIM cards (starting at €10) are available for unlocked cell phones and usually include some talk time before they need to be recharged. Digicel and Orange are the two main SIM card vendors.

Tourist Information

The **Martinique Promotion Bureau** (Comité Martiniquais du Tourisme; www.martiniquetourisme. com) is a good source of information on the island – in English and several other languages. Many towns have at least one small tourism office where the staff will try to speak in English. Pamphlets, mainly in French but with

enough pictures and maps to get the gist, are available at airports and many hotels.

Visas

Citizens of the US, Canada, Australia and New Zealand can stay for up to 90 days without a visa by showing a valid passport. Citizens of the EU can stay in Martinique indefinitely, and just need an official national identity card or a valid passport to enter the country.

Getting There & Away
Entering Martinique

All visitors to Martinique must have a valid passport (or a valid national identity card if you're an EU citizen). A round-trip or onward ticket is officially required of non-EU visitors.

Air

The island's only airport is **Aéroport International Martinique Aimé Césaire** (FDF; ☏05-96-42-18-77; www.martinique.aeroport.fr), near the town of Lamentin in the southeast of Martinique, a short distance from Fort-de-France. Immigration is courteous and efficient, and the airport has ATMs, moneychanging facilities and some basic eateries.

The following airlines service Martinique:

Air Antilles Express (www.airantilles .com) Pointe-à-Pitre (Guadeloupe), St-Barthélemy, St-Martin/Sint Maarten, Santo Domingo (Dominican Republic)

Air Caraïbes (www.aircaraibes.com) Paris, Havana, Pointe-à-Pitre, Port-au-Prince (Haiti), St-Barthélemy, St Lucia, St-Martin/Sint Maarten, San José, Santo Domingo, Cayenne (French Guiana)

Air France (www.airfrance.com) Paris, Pointe-à-Pitre

American Airlines/American Eagle (www.aa.com) San Juan

Corsairfly (www.corsairfly.com) Nantes, Lyon, Paris

LIAT (www.liatairline.com) St Lucia

Sea
FERRY

L'Express des Îles (☏05-96-63-34-47; www. express-des-iles.com) operates large, modern catamarans that have air-conditioned cabins with TVs and a snack bar. There are crossings on Monday, Thursday and Saturday from Fort-de-France to Pointe-à-Pitre, Guadeloupe (one-way/round-trip €67/100, three hours), calling at Roseau in Dominica (one-way/round-trip €67/100, 1½ hours). It is possible to travel from Martinique to Dominica, spend some time there, and then continue to Guadeloupe for a single €67 ticket. In the other direction there are departures from Fort-de-France to Castries in St Lucia on Wednesday, Friday and Sunday (one-way/round-trip €67/100, 80 minutes).

There are discounts of 50% for children aged under two, 10% for students and passengers under 12 years old, and 5% for passengers younger than 26 or older than 60. You can buy tickets in person at the ferry terminal in Fort-de-France, but you'll need your ID and the ID of all travelers to book. Currently, it's not currently possible to book online. Departure days and times for these services change frequently and, due to weather conditions, often bear no relation to the printed schedule. The only way to be sure is to call L'Express des Îles, or check with a local travel agent.

YACHT

The main port of entry is in Fort-de-France, but yachts may also clear at St-Pierre or Marin.

Yachting and sailing are very popular in Martinique and numerous charter companies operate on the island, including **Sparkling Charter** (www.sparkling-charter.com) and **Sunsail Antilles** (www.sunsail.com), which are both based at the marina in Marin, and **Star Voyage** (www.starvoyage.com), based at the Pointe du Bout marina.

Getting Around

Renting a car is the most reliable form of transportation in Martinique. Car rental is a breeze, rates are low and the road network is excellent.

Boat

A regular *vedette* (ferry) between Martinique's main resort areas and Fort-de-France provides a nice alternative to dealing with heavy bus and car traffic; it also allows you to avoid the hassles of city parking and is quicker to boot.

Vedettes Madinina (☎05-96-63-06-46; www.vedettes.madinina.pagesperso-orange.fr) runs a boat between Anse Mitan, Anse-à-l'Ane,

Pointe du Bout and Bourg des Trois-Îlets daily from 6:20am to 6:30pm, and then every hour or so, and costs €4.50/6.50 one-way/round-trip.

There are also countless sailing tours and charters operating around the island. For the latest information, check with the local tourist office or at your hotel.

Bus

Although there are some larger public buses, most buses are minivans marked 'TC' (for *taxis collectifs*) on top. Destinations are marked on the vans, sometimes on the side doors, and sometimes on a small sign stuck in the front window. Traveling by bus is best for shorter distances – and for visitors with a lot of extra time in their itinerary.

Bus stops are marked *'arrêt de bus'* or have signs showing a picture of a bus. Fort-de-France's busy main terminal is at Pointe Simon, on the west side of the harbor. Buses from Fort-de-France to St-Pierre leave frequently Monday to Saturday, but less frequently on Sunday (€3.80, 45 minutes). Other bus fares from Fort-de-France are to Trois-Îlets (€2.90), Diamant (€6.20), Ste-Anne (€8.80) and Grand-Rivière (€6). For buses to Morne Rouge and the gardens of Balata, head to the cemetery south of the Parc Floral in Fort-de-France; they leave about every 30 minutes during the day, Monday to Saturday.

Car

DRIVER'S LICENSE

Your home driver's license is all that you will need to drive legally on Martinique's roads.

RENTAL

There are numerous car-rental agencies at the airport and in Fort-de-France. You'll find the best rates on their websites, and local firms are generally cheaper than international agencies.

It's worth noting that an unlimited mileage rate is generally preferable to a lower rate that adds a charge per kilometer, particularly if you plan on touring the island.

You must be at least 21 years of age to rent a car, and some companies add a surcharge for drivers under the age of 25.

All major international rental companies can be found at the airport, as well as the following local outfits:

Carib Rentacar (☎05-96-42-16-15; www.rentacar-caraibes.com)

Pop's Car (☎05-96-42-16-84; www.popscar
.com)

ROAD CONDITIONS

Roads are excellent by Caribbean standards,
and there are multilane freeways (along
with rush-hour traffic) in the Fort-de-France
area.

ROAD RULES

In Martinique, drive on the right side of the
road. Traffic regulations and road signs are
the same as those in Europe, speed limits

are posted, and exits and intersections are
clearly marked.

Taxi

The taxi fare from the airport is approximately €30 to Fort-de-France, €75 to Ste-
Anne and €45 to Pointe du Bout or Anse
Mitan. A 40% surcharge is added onto all
fares between 8pm and 6am, and all day
on Sunday and holidays. To book a cab, call
24-hour Taxi (☎05-96-63-63-62, 05-96-63-10-
10) or **Les Taxis Martiniquais** (☎05-96-42-
16-66).

Montserrat

Includes »

Best Beaches

» Rendezvous Bay (p596)
» Woodlands Beach (p597)

Best Places to Stay

» Gingerbread Hill (p597)
» Olveston House (p597)

Why Go?

Twenty years ago, Montserrat marketed itself as being 'The way the Caribbean used to be.' Little did anyone know that in a few short years the slogan would become horribly ironic for anyone who harkened back to a pre-Palaeozoic era. A series of volcanic eruptions beginning in 1995 devastated the lower half of the island, turning Plymouth, the capital and only significant town, into an ash-covered wasteland.

Today, most tourists come for volcano-related day trips. Driving down the coast, you quickly get a feel for the island's rich tropical life and take in jaw-dropping vistas of the destruction.

Those who stay overnight get to experience Caribbean culture without the crowds, casinos and cruise ships. They also get the chance to witness the island's rebirth. Hundreds of single-family homes are now dotted across Montserrat's unaffected northern half, while a new capital is slowly but surely taking shape around Little Bay.

When to Go

Help locals paint the island green during St Patrick's Week (March 10 to 17), which celebrates Montserrat's Irish heritage. In November, sweat it out with the other runners or simply cheer 'em on during the Volcano Half Marathon, which skirts the foothills of the occasionally still-belching Soufrière Hills Volcano. The year ends with good vibrations during the raucous Festival, the Montserrat version of Carnival.

Temperatures average between 76°F (24°C) and 88°F (32°C) year-round. The only time that's potentially bad for a visit is during the hurricane season from July to November, when storms may disrupt transport to and from the island.

Fast Facts

» **Area** 39 sq miles

» **Population** 5700

» **Capital** Plymouth (abandoned)

» **Telephone country code** ☑664

» **Emergency** Fire ☑911, police ☑999

Set Your Budget

» **Budget hotel room** US$55

» **Two-course evening meal** EC$50

» **Museum entrance** EC$10

» **Beer** EC$5

» **Bus ticket** EC$1.50 to EC$5

Resources

» **Montserrat Government** (www.gov.ms)

» **Montserrat Tourist Board** (www.visitmontserrat.com)

» **Montserrat Volcano Observatory** (www.mvo.ms)

Itineraries

ONE DAY

It is possible to check off Montserrat's volcano-related highlights on a day trip from Antigua as long as you are motorized. If you rent your own vehicle, a tour might start with a drive down the east coast to Jack Boy Hill, then circle back to see what's happening in Little Bay, Sweeny's, St John's etc. Then follow the west road down to the volcano observatory and check out the ruins of Plymouth from Garibaldi Hill. Olveston House makes a lovely stop for lunch. For a more in-depth experience, consider hiring a car with a local guide. Since some of the roads are unpaved and steep, this may also be a better approach for less experienced drivers.

TWO DAYS

Follow the one-day itinerary, then, for day two, make advance arrangements for the folks from Scuba Montserrat to drop you off on the deserted white sands of Rendezvous Bay beach in the morning for a few hours of sunning, swimming and snorkeling. Pick up a takeaway lunch from John at People's Place and hit the tropical Oriole Walkway to enjoy a picnic with a view from the top of Lawyer's Mountain. Keep an eye out for the elusive Montserrat Oriole. Before leaving the island, meet some friendly locals over a bowl of goat water.

GETTING TO NEIGHBORING ISLANDS

The only island linked to Montserrat is Antigua. There are daily flights aboard tiny prop planes as well as an erratic ferry service. Bad weather may interrupt either.

Essential Food & Drink

» **Goat water** Montserrat's national dish is far more loved than its dubious-sounding name would suggest. 'Got some?' is a frequent conversation starter and refers to the spicy clove-scented broth accented with floating chunks of goat meat. It's eaten hot with a crusty bread roll.

» **Fruit juices** Exotic fruits grow in abundance on Montserrat and make delicious fresh juices. Depending on the season, you'll find mango, guava and papaya as well as the more unusual West Indian cherry and soursop, which tastes a little like a creamy strawberry with hints of pineapple and coconut.

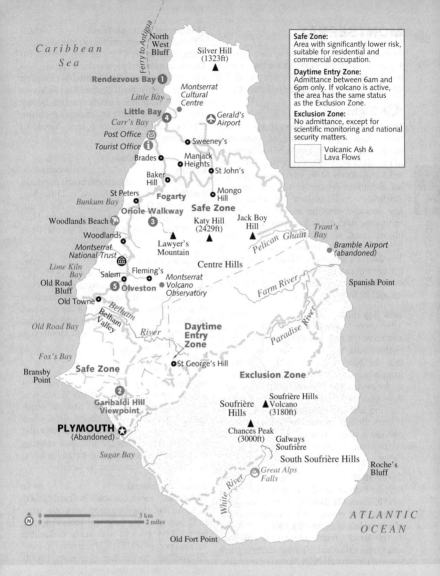

Safe Zone:
Area with significantly lower risk, suitable for residential and commercial occupation.

Daytime Entry Zone:
Admittance between 6am and 6pm only. If volcano is active, the area has the same status as the Exclusion Zone.

Exclusion Zone:
No admittance, except for scientific monitoring and national security matters.

Volcanic Ash & Lava Flows

Caribbean Sea

Ferry to Antigua

North West Bluff

Silver Hill (1323ft)

Rendezvous Bay ❶

Little Bay

Montserrat Cultural Centre

Little Bay ❹

Gerald's Airport

Carr's Bay

Post Office ✉

Tourist Office ℹ

Sweeney's

Brades

Manjack Heights

St John's

Baker Hill

St Peters

Bunkum Bay

Fogarty

Mongo Hill

Oriole Walkway ❸

Woodlands Beach

Safe Zone

Katy Hill (2429ft)

Jack Boy Hill

Trant's Bay

Woodlands

Montserrat National Trust

Lawyer's Mountain

Pelican Ghaut

Bramble Airport (abandoned)

Lime Kiln Bay

Salem

Fleming's

Centre Hills

Montserrat Volcano Observatory

Farm River

Spanish Point

Olveston ❺

Old Road Bluff

Old Towne

Betham Valley

Betham River

Paradise River

Old Road Bay

Daytime Entry Zone

Fox's Bay

St George's Hill

Safe Zone

Bransby Point

Exclusion Zone

Garibaldi Hill Viewpoint ❷

Soufrière Hills

Soufrière Hills Volcano (3180ft)

PLYMOUTH (Abandoned)

Chances Peak (3000ft)

Galways Soufrière

Sugar Bay

South Soufrière Hills

Roche's Bluff

White River

Great Alps Falls

ATLANTIC OCEAN

0 — 3 km
0 — 2 miles

Old Fort Point

Montserrat Highlights

❶ Hike or kayak to secluded **Rendezvous Bay** (p596), Montserrat's only white-sand beach

❷ Marvel at nature's destructive powers from **Garibaldi Hill** (p596)

❸ Keep your eyes open for elusive birds while trekking along the **Oriole Walkway** (p596)

❹ 'Lime' with the locals at **Soca Cabana** (p597) in Little Bay

❺ Enjoy a leisurely lunch at **Olveston House** (p597) in Olveston

MONTSERRAT

Montserrat is divided into a Safe Zone, a Daytime Entry Zone and an Exclusion Zone around the volcano. There are ambitious plans for a new town center in Little Bay.

◉ Sights

Montserrat Volcano Observatory   MUSEUM
(MVO; ☏491-5647; www.mvo.ms; adult/child EC$10/free; ⊙10am-3:15pm Mon-Thu) Scientists at the MVO keep track of the volcano's every belch and hiccup. At the interpretation center, an 18-minute version of the documentary *Pride of Paradise* by local filmmaker David Lea includes riveting live footage of the eruptions and provides insight into the physical and social upheaval they caused. It plays every 15 minutes past the hour. Touchscreen terminals and displays provide further information, while the terrace offers sweeping views of the volcano, Belham Valley and Plymouth.

Jack Boy Hill   VIEWPOINT
After about a 3-mile drive south along the east coast (from where the main road reaches the coast), the badly battered road turns into the hills and leads to this viewpoint, from where you can see ash and mud flows to the south. The contrast of the view over flower-covered trees to the gray expanse that includes the remains of the old airport is stark. Bring a picnic: the flowery grounds provide a nice setting. A nature trail also starts here; it's steep but offers rewarding views.

Garibaldi Hill   VIEWPOINT
Beyond Belham Valley, an extremely rough road leads up Garibaldi Hill, from where you have the best views over the Exclusion Zone of what's left of Plymouth. Once known for its tree-lined streets, colonial-era buildings and grand cathedral, it's now an eerie ghost town of structural shells buried in gray ash.

Belham Valley   LANDMARK
Near Salem the land opens up and you have views of the wide Belham Valley that was covered by 40ft of volcanic debris. If you have a driver or a 4WD vehicle, it's possible to cross what used to be a nine-hole golf course and drive past the top floors of a buried three-story building. On the south side is a surreal scene of abandoned luxury expat mansions. Here and there, owners are staying put, defiantly flying flags in the shadow of the volcano.

Montserrat National Trust   MUSEUM
(☏491-3086; www.montserratnationaltrust.ms; Olveston; admission EC$5; ⊙8:30am-4pm Mon-Fri) Various aspects of Montserrat's culture, history and nature are highlighted in changing exhibits at this small centre. There's also a miniature botanical garden, research library and a gift shop. Staff can arrange for nature hikes and a turtle-watching trek (August to September).

Montserrat Cultural Centre   PERFORMANCE VENUE
(www.themontserratculturalcentre.com) The main building already completed in Little Bay, this stately performance hall is the brainchild of ex-Beatles producer Sir George Martin. It hosts a wide variety of events, from concerts to funerals.

Runaway Ghaut   SPRING
Ghauts (pronounced guts) are steep ravines that send rainwater rushing down from the mountains into the sea. The most famous is Runaway Ghaut, on the side of the road just north of Salem. According to legend, those who drink from it will return to Montserrat time and again.

⚐ Activities

Rendezvous Bay   SECLUDED BEACH
Montserrat's only white sandy beach is a lovely crescent and a perfect base for swimming, snorkeling and diving. It's often deserted since the only access is from the water or via a steep 0.7-mile trail starting behind the concrete block company in Little Bay. There's no shade and no facilities.

Scuba Montserrat   DIVING
(☏496-7807; www.scubamontserrat.com) Based in Little Bay, this dive shop runs boat trips to Rendezvous Bay (one-way/round-trip per boat US$15/25) and also rents two-seater kayaks (per hour US$15) if you want to paddle yourself. Snorkeling gear costs US$10 and one-/two-tank dives are US$55/88.

Oriole Walkway   HIKING
Montserrat's most popular hiking trail cuts for 1.3 miles through the tropical Centre Hills to the top of Lawyer's Mountain, from where you'll have bird's-eye views of the island. Speaking of birds: keep an eye out for the black and yellow Montserrat Oriole, the national bird, that makes its home in the treetops. The tourist office has a map (EC$10) and a comprehensive *Guide to the Centre Hills* (EC$40). Local nature-guide

extraordinaire **James 'Scriber' Daley** (☑492-2943) runs 2½-hour walking tours for EC$135 per person.

Woodlands Beach
FAMILY BEACH

About halfway down the western coast, Woodlands is a dark-sand beach with a covered clifftop picnic area, showers and barbecues. The surf can be rough, so watch the kiddies.

🛏 Sleeping & Eating

Restaurants are few and dinner reservations are recommended. There are also simple cafes, rum shops and small grocers scattered about. The cafe at the airport is something of a community center at flight times.

TOP CHOICE Gingerbread Hill
GUESTHOUSE **$$**

(☑491-5812; www.volcano-island.com; St Peters; d US$55-125; ✳🔁) No matter your budget, Clover and David have a bed with your name on it. Choose from the Backpacker Room with outdoor kitchen, the solar-paneled Eco Cottage or the two large and breezy upstairs apartments with stunning ocean views, spacious verandas, full kitchens and ultra-comfy beds. David is the creator of the seven-volume volcano documentary *Pride of Paradise.*

Olveston House
GUESTHOUSE **$$**

(☑491-5210; www.olvestonhouse.com; Olveston; r US$119-129; ✳🔁🌊) Sting and Eric Clapton slept in the elegant garden villa that belongs to Sir George Martin. Linda McCartney's photographs decorate the skylit corridor leading to the six rooms, some with air-con, others with porch access. The all-day restaurant serves Caribbean-infused English cuisine (mains EC$18 to EC$55). Wednesday barbecue and Friday pub nights are great for eavesdropping on gossiping islanders.

TOP CHOICE Soca Cabana
CARIBBEAN **$$**

(www.socacabana.com; Little Bay; mains EC$30-40; ⊗8am-4pm Sun-Thu, dinner by reservation & 8am-late Fri & Sat) This classic beach shack does dependable chicken, fish and ribs but draws its biggest crowds on Saturday nights for 'Montserrat Idol.' The wooden bar was rescued from Sir George Martin's AIR Montserrat recording studio. Live reggae on Friday nights.

People's Place
CARIBBEAN **$**

(☑491-7528; Fogarty; meals EC$10-25; ⊗8am-6pm) John's blue hilltop shack enjoys a cult

following among islanders, from Rastas to government workers to blue-haired expats. The local food is simple and ample and served with a big smile.

Tina's
CARIBBEAN **$$**

(☑491-3538; Brades Main Rd, Brades; snacks EC$11-18, mains EC$30-65; ⊗8am-midnight) Locals often pack Tina's air-conditioned lair, washing down succulent lobster burgers and finger-licking garlic shrimp with her homemade ginger beer. The coconut cream pie is a divine finish.

Erindell Villa
GUESTHOUSE **$**

(☑491-3655; www.erindellvilla.com; Woodlands; r incl breakfast US$75; @🔁) This friendly guesthouse near the rainforest offers plenty of freebies, including snorkeling gear and cell phones.

Gourmet Gardens
CONTINENTAL **$$**

(☑491-7859; Olveston; mains lunch EC$12-25, dinner EC$30-55; ⊗lunch & dinner) Veal schnitzel, beef Stroganoff and other European classics are served in a charming garden setting.

ℹ️ Information

The hillside village of Brades has a few small shops, government offices, the post office, a library, a pharmacy and the island's only ATM at the Royal Bank of Canada. There's free wi-fi at the library and the airport. You can get maps and brochures at the **Montserrat Tourist Board** (☑491-2230; www.visitmontserrat.com; 7 Farara Plaza, Brades; ⊗8am-4pm Mon-Fri) and at the airport.

UNDERSTAND MONTSERRAT

History

Known to indigenous people as Alliougana, meaning 'Land of the Prickly Bush,' the island lost this colorful moniker in 1493 when Columbus thought the craggy landscape reminded him of the jagged hills above the Monastery of Montserrat near Barcelona.

Irish Catholics were the first European settlers among the indigenous Caribs and Arawaks, arriving in 1632: in flight from English protestant persecution, this time from nearby St Kitts.

Britain has ruled the island since 1632, except for three brief spells of French occupation, the last one in 1782.

A violent, though unsuccessful, slave uprising occurred on March 17, 1768, which happened to be St Patrick's Day. It's now a national holiday and the reason why Montserrat stages the largest and wildest Paddy's Day celebrations outside of Ireland.

The abolition of slavery in 1834 and falling sugar prices in subsequent decades sent Montserrat into economic decline. The island managed to stay self-sufficient in food production, with limes and goats in the north being especially successful.

Hurricane Hugo devastated the island in 1989, and made Montserrat dependent on aid from Britain for reconstruction. Things were mostly back together by 1995, when Montserrat's clichéd yet accurate status as a quiet paradise was forever changed. On July 18 the Soufrière Hills Volcano (now 3180ft) ended its 400 years of dormancy.

A series of ash falls, pyroclastic flows and mud flows destroyed the capital, Plymouth, smaller settlements, farmland and forests. Around 11,000 residents were evacuated and resettled in the north or emigrated to Britain. Still, some farmers continued to use their beloved lands, and on June 25, 1997 the volcano erupted again, requiring 50 helicopter airlifts and causing 19 deaths. Two months later, a superheated pyroclastic flow wiped out the remainder of Plymouth, and its historically significant architecture and character were lost forever.

Eruptions have continued since, with the last major one in February 2010, which buried whatever had been left of the old airport.

Culture

The small population of Montserrat is tightly knit. More than 90% is of African descent with a strong influence of Irish blood. The flag bears Montserrat's coat of arms, which depicts a white woman clutching a harp and hugging a cross.

An increasing number of exiles are returning to the island as new houses are built. Many say that they never felt at home in Britain and miss their lives on the island. Still, the population remains at less than half its total pre-eruption and the economy is still trying to recover.

Quite predictably, cricket is huge and when the national team practices on the pitch near Little Bay, few cars pass without pausing for a critical look. More surprising, perhaps, is the passion for the national soccer team, which plays in a beautiful, brand-new stadium, despite being tied with Papua New Guinea and San Marino for last spot in the FIFA world ranking.

Arts

Montserrat has played a critical role in Caribbean music thanks to the late Alphonsus Cassell (1949–2010) – better known as Arrow – whose soca hit 'Hot, Hot, Hot' has sold over four million copies since its 1982 release. From 1979 to 1989 Montserrat was also home to a famous recording studio, AIR Montserrat, founded by former Beatles producer Sir George Martin. Sting, Elton John, Eric Clapton and Sheena Easton were among the stars who recorded here until the facility was destroyed by Hurricane Hugo. Martin was also the mastermind and key fundraiser behind the sparkling new Montserrat Cultural Centre, which opened in 1987.

Landscape & Wildlife

Volcanic eruptions destroyed about 60% of Montserrat's forest ecosystem, leaving the Centre Hills as the main refuge for flora and wildlife. Laced with hiking trails, they harbor numerous species, including the endemic Montserrat Oriole, the critically endangered 'mountain chicken' (actually a huge frog) and a shy lizard called Montserrat Galliwasp. The island is also home to three species of sea turtle. The Montserrat National Trust arranges turtle-watching treks during nesting time in August and September.

SURVIVAL GUIDE

Directory A–Z

Accommodations

Lodging on Montserrat is limited to a handful of guesthouses, but quality is high and the value is great. Rates listed apply to the peak season (December to April), so expect significant discounts at other times. Following are the price guidelines used in this chapter, based on the cost of a double room with private bathroom.

$	budget	less than US$75
$$	midrange	US$75 to US$200
$$$	top end	more than US$200

Business Hours

In this book we only list opening hours if they differ from the following standards:

Banks 8am-2pm Mon-Thu, to 3pm Fri

Bars noon-11pm or midnight

Businesses 8am-4pm Mon-Fri

Restaurants breakfast 7:30-10am, lunch noon-2:30pm, dinner 6-9:30pm

Shops 9am-5pm Mon-Sat, some close midday on Wed, grocery stores later and on Sun

Food

Price ranges quoted in our restaurant listings in this chapter refer to a meal consisting of an appetizer and a main course. Most places add a 10% service charge; additional tipping is up to you.

$	budget	under EC$30
$$	midrange	EC$30 to EC$60
$$$	eop end	more than EC$60

Health

The US Centers for Disease Control and Prevention recommends avoiding tap water, but the Montserrat Tourist Board claims the island has one of the purest supplies of drinking water and that it's perfectly safe to drink from the tap.

Money

Montserrat uses the Eastern Caribbean dollar (EC$).

US dollars are widely accepted. However, unless rates are posted in US dollars, as is the norm with accommodations, it usually works out better to use EC dollars. There's little to buy using a credit card.

Some restaurant bills already include a 10% service charge, in which case additional tipping is optional. For exceptional service, a small extra amount will be much appreciated. If service is not included, tip 10% to 15%. Housekeeping staff get about US$2 or US$3 per day, while for porters and bellhops a tip of US$1 per bag is appropriate.

Public Holidays

In addition to holidays observed throughout the region (p872), Montserrat has the following public holidays:

St Patrick's Day March 17

Labour Day May 1

PRACTICALITIES

» **Electricity** 220V; 60 cycles; some buildings are wired for both 220V and 110V. Otherwise, transformers are widely available. North American two-pin sockets are prevalent but three-pins are around too, so bring an adaptor.

» **Local Taxes** 10% at hotels, 7% at guesthouses.

» **Newspapers & Magazines** The *Montserrat Reporter* is an enthusiastic compendium of the week's events, as is its website, www.themontser ratreporter.com.

» **Radio** Catch local news, tunes and eruption alerts on ZJB, 91.9FM.

» **Weights & Measures** Imperial system.

Queen's Birthday First, second or third weekend June

Emancipation Day August 1

Safe Travel

The volcano is always a wild card, but there's no need to take precautions. Listen to what locals say regarding ash plumes and other events. And, obviously, respect restrictions of both the Daytime Entry Zone and the Exclusion Zone.

Telephone

Montserrat's country code is ☎664. To call from North America, dial ☎1-664, followed by the seven-digit local number. From elsewhere, dial your country's international access code + ☎664 + the local phone number. When making a call on the island, you only need to dial the seven-digit local number.

For directory assistance, call ☎411.

Getting There & Away
Air

Tiny **Gerald's Airport** (MNI; ☎491-2533) opened in 2005. The runway covers the top of the plateau and the sheer drops at either end add drama to any flight. The only service is provided by **Fly Montserrat** (☎491-3434; www.flymontserrat.com), which makes the 20-minute hop from Antigua in eight-seat

DEPARTURE TAX

The departure tax for stays over 24 hours is EC$55 or US$21 – cash only. If you're just here for the day, you only have to pay the EC$10 security charge.

prop planes for around US$110 each way. Flights often fill up and high winds can halt service for hours or days.

Boat

Ferry service to/from Antigua is an on-again, off-again affair. Check www.visitmontserrat. com for the latest schedule or call ☑496-9912. The trip takes about an hour and costs EC$150 each way (EC$75 for children aged under 12 years).

Tours

Antigua-based **Caribbean Helicopters** (☑268-460-5900; www.caribbeanhelicopters.com) operates flyovers of Soufrière Hills Volcano and the Exclusion Zone. The trip takes 45 minutes and costs US$240 per person.

Getting Around

Bus

Minibuses ply the main road in the daytime from Monday to Saturday. There is no schedule and no official stops, so just hail one as it passes. Fares range from EC$1.50 to EC$5.

Car & Motorcycle

A local driver's license (EC$50) is needed in order to drive on Montserrat and can be obtained at the airport, ferry port or the police stations in Brades or Salem. Rental agencies include the following:

Montserrat Enterprises (☑491-2431; melenter@candw.ms)

Prestige Rentals (☑496-1842; prestigerental smni@gmail.com)

Tours

Unless you're staying for several days, it's easier to hire a car and driver. Rates vary but expect to pay about US$25 per hour. This can be a delightful way to go as you'll learn much about Montserrat while you tour. Check www.visitmontserrat.com for a full list of drivers.

Puerto Rico

Includes »

Best Beaches

» Playa Flamenco (p621)

» Playa Conando (p608)

» Isla Culebrita (p621)

» Playa Luquillo (p617)

» Green Beach/Punta Arenas (p618)

Best Places to Stay

» Gran Hotel El Convento (p610)

» La Concha (p611)

» Hix Island House (p619)

» Mary Lee's By The Sea (p626)

» Blue Boy Inn (p627)

Why Go?

Golden sand, swashbuckling history and wildly diverse terrain make the sun-washed backyard of the United States a place fittingly hyped as the 'Island of Enchantment.' It's the Caribbean's only island where you can catch a wave before breakfast, hike a rainforest after lunch and race to the beat of a high-gloss, cosmopolitan city after dark.

Between blinking casinos and chirping frogs, Puerto Rico is also a land of dynamic contrasts, where the breezy gate of the Caribbean is bedeviled by the hustle of contemporary America. While modern conveniences make it simple for travelers, the condo-lined concrete jungle might seem a bit too close to home. A quick visit for Puerto Rico's beaches, historic forts and craps tables will quicken a visitor's pulse, but the island's singular essence only reveals itself to those who go deeper, exploring the misty crags of the central mountains and crumbling facades of the island's remote corners.

When to Go

With consistent sun and a calendar filled with raucous festivals, visitors enjoy Puerto Rico year-round. Aside from a slump during the late-summer hurricane season, the island has a steady stream of visitors and prices rise marginally during two high seasons – mid-December to mid-April, and July. Like many Latin American destinations, religious festivals on the Catholic calendar are a big deal, particularly around the Dia de los Reyes (Day of the Kings) in January and Lent.

The best time to visit is mid-December through late April. This is when it is sunny (but not too hot) and free from the threat of hurricanes. Skirt the edges of the high season and you could get lucky with both the weather and cut-price rates. The hurricane season runs from June to November, with the highest storm risk in September and October.

Fast Facts

» **Area** 3459 sq miles

» **Population** 4 million

» **Capital** San Juan

» **Telephone country code** ✆787

» **Emergency** ✆911

Set Your Budget

» **Budget hotel room** US$75

» **Two-course evening meal** US$20

» **Museum entrance** under US$10

» **Beer** US$1.50

» **Local intercity público ride** US$1

Resources

» **Escape to Puerto Rico** (http://escape.topuertorico.com)

» **Puerto Rico Tourism Company** (www.prtourism.com)

» **Eye Tour** (www.eyetour.com)

» **Puerto Rico Day Trips** (www.puertoricodaytrips.com)

Itineraries

THREE DAYS

Dive into the cultural waters of Old San Juan, with first-class museums, galleries, monuments and forts. After dark, book a table for world-class fusion dining and go salsa dancing along Fortaleza. Break from beaching to make a rainforest day trip to El Yunque.

ONE WEEK

Follow the three-day itinerary, but make a big day of El Yunque with hiking and river swimming. Check out Playa Luquillo, then head west to karst country and visit the spacey wonder of the Arecibo Observatory.

TWO WEEKS

Follow the one-week itinerary, but sketch out a plan to circumnavigate the island. Spend a couple of days at the bioluminescent bays and amazing beaches of Vieques and Culebra. Next, a day of Ponce museums, before moving up the coast to see surfers shred the perfect waves at Rincón.

GETTING TO NEIGHBORING ISLANDS

Unless you have a yacht (or good people skills with yachters) you'll likely get to and from Puerto Rico via international flights to San Juan's Aeropuerto Internacional de Luis Muñoz Marín (LMM), about 8 miles east of the old city center. Although ferry service sporadically connects the Dominican Republic and San Juan, there is no regularly scheduled service at the time of research. There are several connecting flights between San Juan and the Virgin Islands, though the service regularly changes.

Essential Food & Drink

» **Mofongo** A plantain crust encases seafood or steak in this signature dish.

» **Chuletas Can Can** The house dish at the peerless Restaurante La Guardarraya – a deep-fried bone-in pork chop – is worth going well out of your way for.

» **Brazo Gitano** The 'Gypsy's Arm' is a huge cake roll, filled with fresh, mashed fruit and sweet cheese.

» **Lechón Asado** Smoky, spit-roasted suckling pig is sold at roadside trucks and is a taste of heaven.

» **Medalla** Thanks to low taxes, ice-cold cans can be had for just over US$1 – far and away the cheapest beer in the Caribbean.

» **Ron** The national drink. Though the headquarters of Bacardi are outside San Juan, Puerto Ricans drink locally made Don Q or Castillo.

» **Sorullitos de Maíz** Deep-fried corn-meal fritters make an excellent bar snack.

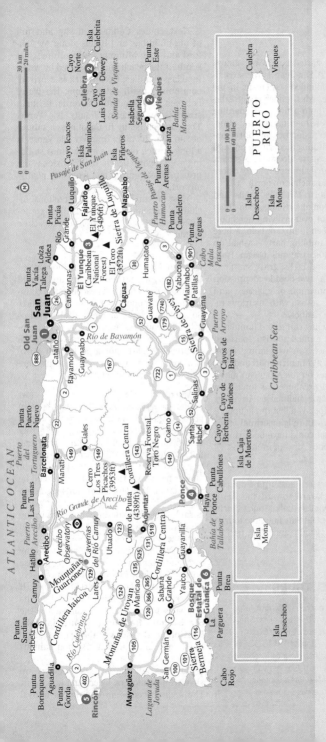

Puerto Rico Highlights

1 Crooked alleys, towering forts, pastel-painted facades and 500 years of history make **Old San Juan** (p604) a must

2 Snorkel and swim at posh, flawless beaches on **Vieques**

(p617) or less-developed **Culebra** (p620)

3 Explore drippy trails and misty waterfalls in the **El Yunque** (p617) rainforest

4 Visit the historic capital of **Ponce** (p623) for its festivals and excellent museums, including Museo de Art de Ponce, the finest of fine-art galleries in the Caribbean

5 Surf perfect tubes in **Rincón** (p626), the well-chilled wave-riding capital

6 Hike the dry forest at **Bosque Estatal de Guánica** (p626), one of the most unique climates in the Caribbean

SAN JUAN

POP 442,447

Modern America started here. Well, almost. Established in 1521 San Juan is the second-oldest European-founded settlement in the Americas and the oldest under US jurisdiction. Shoehorned onto a tiny islet guarding the entrance to San Juan harbor, the atmospheric 'Old City' juxtaposes historical authenticity with pulsating modern energy. And it's all in a seven-square-block grid of streets that was inaugurated almost a century before the *Mayflower* laid anchor up north.

Beyond timeworn 15ft-thick walls and well-polished colonial artifacts, San Juan is also a mosaic of ever-evolving neighborhoods. There's seen-it-all Condado, where Cuba's 24-hour gambling party washed up in the early 1960s; tranquil Ocean Park, with gated villas and B&Bs; gritty Santurce, which suffered a two-decade depression before a recent invasion of galleries; and swanky Isla Verde, awash with luxurious resorts and flashing casinos.

Choked by crawling traffic and inundated with five million annual tourists, parts of San Juan can leave you wondering if you took a wrong turn at Miami airport and never left the big cities on the American mainland. But cultural exchange has long been this city's pragmatic hallmark. For every gleaming office block you'll stumble upon a colorful fiesta, African religious ritual or bit of architecture that could have been ripped out of Seville, Buenos Aires or even Paris.

◉ Sights

Starting at the westernmost tip of the city and working backward toward the Aeropuerto Internacional de Luis Muñoz Marín (LMM), you've got Old San Juan, the tourist center and most visually appealing part of town.

TUNNEL TOURS

Go deeper. And darker. Free hour-long guided tours roam the tunnels at Fuerte San Cristóbal every Saturday (Spanish) and Sunday (English) at 10:30am. Come at least half an hour beforehand (or earlier) to sign up. Guides walk you through three of the fort's tunnels, including one otherwise closed to the public.

Next comes Condado, flashy and full of big buildings and hotels along Av Ashford and then Miramar and Santurce, just south of the beach and populated by working-class families. Ocean Park is a private community (with gates) along the water between Condado and Isla Verde; its main street is Av McLeary. Finally, Isla Verde. Though technically in Carolinas, a suburb of San Juan its main drag, Av Isla Verde, is a long stretch of hotels and casinos standing over a white beach. Its drawback is the proximity of roaring jets from the nearby airport.

Most of San Juan's major attractions, including museums and art galleries, are located in Old San Juan. Most museums close on Mondays.

OLD SAN JUAN

Old San Juan is a colorful kaleidoscope of life, music, legend and history and would stand out like a flashing beacon in any country, let alone one as small as Puerto Rico. Somnolent secrets and beautiful surprises await everywhere. From the blue-toned cobblestone streets of Calle San Sebastián to the cutting-edge gastronomic artistry of SoFo, you could spend weeks, even months, here and still only get the smallest taste.

El Morro
FORT

(Fuerte San Felipe del Morro, San Felipe Fort; Map p606; ☎729-7423; www.nps.gov/saju; adult/child US$3/free; ⊙9am-6pm, free talks on the hour 10am-5pm) A six-level fort with a gray, castellated lighthouse, El Morro juts aggressively over Old San Juan's bold headlands, glowering across the Atlantic at would-be conquerors. The 140ft-high walls (some up to 15ft thick) date back to 1539, and El Morro is said to be the oldest Spanish fort in the New World. It was declared a Unesco World Heritage site in 1983.

The National Park Service maintains the fort and small museum. The lighthouse on the 6th floor has operated since 1846, making it the island's oldest still in use. If you skip the free guided tours, climb the ramparts to the sentries' walks along the **Sta Barbara Bastion** and **Austria Half-Bastion** for the views of the sea, San Juan, El Yunque and the island's mountainous spine.

On weekends the fields by the fort are alive with picnickers, lovers and kite flyers. The scene becomes an impromptu festival with food carts on the perimeter. Combined entry with Fuerte San Cristóbal is US$5.

Fuerte San Cristóbal
FORT

(San Cristóbal Fort; Map p606; ☎729-6777; www.nps.gov/saju; adult/child US$3/free; ☺9am-6pm) San Juan's second fort is one of the largest Spanish military installations in the Americas. In its prime San Cristóbal covered 27 acres, with a maze of six interconnected forts protecting a central core with 150ft-high walls, moats, booby-trapped bridges and tunnels.

The fort was constructed to defend San Juan against land attacks via Puerta de Tierra. Construction began in 1634 in response to an attack by the Dutch, though enlargement continued between 1765 and 1783. The fort became a National Historic site in 1949 and a Unesco World Heritage site in 1983. Facilities include a fascinating museum, military archives, a reproduction of a soldier's barracks and prime city views. You can gain entry to both Fuerte San Cristóbal and El Morro for US$5.

La Fortaleza
MONUMENT

(The Fortress; Map p606; www.fortaleza.gobierno.pr; suggested donation US$3; ☺tours 9am-3:30pm Mon-Fri) A steep climb along Recinto Oeste takes you to the top of the city wall and the guarded iron gates of La Fortaleza. Also known as El Palacio de Santa Catalina, this imposing building is the oldest executive mansion in continuous use in the western hemisphere, dating from 1533. Once the original fortress for the young colony, La Fortaleza eventually yielded its military preeminence to the city's newer and larger forts, and was remodeled and expanded to domicile island governors for more than three centuries. Guided tours include Moorish gardens, the dungeon and the chapel.

Cuartel de Ballajá
MUSEUM

(Map p606; off Norzagaray) Built in 1854 as a military barracks, the Cuartel is a three-story edifice with large gates on two ends, ample balconies, a series of arches and a protected central courtyard. It was the last and largest building constructed by the Spanish in the New World. Facilities included officer quarters, warehouses, kitchens, dining rooms, prison cells and stables. Now its 2nd floor holds the **Museo de las Américas** (Museum of the Americas; www.museolasamericas.org; adult/child US$3/2; ☺10am-4pm Tue-Sat, guided tours by reservation), which

PORT OF CALL – OLD SAN JUAN
605

With a few hours in port:

» Climb the ramparts of El Morro (p604) for great views

» Explore the dripping jungles of El Yunque (p617)

» Splash and gamble at the beaches and casinos of Isla Verde (p609)

» Dine on world-class Caribbean fare in the SoFo dining district (p612)

focuses on cultural development in the New World. Look for an impressive *santos* (religious statuettes) collection.

Paseo de la Princesa
HISTORIC SITE

(Walkway of the Princess; Map p606) With a distinctly European flavor, the Paseo de la Princesa is a 19th-century esplanade just outside the city walls. Lined with antique street lamps, statues, benches and fruit carts, the romantic walk ends at the magnificent **Raíces Fountain**, a stunning fountain depicting the island's Taíno, African and Spanish heritage.

Puerta de San Juan
LANDMARK

(San Juan Gate; Map p606) Spanish ships anchored in the cove just off the ramparts to unload colonists and supplies, all of which entered the city through a tall red portal known as Puerta de San Juan. It marks the end of the Paseo de la Princesa, and stands as one of three remaining gates into the old city (the others lead into the cemetery and the enclave of La Perla). Turn right after passing through the gate to follow the **Paseo del Morro** northwest, paralleling the city walls for approximately three-quarters of a mile.

Museo de San Juan
MUSEUM

(Map p606; ☎723-4317; 150 Norzagaray; donations accepted; ☺9am-4pm Tue-Fri, 10am-4pm Sat & Sun) In a Spanish colonial building at the corner of Calle MacArthur, this museum offers the definitive take on the city's 500-year history. The exhibition showcases pictorial and photographic testimonies from Caparra ruins to modern shopping malls.

Museo del Niño
MUSEUM

(Children's Museum; Map p606; ☎722-3791; www.museodelninopr.org; 150 Calle del Cristo; adult/

Old San Juan

ATLANTIC OCEAN

El Morro

Cementerio de San Juan

LA PERLA

Plaza del Quinto Centenario

Plaza de San José

3

4

1

Parque de Beneficencia

Plazuela Las Monjas

Calle del Cristo

5

7

La Fortaleza

Caleta de San Jaun

Caleta Las Monjas

Calle del Morro

Paseo del Morro

Baiada Matadero

Norzagaray

San Sebastián

Sol

San Justo

Tanca

Luna

14

13

15

10

OLD SAN JUAN

2

20

Cruz

Plaza de Armas

San José

San Francisco

Fortaleza

Parque de las Palomas

6

Presidio

16

O'Donnell

Callejón de la Capilla

9

19

8

12

Plaza de Colón

Av Muñoz Rivera

Fuerte San Cristóbal

Av Ponce de León

Paseo de Covadonga

Bus Terminal

22

18

Plaza del Puerto

Recinto Sur

Comercio

Tetuán

Puerto Rico Tourism Company

17

21

Plaza de la Dársena

La Marina

Autoridad de Transporte Marítimo Ferry

Pier 1

Pier 2

Ferry to Cataño & Hato Rey

Calle La Puntilla

Bahía de San Juan

Pier 3

To Parque de la Ventana al Mar (2.5mi); Condado & Ocean Park (3.4mi)

To Aeropuerto de Isla Grande (2mi)

400 m

0.2 miles

N

PUERTO RICO SAN JUAN

child US$7/5; ◉9am-3:30pm Tue-Thu, 9am-5pm Fri, 12:30-5pm Sat & Sun; ◉) Kids love the three floors of hands-on exhibits on health, natural history and science. Favorites include a walk-through cave explaining bats and echolocation, a magnetic food pyramid, a climbing wall (age five and up) and a dress-up station. One area is designed for children three and under.

Casa Blanca   MUSEUM
(White House; Map p606; ☎924-0700 for tour appt; www.icp.gobierno.pr/myp/museos/m13.htm; adult/child US$2/1; ◉9am-noon & 1-4:30pm Tue-Sat) First constructed in 1521 as a residence of Puerto Rico's pioneering governor, Juan Ponce de León (who died before he could move in), the Casa Blanca is the oldest continuously occupied house in the western hemisphere. Today it's a historic monument and museum with secluded grounds, a chain of fountains and an Alhambra-style courtyard. An animated guide offers a theatrical complementary tour.

FREE Catedral de San Juan   CHURCH
(Map p606; 153 Calle del Cristo; ◉8am-5pm) Noticeably smaller and more austere than other Spanish churches, the city cathedral retains a simple, earthy elegance. After a hurricane in 1529 it was slowly rebuilt into the Gothic-neoclassical-inspired monument seen today. Most people come to see the marble tomb of Ponce de León and the body of religious martyr St Pio, displayed under glass.

SANTURCE

Museo de Arte de Puerto Rico   MUSEUM
(MAPR; Map p608; ☎977-6277, for tours ext 2230 or 3230; www.mapr.org; 299 Av José de Diego; adult/student & senior US$6/3, admission free 2-8pm Wed; ◉10am-5pm Tue & Thu-Sat, 10am-8pm Wed, 11am-6pm Sun) Among the most celebrated art museums in the Caribbean, this splendid neoclassical building was once the city's municipal hospital. It boasts 18 exhibition halls spread over an area of 130,000 sq ft.

This cultural tour de force is more than just a collection of paintings; the facility boasts a 2.5-acre sculpture garden, a conservation laboratory, a computer-learning center and a 400-seat theater. Paths in the lovely gardens pass an excellent sculpture collection.

RÍO PIEDRAS

Mercado de Río Piedras   MARKET
(Paseo de Diego; ◉9am-6pm Mon-Sat) Smells of fish and oranges, the bustle of people, and trading jests in Spanish: this market continues the colonial tradition of an indoor market that spills into the streets and is a feast for the senses.

Next to the Río Piedras stop of the Tren Urbano, the four long blocks of shops and inexpensive restaurants lining Paseo de Diego

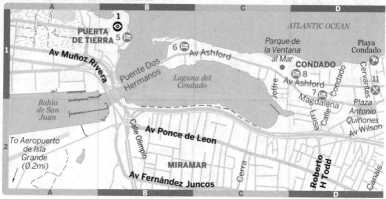

have been closed to traffic, turning the whole area into an outdoor mall. You can shop or watch locals negotiate for everything from *chuletas* (pork chops) to *camisas* (shirts). The area is alive from early morning to late evening.

🏖 Beaches

San Juan has some of the best municipal beaches this side of Rio de Janeiro. Starting half a mile or so east of the Old Town, they go from rustic to swanky in the space of 7.5 miles.

Puerta de Tierra   FAMILY BEACH

(Map p608) Imagine it – a sheltered arc of raked sand, decent surf breaks, plenty of local action and the sight of a 17th-century Spanish fort shimmering in the distance.

Are you really still a stone's throw from Old San Juan and the busy tourist strip of Condado? **Balneario Escambrón** is almost too good to be true, which is probably why so many people miss it. Perched on the north end of the sliver of land that is Puerta de Tierra and abutting majestic Parque del Tercer Milenio, this palm-fringed yet rugged beach might be one of the best municipal options offered anywhere.

Playa Condado   RESORT BEACH

(Map p608) Hemmed in by hotels and rocky outcrops, Condado's narrow beaches are busier than Ocean Park's but less exclusive than Isla Verde's. Expect splashes of graffiti, boisterous games of volleyball and plenty of crashing Atlantic surf. The public beach is a small arc of sand, adjacent to the Dos Hermanos bridge. Lifeguards police the area on weekdays and snack bars open daily, but bathrooms are few.

Parque de la Ventana al Mar (Map p608; Window to the Sea Park) has lovely waterfront views and free jazz concerts the last Sunday of the month.

Ocean Park   ACTIVITIES BEACH

(Map p608) Ocean Park's lesser fame is its hidden blessing. Fronted by leafy residential streets and embellished by the odd luxury B&B, this wide sweep of fine sand is protected by offshore reefs and caressed by cooling trade winds. Although largely the preserve

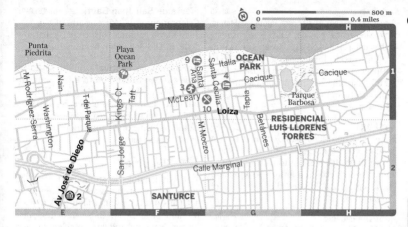

of moneyed residents, anyone can enjoy the ambience here. Just pick a road through the neighborhood's low-rise gated community and follow it towards the water.

Playa Isla Verde RESORT BEACH
Resort pluggers will tell you that Playa Isla Verde is the Copacabana of Puerto Rico, with legions of tanned bodies and dexterous beach bums flexing their triceps around the volleyball net. Regardless of the scene the long wedge of sand between Punta Las Marías and Piñones is an undeniable beauty. The downside is access. Cutting in front of towering condos and plush hotels along Av Isla Verde, the beach is completely obscured from the road and doesn't have the inclusive atmosphere of other municipal beaches.

Activities

One of the best places in the area to buy or rent outdoor gear, including camping equipment, is **Acampa** (706-0695; www.acampapr.com; 1221 Av Jesús T Piñero; 10am-6pm Mon-Fri, 10:30am-5:30pm Sat). It also offers a number of tours around the island, including treks through the rainforest and zip-line expeditions.

Diving & Snorkeling
While Puerto Rico is known for its first-class diving, San Juan isn't the best place for it: strong winds often churn up the water. Condado has an easy dive that takes you between the inner and outer reefs into coral caverns, overhangs, grottoes and tunnels.

Eco Action Tours DIVING
(791-7509; www.ecoactiontours.com) Can do just about any tour imaginable; it offers San Juan area shore dives (US$75, one-tank and all equipment) and dives on the east coast. It also does hiking and rappelling tours.

Caribe Aquatic Adventures DIVING
(Map p608; 281-8858; www.caribeaquaticadventure.com; snorkel/one-tank dive incl equip US$50/90) Dives near San Juan, but also further afield, off Fajardo. Lunch and transportation are included in trips to Fajardo. The company's shore dives from the beach behind the Normandie Hotel are regarded as some of the best on the island.

Surfing & Water Sports
San Juan is no Rincón when it comes to surfing, but the best waves are east of Isla Verde towards Piñones and beyond, where the morning and evening breezes bring a 4ft swell. Popular breaks include Pine Grove, Los Aviónes, La Concha and several low-key local spots along Hwy 187.

WoW Surfing School SURFING
(955-6059; www.gosurfpr.com) Runs surfing lessons from the Ritz-Carlton on Playa Isla Verde, including boards, dry land practice and the real thing. Board rentals (from US$25 per day) are also available.

Tres Palmas SURFING
(Map p608; 728-3377; 1911 McLeary, Ocean Park; short boards/boogie boards per day US$36/25) Has 24-hour surfboard and boogie board rentals and lessons. Both outfitters teach children.

Velauno
SURFING

(www.velauno.com; 2430 Loíza, Punta Las Marías; longboard rental per day US$25, windsurfing equipment per hr US$20) Great for wind-surfing or paddleboarding classes. On Saturday from 9am to 11am, it offers free paddleboarding lessons at the Laguna del Condado near the Conrad San Juan Condado Plaza.

Cycling

Forget the notorious traffic; cycling in San Juan can be good fun, as long as you know where to go. It's feasible to work your way along the safe coastline from Old San Juan out as far as Carolina and the bike paths of Piñones.

Rent the Bicycle
CYCLING

(☑602-9696; www.rentthebicycle.net) This place runs tours and rents sturdy banana-yellow cruisers for US$27 per day, including lock and helmet. Children's bike seats are available. It'll bring the bike to you any-where in San Juan, or you can stop by the shop at Pier 6.

☞ Tours

Forsake the car and **Rent the Bicycle** (☑602-9696; www.rentthebicycle.net). San Juan's reliable bike outfit (p610) does ex-cellent two-wheeled tours of Old San Juan (US$29 to US$49), the Condado beaches (US$37) and Piñones (US$52).

Debbie Molina-Ramos is a well-respected guide for **Legends of Puerto Rico** (☑605-9060; www.legendsofpr.com), whose wildly popular 'Night Tales in Old San Juan' tour (USUS$35 per person) books up pretty fast. She also does 'Legends of San Juan' (US$35 per person) and others, including a culinary tour with rum tasting.

★ Festivals & Events

Aside from Festival San Sebastián, which becomes adults-get-crazy, all the following festivals retain a congenial atmosphere for families. For detailed information, contact the PRTC (p615).

Festival San Sebastián
STREET PARTY

For a full week in mid-January, the old city's famous party street, San Sebastián, hums with semireligious processions, music, food stalls and larger-than-ever crowds. During the day it's all about folk art and crafts; at night it's drunken revelry.

Fiesta de San Juan Bautista
STREET PARTY

Celebration of the patron saint of San Juan and a summer solstice party, Latin-style, in Old San Juan; held on June 24.

SoFo Culinary Festival
FOOD FESTIVAL

This alfresco culinary festival is a semi-an-nual moveable feast that happens in late fall and again in midsummer. For three nights a two-block wedge of Fortaleza is closed to traffic and commandeered by local restaurateurs.

🛏 Sleeping

You'll find ample accommodations in San Juan for every price range except one – bud-get. Outside of a few affordable guesthouses, it's slim pickings for those watching their money. Note that the large hotels tack on a 14% resort fee and charge US$15 to US$20 per night for parking.

OLD SAN JUAN

Gran Hotel El Convento
PARADOR $$$

(Map p606; ☑723-9020; www.elconvento.com; 100 Calle del Cristo; r US$260-325, ste US$535-800; P❄@🛜🏊) Historic monument, tapas res-taurant, meeting place, coffee bar and evoc-ative colonial building...without a doubt El Convento is Puerto Rico's most atmospheric and multifaceted hotel. Built in 1651 as the New World's first Carmelite convent, this baroque beacon oozes old-world relics and subtle Siglo de Oro (Golden Age) charm. El Convento's 58 rooms and six suites are gorgeously decorated with Andalusian tiles, mahogany and thick rugs.

Casablanca Hotel
HOTEL $$

(Map p606; ☑725-3436; www.hotelcasablancapr. com; 316 Fortaleza; r incl breakfast US$95-195; ❄🛜) Cut from the same cloth as its sister property, longtime-favorite Da House, this stylish new SoFo hotel blends together a luxurious mix of colonial and contemporary styles. Five floors of rooms are swathed in vibrant fabrics, and cozy bathrooms sparkle with gorgeous mother-of-pearl sinks from India. Greet the morning with a yoga class on the roof deck with inspirational views of El Morro and El Yunque.

Gallery Inn
INN $$$

(Map p606; ☑722-1808; www.thegalleryinn.com; 204-206 Norzagaray; r incl breakfast US$235-355; P❄@🏊) Get ready to double take: this quirky, artist-owned hotel is like wander-ing onto the set of a Harry Potter movie. Showcasing masks, caged birds, trickling water and paintings, the Gallery Inn's cavernous 18th-century compound has 25 eclectic rooms and a stunning plunge pool. The reception area showcases photos of the Obamas when they overnighted a few years back.

Da House
HOTEL **$$**

(Map p606; ☎977-1180; www.dahousehotelpr.com; 312 Calle San Francisco; r incl breakfast US$80-150; ✴@🖥) One of Old San Juan's funkier hotels is also one of its best bargains, with boutique-style rooms kitted out with chic furnishings and decorated with eye-catching contemporary art. For the musically inclined, one of San Juan's best salsa bars, the Nuyorican, is situated downstairs; for the less enamored (or the sleep-deprived), the reception staff will ruefully give out ear plugs.

Posada San Francisco
GUESTHOUSE **$**

(Map p606; ☎721-7112; 405 Calle San Francisco; r without bathroom US$45; ✴🖥) The paint was barely dry when we visited this excellent family-run budget option, and all eight rooms were already snapped up. Spacious and super-clean (one-use shower mats in the six shared bathrooms), the full and twin rooms have high ceilings, fridges and classic tile floors. Exquisite 5th-floor patio views and a guest kitchen seal the deal. Bookable through www.hostelworld.com.

CONDADO & OCEAN PARK

There are tons of properties and every imaginable American hotel chain in these two neighborhoods. If you're not fussy about where you stay, check with www.priceline. com and bid low.

La Concha
RESORT **$$$**

(Map p608; ☎721-7500; www.laconcharesort. com; 1077 Av Ashford; r US$269-319; P✴@🖥) Recently reopened after being closed for a decade, La Concha will wow you. Spacious and serene white rooms pop with flashes of color, and blue-lit showers exude an otherworldly glow. Add in its three pools (one adults-only), gorgeous indoor and outdoor seating areas, hallways in crayon colors, a 24-hour casino and the drop-dead Perla restaurant (p613) and you'll not venture far. In addition the lobby is the current place to see and be seen in San Juan, with a sophisticated scene on weekends.

Conrad San Juan Condado Plaza
RESORT **$$$**

(Map p608; ☎727-721-1000; www.condadoplaza. com; 999 Av Ashford; r US$140-539; P✴@🖥) Guarding the entrance to Condado like a sparkling sentinel, the Conrad straddles the thin wedge of land that separates the area's eponymous *laguna* from the Atlantic Ocean. Now a Hilton property, it offers stunning views extending in all directions. There's a 24-hour casino with live entertainment, a celebrated gourmet restaurant and a lovely arc of raked sand in view of Fuerte San Gerónimo.

Coral Princess Inn
HOTEL **$$**

(Map p608; ☎977-7700; www.coralpr.com; 1159 Magdalena; r incl breakfast US$137-161; ✴🖥) This independent inn can compete in the quality stakes with the bigger and plusher opposition. The small, 25-room boutique hotel punches way above its weight. Sitting in Condado's midrange bracket, it offers all the luxuries of the fancy resorts – flatscreen TVs, marble floors and original art – but with enough intimacy and Latin flavor to remind you that you're still in Puerto Rico.

SAN JUAN FOR CHILDREN

Traveling in Puerto Rico with children is a breeze and children are welcome at all but a very few exclusive small hotels. You'll rarely encounter icy or disdainful looks when dining out with your child except in the trendiest places in Old San Juan, Condado and Isla Verde.

In and around San Juan there are several attractions that children really enjoy. The Museo del Niño (p605) is always a big hit – as are the stray cats that nap outside it. Isla Verde is the most child-friendly beach, with safe swimming and plenty of beach toys, or you can always head further east to Luquillo (p617).

Alternatively you can hop on one of Old San Juan's two handy trolleys. For an educational but entertaining delve into Puerto Rican history check out the two splendid forts, El Morro (p604) and San Cristóbal (p605). All the larger hotels have vetted babysitters on speed dial – usually staff who are happy to make some extra money on the side.

Caribe Hilton RESORT $$$
(Map p608; ☎721-0303; www.hiltoncaribbean.
com/sanjuan; Rosales; r US$279-479; P✳@
🛜🏊🚣) The Caribe was constructed in 1949
and played host to numerous celebrities
throughout the 1950s and '60s. Its recently
renovated rooms are loaded with ameni-
ties, and the sprawling pool and beach area
includes a lawn chessboard, scores of ham-
mocks and an interesting mini-peninsula
with lounge beds. Though it's a bit of an
island unto itself, there's good beach ac-
cess and Old San Juan is a not-unpleasant
30-minute walk away.

Andalucía Guest House GUESTHOUSE $$
(Map p608; ☎309-3373; www.andaluciapr.com;
2011 McLeary; r US$85-129; P✳@🛜) Within
striking distance of Ocean Park's excellent
restaurants and beaches, this comfortable
guesthouse makes you feel like you're part
of the neighborhood. Its 11 rooms sport pretty tiling and striking boutique-style color
schemes, and some have a kitchen or kitchenette. The super-helpful owners lend out
boogie boards and beach chairs, and there's
a cozy terrace deck and courtyard Jacuzzi.

Número Uno GUESTHOUSE $$
(Map p608; ☎726-5010; www.numero1guesthouse
.com; 1 Santa Ana; r US$149-299; ✳🛜🏊) Pinch
yourself – you're still in the middle of San
Juan: Ocean Park, to be more precise, the
discerning traveler's antidote to Condado
and Isla Verde. Hidden behind the walls of
a whitewashed 1940s beachfront house, and
surrounded by palms and topped by a lumi-
nous kidney-shaped swimming pool, the 12
rooms and four apartments have intimate ser-
vice and there's an exquisite on-site seafood
restaurant.

ISLA VERDE
Ritz-Carlton RESORT $$$
(☎253-1700; www.ritzcarlton.com; 6961 Av Los
Gobernadores; r US$272-1809; P✳@🛜🏊) Ritz
equals posh, so pack trendy slacks and bring
along a platinum card. Decked out in marble
and embellished with Alhambra-esque lions,
this is San Juan at its swankiest and a favorite hangout of visiting celebrities. Rooms
are plush, service heavy on the 'yes sirs and
madams' and the communal areas shimmer
like winning entries in an international design competition. Parceled inside this carefully manicured tropical 'paradise' are a
resident spa, tennis courts, numerous eating
facilities and, yes, that obligatory casino.

El San Juan Hotel & Casino RESORT $$$
(☎791-1000; www.elsanjuanhotel.com; 6063 Av
Isla Verde; r US$259-669; P✳@🛜🏊) Decked
out in Gothic wood, starburst chandeliers
and animal-print sofas, the lobby of El San
Juan is a theatrical backdrop for the veri-
table fashion parade of folks prancing in for
legendary nightly entertainment. Renowned
for its flashy casino, rollicking nightlife and
unlimited water features. All the stylish
rooms have a full or partial ocean view.

Water & Beach Club HOTEL $$$
(☎728-3666; www.waterbeachclubhotel.com; 2 Tar-
tak; r US$195-295, ste US$325-500; P✳@🛜🏊)
Breaking the resort ubiquity of Isla Verde,
the Water Club is one of Puerto Rico's most
celebrated boutique hotels. With a reception
area straight out of *Architectural Digest*
and elevators that sport glassed-in waterfalls, this is the closest San Juan comes to
emulating South Beach, Florida. Rooms are
minimalist, but enjoy spectacular beach
views. There's also a chicer-than-chic pool
on the roof.

El Patio Guesthouse GUESTHOUSE $$
(☎726-6298; 23 Calle Mar de Bering; r US$69-90;
✳🏊) Your average Isla Verde visitor proba-
bly wouldn't poke a stick at this place, but in
the cheaper price bracket it's not a bad bet.
Walking distance to the beach, it is run by
a little old lady who'll bend over backwards
to make sure that your rooms are spick-and-
span. There's a guest kitchen, and rooms
have TVs and fridges.

🍴 Eating

San Juan offers the finest dining in the Ca-
ribbean, with enough cutting-edge restau-
rants to justify a trip in its own right. Calle
Fortaleza in Old San Juan is the eclectic
heart of the city's 21st-century fusion-cuisine
revolution.

OLD SAN JUAN
St Germain Bistro & Café INTERNATIONAL $
(Map p606; ☎725-5830; 156 Sol; dishes US$8-14;
⏰11:30am-3:30pm & 6-10pm Tue-Sat, 10am-3pm &
6-10pm Sun; 🍴) Kudos to the chef for trans-
forming the main-course salads – so often
the dullest dish on the menu – into some-
thing fresh, tasty and filling. Then there's the
aromatic Puerto Rican coffee, the delicious
sandwiches and the homemade, heavenly
cakes. Nestled on the corner of Sol and Cruz,
the St Germain is a bright neighborhood
place with down-to-earth service, interest-

ing clientele and a European feel. Perfect for lunch, a light dinner or Sunday brunch.

Marmalade
FUSION **$$**
(Map p606; ☎724-3969; 317 Fortaleza; dishes US$16-29; ☺6-11pm Sun-Thu, 6pm-midnight Fri & Sat; ☑) Promoted as SoFo's best culinary innovator in a street full of them, this starkly minimalist eating establishment is decked out like the Korova Milk Bar in Stanley Kubrick's *A Clockwork Orange*. Step inside the trendy interior to sample house specialties such as paella bites or grilled pears with Parma ham.

Aguaviva
SEAFOOD **$$**
(Map p606; ☎722-0665; 364 Fortaleza; dishes US$17-34; ☺lunch Fri-Sun, dinner daily) Cerviche's the word at Aguaviva, a trendy SoFo restaurant designed with an arty water/sea-life theme. Everything from the open-view kitchen to the catwalk clientele is slavishly stylish, but the real test is the food: fresh oysters, lobster yucca gnocchi and swordfish steak *frites* with wild mushrooms.

La Bombonera
DINER **$**
(Map p606; ☎722-0658; 259 San Francisco; mains US$5-10; ☺8am-4pm) The old-fashioned coffee machine hisses like a steam engine, career waiters appear like royal footmen at your table and a long line of seen-it-all *Sanjuaneros* populate the row of stools catching up on gossip. La Bombonera is a city institution – it's been around since 1902. Don't leave without trying La Mallorca, the amazing savory and sweet breakfast sandwich.

La Fonda El Jibarito
PUERTO RICAN **$**
(Map p606; ☎725-8375; 280 Sol; dishes US$9-23; ☺11am-9pm) Welcome to the neighborhood, *hermano*. El Jibarito is the kind of salt-of-the-earth, unpretentious place that you should reserve to sample your first *mofongo* or *arroz con habichuelas* (rice and beans). A favorite of local families, in-the-know tourists and passing journalists, the meals are simple but hearty with pork and prawns, or plantains smashed, mashed and fried just about any way you want.

CONDADO & OCEAN PARK
Pikayo
FUSION **$$$**
(Map p608; ☎721-6194; Conrad San Juan Condado Plaza, 999 Av Ashford; dishes US$30-42; ☺dinner) Wilo Benet is the island's very own Gordon Ramsay (without the expletives), a celebrity chef par excellence who has uncovered the soul of Caribbean cooking by infusing colo-

> **DON'T MISS**
>
> ## PERLA
>
> Dine inside a literal architectural oyster, where hand-blown glass lamps cast a flattering glow and pearlescent walls undulate and echo into the nighttime sea. The most romantic **restaurant** (Map p608; ☎977-3285; La Concha, 1077 Av Ashford; dishes US$22-38; ☺dinner) in San Juan and the utmost in tropical modernism, the white seashell is a retro stunner. Not surprisingly, aquatic options feature on the menu, though steak and veggie dishes take a turn. A voluminous wine list highlights French and Californian selections. Reservations recommended, especially for coveted window seats.

nial-era Puerto Rican cuisine with African and Indian elements.

Café Mam
TOP CHOICE
VEGETARIAN **$**
(Map p608; ☎688-6832; 1958 McLeary, ste 103; dishes US$4-7; ☺10am-7pm Mon-Sat; ☜☑⚅) Inside the post office parking lot beside Kasalta's, the welcoming cafe of Mujeres Ayudando Madres (Women Helping Mothers) offers tasty and affordable options to support healthy families and pregnant women. Let the little ones run and play while you recharge with fresh juices, coconut milk shakes and hearty vegetarian (and vegan) dishes like a 'fruity burger' – a lentil burger topped with mango sauce, avocado and papaya – or a tofu and hummus wrap.

Via Appia
ITALIAN **$**
(Map p608; ☎725-8711; 1350 Av Ashford; pizzas US$8-18; ☺11am-11pm) One of a few family-run jewels among all the Starbucks and 7-Elevens, Via Appia is no-nonsense Italian restaurant where the pizza and gentlemanly waiters could seem like props in *The Godfather*. Munch on garlic bread or feast on meatballs alfresco, as the multi-lingual mélange of Av Ashford goes strolling by.

ISLA VERDE
Metropol
SPANISH **$$**
(☎791-5585; Av Isla Verde; dishes US$11-27; ☺dinner) You can't miss this place – it's right next to the cockfighting arena. It's a neighborhood favorite, well known for the plentiful portions and simple (but not plain) Spanish fare. Wandering tourists are sometimes

lured out of their upscale resorts and into its inviting fold.

Don José Café
PUERTO RICAN $

(253-1281; 6475 Av Isla Verde Km 6.3; dishes US$4-18; ⊙24hr) No frills, no formalities, but good food – and it's open 24 hours, though you'd think it wasn't operating at all looking at the heavily tinted windows. Come here for breakfast after one of those exuberant all-night parties and nip your hangover in the bud with two fried eggs, bacon and ham washed down with a strong cup of coffee.

Drinking

Old Harbor Brewery
BREWERY

(Map p606; 202 Tizol; ⊙11:30am-1am) The only microbrewery on the island, Old Harbor concocts a handful of excellent brews, including a Coquí lager, the Kofresí stout, a rotating seasonal variety and a 9% double bock brewed for Christmas. Upscale pub fare and gleaming copper kettles complete the scene. Spent grains become animal feed at local farms or get processed into biofuel.

Los 3 Cuernos
BAR

(Map p606; Calle San Francisco 403; ⊙10:30am-midnight, to 3am Fri & Sat) Wedge your way into this long, packed bar, where students and young hipsters socialize under a wall of Puerto Rican masks and scribbled-on international bank notes. The draw here is the flavored *chichaítos*, an inexpensive Puerto Rican favorite of rum and anise liquor, available at US$1 per shot or US$6 for a *caneca de sabores* (pre-mixed flask-sized bottle).

Entertainment

Old San Juan is the nucleus of the city's nightlife, hosting a high-gloss intersection of Caribbean travelers. For a condensed taste, hit San Sebastián dive bars and clubs, or Fortaleza with its trendy, tasty restaurants.

Isla Verde is an alternative nexus, with most of the action confined to a trio of international-class hotels. Condado plays host to one of the Caribbean's biggest gay scenes.

Nuyorican Café
LIVE MUSIC

(Map p606; 312 San Francisco; ⊙8pm-late) If you came to Puerto Rico in search of authentic salsa music, the legend still lives on at the Nuyorican Café. San Juan's hottest nightspot is a congenial hub of live Latino sounds and hip-gyrating locals that easily emulates its

famous New York namesake. Stuffed into an alley off Fortaleza, you get everything from poetry readings to six-piece salsa bands on the stage. And you'll meet people too – the Nuyorican is refreshingly devoid of pretension or dance snobbery. Things get interesting around 11pm.

Latin Roots
DANCE HALL

(Map p606; Comercio; admission US$5-10 Thu-Sat; ⊙6pm-2am Thu-Sat, 6pm-midnight Mon-Wed, 2pm-midnight Sun) Salseros, need a fix? The Latin Roots is the closest you'll get to 24/7 salsa, with free lessons from 6pm to 10pm daily and live bands every night from 8pm (2pm and 6pm on Sundays). Also a popular Puerto Rican restaurant, you'll find a lively mix of locals and tourists swiveling on the dance floor.

Club Brava
NIGHTCLUB

(www.bravapr.com; El San Juan Hotel & Casino, 6063 Av Isla Verde; admission US$10-20; ⊙10pm-late Thu-Sat) This swinging club frequently gets breathless reviews from celeb spotters and all-night dance fanatics. The two-level interior is small with a mix of dance, reggaeton and salsa. Dress up, bring your credit card and jive to what is touted as the best sound system in the Caribbean.

Shopping

The best arts and crafts shopping is in Old San Juan, though the schlocky t-shirt shops are there too. San Francisco and Fortaleza are the two main arteries in the old city, and both are packed with shops. Running perpendicular at the west end of the town, Calle del Cristo is home to many of the old city's chicest establishments.

Worth looking out for are the jewelry shop and gallery of **Bóveda** (Map p606; Calle del Cristo; ⊙10am-6pm) and **Butterfly People** (Map p606; 257 Cruz; ⊙11am-6pm Sat-Thu), where you'll find unusual art incorporating insects. Cigar fans should stop by the open storefront of **Cigarros Antillas** (Map p606; Edif Intermodal Covadonga, opp Pier 3; ⊙9am-5pm) to see workers roll by hand.

Information

EMERGENCY You may find that telephone directory and tourist publications list nonfunctioning numbers for emergency services. In *any* kind of emergency, call 911.

Medical emergencies (754-2550)

Tourist zone police (911, 726-7020; ⊙24hr) English spoken.

INTERNET ACCESS Internet cafes are hard to come by, but most lodgings have wi-fi. A number of plazas in Old San Juan have free hot spots.

Cybernet Café Condado (1128 Av Ashford; per hr US$9; ⊘9am-10pm Mon-Sat, 10:30am-10pm Sun); Isla Verde (5980 Av Isla Verde; per hr US$9; ⊘10am-10pm Mon-Sat, 6-10pm Sun)

Diner's Internet (311 Tetuán, Old San Juan; per hr US$5)

MEDICAL SERVICES Ashford Memorial Community Hospital (☑721-2160; 1451 Av Ashford) This is probably the best-equipped and most convenient hospital for travelers to visit.

MONEY Banco Popular Old San Juan (☑725-2636; cnr Tetuán & San Justo); Condado (1060 Av Ashford); Isla Verde (Av Isla Verde) Charges no commission to cash up to US$300 in traveler's checks.

POST Old San Juan post office (☑724-2098; 100 Paseo de Colón; ⊘8am-4pm Mon-Fri, to noon Sat) The most convenient for travelers.

TOURIST INFORMATION Departamento de Recursos Naturales y Ambientales (DRNA, Department of Natural Resources; ☑999-2200; www.drna.gobierno.pr, in Spanish; Km 6.3, Rte 8838, Sector El Cinco, Río Piedras) For information on camping, including reservations and permits, contact this department or visit its office.

Puerto Rico Tourism Company (PRTC; ☑800-223-6530, 721-2400; www.seepuertorico.com) LMM airport (☑791-1014; ⊘9am-8pm); Old San Juan (☑722-1709; Edificio Ochoa, 500 Tanca; ⊘8:30am-8pm Mon-Wed & Sat, 8:30am-5:30pm Thu, 8:30am-6:30pm Fri, 9am-8pm Sun) Distributes information in English and Spanish.

ⓘ Getting There & Away

AIR International flights arrive at and depart from Aeropuerto Internacional de Luis Muñoz Marin (LMM), which is about 8 miles east of the old city center. See p631 for information on international flights into San Juan.

Several airlines connect San Juan and other parts of the commonwealth. Many of the commuter flights serving the islands of Culebra and Vieques leave San Juan's original Aeropuerto de Isla Grande, on the Bahía de San Juan in the city's Miramar district. See p632 for details.

BOAT More than a dozen cruise lines include San Juan on their Caribbean itineraries and, as the second-largest port for cruise ships in the western hemisphere, the city is visited by more than a million cruise-ship passengers a year. All ships dock at the piers along Calle La Marina near the Customs House, just a short walk from the cobblestone streets of Old San Juan.

PÚBLICO There is no islandwide bus system; *públicos* form the backbone of public transportation in Puerto Rico and can provide an inexpensive link between San Juan and other points on the island, including **Ponce** (approximately US$20–30) and **Mayagüez** (US$15–20). Prices for these trips depend on space in the vans and the traveler's bartering skills.

In San Juan the major *público* centers include the LMM airport, two large *público* stations in Río Piedras (Centro de Públicos Oeste and Centro de Públicos Este) and – to a lesser extent – the Plaza de Colón in Old San Juan. These are the places you should go first if you want to attempt to understand the intricacies of the fun – but sometimes difficult to fathom – *público* system.

ⓘ Getting Around

TO/FROM THE AIRPORT For the bus look for the 'Parada' sign outside the arrivals concourse at LMM airport. The B40 bus will get you from the airport to Isla Verde or Río Piedras. From Isla Verde you can take bus T5 to Old San Juan and Condado. From Río Piedras take bus T9 to Santurce and Old San Juan. Fares are US$0.75.

For taxis, there's a fixed flat fee per carload (printed on the window) of US$10 to Isla Verde, US$15 to Condado and Ocean Park, and US$19 to Old San Juan. Add another dollar for each piece of luggage, and another buck after 10pm. The taxi reps discourage sharing, but you'll save money by finding someone going your way.

Getting to LMM airport from hotels in the San Juan area is easy. Staff at virtually all of the midrange and top-end hotels will arrange taxis or shuttles to pick you up.

BUS The **Autoridad Metropolitana de Autobuses** (AMA; Metropolitan Bus Authority & Metrobus; ☑294-0500, ext 514 or 524) has a main bus terminal (Map p606) in Old San Juan near the cruise-ship piers. Bus rides cost US$0.75 and run until 10pm. Bus information and maps are hard to come by. These are the routes taken most often by travelers:

T5 Old San Juan, stop 18, Isla Verde (via Loiza)

T9 Old San Juan, Sagrado Corazon (train station), Río Piedras

C10 Sagrado Corazon (train station), Ocean Park (via Loiza), Condado, stop 18, Isla Grande airport/Convention Center

B40 Isla Verde, LMM Airport, Río Piedras

C53 Old San Juan, Condado, Ocean Park (via McLeary), Isla Verde

Old San Juan has a free trolley bus around the old quarter. It starts and finishes just outside the main bus terminal, but you can get on and off at two dozen designated stops.

CAR Though traveling efficiently around the island requires a rental car, traffic, parking and the maze of thoroughfares make having and using a rental car in San Juan a challenge. For information about car hire see p632.

METRO The Tren Urbano connects Bayamón with downtown San Juan as far as Sagrado Corazón on the south side of Santurce, but is little use for travelers. The 16 super-modern stations are safe, spacious and decked out with acres of eye-catching art and polished chrome. The line, which is a mix of sky-train and under-ground, charges US$0.75 for any journey, re-gardless of length. For more information contact **Tren Urbano** (☑866-900-1284; www.dtop.gov. pr, in Spanish).

TAXI A government taxi scheme sets prices in the main tourism zones. From Old San Juan, trips to Condado or Ocean Park cost US$12, and US$19 to Isla Verde. Journeys within Old San Juan cost US$7.

Taxis line up at the south end of Fortaleza in Old San Juan, or you can book at your hotel. Try **Metro Taxi Cab** (☑725-2870) or **Rochdale Radio Taxi** (☑721-1900); they usually come when you call.

AROUND SAN JUAN

You can be three-quarters of the way across the island and still be within an hour or two's drive of San Juan (traffic permitting). Day trips from the capital can thus take you almost anywhere in the commonwealth. If you're keen to probe deeper, it's worthwhile traveling slower and making an overnight stop.

◉ Sights

Bacardí Rum Factory   RUM FACTORY
(☑788-8400; www.casabacardi.org; Hwy 888 Km 2.6; ⊙tours 9am-4:30pm Mon-Sat, 10am-3:30pm Sun) Called the 'Cathedral of Rum' because of its six-story distillation tower, the Bacardí Rum Factory covers 127 acres and stands out like a petroleum refinery across from Old San Juan, near the entrance to the bay. The world's largest and most famous rum-producing family started their business in Cuba over a century ago, but began moving their operation to this site in 1936. Today the distiller produces some 100,000 gallons of rum per day and ships 21 million cases per year worldwide.

In exchange for two free drinks, you'll be escorted on a tram tour that lasts about 45 minutes. To get to the Bacardí factory, take a *público* (about US$3) or walk 15 minutes from the ferry terminal in Cataño along the waterfront on Calle Palo Seco (Hwy 888). At Km 2.6 north of town, look for the Cathedral

of Rum and other Bacardí factory buildings to your left, rising above the landscape.

Arecibo Observatory   OBSERVATORY
(☑878-2612; www.naic.edu; adult/child/senior US$6/4/4; ⊙9am-4pm Dec 15-Jan 15 & Jun-Jul, 9am-4pm Wed-Sun other times) Puerto Ricans reverently refer to it as 'El Radar.' To everyone else it is simply the largest radio telescope in the world. Resembling an extraterrestrial spaceship grounded in the middle of karst country, the Arecibo Observatory looks like something out of a James Bond movie – probably because it is; 007 aficionados will recognize the saucer-shaped dish and cran-ing antennae from the 1995 film *Goldeneye*.

In reality this 20-acre 'dish', set in a sink-hole among clusters of haystack-shaped mogotes, is planet earth's ear into outer space. Involved in the SETI (Search for Ex-traterrestrial Intelligence) programme, the telescope, which is supported by 50-story cables weighing more than 600 tons, is used by on-site scientists to prove the existence of pulsars and quasars, the so-called 'music of the stars.'

Parque De Las Cavernas Del Río Camuy   UNDERGROUND CAVERNS
(☑898-3100; Hwy 129 Km 18.9; adult/child US$12/6, parking US$2; ⊙8am-5pm Wed-Sun & holidays) This park is home to one of the largest cave systems in the world and is defi-nitely worth a stop (but call ahead if it's been raining – too much water causes closures).

Trolleybus trips and ample walking among stalagmites and stalactites make this a fun trip for the whole family. If you come early enough you can visit the caves in the morning and the observatory in the after-noon. They are a 30-minute drive apart.

EL YUNQUE & EASTERN PUERTO RICO

The east coast is Puerto Rico shrink-wrapped; a tantalizing taste of almost ev-erything the island has to offer squeezed into an area not much larger than Manhat-tan. Here in the foothills of the Sierra de Luquillo the sprawling suburbs of San Juan blend caustically with the jungle-like quiet-ness of El Yunque National Forest, the com-monwealth's giant green lungs and biggest outdoor attraction.

Separated from mainland Puerto Rico by a 7-mile stretch of choppy ocean, the two islands of Culebra and Vieques sport unsullied beaches and unblemished countryside that glimmers invitingly with nary a resort, golf course or casino to break the natural vista.

El Yunque

Covering 28,000 acres of land in the Sierra de Luquillo, this verdant tropical rainforest is a shadow of what it was before axe-wielding Spanish conquerors arrived in the 16th and 17th centuries. But, in common with other protected reserves on the island, the ecological degradation has been largely reversed over the past 50 years, and today, under the auspices of the US Forest Service, El Yunque is once again sprouting a healthy abundance of dense tree cover.

Compared to other Puerto Rican reserves, El Yunque is well staffed and crisscrossed by an excellent network of signposted trails, even if they won't thrill the hardcore hiker.

Stop first at **El Portal Visitors Center** (✆888-1880; www.fs.fed.us/r8/caribbean; Hwy 191 Km 4.3; adult/under 15yr/senior US$4/free/2; ⊗9am-5pm, closed Christmas Day) for information and details about its hikes.

If listening to a frog symphony and relaxing on a shady balcony within hammock-swinging distance of a mystical tropical rainforest has you dashing for your jungle apparel, then **Casa Cubuy Ecolodge** (✆874-6221; www.casacubuy.com; Hwy 191 Km 22; r incl breakfast US$90-115; P※🖤🏊) could be your place. Cocooned atop the winding Hwy 191 on El Yunque's wild and isolated southern slopes, Casa Cubuy Ecolodge's 10 cozy rooms offer a welcome antidote to the crowded beaches and spirit-crushing traffic of modern Puerto Rico.

You can get here from San Juan on an organized trip, or by driving along Hwy 3 to the junction with Hwy 191 just past the settlement of Río Grande.

Luquillo

Luquillo is synonymous with its *balneario* (public beach), the fabulous **Playa Luquillo** (Balneario La Monserrate; admission free, parking US$4.50; ⊗8am-5pm). Set on a calm bay facing northwest and protected from the easterly trade winds, the public part of this beach makes a mile-long arc to a point of sand shaded by evocative coconut palms. Although crowds converge on weekends and holidays, Luquillo has always been more about atmosphere than solitude. Its famous food kiosks make it a great place to sample the local culinary culture. There is a bathhouse, a refreshment stand, a security patrol and well-kept bathrooms.

🛏 Sleeping & Eating

Luquillo's famous line of 60 or so *friquitines* (also known as *quioscos, kioskos* or just plain food stalls) along the western edge of Hwy 3 serve some of the tastiest treats around, from outstanding *comida criolla* to top-notch steaks. Some are very basic, others are upscale restaurants, so walk the line and follow your senses – or the locals.

TOP CHOICE **Luquillo Sunrise Beach Inn** HOTEL $$ (✆889-1713; www.luquillosunrise.com; A2 Costa Azul; d incl breakfast US$125-155; P※@🛜) Filling a gap in the midrange market, the Sunrise Beach Inn is caressed by cooling Atlantic sea breezes in each of its 17 spiffy ocean-facing rooms. There's a communal patio and all upper-floor rooms have large balconies. Luquillo plaza is two blocks away and the famous *balneario* and food kiosks a 30-minute stroll along the beach.

❶ Getting There & Away

Públicos run from San Juan (US$5 to US$8) to and from the Luquillo plaza. Aside from that, you'll need your own wheels.

Vieques

POP 10,000

With a name stamped in infamy, Vieques was where Puerto Rico's most prickly political saga was played out in the public eye. For over five decades the US Navy used more than two-thirds of this Spanish Virgin Island for military target practice. The war games ended in 1999 after a misplaced 500lb bomb caused the death of a Puerto Rican civilian and sparked wide protest.

Although it's been developed over the past few years, Vieques remains synonymous with gorgeous beaches, semiwild horses and an unforgettable bioluminescent bay. Neighboring Culebra is less developed still.

◎ Sights & Activities

Bahía Mosquito BIOLUMINESCENT BAY

This bioluminescent bay, a designated wildlife preserve about 2 miles east of Esperanza, has one of the highest concentrations of phosphorescent dinoflagellates in the world. Indeed it's also known as Phosphorescent Bay and it's magnificent.

An evening trip through the lagoon is psychedelic, with hundreds of fish whipping up bright-green contrails below the surface as your kayak or electric boat passes by (never accept a ride in a motorized boat – the engine pollution kills the phosphorescent organisms). But the best part is when you stop to swim: it's like bathing in the stars.

The best way to see the bay is with an organized trip. **Island Adventures** (☏741-0720; www.biobay.com; Rte 996, Km 4.5; tours US$30) offers ecofriendly 90-minute tours in an electric boat just about every night, except when there's a full moon.

TOP CHOICE **Vieques Adventure Company**   KAYAKING
(☏692-9162; www.viequesadventures.com) This company has totally clear kayaks that let you see the action as you glide across the water on its unforgettable bio bay tours (US$45). Groups are small, so reserve well ahead. It also does fly-fishing kayak tours.

Blackbeard Sports   DIVING
(☏741-1892; www.blackbeardsports.com; 101 Muñoz Rivera, Isabel Segunda) The island's main dive operator offers two-tank scuba dives from US$100 and Professional Association of Dive Instructors (PADI) certified basic open-water courses from US$350. You can also rent your own snorkel/scuba gear for US$15/50 a day. It also rents bikes, which make for excellent island transport.

🏄 Beaches

Vieques' beaches are as legendary as Culebra's – and there are more of them. Environmentally, the US occupation was a blessing in disguise, in that it has left many of the island's more remote beaches in an underdeveloped and pristine state. Now protected in a national wildlife refuge, areas such as Bahía de la Chiva, Caracas and Green Beaches are clean, untrammeled and paradisiacal.

Playas La Plata, Caracas, Garcia, Escondida & Bahía de la Chiva
SECLUDED BEACHES
These south-shore beaches, which used to be on Navy land, can be reached by entering the Garcia Gate on Hwy 997. New signage makes it easy to find your way around, and the road's paved as far east as Playa Caracas.

Calm and clear **Playa Caracas** (Red Beach) has gazebos with picnic tables to shade bathers from the sun. **Garcia Beach** is less known and has less shade, and fewer people decamp here. **Playa Escondida** (Secret Beach), also nearby, is a deliciously deserted stretch of sand with absolutely no facilities – just jaw-dropping beauty.

Bahía de la Chiva (Blue Beach), at the east end of the former Camp Garcia road, is long and open, and occasionally has rough surf. If you happen upon this beach during Semana Santa (the Holy Week preceding Easter), you'll see hordes of faithful Catholics camping on the beach, where they pray and party in honor of the death and resurrection of Jesus Christ. **Playa La Plata** (Orchid Beach), further east, is as far as you can go at present. This gorgeously secluded beach has sand like icing sugar and a calm sea in 1000 different shades of turquoise, cobalt and blue.

Green Beach/Punta Arenas   SECLUDED BEACH
Punta Arenas and Green Beach are excellent places for a quiet picnic, family-friendly snorkeling and views of El Yunque. To get here pass through the former Naval Ammunitions Facility (NAF) Gate and head west for about 20 minutes through pastoral fields of wild horses. At the western tip of the island, the road turns to dirt.

The strand here is not very broad and is punctuated with coral outcroppings, but there is plenty of shade. Snorkeling reefs extend for miles, and you can expect to have this place pretty much to yourself, except on summer weekends, when yachts out of Fajardo visit on day trips. Bring bug repellent.

🛏 Sleeping
ESPERANZA

TOP CHOICE **Malecón House**   INN $$$
(☏741-0663; www.maleconhouse.com; 105 Calle Flamboyán; r incl breakfast US$160-250; [P][✷][@][🛜][❄]) With its travertine floors, beautiful fabrics and light wood furniture, this spacious new upmarket inn kicks Esperanza's accommodations up a few notches. Looking over the water from a quiet section of the main street, two of the 10 rooms have private seaside balconies and all have a clean and uncluttered feel. There's a good library and helpful owners, plus a free poolside show in the lush garden – iguanas grazing in the trees overhead.

Esperanza Inn　　　　　　　GUESTHOUSE **$$**

(☎741-2225; www.esperanzainn.com; Calle Hucar; r US$95-100, 1-/2-bedroom apt US$135/200; ❄@ 🛜⛱🛶) A longtime guesthouse with friendly new owners and a coterie of sweet outdoor cats, you'd be hard-pressed to lack anything here. Comfortable rooms are spacious and impeccably clean, and there's the chance to chat with fellow travelers as you whip up something in the guest kitchen, grab a Medalla from the honor bar, or duck in for a morning caffeine fix. Apartments with balconies and full kitchens sleep six to eight people, and an ample grassy backyard contains a small pool.

ELSEWHERE ON THE ISLAND

TOP CHOICE **Hix Island House**　　APARTMENTS **$$$**

(☎741-2302; www.hixislandhouse.com; Hwy 995; apt incl breakfast groceries US$175-310; P🛜⛱) Eco-hip, new-age-minimalist, environmentally austere; to describe the Hix house in a single sentence is nigh-on impossible, suffice to say that the place inspires robust opinions across the spectrum. Designed by cutting-edge Canadian architect John Hix, the guesthouse consists of four industrial concrete blocks that rise out of the surrounding trees like huge granite boulders. Hosting 13 rooms, the ethos here is minimalist, ecological and close to nature – the rooms open up to give the feeling that you are actually living in the forest. Further green credentials come with solar panels, recycled water and natural air-conditioning (trade winds), and daily yoga classes are available. It's a brave and surprisingly attractive experiment.

Inn on the Blue Horizon　　　INN **$$$**

(☎741-3318; www.innontheblehorizon.com; d US$160-370; P❄🛜⛱) Small is beautiful: the Inn on the Blue Horizon was surely invented with such a motto in mind. With only 10 rooms harbored in separate bungalows wedged onto a stunning ocean-side bluff, the sense of elegance here – both natural and contrived – is breathtaking. The luxury continues inside the restaurant and cozy communal lounge, which overlook an infinity pool. Children under 14 not permitted in high season.

TOP CHOICE **Casa de Amistad**　　GUESTHOUSE **$$**

(☎741-3758; www.casadeamistad.com; 27 Calle Benitez Castaño; r US$75-105; ❄@🛜⛱) A fun and comfortable place to crash slap-bang in the middle of town, friendly Casa de Amis-

A hidden blessing of the erstwhile US occupation is that Vieques remains refreshingly undeveloped and ideal for cycling. Free from the main island's traffic jams, this 135-sq-mile sliver of land has become a little-heralded cyclist's paradise.

The island's main bike-rental outlets organize guided rides around the island. A couple of suggestions:

» The main road from Isabel II to Esperanza is Hwy 997, but head west on Hwy 200 and south on Hwy 201 for a quieter, more pleasant route. Halfway along you can detour up Hwy 995, another lovely country road.

» The ultimate Vieques loop involves heading west out of Isabel II on Hwy 200 all the way to Green Beach (the last section is unpaved). After some shore snorkeling and an idyllic picnic lunch, swing south through the old military bunkers to Playa Grande before linking up with Hwy 996 to Esperanza.

tad has seven stylish rooms for rent with air-con and private bathrooms (two of the bathrooms, though private, are separated from bedrooms). Communal areas include an honor bar, sitting room/library, kitchen, landscaped yard and swimming pool, and rooftop deck.

W Retreat & Spa　　　　　RESORT **$$$**

(☎741-4100; www.wvieques.com; Hwy 200 Km 3.2; r from US$499; P❄@🛜⛱) Breathlessly trendy and über-chic, Vieques' only resort has been the darling of the design set since it unfurled its showy feathers in 2010. The lobby lounge is a glammed-out art explosion of color and texture and all 156 rooms have private balconies or patios and hidden TVs. A substantial nightly resort fee (US$60) includes whisking to and from the W's private airport lounge, yoga classes, access to the fitness center and tennis courts and snorkel gear.

✖ Eating

Many of the newer, high-end and American-run restaurants want reservations, especially on weekends in high season.

ESPERANZA

El Quenepo
INTERNATIONAL $$

([phone]741-1215; 148 Calle Flamboyán; dishes US$20-32; [clock]dinner Tue-Sun mid-Nov–Easter & Wed-Sun Easter-Aug) The destination restaurant of Vieques, Esperanza's upscale El Quenepo has a lovely interior and an equally delectable menu. The food's catch-of-the-day is fresh – a family of seven brothers supplies the seafood – and the decor is very chic. A few suggestions to get your mouth watering: whole Caribbean lobsters, *mofongo* made with breadfruit grown in its backyard and a lovely churrasco steak. Reservations highly recommended.

ISABELLA SEGUNDA

Conuco
PUERTO RICAN $$

([phone]741-2500; 110 Calle Muñoz Rivera; mains US$12-20; [clock]lunch Wed-Fri, dinner Wed-Sun) Named for Taíno garden plots, chef Rebecca Betancourt injects culinary magic into his modern take on Puerto Rican cuisine; standouts include the *bacalaítos* (cod fritters), mahimahi with passion fruit and coconut sauce and the *pionono* (sweet yellow plantains stuffed with beef stew). Romantic and refined, this is the north side's best spot for a dinner date.

Barefoot Be'stro
SEAFOOD $$

([phone]340-514-0124; Bravos de Boston; mains US$9-24; [clock]8-11am & 5-9pm Wed-Sat) The open-air dining room is topped by a thatched roof, the patrons dine at mosaic beach tables and benches, and the chef prepares meals in a seascape-festooned food cart. Call it gourmet casual or upscale island, but either way it works.

Shawnaa's
PUERTO RICAN $

([phone]741-1434; 327 Calle Antonio G Mellado; dishes US$6-8; [clock]10:30am-2pm Mon-Fri) Bring a big appetite to Shawnaa's buffet. It's full of superb *comida criolla* dishes that you can take out onto the patio or consume in the shaded interior.

❶ Information

It's a good idea to carry cash on the island (but watch out for petty thieves) as the ATMs have been known to run dry.

Banco Popular ([phone]741-2071; Muñoz Rivera, Isabella Segunda; [clock]8am-3pm Mon-Fri) Has one of two ATMs in Isabella Segunda.

Post office ([phone]741-3891; Muñoz Rivera 97, Isabella Segunda; [clock]8:30am-4:30pm Mon-Fri, 8am-noon Sat)

Puerto Rico Tourism Company (PRTC; [phone]741-0800; www.gotopuertorico.com; Carlos LeBrun 449, Isabella Segunda; [clock]8am-5pm)

❶ Getting There & Away

AIR There are more than 20 flights (25 minutes) a day to/from San Juan's Isla Grande and LMM airports. Round-trip prices start at US$220 from LMM, US$126 from Isla Grande and US$65 from Ceiba (10 minutes).

Vieques Air Link ([link]for San Juan–Vieques flights 888-901-9247, 741-8331, for Ceiba–Vieques flights 741-3266, 534-4222; www.viequesairlink.com) is the major carrier, with an office in Isabel Segunda. It currently flies to Culebra (via Ceiba) for US$70.

Air Sunshine ([link]800-327-8900, 741-7900; www.airsunshine.com) flies directly to St Thomas, St Croix and Tortola in the British Virgin Islands. It also flies between San Juan LMM and Vieques, charging the same rates as the other carriers.

FERRY High-speed passenger ferries run between Fajardo and Vieques four times daily, leaving Fajardo at 9:30am, 1pm, 4:30pm and 8pm; and Vieques at 6:30am, 11am, 3pm and 6pm. Passage takes just over an hour and the round-trip costs US$4.

Confirm the passenger-ferry schedule in advance, as it does change. Frustratingly advance reservations are not taken; the ticket offices usually open one hour before departure. Holiday weekends and summertime are peak times, when tickets can sell out. In these situations Vieques residents get priority and visitors can get bumped. For info try the **Maritime Transportation Authority** ([phone]860-2005, 800-981-2005; www.atm.gobierno.pr; [clock]8-11am & 1-3pm Mon-Fri) or the **Vieques office** ([phone]741-5018; [clock]8-11am & 1-3pm Mon-Fri) at the ferry dock in Isabel Segunda, but good luck; these offices rarely answer their phones.

❶ Getting Around

Vieques is a small island and renting a bike is a great way to get around. *Públicos* and taxis congregate at the ferry terminal, the airport and on 'the strip' in Esperanza.

Culebra
POP 2000

Welcome to Culebra – the island that time forgot; mainland Puerto Rico's weird, wonderful and distinctly wacky smaller cousin that lies glistening like a bejeweled Eden to the east.

Situated 17 miles from mainland Puerto Rico, the culturally isolated island is home to an offbeat mix of rat-race drop-outs, earnest idealists, solitude seekers, myriad eccentrics and others willing to dodge the manic intricacies of modern life. Long feted for its diamond-dust beaches and world-class diving reefs, the place is jaw-droppingly beautiful.

🏖 Beaches

Playa Flamenco   FAMILY BEACH
Stretching for a mile around a sheltered, horseshoe-shaped bay, Playa Flamenco isn't just Culebra's best beach; it is also regarded as the finest in Puerto Rico, and among the best in the Caribbean. Some travel magazines have listed it among the top 10 in the world. There's no denying that this gentle arc of white sand and crystal surf is special. Backed by low scrub and equipped with basic amenities, Flamenco is the only public beach on the island. It is also the only place that allows camping. Facilities include two guesthouses, a kiosk, toilets, outdoor showers, lifeguards, picnic tables and a parking lot. There are snacks but no full-blown restaurants or stores in the area, so visitors should stock up in Dewey before they arrive.

Playa Brava   SECLUDED BEACH
The beauty of Brava lies in the fact that there is no road here; you *have* to hike – make that bushwhack – along a little-used trail that is often overgrown with sea grape and low scrub. The rewards are immense when you finally clear the last mangrove and are confronted with an isolated but stunning swathe of sand that glimmers with a fierce but utterly enchanting beauty. Leatherback sea turtles use isolated Brava as a nesting site from April to June.

Playa Tamarindo   SNORKELING BEACH
A little beyond Melones, this is a very good snorkeling beach. It's accessible by foot by either turning off the Dewey–Flamenco Beach road at the bottom of the hill just before the lagoon, or from an unmarked trail west off the Flamenco parking lot. This place is often overlooked; it's not as flashy and fabulous-looking as others, but there's a good combination of sun and shade, gentle currents and lots of underwater life for good snorkeling.

🏃 Activities

Diving & Snorkeling
Despite reef damage caused during the US Navy testing era and global climate change, Culebra retains some of Puerto Rico's most

WORTH A TRIP

ISLA CULEBRITA

If you need a reason to hire a water taxi, Isla Culebrita is it. This small island, just a mile east of Playa Zoni, is part of the wildlife refuge. With an abandoned and decaying 1880s lighthouse, beaches, tide pools, reefs and nesting seabirds, Isla Culebrita has changed little in the past 500 years. The north beaches, such as the long crescent of Playa Tortuga, are popular nesting grounds for sea turtles. Bring a lot of water, sunscreen, a shirt and a hat if you head for Isla Culebrita because there is little shade here. Ask around in Dewey; hiring a boat to reach the island is easy.

amazing dives, including sunken ships, coral reefs, drop-offs and caves. Highlights include the *Wit Power* tugboat (which sank in 1984), the Geniqui Caves and the fish-filled water-world of Cayo Ratón. Good snorkeling can be accessed from many beaches, in particular Playas Carlos Rosario, Tamarindo and Melones. Don't rely on local maps for accessible entrance spots – ask the locals.

Two-tank dives run from US$90 to US$100 with the island's two main dive operators: **Culebra Divers** (☎742-0803; www.culebradivers.com) and, located across from the ferry dock, **Aquatic Adventures** (☎742-0605; www.diveculebra.com). The latter also offers snorkeling trips (US$50, including equipment and lunch) that go to at least two different locations.

Culebra Divers and Culebra Bike Shop rent snorkeling equipment for US$10 per day; and most boat captains, who are easy to find looking for tourists at the docks, will also arrange snorkel tours.

Hiking
Rejoice! The island is your oyster. The 2.5-mile hike from Dewey to Playa Flamenco is along a paved road with some inclines, but the destination is idyllic. You can veer off to Playa Tamarindo from a junction just before the lagoon. Playa Carlos Rosario is reached via a trail that starts at the west end of Playa Flamenco. The hike to Playa Brava begins at the end of a back road that cuts north from Rte 250 just past the graveyard. The trail rises to a ridge and then drops to the beach via thick bushes. The toughest hike on the

island is the rough trail to Playa Resaca that traverses the eponymous mountain.

🛏 Sleeping & Eating

A host of restaurants line the small main part of Dewey. Though bargains can be had, true shoestringers will save a lot by renting a place with a kitchen and cooking for themselves.

Villa Flamenco Beach   APARTMENTS **$$**
(📞742-0023; www.culebra-island.com; studios US$125-135, apt US$150; ⊙Dec-Sep; 🅿❄) Gentle waves lulling you to sleep, a night sky replete with twinkling stars, and one of the best beaches on the planet just outside your window; this six-unit place would be a winner even if it was just a roof and four walls. To make your stay more comfortable, the management has added self-catering kitchen facilities and inviting hammocks. It's right next to the Culebra Beach Villas.

Palmetto Guesthouse   GUESTHOUSE **$$**
(📞742-0257; www.palmettoculebra.com; r US$95-115; ❄@🛜) Run by two ex–Peace Corps volunteers from New England, this business is a superfriendly and accommodating escape. Five guestrooms have the run of two kitchens, a deck, a handy book exchange and a sporty magazine pile. Situated near the airport, it's a 10-minute stroll to Dewey. Snorkel gear, beach chairs and boogie boards are bonuses.

Villa Boheme   GUESTHOUSE **$$**
(📞742-3508; www.villaboheme.com; Calle Fulladoza; r US$98-139; ❄🛜) A recent remodel has spiffed up this well-situated guesthouse already endowed with a breezy communal patio, lovely bay views, kayak rentals and proximity to town (not to mention the Dinghy Dock restaurant next door). A few of the colorful rooms are equipped with kitchenette for guests who don't care to make use of the shared cooking facilities. Rates dip off-season.

Flamenco Campground   CAMPGROUND **$**
(📞742-0700; www.flamencobeachcampground.com; campsites US$20; 🅿) The only place you can legally camp in Culebra is just feet from the paradisiacal Playa Flamenco. Report to the office at the entrance and you will be assigned a spot. Six people maximum per tent. There are outdoor showers and bathrooms. The campground's pretty safe and reservations aren't usually necessary.

Bahía Marina   RESORT **$$$**
(📞278-5100; www.bahiamarina.net; Punta Soldado Rd, Km 2.4; r US$219-295; 🅿❄🛜⊜) One of the island's newer accommodations is also one of its most luxurious – in fact, it's Buckingham Palace by Culebra standards. Billed as a condo resort, this is not your average high-rise, environmentally unsound concrete block. Abutting a 100-acre nature preserve it has 40 one- and two-bedroom apartments with modern kitchenettes, swimming pools, three restaurants and live music at weekends.

Susie's   CARIBBEAN **$$**
(📞742-0574; dishes US$17-23; ⊙6-10pm Tue-Sun) Beautifully presented Puerto Rican food with Asian accents, this Culebra favorite curates a rotating collection of crowd-pleasing dishes, always including fresh fish like grouper and snapper. Be forewarned: Susie's island mash – a side of yucca, malanga and potatoes – is addictive comfort food.

ℹ Information

Banco Popular (📞742-3572; Pedro Márquez; ⊙8:30am-2:30pm Mon & Wed-Fri) There's an ATM here.

Post office (📞742-3862; Pedro Márquez; ⊙8:30am-4:30pm Mon-Fri, to noon Sat) Right in the center of town.

Tourist office (📞742-3116; Pedro Márquez; ⊙8:30am-3:30pm Mon-Fri) Good islandwide information can be found at this booth outside the *alcaldía* (town hall) on the main street, 200 yards from the ferry terminal.

ℹ Getting There & Away

AIR Culebra gets frequent air service from San Juan (US$65 to US$95 one-way) and Ceiba (US$30 to US$45).

Air Flamenco (📞724-1818; www.airflamenco.net) Has frequent charter flights; call for availability.

Vieques Air Link (📞888-901-9247; www.viequesairlink.com) Flies about four times daily to/from San Juan's Isla Grande.

FERRY Maritime Transportation Authority
Culebra (📞742-3161; www.atm.gobierno.pr; ferry dock, Dewey; ⊙8-11am & 1-3pm Mon-Fri); Fajardo (📞863-0705; ⊙8-11am & 1-3pm Mon-Fri) Ferries travel between Fajardo and Culebra thrice daily and take about 1½ hours. Round-trip passenger fares are US$4.50. Boats leave Fajardo daily at 9am, 3pm and 7pm, and Culebra at 6:30am, 1pm and 5pm. A cargo ferry also visits, but Puerto Rican rental-car contracts prohibit taking cars on any ferries to the islands. Schedules change, so confirm times. Good luck trying

GUAVATE

Puerto Ricans speak of Guavate in reverential tones. During the week it's just an unkempt strip of scruffy, shack-like restaurants abutting the Carite Forest. But on weekends a freewheeling atmosphere united around good food, spontaneous dancing and boisterous revelry earns it the designation as the 'Routa del Lechón,' Hwy 184.

Considered the font of traditional Puerto Rican cooking, Guavate is the spiritual home of the island's ultimate culinary 'delicacy,' *lechón asado*, or whole roast pig, locally reared and turning on a spit. Everyone from millionaire businessmen to cigar-puffing *jíbaros* (mountain villagers) congregate for the best in authentic Puerto Rican cuisine and culture. If it's the island's uninhibited 'soul' you're after, look no further.

Visit on weekends between 2pm and 9pm, when old-fashioned troubadours entertain the crowds and live salsa, meringue and reggaeton brings diners to makeshift dance floors for libidinous grooving. With over a dozen restaurants and stalls all offering similar canteen-style food and service, your best bet is to come hungry and follow the crowds.

If you can't choose which *lechónera*, try **El Rancho Original** (☑747-7296; Rte 184 Km 27.5; plates US$6-7; ☑10am-8pm Sat-Sun, with variations), where they serve consistently perfect pork that's heavenly smoky and covered in crispy skin. But, truth be told, the best *lechón* is a debate that's raged on the island for generations and the standard on the 'Pork Highway' is very high.

To get to Guavate from San Juan, follow expressway 52 to exit 31, halfway between Caguas and Cayey. Turn east onto Hwy 184.

to reach a Maritime Transportation Authority employee by phone.

Ticket offices open one hour before departure; arrive at least 30 minutes in advance of sailing.

ⓘ Getting Around

Most of the island's natural attractions are not near the town, so you will need to organize a ride, by either rental car, taxi, or bicycle. *Público* vans are always waiting at the ferry dock and Playa Flamenco.

Willy (☑742-3537) generally meets every ferry and also arrives at your door when booked. Also try **Ray** (☑225-5717) or **Carlos** (☑975-3513).

SOUTHERN & WESTERN PUERTO RICO

A stunning change of scenery awaits you along the southern coast – particularly west of the main city, Ponce. The central mountains tumble down to denuded plains that held sugar plantations in the 1800s. Now there's little to catch the eye – outside of the colonial charms of Ponce – until you arrive at Bosque Estatal de Guánica, a fabulous 'dry forest' that brings to mind southern Arizona. Unbelievably it's little more than an hour's drive from El Yunque's fecund greenery.

Ponce

POP 194,636

Given its fiercely proud, poetic history as the historic center of Puerto Rico's south, it's little wonder that Ponce is the subject of so many lofty declarations. From the mouths of Puerto Rican statesmen to the inscriptions on public fountains, Ponce is 'a city of initiative, understanding and heart' (Eugenio María de Hostos), a place that 'does not repeat history, but improves it' (Rafael Pon Flores) and a 'land of Camelot: ideal, legendary, dreamlike and real' (Antonio Gautier). The locals put it a bit more succinctly. '*Ponce es Ponce*,' they proudly claim and the rest of Puerto Rico is one great big parking lot.

◉ Sights & Activities

Plaza Las Delicias   PUBLIC SQUARE

Within this elegant square you'll discover the heart of the city and two of its landmark buildings: Parque de Bombas and Catedral Nuestra Señora de Guadalupe. Tolling bells follow churchgoers across the square each morning, children squeal around the majestic Fuente de Leones (Fountain of Lions) under the heat of midday and lovers stroll under its lights at night. Even as the commercial banks and the fast-food joints encroach

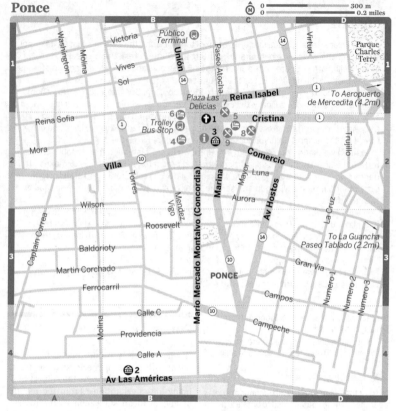

at the edges, reminders of the city's prideful history dominate the plaza's attractions, including marble statues of local *danza* (Victorian parlor music) icon Juan Morel Campos and poet/politician Luis Muñoz Marín, Puerto Rico's first governor. The **Fuente de Leones** was rescued from the 1939 New York World's Fair.

FREE Parque de Bombas   NOTABLE BUILDING
(☎284-3338; ⊙9:30am-5pm) *Ponceños* claim that the eye-popping Parque de Bombas is Puerto Rico's most frequently photographed building – not too hard to believe as you stroll around the black-and-red-striped Arabian-style edifice and make countless, unwitting cameos in family photo albums. The space once housed the city's volunteer firefighters, who are commemorated in a tidy exhibit on the 2nd floor. Today it is a perfect tourist information center – even the most hapless *touristo* can't miss it. Pleasant,

bilingual staff will answer questions and sell you tickets for a trolley that circles the central city's sights.

TOP CHOICE Museo de Arte de Ponce   ART GALLERY
(☎848-0505; www.museoarteponce.org; 2325 Av Las Américas; adult/senior & student US$6/3; ⊙10am-5pm) *Brush Strokes In Flight*, a bold, primary-colored totem by American pop artist Roy Lichtenstein, announces the smartly remodeled MAP, where an expertly presented collection ranks among the best in the Caribbean. It is itself worth making the trip here from San Juan. A US$30-million renovation celebrated the museum's 50th anniversary in 2010 and the smart curation – some 850 paintings, 800 sculptures and 500 prints, presented in provocative historical and thematic juxtapositions – represents five centuries of Western art.

Ponce

🛏 Sleeping

Hotel Meliá　　　　　　　　　HOTEL **$$**
(☑842-0260, 800-44-UTELL; www.hotelmeliapr
.com; 2 Cristina; r incl breakfast US$100-140; P❋
@⊠) Just east of the plaza, this independent, historic hotel might remind you of favorite three-star hotels in Spain and Portugal. The grand lobby is plusher than the basic rooms, but everything is clean and the staff is friendly. Continental breakfast is served on a sunny rooftop deck and the beautifully renovated pool makes an attractive bonus. The 80 rooms are being slowly updated.

Ramada Ponce　　　　　　　　HOTEL **$$**
(☑813-5050; www.ramadaponce.com; cnr Reina Esquina & Av Unión; d incl breakfast US$135-200; P❋🛜⊠) Standing grandly over a corner of the plaza, this historic facade emerged from the scaffolding after years of preservationist dispute. It doesn't escape the bland feel of a chain (cardboard waffles), but the location and clutch of amenities make a great option. The best rooms face the square, with black-and-white tiled floors and balconies; those in the back have tile by way of atmosphere.

Hotel Bélgica　　　　　　　　HOTEL **$$**
(☑844-3255; www.hotelbelgica.com; 122 Villa; r US$70-90; P❋🛜) A travelers' favorite for years, the Bélgica, a 20-room hotel with European-style high ceilings and wrought-iron balconies, is just off the southwest corner of Plaza Las Delicias. Rooms near the front allow you to stare out over the plaza from a private balcony, but be prepared for noise on weekend nights.

✗ Eating 625

TOP CHOICE / Archipielago　　CARIBBEAN FUSION **$$$**
(☑812-882; www.archipielagopr.com; Cristina 76; mains US$15-40; ⊗lunch Wed-Fri, dinner Wed-Sun) With a bird's-eye view above the Parque de Bombas this sleekly designed rooftop restaurant has single-handedly upped the ante on Ponce's fine-dining scene. The blend of Caribbean flavors – chicken and pork stuffed with sweet plantains, an upscale version of local root-vegetable stew and lobster with curry – punch up the menu's more traditional continental plates, like crusted mahimahi. The service is excellent and there's often live music on the weekends. No doubt: Ponce's best.

Cesar's Comida Criolla　　　CARIBBEAN **$**
(near cnr Mayor & Cristina; dishes US$2-14; ⊗lunch) The ultimate hole in the wall for *comida criolla* (traditional Puerto Rican cuisine), this humble joint might be rough around the edges but the savory piles of pork, chicken and seafood (most served with rice and beans) is the city's best home cookin'.

King's Cream　　　　　　　　ICE CREAM **$**
(9223 Marina; cones US$1-3; ⊗8am-midnight) On warm evenings lines stretch down the sidewalk at this institution, located across from Parque de Bombas. Smooth blended tropical licks have big chunks of pineapple, coconut, almond and passion fruit. If the line is too long, there's another location a few blocks north of the plaza on Calle Vives, between Calles Union and Marina.

La Casa de Las Tias　　CARIBBEAN FUSION **$$**
(☑844-3344; 46 Reina Isabel; mains US$15-30; ⊗lunch & dinner) In a cozy historic home, 'the aunts' kitchen is overseen by Wilda Rodriquez, one of Ponce's most creative, least pretentious chefs. The unhurried service and atmosphere may lack a little polish, but whimsical specials (like the fantastic midweek 'Deli & Burger Queens Night') balance traditional and modern Puerto Rican flavors, like the seafood stew and rib eye glazed with a guava reduction.

Café Café　　　　　　　　　　CAFE **$**
(☑841-7185; www.cafecafeponce.com; 2638 Mayor; mains US$15-30; ⊗8:30am-10:30pm Mon-Fri, 11am-3pm Sat) For the best coffee in Ponce and an excellent breakfast, start at this art-filled, bilingual cafe. The coffee beans couldn't be fresher – they're roasted next door – and the egg scrambles are excellent. For lunch try

the *mofongo* 'a caballo,' stuffed with corned beef and topped with a fried egg. When the students are in town, the cobblestone patio is great for mingling.

ⓘ Information

Banks line the perimeter of Plaza Las Delicias, so finding a cash machine is no problem.

Post office (Atocha; ⊘7:30am-4:30pm Mon-Fri, 8:30am-noon Sat)

Puerto Rico Tourism Company (PRTC; ☑284-3338; www.prtourism.com; Parque de Bombas, Plaza Las Delicias; ⊘9am-5:30pm)

ⓘ Getting There & Around

Four miles east of the town center, off Hwy 1 on Hwy 5506, the Aeropuerto de Mercedita (Mercedita Airport) looks dressed for a party, but still waiting for the guests to arrive. **Cape Air** (☑848-2020; www.capeair.net) has four flights a day to San Juan (one-way/return US$87/152) and **jet-Blue** (☑800-538-2583; www.jetblue.com) also services Ponce from a number of American cities.

There's a nice, new *público* terminal three blocks north of the plaza, near Plaza del Mercado, with connections to all major towns. There are plenty of long-haul vans headed to Río Piedras in San Juan (about US$20) and Mayagüez (about US$10).

There are numerous car-rental agencies at the airport.

Bosque Estatal de Guánica

The immense 10,000 acres of the Guánica Biosphere Reserve is one of the island's great natural treasures and its trails are perfect for casual hikes, cycling, bird-watching and broad views of the Caribbean.

The scrubby desert forest is among the best examples of subtropical dry forest vegetation in the world – a fact evident in the variety of flora and fauna. Scientists estimate that only 1% of the Earth's dry forest of this kind remains and the vast acreage makes this a rare sanctuary. It's crossed by 30-odd miles of trails that lead from the arid, rocky highlands, which are covered with scrubby brush, to over 10 miles of remote, untouched coast. Only a two-hour drive from the rainforests of El Yunque, the parched, crumbling landscape makes an unexpected contrast.

To get to the eastern section of the reserve and the **ranger station** (☑821-5706; ⊘9am-5pm), which has trail maps and brochures, follow Hwy 116 south from Hwy 2 toward Guánica town. Turn left (east) onto Hwy 334

and follow this road as it winds up a steep hill through an outlying *barrio* (suburb) of Guánica. Eventually the road crests a hill, ending at the ranger station, a picnic area and a scenic overlook of the forest and the Caribbean.

TOP CHOICE **Mary Lee's by the Sea** (☑821-3600; www.maryleesbythesea.com; 25 San Jacinto; studios from US$120, apt US$250) is one of the most isolated and charming places to stay on the island. On a steep hillside overlooking the Caribbean, each apartment in the guesthouse is appointed with ultra-hip, brightly colored furnishing and many have decks, hammocks, barbecue and sea views. It does not take credit cards.

Rincón

POP 15,000

Shoehorned far out in the island's most psychedelic corner, Rincón is Puerto Rico at its most unguarded, a place where the sunsets shimmer scarlet and the waiters are more likely to call you 'dude' than 'sir.' For numerous California dreamers this is where the short-lived summer of love ended up.

Not surprisingly, Rincón's waves are often close to perfect. Breaking anywhere from 2ft to 25ft, the names are chillingly evocative: Domes, Indicator, Spanish Wall and Dogman's. The crème de la crème is Tres Palmas, a white-tipped monster that is often dubbed the 'temple' of big-wave surfing in the Caribbean.

🏃 Activities

Taíno Divers   DIVING, SNORKELING
(☑823-6429; www.tainodivers.com; Black Eagle Marina; 2-tank dive US$109, snorkeling US$75) Located inside the little marina on the north side of town, this is probably the best outfit on the west coast. Guides are responsible, professional and very environmentally aware. It does almost daily runs to Isla Desecheo (8am to 2pm), a near-uninhabited island off the coast that has very clear water and some of Puerto Rico's best diving. It also does shorter trips to nearby reefs (8am to noon).

West Coast Surf Shop   SURFING
(☑823-3935; www.westcoastsurf.com; 2E Muñoz Rivera) Downtown on the Plaza de Recreo you will find the area's most fully stocked surf shop. Aside from selling all the appropriate gear, the owners have great local knowledge and can organize lessons for any standard or age at short notice.

🛏 Sleeping & Eating

TOP CHOICE **Blue Boy Inn** BOUTIQUE HOTEL $$
(🕿823-2593; www.blueboyinn.com; 556 Black
Eagle St; r US$175-215; P❄🛜) This elegant
little inn near the old marina is an excellent
mid-priced option with very private rooms,
doting staff and the best breakfast around.
It's no good for families (they suggest no
children under 12) or avid surfers (the best
breaks are north of town) but the tiled ter-
races of rooms are tucked hidden among
the leafy gardens and exude a romantic,
secluded atmosphere. In the evening guests
congregate around the outdoor kitchen near
the pool or sit around the fire pit.

Casa Islena BOUTIQUE HOTEL $$
(🕿823-1525; www.casa-islena.com; Hwy 413,
Beach Rd; r incl breakfast US$185-205; P❄@
🛜🏊) A high-class option in the heart of
Rincón's best surfing, Casa Islena is an elegant Mediterranean-style guesthouse on
a magnificent, moody stretch of ocean. A
magnet for discerning, jet-setting surfers,
guests work out the sore muscles at morning yoga under palms and navigate the
walled-in gardens to nine lovely sea-view
rooms. Like all Rinós best, you'll certainly
want to book early.

Lazy Parrot Inn INN $$
(🕿823-5654; www.lazyparrot.com; Hwy 413, Km
4.1; r US$110-155; ❄@🏊) Claiming the mid-
dle ground between high quality and high
quirky, the Lazy Parrot captures the unique
essence of Rincón without scrimping on
home comforts. It occupies the high country
above Rincón Pueblo and offers glimpses of
the sparkling ocean. Rooms are comfortable,
but not flash, and there's a sublime pool and
a great restaurant.

Beside the Pointe HOTEL $$
(🕿823-8550; www.besidethepointe.com; r US$75-
125; P❄🛜) The social centerpiece of Sandy
Beach, this guesthouse has a happening bar
and restaurant, Tamboo Tavern, and rooms
outfitted like small, tiled-floor apartments.
Few have good views, but many have cooking facilities and kitchenettes, and they're
slowly being upgraded with flat-screen TVs.
If you choose a room up front, expect plenty
of background noise after hours.

Horned Dorset Primavera FRENCH FUSION $$$
(🕿823-4030; www.horneddorset.com; Hwy 429
Km 0.3; mains US$30-50; ⊘dinner) Elegant,
exclusive and extraordinary, this is among

Puerto Rico's best fine-dining options –
climb the sweeping staircase to the black-
and-white tiled dining room of billowing
lined drapes and an atmosphere right out
of a colonial Caribbean culinary dream.
The stunning French-influenced food is also
dreamy, relying on a seasonal, daily menu.
Few surf bums turn up here; the clinking
glasses toast marriage proposals and busi-
ness deals, and patrons outfit themselves
accordingly.

☆ Entertainment

TOP CHOICE **Calypso Tropical Café** BEACH BAR
(⊘noon-midnight) Wall-to-wall suntans, svelte
girls in bikini tops, bare-chested blokes
nursing cold beers and syncopated reggae
music drifting out beneath the sun-dappled
palm trees; the Calypso is everything you'd
expect a beachside surfers' bar to be – and
perhaps a little more. On the leafy road to
the El Faro lighthouse, Calypso hosts the
oldest pub scene in Rincón and regularly
books live bands to cover rock, reggae and
calypso classics.

❶ Getting There & Around

Rincón has no airport, but there are two in the
area: Mayagüez and Aguadilla.

The *público* stand is situated just off the town
plaza on Nueva. Expect to pay about US$4 if you
are headed north to Aguadilla or US$1.50 to go
south to Mayagüez (you can access San Juan
from either of these cities).

The easiest way to approach the town is via
the valley roads of Hwy 402 and Hwy 115, both
of which intersect Hwy 2 south of the Rincón
peninsula.

You will pay US$20 or more for a taxi from
either the Aguadilla or Mayagüez airport and you
may prefer a car to move around to the various
attractions in Rincón. There are car-rental sites
at both the Mayagüez and Aguadilla airports.

UNDERSTAND PUERTO RICO

History

Indigenous peoples are thought to have ar-
rived – via a raft from Florida – around the
1st century AD, quickly followed by groups
from the Lesser Antilles. The Taínos created
a sophisticated trading system on the island
they named Borinquen and became the

reigning culture, although they were constantly fighting off Carib invaders.

All that changed forever in 1508, when Juan Ponce de León came back to the island he had glimpsed from one of Christopher Columbus' ships. Driven by a desire for gold, Spanish conquistadores enslaved, murdered, starved and raped natives with impunity. Virtually wiped out by war, smallpox and whooping cough, a few remaining Taínos took to the mountains. Soon Dutch and French traders became frequent visitors, dropping off human cargo from West Africa. By 1530 West African slaves – including members of the Mandingo and Yoruba tribes – numbered about half the population of 3000 in Puerto Rico.

And so it went for several generations. The Spanish-American War of 1898 finally pried Puerto Rico out from under the yoke of the Spanish empire, but it established the small island as a commonwealth of the United States – Borinquen was liberated from Spain, but not quite free.

Operation Bootstrap poured money into the island and set up highways, post offices, supermarkets and a few military posts. Puerto Ricans have accepted the US economic and military presence on their island, with varying degrees of anger, indifference and satisfaction, for more than 100 years now – and the strong *independentista* movement that wanted to cut all ties with the US in the 1950s has mostly receded into the background. The biggest question for Puerto Ricans – a passionately political people who muster at least a 90% voter turnout on election days – is whether to keep the status quo or become, officially, America's 51st state.

In May 2006 a stalemate between Governor Aníbal Acevedo and the Puerto Rican legislature led to a massive budgetary crisis that forced the government to literally shut down after it ran out of funds to pay over 100,000 public-sector employees. The crisis lasted two weeks before a grudging compromise was reached, but it drew intense criticism from business leaders, Puerto Rican celebrities and the general public. Though it was a media sensation on the island, the grand jury investigation that charged Acevedo with corruption eventually found him not guilty.

Today, the global economic crisis has led to devastating unemployment numbers on the island, and the Obama administration has again taken up the long-contentious issue of Puerto Rican statehood.

Culture

As a predominantly Catholic country (albeit widely mixed with African and indigenous practices), Puerto Ricans treasure family values and family pursuits and often have three or more generations living in the same home. But they don't interpret 'family friendly' as being close-minded. They are fiercely and justifiably proud of their mixed European, African and indigenous ancestry – in a country where skin tones range from the darkest coal to freckled white (sometimes even in the same family), it's no mean feat to have created a culture where all are welcome.

Arts

Abundant creative energy hangs in the air over Puerto Rico (maybe it has something to do with the Bermuda Triangle) and its effects can be seen in the island's tremendous output of artistic achievement. Puerto Rico has produced renowned poets, novelists, playwrights, orators, historians, journalists, painters, composers and sculptors. The island's two most influential artists are considered to be rococo painter José Campeche and impressionist Francisco Oller. As well as being a groundbreaking politician, Puerto Rican Governor Luís Moñez Marín was also an eloquent poet. In the world of entertainment Rita Morena is the only Puerto Rican to have won an Oscar, a Grammy, a Tony and an Emmy, while the island's hottest new film talent is actor Benicio del Toro, star of Steven Soderbergh's recent two-part biopic of Che Guevara.

While it's known for world-class art in many mediums, music and dance are especially synonymous with the island.

Landscape & Wildlife
The Land

At 100 miles long and 35 miles wide, Puerto Rico is clearly the little sister of the Greater Antilles (Cuba, Jamaica and Hispaniola). With its four principal satellite islands and a host of cays hugging its shores, Puerto Rico claims approximately 3500 sq miles of land, making the commonwealth slightly larger than the Mediterranean island of Corsica or the second-smallest state in the USA, Delaware.

Puerto Rico has more than a dozen protected wilderness areas, most of which are *reservas forestales* (forest reserves) or *bosques estatales* (state forests). The best known is the 43-sq-mile Caribbean National Forest, generally referred to as El Yunque, which dominates the cloudy-yet-sun-splashed peaks at the east end of the island. Bosque Estatal de Guánica, on the southwest coast, is home to a tropical dry forest ecosystem.

Wildlife

Endangered sea turtles, such as the hawksbill, green and leatherback, nest on Puerto Rican beaches, particularly on the island of Culebra. Puerto Rico's vast coral reefs are the nurseries and feeding grounds for hundreds of species of tropical fish. It offers some of the best places in the world for divers to come face-to-face with large barracudas, manta rays, octopuses, moray eels and nurse sharks.

El Yunque is home to more than 60 species of bird, including the greenish-blue, red-fronted Puerto Rican parrot, which is on the edge of extinction. The coastal dry forest of Guánica features more than 130 bird species, largely songbirds.

Keep your eyes peeled for small-boned Paso Fino horses, brought to the island by the Spanish conquistadores. In many places, but particularly in Vieques, they roam freely across the roads in untamed herds.

SURVIVAL GUIDE

Directory A–Z

Accommodations

There are no hostels in Puerto Rico and very few dorm-style accommodations near local universities. Most options are guesthouses, inns, hotels and *paradores* (midrange to high-end hotels that get regular surprise visits from the tourism board). Rentals are a good idea for long-term guests or big groups. Most hotel rates are for a room where you specify what type of bed you want (double or twin). If you have more than two to a room you'll be charged extra, but solo travelers aren't usually given any price break. National forest camp-

» **Electricity** Puerto Rico has the 110V AC system used in the USA.

» **Newspapers & Magazines** San Juan Star (www.thesanjuanstar.com) is a bilingual daily newspaper. Que Pasa! is a bimonthly magazine put out by the Puerto Rico Tourism Company (PRTC).

» **TV & Radio** American TV is broadcast across the island. Radio is mostly in Spanish; English-language radio station is WOSO San Juan, at 1030AM.

» **Weights & Measures** Puerto Rico follows the imperial system with two exceptions: all distances on road signs are in kilometers and gas (petrol) is pumped in liters.

ground and reservation information can be obtained by calling ☏800-280-2267, but camping is challenging due to the disorganization of the government agencies and poorly maintained facilities.

Accommodations reviews in this chapter are categorized as follows:

$	budget	less than US$75
$$	midrange	US$75 to US$200
$$$	top end	more than US$200

Activities

DIVING & SNORKELING

Three shores of Puerto Rico are surrounded by the Continental shelf and there are plenty of good diving operators scattered around the island. The best places to dive are off Rincón in the south, the scrappy seaside party town of La Parguera in the south and Fajardo in the east, but those short on time will be rewarded with a San Juan shore dive. In San Juan, check out Eco Action Tours and Caribe Aquatic Adventures (p609). In Rincón call by at Taíno Divers (p626). Out east try Culebra Divers (p621) on the island of Culebra, and Blackbeard Sports (p618) in Isabella Segunda on Vieques.

SURFING

Puerto Rico ranks among the best winter surfing locations in the Americas. Close to San Juan surf the beaches east of Isla Verde. For serious surfing go west to Rincón and Isabela.

HIKING

In contrast to national parks in the mainland US, there's no true wilderness in Puerto Rico. The most popular hiking spot is the rainforest at El Yunque (p617), though the paths are short, paved and mild. The commonwealth's *reservas forestales* offer hikes for those who don't mind bushwhacking, but the dry forest in Guánica (p626) is perfect for spotting rare birds. For more adventure hike in the Bosque Estatal Toro Negro, though obtain topographic maps before leaving home.

Business Hours

Reviews in this chapter don't list business hours unless they differ from these standards. Businesses are usually open 8am to 5pm, but there are certainly no hard-and-fast rules.

Banks 8am-4pm Mon-Fri, 9:45am-noon Sat

Bars 2pm-2am Wed-Sat, more days in cities

Government offices 8:30am-4:30pm Mon-Fri

Post offices 8am-4pm Mon-Fri, 8am-1pm Sat

Shops 9am-6pm Mon-Sat, 11am-5pm Sun

Children

Puerto Rico is a safe destination for children, and probably the most comfortable island for families traveling on a modest budget. Some hotels won't take children under a certain age but it's very rare. Several museums and hotels offer child rates. If renting a car, make sure that the agency has a car seat. If taking a taxi any long distance, bring a seat with you. Children should carry ID in case of an emergency.

Dangers & Annoyances

Although street crime is a serious issue in urban areas, visitors need not be obsessed with security. A few commonsense reminders should help keep you secure.

Always lock cars and put valuables out of sight. If your car is bumped from behind in a remote area, it's best to keep going to a well-lit area or service station. Never allow yourself to get in a conflict with another driver in Puerto Rico; road rage can be a serious problem.

Embassies & Consulates

The following are located in San Juan.

Austria (☑766-0799; Plaza Las Américas, Río Piedras)

Canada (☑789-6629; 107 Calle Cereipo Alturas, Guaynabo)

Denmark (☑725-2532; 360 Calle San Francisco, San Juan)

Dominican Republic (☑725-9550; 1612 Ponce de Leon, 7th fl, Hato Rey)

Spain (☑758-6090; Mercantil Plaza, Hato Rey)

UK (☑727-1065; 1509 Calle Lopez Landron, Santurce)

Venezuela (☑766-4255; Mercantil Plaza, Hato Rey)

Food

In this chapter price indicators for Eating reviews are as follows, based on the cost of a main course:

$	budget	less than US$12
$$	midrange	US$12 to US$30
$$$	top end	more than US$30

Gay & Lesbian Travelers

Puerto Rico is among the most gay-friendly places in the Caribbean. San Juan has a well-developed scene, especially in the Condado district, for Puerto Ricans and visitors. Other cities, such as Ponce, have gay-friendly clubs and accommodations as well. Vieques and Culebra are popular destinations for an international mix of gay and lesbian travelers.

Puerto Rico Breeze is a biweekly newspaper on gay nightlife in San Juan.

Health

For emergencies in Puerto Rico call ☑911. Excellent medical facilities are available on the island. A number of hospitals offer emergency rooms and Puerto Rico's *farmacias* are generally well stocked and at North American standards.

There was an outbreak of dengue fever in recent years, but infection rates remain very low. Bring repellent.

Water in Puerto Rico is safe to drink and held to the same purity standards as the mainland United States.

Internet Access

Although internet cafes are quite rare outside San Juan, most public libraries have computers with internet access. Wi-fi is increasingly available in hotels. Popular resort towns such as Rincón, Ponce and Fajardo are extremely well connected.

Language

Both English and Spanish are official languages, although Spanish is primarily spoken. You'll get by in major urban centers with English alone, though a smattering of Spanish will ingratiate travelers with the locals. If venturing to the island's remote corners, take a Spanish phrasebook.

Public Holidays

In addition to holidays observed throughout the region (p872), Puerto Rico also has the following public holidays:

Three Kings Day (Feast of the Epiphany) January 6

Eugenio María de Hostos' Birthday January 10; honors the island educator, writer and patriot

Martin Luther King Jr Day Third Monday in January

Emancipation Day March 22; island slaves were freed on this date in 1873

Palm Sunday Sunday before Easter

Easter Sunday Late March/April

Jose de Diego Day April 18

Memorial Day Last Monday in May

Luis Muñoz Rivera's Birthday July 18; honors the island patriot and political leader

Jose Celso Barbosa's Birthday July 27; honors the father of the Puerto Rican statehood movement

Labor Day First Monday in September

Columbus Day Second Monday in October

Thanksgiving Fourth Thursday in November

Telephone

The Puerto Rican area code is ☎787. To call from North America dial ☎1-787 plus the seven-digit local number. From elsewhere dial your country's international access code followed by ☎787 plus the local number. To call within Puerto Rico, just dial the local number.

American cell phones work on US networks without extra charges.

Travelers with Disabilities

Puerto Rico is generally compliant with the American Disabilities Act. Most modern hotels have at least one room set up for travelers with disabilities.

Visas

US residents don't need visas to enter Puerto Rico. Canadians don't need visas for stays of up to 180 days, as long as they aren't working or studying during that period. Citizens of most European countries, Australia and New Zealand can waive visas through the Visa Waiver program. All non-US and Canadian travelers planning to stay for longer than 90 days need a visa: contact the closest US embassy and be prepared to pay US$140.

Women Travelers

Puerto Rican women crisscross the island all the time by themselves, so you won't be the only solo woman on the ferry or public bus. But as a foreigner you will attract a bit more attention. If you don't want the company, most men will respect a firm but polite 'no thank you.'

Getting There & Away

Entering Puerto Rico

US nationals need proof of citizenship (such as a driver's licence with photo ID) to enter Puerto Rico, but be aware that if traveling to another country in the Caribbean (other than the US Virgin Islands, which, like Puerto Rico, is a US territory), you require a valid passport in order to reenter the US. Visitors from other countries must have a valid passport to enter Puerto Rico.

Air

AIRPORTS

Puerto Rico is the most accessible island in the Caribbean, with three major airports and several small ones.

Luis Muñoz Marín International Airport (http://www.san-juan-airport.com) San Juan's recently modernized airport – commonly shortened to LMM – lies just 2 miles beyond the eastern border of the city, in the beachfront suburb of Isla Verde.

Aeropuerto Rafael Hernández Aguadilla's airport is at the former Ramey Base on the island's northwest tip. It has some international flights from the US, mainly New York.

Aeropuerto Mercedita Ponce's airport has stepped up its number of flights recently, with direct red-eye service to Chicago and New York.

Aeropuerto Eugenio María de Hostos
In Mayagüez, this airport mostly makes regional connections.

AIRLINES

San Juan is served by a number of North American carriers. The most popular routes to Puerto Rico from the US are via New York and Miami, but direct flights from about a dozen other cities in the continental US also serve the island. Some carriers now offer continued service through San Juan to Ponce and Aguadilla, or they fly directly into Aguadilla's airport. Almost all major carriers fly to Puerto Rico; JetBlue is currently the most popular and economical option. British Airways has twice-weekly services from London; Iberia flies from Madrid.

Puerto Rico is linked to Antigua, Barbados, Haiti and Jamaica through the following airlines:

Air Sunshine (www.airsunshine.com)

American Airlines (www.aa.com)

Cape Air (www.flycapeair.com)

Caribbean Air Lines (www.caribbean-airlines .com)

Sea

San Juan is the second-largest port for cruise ships in the western hemisphere (after Miami). Scores of vessels call San Juan their home or departure port and every year new cruise ships either originate sailings from San Juan or make San Juan a port of call.

Getting Around

Air

On an island the size of Yellowstone National Park, getting around by airplane is pretty superfluous (and not particularly en-

vironmentally friendly). The bulk of Puerto Rico's domestic air traffic links San Juan to the islands of Culebra and Vieques.

Air Flamenco (www.airflamenco.net) Flies to destinations in Puerto Rico, including Vieques, Culebra, Ponce and Mayagüez, and other Caribbean islands, such as St Thomas and St Croix.

Vieques Air Link (www.viequesairlink.com) Fares to Vieques are US$63 each way; fares to Culebra are about US$65.

Boat

The **Maritime Transport Authority** (☑800-981-2005, 863-0705) handles the solid and safe ferry service from Fajardo to Vieques and Culebra. Passenger ferries run three to four times daily.

Car

Car rental costs about US$45 to US$75 per day. A valid driver's license issued from your country of residence is all that's needed to rent. Good highways link San Juan to just about every other major point, with a drive of less than two hours. Do not take a rental car on the ferry to Vieques or Culebra, as it will void the contract with your rental agent.

Although drivers are more aggressive than those in the United States, and secondary road conditions can be very poor, Puerto Rico has the same basic rules of the road as the States: cars drive on the right side of the road and drivers sit on the left side of the vehicle. Puerto Rico has more cars per square mile than any other place on Earth, so be prepared for traffic jams.

Público

Públicos – large vans that pick up and drop off passengers with great frequency and little haste – run between a few of the major cities, but it's a very slow (although cheap) way to travel.

Saba

Best Places to Eat

» Eden (p640)

» Swinging Doors (p640)

» Rainforest Restaurant
(p640)

» Saba Coffee House (p641)

Best Places to Stay

» El Momo Cottages (p638)

» Cottage Club (p639)

» Shearwater Resort (p639)

Why Go?

There once was a man and a woman who lived in a perfect garden. They were welcome in this idyllic thicket so long as they didn't eat the fruit of one particular tree. You probably know the rest of the story, but what you didn't know is that although Adam and Eve ruined it for the rest of us, you can still have the chance to find your way back to Eden.

Paradise takes the form of a spiky volcanic peak called Saba (pronounced 'say-bah'), whose winning combination of ocean vistas and white-green-brown architecture sits but a mere 15-minute flight from the garish casinos and condominiums on nearby St-Martin/Sint Maarten. And just when you thought that nothing could be more beautiful than the island's jagged landscape, dive down below to find a colorful kingdom of neon coral that teems with fat reef sharks, sea turtles and slippery fish.

When to Go

From February to April, there are cool Caribbean breezes, and colorful fish spawn below the ocean's surface. From July to September there is surprisingly pleasant weather when compared to the neighboring islands. In October, come for the the islandwide 'Sea & Learn' project. In November, bask in the pre-season rush after the hurricanes clear out.

Fast Facts

» **Area** 13 sq km

» **Population** 1500

» **Capital** The Bottom

» **Telephone country code** ✆599

» **Emergency** ✆111

Set Your Budget

» **Budget hotel room** US$65

» **Two-course evening meal** US$45

» **Two-tank dive** US$104

» **Beer** US$4

» **Taxi from airport to Windwardside** US$12

Resources

» **Saba GIS** (www.sabagis .org)

» **Saba Park** (www.saba park.org)

» **Saba Tourism** (www .sabatourism.com)

» **Sea Saba** (www.seasaba .com)

Itineraries

ONE DAY

First, shed a tear that you only have a day to explore this incredible island. Then meet up with one of the dive boats for a two-tank half-day trip out to some of the finest reefs and submerged pinnacles in the Caribbean. Break for a leisurely lunch amid chatty locals in Windwardside and – if you have enough energy – take a stab at the Sandy Cruz Trail in the late afternoon.

THREE DAYS

Pick a hotel in Windwardside and spend your first day walking around the small town (be sure to stop by Jo Bean's glass studio to say hello), then head out into the bush for a rugged hike up to the top of Mt Scenery. Spend the mornings of the following two days scuba diving with numerous reef sharks around sunken pinnacles; afternoons are best spent curled up with a good novel under the warm Caribbean sun.

ONE WEEK

Spend the greater part of the week blowing bubbles with sharks, rays, barracuda and sea turtles. Take a day off and organize a guided hike through Saba's rugged forests. In the evenings hit up Windwardside's restaurants, then retreat to your cliffside cottage or colonial-style inn and click through your camera's postcard-worthy scenery shots, taken earlier in the day.

GETTING TO NEIGHBORING ISLANDS

Daily flights and regular ferry services connect Saba and St-Martin/Sint Maarten, from where you can take boats or planes to reach the other island destinations in the vicinity.

Essential Food & Drink

» **Homemade rum** Be sure to try one of the many homemade rums, which are often flavored with locally grown banana, mango, vanilla or 'Saba spice.' Most restaurants and hotels have their own special brew.

» **Soursop & Saba lemon** You'll find a mix of interesting fruits growing on the island, including soursop and Saba lemon. Don't miss homemade soursop ice cream. Grab a Saba lemon off a drooping tree, scratch the peel, and take a deep, satisfying whiff of the zest.

» **Themed dinners** The restaurants in Windwardside take turns cooking up themed meals – there's burger night at Tropics Cafe, BBQ night at Swinging Doors and sushi Saturdays at Brigadoon among several other choices.

Flat Point

The aptly named Flat Point is precisely that: a flat point (Saba's only flat point, in fact), and the perfect place to plunk down an airport. The **Juancho E Yrausquin Airport** has the tiniest commercial runway in the entire world, measuring a mere 400m, and

by the time you figure out how to pronounce the airport's name, you'll have already landed on St-Martin/Sint Maarten. There's a small bar called **Flight Deck** inside the airport should you need a couple of frosty ones to ease your jitters before taking off; it's open one hour before and after each flight. Planes departing Saba don't actually lift off

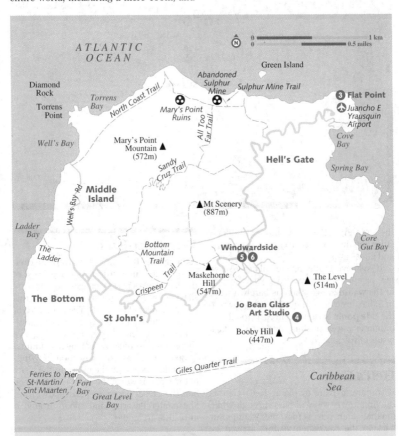

Saba Highlights

❶ Explore the island's dramatic vertical peak and score killer views of the sea below on an afternoon of **hiking** (p638)

❷ Hit the waves and **dive** (p637) among stunning, submerged pinnacles that teem with nurse sharks and large colorful fish

❸ Experience the thrill of **landing on the world's smallest runway** (p635), at Flat Point, then hold your breath when you depart as the plane drives off the side of a cliff

❹ Head to **Jo Bean Glass Art Studio** (p636) – a charming menagerie of colorful doodads – and become a glass-blowing

whiz under the tutelage of the eponymous artist

❺ Savor themed homespun fare during an **evening meal in Windwardside** (p639)

❻ Learn about the island's history and wildlife at a spirited **slideshow presentation** (p638)

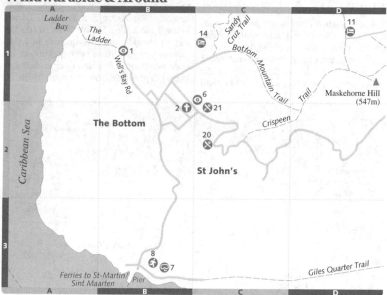

the ground; rather, the runway suddenly stops and the aircraft drives over a sheer cliff and glides away.

If you have a little time to kill before leaving, or after you arrive, leave your luggage in the waiting area ('theft' is barely a word in Saba's lexicon) and quickly hike down to the **tide pools** beside the airport. You'll find dramatic waves crashing against the thick beads of volcanic rock.

Hell's Gate

If you are arriving by plane, Hell's Gate is the first 'town' you will pass through while making your way across the island. But back in the day, when visitors arrived by boat, Hell's Gate was the furthest settlement from the docks. The village earned its infernal name due to the fact that it was absolutely hellish to lug parcels all the way here after they arrived by boat; it would often take an entire day for the residents of Hell's Gate to schlep their shipments across the volcano. Today, this teeny village is mostly residential, with a smattering of private cottages available for holiday rental (see www. sabatourism.com/cottages.html for more information).

Windwardside

Although the Bottom is technically the capital of Saba, Windwardside is where most of the action takes place. Chances are – if you're sleeping on Saba – you'll be staying in this quaint hamlet of red roofs. The main area of town features all of the traveler necessities: banks, convenience stores, a post office, dive shops, a tourist office and many restaurants.

Booby Hill, a small subsection of Windwardside, sits just up the hill from the heart of town and is worth the short trek to check out the stellar views – particularly from Shearwater Resort – and snoop around a nifty little art studio.

◉ Sights

Though light on sights, Windwardside has a couple of gems that are worth checking out when you're in the mood to take a break from reading your book on your balcony.

Jo Bean Glass Art Studio   GALLERY
(☑416-2490; www.jobeanglassart.com; Booby Hill) Local artist, Jo Bean, works out of her colorful studio up on Booby Hill. Discover how she works her magic during a half-day glass-blowing course (US$85), in which you'll be set up with a torch and an unlimited supply

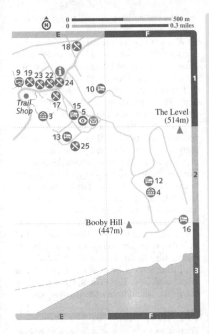

of thin glass shafts that you melt down into swirling balls or cylinders. After you graduate the tutorial, you can start making beads of all shapes and sizes while incorporating gold foil and other quirky objects from around the shop. When the class is done, you'll proudly wear your creations home on a string of leather around your neck.

The best part about the experience is hanging out with Jo Bean, a magnetic character who'll cheer you on as you fumble over your first beads, and dish out an inordinate amount of praise when you finally make a glass pearl that doesn't look like a booger. If you don't have enough time to devote to a course, be sure to pick up a little glass frog, which sits on a rounded bead perfect for a necklace.

Harry L Johnson Museum   MUSEUM
(admission US$2; ⊗10am-noon & 1-4pm Mon-Fri)
This museum sits just down the hill behind Scout's Place, surrounded by wildflowers, including black-eyed Susans, the island's official flower. The small museum sits in a 160-year-old Saban home, which has the typical pearly white facade, green-shuttered windows and earthy, clay-colored roof. The collection features a smattering of vintage B&W photographs, an 'authentic' Saban kitchen, an old piano and scores of antiques from Victorian times.

Lace Ladies   GUILD
(⊗4pm Thu) If you are interested in traditional handicrafts, there is a small legion of older women on the island who spend their leisure hours creating Saban lace, which uses a special stitching technique that has been passed down for a few generations. These women, known locally as the Lace Ladies, gather weekly at the Eugenius Centre, across the street from the RBTT Bank, for their stitching bee and visitors are more than welcome to stop by.

🏃 Activities

Diving
Although it seems hardly possible when you first approach Saba by air or ferry, this stunning volcanic island might even be more scenic below the ocean's surface. Divers and

adventurous snorkelers can find a bit of everything at 26 varied dive sites: steep wall dives just offshore, amazing submerged pinnacles, and varied marine life ranging from sharks to stingrays to turtles.

The Saba Marine Park has protected the area since 1987. It's the only self-supporting marine park in the world, maintained by a US$4 fee charged for each dive; a small price to pay for the pristine conditions. There is no individual diving on Saba; all divers must register with the **Saba Marine Park office** (Fort Bay; ☺8am-noon & 1-5pm Mon-Fri, 8am-noon Sat) and go through a dive operator.

For snorkelers, Well's Bay (p641) and the adjacent Torrens Point are popular spots, and there's even a marked underwater trail. Ladder Bay is also popular, but it's a good 30-minute hike down to the shore from the road and double that back up.

Two of three diving outfits have their offices in Windwardside (the third is based in Fort Bay).

TOP CHOICE **Sea Saba**   DIVING

(☎416-2246; www.seasaba.com; ☺9am-5pm Mon-Sat) This pick of the litter gets our endorsement for its unwavering dedication to its clientele. In addition, it is passionate about marine education and keeping Saba a pristine place to visit.

Saba Divers   DIVING

(☎416-2741; www.sabadivers.com; ☺9am-5pm Mon-Sat) Based at Scout's Place, this is a popular choice and has outgoing staff. The website has detailed listings of dive sites. Offers free nitrox.

Hiking

Saba is a hiker's paradise. Many of the trails have been around for centuries, and were

SABA SLIDESHOWS

For a crash course on all things Saba, look no further than the island's coveted evening slideshows. On Mondays starting at 5:30pm, the folks from Sea Saba discuss the island's history and undersea wonders during a spirited evening session at Brigadoon restaurant. On Wednesday evenings, it's the Ecolodge Rendez-Vous' turn, where discussions lean more towards Saba's wondrously diverse climates and forests that cloak the volcano.

used by the earliest settlers to get from village to village.

When you're hiking, dress in layers, wear sturdy walking shoes and bring water. Some hikers might appreciate a walking stick. Stay on the trails, as they traverse private land.

Before setting out on any hike, start at the Trail Shop (p640) for endless information and maps on Saba's hiking trails.

After Mt Scenery, the most popular hikes include the Sulphur Mine Trail, a moderately strenuous hike past hot springs to an abandoned sulfur mine (exploration of the mine is highly inadvisable), and the relatively easy Sandy Cruz Trail, the locals' favorite trail, which leads past the deserted old village ruins of Mary's Point (p642).

The only trail you shouldn't attempt without a guide is the North Coast Trail. All of the other trails are accessible to experienced hikers. It's not illegal to hike on Saba without hiring 'Crocodile James' Johnson, but it might as well be. This fifth-generation Saban knows the island better than anyone else.

🛏 Sleeping

There are six places to stay in Windwardside, all of which have their own unique flavor. If you're looking for a bit more privacy, there are several holiday cottage rentals scattered throughout town, all of which have the archetypal Saban gingerbread architecture. Check out www.sabatourism.com/cottages/html for more information.

El Momo Cottages   COTTAGES $

(☎416-2265; www.elmomocottages.com; s/d cottage with shared bathroom US$55/65, with private bathroom from US$70/85; ❄@🔊🏊) The small clusters of cottages at El Momo are hidden along a steep, rugged hill smothered in juicy tropical foliage. You'll need a sherpa to haul your luggage up the myriad stone steps to your cabin. Seriously. After cursing under your breath and grabbing your chest to make sure you're not having a heart attack, you'll be rewarded with lovely views of the craggy island and churning sea. The highest cabin – the 'Cottage in the Sky' – is positively breathtaking and oozes rustic romantic charm. Solar-heated outdoor showers, hand built by the previous owners, ensure a clear, private view of the ocean while you suds up, but don't leave your organic soap in the bathroom – it will be devoured by mysterious forest critters during the night.

Shearwater Resort
HOTEL $$$

(☎416-2498; http://shearwater-resort.com; Booby Hill; r US$195-275; ❄@🛜🏊) The highest hotel in the Netherlands, Shearwater Resort is precariously perched atop a craggy cliff with the sea churning 750m below. Run by the affable Paul and his adorable sidekick/dog Maggie, this welcoming spot feels almost Mediterranean with its endless ocean vistas and gentle breezes that flirt with your bedroom's white silk curtains. All modern comforts and conveniences have been accounted for. The hotel also has a small restaurant called **Bistro del Mare**, where you'll be treated to a scrumptious meal overflowing with fresh ingredients.

Cottage Club
COTTAGES $$

(☎416-2386; www.cottage-club.com; s/d/q US$110/120/120; ❄🛜🏊) This quaint collection of spacious, Saba-style cottages sits on a quiet, palm-fringed spot accented by a welcoming swimming pool. Cottages 1 and 2 offer magnificent views of the sea below – you can even catch a glimpse of the airplanes taking their perilous leap off the cliff's edge! In the morning, guests gather around the long wooden table in the lobby for a tasty breakfast with the kind managers, who are keen to dispense valuable info about Saba's sights and activities.

Juliana's
HOTEL $$

(☎416-2269; www.julianas-hotel.com; s/d from US$110/135; ❄@🛜🏊) Juliana's has a sociable vibe centered on the turquoise lap pool, which is also home to the resident giant inflatable swan. The comfortable rooms and prim, private cottages, all in the classic Saban gingerbread-house style, get plenty of sun and offer majestic views of the sea. Each comes with a TV and terrace.

🌿 Ecolodge Rendez-Vous
COTTAGES $

(☎416-3348; www.ecolodge-saba.com; Crispeen Trail; cottages US$95-115; 🛜🏊) If staying deep in the forest at a place powered by solar panels sounds better than having a TV and phone in your room, then these green-conscious cabins might be the perfect place for you. The colorful cottages are covered in beautiful bright murals and all feature individual nature-related themes. One downside to staying at the ecolodge, though, is the lack of awesome ocean vistas available at most of the other accommodations. If you decide that it's a tad too rustic for your taste, be

CROCODILE JAMES

He approaches slowly, raising one eyebrow and wielding a large machete-like knife – he's James Johnson, known as 'Crocodile James,' Saba's official trail ranger. Clad head to toe in khaki (which, according to legend, he only washes twice a year), he quickly plunks down his blade, warmly shakes your hand and whisks you away into the wilds of the island's jungle. A fifth-generation Saban, James knows the terrain oh-so intimately, and his unique tours are a quirky blend of history and biology – be ready for some off-trail trekking and prep your taste buds for sampling local vegetation.

The **guided tours** are US$50 for two people (additional trekkers cost US$15 each), and last anywhere from one to four hours depending on your stamina (James could trek all the way through 'til tomorrow – it's in his Saban genes). Call ☎416-5428 to make arrangements.

sure to swing by the on-site Rainforest Restaurant for an organic/-asmic meal.

Scout's Place
HOTEL $$

(☎416-2740; www.sabadivers.com; d incl breakfast US$109-143; ❄@🛜) This lively 14-room hotel is owned by the same German couple who runs Saba Divers. There are three categories of rooms: the cheapest have a refrigerator, cable TV, wi-fi and ceiling fan, while the spacious private cottages have grand four-poster beds and balconies with ocean views. Ask about renting out the adjacent cottage if you're traveling with your family or a small group. Diving packages are also on offer.

🍴 Eating & Drinking

Windwardside has the largest conglomeration of dining and drinking options on the island.

It's always best to book your dinner plans in advance: Saba's food shipments are sometimes limited and most restaurants only cook enough food each evening for guests with reservations; restaurants also sometimes close unexpectedly for the evening due to a variety of reasons. The hosts at each hotel are always happy to book your dining plans for you.

There's usually one restaurant each evening that offers a special dinner deal of some sort.

Eden
FUSION **$$$**

(☑416-2539; www.edensaba.com; mains US$19-30; ☺dinner Wed-Mon) Gourmet-caliber cuisine on a lonely Caribbean island? Yes, this family-run restaurant has done the impossible with its short list of palate-pleasing dishes. When dusk turns to night soft torch lighting comes on as patrons savor perfected fusion fare. Tax and service are included in the menu's prices.

Swinging Doors
BBQ **$$**

(☑416-2506; mains US$10-20, BBQ dinners US$15; ☺lunch & dinner) Enter through the saloon-style swinging doors and grab a picnic table in the side courtyard for a tasty assortment of dishes that are one step above the usual pub grub. Tuesdays and Fridays feature cheap chicken and ribs, while Sundays are a must – the owner, Eddy, helms the grill and churns out juicy slabs of steak.

Rainforest Restaurant
FUSION **$$$**

(☑416-3348; www.ecolodge-saba.com; Ecolodge Rendez-Vous, Crispeen Trail; mains US$20-27; ☺breakfast, lunch & dinner Tue-Sun) A soul-cleansing meal here is a must. Virtually all of the food is homegrown, and the ever-changing menu features an assortment of international dishes ranging from Asian curries to hearty English breakfasts. Try the tea made from herbs and spices that were plucked minutes earlier from the garden.

Saba Snack
FAST FOOD **$**

(mains US$7-12; ☺lunch & dinner) Billed as a snack stall and loved by the legions of local students, this Dominican-run cantina spins budget-friendly meals of the fast-food variety. Don't miss the succulent chicken burrito, which comes with gut-busting sides of rice and beans.

Brigadoon
INTERNATIONAL **$$$**

(☑416-2380; thebrig@unspoiledqueen.com; mains from US$15; ☺6:30-11pm Wed-Mon) Those who visit the Brig are looking for a quality meal and aren't afraid to drop a few extra bucks on it. Chef Michael Chaamaa brings together an assortment of dishes from all over the world, ranging from fresh lobster to garlicky falafel. Thursday nights feature succulent prime ribs, and Saturday night sushi hour (times vary) is a force to be reckoned with.

Scout's Place
INTERNATIONAL **$$**

(mains US$7-25; ☺breakfast, lunch & dinner) The food isn't anything to write home about, but Friday nights are not to be missed – locals pile in for an evening of karaoke (commonly called 'scary-oke'). Wolfgang, the owner, commandeers the microphone and belts out classics with the utmost seriousness. If you're on the island in October or November, drop by to watch contestants battle it out during 'Saba Idol.'

Tropics Cafe
BURGERS **$$**

(mains US$5-18; ☺breakfast daily, lunch & dinner Tue-Sun) Edging Juliana's lap pool, Tropics has some great eats for very reasonable prices. Friday nights are busy, with a US$10 deal that gets you a delicious burger and drive-in-style movie projected onto a makeshift screen. If you chance upon a 'Caribbean night,' you'll be rewarded with scrumptious lobster pasta worthy of the finest seafood restaurants in the Caribbean.

Saba's Treasure
PIZZA **$**

(pizzas from US$10; ☺lunch & dinner Mon-Sat) The interior of this little cheapie feels like the hull of a wooden frigate. Choose from the assortment of dishes – though the pizza is tops – and wash it down with a beer.

Big Rock Market
SUPERMARKET **$**

(☺8am-7pm Mon-Sat) For a picnic lunch, hit Windwardside's largest grocery store, and browse the relatively impressive selection of international food and wine.

❶ Information

Post office (☺8am-noon & 1-5pm Mon-Fri, to noon Sat)

RBTT Bank (☺8:30am-3:30pm Mon-Fri) Has a 24-hour ATM.

Saba Tourist Bureau (☑416-2231; www.sabatourism.com; ☺8am-5pm Mon-Fri)

Trail Shop (☺10am-4pm Mon-Fri, to 2pm Sat & Sun) Located at the west end of Windwardside, this helpful outpost stocks a large selection of maps, books and souvenirs. It's a nonprofit organization set up by the Saba Conservation Foundation.

Mt Scenery

The tippy top of very-vertical Saba, Mt Scenery (887m) is officially the highest point in the Netherlands. Views from the summit are definitely worth the climb. The peak offers three distinct vistas: Windwardside, the Bottom and Hell's Gate.

The climb to Mt Scenery is the island's most popular hike. It's a three-part climb that starts in the Bottom; the first part is called the Bottom Mountain Trail, while the second leg is the Crispeen Trail. The third and final part of the trail (which is the leg that most people do) starts behind the Trail Shop in Windwardside, and goes straight up until you reach the ethereal cloud forest. The best time to head out is about 9am or 10am, so you can reach the peak at around noon, the least cloudy part of the day, for a view that will make the pain in your calves well worth it.

St John's

Little St John's, straddling a crooked cliff between Windwardside and the Bottom, was created when the locals could not decide where to build the island's school. Residents of each community squabbled over the matter for quite some time, and when no resolution was found, everyone compromised and constructed the school halfway between the villages. A simple cluster of gingerbread houses sits around the classroom buildings; besides that, there's one joint, **Lollipop's Bar and Restaurant** (mains from US$10; ☺infrequent), where you can grab some chow. Hit the restaurant up for mouthwatering fish cakes and excellent ocean scenery, or stop by on a Sunday for the filling brunch.

The Bottom

The Bottom is Saba's official capital, and houses the island's administrative and governmental buildings. The police station is located here (not that the island has any crime); the large bell in the front yard was rung every hour on the hour until the 1990s.

Today, the Bottom is largely the domain of students studying at Saba Medical College, an accredited university offering the first 2½ years of medical education in a course that is on par with those offered at US or Canadian medical schools. The 400 students give the island some much-appreciated revenue. Snoop around the village for cheap eats as prices are slashed for the thrifty wannabe doctors.

◎ Sights

Saba Artisan Foundation   GUILD
(☺8:30am-4pm Mon-Thu, to 3:30pm Fri) Well worth the trip down to the Bottom, the Saba Artisan Foundation is a small guild of women who produce an eclectic assortment

of Saba-specific souvenirs. Standout items include gorgeous silk-screened bags and sheets, and the island's trademark lacework.

Catholic Church   CHURCH
It's worth stopping by the Bottom's Catholic church to check out what the locals refer to as 'Saba's Sistine Chapel.' Heleen Cornet, a respected local artist, spent two long years painting the church's altar with scenes that fuse images from the Saban jungle with biblical themes. Visit her website at www.hele encornet.com.

🛏 Sleeping & Eating

Queen's Garden Resort   HOTEL $$$
(✍416-3494; www.queensaba.com; ste US$250-475; ❄@⸙❄) A 12-unit luxury resort set up a small hill overlooking the Bottom, the beautiful Queen's Garden Resort is the choice retreat for royalty when it visits the island. Gorgeous views accompany rooms equipped with upholstered furniture and a separate living space. The pièce de résistance is the semi-outdoor Jacuzzi in each suite. The hotel's restaurant (open for breakfast and lunch daily, and for dinner Tuesday through Sunday) serves an elegant lineup of dishes – it's pricey, but worth the dough for a romantic soiree.

Saba Coffee House   CAFE $
(mains US$3-9; ☺breakfast, lunch & dinner Sun-Fri; ☏) A welcome addition to Saba's friendly dining scene, Saba Coffee House is geared towards the island's famished medical students who swing by in droves to devour copious cappuccinos. The best part? Everything's under US$10 – even the tasty crabmeat sandwiches and hearty fish-and-chips. Come early in the day before it runs out of stock!

❶ Information

AM Edwards Medical Center (✍416-3239) Offers medical services.

Saba Marine Park Hyperbaric Chamber (✍416-3288; ☺24hr) The region's only hyperbaric facility. On the right side of the road as you enter the Bottom from Windwardside.

Well's Bay

As stunning as Saba is, the spike-shaped island doesn't have a beach to call its own. Well, there's Well's...sort of. After a large storm walloped the island in 1999, a small stretch of grainy sand began to appear and disappear with the tide. Commonly known

MARY'S POINT RUINS

A generation ago Saba was even more isolated than it is now. One village, Mary's Point, was a 45-minute walk from even the next village. In 1934 the Dutch government decided to move every single villager and house to an area behind Windwardside known as the 'Promised Land,' thus lessening the isolation of being so far from any other signs of civilization. You can see the ruins of Mary's Point while hiking on the Sandy Cruz Trail.

among Sabans as 'Wandering Beach,' this cobbled stretch of beach-ish terrain is more of a tourist attraction than a place to recline with a good book. If you plan to walk down to the 'beach' (locals often make the bunny-ear quotation marks with their fingers when referring to Well's Bay), make sure you arrange for someone to pick you up – climbing back up the steep-even-by-Saba-standards hill will be extremely arduous.

While you're visiting, check out **Diamond Rock**, a giant swirling pinnacle bursting skyward from below the waves just offshore. The torpedo-shaped mass is noticeably light in color, the result of years of guano bombardment by resident birds – don't let the locals trick you into thinking that they paint it white to warn watercraft not to crash into it.

Ladder Bay

Before Fort Bay became Saba's official port, everything – from a Steinway piano to Queen Beatrix herself – was hauled up to the Bottom via the **Ladder**, a vertical staircase of over 800 steps. The area is now a moderately difficult trail that heads past an **abandoned customs house** and affords hikers beautiful views.

Fort Bay

A mishmash of concrete structures, electrical parts and oil drums, Fort Bay is Saba's main port and probably the ugliest place on the entire island. Those arriving by ferry will pass through here first before being carted up the crag; divers will also pass through before heading out to sea.

The **Saba Marine Park office** (◷8am-noon & 1-5pm Mon-Fri, 8am-noon Sat) has a few brochures to give away, and it also sells marine-park-logo T-shirts and books on diving.

Saba's third diving outfit, **Saba Deep** (☑416-3347; www.sabadeep.com; ◷9am-5pm Mon-Sat), runs its operation from Fort Bay.

UNDERSTAND SABA

History

Saba was intermittently inhabited by the Siboneys, Arawaks and Caribs before Columbus sailed past the island on his second voyage to the New World. Although English pirates and French adventurers briefly inhabited the island, it wasn't until 1640 that the Dutch set up a permanent settlement, the remains of which are still scattered around the island.

Saba changed hands a dozen times or so over the next 200 years, resulting in mostly Irish and English settlers, but Dutch ownership. Life on Saba was difficult at best. Many of the men made their living from the sea, leaving so many women on the island that it became known as 'The Island of Women.'

Because the steep topography of the island precluded large-scale plantations, colonial-era slavery was quite limited on Saba. Those colonists who did own slaves generally had only a few and often worked side by side with them in the fields, resulting in a more integrated society than on larger Dutch islands.

The close-knit community beat seemingly impossible conditions and thrived in this little outpost. Tourism found Saba when an airport was built in 1959, but it wasn't until 1970 that Saba got uninterrupted electricity.

Saba was a part of the Netherlands Antilles until 2005, when the five islands (Saba, Curaçao, Bonaire, Sint Eustatius and Dutch Sint Maarten) met on the Jesurun Referendum to decide the fate of the Netherlands Antilles. Saba, along with Bonaire, voted overwhelmingly to become administered directly by the Netherlands. In October 2010, after many round-table discussions during the previous two years, the Netherlands Antilles was officially dissolved. Saba, along with Sint Eustatius and Bonaire became 'special municipalities' of the Netherlands, which effectively strengthened the bond between these islands and the mainland. As 'overseas countries and territories' they now share similar rights to those living in Holland and have a more closely linked government system. On January 1, 2011 Saba adopted the US dollar as its currency.

Culture

Most locals are descendants of British, Irish, Dutch and Scandinavian settlers.

Coming to Saba feels more like visiting an 18th-century Celtic village than a Caribbean island. White houses with clay-colored roofs and green-trimmed shutters abound in a *Truman Show* kinda way, but it's all very charming and extremely photogenic. Locals drive leisurely along streets, honking their horns to greet neighbors and friends. After a week of vacationing on the island, you'll be waving at all of the locals as well.

Sabans enjoy a relatively high standard of living. The island is tolerant of differences, an attitude that started hundreds of years ago when slave and master had to work side by side to allow the island to thrive.

Most Sabans attend one of six churches on the island: three Roman Catholic, two Anglican and one Seventh Day Adventist.

Saba has a small handicraft scene, and locals produce and sell beautiful items such as handblown glass, Saban lace and island paintings. In Windwardside you'll have the opportunity to participate in a glass-blowing class at Jo Bean Glass Art Studio.

Saba's most famous craft is lace making, a skill that was brought to Saba in the 1870s by a woman who'd been sent to live in a Venezuelan convent. Older women in the community still weave the lace in their spare time.

Landscape & Wildlife

Six separate temperate zones exist on Saba. Starting with steep cliffs that seem to shoot out of the ocean, the land progresses to grassy meadows, slopes with little vegetation, and up to hilltops, rainforests and the cloud forest covering the top of Mt Scenery.

For a place this small, there is an enormous amount of mammal, fish, bird and plant life on and surrounding the island, both native and introduced. Rare wild orchids peek out along the road or in the rainforest, and oleander and hibiscus flowers are endemic. The elephant-ear plant has shade-bearing leaves as big as...well, elephant ears.

Bird-watchers will enjoy spotting the plethora of avian life overhead as much as

they'll enjoy saying their names: sooty terns, brown boobies, brown noddies, banana quits and pearly eyed thrashers are a handful of the 60 species of birds that call Saba home. Keep an eye out at higher elevations for hummingbirds, and at lower elevations for red-tailed hawks. Saba has its own unique reptile, the skittish little brown anoles lizard, seen scurrying around everywhere.

But perhaps the best thing about Saban wildlife is the obvious lack of a certain pest: mosquitoes are, by and large, absent.

Environmental Issues

Sabans are extremely environmentally aware. The island's water supply mostly comes from rain gathered on rooftop cisterns, or a small desalination plant. Visitors should be mindful about not taking long showers and not running the water longer than absolutely necessary. Latrines on the island are referred to as 'ship toilets' because (gee, how can we put this daintily?) only natural refuse may be flushed away; all paper and other materials are to be placed in the garbage. In the continuous effort to stay 'green,' locals are still grappling with how to reduce the amount of imports to the island (namely food). The Ecolodge Rendez-Vous is pioneering the creation of gardens.

SURVIVAL GUIDE

Directory A–Z

Accommodations

Most of Saba's accommodations are reasonably priced considering the limited number of options: when compared to the other

---

PRACTICALITIES

» **Electricity** Electric current is 110V, 60 cycles. North American–style plugs are used.

» **Newspaper** *St Martin Herald* has one Saban correspondent.

» **Radio & TV** Voice of Saba is at 93.9FM and 1140AM. Radio Transat (broadcast from St-Martin/Sint Maarten and playing reggae and dance tunes) is at 95.5FM. The island has cable TV.

» **Weights & Measures** Metric system.

islands in the Caribbean, sleeping on Saba is a steal. The Saba Tourist Bureau offers help with booking accommodations.

Take a look at www.sabatourism.com/cot tages.html for a list of private vacation rentals. Most cottages are located in Windwardside or Hell's Gate.

Hotels often add a 6% government room tax; the 10% to 15% service charge is usually at the discretion of the visitor. Each guest must also pay a US$1 per day conservation fee.

$	budget	less than US$100
$$	midrange	US$100 to US$150
$$$	top end	more than US$150

Business Hours

General business hours 9am-5pm Mon-Sat

Restaurants breakfast 7-10am, lunch 11:30am-2:30pm, dinner 6-9pm

Embassies & Consulates

There are no embassies on Saba.

Festivals & Events

Saba Summer Festival The island's Carnival is a week-long event in late July that includes a Carnival queen contest, a calypso king competition, a costumed parade around the Bottom and a grand-finale fireworks display.

Sea & Learn (www.seaandlearn.org) In October the entire island becomes a learning center for naturalists, scientists and laypeople, who discover the richness of Saban flora and fauna in a range of activities, from helping out on a shark research project to learning how to use tropical plants to make medicinal teas.

Saba Days Held in the first week in December, this features sporting events, steel bands, dance competitions, donkey races and barbecues.

Food

The following price indicators are used in restaurant reviews in this chapter.

$	budget	less than US$10
$$	midrange	US$10 to US$20
$$$	top end	more than US$20

Gay & Lesbian Travelers

Although it's a complete coincidence that Saba's nickname is the 'Unspoiled Queen,' Saba is one of the most gay-friendly spots in the Caribbean. The island has no nightlife, but it's a good spot for gays and lesbians looking for a relaxed vacation where appropriate displays of affection do not have to be limited to the privacy of their room.

Health

Health risks on Saba are limited. The water, while potable, is best consumed from bottled sources. A teaching hospital in The Bottom can assist with any general issues including diving-related trauma.

Insurance

If you are planning on diving, make sure to register for proper diver's insurance. Try DAN (www.diversalertnetwork.org).

Internet Access

Most of the hotels on Saba have computer terminals and wi-fi.

Money

Although Saba's ties to the Netherlands have tightened over the last year, the currency of choice on the island is the US dollar.

Service charges are generally tacked on to the bill at the end of the meal, thus tipping is not obligatory.

Post

There are no addresses or postal codes on Saba. Simply address correspondence to: Name, Saba, Dutch West Indies.

Public Holidays

In addition to the holidays observed throughout the region (p872; except Whit Monday), Saba has the following public holidays:

Queen's Birthday April 30

Labor Day May 1

Ascension Thursday Fortieth day after Easter

Telephone

Saba's country code is ☎599 and is followed by a seven-digit local number. There are no area codes. If you are calling locally, just dial the seven-digit number. To call the island from overseas, dial your country's international access code + ☑599 + the local number.

Tourist Information

Information can be found at the **Saba Tourist Bureau** (☑416-2231; www.sabatourism.com; ⊙8am-5pm Mon-Fri).

Travelers with Disabilities

Wheelchair-bound travelers may have a difficult time on Saba, as the island is extremely steep and riddled with thousands upon thousands of stairs.

Visas

Citizens of North America, Australia and most European countries do not need a visa to visit Saba. Other nationalities should check with the Dutch representation in their home country.

Getting There & Away

Entering Saba

Valid passports are required by all visitors.

Air

Landing at Saba's **Juancho E Yrausquin Airport** (SAB; ☑416-2255; Flat Point) is the second-most thrilling activity undertaken on Saba. The first is taking off – the runway doesn't end with a comfy grassy meadow or even a fence, but at a sheer cliff. Don't worry, though: your pilot must pass a test every month to be able to fly in and out of Saba.

Currently, the only airline flying into Saba is **Winair** (☑416-2255; www.fly-winair. com). It has five 15-minute flights a day to and from St-Martin/Sint Maarten, as well as a daily flight to and from Sint Eustatius. We strongly recommend having your accommodations or dive outfit call ahead to confirm your flight. Instant flight cancellations and seat changes are known to happen. Also, pack a small overnight kit in your carry-on luggage in case of lost luggage or delayed arrival of bags.

Departure tax to St-Martin/Sint Maarten is US$5.

Sea

There are two ferries that run visitors between St-Martin/Sint Maarten and Saba. Schedules can vary due to waves and boat maintenance; check with your accommodation of choice on Saba before your arrival

and departure. If you plan on visiting Saba with your own boat, check out www.seasaba. com/english_html/why_yachties.htm.

Dawn II (☑416-3671; info@sabactransport. com) Leaves Saba at 7am and returns from Great Bay Marina on St-Martin/Sint Maarten at 5pm.

Edge (☑545-2640) Run by Aqua Mania. Leaves Pelican Marina in Simpson Bay at 9am Wednesday to Sunday, arriving in Saba at about 10:30am. It departs Saba at 3:30pm, arriving at Pelican Marina at 5pm.

Getting Around

There is no bus service on Saba. Most travelers hitchhike, walk or use taxis. Those who prefer walking should get well acquainted with the dirt trails, as they are significantly faster at getting you from point A to point B than following the road.

Car & Motorcycle

Renting a vehicle on relaxing Saba will only give you grief – we do not recommend it. Lifelong residents won't even attempt some driveways (Shearwater Resort's is especially notorious). The only roads are narrow, steep and winding, with tight corners, and driving is difficult in just about every way. The island's sole **gas station** (☑416-3272; ⊙8am-2:45pm Mon-Sat) is located in Fort Bay. If you decide to drive, a driver's license from your home country will suffice. Driving is on the right-hand side of the road. Drivers tend to drive slowly as there are many sharp turns and two-way streets that only fit one car at a time.

Hitchhiking

Hitchhiking is so common and necessary that it's virtually illegal *not* to pick up a hitchhiker. This is the most common method for tourists to get around, although you are highly encouraged to take a taxi to and from the airport so that the cabbies don't go out of business.

Taxi

There is no central taxi dispatch number on Saba, but prices have been set in stone to prevent overcharging (although some drivers will still try to sneak a couple of extra bucks out of you). There is an additional US$1 for transporting luggage. Your hotel or restaurant can arrange a cab; ask for Peddy (☑416-7062) or Garvis (☑416-6114).

Sint Eustatius

Best Dive Sites

» Doobie's Crack (p650)

» Blue Bead Hole (p650)

» Stenapa Reef (p650)

» Charlie Brown (p650)

Best Places to Stay

» Kings Well (p651)

» Old Gin House (p652)

» Statia Lodge (p654)

Why Go?

Pop quiz: which Caribbean island was once the busiest seaport in the world but is unfamiliar to most people today?

Yes, it's true, quiet 'Statia' was the darling of the Caribbean when valuable goods bounced between Europe, Africa and the New World during the 18th century. In fact, the naturally deep harbor was so sought after that the island changed hands 22 times before the Dutch permanently secured their claim.

Today, the island has shed all evidence of its former self, garnering instead an avid cult following among scuba divers and those who enjoy sun-kissed days full of blissful nothingness. Unlike its neighbors, Statia shows no signs of modernization – no grandiose landscaping, no condo development, and barely a hint of urban planning. Oranjestad, the island's only town, is a charming collection of ramshackle structures, each one a quiet homage to a bygone era. Statia lets it all hang out.

When to Go

While neighboring islands swell with visitors during the months of December and January, Statia stays remarkably calm. In April and May savor the last few months of the dry season before the thundershowers plow though. Visit during July to celebrate Carnival with locals amid live music and seafood feasts. Visitors should note that prices remain stagnant throughout the year.

Itineraries

THREE DAYS

Spend your first two days blowing bubbles with rays and sea turtles at various dive sites off the coast. Before leaving, fill up your final morning hiking the Quill all the way down to the heart of the volcanic crater.

ONE WEEK

After following the three-day itinerary, spend another two days exploring additional scuba sites – try a night dive and explore the rougher Atlantic side of the island. Round out the week with an afternoon at the Sint Eustatius Museum, a hike in the Boven, a visit to teeny Zeelandia Beach, and a laid-back walk among Oranjestad's ruins.

ONE MONTH

Popular with travelers staying more than a week is a stint of educational volunteering, such as helping to unearth and restore artifacts from one of the island's 600 documented archaeological sites, maintaining the botanical gardens, or tagging sea turtles.

GETTING TO NEIGHBORING ISLANDS

Daily flights and twice-weekly ferries connect Sint Eustatius to St-Martin/Sint Maarten, from where you can take boats or planes to reach the other island destinations in the vicinity.

Festivals & Events

» **Statia Carnival** With 10 days of revelry in late July, this is the island's biggest festival, culminating on a Monday. Music, dress-ups (including early-morning pajama ones), competitions and local food are the highlights.

» **Statia Day** Fort Oranje is the site of ceremonies held on Statia Day, November 16, which commemorates the date in 1776 when Statia became the first foreign land to salute the US flag. On this date in 2004, Statia adopted a new flag.

» **Golden Rock Regatta** Held in mid-November, this colorful sailing race is held between the nearby islands to commemorate Statia's importance during the American Revolution and the 11-gun salute that was fired from the island on November 16, 1776.

AT A GLANCE

» **Currency** US dollar (US$)

» **Languages** English, Dutch

» **Money** ATMs dispensing US dollars in Oranjestad and at the airport; best to bring cash

» **Visas** Not needed for citizens of North America and most EU countries

Fast Facts

» **Area** 31 sq km

» **Population** 3400

» **Capital** Oranjestad

» **Telephone country code** 599

» **Emergency** 111

Set Your Budget

» **Budget hotel room** US$140

» **Two-course evening meal** US$36

» **Two-tank dive** US$95

» **Beer** US$4

» **Taxi from airport to Oranjestad** US$8

Resources

» **Statia Tourism** (www.statiatourism.com)

» **Stenapa** (www.statiapark.org)

Oranjestad

Little Statia, as Sint Eustatius is commonly known, has but one town: Oranjestad. The rest of the island is made up of rugged, rural terrain.

Sights

FREE **Fort Oranje** RUINS

(⊙24hr) Right in the center of town, Fort Oranje is one of the last remaining bastions of Statia's historic past, an intact fort complete with cannon, triple bastions and a

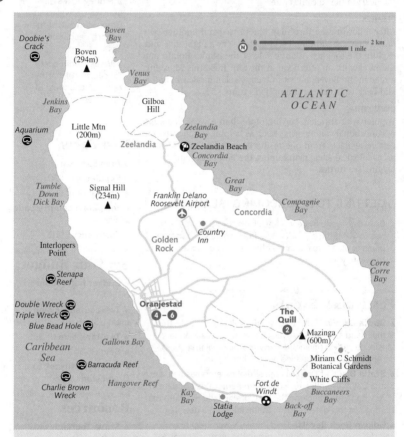

Sint Eustatius Highlights

1 Cavort with reef sharks and sea turtles at one of Statia's many shallow shipwrecks on a **diving adventure** (p650)

2 Ascend **the Quill** (p653), then wind your way down to the bottom of the interior crater, which drips like a rainforest and features impossibly huge trees

3 Uncover the island's rich history, or get closer to Statia's flora and fauna as a volunteer with a **local project** (p656)

4 Walk around the island's only town, **Oranjestad** (p648), to find intriguing ruins in various states of disarray – many untouched for hundreds of years

5 Snorkel between sunken ruins at **Lower Town Beach** (p649) to spot hidden beads and spawning fish

6 Check out the fascinating **Sint Eustatius Museum** (p649) to find a collection of annotated artifacts, including a 2000-year-old skeleton in the basement

cobblestone courtyard. The French erected the first rampart in 1629, but most of the fort was built after the Dutch took the island from the French in 1636. They added to the fort a number of times over the years.

The courtyard has a couple of memorials, including a plaque presented by US President Franklin Roosevelt to commemorate the fort's fateful 1776 salute of the American war vessel *Andrew Doria*. At the time, the British on neighboring Antigua didn't take too kindly to Statia being the first foreign power to officially recognize the new American nation. The British navy later sailed for Oranjestad and, led by Admiral George Rodney, mercilessly bombed it to high heaven, and then took possession of the island and all its wealth.

Sint Eustatius Museum   MUSEUM
(adult/child US$3/1; ☉9am-5pm Mon-Thu, to 3pm Fri, to noon Sat) Chock-full o' history, this museum gives meaning to the Statian tag line 'The Historic Gem.' Set up as an upper-class colonial-era house, the museum also has a pre-Columbian collection of artifacts, and information on slavery, nautical history and colonial relics. The entire venture was funded by private donors, so it's a bit ramshackle; however, the exhibits are thoroughly informative. Head down to the basement and learn about the Saladoids, who came all the way from the Orinoco region in Venezuela to settle here. They had abandoned the island before the arrival of the Arawaks but left behind several burial grounds. The unearthed skeleton of a 60-year-old man sits on display and, if you look closely, you'll notice that his teeth are in remarkably perfect condition – a testament to the indigenous diet before sugarcane was introduced.

Lower Town Beach   BEACH
No one visits Statia for its beaches, which can't compare to those of other islands in the Caribbean. Volcanic Zeelandia Beach, on the east coast, has rough surf and undertows, butts up against the island's landfill, and is not recommended for swimming; nonetheless, it rates as Statia's second beach, the first being the strip of sand in front of Lower Town. From an archaeological perspective, this beach is absolutely fascinating because much of it was once reclaimed land (that has since been re-reclaimed by the sea), and the sturdy stone frameworks of old warehouses are visible beneath the emerald waters.

Government Guesthouse   NOTABLE BUILDING
The Government Guesthouse is the handsome 18th-century stone-and-wood building opposite First Caribbean National Bank. It was thoroughly renovated in 1992 with funding from the EU and is now the government headquarters, with the offices of the lieutenant governor and commissioners on the ground floor and the courtroom on the upper floor. You'll see the lieutenant governor's Mercedes Benz parked out front – the nicest car on the island, by far.

The building, which once served as the Dutch naval commander's quarters, came by its name in the 1920s, when it was used as a guesthouse.

Synagogue Ruins   RUINS
Those with a particular interest in Jewish history or old buildings can explore the roofless and slowly decaying yellow-brick walls of the Honen Dalim (which means 'She Who Is Kind to the Poor'), an abandoned synagogue dating from 1739, which makes it the second-oldest synagogue in the western hemisphere. The synagogue's *mikvah* (a cleansing bath for women) has been left intact. The ruins are 30m down the alleyway with belle epoque lampposts, opposite the south side of the library.

Statia's rising influence as a trade center was accompanied by a large influx of Jewish merchants beginning in the early 1700s. These businessmen were of Sephardic descent and escaped to the Netherlands during the Spanish Inquisition. After the 1781 invasion, British troops stole much of the wealth from the Jewish merchants and by 1847 all of the Jews had been deported or had left.

About 50m south of the synagogue ruins is a **Jewish cemetery**, with gravestones dating from 1742 to 1843. It was here that some Jews tried to avoid British plundering. Troops noticed an extremely large number of funerals for such a small community and, upon opening a casket, found valuables instead of bodies.

Dutch Reformed Church   CHURCH
The thick 60cm stone walls of the old Dutch Reformed Church, built in 1755, remain perfectly intact, but the roof collapsed during a 1792 hurricane and the building has been open to the heavens ever since. The grounds are the resting place of many of the island's most prominent citizens of the past.

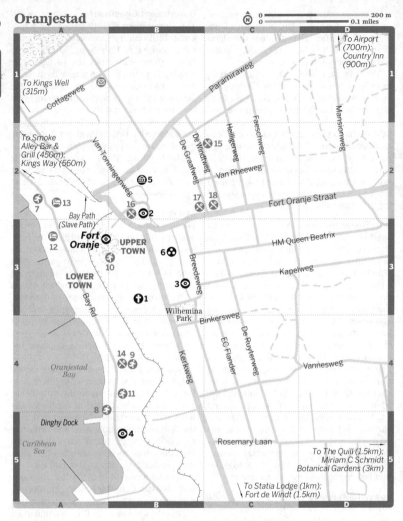

Sint Eustatius Historical
Foundation   MUSEUM
(⊙9am-noon Mon-Sat) The gift shop at this small historical-foundation museum along Lower Town sells secondhand books as well as local art and crafts. Proceeds support the museum and historical research on Statia.

🏃 Activities

The nongovernment organization **Stenapa** (Sint Eustatius National Parks Foundation; ☎318-2884; www.statiapark.org; Lower Town, Oranjestad; ⊙7am-5pm Mon-Fri, 8am-noon Sat & Sun) was started in 1998 to protect Statia's ample nat-

ural resources. It manages the Statia Marine Park, the above-ground national park and the Miriam C Schmidt Botanical Gardens (p653). The office, situated in a traditional *case* building, has detailed information about diving and hiking, as well as everything you need to know about Statian flora and fauna.

Diving & Snorkeling

The waters off Sint Eustatius are blessed with stunning reefs and loads of attractions: reef dives, seahorses, the wrecks of colonial trading ships, giant octopuses, stingrays,

Oranjestad

barracudas, coral, lobster, tropical fish... the list could go on forever. Statia's diving is regarded as among the best in the Caribbean.

Part of what keeps it this way is the US$6 per day or US$30 per year pass fee paid to Stenapa to help the foundation maintain the pristine conditions of the Statia Marine Park. There is an additional US$1 per day harbor fee. Please take only photos and leave all historic objects and marine life alone (fines have been levied at the airport on divers found to have stashed more than just a blue bead or two).

In the last 10 years, Statia has sunk several ships, creating some of the best wreck diving in the world. The *Charlie Brown* was sunk in 2003 and a map of its cavernous hull and quarters now hangs on the Stenapa wall so divers can plan their route beforehand. A dive to *Charlie Brown* is best done before 11am. Several colonial-era wrecks also exist under the waves, but most of them have deteriorated to the point where all that remains are the awesome rusty anchors.

For a deep dive, Doobie's Crack, a large cleft in a reef at the northwest side of the

island, has black-tip sharks and schools of large fish. Try Blue Bead Hole if you're feeling particularly lucky and want to give bead hunting in an underwater sand-dump a go. Adventurous types should do a night dive at Stenapa Reef to check out the creatures that hide during the day.

One-tank dives average US$50, two-tank dives US$95. Night dives, certification courses and multidive packages are also available. PADI Open Water courses will set you back US$425.

Statia has three diving operations, all of which have offices in Oranjestad:

Golden Rock Dive Center   DIVING
(☏318-2964, in the US 800-311-6658; www.gold enrockdive.com) Michele and Glenn run this friendly and professional diving outfitter. With two dive boats and loads of high-quality equipment, Golden Rock guarantees a top-notch scuba experience.

Scubaqua Dive Center   DIVING
(☏318-2160; www.scubaqua.com; Oranjestad) Owned and operated by an international team of scuba pros.

Dive Statia   DIVING
(☏318-2435, in the US 866-614-3419; www. divestatia.com; Oranjestad) Up for sale at the time of research; said to be merging with Scubaqua.

Hiking

The tourist office has a free hiking brochure with descriptions of over a dozen trails, and it can provide information on current trail conditions. Keep your eyes peeled for trail markers, which are usually small orange ribbons.

The most popular hike is to the Quill, Statia's extinct volcano (p653).

Guided tours focusing on native flora and fauna can be organized through Stenapa (p650) or the **Sint Eustatius Tourist Bureau** (☏318-2433; www.statiatourism.com; Fort Oranje).

If you plan on doing any hiking, Stenapa asks that you purchase a 'trail tag' for US$6.

🛏 Sleeping

If none of the accommodations options suit your tastes, you can sign up for a homestay; check out www.statiatourism.com/home stay/index.html for details.

Kings Well   INN $$
(☏318-2538; www.kingswellstatia.com; Van Tonningenweg; s US$125-150, d US$140-165; 🕙🖳) Burst-

ing with character from every vine-draped crevice, Kings Well is a colorful menagerie of horse-sized Great Danes, squawking pet macaws and swirls of hyper goldfish. The owners are some of the most down-to-earth folks you'll ever meet and tend to their B&B-style rooms with love and affection. Wooden furnishings abound, and there's always a new project under way, like adding on an extra bedroom or creating new mosaic art. Lunch and dinner are served only upon request.

Old Gin House HOTEL **$$**
(☎318-2319; www.oldginhouse.com; Bay Rd, Lower Town; s/d US$158/165; ❄@📶≋) This beautiful brick ginning station (no, not the booze – the cotton seeds) has been restored to its 17th-century glory, and makes for a romantic spot to while away the slow Statian day. Most of the hotel accommodations are situated in a two-story complex behind the original structure and feature strong air-con, and plasma TV. The rooms have burgundy and black accents, and although the bathrooms are slightly out of date, the shower nozzles are new and provide excellent water pressure. Rates include continental breakfast.

Golden Era Hotel HOTEL **$$**
(☎318-2345; goldenera@goldenrock.net; Bay Rd, Lower Town; d US$134; ❄@📶≋) 'Golden Era' probably refers to the last time this place had a renovation – it really needs a face-lift. The property sits right along the ocean and a few rooms have private balconies with unobstructed sea views. The grounds are covered with yellow bells and oleander, and the pool bar practically forces guests to lounge on a beach chair with a mystery novel and a piña colada. The brand new menu in the restaurant offers surprisingly decent lunches and dinners.

Eating

Statia's dining scene is dismal. Over the last few years several places have closed their doors as rents rise. There are a few spots serving up local recipes and seafood, but mostly – and bizarrely – you'll find a handful of Chinese restaurants. Decent eats can also be scouted at Golden Era Hotel.

Blue Bead INTERNATIONAL **$$**
(Bay Rd, Lower Town; lunch US$7-10, dinner US$12-26; ⏰lunch & dinner) When you're the best restaurant on an island without any culinary aptitude it's easy to get a big head. Prices are inflated and service may be a tad pretentious, but you'll get fresh-from-the-sea fare in a lovely seaside atmosphere.

Smoke Alley Bar & Grill INTERNATIONAL **$$**
(Bay Rd, Lower Town; meals US$12-25; ⏰lunch & dinner Mon-Sat) Commanding an enviable location directly over the ocean on the turn into Lower Town, this open-air restaurant-nightclub has group bench seating, pulsing music at night (with a DJ and dancing till late on Friday), a questionable pirate theme, an eclectic crowd of medical students and… mediocre food.

Ocean View Terrace INTERNATIONAL **$$**
(Fort Oranje Straat; meals US$11-20; ⏰closed Sun) In the courtyard next to the Government Guesthouse, this place has a quiet open-air setting, and offers stellar views and tasty seafood dishes. Stop by for a li'l drunken karaoke on Friday night.

Super Burger BURGERS **$**
(Fort Oranje Straat; meals US$7-12; ⏰breakfast, lunch & dinner) Skell, the owner, cooks up some (yeah, you guessed it) super burgers, and there's a good assortment of veggie dishes if you aren't in a carnivorous kind of mood.

Sonny's & Cantonese CHINESE **$$**
(Fort Oranje Straat; meals US$7-17; ⏰lunch & dinner) This open-air, lantern-filled joint doesn't win any culinary prizes, but it's a great place to chill with regulars over a few cheap rice dishes. Free delivery available.

Duggins Supermarket SUPERMARKET **$**
(De Windtweg) The main supermarket on Statia, Duggins is packed with low-cost European and American brand names. You'll find loads of Kittitians here, who boat over from next door to stock up on cheap provisions. If Duggins is closed, you'll easily find a smaller rival supermarket with open doors up the street or around the corner.

Information

The two main banks are First Caribbean National Bank and Windward Islands Bank (WIB). There's also an ATM on the corner of Fort Oranje Straat and Breedeweg.

Post office (Cottageweg; ⏰7:30am-4pm Mon-Fri)

Public library (Fort Oranje Straat; internet access per hr US$5; ⏰noon-5pm Mon, 8am-5pm Tue-Fri) Internet.

Queen Beatrix Medical Centre (HM Queen Beatrix) Has quite a good reputation considering the island's remoteness and minuscule population. There are always two doctors on call 24 hours per day.

Sint Eustatius Tourist Bureau (www.statia tourism.com; Fort Oranje; ⏰8am-noon & 1-5pm Mon-Fri)

Around Oranjestad

◉ Sights

The Quill
VOLCANO

Looming large over the rest of the island, the lone photogenic peak, known as the Quill (whose name is derived from the Dutch word *kwil,* meaning pit or hole), spikes high above the rolling terrain below. The once-active volcano now lies perfectly quiet and makes for a fantastic hiking day trip. Follow the markers deep down into the interior crater and witness a thriving rain forest–like environment stocked with dripping foliage and skyscraping trees that are several centuries old.

The Quill, and its surrounding slopes, was designated a national park in May 1998. The trail leading up the mountain begins at the end of Rosemary Laan in Oranjestad and it takes about 50 minutes to reach the edge of the crater. From there you can continue in either direction along the rim. The trail to the right (southeast) takes about 45 minutes and ends atop the 600m-high Mazinga, Statia's highest point. The shorter Panorama Track to the left offers great views and takes only about 15 minutes. A third option is the track leading down into the crater, where there's a thick jungle of tall trees, some with huge buttressed trunks. This steep track, which takes about an hour each way, can be very slippery, so sturdy shoes are essential.

Miriam C Schmidt Botanical Gardens
GARDEN

(☎318-2884) The semiwild botanical gardens grow under the watchful eye of the Quill. Volunteers and Stenapa staff have been busy maintaining them to show residents and visitors alike the rich biodiversity of Statia. Take Rosemary Laan towards the Quill and follow the dirt road that points to the gardens. Take care, as it can be rough riding.

Zeelandia
BEACH

Zeelandia, about 3.2km northeast of Oranjestad, takes its name from Statia's first Dutch settlers, who were from Zeeland province in the Netherlands.

The dark-sand beach at Zeelandia Bay collects its fair share of flotsam and is not ideal for swimming; the Atlantic side of the island is turbulent and there are dangerous currents and undertows. It is a reasonable strolling beach, however, and you can find private niches by walking south toward the cliffs.

For those who are up for a longer walk, a track from the main road leads north to the partly secluded Venus Bay. There's no beach, but it makes for a nice hike, taking about 45 minutes one way.

Forts

Besides the imposing Fort Oranje, there are 18 forts scattered throughout the island, all built in the 18th century. Most of these have been consumed by island foliage, and others lie in various states of disrepair, but a few are worth a glimpse if only for the magnificent views out to sea. Apart from Fort de Windt, all face the gentler Caribbean side of the island

Fort de Windt
RUINS

A couple of rusty cannon atop a cliff-side wall – the fort now looks more like a

---

BLUE-BEAD FEVER

When Peter Minuit purchased the island of Manhattan (the heart of present-day New York City) from its local inhabitants, he paid for the land with 60 Dutch guilders' worth of trinkets, including several alluring blue beads.

These glassy pentagonal balls were produced in Amsterdam and traded throughout all of the Dutch holdings around the world. According to legend, several hundred years ago a large wooden vessel that sank off the coast of Statia was carrying these precious beads by the barrelful. And even today a lonely little bead will, once in a while, wash ashore.

Although the price of the blue beads hasn't risen in value quite like the real estate of New York, these shimmering talismans are considered to be quite a find. They are the only historical artifacts that are allowed to leave the island and, after years of avid plundering, the chance of finding one is slim.

As you walk around Oranjestad, you'll notice that local expats regularly sport their found beads with pride while Zen-fully exclaiming 'you don't find the beads; the beads find you...'

wooden platform. At the southern end of the island, with a fine view of St Kitts to the southeast.

White cliffs LANDMARK

East of Fort de Windt; readily visible from neighboring islands.

🛏 Sleeping

Statia Lodge COTTAGES **$$**

(☑318-1900; www.statialodge.com; s/d/tr US$130/150/230; ❋ 🛜 ⛵) The newest digs on the island, beautiful Statia Lodge opened its doors five years ago and has been getting good reviews ever since. The cluster of quiet wooden cabins is billed as 'ecolodges' and sits on a silent stretch of fenced-in land. A small beach bar and L-shaped pool are on the water's edge. The property is just beyond the limits of Oranjestad on the southern part of the island near Fort de Windt. Single and double rooms come with complimentary scooters; triple and family rooms come with a car.

Country Inn B&B **$**

(☑318-2484; countryinn@statiatourism.com; Concordia; s/d US$50/60; ❋) Within walking distance of the airport, Statia's lowest-priced lodging isn't fancy, but the six quaint rooms are clean and quiet. Breakfast is available for US$5, and Iris Pompier, the dedicated proprietor, will even cook you one of her fabulous lunches or dinners upon request. It's about a 20-minute walk or a quick hitch from town. Credit cards are not accepted.

UNDERSTAND SINT EUSTATIUS

History

Statia has been the Caribbean whipping boy for centuries. Caribs had already left by the time Columbus came across the island, in 1493. Consequently, when the French arrived there was no indigenous population to be devastated by disease or enslavement. The Dutch established the first permanent settlement in 1636. Statia changed hands 22 times among the Dutch, French and British over the next couple of centuries.

Statia was a primary link between Europe and the Atlantic world for much of the later 18th century. As the English and French levied duty after duty on their islands, the Dutch made Statia duty free in 1756. Subsequently, thousands of ships used Oranjestad as their main stopping point between Europe and the American colonies. In its heyday, Statia was home to no fewer than 10,000 full-time residents, both European colonists and African slaves. The population rose to above 25,000 when taking into account the sailors who were in port for months at a time.

On November 16, 1776, Statia's most infamous moment occurred. A member of the rebellious colonies' fledgling navy, the brigantine *Andrew Doria*, sailed into the harbor and fired a 13-gun salute signifying American independence. Statia responded with an 11-gun salute, cementing itself as the first foreign nation to recognize the new United States of America; consequently, the US and the Netherlands have the longest-standing peaceful relationship between two nations in history. Plans are in the works to have a replica of the ship created (see www.andrewdoria.org for more information).

Britain was none too pleased; though, contrary to popular belief, it wasn't the British navy's attack on Statia in 1781 that started the island's downhill spiral. It was taxes imposed by the French in 1795 that eventually drove merchants away to nearby islands.

Since 1954 Statia had been part of the Netherlands Antilles, along with Bonaire, Curaçao, Saba and Sint Maarten. On Statia Day, November 16, 2004, the island adopted a new flag, but in 2005 it voted to remain part of the Netherlands Antilles. However, all four other members voted to disband the island nation group, effactually leaving Statia the sole member. In October 2010, the Netherlands Antilles was officially dissolved and Statia, along with Saba and Bonaire, became a 'special municipality' of the Netherlands. Statians now share similar rights to those living in Holland, and Statia and the Netherlands have a more closely linked government system. On January 1, 2011, Statia adopted the US dollar as its currency.

Culture

Most islanders are descendants of African slaves brought over to work in the warehouses in Lower Town and on the long-vanished plantations. The culture is a mix of African and Dutch heritages with many expats. A recent surge in immigrants has included an influx from the Dominican Republic, resulting in an eclectic Latin addition to the local vibe.

Landscape & Wildlife

The Quill looms above the southern half of the island. This extinct volcano, which reaches 600m at Mazinga, the highest point on the rim, is responsible for the high, conical appearance Statia has when viewed from neighboring islands. Volcanologists maintain the Quill is one of the most perfectly shaped volcanoes in the world.

Cliffs drop straight to the sea along much of the shoreline, resulting in precious few beaches. At the north side of Statia there are a few low mountains, while the island's central plain contains the airport and the town of Oranjestad.

Most of the northern end of the island is dry with scrubby vegetation, although oleander, bougainvillea, hibiscus and flamboyant flowers add a splash of color here and there. The greatest variety of flora is inside the Quill, which collects enough cloud cover for its central crater to harbor an evergreen seasonal forest (which can feel at times like a rain forest), with ferns, elephant ears, bromeliads, bananas, and tall kapok and silk cottonwood trees that are many centuries old. The island also has over two dozen varieties of orchid; new species are still being found today.

There are 25 resident species of bird, including white-tailed tropical birds that nest on the cliffs along the beach north of Lower Town, in Oranjestad. There are also harmless racer snakes, iguanas, lizards and tree frogs. Most other terrestrial animal life is limited to goats, chickens, cows and donkeys. The marine life offers additional diversity, with hundreds of fish species, extensive coral reefs, schools of cuttlefish and large families of Caribbean spiny lobster.

SURVIVAL GUIDE

Directory A–Z

Accommodations

Camping is technically allowed on Statia, although the tourist office has never had a request in its history. Pioneers can call Joshua at ☏526-5027 to pitch a tent on Congo

Preserve – you'll find toilets, showers and kitchen facilities on the premises.

Service and taxes are included in the listed room rates in this chapter.

$	budget	less than US$100
$$	midrange	US$100 to US$150
$$$	top end	more than US$150

Business Hours

The two most common religious groups on Statia are Seventh Day Adventists and Roman Catholics: on Saturday the Seventh Day Adventists' establishments are shut and on Sunday the Catholics close up shop.

Also expect lengthy lunch-break closings and lax hours of operation on weekends.

Grocery stores 7:30am-7pm

Offices & shops 8am-5pm Mon-Fri

Restaurants breakfast 7-10am, lunch 11:30am-2:30pm, dinner 6-10pm

Embassies & Consulates

There are no embassies on Statia.

Food

The following price indicators, based on the cost of a main course, are used in the Eating listings in this chapter.

$	budget	less than US$10
$$	midrange	US$10 to US$20
$$$	top end	more than US$20

Health

There is a medical centre in Oranjestad; see p652. It is best to boil island water before drinking it.

PRACTICALITIES

» **Electricity** 110V/60 cycles; North American–style sockets are common.

» **Newspapers & Magazines** Statia doesn't have its own newspaper but imports St Martin's *Daily Herald*.

» **Radio & TV** Statia's sole radio station is at 92.3 FM. Cable TV comes mostly from the US, but a few channels are from within the Caribbean.

» **Weights & Measures** Metric system.

Insurance

If you are planning on diving, make sure to register for proper diver's insurance. Try DAN (www.diversalertnetwork.org).

Money

US dollars (US$) are used on the island.

Tipping is not necessary or expected.

Public Holidays

In addition to those observed throughout the region (p872), Sint Eustatius has the following public holidays:

Queen's Birthday April 30

Easter Sunday Late March/early April

Labor Day/Ascension Day May 1

Emancipation Day July 1

Antillean Day October 21

Statia Day November 16

Telephone

Statia's country code is ☎599. To call the island overseas, dial your country's international access code followed by ☎599 + the local number. We have included only the seven-digit local number in Statia listings in this chapter.

Tourist Information

The **Sint Eustatius Tourist Bureau** (☎318-2433; www.statiatourism.com; Fort Oranje; ⊙8am-noon & 1-5pm Mon-Fri) has free island maps that show the roads and hiking trails. Also check out the airport's tiny info desk, open when flights are landing. A small walking-tour booklet has been assembled to give visitors a more in-depth perspective of the island, especially the ruins of Oranjestad.

Visas

Citizens of North America and most European countries do not need a visa to visit Statia. Other nationalities should check with the Dutch representation in their home country.

Volunteering

Statia is a good stop for educational volunteering trips. **Stenapa** (☎318-2884; www.statiapark.org; Lower Town, Oranjestad) connects long-and short-term volunteers with opportunities like tagging sea turtles on Zeelandia Beach, maintaining the Miriam C Schmidt Botanical Gardens, staffing the office and cataloguing Statian flora.

Secar (Sint Eustatius Center for Archaeological Research; ☎524-6770; www.secar.org; Oranjestad) is the island's sanctioned organization dedicated to unearthing and restoring relics from the past. Volunteers have the opportunity to work a one of the island's 600 documented archaeological sites.

Getting There & Away

Entering Sint Eustatius

All visitors need a passport and an onward or return ticket.

Air

Franklin Delano Roosevelt Airport (☎316-2887) is Statia's only airport. It's tiny and currently only accommodates the **Winair** (☎318-2303; www.fly-winair.com) puddle jumpers from St-Martin/Sint Maarten. We strongly recommend having your accommodations or dive outfit call ahead to confirm your flight. Instant flight cancellations and seat changes are known to happen.

Departure tax is US$10.

Sea

At the time of research a new ferry service was just starting up. The **Navagante** (☎523-3004; authenticcaribbean@gmail.com; one-way/round-trip US$110/75) cruises between Statia and Simpson Bay in Sint Maarten twice a week (Monday and Friday). The journey takes just under two hours. Save for a few dive boats and the odd small ship, no cruise ships alight here. Virtually all tourist traffic arrives by airplane.

Yachts need to radio the Marine Park at VHF channel 16 or 17 as there are many protected spots around the island and there is only anchorage for about 10 yachts at a time.

Getting Around

Statia has no buses, so renting a car is useful if you want to explore every nook and cranny (which can easily be done in a day). If you're staying in Oranjestad you won't need a car for most of your stay, but expect to do some serious walking, as the town is somewhat spread out. Hiking enthusiasts can easily access the trail up into the Quill from the center of Oranjestad by foot.

Car & Motorcycle

Driving is on the right side of the road. Road conditions are spotty outside of Oranjestad and the road to the Miriam C Schmidt Botanical Gardens can be impassable after rain. Watch out for roaming goats, cows and chickens all over the island, even in town. Also keep an eye out for surprise one-way streets – they tend to appear out of nowhere and the locals can get very upset if you're heading the wrong way.

Little Statia has a ridiculous number of car-rental agencies, including the following. Figure around US$40 to US$55 per day for a car or 4WD, although deals are usually negotiable for weekly rates. Scooters cost around US$30. Just remember, you get what you pay for. Credit cards are usually accepted.

ARC Car & Jeep Rental (☑318-2595)

Brown's Car Rental (☑318-2266)

Reddy Car Rental (☑318-2880)

Rivers Car Rental (☑318-2309)

Hitchhiking

The usual safety precautions apply, but hitchhiking on Statia is considered to be very safe and easy, so it's perfectly fine to stick your thumb out.

Taxi

The island's handful of taxis usually congregate at the airport after flights arrive. If you're looking for a cab, ask a local to call one, or they'll just give you a lift. You can also try the dispatch line (☑318-2205) Figure US$8 to US$15 per person per trip, with an extra US$1 if you're carrying luggage. Tack on an extra US$2 after sunset.

St-Barthélemy

Best Beaches

» Anse de Gouverneur
(p666)

» Anse de Grande Saline
(p666)

» Anse des Flamands
(p663)

» Anse de Colombier (p664)

Best Places to Stay

» Hotel Guanahani & Spa
(p666)

» Salines Garden (p667)

» Le P'tit Morne (p664)

Why Go?

The mere mention of St-Barthélemy conjures up fanciful dreams of cocktails with supermodels, caviar with a four-digit price tag, and dropping some serious bling on a Dior bathing suit...for your miniature schnauzer. Does this stuff really happen in St-Barth? It sure does.

But does St-Barth have anything to offer those of us who haven't won an Oscar? You bet. Beyond its world-famous glitz and glam, there's a quiet community of locals who can trace their ancestry back to the church-studded countryside of Normandy, and even the island's rugged coastal terrain feels bizarrely French.

So, whether you're after the jet-setting lifestyle, or a simple village vibe, St-Barth can supply it. Just remember: while the island's two cultures are almost diametrically opposed, they are ultimately united by their love of the Madonna (albeit different ones...).

When to Go

From late December to mid-January, you'll be sharing the island with a veritable who's who of Oscar winners and oil tycoons. Locals revel in Carnival soon after, and low-season prices start to kick in by April as guests enjoy the end of the *carème* (dry season). July and August signal the beginning of *l'hivernage* (hurricane season) – capitalize on bottomed-out prices before the rains hit.

Itineraries

ONE DAY

Take a puddle jumper or the ferry over from St-Martin/Sint Maarten and spend the day ogling giant yachts in Gustavia. Adventurous types with plenty of energy may consider grabbing a cab to the western lookout point at the end of Colombier and walking back to Gustavia.

FIVE DAYS

Get a room at the Guanahani in Grand Cul-de-Sac (if you've just won the lottery) or at Salines Garden in Anse de Grande Saline and spend three blissful days by the beach. In the evenings try out some of the internationally acclaimed restaurants that pepper the island. On your last two days, undergo some retail therapy in Gustavia, followed by a couple of hours roaming the quiet west coast, particularly around quaint Corossol.

TWO WEEKS

Snag one of the many private villas scattered around the island and spend your first week at a different beach each day. Then get your adrenaline pumping with a sailing day trip and a scuba dive, plus some hiking in the east, and round out the week swiping your plastic at the boutiques in Gustavia.

GETTING TO NEIGHBORING ISLANDS

St-Barth has easy links to St-Martin/Sint Maarten next door by regular ferry and air service. From there you can connect to almost any of the other islands in the region. Direct flights are also available to Guadeloupe.

Essential Food & Drink

» **€29 prix-fixe dinners** Some of St-Barth's finest restaurants offer smaller wallets a chance to play in the big leagues with their three-course set menus.

» **Creole fusion** Elegant nods to the island's eclectic past take the form of flavorful seafood dishes blending French recipes and local spices.

AT A GLANCE

» **Currency** Euro (€)

» **Language** French

» **Money** ATMs aplenty

» **Visas** Not necessary for most residents of North America, the EU and Australia; see p670 for more

---

Fast Facts

» **Area** 21 sq km

» **Capital** Gustavia

» **Population** 8900

» **Telephone area code** ☑590

» **Emergency** ☑16

Set Your Budget

» **Budget hotel room** €150

» **Two-course evening meal** €40

» **Museum entrance** €3

» **Beer** €4

» **Daily car rental** €50

Resources

» **Saint-Barthélemy Tourism Association** (www.saintbarth-tourisme.com)

» **St-Barths Online** (www.st-barths.com)

St-Barthélemy Highlights

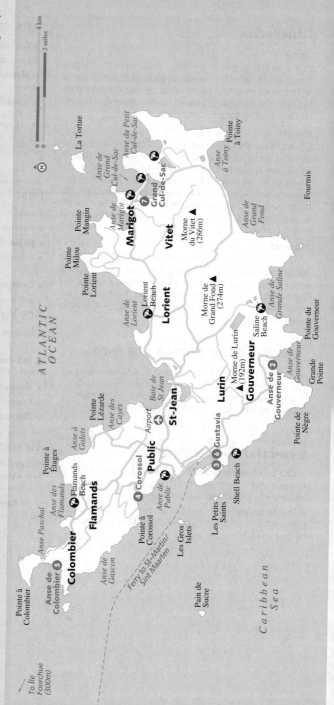

1 Explore the island's dramatic vertical peak and score killer views of the sea below on an afternoon of **hiking**

2 Lay your towel on the perfect stretch of beach at **Anse de Gouverneur** (p666)

3 Strut your stuff window-shopping and yacht-ogling in

St-Barth's stunning fort-flanked capital, **Gustavia** (p661)

4 Step back in time to charming **Corossol** (p663), ripped straight from the tranquil coast of France

5 Peruse powdery white sand at **Anse de Colombier** (p664)

6 Bust out the plastic – the island's chefs dedicate their careers to eliciting a visceral

'mmm!' from guests at **world-class restaurants** (p662)

7 Set your Louis Vuitton luggage down and **stay in style** at an opulent resort or slip away to a hidden cliffside villa (p666)

GUSTAVIA

POP 1500

About 50 years ago, Gustavia was a wind-swept fishing village; today this stunning port town is nothing short of majestic. Although relatively small when compared to other capitals in the Caribbean, Gustavia has plenty of places to 'see and be seen,' including myriad high-end boutiques, upmarket restaurants and a couple of historical sights.

◉ Sights

There aren't loads of sights on St-Barth, but it's worth stopping by the Office Territorial du Tourisme (p663) to grab its small pamphlet, which offers a nuanced caption to some of the older structures in Gustavia, including the **Catholic church**, the **Swedish belfry**, the **Wall House** and the **Anglican church**.

Fort Gustave   RUIN
The site of this ruined fort has a couple of cannons and a slightly bottle-shaped lighthouse, but most people come for the fine view of Gustavia and the harbor. A plaque points out local sights and landmarks. Across the harbor to the south is **Fort Oscar**, which is still used as a military installation, and from there you can see the islands of St Kitts and Sint Eustatius on a clear day.

Musée Territorial   MUSEUM
(admission €2; ⊘8:30am-1pm & 2:30-5pm Mon, Tue, Thu & Fri, 9am-1pm Wed & Sat) Take a look at historical St-Barth, from the Carib settlements to the Swedish occupation, with old photos and traditional clothing.

Le P'tit Collectionneur   MUSEUM
(admission €2; ⊘10am-noon & 4-6pm Mon-Sat) After years of coaxing from his family, André Berry, the island's pack rat, finally opened this museum of oddities. His collection features a diverse array of objects ranging from 18th-century British smoking pipes to the island's first phonograph. In a roundabout way, these items tell the story of St-Barth's colorful history.

🏃 Activities

Operators in Gustavia offer shore and deep-sea **fishing**, where catching tuna, wahoo or blue marlin is common. Renting a 6.5m skippered motorboat for deep-sea fishing starts at about €400 for the day for four to seven people. Half-day trips cost about €65 per person, full-day trips €100 and sunset cruises €55. They usually include a meal or buffet, plus drinks and snorkeling gear.

The island's best snorkeling spot is Île Fourchue (or any of the stoney outcrops around St-Barth), although you'll also find active reefs at Lorient, Anse de Colombier, and Petite de Anse.

Try the following operators:

Big Blue   DIVING
(☏27-83-74) A quality dive center.

Jicky Marine Service   WATER ACTIVITIES
(☏27-70-34; www.st-barths.com/marine.service; Quai du Yacht Club) A full-service center offering snorkeling and diving; shore and deep-sea fishing; and half- and full-day private and public boat charters. One popular boat trip is a half-day snorkeling trip aboard a catamaran.

Ocean Must Marina   FISHING
(☏27-62-25) Offers fishing trips.

Splash   SNORKELING
(☏0690-56-90-24; splash@stbarth.fr) Runs full-day snorkel trips with gourmet buffet to Île Fourchue.

Totem Surf   SURFING
(☏27-83-72) Rents surfing gear.

🛏 Sleeping

Accommodation in Gustavia is focused on the harbor rather than a powdery beach. The two cheapest places on the island are located here, though they cater mostly to yachties.

Sunset Hotel   HOTEL $
(☏27-77-21; www.st-barths.com/sunset-hotel; Rue de la République; s/d from €97/103; ❈ ⊛) The most central hotel in Gustavia, Sunset Hotel is also clean, unpretentious and family run. The 10 rooms all have phones, TVs and refrigerators; the pricier ones have a stunning view of the harbor and sunset but also get a bit of street noise. Rates depend on the season. Book ahead – the owner proudly told us that all his rooms were full every single night in 2010.

La Presqu'île   HOTEL $
(☏27-64-60; La Pointe; s/d €40/60; ❈) Popular with yachties, this hotel is not only a freakishly good deal for St-Barth, but is also reasonably comfortable and central. The rooms are small but clean, and the wraparound patio offers a beautiful spot to have breakfast and admire the Gustavia harbor.

DON'T MISS

THE OTHER SIDE OF ST-BARTH

Pull back the island's satin curtains and link up with Hélène Bernier, whose family has called St-Barth home for 10 generations. Hélène runs **Easytime** (www.stbartheasytime.com), a small tour operator that specializes in showing visitors the real faces of the island. During a **half-day tour** you'll uncover hidden viewpoints, local snack shops and colorful artists' studios. Check the website for details.

✖ Eating

There are loads of amazing restaurants in Gustavia and we highly encourage you to sample any and all, whether or not they appear in the following list. This selection should just whet your appetite, so to speak.

TOP CHOICE Wall House SEAFOOD **$$**
(✆27-71-83; www.wallhouserestaurant.com; La Pointe; set menu €29; ⊘lunch & dinner, closed lunch Sun) Located along the waterfront near the museum, Wall House has plenty of outdoor seating and a view of the harbor that's as good as the exquisitely presented dishes. Service is impeccable, and the €29 three-course dinner is not to be missed. Enjoy a choice of Creole-inspired meat or fish dishes and end the evening with a velvety espresso while sampling the unlimited supply of cavity-makers from the dessert cart.

Le Select FAST FOOD **$**
(cnr Rue de la France & Rue du Général de Gaulle; burgers €4; ⊘lunch & dinner Mon-Sat) When the bombshells were going off in *Casablanca* (the movie), everyone sought refuge at Rick's. Le Select is the equivalent in St-Barth – the bombshells being something more figurative on this star-studded island, of course. Located in the heart of Gustavia, it's a casual place where you can chill out for a few hours with a cold beer and order some greasy grub without breaking the bank.

Eddy's CREOLE **$$**
(✆27-54-17; Rue du Centenaire; mains €12-25; ⊘dinner) This fusion restaurant blends Creole, Caribbean, Cajun and French influences in a Southeast Asian setting. Owner Eddy Stakelborough actually went to Thailand to build

the pavilion, which was then disassembled and shipped to this site for reconstruction. Look for the teeny doorway across from restaurant Le Sapotillier.

L'Entracte INTERNATIONAL **$$**
(✆27-70-11; Rue du Roi Oscar II; mains €10-20; ⊘lunch & dinner Mon-Sat) Toss a few designer chairs and tables into a converted warehouse and you've got this new – and very welcome – addition to Gustavia's dockside dining scene. Stop by during lunch for the catch of the day served with ample sides and fresh-from-the-oven bread. At €12 it's a steal.

L'Isola ITALIAN **$$$**
(www.lisolastbarth.com; Rue du Roi Oscar II; mains €25-60; ⊘dinner) If you've got some cash to burn, let this modern Italian marvel be your pyre. Enjoy an elaborate menu of handcrafted risottos, lavished with an eclectic assortment of fresh ingredients.

La Crêperie SNACKS **$**
(Rue du Roi Oscar II; dishes €6-14; ⊘lunch & dinner, closed Sun lunch) Wholly unpretentious and bearing not an ounce of belabored design, this popular crêperie whips up cheap eats – both savory and sweet – that make the perfect lunch on a budget.

Fish Market MARKET
(Rue de la République; ⊘6am-10pm) If you have your own kitchen, head to the fish market to pick up still-wriggling supplies. Local fisherfolk bring in the catch of the day, including marlin, wahoo, dorado, tuna and langouste.

Produce Market MARKET
(Rue du Roi Oscar II) Stop by this tiny market for local fruits and vegetables.

🔒 Shopping

Gustavia is a duty-free port and features the most exclusive labels in the world: Hermes, Bulgari, Rolex etc. But there is also a slew of small, locally owned boutiques and labels, such as Made in Saint-Barth and Ligne Saint-Barth, which sells name-branded sweatshirts, cloth bags and cosmetics.

ℹ Information

Business hours in Gustavia are typically Monday to Friday from 8am to noon, then from 2pm to 3:30pm.

Gustavia has wi-fi throughout town; buy a wi-fi card and email contact@saintbarth-telecom.com for access.

Public toilets are available behind the Office Territorial du Tourisme, and include showers for boaters.

Banque des Antilles Française Has an ATM.

Banque Nationale de Paris (Rue Bord de Mer) Has an ATM.

Bruyn Hospital (Rue Jean-Bart) A small hospital.

Change Caraibes (Rue du Général de Gaulle) Has an ATM.

Municipal Police (Rue du Roi Oscar II)

Office Territorial du Tourisme (⌨27-87-27; Quai Général de Gaulle; ⊙9am-noon & 2-5pm Mon-Sat) Will help with accommodations, restaurant recommendations, island tours and activities. Has a map for a self-guided Gustavia walking tour.

Pharmacie St-Barth (Rue de la République; ⊙8am-7:30pm Mon-Fri, 8am-1pm & 3:30-7pm Sat & public holidays)

Post office (cnr Rue Jeanne d'Arc & Rue de Centenaire; ⊙8am-3pm Mon, Tue, Thu & Fri, to noon Wed & Sat)

AROUND GUSTAVIA

Check out pretty **Shell Beach**, where you'll find **Dŏ Brazil** (⌨29-06-66; www.dobrazil.com; mains €10-27, set menu €29), a casually trendy sandwich bar fronting the beach. The menu features exotic Brazilian tastes such as *moqueca* (shrimp, lobster and fish marinated in coconut milk). Drinks, snacks and ice creams are available during the day. Go for a Brazilian *saravah* cocktail – a mix of pineapple and ginger with a dash of cachaça.

On the road to Corossol, **Public** (pronounced with a French accent) is the site of a desalination plant and a village, which is centered on a small beach that's popular with locals.

Here you'll also find **Maya's** (⌨27-75-73; www.mayas-sbh.com; mains €30-41; ⊙dinner Mon-Sat), a place that people return to time and time again to enjoy Randy and Maya's personal service; it's like that bar on the TV show *Cheers* where everyone knows your name (because you're either a local or a celebrity). The shabby-chic waterfront restaurant has a menu that changes every day and often includes tropical salads, fish dishes and Maya's world-famous coconut tart. Meal prices are very high, but it's still worth a try – it's advisable to book a table in advance.

WESTERN ST-BARTHÉLEMY

A quaint pastoral vibe is revealed as the cobbled roads curve west of Gustavia. Craggy, windswept cliffs and scrubby green hills with stone fences look like a postcard from the quiet coasts of western France.

Corossol

This is one of the last remaining traditional villages on St-Barth. The villagers still speak in an old Norman dialect; the brown-sand beach is lined with blue and orange fishing boats and stacks of lobster traps; and women still weave the leaves of the latanier palm into straw hats, baskets and place mats, which they line up on the walls in front of their homes to attract buyers.

This is where you'll find **Le Musée International du Coquillage** (International Shell Museum; admission €3; ⊙9am-12:30pm & 3-5pm Tue-Sat), with over 9000 seashells on display. Founder Ingénu Magras started the museum half a century ago, many years after he and his father collected seashells during fishing trips when he was in his teens.

Carib Waterplay (⌨27-71-22; caribwaterplay@wanadoo.fr) offers windsurfing lessons, as well as kayaking, surfing and snorkeling trips.

Flamands

A small village on the northwestern side of the island, Flamands retains a pleasant rural character. The village stretches along a curving bay whose long, broad white-sand beach and clear waters are very popular with beachgoers. There's easy beach access with streetside parking at the westernmost end of Anse des Flamands.

Ranch des Flamands (⌨39-87-01; Merlette) offers 1½-hour **horseback-riding** excursions for beginner and experienced riders. Rides depart most days at 3:30pm and cost about €35 per person.

🛏 Sleeping

Auberge de Terre-Neuve   COTTAGES **$**
(⌨27-75-32; www.auberge-de-terre-neuve.com; cottages €135-145; ❄🛜) On the way down into Flamands, you'll pass a group of flagpoles marking the entrance to quiet Auberge de Terre-Neuve. Technically the front desk is

MONTBARS 'THE EXTERMINATOR'

In addition to having quite possibly the coolest name in history, Monsieur the Exterminator (Daniel Montbars) was a French-born pirate – and not a very nice one at that. He was present when his uncle was killed in a battle with Spanish conquistadores, and he spent the rest of his life exacting revenge (and borrowing a bit of plunder). Legend has it that Montbars buried treasure somewhere between Anse de Gouverneur and Anse de Grande Saline, but it has never been found. If you've been looking for a reason to borrow Grandpa's metal detector...

located at the airport – the owners of this cluster of cottages also run Gumbs Car Rental (p671), and a car rental from its lot is included in the lodging price. The cabins are painted in a pinkish color and the interiors have basic-but-comfy furniture set on sparkling white tiles. Balconies with barbecues abound, and the units higher up on the hill have scenic views.

Auberge de la Petite Anse   COTTAGES $
(☑27-83-09; www.auberge-petite-anse.com; cottages €120-200; ✴) As the snaking stone road starts to peter out at the far end of Flamands, little Auberge de la Petite Anse will emerge. Its clump of green-and-pink semidetached bungalows squats on a small ledge over the cerulean waters many feet below, and from behind the tattered drapes guests can appreciate quiet vistas of rugged, rocky islands. The quirky, shed-like reception area is strewn with curling paperbacks and thousands of brochures lauding the island's merits.

Anse de Colombier

Anse de Colombier is a beautiful secluded white-sand beach that's fronted by turquoise waters and backed by undulating hills. It's reached by boat or via a scenic 20-minute walk that begins at the end of the road in La Petite Anse, just beyond Flamands. The sandy bay is ideal for swimming, and there's fairly good snorkeling on the north side.

Perched high on the hill overlooking the sea, **Le P'tit Morne** (☑52-95-50; www.timorne.

com; cottages from €194; ✴🛜✉) has a fantastic clutch of cliffside cottages managed by a lovely staff. Expect soaring views of the coast and shore, fully equipped kitchens and a welcoming swimming pool.

EASTERN ST-BARTHÉLEMY

East of Gustavia are dramatic sky-scraping mountains, isolated stretches of powder-soft sand and most of the island's opulent hotels. St-Barth's only airport is located northeast of Gustavia.

St-Jean

Many hotels and restaurants line the main stretch of road in this tourist-heavy village, making parking difficult. Once you're off the road, the beach is delightful, the hotels comfortable and the dining eclectic, ranging from delis to tragically hip, techno-infused attitude factories.

 Activities

Carib Waterplay   WATER SPORTS
(☑27-71-22; caribwaterplay@wanadoo.fr) Offers windsurfing lessons, as well as kayaking, surfing and snorkeling trips. It also rents out kayaks.

Hookipa Surf Shop   SURFING
(☑27-71-31) Rents out surfing equipment.

🛏 **Sleeping**

Hotel Le Village St Jean   HOTEL $$
(☑27-61-39; www.villagestjeanhotel.com; r from €220, 1-bedroom cottage from €260; ✴@🛜✉) Comfort, charm and a yummy Italian restaurant: this place has it all. Patriarch André Charneau built the Village himself in 1968, and it has been lovingly run by his family ever since. Accommodations vary from basic hotel rooms to deluxe cottages with kitchenettes and patios (the two-bedroom cottage has its own pool), ensuring good value on any budget – for St-Barth, that is. It's a five-minute walk uphill from the beach.

Emeraude Plage   HOTEL $$$
(☑27-64-78; www.emeraudeplage.com; Rue de St-Jean; r €350-855; ✴@🛜) This gaggle of ghost-white cottages, bungalows and studios is set in a sandy patch directly on St-Jean beach. Tiled suites all have large bedrooms and

come with a private terrace. Room features include funky plasma-TV-cum-computer contraptions, wi-fi and minimalist white-washed decor that looks a bit hospital-like from the wrong angle.

Eden Rock LUXURY HOTEL **$$$**
(📞29-79-89; www.edenrockhotel.com; cottage €615, ste €1095-1750; ✳@🛜🏊) St-Barth's first hotel stretches out and over a rocky promontory down to the white-coral St-Jean beach below. Each suite and cottage is luxuriously appointed with fine antiques, swashbuckling colors and an unbeatable view.

✖ Eating

If you're preparing food at your villa or organizing a picnic, head to **Marché U** (⊘8am-1pm & 3-8pm Mon-Sat, 9am-1pm & 3-7pm Sun), located in the complex across from the airport. Packed with tropical fruit, and European and American food, it's also the best place to pick up reasonable French wines.

Kiki-é Mo CAFE **$**
(Rue de St-Jean; light meals €6-15; ⊘breakfast, lunch & dinner Mon-Sat) In the heart of St-Jean, this full-service deli has delectable pizza, pasta and desserts, but the real draw is the scrumptious paninis.

Sand Bar CAFE **$$**
(Eden Rock; mains €15-45; ⊘lunch) If you're in the mood for a lunchtime splurge, look no further than Sand Bar, the elegant beach bar at the Eden Rock Hotel. The presentation of the food is artful and you'll be nibbling on your gourmet beach grub alongside an assortment of celebrities.

Maya's to Go CAFE **$$**
(www.mayastogo.com; Les Galeries du Commerce; mains €5-20; ⊘breakfast & lunch Tue-Sun; 🛜) Maya's, the oh-so-popular restaurant in Public, has a small *traiteur* (delicatessen) in St-Jean for those who don't have enough time (or money) to visit the legendary restaurant. If you're toying with the idea of doing a beach picnic à la gourmet, it's worth stopping in for some *petits creux* (snacks).

❶ Information

St-Jean has a small branch post office, near the airport.

American Express (La Savane Commercial Center) Handles transactions in euros and dollars.

Pharmacy (La Savane Commercial Center)

Lorient

Lorient, the site of St-Barth's first French settlement (1648), is a small village fronted by a lovely white-sand beach. The town has a charming collection of old stone structures, including a small Caribbean-style convent and one of the island's three Catholic churches. Most of the island's small Portuguese population lives in the area – try the goat stew if you stop by one of the local haunts.

🛏 Sleeping

Les Mouettes COTTAGES **$**
(📞27-77-91; www.st-barths.com/hotel-les-mouettes; cottage €140-199; ✳🛜) Les Mouettes' seven beachy bungalows sit in a row along Lorient's flaxen sands. Prepare a relaxing dinner in your kitchenette and dine on your private terrace, then fall asleep to the sound of crashing waves gently wafting in through your slatted blue shutters.

La Normandie GUESTHOUSE **$**
(📞27-61-66; www.normandiehotelstbarts.com; s/d from €150/175; ✳@🛜🏊) With a fresh coat of paint and a shopping spree at IKEA, this dance hall of yore has been transformed into a quaint stay. Tucked away from the sea in the interior of Lorient, La Normandie is pricy for what you get – a small room and not a whole lot of sunlight – but this spick-and-span spot is a fine choice when the seaside hotels in the same price bracket are booked up.

✖ Eating

K'Fé Massai FUSION **$$**
(📞29-76-78; www.kfemassai.com; set menu from €29; ⊘dinner) With warm orange light emanating from pillars made from adobe and wicker, this restaurant-cum-lounge feels a bit like a hunting lodge at sunset. While the name and decor hint at an African theme, the cuisine is decidedly French. The €29 set dinner is a fantastic deal and features a choice of one starter, main course and dessert. Try the goat's-cheese salad and a main of mahi mahi, then mix things up with a serving of *pain perdu* (French toast) with ice cream for dessert.

Le Ti St Barth FRENCH **$$$**
(📞27-97-71; www.letistbarth.com; mains €25-68; ⊘dinner) Like an evening in Baz Luhrmann's *Moulin Rouge,* Le Ti St Barth is a sumptuous jumble of wrought-iron chandeliers and

gushing velvet drapes. The menu features a mix of upscale barbecue options such as 'Zen tartare' (a tuna steak with guacamole), and in the late evening a local DJ swings by to give the place a li'l edge. It's located between Lorient and Marigot.

Grand Cul-de-Sac

Beautiful Grand Cul-de-Sac yawns across a large horseshoe-like bay, and has a sandy beach with good conditions for water sports. Fronting the open cove are several hotels and restaurants.

This is the island's main windsurfing center with a large protected cover that's ideal for beginners, and some nice wave action beyond the reef for those who are more advanced.

🏃 Activities

There are a couple of activity outfitters in Grand Cul-de-Sac.

Ouanalao Dive   DIVING
(☑0690-63-74-34) Runs diving trips

Wind Wave Power   WINDSURFING
(☑27-82-57; St-Barths Beach Hotel) Offers 1½-hour windsurfing lessons (about €60) and rents kayaks.

🛏 Sleeping

Hotel Guanahani & Spa   LUXURY HOTEL **$$$**
(☑27-66-60; www.leguanahani.com; ste from €580; ✳@🛜🏊) 'Guanahani' can only be uttered with an accompanying sigh of content and relaxation. The ultimate retreat and, with 70 rooms, the island's largest hotel, this stunning resort is a hidden village of brilliantly bright bungalows (with private plunge pools) flung across jungly grounds.

Les Ondines   COTTAGES **$$$**
(☑27-69-64; www.st-barths.com/les-ondines; r €350-690; ✳) You can practically touch the incoming tide from your apartment-style suite at this motel-like structure. When you start dropping €500-plus per night, you should head to the Guanahani next door, but the cheaper rooms aren't bad, especially because they have a full kitchen and a living room, not to mention a prime spot on the sand.

Le Sereno   HOTEL **$$$**
(☑29-83-00; www.lesereno.com; ste/villa from €480/1130; ✳@🏊🛜) Le Sereno is back with a vengeance. After a bit of time off to get a much needed face-lift by Parisian designer Christian Liaigre, the property is now dedicated to relaxation and serenity through Zen-like decoration. Some would say that it's a bit too minimal (and thus not worth the price); others are awestruck at how the staff keeps the sheets so darn crisp and white. Offers wi-fi access.

Eating

Across from the entrance to Le Sereno there's an open area with some picnic tables and a grill. At one time it was called Cocolobo, and since then it's changed hands a couple of times, but it's still worth checking out as there's usually somebody cooking up some cheap barbecue fare. If you get lost, ask someone for directions to **La Gloriette** and they'll almost definitely know the way.

Anse de Gouverneur

This is a gorgeous, sandy beach lining a U-shaped bay that's embraced by high cliffs at both ends. It's one of the broadest and most secluded spots in the region, and it's splendid for sunbathing and picnics. The lack of visitors – even in high season – means you'll often see sunbathers in their birthday suits. Join in and get rid of those tan lines!

Perched high on craggy **Morne de Lurin** (192m), just before the mountain tumbles into beautiful Gouverneur, sits **Santa Fe** (☑27-61-04; mains €12-32; ⊙lunch & dinner). The owner (who was the former sommelier at ritzy Le Sapotillier in Gustavia), has designed a broad menu with a French-Creole twist, and while the food is fantastic throughout the day, it's best to come before sunset so you can appreciate the stunning ocean views. Try the scallops daintily covered in flaky pastry, and the molten chocolate cake with pear sorbet.

Anse de Grande Saline

A long, lovely beach, broad and secluded, Anse de Grande Saline is named after the large salt pond nearby. The locals consider the beach to be one St-Barth's best, and it's a favorite spot for nudists and gay visitors. The nudists go right and the gay visitors go left, and if you're both, well, you can sunbathe in the middle.

🛏 Sleeping & Eating

Salines Garden
GUESTHOUSE $

(☏51-04-44; www.salinesgarden.com; cottages €140-190) Salines Garden is the only accommodation in the area and is, without a doubt, the best deal on the island. Nestled slightly inland on the Grande Saline's parched terrain, five semidetached cottages huddle around a small plunge pool shaded by thick stalks of bamboo. Each unit is styled with knickknacks and drapery from a far-flung destination: Essaouira, Pavones, Padang, Cap Ferret and Waikiki. The owner, Jean-Phillipe, with his gravelly French tones, creates an inviting and friendly ambience.

Le Grain de Sel
CREOLE $$

(☏52-46-05; mains €16-28; ⊘breakfast, lunch & dinner) Bedecked with stone pillars and hidden behind thirsty desert shrubs, Le Grain de Sel is a fantastic spot to savor traditional French and Creole meals before hitting the powdery sand for the day. The chef (who worked for many years at Maya's in Public) prepares a colorful assortment of palate pleasers, such as crab-and-lentil salad (€16), conch fricassee (€25) and homemade lychee-mango ice cream (€8).

UNDERSTAND ST-BARTHÉLEMY

History

Due to its inhospitable landscape and lack of freshwater, St-Barth never had a big Arawak or Carib presence.

When Christopher Columbus sighted the island on his second voyage in 1493, he named it after his older brother Bartolomeo. The first Europeans who attempted to settle the island, in 1648, were French colonists. They were soon killed by Caribs. Norman Huguenots gave it another try about 25 years later and prospered, not due to farming (which was near impossible) or fishing, but by setting up a way station for French pirates plundering Spanish galleons. You can still hear traces of the old Norman dialect in towns such as Flamands and Corossol.

In 1784, the French king Louis XVI gave St-Barth to the Swedish king Gustaf III in exchange for trading rights in Göteburg. There are still many reminders of Swedish rule on the island – such as the name Gustavia, St-Barth's continuing duty-free status,

and several buildings and forts. However, Sweden sold St-Barth back to France in 1878 after declining trade, increasing disease and a destructive fire affected the island.

Throughout the 19th and early 20th centuries, St-Barth wasn't much more than a quaint French backwater, and life was tough for residents. Without the lush vegetation typical of the Caribbean, farming was difficult. Many former slaves emigrated to surrounding islands to find work, leaving St-Barth one of the only islands in the region without a substantial African population.

In the 1950s tourists slowly started arriving at the tiny airport on small planes and private jets. The scrubby island suddenly found new natural resources: beaches, sunsets, quiet. Quick-thinking islanders created laws limiting mass tourism to guard their hard-earned lifestyle; as a result, you won't see casinos, high-rise hotels or fast-food chains, but you will pay for the atmosphere.

On December 7, 2003, an overwhelming 90% of St-Barth's population voted to grant themselves more fiscal and political independence from France and Guadeloupe. As a member of Guadeloupe, St-Barth was part of an overseas *région* and *départment*. After separation, the island became an 'overseas collectivity', which meant that the island gained a municipal council rather than having a single island-wide mayor. Despite the separation, the island has remained part of the EU.

Culture

Most residents of St-Barth fall into one of three categories: descendants of the pioneers from Normandy who have called St-Barth home for over 300 years; mainland French setting up expensive shops and restaurants; or foreigners looking for a more relaxed lifestyle. As tourism blossomed, the first group of residents largely traded in their fishing careers for tourism-related jobs, so virtually everyone is working in hospitality of some sort.

The locals protect their slightly rustic way of life while the glitzy Hollywood types strut around next door – many natives haven't seen their house key for years, and nor do they care whether Beyoncé is being bootylicious at the next table – but neither group seems too bothered about the other's presence.

Despite the island's location, the general atmosphere is much more that of a quiet seaside province in France than a jammin' Caribbean colony.

For hundreds of years, St-Barth's residents were too busy toiling in near-impossible conditions to create much art, thus the traditional handicrafts were largely utilitarian. Head to Corossol, St-Barth's most 'local' area, and you'll find hats and baskets woven by local women from the leaves of latanier palms. These small woven concoctions sit at the front gates to many homes, and make a great, authentic souvenir.

There are about 20 art galleries and spaces around the island devoted to exhibiting local paintings, photography and sculpture. For more information about visiting artists' studios, stop by the **Office Territorial du Tourisme** (p663) for a detailed list.

Landscape & Wildlife

St-Barth's total land area is a mere 21 sq km, although its elongated shape and hilly terrain make it seem larger. The island lies 25km southeast of St-Martin/Sint Maarten.

St-Barth has numerous dry and rocky offshore islets. The largest, Île Fourchue, is a half-sunken volcanic crater whose large bay is a popular yacht anchorage and a destination for divers and snorkelers.

St-Barth's arid climate sustains dryland flora, such as cacti and bougainvillea. Local fauna includes lizards, iguanas and harmless grass snakes. From April to August, sea turtles lay eggs along the beaches on the northwest side of the island. The islets off St-Barth support seabird colonies, including those of frigate birds.

With its numerous bays and coves, St-Barth boasts nearly two dozen beaches – impressive considering the island's miniscule size. Those looking for 'in-town' beaches will find that St-Jean, Flamands, Lorient and Shell Beach all have beautiful sandy strands. The most famous secluded beaches – Colombier, Grande Saline and Gouverneur – are as close to the picture-perfect Caribbean beach as possible, with long white expanses of sand and gently lapping warm waves.

In recent years St-Barth has taken environmental concerns very seriously and has committed to sustainable methods of energy production. The island utilizes a color-coded recycling system; be sure to toss glass in green containers and plastic in blue containers.

In 2001 St-Barth pioneered the first eco-friendly trash incinerator of its kind in the Caribbean. The incinerator is able to simultaneously burn trash, create energy and produce drinkable water, all with less pollution than older incinerators. It comes with a higher price tag, but islanders feel the result is worth it.

SURVIVAL GUIDE

Directory A–Z

Accommodations

St-Barth's largest hotel has a mere 70 rooms and the island's second biggest has barely half that number. The others are small, with usually less than a dozen rooms. This can be a wonderful thing – lots of intimacy and unique design details – but it also means that during high season everything books up fast. Virtually all hotels are priced in euros and there's a 5% tax surcharge added to your quoted rate.

There's no easy way to do St-Barth on the cheap, but with some advance planning you can scout out great deals on private villas, which are almost always a better choice than paying for a hotel room by the night. There are many websites and private brokers offering a variety of villa rental options; try www.stbarth.com or www.wimco.com.

The following price indicators, based on high-season rates, are used for accommodations listings in this chapter.

$	budget	less than €200
$$	midrange	€200 to €400
$$$	top end	more than €400

Activities

Although St-Barth is celebrated for its leisurely pursuits, more active types will have no trouble filling their days – swimming, snorkeling, surfing, diving, fishing, kayaking, hiking and horseback-riding are all possible here.

Surf and dive outfitters are found around the island, but most fishing, diving and snorkeling trips leave from Gustavia (p661). To dive on your own, you must pay a fee and register with the **St-Barth Natural Marine Reserve** (📞27-88-18). The **Mairie** (Town Hall; 🕙9am-noon & 2-3:30pm Mon-Fri) or any dive outfitter will be able to send you through the proper channels. For windsurfers Grand Cul-de-Sac (p666) offers ideal conditions.

Business Hours

The following are normal business hours. Many places shut on Wednesday afternoons and almost everything is closed on Sundays. Shops tend to be open on Thursdays until late and, in high season, may stay open till 5pm on weekdays and may open on weekends.

Reviews don't include hours unless they differ from these standards.

Banks 8am-noon & 2-3:30pm Mon-Fri

Post offices 8-11am Mon-Sat

Restaurants 7-10am for breakfast, 11:30am-2:30pm for lunch, 7-11pm for dinner

Shops 9am-noon & 2-3:30pm Mon-Fri

Embassies & Consulates

Although St-Barthélemey is practically autonomous, consular services are still linked to France. A Swedish diplomatic figurehead is the only foreign representation on the island.

Festivals & Events

A number of festivals are celebrated on St-Barth throughout the year. The **Office Territorial du Tourisme** (p663) has a handy list of important events – it's definitely worth picking it up as it's quite detailed.

St-Barth Music Festival Held in mid-January, this festival features two weeks of jazz, chamber music and dance performances.

Carnival Held for five days before Lent. Includes a pageant, costumes and street dancing, ending with the burning of a King Carnival figure at Shell Beach. Many businesses close during Carnival.

St-Barth Film Festival (www.stbarthff.org) The only festival of its kind, this showcases Caribbean talent in film and documentary. It's held in late April.

Festival of St-Barth August 24, the feast day of the island's patron saint, is celebrated with fireworks, a public ball, boat races and other competitions.

PRACTICALITIES

» **Newspapers & Magazines** Newspapers include the *Weekly*, published in English on Friday from November to April, and *Today*. The latest glossy tourist magazines can be found at the information office in Gustavia.

» **Radio** For local radio, try Radio Transat on 100.3FM, and Radio Saint-Barth on 98.7FM.

» **Electricity** The current used is 220V (50/60 cycles); standard Western Europe plugs are used. Many hotels offer American-style shaver adapters.

» **Weights & Measures** The metric system and 24-hour clock are used.

Food

The following price indicators, based on the the cost of a main course, are used for Eating listings in this chapter.

$	budget	less than €10
$$	midrange	€10 to €20
$$$	top end	more than €20

Gay & Lesbian Travelers

The website www.gay.com points out, 'St-Barth is the most gay-popular spot on earth...without a gay bar,' and this pretty much sums up the nature of the island's gay tourism. Locals and other travelers are very laid-back and it's not uncommon to see gay couples holding hands at the beach or having a romantic dinner. But if you're looking for a bumpin' nightlife scene, you won't find it here.

Health

There are medical facilities in Gustavia (p663) including a small hospital and eight local doctors. There are two pharmacies on the island, one in Gustavia (p663) and one in St-Jean (p665).

Tap water comes from a variety of sources on St-Barth: desalination plants, cisterns, and personalized purification systems (for some small luxury hotels and private villas). Some properties use water from multiple sources. If in doubt, go for bottled water.

Internet Access

Most hotels on the island offer some form of internet access, either via a computer terminal or via wi-fi; upscale venues offer both. There is wi-fi access throughout Gustavia. The tourism office in Gustavia has a list of wi-fi-friendly cafes.

Money

The currency used in St-Barth is the euro. US dollars are sometimes accepted, although you will not find the one-for-one dollar-to-euro trading that occurs on St-Martin/Sint Maarten.

There are six banks around the island, and an American Express office in St-Jean. None of the ATMs on the island accept American Express.

Public Holidays

St-Barth observes the following public holidays, in addition to the standard regionwide holidays (p872):

Easter Sunday Late March/early April

Labor Day May 1

Ascension Thursday Fortieth day after Easter

Pentecost Monday Seventh Monday after Easter

Bastille Day July 14

Assumption Day August 15

All Saints' Day (Toussaints) November 1

All Souls Day November 2

Armistice Day November 11

Telephone

The telephone system has been a bit confusing since a changeover in 1996. The country code is ☑590, but to call St-Barth from abroad, you need to dial your country's international access code + St-Barth's country code *twice,* ie ☑590-590 + the local six-digit number.

Cell phones start with ☑0690; to call a cell phone from overseas, dial ☑590 + the number.

To call from within the French phone system, add '0' in front of the (single) country code, ie ☑0590 + the local number. We have included only the six-digit local number for St-Barth listings in this chapter.

Public telephones take all major credit cards and prices are listed. Prepaid phone cards are available for purchase throughout the island as well.

Visas

Citizens from the US, UK, Canada, Australia, Japan and New Zealand don't need visas. Citizens of several CIS, African and South American countries require visas valid for a French collectivity. Contact the **border police** (☑29-76-76) for more information.

Getting There & Away

Entering St-Barthélemy

Residents of EU countries need only a national identity card to enter St-Barth. Passports are needed for all other nationalities.

Air

Located near the village of St-Jean, St-Barth's only airport, **Aéroport de St-Barthélemy** (SBH; ☑27-65-41), has the second-shortest runway in the world (the shortest is on Saba). Only teeny-tiny puddle jumpers can land on the island, ensuring mass tourism is impossible.

The following airlines fly to and from St-Barth:

Air Antilles Express (www.airantilles.com) Fort-de-France, Pointe-à-Pitre, St-Martin/Sint Maarten

Air Caraïbes (www.aircaraibes.com) Fort-de-France, Havana, Marie-Galante, Panama City, Paris (France), Pointe-à-Pitre, Port-au-Prince, Santo Domingo, St-Martin/Sint Maarten, San José, St Lucia

St-Barth Commuter (www.stbarthcommuter.com) St-Martin/Sint Maarten; charter flights throughout the Caribbean also available

Winair (www.fly-winair.com) Anguilla, Antigua, Barbuda, Montserrat, Nevis, St-Martin/Sint Maarten, St Kitts, Sint Eustatius, Tortola

Sea

FERRY

The ferry service between St-Barthélemy and St-Martin/Sint Maarten often hits choppy water so it's a good idea to take motion-sickness pills beforehand. Your accommodation can usually reserve a seat for you on the boat for a minimal deposit – simply pay the balance when you arrive at the pier for departure.

The main company is **Voyager** (☑St-Martin 87-10-68, Sint Maarten 542-4096; www.voy12.com), which has two modern high-speed boats. One leaves Marigot, St-Martin, at 9am and 6:15pm for the 1½-hour journey; it departs Gustavia at 7:15am and 4:30pm. On Sunday and Wednesday, the boat leaves from Captain Oliver's Marina in Oyster Pond, St-Martin, and the ride is only 40 minutes. Also available is the high-speed catamaran, the **Edge** (✆Sint Maarten 544-2640), which makes the 45-minute trip to Gustavia daily from Pelican Marina on Simpson Bay, Sint Maarten, at 9am; it returns at 4pm. You need to check in 15 minutes in advance. The US$15 departure tax is not included in the ticket price.

Day-trip tickets are significantly cheaper than returning on different days.

YACHT

Those arriving by yacht can clear immigration at the **port office** (✆27-66-97), on the east side of Gustavia Harbor.

Getting Around

There is no bus system on St-Barth. Taxis are pricey, so strongly consider renting a car.

Bicycle

Cycling around the island can be arduous, even for the healthiest individuals, so isn't a recommended way of getting around. The roads can be exceptionally steep.

Car & Motorcycle

DRIVER'S LICENSE

A driver's license from your home country is valid in St-Barth.

FUEL

There are only two gas stations on the island, one in St-Jean and one in Lorient, and both are closed on Sundays. During the week they are open until around 3.15pm (with the obligatory long lunch break from noon until 1pm). If you're desperate, there's an all-night gas pump at the airport, which only works with a credit card (although not usually with American plastic).

RENTAL

There are loads of car- and scooter-rental agencies throughout the island, with about a dozen concentrated in the airport terminal in St-Jean. The others mostly sit around Gustavia, although the cars are kept near the airport. In general, you will be discouraged from renting a scooter or motorcycle as the terrain is quite rugged and steep (and scoot-

ers aren't really that much cheaper than cars, especially as you won't spend that much on gas since the island is so tiny.) Prices between December and April hover around €70 per day for cars, while low-season prices drop to a less outrageous €35 to €40.

Barth'Loc (✆27-52-81) Located in Gustavia; also offers scooter rentals.

Budget (✆27-66-30; budgetsaintbarth@wanadoo.fr) Located at the airport and in Gustavia.

Chez Beranger (✆27-89-00; chezberanger@wanadoo.fr) Located in Gustavia; leases cars and scooters.

Europcar (✆27-74-34; www.st-barths.com/europcar/index.html)

Gumbs Rental (✆27-75-32; gumbs.car.rental@wanadoo.fr) Located at the airport. Is also the front desk for Anse de Terre-Neuve.

Meca Moto (✆52-92-49; mecamoto3@wanadoo.fr) Located in Gustavia. Specializes in motorbikes.

Soleil Caraibes (✆27-67-18; soleil.caraibes@wanadoo.fr) Located at the airport.

Tropic All Rent (✆27-64-76; tropicall.rent@wanadoo.fr) Located in Gustavia; offers cars and motorbikes.

ROAD RULES

Driving is on the right-hand side, and the speed limit is 45km/h, unless otherwise posted. Some of the older roads are quite narrow so be mindful of cars coming in the opposite direction.

Hitchhiking

Hitchhiking is easy and relatively safe in St-Barth, although substantially more difficult the closer one gets to the far corners of the island. As always when hitchhiking, be cautious and obey your instincts.

Taxi

Taxi fares range from pricey to outrageous. There are no set fares, so prices are all over the board, but will generally increase by about 50% when it's dark out. It's around €10 from Gustavia to the airport, or around €25 from Gustavia to Petit Cul-de-Sac.

To book a taxi in Gustavia, call ✆27-66-31; at the airport, call ✆27-75-81. There's a taxi stand in Gustavia. You can also contact drivers directly – a list of drivers and their phone numbers is available at the Office Territorial de Tourisme (p663) in Gustavia.

St Kitts & Nevis

Includes »

Best Beaches

» South Friar's Bay (p682)
» Nisbet Beach (p687)
» Pinney's Beach (p687)
» Lovers Beach (p687)
» South Frigate Bay (p680)

Best Places to Sleep

» Ottley's Plantation Inn (p684)
» Nisbet Plantation Beach Club (p688)
» Banyan Tree (p690)
» Montpelier Plantation Inn (p689)
» Timothy Beach Resort (p681)

Why Go?

Near-perfect packages – that's how you might think of St Kitts and Nevis. The two-island nation combines beaches with beauteous mountains, activities to engage your body and rich history to engage your mind. The legacies of the sugar industry survive in pleasant plantation inns and the local culture is mellow, friendly and infused with a pulsing soca beat.

But if the pair offer much that's similar, they differ in the details. St Kitts is the larger and feels that way, from bustling Basseterre and mighty Brimstone Hill Fortress to the party strip and resorts of Frigate Bay.

Nevis is a neater package, anchored by a single volcanic mountain buttressed by a handful of beaches and a tiny capital, Charlestown. Nature walks take you into the verdant upper reaches of the peak. History here centers on the big names of Horatio Nelson and Alexander Hamilton.

When to Go

High-season rates start from around mid-December and go to mid-April. The best time to visit, price- and weather-wise, is November and early December. Winter days average a temperature of 81°F (27°C), while summers shoot up to 86°F (30°C).

Annual rainfall averages 55in and is fairly consistent throughout the year. The driest months are February to June, and the hurricane (and rainy) season is from July to November.

The four-day St Kitts Music Festival in June brings together top-name performers from throughout the Caribbean. For over 30 years between July and August, Nevis' main event has been Culturama. Starting in mid-December, Carnival is the biggest yearly event on St Kitts.

Itineraries

TWO DAYS

If you only have two days, limit your stay to one island. On St Kitts spend your first morning exploring historic Basseterre, followed by chilling on Frigate Bay or South Friar's Bay beach and partying on the Frigate Bay 'Strip' at night. The next day, take a drive around the northern part of the island and finish with dinner at the Royal Palm at Ottley's Plantation Inn.

On Nevis, spend the better part of day one circling the island, stopping for lunch at a historic plantation inn before winding down the day on Pinney's Beach with a swim and sunset drinks at Sunshine's. The following day, set up a hike or mountain-bike tour for a more intimate look at Nevis' volcano and abundant natural charms, then wrap up with dinner at Bananas Bistro.

FOUR DAYS

Do the two-day highlights for both islands.

ONE WEEK

Split your time between the two islands. Add in a lot more beach time as the extra days let you explore the sandy shores at will, looking for a favorite. Consider overnighting at a romantic plantation inn.

GETTING TO NEIGHBORING ISLANDS

Several passenger ferries and one car ferry link St Kitts and Nevis, but there is no boat service to other islands. Liat has flights to Antigua from both St Kitts and Nevis, while St-Martin/Sint Maarten is served by Liat from St Kitts and Winair from Nevis.

Essential Food & Drink

» **Stewed saltfish** Official national dish; served with spicy plantains, coconut dumplings and seasoned breadfruit.

» **Pelau** Also known as 'cook-up,' this dish is the Kittitian version of paella: a tasty but messy blend of rice, meat, saltfish, vegetables and pigeon peas.

» **Conch** Served curried, marinated or soused (boiled).

» **Cane Spirit Rothschild** More commonly known as CSR, this locally distilled libation is made from pure fermented cane juice and best enjoyed on the rocks mixed with grapefruit-flavored Ting soda.

» **Brinley Gold Rum** Locally blended rum comes in such flavors as vanilla, coffee, mango, coconut and lime. The shop in Port Zante does tastings.

» **Carib** Locally brewed lager.

ST KITTS

St Kitts definitely has a beat, and it's not just the one blasting from the many minibuses hauling folks hither and yon. Basseterre is a fascinating place to wander and very much the commercial heart of the island. Locals bustle shop to shop making their purchases and there's only a bit of compromise offered

for tourists and that's at the cruise-ship dock.

The island's past is very palpable in the northern areas, where abandoned sugar-cane fields climb hills dotted with plantation inns and sleepy villages. The most stunning landmark is Brimstone Hill Fortress National-al Park, a Unesco World Heritage site that

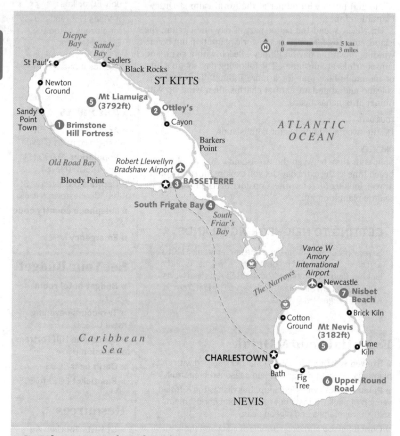

St Kitts & Nevis Highlights

❶ Indulge in a blast from the past at **Brimstone Hill Fortress** (p683)

❷ Laze over lunch at a grand old plantation estate like **Ottley's** (p684)

❸ Stroll around intriguing and vibrant **Basseterre** (p675)

❹ Enjoy a rum-fuelled

party at the 'Strip' of **South Frigate Bay** (p681)

❺ Stare into the crater of a volcano on hikes up **Mt Nevis** (p695) and **Mt Liamuiga** (p695)

❻ Get close to Nevis' nature and history on a trek along the **Upper Round Road** (p689)

❼ Give in to slothdom during a long day at **Nisbet Beach** (p687)

❽ Go local during the Friday night **communal barbecue** (p687)

❾ Take a romantic **sunset cruise** (p695)

preserves a vast 18th-century British hilltop fort.

South of Basseterre a very different vibe rules. The area around Frigate Bay is thick with condos and mega-resorts such as the Marriott. On the west side you're rarely more than a stone's throw from a party, with beach joints rocking on until well after midnight.

But it's on the southeast peninsula where the biggest changes are happening. Until recently, only goats patrolled its sunbaked hillsides and beaches remained largely footprint-free. Now fast-forward to the future and envision an entire snazzy new township called Christophe Harbour, built to lure the ultrarich and catapult St Kitts to the top of the luxury travel market. One island, many faces.

❶ Getting Around

For information about getting to/from St Kitts, see p693.

BUS Buses are privately owned minivans and festooned with hilariously disconcerting names like 'De Punisher' or 'Street Freak.' In Basseterre, most leave from the bus stop on Bay Rd and only when full. Fares range from EC$2 to EC$6.

There's no fixed schedule but they tend to be most plentiful in the early morning and late afternoon. The last bus usually runs between 10pm and midnight. Sunday service is less frequent. To avoid competition with taxis, buses do not normally run to Frigate Bay and beyond.

CAR & SCOOTER Basseterre has quite a few one-way streets, some of which are not clearly marked. Keep an eye out for road signs, and when in doubt, simply follow the rest of the traffic.

Avis (☑465-6507; www.avis.com; S Independence Sq, Basseterre)

Caines Rent a Car (☑465-2366; Princes St, Basseterre)

TDC/Thrifty Auto Rentals (☑465-2991; West Independence Sq, Basseterre)

Islandwide Scooter Rentals (☑465-7841; midasscooter@caribsurf.com; Caunt St) Get at least a 100cc model if you want to make it over Timothy Hill to go to the southeast peninsula.

TAXI A taxi from the airport costs EC$20 to Basseterre, EC$35 to Frigate Bay, and EC$50 to St Paul's.

From the Circus (the main taxi stand in Basseterre), it costs EC$10 to anywhere within town, EC$20 to Frigate Bay and EC$85 to Brimstone Hill round-trip. Rates are 50% higher between 10pm and 6am. There's an EC$3 charge for each 15 minutes of waiting. To call a taxi, dial ☑465-4253 or 465-7818.

POP 12,800

Basseterre (pronounced 'bass-tear') was founded more than 380 years ago as the first French town in the Caribbean. The name combines the French words 'basse' and 'terre,' which roughly translates as lowlands. Leaving behind the cruise-ship terminal at Port Zante plunges you headlong into a vibrant mix of local commerce, history and culture. Nothing in the capital has been overly gussied up, which means that surprises abound. Take time to pick out the surviving colonial buildings with their wide porches and nod to folks lounging on their stoops, Carib in hand.

⊙ Sights

National Museum   MUSEUM

(☑465-5584; Bay Rd; adult/child EC$8/free; ☺9:15am-5pm Mon-Fri, to 1pm Sat) Though modest, this three-room museum is a good place to start your explorations of St Kitts. Displays deal with colonial history, the road to independence and local lifestyle and traditions. It's housed in the 1894 Treasury Building, a stately pile built from hand-cut volcanic limestone.

Circus   SQUARE

The focus of town is the Circus, a roundabout inspired by London's Piccadilly Circus. Anchored by a green clock tower, the Victorian-style Berkeley Memorial Clock, it is surrounded by quaint buildings housing shops and banks.

Independence Square   SQUARE

Locals 'lime' and exchange gossip on this grassy patch anchored by a waterless fountain. Once called Pall Mall Sq, it was used in the 1790s for slave auctions and is flanked by 18th-century Georgian buildings and the dignified cathedral.

Immaculate Conception Cathedral CHURCH

This hulking gray-stone house of worship has a barrel-vaulted wooden ceiling evoking a ship's hull. Sunlight filters through elaborate stained-glass windows above an altar made of multi-hued marble.

St George's Anglican Church   CHURCH

(Cayon St) In a small park behind a fence, this church has a stormy history. French Jesuits built the first one in 1670, but it was destroyed and rebuilt three times, the last time in 1869. The cemetery has some fancy epitaphs.

ST KITTS & NEVIS BASSETERRE

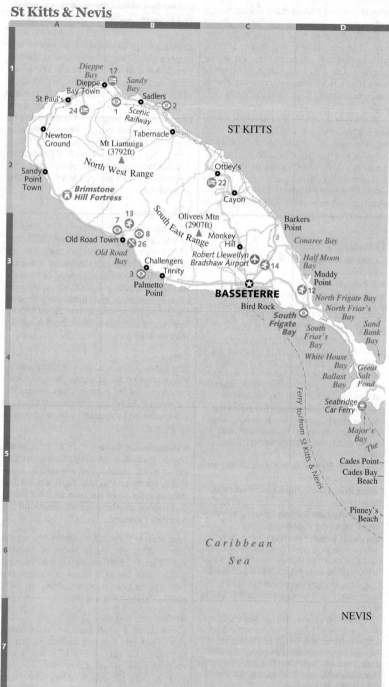

ST KITTS

Dieppe
Bay
Dieppe
Bay Town
St Paul's
Sandy
Bay
Sadlers
Scenic
Railway
Tabernacle
Newton
Ground
Mt Liamuiga
(3792ft)
North West Range
Sandy
Point
Town
Brimstone
Hill Fortress
Ottley's
Cayon
Barkers
Point
Old Road Town
South East Range
Olivees Mtn
(2907ft)
Monkey
Hill
Conaree Bay
Old Road
Bay
Challengers
Trinity
Robert Llewellyn
Bradshaw Airport
Half Moon
Bay
Muddy
Point
Palmetto
Point
BASSETERRE
Bird Rock
North Frigate Bay
North Friar's
Bay
South
Frigate
Bay
South
Friar's
Bay
Sand
Bank
Bay
White House
Bay
Ballast
Bay
Great
Salt
Pond
Ferry to/from St Kitts & Nevis
Seabridge
Car Ferry
Major's
Bay
The
Cades Point
Cades Bay
Beach
Pinney's
Beach
*Caribbean
Sea*
NEVIS

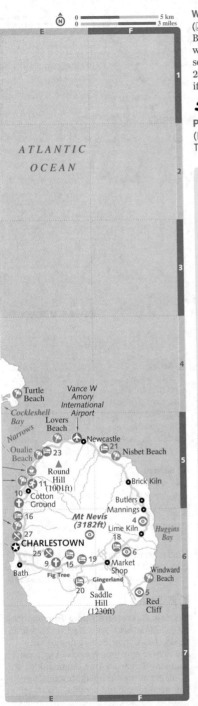

ATLANTIC
OCEAN

Warner Park Stadium   SPORTS STADIUM

(☎466-2007; ⊙office 8.30am-4.30pm Mon-Fri)
Basseterre's cricket and football stadium
was financed with Taiwanese money and
served as one of the match sites during the
2007 Cricket World Cup. Stop by to find out
if any matches are scheduled.

🏃 Activities

Pro-Divers   DIVING
(☎466-3483; www.prodiversstkitts.com; Fort
Thomas Rd; ⊙closed 3 weeks in Aug) Sandy Point

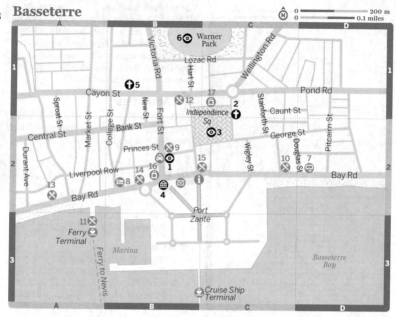

Basseterre

Bay, below Brimstone Hill, is a popular dive spot, as is the dive to the 148ft freighter *River Taw*. This well-established outfit offers single-tank boat dives with equipment (US$70), two-tank dives (US$105), a three-day PADI course (US$420) and a half-day snorkeling trip (US$50). Equipment is available for rent. It's at the Fisherman's Wharf restaurant, about 800 yards west of town.

Kenneth's Dive Centre　　DIVING
(☎465-2670; http://kennethdivecenter.com; Bay Rd) The oldest dive shop on St Kitts offers similar services and rates as Pro-Divers. Clients have included astronaut Buzz Aldrin and underwater explorer Jean-Michel Cousteau.

☞ Tours

Historic Basseterre Audio Tour AUDIO TOUR
(☎662-3445; www.tamarindtreetours.com; tours US$15) Delve into the town's past with the help of this tour conceived by local company Tamarind Tree. Audioguides are available at the National Museum, but you need to call and arrange a pick-up.

Annie Fontaine Walking Tours

(☑668-5425; per person US$50) Get the skinny on Basseterre during Annie's anecdote-filled, two-hour walking tours.

✸✸ Festivals & Events

St Kitts Music Festival
MUSIC

(www.stkittsmusicfestival.com) This four-day festival brings together top-name calypso, soca, reggae, salsa, jazz and gospel performers from throughout the Caribbean. The performances take place at the Warner Park Stadium.

Carnival
CARNIVAL

(www.stkittsneviscarnival.com) Starting around mid-December, Carnival is the biggest yearly event on St Kitts, with 17 days of calypso competitions, costumed street dances and steel-pan music enlivening streets and venues throughout town.

🛏 Sleeping

Ocean Terrace Inn
HOTEL $$

(☑465-2754; www.oceanterraceinn.com; Wigley Ave; r US$132-225; ❄@🛜🏊) Known as OTI, this dignified old-school hotel has 69 units cascading down a bay-front hillside about a 15-minute walk west of central Basseterre. The staff is super-friendly, rooms are classily furnished and there are three smallish pools to compensate for the lack of beach. Rooms 30 to 43 are fronted by a broad lawn and are the most restful. To get here, follow Bay Rd west out of the town center for about 800 yards, go past the hotel, turn right and drive uphill to the reception.

Bird Rock Beach Hotel
HOTEL $$

(☑465-8914; www.birdrockbeach.com; Bird Rock; r US$105-135; ❄🏊🛜) Though not of recent vintage, Bird Rock is a good value-for-money pick. A short drive south of Basseterre, it sits above its own small beach, which has decent diving and snorkeling; a dive shop is on the premises. Many rooms have balconies with ocean views and the studio suites have full kitchens.

Seaview Inn
GUESTHOUSE $

(☑466-1635; Bay Rd; r US$75; ❄🛜) Seaview's 10 dark and small rooms near the ferry terminal are not exactly conducive to hanging out, but they are currently your only in-town lodging option. At least they're reasonably clean and have a TV.

🍴 Eating & Drinking

Fisherman's Wharf
SEAFOOD $$

(☑465-2754; Fort Thomas Rd; mains EC$30-75; ⊘dinner; 👶) With its plank floors, sprawling tables and ocean views, this casual restaurant has a fun vibe and practically gets mobbed during the regular Friday Fish Fry, which has live entertainment. Any night, dinners are cooked to order over an open grill and accompanied by a self-service side buffet. A kids' menu is available, too. The restaurant is about 800 yards west of the town center via Bay Rd.

Caribe Café
CAFE $

(The Sands, Bay Rd; snacks EC$20-30; ⊘7:30am-7pm Mon-Fri, 8:30am-4pm Sat; 🛜) Perk up with a cuppa at this contemporary upstairs cafe. Baked goods, wraps, salads, pizza and other snacks are equally fine and the views over the water may distract you from your laptop.

Ballahoo
INTERNATIONAL $$

(☑465-4197; www.ballahoo.com; Circus; mains EC$30-65; ⊘8am-10pm Mon-Sat; 🛜) If you need a break from exploring Basseterre, Ballahoo's upstairs terrace tables provide a nice people-watching perch. The menu hopscotches around the world, with lobster sandwich, Caesar salad, Madras curry and fettucine marinara all making appearances. There's a full bar and free wi-fi, too.

Kalabash
VEGAN $

(Cayon St; meals from EC$12; ⊘8am-8pm Mon-Sat) Roman, a Rasta from British Columbia, presides over this hole-in-the-wall that dishes out tasty veggie burgers, falafel, lentil soup, roti and other vegan delights. Don't let the fascinating screed about what the pilgrims *really* did to the Caribs (the turkeys got off easy) that's splayed across the wall turn you off.

Redi-Fried Chicken
FAST FOOD $

(Bay Rd; meals EC$13-16; ⊘10am-midnight) Finger-lickin' fried chicken. Tell that to the Colonel.

Ram's Supermarket
SUPERMARKET $

(☑466-6065; S Pelican Dr; ⊘8am-8pm) Ram's is one of the island's best food stores. Get here by following Bay Rd east to the end and then turning left. There's a smaller branch near Port Zante in town.

Public Market
MARKET $

(Bay Rd; ⊘Wed-Sat) Saturday morning is the best time for a spin around Basseterre's tin-roofed market.

ST KITTS & NEVIS BASSETERRE

PORT OF CALL – BASSETERRE

Basseterre is a popular port of call and is a stop on many Eastern Caribbean cruise itineraries.

The St Kitts Scenic Railway (p683) attracts large numbers of cruise-ship passengers, but there are other things to keep visitors occupied with a few hours in port:

» Get your heart pumping on a guided trek up Mt Liamuiga volcano (p695)

» Take a spin around northern St Kitts, stopping at Brimstone Hill Fortress (p683) and for lunch at a plantation inn (p684)

» Catch the ferry to the slow-paced nature isle of Nevis (p685) and hire a cab to explore its lush beauty

» Swim, snorkel, sail and meet a giant pig at Cockleshell Bay (p682)

Dominica Boat PRODUCE **$**

On Mondays, organic produce from fertile Dominica arrives at the ferry terminal.

Shopping

Genuine bargains in duty-free Port Zante next to the cruise-ship dock are as rare as tulips in Tonga, so *caveat emptor*. For a more authentic experience, it's a good idea to stroll into town and see what the locals are buying.

Spencer Cameron Gallery ART, CRAFTS

(☑465-1617; www.spencercamerongallery.com; 10 N Independence Sq; ☺9am-4pm Mon-Sat) An attractive 18th-century colonial cottage showcases the work of local artists, including English transplant Rosey Cameron Smith, who's well known for her paintings of Carnival clowns. Glass artist Leonie makes beautiful jewelry, glass plates and ornaments in her workshop out the back. Quality is high, prices reasonable.

Brown Sugar CLOTHING, ACCESSORIES

(www.mybrownsugar.com; Bay Rd) Kittitian fashion designer Judith Rawlins keeps her studio right above the store that sells her flattering, colorful and sophisticated dresses and shirts for women. There's also a good selection of handbags, sunglasses and other accessories.

Information

A number of international banks and ATMs can be found around the Circus. Only the ATM at the Marriott dispenses US dollars.

City Drug Store (Fort St; ☺8am-7pm Mon-Fri, to 5pm Sat, to 11am Sun) General store with pharmacy.

Compuzone (☑466-8919; cnr Adlam St & Bay Rd; per hr US$8; ☺8am-5pm Mon-Fri, 9am-1pm Sat) Full-service internet access. Places in Port Zante tend to be open later and on Sundays.

Joseph N Francis General (☑465-2551; Cayon St; ☺24hr) Main hospital.

Post office (☑465-2521; Bay Rd; ☺8am-4pm Mon & Tue, to 3:30pm Wed-Fri)

St Kitts Tourism Authority (☑465-4040; www.stkittstourism.kn; Pelican Mall, Bay Rd; ☺7.30am-5pm Mon-Fri) Small office that can answer questions. Sometimes.

Getting There & Around

Besides the main bus stop at the ferry terminal, you can stop minibuses going up the coasts on Cayon St and Wellington Rd.

Frigate Bay

Frigate Bay, located 3 miles southeast of Basseterre, is an isthmus dividing the calm Caribbean side and the rougher Atlantic side, which is dominated by the massive Marriott resort. This is also the center for condo development on St Kitts, and you know you're getting close by the blight of jewelry-store billboards lining the road. The area has some good restaurants, but the key draws are the funky beach bars along South Frigate Bay beach, dubbed 'The Strip'. This is as happening as nightlife gets on St Kitts.

Activities

South Frigate Bay ACTIVITIES BEACH

St Kitts' busiest beach is a sweep of golden sand with mellow waves and warm water. It's great for sunning, snorkeling and water sports, and is backed by bars and casual restaurants attracting a rollickin' party crowd, especially on Thursday, Friday and Saturday nights. Beach chairs rent for around US$5.

D's Watersports WATER SPORTS

(☑465-7043; South Frigate Bay beach; ☺9am-5pm) D's has a full complement of water toys, from snorkeling gear (US$10), Hobie Cat sailboats (per hour US$35), water skiing (three laps US$30) and jet skis (per half-hour US$50).

Royal St Kitts Golf Club   GOLF

(☑466-2700; www.royalstkittsgolfclub.com; greens fee 9/18 holes US$130/180) Tee up in a spectacular setting between the Caribbean and Atlantic at this 18-hole, par 71 championship course that got a recent makeover by Thomas McBroom.

🛏 Sleeping

Timothy Beach Resort   RESORT $$

(☑465-8597; www.timothybeach.com; South Frigate Bay Beach; r US$140-230; ✱🕏✱🕏) The only resort right on a Caribbean-side beach, this simple pad has 60 rooms and suites within stumbling distance of the Frigate Bay 'Strip.' Larger units have full kitchens and can sleep up to four adults and three kids. The cheapest face the hill (avoid!), but most others have large balconies with water views.

Rock Haven B&B   B&B $$

(☑465-5503; www.rock-haven.com; r incl breakfast US$155-175; ✱🕏) This lovely Caribbean home is a great find if you're not the type in need of buckets of privacy. There are just two beautifully decorated suites, one with a full kitchen and a flower-filled terrace with views of the Atlantic. The warm host, Judith, makes memorable breakfasts and can happily help you plan your day.

St Kitts Marriott Resort   RESORT $$$

(☑466-1200; www.marriott.com; 858 Frigate Bay Rd; r from US$200; ✱@🕏✱🕏) Utterly out of scale from the rest of Frigate Bay, this 513-room resort exudes cookie-cutter sophistication and is like a small village unto itself, with multiple pools, restaurants and bars, a gym, spa, nightclub, shops and even a casino. It also comes with plenty of time-share buying opportunities. Check the web for discounts.

🍴 Eating & Drinking

The string of beach joints along the Frigate Bay 'Strip' should be a top destination no matter where you stay on St Kitts. Hours are as casual as the vibe – some close at 10pm, others at dawn. The Atlantic side of Frigate Bay has several excellent restaurants. The island's best breakfast is the giant buffet at the Marriott (US$25).

Rainbow Bar & Grille   CARIBBEAN $

(www.rainbowbeachbar.com; The Strip; meals EC$10-45; ⊙10am-late) Dave and Patsy serve the most authentic and best-value food along the Strip. The baby back ribs and grilled mahi mahi are standouts, and local dishes such as bullfoot soup or 'cook-up' (rice, veg and meat pilaf) are a taste worth acquiring.

Marshall's   CONTINENTAL $$$

(☑466-8245; www.marshalls-stkitts.com; Horizons Villas; mains US$20-40; ⊙dinner Mon-Sat) Views from this elegant hilltop villa compete with the creative Caribbean-style continental fare, at least if you come by sunset. The menu here has few false notes and features such standouts as conch chowder, grilled rack of lamb and pan-seared duck breast. It's uphill at the second roundabout.

Mr X's Shiggidy Shack Bar & Grill   CARIBBEAN $$

(www.mrxshiggidyshack.com; The Strip; mains lunch EC$8-18, dinner EC$35-50; ⊙10am-late) Lanterns on battered picnic tables on the sand put you in instant party mood at this popular joint. On many nights bands hook up to the generator and jam; on others, karaoke drives many to drink (more). Thursday is bonfire night.

Monkey Bar   SEAFOOD $$

(☑465-8050; www.monkeybarstkitts.com; The Strip; meals from EC$40) An octagonal wooden bar gives way to a dining deck where tables even feature tablecloths. That still doesn't mean anybody is wearing shoes. Monkey Sex at sundown (the signature drink!) is a great way to kick off a party night.

Rock Lobster   SEAFOOD $$

(☑466-1092; mains US$15-30; ⊙dinner Thu-Tue) Like the clam shells, you'll be clappin' for the Mediterranean-style seafood and tapas dishes at this relaxed open-sided patio and bar. Start with a plate of crispy calamari, follow up with the silky lobster bisque or maybe hold off for the namesake menu star. Rock Lobster is to the left at the third roundabout, going towards the Marriott.

Ziggy's   CARIBBEAN $

(☑662-3104; The Strip; meals from EC$35) The party starts early at this jamming shack and goes late. Always a must-stop on a South Frigate Bay bar hop.

Southeast Peninsula

St Kitts' south is a scrubby wild plain filled with sandy beaches, grassy hills, barren salt ponds and the occasional meandering goat. However, this will soon be changing dramatically now that construction has begun on Christophe Harbour, a 2500-acre development that will include fancy residences, five-star hotels, a megayacht marina, a members-only beach club and a Tom Fazio–designed golf course. Come now. The idyllic beaches that brought many to the Caribbean in the first place are vanishing.

Heading south on the main road, which runs for 8 miles from Frigate Bay, you cross over St Timothy's Hill with good views back to Frigate Bay. Further on, the road curves around the **Great Salt Pond**; watch the sides of the road for the island's greatest concentration of green vervet monkeys.

🏖 Beaches

South Friar's Bay
ACTIVITIES BEACH

This lovely golden strip of sand backed by palm trees and sea grapes tends to get deluged on cruise-ship days. A few salty beach bars rent out lounge chairs and snorkeling gear, prepare simple meals and whip up brain-numbing cocktails. Great at sunset. Follow the signs to Shipwreck Bar & Grill. Locals come out for the live bands on Sundays.

North Friar's Bay
SURFING BEACH

On the Atlantic side, this beach is utterly wild, with stiff bodysurfing swells and not so much as a cold-beer vendor in sight. Park along the road and search out one of the narrow trails for access.

White House Bay
SNORKELING BEACH

About 1½ miles past South Friar's Bay, this is a favorite snorkeling beach thanks to offshore reefs and a couple of sunken wrecks (marked by buoys), including an 18th-century British troop ship, which attracts lots of fish. It's a rocky beach, though, so not so good for sunning and relaxing.

Cockleshell Beach
ACTIVITIES BEACH

On the southern tip of the island, this is a pretty but busy beach with views across to Nevis and calm waters that are great for splashing. Several bars, restaurants and water-sports concessionaires help create a party vibe from about midday onward. Local women offer massages in the tree shade. If you like it quieter, head to Banana Bay, the next beach to the right (behind the Spice Mill restaurant).

🍴 Eating & Drinking

TOP CHOICE **Beach House**
INTERNATIONAL **$$$**

(☑469-5299; www.stkittsbeachhouse.com; Turtle Beach; mains lunch US$11-35, dinner US$30-42; ⊗lunch Tue-Sat, dinner Mon-Sat) This hip, sultry pavilion overlooking silvery Turtle Beach scores a perfect 10 on the 'romance meter.' But even if your date doesn't make you swoon, Lionel Garnier's culinary magic ensures a memorable meal. The lobster avocado sandwich is a lunchtime favorite, while the grilled yellowfin tuna is a stellar dinner choice.

Reggae Beach Bar
CARIBBEAN **$$**

(☑762-5050; www.reggaebeachbar.com; Cockleshell Beach; mains US$7.50-32; ⊗10am-6pm; ⊞) This sprawling beach bar is a darling with the cruise-ship crowd for good reason: the food's excellent (the conch fritters get top marks, as does the banana bread pudding with rum-soaked raisins), the drinks inventive and strong (try the BBC, or Banana Baileys Colada) and the staff charming. Beach chairs and all sorts of water-sports equipment are available for rent. Don't leave without saying hi to Wilbur, the 700lb pig.

Spice Mill
CARIBBEAN FUSION **$$$**

(☑469-6455; www.spicemillrestaurant.com; Cockleshell Beach; mains lunch US$14-22, dinner US$30-40; ⊗lunch Tue-Sat) With its canopied daybeds, crayfish-trap lamps and dugout canoe bar, Spice Mill gives the rustic beach shack a hipster makeover. The menu is just as boundary-pushing and may feature Cajun shrimp with caper-olive tapenade or pan-seared mahi mahi with butternut-ginger sauce. The bar has pizzas and salads.

Lion Rock Beach Bar
CARIBBEAN **$$**

(Cockleshell Beach; meals US$15; ⊗10am-dusk) At this low-key alternative you can feast on platters of fresh fish or ribs in between volleyball matches.

Northern St Kitts

A drive around the northern part of the island is a must. The entire circuit is about 35 miles and, with various stops and lunch at one of the plantation houses, can easily fill a day. The key sight is majestic Brimstone Hill Fortress, a quick drive northwest of Basseterre. Beyond here lowlands covered with abandoned sugarcane fields run up the hills to Mt Liamuiga, the 3792ft dormant volcano that dominates the interior. It's possible to hike to the top of the crater, but a guide is recommended (see p695).

In the far north, **Dieppe Bay Town** was first settled by French Huguenots fleeing from religious persecution in the 17th century. It is the northern gateway to the island's Atlantic side where the surf can often be spectacular.

Much of the east coast is thinly populated. Endless fields of sugarcane wave in the trade winds, never to decay a tooth again. The constant rustle of the leaves and the underlying roar of the surf are punctuated by the calls of songbirds. Signs reading 'Disasters... Swift, Sudden, Deadly. Let's get ready now!!!' add a sense of foreboding (we assume they mean hurricanes, but...).

The best way to make this trip is by car. Note that the only gas station along the loop is near Brimstone Hill Fortress. Without a car, you can use minibuses, but they stick to the main coast road and many of the places worth visiting are a hike inland. You can also take a tour (there are many) or hire a driver.

◉ Sights & Activities

TOP CHOICE/ **Brimstone Hill Fortress** FORT
(www.brimstonehillfortress.org; foreign visitors adult/child US$8/4; ◷9:30am-5:30pm) St Kitts' historical highlight was made a Unesco World Heritage site in 1999 for being an exceptionally well-preserved example of 17th- and 18th-century military architecture. Far larger than you'd think, this vast old military stronghold was built by the British with slave labor and offers insight into the violent and tumultuous past of the former Caribbean colonies.

Budget at least an hour, better yet two, to explore this rambling compound. Start by watching a brief video on the fort's history in the small theater next to the gift shop or invest US$5 in the excellent audioguide, available at the entrance, for a more in-depth experience.

Nicknamed the 'Gibraltar of the West Indies,' Brimstone Hill perches atop an 800ft volcanic cone and is one of the largest forts in the Caribbean. As a major British garrison, it played a key role in battles with the French, who seized the fort in 1782 after the 1000 British soldiers inside were besieged for 30 days by 8000 French troops. The British regained it through the Treaty of Paris the following year. By the 1850s the fort was abandoned.

After a fire swept through Basseterre in 1867, some of the fort structures were partially dismantled and the stones used to rebuild the capital. In the 1960s major restoration was undertaken, and much of the fortress has been returned to its earlier grandeur. Queen Elizabeth II inaugurated it as a national park during her visit to St Kitts in October 1985.

The main hilltop compound, the Citadel, is lined with 24 cannons and provides excellent views of Saba and Sandy Point Town. Inside the Citadel's old barracks are displays on colonial history that do a fine job of documenting life back in the day. Additional displays are scattered throughout the complex.

Also worthwhile is the short stroll above the cookhouse to the top of **Monkey Hill**, which provides excellent coastal views.

It is a 2-mile steep and winding uphill drive to the fort from the coastal road. If you want to use public transportation, minibuses from Basseterre to Sandy Point Town can drop you off at the access road from where it's a heart-pumping walk up to the fort. There's a good little cafe near the parking area.

Romney Manor HISTORIC MANSION
(☑465-6253; www.caribellebatikstkitts.com; Old Road Town; ◷8:30am-4pm Mon-Fri) Just above Old Road Town, the 17th-century Romney Manor sugar estate once belonged to the great-great-great-grandfather of Thomas Jefferson. Since 1964 it has been the home of **Caribelle Batik**, which sells handmade batik wraps, dresses, wall hangings and other items. There is also a small workshop where you can watch the colorful fabric being made. Don't leave without a stroll amid the palms and poinsettias of the glorious gardens, which are guarded by a magnificent 350-year-old saman tree.

The short drive to the batik shop on Wingfield Rd goes past some large black stones with **petroglyphs** left by Amerindians; they're just past the nursery.

Bloody Point HISTORIC SITE
It was a grisly moment in Kittitian history: in 1626 joint British and French forces massacred more than 2000 Caribs in a site about 4 miles west of Basseterre, along Old Rd. Legend has it that so much blood was spilled that it ran for three days straight – hence the name Bloody Point.

A short drive further northwest, the road swings down to **Old Road Town**, the landing site of the first British settlers in 1623.

St Kitts Scenic Railway TRAIN
(☑465-7263; www.stkittsscenicrailway.com; adult/child from US$89/44.50; ◷Dec-Apr) This tourist train follows the tracks of the old narrow-gauge sugar railway that circled the island. Sadly, the train only runs on 18 miles of the tracks along the east and north coasts. The other 12 miles is by bus, but this lets the attraction sell tickets in both directions. Passengers ride in custom double-decker cars. You can sightsee from the open-sided upper

deck or kick back with rum punch on the air-con lower deck. The tour takes three hours in total and is hugely popular with cruise-ship passengers, which is why the train schedule is calibrated to when ships are in port. Independent travelers can buy tickets at their hotel or by calling the railway's office. The train station is close to the airport.

Sky Safari
ZIP-LINING

(☑466-4259; www.skysafaristkitts.com; Wingfield Rd, Old Road Town) 'Speed junkies' will leap at the chance to whoosh through the rainforest treetops at speeds of up to 50mph while suspended on a cable high in the air. The longest of the five lines is an exhilarating 1350ft and puts you 250ft above the ground. Budget two to 2½ hours for the full tour (US$89) and one hour for the half tour (US$50). It's as close to flying as you can get without growing wings.

Black Rocks
NATURE SITE

In the northeast, near the village of **Sadlers**, wind and water have chiseled lava belched up eons ago by Mt Liamuiga into fanciful coastal rock formations. Look for the turnoff after the road passes an old stone church. In the parking lot, vendors hawk souvenirs, while the 'Black Rock Pub' supplies lubrication.

Beaumont Park
RACETRACK

(☑465-1627; www.beaumontpark.kn; Whitegate) Thoroughbred horses and greyhounds have hit the track once or twice every month since this sparkling facility opened in December 2009. It's in the northeast, at the foot of Mt Liamuiga, just past Dieppe. Locals turn out by the thousands for the races, which conclude with a concert under the stars. Check the website for upcoming meets, usually held around major holidays.

Kate Design Studio
GALLERY

(☑465-7740; www.katedesign.com) Just outside the Rawlins Plantation Inn, British-born Kate Spencer has a dream studio-gallery that enjoys fine views out to sea. Spencer's work embraces a variety of styles, and the results range from lush to stark. Call ahead if you want to visit the studio. Otherwise, her work can also be seen in the gallery at the Marriott (p681).

Sleeping & Eating

Ottley's Plantation Inn
TOP CHOICE

PLANTATION INN $$$

(☑465-7234; www.ottleys.com; Ottley's Village; r incl breakfast US$180-550, cottages US$415-830; ✱@🕏🗷) An ambience of old-time sophis-

tication hangs over the most romantic of St Kitts' plantation inns. The immaculately restored Great House, where the planters lived, gives way to a sprawling manicured lawn dotted with villas and cottages. Rooms are spacious and furnished with antiques (love those planters' chairs!), cheerful chintzes and shiny wicker. Some rooms have a private plunge pool. Though tranquility rules the grounds, tennis courts, a nature trail, croquet and mountain bikes beckon more active types.

Rawlins Plantation Inn
PLANTATION INN $$$

(☑465-6221; www.rawlinsplantation.com; St Paul's; r incl breakfast & afternoon tea from US$300; @🕏🗷) Driving along the north coast, signs point you through the cane fields on a 1-mile dirt road to this grand old inn. The gingerbread-trimmed cottages easily recall elegant 18th-century living with their mahogany floors, four-poster beds and separate sitting rooms or verandas. The stunning Honeymoon Suite is in an old sugar mill itself. Day-trippers descend at lunchtime for the West Indian buffet (US$30), best enjoyed on the broad veranda with views down to the coast and beyond to Sint Eustatius. Dinner (mains US$35 to US$50) features seafood, chicken and beef creatively paired with whatever grows in the kitchen garden.

Golden Lemon
INN $$$

(☑465-7260; www.goldenlemon.com; Dieppe Bay Town; r incl breakfast from US$270, villas from US$295; @🗷) Near a tiny fleck of charcoal-colored beach in the far northern village of Dieppe, the Golden Lemon is one of St Kitts' more storied inns, a slice of the Old Caribbean with grandly decorated rooms and refined ambience. It's the life work of Arthur Leaman, a dapper octogenarian and former editor at *House & Garden*, whose immaculate taste is reflected in the decor throughout. Alas, these days the inn is struggling and, quite frankly, in bad need of rejuvenation. On our visit, there was not a single guest. That may change now that Leaman has sold the property to the owners of the Rawlins Plantation Inn. Stay tuned.

Royal Palm
MODERN CARIBBEAN $$$

(☑465-7234; Ottley's Plantation Inn; lunch mains US$12-40, 3-course dinner US$66; ◷breakfast, lunch & dinner) The historic stone walls of the old sugar boiling house hem the fine-dining restaurant at Ottley's Plantation Inn. It regularly gets showered with accolades and would make a fine lunch stop on an island tour. Choices include lobster wraps and inventive sandwiches. Dinner is a more formal affair with fine steaks and seafood. Great Sunday brunch, too (US$36).

Sprat Net Bar & Grill CARIBBEAN $$
(☑465-7535; Old Road Town; meals from EC$60; ☺dinner Wed-Sun) In Old Road Town on the western shore, Sprat is a Kittitian waterfront institution. At sunset visitors and locals start swarming the picnic tables for rum drinks and the honest-to-goodness menu of chicken, fish or lobster paired with coleslaw, corn and rice.

NEVIS

Coin-shaped Nevis (pronounced 'nay-vis') is a smaller, neater version of St Kitts. It combines history, beauty and beaches in one tidy package sprinkled with rustic charm and a keen historical awareness and appreciation. Many visitors come here just for the day but those in the know stay much longer.

Sorting through the sights and activities, there's just enough to add spice to the day but not so much that important rest and relaxation are impeded. Circling the island by car takes only about two hours. Stop to see the sights and have lunch at a plantation house and it can take all day.

There are good hikes in the hills and plenty of water sports at the beaches. The forested interior rises to scenic Mt Nevis, which is often cloaked in clouds. It's possible to hike to the top of the rim but the trail leads through a patchwork of private property and should ideally be done with a guide.

The coastal lowlands, where the larger villages are located, are much drier and support bougainvillea, hibiscus and other flowering bushes that attract numerous humming-birds. It's a beautiful place.

❶ Getting There & Away
For details on transport options to/from Nevis, see p693. There are ferry services between Nevis and St Kitts; for details, see p694.

❶ Getting Around
BUS Buses leave from Memorial Sq in Charlestown. They're privately owned minivans sporting a green license plate starting with the letter H or HA. There is no fixed schedule but departures are most frequent in the morning and the after-noon. You're free to flag down passing buses and request stops along the main road. Fares range from EC$1 to EC$5.

CAR & SCOOTER 1st Choice Car Rental (☑469-1131; www.neviscarrental.com; New-castle)

Forbes Scooter Rental (☑469-2668) Call to arrange scooter drop-off.
Nevis Car Rental (☑469-9837; Newcastle)
TDC/Thrifty Auto Rentals (☑469-5430; Bay Rd, Charlestown) Near the ferry dock.
TAXI There are taxi stands at the airport and near the ferry dock in Charlestown. Service be-tween 10pm and 6am adds 50% extra. To order a taxi call ☑469-1483 or have your hotel arrange one. Sample taxi fares:

Airport to Pinney's Beach or Charlestown US$20

Airport to Montpelier Plantation Inn US$32

Charlestown to Four Seasons Resort US$10

Charlestown to Oualie Beach US$15

Charlestown
POP 1800
The ferry from St Kitts docks right in the pint-size center of Charlestown, Nevis' cute little capital, where banks and businesses co-exist with tourist facilities and gingerbread Victorians. It's a fun spot for a stroll and is rarely overcrowded as large cruise ships by-pass Nevis. Tourist tat is refreshingly limited.

The greater Charlestown area can be readily explored on foot – the museums and the Bath Hotel are within walking distance. Just a 15-minute jaunt north of the center will put you on lovely Pinney's Beach.

Charlestown is also the starting point of the **Nevis Heritage Trail**, which links 25 sites of historical importance throughout the island, including churches, sugar estates, military installations and natural sites. Look for the blue and green markers or pick up a leaflet at the tourist office or the museums.

◎ Sights & Activities
Alexander Hamilton Museum MUSEUM
(www.nevis-nhcs.org; Main St; adult/child US$5/2; ☺9am-4pm Mon-Fri, to noon Sat) American statesman Alexander Hamilton (1757–1804) was many things in his short life: soldier, lawyer, author of the *Federalist Papers*, US founding father, the country's first Secretary of State and, finally, the victim of a fatal duel with his political nemesis Aaron Burr. He was also born – scandalously out of wedlock – on Nevis, close to the site of this modest museum that chronicles his amazing rags-to-riches career. Shady grounds and a cafe offer a lovely picnic and rest spot.

Nelson Museum MUSEUM
(www.nevis-nhcs.org; Building Hill Rd; adult/child US$5/2; ☺9am-4pm Mon-Fri, 10am-1pm Sat)

About 100yd east of the old Bath Hotel, this museum contains memorabilia relating to Lord Nelson (1758–1805), the dashing British sea captain whose fateful visit to the island in 1787 led to his unhappy marriage to Fanny Nisbet, the niece of the island's governor. Among the items on display is a plate from their wedding. It has a crack. The exhibit was expected to move to the grounds of the Alexander Hamilton Museum in 2011 or 2012.

Hamilton Estate
HISTORIC SITE

Enjoy views of Charlestown from this romantically ruined sugar estate, which is being reclaimed by the jungle. Wander among the foundations of the Great House, the windmill, the boiling house and the chimney.

Jewish cemetery
CEMETERY

In the early 18th century, about a quarter of Nevis' nonslave population were Jews who'd fled to the Caribbean after getting kicked out of Brazil. They brought with them knowledge about the cultivation of sugarcane and thus changed the local economy forever. The modest cemetery is all that's left of the Jewish legacy. The oldest gravestone dates to 1679.

Bath Hotel & Spring House
HISTORIC SITE

In the late 18th century, a who's who of politicians, crowned heads and the merely moneyed came to 'take the cure' in the 107°F hot mineral springs of this palatial hotel. The main building now houses government offices, but the Spring House below the hotel had to close because of hurricane damage. An outdoor pool was recently constructed nearby in case you wish to soothe aching bones. Water filters in through layers of crushed stones through the bottom of the pool and flows out via a pipe into the stream.

🎉 Festivals & Events

Culturama
CULTURAL FESTIVAL

(www.nevisculturama.net) For over 30 years, Nevisians have celebrated their heritage

---

PORT OF CALL – CHARLESTOWN

Nevis doesn't have a dock that can accommodate enormous boats. Passengers are brought to port by tender from small ships anchored offshore, or as part of excursions from St Kitts. With its museums, Charlestown is good for a couple of hours of wandering.

---

with a joyous program of street jams, calypso tents, fashion shows, boat rides, parties and dance, all culminating in the Calypso King and Miss Culture Queen competitions. The event is held from late July to early August.

👁 Sleeping

Charlestown is home to the only budget options on Nevis.

Pinney's Beach Hotel
HOTEL $$

(☎469-5207; www.pinneyshotel.com; d US$104-154; ❋🛜🏊) Close to town, rooms are pretty plain but clean and comfortable enough for gearing up for a day of sightseeing or vegging on the beach. The south end of Pinney's Beach is steps away.

JP's Guest House
GUESTHOUSE $

(☎469-0319; jpwalters@caribsurf.com; Lower Prince William St; r US$72; ❋🛜) Two minutes from the ferry dock, this tidy upstairs place in a modern building has 10 rooms that are a tad twee but spotless and outfitted with cable TV and a fridge. Self-caterers can make use of the communal kettle and microwave.

🍴 Eating

Aside from a few Chinese eateries, there's a dearth of restaurants in Charlestown.

Seafood Madness
SEAFOOD $$

(☎469-0588; mains lunch US$5-11, dinner US$13-25; ☺lunch & dinner; 🚤) The name pretty much sums it up: this place is all about fish. With its cafeteria looks and roadside location, it's often bypassed by visitors, yet packed to the gills with locals in the know. You can't go wrong with ordering the catch of the day (prepared as you like it). Call ahead to double-check if it's open. It's about a 10-minute walk north of town, oppostive Pinney's Beach Hotel.

Tea House
CHINESE $

(☎469-7033; Memorial Sq; mains EC$15-40; ☺9am-11pm) Right in town, Tea House doles out big portions of decent Chinese standards. Since the dining room has zero ambience, most come for take-out.

Mnandi Bake Shop
BAKERY $

(Main St; dishes EC$15-30; ☺8:30am-4:30pm Mon-Fri, to 1pm Sat) Inside the Superfoods supermarket, pastry chef Anneliese Leibbrandt makes fresh sandwiches and possibly the best bread on Nevis.

Superfoods
SUPERMARKET $

(Main St; ☺8am-8pm Mon-Fri, to 9pm Sat, 9am-noon Sun) Full-service, reasonably priced supermarket with an extensive liquor selection. About a quarter-mile south of the ferry dock.

Public Market SUPERMARKET $
(Market St; ☉7am-4:30pm Mon-Sat) A few stalls selling local fruit and vegetables; busiest on Saturday morning.

Chinese supermarket SUPERMARKET $
(Memorial Sq; ☉8am-11pm) Expensive and basic but open when everything else is closed.

ⓘ Information

Main St north of the tourist office is lined with banks.

Alexander Hamilton Museum (Main St; ☉9am-4pm Mon-Fri, to noon Sat) Internet costs EC$10 per hour or EC$25 all day

Alexandra Hospital (☑469-5473; Government Rd)

City Drug Store (☉8am-7pm Mon-Sat) Pharmacy, drugstore and general store.

Nevis Tourist Office (☑469-7550; www. nevisisland.com; Main St; ☉8am-4pm Mon-Fri) Two minutes from the ferry pier.

Post office (Main St; ☉8am-3:30pm Mon-Fri)

Public Library (Memorial Sq) Free wi-fi.

ⓘ Getting Around

Charlestown is tiny so everything can be reached on foot.

Northern Nevis

The coast north of Charlestown has Nevis' best beaches, from long and lovely Pinney's and busy Oualie to romantic Lovers and picture-perfect Nisbet, which is home to a grand seafront plantation inn. The island's only major luxury resort, the Four Seasons, is also here, at Pinney's, and the Seabridge car ferry leaves from Cades Bay. Some of Nevis' best dive sites are a short boat ride off the west coast, including Monkey Shoals, Thermal Vents and Fish Bowl.

⊙ Sights & Activities

[TOP CHOICE] **Nisbet Beach** RESORT EACH
Backed by the eponymous plantation resort, this is perhaps the loveliest strand on Nevis, with palm-lined powdery white sand, crystal-clear water and great views across to St Kitts.

Pinney's Beach FAMILY BEACH
Reef-protected Pinney's Beach is a 4-mile-long lovely stretch of tan sand within walk-

ing distance of Charlestown. Backed by spiky coconut palms, it has lovely views of St Kitts across the channel. There's decent snorkeling right offshore. Despite several beach bars and the splashy Four Seasons Resort, private patches of sand abound.

Oualie Beach ACTIVITIES BEACH
Nevis' most popular, though not nicest, beach, Oualie is a long, laid-back strip of gray sand backed by palms and sea-grape plants. Waters are generally calm and good for swimming. It's great for families and active types as there is a dive, water-sports and bike shop. Tan junkies can just rent a beach chair and look out over to St Kitts.

Lovers Beach SECLUDED BEACH
North of Oualie Beach, tranquil Lovers Beach does its name justice. It's about a mile long with golden sand, never crowded and lapped by some pretty sizable waves.

Windsurf 'n Mountain Bike

WATER SPORTS, CYCLING
(☑469-9682; www.bikenevis.com; Oualie Beach) Run by the ebullient Winston Crooke, this shop rents out bikes (from US$15 per day), kayaks (per hour US$15), windsurfing boards (per hour US$20) and Hobie Cats (per hour US$50). Winston also offers windsurfing lessons from US$20 per hour, hike-and-bike combination tours (US$85) and guided kayak trips (US$55).

Scuba Safaris DIVING
(☑469-9518; www.scubanevis.com; Oualie Beach) Nevis' diving scene is a low-key affair and features undisturbed coral reefs such as Monkey Shoals close to Oualie Beach, and Devil's Caves, off the western coast, with coral grottoes and underwater lava tubes. This five-star PADI outfit charges US$69 for single-tank boat dives and US$95 for two-tank

dives, including all equipment. Its half-day snorkeling trip costs US$49. Reserve ahead.

Four Seasons Golf Course GOLF
Designed by Robert Trent Jones II, this 18-hole, par 71 course ranks among the most acclaimed in the Caribbean. The greens fee is US$205 for non-resort guests.

Nevis Equestrian Centre HORSEBACK RIDING
(☑662-9118; www.nevishorseback.com; Cotton Ground) Saddle up and explore the verdant and sandy scenery on a variety of rides, including the popular 90-minute Beach & Trail Ride (US$55).

St Thomas Anglican Church CHURCH
About 3 miles north of Charlestown, Nevis' oldest church (1643) stares serenely out to sea from its hilltop perch. Goats keep the cemetery grounds trimmed.

🛏 Sleeping

TOP CHOICE Nisbet Plantation
Beach Club PLANTATION INN $$$
(☑469-9325; www.nisbetplantation.com; Nisbet Beach; r US$350-680; ✽@❋) Just south of the airport, Nisbet is a class act all around and the Caribbean's only plantation inn with a beachfront location. And what a beach it is! The 36 sunny and cheery rooms are infused with casual plantation glam inspired by the site's history: this is, after all, the ancestral home of Fanny Nisbet, Horatio Nelson's gal. Rates include cooked breakfast, afternoon tea and gourmet dinner.

Four Seasons Resort RESORT $$$
(☑469-1111; www.fourseasons.com; Pinney's Beach; r from US$700; ✽@❋❋) Reopened in late 2010, two years after being leveled by Hurricane Omar, this luxury abode curries favor with deep-pocketed leisure hounds who like their surrounds pretty but predictable. The 196 luxurious rooms are discreetly set in low-rise buildings deeply spaced on the lush ground fronting the beach. Amenities are many: three free-form pools, 10 tennis courts, a championship 18-hole golf course, full spa and several restaurants. Check the web for specials and discounts.

Oualie Beach Resort RESORT $$$
(☑469-9735; www.oualiebeach.com; Oualie Beach; r from US$300; ✽@❋❋⚓) The family who runs this beachfront resort has been on Nevis for over 350 years. Rooms are scattered in several low-rise buildings and comfortable enough, though somewhat overpriced for

what they are. It's a good base for families and water rats.

🍴 Eating & Drinking

Sunshine's BAR, RESTAURANT $$
(☑469-5817; mains lunch US$8-15, dinner US$15-20; ⊙11am-late) This Rasta-run rum-and-reggae joint has been getting people in a party mood for decades. A cold Carib goes well with the tasty sandwiches and seafood platters or go local and order the signature drink, the much-hyped Killer Bee. Its sting has been recorded in the hundreds of photos on the walls, some featuring such A-listers as Beyoncé and John Travolta.

Chrishi Beach Club RESTAURANT $$
(☑662-3959; www.chrishibeachclub.com; Cades Bay beach; mains US$10-18; ⊙lunch Tue-Sun, dinner Fri; ❋⚓) This stylish white beachfront pavilion has a decidedly European flair (check out the canopied lounge beds in the sand), which is no surprise given that the owners hail from Norway. The menu is a light and satisfying potpourri of salads, sandwiches, pasta and pizza. Right on beautiful Cades Bay beach, it also has a kids' menu and a full complement of toys, games and costumes for borrowing. The Friday-night sunset dinners feature a live jazz band.

Gallipot BAR, RESTAURANT $$
(☑469-8230; www.gallipotnevis.com; mains lunch US$11-19, dinner US$16-29; ⊙lunch Thu-Sun, dinner Thu-Sat) Gallipot catches and smokes its own fish, bakes its own quiches and makes its own desserts. It's a favorite of the expat set, who knock back Heinekens while exchanging the latest gossip at the circular bar. It's located north of Oualie Beach.

Chevy's BAR
(Pinney's Beach; ⊙3pm-late) The beach boozer for a new generation, the reggae shack/bar gets a good mix of locals and visitors who party 'til late just south of Sunshine's.

South Nevis

The circular road crosses the southern part of Nevis between cloud-shrouded Mt Nevis and Saddle Hill, passing through the districts of Fig Tree and Gingerland. As the hub of Nevis' sugar industry in colonial days, there are many crumbling sugar-mill stacks to evoke that era. A few of the former plantation estates have been converted into romantic retreats. The entire area is lush and green; watch for mongooses darting across the road in search of rodents.

As the main road hits the east coast, the population thins out and the sloping, green flatlands – once sugarcane plantations – run down to the turbulent Atlantic. It's desolate and dramatic.

◎ Sights

Botanical Gardens of Nevis GARDEN
(✆469-3509; adult/child US$10/7; ☺9am-5pm Mon-Sat, closed mid-Aug–mid-Oct) Near Montpelier Plantation Inn, these glorious gardens are a perfumed symphony of trees, vines, orchids, roses and other flora. The centerpiece is the Rainforest Conservatory, which shelters huge tropical plants and Mayan-type sculpture.

St John's Fig Tree Church CHURCH
St John's, on the main road in the village of Fig Tree, is a stone church that dates from 1680. A glass case in the back displays a copy of the church register, dated March 11, 1787, which records the marriage of Horatio Nelson and Fanny Nisbet. If you peek beneath the red carpet in the center aisle you'll find a continuous row of tombstones of island notables who died in the 1700s.

Nevisian Heritage Village MUSEUM
(✆469-5521; Stoney Grove; adult/child US$3/1; ☺9am-3:30pm Mon-Sat) This ever-expanding open-air museum illustrates Nevisian social history, from Carib times to the present, through a collection of re-created buildings furnished with period relics. Exhibits include a Carib chief's thatched hut, slave houses and a blacksmith's shop.

Eden Brown Estate HISTORIC SITE
(btwn Mannings & Lime Kiln) On the remote east coast, this 18th-century sugar plantation has the dubious distinction of being Nevis' spookiest site. The year was 1822 and Julia Huggins was about to get married when her husband-to-be and her brother (his best man) decided to resolve a quarrel with a dual that left them both dead. Heartbroken, Julia became a recluse and can allegedly still be heard roaming the grounds at night. The grounds are always open to visitors.

🏃 Activities

Golden Rock Nature Trail HIKING
The Golden Rock Inn is the departure point for this easy rainforest hike along a ridgeline and down a gentle ravine. Keep an eye out for troops of vervet monkeys. Maps are available at the inn.

Windward Beach SECLUDED BEACH
Remote Windward Beach, also known as Indian Castle Beach, has views across to Montserrat and is the only easily accessible beach on Nevis' southern shore. Backed by beach morning glory and low scrubby trees, it has fine gray sand and Atlantic surf suited for bodysurfing and boogie boarding. Unless it's a weekend, the odds are good that, with the exception of a few rummaging goats, the sands are footprint-free. To get to the beach, turn south at the Gingerland post office and follow the signs. Along the way, you pass Nevis' horse-racing track.

Indian Castle Race Track HORSE RACING
(✆469-3477; www.ntajc.com) Aside from cricket, there are few things that get the locals more excited than a 'day at the races.' Several times a year, usually around major holidays, the Nevis Turf and Jockey Club sponsors thoroughbred races starring mostly local equines. The dirt track is basic but beautifully located above the Atlantic with views out to Montserrat. Hilarious moments ensue when stray donkeys or goats join the races. Live music, barbecue chicken and rum punches keep the party going well into the evening.

Upper Round Road HIKING
Originally built in the late 1600s, this road once linked the sugar estates, cane fields and villages surrounding Mt Nevis. Today, it travels 9 miles from Golden Rock Inn in the east to Nisbet Plantation Beach Club in the north, past farms, orchards, gardens and rainforest. Along the way, sample fresh fruit and observe monkeys and butterflies. Budget about five hours for the entire trek or walk a shorter section.

🛏 Sleeping & Eating

Three plantation estates offer elegant stays that are among the finest on the island. You can sample some of the vintage atmosphere at a casual lunch.

TOP CHOICE Montpelier Plantation Inn PLANTATION INN $$$
(✆469-3462; www.montpeliernevis.com; r incl breakfast & afternoon tea from US$445; @🛜🏊) This 17th-century inn hosted Nelson's wedding to Fanny Nisbet in 1787 and much later, the equally doomed Princess Diana. Happily, the past is past and this beautiful estate

evokes a relaxed contemporary elegance alongside its long history. The luxuries are real but understated – you can select a book from the library, use the wi-fi and then loll back for a snooze in the gazebo. There are several worthy eating options, including poolside tapas at the pleasantly informal Indigo (Thursday to Saturday).

TOP CHOICE / Banyan Tree B&B $$

(☑469-3449; www.banyantreebandb.com; r incl breakfast US$135-185; 🔊) A centuries-old Banyan tree surrounded by jungly gardens is the namesake of this tranquil hideaway tucked beneath the leafy skirts of Mt Nevis. Days start with home-cooked breakfasts featuring herbs, fruit and vegetables straight from the kitchen garden and might continue with a vigorous volcano hike or a restorative slumber in the hammock. There are just two guest rooms and one cottage, so you can be assured of personal attention from your delightful hosts, Anne and John. No phone or TV.

Hermitage PLANTATION INN $$$

(☑469-3477; www.hermitagenevis.com; Gingerland; r incl breakfast from US$395; @🔊🏊) At this 260-year-old plantation inn, you can't help but feel transported to another era as you sit on the porch of your gingerbread cottage taking in the views from an 800ft elevation. Lunch (US$15 to US$25) here is the usual casual affair, with fresh fare such as salads and sandwiches served on a lovely veranda. Dinner (four courses US$65) is more elaborate and marries the Mediterranean with the Caribbean, usually with pleasing results.

Golden Rock Inn PLANTATION INN $$$

(☑469-3346; www.golden-rock.com; d from US$200; ⊘closed mid-Aug–mid-Oct; 🔊🏊) The funkiest choice among the plantation inns, the owner's great-great-great-great-grandfather built this lava-stone plantation by hand in the 1810s. The 11 rooms in seven cottages stress casual comfort over elegance and vary in size and style. The nicest is in the romantic Sugar Mill. A recent overhaul has added a spectacular terraced deck with a fountain and an open-air, glass-top roof dining area. Guests can use a shuttle to Charlestown and the beaches. The restaurant makes inventive sandwiches and salads at lunchtime (mains US$9 to US$30) and creatively calibrated fish and meat dishes at dinner (US$22 to US$32, reservations required). Work off the carbs by hitting the Golden Rock Nature Trail.

TOP CHOICE / Bananas Bistro INTERNATIONAL $$

(☑469-1891; mains lunch US$16-25, dinner US$20-30; ⊘lunch & dinner Mon-Sat) Perched way up the mountains, Bananas is a perennial pleaser run by former dancer Gillian Smith. The veranda of her hand-built plantation-style house is perfect for slurping smooth tropical drinks and tucking into food inspired by her travels around the world. Think guava-barbecued shrimp, curried conch and masala lamb. Expect your taste buds to do cartwheels throughout the evening. Reservations required.

UNDERSTAND ST KITTS & NEVIS

History

The island known today as St Kitts was called Liamuiga (Fertile Island) by the Caribs, who arrived about AD 1300 and chased out the peaceable agrarian bands who'd been in the area for hundreds of years. When Columbus sighted the island on his second voyage to the New World, in 1493, he named it St Christopher after his patron saint, later shortened to 'St Kitts.'

Columbus used the Spanish word for 'snow,' *nieves,* to name Nevis, presumably because the clouds shrouding its mountain reminded him of a snowcapped peak. Caribs knew the island as Oualie (Land of Beautiful Waters).

Colonial Times

St Kitts and Nevis are the oldest British colonies in the Caribbean. Sir Thomas Warner founded a colony way back in 1623, only to be joined soon after by the French, a move the British only tolerated long enough to massacre the Caribs. In one day, 2000 of them were slaughtered, causing blood to run for days at the site now known as Bloody Point.

A century and a half of Franco-British battles culminated locally in 1782, when a force of 8000 French troops laid siege to the important British stronghold at Brimstone Hill on St Kitts. Although they won this battle, they lost the war and the 1783 Treaty of Paris brought the island firmly under British control. During this era sugar plantations thrived on the islands.

Nevis had a colonial history similar to St Kitts. In 1628 Warner sent a party of about

100 colonists to establish a British settlement on the west coast of the island. Although the original settlement, near Cotton Ground, fell to an earthquake in 1680, Nevis eventually developed one of the most affluent plantation societies in the Eastern Caribbean. As on St Kitts, most of the island's wealth was built upon the labor of African slaves who toiled in the island's sugarcane fields. Sugar continued to play a role in the local economies until the last plantation closed in 2005.

By the late 18th century, Nevis, buoyed by the attraction of its thermal baths, had become a major retreat for Britain's rich and famous.

In 1816 the British linked St Kitts and Nevis with Anguilla and the Virgin Islands as a single colony. In 1958 these islands became part of the West Indies Federation, a grand but ultimately unsuccessful attempt to combine all of Britain's Caribbean colonies as a united political entity. When the federation dissolved in 1962, the British opted to lump St Kitts, Nevis and Anguilla together as a new state. Anguilla, fearful of domination by larger St Kitts, revolted against the occupying Royal St Kitts Police Force in 1967 and returned to Britain as an overseas territory.

Independence & Rivalries

In 1983 St Kitts and Nevis became a single nation within the British Commonwealth, with the stipulation that Nevis could secede at any time. In the 1990s, a period of corruption on St Kitts and pro-independence on Nevis almost brought an end to the federation. A referendum held on Nevis in 1998, however, failed to produce a two-third majority needed to break away.

Nevis – a major offshore tax haven – now has an economy stronger than that of its larger neighbor. This, coupled with the constant irritation of having only three members in the 11-member governing assembly, continues to fuel calls for secession, although the movement has flagged since the election of Joseph Parry as Nevis premier in 2006.

Looking Ahead

St Kitts' future is quite literally under construction as much of the unpopulated southern part of the island is being developed into a high-end residential area, complete with fancy hotels, private clubs and a marina that can accommodate giant yachts. Nevis, on the other hand, is looking to the past

as its greatest asset. It has created a Nevis Heritage Trail and is extending major efforts towards education and heritage preservation. The island is also embarking on several green initiatives. A wind farm started operating in August 2010 and a new geothermal power plant is expected go online in 2011.

Culture

Although the population is predominantly (90%) of African descent, culturally the islands draw upon a mix of European, African and West Indian traditions. Architecture is mainly British in style and cricket is the national sport.

Both islands feel like places where people live and work, rather than just a tourist destination. Walk through a residential area on St Kitts on any given night and locals will be out in the streets, listening to reggae or calypso blaring out of homes and chatting with friends. On weekend nights, many villages on Nevis have communal barbecues.

St Kitts and Nevis have an interesting mixture of leniency and propriety. You can get fined for using foul language in public, but you can drink while driving (note that doesn't mean you can drive drunk!), so keep an eye out on the road at night. Swimwear should be restricted to the beach and pool areas of resorts.

Landscape & Wildlife

Both islands have grassy coastal areas, a consequence of deforestation for sugar production. Forests tend to be vestiges of the large rainforests that once covered much of the islands, or they are second-growth.

Away from developed areas, the climate allows a huge array of beautiful plants to thrive. Flowers such as plumeria, hibiscus and chains-of-love are common along roadsides and in garden landscaping.

Nevis is fairly circular and the entire island benefits from runoff from Mt Nevis. St Kitts' shape resembles a tadpole. The main body is irrigated by water from the mountain ranges. However, this is of little value to the geographically isolated, arid southeast peninsula which is covered with sparse, desertlike cacti and yucca.

Aside from the vervet monkey, another ubiquitous creature is the mongoose, imported from Jamaica by plantation owners to rid their sugarcane fields of snakes. Both

MONKEY SEE, MONKEY DO

Mischievous vervet monkeys were brought to St Kitts and Nevis by French settlers from Africa and have since flourished so well that they outnumber humans two to one. Traveling in packs of up to 30, they can be spotted in the rainforest and on St Kitts' southeast peninsula. They may look cute but residents consider them a major pest because they raid fruit and vegetable crops and destroy birds' nests. A biomedical research facility on St Kitts uses the monkeys for experiments in their research for a cure for Parkinson's disease and to do preclinical testing of a new dengue-fever vaccine.

islands provide plenty of avian life for bird-watchers.

Reefs around the two islands face the same threats as elsewhere in the region. On St Kitts, some of the best reefs ring the southeast peninsula. A new project is underway to limit the range of feral goats, whose overgrazing leads to increased runoff of reef-killing silt and organic matter.

SURVIVAL GUIDE

Directory A–Z
Accommodations

There are large resorts on each island, but most accommodations are still small-scale hotels, plantation inns, guesthouses and condominiums. Camping is technically allowed, but neither island is set up with facilities. Contact the tourist office on either island to inquire.

$	budget	less than US$75
$$	midrange	US$75 to US$200
$$$	top end	more than US$200

Business Hours

In this chapter we only list opening hours if they differ from the following standards:

Banks 8am-2pm Mon-Thu, to 4pm Fri

Bars noon-11pm or midnight

Businesses 8am-5pm Mon-Fri, some to 2pm Sat

Restaurants breakfast 7-10am, lunch noon-2pm, dinner 6-9:30pm

Shops 9am-5pm or 6pm Mon-Fri, to 4pm Sat, later and on Sun for touristy places and supermarkets

Embassies & Consulates

Consular affairs for US citizens are handled by the US embassy in Bridgetown, Barbados.
Germany (☏465-8857; Frigate Bay)
UK (☏466-8888; Basseterre)

Food

Price indicators given in Eating listings in this chapter are based on the cost of a meal, consisting of an appetizer and a main course.

$	budget	less than EC$30
$$	midrange	EC$30 to EC$80
$$$	top end	more than EC$80

Gay & Lesbian Travelers

While there is no real gay and lesbian scene on St Kitts and Nevis, there is no overt discrimination either. However, homosexual 'acts' are officially punishable with up to 10 years imprisonment. Even though the law is not enforced, discretion is advised, so no public displays of affection and, in hotels, no advertising that you'll be sharing one bed.

Health

Many people drink the local tap water, but the CDC recommends using bottled water, which is cheap and widely available.

Internet Access

Basseterre has internet cafes and most hotels offer wi-fi or computers in the lobby. Public libraries also offer free wi-fi.

Maps

On St Kitts, the tourist office's free *Road Map & Guide* will suffice for most visitors. On Nevis, the excellent *Journey Map* sells for US$5 and has a detailed road map of both the island and Charlestown. Both maps are available at most hotels, the tourist offices and many shops.

Money

The official currency is the Eastern Caribbean dollar, and although US dollars are accepted almost everywhere, ATMs don't dispense them.

Hotels and restaurants add a 12% tax and a 10% service charge as well. When a restaurant doesn't add a service charge, a 10% tip is appropriate.

Post

When mailing a letter to the islands, follow the addressee's name with the town and 'St Kitts, West Indies' or 'Nevis, West Indies.'

Public Holidays

Islanders celebrate the following local holidays, in addition to those observed throughout the region (p872).

Labour Day First Monday in May

Emancipation Day First Monday in August

National Hero's Day September 17

Independence Day September 19

Safe Travel

Common sense should prevail while walking around Basseterre at night. If the area looks dodgy, it is. In November 2010, the armed robbery of a busload of tourists made international headlines, but it seems that this was an isolated incident.

Greater danger lurks on the road, especially when driving at night: kids, dogs, goats and, yes, enormous potholes, can appear out of nowhere. And beware that drivers are allowed to drink (although not be drunk) behind the wheel.

Telephone

The St Kitts and Nevis area code is ☎869. To call from North America, dial ☎1-869, followed by the seven-digit local number. From elsewhere, dial your country's international access code + ☎869 + the local phone number. If making a call within or between the islands, you only need to dial the seven-digit local number. St Kitts numbers start with 465 or 466 and Nevis numbers with 469. Mobiles begin with a 7.

Phone calling cards are widely available. Local cell phones use the GSM system.

Avoid credit-card phones, as they charge a rapacious US$2 per minute or more lo-cally, US$4 to other Caribbean islands or the US, and up to US$8 elsewhere.

For directory assistance, dial ☎411.

Travelers with Disabilities

International resorts generally have good accommodations for people with disabilities. Otherwise, much of the islands are something of a challenge. Fortunately, almost everything of interest can be reached directly by car. The must-see Brimstone Hill Fortress has both accessible and inaccessible areas.

Getting There & Away
Entering St Kitts & Nevis

Visitors from most countries need only a passport to enter St Kitts or Nevis, as well as a round-trip or onward ticket.

Air

St Kitts has regional services plus nonstop flights to the US, while Nevis has services that are mostly regional; to get here you'll need to change planes somewhere.

NEVIS

Vance W Amory International Airport (NEV; ☎469-9040), in Newcastle, is a small operation with an ATM.

The following airlines connect Nevis with the places listed (some services are seasonal and only weekly):

American Eagle (www.aa.com) San Juan

PRACTICALITIES

» **Electricity** 220V, 60 cycles; North American–style two-pin sockets.

» **Local Taxes** Hotels and restaurants add 10% VAT, 2% IET (island enhancement tax) and a 10% service fee. The VAT on goods and services is 17%.

» **Newspapers & Magazines** Publications include the daily *Sun St Kitts/ Nevis*, the weekly *Democrat* and *Observer* and the biweekly *Labour Spokesman*.

» **Radio** 90.3FM, 96FM and 98.9FM play reggae, soca, calypso or island music.

» **Weights & Measures** Imperial measurements are used. Speed-limit signs are in miles, as are rental-car odometers.

DEPARTURE TAX

The departure tax is EC$60 (US$22), payable in cash or by credit card at the airport. If you're leaving from Nevis, it's EC$54 (US$20.50).

LIAT (www.fly-liat.com) Antigua

Winair (www.fly-winair.com) The only direct flight from Nevis is to St-Martin/Sint Maarten. Service to St-Barths, Guadeloupe, Sint Eustatius and Saba requires a change in St-Martin/Sint Maarten.

ST KITTS

St Kitts' modern international airport, **Robert Llewellyn Bradshaw Airport** (SKM; ☑465-8121), is located on the northern outskirts of Basseterre. The departure area is bright and airy but amenities are limited to a bare-bones snack bar. There is an ATM before security.

The following airlines connect St Kitts with the places listed (some services are seasonal and only weekly):

American/American Eagle (www.aa.com) Miami; New York (Kennedy); San Juan, Puerto Rico

Delta (☑www.delta.com) Atlanta

LIAT (www.fly-liat.com) Antigua, St Thomas, St-Martin/Sint Maarten

US Airways (www.usairways.com) Charlotte, NC

Sea

CRUISE SHIP

Scores of cruise ships on Eastern Caribbean itineraries visit St Kitts, docking at Basseterre's deep-water harbor. It can be a good idea to email the tourist office when you know your travel dates to get the cruise schedule, as certain places, such as the beaches in the south or the St Kitts Scenic Railway, are mobbed when ships are in port. Nevis lacks a dock that can handle the enormous boats so visits are limited to passengers brought ashore by tender from small ships (usually under 300 passengers) anchored offshore or those on flying visits as part of excursions from St Kitts.

YACHT

St Kitts and Nevis are right on the Eastern Caribbean yachting circuit, although their lack of natural harbors like those on Antigua keep the numbers of people mooring for any period of length low.

The two ports of entry are Basseterre and Charlestown. On both islands, customs is near the ferry dock and is open from 8am to noon and 1pm to 4pm Monday to Friday. Boaters will need permits to visit other anchorages and a special pass to go between the two islands.

Getting Around

Boat

Several passenger ferries shuttle between Basseterre and Charlestown. The trip takes about 45 minutes and is both a pleasant and scenic way to travel. Fares are set at adult/child EC$25/15 one-way. In each port, be sure to pay the EC$1 port tax before you depart. Tickets are sold from about 30 minutes before sailings. It's a good idea to arrive early as some boats sell out.

Each ferry company operates by its own schedule. Since it may change at any time, it is best to confirm departures in advance, which you can do at the ferry terminal, the tourist offices or by checking the online Leyton Ferry Schedule (http://boatschedule .leytonms.com). Between the various boats there's a service every one to two hours (less frequently on Sundays).

Companies operating at press time:

Carib Breeze/Carib Surf (☑466-6734; mmtscaribe@hotmail.com) The most reliable service. Both boats are large, with enclosed cabins and large, sunny upper decks.

Mark Twain (☑469-0403) No open deck.

Sea Hustler (☑469-0403) No Sunday service; children under five free.

People with cars can use the **Seabridge** (☑662-9565/7002) car-ferry service. It links Major's Bay in the south of St Kitts with Cades Bay on Nevis. The first ferry leaves Cades Bay at 8:30am, and at 9am from St Kitts, and continues on the even hour from Nevis and the odd hour from St Kitts until the last ferry leaves St Kitts at 7pm. The trip takes 20 minutes. The fare for one car and a driver is EC$75 one-way and EC$125 round-trip. Additional passengers cost EC$20. If you have a rental car on one island, this can be a good way to explore the other island on a day trip without having to rent another car.

Water-taxi service between the islands is provided by Scuba Safaris (p687) and Nevis Water Sports (⌀662-9166) on Nevis, and Kenneth's Dive Centre (p678) on St Kitts. Rates are between US$20 and US$30 per person, usually with a four-person minimum.

You can also freelance your way across the 2 miles that separate the islands. At most of the southern beaches on St Kitts you're likely to find a fisherman willing to run you over to Nevis or even St-Barthélemy or Sint Eustatius for very negotiable rates that start at US$30. The rides can be wet and wild.

Bus

Buses on both islands can resemble minivan taxis, so check the front plate to be sure. An 'H' means private bus and a 'T' means taxi (an 'R' is a rental car and a 'P' or 'PA' is a resident's car).

Car & Motorcycle

Foreigners must purchase a visitor driver's license, which costs EC$62.50 (US$24) and is valid for 90 days. Rental companies will issue you one when you fill out your contracts, and a license on one island is good for the other.

Rental companies will usually meet you at the airport, ferry port or your hotel. Daily rates start at about US$40. You really won't need a 4WD for going anywhere – unless it's rainy season. Most of the major firms have local affiliates.

Drive on the left side of the road, often around goats, cows and pedestrians. Speed limits are posted in miles per hour, and are generally between 20mph and 40mph. There are no traffic lights on either island, but there are several traffic circles where you yield to cars already in the circle. Gas costs over EC$12 per gallon.

Taxi

Taxis meet scheduled flights on both islands. See p675 and p685 for sample fares.

Taxi island tours on both islands cost around US$80. Those short on time can take a three-hour half-island tour for US$60.

Tours

NEVIS

Sunrise Tours (⌀469-2758; www.nevisnature tours.com) Lynell Liburd leads a variety of guided walks, including the strenuous trek up Mt Nevis and a moderate hike to the haunted Devil's Copper area with its volcanic vents and waterfalls. Prices depend on group size and tour length.

Windsurf 'n Mountain Bike (⌀469-9682; www.bikenevis.com; Oualie Beach) Winston Crooke leads a Nevis mountain-bike team and also gets visitors in the saddle on guided tours. The most popular is the Island Discovery Tour (US$65), an easy two-hour spin along historic sugarcane trails with stops in small villages and at plantations. Hike-and-bike combination tours (US$85) as well as guided kayak trips (US$55) are also available.

ST KITTS

Blue Water Safaris (⌀466-4933; www.blue watersafaris.com) Full-day catamaran cruises for US$95, with snorkeling, lunch on Pinney's Beach and an open bar thrown in. Sunset and moonlight cruises are US$50 per person.

Greg's Safaris (⌀465-4121; www.gregsafaris. com) Greg Pereira leads a half-day hike into the rainforest of St Kitts for US$65. The trek moves at a measured pace, identifies flora and fauna, and stops to sample fruits along the way. Considerably more challenging is the rugged all-day tour up to the Mt Liamuiga volcano crater rim for US$95, including lunch.

Leeward Islands Charters (⌀465-7474; www.stkittsleewardislandscharters.com) This class act offers a range of options, including a three-hour Sail and Snorkel trip for US$45 (Nevis departures US$62), a full day of sailing, snorkeling, drinks and beach barbecue for US$87, and two-hour sunset cruises for US$50. Boats leave from Port Zante on St Kitts or Oualie Beach on Nevis.

St Lucia

Why Go?

Rising like an emerald tooth from the Caribbean Sea, St Lucia definitely grabs your attention. While it fits the image of a glam honeymoon spot, this mountainous island has more to offer than sensuous beaches flanked by sybaritic lodgings.

Diving, snorkeling, sailing and kitesurfing are fabulous. On land there's no better ecofriendly way to experience the rainforest-choked interior than on foot, on horseback or suspended from a zip line. Wildlife lovers will get a buzz, too. Whales, dolphins, turtles and endemic birds can easily be approached, with the added thrill of a grandiose setting. Near Soufrière, the awesomely photogenic Pitons rise from the waves like pyramids of volcanic stone.

Bar the island's northeast, where most tourist facilities are concentrated, the rest of St Lucia is definitely a back-to-nature haven, making it possible to find a deserted bay, secluded waterfall, character-filled fishing community or odd colonial-style plantation.

Best Beaches

» Anse Chastanet (p708)
» Anse Mamin (p709)
» Sandy Beach (p712)
» La Toc Beach (p701)
» Smugglers Cove (p705)

Best Places to Stay

» Crystals (p710)
» Anse Chastanet Resort (p710)
» Fond Doux Holiday Plantation (p710)
» Ladera (p711)
» Balenbouche Estate (p712)

When to Go

As with most Caribbean destinations the winter season is the most popular time to visit St Lucia. The very unwintry weather brings the crowds and jacks up the prices, especially during the driest period from December to March. Winter weather is sublime with average temperatures around 81°F (27°C). Summer is quiet and hot with the July temperatures averaging 85°F (29°C). Hurricane season falls between June and October – expect more rain this time of year and maybe the odd storm.

Itineraries

ONE WEEK

Basing yourself in Soufrière, spend a day exploring the town and the surrounding beaches. Allow two to three days for some adventure options, including diving, cycling, hiking and zip-lining. Travel north to the lively city of Castries. Spend a couple of days exploring the area around Gros Islet, Pigeon Island and Rodney Bay before returning south to unwind for a day in the thermal pools in Soufrière.

TEN DAYS

After the one-week tour, head south for a day of kitesurfing on the south coast. Next, sample the delights of the Atlantic-battered east coast. Be sure to spare some cash for your last day – with its great shopping options, Castries will torment the weak-willed.

GETTING TO NEIGHBORING ISLANDS

There are frequent direct flights to Martinique, Barbados, St Vincent, Trinidad, Puerto Rico and Antigua. For other Caribbean destinations, you'll have to connect through one of these islands.

There's a regular high-speed catamaran service between St Lucia and Martinique. At certain times of the year it also operates between St Lucia and Guadeloupe.

Essential Food & Drink

» **Seafood** Dorado (also known as mahi mahi), kingfish, marlin, snapper, lobster, crab and shellfish feature high on the menu.

» **Meat dishes** Chicken and pork dishes are commonly found.

» **Local specialties** Try callaloo soup, *lambi* (conch) and saltfish with green fig (seasoned salt cod and boiled green banana).

» **Piton** The beer of St Lucia; crisp and sweet, it's perfectly light and refreshing.

» **St Lucian rum** The island's sole distillery produces white rums, gold rums and flavored rums.

AT A GLANCE

» **Currency** Eastern Caribbean dollar (EC$); US dollar (US$) widely accepted

» **Language** English, Creole

» **Money** ATMs all over; dispense only Eastern Caribbean dollars

» **Visas** Not required for US, EU or most Commonwealth citizens for stays under 28 days; see p716

Fast Facts

» **Area** 238 sq miles
» **Population** 170,000
» **Capital** Castries
» **Telephone country code** ☑758
» **Emergency** ☑999

Set Your Budget

» **Budget hotel room** EC$170

» **Two-course evening meal** EC$110

» **Museum entrance** EC$25

» **Beer** EC$5

» **City Transport Ticket** EC$1.75

Resources

» **Intimate Inns** (www.inntimatestlucia.org) A list of affordable accommodation options

» **St Lucia Star** (www.stluciastar.com) A weekly online newspaper

» **Tourist office** (www.stlucianow.com) The official tourist-board site with great general information; a good place to start

Ferry to Fort-de-France

Pointe
du Cap

Smugglers
Cove

Pigeon Island
National Landmark
Pigeon Point

Cap
Estate

Cas En Bas

Anse Lavoutte

*Caribbean
Sea*

Rodney Bay
Reduit Beach

Labrellotte
Bay

Gros Islet
Rodney Bay
Marina

Monchy

Choc Beach
Vigie Beach
Vigie Peninsula
La Toc Bay

Monier

Marquis

Morne
Fortune
(853ft)

George FL
Charles Airport

CASTRIES

Babonneau

Grande Anse

Cul de Sac River

Forestiere

3 Chassin

Marigot
Bay

Roseau Bay

Roseau River

Piton Flore
(1871ft)

2 Anse
La Raye

Grand
Rivière

Anse Cochon

Canaries

Millet

Nature
Reserve

*Treetop
Adventure
Park*

Fond d'Or Bay

Dennery

Dennery Island

Sault
Waterfalls

6

Anse Mamin **1**
Anse Chastanet **4**

Mt Gimie
(3118ft)

Diamond
Botanical
Gardens

Soufrière **5**

Malgretoute

Jalousie Beach
Anse des Pitons

Gros Piton
(2617ft) **8**

Petit Piton
(2460ft)

Fond
St Jacques

Sulphur Springs

Quilesse
Forest
Reserve

Edmond Forest
Reserve

*Descartiers
Rainforest Trail*

Troumassée River

Etangs
*Tet Paul
Nature Trail*

*Mamiku
Gardens*

Praslin

Frigate Islands
Nature Reserve

Mon Repos

*ATV Paradise Tours &
Rainforest Parrot Trail*

*La Tille
Waterfalls*

Micoud

Desruisseaux

Canelles River

*Balenbouche
Estate*

Laborie

*Hewanorra
International
Airport*

Anse l'Islet

*ATLANTIC
OCEAN*

Vieux Fort
Vieux Fort Bay

Maria Islands
Nature Reserve

Sandy Beach

7

Cape Moule
à Chique

Gros Islet Rd

0 ——— 6 km
0 ——— 4 miles

St Lucia Highlights

1 Sun and splash on the idyllic beach of **Anse Mamin** (p709)

2 Lose your inhibitions and dance to calypso at **Anse La Raye** (p708) on Friday

3 Swing through the trees with **Rain Forest Sky Rides** (p707)

4 Snorkel or dive at **Anse Chastanet** (p708)

5 Go heritage hunting among the colonial buildings of the estates near **Soufrière** (p708)

6 Take a drive through the fishing villages along the less-explored **east coast** (p712)

7 Try kitesurfing at **Sandy Beach** (p712)

8 Huff and puff up the steep trail to the iconic **Gros Piton** (p710) for astounding views

Castries

Walking along the crowded streets of Castries, you are bombarded with the kinetics of a city that is bustling with life. The throbbing heart of the city is the market area – it heaves and vibrates, with the locals scurrying to fetch their wares and sell their goods.

Castries' setting couldn't be more photogenic. Think massive cruise ships anchored in a sheltered bay, with the soaring Morne Fortune (2795ft) as the backdrop. Although most of the city's historic buildings were destroyed by major fires between 1785 and 1948, a smattering of appealing colonial-era edifices in the center will transport you back in time.

Come with maximum overdraft – if you love shopping you've come to the right place.

◉ Sights & Activities

Cathedral of the Immaculate
Conception   CATHEDRAL
(Laborie St) The city's Catholic cathedral, built in 1897, is a grand stone structure that has a splendidly painted interior of trompe l'oeil columns and colorfully detailed biblical scenes. The island's patron saint, St Lucia, is portrayed directly above the altar. The church richly incorporates both Caribbean and African influences, including images of a Black Madonna and child, and the liberal use of bright red, green and yellow tones.

Castries Central Market   MARKET
(Jeremie St) For a peek at local life, nothing beats an immersion in the bustling alleyways of the central market. The most fun time to visit is early Saturday morning when local residents flock in and farmers bring their fresh produce to town.

Derek Walcott Square   SQUARE
A lovely space in the middle of the city, Derek Walcott Sq is a quiet park surrounded by a handful of 19th-century wooden buildings with gingerbread-trim balconies, an attractive Victorian-style library and the imposing Cathedral of the Immaculate Conception.

Morne Fortune   MOUNTAIN, FORT
Sitting atop the 2795ft Morne Fortune, about 3 miles south of Castries center, is Fort Charlotte, whose construction began under the French and was continued by the British. Because of its strategic hilltop vantage-point overlooking Castries, the fort

was a source of fierce fighting between the French and British in colonial times. The fort buildings have been renovated and given a new life as the Sir Arthur Lewis Community College.

At the rear of the college, a small obelisk monument commemorates the 27th Inniskilling Regiment's retaking of the hill from French forces in 1796. Near the monument you'll also find a couple of cannons and a fairly good view of the coast north to Pigeon Point.

Deep-Sea Fishing & Whale-Watching
Between February and May it's common to see humpback whales offshore from the west coast, as well as pilot whales, sperm whales and pods of dolphins year-round.

Castries is also a good base for fans of Ernest Hemingway. Billfish, marlin and yellowfin tuna can be caught from November to January, while the wahoo and dorado season is around February to May.

Hackshaw's (☎453-0553; www.hackshaws. com; Vigie) runs whale- and dolphin-watching outings (from US$50) as well as deep-sea fishing trips (half-day from US$450, up to eight people).

✯✯ Festivals & Events

St Lucia Jazz Festival   JAZZ
(www.stluciajazz.org; May) Concerts and jam sessions featuring big names from the international jazz scene.

Carnival   MUSIC, PARADE
(www.luciancarnival.com; July) The biggest show on the island's calendar. Castries' streets buzz with music, costume parade and calypso.

Atlantic Rally for Cruisers   BOAT RACE
(www.worldcruising.com; November-December) A fun 'race' across the Atlantic starting off the coast of Spain and ending in St Lucia.

🛌 Sleeping

With a range of resorts so close to the city, accommodations in Castries itself are thin on the ground.

Auberge Seraphine   INN $$
(☎453-2073; www.aubergeseraphine.com; Pointe Seraphine; s/d from US$130/177; ❄🛜🏊) This inn has a heavy focus on regional businesspeople, so it's not exactly a vacation environment, but it's convenient to downtown Castries and the airport. All the rooms are functional and clean. Be sure to ask for one

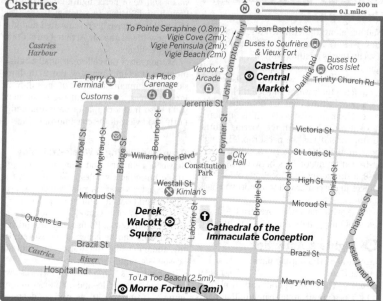

with a marina view – rooms 301 to 304 are the best. There's also an on-site restaurant.

Eudovic's Guesthouse GUESTHOUSE $
(✆452-2747; www.eudovicart.com; Morne Fortune; d US$50; ❀☎⛱) Everything is simple and ultra-laid-back at this low-key guesthouse run by master artisan Eudovic. The four fan-cooled, fully equipped rooms are clean and utilitarian, and open onto a jungle-like garden. Rooms 1 and 2 get more light. Downtown Castries is a five-minute bus ride away.

✗ Eating

For good rotis and local dishes, try the stalls at the south side of Castries Central Market.

Coal Pot FRENCH-CARIBBEAN $$$
(✆452-5566; Vigie Cove; mains EC$80-120; ⊙lunch & dinner Mon-Sat) Follow the road around the harbor to find this little hidden gem run by a French chef. It's right on the water and far enough from town that the tranquility of the sea lulls you into a diner's dream. The cooking is decidedly French, with fresh produce and local spices creating a fusion cuisine.

Pink Plantation House CREOLE $$
(✆452-5422; Chef Harry Dr, Morne Fortune; mains EC$40-75; ⊙lunch Sun-Fri, dinner Thu-Sat) This art gallery housed in a splendid colonial mansion

(see p701) sitting on a lush property doubles as a restaurant. The views from the veranda are to die for. The Sunday brunch, at EC$60, is brilliant value. Wonderful cocktails, too.

Kimlan's CARIBBEAN $
(✆452-1136; Micoud St; mains EC$11-20; ⊙lunch Mon-Sat) It's not love, but it hits the spot. Plates brim high with rotis and Creole dishes at wallet-friendly prices. It offers seating on a shaded balcony that overlooks Derek Walcott Sq.

🛍 Shopping

Both **Pointe Seraphine** (⊙9am-5pm), on the north side of the harbor, and **La Place Carenage** (Jeremie St; ⊙9am-5pm) have a duty-free shopping complex catering to cruise-ship passengers; there's a raft of shops selling liquor, jewelry, perfume and the usual duty-free items.

TOP
CHOICE **Eudovic's Art Studio** WOODCARVINGS
(✆452-2747; www.eudovicart.com; Morne Fortune; ⊙8am-4:30pm Mon-Fri, 8am-2pm Sat & Sun) Vincent Joseph Eudovic is an internationally renowned master carver, and his studio at Morne Fortune is a magnificent art gallery. He uses only local woods, and no two carv-

ings are alike. His commitment to training young St Lucians deserves to be mentioned.

Bagshaws Shop SILK-SCREENED ITEMS

(☑451-9249; www.bagshawsstlucia.com; La Toc Beach; ◷8:30am-4pm Mon-Fri) For quality silk-screen products, head to this welcoming boutique. Signature items include exquisitely colored shirts, placemats, hotpads and wall hangings, all made locally. The main studio, where you can watch the printers at work, is scenically located at La Toc Beach. There are also Bagshaws boutiques at La Place Carenage and Pointe Seraphine.

Pink Plantation House PAINTINGS, CERAMICS

(☑452-5422; Chef Harry Dr, Morne Fortune; ◷11:30am-3pm Mon-Sat, 10am-3pm Sun) Michelle Elliot's eye-goggling paintings and hand-painted ceramics are sure to enliven your bedroom. This place is also famous for its good-value **restaurant** (p700) and wrap-around views of Castries.

Caribelle Batik BATIK

(☑452-3785; www.caribellebatikstlucia.com; Old Victoria House, Morne Fortune; ◷8am-5pm Mon-Sat) Housed in an enticing Victorian Caribbean mansion nestled amid lush tropical gardens, this working batik studio is a feast for the eyes. Each product (purses, hats, bags, T-shirt, sarongs, wall hangings) is handmade and incorporates tropical motifs.

Castries Central Market SOUVENIRS, FOOD

(◷Mon-Sat) Sprawling in size and impossible to miss from the center of town, you can get almost anything here from fruit and vegetables to souvenirs and household items.

Vendor's Arcade CLOTHING, SOUVENIRS

(Peynier St; ◷Mon-Sat) Across the road from the Central Market is this shopping arcade, which backs onto the waterfront. Load up on colorful textiles, rum, spices, handicrafts, basketwork and jewelry.

❶ Information

Most banks have branches with ATMs in the center.

Tourist office (☑452-4094; www.stlucianow. com; La Place Carenage, Jeremie St; ◷8am-4:30pm Mon-Fri)

❶ Getting Around

TO/FROM THE AIRPORT Taxis are plentiful at George FL Charles Airport, which is very close to downtown. Rates from the airport are roughly EC$25 to Derek Walcott Sq in central Castries; EC$45 to Reduit Beach; EC$60 to Rodney Bay Marina; and EC$90 to Marigot Bay.

There are no direct buses; the nearest bus stop is about 1 mile away, at the northern end of the airport runway.

TAXI You can hail a taxi on the street, or ask your hotel to book one for you. Always agree on a fare before you depart.

Around Castries

Going north along Gros Islet Rd from Vigie Peninsula the oceanside highway snakes its way to Rodney Bay. This stretch is far busier and more built-up than any other areas in St Lucia, but it's not too hard to discover a few nooks that remain largely untouched by development.

On the southern shore of Castries Bay, La Toc Beach is well worth a peek (and a dip).

🏖 Beaches

TOP CHOICE Labrellotte Bay FAMILY BEACH

This quiet, sheltered bay is fringed by a broad strand of golden sand backed by steep hillsides. It has shallow, calm waters, making it an ideal location for families. The southern section fronts the East Winds Inn (and is appropriately dubbed 'East Winds Inn Beach'), while the northern swath of sand is occupied by the Windjammer Landing Villa Beach Resort (and is also accordingly called 'Windjammer Beach'). To get to the beach, follow the road to the East Winds Inn, then take the rough road that skirts the hotel and descends to the beach.

Vigie Beach FAMILY BEACH

This 2-mile beach runs parallel to the George FL Charles Airport runway. Vigie Beach is where you can find locals taking a quick dip on hot days. The color of the sand? Brown-gray.

Choc Beach FAMILY BEACH

A promontory separates Vigie and Choc Bays. The southern section of this long swath of honey-colored sand is flanked by the highway (noise!) but if you walk to the north it gets much quieter.

La Toc Beach RESORT BEACH

South of Castries, this splendid golden-sand beach remains largely off the tourist radar, not least because it's a bit hard to find. Go the direction of Morne Fortune, then head to the gate of the Sandals Regency Golf Re-

PORTS OF CALL

Cruise ships dock in Castries, at Pointe Seraphine. Smaller vessels call at Soufrière; they anchor offshore and bring passengers ashore via tenders.

With a few hours in the ports, you can do the following:

Castries

» Hunt for souvenirs and gifts at Castries Central Market (p699) or Bagshaws (p701)

» Lay your towel at Reduit Beach or Pigeon Island National Landmark (p705)

» Experience the thrills of zip-lining in the rainforest (p707)

Soufrière

» Mosey around the Botanical Gardens (p709)

» Immerse yourself in the Martian landscape of Sulphur Springs (p709)

» Discover an 18th-century plantation at Morne Coubaril Estate (p709)

» Dive or snorkel (p710) in the marine park off Soufrière

» Take a guided walk along Tet Paul Nature Trail (p709) for gorgeous views of the Pitons

sort & Spa, where the guards will show you the path that leads down to the beach.

Rodney Bay & Gros Islet

About 10km north of Castries, the vast horseshoe of Rodney Bay is the eye of the tourist storm, boasting the island's most diverse tourist facilities. Within the bay is a large, man-made, completely protected inner lagoon. It's flanked to the east by the Rodney Bay Marina, which is rated as one of the Caribbean's premier yachting centers, and to the west by Reduit Beach, which is home to a cluster of low-rise resorts. To the south, Rodney Bay Village is chockablock with restaurants, bars, clubs, vacation condos and shopping malls.

The contrast with the neighboring fishing village that is Gros Islet, to the north, is astounding. Walking along the streets lined with weather-beaten cottages, unassuming rum shops and the odd fishing shacks draped with drying nets, it's hard to fathom that the bustling marina is just up the road. Brimming with character, Gros Islet is a great insight into the reality of St Lucia.

◉ Sights

Reduit Beach   RESORT BEACH

This stellar stretch of white sand is by far the most popular beach on the island, and it's easy to see why. The sea ranges from turquoise to azure; the waves are benign; Pigeon Island, to the north, and Mt Pimard,

to the south, scenically frame the horizon; and there are plenty of dining options and bars nearby.

That said, the beach is fairly narrow and it's fronted by a couple of sprawling resorts. Tip: head to the southernmost section of the beach. It's less congested and you'll find more shade, a good beach bar and restaurant, and excellent snorkeling options.

Rodney Bay Marina   MARINA

The state-of-the-art marina is the stomping ground of sailors and the well-heeled. The expansive floating parking lot sits adjacent to a series of shops, restaurants, trendy bars and just about anything else a mariner might need. It's a lovely place for an evening stroll.

🏃 Activities

Tours R Us   SEGWAY TOURS

(☏724-8200; www.stluciasegway.com; Rodney Bay Village; tour US$69; ⊘daily) This outfit offers Segway tours to Mt Pimard. They follow a dirt track leading to various lookouts and last two hours, including a 15-minute practice session. The guide gives insights into the local flora and fauna, and you'll stop at interesting historical relics.

Saluna Watersports   WATERSPORTS

(www.saluna-watersports.com; Reduit Beach; ⊘8:30am-4pm) Right on Reduit Beach, this watersports center rents paddleboats, kayaks and sailboats (from EC$54 per hour), and offers water-taxi services to Pigeon

Island National Landmark (US$20 round-trip).

Diving & Snorkeling

There are several dive sites and snorkeling spots of note off the northwestern coast of St Lucia (see also p45).

Eastern Caribbean Diving
DIVING & SNORKELING

(☑456-9581; www.easterncaribbeandivingstlucia.com; Reduit Beach) Based at Bay Garden Beach Resort & Spa. Also offers dive outings to Anse Cochon and Soufrière, as well as snorkeling trips. A two-tank dive costs from US$105 (gear included).

Scuba Steve's Diving
DIVING & SNORKELING

(☑450-9433; www.scubastevesdiving.com; Gros Islet; ⦿) Also offers dive trips to Anse Cochon and Soufrière, as well as snorkeling trips. A two-tank dive costs from US$90 (gear included). Runs a dedicated PADI Bubblemaker programme for kids.

Boat Trips

Seeing St Lucia from the sea is a real treat. The following operators organise day sails and boat trips (from US$100) along the west coast:

Endless Summer Cruises
CRUISES

(☑450-8651; www.stluciaboattours.com; Rodney Bay Marina) Day sail and sunset cruises.

SunLink Tours
CRUISES

(☑456-9100; www.sunlinktours.com) Day sail and sunset cruises on a replica pirate ship.

🛏 Sleeping

Ginger Lily Hotel
HOTEL $$

(☑458-0300; www.thegingerlilyhotel.com; Reduit Beach Ave; d from US$180; ❄☎⛱) An excellent alternative to the bigger resorts nearby, Ginger Lily Hotel is functional, intimate and blissfully quiet. The 11 rooms are equipped to a high standard but have no sea views. Tropical charm is manifested through exuberant gardens and an inviting pool. Reduit Beach is just across the road.

Bay Guesthouse
GUESTHOUSE $

(☑450-8956; www.bay-guesthouse.com; Gros Islet; s US$35-45, d US$40-50; ☎) On the waterfront it's hard to miss the safety-orange building that is the Bay Guesthouse. This great property is run by a charming couple who have a great insight into the needs of the budget traveler. Smallish but cozy rooms enjoying good views of the sea (bar the street-facing room, at the back), hammocks in the garden and a congenial atmosphere make it a great budget option.

La Terrasse
GUESTHOUSE $

(☑572-0389, 721-0389; www.laterrassestlucia.com; Rodney Bay Village; d from US$60; ❄☎) This delightful guesthouse run by a French couple feels remarkably homey. It has a tropical courtyard and dining deck (see p704) and there are four rooms that are handsomely decorated with an eclectic mix of rustic wooden touches and thoroughly modern fixtures. It's in a quiet street off the main avenue and a five-minute walk to the beach.

Bay Gardens Beach Resort & Spa
RESORT $$

(☑457-8500; www.baygardensbeachresort.com; Reduit Beach Ave; d from US$180; ❄☎⛱♿) An excellent choice if you prefer a full-service resort, the BGBR has an idyllic beachfront location, and it's competitively priced. Rooms are in three-story buildings designed with a neoclassical flair; most overlook the large cloverleaf pool or the beach. All units have good-sized kitchens, making this a great choice for families.

Bay Gardens Hotel
HOTEL $$

(☑457-8006; www.baygardenshotel.com; Rodney Bay Village; d from US$110; ❄☎⛱♿) Bay Gardens Hotel is a colony of attached cottages that are trimmed in the perky pastels typical of the Caribbean and cloistered around a small pool. The good-sized rooms are basic in style but are kept clean. It's not on the sands but guests have full access to the facilities at Bay Gardens Beach Resort & Spa, a sister property that faces the beach, just two minutes away via the hotel's free shuttle.

> **DON'T MISS**
>
> ## TURTLE-WATCHING
>
> Between March and August the long stretch of Grande Anse on the northeast coast is a favorite nesting ground for hundreds of leatherback turtles. Visitors are allowed to check out the turtle rookeries at night and observe eggs being laid or hatching – a fantastic spectacle. A licensed guide must accompany all visitors. Contact **Heritage Tours** (☑458-1454, 451-6058, 285-6058; www.heritagetoursstlucia.org). Note that Grande Anse beach is only accessible by 4WD.

Coco Palm
HOTEL **$$**

(☑456-2800; www.coco-resorts.com; Rodney Bay; d from US$150; ✳︎☎✉♨) A harmonious blend of modern lines and Creole styling. Although the Coco Palm is not right on the beach, it provides an intimate setting on a grassy terrace overlooking Rodney Bay Village. With its varied accommodations, it's appropriate for singles, couples and families alike. All the action of Rodney Bay Village is within walking distance, as is the beach.

✗ Eating

The Edge
FUSION **$$**

(☑450-3343; www.edge-restaurant.com; Rodney Bay Village; mains EC$50-140; ⊘breakfast, lunch & dinner) Swedish chef Bobo Bergström conjures up high-flying creative 'Eurobbean' dishes (European-inspired specialties combined with Caribbean traditions) and tempting sushi. Nice views of the marina from the dining room help to wash down the tasty (and expensive) food. To some, it may feel a bit pretentious. On the waterfront, inside Harmony Suites hotel.

Cafe Ole
CAFETERIA **$**

(Rodney Bay Marina; mains EC$14-30; ⊘6am-10pm) This sprightly eatery sitting on a wood-planked covered deck overlooking the marina is the perfect venue to enjoy a drink, a snack or a meal – and to people-watch.

The Charthouse
GRILLED DISHES **$$**

(☑452-8115; Rodney Bay Village; mains EC$65-120; ⊘dinner) Carnivores, you'll find nirvana here: the well-respected Charthouse majors on flawlessly cooked, charcoal-broiled beefsteak. It also offers a good selection of seafood dishes. The decor is embellished with mahogany wood and tropical plants, and the breezy terrace is right on the waterside.

Starfish
CARIBBEAN **$**

(☑452-0100; Rodney Bay Marina; mains EC$18-35; ⊘lunch & dinner) Next door to Cafe Ole, Starfish is the sister restaurant of The Edge, but with a much more affordable price tag. Let the wok noodles and daily specials, such as fresh fish in white-wine sauce, tingle your taste buds.

Spinnakers Beach Bar & Restaurant
CARIBBEAN **$**

(☑452-8491; Reduit Beach; mains EC$25-90; ⊘lunch & dinner) Right on Reduit Beach, this venue with a casual atmosphere is a catch-all for locals, cruise shippers and seemingly everybody else. After a morning spent in the waves, re-energize with pork ribs, curried lamb or a prawn and pineapple salad.

Flavours of the Grill
CARIBBEAN **$**

(☑450-9722; Gros Islet; mains EC$18-35; lunch buffet EC$20; ⊘lunch & dinner Mon-Sat) This intimate eatery, in a colorful, quirky Creole home in the center of Gros Islet, offers simple yet toothsome dishes. Pounce on its excellent-value lunch buffet and you'll leave perfectly sated.

Rituals Coffee
CAFETERIA **$**

(Rodney Bay Village; snacks EC$15-40; ⊘7am-10pm) A sleek venture with an appetizing selection of bagels, sandwiches, pastries, burgers and salads. The coffee earns top marks and it's a great place to escape the heat with cool blasts of air-con.

The Fire Grill
GRILLED DISHES **$$$**

(☑451-4745; Rodney Bay Ave; mains EC$75-150; ⊘dinner daily, lunch Sun-Fri) If you're in the mood for a perfectly cooked Angus beefsteak – or seafood – head to this eatery. Side dishes are expensive, though.

La Terrasse
FRENCH **$$**

(☑572-0389; Rodney Bay Village; mains EC$55-85; ⊘lunch & dinner) *Gratin dauphinois* (potatoes baked in cream and crusted on top) and *fondue bourguignonne* (Burgundy fondue) in St Lucia? Yes, it's possible in this French restaurant.

Elena's
ICE CREAM **$**

(Rodney Bay Marina; snacks EC$18-35; ⊘8am-9pm) Elena's whips up a scrumptious assortment of flavors to cool you down after a day in the sun. Also serves up snack options and pasta.

Razmataz
INDIAN **$**

(☑452-9800; Rodney Bay Ave; mains EC$40-85; ⊘lunch & dinner) Fantastic Indian curries and vegetarian options.

Golden Taste
CARIBBEAN **$**

(☑450-9792; Gros Islet; mains EC$30-75; ⊘lunch & dinner Wed-Mon) This popular joint is worth visiting for its good, cheap and wholesome Caribbean staples.

☕ Drinking & Entertainment

Rodney Bay is the most 'happening' area in St Lucia. Most restaurants feature a bar section. You can also check out the bars in the large hotels. A few recommended watering holes:

Tequila Joe's
BAR

(Rodney Bay Ave; ⊘daily) Kick off the night with a few tequila shots at this cheerful hangout decked in wood. Also serves food.

Delirious　　　　　　　　　　　　BAR
(Rodney Bay Village; ⊘Mon-Sat) St Lucia's hottest spot at the time of writing. Come for the good fun, good mix of people and good cocktails. There's also a restaurant.

Boardwalk　　　　　　　　　　　　BAR
(Rodney Bay Marina; ⊘daily) A cool spot where you can cut loose over some sunset cocktails in pleasant surrounds. At the marina, on the waterfront.

Gros Islet heats up on Friday nights when the weekly jump-up gets going. Street stalls sell fresh fish, grilled chicken and other delights. The music plays at full volume and the dance moves flow more readily as the rum punch starts to take effect. For visitors it's a great opportunity to catch local vibes.

Pigeon Island National Landmark

Don't expect an island here, but a small peninsula jutting out from the northwest coast. In the 1970s a sandy causeway was constructed between Gros Islet and Pigeon Island, but it's still designated as an 'island'.

Pigeon Island is of significant historical importance, with a number of ruins scattered around the grounds. Its spicy history dates back to the 1550s, when St Lucia's first French settler, Jambe de Bois (Wooden Leg), used the island as a base for raiding passing Spanish ships. Two centuries later, British admiral George Rodney fortified Pigeon Island, using it to monitor the French fleet on Martinique. Rodney's fleet set sail from Pigeon Island in 1782 for his most decisive military engagement, the Battle of the Saintes. With the end of hostilities between the two European rivals, the fort slipped into disuse in the 19th century, although the USA established a small signal station here during WWII.

It's also a venue for concerts, festivals – including the famous St Lucia Jazz Festival – and weddings. It's popular with picnicking families and sunbathers.

◎ Sights & Activities

Ruins　　　　　　　　　　　　　　RUINS
(admission EC$13.50; ⊘9am-5pm) Pigeon Island is a fun place to explore, with paths winding around the remains of barracks, batteries and garrisons whose partially intact stone buildings create a ghost-town effect. The grounds are well endowed with lofty trees,

manicured lawns and fine coastal views. Near the gate is a kitchen dating from 1824 and further on are the main fortress and a small **interpretative center**. At the top of Fort Rodney Hill, you'll find a small but well-preserved **fortress**, a few rusting cannons and cardiac-arresting views. For more views, continue north past the stone foundations of the ridge battery to the top of the 359ft **Signal Peak**, about a 20-minute walk.

Beaches　　　　　　　　　　　BEACHES
Most of the coastline around Pigeon Island is rocky, but you'll find two small sandy beaches pricked with palm trees. The water is safe for swimming and snorkeling.

Snuba　　　　　　　　　　　　DIVING
(⌨456-5006; www.snubastlucia.com; US$55; ⊘four times a week, by appointment; 🚼) Bridging the gap between snorkeling and diving, Snuba's a great chance to get really acquainted with marine life. At a depth of about 3m, you breathe in a regulator that provides a supply of air connected to an air tank mounted on a raft at the surface. You'll enter the water directly from one of the park's two beaches before being taken on a guided underwater tour along the coast. It's fun and easy – families will love it.

✕ Eating

ᴛᴏᴘ⁄ᴄʜᴏɪᴄᴇ **Jambe De Bois**　　　CARIBBEAN $
(Pigeon Island; mains EC$10-25; ⊘breakfast, lunch & dinner) This is a casual restaurant where locals, yachties and frequent visitors know they'll get a delicious, reasonably priced meal. Pick out a table on the breezy veranda and savor the views onto the bay. On Saturday and Sunday night it has live music to soothe the soul.

The Northern Tip

Once you've left bustling Rodney Bay and Pigeon Island National Landmark, life becomes more sedate as you head towards the island's northernmost reaches. On Cap Estate the hilly terrain is dotted with chichi villas, large estates and the island's only public golf course. From there it's an easy drive downhill to secluded Cas En Bas beach.

◎ Sights & Activities

ᴛᴏᴘ⁄ᴄʜᴏɪᴄᴇ **Smugglers Cove**　SECLUDED BEACH
Close your eyes and imagine the quintessential Caribbean cove, framed on three sides

by steep sheltering cliffs. You've just pictured Smugglers Cove, a secluded crescent of brown sugary sand. You'll find a lifeguard on duty (ideal if you're with the little 'uns) and a beach bar that doubles as a water-sports center.

Cas En Bas
ACTIVITIES BEACH

This wide curve of gray sand sees few visitors because it's a bit off the beaten track. It's a stunning beach to sun yourself on.

St Lucia Golf & Country Club
GOLF

(☑450-8523; www.stluciagolf.com; Cap Estate; ⊙daily) This challenging 18-hole championship course (6836 yards, par 71) is the island's only public course. Green fees start at US$95 for nine holes. The clubhouse has a good restaurant.

Horseback Riding
HORSEBACK RIDING

Trims National Riding Academy (☑450-8273; ⊙by reservation) and **International Pony Club** (☑450-8665; ⊙by reservation) both offer countryside trail rides as well as beach canters along Cas En Bas beach. Expect to pay US$65 for two hours. Free pick-up services can be arranged from most hotels in the Rodney Bay area. Children are welcome.

Water Sports

Cas En Bas beach and Smugglers Cove both have a small water-sports center that rents out sailboats, kayaks, windsurfers and snorkeling gear (from US$25 per hour).

Cas En Bas always has a stiff breeze, which makes it an excellent (yet largely undiscovered) kitesurfing spot. **Kitesurfing St Lucia** (☑714-9589; www.kitesurfingstlucia.com; ⊙by reservation) offers lessons (from US$80 for two hours) and rentals (from US$35).

🛏 Sleeping & Eating

TOP CHOICE / Cap Maison
BOUTIQUE HOTEL $$$

(☑457-8679; www.capmaison.com; Cap Estate; d incl breakfast from US$480; ❄🐝☁🍴) Privacy, luxury and service are hallmarks of this sanctuary built on a seaside bluff. The elegant Moroccan-Caribbean architecture features suites that are elegantly furnished and decorated. Another draw is the superb Cliff at Cap restaurant (open to nonguests). Downside: the nearest beach, Smugglers Cove, requires hiking down (and back up) 92 steps. Cap Maison appeals to couples but also caters to families at certain times of year.

Cotton Bay Village
RESORT $$$

(☑456-5700; www.cottonbayvillage.com; Cas En Bas; d from US$310; ❄🐝☁🍴) This complex overlooking Cas En Bas beach is large enough to cater to sophisticated couples and active families while, at the same time, offering cozy privacy to honeymooners. It features luxurious villas, a huge pool, a spa and excellent dining options. The main draw: it feels secluded.

Smuggler's Cove Resort & Spa
RESORT $$$

(☑457-4140; www.smugglersresort.com; Cap Estate; per person all-inclusive from US$260; ❄🐝☁🍴) Families flock to Smuggler's Cove because it fronts a sandy bay and offers enough included activities for everyone to enjoy. Spread out over 60 acres on a greenery-shrouded hillside, the sprawling resort has a host of facilities and amenities, including six swimming pools, four restaurants and four kids' clubs. The 357 rooms are all ground floor.

Marjorie's Beach Bar & Restaurant
CARIBBEAN $

(☑520-0001; Cas En Bas; mains EC$35-50; ⊙lunch) Feel the sand between your toes at this modest eatery on Cas En Bas beach. It's noted for its well-prepared Creole dishes and its wicked rum cocktails.

Western St Lucia

As the road heads south from Castries, it encounters the rising topography of the island – twisting and turning around hairpin corners and steep hills – and uncluttered ocean views. Passing through the tiny fishing villages of Anse La Raye and Canaries, and the banana plantations that surround them, the real St Lucia comes to the fore.

The jade-green jungle expands to the interior, and as the road nears Soufrière the iconic Pitons emerge on the horizon and dominate the skyline.

MARIGOT BAY

Deep, sheltered Marigot Bay is a stunning example of natural architecture. Sheltered by towering palms and the surrounding hills, the narrow inlet is said to have hidden the entire British fleet from its French pursuers. Yachts play the same trick these days – the bay is a popular place to drop anchor and hide away for a few nights. Even if you don't have a ship to hide, it's still a great place to get lost for the day.

When it comes to fun in, on and under the water, Marigot Bay is an excellent base. It's an obvious launching pad for diving and snorkeling trips to Anse Cochon and Soufrière, to the south.

Sights & Activities

Millet Bird Sanctuary   NATURE RESERVE
(☏519-0787; Millet; walking EC$25, bird-watching EC$75; ◷8:30am-3pm Mon-Fri) This nature reserve lies about 10km inland from the west-coast highway, in Millet. Here's your chance to spot endemic species, including the St Lucia parrot and the St Lucia warbler. A knowledgeable forest ranger will take you on a tour. There's also a scenic 2-mile loop trail that alternates between thick forests and wide-open hilltops.

LaBas Beach   BEACH
Studded with a strand of palms, this small sliver of sand that juts out into the bay is the picture-perfect place for sunbathing, swimming, snorkeling or simply watching yachts quietly slipping by. One downside: it's fairly narrow due to sand erosion. Water sports are available with Aquarius.

LaBas beach is accessible by a small ferry (EC$5 round-trip) that grinds a groove from one side of the bay to the other as it makes dozens of trips a day.

St Lucia Rum Distillery   DISTILLERY
(☏456-3148; www.saintluciarums.com; EC$26; ◷9am-4pm Mon-Fri) On this popular tour you learn the colorful story behind the island's only remaining distillery and about the the rum-making procedure. The one-hour tour runs hourly or so and concludes with a tasting and an opportunity to purchase bottles of rum at factory prices. It's off the road to Anse La Raye, in Roseau, south of Marigot Bay.

Dive Fair Helen   WATER SPORTS
(☏451-7716; www.divefairhelen.com; ◷Mon-Sat;) Based at Marigot Beach Club, Dive Fair Helen charges US$120 for a two-tank dive, including equipment, and US$66 for a snorkeling excursion (US$46 for kids). It also offers kayaking tours along the coast and up a river (US$60), with a focus on fauna, flora and history.

Aquarius   WATER SPORTS
(◷8am-5.30pm) Based on LaBas beach, Aquarius rents snorkeling gear (US$10) and Hobie Cats (US$30). It also runs snorkeling trips to Anse Cochon (US$25) and kayaking excursions (US$45).

Sleeping

TOP CHOICE Inn On The Bay   B&B $$$
(☏451-4260; www.ste-lucie.com; d incl breakfast US$218-277; ☎☒; ◷Sep-Jun) Outstandingly

WORTH A TRIP

707

INLAND THRILLS

Why not see the beautiful rainforest from a Tarzan perspective? In the hamlet of Chassin, 30 minutes east of Rodney Bay, **Rain Forest Sky Rides** (☏458-5151; www.rfat.com; tram ride US$72, zip line US$85, combination US$100; ◷9am-3pm) is an ecofriendly outfit that has set up 11 zip lines in the trees. For the less adventurous, it offers a 1½-hour aerial 'tram' ride over the canopy. A tour guide provides insight into the local flora and fauna.

On the way to Chassin, make a beeline for **Union Nature Trail & Zoo** (☏468-5649; EC$5; ◷8am-4pm Mon-Fri), where you can wander amid a botanical garden. The small zoo section has an interesting collection of local species, including iguanas, boa constrictors and St Lucian parrots. Kids will love it.

positioned atop a secluded hill (views!), this peach of a place, run by a Canadian couple, features five bright, spacious and immaculate rooms that open onto a pool and a sunset-friendly deck. A free shuttle takes you to the bay. Alternatively you can take the 300 steps down to a secluded cove that offers great snorkeling ops.

Nature's Paradise   B&B $$
(☏458-3550; www.stluciaparadise.com; d US$155-207, cottage US$207-230, incl breakfast; ☎☒) Nature's Paradise is magical, if you don't mind the bone-crushing dirt road between the bay and the B&B (a 4WD is a must). Poised on a greenery-shrouded promontory, it proffers cracking views of the sea and the bay. The two rooms in the main building are a tad small, while the two cottages nestled in a Garden of Eden are roomy and fully equipped. A real hit is the pool, a dazzling mirage that seems to melt into the sea on the horizon.

Mango Beach Inn   B&B $$
(☏458-3188; www.mangobeachmarigot.com; s US$80-120, d US$120-160, incl breakfast; ✳☎☒⊞) The owner, the affable Judith Verity, a native from England, dotes upon her guests with effortless charm. The historic stone house is soothingly positioned on a velvety emerald hillside just above the Rainforest Hideaway restaurant. The five rooms are well appointed yet on the small side, but

DON'T MISS

ANSE LA RAYE

Heading south along the coast from Marigot Bay, the winding road snakes its way through the tiny village of Anse La Raye. The smattering of colorful buildings is typical of every St Lucian fishing community, and the village itself gives a good insight into the daily lives of the locals. On a Friday night Anse La Raye wakes up big time. 'Seafood Friday' has become one of the highlights for St Lucians and in-the-know tourists. Street stalls sell fish of every variety at unbeatable prices. The party gets a bit wild and goes most of the night. It will definitely be memorable, filled with food, refreshments (expect plenty of rum and beer) and dance.

you'll be too busy lounging by the pool or soaking up the fabulous views from the vast living room to mind. Families are welcome; cribs and high chairs are available.

Marigot Bay Hotel　　　　RESORT **$$$**
(☑458-5300; www.marigotbay.com; r incl breakfast from US$400; ❉ ❡ ☲) Occupying a nicely landscaped plot on the southern shore of the bay, this upmarket resort offers 122 smartly finished rooms with dark-wood fixtures, clean lines, ample space and heaps of amenities.

✖ Eating

TOP CHOICE ⟩ Rainforest Hideaway　　FUSION **$$$**
(☑451-4485; www.rainforesthideawaystlucia.com; menus EC$145-180; ⊙dinner Wed-Mon) Marigot Bay's most stylish restaurant is perfect for a tête-à-tête. Subdued lighting, elegant furnishings and a breezy deck overlooking the bay will rekindle the faintest romantic flame. The emphasis is on local dishes with a contemporary twist. There's live jazz on Wednesday and Saturday evening. It's accessible by a small ferry.

Chateau Mygo　　　　　　　CREOLE **$$**
(☑458-3947; mains EC$20-70; ⊙breakfast, lunch & dinner) This unfussy little eatery could hardly be better situated: the dining deck is right on the waterfront. The menu concentrates on simply prepared seafood and meat dishes served in generous portions.

Julietta's Restaurant & Bar　　CARIBBEAN **$$**
(☑458-3224; mains EC$25-80; ⊙lunch & dinner) At the lookout at the top of the hill, before the road descends to the waterfront, Julietta's offers exceptional views of the bay. It's renowned for its fresh fish (check out the day's catch) and coconut shrimps. Even if you aren't dining, do pause for a drink.

Rowley's Baguet Shop　　　CAFETERIA **$**
(mains EC$25-40; ⊙breakfast & lunch; ☎) Tasty snacks, light meals, ice creams and all sorts of crumbly goods are the order of the day at this modern venture opening onto the marina. Excellent breakfasts, too.

Hurricane Hole　　　　　CARIBBEAN **$$**
(☑458-5300; mains EC$40-120; ⊙lunch & dinner; ☎) A cool spot and a superb setting by the pool of the Marigot Bay Hotel.

SOUFRIÈRE & THE PITONS

If one town were to be the heart and soul of St Lucia, it would have to be Soufrière. Its attractions include a slew of colonial-era edifices scattered in the center and a bustling seafront.

The landscape surrounding the town is little short of breathtaking. The sky-scraping towers of rock known as the Pitons stand guard over the town. Jutting from the sea, covered in vegetation and ending in a summit that looks otherworldly, these iconic St Lucian landmarks are the pride of Soufrière.

If you think the above-ground scenery is spectacular, you should see it under the sea. A few fin strokes from the shore unveil a magical underwater world, pocketed with healthy reefs and teeming with sea life – heaven for divers and snorkelers. For those who've got itchy feet, a number of nature trails await.

But there's no obligation to overdo it: a smattering of historical and cultural sights, as well as a good selection of attractive dining and lodging options, mean this incredible dose of natural magnificence can be appreciated at a more relaxed pace.

◎ Sights

TOP CHOICE ⟩ Anse Chastanet　　　DIVING BEACH
Stretched out in front of the resort of the same name, Anse Chastanet could be the quintessential St Lucian beach experience. Though only a mile or so from Soufrière, it feels like a lost tropical world. The sheltered bay is protected by high cliffs, with towering palms on the shore. The sparkling ash-gray beach is great for a dip and the snorkeling

just offshore is some of the best on the island. Access to the beach is through the resort (nonguests are admitted without fuss).

You'll find a dive shop here (p710) to take you deeper. For refueling, the resort's restaurant and bar are open to the public.

From Soufrière, the road is in bad shape but is still passable with a standard vehicle.

TOP CHOICE **Anse Mamin**   SECLUDED BEACH
This dreamy enclave of golden sand edges a gently curved cove immediately north of Anse Chastanet. It's accessible by a 10-minute coastal walk or by water taxi from Anse Chastanet. Mountain biking (p709) is available, and there's a beachfront restaurant.

Sulphur Springs   SULPHUR SPRINGS
(☑459-7686; admission EC$20, with thermal baths EC$27.50; ☺9am-5pm) Looking like something off the surface of the moon, the Sulphur Springs are saddled with the unfortunate tagline of being the world's only drive-in volcano. The reality is far from the garish description. There isn't a crater, or a cauldron of magma, to check out – you'll have to be content with a bit of stinky, boiling muck. Bubbling mud is observed from platforms surrounded by vents releasing sulfur gas. It's a couple of miles south of Soufrière, off the Vieux Fort road.

Morne Coubaril Estate   PLANTATION
(☑459-7340; adult/child EC$18/9; ☺10am-4pm) This 18th-century estate, on the Vieux Fort road, about half a mile north of Sulphur Springs, offers a great insight into the plantation world that dominated this country for so long. You can wander through the working coconut and cocoa plantation; and have a gander at the ruins of an old sugar mill. An additional incentive to spend time here is **zip-lining** (US$69). Eight zip lines have been set up in a sensational setting, with the Petit Piton forming a perfect backdrop. Kids over eight are welcome.

Diamond Mineral Baths & Botanical Gardens   GARDEN
(☑459-7565; www.diamondstlucia.com; adult EC$25; ☺10am-5pm Mon-Sat, 10am-3pm Sun & holidays) The Diamond Estate's botanical gardens, waterfall and mineral baths are all at the same site.

Well-marked paths wind through the manicured gardens, which are planted with tropical flowers and trees, including numerous heliconia and ginger specimens. At the

back of the gardens a small **waterfall** drops down a rock face that is stained a rich orange from the warm mineral waters.

The **mineral baths** date from 1784, when they were built atop hot springs so that the troops of King Louis XVI of France could take advantage of their therapeutic effects. The baths were largely destroyed during the French Revolution, but in recent times a few have been restored and are open to visitors.

The Diamond Estate is 1 mile east of the Soufrière town center.

Malgretoute & Jalousie Beach   RESORT BEACH
Heading south from Soufrière along the coastal road you soon come upon the tranquil beach of Malgretoute (take the road to Jalousie Plantation). It's a pleasant stretch of dark-sand beach with some good snorkeling just offshore.

The sand is white at Jalousie Beach, which stretches out in front of Tides Sugar Beach – Jalousie Plantation (p711). Public access is permitted through the hotel.

Pitons Waterfall   WATERFALL
In the mood for a dip in tepid waters? Make a beeline for this picturesque cascade fed by a mix of natural streams and underground thermal sulfur springs from Soufrière volcano. On the road to Jalousie Plantation.

Fond Doux Holiday Plantation   PLANTATION
At this bijou hideaway (p710) you can catch an informative one-hour walking tour that allows you to take in military ruins built by the French, and a cocoa fermentary.

🏃 Activities

TOP CHOICE **Jungle Biking**   CYCLING
(☑457-1400; www.bikestlucia.com; Anse Mamin; 2½hr trip US$65; ☺8am-3:30pm Mon-Sat) This outfit, which is part of the Anse Chastanet Resort (nonguests are welcome), offers mountain-biking tours along trails that meander through the remnants of an old plantation, just next to Anse Mamin beach. It's suitable for all fitness levels. Various stops are organized along the way, where the guide will give you the lowdown on flora, fauna and local history.

Tet Paul Nature Trail   NATURE TRAIL
(www.soufrierefoundation.org; EC$25; ☺9am-5pm) This community-run nature trail is a treat. During the 45-minute tour, a guide will show you an organic farm and take you to

CLIMBING GROS PITON

If you have time for only one walk during your stay, choose the Gros Piton (2617ft) climb, because it's the most scenic. Starting from the hamlet of Fond Gens Libres, you walk almost all the way through a thick jungle, with lots of interesting fauna and flora. Approximately halfway the path goes past a lookout that affords fantastic vistas of Petit Piton and the ocean. The final section is very steep, but the reward is a tremendous view of southern St Lucia and the densely forested mountains of the interior. Allow roughly four hours there and back. A guide (US$30) is mandatory; contact **Gros Piton Nature Trail Guides** (✆286-0382).

Climbing Petit Piton is discouraged by local authorities because some sections involve clambering on near-vertical slabs of rock.

a lookout; the view of the Pitons that jab the skyline will be etched into your memory forever. It's signposted, a few miles south of Soufrière.

Mystic Man Tours   BOAT TRIPS
(✆459-7783; www.mysticmantours.com; Soufrière; ☺Mon-Sat) This well-established operator organizes a variety of boat excursions in the area, from whale-watching and snorkeling trips to sunset cruises and deep-sea fishing outings.

Diving   DIVING
The waters off Soufrière, which have been designated a marine park, are a magnet for divers of all levels. There's a good balance of reef dives, drop-offs and easy dives, as well as a couple of wrecks. For snorkeling, Anse Chastanet, Anse Mamin and Jalousie Beach offer optimal conditions. **Action Adventure Divers** (✆459-5599; two-tank dive US$80; ☺Sun-Fri) is a friendly crew running daily trips. It's just in front of the Hummingbird Beach Resort. Well-organized **Scuba St Lucia** (✆459-7000; www.scubastlucia.com; Anse Chastanet Resort; single dive US$47) is right on the beach at Anse Chastanet.

🛏 Sleeping

Most places to stay are fairly isolated, so a rental car is advised. Some hotels provide shuttle services to nearby beaches.

TOP
CHOICE ◢ **Crystals**   B&B **$$**
(✆285-1984; www.stluciacrystals.com; Soufrière; d incl breakfast from US$180; ❈❊) After something extra-special? Here you'll go giddy over the exuberant, ever-so-slightly OTT interior, which blends Indian and Caribbean touches – think red and orange linens, woodcarved furnishings, a treehouse bar – but it does the trick if you want to disconnect from it all. No two cottages are alike and they all come with a private plunge pool. The views of the Pitons and the valley of Soufrière are mesmerizing. It's nestled on a hillside on the northern outskirts of Soufrière.

Anse Chastanet Resort   RESORT **$$$**
(✆459-7000; www.ansechastanet.com; Anse Chastanet; d from US$390; ❈❊❆) The hillside-beachside location is supremely enjoyable. Whether you want to dive, snorkel, cycle, get pampered, experience fine dining or simply do nothing, this resort has it all.

◢ **Fond Doux Holiday Plantation**   RESORT **$$**
(✆459-7545; www.fonddouxplantationresortstlucia.com; cottages from US$170; ❈❊❆☀) Hidden in the hills to the south of Soufrière, this 250-year-old working cocoa plantation is a great place to engage in local culture. The proprietors have made the most of the exquisite landscape, with 11 tastefully refurbished historic cottages deployed over several acres of tropical gardens. There are botanical gardens and military ruins to explore, nature trails to follow and a three-level pool in which to cool off.

◢ **Stonefield Estate Villa Resort**   RESORT **$$$**
(✆459-7037; www.stonefieldvillas.com; off Vieux Fort road; villas from US$366; ❈❊❆) This historic plantation estate sports a cache of well-proportioned gingerbread-style cottages scattered amid a lush property, with glorious views over Petit Piton. Perks include an on-site restaurant, a spa and a pool. The property also has a superb petroglyph inscribed on a big basaltic boulder. On the southern outskirts of Soufrière.

Hummingbird Beach Resort   RESORT **$$**
(✆459-7232; www.istlucia.co.uk; Soufrière; d incl breakfast from US$85; ❈❊❆☀) Friendly, low-key and peaceful are good descriptions of the day-to-day atmosphere that prevails in this compact resort perched only a few feet from the beach. Rooms are simply furnished

and without frills. The attached restaurant is a winner.

Downtown Hotel
HOTEL $$

(☏459-7252; www.thedowntownhotel.net; d from US$75; ❄🛜♿) The Downtown doesn't exactly scream vacation (it's within a small shopping mall), but it's very central, convenient, well-maintained and affordable. Aim for a room at the back to avoid the road noise.

The Soufrière area is also famous for its grandiose resorts:

🏆 Ladera
BOUTIQUE RESORT $$$

(☏459-7323; www.ladera.com; ste incl breakfast from US$460; ❄🛜🏊) The location is one of the best in St Lucia: a ridge with full-frame views of the Pitons and the ocean. Rooms have their own plunge pools. It has a green ethos, too.

Jade Mountain
BOUTIQUE RESORT $$$

(☏459-4000; www.jademountainstlucia.com; Anse Chastanet; ste incl breakfast from US$1120; ❄🛜🏊) Sitting castle-like atop a hill, this exclusive resort offers stadium-sized suites (called 'sanctuary') that come with their own private infinity pool. Each unit has an open fourth wall with a heavenly view of the Pitons.

🏆 Hotel Chocolat
BOUTIQUE RESORT $$$

(☏+44 844 544 1272 (UK); www.thehotelchocolat .com; d incl breakfast US$300-800; ❄🛜) What sets this place apart is the design scheme; cocoa is the dominant theme, and it's no wonder – the resort is set in a cocoa plantation. The hotel prides itself on its engaged ethics.

Tides Sugar Beach – Jalousie Plantation
BOUTIQUE RESORT $$$

(☏456-8000; www.tidesresort.com; Anse des Pitons; d incl breakfast from US$850; ❄🛜🏊) Stunning location – it's nestled in a coconut grove smack between the Pitons, and opens onto a white-sand beach (the sand was imported from abroad).

🍴 Eating & Drinking

Most hotels and resorts have in-house restaurants and bars that are also open to non-guests. Given the high-quality cuisine, the location and the views, they're good value.

Hummingbird Beach Resort
CARIBBEAN $$

(☏459-7232; Soufrière; mains EC$40-85; ⊙breakfast, lunch & dinner) Mouth-watering local dishes are intermixed with old favorites to form a perfect culinary balance. The fish is prepared with style and flavor and served up with a great view. Don't miss out on beach-barbecue Saturdays (EC$85).

Petit Peak Bar & Restaurant
CARIBBEAN $

(☏459-7838; Soufrière; mains EC$15-100; ⊙lunch & dinner) Another great-value option, with a breezy terrace right on the waterfront. Choose from frondy salads, mouth-watering rotis and flawlessly grilled fish.

Waterfront De Belle View Restaurant & Bar
CARIBBEAN $$

(☏712-3663; Soufrière; mains EC$35-70; ⊙lunch & dinner) Blink and you'll miss the tiny entrance of this funky little den on the waterfront. It whips up well-priced Caribbean staples.

Big Bamboo
CARIBBEAN $

(Soufrière; set menu EC$25; ⊙lunch & dinner) Simple and satisfying are words that come to mind when dining at Big Bamboo. The set menu, consisting of Caribbean dishes prepared from fresh, simple ingredients, is unbeatable value.

Boucan Restaurant & Bar
FUSION $$

(☏457-1624; Hotel Chocolat; mains US$17-31; ⊙breakfast, lunch & dinner) Succulent cocoa-inspired cuisine in contemporary surrounds. Hmm, the *crème brûlée* flavored with cocoa...

Dasheene
CARIBBEAN $$

(☏459-7323; Ladera; mains US$17-40; ⊙lunch & dinner) This place serves excellent Caribbean fare in magical surrounds, and has incomparable Pitons views.

🏆 Jardin Cacao
CARIBBEAN $$

(☏459-7545; Fond Doux Holiday Plantation; mains EC$30-60; ⊙lunch & dinner) The emphasis is on local cuisine, using vegetables that are organically grown on the estate. Some desserts are prepared with cocoa.

🛍 Shopping

Zaka Masks
MASKS

(☏457-1504; www.zaka-art.com; Malgretoute; ⊙9am-5pm Mon-Sat) On the road to Tides Sugar Beach – Jalousie Plantation, you can't miss this quirky studio right by the road. You'll be welcomed by friendly Zaka, who creates lovely wooden masks that are painted in vivid colors. His works embellish a number of hotels on the island. They are irresistible and highly collectable, so bring plenty of cash (or a credit card) if you're thinking of buying.

THE (UNEXPECTED) JOYS OF THE EAST COAST

What a difference a few miles can make! A 30-minute drive from Castries transports you to yet another world, along the Atlantic-battered east coast, where you can experience St Lucia from a different perspective. In both landscape and character, this region is distinct. It feels very Creole and laid-back.

While this coast lacks the beaches of the west, it makes up for it with lovely bays backed by spectacular cliffs, a rocky shoreline pounded by thundering surf, and a handful of picturesque fishing towns, including **Dennery** and **Micoud**. Garden fans and history buffs will enjoy a visit to the **Mamiku Gardens** (455-3729; EC$20; 9am-5pm), between Mon Repos and Praslin. Wander among orchids, rock pools and aromatic plants, or visit the medicinal herb garden. If you need to cool off, there's no better place than **La Tille Waterfalls** (EC$10; 9am-4pm), signposted north of Micoud. For a more off-the-beaten-track experience, you can tackle the **Descartiers Rainforest Trail** (715-0350; Desruisseaux; EC$25; 8am-3pm Mon-Fri), an easy 4km loop.

If you want to get a buzz, try **zip-lining** at **Treetop Adventure Park** (458-0908; www.adventuretoursstlucia.com; from US$65; 8am-4pm). Here you'll find the island's longest zip line – 240m! Treetop Adventure Park also arranges **mountain biking tours** (from US$30) in the forest. North of Micoud, **ATV Paradise Tours & Rainforest Parrot Trail** (455-3245; www.atvstlucia.com; quad ride US$120, nature trail US$25; 9am-4:30pm) offers exhilarating quad rides in a lush, 500-hectare working plantation. All rides are guided and include stops at scenic spots. The domain also features an enjoyable four-hour walking trail that takes in a few waterfalls.

Accommodations are thin on the ground in this less-visited part of the island, but you can set up a base at the **Fox Grove Inn** (455-3800; www.foxgroveinn.com; Mon Repos; d incl breakfast US$75-86;), which sports 12 simple yet luminous rooms, a large pool and a well-regarded restaurant.

The South Coast

CHOISEUL

Choiseul, a little village south of Soufrière, has an active handicraft industry, and its roadside arts-and-crafts center is a good place to pick up locally made dolls, baskets, pottery and woodcarvings.

TOP CHOICE **Balenbouche Estate** (455-1244; www.balenbouche.com; Balenbouche; d from US$80;), between Choiseul and Laborie, is a tranquil 18th-century estate home with an eco-bent, comprising four simple yet delightful all-wood garden cottages. You really feel that you've stepped back in time here; complete the experience with a stroll round the grounds and truly atmospheric jungle-covered mill ruins. There is no pool, but there are two dark-colored sandy beaches nearby. Meals are available on request.

VIEUX FORT
POP 4900

St Lucia's second-largest town lies on a vast plain at the southern tip of the island. This is where the azure waters of the Caribbean Sea blend with those of the rough Atlantic Ocean. Vieux Fort won't leap to the top of your list of preferred destinations in St Lucia but the coastal area is scenic; the town fronts a lovely bay with Maria Islands in the distance. The bay is recognized as a prime destination for kitesurfing and windsurfing.

Sights & Activities

Sandy Beach KITESURFING BEACH
At the southern tip of the island, Sandy Beach is a beautiful strand of white sand that always has a stiff breeze, which makes it a hot spot for kitesurfers. It's also suitable for swimming – on a calm day. It's never crowded.

Reef Kite & Surf WATER SPORTS
(454-3418; www.kitesurfstlucia.com; Sandy Beach, Anse des Sables, Vieux Fort) The combination of constant strong breezes, protected areas with calm water, and a lack of obstacles make the bay of Anse de Sables a world-class destination for kitesurfers and windsurfers. A two-hour 'taster session' is US$80; a three-hour course costs US$250.

It also rents kayaks that can be paddled around Maria Islands.

🛏 Sleeping & Eating

The Reef Beach Resort
& Café   GUESTHOUSE **$**
(☑454-3418; www.kitesurfstlucia.com; Sandy Beach, Anse de Sables, Vieux Fort; s/d incl breakfast US$50/60) There are four rooms adjacent to Reef Kite & Surf, and there's a wonderful beachside **restaurant** (mains EC$20-40; ⊙breakfast, lunch & dinner).

Kimatrai Hotel   HOTEL **$**
(☑454-6328; Vieux Fort; s/d from US$55/65) A good port of call overlooking the marina. The motel-like rooms are not fancy but are adequate in comfort and cleanliness. The attached **restaurant** (mains EC$40-70; ⊙lunch & dinner) serves delectable meat and fish dishes.

UNDERSTAND ST LUCIA

History

Archaeological finds on the island indicate that St Lucia was settled by Arawaks between 1000 BC and 500 BC. Around AD 800 migrating Caribs conquered the Arawaks and established permanent settlements.

St Lucia was outside the routes taken by Columbus during his four visits to the New World and was probably first sighted by Spanish explorers during the early 1500s. Caribs successfully fended off two British attempts at colonization in the 1600s, only to be faced with French claims to the island a century down the road, when they established the island's first lasting European settlement, Soufrière, in 1746 and went about developing plantations. St Lucia's colonial history was marred by warfare, however, as the British still maintained their claim to the island.

In 1778 the British successfully invaded St Lucia and established naval bases at Gros Islet and Pigeon Island, which they used as staging grounds for attacks on the French islands to the north. For the next few decades possession of St Lucia seesawed between the British and the French. In 1814 the Treaty of Paris finally ceded the island to the British, ending 150 years of conflict during which St Lucia changed flags 14 times.

Culturally the British were slow in replacing French customs, and it wasn't until 1842

that English nudged out French as St Lucia's official language. Other customs linger, and to this day the majority of people speak a French-based patois among themselves, attend Catholic services and live in villages with French names.

St Lucia gained internal autonomy in 1967 and then achieved full independence, as a member of the Commonwealth, on February 22, 1979. Politics has stabilized in recent times, with election results usually coming in the form of landslide victories for the opposing party. The downturn in the banana industry has meant that a diversification of industry is vital for economic prosperity. Tourism is now the main source of revenue.

In late 2010 the island was severely hit by a hurricane, which caused much damage in the Soufrière area.

Culture

St Lucians are generally laid-back, friendly people influenced by a mix of their English, French, African and Caribbean origins. For instance, if you walk into the Catholic cathedral in Castries, you'll find a building of French design, an interior richly painted in bright African-inspired colors, portraits of a Black Madonna and child, and church services delivered in English. About 85% of St Lucians are Roman Catholics.

The population is about 170,000, one-third of whom live in Castries. Approximately 85% are of pure African ancestry. Another 10% are a mixture of African, British, French and Indian ancestry, while about 4% are of pure Indian or European descent.

The predominantly African heritage can be seen in the strong family ties that St Lucians hold and the survival of many traditional customs and superstitions. Obeah (Vodou) is still held in equal measures of respect and fear in places like Anse La Raye.

The local snakeman is visited by islanders for his medicinal powers. One such muscular remedy he uses involves massaging the thick fat of the boa constrictor on aching limbs.

There is an eclectic mix of cultural ideologies within St Lucia. Economic disparity has had a negative effect on the cultural identity of young people. Disenfranchised youth have turned to imported movements to find acceptance. There's a Rastafarian influence within the culture and an increasing alliance with urban-American ghetto-thug-style

BIRD-WATCHING

Twitchers are sure to get a buzz in St Lucia – there are a number of desirable new ticks for their list, including five endemic species: the St Lucia parrot, the St Lucia warbler, the St Lucia oriole, the St Lucia peewee and the St Lucia black finch. The St Lucia parrot (*Amazona versicolor*), locally called the Jacquot, is the national bird and appears on everything from T-shirts to St Lucian passports.

Good bird-watching spots include Millet Bird Sanctuary (p707), Descartiers Rainforest Trail (p712) and ATV Paradise Tours & Rainforest Parrot Trail (p712).

culture. Violent crime, mostly drug-related, is on the rise.

Arts

In the art world St Lucia's favorite son is writer Derek Walcott. The gifted poet and playwright won the Nobel Prize for literature in 1992. Strongly influenced by Tolstoy, Homer and Pushkin, his writing is literate, intense and sweeping. His 1990 epic poem *Omeros* is a shining example of his work. The ambitious project, retelling Homer's *Odyssey* in the modern-day Caribbean, was praised for its panache, scope and success.

The musical sounds of the Caribbean are alive in St Lucia – calypso, reggae and dancehall all play an important role in the lives of locals. Though few artists are local, the grooves are a way of life and provide a soundtrack for everyone on the island.

Landscape & Wildlife

The Land

The striking landmass of St Lucia is one of its defining features. At only 27 miles long the teardrop-shaped island packs a variety of topography into its 238 sq miles. Standing nearly as tall as they are long, the rolling hills and towering peaks of the interior make this green island an apparition of altitude rising from the sea.

Banana plantations dominate every flat section of land, and some not so flat. The Caribbean cash crop is a staple industry for St Lucia. Lush tropical jungle forms a rat's

nest of gnarled rainforest, filling the interior of the island with thick bush.

In the north the island flattens out a little and the beaches get a bit wider – allowing infrastructure to get a foothold. In the south the land rises sharply and continues in folds of green hills that stretch right to the shoreline. It's in this portion of the island, near Soufrière, that St Lucia's iconic landmarks are found. The twin peaks of the Pitons, which are extinct volcano cones, rise 2600ft from the sea and dominate the horizon.

Wildlife

St Lucia's vegetation ranges from dry and scrubby areas of cacti and hibiscus to lush, jungly valleys with wild orchids, bromeliads, heliconia and lianas.

Under the British colonial administration much of St Lucia's rainforest was targeted for timber harvesting. In many ways the independent St Lucian government has proved a far more effective environmental force, and while only about 10% of the island remains covered in rainforest, most of that has now been set aside as nature reserve. The largest indigenous trees in the rainforest are the gommier, a towering gum tree, and the chatagnier, a huge buttress-trunked tree.

Fauna includes endemic birds, bats, lizards, iguanas, tree frogs, introduced mongooses, rabbitlike agouti and several snake species, including the fer-de-lance and the boa constrictor.

SURVIVAL GUIDE

Directory A–Z

Accommodations

St Lucia has a pretty wide range of accommodations options. In addition to swish hotels and all-inclusive resorts, which form the core of the market, it offers a range of more intimate ventures, boutique inns and self-catering villas – check out www.inntimatestlucia.org for a list of such options. Most accommodations are concentrated in the northeast and Marigot Bay. If you prefer a quiet retreat, opt for the Soufrière area. Most hotels have an on-site restaurant.

Taxes, which include a 10% service charge and an 8% government tax, are included in our listed prices. Watch out, though, because most places will quote before-tax prices.

Following are the price indicators used in the accommodations listings in this chapter:

$	budget	less than US$75
$$	midrange	US$75 to US$200
$$$	top end	more than US$200

Business Hours

The following are common business hours in St Lucia; exceptions are noted in reviews.

Banks & post offices 8:30am-3pm Mon-Thu, to 5pm Fri

Bars to midnight

Restaurants breakfast from 8:30am, lunch from noon, dinner 6:30-9pm

Shops 8:30am-12:30pm, 1:30-4:30pm Mon-Fri, 8am-noon Sat

Children

Although purpose-made kids' attractions are scarce, St Lucia is an eminently suitable destination if you're traveling with children. With its abundance of beaches and opportunities for outdoor activities, including horseback riding, snorkeling, zip-lining and diving, there's plenty to do in a generally safe environment. Whale- and dolphin-watching excursions are also popular with families.

There are some hotels that won't take children under a certain age, but a number of all-inclusive resorts cater specifically to families and have an impressive range of amenities for children. Most hotels also offer reduced rates for children staying in their parents' room.

Embassies & Consulates

Germany (☑450-8050; Care Service Bldg, Massade Industrial Estate, Gros Islet)

UK (☑452-2484/5; NIC Waterfront Bldg, 2nd fl, PO Box 227, Castries)

Food

In this chapter we indicate the prices of mains, inclusive of taxes. Eating places have been categorized according to the following price brackets, and are based on the cost of the cheapest main meal:

$	budget	less than EC$35
$$	midrange	EC$36 to EC$70
$$$	top end	more than EC$70

Gay & Lesbian Travelers

As with most destinations in the region, St Lucia isn't all that friendly to those with 'alternative' lifestyles. Gay men should be especially aware that homosexuality is generally not accepted.

Health

You'll find medical facilities in Castries, Vieux Fort and Rodney Bay.

Tap water is safe to drink in St Lucia.

Internet Access

Internet cafes are not widespread, but most accommodations offer wi-fi. Connection speeds vary, but are generally fast.

Money

The Eastern Caribbean dollar (EC$) is the island currency. US dollars are often accepted by taxi drivers, shops, restaurants and larger hotels. Traveler's checks can be exchanged in banks and in larger hotels without issue.

Visa, American Express and MasterCard are widely accepted at hotels, car-rental agencies, shops and restaurants. ATMs are available at bank branches and shopping centers throughout the island. They dispense Eastern Caribbean dollars.

An 8% tax and 10% service charge are added to the bill at all but the cheapest hotels and restaurants; there's no need for additional tipping.

Public Holidays

In addition to holidays observed throughout the region (p872), St Lucia has the following public holidays:

New Year's Holiday January 2

Independence Day February 22

MONEY MATTERS

Prices for most tourist services, including accommodations, activities, excursions and car hire, are often quoted in US dollars and can be paid in US dollars. But you can also pay in the equivalent EC dollars or with a major credit card. Prices in this chapter are quoted in Eastern Caribbean dollars or in US dollars, depending on which currency is used by the business being reviewed.

PRACTICALITIES

» **Electricity** 220V (50 cycles); three-pronged, square European-style plugs.

» **Newspapers & Magazines** *The Voice* (www.thevoiceslu.com) is the island's main, tri-weekly newspaper.

» **Radio** Tune into music, news and patois programmes on Radio Caribbean International (101.1FM).

» **Weights & Measures** Imperial system.

Labour Day May 1

Corpus Christi Ninth Thursday after Easter

Emancipation Day August 3

Thanksgiving Day October 5

National Day December 13

Telephone

St Lucia's area code is ☎758. To call from abroad, dial your country's international access code plus ☎758 and the seven-digit local number. We have included only the seven-digit local number for listings in this chapter.

Your cell phone can be used in St Lucia. If you have a GSM phone that is unlocked, you can purchase a new SIM card for about EC$25 from any **Lime** (www.time4lime.com/lc) or **Digicel** (www.digicelstlucia.com) branch. This gives you a local number to call from and is much cheaper than global roaming in the long run.

Travelers with Disabilities

Most resorts have some facilities for disabled travelers, but it is best to enquire before heading out.

Visas

For all foreign visitors, stays of over 28 days generally require a visa. Note that Australian citizens need a visa to enter St Lucia.

Getting There & Away

Entering St Lucia

Most visitors must show a valid passport. Visitors are required to fill in an immigration form on arrival detailing the length, purpose and location of their stay, plus any customs declarations they may have. An on-ward or round-trip ticket, or proof of sufficient funds, is officially required.

Air

St Lucia has two airports: **Hewanorra International Airport** (UVF), in Vieux Fort at the remote southern tip of the island; and **George FL Charles Airport** (SLU), also known as 'Vigie', in Castries near the main tourist area.

Scheduled international flights land at Hewanorra, which has a longer runway, while flights from within the Caribbean generally land at the more-central George FL Charles Airport.

Both airports have tourist information booths, exchange facilities, taxi stands and booths for car-rental agencies.

Offices for the main airlines serving St Lucia are in central Castries.

St Lucia is served by regular flights with major airlines to/from cities in the US and Canada with Air Canada, American Airlines, Delta, JetBlue and Sunwing. There are flights to/from London with British Airways and Virgin Atlantic. Condor flies from Frankfurt between January and April. Airlines serving local destinations:

LIAT (www.liat.com) Barbados, St Vincent, Trinidad, Antigua

Air Caraïbes (www.aircaraibes.com) Fort-de-France (Martinique) daily

Sea

CRUISE SHIP

Cruise ships dock in Castries, at Pointe Seraphine. Smaller vessels call at Soufrière; they anchor offshore and bring passengers ashore via tenders.

FERRY

The fast-ferry service **L'Express des Îles** (☎456-5022; www.express-des-iles.com) operates a daily 80-minute express catamaran between Castries and Fort-de-France on Martinique. It also has occasional service to Guadeloupe (six hours). Departure days and times change frequently; check in advance.

See also p590.

YACHT

Customs and immigration can be cleared at Rodney Bay, Castries, Marigot Bay, Soufrière or Vieux Fort. Most yachties pull in at Rodney Bay, where there is a full-service marina and a couple of marked customs slips opposite the customs office.

It's easy to clear customs and immigration at Marigot Bay, where you can anchor in the inner harbor and dinghy over to the customs office. Castries is a more congested scene, and yachts entering the harbor are required to go directly to the customs dock. If there's no room you should head for the anchorage spot east of the customs buoy. In Soufrière the customs office is right on the waterfront. At Vieux Fort you can anchor off the big ship dock, where customs is located.

Popular anchorages include Reduit Beach, the area southeast of Pigeon Island, Rodney Bay Marina, Marigot Bay, Anse Chastanet, Anse Cochon and Soufrière Bay.

Yacht charters are available from the following companies:

Bateau Mygo (☑458-3947; www.bateaumygo. com) At Marigot Bay.

Caribbean Yachting (☑458-4430; www. caribbeanyachtingbj.com) At Rodney Bay Marina.

DSL Yachting (☑452-8531; www.dsl-yachting. com) At Rodney Bay Marina.

Moorings (☑451-4357; www.moorings.com) At Marigot Bay.

Getting Around

Bus

Bus service is via privately owned minivans. They're a cheap way to get around, and the means by which most islanders get to town, school and work. St Lucia's main road forms a big loop around the island, and buses stop at all towns along the way. They're frequent between main towns (such as Castries and Gros Islet) and generally run until 10pm (later on Friday); however, there is no scheduled timetable. Very few buses run on Sunday.

If there's no bus stop nearby, you can wave buses down as long as there's space for the bus to pull over. Pay the fare directly to the driver.

In Castries, buses going south to Soufrière and Vieux Fort, or north to Gros Islet, can be found east of the market on Darling Rd. Sample fares from Castries to Gros Islet or Marigot Bay are EC$2.50, and to Soufrière, EC$10.

Route numbers are displayed on the buses, but it's best to check with the driver, just in case.

Car & Motorcycle

DRIVER'S LICENSE

Drivers must purchase a local driving permit (US$22), which is valid for three months. For one day it costs US$12. It's available from the car-rental companies.

RENTAL

You can rent a car when you arrive in St Lucia, be it at the airport or in town. Most companies require the driver to be at least 25 years old and to have had a driver's license for at least three years.

The cheapest cars, those without air-conditioning, rent for about US$60 a day; you'll find the best rates on the internet. Nearly all car-rental agencies offer unlimited mileage. If you're planning an extensive tour of the island, it's advisable to hire a 4WD, as many of the roads are steep and smaller ones can become little more than potholed mudslides after a bout of rain.

Some of the major operators in St Lucia:

Avis (www.avis.com)

Cool Breeze Car Rental (www.coolbreeze carrental.com)

Courtesy Car Rentals (www.courtesycar rentals.com)

National (www.caribbeancars.com/slunational)

Sixt (www.sixt.com)

West Coast Jeeps (www.westcoastjeeps.com)

ROAD CONDITIONS

Roads vary greatly around the island, with some sections being newly surfaced and others peppered with abyssal potholes. Make sure you have a workable jack and spare tire available. Many of the interior and southern roads are also very winding and narrow. Gas (petrol) stations are distributed around the island.

ROAD RULES

Drive on the left-hand side. Speed limits are generally 15mph (24km/h) in towns and 30mph (48km/h) on major roads.

Taxi

Taxis are available at the airports, the harbor and in front of major hotels. They aren't metered but adhere to standard fares. As an indication of price, a ride between Castries and Rodney Bay will set you back US$22, and US$90 between Castries and Soufrière. It's always best to confirm the fare before getting in.

St-Martin/Sint Maarten

Best Beaches

» Orient Beach (p729)
» Maho Beach (p724)
» Happy Bay (p726)

Best Places to Stay

» Les Balcons d'Oyster Pond (p730)
» Hotel L'Esplanade (p727)

Why Go?

For hundreds of years the Caribbean was the playground of imperialists who transported rum, slaves and gold between worlds. These faraway kingdoms repeatedly conquered and retreated, radically changing the area's political geography with the spark of a cannon. After years of divvying up these sand-strewn paradises, only one of the Caribbean's 7000 islands remained so dear to two separate empires – the French and the Dutch – that they decided to share it.

This arbitrary division of land has given the scrubby island two very distinct personalities, like a set of Siamese twins. At times they work as one, but in other instances they become a caricature of themselves by exaggerating the traits that makes them unique: the French cling to their European roots, while the Dutch side plays up its jammin' vibe. Although neither side likes to admit it, the whole really is greater than the sum of its parts.

When to Go

St-Martin/Sint Maarten averages an annual temperature of a perfect 26°C. Come in March when the party's in full swing with the Heineken Regatta and Carnival festivities. In May and June, capitalize on reduced prices and quieter beachscapes before hurricane season roars up. The best times to visit St-Martin are November and early December – stop by just before the massive crowds roll in for the holiday season.

Itineraries

ONE DAY

Rent a car and make a beeline for Grand Case for an early lunch of sweet barbecue ribs at one of the Creole open-air *lolos*. Next, hit Orient Beach for some sand and sun, and before the day is done stop at the Dutch side's Sunset Beach Bar to nurse a beer as the jumbo jets make a dramatic (and noisy) landing right over your head.

FIVE DAYS

Spend half your time roaming around Orient Beach, Marigot and Grand Case on the French side, then bop around Philipsburg and the casino-riddled area near the airport on the Dutch half. A rental car is a must.

TWO WEEKS

Scout out one of the myriad private villas on the island and spend your first week recharging your batteries along one of the quieter beaches like Friar's Bay, Baie Longue or Le Galion. When you start feeling antsy, hit the fine dining in Grand Case, the lively bar scene at Maho Beach and, now that you've worked up the courage, wear your birthday suit to Orient Beach to get rid of those pesky tan lines.

GETTING TO NEIGHBORING ISLANDS

St-Martin/Sint Maarten acts as a hub for many of the surrounding islands – short puddle-jumper flights link Saba, Sint Eustatius, St-Barthélemy, St Kitts, St Croix, St Thomas, Antigua and Montserrat. Ferries also run frequently to Anguilla and St-Barth. Less frequent service departs for Saba and Sint Eustatius.

Essential Food & Drink

» **Lolos** Savor local faves like BBQ pork and ribs at these open-air cantinas, namely the ones in Grand Case.

» **Gourmet in Grand Case** Taking its cue from the motherland, the French side's gourmet capital, Grand Case, features a handful of high-end hotspots that stretch over the curling tide; dishes proudly fuse European and Caribbean influences.

» **Rum** Caribbean rum is not in short supply; you'll find Guavaberry stores selling a black-faced bottle of the island's signature liqueur.

St-Martin/Sint Maarten Highlights

1 Head to **Simpson Bay** (p723) for the odd juxtaposition of cerulean waters and careening jumbo jets

2 Gorge on sticky ribs at a beachside *lolo* shack in **Grand Case** (p727) or kick it up a notch and go for a shmancy dinner that will transport your taste buds all the way to Paris

3 Hop on a catamaran or sailboat and visit one of the island's scrubby satellites, such as **Îlet Pinel** (p728)

4 Visit jammin' Sunset Beach Bar in **Maho** (p724), a rite of passage for any visitor: drink a piña colada and don't forget to duck when the planes come in for landing at Juliana airport

5 Go *au naturel* on gorgeous **Orient Beach** (p729)

6 Take a Rastafari satari at **Friar's Bay** (p727) then sneak over the cape to find the cove at **Happy Bay** (p726)

7 Stop by remote **Oyster Pond** (p730) for a relaxed atmosphere – it's half French, half Dutch and all great

SINT MAARTEN

If you're arriving on the island from a far-flung destination, chances are you'll be landing on the Dutch side's Juliana International Airport – one of the largest airports in the Caribbean and a transfer hub to many of the smaller islands orbiting nearby.

As the *Sint*illating side of the border, Holland's land claim gets continuously tweaked and tuned as it strives to be the ultimate holiday destination for adults. The construction laws are not particularly stringent, so the artificial landscape feels a bit Vegas-in-the-'80s. The capital of the Dutch side is Philipsburg, a gridiron town along a wide arcing bay that mostly functions as an outdoor shopping mall for cruise-goers with cash to burn.

Those in the know used to say 'sleep on the Dutch side, eat on the French side', but this no longer holds true. In the last few years many excellent restaurants have opened their doors here, giving the more traditional French dining venues a run for their money. Similarly, many boutique businesses have moved to the Dutch side from the French side to regain their large American client base. Although, on the other side of the equation, accommodation in Sint Maarten is gradually turning into one big mess of timeshares, so have a look at the lodging choices on the French side – even though they are priced in euros, you can still snag an excellent deal.

This section starts at the far end of the Dutch holding (relative to the airport) and works its way back from Philipsburg along the winding cobbled coast, past Simpson Bay and on through Maho Bay, Mullet Bay and Cupecoy Beach before crossing over onto the French half. For information about Oyster Pond, which is split between both colonies, see p730.

Philipsburg

POP 18,000

Philipsburg, Dutch Sint Maarten's principal town (and often simply referred to as 'Town'), is centered on a long, narrow stretch of land that separates Great Salt Pond from Great Bay. There are some older buildings mixed among the new, but overall the town is far more commercial than quaint. Most of the action is along Frontstreet, the bayfront road, which is lined with boutiques, jewelry shops, restaurants, casinos and duty-free

shops selling everything from Danish porcelain to Japanese cameras and electronics.

Four streets run east to west, and numerous narrow lanes (called *steegjes*) connect them north to south. Frontstreet has one-way traffic that moves in an easterly direction, and Backstreet has one-way traffic heading west. The north side of Philipsburg is sometimes referred to as Pondfill, as much of this area is reclaimed land. Parking is extremely limited and there are always twenty cars vying for a place to pull over. It's best to stop along the interior and walk up to Frontstreet.

⊙ Sights

Sint Maarten Museum   MUSEUM
(Frontstreet 7; admission by donation; ⊙10am-4pm Mon-Fri, to 2pm Sat) This little museum has displays on island history, including Arawak pottery shards, plantation-era artifacts, period photos and a few items from HMS *Proselyte*, the frigate that sank off Fort Amsterdam in 1801. The little shop downstairs sells an assortment of Caribbean arts and crafts.

Sint Maarten Park   ZOO
(admission US$5; ⊙9:30am-5pm) The largest zoo in the Caribbean features over 80 kinds of indigenous species. It's located at the northern edge of the Great Salt Pond.

🏃 Activities

The most popular dive spot is at Proselyte Reef, a few miles south of Philipsburg, where in 1802 the British frigate HMS *Proselyte* sank in 50ft (15m) of water.

In addition to the remains of the frigate, there are 10 dive sites in that popular area, including fascinating coral reefs with caverns.

See www.vacationstmaarten.com for a list of dive shops around the island. Serious divers should consider a day trip to the neighboring island of Saba.

Sint Maarten 12 Metre Challenge   BOATING
(☑542-0045; www.12metre.com) At Bobby's Marina, the 12 Metre Challenge has three-hour excursions on America's Cup racing yachts, which are large, fast and sleek. Its fleet includes *Stars & Stripes*, the very yacht Dennis Conner used in the 1987 challenge for the America's Cup in Australia.

🛏 Sleeping

Philipsburg is largely the domain of cruise-ship folk who stroll the boardwalk souvenir shops, so it's not the best place if you're looking for a secluded paradise. But there are, a couple good reasons for staying within a stone's throw of the cruise docks. The area has recently received a much-needed facelift and the prices are reasonable compared to the rest of the island. You can also save a bit on car rental, since decent restaurants and bars are only a quick walk away.

Pasanggrahan Royal Guest House
HOTEL **$$**

(✆542-3588, in the US ✆800-223-9815; 19 Frontstreet; r from US$175; ✼🛜) The restaurant and lobby are in a former governor's residence that feels like a Cuban plantation house, but most rooms are in less-distinguished side buildings. The standard rooms here are simple and small with a shared seaside balcony. The deluxe rooms are larger and fancier, with private balconies and a view of Great Bay.

Holland House Beach Hotel
HOTEL **$$**

(✆542-2572, in the US ✆800-223-9815; www.hollandhousehotel.com; d from US$230; ✼@🛜) Has a central beachfront location in the heart of Philipsburg and 54 spacious rooms. Overall, they're Philipsburg's nicest, featuring hardwood floors, subtle trendy design details, balconies, cable TV, wi-fi, phones and, in most cases, a kitchenette. Top-floor suites have the best views.

Joshua Rose Guest House
GUESTHOUSE **$**

(✆542-4317; www.joshuaroseguesthouse.com; Backstreet 7; standard s/d/tr/q US$55/70/90/100; ✼🛜) Nothing to write home about, but the small rooms are central and it has private baths, TV and refrigerator.

Seaview Beach Hotel
HOTEL **$**

(✆542-2323; www.seaviewbeachhotel.com; Frontstreet; s/d from US$99/121; ✼🛜) Good prices, friendly service and a beachfront location make this a good bet all round. Rooms aren't particularly inviting, but they're comfortable and come with refrigerators and cable TV. There's a predictably tacky casino on the 1st floor.

✖ Eating & Drinking

If you have the time (and a car) head away from the waterfront area and explore the inland communities for cheap local eats. There's a great little shwarma joint up in Madame Estate – ask a local for directions to the bowling alley (there's only one) and you'll find a white-and-red truck-cum-kitchen parked across the street. The hard-to-miss **Heineken airplane** along the main road to Cole Bay is worth a peek as well.

The cheapest grocery store on the island, **Sang's Super Center** (✆542-3447; 3 Juancho Irausquin Blvd) is located near the outlet of Frontstreet toward the cruise ship marina.

Get Wet
BURGERS **$**

(Board Walk; mains from US$4; ☺lunch & dinner) Owned and operated by a gang of canucks, this friendly yellow hut offers cheaper-than-cheap beer and hearty *poutine* – a traditional Canadian dish of french fries, chicken gravy and melted cheese.

Taloula Mango's
BURGERS **$**

(cnr Board Walk & St Rose Arcade; mains from US$7; ☺lunch & dinner) A local favorite, this relaxed beachside joint is a great place to while away the afternoon over a few beers and some excellent American pub food. Head upstairs to **Blue Bitch Bar** and order Ruff Sex on the Beach or any of the other cleverly coined cocktails.

Kangaroo Court
CAFE **$**

(6 Hendrickstraat; mains from US$7; ☺breakfast & lunch) This vine-draped cloister near the courthouse is a great place for a light bite. Choose from a tasty assortment of sandwiches, salads and homemade pastries.

Greenhouse
INTERNATIONAL **$$**

(mains US$10-28; ☺breakfast, lunch & dinner) This lively spot with a charismatic staff pulls in the punters during its happy hour from 4:30pm to 7pm, which has two-for-one drinks as well as half-price snacks. At lunch there are burgers, sandwiches, barbecued ribs and chicken; at dinner, meat and seafood dishes are served.

ⓘ Information

Banks are plentiful along Frontstreet, and all deal in US dollars or Netherlands Antillean guilders.

Hospital (Cay Hill) East of Philipsburg in the Cay Hill area.

Post office (☺7:30am-5pm Mon-Thu, to 4:30pm Fri) At the west end of E Camille Richardson St.

Public library (Vogessteeg; internet access per 30min US$4; ☺9am-12:30pm Tue, Wed & Fri, 4-6:30pm Mon, Wed & Fri, 4-9pm Tue & Thu, 10am-1pm Sat)

Sint Maarten Tourist Bureau (www.st-maarten.com; 33 WG Boncamper Rd; ☺8am-5pm Mon-Fri)

Simpson Bay

Beautiful Simpson Bay has some of the most captivating crystal tidewater out of all the beaches on the island. At first glance it may seem surprising that the sleeping spots in the area are well priced compared to other parts of the island – then you'll hear the roaring jet engines of a plane getting ready to take off at Juliana airport. Those who enjoy staying along Simpson Bay claim that they don't even realize that jumbo jets are careening through; if you are sensitive to noise, this area is not for you.

Activities

Random Wind BOATING
(☎52-02-53; www.randomwind.com) Random Wind runs a small sailboat out to some of the quieter bays around the island. Day trips run on Tuesdays through Fridays.

Sleeping

Horny Toad Guesthouse APARTMENTS $$$
(☎545-4323, in the US ☎800-417-9361; www. thtgh.com; 2 Vlaun St; ste from US$218; ❋@🛜🏊) Run by Betty, a lovely American woman with a tinge of the '*pahk the cah*' Boston accent, this charming guesthouse right along the sea features a handful of apartment-style rooms sporting loads of wicker furniture.

Mary's Boon HOTEL $$
(☎545-7000, in the US ☎866-978-5899; www. marysboon.com; r from US$135, ste from US$270; ❋@🛜🏊) A stone's throw from Juliana's runway, this freshly restored plantation-style inn offers beautiful rooms draped in upscale Caribbean design details. Expect four-poster beds, curios made from coconuts and charming wooden beams.

Eating & Drinking

The row of restaurants between the airport and the drawbridge features a flashy mix of fried foods from burritos to juicy burgers. You can't go wrong if you're looking for a cheap place to coat your stomach with grub and grog.

Karakter BAR $$
(Simpson Bay; mains US$8-20; ⊙lunch & dinner Wed-Mon) Built amid the ruined foundations of an old condo complex, Karakter gives the Sunset Beach Bar in Maho a run for its money, with its own slice of scenic beach located uncomfortably close to landing planes. Snag drinks from the dilapidated bus-turned-bar and enjoy daily specials like 'Sushi Saturday'. There's live jazz on Friday evenings.

Stone FUSION $$$
(☎526-2037; www.thestonerestaurant.com; mains US$20-30; ⊙dinner) The Stone distinguishes itself from other restaurants on the island

---

PORTS OF CALL

Philipsburg

After alighting in Philipsburg, spend your half-day ogling souvenirs or toting a beer with the other cruise-goers on the boardwalk, or you can do the following:

» Go to the rugged east side of the island for postcard-worthy snaps of quiet coastline

» Enjoy barbecue beach fun at Orient Beach (p729) and strip to your birthday suit if you dare

» Visit Oyster Pond (p730) and plunk one foot down in France, the other in the Netherlands

Marigot

Private yachties and day-trippers from Anguilla can alight in Marigot, where they'll find the charming trappings of a European village lost in the Caribbean. Shop for colorful island wares while nibbling on a baguette, or set your sights further afield:

» Rent a car near the ferry terminal and go to secluded Friar's Bay (p727) and Happy Bay (p726)

» Enjoy succulent fusion fare in Grand Case (p728) – the next village over – often called the 'culinary capital of the Caribbean'

» Visit the crumbling fort ruins perched high atop a hill overlooking central Marigot (p725)

in two ways. First, everything is served on a steaming slab of granite. Not only is this a great gimmick, but it allows customers to cook their steaks as long or as little as they want. Second, the enterprising owner and head chef opened the restaurant before his 22nd birthday. Try the biltong soup – a South African mix of jerked beef and thick cheddar. Live classical guitar on Tuesdays.

Top Carrot CAFE $
(Simpson Bay Yacht Club; mains US$5-10; ⊙breakfast & lunch Mon-Sat) A refreshing change from the usual greasy haunts, Top Carrot serves up scrumptious veggie options in a chilled out cushion-clad ambience stuffed with fashion magazines.

Lal's INDIAN $$
(126 Airport Rd; mains US$10-18; ⊙dinner daily, lunch Sat-Sun) Lost in the mess of car-rental lots by the airport, Lal's rarely beeps on the tourist radar, but locals come here time and time again for delicious Indian fare. Try the rich butter chicken.

Maho & Mullet Bay

If you have a few hours to kill before a connecting flight, make your way to Maho. The beautiful beach is situated at the end of Juliana airport's runway, and perhaps the world's lone stretch of sand with a sign that reads: 'Low flying and departing aircraft blast can cause physical injury' (with the obligatory picture of a stick figure getting blown away).

If you aren't into waving at passengers as they land on the island, this flashy area of St-Martin/Sint Maarten offers countless casinos, clubs and restaurants.

🏃 Activities

Mullet Bay Golf GOLF
(☑545-2801) The island's golf course, the 18-hole Mullet Bay, has greens fees of around US$100, cart included. The old resort that winds its way through the course has been closed for around 15 years and desperately needs to be torn down – it is unsightly and quite distracting.

🛏 Sleeping

Sleeping in the Maho area used to be much more popular than it is today. The hotels here could use a renovation and they rely heavily on tourists who book cheap package vacations. Construction has already started on myriad timeshares in the area – a fate that seems unavoidable for most of the Dutch side.

Maho Beach Hotel HOTEL $$
(☑545-2115, in the US ☑800-223-0757; www.mahobeach.com; r from US$135; ✳@🛜🏊) This 600-room behemoth sits within waving distance of the Juliana airport. The resort grounds include a casino, several restaurants, fitness center, indoor parking garage and a 1000-seat Vegas-style showroom.

🍴 Eating & Drinking

TOP CHOICE Sunset Beach Bar BAR $
(www.sunsetbeachbar.com; 2 Beacon Hill Rd; mains US$7-19; ⊙breakfast, lunch & dinner; 🛜) When you arrive at Sunset Beach Bar, grab a beer and check out the surfboard/chalkboard that lists the arrival times of the jumbo jets. As the minutes draw near, everyone rushes out onto the sand to get under the whooshing plane as it lands. Once you've mastered the landing, then try the take-offs. As the jets rev their engines, huge gusts of gale-force winds shoot across the beach, right beside the bar. Savvy daredevils wear snorkel masks so as to not inhale copious amounts of sand, others simply hold on to the chain-link fence for dear life while their personal effects are blown into the sea. Topless girls drink free and if you come on a Monday or Friday, there's a body artist that will paint you a bikini top. Hint: check in early at the airport, then hitch or catch a US$6 taxi to the bar.

Bliss FUSION $$$
(☑545-3996; breakfast/lunch/dinner around US$10/18/35; ⊙practically 24hr; 🛜) This experience is not for the faint of heart. The restaurant serves breakfast and Sunday brunch with main meals consisting of dishes like duck *confit* baguette and dorado filet with coconut carrot sauce. House music kicks up at about 11pm each night on the open-air dance floor, Tuesday is Martini Night, and Thursday to Saturday is DJ dancing to an international groove. Don't worry if all that dancing makes you get the munchies: the grill is open until 4am.

Bamboo Bernie's SUSHI $$$
(☑545-3622; sushi US$6-20; ⊙lunch & dinner) Hidden just beyond Bliss, Bamboo Bernie's is a chic, tiki-torched hangout spot that specializes in Asian fusion cuisine. Try the 'sexy salmon' or ask about the secret Saavo sushi roll that isn't even marked on the menu.

Wednesday is the night to come if you're looking for a more raucous affair.

Cupecoy Beach

If you're looking for a beach that's quiet but not totally secluded, Cupecoy is a good choice. This pleasant white-sand beach is backed by low sandstone cliffs that eroded in such a way that they provide a run of small semiprivate coves. There's beach parking down an unmarked drive at the north side of the Ocean Club in Cupecoy.

ST-MARTIN

While the Dutch side embraces every Caribbean cliché, the French half clings to its European roots and holds on for dear life. Noticeably devoid of casinos and skyscraping timeshares, the quieter French side is a charming mix of white-sand beaches, cluttered town centers and stretches of bucolic mountainside.

As the euro continues to outperform the American dollar, many businesses are having a hard time keeping up with their neighbors on the Dutch lands. Restaurants sometimes advertise one-for-one euro-to-dollar exchange rates on their meals, and hotels keep their prices as low as possible in order to compete with the big-name resorts on the other side.

This section starts where the Dutch coverage ends – in Marigot, the French side's capital, and the neighboring Terres Basses. Then we head across the island toward Grand Case, Orient Beach and down to Oyster Pond (which links back up to the beginning of the Dutch sub-chapter at Philipsburg).

Marigot

POP 12,500

The capital of French St-Martin, Marigot is a bustling port town dominated by a stone fort high up on the hill. A distinctive European flavor is palpable here – there's a produce market, a gaggle of *boulangeries* (bakeries), and a few buildings with iron-wrought balconies and Belle Epoque lamp-posts.

⊙ Sights

Fort Louis   RUINS
Fort Louis was constructed in 1767 by order of French King Louis XVI to protect Marigot from marauding British and Dutch pirates. It's been abandoned for centuries and contains only remnants from bygone eras, but the view alone is worth the 15-minute hike up (past the old hospital) to the ruins.

St-Martin Archaeological Museum   MUSEUM
(⊙9am-4pm Mon-Fri, 9am-1pm Sat) This museum covers everything from the Arawak period to island fashion in the 1930s, and features period photography, historical displays and artifacts from the pre-Colombian period.

🛏 Sleeping

The hotels in the center of Marigot cater to island folk who live on smaller islands and need a place to crash while they do their bulk grocery shopping on St-Martin. Although they are priced in euros, these spots are still some of the cheapest places on the island.

Le Cosy   GUESTHOUSE $
(☎87-43-95; 8 Rue du Général de Gaulle; s/d €58/78; ✳🛜) Up a flight of stairs, little Le Cosy has 11 rooms set around a small open-air courtyard. The freshly painted rooms are quite large, although sparsely decorated. Reception is open only from 9am until noon.

Centr'Hotel   GUESTHOUSE $
(☎87-86-51; centrhotel.sxm@wanadoo.fr; Rue du Général de Gaulle; s/d €45/55; ✳) This 21-room hotel has large, adequate rooms with TV, aircon, room safes, balconies and minibars.

✕ Eating

For all your self-catering needs, there's **Match** (⊙9am-8pm Mon-Sat, to 1pm Sun) on the north side of Marigot.

PORT LA ROYALE
Port La Royale Marina has a waterfront lined with restaurants offering everything from pizza and burgers to seafood and nouvelle cuisine. There's fierce competition, with some of the island's lowest menu prices and lots of chalkboard specials. The best bet is just to wander around and see what takes your fancy.

Serafina   BAKERY $
(mains €4-10; ⊙breakfast & lunch) In the heart of Marigot between the two ports, Serafina lures peckish pedestrians off the sun-soaked streets with its authentic spread of French baked goods that come in sweet and savory forms. Wash it all down with a smooth espresso and you're good to go.

HAPPY BAY

If you thought that Friar's Bay was a quaint little speck of sand, head to the northernmost point of the beach and you'll discover a dirt path that twists over a bumpy headland to the perfectly deserted Happy Bay. Equidistant from bustling Marigot and Grand Case, this surprisingly serene strip of powdery sand is completely bare (as are those who like to hang out here). The beach doesn't even get boat traffic because there isn't enough of a curvature in the bay to block the tidewater from dizzying swells.

La Croissanterie　　　　　　BAKERY $
(mains €5-13; ⊘lunch & dinner) Enjoy the flakiest croissants around in a breezy marinaside setting. Go for the ham and cheese sandwich.

Le Saint Germain　　　　　　FRENCH $$
(mains €10-12; ⊘lunch & dinner) Bite into savory and sweet crepes and a fantastic view of the marina.

La Belle Epoque　　　　　　FRENCH $$
(☑87-87-70; mains €10-17; ⊘breakfast, lunch & dinner Mon-Sat, dinner Sun) A charming harborside spot with decorations plucked straight from a car boot sale.

Tropicana　　　　　　CARIBBEAN $$$
(☑87-79-07; mains €16-30; ⊘lunch & dinner) Great service and delicious food. Worth the splurge.

PORT ST-LOUIS

The **produce market** (⊘sunrise-2pm Sat) on Marigot's waterfront has tropical fruit such as passion fruit and bananas as well as local root vegetables.

Ô Plongeoir　　　　　　FUSION $$
(mains €10-15; ⊘lunch & dinner) At the far end of Port St-Louis (north of the shopping mall), this open-air joint is a great place to sit back with a coffee and spy on Anguilla in the distance. The food is excellent as well – try an assortment of fusion favorites like tuna tartare and fried Camembert.

La Vie en Rose　　　　　　FRENCH $$$
(Blvd de France; mains €15-20; ⊘lunch & dinner) One of the oldest eateries in Marigot, this fashionable French restaurant sits in a prime location near the harbor. Lunch is either on the patio or the casual 1st floor while dinner is served in the graceful upstairs dining room.

ℹ Information

State-of-the-art bathrooms (US$1) are available in the West Indies Mall; they were designed by noted architect Philippe Starck.

Bibliothèque Municipale (Rue du Palais Justice; internet per 15/30min €1.50/3; ⊘2-7pm Mon & Tue, 9am-7pm Wed, 11am-7pm Thu & Fri, 9am-1pm Sat)

Change Point (⊘7:30am-7pm Mon-Sat) A forex bureau near the marina.

Post office (25 Rue de La Liberté; ⊘7am-5:30pm Mon-Fri, 7:30am-noon Sat)

Tourist office (Port La Royale; ⊘8:30am-1pm & 2:30-5:30pm Mon-Fri, 8am-noon Sat) Southwest of the marina.

Terres Basses

Terres Basses (pronounced 'tair boss'), also called the French Lowlands, is a verdant clump of lush, low-lying acreage connected to the larger part of the island by two thin strips of land. This quiet area is dominated by three gorgeous beaches and consists mostly of large private villas.

BAIE LONGUE (LONG BAY)

Long Bay, or Baie Longue, embraces two splendid miles of seemingly endless white sand and rocky outcrops. It's very wide and well off the beaten path, making it a great place for long strolls and enjoying quiet sunsets.

The only commercial development along the shoreline is the **La Samanna** (☑87-64-00, in US 800-854-2252; www.lasamanna.com; r from US$995, ste from US$1825; ❄@🤙≋), St-Martin's most expensive resort, located at the extreme southern tip of the beach.

To get there, after Cupecoy head to Baie aux Prunes then enter the seemingly private entrance and take an immediate left.

BAIE AUX PRUNES (PLUM BAY)

The remote and unspoiled Baie aux Prunes is a gently curving bay with polished shell-like grains of golden sand. The beach is popular for swimming and sunbathing, and it's backed by a little grove of white cedar trees with pink blossoms that attract hummingbirds.

The bay can be reached by turning right 1.3km south of Baie Rouge and immediately taking the signposted left fork. After 2km you will come to a junction; veer right and continue for another 300m, where there's a parking area and a short walkway to the beach.

BAIE ROUGE

Baie Rouge, 3.2km west of Sandy Ground, is a long, beautiful sandy strand with good swimming, though if you have children be aware that the ocean floor drops off quickly to overhead depths. Although this golden-sand beach is just 150m from the main road, it retains an inviting natural setting. For the best snorkeling, swim to the right toward the rocky outcrop and arch. There are a few beach shacks renting snorkel gear or selling barbecued chicken, but this is a fairly secluded spot.

Sandy Ground & Baie Nettlé

Sandy Ground is the long, narrow, curving strip of land that extends west from Marigot, with Baie Nettlé (Nettle Bay) on one side of the road and Simpson Bay Lagoon on the other. Sandy Ground itself is nothing special, featuring scores of uninspired accommodations, but the beach at Baie Nettlé is a lovely place to spend the day.

For a tasty meal, try **Layla's** (mains US$10-20; ⊙lunch & dinner); walk through the rainforest-like path to discover the atmospheric open-air restaurant, where chic Paris meets beach-bum fish shack.

Friar's Bay

Friar's Bay, north of Marigot, is a postcard-worthy cove with a broad sandy beach. This popular local swimming spot is just beyond the residential neighborhood of St Louis and the road leading in is signposted.

A stop at **Kali's Beach Bar** (☎72-62-05; www.kali-beach-bar.com; mains €10-15; ⊙lunch winter, lunch & dinner summer) is a must. Decked out in the trademark Rastafarian greens, yellows and reds, this happenin' hangout serves up tasty dishes from the Creole kitchen and rents out water-sports equipment and lounge chairs (€16 for two beach chairs and an umbrella). On the evenings of the full moon, Kali's is the place to be for a rowdy evening of live music, dancing and drinks.

Pic Paradis

The 424m Pic Paradis, the highest point on the island, offers fine vistas and good hiking opportunities. The peak is topped with a communications tower and is accessible by a rough maintenance road that doubles as a hiking trail. You can drive as far as the last house and then walk the final 1km to the top.

A must for hikers and foodies, the **Loterie Farm** (☎87-86-16; Rte Pic Paradis; mains €10-20; ⊙closed Mon) on the way up to the peak, is an excellent place to spend the afternoon. The quiet plantation features a couple of hikes, a ropes course high in the trees and a great restaurant that gets rave reviews.

The road to Pic Paradis is 500m north of the 'L' in the road between Friar's Bay and Grand Case that splinters off to the inland community of Colombier. Take the road inland for 2km, turn left at the fork (signposted 'Sentier des Crêtes NE, Pic Paradis') and continue 500m further to the last house, where there's space to pull over and park (do not leave anything in your car).

For those who don't want to trek off on their own, guided hikes are offered by Sint Maarten's **Heritage Foundation** (☎542-4917), which is affiliated with the Sint Maarten Museum in Philipsburg.

Grand Case

The small beachside town of Grand Case (pronounced '*grond kaz*') has been dubbed the 'Gourmet Capital of the Caribbean.' The beachfront road is lined with an appealing range of places to eat, from local *lolos* to top-notch French restaurants. While dining is the premier attraction, there's also a decent beach and several cheap places to hang your hat.

🏃 Activities

Scoobidoo   BOATING
(☎52-02-53; www.scoobidoo.com) Scoobidoo offers excellent catamaran trips that go to Prickly Pear in Anguilla, Tintamarre or St-Barthélemy for around US$110 per person. It also offers sunset cruises and snorkeling trips (US$55 per person). Boats may also leave from Anse Marcel, depending on the trip.

🛏 Sleeping

Hotel L'Esplanade   B&B $$$
(☎87-06-55; www.lesplanade.com; r from US$245;) This romantic, impeccably run

ÎLET PINEL

This little islet just 1km from French Cul-de-Sac is a great spot to spend a sun-soaked afternoon. Totally undeveloped (it's protected by the national forest system), Pinel is the domain of day-trippers, who are deposited on the island's calm west-facing beach, where there's good swimming, snorkeling (snorkel gear €10) and three drink-wielding restaurants.

It's easy to get to Pinel – simply go to the dock at the road's end in French Cul-de-Sac, where you can catch a small boat that departs roughly every 30 minutes. The five-minute ride costs US$7 round-trip and runs 10am to 5pm.

hillside hotel is a quick hop from the hustle of Grand Case. The beautiful lofts and suites are sumptuous yet homey, and have fully equipped kitchens and private terrace, as well as a pool and swim-up bar. It'll be tough to leave. Check out l'Esplanade's equally charming sister property, **Le Petit Hotel** (✆29-09-65; www.lepetithotel.com; r from US$265; ✳️🛰), on the other side of town.

Grand Case Beach Club   HOTEL **$$**
(✆87-51-87, in the US ✆800-447-7462; www.grandcasebeachclub.com; ste from €330; ✳️@🛰🏊🍴) On the quiet northeast end of the beach, this gently sprawling place has 73 pleasant condo-like units with full kitchen and balcony. It's a great place to bring children, as those aged 12 years and under stay free in all rooms other than the studios. Plus, there's an onsite pool, recreation room and tennis courts. Rates include continental breakfast at the well-regarded restaurant.

Hotel Hevea   GUESTHOUSE **$**
(✆87-56-85; hevea@outremer.com; 163 Blvd de Grand Case; s/d from €50/60; ✳️) The rooms at Hotel Hevea feel like Parisian studio apartments from the 1950s. A scruffy dog guards the calm inner courtyard, which features plenty of patio furniture and a barbecue.

✗ Eating & Drinking

Each evening, a ritual of sorts takes place on Grand Case's beachfront road, with restaurants placing their menus and chalkboard specials out front, and would-be diners strolling along the strip until they find a place that strikes their fancy. Tuesday nights are when all the locals descend on the town.

Calmos Cafe   CAFE **$$**
(✆29-01-85; Blvd de Grand Case; mains €10-20; ⏱lunch & dinner) Bury your feet in the sand while hanging out at this casual local fave. Whether you've come for a drink or for one of the overflowing international dishes (go for the ribs!), Calmos is a great spot to escape the parade of fine-dining tourists.

L'Estaminet   FRENCH **$$$**
(✆29-00-25; 103 Blvd de Grand Case; mains around €25; ⏱dinner) Traditional French fare in Grand Case? L'Estaminet is anything but! Take your taste buds on a gustatory adventure through the twisted mind of the owner and chef. Sample couplings of untraditional ingredients that prove that *haute cuisine* can be playful instead of pretentious.

Lolos   BBQ **$**
(mains €6-14) The big draw here for penny-pinchers is the collection of *lolos* between the main drag and ocean. These Creole barbecue shacks sit clustered around wooden picnic tables. There are six unique establishments (with oddly idiomatic names like Talk of the Town or Sky's the Limit) comprising this steamy jungle of smoking grills – each one with its own specialty. Try succulent ribs or chicken legs, with a side of rice and peas.

Le Tastevin   FRENCH **$$$**
(✆87-55-45; 86 Blvd de Grand Case; mains from €25; ⏱lunch & dinner) The full Parisian experience: excellent food served by slightly curt waiters. The white tablecloths gently flutter under your plate of mouthwatering pork tenderloin as the breezy ocean air swooshes through.

Le Pressoir   FRENCH **$$$**
(✆87-76-62; 30 Blvd de Grand Case; mains €24-30; ⏱dinner) Set in a beautiful bright yellow house with charming clapboard shutters – one of the last remaining traditional Creole houses – this fantastic restaurant gets loads of well-deserved praise for its warm atmosphere and scrumptious dishes. Prices are steep, but this is the place to splurge.

Le Shore   BAR **$$**
(28 Blvd de Grand Case) A fierce new arrival to Grand Case's beachside scene, Le Shore sits along the sea in a Kasbah-like setting that glistens in the sun after a brilliant renovation. Not just a place to slurp a cocktail or grab some Franco-Caribbean fare, Le Shore

is a full-day affair with a swimming pool, soft sand, and live music.

Anse Marcel

Beautiful Anse Marcel is first glimpsed from high up in the mountains as you gently descend into this hidden bay. This quiet port is the stomping ground for wealthier vacationers, as some of St-Martin/Sint Maarten's fancier properties are located here. One of the island's top hidden beaches, **Petites Cayes** is accessible via a small trail at the north end of Anse Marcel. Follow the path along the rugged headland – it's a bit of a walk, but definitely worth it.

Scoobidoo (☎52-02-53; www.scoobidoo.com) has catamaran trips, plus sunset cruises and snorkeling trips. Boats also leave from Grand Case, depending on the trip.

Hidden behind iron gates, **Le Domaine** (☎52-35-35; www.hotel-le-domaine.com; r from €310; ❄@📶🏊) is one of St-Martin's most private hideaways. The stunning lobby opens up onto the perfectly manicured grounds set along the sea.

Up the hill, the **Marquis Hotel Resort & Spa** (☎29-42-30; www.hotel-marquis.com; Pigeon Pea Hill; r from €380; ❄@📶🏊) is a stunning property featuring 17 brightly colored rooms with stunning views of the port down below.

French Cul-de-Sac

French Cul-de-Sac is a small but spread-out seaside community just east of Anse Marcel and north of Orient Bay. This is the jumping-off point for the fun-filled Îlet Pinel – local fishers run boats back and forth all day to the islet's soft white sands.

The **Plantation Mont Vernon** (admission US$12; ⏱9am-5pm) is also located in the quiet headland. This restored plantation offers visitors a glimpse of the past (specifically gin and coffee in the 18th century) with recreated distilleries and mills set around a scenic garden. Lunch is available on Sundays.

Orient Beach (La Baie Orientale)

Although this most perfect of beaches has become somewhat of a tourist settlement, it still retains a breezy Caribbean atmosphere. Snorkel-friendly reefs protect 5.5km of inviting white-sand beach. Restaurants, bars, water sports and an *au naturel* resort all call Orient Beach home.

Sleeping

Within the gates of Orient Beach you'll find a handful of hotels – most priced in the high-end bracket.

Club Orient Naturist Resort RESORT **$$**
(☎87-33-85; www.cluborient.com; 1 Baie Orientale; studios from €200, ste from €330; ❄@🏊) Walking around this ranch-style resort is like watching *Animal Planet* or the Discovery Channel: 'come see the elusive middle-aged male, with swinging beer belly in tow, as he plays boccie ball in the buff.' Club Orient offers a range of activities, all done in the nude – fine dining, water sports, sunbathing and sailing cruises. Six different levels of accommodations all feature fully equipped kitchens in semidetached cottages. And there's a completely stocked general store and car-rental agency available.

L'Hoste Hotel APARTMENTS **$$**
(☎87-42-08; www.hostehotel.com; Parc de La Baie Orientale; r from €250; ❄@📶🏊) Set slightly away from the sand, L'Hoste is the best bang for your buck near the booming Orient Beach. Rooms are cheered with bright colors and Caribbean knick-knacks.

Eating & Drinking

The tiny village square just off of Orient Beach is one of the most charming spots on the entire island. Each restaurant offers overflowing patio seating that spills out the sides of each restaurant and onto the cobblestone roads. You'll find loads of beach bars on the sand as well.

Côté Plages FRENCH **$$$**
(☎52-47-37; mains €20-29; ⏱dinner) Ignore the touristy implications of the giant French flag outside; this is one of the best restaurants around. The prices might be slightly higher than the other restaurant's in Orient Beach's village square, but as the old adage goes – you get what you pay for. Feast on brilliantly prepared salmon tartare, foie gras or freshly caught fish, wash it down with a glass of imported wine, and don't miss the triple chocolate platter for dessert.

Le Piment FRENCH **$$**
(mains €11-26; ⏱dinner) A wide selection of international eats and everything's delicious. Be sure to listen to the amicable hostess as she lists off the daily specials with gusto –

then go for one of the homemade treasures like baked Camembert or seafood risotto.

Kontiki
FRENCH $$

(mains from €9; ☺lunch) A maze of driftwood and booth seating, Kontiki is a great spot for a shaded lunch break during a dedicated day of beach lazing. Don't miss the signature Sunday night parties that stretch out across the sand.

Safari
FRENCH $$

(mains €8-17; ☺dinner) A mix of European standards (think pizza and steak), along with scrumptious Creole cuisine is served at this anything-goes joint with a subtle African open-air theme.

Le Galion

Near the party on Orient Beach but with about one-tenth of the bustle, Le Galion is a quiet spot with plenty of shallow water and offshore reefs. A top stop for families, this sandy patch remains untouched by development as it is protected by the national marine reserve. Stop by **Tropical Wave** (✆87-37-25), the local water-sports outfitter, which will hook you up with windsurfing equipment or kayaks. **Bayside Riding Club** (✆in St-Martin 87-36-64, in Sint Maarten 547-6822) is located along a bucolic stretch between Le Galion and Oyster Pond. The **OK Corral** (✆87-40-72), located at Baie Lucas, also has horseback rides.

Adults and children alike will walk away feeling like veritable lepidopterists after a visit to the **Butterfly Farm** (✆87-31-21; www.thebutterflyfarm.com; adult/child US$15/10, admission valid for repeat visits; ☺9am-3:30pm), on a turn-off from the N7 in Quartier d'Orleans. Peer into cocooning chrysalises as butterflies flit above, adding to the magical wonderland feel. Guided tours cover biology, conservation and fun facts. Come early to see the butterflies at their most active.

Signposts between Orient Beach and Oyster Pond clearly point the way, although the road to the beach is ridiculously bumpy – the road feels almost impassible at times due to crater-sized divots.

Oyster Pond

The Dutch–French border slices straight across Oyster Pond, which actually isn't a pond at all but a stunning sunken bay nes-tled between two jagged hills. Oyster Pond's biggest draw used to be **Dawn Beach**, on the Dutch side, however the recent completion of the clunky Westin hotel has transformed this charming scrap of sand into a bustling compound of roasting tourists. Most of the area's accommodations fall on the French side while the Dutch half features condos and vacation rentals.

TOP
CHOICE **Les Balcons d'Oyster Pond** (✆29-43-39; www.lesbalcons.com; 23 Av du Lagon; bungalow from €85; ✳☎☒) is, without exaggeration, one of the best deals in the Caribbean. Sitting on the French side, this charming collection of villas gently spreads across a scrubby hill, and offers excellent views of the bay and quiet marina below. Although it's run like a hotel (by a lovely French couple), each cottage is privately owned and thus each has a completely different decor – some have a Balinese-style darkwood theme, others are a cheery mix of Caribbean colors. Splurge on cottage 23 – a two-bedroom suite – which offers commanding views of the harbor and features an inviting hot tub. Advance bookings are imperative.

Just a few minutes' walk from the marina, **Columbus Hotel** (✆87-42-52; r incl breakfast from €120; ☎) offers condo-type units featuring TVs, phone, kitchenette and a terrace or balcony. **Captain Oliver's** (✆87-40-26; www.captainolivers.com; d incl breakfast from US$180; ✳@☒), at the marina, is perhaps the only hotel in the world where you can be in two different countries at once. The rooms are technically on the French side, while the floating bar is in Dutch waters. Service is a bit muddled, and rooms feel rather soulless. Nonetheless, they each come with balconies and some have splendid marina and ocean views. The open-air restaurant features burgers with fries, seafood and steaks, and once a week there's an all-you-can-eat lobster buffet.

Quai Ouest (meals from US$8-16; ☺breakfast, lunch & dinner Mon-Sat), a small spot with no more than 10 tables, serves up mostly pizzas and a few meaty mains.

The big draw at the **Dinghy Dock Bar** (mains from US$8) is happy hour (5pm to 7pm), when customers get to mix their own drinks. Otherwise this snack bar with picnic tables on the marina dock serves up mediocre sandwiches, hot dogs and full meals, and has Foster's on tap for some strange reason.

UNDERSTAND ST-MARTIN/SINT MAARTEN

Maarten toward independence when it officially became recognized as a 'constituent country' of the Kingdom of the Netherlands.

History

For a thousand years, St-Martin/Sint Maarten was sparsely populated by the Arawaks and later the fiercer Caribs. They named the island Sualouiga after the brackish salt ponds that made it difficult to settle.

Columbus sailed past on November 11, 1493, which happened to be the feast day of St Martin of Tours, after whom he named the island. But it was the Dutch who were the first to take advantage of the land, a nice stopping-off point between Holland and their colonies in Brazil and New Amsterdam (New York City). After a few abortive attempts by the Spanish to regain the island, now found to be brimming with lucrative salt deposits, the French and Dutch ended up fighting for control of it.

As the legend has it, the Dutch and the French decided to partition St-Martin/Sint Maarten from a march originating in Oyster Pond. The French walked northward, the Dutch south. While the French quenched their thirst with wine, the Dutch brought along dodgy gin. Halfway through, the Dutchmen stopped to sleep off the ill effects, effectively giving the French a greater piece of the pie.

St-Martin became a plantation island much like many of its neighbors. The end of slavery brought an end to the plantation boom and by 1930 the population stood at just 2000 hearty souls. Ironically, it was WWII that brought tourism to St-Martin/Sint Maarten. In 1943 the US Navy built large runways on the island to use as a base in the Caribbean. The French capitalized by using the runways to fly in tourists, by the 1950s bringing the population of St-Martin/Sint Maarten up to about 70,000 and making tourism the number one industry on both sides of the island.

In the 1980s, Aruba's secession from the Netherland Antilles sparked movements on St-Martin/Sint Maarten toward greater independence from their parent entities. The Dutch were first in 2000, when they received a 'status aparte' with mother Holland. The French side followed in 2003, voting to secede from Guadeloupe to form their own separate overseas colony. In 2010, the Netherland Antilles dissolved, propelling Sint

Culture

St-Martin/Sint Maarten is a melting pot of ethnicities like no other place in the Caribbean. The island culture has its roots largely in African, French and Dutch influences, though scores of more recent immigrants – including many from the Dominican Republic, Haiti and China – have added their own elements to this multicultural society. Today, the island proudly claims that 80 different languages are spoken throughout, although French dominates St-Martin and English dominates Sint Maarten.

St-Martin/Sint Maarten has adapted to tourism better than any other island nearby. You'll rarely meet someone who was actually born on the island. As the smallest area of land in the world divided into two nations, each side functions symbiotically while attracting tourists in very different ways. The French side embraces its European roots and seeks to recreate a certain amount of 'Old World' atmosphere along the cobble sands. The Dutch side is a mixed bag of Caribbean clichés. Residents coexist with the constant hum of low-lying debauchery that accompanies the dozens of gentlemen's clubs, casinos and thriving discos. Some ignore it, some join in, but most simply accept that their beautiful island home plays host to one long adult spring break.

Topless sunbathing is customary on both sides of the island and nude sunbathing is sanctioned at Orient Beach.

Landscape & Wildlife

The west side of the island is more water than land, dominated by the expansive Simpson Bay Lagoon, which is one of the largest landlocked bodies of water in the Caribbean and has moorings for a large array of boats. The island's interior is hilly, with the highest point, Pic Paradis, rising 424m from the center of French St-Martin.

Herons, egrets, stilts, pelicans and laughing gulls are among the plentiful shorebirds in the island's brackish ponds. Frigatebirds can be spotted along the coast, and hummingbirds and bananaquits in gardens. Lizards also are abundant.

Directory A–Z

Accommodations

There are plenty of places to hang your hat on the island, but it's best to book in advance, especially during high season. Despite the difference between the US dollar and the euro, rooms on both sides come in at around the same price, even when factoring in the steep exchange rates. Most of the lodging on the Dutch side is being turned into timeshares or large-scale resorts, while French properties tend to be much more quiet and quaint.

$	budget	less than US$150
$$	midrange	US$150 to US$300
$$$	top end	more than US$300

Activities

St-Martin/Sint Maarten is a great destination for families, couples and those seeking a bit of adventure. The usual assortment of water sports are the most popular activities – scuba diving, windsurfing, speedboating, yachting, sailing, waterskiing, wakeboarding, deep-sea fishing, kayaking and snorkeling – but visitors will be pleased to find a variety of other activities as well, including horseback riding, hiking, paragliding, golf and cycling.

Business Hours

Banks 8am-3pm Mon-Fri

Restaurants breakfast 7-10:30am, lunch 11:30am-2:30pm, dinner 5-11pm; French restaurants tend to open for dinner slightly later

Festivals & Events

Carnival On the French side, celebrations are held during the traditional five-day Mardi Gras period that ends on Ash Wednesday. It features the selection of a Carnival Queen, costume parades, dancing and music. On the Dutch side, which has the larger Carnival, activities usually begin the second week after Easter and last for two weeks, with steel-pan competitions, jump-ups, calypso concerts, beauty contests and costume parades. Events are centered at Carnival Village on the north side of Philipsburg.

Heineken Regatta (early March) This annual event bills itself as 'serious fun' and features competitions for racing yachts, large sailboats and small multihulls.

Food

The following price indicators, based on the cost of a main meal, are used in Eating reviews in this chapter.

$	budget	less than US$10
$$	midrange	US$10 to US$20
$$$	top end	more than US$20

Health

Medical services can be easily scouted in the capital towns on each side of the island: Marigot and Philipsburg.

Tap water on both sides of the island come from desalination plants and it is generally safe to drink, though sometimes it is not particularly tasty.

Internet Access

Wireless hot spots can be easily scouted throughout the island; even Juliana Airport has wi-fi. Most hotels offer wi-fi services and many have computer terminals as well.

Money

On the French side, everything is priced in euros, while on the Dutch side (despite the currency being the Netherlands Antillean guilder) items are always posted in US dollars. If you are paying with cash, it never hurts to ask the businesses on the eurocentric French side if they'll take one-for-one dollars to euros – often times you'll get a reluctant-yet-positive response.

Note that at the time of writing plans were being debated to switch the official currency of Sint Maarten from NAf to either US dollars, or use a new currency, the Caribbean guilder (CMg). A decision could be made by 2012, later or not at all. Check on the latest currency news before you travel.

ATMs blanket the island and transaction fees will cost substantially less than using the exchange bureaus. Note that American Express cards are rarely accepted on the island, especially on the French side.

Public Holidays

In addition to those observed throughout the region (p872), St-Martin/Sint Maarten has the following public holidays:

Queen's Day April 30 (Dutch side)

Labor Day May 1

Government Holiday The day after the last Carnival parade, about a month after Easter (Dutch side)

Ascension Thursday Fortieth day after Easter

Pentecost Monday Eighth Monday after Easter (French side)

Bastille Day July 14 (French side)

Assumption Day August 15 (French side)

Sint Maarten Day November 11 (both sides)

Safe Travel

In the evenings, muggers have been known to follow cars home, and when the victim is driving through a quiet area, the assailants will purposefully bump the car. After you pull over to check for damages, the thief will mug you and take off. Petty criminals have also followed victims all the way back to the victim's hotel and robbed them as they walked from the car to their lodging. Be mindful of who is behind and in front of you. If you feel like you are being followed, simply pull into a very public place, or continue driving past where you are staying until the driver goes in another direction. If you are bumped by another car, just continue driving. The highest concentrations of these crimes have occurred in the quiet area of Oyster Pond.

During bottleneck traffic jams, particularly in congested Marigot, druggies and derelicts may start banging on the window of your 'parked' car begging (and sometimes threatening you) for money. Simply ignore them.

A good ole fashioned 'hold-up' is another petty crime that often makes the papers. In the last few years Grand Case has developed a bit of an edge, and once in a while a robber will hold up one of the posh restaurants, collect everyone's wallets and zoom out the door.

Telephone

St-Martin's area code is ☎590 and Sint Maarten's is ☎599. Calls between the two sides are (annoyingly) treated as international calls. To call the Dutch side from the French side, dial ☎00-599 + 54, then the seven-digit number. To dial the French side from the Dutch side, dial ☎00-590-590 + the six-digit number (that's the area code dialed twice).

» **Electricity** French side: 220V, 60 cycles; standard two- and three-pronged plugs as found in the US; Dutch side: 220V, 60 cycles; standard European two-pin plugs.

» **Newspapers & Magazines** French side: *Saint-Martin's Week, Fax Info, Pelican;* Dutch side: *The Daily Herald, Today* (both in English); also *Discover Saint Martin/Sint Maarten, Sint Maarten Events* and *Ti Gourmet.*

» **Radio & TV** For island music try Radio Calypso 102.1, or Radio 101.5 for reggae and dance music. Radio Transat is at 106.1FM. SXM-TV6 broadcasts from Philipsburg in English.

» **Weights & Measures** Metric system.

To dial within the French telephone system, dial ☎0590 + the six-digit number. To dial within the Dutch telephone system, dial ☎0599 + the seven-digit number. We have included only the six- and seven-digit local numbers in the listings here. For French cell phones, the second 590 is replaced with 690.

Travelers with Disabilities

Although St-Martin is rugged and quite mountainous, the massive amount of tourist development has made it relatively hassle-free for disabled travelers to experience the island.

Visas

Visas are not necessary for North Americans, EU nationals and Australians. Some former Soviet states, Latin American countries and many African nationals will need visas, especially for the French side. Always remember that different visa situations apply for the neighboring islands, so read up on the red tape before planning a day trip.

Getting There & Away

Entering the Island

Citizens of the EU need an official identity card or valid passport. Citizens of other foreign countries need a valid passport.

A round-trip or onward ticket is officially required of Americans, Canadians and all non-EU citizens, regardless of whether one enters on the French or Dutch side.

Air

There are two airports on the island: **Juliana International Airport** (☑545-2060; www.pjiae.com; Sint Maarten) and **L'Espérance Airport** (☑87-53-03; Grand Case, St-Martin). All international flights arrive at Juliana Airport and it is a major hub for the region. Prop planes head from L'Espérance to St-Barthélemy, Guadeloupe and Martinique.

International departure tax is US$30, although most tickets already include the fee.

Note that Juliana is either a crowded tedious experience, or a lovely, no-lines hop through – if you're passing through the airport around 2pm expect the former. Your best bet is to arrive well before your flight, check in and, if you end up with plenty of time, take a US$6 taxi to the Sunset Beach Bar (p724).

Major airlines fly to the island from the US, including Air Canada, American, Continental, Delta, JetBlue, United and US Airways. Air France and Alitalia connect the island with Paris and KLM has flights from Amsterdam. Other airlines operating in the region:

Insel Air (www.caribbeanjet.com) Aruba, Bonaire, Curaçao

LIAT (www.liatairline.com) Antigua, Beef Island, Nevis, St Kitts, St Crois, St Thomas, Tortola

St Barth Commuter (www.stbarthcommuter .com) St-Barthélemy

Spirit (www.spiritair.com) Fort Lauderdale

Winair (www.fly-winair.com) Saba, St Kitts, St-Barthélemy, Sint Eustatius, Tortola, Santo Domingo, Beef Island

Sea

CRUISE SHIP

No less than 12 major companies land in Philipsburg and Marigot. Passengers arriving at Philipsburg can disembark directly onto land. Day-trippers head to duty-free shopping in the main towns or to beach excursions. Sometimes up to four ships a day are in port.

FERRY

Ferries depart from Marigot, Oyster Pond, Philipsburg and Simpson Bay for Anguilla, St-Barthélemy and Saba. Schedules and departure points are prone to change so call the **main ferry line** (☑87-53-03) in St-Martin for the most up-to-date information.

Ferries make the 25-minute journey from Marigot Bay in St-Martin to Blowing Point in Anguilla an average of once every 45 minutes during daylight hours. The one-way fare is US$15. The fare for the passage is paid onboard the boat.

YACHT

There are marinas at Philipsburg, Marigot, Simpson Bay Lagoon, Oyster Pond and Anse Marcel.

People arriving by yacht can clear immigration at the **office** (☑542-2222) based in Philipsburg, Sint Maarten.

On the French side, yachts can dock at one of the two marinas in Marigot – Fort Louis (www.caribbean-marinas.com/fort louis) or Port La Royale (www.caribbean -marinas.com/portlaroyale).

Visit www.stmartinisland.org/st-martin -st-maarten-activities/boating-and-marinas-st-martin-st-maarten.html for a detailed timetable of when the island's two bridges are raised to allow boats to enter the coves at Simpson Bay and Sandy Ground.

Getting Around

Although the island is divided into two separate land claims, there are no official borders or border crossings (besides a couple of cheesy billboards welcoming drivers to each side of the island). Traffic moves as freely across both sides of the island as if it were one entity.

Bicycle

Frog Legs Cyclery (☑87-05-11), next to the Match supermarket in Marigot, St-Martin, rents out mountain bikes from US$15 a day and organizes island cycling tours for US$20.

Bus

Buses are by far the cheapest method of transportation, but if you need to be somewhere fast, take a taxi, or better yet rent a car. Buses do not have any set schedule and they come and go as they please until around 10:30pm. Buses charge US$2 for every town you pass through along your journey. Service mostly moves through Philipsburg, Mullet Bay, Simpson Bay, Marigot and Grand Case. When you need to get off, simply yell 'stop.'

In the capitals you have to stand at bus stops, which are called 'Bushalte' in Philipsburg. In rural areas you can flag down buses anywhere along the route. Buses have their final destination posted on the front shield, but most are bound for either Philipsburg or Marigot.

Car & Motorcycle

RENTAL

When you arrive at Juliana airport, you'll exit the international terminal into a large foyer filled with car rental agencies. Due to the abundance of service providers you can easily play one agency off of the next asking for small discounts (especially if you're planning to rent your vehicle for a week or more). This method can usually work to your advantage – especially during the quieter months – but if it's the height of high season you might find yourself at the opposite end of the equation: begging for a vehicle.

During low season you'll usually find wheels for around US$22 to US$28 per day. In high season, expect to pay around US$32 to US$40 for a small car depending the length of your rental. If you do try the bargaining tactic make sure you take a good look at your vehicle before leaving the lot – there are a lot of shoddy cars on the island.

If this all sounds too hectic, we recommend two operators on the island that promise excellent service and have quality automobiles. First, try **Banana Location** (☑0690-71-91-05; bananalocation@orange.fr) and you'll be guaranteed a clean, comfortable vehicle at a very reasonable price (€30 to €35). The affable owner delivers some of the top customer service on the island – he'll meet you at the airport to make sure you start your holiday off on the right foot. **Coastal Car Rental** (☑543 0244; www.coastalcarrental.com), based on the Dutch side, offers ultra-efficient service with polite staff. Their armada of cars is in excellent condition. Prices hover around US$35.

Other companies at Juliana airport:

Avis (☑545-2316)

Budget (☑545-4030)

Dollar (☑545-3061)

Hertz (☑545-4440)

Paradise Island (☑545-2361)

Sunshine (☑545-2685)

Safety

Be aware that all leased cars on the Dutch side of the island have an 'R' marking on the license plate that show they are rentals, making them easy targets for petty thieves. Do not leave anything whatsoever in your car when you leave it parked. Certain spots on the island are a bit more dangerous than others, such as Pic Paradis, where every single car will be scoped out no matter how dingy it looks. But it's not worth taking a chance anywhere or at anytime. Even if you don't mind that something minor was stolen, you might end up paying through the nose to repair your smashed-in window. Before taking your rental car off the lot, check the car doors – many have had the locks jimmied open at some point in their lives.

ROAD RULES

Driving is on the right side of the road on both sides of the island, and your home driver's license is valid. Road signs and car odometers are in kilometers.

The amount of traffic in Marigot, Grand Case and Philipsburg can shock visitors expecting a peaceful getaway. Traffic jams occur regularly.

Hitchhiking

You'll see many locals with their thumbs out, but tourists shouldn't follow suit. Petty theft and violent crime is on the rise all over the island.

Taxi

The government-regulated fares should be posted in each taxi. Rates increase in the evening or if there are more than three passengers. From Juliana airport it's US$6 to Maho, US$18 to Marigot and US$25 to Grand Case.

To book a taxi, call ☑147 anytime day or night.

St Vincent & the Grenadines

Best Beaches

» Princess Margaret Beach (p747)

» Friendship Bay (p749)

» Britannia Bay Beach (p750)

» Twin Bay (p751)

» Saltwhistle Bay (p752)

Best Places to Stay

» Firefly (p750)

» Palm Island Beach Club (p755)

» Petit St Vincent Resort (p755)

» Frangipani Hotel (p747)

» Young Island Resort (p742)

Why Go?

Just the name St Vincent and the Grenadines evokes visions of exotic, idyllic island life. Imagine an island chain in the heart of the Caribbean Sea, uncluttered by tourist exploitation; with white-sand beaches on deserted islands, sky-blue water gently lapping the shore and barely a soul around.

Once you get off the big island, with its traffic, hustle and noise, and out into the Grenadines, everything changes. There are 31 Grenadines, each one more tranquil than the next and each begging to be explored. Beaches stretch out before you, the pace of life slows to a crawl and the desire to go home vanishes.

These islands have enchanted sailors for centuries, and continue to do so. Whether you have your own vessel, are happy to hitch a ride or take one of the new ferries, the island-hopping opportunities are irresistible.

When to Go

The climate varies between the islands, as the Grenadines to the south are slightly drier and marginally warmer than St Vincent. In St Vincent the dry season runs approximately from January to May. In July, the wettest month, rain falls for an average of 26 days, while in April, the driest month, it averages only six days. In January the average daily high temperature is 29°C (85°F), while the nightly low is 22°C (72°F). In July the average high is 30°C (86°F), while the nightly low is 24°C (76°F).

Itineraries

ONE WEEK

Spend a day or two in St Vincent, exploring the busy streets. Then head south and get ready to relax. Take the boat to Bequia and settle into the beach life. Go for a wander, if the mood takes you, and compare stretches of sand. Be sure to factor into your plans a day trip to the Tobago Cays aboard Bequia's *Friendship Rose*.

TWO WEEKS

Start your journey in St Vincent and spend a few days on on the big island, then jump on a ferry and head to Bequia, where you'll be overwhelmed by the change of pace. After decompressing, catch the ferry further south to Mustique, then onwards to Canouan, Mayreau, the Tobago Cays, Palm Island and finally to Union Island. Take as much time as you can – the slower the better.

GETTING TO NEIGHBORING ISLANDS

St Vincent and the Grenadines are the ultimate island-hopping adventure. As you'll read often in this chapter, there are myriad opportunities for getting a boat to another island. It's no problem catching a ferry or hiring a boat within the 32 main islands of SVG. Reaching Grenada is not a problem either. It's a short trip by hired fishing boat to Carriacou where you can get a ferry to Grenada proper.

Reaching Barbados, however, still requires a plane ticket; it's the same for St Lucia and neighboring islands. Airline service is fast and frequent.

Essential Food & Drink

As far as West Indian food goes, SVG is one of the better destinations for enjoying its unique flavors.

» **Fresh produce** St Vincent produces top quality and delicious fruits and vegetables.

» **Seafood** Lobster, shrimp, conch and fish are all popular and readily available.

» **Callaloo** A spinachlike vegetable used in soups and stews. Many vitamins!

» **Savory pumpkin soup** More squash-like than the American Thanksgiving staple; often like a rich stew.

» **Saltfish** Dried fish that has been cured, delicious when made into fishcakes.

» **Rotis** Curried vegetables, potatoes and meat wrapped in a flour tortilla are a national passion.

» **Hairoun** (pronounced 'high-rone') The light and tasty local lager.

AT A GLANCE

» **Currency** Eastern Caribbean dollar (EC$)

» **Language** English

» **Money** ATMs in main tourist areas, not on smaller islands; most dispense only EC$

» **Visas** Not required for citizens of the US, Canada and most European and Commonwealth countries

Fast Facts

» **Area** 150 sq miles

» **Population** 104,000

» **Capital** Kingstown

» **Telephone country code** ☑1

» **Telephone area code** ☑784

» **Emergency** ☑999

Set Your Budget

» **Budget hotel room** EC$50

» **Two-course evening meal** EC$30

» **Beer** EC$5

» **Ferry from St Vincent to Bequia** EC$20

» **Villa for the week on Mustique** US$40,000

Resources

» **Bequia Tourism Association** (www.bequia tourism.com)

» **Ins & Outs** (www.insand outsofsvg.com) An excellent online magazine

» **St Vincent & the Grenadines** (www.discoversvg .com) Official tourism site

St Vincent & the Grenadines Highlights

1 Visit **Tobago Cays** (p754): five picture-perfect islands that are the essential SVG snorkeling experience

2 Toss away your return ticket when you reach **Bequia** (p746), one of the region's best small islands

3 Explore the undeveloped half of picturesque **Canouan** (p751), especially its beaches

4 Cruise the ocean, vagabond around the islands, find your own perfect beach and play pirate **island hopping the Grenadines**

5 Cruise the cobblestone streets of SVG's biggest city and capital, **Kingstown** (p739), a vibrant and decidedly nonupscale mélange

6 Get wet under the amazingly beautiful waters at the **Falls of Baleine** (p745) on St Vincent

7 Kick up your heels with rock stars at impossibly beautiful and expensive **Mustique** (p750)

ST VINCENT

POP 105,000

St Vincent is the largest island and the hub that most travelers will pass through on their visit to SVG. Though not uninspiring, the allure of the Grenadines pulls most visitors away from here quickly.

The beaches are on the average side and the frenetic pace of Kingstown and its unpolished edges inspires many to head out to the calm of the Grenadines. But the island is fascinating for exploring. The verdant rainforested interior has good hiking options and vast banana plantations provide a timeless spectacle.

This is not the polished Caribbean of Barbados or other heavily touristed islands, rather it is a lush and raw place where people are working hard every day to get by.

It's easy for independent travelers to witness traditional Vincy life, as the towns and villages are unspoiled by tourism. Those staying within the resorts around the island's coast, though, are for the most part insulated from the realities of local life on St Vincent.

ℹ Getting There & Away

AIR The short runway at ET Joshua Airport (SVD) near Kingstown receives regular flights (with connections further afield) from nearby islands such as Barbados and Grenada. See p758.

BOAT Several ferries depart from Kingstown for other islands. It's very important to confirm schedule details in advance as they change frequently. The best choices for **Bequia** are:

Bequia Express (☑458-3472; www.bequiaexpress.net) Car ferry; one-way/return EC$20/EC$35; one hour; several times daily

MV Admiral (☑458-3348; www.admiralty-transport.com) Car ferry; one-way/return EC$20/EC$35; one hour; several times daily

Options for ferries to/from the **Grenadines** include (see the individual island sections for more details):

Jaden Sun (☑451-2192; www.jadeninc.com) Fast ferry, serves Bequia, Canouan (EC$85), Mayreau, Union Island (EC$115), up to three times daily, never Tue

MV Barracuda (☑455-9835) Slow cargo boat, serves Bequia, Canouan, Mayreau, Union Island (EC$40), three trips each way each week

MV Gem Star (☑457-4157) Slow cargo boat, serves Canouan, Mayreau, Union Island, two trips each way each week

ℹ Getting Around

BUS Buses are a good way to get around St Vincent, with fares ranging from EC$1 to ED$6, depending on the destination. Taxis are available at the airport and at a couple of stands in central Kingstown. Fares from the airport to Kingstown and Villa are EC$20. Other fares, while set, are actually negotiable.

CAR Car rental companies will deliver cars to the ferry dock in Kingstown or the airport. **Avis** (☑456-4389; www.avis.com) and **Lewis Auto World** (☑456-2244; www.lewisautoworld.com) have airport offices.

Kingstown

POP 32,000

Rough cobblestone streets, arched stone doorways and covered walkways conjure up a Caribbean of banana boats and colonial rule. The city of Kingstown heaves and swells with a pulsing local community that bustles through its narrow streets and alleyways. Steep hills surround the town, amplifying the sounds of car horns, street vendors and the music filtering through the crowd.

For nearly all visitors to SVG, Kingstown is the gateway to exploring the outer islands of the Grenadines. Travelers come here to use the bank, stock up on supplies and have a taste of town before heading out into the quiet of the surrounding islands. The one time to make sure you visit Kingstown is on Saturdays when the streets and market heave.

There is more tourist infrastructure a few miles down the road from Kingstown in the towns of Villa and Indian Bay – this is where you will find the majority of the resorts on the island.

The city is hemmed in by the island's hilly topography, and the center consists of only about a dozen dense blocks. Ferries from the Grenadines arrive at the jetty just south of the city center.

☉ Sights

The cobblestone streets, shipping agencies and rum shops around Sharpe St feel unchanged in a century.

Save your real beach time for the idyllic white sands of the Grenadines, but for a local dip, look for the narrow strips of sand amidst small coves at **Villa Beach**. About the best spot is directly in front of the Beachcombers Hotel.

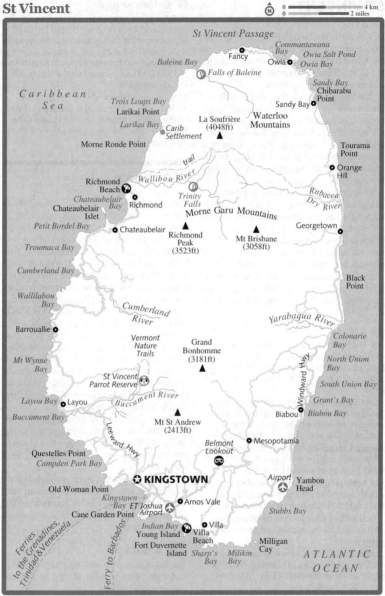

TOP CHOICE **Public Market**   MARKET

(⊙6am-3pm) Kingstown is at its frenetic best in and around the Public Market near the junctions of Hillsboro, Upper Middle and Bedford Sts. There's some permanent stalls in the market building but the real action is on the streets outside. The fertile bounty of the island is sold from tables and blankets on the ground. Huge breadfruit and melons are displayed along with tiny chilies and spices of all flavors. Bananas in shapes and sizes that will never get slapped with a multinational brand label are found in profusion. Household goods, cheap toys, plastic sandals and much more are on offer.

There is selling every day but the real action is on Saturday when vendors fill block after block with their wares and the crazy energy of the crowds is at once bewildering, confounding and seductive.

Fort Charlotte
FORT

(☉daylight) Just north of the city and standing proudly atop a 660ft ridge, Fort Charlotte offers commanding views of both town and the Grenadines to the south.

Built in 1806 and named after King George III's wife, the fort was built to repel the French navy. In its heyday it was home to 600 troops and 34 cannons. These days it's a fair bit quieter, but the walls and a few of the guns remain. It's a steep 30-minute walk from town or you can hop on a bus that will drop you off near the fort; then you only have to contend with the last 10 minutes uphill.

St Vincent Botanic Gardens
GARDEN

(Montrose; ☉6am-6pm) The oldest botanical gardens in the western hemisphere, the St Vincent Botanic Gardens are lovingly tended and provide an oasis of calm that's only half a mile north from the frenzy of Kingstown. Originally established in 1762 to propagate spices and medicinal plants, the gardens now comprise a neatly landscaped 20-acre park with lots of flowering bushes and tall trees. There's a small **aviary** that is intermittently home to some of the island's remaining 500 endangered St Vincent parrots. Guided tours are sometimes available.

Belmont Lookout
VIEWPOINT

On the road to Mesopotamia – the SVG version – there is an excellent lookout when you crest the peak and leave the coast behind while the impossibly green Mesopotamia Valley unfolds before you. Signs detail the area's history and features. Continue on the narrow, twisting roads through the verdant valley to the coast road.

🏃 Activities

Snorkeling can be OK a little way off Indian Bay Beach and Villa Beach. Most boat trips to the Falls of Baleine include stops along the very good west coast for snorkeling. For more on diving in SVG, see p754.

Dive St Vincent (☑457-4714; www.divest vincent.com; Young Island dock, St Vincent) offers dive trips, rentals and instruction, as well as snorkeling trips.

✷ Festivals & Events

Vincy Mas
CARNIVAL

For more than 30 years, Vincy Mas has been *the* big yearly event in St Vincent. This enormous carnival takes place at the end of June or in early July. The calypso and soca competitions culminate in a street party in Kingstown with steel bands, dancers and drinks.

🛏 Sleeping

The majority of options are in the beachside communities of Indian Bay and Villa. There are a few places to stay in Kingstown itself; none are more than 15 minutes drive from the airport or ferry dock. Overall, prices reflect excellent value.

KINGSTOWN

TOP CHOICE **Cobblestone Inn**
HOTEL **$$**

(☑456-1937; www.thecobblestoneinn.com; Upper Bay St, Kingstown; r US$75-95; ❄@🛜) The Cobblestone Inn was built from the shell of an 1814 cobblestone warehouse and modernized into a comfy urban hotel. Arched stone passageways connected with narrow stairs form a labyrinth that's as enticing as it is aesthetic. The 26 rooms are nicely fitted out with Renaissance-style curtains and shiraz-colored hardwood. The alluring rooftop cafe is a bonus for an establishment that truly leaves no (cobble)stone unturned.

Grenadine House
BOUTIQUE HOTEL **$$$**

(☑458-1800; www.grenadinehouse.com; Kingstown; r US$180-300; ❄@🛋) High in the hills overlooking Kingstown, like a fortress of whitewashed luxury, Grenadine House is a step in a different direction compared to most properties on the island. Away from the beach and near the genteel district of the botanical gardens, the property offers fantastic views of town and the Grenadines. White linen with thread-counts to brag about, wicker headboards and fresh flowers complement the bedrooms. The food and drink options are excellent. The French Governor General, the original resident in the 1760s, would still approve.

INDIAN BAY & VILLA

TOP CHOICE **Beachcombers Hotel**
RESORT **$$**

(☑458-4283; www.beachcombershotel.com; Villa; r US$100-200; @🛜🛋) This is a real find on the west side of Villa. Multicolored buildings dot

ST VINCENT & THE GRENADINES KINGSTOWN

ST VINCENT & THE GRENADINES ST VINCENT

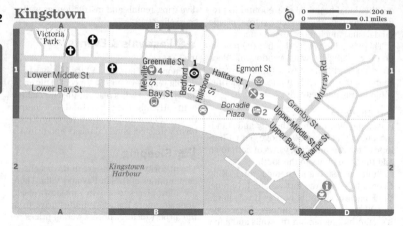

Kingstown

◎ Sights
1 Public Market B1

🛏 Sleeping
2 Cobblestone Inn C1

🍴 Eating
Basil's Bar & Restaurant .... (see 2)
3 Bounty C1
Cobblestone Inn Rooftop Bar .... (see 2)

🍷 Drinking
4 Attic B1

the landscape in true Caribbean style. The basic rooms are just that, but things get markedly better as you climb the rate card. Spacious rooms with large verandas over-looking the harbor and islands are the top pick. Spacious grounds with an oceanside pool, plus a fun bar and restaurant, clinch the deal.

Grand View Beach Hotel RESORT **$$**
(☎458-4811; www.grandviewhotel.com; Villa; r US$120-250; ❄@🛜☒) Sweeping views of the island-dotted waters and curvaceous shore in front of Villa are reason enough to stay at this modest hillside resort with truthful name. The 19 rooms are split between cozy ones in an old plantation house and larger ones in a modern Spanish-style wing. The grounds are lovely and the beach a short stroll away.

Skyblue Apartments APARTMENTS **$$**
(☎457-4394; www.skybluebeach.com; Indian Bay; r from US$80; ❄@🛜) Nestled in the suburban neighborhood of Indian Bay, this place has quirky extras aplenty, with turtles in the yard

and a miniature golf course. The tranquil rooms are tidy, basic and not liable to win design awards; all come equipped with kitchens.

Villa Lodge Hotel HOTEL **$$**
(☎458-4641; www.villalodge.com; Indian Bay; r US$120-150; ❄@🛜☒) Luscious landscaped grounds, large rooms and friendly staff make this a popular place for retuning guests. Just off the succulent sands of Indian Bay, each of the 19 rooms sports a balcony and some have sea views too. Nearby full apartments are only slightly more expensive.

YOUNG ISLAND
It's only 200yds offshore from Villa, but the vaguely heart-shaped private Young Island is a whole world away. Swaying palms line the beach and shade the attractive tropical retreats that speckle the hillside. To enjoy the island you need to enjoy the resort, they are one and the same.

TOP CHOICE Young Island Resort RESORT **$$$**
(☎458-4826; www.youngisland.com; Young Island; r incl meals US$450-1200; ❄@☒) Abundant gardens of native plants delight the senses and the bar on stilts perched among the breakers teases your imagination. The 29 units include sexy villas, some with plunge pools, killer views and everything you need to forget about the little hotel ferry back to St Vincent.

🍴 Eating & Drinking

The larger hotels and resorts have some fine eating and drinking options. There are some good, simple restaurants in Kingstown serving local fare but there is a paucity of high-style restaurants.

KINGSTOWN

Impromptu bars rule the streets as the Saturday market wanes in the afternoon. Vendors sell Hairouns from ice buckets, the raucousness is proportional to the number of bottlecaps covering the pavement.

TOP CHOICE Sapodilla Room
CARIBBEAN $$$

(458-1800; Grenadine House, Kingstown; mains US$20-40; lunch & dinner) The fine dining room of the Grenadine House lives up to the high standards of the hotel. Locally sourced produce is used in inventive creations that combine Creole, Caribbean and American flavors. Start your night in the elegant Mayfair-style British pub and segue into the elegant dining room. For casual fare outside with great views, try the **Terrace** (breakfast & lunch).

Basil's Bar & Restaurant
INTERNATIONAL $$

(Cobblestone Inn, Upper Bay St; mains from EC$30; 8am-10pm) Downstairs in the Cobblestone Inn you'll find the passage to this atmospheric bar and grill. If the food weren't so good you might think you'd entered a pirate's dungeon, given the moody lighting and stone walls. From breakfast to dinner, the food spans American and Caribbean favorites, although many simply avail themselves of Kingstown's classiest bar. You'd be hard-pressed to guess that this Basil's is a sibling of the legendary Basil's beach bar on Mustique.

Bounty
CARIBBEAN $

(Egmont St; meals from EC$10; 7:30am-4pm Mon-Sat) Looking down on the bustle of Kingstown from this simple cafe is the perfect escape from the Saturday market madness. Rotis, mac and cheese, and other island favorites populate the menu. Finish your break with some fruity ice cream and pause to peruse the local arts and crafts on display.

Cobblestone Inn Rooftop Bar
AMERICAN $$

(Cobblestone Inn, Upper Bay St; meals EC$12-20; 7am-3pm) Stare out to sea across Kingstown's historic rooftops from the hotel's airy top-floor cafe. Serves pancakes, omelettes, burgers, salads and more. The ice cream sundaes are a good mid-afternoon treat.

Attic
BAR & GRILL $

(Melville St; meals EC$10-20; 7am-late) As the sign says, 'We are at the top of the stairs.' Make your way up to this jovial bar atop a beautiful old stone building for some live music ('Wild Meat' Saturdays can feature a soca band) and bonhomie.

INDIAN BAY & VILLA

French Veranda
FRENCH $$$

(458-4972; www.marinershotel.com; Mariners Hotel, Villa; mains US$20-40) The name says it all: the food is French and it's served on a lovely veranda. Right down on the waterfront at Villa Beach, this casually gracious bistro sets the mood with candles on the tables. While ship's bells ring in the distance, enjoy classics such as shrimp in garlic butter, poached salmon and grilled beef.

Lime N' Pub
BAR & GRILL $$

(Villa; mains EC$25-90; 9am-midnight) A classic yachties' bar complete with '80s beer posters on the wall, signed undies and hand-drawn maps to secret islands. This Villa establishment does burgers and pizza in the barebones pub area; the more refined dining room (no beer posters) has fresh seafood and Caribbean fare.

YOUNG ISLAND

Young Island Resort
FUSION $$$

(458-4826; www.youngisland.com; mains US$20-50; breakfast, lunch & dinner) There are few places that can boast that their specialty is bread, but here at Young Island the proof is in the pumpernickel. Every meal comes with a barge full of fresh bread to accompany the equally fresh seafood and other dishes prepared with some of St Vincent's best bounty. Tables are set in beautiful gardens by the beach. Nonguests are welcome, reserve in advance. The little hotel boat takes five minutes to reach the resort.

PORT OF CALL – KINGSTOWN

Traveling on foot from the cruise-ship dock, you can spend an intriguing day exploring the traditional Caribbean port town of Kingstown. It's little changed since the days when the wharves were lined with tramp steamers and banana boats.

Further afield, you can...

» Take a day trip by boat to the Falls of Baleine (p745)

» Tour St Vincent's lush interior on a hike or a drive

» If it's Saturday, lose yourself in the chaos of the public market (p740)

» Jump on a ferry to the stunning island of Bequia (p746)

ST VINCENT TOURS

Tours that include St Vincent's coast, the remains of *The Pirates of the Caribbean* sets and stunning Falls of Baleine are very popular. Longer ones usually include refreshments and lunch. Pickups at the cruiseship dock or at hotels are either included or can be arranged.

Wayne's Tours (☑457-4089, 315-608-7118; www.sites.google.com/site/whalbich/home; adult/child US$80/40) is a much-lauded outfit that takes people on a boat along the west coast for a day that includes swimming at the Falls of Baleine, lunch at a *Pirates of the Caribbean* site and other stops on the lush and wild shore. The boats leave from the cruise ship dock or by other arrangement. Other trips are available, as are custom outings.

Fantasea Tours (☑457-4477; www.fantaseatours.com) arranges day tours of the St Vincent coast, including Baleine Falls from US$80.

HazEco Tours (☑457-8634; www.hazecotours.com) offers a wide range of tours with an emphasis on the outdoors. Options include a half-day outing to the Vermont Nature Trails or a hiking trip to the summit of La Soufrière. Tours run from US$60 per person.

Sailor's Wilderness Tours (☑457-1274; sailortours@hotmail.com) offers mountain-bike tours and also rents bikes from US$25 per day.

Sam's Taxi Tours (☑456-4338; www.samtaxiandtours.com) offers a variety of land-based tours that take in the sights of St Vincent from around US$40 to US$50 per hour for up to two people.

Shopping

Looking to get a cheap T-shirt, a mix CD of local reggae favorites or perhaps a dubious DVD of the latest Hollywood release? Look no further than Upper Middle St. If nothing else, this lane of street stalls and tiny shops is a great spot to hang out with the locals, in their element, and find some real bargains.

Otherwise, outside of the obvious appeal of market days, just wander the small shops along the streets and enjoy the kind of shopping that was universal before the big box stores.

ℹ Information

Ferry Terminal internet (per hr US$2) A great way to kill some time while waiting for the ferry and also a good option if you're in this end of town. Good computers and a pretty fast connection.

Kingstown General Hospital (☑456-1185; ⏰24hr) On the Leeward Hwy. For serious illness or decompression sickness you will be sent to Barbados.

General post office (☑456-1111; Halifax St; ⏰8:30am-3pm Mon-Fri, to 11:30am Sat)

Tourist office (☑457-1502; www.discoversvg.com; Cruise Ship Terminal; ⏰8am-noon & 1-4:15pm Mon-Fri)

ℹ Getting Around

The Cruise Ship Terminal and Ferry Terminal at the south end of Kingstown Harbour receives international cruise ships and has tourist facilities, including information and shops.

The bus station is near the Little Tokyo Fish Market on Bay St, although buses can also be hailed along the road.

It is easy to walk around Kingstown, which is surprisingly small. A taxi from the airport to Kingstown costs a negotiable EC$20.

Windward Highway

The windward (east) coast of St Vincent is a mix of wave-lashed shoreline, quiet bays and small towns. As it's away from the tourism that dominates the southern coast of the island, it's a fine place to visit for those wanting to experience a more sedate version of St Vincent. The black-sand **beaches** meld into the banana plantations and the lush vegetation grows up into the hilly interior. Humble villages pop up from time to time, filled with down-to-earth locals and ramshackle buildings.

Buses from Kingstown to Georgetown are fairly regular (except on Sunday) and cost EC$4. Buses driving north from Georgetown are irregular, so get information from the Kingstown bus station before heading off. Note also that the beaches along the entire east coast are generally not safe for surfing.

As you head further north along the east coast, you really start to get off the beaten track. The jungle gets a bit thicker, the road a bit narrower, and towering **La Soufrière** volcano (4048ft) begins to dominate the skyline. Still active and slightly ominous, this striking feature is the hallmark of the northern end of St Vincent. About a mile north of Georgetown the road passes over an old lava flow from the 1902 eruption – a solemn reminder of the power of the volcano.

Heading yet further north the rough track turns inland near **Orange Hill** and, amid the coconut palms and the banana plantations, the **hiking trail** to La Soufrière's crater begins. This 3.5-mile hike will take you up to the crater, where you can see the lake and, on a clear day, spectacular views of the island and the Grenadines.

Getting to the hike is a bit of mission in itself. The trailhead is 2 miles off the main road and bus access this far north is a bit sporadic. If you don't have your own wheels you can either arrange for a taxi, which will cost you over US$100 from Kingstown, or join a guided tour, especially those by HazEco Tours (see p744).

Also at Orange Hill, look for the **Youroumei Heritage Village**, a somewhat restored old sugar plantation that still stands thanks to its stout stone construction.

Continuing north you will hit **Sandy Bay**, a sizable village that has the island's largest concentration of Black Caribs. North of Sandy Bay is Owia Bay and the village of **Owia**, where you'll find the **Salt Pond**, a group of tidal pools protected from the crashing Atlantic by a massive stone shield. This is a popular swimming hole with crystal-clear waters and a view of St Lucia to the north. There are thatched shelters, picnic tables and restrooms here.

Leeward Highway

The Leeward Hwy runs north of Kingstown along St Vincent's west coast for 25 miles, ending at Richmond Beach. Offering some lovely scenery, the road climbs into the mountains as it leaves Kingstown, then winds through the hillside and back down to deeply cut coastal valleys that open to coconut plantations, fishing villages and bays lined with black-sand beaches.

The drive from Kingstown to Richmond Beach takes about 1½ hours. There are weekday buses roughly every 15 minutes from Kingstown to Barrouallie (EC$4, 45 minutes). From there it is a 1-mile walk to Wallilabou Bay, and about four buses per day continue north to Richmond.

VERMONT NATURE TRAILS
About a 3-mile drive north of Kingstown is a sign along the Leeward Hwy, pointing east to the **Vermont Nature Trails**, 3.5 miles inland. Here you'll find the Parrot Lookout Trail, a 1.75-mile loop (two hours) that passes through the southwestern tip of the **St Vincent Parrot Reserve**, which is a thick **rainforest**.

The turn to the reserve is at **Buccament Bay**, which has been designated for new resort development. At great expense the natural black sand is being covered with imported white sand for color-conscious sunbathers.

WALLILABOU BAY & FALLS
Just a few years ago, the small village of Wallilabou was one of the most recognizable places in all of SVG. Various parts of the first *Pirates of the Caribbean* movie were filmed here in 2002, in the process creating a full-scale seaside pirate village for scurvy dogs and old sea salts to call home. For a few years afterwards, the old sets were a huge attraction, and were reused for brief scenes in later installments in the franchise. But now, these temporary facades are falling fast and will soon return to the jungle.

DON'T MISS

FALLS OF BALEINE

It's the stuff of tropical fantasies: a 60ft waterfall crashes down a fern-dappled rock in a silvery arc into a lovely wide freshwater pool below. The gorgeous Falls of Baleine, at the isolated northwestern tip of the island, are accessible only by boat. A few minutes' walk from the beach where your boat anchors, listen for the cascade amidst the rainforest.

Most tour companies charge US$60 to US$80 for a day trip that includes the falls, a stop for lunch at Wallilabou Bay and some afternoon snorkeling. Among the operators (see p744), Wayne's Tours wins much praise.

Wallilabou Falls are near the inland side of the main road, about a mile north of Wallilabou Bay. Although only 13ft high, the falls are beautiful and drop into a waist-deep bathing pool.

Wallilabou Anchorage INN $$$
(☎458-7270; www.wallilabou.com; Wallilabou; r US$50-65; ☎) The mooring facilities are popular with yachts and there's a small inn, and a pleasant bayside **restaurant** (⊙7am-9pm) and bar. Seafood caught in the bay is the big draw.

RICHMOND BEACH

Nearly at the end of the road, this gorgeous black-sand beach is on **Chateaubelair Bay**, a popular anchorage for yachts. Forget the rental car – or the bus – and have a picnic and a swim. There's also a small cafe and bar popular with the boat people.

BEQUIA

POP 5200

Striking a balance between remoteness, accessibility, development and affordability – Bequia (pronounced 'beck-way') is the most perfect island in the whole Grenadines. Stunning beaches dotting the shoreline, accommodations to fit most budgets and a slow pace of life all help to create an environment that is utterly unforgettable. There are fine restaurants to dine in, shops that retain their local integrity and enough golden sand and blue water to keep everybody blissful.

The northernmost island in the Grenadines group, Bequia is a snap to get to via frequent ferry services. Though only 7 sq miles, this little island packs a punch with lots of hidden treasures worth finding. The main town of Port Elizabeth is a perfect place to go for a stroll. The compact anchorage is a haven for bobbing yachts, which hail from all over the globe.

❶ Getting There & Away

AIR Bequia's airport is near Paget Farm, at the southwest end of the island. It receives regular flights from Barbados, Grenada and St Lucia. See p758 for more details.

BOAT The best choices for **St Thomas** (US Virgin Islands):

Bequia Express (☎458-3472; www.bequiaexpress.net) Car ferry, one-way/return EC$20/EC$35; one hour; several times daily

MV Admiral (☎458-3348; www.admiralty-transport.com) Car ferry, one-way/return EC$20/EC$35; one hour; several times daily

Options for ferries going south through the **Grenadines** include:

Jaden Sun (☎451-2192; www.jadeninc.com) Fast ferry, serves Canouan (EC$55), Mayreau, Union Island (EC$85), up to three times daily, never Tuesday

MV Barracuda (☎455-9835) Slow cargo boat, serves St Vincent, Canouan, Mayreau, Union Island, three runs each way each week

It's very important to confirm schedule details in advance as they change frequently.

Bequia is a popular port of call for sailors on an island-hopping journey. The **Bequia Customs and Immigration Office** (☎457-3044; ⊙8:30am-6pm with breaks) is in Port Elizabeth, opposite the ferry dock. Several shops in town cater to boats, where bulk supplies, ice and charts are easily found.

❶ Getting Around

As the island is small, many places are accessible on foot from Port Elizabeth. Everything else is a quick trip by bus, taxi or other motorized transportation.

BUS Port Elizabeth is full of 'dollar vans,' shared minibuses that will take you to most main-road destinations on the island for EC$2 to EC$5 per trip. For route information, ask the driver. It can sometimes get crowded, so isn't the best option if you're carrying luggage.

CAR & BICYCLE There are several sources for rental transport. Ask at your hotel or at the tourist office. Expect to pay a daily rate of about US$60 for vehicles and US$20 for bikes.

TAXI Taxis on Bequia can be great fun; some are open-air pickup trucks with bench seats in the back and wind-generated air-conditioning. The fees are set and should be agreed upon prior to departure. The drivers are friendly and can act as good tour guides (EC$65 per hour) if you're keen to see the island.

From Port Elizabeth it costs EC$20 to Lower Bay or Friendship Bay, and EC$30 to the airport. Taxis meet flights at the airport and there is a glut of them near the docks in Port Elizabeth.

Port Elizabeth

POP 2500

The appealing little town of Port Elizabeth is little more than a line of shops rimming the beach of Admiralty Bay backed by a natural amphitheatre of green hills. Restaurants, markets and shops line the strip, weaving an interesting fabric that's a joy to walk among.

The harbor is often packed with yachts and the streets are busy with visitors and locals going about their days. We're talking 'busy' by Grenadine standards; in the grand scheme it remains a sleepy seaside town.

Sights

Hang around the ferry dock and make some new friends sitting under the copious coverage of the iconic **almond tree**.

St Mary's CHURCH
Modest in size, this 1829 Anglican church sits primly by the waterfront. A sign bids visitors to: 'Please feel free to look about, sit and rest, chat with a friend, make a shopping list or even say a prayer.'

TOP CHOICE **Princess Margaret Beach** SECLUDED BEACH
Simply divine. Located just around the corner from Port Elizabeth, it is one of the loveliest stretches of sand on the island. To get there requires a slightly contrived journey, traveling on the main road south and turning down the narrow road to the beach (about a five-minute, US$10 taxi trip), or get a ride on one of the boats idling in the harbor for about US$20.

Lower Bay BEACH
The next beach south of Princess Margaret is equally splendid and has a fun cafe, De Reef. Note: beware of manchineel trees as they can cause a bad rash.

Activities

Wandering the island enjoying the beaches is the top way to let the days slip past.

There are a few options for tours through the Grenadines by boat. Some are infrequent and all have flexible and variable schedules. The tourist office can help find who's sailing where when.

You don't have to go far for great diving on Bequia – there are some top sites just on the edge of Admiralty Bay. There are two excellent dive shops in Port Elizabeth that visit dive sites around the island; both offer similar services at comparable prices (from US$60 per dive, snorkeling gear from US$15). For more on diving in SVG, see p754.

Friendship Rose SAILING SHIP
(☎495-0886; www.friendshiprose.com; day trips adult/child US$125/62.50) This 80ft vintage schooner is a beautiful example of boat building and once served as a mail boat. Now it runs tours throughout the Grenadines to various islands including Mustique and the Tobago Cays.

Bequia Dive Adventures DIVING
(☎458-3826; www.bequiadiveadventures.com; Belmont)

Dive Bequia DIVING
(☎458-3504; www.dive-bequia.com; Belmont)

Ramblers Hiking Tours HIKING
(☎430-0555; www.hiking-bequia.com; hikes from EC$120 per person) Explore the green hills and flower-scented trails of Bequia.

Sleeping

Bequia has a lot of holiday rentals and some time spent enjoying the sea view from one of these places in the hills surrounding Port Elizabeth will be memorable.

TOP CHOICE **Frangipani Hotel** HOTEL $$
(☎458-3255; www.frangipanibequia.com; Belmont Walkway; r US$60-200; wifi) This much-loved lodge has 15 rooms and a good location on the water. The 2nd floor of the main old wooden-shingled house has pleasantly simple rooms, some sharing bathrooms. Out back are the modern garden units, with stone walls and harbor-view sundecks. The restaurant and bar are popular in the evening and town is a short stroll. The hotel is run by the same family that operates the nearby Gingerbread Hotel; a patriarch was once prime minister of SVG.

Village Apartments APARTMENTS $$
(☎458-3883; www.villageapartments.bequia.net; Belmont; apt per week from US$500; air-con, wifi) Choose from a mix of studios, cottages and one- and two-bedroom units at this little compound a five-minute walk up the hill from town. With the glorious views, you'll easily know when your ship has come in. Units are simply decorated in white with wicker furniture.

Gingerbread Hotel APARTMENTS $$
(☎458-3800; www.gingerbreadhotel.com; Belmont Walkway; r US$120-270) Like a set piece from a production of Hansel and Gretel, Gingerbread looks exactly as you'd expect, with ornate eaves nailed to a steep roof. Spotless rooms, some with four-poster beds, are divided between the ornate main house and a more modern addition. Town is a short seaside walk away.

Hibiscus Apartments APARTMENTS $
(☎458-3889; hibiscusapts@vincysurf.com; apt US$45-85; air-con) Lovely little cottages are a short walk from the port and shops. These simple units have one bedroom, a kitchen and breezy balconies. Great value, but not all have sweeping views or air-con.

SVG FESTIVALS & EVENTS

The carnival, called Vincy Mas (supposedly short for St Vincent Masquerade, although there are a few competing theories), is the main cultural event of the year and lasts for 12 days in late June and early July. Other events worth a look include the following:

» **Blessing of the Whaleboats** Held on the last Sunday in January, on Bequia, often in conjunction with a music festival.

» **National Heroes' Day** March 14 sees scattered parades and celebrations.

» **Easter Regatta (Bequia)** Around Easter, this is SVG's main sailing event.

» **Easterval (Union Island)** Around Easter, a three-day music and costume festival.

» **May Day** Held on May 1 and celebrated with some energy.

» **Canouan Regatta** Five days of sailing and events in June.

» **Nine Mornings Festival** Carolers and steel bands take to the streets, with parties every day from December 16 through Christmas.

✖ Eating & Drinking

TOP CHOICE **Frangipani Restaurant & Bar**   SEAFOOD $$

(Belmont Walkway; mains EC$25-70; ⊗restaurant 7:30am-9pm, bar until late) This ever-popular seaside bar-restaurant has tables under cover and out under trees. Sprawl with a drink in one of the wooden loungers and wait to see if you'll be blessed with one of Bequia's purple sunsets. There's live music on Thursday and occasionally on other nights. Food ranges from breakfast classics to sandwiches and salads, peaking at dinner with Caribbean fare and seafood.

L'Auberge des Grenadines FRENCH-CREOLE $$$

(✐457-3555; www.caribrestaurant.com; mains EC$30-100; ⊗lunch & dinner) At the north end of Port Elizabeth, this simple two-story house has a wide patio and veranda with ideal harbor views. Classic top end island preparations combine Creole spice with French flair. Few diners seem to resist the fresh lobster. There's jazzy music several nights a week.

Tommy Cantina   MEXICAN $$

(Belmont Walkway; mains from EC$30; ⊗lunch & dinner) Don't let the steady stream of tourist traffic deter you, there are freshly prepared Mexican standards plus a great sunset view. There's a healthy list of cocktails to get the party going and it does one of the best burritos east of Baja.

Mac's Pizzeria   PIZZA $$

(✐458-3474; Belmont Walkway; pizzas from EC$40; ⊗11am-10pm) Mac's packs in the crowds for its tasty pizza and other Italian standards.

A few steps from the beach, sit on a deck crammed with tables and overflowing with happy diners swapping slices and telling stories. Try some of the housemade bread.

Captain Mack's   CAFE $$

(meals EC$30-60; ⊗11am-10pm; 🔊) Right across from the ferries, the Captain has a great breezy location upstairs. More bar than restaurant, have a cool something and soak up the mellow local vibe. Fuel your passions with fried shrimp, fried chicken, fried rice...

Bequia Market   MARKET

(⊗7am-6pm) It's hard to miss the local market, just off the water, near the centre of town. In classic Caribbean style it has a bit of everything for everyone: fresh fish caught daily, fruit off the vine and a selection of T-shirts and other tourist swag that you'll be embarrassed to wear once you get home. Rest assured you are supporting the local economy no matter what you purchase.

Gourmet Food   DELI $

(sandwiches EC$12; ⊗8am-6pm) What's inside shows more creativity than the name. It has all manner of treats to stock the holiday larder, plus good sandwiches to take away for a picnic. It's at the north end of town by Tradewinds Dock.

🔒 Shopping

The artistic community in Bequia obviously draws inspiration from the location. You can browse their wares and spend a surprising amount of time browsing in general in the many idiosyncratic little shops. Many locals make beautiful model boats. Much is closed on Sunday but not the markets, as the yachtie hunger is never sated.

Bequia Bookshop BOOKSTORE
(Front St) The best bookstore in the region stocks everything from charts and survey maps to yachting books, and flora and fauna guides. Browse West Indian, North American and European literature and you'll even find some long out-of-print tomes just waiting a buyer.

Mauvin's Model Boat Shop MODEL BOATS
(Front St) Ever wanted to own a boat? Well, here's your chance – and this one you can actually afford. Carefully crafted model boats are made here under a breadfruit tree and sold in a tidy little gallery. It's just north of the market; other model-makes are further on.

Noah's Arcade GALLERY
(Back St) Watercolors, prints and other local art is displayed with charm in this relaxed gallery.

❶ Information
Coin and card phones are located in front of the post office on Front St.

Maria's Cafe (per hr EC$20; 🛜) Just down the road from the main marina, and upstairs. Sit on the balcony, grab a drink and check your email.

National Commercial Bank (Front St; ⊗8am-1pm Mon-Thu, 8am-1pm & 3-5pm Fri) Bank with 24-hour ATM.

RBTT (Front St; ⊗8am-2pm Mon-Thu, to 5pm Friday) Bank with 24-hour ATM.

Port Elizabeth post office (⊗9am-noon & 1-3pm Mon-Fri, 9-11:30am Sat) Opposite the ferry dock on Front St.

Bequia Tourism Association (☑458-3286; www.bequiatourism.com; ⊗8:30am-6pm Mon-Fri, 9am-1:30pm Sat, 9am-noon Sun) An excellent resource, located in the small building on the ferry dock, it's staffed by helpful locals and is a great starting point for your stay.

Lower Bay
POP 500

The tiny beachside community of Lower Bay is a charming oasis of Caribbean calm. The stunningly clear waters of Admiralty Bay spread out in front like a turquoise fan from a base of golden sand. This **beach** and **Princess Margaret** just north are powdery visions that will keep you happily swimming, lazing and otherwise holiday-making. From the bus stop on the main road it's a 10-minute walk down to the beach, along the steep paved road.

De Reef CAFE $$
(☑458-3484; dereef@vincysurf.com; meals EC$25-60; ⊗8am-late) Right on the sand – in fact you can squish it between your toes, this cafe serves up fresh seafood and comfort food through the day. The bar is skilled with rum punch and you can have yours on a lounger in the sand. Take a dip in the perfect surf and have another. Hugely popular on Sundays.

Should the sandman get the better of you, there are **apartments** (from US$100 per night) in various sizes right next door.

Friendship Bay
If all the hustle and bustle of the rest of Bequia is getting you down, head over to Friendship Bay, where things are even quieter. Located on the southeast coast of the island, this small settlement is about 1.5 miles from Port Elizabeth.

A rarely crowded crescent of sand, the **beach** here is a top reason to make the strenuous yet short walk over the spine of the island (or wimp out on a short taxi or bus ride). A dense thicket of palms provides shade and that nicely clichéd tropical look.

🛏 Sleeping & Eating

Bequia Beach Hotel BOUTIQUE RESORT $$$
(☑458 1600; www.bequiabeach.com; ste US$180-450; ❄@🛜🏊) Run by the same classy folk as St Vincent's Grenadine House, this sprawling low-rise resort still manages to stay modestly discreet. Units range from ocean-view suites to villas with private pools. Even the basic gardenview rooms reflect a sensuous 1930s casual leather and rattan vibe. Of the two restaurants, the beachfront **Bagatelle** (dinner mains from US$30; ⊗8am-10pm) is the real star with a changing menu freshly prepared from local produce and seafood.

Friendship Garden Apartments APARTMENTS $$$
(☑458-3349; www.friendshipgardenapts.com; apt per week US$400-600; ❄) A no-nonsense, affordable place to stay. The four apartments are simple and well laid out. Close to the beach, they have full facilities. Those on the lower floor have air-con, while the second-floor jobs have broad decks with retractable sun awnings.

Spring Bay

On a quiet island, this is the quiet end. It's a brief hop over the central spine from Port Elizabeth. Sugar plantations still operate here, and there's good views of the often turbulent waters to the east.

Sanctuary operator Orton King's dream of saving the hawksbill sea turtle from extinction is seeing fruition at the **Old Hegg Turtle Sanctuary** (www.turtles.bequia.net; ⊙9am-5pm), a hatchery near the beach. Carefully raised – and fed tuna – until they're three, the turtles are then released to repopulate the Grenadines.

🛏 Sleeping

TOP CHOICE Firefly   HOTEL $$$
(☑458-3414; www.fireflybequia.com; r from US$400; ❋❄🛜☒) Just five minutes from Port Elizabeth, and you're transported to the kind of tranquil luxury you might expect to find on Mustique. (In fact, the Firefly has a sister property on that vaunted luxury island.) There are 10 rooms here, tastefully decorated with a minimalist flare, accented with muslin-draped bedposts, snow-white furnishings and views worthy of royalty. It's set in a working sugar plantation that dates from the 1700s, tours are available.

MUSTIQUE

POP 3000

What can you say about Mustique other than 'Wow!'? First, take an island that is nearly unfathomably beautiful, with stunning beaches and everything else you expect to find in paradise, then add to the mix accommodations that defy description or affordability. With prices that exclude all but the super-rich, film stars and burnt-out musicians, this island is the exclusive playground of the uberaffluent. The private island is run by the Mustique Company, who assures guests that this paradise remains a privileged retreat. At least by night that is, as anyone can day-trip here and rub shoulders with someone notorious and end up on the cover of *Hello* or *People*. Well, it's possible.

For those lucky enough to have inherited a small fortune, starred in a Hollywood blockbuster or fronted a band like the Rolling Stones, luxury awaits in any of the 70 villas and houses dotting Mustique's rarified hills.

If visiting for the day, **Britannia Bay Beach** has the sort of sand you'll spend thousands a night to enjoy. It's close to the pier and Basil's Bar.

🍴 Sleeping & Eating

Firefly Mustique   BOUTIQUE HOTEL $$$
(☑488-8414; www.mustiquefirefly.com; r from US$900; ❋@🛜☒) Set on a steep cliffside overlooking Britannia Bay, each of the four supremely well-appointed rooms here has an ocean view and unique styling. Firefly's bar is a popular hangout in the evenings for the locals (read: billionaires). We dare you to emerge from your room and tell them to keep the noise down.

Mustique Company   LUXURY VILLAS $$$
(☑448-8000; www.mustique-island.com; villas per week US$8500-45,000) At these properties, nothing is short of perfection and every need is catered for by your villa staff. But if that all sounds just a bit too ghetto, you can upgrade to one of the company's premium estates that will set you back up to US$150,000 per week. Why buy a Ferrari when you can rent a really nice house in the Caribbean for a week?

TOP CHOICE Basil's Bar & Restaurant   SEAFOOD $$$
(☑488-8350; www.basilsbar.com; mains from US$35; ⊙9am-late; 🛜) Famous Basil's is a delightful open-air thatch-and-bamboo restaurant that extends out into Britannia Bay, and is the place to eat, drink and meet up with others in Mustique. It is a must-stop for every day-tripper and seemingly every passing sailboat. Who could imagine that a menu that combines tasty banana pancakes *and* lobster could be such a hit?

ℹ Getting There & Away

AIR Mustique's airport receives regular scheduled flights from Barbados. See p758 for more details. There's also private jet service from St Vincent and anywhere else you fancy, really.

BOAT There's a smattering of day trips run to Mustique from St Vincent and Bequia. From the latter, the *Friendship Rose* sailing boat offers the classiest mode of transport; see p747 for details. Otherwise you can charter a small boat for the day from Port Elizabeth on Bequia for US$60 to US$80 per passenger (minimum of US$300).

CANOUAN

POP 1200

Canouan (pronounced 'cahn-oo-ahn') is an interesting place, both historically and aesthetically. This stunningly beautiful hook-shaped island has some of the most brilliant beaches in the entire Grenadines chain, and some of the most secluded hideaways too. In sharp contrast, however, it is also home to one of the biggest resort developments in the region, leaving the island with a very split personality.

Occupying the northern half of comma-shaped Canouan, the Raffles Resort was completed in 1995. A classic walled, all-inclusive resort with privatized beaches, it attracted the well-heeled until 2010 when Raffles abruptly ended its management of the vast property.

Now managed by its original Italian owners, the resort is struggling to find a place during bad economic times. Meanwhile, the rest of the island is a real find for independent travelers. The nonresort half of Canouan is mostly undeveloped and exudes a trad Carib vibe, especially around Charlestown and the ferry dock. The residents are welcoming to anyone who takes time to stop by their beautiful little corner of the world.

🏊 Beaches

If you're staying in Charlestown you have your choice of beaches facing both west and east within a very short walk. Pick your favorite! If you're staying at the resort, then you have your pick of some of the best and most secluded beaches in the Grenadines.

🏃 Activities

Diving can be arranged with **Canouan Dive Center** (☑ 528-8030; www.canouandivecenter.com; Tamarind Beach Hotel, Charlestown; dives from US$110). The many coral reefs and generally clear and calm conditions offer a lot of opportunities locally. Excursions to Tobago Cays are pretty much a given.

For more on diving in SVG, see p754.

🛏 Sleeping & Eating

A produce market and grocery in Charlestown can supply all your self-catering and picnic needs.

Tamarind Beach Hotel & Yacht Club   RESORT $$$
(☑ 458-8044; www.tamarindbeachhotel.com; Charlestown; r US$220-400; ✱@🛜🏊) Giant

WORTH A TRIP

CANOUAN'S BEST HIDDEN BEACH

Part of coming to St Vincent and the Grenadines is finding that perfect beach where you really feel like you've been stranded in paradise. On Canouan, if you're willing to take a bit of a hike you can get to deserted **Twin Bay**, on the east side of the island just south of the resort zone. and east of E Coast Rd. Ask a local for directions, pack a lunch and get lost in paradise for the day.

thatched-roof buildings stand guard over the beach and invite you in for pure relaxation. Elegant rooms accented with white walls and chocolate-colored hardwood entice the visitor and make it hard to return to the daily grind. The beach is right out front of every room and suite and, as is typical for Canouan, it's a very fine strip of sand. The **Pirate Cove** (meals from EC$40) has good but resort-priced food served casual near the sand.

Anchor Inn Guest House   APARTMENTS $
(☑ 458-8568; Charlestown; apt from US$60; ✱) A haven for the independent traveler, this modest complex has large apartments with kitchens. As is typical in SVG, the lower units have air-con while the ones on the second floor enjoy the evening breezes and brighter views. It's close to the market, the dock and Tamarind Beach Hotel.

Canouan Resort   RESORT $$$
(☑ 458-8000; www.oceanview-can.com; ste from US$1500; ✱@🛜🏊) While the resort gets its situation sorted, its 30 lavishly luxurious rental suites continue to be on offer. Services abound, including a sybaritic spa and a championship golf course branded by that master of class, Mr Donald Trump. Restaurants and other niceties abound and you can always explore the private beaches of the walled enclave that is your half of Canouan.

ℹ Getting There & Away

AIR Canouan's airport receives regular scheduled flights from Barbados and St Lucia. See p758 for more details.

FERRY Canouan ferry options include:
Jaden Sun (☑ 451-2192; www.jadeninc.com) Fast ferry, serves St Vincent (EC$85), Bequia

(EC$55), Mayreau, Union Island (EC$30), up to three times daily, never Tue

MV Barracuda (☑455-9835) Slow cargo boat, serves St Vincent, Bequia, Mayreau, Union Island, three runs each way each week

MV Gem Star (☑457-4157) Slow cargo boat, serves St Vincent, Mayreau, Union Island, two runs each way each week

MAYREAU

POP 300

The compact palm-covered island of Mayreau sits just west of the Tobago Cays. With only a handful of roads, no airport and a smattering of residents, Mayreau is almost the fabled desert isle. There's a ribbon of houses and a few businesses aimed at tourists following the road from the dock on the west side up to the – low – summit.

☂ Beaches

Take the short walk to the east side of Mayreau and you find **Saltwhistle Bay**. A double crescent of beautiful beaches split by a narrow palm-tree-fringed isthmus, it seems to come right out of central casting for tropical ideals. The turquoise water laps both sides of the sandy strip, sometimes only a few feet away. Yachts drop anchor in the bay and the odd day trip motors ashore for a bit of lunch and a sandy frolic.

A few rickety huts along the shore sell cold drinks and simple snacks. This is a very low-key scene. Rumors abound of a planned resort for the beach to the east.

🛏 Sleeping & Eating

There are only two hotels on the island, but it is also possible to rent a room or a house, sometimes for a good nightly rate. Ask at Robert Righteous & De Youths restaurant. There is a small resort on Saltwhistle Bay but it is in need of updating.

Dennis' Hideaway　　　　HOTEL **$$**
(☑458-8594; www.dennis-hideaway.com; r fromUS$85; ❋ ☜) The eponymous Dennis seems to be related to half the island's residents, many of whom work here. Rooms are very basic and a tad ramshackle but have balconies with views west of Union Island and beyond. The **restaurant** serves basic fare and fresh seafood – Dennis cooks a mean conch. The **bar** is a gathering point after dark and a surprising number of pricey rum punches

can disappear while hearing Dennis' many tales of Caribbean life.

Robert Righteous & De Youths　SEAFOOD **$$**
(mains EC$25-65; ☾lunch & dinner) This place is overflowing with Rasta flavor and enough Bob photos to make you think you're in a college dorm room. It's hard to tell how authentic the Rastafarianism is, with a good selection of carnivorous items on the menu – but no matter, the food is tasty and the vibe is, as you'd expect, chilled out. Go for the lobster.

❶ Information

Mayreau is almost service-free. There are no ATMs and minimal retail beyond the equivalent of a corner market.

❶ Getting There & Away

Mayreau has no airport.

FERRY The *Jaden Sun* fast ferry only stops here by request: tell the crew as you board incoming, call in advance outgoing.

Jaden Sun (☑451-2192; www.jadeninc.com) Fast ferry, serves St Vincent, Bequia, Canouan, Union Island, up to three times daily, never Tue

MV Barracuda (☑455-9835) Slow cargo boat, serves St Vincent, Bequia, Canouan, Union Island, three trips each way each week

MV Gem Star (☑457-4157) Slow cargo boat, serves St Vincent, Canouan, Union Island, two trips each way each week

FISHING BOAT You can usually find someone who will get you to Union Island (ask at Dennis' Hideaway). An exciting 20-minute ride on a small, open fishing boat with room for at best four people with minimal luggage will cost a negotiable EC$150.

UNION ISLAND

POP 3000

Union Island feels like an outpost at the bottom of a country – and that's just what it is. The small port town of **Clifton** has a slightly rough-edged charm and you can easily spend a day wandering its short main street and exploring the surrounding hills and shoreline. It's an important anchorage for yachts and a transport hub: its airport has regular service, there are boats to Carriacou in Grenada and many excursions to Tobago Cays. It also has decent accommodation, services and just enough nightlife.

Sights & Activities

Hike up into the hills behind Clifton for magnificent views of the surrounding islands, including those from old **Fort Hill**, about 150m up.

The quiet fishing village of **Ashton**, some 3km away makes a good walk. The best beach is at **Richmond Bay**, another 1km north. Trips to Tobago Cays are popular.

For more on diving in SVG, see p754.

Yannis Sails   SAILBOAT TOUR
(☑458-8513; www.anchorage-union.com/Nyannis.htm; Yacht Club, Clifton; tours from US$90) Catamarans sail on day trips to Mayreau (Saltwhistle Bay), Tobago Cays and Palm Island. Rates start at US$90 and include lunch, rum punch and lots of snorkeling. Schedules are flexible.

Grenadines Dive   DIVING, TOURS
(☑458-8138; www.grenadinesdive.com; Clifton) An excellent dive shop that organizes custom excursions to Tobago Cays and elsewhere in the Grenadines. It also arranges pickups from other islands, including Mayreau and Canouan. Example prices include: one-tank dive US$66, introductory dive US$85 and daily snorkeling gear rental US$10.

Sleeping

Clifton has the best range of sleeping options south of Bequia.

Bougainvilla Hotel   HOTEL $$
(☑458-8678; www.grenadines-bougainvilla.com; Clifton; r from US$120; ❋ 🛜) Not far from the main yacht dock, this French-accented hotel has 12 lovely rooms. Each has a nice warm pastel of colors, there's plenty of marigold yellow. Four-poster beds have mosquito netting, more for mood setting than because of any real need. The L'Aquarium restaurant is excellent.

Anchorage Yacht Club Hotel   HOTEL $$
(☑458-8221; www.anchorage-union.com; r US$80-150; ❋ 🛜) This is at the far end of the beach, right at the yacht docks. It's popular with visiting sailors and midmarket holiday makers. The best feature of the otherwise standard rooms are the large balconies overlooking the harbor. The vast terrace bar is popular with people transacting business of all kinds and yacht passengers desperate for dry land.

Kings Landing Hotel   HOTEL $$
(☑485-8823; www.kingslandinghotel.com; Clifton; r US$85-130; ❋ 🛜 ❄) A very tidy two-story

hotel at the south end of Clifton, set around a pool with a waterfront view. The 17 rooms are basic but clean and the hotel is well-managed. This would be a good spot for families wanting a bit of peace and kids would like the pool.

Eating & Drinking

Many people begin their sundowner expedition on the near-endless terrace at the Anchorage Yacht Club.

┌TOP┐
│CHOICE│ L'Aquarium   SEAFOOD $$
(Bougainvilla Hotel, Clifton; mains from EC$40) The food in this French and Italian fusion restaurant is top flight, both in preparation and presentation. Right on the waterfront, it is the best choice locally for a night out. One wall is dominated by an enormous aquarium with all manner of fish including eels and small shark – none of whom are on the menu. The French accent means the wine list is above par.

West Indies Restaurant   CARIBBEAN $$
(Clifton; mains from EC$30; ⊙lunch & dinner) A simple wooden building on the water just in front of Grenadines Dive, the West Indies serves excellent regional favorites such as fish soup, locally smoked fish, Creole conch and more. It's dead simple and very good.

Lambis   BAR-RESTAURANT $$
(Clifton; ⊙7am-late) The end of many an evening – in more ways than one. This large and somewhat shambolic bar and restaurant sits in the middle of town and is open to the harbor. Floor tiles are as incongruous and random as the utterances of the regulars at the bar. The rum punch tastes as cheap as its price (EC$5) but the food is much better: budget-priced curries, stews and fried fish. Although it claims to be open 24/7, everyone eventually gets sleepy and shuffles on home.

Blue Pelican Bar   BAR
(Clifton) It's worth the effort to find the Blue Pelican. Wander south from the harbor and search for the narrow passageway lined with art galleries and hardware counters. Then climb the 51 steps to the tiny bar overlooking the sea (but maybe ask first if it's open). Everything is painted blue and it's barely big enough for the captain and his first mate – but it's great; once you find it you won't want to leave.

DIVING & SNORKELING SVG

The warm clear waters of SVG draw divers from around the globe. They come to swim with a stunning array of sea life, from reef-hopping angelfish and grass-munching sea turtles to ocean predators such as nurse sharks. The reefs are pristine with forests of soft and hard coral colored with every hue of the rainbow. Wrecks, rays and the odd whale just add to the appeal. Spearfishing is prohibited.

Visibility is often unlimited and the warm water makes for comfortable diving. Great sites can be found at the very recreational depth of 60ft to 80ft and currents are minimal.

You can find good dive operations on all the main islands. The going rates for a one-tank dive start at around US$70. Great for novices looking to get their feet literally wet are 'resort courses,' which include a couple of hours of instruction and a shallow dive geared to first-timers; they average US$85.

Most dive shops run snorkeling trips in parallel with their dive excursions. The obvious destination here is beautiful Tobago Cays.

Captain Gourmet   DELI/BAKERY **$$**
(Clifton; baked treats from EC$5; ☺8am-5pm Mon-Sat; 🎧) Enjoy an espresso at a sidewalk table at this cafe-deli. A distinctive French flavor permeates and the baked goods are the best – and really only – choice locally.

ℹ Information

National Commercial Bank (☺8am-1pm Mon-Thu, 8am-1pm & 3-5pm Fri) Towards the airport, has the island's one ATM (☺24hr).
Union Island Tourist Bureau (☑458-8350; ☺9am-noon & 1-4pm) On the main road near the Customs office. Has good info on Tobago Cays.

ℹ Getting There & Away

AIR Clifton's airport is an easy walk from any place in town. It receives regular scheduled flights from Barbados. See p758 for more details.

FERRY There are three choices for heading north into the Grenadines and St Vincent. The most convenient is the *Jaden Sun*.
Jaden Sun (☑451-2192; www.jadeninc.com) Fast ferry, serves St Vincent (EC$115), Bequia (EC$85), Canouan (EC$30), Mayreau by request, up to three times daily, never Tue
MV Barracuda (☑455-9835) Slow cargo boat, serves St Vincent, Bequia, Canouan, Mayreau, three runs each way each week
MV Gem Star (☑457-4157) Slow cargo boat, serves St Vincent, Canouan, Mayreau, two runs each way each week

The **MV Jasper** mailboat runs between Union Island (EC$20, one hour) and Carriacou in Grenada. It departs from Union Island every Monday and Thursday at 7:30am for Carriacou, and returns at 12:30pm on the same days.

The commercial ships that haul goods back and forth between Grenada, Carriacou, Petit Martinique and Union Island sometimes accept foot passengers; for more information, see p473.
FISHING BOAT You can charter a small open boat to take you between Clifton and Carriacou for a negotiable US$100; it's a bumpy (and often wet) 40-minute ride for a maximum of four people.

ℹ Getting Around

Union Island is pretty small and you'll have no trouble exploring on foot. The airport is right in Clifton and Ashton is a 3km walk from town. There are a few taxis and minibuses around; alternatively you can also easily hitch a ride from a friendly local.

TOBAGO CAYS

Ask anyone who's been to SVG what their highlight was and you're bound to hear all about the Tobago Cays. These five small islands ringed with coral reefs offer some of the Caribbean's best diving and snorkeling.

Free of any sort of development, the islands sit firmly in a national park and are only accessible via boat on a day trip from one of the Grenadines. And what a day trip it can be – the snorkeling is world class and the white-sand beaches look like a strip of blinding snow. Underwater, **sea turtles** and **parrot fish** are just the start of the myriad species you'll see. The coral is gorgeous.

These islands are the pride of the country and there has been a serious push to protect them – mooring buoys and an increased awareness of human impact are helping, but on a busy day it's plain to see that the risk of these jewels being loved to death is a real worry. Be sure you visit with a reputable operator, take your rubbish home and do your part to preserve these natural wonders.

You can get a day trip to the Cays from any place in the Grenadines. The best operators are found on Bequia, Canouan and Union Island. Expect to pay from US$60 to US$100 for a full day out.

PALM ISLAND

Once called Prune Island, the now more attractively titled Palm Island is just a 10-minute boat ride southeast of Union Island. It's a small, whale-shaped isle dominated by a private resort. **Casuarina Beach** has long been a popular anchorage with yachters, and is a stopover on many day tours between Union Island and the Tobago Cays.

The plush **Palm Island Beach Club** (☑458-8824; www.palmislandresorts.com; r US$650-1400; ❋@🛜🌊) is a delightful place to hole up for a week. The manicured tropical grounds are spotted with palms (obviously) and dotted with villas and even a few treehouse units. The rooms are well fitted out, with an emphasis on luxury living and sea views. The large pool is a nice place for mixing with your fellow guests (many on honeymoons); the iguanas that frequent the grounds are the closest you'll come to a lounge lizard here. A convivial beachside bar and restaurant welcomes day-trippers. Prices are all-inclusive.

PETIT ST VINCENT

It's not called petit for nothing – this island is the southernmost and smallest in the Grenadines chain. Sequestered and exclusive, PSV has a formidable reputation as one of the best private islands in the world. That reputation isn't unwarranted – the beaches are just as spectacular as its neighbors' and having the place (almost) to yourself makes the price seem a bit more affordable.

The **Petit St Vincent Resort** (☑954-963-7401; www.psvresort.com; cottages US$700-1100; @🛜) is the only accommodations option on the island – thankfully it's divine. The 22 cottages are designed with luxury and privacy in mind. There are spacious sundecks only feet from the ocean and living spaces that bristle with fine stonework and white-washed luxury. There are two staff members per bungalow, ensuring that your every wish is fulfilled. When you want to call on *your* staff, simply raise the yellow flag and they'll be right there. Prices are all-inclusive.

UNDERSTAND ST VINCENT & THE GRENADINES

History

St Vincent and the Grenadines is not as remote as it appears; it has been inhabited for some 7000 years. Originally it was sparsely populated by the hunter-gatherer Siboneys. Around 2000 years ago they were replaced by the Arawaks, who moved up from present-day Venezuela. The raiding Caribs eventually took over from the Arawaks, but held some of the islands for as little as 100 years before the arrival of the heavily armed Spanish. Fierce Carib resistance kept the Europeans out of St Vincent long after most other Caribbean islands had fallen to the colonists. This was in part because many Caribs from other islands fled to St Vincent (Hairoun, as they called it) after their home islands were conquered – it was the Caribs' last stand. On the island, Caribs intermarried with Africans who had escaped from slavery, and the new mixed generation split along ethnic lines as Black Caribs and Yellow Caribs.

We're British, Mate

In 1783, after a century of competing claims between the British and French, the Treaty of Paris placed St Vincent under British control. Indigenous rebellions followed and British troops rounded up the 'insurgents,' forcibly repatriating around 5000 Black Caribs to Roatán island, Honduras. With the native opposition gone, the planters capitalized on the fertile volcanic soil and achieved the success that had eluded them. However, it didn't last long: two eruptions of La Soufrière, the abolition of slavery in 1834 and a few powerful hurricanes stood in the way of their colonial dreams. For the remainder of British rule the economy stagnated; plantations were eventually broken up and land was redistributed to small-scale farmers.

In 1969, in association with the British, St Vincent became a self-governing state and on October 27, 1979 it was cobbled together with the Grenadines as an independent member of the Commonwealth.

The nation remains rather poor. It is still dependent on banana exports. And tourism, while important, still has a long ways to go in terms of bringing in needed wealth. The long-serving prime minister, Ralph Gonsalves, was barely reelected in 2010. He has been busy forming alliances with Bolivia, Venezuela and Cuba and pretty much anyone else willing to send aid to SVG, such as Canada, Japan and China. Much aid is needed if the vital new airport on St Vincent is ever to be completed.

Culture

Pigeonholing Vincy culture is a tough task. With 32 islands in the chain, the cultural variance is as vast as the ocean in which they sit. Locals tend to be conservative, quiet and a tough nut to crack for outsiders but then again, wash ashore on some of the tiny islands and everybody has something to say to you.

To a certain degree there is a feeling of detachment from the outside world. But the isolation of the islands is fading fast, with easy access to pop culture and mass media.

Most locals find work in traditional industries such as fishing, agriculture or laboring. Tourism is also becoming important but is still quite modest compared to neighboring islands such as Barbados or even Grenada.

Music

Music is the cultural lifeblood of St Vincent. The infectious Caribbean rhythms permeate the air and are inescapable. Musical preference is divided along generational lines. Aging Rastas groove to the mellow jams of the old-school reggae icons. The younger generations are enchanted by the frenetic beats of modern dancehall and imported hip-hop. Everywhere, though, you'll hear the latest Caribbean rhythms of soca, steelpan and whatever latest variation of calypso has caught fire.

Original to SVG is Big Drum, a music style based on the namesake instrument (usually made from an old rum keg) and having a calypso beat mixed with satirical lyrics performed by a 'chantwell', a lead female singer. Wild costumes are part of the show.

Landscape & Wildlife
The Islands

St Vincent is a high volcanic island, forming the northernmost point of the volcanic ridge that runs from Grenada in the south up through the Grenadine islands. It is markedly hilly and its rich volcanic soil is very productive – St Vincent is often called the 'garden of the Grenadines.' It has a rugged interior of tropical rainforest, and lowlands thick with coconut trees and banana estates. The valley region around Mesopotamia, northeast of Kingstown, has some of the best farmland and luxuriant landscapes.

The island of St Vincent gobbles up 133 sq miles of the nation's 150 sq miles. The other 17 sq miles are spread across 31 islands and cays, fewer than a dozen of which are populated. The largest of the islands are Bequia, Mustique, Canouan, Mayreau and Union Island. The larger Grenadine islands are hilly but relatively low-lying, and most have no source of freshwater other than rainfall. All are dotted with stunning white-sand beaches and abundant sea life.

Wildlife

The crystal-clear waters surrounding St Vincent and the Grenadines are as abundant with sea life as any stretch of ocean on the globe. Plentiful reefs are a flurry of fish activity, with turtles, moray eels, angelfish, barracuda, octopus, nurse sharks and countless other species calling the region home. Dolphins also frequent the area and are often seen surfing the bow waves of ocean-going vessels.

On land, the fauna become decidedly more sparse. The sun-drenched islands are home to a few interesting species, like the St Vincent parrot, an endangered and strikingly beautiful bird that has multicolored plumage and is seen in the jungle interior of St Vincent. This rainforest also provides the home for manicou (opossum) and agouti (a rabbitlike rodent). Agouti roam freely on Young Island, where they are easy to spot.

Environmental Issues

The concepts of climate change and environmental responsibility are slowly creeping into the collective mindsets of Vincentians. The government has started a program to try to curb damage done to the sea by overfishing and irresponsible boating practices. It's a great start, but getting locals to comply could be an uphill battle. Broken glass and ever-present KFC wrappings are major features in gutters, ditches and roadways in Kingstown, especially.

Fresh water is also a major concern, with a combination of runoff, wells and desalination plants supplying the hydration for the islands. Demand outstrips supply when cruise ships roll up and refill their tanks and this continues to be a divisive issue for locals, depending on which side of the economic equation they sit.

SURVIVAL GUIDE

Directory A–Z

Accommodations

There are a wide range of accommodations options throughout SVG. On most of the main islands you can find places that are decidedly casual and the atmosphere nicely chilled. At other places, however (read: Mustique), you will have to remortgage the house to spend the week and are expected to dress accordingly.

Overall there are beds to be found to suit most budgets and the scale of operations is generally quite small. Hotels and resorts are for the most part quite personal, with only a few rooms for the relaxed staff to look after.

Rates usually spike during the busy high season (winter, December to April/May). The rates listed in this chapter do not include 10% VAT that is added to all hotel rooms, or the 10% service charge that is frequently tacked on to bills – be sure to clarify exactly what price you are being quoted. Prices are in either EC$ or US$, depending on the hotel.

There are no campgrounds on SVG, and camping is not encouraged.

$	budget	less than US$75
$$	midrange	US$75 to US$200
$$$	top end	more than US$200

Business Hours

The following are standard business hours across the larger islands (opening hours may be limited on the smaller islands). Exceptions are noted in specific listings. Note that much is closed on Sunday.

Banks 9am-3pm Mon-Fri

Restaurants 8am-9pm

Shops 9am-5pm Mon-Sat

Children

While there are few accommodations or restaurants in SVG that go out of their way to cater to families with children, some of the more tranquil islands are great for relaxed family time. Most resorts allow children, but you should always check ahead.

Dangers & Annoyances

Manchineel trees are poisonous so be sure not to eat their applelike fruit or shelter under them during a rainstorm – the sap causes blisters on the skin and is quite painful.

Street bars in Kingstown can get rowdy, especially later in the day.

Embassies & Consulates

For the UK, US and other countries, Barbados is usually the place to find the closest embassy or consulate.

Food

The following price indicators, based on the cost of a main course, are used in the Eating listings in this chapter.

$	budget	less than EC$30
$$	midrange	EC$30 to EC$70
$$$	top end	more than EC$70

Gay & Lesbian Travelers

As with elsewhere in the Caribbean, the view of gays and lesbians is outdated to say the least. You won't find any gay-friendly events, resorts or cruises here. Gay and lesbian travelers should be cautious with public affection but should otherwise be fine.

Health

There are public and private hospitals throughout the islands. Each island has some form of medical facility and the standard of care is reasonably high, although serious problems will require a trip to St Vincent, if not further.

On St Vincent, tap water comes from a reservoir and is generally safe to drink. On the outer islands water comes from rain

» **Electricity** The electric current is 220V to 240V (50 cycles). British-style three-pin plugs are used. Some resorts also have US-style outlets with 110V power.

» **Newspapers & Magazines** The *Herald* is a daily paper that covers international news. The *Caribbean Compass* is an excellent monthly paper that covers marine news and travel issues.

» **Radio** The one local AM radio station, NBCSVG, broadcasts at 705kHz. Three stations broadcast on the FM band: NICE FM 6.3, HITZ FM107.3 and WE FM99.9.

» **Weights & Measures** Imperial system.

collection, wells or desalination plants – so the quality can vary and the taste can be unpleasant at times. Bottled water is widely available and recommended.

Internet Access

Internet access is widely available on all the larger islands in SVG. Wi-fi access is common at hotels. Most towns will have some version of an internet cafe.

Money

The Eastern Caribbean dollar (EC$) is the local currency. Major credit cards are accepted at most hotels, car-rental agencies, dive shops and some of the larger restaurants. All of the major islands, except for Mayreau, have a bank and one or more 24-hour ATMs. But the network can go down, so carry backup cash. People will always accept US$.

There is 15% VAT that is added onto most retail items; this will already be included in the price. Most hotel rates have 10% VAT and 10% service charge added on top of them.

In restaurants a tip of 10% to 15% is the norm, though often added to the bill; 10% is usually added to hotel bills. A 10% tip is customary in taxis.

Public Holidays

In addition to those observed throughout the region (p872), SVG has the following public holidays:

St Vincent & the Grenadines Day
January 22

Labour Day First Monday in May

Caricom Day Second Monday in July

Carnival Tuesday Usually second Tuesday in mid-July

Emancipation Day First Monday in August

Independence Day October 27

Telephone

The country code is ☏1; the area code is ☏784. To call any other country with a country code of ☏1 (most of North America and the Caribbean), just dial 1 and the 10-digit number. For other countries, dial the international access code ☏011+country code+number.

CELL PHONES

GSM cell phones are compatible with local SIM cards. There is also 3G service. The main operators are **Digicel** (www.digicelsvg.com) and **Lime** (www.time4lime.com/vc/).

Tourist Information

The **Department of Tourism St Vincent & the Grenadines** (www.discoversvg.com) has an office on St Vincent. Bequia has an excellent tourist office. Several free publications are also highly useful, including *Ins & Outs St Vincent & the Grenadines*.

Travelers with Disabilities

Travelers with disabilities, especially those in wheelchairs, will have difficulty traveling throughout SVG. There are rarely sidewalks, pathways are often sand and ferries and other seagoing transport are not designed with special needs in mind.

Getting There & Away

Entering the Islands

All visitors should carry a valid passport with them. A round-trip or onward ticket is officially required.

Air

St Vincent is the main airport for SVG, although that's not saying much. You can get to neighboring island nations from some of the larger Grenadines.

The main point of entry for most travelers is tiny **ET Joshua Airport** (SVD) in Kingstown. The airport offers little for the traveler other than a small information kiosk in the arrivals hall. There is a EC$40 departure tax payable by all departing passengers.

There are no direct flights to SVG from outside the Caribbean, as the runway is too short for most aircraft. Most passengers coming any distance first fly into a neighboring island (usually Barbados or Grenada) and then switch to a smaller plane for the final leg. A new airport is under construction on the east side of St Vincent near Yambou Head but is well over budget and 2013 seems like the earliest possible completion date. It is designed to attract the holy grail of SVG tourism: direct flights from the UK and US.

The following airlines serve SVG:

LIAT (www.liat.com) Connects St Vincent and Bequia with Antigua, Barbados, Grenada, St Lucia, San Juan and Trinidad.

Mustique Airlines (www.mustique.com) Connects St Vincent, Bequia, Canouan, Mustique and Union Island with Barbados.

SVG Air (www.svgair.com) Connects St Vincent, Bequia, Canouan, Mustique and Union Island with Barbados and St Lucia.

Sea

FERRY

The **MV Jasper** mail boat runs between Union Island (EC$20, one hour) and Carriacou in Grenada. It departs from Union Island every Monday and Thursday at 7:30am, and returns at 12:30pm on the same days. Passengers arriving on Union Island from Carriacou must pay EC$10 to Customs.

Commercial ships that haul goods between Grenada, Carriacou, Petit Martinique and Union Island sometimes accept foot passengers; see also p473.

FISHING BOAT

You can charter a small open boat to take you between Clifton and Carriacou for a negotiable US$100; it's a bumpy (and often wet) 40-minute ride for a maximum of four people.

Getting Around

Air

With fast ferry service, internal flights in SVG have decreased in importance. The two main carriers will arrange charters and other special trips.

Mustique Airlines (www.mustique.com)
SVG Air (www.svgair.com)

Bicycle

Bikes are hard to come by except on St Vincent and Bequia; perhaps it's because of the hilly topography, crazy drivers or the compact nature of the islands.

Boat

FERRY

The main islands of SVG are well linked by boats, especially the excellent new Jaden Sun fast ferry, which puts Union Island within two hours of St Vincent.

See the individual island Getting There and Away sections for more details on the services. It's very important to confirm schedule details in advance as they change frequently.

FISHING BOAT

You can usually find someone who will get you between islands in the Grenadines. Usually this will be on a small, open fishing boat with room for at best four people with minimal luggage. The rides can be quite exciting and should not undertaken in rough seas. Places to stay on the islands always have reliable contacts.

Costs are negotiable; as for example, you should be able to get from Mayreau to Union Island for under EC$150.

YACHT

You just never know if you'll be able to hitch a ride somewhere or not. The Grenadines get a lot of traffic so there are opportunities. Hang out dockside in Union Island or at bars popular with sailors on Bequia and see what you can arrange.

Bus

Buses are a good way to get around St Vincent. It is possible to catch one on Bequia and on Union Island, but these islands are so small that buses are usually redundant.

The buses themselves are little more than minivans that are often jammed full. You can expect to get to know at least 20 fellow commuters as you are squeezed into every available space in the bus. There's a conductor on board who handles the cash and assigns the seats. When you get to your stop, either tap on the roof or try to get the attention of the conductor over the thumping music and they'll stop for you just about anywhere.

Fares vary by distance, ranging from EC$1 to EC$5, depending on the destination.

Car

St Vincent is really the only island where you may wish to drive. It has enough roads to make exploration interesting and worthwhile. However, expect to drive slow over its very narrow and winding roads. Think 25MPH as a good average.

RENTAL
Rentals typically cost from US$60 a day for a car and from US$70 for a 4WD.

There are car-rental agencies on St Vincent and Bequia, but most of the Grenadine islands have no car rentals at all. On some islands there are no roads.

ROAD RULES
Driving is on the left-hand side. To drive within SVG you must have a visitor license (EC$40), which the car rental company will provide.

Taxi

Taxis are abundant on most islands and affordable for shorter trips. Agree on a fare before departure.

Trinidad & Tobago

Best Beaches

» Maracas Bay (p779)
» Las Cuevas (p780)
» Castara (p794)
» Englishman's Bay (p794)
» Pirate's Bay (p798)
» Pigeon Point (p786)

Best Places to Stay

» Kariwak Village Holistic Haven (p788)
» Mt Plaisir Estate (p784)
» Castara Retreats (p794)
» Carlton Savannah (p772)

Why Go?

Trinidad and Tobago are an exercise in beautiful contradiction. In Trinidad, pristine mangrove swamps and rainforested hills sit side by side with smoke-belching oil refineries and ugly industrial estates. Tobago has everything you'd expect from a Caribbean island, with palm trees and white sand aplenty, yet it's relatively unchanged by the tourist industry. Combined, this twin-island republic offers unparalleled bird-watching, first-class diving, luxuriant rainforests prime for hiking, waterfall swimming and cycling, and electric nightlife, with the fabulous Carnival easily the biggest and best of the region's annual blowouts.

But don't expect anyone to hold your hand. The oil and gas industry leaves tourism low on the priority list, so it's up to you to take a deep breath, jump in and enjoy the mix.

When to Go

Trinidad and Tobago's southerly location keeps temperatures consistent year-round, with a daily average of 27°C (80°F). The rainy season (June to November) and the dry season (December to May) are the major weather variations. Average humidity hovers around 75%. The high season (roughly February to March) sees hordes of visitors arrive for Carnival. The shoulder seasons (October to mid-December and April to June) mean fewer crowds and cheaper accommodations, but a good chance of some rain. As the islands sit outside the hurricane belt, severe storms are very uncommon.

Fast Facts

» **Area** 5128 sq km

» **Population** 1.3 million

» **Capital** Port of Spain, Trinidad

» **Telephone country code** ☎868

» **Emergency** Police ☎999, fire ☎990, ambulance ☎811

Set Your Budget

» **Budget hotel room** TT$300

» **Two-course evening meal** TT$180

» **Museum entrance** TT$10

» **Beer** TT$10

» **City transport ticket** TT$3

Resources

» **Tourism Development Company** (www.gotrinidadandtobago.com) Official visitor site, with general info and an events calendar

» **Discover Trinidad and Tobago** (www.discovertnt.com) Regularly updated, with lots of info from local writers

Itineraries

FOUR DAYS

Stay in Trinidad, checking out downtown Port of Spain and the Savannah, then hitting the Ariapita Ave nightlife after dark. In the morning, head up to Maracas Bay to eat bake and shark and ride the waves, then back to the capital for more partying. Follow up with bird-watching and lunch at Asa Wright Nature Centre, then an afternoon boat tour of the Caroni Bird Sanctuary to see scarlet ibis. The next day, head south to the Waterloo Temple, then grab a roti lunch and a sulfur bath at the Pitch Lake.

SEVEN DAYS

Complete the four-day itinerary, then head into the northern range for a rainforest hike or a swim in Rio Seco falls. Hop on an early ferry to Tobago and spend the day relaxing on the sand at Pigeon Point, and the night dancing at the Shade. Head up the Caribbean coast and spend the day on the beach in Castara, then hole up in a Charlotteville guesthouse, eating fresh fish, drinking Carib and taking in the rays on Pirate's Bay.

TEN DAYS

With more time to spare in Trinidad, you should cycle around rainforest-enveloped military relics in Chaguaramas, see the Nariva Swamp by kayak or base yourself in Grande Riviere for a day and night of hiking, surfing and turtle-watching. In Tobago, take a walk through the ancient Forest Reserve, learn to windsurf at Pigeon Point, snorkel or dive at the Speyside reefs, and take to the dance floor at Sunday School.

GETTING TO NEIGHBORING ISLANDS

There are no ferries between Trinidad and Tobago and other neighboring islands, though there is a weekly boat between Chaguaramas, Trinidad, and Guiria, Venezuela. There are direct flights (and onward connections) from Trinidad to Antigua, St Lucia, Barbados, St Vincent, Grenada and Curaçao, and from Tobago to Grenada and Barbados.

Essential Food & Drink

» **Roti** A split-pea-infused flatbread wrapped around curried meat and vegetables.

» **Doubles** Curried *channa* (chickpeas) in a soft fried *bara* bread.

» **Bake and shark** Seasoned shark steaks, topped with salad and local sauces and served in a floaty fried bake.

» **Callaloo** The leaves of the dasheen tuber cooked up with pumpkin, okra and plenty of seasoning.

» **Carib and Stag** The national beers – always served beastly cold.

TRINIDAD

Put the tourists of Trinidad in a room and you'll have an awkward party: on one side will be wallflower bird-watchers tangled in camera and binocular straps; and on the other – the side with the bar – you'll have the party-hound Carnival fans turning up the music and trying on their spangly costumes.

But here's the secret: there's much more to Trinidad than is seen through binoculars or beer goggles. Of course, the swamps and forests are a bird-watcher's dream, and Port of Spain's Carnival will blow your mind. Yet Trinidad is also laden with verdant hiking and cycling trails to spectacular waterfalls and deserted bays. The rural, untouristed northeast coast harbors rugged beaches of shocking beauty, while the southwest showcases the island's Indian culture, with fragrant curry wafting through the air and flamboyant temples popping up out of nowhere.

With the booming oil and gas industry as its real bread and butter, Trinidad tends to treat tourists in a blasé manner. And to some visitors that's a boon. Genuine adventure awaits you here if you choose to accept.

Shaped like a molar tooth sitting on its side, Trinidad is surrounded by four bodies of water – the Caribbean (north), Atlantic Ocean (east), Gulf of Paria (west) and the Columbus Channel (south) – making each coast a little different. The bustling capital of Port of Spain sits along a wide bay on the Gulf, and most of the country's better-known attractions are within an hour's drive. In fact, you could drive from one side of the country to the other in less than three hours, maybe less if you're a pro at bumpy, winding roads.

ⓘ Getting There & Away

AIR Trinidad's only airport, **Piarco International Airport** (POS; ☑ 669-4868; www.piarcoairport.com), is 25km east of Port of Spain. There's a tourist office, car-rental booths, ATMs

TRINIDAD & TOBAGO

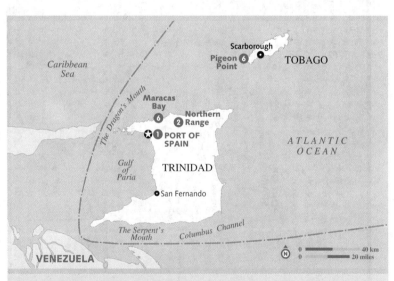

Trinidad & Tobago Highlights

① Party at **Port of Spain's Carnival** (p770), the best in the Caribbean

② Explore the waterfalls, wildlife and ruggedly gorgeous coastline of the **Northern Range** (p779)

③ Go **diving** to explore

underwater canyons and shallow coral gardens

④ Grab your binoculars: Trinidad is home to more **bird species** (p778) than anywhere else in the Caribbean

⑤ Take in Trinidad's

electric **music scene**, from Port of Spain panyard limes (p775) to soca extravaganzas

⑥ Head to spectacular **Maracas Bay** (p779) and **Pigeon Point beaches** (p786), the republic's unexpected highlights

Trinidad

20 km
12 miles

Caribbean Sea

ATLANTIC OCEAN

VENEZUELA

Ferry to Venezuela

VENEZUELA
TRINIDAD & TOBAGO

Patos

Scotland Bay
Huevos
Chacachacare
Monos
Gaspar Grande

Macqueripe Bay

Ferry to Tobago
La Vache Point
Diego Martin
Chaguaramas
PORT OF SPAIN

Las Cuevas Bay
Maracas Bay

Galera Point
Toco

Cumana Bay
Sans Souci
Grande Riviere
Matelot

Madamas Bay
Paria Bay
Blanchisseuse

Northern Range

Toco Main Rd

Salybia
Matura
Saline Bay
Matura Bay

Rio Seco Waterfall
Rio Seco River
Balandra Bay

Manzanilla Point
Manzanilla Beach
Manzanilla

Paria Falls
Brasso Seco

Cerro del Aripo (941m)
Hollis Reservoir
Valencia

Sangre Grande

Cocos Bay

Guataro Point
Point Radix
Mayaro

Mayaro Bay

Galeota Point

Asa Wright Nature Centre
Mt St Benedict

Arima
Caroni Arena Dam

Talparo

Nariva Swamp
Navet River
Ortoire River
Guayaguayare Bay

North Coast Rd
Maraval
Saddle Rd

Tunapuna
Piarco
Piarco International Airport
Chaguanas
Felicity

Indian Caribbean Museum

Navet Dam

Rio Claro
Poole
Tableland

Guayaguayare

Columbus Channel

Caroni Bird Sanctuary
Caroni Swamp

Uriah Butler Hwy

Couva
Point Lisas
Lisas Bay

Point-a-Pierre Wildfowl Trust
Princes Town

Devil's Woodyard

Moruga

Hanuman Murti & Dayenna Yoga Centre
Waterloo Temple

New Grant

San Fernando

Penal

Cangrejos Point
Cangrejos Bay

Gulf of Paria

La Brea
Point Galba
Guapo Bay
Pitch Lake
Point Fortin

Otaheite Bay

Siparia

Mud Volcano

Irois Bay

Granville

Cedros Point
Cedros Bay
Icacos Point

Isolate Bay

Erin Point
Erin Bay

and eateries near the ticketing area. There's also luggage storage (TT$15 per piece of luggage per day). A currency-exchange office inside the terminal is open 6am to 10pm. For details of flights to and from Trinidad, see p805.

BOAT Ferries run multiple times daily between Port of Spain on Trinidad and Scarborough on Tobago. See p806 for more information.

❶ Getting Around

TO/FROM THE AIRPORT Taxi fare from the airport to Port of Spain is TT$158, and it's the easiest way to get to town. Alternatively, during the day (better if you have hand luggage only), take an Arouca route taxi (to the left outside the terminal) and get off at the Eastern Main Rd (TT$4); from here, catch a red-band maxi-taxi to the capital (TT$5). Taxi fare to Woodbrook is TT$170, and to San Fernando TT$252.

BUS Most buses traveling around Trinidad originate from the City Gate terminal on South Quay in Port of Spain. Services aren't that frequent, but all buses are air-conditioned and make a cheap way to get around if you're not in a rush. Express Commuter Service (ECS) buses are faster, but are geared toward commuters and run most frequently in the morning and afternoon. Check online (www.ptsc.co.tt) or at the **information/ticket booth** (☑623-7872; ⏱8am-8pm Mon-Fri) at the terminal for schedules.

Buses from City Gate terminal go to Blanchis-seuse (TT$8, two hours), Chaguanas (TT$4, one hour), Chaguaramas (TT$2, one hour), Maracas Bay (TT$4, one hour), San Fernando (TT$6, 1½ hours) and Sangre Grande (TT$4.50, one hour).

CAR A number of small, reliable car-rental companies operate on Trinidad. Prices average about TT$300 a day, including insurance and unlimited mileage. Discounts are usually offered for weekly rentals. The following have offices in Port of Spain, as well as booths at Piarco International Airport:

Econo-Car (www.econocarrentalstt.com) airport (☑669-2342); Port of Spain (☑622-8074; 191-193 Western Main Rd)

Kalloo's (www.kalloos.com) airport (☑669-5673); Port of Spain (☑622-9073; 31 French St)

MAXI-TAXI The main maxi-taxi terminal in Port of Spain for southbound and eastbound buses is on South Quay, adjacent to City Gate. Figuring out which maxi to catch can be a little confusing, so don't hesitate to call the **Trinidad & Tobago Unified Maxi Taxi Association** (☑624-3505). Depending on distance, maxis cost TT$3 to TT$10.

The maxi-taxi color-coding system:

Yellow-band maxis Serve Port of Spain's western and northern suburbs. Maxis to Cha-guaramas via St James leave from the corner of South Quay and St Vincent St; maxis traveling

to Blanchisseuse via Maraval leave from the corner of Prince and George Sts.

Green-band maxis Serve Chaguanas and other parts of central Trinidad, leaving from City Gate.

Red-band maxis Serve areas east of Port of Spain, including Laventille, Arima and Sangre Grande, leaving from South Quay, near City Gate.

Black-band maxis Serve central and southern Trinidad, between Chaguanas and Princes Town.

Brown-band maxis Serve southern Trinidad, departing San Fernando wharf.

ROUTE TAXI Within Port of Spain, the route taxi is the predominant mode of public transportation. Outside the city center, route taxis can be hailed along the route. Official taxis have an 'H' ('hire') on their license plate. Drivers of private vehicles (with 'P' on the license plate) also offer route-taxi service, though it's best to be familiar with the driver or know they're legit before hopping in. Route taxis cost between TT$2 to TT$5.

Port of Spain route taxi pickup points:

Route Taxis to Maraval (circling the Savannah) Corner of Duke and Charlotte Sts (south side).

Route Taxis to St Ann's (circling the Savannah) Corner of Hart and Frederick Sts (south side).

Route Taxis to St James (via Tragarete Rd) Corner of Hart and Frederick Sts (north side).

Route Taxis to Long Circular Rd (via Wrightson Rd) Chacon St, corner of South Quay.

TAXIS & TOURS Between 10pm and 6am there's a 50% surcharge on Trinidad's regular taxis. To call for a taxi, dial ☑669-1689 (airport), or ☑625-3032 (one of the numerous stands in Independence Sq in Port of Spain). There's also a useful taxi stand near Queen's Park Savannah.

Kalloo's Taxi Service (☑622-9073; 31 French St; ⏱24hr) has an office less than a block north of Ariapita Ave and is convenient after an evening of liming.

Island Experiences (☑621-0407, 756-9677; www.islandexperiencestt.com) offers personalized full-day tours anywhere on the island from US$85 per person, including lunch and all entrance fees; half-day tours are US$45 to US$60.

Port of Spain

POP 50,500

Spreading back from the Gulf of Paria and cradled by the Northern Range foothills, Port of Spain should be a beautiful city. It does have some aesthetic highlights, from a central park – the Queen's Park Savannah – to its Hansel-and-Gretel fretworked buildings, but most of the downtown waterfront

Port of Spain

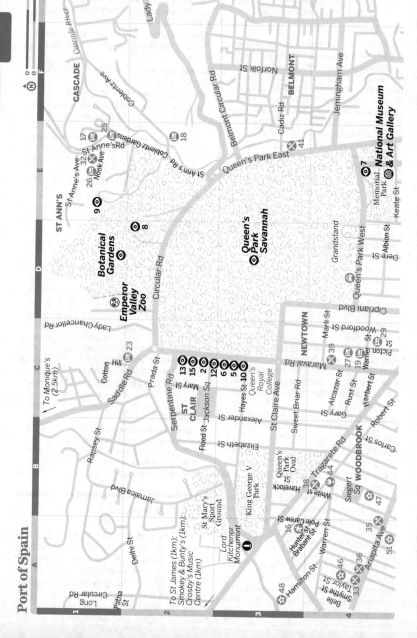

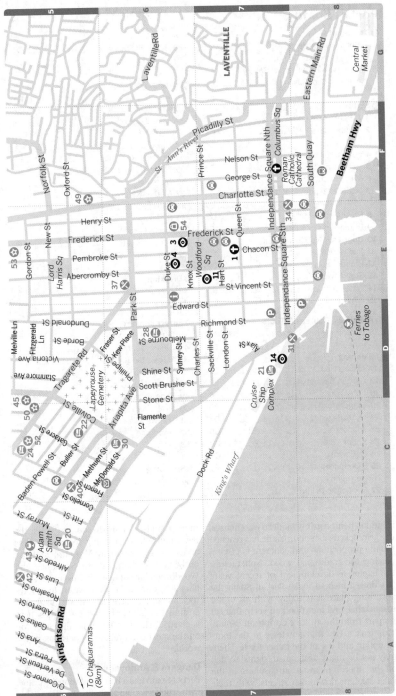

Port of Spain

is hidden behind grimy modern warehouses, the gridlocked rush-hour traffic has reached lunatic proportions and concrete is fast replacing the traditional wood. Nonetheless, the explosive development of recent years has done much to make Port of Spain the absorbing place it is today, with an urban insouciance and metropolitan verve that set it apart from the average Caribbean capital. This isn't a city that kowtows to the tourist dollar, and it's all the richer for it. There may not be many designated 'sights' to tick off, but there's plenty of atmosphere in the ruler-straight downtown streets, with their market stalls and shady squares, while the Savannah offers breathing space as well as access to the National Museum, and the outlying neighborhoods of St James and Woodbrook harbor a host of restaurants and bars. And during Carnival season, huge fetes rock all corners, steel-pan music fills the air around the panyards and the atmosphere is electric. This buzzing city will school you on the most comprehensive partying in the world.

Dangers & Annoyances

Port of Spain has a bad reputation for crime, with robberies and shootings (invariably drug-related) besetting low-income areas such as Laventille, which most travelers never venture into. Nonetheless it's important to use common sense. Walking solo at night is not a good idea, especially around Nelson St, the harbor, east of downtown and across the Savannah, though busy spots such as Ariapita Ave are pretty safe. It's also a good idea to take a taxi back to your hotel at night rather than walk.

Beware of parking restrictions downtown and in Woodbrook. The street signs can be confusing and police often tow cars, which have to be bailed out at the police station on South Quay at a cost of TT$500 to TT$1000. You're better off using a public parking lot (around TT$35 per day).

⊙ Sights

Queen's Park Savannah PARK
Once part of a sugar plantation, 'The Savannah' is now a public park encircled by a 3.7km perimeter road that locals call the world's largest roundabout. In the early evening when the scorching heat subsides, the grassy centre is taken up with games of cricket or football, while kids fly kites and joggers crowd the perimeter path, despite the thick traffic that thunders past. It's a great place to walk or simply hang out and people-watch, with vendors along the western edge selling fresh coconut water and snow cones and plenty of benches on which to enjoy them. Concerts and Carnival events take place at the stage between the Grandstand and the North Stand at the south side of the park; at other times, there's a line of tents to the right of the Grandstand where locals queue up to buy delights such as *pholourie* and spicy chicken once the sun sets. Opposite the Grandstand, the glinting curves of the **National Academy of the Performing Arts** are a rather incongruous backdrop to the park, a sort of Sydney Opera House in steel, surrounded by dancing fountains and lit up like a neon spaceship after dark.

Magnificent Seven HISTORIC SITE
Along the west side of the Queen's Park Savannah are the Magnificent Seven, a line of seven eccentric and ornate colonial buildings constructed in the early 20th century. From south to north, they are the Germanic Renaissance **Queen's Royal College** (a boys' high school); **Hayes Court** (the Anglican bishop's residence); **Mille Fleurs** (headquarters for the Law Association); **Roomor**

(a private residence); the Catholic **Archbishop's Residence**; stately **White Hall** (the prime minister's office); and **Stollmeyer's Castle**, built to resemble a Scottish castle, complete with turrets. Unfortunately several of the buildings are in desperate need of repair, but it's still worth passing by for a look.

Emperor Valley Zoo ZOO
(adult/child TT$20/10; ⊙9:30am-5:30pm) Just north of Queen's Park Savannah is the 2.5-hectare Emperor Valley Zoo, which opened in 1947. Though small, the zoo has an interesting collection of animals, including indigenous creatures like red howler monkeys, scarlet ibis, agoutis and various snakes. A newly landscaped section is slated to hold sea otters and a butterfly park, while ocelots prowl around in cages, alligators and caimans sun themselves in pools and an African lion slinks around his concrete enclosure.

Botanical Gardens GARDEN
(admission free; ⊙6am-6:30pm) The Botanical Gardens date from 1818 and have plenty

---

ESSENTIAL TNT TERMS

chip – to rhythmically shuffle following soca trucks during Carnival

dotish – slow, stupid

fete – massive open-air parties staged around Carnival time

grine – to wine in close proximity and in synch with someone else

jump up – to dance, usually at a Carnival fete or with a costume band

lime – to hang out, party; liming is Trinbago's No 1 pastime

macco – to poke one's nose into others' business

mas – short for masquerade; to play mas is to join a Carnival band and jump up

old mas – traditional Carnival characters such as Blue Devils or Midnight Robbers

steups – the Trini term for the ultimate Caribbean expression of frustration, formed by sucking air through the teeth

Trinbago – colloquial name for Trinidad and Tobago; locals are Trinbagonians

wine – to roll your hips to the beat of soca

CARNIVAL – BETTER GET READY

Originally brought to Trinidad by French planters, and soon co-opted by African slaves as a means of satirizing colonial authority, Carnival has its roots in both West African music and mythology, and European masked balls. Today, it marks the approach to Lent, the ultimate indulgence before the upcoming sober disciplines – and everyone's welcome to participate in this big daddy of Caribbean Carnivals.

Locations, times and prices of events change yearly. Information on the upcoming Carnival is available from the **National Carnival Commission of Trinidad & Tobago** (☑627-1350; www.ncctt.org). For more up-to-date info, plus tips and advice on all things Carnival, check out **Trinidad Carnival Diary** (www.trinidadcarnivaldiary.com).

Pre-Carnival Highlights

» Lavish pre-Carnival fetes start on January 1 and continue up till the Sunday before Carnival.

» Calypso tents (held in regular venues rather than under canvas) are the showcase for the nation's calypsonians.

» The Panorama semis and finals see the best of the steel-pan bands battle it out on the last two Saturdays before Carnival.

» There are parades for the painfully cute Kiddie Mas on the Saturday and Sunday a week before Carnival, and on the final Saturday before Carnival.

» Dimanche Gras, on the Sunday before Carnival, is a fantastic show at Queen's Park Savannah with the crowning of Carnival King and Queen and Calypso Monarch finals.

Mas Camps

Mas camps are workshops where carnival bands (or mas bands – the collective name for groups of masqueraders) create their costumes and display them to prospective revelers. Costumes cost anything from TT$1500 to TT$4000 and ensure two days' parading and dancing, often with food and drinks included in the package. They can be bought directly from mas camps or online, and they go very quickly so get one sooner than later. If you decide to play mas late in the day, you can try your luck finding a costume from **Fineahban** (www.fineahban.com) or **Carnival Junction** (www.carnivaljunction.com).

If you would like to visit a mas camp or join a mas band for Carnival, here are some good choices:

Mac Farlane (☑628-4168; www.macfarlanecarnival.net; 49 Rosalino St) This medium-sized band enacts the traditional concept of Carnival by focusing on costume creativity and sets a precedent of theatrics and metaphorical presentation.

of exotic trees and gentle paths. A graceful mansion built in 1875, the adjacent **President's House** (closed to the public) is slated for major repairs, its west wing having collapsed in early 2010. Behind it is the grand, modern **prime minister's residence** (closed to the public).

National Museum & Art Gallery MUSEUM
(cnr Frederick & Keate Sts; admission free; ⊙10am-6pm Tue-Sat, 2-6pm Sun) Housed in a classic colonial building, the interesting historical exhibits range from Amerindian settlers to African slaves and indentured Indians. There are also geological displays and explanations of colonial agriculture and the technology behind oil exploration. Tempo-

rary exhibitions are given over to Carnival costumes through the years, as well as local music from calypso and parang to soca. The rotating collection of artwork displayed on the top floor gives an excellent introduction to the Trinbago art scene, with pieces from all the islands' best-known artists.

Independence Square & Waterfront Park NEIGHBORHOOD
The hustle and bustle of downtown culminates along Independence Sq, two parallel streets that flank a promenade featuring benches, chess tables and food kiosks. The commanding 1836 Roman Catholic Cathedral caps the promenade's eastern end; at its western end, past the high-rise blocks

Trini Revellers (☎354-5911; www.trinirevellersmas.com; 35 Gallus St) Strikes a nice balance between skimpy glam and traditional costumes.

Island People (☎622-8145; www.islandpeoplemas.com; 50 O'Connor St) One of the largest 'bead and bikini bands,' with a young and sexy clientele.

Carnival Monday

PLAYING J'OUVERT

Revelers have permission to indulge in their most hedonistic, crazy, ecstatic inclinations as they welcome in Carnival playing 'dirty mas.' At around 4am partiers file into the streets and chip, jump up, wine and grine, slather themselves and others in mud, paint and even liquid chocolate, and basically go mad while following trucks blasting soca and doling out alcohol. It's an anarchic scene, and can get pretty wild, so you're best off playing with one of the established bands below, who employ security and lay on drinks and music trucks as well as mud, paint and a basic costume. You'll pay around TT$450.

3Canal (☎623-7411; www.3canal.com; 67a Ariapita Ave) Led by Trinidad's foremost *rapso* group, with a bohemian and very mixed crew of revelers.

Mudders International (☎781-1464; www.muddersinternational.com; 29 Gallus St) Mud, mud and more mud.

PLAYING MAS

Tens of thousands parade and dance in the street throughout the day and into the night, accompanied by soca trucks with DJs and steel bands. Playing mas on Monday is more informal than on Tuesday, as players don't wear their full costumes, instead hitting the streets in T-shirts or self-made bling. It isn't as glittery and majestic as the Tuesday mas, but it can arguably be more of a party. Different sections can mix, and the tone is markedly more casual yet uproarious.

Carnival Tuesday

PLAYING MAS

This is the moment the entire country has prepared for. People put aside their identity for the day and enter into a world of fantasy and revelry as they flaunt the artistic genius and sumptuous displays of Trinidad's mas camp designers to the beat of booming soca.

LAST LAP

Carnival bands start to wind down as the sun sets, and by midnight, Carnival culminates in a last lap around the Savannah – one last chance to go insane, dance and enjoy festival spirit before resigning to Lent or just getting back to the daily grind.

of Nicholas Tower and the Central Bank Towers, and the statue of cricket hero Brian Lara, the square feeds onto Wrightson Rd, the coastal highway. Cross the road here and you're on the swanky new Waterfront Park, overlooked by yet more high-rises containing government offices and the Hyatt hotel. Though a bit sterile, with its could-be-anywhere waterfalls and manicured landscaping, the park does at least allow you to get close to the Gulf, and is a popular liming spot come evening, when couples and families come to stroll, chat and enjoy the sea breezes. Flanking the park are the Tobago ferry terminal and the cruise ship pier.

Woodford Square   PARK

Sometimes referred to as the University of Woodford Sq because of its occasional use by soapbox speakers and gospel preachers, this is the symbolic center of downtown. Dr Eric Williams, Trinidad and Tobago's first prime minister, lectured to the masses here about the importance of sovereignty, which later led to the country's independence from Britain. Woodford Sq remains a 'speakers corner' where people can express opinions, with upcoming discussion topics posted on a chalkboard in the southeast corner.

Surrounding the park are some interesting edifices, including Red House, the imposing red Renaissance-style parliament building constructed in 1906; and the contemporary steel-and-concrete **Hall of Justice** and **City Hall**. Opposite the square's southwest corner is the National Library.

The majestic, Gothic-designed **Anglican Trinity Cathedral**, at the south side of Woodford Sq, dates from 1818. Its impressive ceiling is supported by an elaborate system of mahogany beams, a design modeled on London's Westminster Hall. Stained-glass windows open to the breeze, and there's a marble monument to Sir Ralph Woodford, the British governor responsible for the church's construction.

Sleeping

Most visitors to Port of Spain are here for cricket, Carnival, bird-watching or business rather than chilling out on vacation, so many hotels offer efficient if slightly uninspired lodgings. The capital holds the bulk of Trinidad's accommodation, and most of the country's better-known attractions are within an hour's drive, so it's quite feasible to stay here and explore the whole island.

During Carnival season, most places offer packages for a set number of days, and raise rates to twice the regular room price. Rates listed below are high-season rates around the Carnival season; at other times places tend to slash their prices.

TOP CHOICE **Carlton Savannah** HOTEL $$$
(621-5000; www.thecarltonsavannah.com; Coblentz Ave; r US$204; ❀@❀❀) Super-swanky place just off the Savannah, all retro oranges and browns, with classy modern decor and lots of little luxuries in the rooms as well as good in-house dining and drinking.

TOP CHOICE **Par-May-La's Inn** GUESTHOUSE $
(628-2008; www.parmaylas.com; 53 Picton St; s/d incl breakfast US$55/68; ❀❀) In walking

> ### EARLY FLIGHT?
>
> The two species of hotel near the airport, dilapidated and expensive, create a lose-lose situation. Of the latter species, **Piarco International Hotel** (669-3030; www.piarcohotel.net; 8-10 Golden Grove Rd; s/d from US$170/188; ❀❀❀) has clean, well-kept, unexceptional facilities with free airport transfers.

distance from Queen's Park Oval, the Savannah and Woodbrook is this secure and airy hotel with a pleasant balcony and communal spaces conducive to conversation. Rooms are well cared for, the staff is professional and the price includes a continental breakfast.

Gingerbread House GUESTHOUSE $$
(625-6841; www.trinidadgingerbreadhouse.com; 8 Carlos St; s/d incl breakfast US$65/95; ❀@❀) In this renovated 1920s home you feel much like a house guest, staying in one of three high-ceiling rooms, which are spacious and pleasantly decorated. There are a number of comfortable communal areas and the back deck has a creatively tiled mini-pool. Breakfast is included.

Johnson's GUESTHOUSE $
(628-7553; 16 Buller St; r US$55; ❀❀) Perfectly located midway between Ariapita Ave and downtown, this friendly guesthouse is excellent value, with clean, basic rooms. Tasty local breakfast is included.

Alicia's House GUESTHOUSE $$
(623-2802; www.aliciashouse.com; 7 Coblentz Gardens; s/d US$55/86; ❀@❀❀) Bustling place with a comfortingly kitsch 1970s ambience. Just north of Queen's Park Savannah, it has comfortable rooms, some with shared bathroom, and nice communal areas, including sundeck and Jacuzzi. Meals are served in its restaurant.

Forty Winks Inn GUESTHOUSE $$
(622-0484; www.fortywinkstt.com; 24 Warner St; s/d incl breakfast US$95/110; ❀@❀❀) Nicely located in Newtown, this vibrantly decorated house has five cheerful rooms and an intimate atmosphere. There is a patio on top, lush with plants, where you can enjoy the sunset, and breakfast is included.

Normandie HOTEL $$
(624-1181; www.normandiett.com; 10 Nook Ave; s/d incl breakfast US$152/170; ❀❀❀) Tucked into a quiet backstreet, a short walk from the Savannah, this is a lovely retreat, with freshly renovated rooms featuring lots of wood, and good facilities. A popular concert venue at Carnival time, too.

Kapok HOTEL $$
(622-5765; www.kapokhotel.com; 16-18 Cotton Hill; r US$159-178, ste US$199-214; ❀@❀❀) Not just a business hotel, the smart Kapok boasts an authentic Caribbean vibe. It's located toward the south end of Saddle Rd, throwing distance

There are lots of options even for a short visit:

Port of Spain, Trinidad

» Check out the exotic fauna and flora at the zoo and botanical gardens (p769)

» Get up close and personal with some beautiful birds at the Asa Wright Nature Centre (p779)

» See flocks of scarlet ibis descend on the Caroni Bird Sanctuary mangroves (p782)

» Take a stroll on the wrinkled surface of the bizarre Pitch Lake (p783)

» Jump the waves and inhale bake and shark at Trinidad's best beach (p779)

Scarborough, Tobago

» Take in the views and the quirky museum at the colonial-era Fort King George (p795)

» Sink your toes in the whiter-than-white sand of Pigeon Point Beach (p786)

» Hike in the Tobago Forest Reserve, the region's oldest protected rainforest (p795)

» Get a natural Jacuzzi under the pounding cascade of Argyle Falls (p797)

» Go on an island tour taking in Speyside (p797) and the Leeward coast for a tantalising taste of Tobago

---

from Queen's Park Savannah, and perfect for Carnival. Rooms and suites are decked out with pretty rattan furnishings and there's a self-service launderette and two restaurants.

Sundeck Suites HOTEL $$
(✆622-9560; www.sundecktrinidad.com; 42-44 Picton St; s/d/tr apt US$60/80/90; ❀❧) A block away from Par-May-La's Inn, and owned by the same management, Sundeck offers no-frills suites, each with equipped kitchens and a small deck. Guests can enjoy mountain views from atop its broad 130-sq-meter rooftop deck.

L'Orchidée GUESTHOUSE $$
(✆621-0618; www.trinidadhosthomes.com; 3 Coblentz Gardens; s/d $132/165; ❀@❧) Smart 12-bedroom inn, popular with business travelers, with bright, well-appointed rooms in vibrant colors. Breakfast is included in the rates, and it's walking distance from the Savannah.

Hyatt Regency HOTEL $$$
(✆623-2222; www.trinidad.hyatt.com; 1 Wrightson Rd; r from US$189; ❀@❧❧) Taking up a fat piece of oceanside real estate next to the ferry terminal, this is the most luxurious choice in Port of Spain. Its army of staff presides over a huge array of amenities, from stunning rooftop pool and spa to multiple restaurants and bars.

Monique's GUESTHOUSE $$
(✆628-3334; www.moniquestrinidad.com; 114-116 Saddle Rd; s/d/tr US$84/90/102, with kitchen

US$90/108/120; ❀❧) In Maraval, 3km north of Queen's Park Savannah, Monique's has 10 pleasant rooms. Its hillside annex has 10 large studios with cooking facilities and balconies overlooking the hills, and the friendly owners organize nature tours for guests.

Pearl's GUESTHOUSE $
(✆625-2158; 3-4 Victoria Sq; r US$20) Bare-bones, cheap and perfect for Carnival, this basic accommodation has a shared bathroom and kitchen, and a communal balcony overlooking Victoria Sq.

Tourist Villa GUESTHOUSE $
(✆627-5423; caribbeantouristvilla@gmsil.com; 7 Methuen St; s/d/tr US$55/65/75; ❀❧) This well-worn place on a quiet street has lots of balconies and a small pool. The rooms are unexceptional but acceptable, with fridge, and are all you'd need for a budget Carnival bolt-hole.

La Calypso GUESTHOUSE $
(✆622-4077; lacalypso@tstt.net.tt; 46 French St; r without bathroom US$41, with bathroom US$51-65; ❀) A short walk from Woodbrook's entertainment zone, this ultrasecure, nonlinear structure has 18 basic, clean rooms in its crooks and crevices, some with balconies.

Eating

Street food is a big deal in Port of Spain, with Trini treats available from dusk until late into the night on Independence Sq, along Western Main Rd in St James, Ariapita

Ave in Woodbrook and the paved area on the southern Savannah. The mom-and-pop lunch spots all over town tend to sell out by 3pm; the food courts of Long Circular and Westmall malls are a good bet, too.

Patraj
CARIBBEAN $

(161 Tragarete Rd; roti TT$15-30; ☺8am-5pm Mon-Sat; ✳) Right before entering St James, Patraj serves some of the most mouth-watering roti in the city, with a huge array of fillings from shrimp to beef and plenty of veggies.

Breakfast Shed
CARIBBEAN $

(Wrightson Rd; mains TT$40; ☺breakfast & lunch) Right on the water, Trini women sell home-made food from stalls around the perimeter of an open-air, picnic-benched eating area. The large servings of Trinidadian fare include fish or chicken with macaroni pie, callaloo, plantain and rice. You can grab a fresh cane juice or sea moss shake at Mr Juice's stall.

More Vino
JAPANESE/FUSION $$

(☎622-8466; www.morevino.com; 23 O'Connor St; sushi TT$68, mains from TT$90; ☺11am-midnight Mon-Wed, 11am-1am Thu-Sat ✳) This popular wine bar serves up some of the best sushi in town, with all the familiar rolls plus local flavors such as the spicy Maracas, all made right in front of your eyes. Seafood and pasta dishes are also on offer, the wine list is excellent and it's a great spot for a cocktail, too.

Veni Mangé
CARIBBEAN $$

(☎624-4597; 67A Ariapita Ave; mains TT$90-150; ☺11am-3pm daily, dinner from 7pm Wed & Fri; ✎) West Indian flavor, art, foliage and enthusiasm infuse this vibrant restaurant. Serving Caribbean cuisine with classic French influences, it's one of the best spots for lunch. Try the beef dumplings, the grilled fresh fish with tamarind sauce, or the excellent veggie options.

Mother Nature's
VEGETARIAN $

(cnr Park & St Vincent Sts; mains TT$20-50; ☺5am-4pm Mon-Sat; ✳✎) Whole wheat roti? Yes, it exists here as well as dairy-free desserts (including a showcase of ice creams) and vegetarian dishes sieved from the local repertoire.

Ciao Café
ITALIAN/CARIBBEAN $$$

(☎624-1181; 10 Nook Ave; mains TT$85-240; ☺11:30am-3pm & 6-10:30pm; ✳) If you're looking for a quiet romantic dinner, take a table on the pretty terrace and settle back to enjoy excellent service and great Italian food with a Caribbean twist. Menu choices include veal, fish and seafood, plus fresh and yummy desserts.

Hakka
ASIAN FUSION $$

(☎221-0800; 4 Taylor St; mains from TT$50; ☺lunch & dinner, closed Sun; ✳) Buzzing place offering delectable Chinese cuisine with an Indian flavor. Eating in can build up the bill, but inexpensive takeaway is also on offer, and the terrace out front fills up with drinkers on the weekends.

Rituals
CAFE $

(cnr Marli St & Maraval Rd; sandwiches TT$30; ☺6:30am-7pm; ☎) This coffeehouse chain (one of many Port of Spain branches) serves smoothies, coffee drinks, paninis, bakery goods and bagel sandwiches. Tap into the free wi-fi and take refuge from the heat in the blasting air-conditioning.

Mangoes on the Avenue
CARIBBEAN $$

(40 Gallus St, cnr Ariapita Ave; lunch from TT$50; ☺breakfast, lunch & dinner; ✳) Reliable place for an inexpensive local meal. Food is laid out buffet-style, and servers fill you up with a plate of goodies, from fish and chicken to noodles, veggies and salads. There's also a branch on Independence Sq (cnr Chacon St).

Hosein's Roti Shop
CARIBBEAN $

(cnr Independence Sq South & Henry St; rotis TT$15-30; ☺lunch & dinner) On the south side of town, this is a hugely popular carryout, with hungry workers queuing up for the tasty and generously sized rotis.

Chaud Creole
CARIBBEAN $$$

(☎621-2002; 6 Nook Ave; mains from TT$125; ☺11am-3pm & 6-10:30pm, closed Sun lunch) The newest project of local superchef Khalid Mohammed, this place offers a sophisticated take on Trini food, with local dishes spiced up in inventive and delicious ways. Fresh ingredients and truly high-class cooking.

Sweet Lime
CARIBBEAN $$

(cnr Ariapita Ave & French St; mains TT$60-190; ☺lunch & dinner; ☎✎) This restaurant-bar has an open-air kitchen, plant-laden outdoor seating and free wi-fi. The set-menu lunch is economical, local and generous. The expensive dinner menu includes salads, grilled meats and fish or seafood.

Tamnak Thai
THAI $$$

(13 Queen's Park East; mains TT$70-300; ☺11am-3pm & 6-11pm Mon-Fri, dinner only Sat & Sun) The outside patio has lovely tropical wood tables

and a lily-pad pond while the inside is quiet and cool. Dishes include lemongrass-infused soups; seafood salad; vegetable, lamb and shrimp curries; and spicy tofu with vegetables.

Apsara
INDIAN $$$

(13 Queen's Park East; mains TT$90-250; ☺lunch & dinner Mon-Sat; ❀) Specializing in North Indian cuisine, Apsara is named after the dancers of the court of Indra, who, it's said, could move freely between heaven and Earth. The curries and tandoori meats and fish will melt in your mouth, and vegetarians have many options.

🍷 Drinking

Port of Spain's drinking scene is concentrated along Ariapita Ave in Woodbrook, with a string of bars pulling in the crowds most nights. Places change quite quickly, so the best plan is to start at Crobar and work your way west.

Crobar
BAR

(cnr Ariapita Ave & Carlos St) Right on trendy Ariapita, this open-air bar has a nice sound system and serves them cold. It's a good place to start a bar crawl of the many drinking joints along the Avenue.

Drink
BAR

(63 Rosalino St, cnr Roberts & Warren Sts) A block back from the Avenue, this cool little wine bar is a popular hangout for arty types, with a host of cultural happenings, great finger food and, of course, an excellent selection of wine.

Smokey & Bunty's
BAR

(97 Western Main Rd) The suburb of St James, just west of central Port of Spain, becomes a hub of activity almost any evening, and this hole-in-the wall watering hole is the center of the action. It's a brilliantly seedy scene, and a myriad of busy bars surround it if you want to hop around.

☆ Entertainment

Port of Spain's nightlife is especially happening Thursday through Saturday, but the St James neighborhood is known to always be rocking and the place to find a proper lime when all else fails. Many times bars have live music or DJ's.

If you'd like someone to accompany you on your first night on the town, contact Gunda Harewood for an **evening entertainment tour** (☎625-2410, 756-9677; www.island experiencestt.com), which might include visits to a couple of panyards, a local live band and guidance in choosing the best street snacks. About three hours of fun and transportation costs US$55 per person.

Zen
NIGHTCLUB

(www.zen.tt; Keat St; cover from TT100; ☺10pm-late Wed, Fri & Sat) Just behind the museum, this three-tier club is replete with slick modern decor and Buddha statues. There's a VIP Champagne room, make-out nooks, myriad dance floors, and plenty of pretty young things who shake it all night to soca, hip-hop and other popular beats. A dress code is in effect.

PANYARDS

For much of the year, panyards are little more than vacant lots where steel bands store their instruments. Come Carnival season, they become lively rehearsal spaces, pulsating with energy and magnificent sound, with pan lovers crowding in to buy drinks from the bar and take in the music. It's a window into one of the most important and sacred parts of Trinidad's urban landscape, with aficionados discussing every note and tempo change, and the excitement builds as the Panorama competition (see p770) gets closer.

Steel bands start gearing up for Carnival as early as late September, sometimes rehearsing and performing throughout the year. The best way to find out about practice and performance schedules is by asking around. You can also contact **Pan Trinbago** (☎623-4486; www.pantrinbago.co.tt).

Some popular panyards that welcome visitors:

Phase II Pan Groove (☎627-0909; Hamilton St)

Renegades (☎624-3348; 138 Charlotte St)

Silver Stars (☎633-4733; 56 Tragarete Rd)

Woodbrook Playboyz (☎628-0320; 27 Tragarete Rd)

Fifty One Degrees
NIGHTCLUB

(www.51degrees.biz; 51 Cipriani Blvd; weekend cover charge TT$120-150; ☺7pm-very late Tue-Sat) Not just a dance club, this Port of Spain nightlife waypoint has games nights, karaoke, live bands and some of the city's best club nights. Dress code is in effect.

Mas Camp Pub
LIVE MUSIC

(cnr French St & Ariapita Ave) A taste of oldschool Port of Spain, with live calypso several times a week (cover charge varies) often featuring the nation's most celebrated calypsonians. Other nights see anything from karaoke to Latin dance, and there are pool tables out back, too. It has been renamed as the Nu Pub, but it's universally referred to by its original name.

MovieTowne
CINEMA, BAR, RESTAURANT

(☑627-8277; www.movietowne.com; Audrey Jeffers Hwy, Invaders Bay; tickets adult/child TT$45/35; ✳) Besides 10 wide-screen movie theaters, there's also video arcades, a shopping mall, and restaurants and bars arranged around a central courtyard that is a popular liming spot – though it could be in any American suburb. It's west of the center.

🛍 Shopping

The central area of Port of Spain, especially around Independence Sq, Charlotte St and Frederick St, is filled with malls and arcades selling everything from spices to fabric by the yard. Music is one of the best local souvenirs. Head for **Crosby's Music Centre** (☑622-7622; 54 Western Main Rd) in St James, opposite Smokey & Bunty's, or **Cleve's One Stop Music Shop** (☑624-0827; 58 Frederick St), in a small shopping center downtown. You can also pick up CDs at the airport.

Reader's Bookshop
BOOKSTORE

(☑628-7221; 1 Middle St; ☺10am-6pm Mon-Sat) Brilliant bookshop with a great selection of Caribbeana and international writers. Located off Long Circular Rd.

ℹ Information

INTERNET ACCESS International Calling Center (City Gate, South Quay; per hr TT$10; ☺6am-11pm)

L and C Internet Services (26 Maraval Rd; per hr TT$10; ☺7am-7pm Mon-Fri, 10am-5pm Sat & Sun)

MEDICAL SERVICES General Hospital (☑623-2951; 56-57 Charlotte St) A large fullservice public hospital.

St Clair Medical Centre (☑628-1451; 18 Elizabeth St) A private hospital preferred by expatriates.

MONEY The major banks – RBTT, Republic Bank, Royal Bank and First Citizens – all have branches on Park St east of Frederick St, and on Independence Sq. There are also banks in West Mall, Long Circular Mall and on Ariapita Ave. All have 24-hour ATMs.

POST Main post office (☑669-5361; www.ttpost.net; Wrightson Rd; ☺8am-4pm Mon-Fri) TT Post has outlets all over town.

TELEPHONE bmobile (☑824-8788; www.bmobile.co.tt; cnr Chacon & Independence Sq South; ☺8:30am-4:30pm Mon-Fri, 8am-1pm Sat) For around TT$125 you can buy a cell phone and use prepaid phone-card inserts (TT$0.50 to TT$1.30 per minute within Trinidad and Tobago and TT$1 to TT$1.25 per minute to the US). There are bmobile outlets throughout Port of Spain.

International Calling Center (City Gate, South Quay; ☺6am-11pm) This center has private calling booths for making international calls (TT$1 per minute to the US, Canada, UK and Europe).

TOURIST INFORMATION Tourism Development Company (TDC; ☑675-7034; www.gotrinidadandtobago.com) Has a helpful outlet at **Piarco International Airport** (☑669-5196; ☺8am-4:30pm).

Ministry of Tourism (☑624-1403; www.tourism.gov.tt; cnr Duke & St Vincent Sts; ☺8am-4:30pm Mon-Fri) Provides useful information and brochures.

Around Port of Spain

CHAGUARAMAS

A 30-minute drive from the capital, the Chaguaramas (sha-gah-*ra*-mus) peninsula was the site of a major US military installation during WWII, and it was fully handed back to Trinidad only in the 1970s. Today the string of marinas along the ocean is a hot spot for yachters, who come here to take advantage of the comparatively inexpensive marina and dry-docking facilities, or wait out the weather – Trinidad lies safely south of the hurricane belt. While you're there, you might want to check out the interesting **Chaguaramas Military History & Aerospace Museum** (☑634-4391; adult/child TT$20/10; ☺9am-5pm), which explains Trinidad and Tobago's complex military history. Another popular activity is to rent a kayak from the **Kayak Centre** (☑633-3348; per hr TT$40) and paddle around the calm waters of Williams Bay.

CYCLING TRINIDAD

The traffic, crazy drivers and narrow roads are out of hand near cities. However, if you love cycling and have an adventurous streak, you can enjoy some spectacular rides in the more remote areas and back roads. While riding, beware of dogs (usually all bark), narrow roads, blind corners, honking (not malicious, usually jovial, but disconcerting) and opportunists (go with a guide or in a group, especially if you're female).

Best Road Rides

» Toco to Matelot (out and back about 48km) – Absolutely stunning coastal scenery with lots of hills and very little traffic (the road ends in Matelot).

» Blanchiseusse Rd (39km) – Once you're out of Arima, any part of this road is gorgeous: it heads straight through the heart of the Northern Range, passing through rainforest and by small farms. Asa Wright Nature Centre is great for lunch, with the turnoff to Petite Marianne Waterfall halfway back down to Blanchisseuse. There are big ascents and descents.

» Chaguaramas – There are some beautiful, flat roads with little traffic in Tucker Valley National Park.

Guides & Rentals

Anton Roberts (☎763-2013) A cycling guide who will show you Trinidad's road rides.

Geronimo's (☎622-2453; 15 Pole Carew St) A reliable bike shop in Port of Spain that rents good bikes and sells quality merchandise.

Paria Springs Tours (☎622-8826; www.pariasprings.com; tours per person US$75-100) Run by an enthusiastic biker with an exhaustive knowledge of Trini trails and quality bikes to rent, this is the company to go to for cycling.

Chaguaramas is also the launching point for tours to a chain of offshore islands, the **Bocas**. Boat tours, as well as hiking, swimming and historical excursions, can be arranged by the **Chaguaramas Development Authority** (☎634-4227; www.chagdev.com). Popular tours include the boat trip out to **Gasparee Island** (TT$125, three hours), at the south side of Chaguaramas Bay, where you can swim in tidal pools and visit caves that drip with stalactites. The most distant island, 360-hectare **Chacachacare**, was once a leper colony; camping is permitted on the now-deserted isle, replete with beaches and stunning cliff views of Venezuela. You can also arrange independent boat trips with boatmen at the Island Property Owners' jetty, on the west side of Chaguaramas. Expect to pay at least TT$195 per person for Gasparee Island. For fishing charters around the area contact **Classic Sport Fishing Charters** (☎680-1357; per day US$750).

Just inland of Chaguaramas town, the 6000-hectare **Tucker Valley National Park** is a popular recreation spot, with picnic grounds, a golf course and around 20km of mountain-bike trails through the rainforest and bamboo groves. Local guide Courtney Rooks of Paria Springs Tours knows the trails in and out, and also rents suspension mountain bikes.

The main road through Tucker Valley ends at **Macqueripe**, formerly the swimming spot of American troops and now a pretty place to dive into cool green waters, with views over to the misty Venezuelan coastline. There are changing rooms (TT$1, open 10am to 6pm), but no food or drink outlets.

Sleeping

Bight GUESTHOUSE **$$**
(☎634-4427; www.peakeyachts.com; 5 Western Main Rd; r US$75; ❄📶) Simple, tidy rooms overlooking the bay make the Bight good value for the price. Its **restaurant** (mains from TT$75; ⏰breakfast, lunch and dinner) has terrace dining where people drink colorful cocktails. Inside there's a pool table, darts and big-screen TVs.

Coral Cove Hotel HOTEL **$**
(☎634-2040; www.coralcovemarina.com; Western Main Rd; r US$70; ❄📶) This is another little hotel near the water that is unremarkable but clean and near a handful of restaurants. Rooms have kitchenette.

CrewsInn
HOTEL $$$

(☑634-4384; www.crewsinn.com; Point Gourde; r US$198; ❄@❊❅) As the highest-end option in town, its bright rooms all have patios and complete amenities, though are very overpriced. This hotel-and-marina complex houses the open-air, upscale **Lighthouse Restaurant** (mains from TT$100; ☺breakfast, lunch and dinner), the main draw of which is the covered deck overlooking the marina.

✖ Eating & Drinking

Most of the marinas have somewhere to munch seafood and sip a Carib. The area's clubs are only rented out for events, especially at Carnival time, so the liming is low-key, but the waterside restaurants are a great alternative to Port of Spain.

TOP CHOICE Sails
RESTAURANT $$

(Power Boats Marina; mains from TT$50; ☺11am-midnight) This popular hangout has seating on the water, pool tables inside and steel pan on Sundays. You can get bar and grilled food here as well as shepherd's pie and local dishes such as callaloo soup and fresh fish.

Roti
CARIBBEAN $

(Power Boats Marina, Western Main Rd; rotis from TT$18; ☺11am-1pm) There's a nameless blue roti hut tucked in a corner of the Power Boats Marina that serves terribly famous roti and 'buss up shut' (paratha roti). The hut serves food until it runs out, so get there sooner than later.

Barracuda
BAR

(CrewsInn Marina; ☺10am-late daily) Right on the water, with tables in the air-conditioned interior or on a deck overlooking the marina's bobbing masts, this is a cool spot for a drink, with karaoke every Thursday evening, DJs on Friday and Saturday and a weekday happy hour (5pm to 7pm).

Caffé del Marre
CAFE $$

(CrewsInn Marina; quiche from TT$40; ☺8am-8pm Mon-Thu & Sun, 8am-9pm Fri & Sat; ❊) A great stop off for an ice cream, gooey cake, sweet or savory pastry or slice of quiche. Smoothies, coffee, wine and beer, too, with tables inside or out on the marina front.

Lure
SEAFOOD $$$

(☑634-2783; Sweet Water Marina; mains from TT$90; ☺11am-11pm Tue-Sat, 11am-9pm Sun) A lovely waterside setting, this is a great alternative to Port of Spain for a nice dinner out. Its international fusion menu features a variety of seafood, meat and pasta dishes. Check out the saltwater pool (not for swimming), inhabited by local varieties of fish and a small shark.

MT ST BENEDICT

A Benedictine **monastery** sits on 240 hectares on a hillside north of Tunapuna, 13km east of Port of Spain. Though not a major sight in itself, the monastery attracts people who want to stay or eat at its secluded guesthouse, bird-watch or walk in the surround-

---

WORD ON THE BIRD

Trinidad and Tobago is excluded from many Caribbean birding books because of the sheer magnitude of additional species here – about 430 in total. Torn from Venezuela, these islands share the diversity of the South American mainland in their swamps, rainforests, ocean islets, lowland forests and savannahs, and the bird-watching is some of the best in the Caribbean.

For references, try *A Guide to the Birds of Trinidad and Tobago* by Richard Ffrench, which has good descriptions but limited plates; or *Field Guide to the Birds of Trinidad and Tobago* by Martyn Kenefyk, Robin Restall and Floyd Hayesm, which has a few more. Detailed plates can also be found in *Birds of Venezuela* by Steven L Hilty.

Best birding spots in Trinidad are Asa Wright Nature Centre, Caroni Bird Sanctuary, Pointe-a-Pierre Wildfowl Trust, Mt St Benedict and Brasso Seco. In Tobago: Little Tobago, St Giles Island, Grafton Caledonia Wildlife Sanctuary and Tobago Forest Reserve.

Accommodations

Trinidad and Tobago have a number of lovely accommodations at prime birding sites. These quiet and peaceful retreats connect you with savvy guides, and you can practically bird-watch from your room. Good bets include Pax Guest House (p779) and Asa Wright Nature Centre (p779) in Trinidad; and Cuffie River Nature Retreat (p794), Adventure Eco-Villas (p793) and Arnos Vale Hotel (p793) in Tobago.

ing forest. Today, the monastery is home to just 20 aging monks.

The thickly wooded hills behind the monastery provide hiking opportunities and possible glimpses of hawks, owls and numerous colorful forest birds, and maybe a monkey. A favorite **hike** is to the fire tower, which offers good views and birding. It takes about 30 minutes one-way from the guesthouse.

Pax Guest House (662-4084; www.paxguesthouse.com; s/d incl breakfast US$50/75, dinner TT$150; ✷) is a handsomely restored colonial house. Hosts Gerard and Oda welcome everyone as though they're family, and bend over backwards to arrange day trips, transportation and bird-watching hikes. A peaceful retreat, the guesthouse's 18 rooms feature teak floorboards and antique four-poster beds; some have private bathrooms. Unless you have a car, however, it's inconvenient to get around. Nonguests can come for a delicious local dinner or a delightful **afternoon tea** with scones, pastries or Trinidadian sweet bread. Reservations are essential for dinner but not for tea (served 2pm to 6pm).

To get to Mt St Benedict from Port of Spain, take the Eastern Main Rd, then St John's Rd 3.3km north. For public transportation, take a maxi to Tunapuna and get off at St Johns Rd, where you will usually get a maxi up to Pax within an hour before 5pm. Leaving Pax, maxis start around 6am.

ASA WRIGHT NATURE CENTRE

A former cocoa and coffee plantation transformed into an 80-hectare nature reserve, the **Asa Wright Nature Centre** (667-4655; www.asawright.org; adult/child US$10/6; ⊙9am-5pm) blows the minds of bird-watchers, and makes a worthwhile trip even if you can't tell a parrot from a parakeet. Located amid the rainforest of the Northern Range, the center has attracted naturalists from around the world since its founding in 1967. The property has a central lodge catering to birding tour groups, a research station for biologists and a series of hiking trails. Day visitors can only explore on a guided tour (10:30am and 1:30pm); reservations should be made at least 24 hours in advance. Nonguests can also have **lunch**, with an excellent hot buffet (TT$140, Sunday TT$200).

Bird species found at the center include blue-crowned motmots, chestnut woodpeckers, channel-billed toucans, blue-headed parrots, 14 species of hummingbird and numerous raptors. The sanctuary is also home

---

AMERINDIAN LEGACY

In Arima there remains a small community of Amerindian descent who still follow some traditional customs. Arima has the **Amerindian Museum** (Cleaver Woods; admission free; ⊙8am-6pm) displaying artifacts, and local shaman **Cristo Adonis** (395-0999) can show you around or take you on an educational hike to learn about the medicinal plants and spirituality of the Amerindians.

---

to the elusive nocturnal guacharo (oilbird). To protect the oilbirds, tours are limited. Guests staying at the center's lodge can view them for free (nonguests TT$150).

The **lodge** (667-4655, in the US 800-426-7781; s/d per person US$295/215; ✷) has some rooms in the weathered main house and others in nearby cottages; all are quite simple with private bathrooms. Rates are high but include three ample meals a day, afternoon tea and rum punch each evening.

The centre is about a 1½-hour drive from Port of Spain. At Arima, 26km from Port of Spain, head north on Blanchisseuse Rd, turning left into the center after the 7½-mile marker sign. A taxi there and back to Asa from Port of Spain (essentially an all-day affair) will cost between TT$400 and TT$600; one-way is about TT$250. For public transportation, take a maxi to Arima and catch another maxi going up Blanchisseuse Rd; they are most frequent during commuting hours.

North Coast

Winding north from Port of Spain, Saddle Rd becomes the North Coast Rd, climbing over the jungle-slathered mountains of the Northern Range and descending to the Caribbean coastline at Maracas Bay. The road then hugs the seafront for about 15km to the small settlement of Blanchisseuse, after which it passes over a small suspension bridge and narrows into impassability.

Maxi-taxis and route taxis travel to Maracas Bay, but transport to Blanchisseuse is far less frequent.

MARACAS BAY

Just 40 minutes' drive from Port of Spain, Maracas Bay has Trinidad's most popular beach. The wide, white-sand beach, thick with palm trees contrasting against the backdrop of verdant mountains, remains an irresistible lure for both locals and travelers.

Despite the curving headland, the sand is often pounded by waves that serve up good bodysurfing. There are lifeguards, changing rooms (TT$1, open 10am to 6pm), showers, picnic shelters and huts selling cold beers and shark and bake. On weekends the beach gets pretty crowded, but during the week it can feel almost deserted.

Right on the bay, **Maracas Bay Hotel** (☑669-1914; www.maracasbay.com; r US$87; ❋ @) is the only hotel in Maracas and is accordingly overpriced. Its rooms are simple, a bit musty, face the ocean and have balconies. Its restaurant (mains TT$75 to TT$150) is under a giant pagoda and has both bar food and seafood and meat dishes. To grab a beer and lime with the locals, head to **Uncle Sam's** (beer TT$10), on the eastern side of the bay, which often has a DJ on Sundays.

LAS CUEVAS

Just east of Maracas Bay, quieter and less commercial Las Cuevas is another beautiful bay, its wide sweep of sand overhung by cliffs and forest. There's usually good surfing at its west end, and calmer conditions at its center, where lifeguards patrol. The car park above the sand has changing rooms (TT$1, open 10am to 6pm) and a restaurant serving cold drinks, beers and basic fish or chicken lunches.

BLANCHISSEUSE
POP 800

The road narrows east of Maracas Bay, ending at the tiny village of Blanchisseuse (blan-she-*shuhze*), where beautiful craggy coastline dotted with weekend homes can seem romantic or harsh, depending on your mood. The three beaches aren't the best for swimming, especially in the fall and winter, but the surfing can be pretty good. The town's name stems from the time of Trinidad's French occupation, when local women washed clothes in the river here; *blanchisseuse* is the French word for 'launderer.'

Blanchisseuse makes a great base for **hiking**, especially to **Paria Bay**. The trailhead starts just past the suspension bridge that spans the Marianne River, just before the end of the North Coast Rd. About two hours each way, the hike winds through the forest, over the Jordan River to the spectacular and completely undeveloped Paria Beach. Head inland for 20 minutes along a trail from the beach and you'll hit **Paria Falls**, where you're greeted with a clear, refreshing bathing pool. Continuing east will lead you on a scenic coastal hike that dumps you out in Matelot. From Blanchisseuse to Matelot is around 32km. Backpacking is possible and having a guide is suggested because parts of the trail aren't well marked and in the past there have been reports of assaults on foreigners. **Eric Blackman** (☑669-3995) can arrange a guide or short kayaking trips to the Three Pools, three luscious pools found less than 1.5km up the Marianne River from Blanchisseuse. There are trails flanking the river if you want to meander up there yourself.

If hiking is not your thing, you can go to Blanchisseuse Fishing Port and hire a fisherman to take you (from TT$250) to and from Paria Bay or **Madamas Bay**, which will most likely be deserted.

Hotels in Blanchisseuse don't have a stringent service-industry standard, but you can hear or see the ocean from most. The best choice in the area is **Second Spring** (☑669-3909; www.secondspringtnt.com; Lamp Post 191, Paria Main Rd; studio/cottage US$70/120), three comfortable, endearing self-contained cottages by a rocky yet gorgeous section of coast. Local breakfasts are available (US$10).

A professional, well-run place, German-operated **Laguna Mar** (☑669-2963; www.lagunamar.com; 65½-mile marker, Paria Main Rd; r TT$440; ❋) comprises three buildings on the hillside at the end of the road, plus a four-bedroom cottage. Try to snag a room in the far building, which has a righteous common room with shared kitchen and deck.

Casual and comfortable, **Almond Brook** (☑758-0481; Lamp Post 16, Paria Main Rd; r incl breakfast US$50) has three pleasant, clean rooms. The appealing communal deck outside the rooms looks to the ocean. There's a large shared kitchen and meals can be arranged.

Cocos Hut (meals from TT$90; ⊙7am-7pm), a small, cozy place near the end of the road and under the same ownership as Laguna Mar, is about the only restaurant in town. It serves up tasty fresh fish or chicken platters.

If you are planning to stay in Blanchisseuse for a while, shop for provisions before coming, as the nearest grocery store is in Maraval. Booths here will sell you basics.

Brasso Seco

Plum in the middle of the lush rainforest that smothers the Northern Range, Brasso Seco is a quiet little village that once made its living from growing cocoa and other crops. Today, it has reinvented itself as a low-key base for nature lovers in search of hiking, bird-watching or just a bit of insight into the slow, slow pace of life in rural Trinidad.

There are some spectacular day **hikes** of varying lengths to waterfalls: Double River Waterfalls, Madamas Falls and Sobo Falls. The 13km trek to Paria Bay from Brasso Seco is one of the most gorgeous in Trinidad, passing the famous Paria Falls. You can make this hike into a fine coastal backpacking trip with camping on beautiful bays by continuing all the way to Matelot to the east. If you're a very hardy hiker, you might want to attempt the scramble up Cerro del Aripo, the tallest mountain in Trinidad (941m).

Guides can be arranged through the **Tourist Action Committee** (☑669-6218; www.brassosecoparia.com; half-/full-day hikes TT$360/540). Of these, **Carl Fitzjames** (☑669-6054) knows all the local trails and can also arrange multiday camping treks. Stephen Broadbridge of Caribbean Discovery Tours (see p807) also offers local tours, including the gentle stroll to Avocat Waterfall and a stop in Brasso Seco for cocoa tea. He can also arrange a night in the remote coastal **campsite** (per person incl boat transfers and meals US$100) at Tacarib Bay, 11 miles from Brasso Seco; you can walk there or take a boat from Blanchisseuse.

Brasso makes a lovely place to stay as long as you don't mind fairly basic accommodations. You'll get a friendly welcome at the **Pachenco's** (☑669-6139; per person incl 2 meals TT$300), whose neat and tidy house, with three bedrooms and a sitting area, is by the church. It's basic and does the trick, and Mrs P's homemade meals and cocoa tea (hot chocolate) are delicious. Another alternative is a stay at **Rosa's** (☑669-2244; r TT$200), with a smart single bedroom and yummy meals available (TT$30 to TT$60).

West Coast

CHAGUANAS

Easily accessed from the north by the Uriah Butler Hwy and the Southern Main Rd, Chaguanas (sha-*gwaan*-as) is a sprawling town known for its excellent shopping, with

plenty of Indian clothing and jewelry on sale along the main street. South of town, at Felicity, the Chaguanas **potteries** use traditional methods to make beautiful ceramic items including *deyas*, tiny earthenware lamps that are lit during the annual Hindu Divali festival each October, when crowds of people from around the country descend on Felicity to see the beautiful glowing displays.

CARAPICHAIMA

Between Chaguanas and Couva, the Carapichaima area is the heartland of Trinidad's Indian population, whose forebears mostly came to Trinidad between 1845 and 1917 as indentured workers to fill the labor gap when slavery was abolished. Today, Indo-Trinidadian culture dominates, with endless restaurants and street stalls selling delicious roti, doubles and Indian snacks, and Hindi temples adding a splash of color to the landscape.

◉ Sights

Waterloo Temple   HINDU TEMPLE
(donation suggested; ⊗8am-3pm Tue, Thu & Sat, 9-11am Sun) This tranquil, almost surreal Hindu temple sits at the end of a causeway jutting 90m off the central west coast. Its formal name is Sewdass Sadhu Shiv Mandir, after its creator. Grateful for his safe return from India through the WWII-embattled waters of the Pacific, Sadhu committed himself to building a temple. Construction began in 1947 on state-owned land. When the state demolished his efforts, Sadhu began building out in the sea, carrying each foundation stone on his bicycle to the water's edge. When he died in 1970, his work was still incomplete; the temple was finally finished by the Hindu community in 1995. It's a beautiful place, surrounded by the shallow waters of the Gulf at high tide and with prayer flags fluttering in the air. The site is sacred to Hindus (as is the adjacent creation site), but visitors are welcome; remove your shoes before entering.

To get to Waterloo, travel south from Port of Spain on the Uriah Butler Hwy to Chaguanas, then take the signposted turnoff onto the Southern Main Rd. At St Mary's (near the big KFC), Waterloo Rd heads west to the temple. Alternatively, take a maxitaxi to Chaguanas (TT$6), then another to St Mary's (TT$3), from where you can get a route taxi (TT$3) to the temple.

Indian Caribbean Museum   MUSEUM
(admission free; ⊗10am-5pm Wed-Sun) Just inland from Waterloo Temple, this absorbing

DON'T MISS

CARONI BIRD SANCTUARY

Caroni Bird Sanctuary is the roosting site for thousands of scarlet ibis, the national bird of Trinidad and Tobago. At sunset the birds fly in to roost in the swamp's mangroves, giving the trees the appearance of being abloom with brilliant scarlet blossoms. Even if you're not an avid bird-watcher, the sight of the ibis flying over the swamp, glowing almost fluorescent red in the final rays of the evening sun, is not to be missed.

Long, flat-bottomed motorboats, some holding up to 30 passengers, pass slowly through the swamp's channels. To avoid disturbing the birds, the boats keep a fair distance from the roosting sites, so bring a pair of binoculars. Expect to also see herons and egrets, predominant among the swamp's 150 bird species. Note that during summer very few ibis are sighted, but the trip is still worthwhile.

The main companies offering tours of the swamp are **Nanan** (☑645-1305; www. cvmtravel.com; TT$60) and **Sean Madoo** (☑663-0458; www.madoobirdtours.com; TT$90). Both offer 2½-hour tours, starting at 4pm daily; Nanan is the bigger operator, with larger boats; Madoo's tours are better for serious bird-watchers, with smaller numbers. Reservations for the tours are recommended, but if you just show up you'll probably be able to find space on one of the boats. If your main interest is photography, the light is more favorable in the morning. Morning tours, which leave at 4:30am, can be arranged with both companies.

The sanctuary is off the Uriah Butler Hwy, 14km south of Port of Spain; the turnoff is marked. Many guesthouses and hotels in Port of Spain also arrange trips; a taxi will cost around TT$100.

museum is dedicated to the Indian history and experience in Trinidad. Some gorgeous antique sitars and drums are displayed as well as photographs and informational displays about early Indian settlers. Other highlights include local art, traditional Hindi clothing, a display of a traditional Indian Trini kitchen (replete with a *chulha*, the earthen stove where roti is made) and crazy pictures of Brits with their Indian indentured servants.

Hanuman Murti and Davenna Yoga Centre   HINDU TEMPLE

Towering 26m over the Davenna Yoga Centre and Ashram, the richly decorated Hanuman Murti is another potent icon of Trinidad's Hindu community. Devotees from all over the country come here to pray and walk devotional circles around the statue. The only Southern Indian–style temple in the western hemisphere, the pink-painted yoga centre is equally ornate and is an incredible sight to behold in the middle of a small Trinidadian town. Take the Chase Village exit from the highway and 1km down the road you'll see the turnoff for Orange Field Rd; the site is a couple of kilometers down. Call ☑673-5328 for information on attending yoga classes here.

POINTE-A-PIERRE WILDFOWL TRUST

Despite being in the midst of the island's sprawling oil refinery, the wetland sanctuary of the **Pointe-a-Pierre Wildfowl Trust** (☑658-4200, ext 2512; www.petrotrin .com/wildfowlweb; adult/child/teen TT$10/3/6; ☺8am-5pm Mon-Fri, 10am-5pm Sat & Sun) has an abundance of birdlife in a highly concentrated 26 hectares. There are about 90 bird species, both wild and in cages, including endangered waterfowl, colorful songbirds, ibis, herons and other wading birds. In a 20-minute stroll around the grounds, you can easily spot a few dozen species; guided tours also take place at 9:30am and 1:30pm.

A nonprofit organization, the trust is an environmental education center that rehabilitates and breeds endangered birds, which are then released into the wild, where they bolster natural populations. The visitor center has small exhibits and a gift shop.

Reservations should be made in advance, so the refinery guards know you're coming. Several entrances lead into the surrounding PetroTrin Oil Refinery, and gate access to the sanctuary occasionally changes, so get directions when you call to book.

SAN FERNANDO

POP 75,300

Trinidad's second-largest city, San Fernando is also the center of the island's gas and oil industries. Anyone looking for real cultural immersion will enjoy San Fernando, as few tourists come through the town. Most of the action happens at shops and stands around Harris Promenade, or you can find great views from **San Fernando Hill**.

As the transportation hub for the region, maxi-taxis and route taxis run regularly to Port of Spain and other outlying areas. Most of the town's hotels cater to visiting oil and gas types in town on business.

The 40-room, family-owned **Tradewinds Hotel** (☑652-9463; www.tradewindshotel.net; 36-38 London St; s/d US$119/129, ste s/d US$159/169, all incl breakfast; ❄@🌐✈) is the best place to stay, with an outdoor pool, bar, restaurant, spa and gym. Room configurations range from a small standard room to the deluxe suite with kitchen and Jacuzzi. The hotel's **Driftwood Restaurant** (dinner mains US$110-300; ⊙5am-midnight) serves up good breakfasts, sandwiches, seafood and meat dishes. Views from the patio are spectacular.

PITCH LAKE
Some 22km southwest of San Fernando, near the town of La Brea, is **Pitch Lake** (☑651-1232; tours TT$50; ⊙9am-5pm). Once thought of by the Amerindians as a punishment of the gods, this bubbling lake of pitch is perhaps Trinidad's greatest oddity. The 40-hectare expanse of asphalt is around 75m deep at its center, where hot bitumen is continuously replenished from a subterranean fault. One of only three asphalt lakes in the world, it has the single-largest supply of natural bitumen, and as much as 300 tons are extracted daily. The lake's surface looks like a clay tennis court covered with wrinkled, elephant-like skin; tour guides sagely take you across via the solid parts. High heels are not recommended. During the rainy season, people sit in its warm sulfurous pools, said to have healing qualities. A visitor center gives some background on the history of the lake.

East Coast

Trinidad's east coast is wild and rural. The mix of lonely beaches with rough Atlantic waters, mangrove swamps and seaside coconut plantations creates dramatic scenery. It's deserted most of the year, except for holidays and weekends, when people flood in for beachside relaxation, packing coolers with food and even camping by the sand.

Few hotels operate on the east coast. Sometimes locals will come down for a weekend beach lime, but places are mainly patronized the week after Carnival. Rates listed here are for the high season (January to May) and drop dramatically in the low season.

MANZANILLA & MAYARO
Long, wide and windswept, **Manzanilla Beach** has caramel-colored sand, palm trees and rather murky, choppy waters. The strong winds and tempestuous seas make swimming a challenge, though the beach shelves so gently that paddling can be fun. A public beach facility at the northern end has changing rooms, food and drink and lifeguards. Around the headland to the south of Manzanilla, **Mayaro Beach** offers more of the same, though the waters are a bit calmer.

The immaculate 16-room family-run **Hotel Carries on the Bay** (☑668-5711; r TT$400; ❄) sits on the main road as you approach Manzanilla Beach. Just steps from the beach, its bright, spacious rooms are some of the best-maintained in the area. The **restaurant** (TT$30-50) here serves three meals a day.

Mayaro has a smattering of accommodation options on the beach. **Queen's Beach Resort** (☑630-5532; www.queensbeachresort.com; Church Rd, Radix Village; r/ste TT$400/900; ❄) is the closest Mayaro comes to a resort hotel, with a good restaurant serving local food.

THE COCAL & NARIVA SWAMP
Running parallel to the beach, the Manzanilla–Mayaro Rd makes for a beautiful drive. It passes through the Cocal, a thick forest of coconut palms whose nuts are shipped all around the island. Fringed with clusters of orange heliconia, the trees harbor some interesting birds, including red-chested macaws.

Inland of the Cocal, the freshwater Nariva Swamp is a Ramsar-protected site with more than 6000 hectares of wetlands of international importance. A few tour guides offer boat trips through the swamp but tours must be arranged ahead of time. **Paria Springs** (☑622-8826; www.pariasprings.com; US$115) offers kayaking tours of the swamp coupled with expert birding guides. It's one of the best ways to experience the swamp, and tours include a curry lunch at a local home. **Caribbean Discovery Tours** (☑624-7281; www.caribbeandiscoverytours.com; US$100-150) also offers day-long kayak and walking tours, as does local operator Kayman Sagar of **Limeland Tours** (☑668-1356; www.limeland -tours.com; US$95), based in Manzanilla.

Northeast Coast

'When you out, you out. When you in, you in,' is what they say about this remote area. Despite the ruggedly beautiful coastline, the waterfalls, hiking trails, swimming holes and rivers – and the leatherback turtles that lay eggs on the beaches – tourism remains low-key in the northeast. Inaccessible from Blanchisseuse, where the north-coast road ends, this quiet region is bounded by Matelot in the north and Matura in the southeast. It's accessed via Arima or Sangre Grande (known as Sandy Grandy), where the Eastern Main Rd forks and the Toco Main Rd extends northeast along the coast. Getting here is easiest by far with your own vehicle, but it's possible to arrive on public transportation through the Sangre Grande hub.

MATURA & AROUND

The northeast is the epicenter of Trinidad's **turtle conservation programme**. With a wild, undeveloped beach that offers perfect conditions for leatherbacks to lay their eggs, Matura is the natural home for **Nature Seekers** (☑727-3933; www.natureseekers.org), a nonprofit community organization that runs educational programmes and evening turtle tours (US$10), where you can watch leatherbacks laying eggs close up – a magical experience. You can come just for the turtle-watch or stay on at Nature Seekers' **guesthouse** (dm/r TT$250/350, incl meals TT$375/475).

A couple of kilometres past Matura, a roadside sign marks the start of the **Rio Seco Waterfall Trail** in Matura National Park, which leads to a stunning swimming hole and a waterfall. It's a 45-minute hike from the trailhead.

TOCO

Sleepy to the point of catatonic, tiny Toco is an attractively battered fishing village of weathered wooden homes. From the main road, Galera Rd heads toward the sea, passing a tiny cultural **museum** (adult/child TT$5/3; ◷8am-3:30pm Mon-Fri) located in the school. Beyond this is the **beach**, a pretty stretch of gleaming sand and calm, clear water, with drinks and snacks sold from a stall. The road ends at the lighthouse that marks **Galera Point**, from which you can see the blue Caribbean sea meeting the green Atlantic.

SANS SOUCI

A short drive west of Toco, the small village of Sans Souci has several good beaches, though as they're all lashed by pounding waves, most people come here to surf rather than swim. The best (and the largest) is **Big Bay**, a wide sweep of smooth yellow sand that's usually all but deserted. There are one or two mom-and-pop places in the village serving local food and drinks.

GRANDE RIVIERE
POP 350

The closest the northeast gets to a resort town, Grand Riviere is still a far cry from most Caribbean holiday spots. It's a quiet and peaceful place, rich in natural attractions, from a stunning beach where leatherbacks lay eggs to surrounding rainforest studded with waterfalls and hiking trails and offering plenty of good bird-watching. A few small-scale nature-oriented resorts have sprung up to cater to lovers of the outdoors, and the village is a fantastic place to get away from it all. The long, wide **beach** shelves steeply down to turbulent waters, but there's calmer swimming to be had at the eastern end, where a clear river flows into the sea.

For other activities, hit up the office of the community-run **Grand Riviere Nature Tour Guide Association** (☑670-4257), in the middle of the village. From March to August, it offers night-time **turtle-watching** (TT$70, including the required permit) on the beach, as well as year-round **bird-watching** excursions and **hiking** tours (from TT$100) to waterfalls, swimming holes and seldom-visited natural wonders in the area.

Some locals rent rooms in their homes, which are great if you're on a budget. Otherwise, head for the beachside **Mt Plaisir Estate** (☑670-1868; www.mtplaisir.com; r incl breakfast TT$788), the first hotel in the area. Local art, murals and handcrafted furnishings adorn the quirky but comfortable rooms, and the **restaurant** (mains TT$90-150) cooks up divine seafood and local dishes featuring organic fruits and vegetables, plus great homemade bread.

Next door, the adorable, well-done rooms at **Le Grande Almandier** (☑670-1013; www .legrandealmandier.com; s/d TT$660/864; ❋@) have quaint balconies overlooking the sea, and the laid-back cafe has rooftop seating. Of Grand Riviere's beachside accommodations, this is the best value.

The five bungalows dappling **Acajou** (☑670-3771; www.acajoutrinidad.com; bungalow incl breakfast TT$900) are beside the mouth of the river. The decor is simple and fresh with rich wood and bright-white linens and cushions. French doors open to hammocked patios that look towards the ocean. No air-conditioning, TV or phones make this a fantastic retreat.

TOBAGO

While Trinidad booms with industry and parties all night, tiny Tobago (just 42km across) slouches in a deck chair with a beer in hand watching its crystalline waters shimmer in the sun. Though Tobago is proud of its rainforests, fantastic dive sites, stunning aquamarine bays and nature reserves, it's OK with not being mentioned in a Beach Boys song. It accepts its tourists without vigor, but rather with languor, and allows them to choose between plush oceanside hotels or tiny guesthouses in villages where you walk straight to the open-air bar with sandy bare feet, and laugh with the locals drinking rum.

When Hurricane Flora ripped by in 1963, she blew away the agro-based plantation economy, and the government turned its rebuilding efforts to tourism. Though there's enough infrastructure to make navigating Tobago easy, it's not overrun...yet. Don't dally in visiting because times are changing. Sleepy Tobago is increasingly being woken by a jostling tourism industry that loves its great value, beauty and genuinely friendly culture.

Most of the white-sand beaches and tourist development are centered on the southwestern side of Tobago, starting at Crown Point and running along a string of bays up to Arnos Vale. The lowlands that predominate in the southwest extend to Tobago's only large town, Scarborough. The coast beyond is dotted with small fishing villages and the interior is ruggedly mountainous, with thick rainforest. Divers and snorkelers, and those seeking mellow days, visit the easternmost villages of Speyside and Charlotteville. The nearby uninhabited islets of Little Tobago, Goat Island and St Giles Island are nature reserves abundant in both bird and marine life.

⊕ Getting There & Away

AIR Most people get to Tobago by taking the 20-minute flight from Trinidad (see p806), or fly in direct from Europe. The ANR Robinson International Airport, like Tobago, is small, relaxed and rarely rushed.

BOAT A slower, less expensive alternative to flying to Tobago is to take the catamaran ferry from Port of Spain, Trinidad, to Scarborough, Tobago (see p806).

⊕ Getting Around

Getting around any of Tobago's small towns is easy on foot. Buses and route taxis aren't as readily available as they are on Trinidad, but there are enough to get you from A to B.

TO/FROM THE AIRPORT Taxis from ANR Robinson International Airport charge about TT$33 to hotels around Crown Point, TT$40 to Pigeon Point, TT$60 to Scarborough, TT$60 to Mt Irvine or Buccoo and TT$330 to Charlotteville.

BICYCLE There are rental places on the island, and cycling is a fine way to navigate around the towns, and sometimes town to town, on Tobago.

BUS The Scarborough bus terminal is a short walk from the ferry terminal, off Milford Rd on Sangster Hill Rd. Buses to/from Crown Point (TT$2) and Plymouth (TT$2), via Buccoo and Mt Irvine, run hourly from 5am to 8pm. Service decreases at night and on weekends. Other departures from Scarborough are: Charlotteville via Speyside (TT$8, 1½ hours, seven departures from 4:30am to 6.30pm), and Parlatuvier via Castara (TT$6, 45 minutes, 6am, 2:30pm, 4pm and 6pm).

Note that buses aren't reliable. For more information on services, call ☑639-2293.

CAR If you want a leisurely drive around the island, you could consider renting a car for a day or two, though rates can be slightly higher than on Trinidad. Gas stations are fairly widespread in the southwest, less so elsewhere, so it's wise to fill up when you can. The following agencies are reliable operators.

Baird's Rentals (☑639-2528; airport)

Econo Car (☑660-8728; www.econocarrental stt.com; airport)

Spence's Car Rental (☑639-7611; Store Bay Rd, Crown Point)

Thrifty Car Rental (☑639-8507; www.thrifty. com; airport)

MAXI-TAXI Tobago's maxi-taxis have a blue band. They mostly serve locals and travel can be excruciatingly slow.

ROUTE TAXI In lower Scarborough, taxis to Plymouth, Castara and Parlatuvier (TT$5 to TT$8) depart from opposite the market, and taxis to Crown Point (TT$6) leave from in front of the ferry terminal. In upper Scarborough, taxis to Speyside and Charlotteville (TT$12) leave from Republic Bank by James Park.

TAXI There's a taxi stand at Club Pigeon Point.

Crown Point

Spread over Tobago's southwest tip, Crown Point is the island's tourist epicenter, offering a relatively wide range of accommodations, restaurants, and some nightlife. The attractive beaches and extensive services make many tourists stay put, but anyone wanting a deeper appreciation of Tobago's charms should plan to push eastward to explore other parts of the island.

◉ Sights

Store Bay   FAMILY BEACH
You'll find white sands and good year-round swimming at Store Bay, a five-minute walk from the airport. As well as a place to suntan on a sun lounger, Store Bay is the main departure point for glass-bottom boat trips to the Buccoo Reef, with hawkers offering these and rides on Jet Skis and banana boats. Facilities include a clean toilet (TT$1) and a row of huts serving up delicious local food.

Pigeon Point   FAMILY & ACTIVITIES BEACH
You have to pay to get access to **Club Pigeon Point** (admission TT$18, weekly pass TT$75; ⊙9am-7pm), the fine dining of Tobago's beaches, with landscaped grounds, bars, restaurants, snack bars, toilets and showers spread along plenty of beachfront. The postcard-perfect, palm-fringed beach has powdery white sands and clear aqua water. Vendors rent out beach chairs for TT$20 per day.

The main beach is calm and limpid, but around the headland, choppy waters and constant breezes make perfect conditions for windsurfing and kitesurfing. **Radical Watersports** (☑631-5150; www.radicalsports tobago.com; windsurf boards per hr TT$250, kitesurfing TT$150 per upwind drop-off; ⊙9am-5pm), at the northernmost end, is the center of these wind sports, providing quality rental and lessons. It also rents kayaks that can be paddled east towards the mangrovey 'No Man's Land' and deserted beaches.

Pigeon Point is 1.5km north of Store Bay, about a 15-minute walk from the airport.

Canoe Bay   SECLUDED BEACH
(adult/child TT$15/10) Accessed by a turnoff from the main highway a few kilometers

east of Crown Point, Canoe Bay is a gorgeous shallow bay that's popular with picnicking families. The lone hotel here is Canoe Bay Beach Resort (p788). A bar serves drinks and snacks.

⚡ Activities

Diving
Stupendous water clarity, giant shoals of tropical fish, stunning corals, a variety of dive sites and excellent operators make diving on Tobago some of the best in the Caribbean. Whether you want to do mellow coral-viewing dives or current-zipping drift dives past huge turtles and sharks, Tobago's got it all. Although serious divers tend to stay at Speyside and Charlotteville, dive operators in Crown Point run trips all over the island. There is one recompression chamber on the island, in the east-coast village of Roxborough.

Numerous dive operators vie for your business here. With diving you often get what you pay for, so be wary of operators offering cheap trips – it can mean shoddy equipment and unprofessional dive masters.

R&Sea Divers (☑639-8120; www.rseadivers. com; Toucan Inn, Store Bay Rd; dive US$45) is safe, professional and friendly. R&Sea is a Professional Association of Diving Instructors (PADI) facility that's been around for a long time. Staff will pick up divers at any hotel.

Wild Turtle Dive Safari (☑639-6558; www. wildturtledive.com; Pigeon Point Rd; dive US$40) is certified by PADI and diver recommended. It offers open-water dive certification (US$375) as well as refresher, advanced and dive master classes. The overnight Dive Safari (US$325) includes five dives and camping on a remote beach.

Other Activities
Rent a bike from James Percy of **First Class Bicycle Rentals** (☑494-2547; per day TT$70) by Café Iguana. He even has tandems. It's a fantastic way to tool around the area. Prices decrease when renting for multiple days.

Near Canoe Bay, **Friendship Riding Stables** (☑620-9788; www.friendshipridingstables. com; 75min ride TT$300) will take you on an equestrian adventure down to the sea.

🛏 Sleeping

Crown Point has inexpensive guesthouses and luxury resorts and most accommodations have a kitchenette or access to one. Unless otherwise indicated, all places to stay

Tobago

5 km
3 miles

St Giles
Island

Iguana
Bay

Flagstaff
Hill (350m)

Charlotteville

Batteaux Bay

Little
Tobago

Speyside

Goat
Island

Lucy Vale Bay

North
Point

Fort
Cambleton

Pirate's
Bay

Tyrrel's
Bay

Pigeon Peak
(576m)

Cape
Gracias-a-Dios

Pedro Point

Corvo
Point

Booby
Island

Roxborough–
Parlatuvier Rd

Delaford

Roxborough

Prince's
Bay

Queen's
Island

L'Anse
Fourmi

Lookout
Hut

Argyle River

Queen's
Bay

Richmond
Island

Brothers
Rocks

Bloody
Bay

Parlatuvier

Tobago Forest
Reserve

Argyle Falls

Richmond

ATLANTIC OCEAN

Sisters
Rocks

Parlatuvier Bay

Englishman's
Bay

Rainbow
Waterfall

Hillsborough
Dam

Goldsborough
Bay

Windward Rd

Fort
Granby

Smith's
Island

Castara

Northside
Rd

Mason Hall

Mt St George

Barbados
Bay

Granby
Point

Castara Bay

Moriah

Caribbean
Sea

King Peter's Bay

Amos Vale Rd

Adventure Farm
and Nature
Reserve

Plymouth Rd

Black Rock

Scarborough

Fort King
George

Minister
Point

Rockly
Bay

Bacolet
Point

Culloden Bay

Amos
Vale

Plymouth

Grafton Caledonia
Wildlife Sanctuary

Claude Noel Hwy

Old Milford Rd

Bacolet
Bay

Fort James

Turtle Beach

Golf
Course

Buccoo Rd

Tobago
Art
Gallery

Little
Rockly
Bay

Ferry to Trinidad

Amos Vale Bay

Fort Bennett

Stonehaven Bay

Mt Irvine

Pleasant Prospect

Shirvan Rd

Petit Trou
Lagoon

Buccoo
Reef

Buccoo

Buccoo
Bay

Milford Rd

Store Bay Rd

Canoe
Bay

Columbus
Point

Pigeon
Point

Store
Bay

Fort Milford

ANR Robinson
International
Airport

Crown
Point

Milford Rd

YOGA, ANYONE?

Some upscale hotels on Tobago offer yoga classes free to guests, but the best place to take a stretch is the Kariwak Village Holistic Haven, which has a lovely open-air yoga studio, the Ajoupa, where regular Iyengar and Hatha classes are staged, alongside tai chi. Classes cost about TT$50.

are less than a 1.5km walk to the airport and the Store Bay beach.

TOP CHOICE Kariwak Village Holistic Haven
HOTEL $$

(☎639-8442; www.kariwak.com; r from US$150; ❋@🛜🏊) Off Store Bay Rd, just a two-minute walk from the airport, Kariwak nestles in lush landscaping. The duplex cabanas line paths that wind through tropical gardens. It's both rustic and refreshing. There's an organic herb garden, two pools (one with waterfall), free yoga and tai chi classes and an excellent restaurant.

Mike's Holiday Resort
GUESTHOUSE $

(☎639-8050; Store Bay Rd; apt TT$300; ❋) Centrally located in the heart of Crown Point, Mike's has 12 clean, modern apartments with large kitchens that are updated and cheerful. In a town of skyrocketing prices, this is a deal.

Canoe Bay Beach Resort
HOTEL $

(☎631-0367; www.canoett.com; Canoe Bay; r US$70; ❋🏊) Set on 17.6 hectares in Canoe Bay, this resort is a quiet, low-key place featuring 18 apartment-style villas, a bar, restaurant and several huts along the adjacent beach. Perfect for families.

Bananaquit
GUESTHOUSE $

(☎639-9733; www.bananaquit.com; Store Bay Rd; studio/loft US$67/75; ❋@🏊) The arrangement of these spacious 14 apartments around the courtyard garden creates a community feel. The lofts upstairs can sleep up to six people and are clean, comfortable and attractively decorated. It's a five-minute walk to Store Bay beach.

Sandy Point Beach Club
HOTEL $$

(☎639-0820; www.sandypointbeachclub.com; Sandy Point; apt US$124-355; ❋❄🛜🏊) A good-value option, this resort mostly rents its comfortable, well-attended studios and apartments for week-long stays. Facilities

are excellent, including a sauna, tennis court, playground and games room. The apartments range in size from studios to four-bedroom units that sleep 10. Free shuttles to other beaches run daily.

Coral Inn Guesthouse
GUESTHOUSE $

(☎639-0967; John Gorman Trace; apt US$70; ❋🏊) This clean guesthouse quietly set back from Store Bay Rd has self-contained apartments with two bedrooms each. The friendly owner, Veda Gopaul, lives upstairs. Rates are negotiable for longer stays.

Johnston Apartments
GUESTHOUSE $$

(☎639-8915; www.johnstonapartments.com; Store Bay Rd; r US$105; ❋@🛜🏊) A great location, perched on the cliffs above Store Bay Beach and in walking distance of the Crown Point restaurants and bars. Rooms are neat, clean and modern. Popular with visiting Trinis.

Conrado Beach Resort
HOTEL $$

(☎639-0145; www.conradotobago.com; Pigeon Point Rd; r US$85-130; ❋🛜🏊) A short walk from Pigeon Point, this no-frills beach resort proves to be excellent beachside value. Sand and surf are at stumbling distance. The rooms are clean and bright, many with ocean-view balconies. There is a restaurant and bar on site.

Sandy's Guesthouse
GUESTHOUSE $

(☎639-9221; Store Bay Rd; r with fan/air-con TT$250/300; ❋) Stay with Valerie and Hugh Sandy and you're a guest in a welcoming Tobagonian home. The rooms and shared kitchen facilities are scrubbed attentively.

Crown Point Beach Hotel
RESORT $$

(☎639-8781; www.crownpointbeachhotel.com; d studio US$115, cabana US$130, 1-bed apt US$165; ❋@🛜🏊) Somewhat clinging to yesteryear, this hotel enjoys a good beachfront location next to Fort Milford. All rooms have kitchenettes and views of the ocean. There's also a pleasant pool, tennis courts and a restaurant.

Crusoe's Apartments
HOTEL $

(☎639-7789; www.crusoes.net; Store Bay Rd; TT$400; ❋@🛜🏊) A spacious complex with smart, squeaky-clean apartments with kitchenettes ranged around grassy lawns. Great value, though not right in the middle of Crown Point.

Coco Reef Resort
RESORT $$$

(☎639-8572; www.cocoreef.com; d US$236-617; ❋@🏊) Coco Reef pays elegant homage to luxurious colonial architecture, but a real highlight is the gorgeous Cuban art that lavishes the entire facility. Rooms overlook the white sand of a private beach, and guests enjoy top-tier amenities and excellent service. The resort is just next to the Store Bay parking lot off Milford Rd.

Toucan Inn
HOTEL $$

(☎639-7173; www.toucan-inn.com; Store Bay Rd; r US$110-130; ❄@☒) This 20-room hotel creates an intimate, relaxing atmosphere with four circular duplex cabins arranged around a pool and a section of rooms wrapped around a lush garden. All have teak furnishings and comfortable beds. Also on the grounds is the Bonkers bar-restaurant. It's a 10-minute walk to Store Bay.

Summerland Suites
HOTEL $$

(☎631-5053; www.summerlandsuites.info; Roberts St, Bon Accord; 1-/2-bed apt US$65/80; ❄@�奈☒) Set in a quiet Bon Accord neighborhood, these self-contained suites are slickly laid beside a long skinny pool. The apartments are well maintained with updated, tasteful furnishings.

Surfside Hotel
HOTEL $

(☎639-0614; www.surfsidetobago.com; Pigeon Point Rd; studio TT$300; ❄奈☒) This hotel used to be a good deal for travelers on a budget. Now it's still a good place to meet people from all corners, even if prices have risen, and the self-catering rooms are good value. Extra Dive Shop makes its base here.

✖ Eating

The best place to each lunch is at the row of **food huts** opposite the beach at Store Bay, where local women offer delicious dishes like rotis, shark and bake, crab and dumplin' and simple plate lunches for TT$30 to TT$60. They're all pretty similar, so the best plan is to head for the stall with the longest queue. Also, local chefs set up barbecues, cooking up smoking chicken and ribs on weekend evenings, and there's a **mobile stall** on the road between the airport and Store Bay Beach that sells doubles, pies, roti and other Trini Indian delights.

TOP
CHOICE **La Cantina**
ITALIAN $$

(☎639-8242; http://lacantinapizzeria.com; RBTT Compound, Milford Rd; pizza from TT$40; ◷lunch & dinner, closed Wed & Sun lunch) Tucked into a bank compound off Milford Rd, this buzzing pizza joint cooks up a huge range of pizzas in its wood-fired oven – you can watch the chef spinning dough and adding toppings. Good salads and fast service.

789

TOP
CHOICE **Kariwak Village**
CARIBBEAN $$

(☎639-8442; Kariwak Village Hotel; breakfast TT$70, dinner from TT$150; ◷breakfast, lunch & dinner; ✎☙) Beneath the thatched roof and coral-stone walls of this open-air restaurant, the Kariwak chefs create masterpieces of Caribbean and Creole cuisine using fresh ingredients, including organic herbs and vegetables from the garden. Breakfast includes a healthy bowl of fresh fruit, eggs, fish, homemade granola and bread. At lunch and dinner, you can do no wrong with the set menus, usually featuring grilled fish and seafood.

Marcia's
CARIBBEAN $$

(Milford Rd; mains from TT$50; ◷lunch & dinner) A great place to have a sit-down meal of Tobagonian classics, from fresh fish to curried conch or baked chicken with callaloo, macaroni pie and salad. Friendly and good value.

House of Pancakes
BREAKFAST $

(Milford Rd, behind Colours restaurant; mains TT$40-80; ◷breakfast) Service is slow, but the chef cooks up the best breakfast in town, with fresh juices, smoothies and huge omelets served until noon on a pleasant wooden deck.

Dillons
SEAFOOD $$

(Milford Rd; mains from TT$100; ◷5-11pm) Locally owned seafood place with tables on the lawn out front or a covered patio at the back. The cooking is reliably good, with highlights such as fish in coconut sauce with pawpaw salsa.

Backyard
CARIBBEAN $$

(Milford Rd; mains TT$35-150; ◷noon-7pm Mon-Fri, plus dinner Tue-Fri; ✎) It's a treat to visit this colorful roadside cafe that brings a European spin to local ingredients. The dishes are light and flavorful and the juices – like papaya guava (TT$18) – are lovely.

Bonkers
RESTAURANT $$

(Toucan Inn, Store Bay Rd; breakfast & lunch mains TT$40-70, dinner mains TT$70-200; ◷breakfast, lunch & dinner) This veranda restaurant and bar serves tasty breakfasts, sandwiches, salads and fish and chips, and sometimes has live music at weekends.

Café Coco
CARIBBEAN $$

(Old Store Bay Rd; mains TT$80-275; ◷dinner) Candlelit and breezy, with waterfalls and greenery, the wistful ambience, complemented by friendly staff, leads you to a lovely

BUCCOO REEF

Stretching offshore between Pigeon Point and Buccoo Bay, the extensive Buccoo Reef was designated as a marine park in 1973 and a Ramsar site in 2006. The fringing reef boasts five reef flats separated by deep channels. The sheer array of flora and fauna – dazzling sponges, hard corals and tropical fish – makes marine biologists giddy.

Glass-bottom-boat reef tours are an accessible way to explore Tobago's incredible treasure. Tours leave from Store Bay, Pigeon Point and the village of Buccoo. Most operators charge US$20 per person for a two-hour trip. The boats pass over the reef (much of which is just a meter or two beneath the surface), stop for snorkeling and end with a swim in the **Nylon Pool**, a calm, shallow area with a sandy bottom and clear turquoise waters. All the operators are pretty similar, often playing loud soca and selling drinks on board; you'll be repeatedly approached by touts when on Store Bay beach.

Despite the efforts of conservation groups like the **Buccoo Reef Trust** (www.buc cooreeftrust.org), Buccoo Reef has unfortunately been battered by too much use and not enough protection. In addition to anchor damage, reef walking and overfishing, polluted runoff from sewage, construction and agricultural activities floods the water and smothers the reef.

Do your part and never walk on or touch coral and avoid products made from coral or marine species (like turtle-shell jewelry).

experience. You won't go wrong choosing from its cocktail or seafood menus.

Shirvan Watermill RESTAURANT $$$
(☏639-0000; Shirvan Rd; mains TT$105-220; ⊙dinner from 6:30pm Tue-Sun) Between Crown Point and Buccoo Bay, this long-time popular restaurant sits under a coral-columned gazebo beside the mill of a former sugar estate. It has lovely outdoor dining and some of the island's best food, such as delicate soups and salads, meats, chicken Creole and lobster.

Vie de France BREAKFAST $
(☏631-8088; mains TT$17-43; ⊙6:30am-8pm) Don't let the name fool you. This is the closest thing in Tobago to an American diner, replete with breakfast faves from bagels and French toast to bacon and eggs. Just across from the airport, it's a great place for a pre-flight bite, with the coffee shop Rituals attached for your caffeine fix.

Skewers MIDDLE EASTERN
(cnr Milford & Pigeon Point Rds) For something a bit different, try the Middle Eastern goodies here, from falafel and fattoush to grilled halal chicken.

Pennysaver's GROCERIES
(Milford Rd) There are several minimarts on Store Bay Rd but for big grocery shops head east of Crown Point to Pennysaver's, near Canaan.

🍷 Drinking

Afterhours BAR
(⊙10am-late) This is a reliable bar-restaurant just back from the airport, serving food and drinks when most of quiet little Tobago is head to pillow.

Bago's BAR
(⊙10am-late) Right on the sand where Pigeon Point beach road forks right, this cool little beach bar serves them cold and mixes a mean rum punch. Great for sunset.

☆ Entertainment

TOP CHOICE Shade NIGHTCLUB
(Bon Accord; ⊙6pm-late Wed-Sat) Locals, foreigners and tourists all flock to Shade for a proper party lime. It's probably the hippest place on the island to wine and grine. Small cover charge Friday and Saturday.

Café Iguana LIVE MUSIC
(www.iguanatobago.com; cnr Store Bay & Milford Rds; ⊙6-10pm Thu-Tue) This stylish, casual hangout serves up good cocktails and live, jazz-inspired tunes. The menu offers good local cuisine, but most folks come for the Friday and Saturday night jazz music.

The Deep NIGHTCLUB
(Sandy Point Beach Club, Sandy Point; cover charge TT$50; ⊙10pm-late Thu-Sat) DJs spin soca, salsa and alternative beats at this indoor nightclub.

ℹ️ Information

In Crown Point, Republic Bank (at the airport), and RBTT (next to the Clothes Wash Cafe), have 24-hour ATMs. You'll also find banks and ATMs in Scarborough, and ATMs in Pleasant Prospect, Roxborough, Castara and Charlotteville.

INTERNET ACCESS Clothes Wash Cafe
(✉639-0007; Airport Rd; per hr TT$20; ⊘8am-9pm) Check your email during the spin cycle at this internet cafe/laundry. You can use the coin-operated washers and dryers (about TT$30 each load), or drop the clothes off and they'll do it for you for around twice as much.

RCS (✉631-8597; Spence Plaza, Milford Rd; per 30min TT$10; ⊘9am-6pm Mon-Fri, to 2pm Sat) On the 2nd floor in Spence Plaza, you'll find flat-screen computers.

MEDICAL SERVICES Scarborough General Hospital (✉639-2551; Calder Hall Rd; ⊘24hr) A 15-minute drive from Crown Point.

TOURIST INFORMATION Tourist office (✉639-0509; ANR Robinson International Airport; ⊘8am-10pm) The staff provide basic information and can help you book a room or find hiking and bird-watching tour guides.

Buccoo

The narrow tan-sand beach of Buccoo Bay doesn't compete with the generous white sands of Store Bay, and its amenities aren't as refined, but tiny Buccoo offers a taste of true local flavor: friendly folks who define laid-back, breathtaking sunsets over the bay, and the infamous Sunday School party every week.

🏃 Activities

Being with Horses (✉639-0953; www.being-with-horses.com; rides from US$50) is a small-scale stable offering rides along Buccoo Point and beach. Great for kids, with an intuitive, holistic approach to things equestrian.

🎉 Festivals & Events

Easter weekend is a huge deal in Tobago, when everyone flocks to Buccoo for a series of open-air parties and – the highlight of it all – goat races. Taken very seriously, goat racing draws more bets than a Las Vegas casino. The competing goats get pampered like beauty contestants and the eventual champion is forever revered. The partying stretches throughout the weekend and the big races happen on Tuesday.

🛏️ Sleeping

Miller's Guesthouse GUESTHOUSE $
(✉660-8371; www.millersguesthouse.com; 14 Miller St; dm US$17, s/d US$30/50; ❄🐾🤶) The basic singles and doubles are great for budget travelers, and there are also hostel dorms and even a self-contained villa. A great place for meeting people.

Seaside Garden Guesthouse GUESTHOUSE $$
(✉639-0682; www.tobago-guesthouse.com; Buccoo Bay Rd; r US$42-58, apt US$100; ❄) One of the nicest small guesthouses in Tobago and stumbling distance from Sunday School, with rooms and apartments that are meticulously cared for. A tastefully decorated sitting room with a bay window enhances the serenity of the place, while the communal kitchen is well equipped.

🍴 Eating & Drinking

The main Buccoo Bay Rd has several places selling inexpensive local lunches and dinners, usually based around fish and chicken. There are also a few friendly rum shops dotted around town – just drop in wherever you see a crowd.

TOP CHOICE La Tartaruga ITALIAN $$
(✉639-0940; www.latartarugatobago.com; Buccoo Bay Rd; mains TT$30-245; ⊘dinner Mon-Sat; 🐾) It's surprising to find this authentic fine Italian restaurant with scrumptious homemade pastas and delectable wine (it has the second-largest Italian wine cellar in the Caribbean) tucked away in tiny Buccoo. But it's a treat indeed. The ambience melds lively Caribbean colors and art with a candlelit patio fit for a romantic Italian cafe.

El Pescador CARIBBEAN FUSION $$
(Buccoo Bay Rd; breakfast TT$25-45, lunch & dinner TT$35-300; ⊘breakfast, lunch & dinner) Attached to Miller's Guesthouse, and with tables overlooking Buccoo Bay (with great sunset views), this friendly place cooks up excellent seafood and meat dishes with a South American twist. Great for a drink, too, with a nice cocktail list.

⭐ Entertainment

Sunday School LIVE MUSIC
Lacking any religious affiliation, Sunday School is the sly title for a street party held in Buccoo every Sunday night. Until around 10pm, partygoers are mostly tourists enjoying rum drinks and steel pan, plus barbecue and snacks. Later in the night, folks from

CYCLING TOBAGO

Tobago has less traffic than Trinidad, especially on the remote eastern part of the island. There are some nice roads, usually hilly, that bring you through amazing landscapes: Roxborough–Parlatuvier Rd, which passes straight through the Tobago Forest Reserve; Arnos Vale Rd to Mason Hall; Buccoo to Charlotteville along the northern coast. If cycle touring is your shtick, it's possible to circumnavigate the island.

For mountain biking, a guide is suggested. Contact **Mountain Biking Tobago** (☎681-5695; www.mountainbikingtobago.com; per person US$40-50). Owner Sean de Freitas is a straight-shooting guide who provides solid rentals and cycling equipment. His Highland Falls ride is particularly awesome, ending at a splendid swimming hole and waterfall. He also guides road rides.

Besides renting from Mountain Biking Tobago, beater bikes are rented near the Crown Point area; you can also rent one in Trinidad and bring it over on the ferry, or BYO. You'll be limited with skinny tires due to road conditions.

Buccoo and all over the island come to 'take a wine' or just hang out, with DJs spinning everything from reggae to soca.

Leeward Road

The stretch of coastline from Mt Irvine Bay to Plymouth has several lovely beaches, a few sizable hotels and a slew of fancy villas hugging the greens of the golf course. Like a sloppy adolescent propping its feet on the table in a fancy living room, Black Rock's tiny Pleasant Prospect is right in the middle. It's a teeny surfer haunt: a cluster of cheap unofficial accommodations, eateries and a few good places to lime.

◉ Sights & Activities

Mt Irvine Beach　　　　　　FAMILY BEACH
This pretty public beach, 200m north of Mt Irvine Bay Hotel, has sheltered picnic tables and changing rooms, plus a good beachside **restaurant** (see Surfer's Restaurant & Bar, p793), roti shacks and plenty of shade trees. Surfers migrate here from December to March. You can rent sun loungers, sit-on-top kayaks and surfboards on the beach.

Just before the main beach, closer to the hotel, a turnoff from the main road leads to an adjoining swathe of sand, where swimming is a little better. A hotel-run bar and restaurant sells snacks and drinks, and rents loungers.

Kimme's Sculpture Museum　　　MUSEUM
(☎639-0257; www.luisekimme.com; Bethel; admission TT$20; ⊙10am-2pm Sun or by appointment)
Turn right off the main road by the golf course and you'll see signs leading you to the home of German eccentric Luise Kimme,
who sells and displays fantastic, 2m to 3m wood-and-metal Caribbean-themed sculptures from her blinged-out mansion.

Stonehaven Bay　　　　　　FAMILY BEACH
The next beach northeast of Mt Irvine, this fabulous sweep of coarse yellow sand (also known as Grafton Bay) offers some good swimming and bodyboarding. A couple of large-scale hotels overlook the sand, one of which has a beach bar selling lunch and drinks; the eastern end has calmer waters.

Fort Bennett　　　　　　　HISTORIC SITE
Built by the British in 1778 to defend against US enemy ships, little remains of Fort Bennett other than a couple of cannons, but there's a good view of the coast. It's on a rocky hill at the north side of Stonehaven Bay, about 500m west of a marked turnoff on the main road.

Grafton Caledonia Wildlife Sanctuary　　　　　　NATURE RESERVE
After Hurricane Flora in 1963, Brit Eleanor Alefounder converted her 36 hectares into a bird sanctuary. There are some short **hiking** trails and excellent **bird-watching**. Visitors can come to the reserve any time, but the best time to come is around the 4pm feeding time. To get there, follow signs inland opposite the Grafton Beach Resort.

Turtle Beach　　　　　　　　BEACH
Another long stretch of yellow-brown sand, with wave-whipped waters shelving sharply off from the beach, this is also one of Tobago's main nesting sites for leatherback turtles, though the all-inclusive hotel right on the sand doesn't help matters much. A couple of the tour companies listed on p805

offer turtle-watching tours in the March-August season.

🛏 Sleeping

Resorts and rental villas dominate on this stretch of coastline, but Pleasant Prospect has a handful of unofficial guesthouses; just ask around.

Seahorse Inn GUESTHOUSE $$
(🖉639-0686; www.seahorseinntobago.com; Stone Haven Bay; r incl breakfast summer/winter US$94/110; ❄) A nice contrast to the big resorts, this lovely guesthouse, just below the Grafton Beach Resort, is a low-key establishment with four spacious rooms with teak floors and broad balconies facing Stonehaven Bay.

Plantation Beach Villas RESORT $$$
(🖉639-9377; www.plantationbeachvillas.com; villas from US$300; ❄) Right on Stonehaven Beach, this is the nicest of the villa resorts in the area, with tastefully appointed three-bedroom villas, a communal pool and a cute little restaurant and bar. All villas come with a housekeeper who cleans daily and will cook for guests.

The two large resorts sitting side-by-side overlooking Stonehaven Bay should be bustling with visitors, but intermittent closures mean they tend to be very quiet. Both have extensive facilities, though they're often under repair or out of action. Of the two, **Grafton Beach Resort** (🖉639-0191; r from US$110; ❄@🛜❄) is the less expensive; next door, **Le Grand Courland Resort & Spa** (🖉639-9667; www.legrandtobago.com; r from US$139; ❄@🛜❄) is more exclusive.

🍴 Eating & Drinking

Pleasant Prospect has a cluster of local bars, eateries, and even a Rituals coffee shop and Pizza Boys takeaway. The **Oceanview Bar** is an unpretentious bar nooked into a cliff overlooking the ocean. It's a great place to snag a beer after a day of sand and surf. It has barbecue Fridays as well. Right across the road, **Moon Over Water** is also a good place to hang with folks, while the **Signature Lounge**, above Rituals, has regular spoken word and karaoke nights.

TOP CHOICE **Fish Pot** SEAFOOD $$
(🖉635-1728; Pleasant Prospect; mains TT$40-100; ⊙lunch Mon-Sat, dinner Wed-Fri) Very reasonable, this laid-back restaurant specializes in

super-fresh, simply prepared seafood (with some chicken and steak dishes), and is equipped with an open-air patio. Excellent homemade bread, too. Live music on Friday nights.

Surfer's Restaurant & Bar CARIBBEAN $
(Mt Irvine Beach; mains TT$30-70) This casual spot serves up delicious fish and bake, sandwiches and daily local specials.

Seahorse Inn Restaurant & Bar CARIBBEAN $$$
(Seahorse Inn, Stone Haven Bay; mains TT$70-200; ⊙lunch & dinner) Sitting alfresco amid a tropical setting overlooking the water, with the sound of waves crashing below, this special restaurant specializes in gourmet Creole cuisine.

Arnos Vale Road

You could just call it the Rodeo Dr of bird-watching. There is a smattering of nature reserves as well as lovely higher-end accommodations that cater to nature lovers and bird-watchers.

Though it has seen better days, **Arnos Vale Hotel** (🖉639-2881; www.arnosvalehotel.com; Arnos Vale Rd; r from US$80; ❄@🛜❄) is frequented by nature lovers wanting retreat and premium bird-watching. Rooms are dated but clean and serviceable, with balconies. Amenities include a pool, bar, gym and a pleasant strip of beach with excellent snorkeling. The lovely veranda restaurant is known for its afternoon tea (TT$60).

Adventure Farm and Nature Reserve (🖉639-2839; TT$30; ⊙9am-5pm) is a 5-hectare working organic estate that has retained about 1 hectare of wild area. This is home to a wealth of bird species and revered for its hummingbirds, which cluster around feeders at the main house. You can also come to learn about tropical agriculture practices, buy organic fruit, or take short hikes around the estate.

TOP CHOICE **Adventure Eco-Villas** (🖉639-2839; www.adventure-ecovillas.com; Arnos Vale Rd, Adventure; s/d/ste US$105/140/170; ❄), at the reserve, has two lovely wooden cottages with kitchens, hardwood floors, tons of windows that open into the forest and a spacious deck. You feel a part of the environment as if you were camping, but you're actually in a styled-out cottage.

Follow signs off Arnos Vale Rd down a rough road for 20 minutes to the charming, secluded **Cuffie River Nature Retreat** (☑660-0505; www.cuffieriver.com; Runnemede; r incl breakfast US$207, with 3 meals US$345; ☀) at the edge of the rainforest. Utterly designed for bird-watching fanatics, it has a highly trained birding guide on hand to lead hikes around the area. The spacious, comfortable rooms, equipped with balconies, are flooded with natural light. There is also an ecofriendly swimming pool and a number of freshwater springs nearby.

Castara

About an hour's drive from Plymouth, Castara is a working fishing village that has become popular with tourists not wanting the inundated Crown Point scene. People love the wide, sandy beach, relaxed atmosphere and picturesque setting, but the village is on the cusp of feeling overcrowded itself during high season. Snorkeling is good in the calm Heavenly Bay to the right of the main beach. **King David Tours** (☑660-7906; www.kingdavidcastaratobago.com) is based here, providing hiking and boating tours.

🛏 Sleeping

There are scores of accommodation options in and around town; if the places below are full, just ask around.

Castara Retreats RESORT $$
(☑766-3656; www.castararetreats.com; r incl breakfast US$170-260; ☀) Beautifully designed wooden villas on a lushly landscaped hillside that offers lovely views of the beach. Each is kitted out in stylish modern decor, and there are even sea views from the beds. Friendly, helpful staff and plenty of privacy.

Castara Cottage GUESTHOUSE $$
(☑757-1044; www.castaracottage.com; apt US$75-110) Decked out in rich tropical colors, these three simple apartments are perched on a hillside between Big and Heavenly Bays. Each is equipped with all you need to self-cater, and has pleasant outdoor areas for liming and lounging.

Castara Bliss GUESTHOUSE $
(☑352-5727; castarabliss@ymail.com; r US$50-60) Set on a hillside and with distant sea views, these cool little self-contained studios are great for budget travelers, with netted beds and lots of local info from the helpful owner.

Naturalist Beach Resort GUESTHOUSE $$
(☑639-5901; www.naturalist-tobago.com; d apt US$50-90; ☀@🛜) This cheerful, family-run place is at beach level, and its cozy apartments include kitchens, fans and air-con, and are all different; some have water views. The newer upstairs units feature lots of local wood and are quite a bit nicer, with shared balconies. There's an internet cafe and restaurant on site.

Alibaba's Beach Apartments GUESTHOUSE $$
(☑686-7957; www.alibaba-tours.com; Depot Rd; r US$85; ☀) This well-run bunch of apartments has magnificent beach-facing balconies, kitchens and comfortable rooms with bamboo and seashell details. Alibaba's Tours is run out of the hotel and will take you on boat, 4WD, rainforest or island tours for US$70 to US$95 per person.

🍴 Eating & Drinking

Margarite's CARIBBEAN $
(mains from TT$65; ◷lunch & dinner) This cute eatery right off the main road serves up local specialties. The menu changes regularly.

L&H Restaurant CARIBBEAN $
(mains from TT$20; ◷lunch) Right next to the Fishermen's Co-op, this is the eatery of choice for the local fishermen, with delicious plates of fresh fish and chicken served on a balcony overlooking the water.

Cheno's CARIBBEAN
(breakfast from TT$25) The best breakfast in town, from saltfish buljol and coconut bake to bacon and eggs. Local lunch and dinner is also available.

Boat House RESTAURANT $$
(mains from TT$60; ◷breakfast, lunch & dinner Sun-Fri) Between the colorful decor, bamboo detailing and beachside ambience, this restaurant achieves a festive atmosphere. The seafood dishes are accompanied by fresh vegetable side dishes and salad. On Wednesday it has a popular steel-pan night with a set menu that includes free rum punch.

Englishman's Bay

North of Castara, the road winds past a stretch of coast that's punctuated by pretty beaches and villages, unhurried places with kids playing cricket on the road. The best place to stop is Englishman's Bay, a superb undeveloped beach shaded by stands of bamboo and coconut palms, which draws snorkelers to its gentle waters – a coral reef lies 20m offshore. **Eula's Restaurant**, serving overpriced roti and fat plates of local fare, caters to the handful of visitors. Rustic latrines are provided.

Parlatuvier

Just west of Bloody Bay is Parlatuvier, a tiny fishing village on a striking circular bay. On the hillside just before the village, a small car park provides a perfect view of the horseshoe bay below.

Further east, at Bloody Bay, is the Roxborough–Parlatuvier Rd through the Tobago Forest Reserve.

Scarborough

POP 16,800

Located 15 minutes' drive east of Crown Point, Scarborough is the island's only city, a crowded port with bustling one-way streets and congested traffic. Tobagonians come here to bank, pay bills or send packages. There are some good places to grab a bite and a neat public market, but most people will want to push onward. If you arrive late or leave early, there are fine accommodations.

◉ Sights & Activities

Botanical Gardens   GARDEN
(admission free; ⊘dawn-dusk) A pretty place to duck out of the heat, with a variety of flowering trees and shrubs, including flamboyants, African tulips and orchids (in an orchid house) laid out over 3 hectares of a former sugar estate.

Fort King George   FORT
(admission free) Immediately beyond the hospital, atop a hill at the end of Fort St, this sizable fort was built by the British between 1777 and 1779. It's the only intact colonial fortification remaining in Tobago and is worth a visit for its history and magnificent coastal view. Benches under enormous trees allow you to gaze out over the harbor, while cannons line the fort's stone walls.

The officers' quarters now contain the small but worthy **Tobago Museum** (☑639-3970; tobmuseum@tstt.net.tt; admission TT$10; ⊘9am-4:30pm Mon-Fri), which displays a healthy collection of Amerindian artifacts, maps from the 1600s, military relics, a small

WORTH A TRIP

TOBAGO FOREST RESERVE

The paved Roxborough–Parlatuvier Rd crosses the island from Roxborough to Bloody Bay, curving through the Tobago Forest Reserve, which was established in 1765, making it the oldest forest reserve in the Caribbean. The 30-minute drive through completely undeveloped jungle passes pretty valleys and mountain views, and is one of the most scenic on the island.

A number of **trailheads** lead off the main road into the rainforest, where there's excellent **bird-watching**. Three-quarters of the way from Roxborough, **Gilpin Trace** branches northeast to Bloody Bay, a 5km walk through the rainforest. Authorized guides at the trailhead charge around TT$160 for a 1½-hour walk, or TT$240 for a two-hour hike to the Main Ridge lookout hut, which affords scenic views of Bloody Bay and the offshore Sisters Rocks; on a clear day you can see Grenada 120km away. All guides provide interesting commentary on the forest ecosystem and inhabitants.

geology exhibit and a very interesting collection of watercolor paintings by Sir William Young that depict Tobago from 1807 to 1815.

Bacolet Bay   FAMILY BEACH
Around the headland to the east of Scarborough is the suburb of Bacolet, a pretty enclave of well-to-do homes, with a couple of hotels overlooking the lovely Bacolet Bay beach, a pretty horseshoe of yellow sand backed with palm trees. Steps lead down to the bay, and a beach bar sells refreshments.

🛏 Sleeping

Those arriving on the evening ferry will find a couple of cheap guesthouses a short distance from the waterfront.

Sandy's Bed & Breakfast   GUESTHOUSE $
(☑639-2737; www.tobagobluecrab.com; cnr Robinson & Main Sts; r incl breakfast US$70; ❄) Behind the Blue Crab Restaurant, amicable owners Ken and Alison Sardinha rent out three rooms in their home. The rooms are pleasantly simple with pine floors, nice furniture and views overlooking Rockly Bay.

Hope Cottage
GUESTHOUSE $

(☑639-2179; hcghtobago@hotmail.com; Calder Hall Rd; s TT$100-150, d TT$200-250) A solid budget option near Fort King George, a half-hour walk uphill from the dock. Within this former home of 19th-century governor James Henry Keens (acting governor from 1856 to 1857 and buried in the backyard), guests have access to a big kitchen, TV room, dining room, backyard and front porch; the more expensive rooms have private bathroom and cable TV.

Blue Haven Hotel
HOTEL $$$

(☑660-7400; www.bluehavenhotel.com; Bacolet Bay; low/high season d US$185/238, ste US$275/355; ❄@🛜🏊) Robinson Crusoe supposedly was stranded at this beach, but today it's home to the Blue Haven, a romantic, tastefully done resort hotel. Amenities here include a beachside pool, tennis courts and spa services, and each room has an oceanfront balcony.

🍴 Eating & Drinking

TOP CHOICE Ciao Café and Pizzeria
ITALIAN $

(Burnett St; mains from TT$35, ice cream from TT$15; ❂lunch-late Mon-Sat, lunch only Sun) Both locals and foreigners come to lime at this adorable cafe, side by side with an authentic Italian pizzeria. You'll find the best homemade gelato in Trinidad and Tobago here.

TOP CHOICE Shore Things
CARIBBEAN $$

(Old Milford Rd, Lambeau; mains TT$50-120; ❂10am-6pm Mon-Sat, plus 8-11am Sat Eve) Even though it's a couple of kilometers west of the city, this is one of the most pleasant oceanside cafes on the island, serving soups, fresh seafood and local dishes in a lovely setting overlooking the ocean. Great for teatime cakes, too.

Salsa Kitchen
MEDITERRANEAN $$$

(☑639-1552; 8 Pump Mill Rd; tapas from TT$60, mains from TT$150; ❂lunch & dinner Tue-Sun) A tiny place on a hillside verandah of Wilson Rd, Salsa Kitchen cooks up delicious tapas bites from lobster dumplings to eggplant mozzarella, and more substantial fare such as saddle of lamb and even pizza. Book ahead, as there are only five tables and it often gets busy.

Blue Crab Restaurant
CARIBBEAN $$

(☑639-2737; www.tobagobluecrab.com; cnr Main & Robinson Sts; lunch TT$55, dinner mains TT$85-165; ❂lunch Mon-Fri, dinner Mon, Wed, Fri by reservation) A family-run restaurant with pleasant alfresco seating (and an air-conditioned dining room) and good West Indian food. You'll have a choice of fresh juice and main dishes such as Creole chicken, fresh fish or garlic shrimp.

Barcode
BAR

(www.barcodetobago.com; cover varies; ❂7pm-late) Cooled by sea breezes and overlooking the ocean, this popular bar and nightspot has pool tables, a wide variety of rums and regular special events that draw a big crowd. The karaoke on Thursday is usually pretty popular.

Lal's Roti
CARIBBEAN $

(☑639-3606; Dutch Fort; roti TT$12-25; ❂8am-5pm Mon-Sat) Locals say the tasty rotis here are the best in town, and there's an open-air space to munch on your hot curried feast.

Patsy's Doubles
CARIBBEAN $

(doubles TT$3.50; ❂from 4pm most days) Found in the parking lot just east of the ferry terminal, Patsy is known throughout the island for her lovely bundles of garbanzo and flatbread goodness.

Ma King's Dinette
CARIBBEAN $

(Wilson Rd; mains TT$35-65; ❂10am-5pm Mon-Sat) Opposite the market, this popular eatery offers all sorts of local specialties, such as cassava and fried fish. Plus, it has fresh-squeezed juices and a soy-dish option.

ℹ Information

There are branches of Republic Bank and Scotiabank just east of the docks, both equipped with ATMs. There's another ATM right outside the ferry terminal.

MG Photo Studios (☑639-3457; Scarborough Mall; per 30min TT$10; ❂8:30am-6pm Mon-Fri, to 2pm Sat) Fast internet access across from the ferry terminal.

Post office (Post Office St; ❂7:30am-6pm Mon-Fri, 9am-1pm Sat) There's also a TT Post postal outlet in the ferry terminal.

Scarborough General Hospital (☑639-2551; Calder Hall Rd; ❂24hr) En route to Fort King George, it handles most emergencies and medical issues on Tobago.

Tobago House of Assembly Tourism Branch (☑639-4636; www.visittobago.gov.tt; 12 Sangster's Hill; ❂8am-4pm Mon-Fri) The main office is just west of the esplanade and ferry terminal; there's also an office at the cruise ship terminal (adjacent to the ferry terminal).

Windward Road

Just east of Scarborough is the more rural part of the island. It is less appealing to tourists because the beaches have darker sand and tend to be rough. The Windward Rd, which connects Scarborough with Speyside, winds past scattered villages, jungly valleys and white-capped ocean. The further east you go, the more ruggedly beautiful the scenery becomes. Although much of the road is narrow and curvy with a handful of blind corners, it's drivable in a standard vehicle and cyclable if you're gutsy and fit. Driving straight through from Scarborough to Speyside takes about 1½ hours.

Eight kilometers east of Scarborough is Granby Point, a jut of land separating Barbados Bay from Pinfold Bay. In 1764 the British established a temporary capital on the east side of Barbados Bay and built **Fort Granby** at the tip of the point. Little remains other than a solitary soldier's gravestone, but day-trippers will find a couple of hilltop picnic tables, a gorgeous ocean view and a brown-sand beach with changing rooms.

Just west of Roxborough, the triple-tiered **Argyle Falls** (admission TT$40; ☉7am-5:30pm) are a far busier affair; go early to skip crowds. On top of admission, you pay one of the resident guides US$10 to lead you on the 20-minute hike up to the falls. Guides swarm the entrance; official guides wear khaki uniforms and carry ID. At 54m, this is Tobago's highest waterfall, cascading down four distinct levels, each with its own pool of spring water. Roxborough has a gas station and a few stores where you can pick up snacks.

Speyside

The small fishing village of Speyside fronts Tyrrel's Bay, and attracts divers and birders. It's the jumping-off point for excursions to uninhabited islands, including Little Tobago, a bird sanctuary 2km offshore, and St Giles Island. Protected waters, high visibility, abundant coral and diverse marine life make for choice diving. Nondivers can take glass-bottom boat/snorkel tours. Speyside funnels visitors into high-end, diver-oriented hotels much more than its neighbor Charlotteville, where mixing with the locals is more of a possibility. There's a thin public beach with facilities at the south end of the bay; and above Speyside, the off-road

lookout has panoramic views out over the islands and reef-studded waters.

◉ Sights & Activities

Little Tobago   NATURE RESERVE
Also known as Bird of Paradise Island, Little Tobago was the site of a cotton plantation during the late 1800s. In 1909 Englishman Sir William Ingram imported 50 greater birds of paradise from the Aru Islands, off New Guinea, and established a sanctuary to protect them, but in 1963 Hurricane Flora devastated the habitat and decimated the flock.

Now managed by the government, Little Tobago remains an important seabird sanctuary and offers rich pickings for bird-watchers. Red-billed tropic birds, magnificent frigate birds, brown boobies, Audubon's shearwaters, laughing gulls and sooty terns are some of the species found here. The hilly, arid island, which averages just 1.5km in width, has a couple of short hiking trails with captivating views.

Several operators run glass-bottom boat trips for US$25. The trip to Little Tobago, a 15-minute crossing, includes bird-watching on the island and snorkeling at Angel Reef. Masks and fins are provided. **Frank's** (☏660-5438; Batteaux Bay; ☉10am & 2pm), based at Blue Waters Inn, and **Top Ranking Tours** (☏660-4904), departing from the beach near Jemma's restaurant, are recommended.

The diving at Little Tobago is some of the region's best; see p45.

☕ Sleeping

Top Ranking Hill View Guest House   GUESTHOUSE $
(☏660-4904; www.toprankingtobago.com; r from US$50; ✽☎) Reached via a series of steps from Top Hill St, about a 10-minute walk from the beach, this guesthouse is a quiet retreat that has clean, nicely furnished rooms with one or two double beds. Wraparound balconies provide excellent views of both the ocean and rainforest.

Speyside Inn   HOTEL $$
(☏660-4852; www.speysideinn.com; 189-193 Windward Rd; s/d from US$79/116; ✽@☎) Quite lovely, this butter-yellow hotel houses bright balcony rooms looking over the ocean, and cottages nestled out back in the jungly landscaping. Extra Divers shop makes its home here, there's a restaurant and bar, and it's often the most animated spot in town (though that's not saying much in quiet Speyside).

Manta Lodge   HOTEL **$$**
(📞660-5268, in the USA 954 453-5028; www.mantalodge.com; s & d US$95-110; ✳🔝🌐⛱) Catering to divers, this is a plantation-style house fronting the beach. Its airy rooms have wicker furniture and ocean-view balconies, and the ground-level bar-restaurant opens onto the small pool. The hotel is also home to the reliable Tobago Dive Experience dive shop.

Blue Waters Inn   HOTEL **$$$**
(📞660-2583; www.bluewatersinn.com; Batteaux Bay; r incl breakfast from US$210; ✳🌐⛱) The most upscale place to stay and geared to divers, Blue Waters sits on pretty Batteaux Bay, just 1km from the main road. The rooms all have patios and great views. Guests get use of tennis courts, beach chairs and kayaks. There's also a restaurant, bar, spa services and Aquamarine Dive, a full-service PADI dive center.

Eating

Redman's   CARIBBEAN **$**
(mains from TT$50; ⊘lunch & dinner Mon-Sat) A raised-deck affair, this local hangout is cheaper and less refined than Jemma's and Birdwatchers.

Jemma's   CARIBBEAN **$$**
(mains from TT$60; ⊘breakfast & lunch Sun-Fri, dinner Sun-Thu) Nestled in a tree-house setting and blessed by sea breezes, Jemma's is a standard stop for tour groups. It boasts excellent atmosphere and fresh local food, including fish, chicken and shrimp dishes, and prices are on the higher end. It doesn't serve booze but you are welcome to bring your own.

Birdwatchers Restaurant & Bar   CARIBBEAN **$$**
(mains TT$70; ⊘lunch & dinner) Kick back on the candlelit deck and enjoy fresh seafood and cold beers at this friendly place. The menu changes with the catch of the day.

Veryln's Roti Shop   CARIBBEAN **$**
(roti TT$15; ⊘lunch) Coming into town from the west, there's a bright-yellow shack right before the beach facilities where Veryln sells her delicious roti and homemade baked goods.

Charlotteville

There are about four winding kilometers over the mountains from Speyside to Charlotteville, a delightful little fishing village nestled in aquamarine Man of War Bay. This secluded town accepts the trickle of off-the-beaten-track tourists with mostly jovial spirits and occasionally apathy. Less hoity-toity than Speyside, the tourist services are still good, including a sprinkling of places to stay and eat, an internet cafe and an ATM. Tickets for an unreliable bus to Scarborough can be bought at the gas station (TT$8). A maxi taxi (TT$12) might come before, so you can wait till you see the bus, then join the rushing crowd to buy your ticket.

🔾 Sights

Man of War Bay   FAMILY BEACH
The large, horseshoe-shaped Man of War Bay is fringed by a palm-studded brown-sand beach with good swimming. Roughly in the middle of the beach, you'll find changing facilities (TT$1) and a beach bar. The pier towards the eastern end is a nice spot for fishing or sunset-watching.

Pirate's Bay   SECLUDED BEACH
Walk to the north end of the village, and take the dirt track winding up and around the cliff, and a 10-minute walk brings you to the top of the concrete steps that descend to Pirate's Bay, which offers excellent snorkeling and fantastic beach liming, with locals and visitors making a day of it with coolers and games of beach football. There are no facilities, so bring your own drinks and food.

🏃 Activities

Workshop Sea Tours (📞660-6281; www.workshopseatours.com; Bay St), based right in town, offers **fishing charters** (US$250), **snorkel** (per person US$40) and island tours and **bird-watching** excursions. The office has laundry and internet services.

Scuba divers should contact **Shark Shacks** (📞757-3666; www.shark-shacks.com; dive US$45). Right on Man of War Bay, the full-service, PADI-certified dive center rents out full gear and offers a variety of dive trips and certification. Packages include quaint, colorful, clean accommodations.

If you are up for some exploring on dry land, take a walk to the site of the old **Fort Cambleton**, on the west side of the bay, which offers a good coastal view; or take a more substantial hike (or drive) up **Flagstaff Hill**, a popular spot to picnic and watch the birds circling St Giles Island.

🛏 Sleeping

Besides the following listings, there are several small, unofficial guesthouses.

Top River Pearl GUESTHOUSE **$**

(🖉660-6011; www.topriver.de; 32-34 Spring St; r from US$70, 2-bed apt from US$140; ❋🖥) Although it's not on the beach, this guesthouse, just 180m up from the waterfront, is a treat with its laid-back coffee bar, hammocks and expansive bay views. With furnishings built from local teak, mahogany trimmings and red-tiled floors, each of the four immaculate rooms has a balcony with ocean views, plus minikitchen.

Man-O-War Bay Cottages CABINS **$**

(🖉660-4327; www.man-o-warbaycottages.com; Charlotteville Main Rd; 1-/4-bedroom cottage US$60/135; ❋) Plotted in a little botanical garden, with lots of tropical trees, ferns and flowering plants, these 10 simple cottages with kitchens and screened, louvered windows are open to the breeze and sounds of the surf. You'll find them beachside, about five minutes' walk south of the village.

Charlotte Villas GUESTHOUSE **$**

(www.charlottevilla.com; d US$80) In the south part of town, these three fully equipped, high-ceiling apartments are spacious, simple and relaxing with verandahs and tons of natural light flooding in.

Cholson Chalets GUESTHOUSE **$**

(🖉639-8553; 74 Bay St; apt US$40-88; ❋) Cholson Chalets is a clean, well-run place just steps from the ocean. The fresh green-and-white beach-house exterior complements the fishing-town vibe. It has nine units of varying size, equipped with kitchens.

🍴 Eating & Drinking

A handful of family-run restaurants in Charlotteville offer good, economical lunch and dinner, though their opening hours can be sporadic. Jane's Quality Kitchen provides seating in the shade of an almond tree with excellent views of the bay and local liming, and the bar at the beach facility dishes up all the local favorites as well as cocktails; it also has DJs on the weekend.

There are a couple of minimarts in town. Along the waterfront are small huts selling rotis, baked goods and fresh produce.

TOP CHOICE Sharon's & Pheb's CARIBBEAN **$$**

(Bay St; mains TT$60-140; ⊘lunch & dinner) Doing amazing things with fresh fish, shrimp,

beef, chicken and vegetables, chef Sharon cooks up truly fantastic local cuisine. Don't miss out on barbecue Wednesdays. There's indoor or outdoor seating.

G's CARIBBEAN **$**

(Bay St; ⊘lunch & dinner) Open when other places in town are closed, this hole-in-the wall eatery opposite Sharon's & Pheb's has a breezy seaside patio for enjoying the simple meals of fish or chicken and chips or more elaborate plates with all the local trimmings. Blaring music at weekends, too.

Gail's CARIBBEAN **$**

(mains from TT$50; ⊘7pm-late Mon-Sat) Located at the northern end of the waterfront, Gail's serves up freshly caught fish with fantastic local side dishes. Many of the ingredients come straight from Gail's garden.

Top River Pearl Cappuccino Cafe CAFE **$**

(32-34 Spring St; cappuccino TT$20; ⊘8:30am-6:30pm Mon-Sat) Within a guesthouse, this breezy outdoor cafe provides proper cappuccino and espresso, light meals and wi-fi access.

UNDERSTAND TRINIDAD & TOBAGO

History
Early History

Caribs and Arawaks were Trinidad's sole inhabitants until 1498, when Columbus arrived and christened the island La Isla de la Trinidad, for the Holy Trinity.

Initially, gold-hungry Spain gave only scant attention to Trinidad, which lacked precious minerals, but in 1592 a Spanish capital was finally established at San José, just east of present-day Port of Spain, and enslavement of the Amerindian population began in earnest. French planters descended en masse to assist the Spanish with development of the island, and West African slaves were brought in to supplement the labor forces toiling on tobacco and cocoa plantations.

British forces took the island from the Spanish in 1797. With the abolishment of slavery in 1834, slaves abandoned plantations; this prompted the British to import thousands of indentured workers, mostly from India, to labor in the cane fields and service the colony. The indentured labor system remained in place for over 100 years.

Tobago's early history is a separate story. Also sighted by Columbus and claimed by Spain, it wasn't colonized until 1628, when Charles I of England decided to charter the island to the Earl of Pembroke. In response, a handful of nations took an immediate interest in colonizing Tobago.

During the 17th century Tobago changed hands numerous times as the English, French, Dutch and even Courlanders (present-day Latvians) wrestled for control. In 1704 it was declared a neutral territory, which left room for pirates to use the island as a base for raiding ships in the Caribbean. The British established a colonial administration in 1763, and within two decades slave labor established the island's sugar, cotton and indigo plantations.

Tobago's plantation economy wilted after the abolition of slavery but sugar and rum production continued until 1884, when the London firm that controlled finances for the island's plantations went bankrupt. Plantation owners quickly sold or abandoned their land, leaving the economy in a shambles.

A Free Colony

In 1889 Tobago joined Trinidad as a British Crown Colony. Even though Trinidad and Tobago's demand for greater autonomy grew and anticolonial sentiment ripened, the British didn't pay attention until 1956, when the People's National Movement (PNM), led by Oxford-educated Dr Eric Williams, took measures to institute self-government. The country became a republic of the Commonwealth in 1976.

Frustration with the leftover colonial structure led to the Black Power movement, which created a political crisis and an army mutiny, but ultimately strengthened national identity. Bankrupt and without prospects, the country's luck changed in 1970 with the discovery of oil, which brought instant wealth and prosperity. During the 1980s, when oil prices plummeted, a recession hit and political unrest ensued. Accusations of corruption and complaints from an underrepresented Indian community led to the PNM's defeat in 1986 by the National Alliance for Reconstruction (NAR).

Corruption blossomed in a judicial system congested with drugs-related trials (the country is a stopover in the South American drug trade). In July 1990 members of a minority Muslim group attempted a coup, stormed parliament and took 45 hostages, including Prime Minister ANR Robinson. Though the coup failed, it undermined the government, and the PNM returned to power.

Trinidad & Tobago Today

Vast petroleum and natural gas reserves discovered in the late 1990s helped stabilize the economy. In 1995 Basdeo Panday of the United National Congress (UNC) beat the PNM's Patrick Manning in a controversial election, seating the first prime minister of Indian descent. A stalemated political process led Manning again to win the 2002 and 2007 elections. With his popularity failing amid a slew of corruption scandals, Manning called an early election in 2010 and was trounced by the People's Partnership (PP), a coalition of the UNC and COP parties led by Kamla Persad-Bissessar, who became the Republic's first female prime minister. Trinidad and Tobago's party politics had long been divided along ethnic lines, with the PNM being the predominant party of Afro-Trinidadians and the UNC representing the Indian community, and for many, the PP government represented a new start. Whether the PP will be any more successful than the PNM in dealing with the key issues of high crime and deep-seated corruption remains to be seen.

Social inequality is also a huge issue for the PP. Over the past decade the Trinidad and Tobago economy has grown steadily, thanks especially to foreign investment and the oil and gas industry. But despite Port of Spain's new skyscrapers and shopping malls, and a booming energy sector, some 21% of Trinbagonians still live in poverty, many without easy access to adequate housing or quality health care. There are government programs in place to try and address poverty, such as CEPEP, which pays the unemployed to do half-days of manual labor, but breaching the gap between rich and poor remains a huge challenge.

Culture

Trinidadians and Tobagonians love to party and take every opportunity to lime (hang out) whenever the whim hits. Official and unofficial celebrations are plentiful, usually with lots of great food and rum. Most revolve around calypso, soca, or steel pan (see p801), great food and large amounts of rum.

Like other Caribbean destinations, the pace is slow here. Though their energy is bountiful, Trinbagonians see rushing and stress as entirely unnecessary, and take time to visit with one another and discuss everything from politics to the lyrics of the new soca tune dominating the airwaves.

Traditional roles still dominate in Trinbagonian homes. Women cook, clean and take care of the kids, and the inequality between women and men remains depressingly Stone Age. While women generally receive a higher level of education and fill about half the professional and management jobs, they earn about 50% less than men in equitable roles. Many men think it's natural for a man to 'stray' from a committed relationship, but they'd think it an unforgivable sin if a woman were to do the same. Things are slowly changing, however, with Kamla Persad-Bissessar the most prominent of the sassy Trinbagonian women gaining more vital roles in government and demanding better standards of treatment.

Of the country's 1.3 million inhabitants, just 54,000 live on Tobago. Trinidad has one of the most ethnically diverse populations in the Caribbean, a legacy of its checkered colonial history. The majority is of Indian (40.3%) and African (39.5%) descent. The remaining 20% are of mixed ancestry, but there are also notable European, Chinese, Syrian and Lebanese communities, while a few hundred native Caribs live in the Arima area.

Roughly one-third of all islanders are Roman Catholic. Another 25% are Hindu, 11% are Anglican, 13% are other Protestant denominations and 6% are Muslim. Traditional African beliefs also remain strong in some areas, as does Rastafarianism.

Cricket

Introduced by the British in the 19th century, cricket isn't just a sport in Trinidad and Tobago, it's a cultural obsession. International cricket star Brian Lara – the 'Prince of Port of Spain' – hails from Trinidad and his popularity ranks up there with Jesus. And despite their failing fortunes, the arrival of the West Indies team for a test match still sees everything grinding to a halt as people stick to their TVs to capture the action.

The main venue is the Queen's Park Oval, home to the **Queen's Park Cricket Club** (☎622-4325; www.qpcc.com; 94 Tragarete Rd), a few blocks west of the Queen's Park Sa-vannah in Port of Spain. Originally built in 1896, with the northern hills as a spectacular backdrop, it's the site of both regional and international matches and holds 25,000 spectators who pack out the stands and create a party atmosphere at matches. It also has a small museum dedicated to cricket heritage; call to arrange a visit.

Music

Stop for a moment on the streets of Trinidad and Tobago and listen. You'll likely hear the fast beat of soca playing on a maxi-taxi radio, or the sound of steel drums drifting out from a panyard. Often festive, sometimes political or melancholy, music digs deep to the emotion of island life.

Although Carnival happens in February, there's always plenty of great live music happening, especially in the months leading up to Carnival.

CALYPSO

A medium for political and social satire, calypso hearkens back to the days when slaves – unable to chat when working – would sing in patois, sharing gossip and news while mocking their colonial masters. Mighty Sparrow, long acknowledged the king of calypso, has voiced popular concerns and social consciousness since the 1950s, as did his contemporary, the late, great 'Grand-master,' Lord Kitchener. Another famous calypsonian, David Rudder, helped revive the musical form in the mid-1980s by adding experimental rhythms, unearthing both the cultural importance and flexibility of calypso.

SOCA

The energetic offspring of calypso, soca was born in the 1970s, and uses the same basic beat but speeds things up, creating danceable rhythms with risqué lyrics, pointed social commentary and verbal wordplay. Soca dominates the nightclub and Carnival scene and rules the airwaves.

CHUTNEY

This up-tempo, rhythmic music of Indian Trinis is accompanied by the *dholak* (Northern India folk drum) and the *dhantal* (a metal rod played with a metal striker). Chutney songs celebrate social situations – everything from women witnessing a birth to men partying at a bar. It's a fusion of classical Hindu music with more contemporary soca.

STEEL PAN

Rhythm and percussion are the beating heart behind Carnival. Traditionally percussionists banged together bamboo cut in various lengths, or simply drummed on whatever they could – the road, sides of buildings, their knees. When African drums were banned during WWII, drummers turned to biscuit tins, then oil drums discarded by US troops. Today, steel pans come in a variety of sizes, each producing a unique note. Heard together, they become a cascading waterfall of sound. During Carnival, some bands are transported on flatbed trucks along the parade route. All bands aim to win Panorama, the national competition that runs throughout Carnival season.

PARANG

Heard mostly at Christmas time, parang originated in Venezuela. Lyrics are sung in Spanish and accompanied by guitars and maracas. At first heard only in rural areas inhabited by Hispanic Trinis, parang has evolved into a nationwide phenomenon. At Christmas time, groups of *parranderos* play at bars and clubs throughout the islands.

Landscape & Wildlife

The Land

Boot-shaped Trinidad was once part of the South American mainland. Over time a channel developed, separating Trinidad from present-day Venezuela. The connection to South America is noticeable in Trinidad's Northern Range, a continuation of the Andes, and in its abundant oil and gas reserves, concentrated in southwestern Trinidad.

The Northern Range spreads east to west, forming a scenic backdrop to Port of Spain. The rest of the island is given to plains, undulating hills and mangrove swamps. Trinidad's numerous rivers include the 50km Ortoire River, and the 40km Caroni River dumping into the Caroni Swamp.

Tobago, 19km northeast of Trinidad, has a central mountain range that reaches almost 610m at its highest point. Deep, fertile valleys run from the ridge down toward the coast, which is niched with bays and beaches.

Wildlife

Because of its proximity to the South American continent, Trinidad and Tobago has the widest variety of plant and animal life in the Caribbean: 430 species of birds,

600 species of butterfly, 70 kinds of reptiles and 100 types of mammals, including red howler monkeys, anteaters, agouti and armadillos.

Plant life is equally diverse, with more than 700 orchid species and 1600 other types of flowering plants. Both islands have luxuriant rainforests, and Trinidad also features elfin forests, savannas and both freshwater and brackish mangrove swamps.

Environmental Issues

Water pollution is a huge environmental concern on Trinidad and Tobago. Agricultural chemicals, industrial waste and raw sewage seep into groundwater and eventually the ocean. Reef damage is due mostly to pollution, as well as overuse.

Unsustainable development is rampant in this eco-destination. Deforestation and soil erosion are direct results. Sand erosion is a special concern on the northeast coast of Trinidad, where leatherback turtles lay eggs. **Environmental Management Authority** (☑628-8042; www.ema.co.tt) is charged with monitoring environmental issues but, as in other developing countries, the pressure of 'progress' trumps preservation. **Environment Tobago** (www.environmenttobago.net) is an informative source about issues facing Tobago.

SURVIVAL GUIDE

Directory A–Z

Accommodations

Both islands have good-value guesthouses and small hotels. Finding a room is seldom a problem, except during Carnival season when reservations should be made far in advance (and rates increase dramatically). Places in Tobago also raise rates during the winter high season (mid December to mid April).

Trinidad and Tobago is less expensive than many places in the Caribbean, so budget options abound (from US$20 a night), especially in the low or shoulder seasons (roughly April to early December).

Each year, the **TDC** (☑675-7034; www.go trinidadandtobago.com) publishes a small *Accommodation Guide* and it also features updated listings of B&Bs, guesthouses and hotels on its website. It's also worth checking the classified sections of local papers, in print and online.

A 10% service charge and a 15% value-added tax (VAT) can add 35% more to your bill. Most advertised accommodations rates include the tax and service charge, but not always.

$	budget	less than US$75
$$	midrange	US$75 to US$200
$$$	top end	more than US$200

Activities

Some of Trinidad's best bird-watching areas, such as Aripo Savannah and Arena Dam, are very ecologically sensitive and all visitors need a permit to enter. These can be obtained independently, but it's time-consuming and difficult. Far better to let one of the tour operators listed on p805 handle it for you.

During turtle nesting season (March to August) you must have a permit to enter key nesting sites such as the beaches at Matura and Grande Riviere after dark. These are available from Nature Seekers in Matura (p784) and the Grand Riviere Nature Tour Guide Association (p784).

Business Hours

Bars noon-midnight, or when last customer leaves

Banks 8am-2pm Mon-Thu, 8am-noon & 3-5pm Fri

Offices 8am-4pm Mon-Fri

Post offices 7.30am-5pm Mon-Fri

Restaurants 11am-10pm; nontourist restaurants close at 3pm

Shops 8am-4pm Mon-Wed, to 6pm Thu & Fri, to noon Sat; most malls are open later and all day Sat

Children

Kids of all ages flock with their parents to Tobago's beaches, and most facilities are family-oriented. In Trinidad, the tourism is less family-oriented, but higher-end hotels usually accommodate children. During Carnival, Kiddie Mas is a sight not to miss, whatever age.

Dangers & Annoyances

Tobagonians warn of rampant lawlessness in Trinidad, and Trinidadians say crime is increasing in Tobago. While such claims substantiate a real crime increase, they tend to exaggerate the dangers of travel on the islands. Avoid walking alone at night, especially around dark, desolate areas and particularly in Port of Spain. Theft can be a problem, especially in touristy parts of Tobago, so keep an eye on your valuables and don't bring them to the beach.

Some travelers find the aggressive tactics of souvenir hawkers or boat-ride sellers annoying. Just be firm but polite and you'll usually be left alone. Women may also feel frustrated by the overt attention of men, but – again – be firm but polite. While flirting will invite more hassle, a friendly, formal greeting can be disarming. Whether you're male or female, a 'good morning' is the first step to befriending a local.

Trinidad and Tobago gets its share of no-see-ums (tiny sandflies that munch on your skin), especially in the afternoon and early evening. Mosquitoes can also be a bother. A good, strong bug spray will make you a much happier person.

If you've traveled around other Caribbean islands you may have encountered a lax attitude toward drugs. Beware – smoking pot in Trinidad and Tobago is a serious offense and getting caught can quickly ruin your holiday.

Embassies & Consulates

All of the following are located in Port of Spain:

Australia (☑822-5450; www.trinidadandtobago. embassy.gov.au; 18 Herbert St)

Canada (☑622-6232; www.trinidadandtobago. gc.ca; Maple Bldg, 3-3A Sweet Briar Rd)

France (☑622-7446; www.ambafrance-tt.org; Tatil Bldg, 11 Maraval Rd)

Germany (☑628-1630; www.port-of-spain.diplo. de; 7-9 Marli St)

Netherlands (☑625-1201; Life of Barbados Bldg, 69-71 Edward St)

UK (☑622-2748; http://ukintt.fco.gov.uk; 19 St Clair Ave)

USA (☑622-6371; http://trinidad.usembassy. gov; 15 Queen's Park West)

Venezuela (☑627-9821; 16 Victoria Ave)

Food

Eating places in this chapter have been categorized according to the following price indicators, which relate to the cost of a main meal:

PRACTICALITIES

» **Electricity** Electrical current 115/230V, 60hz; US-style two-pin plug.

» **Newspapers & Magazines** There are three daily newspapers: *Trinidad Express*, *Newsday* and *Trinidad Guardian*. *Discover Trinidad & Tobago* is a helpful free tourist magazine found at tourist offices and hotels.

» **Radio & TV** There are three local TV stations: TV6 (channel 5), CVM (channel 6) and Gayelle (channel 7), the latter broadcasting only local programming. Cable channels include CNN and BBC World News. About 15 independent radio stations blast the airwaves.

» **Weights & Measures** Metric system. Highway signs and car odometers are in kilometers, but some road markers still measure miles.

$	budget	less than TT$30
$$	midrange	TT$30 to TT$100
$$$	top end	more than TT$100

Gay & Lesbian Travelers

Though more progressive than some other Caribbean islands, Trinidad and Tobago remains pretty closed to the idea of same-sex relationships. There are enclaves, such as the more touristy spots or upper-echelon districts in metropolitan areas, where being out and expressing affection is OK, but on beaches and in rural areas you may get negative repercussions.

Health

Tap water is heavily chlorinated in Trinidad and Tobago, though tastes better boiled than fresh from the tap. It can still cause upsets for those unused to it, though, so it's best to stick to bottled water.

Internet Access

Internet service is widely available in bigger cities and in most smaller towns as well. The rate is about TT$10 per half-hour. Most accommodations have access for guests, and wi-fi too, which is increasingly offered by bars and restaurants.

Money

The official currency is the Trinidad and Tobago dollar (TT$). Banks will exchange a number of foreign currencies, but you'll generally get better rates for US dollars or euros. Most restaurants, hotels, dive shops, car-rental companies and more established guesthouses accept credit cards. In this book, we quote rates as they are given in Trinidad and Tobago, whether it be in TT$ or US$.

Many restaurants add a 10% service charge to bills; if not, a tip of 10% to 15% is customary.

Public Holidays

Carnival Monday and Tuesday are unofficial holidays, with banks and most businesses closed. In addition to those observed throughout the region (p872), Trinidad and Tobago has the following public holidays:

Spiritual Baptist/Shouter Liberation Day March 30

Indian Arrival Day May 30

Corpus Christi Ninth Thursday after Easter

Labour Day June 19

Emancipation Day August 1

Independence Day August 31

Republic Day September 24

Eid al Fitr (Muslim New Year) Dates vary

Telephone

The country's area code is ☑868. When calling from North America, dial ☑1-868 plus the local number. From elsewhere dial your country's international access code plus ☑868 plus the local number. Within the country, just dial the seven-digit local number (as we have listed in this chapter).

Public phones are numerous but many nonfunctional. Your best bet is to purchase a Telecommunications Services of Trinidad and Tobago (TSTT) phonecard, use calling centers or, if you're needing to make calls frequently, it's easiest and cheap to get a local SIM card (around TT$100) and use a cell phone.

Tourist Information

Tobago House of Assembly Tourism Branch (☑639-4636; www.visittobago.gov.tt; 12 Sangster's Hill; ⊙8am-4pm Mon-Fri)

Tourism Development Company (TDC; ☑675-7034; www.gotrinidadandtobago.com)

Travelers with Disabilities

With tourist infrastructure already wobbly here, Trinidad and Tobago doesn't have extensive facilities for travelers with disabilities. However, the higher-end hotels and resorts are equipped to accommodate.

Visas

Visas are not necessary for citizens of the US, Canada, the UK or most European countries for stays of less than three months.

Visas are required by citizens of Australia, New Zealand, South Africa, India and some other Commonwealth countries (including Nigeria, Papua New Guinea, Sri Lanka, Tanzania and Uganda). In most countries visas are obtained through the Trinidad and Tobago or British embassy, and cost TT$200. For more, contact **Trinidad and Tobago Immigration** (✆669-5895; www.immigration.gov.tt).

Women Travelers

A woman traveling alone, especially on Trinidad, is about as common as snow. Men will stare, make kissy noises, hiss or offer to be anything from your protector to your sex slave. Says one Trini woman, 'Trini men feel compelled to let women know they are noticed and appreciated.' While the constant attention can wear on your nerves, most men are harmless. Your best bet is to smile politely, or ignore it altogether and move on.

Getting There & Away

Entering Trinidad & Tobago

Provided you have a valid passport (US citizens, see p875), coming and going from Trinidad and Tobago is easy. When you arrive, you'll fill out an Immigration Arrival Card. Customs officials require that you fill out the line asking where you are staying; if you don't know, list any local hotel.

Air

Airports in both Trinidad and Tobago handle international air traffic, but the bulk of international flights arrive and depart from Trinidad.

AIRPORTS

ANR Robinson International Airport (TAB; ✆639-8547; www.crownpointairport.com) Located in Crown Point, 11km southwest of Scarborough, on Tobago.

Piarco International Airport (POS; ✆669-8047; www.piarcoairport.com) Located 25km east of Port of Spain, on Trinidad.

AIRLINES

Air Canada, American, Continental and Delta fly to Trinidad from cities in the US and Canada. British Airways has flights from London to Trinidad and Tobago via St Lucia; Monarch and Virgin Atlantic also fly to Tobago from London. The following airlines also serve Trinidad and Tobago:

Caribbean Airlines (www.caribbean-airlines.com) Antigua, Barbados, Caracas, Fort Lauderdale, Grenada, New York, Toronto

LIAT (✆625-9451; www.liatairline.com) **Connections with Trinidad**: Anguilla, Antigua, Barbados, Curaçao, Dominica, Grenada, Guadeloupe, Martinique, Nevis, St Kitts, St Vincent, San Juan, Santo Domingo, St-Martin/Sint Maarten, St Croix, St Lucia, St Thomas, Tortola; **Connections with Tobago**: Antigua, Barbados, Grenada, St-Martin/Sint Maarten, St Kitts, St Lucia, St Vincent, Tortola

Travelspan (www.travelspan.com) Miami, New York

Sea

CRUISE SHIP

In Trinidad ships dock at the King's Wharf, on ugly Wrightson Rd in Port of Spain, from where you can walk onto Independence Sq and the downtown area. In Tobago, the cruise ship terminal is adjacent to the ferry terminal in downtown Scarborough. See p773 for more information on what to see during your stop off.

FERRY

A ship leaves for Guiria, Venezuela (TT$552 plus TT$75 departure tax, 3½ hours), at 9am on Wednesday (arrives at 7am) from **Pier One** (✆634-4472) in Chaguaramas. It returns from Guiria at 4pm on the same day.

YACHT

Out of the hurricane path, Trinidad and Tobago is a safe haven for yachters. Chaguaramas has the primary mooring and marina facilities as well as an immigration and customs office for yachters. Tobago is an upwind jaunt, but sometimes yachts moor at Charlottesville or Scarborough. For more information, contact the **Yacht Services Association of Trinidad and Tobago** (✆634-4938; www.ysatt.org).

Getting Around

Air

Caribbean Airlines (☎625-8246; www.caribbean-airlines.com) operates the 20-minute flight between Trinidad and Tobago (one-way TT$150). The checked baggage weight allowance is 20kg. While it's wise to book in advance, it is often possible to buy tickets at the airport on the day of departure.

Boat

Fast catamaran ferries make the trip between Queen's Wharf in Port of Spain, Trinidad, and the main ferry dock in Scarborough, Tobago (TT$50, 2½ hours). It's a cheaper, comfortable way to travel (unless you're prone to seasickness), with the added bonus of not having to travel all the way to Piarco airport. There is a bar, cafeteria and deck, and movies are played in the air-conditioned interior.

There are two to four departures daily from both islands, in the morning and afternoon. Around the Carnival season it's best to buy tickets as far as possible in advance; these are available from travel agents on both islands. The **Port Authority** (☎Trinidad 625-3055, Tobago 639-2181; www.patnt.com) has schedules and a list of outlets.

Bus

Buses offer travelers an inexpensive way to get around, especially on longer cross-island trips, but can be infrequent and unreliable. For shorter distances, travelers are better off taking maxi-taxis or route taxis. Check the bus information for Trinidad (p765) and Tobago (p785).

Car

RENTAL

Driving yourself can be a great way of getting around the islands. Car rentals start at about TT$300 a day, and include insurance and unlimited mileage. For more information on rentals, see p765 for Trinidad and p785 for Tobago.

ROAD RULES

Cars drive on the left, and the car's steering wheel is on the right (as in the UK). Your home driver's license is valid for stays of up to three months.

Twisting, narrow roads and fast, horn-happy drivers can make driving on the islands an adventure; in Port of Spain, traffic complicated roads and poor signage can make for a white-knuckle experience. Your best bet is to study a map before you get in the car, take a deep breath and practice Zen-like patience. You will get the hang of it, and you'll find driving much easier if you simply relax a little and follow the flow. Be aware that fellow road users will stop suddenly to drop off a friend, say 'hi' to a neighbor or pick up a cold beer. Sometimes they'll simply stop, while other times they'll wave an arm up and down to signal they are about to do something.

The ignored speed limit on highways is 80km/h, and 50km/h to 55km/h on city streets. Gas (petrol) is about TT$2.75 a liter for regular.

Hitchhiking

Hitching is very common among locals, particularly in rural areas, but it's not a safe mode of transportation for foreign visitors, especially women (your want of a ride will be misconstrued as a want of other things).

Maxi-Taxi

Maxi-taxis are 12- to 25-passenger minibuses that travel along a fixed route within a specific zone. They're color-coded by route, run 24 hours, are very cheap and are heavily used by the locals. Rides cost TT$2 to TT$12, depending on how far you go. You can flag a maxi at any point along its route, or hop on at the appropriate taxi stand. Keep in mind that, due to their frequent stops, maxi-taxis will take a long time to get from A to B.

On Trinidad, many maxi-taxis operate out of the maxi-taxi terminal adjacent to City Gate. For information on Trinidad's maxi-taxi color-coding system, see p765. On Tobago, all maxis have a blue band.

For information about maxi-taxi routes, contact **Trinidad & Tobago Unified Maxi Taxi Association** (☎624-3505).

Route Taxi

These taxis are shared cars that travel along a prescribed route and can drop you anywhere along the way. They look like regular cars, except that their license plates start with an 'H' (for 'hire'). See p765 (Trinidad) and p785 (Tobago) for island-specific info.

Taxi

Regular taxis are readily available at the airports, cruise-ship and ferry terminals and at hotels. All are unmetered but follow rates established by the government; hotel desks and airport tourist offices have a list of fares. Make sure to establish the rate before riding off, and note that fares increase after 10pm. For island-specific taxi information, see p765 (Trinidad) and p785 (Tobago).

Tours

TOBAGO

Alibaba (✆635-1017; www.alibaba-tours.com; Heavenly Bay, Castara; per person US$65-95) Professional outfit offering boat trips and land tours throughout the island.

Frankie's (✆631-0369; www.frankietours.com; Mt Irvine Beach; per person US$20-110) Offers turtle, bird-watching and rainforest tours as well as glass-bottom/snorkel tours around the island, 24-hour taxi service and car rentals.

Grand Slam Charters (✆639-9961; http://grandslamtobago.com; Crown Point) Offshore fishing charters (US$400 to US$600 for up to four people) and inshore fly-fishing trips (US$200 to US$400 for one to two people).

Peter Cox Nature Tours (✆751-5822; www .tobagonaturetours.com; per person US$75-90) A good choice for serious bird-watchers, with avian-oriented trips islandwide, plus hiking and turtle-watching.

TRINIDAD

The following companies are recommended for islandwide tours and activities:

Caribbean Discovery Tours (✆620-1989; www.caribbeandiscoverytours.com) A good choice for island and city tours, hiking, kayaking and bird-watching.

Island Experiences (✆625-2410, 756-9677; www.islandexperiencestt.com) Highly recommended. Gunda Harewood offers 'ecocultural tours' (TT$75 to TT95 per person) throughout the island, which aim to show the country's underbelly and to impart local knowledge and lore.

Paria Springs (✆622-8826; www.pariasprings .com) Run by a local mountain biker and wildlife expert, tours include bird-watching, cycling, hiking and kayaking.

Turks & Caicos

Best Beaches

» Grace Bay Beach (p812)

» Mudjin Harbor (p821)

» Bambarra Beach (p821)

» Governor's Beach (p824)

Best Places to Eat

» Grace's Cottage (p816)

» Terrace (p819)

» Coyaba (p817)

» Osprey (p825)

Why Go?

The Turks and where? That's the reaction most people have when you mention these tropical isles. Like all great Shangri-Las, this one is hidden just under the radar. Be glad that it is, as this tropical dream is the deserted Caribbean destination you've been looking for. And the best part – it's only 90 minutes by plane from Miami.

So why would you want to go there? How about white-sand beaches, clear blue water and a climate that defines divine. Secluded bays and islands where you'll see more wild donkeys than other travelers. Historic towns and villages where life creeps along at a sedate pace.

Divers and beach aficionados will rejoice: clear warm waters teem with marine life, yet are devoid of crashing waves. Islands like Grand Turk – set in a time long since past, with its dilapidated buildings, salt ponds and narrow lanes – contrast with the ever expanding Providenciales. While development is on the rise, all one has to do is catch a boat to the next island over and the solace of solitude returns.

When to Go

January to April is the islands' high season and is rightly popular – the weather is normally dry and warm. In July, the country's biggest fishing competition, the Grand Turk Game Fishing Tournament, arrives. Come in November to blow a conch shell or just head for the tasting tent at the Turks & Caicos Conch Festival.

Itineraries

THREE DAYS

Spend the day admiring Grace Bay on Providenciales then wake up the next day to go for a snorkeling trip to French Cay to frolic with some stingrays. On the last day rent a bike and explore the island under your own steam.

ONE WEEK

Add on a trip to the islands of North Caicos and Middle Caicos and discover what solitude is really all about. Complete the trip by heading to Grand Turk to explore the town, do some great diving and spend a day or two on Salt Cay – the best-kept secret in the country.

GETTING TO NEIGHBORING ISLANDS

There are no scheduled ferry services to neighboring islands from the Turks and Caicos. Flying is the way to get around and there are regular flights to Nassau (Bahamas), Puerto Plata and Santiago (Dominican Republic), Cap-Haïtien and Port-au-Prince (Haiti) and to Kingston (Jamaica).

Essential Food & Drink

» **Conch** This grilled gastropod remains the dish of choice across the islands, and rigorous controls on the fishing industry mean that its numbers are not declining here.

» **Lobster** Don't miss tasting the fresh lobster during your stay – traditionally served in a butter sauce with lime, it's the culinary highlight of the country.

» **Turk's Head** The local brew is a great way to cool down in the height of the Caribbean afternoon.

AT A GLANCE

Currency US$

Language English

Money ATMs abundant on Providenciales, less common elsewhere

Visas Not required for citizens of the US, Canada or Western Europe

Fast Facts

» **Area** 430 sq miles

» **Population** 44,800

» **Capital** Cockburn Town

» **Telephone country code** ☑649

» **Emergency** ☑911

Set Your Budget

» **Budget hotel room** $80

» **Two-course evening meal** $50

» **Museum entrance** $5

» **Beer** $3

Resources

» **Official tourism website** (www.turksandcaicostourism.com)

» **Government website** (www.tcgov.tc)

» **Time of the Island** (www.timespub.tc)

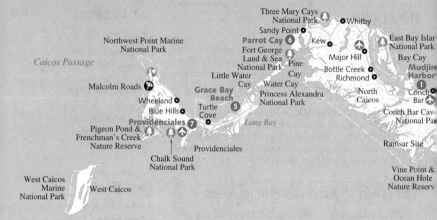

Turks & Caicos Highlights

1 Seeking out stunning **Mudjin Harbor** (p821) – one of the best beach entrances anywhere in the Caribbean

2 Joining a **whale-watching trip** (p824) in Salt Cay and see huge humpback whales breaching the ocean, an unforgettable experience

3 Diving into the water at **Grand Turk** (p824), where the fish are plentiful and the reef pristine

N
0 ——————————— 50 km
0 ——————————— 30 miles

ATLANTIC

OCEAN

uniper Hole

● Bambarra

● Lorimers

ddle Caicos   *Crossing Place Trail*

● Jacksonville

East Caicos

Caicos Bank

Belle Sound & Admiral Cockburn Cays Nature Reserve   South Caicos

Six Hill Cays

● Cockburn Harbour

Long Cay

Turks Island Passage

Grand Turk ❸ ❹
● Cockburn Town

● Waterloo

Long Cay

Grand Turk Cays Land & Sea Park

Cotton Cay

Fish Cays

Balfour Town ●
Salt Cay ❷

Big Ambergris Cay

Little Ambergris Cay

Seal Cays   Bush Cay

Sand Cay

● *HMS Endymion Wreck*

❹ Finding your own slice of heaven on miles of white powder sand at **Grace Bay Beach** (p812)

❺ Pampering yourself by booking a room at the sumptuous **Parrot Cay** (p819), for the ultimate in Caribbean elegance and luxury

❻ Enjoying cosmopolitan pursuits in **Providenciales** (p812) – shopping in its many malls, eat in its great restaurants and enjoy cocktails on the beach

CAICOS ISLANDS

The fan of islands that form the main landmass of this nation are the Caicos Islands, made up of West Caicos, Providenciales, North Caicos, Middle Caicos, East Caicos, and South Caicos, plus numerous other tiny islands both inhabited and deserted. Nearly everyone arrives in Providenciales. Whether or not they stay there depends on what kind of holiday they want.

ℹ Getting There & Around

Providenciales International Airport is the main point of entry for the Caicos Islands as it is for the entire country. There are connecting flights to the rest of the Caicos Islands from here, too, with daily connections to South Caicos, as well as to Grand Turk and Salt Cay in the Turks Islands.

The most normal way to get around Providenciales itself is by rental car, which can be picked up at the airport or rented through hotels.

There is a ferry connecting Providenciales to North Caicos several times a day from the western tip of the island.

Providenciales

POP 8900

Providenciales, or Provo as it's known locally, is the tourism capital of the Turks and Caicos. It's home to a busy international airport, some fairly rampant development and its crowing glory, miles of beautiful white-sand beaches along its northern coast. While it's a great place for those wanting a large choice of eating and sleeping options, you certainly won't be alone in heading here – and development continues at an impressive pace as the last beachfront plots are divided and sold.

But there are still pockets of the island that haven't succumbed to the developers' attentions, and thankfully much of the island's western side is protected land, including the Pigeon Pond & Frenchman's Creek Nature Reserve and the Chalk Sound National Park.

◉ Sights

Grace Bay Beach   BEACH

The biggest attraction on the island is this world-famous stretch of sand, notably long and beautiful even by Caribbean standards. This stunning stretch of snow-white sand is perfect for relaxing, swimming and evening up your sunburn. Though it's dotted with hotels and resorts, its sheer size means that finding your own square of paradise is a snap.

Chalk Sound National Park   NATIONAL PARK

The waters of this 3-mile-long bay, 2 miles southwest of downtown, define 'turquoise.' The color is uniform: a vast, unrippled, electric-blue carpet eerily and magnificently studded with countless tiny islets.

A slender peninsula separates the sound from the sea. The peninsula is scalloped with beach-lined bays, notably **Sapodilla Bay**. A horribly potholed road runs along the peninsula; although it is accessible, drive carefully. Unfortunately, large vacation homes line both sides of the peninsula from top to toe, which clip the views and hinder some public access from the roads to the water and beaches.

At the far eastern end of the Sapodilla Bay peninsula, a rocky hilltop boasts **rock carvings** dating back to 1844. The slabs of rock are intricately carved with Roman lettering that records the names of sailors apparently shipwrecked here and the dates of their sojourns. The carvings are reached via a rocky trail that begins 200yd east of the Mariner Hotel; it leads uphill 200yd to the summit, which offers wonderful views over the island and Chalk Sound.

Provo Conch Farm   CONCH FARM

(☏946-5643; tour adult/child $10/5; ⊗9am-4pm Mon-Fri, until noon Sat) If you want to see what you've been chowing down on, head to the northeast corner of Provo and have a look at this working conch farm. Slightly ramshackle (it was battered by Hurricane Ike in 2008 and is still rebuilding) and more than a little strange, it has a speedy 20-minute tour to show you how they grow the Caribbean Queens. There are also green turtle feeding sessions each day at 9.30am and 3.30pm and at 10am Saturday.

Other Sights

If you feel inclined to tear yourself away from the beach and see some other sights, there are a few worth taking in. Though the options are limited, there are some historic points that should perk scholarly interest. Check out the ruins of **Cheshire Hall** (Leeward Hwy), a plantation house constructed in the 1790s by British Loyalists.

If you've got a rental car that can handle a bit of dirt road, be sure to check out the lighthouse at **Northwest Point**, 8 miles from Providenciales. Caution is the word as the road has been known to swallow cars whole.

Once you get all that history out of your system go for an anti-intellectual cleanse and seek out the sparkling beach at **Malcolm Roads**. From the settlement of Wheeland, northwest of downtown, a rough dirt road leads to this top-notch sandy spot.

Protecting reefs off of Provo's west shore, Northwest Point Marine National Park also encompasses several saline lakes that attract breeding and migrant waterfowl. The largest is **Pigeon Pond**, inland. This part of the park is the Pigeon Pond & Frenchman's Creek Nature Reserve. Other ponds – notably **Northwest Point Pond** and **Frenchman's Creek** – encompass tidal flats and mangrove swamps along the west coast, attracting fish and fowl in large numbers. You'll have to hike here, and come equipped with food and water.

🏃 Activities

Diving & Snorkeling

All the dive operators offer a range of dive and snorkel options, from introductory 'resort courses' to PADI certification ($350 to $395).

Most offer free hotel pick-up and drop-offs. Dive sites include the other Caicos islands and cays.

Art Pickering's Provo Turtle Divers DIVING
(☑946-4232; www.provoturtledivers.com; Turtle Cove Marina) Has been going strong for 35 years now; it offers two-tank/night dives for $119/85. Visits all the major dive sites – the company is all about service.

Dive Provo DIVING
(☑946-5040; www.diveprovo.com; Ports of Call plaza, Grace Bay Rd) Has two-tank/night dives ($119/85) at sites around the island, plus photo and video services.

Ocean Vibes DIVING
(☑231-6636; www.oceanvibes.com; Leeward Marina) Is the only dive operation on the island run by Belongers. It specializes in small groups and an intimate feel to its aquatic adventures. Two-tank dives are $125 and there's a host of good deals on the website.

Fishing

Boat charters and trips can be arranged from Leeward and Turtle Cove Marinas. Try the following:

Catch the Wave Charters FISHING
(☑941-3047; www.catchthewavecharters.mobi; Leeward Marina) Runs a variety of boat charters to suit your taste. Fishing costs $500 for half a day. Deep-sea/bottom fishing is $750 for a half-day rental of a boat that will fit four fishers.

Bite Me Sportfishing FISHING
(☑231-0366; biteme@tciway.tc) Is not just a great name, but a good group of folks to help you land the big one.

Grand Slam Charters FISHING
(☑231-4420; www.grandslam-fishing.com) Offers the biggest charter boat on the Turks and Caicos for some serious deep-sea fishing!

Boat Trips

Undersea Explorer Semi Submarine BOAT TRIP
(☑231-0006; www.caicostours.com; Turtle Cove Marina; adult/child $55/40; 🅓) This is a moving underwater observatory that's a big hit with kids and those with a phobia of actually getting wet. It's a cool way to see three different sections of the reef – as long as you're not claustrophobic. There are tours leaving at 10am, noon and 2pm each day, and your ticket includes a free pick-up and drop-off at any hotel in the Grace Bay area.

Water Sports

Windsurfing Provo WINDSURFING
(☑241-1687; www.windsurfingprovo.tc; Ocean Club, Grace Bay) Has windsurfing ($40 per hour), sailing ($150 per day) and kayaking ($25 per hour) on offer.

🛌 Sleeping

Provo most definitely isn't lacking in places to spend the night. Hotels, condos and resorts dot the island with a frequency that may make you wonder if there really are possibly enough tourists to fill all these rooms. Most budgets are accommodated for, but there is a skew to the higher end so those with deeper pockets will be spoilt for choice. At present, supply outnumbers demand so there are some good deals to be found, especially in the low season.

DOWNTOWN & TURTLE COVE

Coral Gardens BEACH HOTEL $$$
(☑941-5497; www.coralgardensatgracebay.com; Turtle Cove; r from $249; ❄🅢🅢) This modern and sleek resort right on the beach manages to feel both relaxed and classy. All rooms,

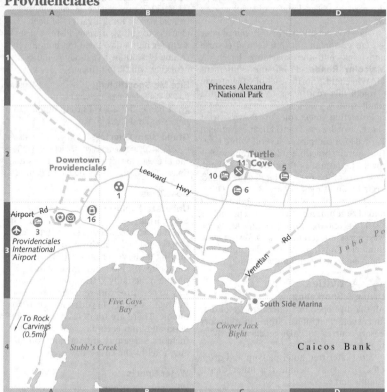

from the modest garden category to the three-bedroom ocean-front suites, are very plushly appointed and on top of that there's a fantastic and unusually social beach bar and restaurant.

Turtle Cove Inn   INN **$**

(✆946-4203; www.turtlecoveinn.com; Turtle Cove Marina; r from $79; ❄️🛜🏊) If you're here to dive and lounge by the pool, this older but friendly and well-run property in the heart of the Turtle Cove Marina is a good option. The rooms have fridge and a safe, but are otherwise frill-free, but staying here puts you in a great location. There are numerous restaurants a few steps away, and dive boats, fishing charters and rental cars all leaving from the doorstep.

Miramar Resort   RESORT **$**

(✆946-4240; www.miramar.tc; Turtle Cove; r $89; ❄️🛜🏊) Has bright, clean and spacious rooms with patio, fridge and good views of Turtle Cove from the hill above. It does lack a bit of character and there are some quirks to the place. It's also a fair trek from the beach. But it has a pool, tennis courts and a gym to keep you busy, and there is the excellent Magnolia Restaurant & Wine Bar in the adjacent building. Note also that there's a three-night minimum stay requirement.

Airport Inn   HOTEL **$$**

(✆941-3514; www.airportinntci.com; Airport Plaza; s/d $130/140; ❄️🛜) Sporting unencumbered views of the runway, the Airport Inn isn't the sort of place to spend your holiday, but is worth considering if you have an early flight. It is also actually a great option if you're not here for the beach – the rooms are huge and very comfortable given the price. There are also plenty of eating options nearby, all with a local flavor.

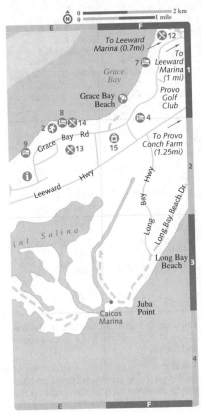

cottages are clustered around the pool in blocks of four, and still afford generous privacy and space. The entire place feels far removed from the bustle of the other resorts and this makes it a great place to escape to.

Comfort Suites
SUITES **$$**

(☏946-8888; www.comfortsuitestci.com; Grace Bay; r from $105; ❄️🛜🏊) If you're searching for an affordable resort and are willing to accept that it isn't beachfront (though not far off!), this is a great option. Clean and spacious rooms stack in three stories above the pool and chilled poolside bar. Couches in the rooms and chilled-out staff are thrown in. There are even designated chairs on the beach for guests. Nothing too special, but if you're here to dive, lie on the beach or not liquidate your finances, this is the place to stay.

Ocean Club West
RESORT **$$$**

(☏946-5880; www.oceanclubresorts.com; Grace Bay; r from $289; ❄️🛜🏊) With a great location in the heart of Grace Bay, the OC is a safe bet. The wonderful pool is complete with an arch-bridge-appointed 'river' and the requisite swim-up bar. Rooms are a bit cramped, but the kitchenettes and balconies more than make up for it. Guests here are also able to use the facilities at the nearby Ocean Club, effectively giving you access to two resorts for the price of one.

Sands
RESORT **$$$**

(☏946-5199; www.thesandstc.com; Grace Bay; r from $285; ❄️🛜🏊👶) This mammoth place is a great family option with a kiddy pool, and kitchenettes in every room. The 118 suites cluster around the superb pool area or face onto the beach where there are tiki huts, for the sun worshippers and the excellent Hemingway's Bar and Grill on-site.

🍴 Eating & Drinking

Provo has by far the best eating options in the country: those on a budget have the choice of some fun pubs and family-style restaurants, while those looking for a truly memorable experience have several excellent options.

GRACE BAY & EAST PROVIDENCIALES

TOP CHOICE Sibonné Beach Hotel   BEACH HOTEL **$$**
(☏946-5547; www.sibonne.com; Grace Bay; r incl breakfast $125-235, apt $350; ❄️@🛜🏊) Deservedly popular and occupying a divine stretch of sand on Grace Bay, Sibonné is a real anti-resort and it gets our vote. With five room categories ranging from comfortable to luxurious and a friendly relaxed feel (no officious security guards here) this is a great place to enjoy the beach in a low-key surrounding.

Point Grace Luxury Resort & Spa
RESORT **$$$**

(☏946-5096; www.pointgrace.com; Grace Bay; r $475, ste from $915; ❄️🛜🏊) The 28 rooms and cottages at this very up-market resort right on the beach are all very sophisticated and luxurious with freestanding bathtubs and vast four-poster beds. The very best suites are right on Grace Beach, while the cheaper

DOWNTOWN & TURTLE COVE
Baci Ristorante   ITALIAN **$$**
(☏941-3044; Harbour Towne Plaza, Turtle Cove; mains $10-30; ⏰lunch & dinner) Maritime chic at its best with wrought-iron scrollwork lining the ceilings, all with an authentic

TURKS & CAICOS PROVIDENCIALES

Italian-infused flavor overlooking the marina. There's a cheap lunch menu offering paninis and pasta ($10 to $14), while the evening menu is more traditionally Italian (carpaccio, *scaloppini al limone*, steaks). Book ahead for the evening.

Magnolia Restaurant &
Wine Bar   MODERN CARIBBEAN $$$
(🕿941-5108; Turtle Cove; mains from $22-35; ⊘dinner Tue-Sat) Sitting on the hill overlooking Turtle Cove, Magnolia is a great place for a romantic meal, with superb (if pricey) cooking and an equally lovely view over the lights of the cove. The fairy-light-rimmed balcony is the perfect setting for the signature dish, a cracked-pepper and sesame-encrusted rare-seared tuna, which is so tender it melts in your mouth. The restaurant has an ample wine list to choose from and the service is impeccable. Book ahead to get a table with a good view. The wine bar is open from 4pm daily, so this is also a great spot for a sundowner cocktail, even if you don't plan to eat.

Somewhere Café & Lounge   MEXICAN $$
(Coral Gardens, Leeward Hwy, Turtle Cove; mains $12-25; ⊘breakfast, lunch & dinner) This charmingly laid back two-floor beach cabaña is a treat any time of the day. Good breakfasts, spicy Mexican dishes, delicious pastries

and a lively bar make this one of the few places in Provo where you'll meet a young and fun crowd.

Tiki Hut   INTERNATIONAL $$
(Turtle Cove Marina; mains from $16; ⊘11am-10pm Mon-Fri, 9am-10pm Sat & Sun) Set right on the wharf at Turtle Cove Marina, this popular spot is where you can sit with a cold beer and watch the boats returning to port. There are cheap sandwiches and burgers ($10 to $12) or more substantial dishes such as baby ribs, cracked conch or lobster pasta.

Carambola Grill & Lounge   GRILL $$
(🕿946-8122; Airport Hotel Plaza; mains $16-26; ⊘lunch & dinner) The huge menu at this popular downtown spot can be overwhelming, but it's safe to say you'll find something you want, from lobster thermidor to Cajun shrimp and chicken pasta. It offers a pick-up service from Grace Bay hotels, simply call ahead.

GRACE BAY & EAST PROVIDENCIALES
There is a wide choice of dining options in this neck of the woods. The Ports of Call shopping plaza has a stack of midrange options and nearly all hotels and resorts in this area have restaurants that are open to the public.

TOP
CHOICE **Grace's Cottage**   INTERNATIONAL $$$
(🕿946-8147; Point Grace Luxury Resort & Spa, Grace Bay; mains $25-50; ⊘dinner) Tucked

out of the way from the main road, this charming cottage has tables spread out among the trees and in romantic hidden enclaves. Crisp white-linen tablecloths adorn the surfaces and service is excellent. The menu encompasses inventive seafood dishes and pasta, and vegetarians are well catered for. There's also a superb wine list. Reservations are usually essential.

TOP CHOICE Coyaba   CARIBBEAN $$$
(☑946-5186; www.coyabarestaurant.com; Paradise Inn; mains from $35; ☺dinner Wed-Mon) Off Grace Bay Rd, Coyaba somehow treads the line of fine dining while retaining a relaxed atmosphere. The food is a clever fusion of Caribbean flavors and faithful classics. The legendary chef shows his skills with daily specials that outnumber the menu standards. This is a real food-lovers' paradise. Be sure to make a reservation – word's out about this one.

Green Bean   CAFE $
(Leeward Hwy, Turtle Cove; mains $8-15; ☺7am-6pm) This excellent initiative pairs up healthy eating and environmental awareness and is leading where hopefully others will follow, using organic produce, compostable packaging and, where possible, locally sourced ingredients. Try its excellent salads or make your own, get a fresh smoothie or panini to go, or just chill out with a range of tea and coffee.

O'Soleil   SEAFOOD $$$
(☑946-5900; The Somerset, Princess Dr; mains $26-40; ☺dinner) Fresh seafood is the specialty in this stylish eatery. The Mediterranean-influenced architecture provides the perfect backdrop for the culinary designs created in the kitchen. Be sure to try the Turks and Caicos chowder: it's loaded with fresh seafood and the secret ingredient that makes it nearly irresistible – Caribbean rum.

Calico Jack's   BAR & GRILL $$
(Ports of Call plaza; mains from $12; ☺dinner) Comes with a generous helping of nautical paraphernalia and is named after the English pirate who popularized the skull and crossbones flag. Nightly drink specials, Spanish armada–sized portions and a friendly atmosphere make it a locals' favorite. The conch is awesome, and be sure to swing by on a Thursday when the place really hops to the sounds of live music.

Danny Buoy's Irish Pub & Restaurant   PUB $
(Grace Bay Rd; mains from $10; ☺lunch & dinner) This dark but lively pub offers up traditional Irish fare mixed with Caribbean classics. The Guinness on tap is good, but you'll need a lot of them to believe you're in the old country!

Island Scoop Ice-Cream   ICE CREAM $
(Grace Bay Plaza, Grace Bay Rd; ice cream $3; ☺10am-9pm) When the sun is shining and it's all starting to get just a bit too hot, slide into Island Scoop for the therapy you need. Twenty-four flavors of goodness to choose from, piled into homemade waffle cones.

The best supermarket in Providenciales is **Graceway Gourmet**, just next to the Scotiabank and Comfort Suites in Grace Bay. It may be eye-wateringly expensive, but its selection of fresh fruit and vegetables can't be beaten anywhere else in the country.

🔒 Shopping
Providenciales has a large selection of shopping malls spread out along the Grace Bay Rd. These largely contain international brand shops and prices aren't particularly

JOJO: A NATIONAL TREASURE

Since the mid '80s a 7ft bottle-nosed male dolphin called JoJo has cruised the waters off of Provo and North Caicos. When he first appeared, he was shy and limited his human contact to following or playing in the bow waves of boats. He soon turned gregarious and has become an active participant whenever people are in the water.

JoJo is now so popular that he has been named a national treasure by the Ministry of Natural Resources. This treasure is protected through the **JoJo Dolphins Project** (☑941-5617; www.deanandjojo.com; PO Box 153, Providenciales, Turks and Caicos). In addition to looking out for JoJo, it educates and raises awareness of issues affecting the ocean.

JoJo, as with any wild dolphin, interprets attempts to touch him as an aggressive act, and will react to defend himself, so please bear that in mind if you're lucky enough to experience his playfulness and companionship for a while.

GO FLY A KITE

The steady winds that buff the coast-line of the Turks and Caicos mixed with the reef-sheltered shoreline are the perfect combination for the snowboarding of the aquatic world – **kitesurfing**. The bastard child of stunt kite flying, wakeboarding and windsurfing, this sport is going off right now. Imagine flying the biggest kite you've ever seen, strapping yourself onto a wakeboard and holding on for dear life. Depending on how much sugar you like in your tea, it either sounds terrific or terrifying. The warm T&C waters are already on the radar of the sport's elite – but don't be put off, it's also a great place to learn. Chat to Mike at **Windsurfing Provo** (☎241-1687; www.windsurfingprovo.tc; Ocean Club, Grace Bay) to get hooked up with the how-to ($150 for a two-hour lesson). Who said all there is to do in the Caribbean is lie on the beach?

good, as everything has been imported. Locally produced items are generally of very little interest to travelers, there are few local arts and crafts, and most items on sale come far more under the heading of 'tourist tat' that genuine souvenirs.

A large selection of beachy items, casual clothing and batiks is offered at Tattooed Parrot, Marilyn's Crafts and the Night & Day Boutique, all in the Ports of Call plaza.

Information

Associated Medical Practices Clinic (☎946-4242; Leeward Hwy) Has several private doctors. The clinic has a recompression chamber.

Cable & Wireless (☎111; Leeward Hwy) Make calls here. It has telephone information and can sort you out with a cell phone. There are also public phone booths at several roadside locations. You dial ☎111 to place credit-card calls.

Fire (☎946-4444)

Police (☎946-4259; Old Airport Rd)

Post office (Old Airport Rd; ☻8am-noon & 2-4pm Mon-Thu, 8am-12:30pm & 2-5:30pm Fri) Next to the police station.

Provo Discount Pharmacy (☎946-4844; Central Sq Plaza, Leeward Hwy; ☻8am-10pm)

Tourist information booth (Arrivals Hall, Providenciales International Airport)

Turks & Caicos Tourism (☎946-4970; www

.turksandcaicostourism.com; Stubbs Diamond Plaza, ☻9am-5pm Mon-Fri)

 Getting There & Around

Air

For flight information to and from the Caicos Islands, see p831.

There is no bus service from Providenciales International Airport. A taxi from the airport to Grace Bay costs $20 one way for two people; each extra person costs $5. Some resorts arrange their own minibus transfers.

Bicycle

Both **Scooter Bob's** (☎946-4684; scooter@provo.net; Turtle Cove Marina Plaza) and **Caicos Cyclery** (☎941-7544; www.caicoscyclery.com; Grace Bay Rd) rent out bikes for $25 per day.

Boat

A plethora of boat charters and trips can be arranged to the islands and cays from Turtle Cove and Leeward Marinas (see p831).

Car & Motorcycle

You'll find the following rental agencies on the island:

Budget (☎946-4079; www.budget.com; Providenciales International Airport)

Hertz (☎941-3910; www.hertztci.com; Providenciales International Airport)

Rent-a-buggy (☎946-4158; www.rentabuggy.tc) Specializes in 4WD rentals.

Scooter Bob's (☎946-4684; scooter@provo.net; Turtle Cove Marina Plaza) Rents out cars and 4WDs from $75 per day and scooters from $50 per day. It also rents out bicycles for $25 per day and snorkeling gear for $15 per day.

Taxi

Taxis are a popular way of getting around the island. Most are vans and although unmetered the pricing is consistent. It's best not to be in a hurry as they often take forever to come pick you up. Your hotel can arrange a taxi for you and they meet all flights at the airport. Here are a couple of good options:

Nell's Taxi Service (☎941-3228)

Provo Taxi & Bus Group (☎946-5481)

The Cays

The smaller islands around Providenciales are known simply as the Cays, and most of them boast superb beaches and total isolation, being accessible only by a private boat charter.

Northeast of Provo and separated from it by the 400yd-wide channel, **Little Water Cay** is a nature reserve within Princess

Alexandra National Park and is the home of about 2000 endangered rock iguanas. If you land here, do not feed or touch the iguanas, even though they are generally easy to approach. Also keep to the trails to avoid trampling their burrows and the ecologically sensitive plants. Next door **Pine Cay**'s primary residents are celebrities. The 2 miles of ocean separating it from the northeast edge of Provo is plenty of moat to keep the riffraff out.

Fort George Cay is home to the remnants of an 18th-century British-built fort built back in the day to protect the islands. Now the only invaders are divers and snorkelers there to inspect the gun emplacements slowly becoming one with the sea bottom. The site is protected within Fort George Land & Sea National Park, which is also home to a protected iguana population. **Dellis Cay** has some of the best shells around on its beautiful beaches, but being in the park precludes you from taking them home.

Parrot Cay is home to the Turks and Caicos' most luxurious and famous hotel and is very private indeed.

Some way south of Providenciales, the old pirate hideaway of **French Cay** is now more frequented by migrating birds than swashbuckling scoundrels. Uninhabited and a permanent wildlife sanctuary, this small island 15 miles south of Provo is home to a staggering number of bird species. Just offshore the waters are teeming with stingrays who use the calm waters as a nursery. Nurse sharks (entirely harmless creatures) gather here in summer where they feed, breed and scare swimmers. You can snorkel among the menagerie of sea life on a day trip from Provo.

North Caicos

POP 1500

There was a time a century ago when bountiful North Caicos, with its lush farmland and bustling towns, was the center of action in the island chain. These days there are only stone ruins and a few small towns to show for these early expansions, but there remains a pristine tropical isle that is a joy to visit.

While there is a distinctive lost-world feel to this island, change is coming – a number of projects are underway, including a deep-water harbor that will make bringing building materials to the island much easier. It does signal the end of a very quiet era on NC, so enjoy the empty roads, shell-strewn beaches and green interior in the relative quiet while you still can.

◉ Sights & Activities

The Kew area has several historic ruins, including the interesting **Wades Green Plantation**, granted to a British Loyalist by King George III. The owners struggled to grow sisal and Sea Island cotton until drought, hurricanes and bugs drove them out. The plantation lasted a mere 25 years; the owners abandoned their slaves and left. It's a sobering place to visit and worth the effort.

Beaches along the north coast of North Caicos include **Pumpkin Bluff**, **Horsestable** and most importantly, **Whitby Beach**. On any one, yours will be the only Robinson Crusoe footprints. Pumpkin Bluff beach is especially beautiful and the snorkeling is good, with a foundered cargo ship adding to the allure.

Cottage Pond, a 150ft-deep blue hole on the northwest coast, attracts waterfowl such

---

PARROT CAY

Look no further for true indulgence than **Parrot Cay** (☏941-7544; www.parrotcay.como.biz; r from $938; ❋@🛜🌊), which is definitely the best hotel in the Turks and Caicos, and one of the very best in the Caribbean. On its own eponymous private island, Parrot Cay is part resort with its infinity pool, water sports, diving school and superb restaurants, and part spa, with a firm emphasis on healthy treatments, yoga and 'wellness' provided by the international spa brand Como Shambala. The rooms, which run from simple but sublime one-room garden-view rooms to the incredible five-bedroom Residence, are done in beautifully understated teak furnishings and white timbered walls. The main restaurant, **Terrace**, is a sublime experience catering for all needs with cuisines ranging from macrobiotic to gourmet. Of course, if you need to ask about the price, you probably can't afford it, but if you're looking for a once-in-a-lifetime splurge or you happen to be a Wall Street banker, then this is the place for you.

as West Indian whistling ducks, grebes and waders. Bellfield Landing Pond, Pumpkin Bluff Pond and Dick Hill Creek also attract flamingos, as does a large brine lake, **Flamingo Pond**, which floods the center of the island. Here the gangly birds strut around in hot pink. The ponds are protected as individual nature reserves.

A series of small cays off the northeast shore are protected within **East Bay Islands National Park**, and a trio of cays to the northwest form **Three Mary Cays National Park**, another flamingo sanctuary and an osprey nesting site. The **snorkeling** is good at Three Mary Cays and further west at Sandy Point Beach.

🛏 Sleeping

Generally accommodations on North Caicos are set up with self-catering in mind. All the options listed here come standard with kitchenettes, except for the Pelican Beach Hotel, which cooks for you.

Ocean Beach Hotel   BEACH HOTEL **$$$**
(📞946-7113; www.turksandcaicos.tc/ocean beach; r $225-275; ❄️🛜🍴) Popular with families and often full of returning guests, Ocean Beach is a treat. Beautifully maintained with simple homely touches, it feels like you're staying at a friend's cottage – with the best view money can buy. There are rooms here accommodate every type of group; big or small it will sort you into the right spot, while the complimentary local cell phone will make organization that much easier. Ocean Beach has been a trendsetter in sustainability from its inception: the 'so simple it's clever' solar-heated rooftop water-collection system provides all the water for the hotel. It doesn't stop there: compact fluorescent lighting, room orientation to take advantage of the wind and avoid air-con use, and a commitment to reducing linen and towel washing. Big hotels around the world could learn a lot from this little inn on North Caicos.

Pelican Beach Hotel   BEACH HOTEL **$$**
(📞946-7112; www.pelicanbeach.tc; r $145, s/d half board $160/225; ❄️🛜) For those looking for a relaxed, back-to-basics place to stay, this is an excellent option. Suzie and Clifford's place is getting a bit old and tired, but the old-school feel adds to the experience. There is nothing fancy here; plain TV-less rooms sit in a row only a few feet from the beach. It's well worth taking the half-board option

as Suzie is a legend in the kitchen! There are also free bicycles for guests.

Hollywood Beach Suites   BEACH HOTEL **$$$**
(📞231-1020; www.hollywoodbeachsuites.com; ste from $235; ❄️🛜) Housing just eight guests, finding space on the beach won't be an issue. The rooms are tidy, modern and well set up for a relaxing holiday, with couches, TV and DVD player for when the stress of sun worshipping just gets to be too much. There are complimentary kayaks and bikes for guests. Your dinner is cooked for you the first night of your stay too – go for the lobster!

🍴 Eating

You can buy produce and groceries at KH's Food Store in Whitby and at Al's Grocery in Bottle Creek.

Silver Palm   CARIBBEAN **$$**
(📞946-7113; Ocean Beach Hotel; mains $10-18; ⏰breakfast, lunch & dinner) Lobster and conch are the specialties here – all of course sourced locally. Informal and friendly, small and intimate, this place epitomizes the North Caicos experience: simple and delicious.

Frank's Café   GRILL **$$**
(📞243-5256; mains from $15; ⏰10am-10pm Mon-Sat) Some way down the coast away from much of the development on the rest of the island, this friendly place serves up great seafood dishes as well as a mixture of international cuisine, from Italian dishes to burgers.

ℹ Information

There's a post office in Kew, and Bottle Creek has a small public library. The nearest hospital is in Provo.

Government clinic Bottle Creek (📞946-7194); Kew (📞946-7397)

Police Bottle Creek (📞946-7116); Kew (📞946-7261)

ℹ Getting There & Around

For information on getting to/from the island by air or boat, see p831.

A taxi from the airport to Whitby costs $10 or about $40 from the ferry landing, one way. **M&M Tours** (📞231-6285) will pick you up; be sure to prebook. Most hotels and condos offer complimentary bikes to their guests.

Car rental costs are around $80 per day. Try the following options:

Al's Rent A Car (📞946-7232)

Pelican Car Rentals (📞241-8275)

Middle Caicos

POP 300

If you're really looking to get away from it all, treat yourself by checking out Middle Caicos. With an area the size of North Caicos and with such a small population you'll be lucky to see *anyone*. The topography is much the same as North Caicos, with a green, lake-filled interior surrounded by white-sand beach and azure water. Recently a causeway has been completed connecting North and Middle, making the visiting process a whole lot easier. There are few places to stay on the island and even fewer places to eat, so those not intending on a self-catered, pre-arranged stay would do well to plan a day-trip. But for those who do decide to stay, your efforts will most certainly be rewarded – this is the way the Caribbean used to be.

◉ Sights & Activities

There are a few tiny settlements dotted along the island; Conch Bar and Bambarra are the largest, but there still isn't much to them. **Bambarra Beach**, however, is possibly the Caribbean beach you've been dreaming about. Impossibly white sand, robin egg–blue water and not a soul around. On the quiet end of a blissfully uninhabited island, this beach sees little traffic of any sort.

The aim of the game on Middle is to relax – but if you're keen to get the blood flowing a bit there are a few options worth checking out. Five miles west of Bambarra Beach, directly in front of Blue Horizon Resort, is

Mudjin Harbor – the rocky shore rears up to form a bit of rare elevation. Walking along the cliff top you'll be surprised to see a staircase appear out of nowhere, leading into the earth. Take it down through the cave and emerge on a secluded cliff-lined beach. Looking seaward you'll be entertained by the waves crashing into the offshore rocks in spectacular fashion.

A great way to get a feel for the island is to go for a walk on the **Crossing Place Trail**. Hugging the northern edge of Middle Caicos and crossing into North Caicos, this easy-to-follow and straightforward track supports good ocean views and birdwatching opportunities. It's easily picked up from Mudjin Harbor or from other points along the main road – keep an eye open for the signs.

🛏 Sleeping

At present there are only a couple of sleeping options on Middle Caicos. The emphasis is on longer-term stays where self-catering is a must.

TOP CHOICE **Dreamscape Villa** VILLA $$$
(☎946-7112; www.middlecaicos.com; Bambarra; per week $2000; ❋☷) OK so its interior design won't win any prizes, but this villa is magnificently located on a pristine section of Bambarra Beach, just a few yards from the sea. The house itself has three bedrooms and is set up to sleep four comfortably. It has all the modern conveniences and is perfectly arranged for a week of relaxation. There are bikes and sea kayaks to keep you busy, and great snorkeling, right out front, if the mood strikes. Nice touches such as an outdoor

BEST OF THE REST

If you really want an adventure and want to escape from any sort of tourist infrastructure, then all you have to do is head to either South or East Caicos. These islands are a paradise for those with a phobia of development, tourism or other people.

East Caicos is the least inhabited island in the chain. There is a Haitian immigrant community on the island but little else. The beaches are renowned and odds are you will have them all to yourself. East Caicos is not linked by air or a ferry service to elsewhere in the country, however, so the only way to get here is by boat charter or your own yacht. As there is almost no infrastructure on the island, the latter is far preferable.

South Caicos is the place to go for unspoilt scuba diving. The waters are pristine and prized for the effort required to get there. The land itself is a windswept wasteland of sand and scrub. The towns are microscopic and you really will find more donkeys than people here. Each May things spark up a bit for the annual **Big South Regatta** – but don't worry, this is still way off the radar of most T&C visitors. South Caicos is connected by two daily flights from Providenciales (from $48 one way).

shower, hammocks and a barbecue add up to make this great for a family holiday.

Blue Horizon Resort
RESORT $$$

(☎946-6141; www.bhresort.com; Mudjin Harbor; cabins from $230; ❉) This beautiful property at Mudjin Harbor boasts its own 2200ft stretch of private beach and a wonderful setting amid the foliage. The five cabins are spread out among the greenery, all with prime ocean views. The decor is nothing special, but the views and the seclusion more than make up for the slightly dated sense of style. The units all have kitchens and you can provide a shopping list so the cupboards are full for you when you arrive.

ℹ Information

There are few services to speak of on the island, save the odd seemingly abandoned gas pump (which may or may not have gas) and a few phone booths that have seen better days. The proximity to North Caicos dictates that traveling over to the neighboring island is the way to go if you want to buy groceries or head out for a meal.

TURKS ISLANDS

The Turks group comprises Grand Turk and its smaller southern neighbor, Salt Cay, in addition to several tiny cays. The islands lie east of the Caicos Islands, separated from them by the 22-mile-wide Turks Island Passage.

ℹ Getting There & Away

For flight information, see p831.

ℹ Getting Around

TO/FROM THE AIRPORT

Taxis meet incoming flights; to Cockburn Town (1 mile north of the airport) costs about $10. There are no buses, but pre-booked rental cars will meet your plane.

BICYCLE

Most, if not all, hotels on Grand Turk provide bikes for their guests as they are the perfect way to get around the tiny island. On Salt Cay, **Trade Winds Guest Suites** (☎946-6906; www.tradewinds.tc; Victoria St, Salt Cay) will get you pedaling for $15 per day.

BOAT

A ferry runs biweekly from Grand Turk to Salt Cay (round trip $12). Contact **Salt Cay Charters** (☎231-6663; piratequeen3@hotmail.com). Arrangements can also be made with any of the Grand Turk dive companies to take you over to Salt Cay; costs vary depending on numbers.

CAR & SCOOTER

Car hire is very simple to arrange on both Grand Turk and Salt Cay. Expect to pay around $70 per day. All hotels can either arrange car rental or point you in the direction of local companies.

TAXI

Taxis are an inexpensive and reliable way to get around Grand Turk. A taxi from the airport to town will cost you about $10 though prices vary according to distance; the entire island can be reached from the airport for up to $25. Be sure to settle on a price before you head out as the cabs are unmetered. Your hotel can easily sort you a cab, or call **Carl's Taxi Service** (☎241-8793).

Grand Turk

Happily lacking the modern development that has enveloped Provo, Grand Turk is a step back in time. At just 6½ miles long, this dot amid the sea is a sparsely populated, brush-covered paradise. Cockburn Town, the main settlement, is still the capital of the country and is lined with buildings that date back to colonial times. Narrow streets are frequented by wild donkeys and the odd local cruising by. That of course can change in an instant if a large cruise ship docks off Grand Turk and several thousand day visitors crowd out this tiny Caribbean town.

Where salt was once the main industry, tourism has taken over and you are blessed with a slew of charming guesthouses to choose from. Beaches rim the land and calm blue water invites you in for a refreshing swim. There is a quiet peace to the island and a feel among the locals, discovered long ago, that this is the place to be.

COCKBURN TOWN
POP 5500

Without knowing beforehand you'd be hard pressed to guess that sleepy Cockburn is the capital city of the Turks and Caicos. What it lacks in polish and sophistication it more than makes up for in rustic charm. The town itself comprises two parallel streets that are interconnected with narrow laneways. Colonial-era houses line the tiny streets and former salt-storage sheds hark back to a bygone era of dusty roads and donkey-filled lanes.

The heart of town is sandwiched between the ocean and the salt pond named Red Salina.

Grand Turk

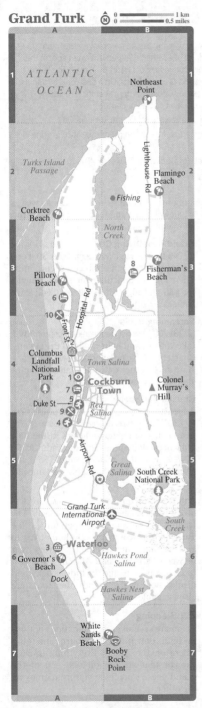

Sights

The Turks & Caicos Island Tourist Board, the museum and most hotels have free *Heritage Walk* pamphlets. **Front St**, which runs along the waterfront, has some magnificent buildings. The salt air and the rough treatment of time have not been kind to many of these structures and some have begun the slip into dilapidation. But there are still highlights here, and a walk among the architecture is recommended.

The **General Post Office** is a relic of a forgotten era, and still shines brightly. Nearby, four large cannons point to sea, guarding the site that Columbus supposedly set foot upon land – the reality of that claim is still up for grabs, but it does make for a nice photo. The fringing coral reef just offshore is protected within the confidently named **Columbus Landfall National Park**.

The little **Turks & Caicos National Museum** (www.tcmuseum.org; Front St; admission nonresidents $5; ⊙9am-4pm Mon, Tue, Thu & Fri, to 6pm Wed, to 1pm Sat) boxes above its weight with a great selection of displays. Everything from shipwrecks to messages in bottles and crash-landing spacecraft are covered – be sure to ask to see the cabinet of cannons.

South of the heart of downtown, Duke St narrows off to form a twisting lane of old buildings. Even the most jaded of futurists will be left enchanted by the colonial-era structures.

The long and pothole-covered road to Northeast Point is the way to get to the old cast-iron **lighthouse**. It's open when

TURKS & CAICOS GRAND TURK

Grand Turk

The building of a cruise-ship harbor and an accompanying leisure complex (with shops, eateries, pool and beach) in the south of the island has rather changed this quiet spot in the Eastern Caribbean. It's certainly changed the economic face of Grand Turk, too – this is the port of call for most cruises coming to the Turks and Caicos Islands. On a busy day, two ships will be in port – off-loading nearly 7000 people, who suddenly outnumber local residents.

If you want to see a bit more of the island outside the cruise center:

» Book a snorkeling or diving trip in the pristine waters off Grand Turk (p824)

» In February and March join a whale-watching trip to see the magnificent migrating humpbacks (p824)

» Wander the charming old Caribbean streets of Cockburn Town (p822)

cruise ships are in port and offers a good vantage point of the crashing waves.

Waterloo (1815) is the official Governor's residence. The island's dock is here, and the old US missile-tracking station sits as a reminder of the Cold War. In 1962 Grand Turk was briefly put on the world stage when astronaut John Glenn splashed down in his Mercury spacecraft off the coast of the island. He made landfall at this dock and was debriefed at the missile-tracking post.

🏕 Beaches

A dirt road leads south to **White Sands Beach**, which is great for snorkelers, and on to lovely pine-shaded **Governor's Beach**, 1½ miles south of town, a popular place for a picnic and a dip in the sea.

Dirt roads lead east to three prime **bird-watching spots**: Hawkes Pond Salina, Hawkes Nest Salina and South Creek National Park, which protects the mangroves and wetlands along the island's southeast shore.

To the north of Cockburn Town are remote **Corktree** and **Pillory Beaches**. Both are good for bathing and out of the way enough that you'll have the sand to yourself.

🏃 Activities

Diving is the main reason to come to Grand Turk. The following diving operators will take you snorkeling if you're not a diver, and run courses if you want to learn.

Oasis Divers   DIVING, SNORKELING
(☑946-1128; www.oasisdivers.com; Duke St) Will take you down on a two-tank dive ($85), a single tank in the afternoon ($55) or a night dive ($60). It rents out gear at good rates and has a great reputation for service and professionalism. It also runs trips to Gibbs Cay, where you can hand-feed

stingrays ($60 plus diving rates), as well as whale-watching and kayak trips and renting snorkeling equipment.

Grand Turk Diving Co   DIVING, SNORKELING
(☑946-1559; www.gtdiving.com; Duke St) Local legend Smitty runs this excellent outfit. There are two-tank dives for $75 and singles for $50 and night dives for $60. Full PADI courses are offered for $450.

Screaming Reels   FISHING
(☑231-2087; www.screamingreelstours.com) Will take you out and help you land the big one. Charters are based on a per-boat basis and start at $500 per day, but that cost can be shared between up to eight people.

**Chukka Caribbean
Adventures**   ADVENTURE, SAFARI
(☑232-1339; www.chukkacaribbean.com) This is a great one for horse lovers as there's a horseback ride and swim tour (adult/child $74/52) as well as a kayak safari ($65) and river tubing ($64/45) available, to name just a few.

Salt Cay Charters   WHALE-WATCHING
(☑231-6663; piratequeen3@hotmail.com) The leading whale-watching operator in the Turks and Caicos offers 2½-hour trips to see the migrating humpbacks every year between February and March. Trips cost $125 per person and include snacks and drinks. Boat charters and other tours are also available.

🛏 Sleeping

There are several accommodations options in both downtown Cockburn and elsewhere on the island. Everything is close enough that staying on one end of the island doesn't preclude you from enjoying the other.

Island House
GUESTHOUSE $$

TOP CHOICE (☑946-1388; www.islandhouse.tc; d $190; ❄️📶🏊) Walking through the doors at Island House you'll be met with Mediterranean-influenced architecture, whitewashed walls and arched doorways. Further in you'll discover the inviting pool and opulent courtyard. The rooms are airy and nicely put together. Guests, who mostly come here to dive and purchase packages when they book, have free use of a car while staying and there are bikes too, if you're feeling energetic.

Grand Turk Inn
GUESTHOUSE $$$

(☑946-2827; www.grandturkinn.com; Front St; ste $300; ❄️📶) This beautifully restored Methodist manse is definitely Grand Turk's most atmospheric place to stay. The Balinese bamboo furniture sets the tone and the owners, two sisters, make you feel immediately at home. There are full kitchens in each of the five suites and its central location in Cockburn Town is hard to beat.

Bohio Dive Resort & Spa
DIVING RESORT $$

(☑946-2135; www.bohioresort.com; Front St; r $190; ❄️📶🏊) Boasts a prime location on a stunning stretch of sand, excellent value dive packages and a friendly atmosphere. The staff here is top notch and the rooms are pleasant and clean. There are kayaks, sailboats, snorkeling gear and even yoga classes available. The resort is just north of the town center.

✕ Eating

Osprey
INTERNATIONAL $$

(☑946-2666; Duke St; mains from $10-25; ☺lunch & dinner) Make sure you drop by on Wednesday or Sunday night for the legendary barbecue: amazing seafood, poultry and beef grilled before your eyes, bombarded with salads and served up poolside. There are great ocean views and the band gets going after dinner so you can dance off that dessert.

Taste of the Island
CARIBBEAN $

(West St; mains from $10; ☺lunch & dinner) Come to this locals' beachside restaurant and bar to work on your Creole or enjoy a swim in the sea while you wait for your food. The offerings are simple, fresh and cheap and it can get loud and a little crazy, making it a real taste of the island. It's just north of the town center.

Sand Bar
BAR & GRILL $

(☑946-1111; Duke St; mains $8-15; ☺noon-1am) This small yet lively bar is a popular hot spot with locals, expats and tourists alike. It has yummy burgers if you've got the munchies, and the potential for spotting the green flash (a Caribbean phenomenon where you can see a green flash as the sun sets into the ocean) is great, especially if you've had a few Turk's Heads first.

🛍 Shopping

The best shopping to be found on the island is in the street stalls that open up on Duke Street when the cruise ships are in port. There is a good variety of locally made goods, Haitian artwork and hand-drawn maps. Conversely if you are seeking cheap T-shirts, snow globes and shot glasses, head to the cruise-ship center (opposite) where you will be inundated with an ocean of cheap rubbish.

ℹ Information

Businesses and government offices close at 3pm on Friday. Some businesses open from 9am to 1pm on Saturday. Public phones can be found at most central places.

General Post Office (☑946-1334; Front St)

Grand Turk Hospital (☑946-2333; Hospital Rd)

Turks & Caicos Islands Tourist Board (☑946-2321; www.turksandcaicostourism.com; Front St)

ℹ Getting There & Around

The town center is 1 mile north of the Grand Turk International Airport; a taxi ride from the airport into town costs about $10. Bikes are often provided to hotel guests and are a great way to get around. You're hardly likely to need a car in town, but do pay attention anyway to the one-way system along Duke and Front Sts. You can rent cars ($70 per day) from **Tony's Car Rental** (☑946-1879; www.tonyscarrental.com; Airport Rd), located at the airport.

For details about getting around Grand Turk, see p822.

Salt Cay

If you can't quite envision what the Turks would have been like in the 19th century, take a trip to Salt Cay. Like stepping into a time machine, this picturesque island is the sort of hideaway that you search your whole life to discover. A few dusty roads interconnect the handful of structures, and donkeys wander aimlessly through the streets intermixed with friendly locals. While the land is quiet, the sea surrounding the island is awash with life. Turtles, eagle rays and the majestic humpback whale all frequent the waters.

Hard to get to and even harder to leave, this place is a true haven for scuba divers and for those seeking an escape from the modern world.

Salt Cay Divers (⏺241-1009; www.saltcaydivers.tc) is a one-stop dive shop. The owner is a long-term local who has her finger in most pies on the island. The staff can take you out for a dive ($45 per tank), and sort you out with accommodations and a hearty meal too. The annual humpback whale migration (February to March) is a big draw, and this operation takes pride in showing off the whales yet not disturbing them ($75 for divers, $95 for non-divers).

For details on getting to/from Salt Cay, see p822.

🛏 Sleeping

Pirate's Hideaway Guesthouse   GUESTHOUSE **$$$**
(⏺244-1407; www.pirateshideaway.com; Victoria St; r from $200; ❄🎧🛋) The colorful owner Nick goes out of his way to make you feel at home here. Cool features include an 'infinity bed' in the crow's-nest room and a new freshwater pool to cool you off. You can see the whales from the upstairs rooms as they pass by, or just hang out with the parrots – it is a pirate's place after all.

Trade Winds Guest Suites   RESORT **$$**
(⏺241-1009; www.tradewinds.tc; Victoria St; r $190; ❄🎧) Right on the beach, just a few steps from town. Trade Winds is a great spot to base yourself for an extended stay: there are weekly rates and the location is tops. There are complimentary bikes and dive packages available, too. The rooms are tidy, ocean-facing and good value.

A WHALE OF A TALE

Salt Cay could very well be one of the best places on earth to see humpback whales – by the thousands. Every winter the gentle giants make their annual pilgrimage to the warm seas of the Caribbean to mate and give birth. From the sandy shores of Salt Cay you can watch the majestic beauties of the sea saunter past from February to March. They are plain to see from the beach but you can also get among it on a whale-watching trip or dive trip organized from either Grand Turk or Salt Cay.

🍴 Eating

 Island Thyme Bistro   BISTRO **$$$**
(⏺242-0325; mains from $20; ⏱breakfast, lunch & dinner) This little restaurant and bar is set to be the big memory of your Salt Cay stay. The food is great and is prepared and presented with a sense of fun. There's also a popular guest-chef night, where you get to strut your stuff in the kitchen. Friday is pizza night and the restaurant prides itself on a flexible menu – try the Filipino roast sucking pig if you really want a treat.

Green Flash Cafe   GRILL **$$**
(Main Dock; mains from $12; ⏱lunch & dinner) Right off the main dock and the perfect vantage point to watch out for its namesake. Nothing pretentious here, just simple food enjoyed on picnic tables in a beautiful setting. Great burgers, conch and cold beer – what more could you want?

UNDERSTAND TURKS & CAICOS

History

Recent discoveries of Taíno (the indigenous population) artifacts on Grand Turk have shown that the islands evolved much the same indigenous culture as did their northern neighbors. Locals even claim that the islands were Christopher Columbus' first landfall in 1492.

The island group was a pawn in the power struggles between the French, Spanish and British, and remained virtually uninhabited until 1678, when some Bermudian salt rakers settled the Turks islands and used natural *salinas* (salt-drying pans) to produce sea salt. These still exist on several islands.

Fast forward to the mid-20th century: the US military built airstrips and a submarine base in the 1950s, and John Glenn splashed down just off Grand Turk in 1962, putting the islands very briefly in the international spotlight.

Administered through Jamaica and the Bahamas in the past, the Turks and Caicos islands became a separate Crown colony of Great Britain in 1962, then an Overseas Territory in 1981. In 1984 Club Med opened its doors on Providenciales (Provo), and the Turks and Caicos started to boom. In the blink of an eye, the islands, which had previously lacked electricity, acquired satellite TV.

The Turks and Caicos relied upon the exportation of salt, which remained the backbone of the British colony until 1964. Today finance, tourism and fishing generate most of the income, but the islands could not survive without British aid. The tax-free offshore finance industry is a mere minnow compared with that of the Bahamas, and many would be astonished to discover that Grand Turk, the much-hyped financial center, is really just a dusty backwater in the sun.

Illegal drug trafficking, a major problem in the 1980s, has also been a source of significant revenue for a few islanders.

Relations between islanders and British-appointed governors have been strained since 1996, when the incumbent governor's comments suggesting that government and police corruption had turned the islands into a haven for drug trafficking appeared in the *Offshore Finance Annual,* and opponents accused him of harming investment. Growing opposition threatened to spill over into civil unrest.

Things were made far worse in 2009, when the Governor of the Turks and Caicos imposed direct rule on the country following a series of corruption scandals that rocked the islands in 2008. The scandals concerned huge alleged corruption on the part of the Turks and Caicos government, including the selling off of its property for personal profit, and the misuse of public funds.

The imposition of direct rule from London was attacked by members of the suspended Turks and Caicos government, who accused the UK of 'recolonizing' the country, but the general reaction across the country was a positive one, as faith in the local political system had been extremely low in the years leading up to the suspension.

The British government is looking to hold elections for a new Turks and Caicos government at some time in 2011. Despite the ongoing problems of corruption, it's likely to create a resurgence in calls for independence, or even a slightly wackier idea that has been kicking around the country for some time: a union with Canada.

Culture

The culture of the Turks and Caicos is that of a ship that is steadied by a strong religious keel. There is a very strong religious core to these islands, and the populace is friendly, welcoming and a bit sedate. Native Turks and Caicos islanders, or 'Belongers' as they are locally known, are descended from the early Bermudian settlers, Loyalist settlers, slave settlers and salt rakers.

There are a few expats lurking about calling the Turks home; Americans because of the proximity, Canadians because of the weather and Brits because of the colonial heritage. Some have come to make their fortunes, some to bury their treasure like the pirates of old and others to escape the fast-paced life that permeates much of the developed world.

More recently hundreds of Haitians have fled their impoverished island and landed on the Turks and Caicos Islands; for some this is only a port of call on their way to America, while others are happy to stay. Some Belongers are wary of these new immigrant communities, while some locals are sympathetic or even indifferent.

Nightlife in the Turks and Caicos is of the mellow variety for the most part. There are a few night spots in Provo, and some beachside bars on the outer islands. Those seeking a roaring party of a holiday should look elsewhere – having said that, the local rake 'n' scrape music can really get the crowd going. For those not in the know, rake 'n' scrape or ripsaw (as it is locally known) is a band fronted by someone playing a carpenter's saw by rhythmically scraping its teeth with the shaft of a screwdriver; sometimes other household objects are used as percussion.

The art scene in the Turks and Caicos is slowly evolving. Traditional music, folklore and sisal weaving evolved during colonial days, have been maintained to this day. Paintings depicting the scenery are popular and the quality appears to be improving. The Haitian community has had a strong influence on the Turks and Caicos art scene.

There are a few shops in Provo that have a good selection of locally produced art; unfortunately, except for a few choice locations, most of the art that's available outside Provo is tourist paraphernalia, made in China and slapped with a T&C sticker.

Landscape & Wildlife

Much of the Turks and Caicos can be described as flat, dry and barren. The salt industry of the last century saw fit to remove much of the vegetation from Salt Cay, Grand Turk and South Caicos. Low-lying vegetation now covers the uninhabited sections of these islands. The larger islands are in a much more pristine state, with vegetation and a higher degree of rainfall prominent on North, Middle and East Caicos. Small creeks, inland lakes – often home to flamingos – and wetlands make up the interior of these larger land masses.

On Providenciales the most common sight on land is not anything natural but the explosive degree of development. Everywhere you look, there seems to be another new property and resulting heap of construction garbage. The scrubby landscape is still visible among the fresh buildings – but for how long?

All the islands are rimmed with stunning beaches. Most are great and some are exceptional – truly world-class stretches of sand worthy of every accolade and hyperbolic description of sun, sand and gentle surf.

Walking down a dusty laneway and coming upon a donkey is a quintessential T&C experience. Their forebears once carried 25lb burlap bags of salt from the ponds to the warehouses and docks.

Iguanas once inhabited much of the Turks and Caicos until they lost their lives to introduced dogs and cats, and their habitats to development. Now Little Water Cay, Fort George Cay and the Ambergris Cays are all protected iguana reserves.

The waters are favored by four species of turtle: hawksbills (an internationally endangered species, although sadly not recognized in this region), green, loggerheads and, occasionally, leatherbacks.

Countless species of sea birds and waders have been sighted, both migratory and nonmigratory. Ospreys are numerous and easily spotted, as are barn owls and sparrow hawks. Flamingos – once numerous throughout the chain – are now limited to West, North and South Caicos, where you may also see Cuban herons.

A flourishing population of bottlenosed dolphins lives in these waters. Also, some 7000 North Atlantic humpback whales use the Turks Island Passage and the Mouchoir Banks, south of Grand Turk, as their winter breeding grounds between February and March. Manta rays are commonly seen during the spring plankton blooms off of Grand Turk and West Caicos.

SURVIVAL GUIDE

Directory A–Z

Accommodations

Accommodations in the Turks and Caicos are mostly in hotels, resorts and the odd smaller establishment. On Provo you'll mostly find larger resorts, but there are still a large number of smaller hotels and guesthouses, most of which are well established and reasonably priced. As you head out to the less populated islands the establishments get more intimate.

The **Turks & Caicos Hotel Association** (www.turksandcaicoshta.com) has a useful website with an exhaustive list of accommodations options, while the following agencies arrange villa rentals:

Coldwell Banker (www.coldwellbankertci.com)

Grace Bay Realty (www.gracebayrealty.com)

Prestigious Properties (www.prestigious properties.com)

Turks & Caicos Sotheby's (www.turksand caicossothebys.com)

Prices quoted for accommodations in this chapter are for high season.

$	budget	$80 to $100
$$	midrage	$100 to $200
$$$	top end	more than $200

Activities

The most popular activities are diving and snorkeling, fishing and boating. Diving highlights include Salt Cay (p825) where you can dive with humpback whales during their annual migration. Grand Turk (p822) has pristine reefs and spectacular wall-diving. And then there is diving off Provo (p812), where you might just get the chance to share the sea with JoJo the dolphin.

In Caicos, a two-tank dive typically costs around $100 and a half-day snorkeling trip is around $65. Fishing can cost $400 to

$800 per half-/full day, while windsurfing averages $30 to $40 per hour.

A two-tank dive in the Turks typically costs from $40 to $80 and snorkeling around $50 per half-day. Fishing is around $300 to $400 per half-/full day.

Business Hours

We've only listed business hours where they differ from the following standards. Expect limited hours away from Provo or touristy areas.

Bars to 1am or 2am

Businesses 9am-5pm Mon-Sat

Restaurants breakfast from 8am, lunch from noon, dinner 6:30pm-9pm

Children

The Turks and Caicos is a fantastic kid-friendly destination, although you will struggle to find specific programs and activities aimed at younger travelers. Crime is low, traffic is sparse, waves are tiny and the locals are friendly. Some hotels are specifically non-kid-friendly so it's a good idea to check with your hotel beforehand.

Embassies & Consulates

There are no foreign embassies or consulates in the Turks and Caicos. Contact the relevant officials in Nassau in the Bahamas (see p191).

Festivals & Events

Big South Regatta Held on South Caicos in late May, this regatta is a classic for the sea dogs.

Annual Music & Cultural Festival Held in July and August, this annual event is the islands' biggest party – good times and hangovers guaranteed.

Grand Turk Game Fishing Tournament Held end July/early August. I once caught a fish that was this big...

Marathon Run Held each December. Why relax when you can run 26.2 miles?

Christmas Tree Lighting Ceremony Grand Turk hosts this special event in mid-December for kids of all ages.

Food

In restaurant reviews in this chapter, we've used the following price indicators, based on the cost of a main dish.

» **Newspapers & Magazines** There are two newspapers in the Turks and Caicos: the biweekly *Free Press* and the weekly *Turks & Caicos News*.

» **Radio & TV** The official Turks and Caicos government radio station is Radio Turks and Caicos (106FM) on Grand Turk. For contemporary light rock, try 92.5FM; country and western 90.5FM; easy listening 89.3FM; and classical music 89.9FM. Multichannel satellite TV is received from the USA and Canada. The islands have one private TV station.

» **Electricity** Hotels operate on 110V (60 cycles), as per the USA and Canada. Plug sockets are two- or three-pin US standard.

» **Weights & Measures** Imperial and metric systems are both in use.

$	budget	less than $10
$$	midrange	$10 to $20
$$$	top end	more than $20

Gay & Lesbian Travelers

As in most Caribbean destinations, the attitude toward gay and lesbian travelers in the Turks and Caicos is far from progressive. While totally legal, gay sex remains a taboo subject here, particularly with reference to gay men. That said, as more gay and lesbian cruise ships enter port and mix with the locals, some degree of acceptance has been forthcoming. There is however, no openly gay scene or gay bars to speak of.

Health

There are small hospitals on Provo and on Grand Turk. There are clinics on the smaller islands and a recompression chamber in Providenciales.

Internet Access

Internet access in the Turks is getting easier all the time. Wireless internet is offered free of charge in nearly all hotels and many restaurants and bars, while internet cafes and in-house terminals are getting rarer. It's a good idea to bring a smart phone or laptop with you to guarantee ease of access.

Money

The Turks and Caicos are unique as a British-dependent territory with the US dollar as its official currency. The treasury also issues Turks and Caicos crowns and quarters. There are no currency restrictions on the amount of money that visitors can bring in.

The country is pricey, with a hefty 30% duty slapped on all imports. When you consider how much is imported to this tiny and barren group of islands, the high price of food suddenly makes sense. Credit cards are readily accepted on Provo and Grand Turk, as are travelers checks. Elsewhere, you may need to operate on a cash-only basis. Foreign currency can be changed at banks in Provo and Grand Turk, which can also issue credit-card advances and have ATMs. Major credit cards are widely accepted in the Caicos and Grand Turk. However, credit cards are not widely accepted for small transactions in the more remote cays and islands. Travelers checks are accepted in the Caicos and Grand Turk, but you may be charged a transaction fee of 5%.

It's customary to tip 10% to 15% of the bill in restaurants and a similar amount for taxi drivers. However, do check your bill first, as many restaurants add a service charge automatically.

Public Holidays

Turks and Caicos national holidays:

New Year's Day January 1

Commonwealth Day March 13

Good Friday Friday before Easter

Easter Monday Monday after Easter

National Heroes' Day May 29

Her Majesty the Queen's Official Birthday June 14 (or nearest weekday)

Emancipation Day August 1

National Youth Day September 26

Columbus Day October 13

International Human Rights Day October 24

Christmas Day December 25

Boxing Day December 26

Telephone

The Turks and Caicos country code is ☏649. To call from North America, dial ☏1-649 + the local number. From elsewhere, dial your country's international access code + ☏649 + the local number. For interisland calls, dial the seven-digit local number. We've included only the seven-digit local number in Turks and Caicos listings in this chapter.

Phone calls can be made from **Cable & Wireless** (☏1800-804-2994), which operates a digital network from its offices in Grand Turk and Provo.

Public phone booths are located throughout the islands. Many booths require phonecards.

Hotels charge $1 per local call. Frustratingly, some also charge for unanswered calls after the receiving phone has rung five times.

Some useful telephone numbers:

Directory Assistance (☏118)

International Operator Assistance (☏115)

Local operator (☏0)

CELL PHONES

Most cell phones will work in the Turks and Caicos; you can either set your phone up for global roaming prior to leaving home or purchase a SIM card for it once you get here. Global roaming is both easier and more expensive; be sure to check rates with your phone company prior to dialing. If you have a GSM phone that is unlocked you can purchase a new SIM card for it ($10 from Cable & Wireless outlets). This gives you a local number to call from and is much cheaper in the long run.

PHONECARDS

Phonecards cost $5, $10 or $15, and can be bought from Cable & Wireless outlets, as well as from shops and delis. You can also bill calls to your Amex, Discover, MasterCard or Visa card by dialing ☏1-800-744-7777 on any touchtone phone and giving the operator your card details (there's a one-minute minimum).

Tourist Information

Turks & Caicos Tourism (www.turksand caicostourism.com; ⊙9am-5pm Mon-Fri); Grand Turk (☏946-2321; Front St, Cockburn Town); Providenciales (☏946-4970; www.turksandcaicos tourism.com; Stubbs Diamond Plaza)

Travelers with Disabilities

Some of the larger hotels have rooms that are wheelchair accessible, but it's best to enquire before arriving.

Visas

No visas are required for citizens of the US, Canada, UK and Commonwealth countries, Ireland and most Western European countries. Citizens from elsewhere require visas, which can be obtained from British representation abroad.

Getting There & Away

Entering Turks & Caicos

All visitors, including US citizens, need a valid passport to enter the country. Proof of onward transportation is required upon entry, so make sure you have your return flight confirmation to show immigration officers if they ask.

Air

AIRPORTS

There are three airports handling international traffic to Grand Turk and Provo, but nearly all international flights arrive at Provo. The Provo airport has a tourist information booth in arrivals, car rental offices, a restaurant and not much else. Other islands just have airstrips with no amenities.

Grand Turk International Airport (GDT; ☎946-2233)

Providenciales International Airport (PLS; ☎941-5670)

South Caicos International Airport (XSC; ☎946-4255)

AIRLINES

There are good air connections elsewhere within the Caribbean from Turks and Caicos, including to Jamaica, the Bahamas, Haiti and the Dominican Republic. To get to elsewhere in the region, you may have to hop to Miami. The following airlines fly into Turks and Caicos:

Air Canada (www.aircanada.com)

Air Turks & Caicos (www.airturksandcaicos.com)

American Airlines (www.aa.com)

Bahamas Air (www.bahamasair.com)

British Airways (www.ba.com)

Delta Airlines (www.delta.com)

US Airways (www.usairways.com)

West Jet (www.westjet.com)

Getting Around

Air

Following are airlines flying within the Turks and Caicos:

Air Turks & Caicos (☎946-4999; www.airturksandcaicos.com) Flies from Providen-

ciales to Grand Turk six times daily, North Caicos (airport is just north of Major Hill) three times daily, Middle Caicos (near Conch Hill) four times per week, South Caicos twice daily and Salt Cay daily. It also flies from Grand Turk to Salt Cay daily.

Bicycle

Cycling is a cheap, convenient, healthy, environmentally sound and above all fun way to travel. Bicycles are complimentary to guests at many hotels or can be rented at concessions for around $20 per day.

Boat

TCI Ferry Service (☎946-5406) is a small passenger ferry operation taking people from the Leeward Marina on Providenciales to North Caicos (round trip $30), eliminating the need for the expensive and inconvenient flight. There are four departures each way daily, leaving Leeward Marina daily at 10.30am, 12.30pm, 3pm and 4.30pm. On Sunday there are just two services in each direction each day.

A ferry runs biweekly trips from Grand Turk to Salt Cay (round trip $12); contact **Salt Cay Charters** (☎231-6663; pirate queen3@hotmail.com) for details.

Car, Motorcycle & Scooter

Taxis get expensive in the long run so renting a car makes sense if you plan to explore Provo or Grand Turk. The local companies are very good, and may be cheaper than the internationals. Rentals average around $80 per day and the cars are generally in good nick; most rental companies offer free drop-off and pick-up. A government tax of $15 is levied on car rentals ($8 on scooter rentals). Mandatory insurance costs $15. A minimum age of 25 years may be required.

Driving is on the left-hand side. At roundabouts (traffic circles), remember to circle in a clockwise direction, entering to the left, and give way to traffic already on the roundabout.

Speed limits in the Turks and Caicos are 20mph (around 32km/h) in settlements and 40mph (around 65km/h) on main highways.

Please refer to island destinations for rental companies.

DRIVER'S LICENSE

To rent a car, citizens of the US, Canada, and the UK and Commonwealth countries are required to have a valid driving license for stays of up to three months. Everyone else requires an International Driving Permit. You must get this permit before you arrive on the Turks and Caicos Islands.

FUEL

Gas stations are plentiful and usually open from 8am to 7pm. Some close on Sunday. Gasoline costs about $5.50 per US gallon – luckily most destinations are pretty close. Credit cards are accepted in major settlements. Elsewhere, it's cash only, please!

Taxi

Taxis are available on all the inhabited islands. Most are minivans. They're a good bet for touring, and most taxi drivers double as guides. The cabs are unmetered (though pricing is consistent), so be sure to negotiate an agreeable price before setting out.

US Virgin Islands

Why Go?

Hmm, where to go for consistent 80°F (27°C) weather, ca-lypso-wafting beach bars and a taste of West Indian culture, but without any border crossing or passport hassle? The US Virgin Islands (USVI) have your back, mon.

St John is the greenest island, literally and figuratively. Two-thirds of its area is cloaked in parkland and sublime beaches, ripe for hiking and snorkeling. It also leads the way in environmental preservation, with several low-impact tent-resorts for lodging. Dizzying cruise-ship traffic and big resorts nibbling its edges make St Thomas the most com-mercialized island. St Croix is the odd island out, floating far from its siblings and offering a mix of rainforest, sugar plan-tations, old forts and great scuba diving. And wait – there's a fourth Virgin that often gets overlooked. That's Water Is-land, a stone's throw from St Thomas' airport but a world away in its taxi-less, shop-less atmosphere.

Best Beaches

» Lindquist Beach (p843)
» Magens Bay (p840)
» Salt Pond Bay (p851)
» Cinnamon Bay (p850)
» Cane Bay (p849)

Best Places to Stay

» Green Iguana (p839)
» Concordia Eco-Tents (p851)
» St John Inn (p847)
» Garden by the Sea B&B (p847)
» Hotel on the Cay (p855)

When to Go

Mid-December through April is the dry and sunny high sea-son, when activities are in full swing. St Thomas' big bash is the whopping, party-hearty St Thomas Carnival from mid-April to early May. St Croix throws a cheery Cruzan Christ-mas Fiesta from mid-December until early January. Sailors, swimmers and snorkelers might like spring best, when the water is calmest. May and November are shoulder-season months for bargains and decent (if wet) weather; early De-cember is the best of all for fair weather and fare deals.

Fast Facts

» **Area** 136 sq miles

» **Population** 109,700

» **Capital** Charlotte Amalie

» **Telephone country code** ☑1

» **Telephone area code** ☑340

» **Emergency** ☑911

Set Your Budget

» **Budget hotel room** US$90

» **Two-course dinner** US$30

» **Coral World admission** US$19 (adult)

» **Bottle of beer** US$3

» **St John ferry** US$6

Resources

» **USVI Department of Tourism** (www.visitusvi .com) Official tourism site with a 'hot deals' page

» **Virgin Islands Now** (www.vinow.com)

» **St Thomas/St John This Week** (www.virgin islandsthisweek.com)

» **St Croix This Week** (www.stcroixthisweek.com)

» **See St John** (www.see stjohn.com)

Itineraries

FOUR DAYS

Start on St John. Spend day one at the North Shore beaches: Cinnamon Bay with wind surfing and trails through mill ruins; Maho Bay, where sea turtles swim; or Leinster Bay/ Waterlemon Cay, where snorkelers can jump in amid rays and barracudas. Toast your beach in rollicking Cruz Bay.

Spend day two on the South Shore at Salt Pond Bay, where hikes, beachcombing and snorkeling await. Drink, dance and dine with the colorful characters in Coral Bay afterward.

Devote day three to hiking the Reef Bay trail, kayaking along coastal reefs or another favorite activity. Hop on a ferry on day four to check out St Thomas' East End.

SEVEN DAYS

Spend the first day in Charlotte Amalie, St Thomas, strolling downtown and making a dent in your US$1600 duty-free allowance. The next day ferry over to the fourth Virgin, Water Island, to swim and snorkel at Honeymoon Beach.

Take the seaplane to Christiansted, St Croix. Over the next three days drink at old windmills turned gin mills on Christiansted's wharf, dive the north-shore wall, sip at west-end rum factories and paddle through Salt River Bay in a see-through kayak.

Return to Charlotte Amalie, then catch the ferry to Cruz Bay, St John. You can't beat the green island for beaching, snorkeling and hiking trails that wind by petroglyphs, sugar mill ruins and wild donkeys.

GETTING TO NEIGHBORING ISLANDS

Ferries run between St Thomas and St John hourly (a 20-minute trip). They glide between St Thomas, St John and the British Virgin Islands (BVI) frequently each day; trips average between 30 and 60 minutes. Seaplanes fly the 20-minute route between St Thomas and far-flung St Croix at least once per hour. Regional airlines make daily runs to Puerto Rico, Tortola, Antigua, Anguilla and St Kitts from St Thomas, and to St-Martin/Sint Maarten from St Croix.

Essential Food & Drink

» **Callaloo** Spicy soup stirred with okra, various meats, greens and hot peppers.

» **Pate** (*paw*-tay) Flaky fried dough pockets stuffed with spiced chicken, fish or other meat.

» **Fungi** (*foon*-ghee) A polenta-like cornmeal cooked with okra, typically topped by fish and gravy.

» **Mango Pale Ale** Fruit-tinged microbrew by St John Brewers.

» **Cruzan Rum** St Croix's happy juice since 1760, from light white rum to banana, guava and other tropical flavors.

US Virgin Islands Highlights

1 Trek to petroglyphs, sugar mill ruins and isolated beaches rich with marine life in **Virgin Islands National Park** (p846)

2 Snorkel with barracudas, turtles and nurse sharks at **Leinster Bay/Waterlemon Cay** (p850)

3 Sip microbrews and explore the cannon-covered fort in historic **Christiansted** (p852)

4 Dive the wall and peer into the deep at **Cane Bay** (p854)

5 See where Columbus landed, then kayak the bioluminescent water at **Salt River Bay** (p856)

6 Drink the Virgin Islands' favorite attitude adjuster at its source at the **Cruzan Rum Distillery** (p859)

7 Raise a glass to happy hour in **Cruz Bay** (p848)

8 Slow down on a jaunt to wee **Water Island** (p843)

9 Shop for rum, pirate gear and fiery hot sauces in historic **Charlotte Amalie** (p842)

ST THOMAS

POP 52,200

Most visitors arrive at the US Virgin Islands via St Thomas, and the place knows how to strike a first impression. Jungly cliffs poke high in the sky, red-hipped roofs blossom over the hills, and all around the turquoise, yacht-dotted sea laps. St Thomas is the most commercialized of the Virgins, with several cruise ships bellowing into port daily and big resorts spread all along its perimeter. But this is also a fine island to sharpen your knife and fork. Curried meats and hot-spiced callaloo soup fill local tables. Beaches pretty enough to star in Hollywood movies beckon. And opportunities for surfing, kayaking through mangrove lagoons and getting face-to-face with sea turtles pop up, too.

ⓘ Getting There & Around

See p864 for further details on airlines and ferries to and from the island.

AIR St Thomas' **Cyril E King Airport** (STT; www.viport.com) is the region's main hub; it's located 2.5 miles west of Charlotte Amalie. Taxis (ie multipassenger vans) are readily available. The fare to downtown is US$7; it's US$11 to US$15 to Red Hook. Luggage costs US$2 extra per piece.

BOAT St Thomas has excellent ferry connections to the rest of the Virgins. The two main marine terminals are at Charlotte Amalie (ferries to St Croix and the British Virgin Islands) and Red Hook (ferries to St John). St Thomas also has two cruise ship terminals: Havensight and Crown Bay.

BUS Vitran (fare US$1) operates buses over the length of the island. Look for the bus stop signs on Rtes 30 and 38.

'Dollar' buses (aka 'safaris' or 'gypsy cabs') also stop along the routes. These vehicles are open-air vans that hold 20 people. They look like taxis, except they're filled with locals instead of sunburned tourists. Flag them down by flapping your hand, and press the buzzer to stop them when you reach your destination. The fare is US$2.

CAR Most of St Thomas' rental agencies have outlets at the airport and resort hotels. Prices start around US$60 per day.

Avis (☏800-331-1084; www.avis.com)

Budget (☏776-5774, 800-626-4516; www.budgetstt.com)

Dependable Car Rentals (☏800-522-3076; www.dependablecar.com)

Discount Car Rentals (☏776-4858, 877-478-2833; www.discountcar.vi)

Hertz (☏800-654-3131; www.hertz.com)

TAXI Territorial law requires taxi drivers to carry a government-set rate sheet, and prices are listed in the readily available and free tourist guide *St Thomas/St John This Week*.

Many taxis are vans that carry up to 12 passengers. These service multiple destinations and may stop to pick up passengers along the way, so their rates are usually charged on a per-person basis. The following are per-person rates from Charlotte Amalie.

Frenchtown US$4
Havensight US$6
Magens Bay US$10
Red Hook US$13

PORTS OF CALL

There are plenty of options for even a short visit:

Charlotte Amalie

» Stroll downtown and check out historic sites such as sand-floored St Thomas Synagogue (p837) and Emancipation Garden (p837)

» Browse the town's famous shops (p842) for a Rolex or pirate eye patch

» Grab a taxi to Magens Bay (p840), the island's beach hot spot

» Taxi to Red Hook, then ferry over to St John and its North Shore beaches (p849)

» Get off the beaten path on Water Island (p843) if you're docking at Crown Bay

Frederiksted

» Visit the Cruzan Rum Distillery (p859), St George Village Botanical Garden (p859) and Estate Whim Plantation Museum (p859) en route to Christiansted (p852)

» Go off the rails with a rainforest trail ride from Freedom City Cycles (p858)

Charlotte Amalie

With two to six Love Boats docking in town daily, Charlotte Amalie (a-*mall*-ya) is one of the most popular cruise ship destinations in the Caribbean. Downtown buzzes with visitors swarming the jewelry shops and boutiques by day. By early evening, the masses clear out, the shops shutter, and the narrow streets become shadowy.

Sure, the scene here can overwhelm, but why not take a deep breath and focus on the town's lip-licking West Indian cuisine,

Frenchtown wine bars and proximity to white-sand beaches?

◎ Sights

Charlotte Amalie stretches about 1.5 miles around St Thomas Harbor from Havensight on the east side (where cruise ships dock) to Frenchtown on the west side. Around the peninsula from Frenchtown lies Crown Bay, another cruise-ship-filled marina and the jump-off point to Water Island.

Street signs are labeled with original Danish names. North St, for example, is Norre Gade (*gaa*-da, which is 'street' in Danish). Main St and Back St are generally called by their English names.

Emancipation Garden   PARK
(btwn Tolbod Gade & Fort Christian) Emancipation Garden is where the emancipation proclamation was read after slaves were freed on St Croix in 1848. Carnival celebrations and concerts take place here, but mostly folks kick back under trees with a fruit smoothie from the **Vendors' Plaza**, where sellers also hawk batik dresses, T-shirts and Prada knock-offs under blue-canopied stalls.

Fort Christian   FORT
(Waterfront Hwy; admission by donation; ◎8:30am-4:30pm Mon-Fri) Red-brick Fort Christian is the oldest colonial building in the USVI, dating back to 1666. Over the years, it has functioned as a jail, governor's residence and Lutheran church. At press time, the fort and its artifact-rich museum were closed and undergoing renovations. The reopening date for the multi-year project has not been determined.

Frederik Lutheran Church   CHURCH
(Norre Gade) Located near the fort, this is one of Charlotte Amalie's architectural gems. During the 19th century the church had segregated congregations – one West Indian, the other Danish. The church is open sporadically during the week, and you can attend services on Sunday at 9am.

Government House   HISTORIC BUILDING
(21-22 Kongens Gade; ◎9am-noon & 1-5pm Mon-Fri) Ascend the hill behind the church and you'll come to a grand white mansion, where the territorial governor has his offices. It was built between 1865 and 1867, and restored in 1994. You can walk around the 1st floor, though there's not much to see.

Blackbeard's Castle   HISTORIC SITE
(www.blackbeardscastle.com; admission US$12; ◎9am-3pm when cruise ships in port) Black-

ⓘ **CRUISE SHIP LOWDOWN**

Many attractions are only open when cruise ships are in port. Check **VI Now** (www.vinow.com) to see how busy it'll be on the day you're visiting. Tuesdays and Wednesdays typically see the most traffic, Fridays the least. If it's an off day, consider heading to the beach instead.

beard's Castle watches over the town from atop Government Hill. In the 18th century this five-story masonry watchtower was said to be the lookout post of pirate Edward Teach, alias Blackbeard. Actually, historians don't lend much credence to the tale. What's known for certain is that colonial Danes built the tower as a military installation in 1678. You can climb up for good harbor views.

The admission fee includes use of the three pools on the grounds, photos with the myriad pirate statues that dot the property, and entrance to **Villa Notman, Britannia House** and **Haagensen House** – three colonial homes furnished with West Indian antiques and/or jewelry shops. It also includes entry to the **World Caribbean Amber Museum**, guarded by a hokey mechanical dinosaur; the **amber waterfall**, studded with 12,000 yellowy gems; and a **rum factory**, where a guide explains the distilling process, though there isn't much to see. The whole thing is kind of a hefty price without much payoff.

A better idea is to attack Government Hill from below and ascend the steep set of stairs – the so-called **99 Steps** – that lead from the commercial district near Kongens Gade up into a canopy of trees. These steps, of which there are actually 103 (though you'll be too out of breath to count), were constructed using ship-ballast brick in the mid-18th century. At the top of the 99 Steps, and about halfway up to the watchtower, you'll see Haagensen House, which you can sometimes peek in for free. Explore the area in the cool of the morning, before the cruise-ship crowds arrive.

St Thomas Synagogue   HISTORIC BUILDING
(www.stthomassynagogue.com; 16A&B Crystal Gade; ◎10am-4pm Mon-Thu, to 3pm Fri) The second-oldest Hebrew temple in the western hemisphere (the oldest is on the island of Curaçao), peaceful St Thomas Synagogue is a National Historic Landmark. The current building dates from 1833, but Jews have

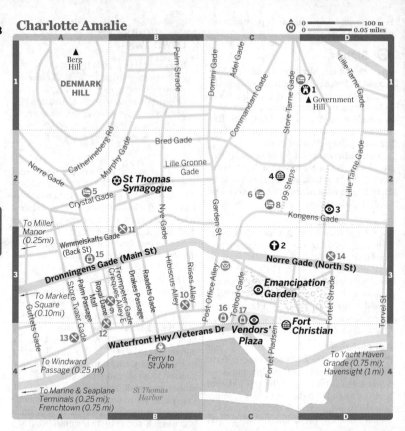

worshipped here since 1796, from Sephardic Jews from Denmark to today's 110-family Reform congregation. The temple floor is made of sand to symbolize the flight of the Israelites out of Egypt and across the desert. There's a tiny museum in the back room.

Frenchtown NEIGHBORHOOD

The island's 'Frenchies,' aka Huguenots who immigrated to St Thomas from St-Barthélemy during the mid-19th century, populated this community of brightly painted frame houses on the harbor's western side. Nowadays the fishermen's neighborhood has several good restaurants that overlook the water.

To get here from town, take a taxi (per person US$4), or walk west on Waterfront Hwy past the Seaplane Terminal and turn left just past the post office. The 1.25-mile walk takes about 25 minutes from Emancipation Garden.

Havensight NEIGHBORHOOD

A hundred years ago, the area on the east side of St Thomas Harbor (known today as Havensight) was a bustling steamship wharf and coaling station. Today it's still busy, but with behemoth cruise ships that tie up to the West Indian Company Cruise Ship Dock.

When passengers disembark, they find **Havensight Mall**, a compound with row upon row of shops and restaurants. They also find **Paradise Point Skyride** (☎774-9809; www.stthomasskyride.com; adult/child US$21/10.50; ☺9am-5pm when cruise ships in port). From a base station across the street from the mall, gondolas whisk visitors 700ft up Flag Hill to a scenic outlook; the ride takes seven minutes. At the top a restaurant, bar, gallery of shops and a short nature trail await. The skyride stays open later on some Tuesdays and Wednesdays.

The **Butterfly Farm** (☎715-3366; adult/child US$15/9; ☺8:30am-4pm) lies at the cruise-ship dock's far south end. Amid the garden full of fluttering beasties, you'll learn about metamorphosis during a 25-minute guided tour. Wear bright colors and perfume if you want the butterflies to land on you. The attraction often has discount coupons in the free tourist guides.

Taxis travel to and from Havensight regularly (US$6 per person).

Yacht Haven Grande   SHOPPING COMPLEX
Next door to Havensight is this marina and chic shop complex. Gucci and Louis Vuitton headline the tony roster, along with a hookah bar and several waterfront bistros where you can sip cosmos and watch mega-yachts drift in to the dock. A **farmers' market** (www.growvi.org; ⊙10am-2pm, 1st & 3rd Sun) with produce and crafts sets up on the grounds on the first and third Sunday of the month.

🎊 Festivals & Events

International Rolex Cup Regatta   REGATTA
(www.rolexcupregatta.com; ⊙late Mar) World-class racing boats gather.

St Thomas Carnival   CULTURAL
(www.vicarnival.com; ⊙mid-Apr–early May) It's the second-largest carnival in the Caribbean after the one at Port of Spain, Trinidad.

🛏 Sleeping

The rates listed do not include the 18% tax. Some places require a two- or three-night minimum stay in high season. For local villa and condo rentals try **Calypso**

Realty (☑774-1620; www.calypsorealty.com) or **McLaughlin Anderson Luxury Villas** (☑776-0635, 800-537-6246; www.mclaughlinanderson.com). Many St Thomas visitors also swear by **VRBO** (www.vrbo.com).

┌─────┐
│ TOP │ **Green Iguana**   HOTEL $$
│CHOICE│
└─────┘
(☑776-7654; www.thegreeniguana.com; 1002 Blackbeard's Hill; r US$140-170; ❄@🛜) Way the heck up the hill behind Blackbeard's Castle, this homey place is set in lush gardens and overlooks St Thomas Harbor. The nine rooms come in several configurations, but all have free wi-fi access, satellite TV, a microwave, refrigerator and bright, welcoming decor; some also have a fully equipped kitchen and private balcony. It's great value if you don't mind the steep walk.

Miller Manor   GUESTHOUSE $$
(☑774-1535, 888-229-0762; www.millermanor.com; 26 Prindsesse Gade, Frenchman's Hill; r US$91-145; ❄🛜) This 26-room hillside establishment has the feel of your Aunt Josie's summer place. A 150-year-old Danish townhouse anchors the complex, with a bar (with free wi-fi) overlooking the town and harbor. Rooms range from singles with a shared bathroom to large rooms with water-view balconies. While the manor is in a safe neighborhood, the dicey Savan district lies between here and the heart of town. Take a cab at night.

Crystal Palace   B&B $$
(☑777-2277, 866-502-2277; www.crystalpalaceusvi.com; 12 Crystal Gade; r incl breakfast US$119-149; ❄🛜) Ronnie Lockhart owns this five-room

DON'T MISS

TOP THREE OUTLYING BEACHES

To reach the sweetest stretches of sand, you'll need to motor beyond Charlotte Amalie.

Magens Bay

The sugary mile that fringes heart-shaped Magens Bay, 3 miles north of Charlotte Amalie, makes almost every travel publication's list of beautiful beaches. The seas here are calm, the bay broad and surrounding green hills dramatic, and tourists mob the place to soak it all up. The **beach** (adult/child US$4/2; ⊙6am-6pm; 🚻) has lifeguards, picnic tables, changing facilities, food vendors and water-sports operators renting kayaks and paddle boats (US$20 to US$30 per hour). A taxi from Charlotte Amalie costs US$10 per person. Parking costs US$2. On the road down, stop for a milkshake at **Udder Delite Dairy Bar** (📞777-6050; milkshakes US$5; ⊙1-6:30pm Mon, 10am-6:30pm Tue-Sat, 11:30am-6:30pm Sun; 🚻), part of a working farm. Adults can get their creamy goodness spiked with booze.

Hull Bay

Also on the north coast and just west of Magens Bay, Hull Bay is the island's most popular surfing beach and usually a gem of solitude when Magens is overrun. The shady strand lies at the base of a steep valley and has a restaurant, bar and changing facilities. **Homer's** (📞774-7606, 866-719-1856; www.nightsnorkel.com; ⊙10am-5pm) rents surfboards (US$50 per half-day) and kayaks (US$40 per half-day) and conducts raved-about night snorkel tours (US$38 per person). Taxis are scarce, so you'll need a car to get here.

Brewers Bay

This beach, located behind the University of the Virgin Islands, is beloved by students, local families and shell spotters alike. There are no facilities other than snack vans serving *pates* and cold Heineken beers. It gets deserted fast come nighttime. Brewers is right by the airport and accessible by taxis and public buses.

property in a colonial mansion that has been in his family for generations. Two rooms have private bathrooms; the other three share a bathroom. Antique West Indian decor pervades, and there's a view-tastic patio on which to eat the continental breakfast or swill a drink from the honor bar. Ronnie is a fountain of local lore; he'll pick you up at the airport or ferry dock for free.

Hotel 1829   HOTEL $$

(📞776-1829, 800-524-2002; www.hotel1829.com; 30 Kongens Gade; r incl breakfast US$105-190; 🕸🌐🚻) Built in 1829, this seven-room inn blends the atmosphere of a Victorian gentlemen's club and a colonial villa. Exposed rubble walls, beamed ceilings and period West Indian furnishings characterize the rooms. The result is a romantic, Old World island vibe. Be aware the 'moderate' rooms are tiny.

Galleon House   HOTEL $$

(📞774-6952, 800-524-2052; www.galleonhouse.com; 31 Kongens Gade; r incl breakfast US$85-155; 🕸@🌐🚻) The 'harbor view' rooms are the winners at friendly Galleon House, with wood doors that open onto a balcony over-

looking the waterfront. The 'shared bathroom' and 'interior private bathroom' rooms are confining and not recommended unless you're truly strapped for dough. The veranda and pool are good for hanging out and munching breakfast.

Windward Passage   HOTEL $$$

(📞774-5200, 800-524-7389; www.windwardpassage.com; Waterfront Hwy; r US$210-275; 🕸@🌐🚻) The four-story Windward Passage is primarily a business hotel. It's useful for those seeking free in-room wi-fi access, a fitness center, on-site eateries and quick taxi access. It's also right across from the Marine Terminal, and super convenient if you're catching an early morning ferry or seaplane. It's less beneficial to those seeking good value, since the peach-colored, cookie-cutter rooms are overpriced. However, when other hotels are booked, there's usually room here. The hotel is located at the edge of downtown, not far from Frenchtown.

Inn at Villa Olga   HOTEL $$

(📞715-0900, 800-524-4746; www.villa-olga-inn.com; r US$150-175; 🕸@🌐🚻) Villa Olga offers

12 motel-like rooms off the beaten path in Frenchtown. While the faded rooms have seen better days, they are spacious and scattered over pretty, palm-shaded grounds. The bonus here is free access to the beach and water-sports equipment at Bolongo Bay Beach Resort, Olga's sister property. It's on the waterfront, on a road that runs behind Frenchtown's cluster of restaurants.

Best Western Emerald Beach Resort
HOTEL **$$$**

(☎777-8800; 800-233-4936; www.emeraldbeach.com; 8070 Lindbergh Bay; r US$260; ✳@🖥🌊) This property, near the airport, offers 90 snazzy rooms, with private beachfront balconies, flat-screen TVs and free in-room wi-fi.

Best Western Carib Beach Hotel
HOTEL **$$**

(☎774-2525, 800-792-2742; www.caribbeachresort.com; 70C Lindbergh Bay; r US$159-179; ✳🖥🌊) As close as you'll get to the airport, just 0.25 miles away. Rooms are fine but nothing special. You're on the waterfront, but not on the beach.

✖ Eating & Drinking

Downtown is good for breakfast and lunch, though dinner options are scarce. Frenchtown holds several great restaurants that buzz in the evening. Havensight is touristy and chain-oriented but offers a fun, high-energy atmosphere. Stylish Yacht Haven Grande works well for a happy-hour martini.

DOWNTOWN CHARLOTTE AMALIE

[TOP CHOICE] **Gladys' Cafe**
CARIBBEAN **$$**

(☎774-6604; Royal Dane Mall; mains US$13-21; ☉7am-5pm Mon-Sat, 8am-3pm Sun) With the stereo blaring beside her, Gladys belts out Tina Turner tunes while serving some of the best West Indian food around. Callaloo, fungi, Ole Wife (triggerfish), fried plantains and sweet potatoes hit the tables along with Gladys' homemade hot sauce (for sale at the front, making a fine souvenir).

Cuzzin's Caribbean Restaurant & Bar
CARIBBEAN **$$**

(☎777-4711; 7 Back St; mains US$10-21; ☉11:30am-4:30pm Tue-Sat) With exposed brick walls, burnished wood furnishings and red-clothed tables, classy-but-casual Cuzzin's is everybody's favorite stop for West Indian cuisine. Try the conch (a local shellfish) curried, buttered or Creole style, or the Ole Wife

(triggerfish) alongside fungi, johnnycakes and a Blackbeard Ale.

Green House
BURGERS, SEAFOOD **$$**

(www.thegreenhouserestaurant.com; cnr Waterfront Hwy & Store Tvaer Gade; mains US$12-24; ☉lunch & dinner; 🖥) Cavernous, open-air Green House overlooks the harbor and rocks hard during happy hour (4:30pm to 7pm, when drinks are two for the price of one) and evenings after 10pm. The cuisine is predictable American pub fare, but the menu is extensive, with burgers, pizzas and seafood.

Natural Livity
VEGETARIAN **$**

(www.naturallivitykulchashop.com; 9A Norre Gade; mains US$6-12; ☉8am-8pm Mon-Sat; 🖥) Lentil burgers, pumpkin soup, scrambled tofu and other healthy vegan dishes are on the menu at this Rasta cafe/shop. The best thing to do is to pick and mix a platter of daily specials (stewed eggplant, soy duck, veggie lasagna) from the glass case. The space is tiny, so carry out and have a picnic at Veteran's Memorial Park, which offers shaded benches a block to the east.

Bumpa's
CAFE **$**

(☎776-5674; Waterfront Hwy; mains US$9-14; ☉breakfast & lunch) Climb the stairs to the 2nd floor, order at the counter, then carry your hearty oatmeal pancakes, pumpkin muffin, veggie burger, chicken *pate* or grilled fish wrap to the small patio overlooking the street.

Beans, Bytes & Websites
CAFE **$**

(5600 Royal Dane Mall; sandwiches US$6-8; ☉breakfast & lunch; @🖥) This chic little cyberbistro pours Charlotte Amalie's best java to go with bagels and toasted sandwiches.

FRENCHTOWN

Frenchtown's restaurants are all within a few minutes' walk of each other, so you can peruse the options. Dinner reservations are a good idea.

[TOP CHOICE] **Pie Hole**
ITALIAN **$$**

(☎642-5074; mains US$13-17; ☉lunch Mon-Fri, dinner Mon-Sat) Six tables and nine bar stools comprise this cozy eatery. The 13in, crisp-crusted, brick-oven pizzas are the claim to fame. Super-fresh ingredients, ie spinach and ricotta or mozzarella and basil, top the white or wheat crust. Several house-made pastas and a robust beer list raise Pie Hole to near perfection.

Craig & Sally's
FUSION $$$

(☏777-9949; www.craigandsallys.com; mains US$22-40; ⊙lunch Wed-Fri, dinner Wed-Sun) Chef Sally Darash lives up to the claims that she is a 'kitchen witch.' Her fusion cooking draws a crowd every night to the open-air alcoves of this 'Frenchie' cottage. The menu changes according to Sally's whim, but expect dishes such as pan-seared jumbo scallops with avocado slices and mozzarella mashed potatoes. Eclectic small plates are available too, such as lamb-burger sliders and barbecue eel.

Hook, Line & Sinker
BURGERS, SEAFOOD $$

(☏776-9708; www.hooklineandsinkervi.com; mains US$13-25; ⊙lunch & dinner Mon-Sat, brunch Sun) This open-air, mom-and-pop operation feels like a real sea shack, where you smell the salt water, feel the ocean breeze and see sailors unload their boats dockside. The menu mixes sandwiches, salads, pastas and seafood mains, such as the almond-crusted yellowtail, with plenty of beers to wash it down.

🛍 Shopping

Jewelry is the big deal in town. Shops fill the alleys between Waterfront Hwy and Main St, west of Emancipation Garden. US citizens can leave with up to US$1600 in tax-free, duty-free goods.

The Vendors' Plaza (p837) is interesting to wander, as are the following places.

Camille Pissarro Gallery
FINE ARTS

(14 Main St) Located in Pissarro's boyhood home (a display case outside summarizes the family's history), the gallery sells a few reproductions of the famous impressionist's St Thomas scenes, but mostly focuses on works by contemporary artists.

Pirates in Paradise
SOUVENIRS

(38A Waterfront Hwy) Argh! Here's your treasure trove of pirate gear, including eye patches and fake doubloons. The shop is underneath Bumpa's restaurant.

Native Arts & Crafts
SOUVENIRS

(Tolbod Gade) This is the place to buy local hot sauces, straw dolls and painted gourd bowls made by island craftspeople, as well as books by local authors.

ℹ Information

There is no official tourist office downtown, but the free St Thomas/St John This Week magazine has maps and everything else you'll need.

DANGERS & ANNOYANCES Charlotte Amalie has some big-city issues, including drugs, poverty, prostitution and street crime. Waterfront Hwy and Main St in the town center are fine at night, but move a few blocks away and the streets get deserted quickly. Avoid the Savan area, a red-light district that surrounds Main St west of Market Sq and north of the Windward Passage hotel; this is where the island's underworld takes root. In general, savvy travelers who take reasonable precautions should have no problems.

INTERNET ACCESS Some restaurants and bars have free wi-fi, such as Green House.

Beans, Bytes & Websites (5600 Royal Dane Mall; per half-hr US$4.50; ⊙7am-6pm Mon-Sat, to 1pm Sun) Connect with your electronic mailbox at the 12 or so terminals, plus wi-fi and data ports for laptops.

MEDIA St Thomas/St John This Week (www.virginislandsthisweek.com) Widely available free monthly magazine that has events listings, maps and the cruise-ship schedule. The website has happy-hour drink coupons.

VI Daily News (www.virginislandsdailynews.com) The main newspaper.

MEDICAL SERVICES Roy Schneider Community Hospital (☏776-8311; 48 Sugar Estate Rd at Rte 313; ⊙24hr) On the east side of Charlotte Amalie, this full-service hospital has an emergency room, recompression chamber and doctors in all major disciplines.

MONEY FirstBank, Scotiabank, Banco Popular and other banks are on Waterfront Hwy.

POST Main post office (☏774-3750) It's on the west side of Emancipation Garden.

Red Hook & East End

The East End holds the bulk of the island's resorts. Red Hook is the only town to speak of, though it's small and built mostly around the St John ferry dock and American Yacht Harbor marina.

👁 Sights & Activities

Coral World Ocean Park
MARINE PARK

(☏775-1555; www.coralworldvi.com; 6450 Estate Smith Bay; adult/child US$19/10; ⊙9am-4pm; 🚼) This 4.5-acre marine park, at Coki Point, is the most popular tourist attraction on St Thomas. Pick up a schedule when entering – staff feed the sea creatures and give talks about marine biology and conservation throughout the day, and it's during these times that you'll engage in behaviors you never thought possible, such as petting baby nurse sharks, touching starfish and feeding raw fish right into a stingray's mouth. Many of the creatures have been rescued (for example the sea turtles were orphans; and the sea lions were in harm's way in Uruguay, where

WATER ISLAND

Do the Charlotte Amalie crowds have you pining for peace and seclusion? Water Island is your answer. Sometimes called the 'Fourth Virgin,' it floats spitting distance from town. But with only about 100 residents and very few cars or shops, it feels far more remote.

At 2.5 miles tip to tip, it doesn't take long to walk the whole thing. **Honeymoon Beach** offers fine swimming and snorkeling – it's a 10-minute walk from the ferry dock. Follow the road uphill from the landing; when the road forks, go right and down the hill to the sand.

Water Island Adventures (www.waterislandadventures.com; 3hr tours US$60) offers bicycle tours of the island, including swim time at the beach.

Virgin Islands Campground (☑776-5488, 877-502-7225; http://virginislandscampground. com; cottages US$170; @🔊) is the only option if you want to spend the night, but it's an eco-winner. Each wood-frame-and-canvas cottage has beds, linens, electrical outlets and a table and chairs inside. Guests share the communal bathhouse, cooking facilities and hot tub. Captured rainwater runs through the sinks and showers; solar energy heats it.

The **Water Island Ferry** (☑690-4159; one way US$5) departs roughly every hour from outside Tickle's Dockside Pub at Crown Bay Marina. The journey takes 10 minutes. Taxis from downtown to the marina cost US$4 to US$5 per person.

fishermen were shooting them as pests). Pay an extra US$40 to US$125, and you can swim with the sharks, turtles or sea lions.

The site has restaurants and gift shops, along with changing rooms if you want to visit nearby Coki Beach. Look for Coral World discount coupons in the free tourist guides.

Sapphire Beach　　ACTIVITIES BEACH
The Sapphire Beach Resort, just off Smith Bay Rd (aka Rte 38), is perhaps the most welcoming of all the island's resorts to transient beach visitors. The volleyball games here can get spirited, as can the party scene on Sunday afternoons. Virtually every conceivable type of water-sports equipment is available for rent, from kayaks to jet skis to Sunfish sail boats (about US$15 to US$20 per hour).

Secret Harbour Beach　　ACTIVITIES BEACH
This west-facing beach in front of the eponymous resort could hardly be more tranquil. It's an excellent place to snorkel or to learn to windsurf with equipment rented from the resort's water-sports operation. A platform floats in the middle of the bay that children enjoy swimming to and jumping off.

Lindquist Beach　　SECLUDED BEACH
(admission $2) Part of protected Smith Bay Park, this narrow strand is probably the largest piece of undeveloped beach property on the island. It's a beauty all right: calm, true-blue water laps the soft white sand, while several cays shimmer in the distance. Hollywood has filmed several commercials

here. There are lifeguards on duty, chairs for rent and portable toilets, but no other amenities. Access is via dirt road off Smith Bay Rd (aka Rte 38), north of Sapphire Beach.

Coki Beach　　DIVING & SNORKELING BEACH
This beach is on a protected cove right at the entrance to Coral World. The snorkeling is excellent with lots of fish action, and you can dive from the shore with the Coki Beach Dive Club. Coki is the one beach on St Thomas with touts – as soon as you arrive someone will quickly become your 'friend'. You'll likely see police here keeping an eye on things, as Coki has had issues with violent crime in the past. Despite it all, the festive little beach gets quite crowded.

Virgin Islands Ecotours　　TOURS
(☑779-2155, 877-845-2925; www.viecotours.com; 2½hr tours adult/child US$77/43; ⊙10am & 2pm) offers a guided kayak-and-snorkeling expedition where you'll paddle through a mangrove lagoon to a coral rubble beach. Tours depart just east of the intersection of Rtes 30 and 32, at the entrance to the Inner Mangrove Lagoon Sanctuary. There's also a three-hour tour that adds hiking to the mix.

Diving & Snorkeling

St Thomas features several premier dive sites, and most resort hotels have a dive service on the property. Dive centers charge about US$90 for a one-tank dive, or US$125 for two. They also rent snorkeling gear for US$10 to US$15 per day. Recommended dive shops include the following:

Red Hook Dive Center

DIVING

(777-3483; www.redhookdivecenter.com) The retail center is at American Yacht Harbor. It offers mostly boat dives out of the Wyndham Sugar Bay Resort, as well as night dives and trips to the British Virgin Islands' wreck RMS *Rhone*.

Coki Beach Dive Club

DIVING

(775-4220; www.cokidive.com; ⊘closed Sun) Just steps away from Coki Beach, it offers shore and night dives, plus Professional Association of Diving Instructors (PADI) courses.

Fishing

Troll for wahoo, or get the live bait ready for yellowfin tuna. Add blue marlin to the list from May through October. Most trips depart from American Yacht Harbor. Expect to pay about US$800 for a half-day excursion, and US$1450 for a full day.

Marlin Prince

FISHING

(779-5939; www.marlinprince.com) Captain John Prince operates this 45ft vessel. He also offers saltwater fly-fishing for marlin.

Nate's Custom Charters

FISHING

(244-2497; www.natescustomcharters.com) Hit the waves in a 27ft ProKat.

🛏 Sleeping

Resorts are the East End's only option. **Antilles Resorts** (www.antillesresorts.com) manages

OLD STONE FARMHOUSE

The 200-year-old **Old Stone Farmhouse** (777-6277; www.oldstonefarmhouse.com; Mahogany Run Golf Course; mains US$24-36; ⊘dinner, closed Tue) lies high on a hill overlooking St Thomas' only golf course. The rustic, low-lit room impresses with its arched stone walls and mahogany ceiling. The chef invites guests back to the kitchen to select their own meat and fish and discuss their preferences; he then prepares the dish accordingly. The Caribbean-style menu changes, but local fish (snapper, wahoo, mahi mahi, live lobster) are always available, as well as a vegetarian option. The stellar service, setting and chef make this a one-of-a-kind evening. The restaurant is on the north shore, en route to Magens Bay from the East End.

six properties here, including Sapphire Beach Resort, Pavilions and Pools, and Point Pleasant Resort. Many units are privately owned condos, and they vary widely in quality. Savvy visitors say they have better luck booking through **VRBO** (www.vrbo.com), where they deal with the condo owners directly.

Bolongo Bay Beach Resort

RESORT $$$

(775-1800, 800-524-4746; www.bolongobay.com; 7150 Bolongo Bay; r US$230-395; ❋❄) Family-owned Bolongo is a fun, casual resort. Its beach offers a full array of free water sports, and tennis courts, a pool and fitness center are on site. Oceanview rooms are on the 2nd and 3rd floors, while beachfront rooms are on the 1st floor – all have sea views and private patios. The 'value' rooms are in a building across the street. The interiors won't win any awards for size or decor, but who cares? You'll be outside enjoying fun in the sun. Bolongo is located between Red Hook and Charlotte Amalie.

Secret Harbour Beach Resort

RESORT $$$

(775-6550; www.secretharbourvi.com; 6280 Estate Nazareth; ste US$345-625; ❋@❄❄) Secret Harbour is a family favorite. Of the 60 suites, 42 units sit on the beach and the rest are up a hill behind the beach, with sea views. Suites come in three sizes: studio (600ft), one bedroom (900ft) and two bedroom (1300ft). All have a kitchen and a balcony or patio. You can get your exercise at the pool, fitness center and three tennis courts, but the calm, shallow beach is the main draw.

Sapphire Beach Resort & Marina

RESORT $$$

(775-6100, 800-874-7897; www.antillesresorts.com; 6720 Estate Smith Bay; ste $335-495; ❋❄) The draw for this condo resort is being on gorgeous Sapphire Beach itself. It's also handy to be so close to Red Hook – a five-minute drive or a 15-minute walk (along the busy road) – where restaurants and bars abound. The condos themselves are studio-style suites that vary in quality. Check VRBO for this one, to have more control over what you're getting.

Pavilions and Pools

RESORT $$$

(775-6110, 800-524-2001; www.pavilionsandpools.com; 6400 Estate Smith Bay; ste incl breakfast US$325-350; ❋@❄❄) The cool thing about this small hotel is that each of the 25 suites has its own pool – yeah, you read that right! Suites have full kitchens, wi-fi access and separate bedrooms with sliding doors that open to your own pool. Staff will shuttle you to nearby Sapphire Beach.

Point Pleasant Resort
RESORT $$$

(☎775-7200, 800-524-2300; www.pointpleasantre
sort.com; 6600 Estate Smith Bay; ste US$300-550;
❋❋) On a steep hill overlooking Water Bay,
the property has lots of charm though the
rooms are somewhat dated. The 128 suites
are in multi-unit cottages tucked into the hill-
side forest. Each unit has a full kitchen, sepa-
rate bedroom and large porch. The grounds
have walking trails, three pools and a beach.

✗ Eating & Drinking

Lots of party-hearty bars and restaurants
cluster in Red Hook near the ferry dock.

Duffy's Love Shack
BURGERS $$

(www.duffysloveshack.com; 650 Red Hook Plaza;
mains US$9-16; ⊘lunch & dinner) It may be a
frame shack in the middle of a paved parking lot, but Duffy's creates its legendary
atmosphere with high-volume rock and
crowds in shorts and tank tops. The food is
classic, burger-based pub fare. The big attractions here are the people-watching and
killer cocktails, like the 64oz 'shark tank.'
Cash only.

Latitude 18
BURGERS, SEAFOOD $$

(☎779-2495; www.latitude18usvi.com; Vessup Bay
Marina; mains US$20-28; ⊘lunch & dinner) This
funky sea ramblers' place is a patio protected
by a roof of old sails and tarps. Locals rave
about the flavorful dishes coming from the
little kitchen, such as seared tuna roll with
papaya salad. Most nights during the week,
Latitude brings in fiddlin' bands that fire up
the crowd. It's located down a bumpy dirt
road around the south side of Vessup Bay.

Molly Malone's
BURGERS, SEAFOOD $$

(www.mollymalonesstthomas.com; American Yacht
Harbor, Red Hook; mains US$13-27; ⊘breakfast,
lunch & dinner) A re-creation of a friendly Irish
pub, Molly's has a huge menu, from omelets
to shepherd's pie to veggie lasagna. It's a
great place to watch sports on overhead TVs,
or cool off with a brew at the bar.

Agavé Terrace & Bar
SEAFOOD $$$

(☎775-4142; www.agaveterrace.com; 6600 Estate
Smith Bay, Point Pleasant Resort; mains US$22-38;
⊘dinner) The deck hangs out in thin air over a
steep slope, giving diners a breathtaking view
of St John and the British Virgin Islands. It
specializes in fish, lobster and crab legs.

Fungi's on the Beach
CARIBBEAN $$

(Point Pleasant Resort; mains US$9-18; ⊘lunch & din-
ner) The Point Pleasant Resort's Rasta-colored
beach bar is a fun, waterside place to try local
dishes such as conch or the namesake fungi.

ST JOHN

POP 4300

Outdoor enthusiasts and ecotravelers: welcome to your island. Two-thirds of St John is
a protected national park, with gnarled trees
and spiky cacti spilling over its edges. There
are no airports or cruise-ship docks, and the
usual Caribbean resorts are few and far between. Instead, the island hosts several tent-
resorts (aka campgrounds with permanent
canvas structures), keeping costs reasonable
and the environment intact.

Hiking and snorkeling are the big to-dos.
Trails wind by petroglyphs and sugar-mill
ruins, and several drop out onto beaches
prime for swimming with turtles and spotted eagle rays.

Two towns bookend the island: Cruz Bay,
the ferry landing and main village that hosts
a helluva happy hour; and Coral Bay at the
East End, the sleepy domain of folks who
want to feel like they're living on a frontier.

ℹ Getting There & Around

BOAT All ferries arrive in Cruz Bay. Check **See
St John** (www.seestjohn.com) for schedules.
Boats from St Thomas and the British Virgin
Islands arrive at separate docks, though they are
within steps of each other. Main routes:
Red Hook, St Thomas US$6 one way, 20
minutes, hourly (big pieces of luggage cost
US$2.50 extra)
Charlotte Amalie, St Thomas US$12 one way,
45 minutes, three daily
West End, Tortola US$45 round trip, 30
minutes, three daily
Jost Van Dyke US$70 round trip, 45 minutes,
two daily (except none Wednesday or Thursday)
BUS Vitran (fare US$1) operates air-con buses
over the length of the island via Centerline
Rd. Buses leave Cruz Bay in front of the ferry
terminal at 6am and 7am, then every hour at 25
minutes after the hour until 7:25pm. They arrive
at Coral Bay about 40 minutes later.
CAR St John has a handful of rental agencies.
Most provide 4WDs and SUVs to handle the
rugged terrain. Costs hover near US$80 per day.
The following agencies have outlets in Cruz Bay
near the ferry terminals:
Cool Breeze Jeep/Car Rental (☎776-6588;
www.coolbreezecarrental.com)
Denzil Clyne Car Rental (☎776-6715)
St John Car Rental (☎776-6103; www.st
johncarrental.com)

TAXI Territorial law sets the island's taxi rates. They're listed in *St Thomas/St John This Week* magazine. From Cruz Bay it costs per person US$7 to US$9 to Cinnamon Bay, and US$9 to US$16 to Coral Bay. Call the **St John Taxi Commission** (✆774-3130) for pickups.

Cruz Bay

Nicknamed 'Love City,' St John's main town indeed wafts a carefree, spring-break party vibe. Hippies, sea captains, American retirees and reggae worshippers hoist happy-hour drinks in equal measure, and everyone wears a silly grin at their great good fortune for being here. Cruz Bay is also the place to organize your hiking, snorkeling, kayaking and other activities, and to fuel up in the surprisingly good restaurant mix. Everything grooves within walking distance of the ferry docks.

◉ Sights

FREE **Virgin Islands National Park** PARK (www.nps.gov/viis) In the early 1950s, US millionaire Laurence Rockefeller discovered and fell in love with St John, which was nearly abandoned at the time. He purchased large tracts of the land, built the Caneel Bay resort, and then donated more than 5000 acres to the US government. The land became a national park in 1956, and over the years the government added a couple of thousand more acres. Today Virgin Islands National Park covers two-thirds of the island, plus 5650 acres underwater.

It's a tremendous resource, offering miles of shoreline, pristine reefs and 20 hiking trails. The **park visitors center** (✆776-6201; ⊗8am-4:30pm) sits on the dock across from the Mongoose Junction shopping arcade. It's an essential first stop to obtain free guides on hiking trails, snorkeling spots, bird-watching lists and daily ranger-led activities.

For the record: more than 30 species of tropical birds nest in the park, including the bananaquit, hummingbird and smooth-billed ani. Green iguanas, geckoes, hawksbill turtles, wild donkeys and an assortment of other feral animals roam the land. Largely regenerated after 18th-century logging, the island flora is a mix of introduced species and native plants, with lots of spiny cacti.

A great way to give back to the park is by volunteering for trail or beach **clean-ups** (⊗8am-1pm Tue & Thu Nov-Apr); meet at the maintenance parking lot (it's well marked) by the visitors center. Clean-ups also take place at Maho Bay and Cinnamon

---

BEST HIKING TRAILS

St John's greatest gift to visitors (aside from the awesome snorkeling, feral donkeys, eco-camps and happy-hour booze) is its hiking trails. The national park maintains 20 paths, and any reasonably fit hiker can walk them safely without a local guide. The park visitors center provides trail details in the helpful free *Trail Guide for Safe Hiking* brochure. Über-enthusiasts should also buy the **Trail Bandit map** (www.trailbandit.org; US$4) that lists several additional footpaths; it's available at the Maho Bay Camps store or online.

If you prefer guided hikes, the National Park Service sponsors several free ones, including birding expeditions and shore hikes, but its best-known offering is the **Reef Bay Hike** (✆776-6201, reservations ext 238; hikes US$21; ⊗9:30am-3pm Mon & Thu year-round, plus Fri Dec-Apr). This begins at the Reef Bay trailhead, 4.75 miles from Cruz Bay on Centerline Rd. The hike is a 3-mile downhill trek through tropical forests, leading past petroglyphs and plantation ruins to a swimming beach at Reef Bay, where a boat runs you back to Cruz Bay (hence the fee). It's very popular, and the park recommends reserving at least two weeks in advance.

These other favorite trails are each less than 3 miles round trip; all have identifying signs at the trailheads and small lots to park your car.

» **Lind Point** Departs from behind the visitors center, past the occasional donkey and bananaquit, to secluded Honeymoon Beach.

» **Leinster Bay** Goes from the Annaberg sugar-mill ruins to fantastic snorkeling at Waterlemon Cay.

» **Ram Head** Rocky, uphill slog to a worth-every-drop-of-sweat clifftop view.

» **Cinnamon Bay Loop** Easy trail from the campground that swings through tropical forest and mill ruins.

Bay beaches during the same timeframe on Thursdays.

 Activities

For hiking, see the boxed text on p846. Also see 'Diving & Snorkeling St John' (p850).

Arawak Expeditions KAYAKING, SNORKELING
(☑693-8312, 800-238-8687; www.arawakexp.com; half/full day trips US$65/110) Departs out of Cruz Bay; snorkel gear not included. Offers mountain-biking tours (similar prices), as well.

Hidden Reef Eco-Tours KAYAKING, SNORKELING
(☑877-529-2575; www.hiddenreefecotours.com; 3hr/5hr tours US$65/115) Departs from Haulover Bay at the island's more remote east end; snorkel gear is included. Also offers night paddles.

Friends of the Virgin Islands National Park MULTI-SPORT
(www.friendsvinp.org; trips US$25-85) The nonprofit group offers hiking, snorkeling and sailing trips around the island, as well as cooking, painting, jewelry-making and West African drumming workshops.

✦✦ **Festivals & Events**

8 Tuff Miles ROAD RACE
(www.8tuffmiles.com; ⊙late Feb) Popular foot race from Cruz Bay to Coral Bay.

St John Blues Festival MUSIC
(www.stjohnbluesfestival.com; ⊙mid-Mar) Music bash in Coral Bay; tickets cost US$30 per night.

St John Carnival CULTURAL
(⊙early Jul) The island's biggest celebration; surrounds Emancipation Day (July 3) and US Independence Day (July 4).

🛏 **Sleeping**

Adventure travelers keen on eco-camping (and lower-priced lodging) should head to the North Shore. Properties add an 8% hotel tax, and many also charge a 10% service fee (sometimes called an 'energy surcharge') on top.

Villa rentals can be reasonable, especially if you're accommodating more than two people and staying a week or longer. One-bedroom villas could cost US$1600 to US$2700 per week from these companies: **Carefree Get-Aways** (☑779-4070, 888-643-6002; www.carefreegetaways.com), **Caribbean Villas** (☑776-6152, 800-338-0987; www.caribbeanvilla.com), **Catered To** (☑776-6641, 800-424-6641; www.cateredto.com), **Coconut Coast**

Villas (☑693-9100, 800-858-7989; www.coconutcoast.com).

🏆 **St John Inn** HOTEL $$
(☑693-8688, 800-666-7688; www.stjohninn.com; r incl breakfast US$175-225; ❉🐾) Rooms at the popular St John Inn are decked out with tiled floors, handcrafted pine furniture and iron beds. Many also have water views or a kitchen. A homey atmosphere pervades, and guests grill fresh fish on the communal barbecue, laze on the sun deck or dip in the small pool.

🏆 **Garden by the Sea B&B** B&B $$$
(☑779-4731; www.gardenbythesea.com; r incl breakfast US$250-275; ❉🐾) B&Bers swoon over this place. The owners live on-site and have splashed the three rooms in bright hues of sea green, lavender and blueberry, each with a sturdy, four-post canopy bed and private bathroom. Solar panels provide the electricity. Cash or traveler's checks only.

Samuel Cottages APARTMENTS $$
(☑776-6643; www.samuelcottages.com; 4-person apt US$125; ❉) These three peach-colored cottages are a stiff 10-minute walk uphill from the ferry dock, but you'll be hard-pressed to beat the value. They are sort of like state park cabins – nothing fancy, but clean and spacious enough, with a fully equipped kitchen and deck for sitting and contemplating how much cash you're saving.

Inn at Tamarind Court HOTEL $$
(☑776-6378, 800-221-1637; www.innattamarindcourt.com; s/d/q US$75/148/240; ❉🐾) The rooms are small, thin-walled and lack frills such as private decks and water views, but Tamarind Court does try hard with its friendly staff, bamboo-and-tiki decor and jumpin' courtyard bar-restaurant. A separate building holds six single rooms sharing two bathrooms.

✖ **Eating**

Window-shopping for a place to eat is one of the joys of dining out in Cruz Bay. Everything is located in a compact core.

Jake's BREAKFAST, BURGERS $$
(☑777-7115; Lumberyard; mains US$10-17; ⊙7am-4am) All-day breakfast is Jake's forte, including well-stuffed omelets, crispy home fries and strong coffee. Ceiling fans whir, newspapers rustle and reggae drifts from the speakers – then the couple next to you orders a

triple shot of Jack Daniel's to accompany their pancakes. Jake's is that kind of place. The open-air cafe is up the hill across from the BVI ferry dock, on the 2nd floor.

Shela's Pot
CARIBBEAN $$

(cnr Prince & Strand Sts; mains US$10-15; ☺lunch Tue-Sat) This is where the locals go for home cookin'. Shela takes shrimp, conch, fish and chicken, stirs them up in her big pots, and scoops them into takeaway boxes along with side dishes such as mashed sweet potato and fried plantains. It's a small shack across from the ferry landing; look for the spot where all the taxi drivers are hanging out. Cash only.

Rhumb Lines
ASIAN FUSION $$

(☑776-0303; www.rhumblinesstjohn.com; Meada's Plaza; mains US$16-30; ☺dinner, closed Tue; ☑) Tucked in a lush courtyard, this little restaurant has superb salads, sandwiches and fresh, healthy tropical cuisine served by happy, friendly hippies. Try selections from the 'pu pu' menu, a mix of tapas-like treats. There's air-conditioned indoor seating, or outdoor seating under palms and umbrellas.

Da Livio
ITALIAN $$

(☑779-8900; King St; mains US$17-32; ☺dinner Mon-Sat) Fork into authentic northern Italian food lovingly cooked by a chef-transplant from the motherland. Staff makes all the pasta, gnocchi and bread from scratch, and it goes down nicely with the hearty wines. Corks dot the ceiling, and the black-and-white decor gives the trattoria a sleek-casual ambience.

Joe's Diner
BREAKFAST $

(cnr Prince & King Sts; mains US$5-10; ☺6am-6pm) This hole-in-the-wall, with about six streetside tables, is a Cruz Bay institution. It's a favorite place for locals and travelers to catch a fast bite, especially at breakfast, when you'll see a queue of folks at the window ordering coffee, beer, bagels or egg sandwiches.

Lime Inn
SEAFOOD $$

(☑776-6425; www.limeinn.com; King St; mains US$20-30; ☺lunch Mon-Fri, dinner Mon-Sat) Lime Inn is a travelers' favorite for quality cuisine, ambience and service at moderate prices. The New England clam chowder and the shrimp dijon get rave reviews. Reservations are a good idea.

🍷 Drinking

TOP CHOICE Joe's Rum Hut
BAR

(Wharfside Village) Around 11am, a bartender materializes with rum and a whopping bowl of limes at this beachfront boozer. After that, it's all about sitting at the open-air counter, clinking the ice in your mojito and watching the boats bob in the bay out front. To find Joe's, head through the Wharfside Village mall in the opposite direction of the ferry dock; it's on the 1st floor fronting the water.

Woody's Seafood Saloon
BAR

(www.woodysseafood.com) St John's daily party starts here at 3pm, when the price on domestic beers drops precipitously. By 4pm the crowd in this tiny place has spilled over onto the sidewalk. Bartenders pass beers out a streetside window. While lots of folks just show up to cram in and whoop it up with fellow tanned bodies, you can actually get some reasonable pub food, such as grilled fish or corn-crusted scallops.

Tap Room
MICROBREWERY

(www.stjohnbrewers.com/taproom.html; Mongoose Junction; ☺noon-9pm Mon-Sat, 2-9pm Sun; 🛜) St John Brewers taps its sunny, citrusy suds here (the actual brewing takes place stateside). Sip a flagship Mango Pale Ale, or try the alcohol-free options, including house-made root beer, ginger beer and Green Flash energy drink.

🛍 Shopping

Starfish Market
FOOD

(Marketplace Bldg; ☺7:30am-9pm) Self-caterers can stock up at this full-service supermarket. Beer, wine and cheese are in a separate shop across the hall from the main market's front door. It's about a 15-minute walk northeast from the ferry dock.

🌿 Friends of the Park Store
SOUVENIRS

(Mongoose Junction) Looking for paper made out of local donkey poo? Thought so. It's here, along with shelves of other ecofriendly wares. Proceeds go to the Virgin Islands National Park.

ℹ Information

CUSTOMS & IMMIGRATION US Customs & Immigration (☑776-6741; ☺8am-noon & 1-5pm) Adjoins the British Virgin Islands ferry dock. If you arrive on a ferry or on a yacht from the BVI, you must clear immigration here (typically a no-hassle process) before you head into town.

INTERNET ACCESS There's free wi-fi in some of the popular drinking establishments. Also, if you sit in the park behind Connections, you can usually pick up free wi-fi from Computer Express, which makes its signal available to the public.

Connections (www.connectionsstjohn. com; cnr Prince & King Sts; per 30min US$5; ☺8:30am-5:30pm Mon-Sat) An all-purpose communications center where you can use the internet terminals, print, send packages, etc.

MEDIA & WEBSITES See St John (www. seestjohn.com) Excellent resource by local author Gerald Singer, with detailed hiking-trail directions and beach guides.

St John Sun Times (www.facebook.com/ suntimesmag) Free biweekly magazine with restaurant and event listings.

MEDICAL SERVICES Myrah Keating Smith Community Health Center (☏693-8900; ☺8am-8pm Mon-Fri) About 2 miles east of Cruz Bay on Centerline Rd.

MONEY There's a FirstBank branch with ATM near Woody's Seafood Saloon.

POST Post office (☏779-4227) Across the street from the British Virgin Islands ferry dock.

TOURIST INFORMATION Most businesses offer free island maps.

Visitors center (☺8am-4:30pm) A small building next to the post office with brochures and whatnot.

North Shore

Life's a beach on the tranquil North Shore. A rental car is the easiest way to see the area via North Shore (Rte 20) and Centerline (Rte 10) Rds, but taxis will also drop you at the beaches for between US$6 and US$13 per person.

◉ Sights & Activities

FREE **Annaberg Sugar Mill**
Ruins   HISTORIC SITE
(www.nps.gov/viis; North Shore Rd; ☺9am-4pm) Part of the national park, these ruins near Leinster Bay are the most intact sugar plantation ruins in the Virgin Islands. A 30-minute, self-directed walking tour leads you through the slave quarters, village, windmill, rum still and dungeon.

The schooner drawings on the dungeon wall may date back more than 100 years. Park experts offer **demonstrations** (☺10am-2pm Tue-Fri) in traditional island baking, gardening, weaving and crafting.

When you're finished milling around, hop on the **Leinster Bay Trail** that starts near the picnic area and ends at, yep, Leinster Bay. It's 1.6 miles, round trip.

🏖 Beaches

Most beaches have rest rooms and changing facilities, and most are excellent for snorkel-

ing. You can rent gear at tourist-favorites Trunk and Cinnamon Bays, or at dive shops in Cruz Bay (see the boxed text, p850). We've listed the following sand patches starting from Cruz Bay and moving eastward.

Honeymoon Beach   SECLUDED BEACH
Honeymoon is a mile hike from the park visitors center along the Lind Point Trail. The handsome white-sand strand has no facilities, other than sea-grape trees to hang your clothes on. It's often empty and quiet – except on days when charter boats arrive between mid-morning and mid-afternoon.

Caneel Bay   ACTIVITIES BEACH
This is the main shore in front of Caneel Bay resort, which actually has seven beaches, but this is the one it permits visitors to use. It's a lovely place, with fair snorkeling off the east point. You must sign in at the guardhouse when you enter the resort property, and pay US$10 if you're parking.

Hawksnest Bay   PICNIC BEACH
The bay here is dazzling to behold, a deep circular indentation between hills with a broken ring of sand on the fringe.

Jumbie Bay   SECLUDED BEACH
Jumbie is the word for ghost in the Creole dialect, and this beach has a plethora of ghost stories. Look for the parking lot on North Shore Rd that holds only three cars. From here, take the wooden stairs and a short trail down to the sand.

Trunk Bay   ACTIVITIES BEACH
This long, gently arching beach is the most popular strand on the island and charges a US$4 fee. The beach has lifeguards, showers, toilets, picnic facilities, snorkel rental, a snack bar and taxi stand. No question, the sandy stretch is scenic, but it often gets

WORTH A TRIP

PEACE HILL

Pull over when you see the Peace Hill sign shortly after driving past Hawksnest Bay. If you're willing to walk 0.1 miles you'll be rewarded with moody ruins of an old windmill and superb views out to sea. A statue of Jesus once lorded (pun!) over the hill, but Hurricane Marilyn in 1995 proved to be the stronger force. Look for the plaque marking his former post.

St John offers loads of snorkel hot spots that are accessible from shore. The park service publishes an oft-photocopied but useful brochure called *Where's the Best Snorkeling?* – pick it up at the park visitors center. Gold stars go to Leinster Bay/Waterlemon Cay and Salt Pond Bay.

The island also has cool dive sites, all of which are accessed by boat, including wreck dives on the *General Rogers* and RMS *Rhone*. A two-tank trip including gear costs US$95 (about US$160 to the *Rhone*). The following shops in Cruz Bay also offer dive certification, snorkel gear rental (US$8 to US$10 per day for a full set) and boat trips to the BVI (about US$130 plus US$25 in customs fees for a full day): **Cruz Bay Watersports** (☑776-6234; www.divestjohn.com; Lumberyard; ⊙8am-6pm) and **Low Key Watersports** (☑693-8999; www.divelowkey.com; Wharfside Village; ⊙8am-6pm).

packed. Everyone comes here to swim the underwater snorkeling trail, though experienced snorkelers will likely not be impressed by the murkiness or quality of what's on offer beneath the surface.

Cinnamon Bay
ACTIVITIES BEACH

The mile-long beach, St John's biggest, is home to the Cinnamon Bay Campground. The beach has showers, toilets, a restaurant, grocery store, taxi stand and – something you don't see at every beach – an archaeological dig. It also offers a full slate of activities through its **Water Sports Center** (⊙8:30am-4:30pm), where you can rent sailboats, windsurf boards, stand-up paddleboards and sea kayaks (US$20 to US$35 per hour). Lessons including equipment cost around US$65 per hour.

Maho Bay
SNORKELING BEACH

The water is shallow and less choppy than elsewhere, and it's a good bet you'll see green sea turtles in the early morning or late afternoon. There are no facilities and no parking lot; just pull over at the side of the road and voilà – you're at the beach.

Leinster Bay
SNORKELING BEACH

This bay adjoins the Annaberg mill ruins. Park in the plantation's lot and follow a dirt road/trail around Leinster Bay. Some of St John's best snorkeling is at the bay's east end, offshore at Waterlemon Cay, where turtles, spotted eagle rays, barracudas and nurse sharks swim. Be aware that the current can be strong.

🛏 Sleeping

Travelers unenthused by big swanky resorts will love the two low-key options here. Bring the insect repellent.

🏕 Maho Bay Camps
ECO-TENTS $$

(☑776-6226, 800-392-9004; www.maho.org; tents US$135, condos US$225-250; @🏕) Stanley Selengut's mega-popular, ecosensitive tent resort lies 8 miles east of Cruz Bay on North Shore Rd (Rte 20). The complex offers 114 'tents,' akin to fabric-lined cabins, which sit on wood platforms on a steep, forested hillside. Each unit has a sleeping area with twin beds, a propane stove, electrical outlets and an open-air terrace.

The tents are so far off the ground, and the surrounding vegetation is so thick, it's like living in a tree house. Prepare for lots of stair climbing. To conserve water, guests use low-flush toilets and solar-heated (frequently cold) showers in bathhouses sprinkled around the grounds.

For those seeking higher-grade amenities, the resort's adjoining Harmony Studios are condos with a private bathroom, kitchen and deck, plus solar-generated electricity and rainwater collection.

Now for the sad news: Maho sits on leased land, and the lease runs out in 2012. At press time, it was taking reservations only through May 2012. But the **Trust for Public Land** (www.tpl.org) is fighting hard to acquire the property and keep the camp going; check the website for updates.

Cinnamon Bay Campground
CAMPGROUND $

(☑776-6330, 800-539-9998; www.cinnamonbay. com; campsites/equipped tents US$32/93, cottages US$126-163; ⊙closed Sep) About 6 miles east of Cruz Bay on North Shore Rd (Rte 20), this campground-ecoresort sits along a mile-long crescent beach at the base of forested hills. It's really a campers' village with a general store, snack bar and restaurant, but with thick vegetation giving plenty of privacy. There are three accommodations options. You can use your own tent; stay in a 10ft by 14ft tent that sits on a solid wood platform and comes equipped with four cots, a lantern, ice chest, charcoal grill and gas stove; or stay in a cottage – a 15ft by 15ft concrete shelter with two screened sides, electric lights, grill, stove and ceiling fan. The best bets are using your own tent or the cottages; the equipped tents are a bit gloomy. Everyone uses the public toilet facilities and cold-water showers.

Caneel Bay RESORT $$$
(☎776-6111, 888-767-3966; www.caneelbay.com; r from US$550; 🏵@🛜🌊✈🏄) It's the resort that started it all, back in 1955. Located 2 miles north of Cruz Bay, Caneel Bay is where folks such as Angelina Jolie and Brad Pitt come when they need seven beaches, 11 tennis courts, five restaurants and all-round elegance. There are no phones or TVs in rooms.

Coral Bay & Around

Coral Bay, St John's second town, is really just a handful of shops, restaurants and pubs clustered around the 1733 hilltop Emmaus Moravian Church. Two hundred years ago, it was the largest settlement on the island. Known then as 'Crawl Bay', presumably because there were pens or 'crawls' for sea turtles here, the settlement owes its early good fortune to being the largest and best-protected harbor in the Virgin Islands. Today it serves as the gateway to the island's most remote beaches and coastal wilderness, ripe for hiking, horseback riding and ecocamping.

⊙ Sights & Activities

Strap on your walking shoes for two essential **hikes** near Coral Bay. The first one is at **Salt Pond Bay**, a few miles from town down Rte 107 and a 10-minute walk from the road. The bay itself provides excellent snorkeling; keep an eye out for turtles and squid. At the beach's south end, the **Ram Head Trail** takes off and rises to a windswept cliff jabbing out into the sea. The trek is a 2-mile round trip through rocky exposed terrain, so bring ample water and sun protection.

The second cool hike is the **Brown Bay Trail**, which starts a mile east of Coral Bay. The path runs for 3.2 miles, round trip, going over a small ridge and past a conch-scattered beach; sweet viewpoints and butterflies pop up en route.

Horseback riding enthusiasts can saddle up a trusty steed or donkey with **Carolina Corral** (☎693-5778; www.carolinacorral.vi; Rte 107; rides adult/child US$75/65; ⊙10am & 3pm Mon-Sat) for a 1½-hour jaunt on mountain trails.

🛏 Sleeping & Eating

TOP CHOICE **Concordia Eco-Tents** ECO-TENTS $$
(☎693-5855, 800-392-9004; www.maho.org; tents US$155-185, apt US$150-225; ✺) Concordia is the sister resort to Maho Bay Camps. Only here, each 16ft-by-16ft unit has a 2nd-floor loft and a private bathroom, with composting toilet and solar-heated shower (still a bit chilly). A kitchen (small refrigerator and two-burner propane stove) and sea view complete the package. The camp also offers studio apartments with slightly upgraded amenities, plus a cafe, activities center (for yoga and water sports), swimming pool and store for everyone to use. It's all strung together by boardwalks and steps up the steep hillside. About 2.5 miles south of Coral Bay, Concordia is quiet and remote. You'll likely want a rental car, though patient souls can access it by public bus.

Skinny Legs BURGERS $
(☎779-4982; www.skinnylegs.com; Rte 10; mains US$8-13; ⊙lunch & dinner) Salty sailors, bikini-clad transients and East End snowbirds

---

MONGOOSES, DONKEYS & GOATS – OH MY!

Whether you are camping, hiking or driving on St John, it won't be long before you have a close encounter with the island's odd menagerie of feral animals. According to National Park Service estimates, 500 goats, 400 donkeys, 200 pigs and hundreds of cats roam the island, descendants of domestic animals abandoned to the jungle eons ago. White-tailed deer and mongooses are two other introduced species that multiplied in unexpected numbers.

Do not tempt the animals by offering them food or leaving food or garbage where they can get at it. And do not approach them for petting or taking a snapshot. While most have a live-and-let-live attitude and don't mind you stepping around them on the trails, they are all capable of aggression if provoked.

mix it up at this open-air grill just past the fire station. Overlooking a small boatyard, it's not about the view, but the jovial clientele and lively bar scene. Burgers win the most raves, so open wide for a cheeseburger, or try a grilled mahi mahi fish sandwich. Live music and dancing rock weekend nights.

Vie's Snack Shack
CARIBBEAN $

(☑693-5033; Rte 10; mains US$7-13; ⊙10am-5pm Tue-Sat) Vie Mahabir opened this plywood-sided restaurant next to her house in 1979, just after the government paved the road. She wanted to make a living while raising her 10 children. In the process, she perfected the art of conch fritters, garlic chicken with johnnycakes and coconut tarts. Vie will also let you lounge (US$2.50 per day) or camp (US$35 per night) on her low-key beach. She's located east of town (on East End Rd) by Hansen Bay. Cash only.

Miss Lucy's
CARIBBEAN $$

(☑693-5244; Rte 107; mains US$16-25; ⊙lunch & dinner Tue-Sat, brunch Sun) Miss Lucy, the island's first female cab driver and one heck of a cook, passed away in 2007 at age 91. Her restaurant lives on, as famous for its Sunday jazz brunch and piña colada pancakes as for its weekday conch chowder, jumbo crab cakes and toasted goat-cheese salad – all served at water's edge under the sea-grape trees. Take Rte 107 to Friis Bay; it's en route to Concordia.

ST CROIX

POP 53,200

St Croix is the USVI's big boy – it's more than twice the size of St Thomas – and it sports an exceptional topography spanning mountains, a spooky rainforest and a fertile coastal plain that, once upon a time, earned it the nickname 'Garden of the Antilles' for its sugarcane-growing prowess. Today the island is known for its scuba diving, rum making, marine sanctuary and, dare we say it, beer-drinking pigs.

St Croix is also distinguished by the fact that tourism is not its main income source. That honor goes to the Hovensa Oil refinery on the south shore, one of the world's largest processors. With so many locals working in 'regular' jobs, the vibe on St Croix is more suburban than bash-you-over-the-head idyllic, which actually makes

for a refreshing, less-congested change of pace.

St Croix drifts by its lonesome 40 miles south of the other Virgins. It has two main towns: Christiansted, the largest, sits on the northeast shore. Frederiksted, its much sleepier counterpart, resides on the west end, where a large Puerto Rican community has grown over the last few generations.

❶ Getting There & Around

AIR Henry E Rohlsen Airport (STX; www.viport. com) is on St Croix's southwest side and handles flights from the US, many connecting via San Juan, Puerto Rico or St Thomas.

Seaborne Airlines (www.seaborneairlines. com) flies seaplanes between St Thomas and St Croix – a sweet little ride (one way US$80, 20 minutes). They land in Christiansted's downtown harbor.

BOAT VI Seatrans (☑776-5494; www.go viseatrans.com) operates a passenger ferry between Christiansted and Charlotte Amalie, St Thomas (one way US$50, 90 minutes). It sails twice on Friday and Saturday, and once on Sunday and Monday. Departures are from Gallows Bay, about 0.75 miles east of downtown Christiansted.

The cruise-ship dock is in Frederiksted on the island's west end.

BUS Vitran (fare US$1) buses travel along Centerline Rd between Christiansted and Frederiksted. The schedule is erratic; buses depart roughly every hour or two.

CAR Rentals cost about US$55 per day. Many companies, including the following, will pick you up at the airport or seaplane dock.

Budget (☑778-9636; www.budgetstcroix.com)

Centerline Car Rentals (☑778-0450, 888-288-8755; www.ccrvi.com)

Hertz (☑778-1402; www.rentacarstcroix.com)

Olympic (☑773-8000, 888-878-4227; www.olympicstcroix.com)

TAXI Taxis are unmetered, but rates are set by territorial law. Prices are listed in the readily available free tourist guide St Croix This Week. Taxis from the airport to Christiansted cost US$16 per person.

Christiansted

Christiansted evokes a melancholy whiff of the past. Cannon-covered Fort Christiansvaern rises up on the waterfront, and arcaded sidewalks connect several other colonial buildings. They abut Kings Wharf, the commercial landing where, for more than 250 years, ships landed with slaves and set off with sugar or molasses. Today the wharf is fronted by a boardwalk of restaurants, dive shops and bars. It all comes together as a well-provisioned base from which to explore the island.

◉ Sights

Several painters, jewelry makers and photographers have galleries in town, with most on Company St near Queen Cross St. The **Art Thursday** (www.artthursday.com; ☺5-8pm, 3rd Thu of month) gallery hop takes place November through June.

Christiansted National Historic Site   HISTORIC SITE

(☑773-1460; www.nps.gov/chri; ☺9am-5pm) This historic site includes several structures. The most impressive is **Fort Christiansvaern** (admission $3), a four-point citadel occupying the deep-yellow buildings on the town's east side, and the best-preserved Danish fort in the West Indies. Built between 1738 and 1749 out of Danish bricks (brought over as ships' ballast), the fort protected citizens from the onslaught of pirates, hurricanes and slave revolts, but its guns were never fired in an armed conflict. After 1878, the fort served as a prison and courthouse for the island. Cannons on the ramparts, an echoey claustrophobic dungeon and latrines with top-notch sea views await visitors who tour the site.

Other historic buildings nearby include the **Scale House**, where the Danish weighed hogsheads of sugar for export (the building now houses a National Park Service visitors center). The **Customs House**, recognizable by its sweeping 16-step stairway, served as the Danes' customs house for more than a century. Nearby, the three-story neoclassical **Danish West India and Guinea Company Warehouse** served as company headquarters; slaves were auctioned in its central courtyard. Next door, the 1753 **Steeple Building** (admission $3, free with fort ticket) was the island's first house of worship; it's now a museum of Taíno relics and sugar-plantation exhibits.

Protestant Cay   BEACH

This small triangular cay, located less than 200yd from Kings Wharf, is a little oasis. It's the site of a mellow resort whose wide, sandy beach and bar-restaurant are open to the public. The **St Croix Water Sports Center** (www.stcroixwatersports.com) rents out snorkel gear, kayaks, sailboats and windsurfers. Some swimmers rave you can see just as much underwater life here as at Buck Island. The ferry (US$4 round trip, five minutes) departs from the wharf in front of the Customs House; look for a step labeled Hotel on the Cay.

🏃 Activities

Christiansted is chock-full of operators that book diving trips, and Buck Island tours (see the boxed text, p857).

World Ocean School   BOAT TRIPS

(☑626-7877; www.worldoceanschool.org; 2½hr tours adult/child US$45/30; ☺4:30pm Dec-May) Head out to sea aboard the sharp-looking, historic schooner *Roseway*. Added bonus: sailing with these folks supports their non-profit group that teaches local students sailing and leadership skills. Departures are from Gallows Bay.

Hiking

Hikers will love the guided ecowalks available. They depart from sites around the island. Fees vary.

St Croix Environmental Association   HIKING

(☑773-1989; www.stxenvironmental.org) Offers hiking, bird-watching and snorkeling trips, plus programs to help count sea turtles.

Ay-Ay Eco-Hikes   HIKING

(☑277-0410, 772-4079; eco@viaccess.net) Herbalist Ras Lumumba offers tours to Maroon Ridge, Annaly Bay, Salt River Bay and more.

St Croix Hiking Association   HIKING

(www.stcroixhiking.org) Sponsors a couple of guided hikes per month.

GO GREEN

For those watching their eco-footprint, the US Virgins offer several places where you can tread gently on the earth:
» Virgin Islands Campground, Water Island
» Maho Bay Camps, St John
» Concordia Eco-Tents, St John
» Mt Victory Campground, St Croix
» Northside Valley, St Croix
» Friends of the Virgin Islands National Park, St John
» Eco-hikes, St Croix

If you are a scuba enthusiast worth your sea salt, you'll be spending lots of time underwater in St Croix. It's a diver's mecca thanks to two unique features: one, it's surrounded by a massive barrier reef, so turtles, rays and other sea creatures are prevalent; and, two, a spectacular wall runs along the island's north shore, dropping at a 60-degree slope to a depth of more than 12,000ft. It gives a true look into 'the deep,' and there's nothing quite like it anywhere in the world.

The best dives on the north shore are at Cane Bay Drop-Off, North Star Wall and Salt River Canyon. The top west island dives are at the Butler Bay shipwrecks (including the *Suffolk Maid* and *Rosaomaira*) and at Frederiksted Pier. While almost all dive operators offer boat dives, many of the most exciting dives, such as Cane Bay, involve beach entries with short swims to the reef.

The operators listed here go to the various sites around the island and charge about US$75 for one-tank dives and about US$100 for two tanks (including equipment).

Anchor Dive Center
DIVING

(☎778-1522, 800-532-3483; www.anchordivestcroix.com; Salt River Marina) Specializes in dives in Salt River Canyon (where the shop is located).

Cane Bay Dive Shop
DIVING

(☎773-9913, 800-338-3843; www.canebayscuba.com; Cane Bay) A friendly five-star PADI facility, across the highway from the beach and the Cane Bay Drop-Off, and with shops in both Christiansted and Frederiksted.

Dive Experience
DIVING

(☎773-3307, 800-235-9047; www.divexp.com; 1111 Strand St) This woman-owned shop has a strong environmental commitment and offers 'green' diving courses. The shop is in Christiansted.

N2 The Blue
DIVING, SNORKELING

(☎772-3483; www.n2theblue.com; Frederiksted) Specializes in west-end wreck dives and Frederiksted Pier snorkel trips.

Scuba West
DIVING

(☎772-3701, 800-352-0107; www.divescubawest.com; Frederiksted) Specializes in west island dives, including awesome night dives on Frederiksted Pier (located across from the shop).

St Croix Ultimate Bluewater Adventures
DIVING, SNORKELING

(☎773-5994, 887-567-1367; www.stcroixscuba.com; 81 Queen Cross St) Another ultra-professional company that offers dives all over the island; it also offers west-end snorkel trips. The shop is in Christiansted.

☞ Tours

Tan Tan Jeep Tours (☎773-7041; www.stxtan tantours.com) goes four-wheeling to the Annaly Bay tide pools, deep into the rainforest and to other hard-to-reach destinations. Tours range from 2½ hours (US$70 per person) to eight hours (US$140 per person).

✯ Festivals & Events

In addition to the events below, Jump Ups (music-filled street carnivals) take place four times per year.

St Croix Agricultural Festival CULTURAL FAIR (www.viagrifest.org; ☺mid-Feb) The three-day event features island crafters, food stalls with superb examples of West Indian and Puerto Rican cooking, bands and livestock contests.

St Croix Half-Ironman Triathlon TRIATHLON (www.stcroixtriathlon.com; ☺early May) Participants strive for Ironman qualification.

Cruzan Christmas Fiesta CULTURAL FAIR (www.stxfestival.com; ☺early Dec-early Jan) It's a month of pageants, parades and calypso competitions, putting a West Indies spin on the Christmas holidays.

⌂ Sleeping

Tax is an additional 18%, and some places tack on an energy surcharge (about US$4).

Hotel on the Cay

HOTEL **$$**

(☑773-2035, 800-524-2035; www.hotelonthecay.com; r US$150-190; ❋@🐾❄) A truly cool place to stay, this hotel sits just offshore on its own little island called Protestant Cay, accessible by a five-minute ferry ride (free for guests). It's good value for the spacious rooms with full kitchenettes, cooking utensils and bright furnishings. The pièce de résistance: private balconies for taking in cool breezes, hearing waves lap the shore and watching pelicans dive-bomb for fish.

Company House Hotel

HOTEL **$$**

(☑773-1377; www.companyhousehotel.com; 2 Company St; d incl breakfast US$115; ❋@🐾❄) Company House is the budget pick of the downtown hotels. It is the sister property of King Christian Hotel, and as such guests have access to that entity's fitness center and continental breakfast. Rooms at Company House don't have views, a private deck or waterfront locale, but they are newly renovated, well maintained and offer free in-room wi-fi.

Club Comanche Hotel

HOTEL **$$**

(☑773-0210; www.clubcomanche.com; 1 Strand St; r US$135-165; ❋🐾❄) This downtown property is set in a 250-year-old Danish mansion. The 23 rooms have been renovated recently with West Indian antique decor, new beds, flat-screen satellite TVs and in-room internet access, and the place now has a boutique-hotel vibe. The good news is it's in the heart of Christiansted's entertainment district, right by the boardwalk; the bad news is the area can be noisy.

King Christian Hotel

HOTEL **$$**

(☑773-6330, 800-524-2012; www.kingchristian.com; 59 Kings Wharf; r incl breakfast US$120-155; ❋@🐾❄) You can't miss this three-story, peach-colored building that looks like a Danish warehouse (which it was 200 years ago) right next to the National Park Service sites. The 39 rooms are typical midrange, flowery-bedspread types; opt for a 'superior' room with harbor view, which will brighten up the scene considerably.

Hotel Caravelle

HOTEL **$$**

(☑773-0687, 800-524-0410; www.hotelcaravelle.com; 44A Queen Cross St; d US$170-190; ❋❄) Located on the waterfront, this 43-room property is similar in spirit to, though a bit fancier than, the King Christian Hotel. The more expensive rooms have harbor views. You can also get a harbor view by heading out to the pool and sundeck.

✖️ Eating

855

Harvey's

CARIBBEAN **$$**

(☑773-3433; 11B Company St; mains US$11-22; ⊙11am-4pm Mon-Sat) At breezy, 10-table Harvey's, a classic tropical cafe, you half expect Humphrey Bogart from *Casablanca* to walk in and order a drink at the bar. Conch in butter sauce, delicate grouper, sweet potato–based Cruzan stuffing, rice and peas and many more West Indian dishes arrive heaped on plates. Look for the big mural outside of NBA star Tim Duncan; he used to wait tables here before achieving his hoop dreams.

Sale e Miele

ITALIAN **$$**

(☑719-0510; 57C Company St; mains US$14-23; ⊙lunch Tue-Sat, dinner Thu-Sat) This amiable trattoria serves authentic Tuscan cuisine at tables scattered in a shady courtyard. Calamari, lasagna, and ricotta and spinach quiche are some of the dishes written on the blackboard menu. The Italian owner and her husband source much of their produce from the local farmers market and use those ingredients as a starting point for the menu each week.

Savant

INTERNATIONAL **$$**

(☑713-8666; 4C Hospital St; mains US$17-28; ⊙dinner Mon-Sat; 🍴) Cozy, low-lit Savant serves upscale fusion cookery in a colonial townhouse. The ever-changing menu combines spicy Caribbean, Mexican and Thai recipes; sweat over them indoors in the air-conditioning or outdoors in the courtyard. Reservations recommended.

Singh's Fast Food

CARIBBEAN **$**

(☑773-7357; King St; mains US$6-12; ⊙lunch & dinner; 🍴) When the roti craving strikes – and it will – Singh's will satiate with its multiple meat and tofu varieties. The steamy, four-table joint also serves shrimp, conch, goat, turkey and tofu stews – all while island music ricochets off the pastel walls. Cash only.

Avocado Pit

CAFE **$**

(☑773-9843; 59 Kings Wharf; mains US$6-12; ⊙breakfast & lunch) Young staff pour strong coffee and fruity smoothies at this wee cafe overlooking the fort and harbor. The granola-and-yogurt wins raves for breakfast, while the wraps (spicy tuna, tofu or avocado) make a delicious lunch or Buck Island picnic fare.

Lalita

VEGETARIAN **$$**

(☑719-4417; www.kalimacenter.org; 54 King St; mains US$8-16; ⊙9:30am-9pm; 🐾🍴) Raw-food nuts and vegans: Lalita is your place, serving

US VIRGIN ISLANDS CHRISTIANSTED

everything from organic muesli to seaweed salad to hummus plates.

Drinking

Places to pop in for a drink line the board-walk.

Fort Christian Brew Pub MICROBREWERY
(www.fortchristianbrewpub.com; boardwalk at King's Alley) Right on the boardwalk overlooking yachts bobbing in the sea, this open-air pub is primo for sampling the VI Brewing Company's small-batch suds. Try the flagship Blackbeard Ale or Foxy's Lager (the brewmaster here doubles as the suds-maker at Foxy's place on Jost Van Dyke in the BVI).

Comanche Mill Yacht-less Club BAR
(www.comanchemillyacht-lessclub.com; boardwalk at Comanche Walk) Set around an old windmill at the water's edge, the Yacht-less Club is hard to miss. It hosts a crowd of grizzled regulars in the afternoon, then morphs into a younger, clubbier group at night. The windmill used to pump sea water to the old pool at the Comanche Hotel. These days, the bar mostly pumps rum and beer.

Information

INTERNET ACCESS Strand Street Station (Pan Am Pavilion; per half-hr US$5; ⊙10am-5pm Mon-Sat, to 3pm Sun) Internet cafe with eight terminals; you can print and burn CDs.

INTERNET RESOURCES St Croix Landmarks Society (http://heritagetrails.stcroixlandmarks.org) Maps to ruins and cultural sites island-wide.

Go to St Croix (www.gotostcroix.com) Comprehensive event and nightlife information.

MEDIA St Croix This Week (www.stcroixthisweek.com) Widely available free monthly magazine with events listings.

St Croix Avis The island's daily newspaper.

MEDICAL SERVICES Governor Juan F Luis Hospital (☎776-6311; ⊙24hr) On Centerline Rd, 2 miles west of Christiansted.

MONEY There are a couple of banks with ATMs on King St near Prince St.

TOURIST INFORMATION Visitors center (☎773-1460; King St; ⊙10am-5pm) Pick up maps and attraction information in the historic Scale House.

Point Udall & Around

Point Udall is the easternmost geographic point in the US territory. As you face into a 25-knot trade wind, the vista from the promontory high above the surf-strewn beaches is enough to make you hear symphonies. Hikers will like the challenge of taking the steep trails down the hillside to isolated **Jack and Isaac Bays**, which are ecoreserves for green and hawksbill turtles; look for the trailhead near the Millennium Monument.

Some of St Croix's splashiest resorts take up the beachfront en route to Point Udall. **Divi Carina Bay Beach Resort** (☎773-9700, 877-773-9700; www.divicarina.com; 25 Estate Turner Hole, Grapetree Bay; r incl meals from $400; ✳@🛜🏊❄), on the southeast shore, draws visitors and locals alike. The former come to stay at the 180 mod, wicker-furnished rooms. The latter come to win big at the island's only **casino**.

North Shore

Luminescent bays, Chris Columbus' landing pad and hot dive sites await along the north shore.

About 4 miles west of Christiansted on Rte 80, **Salt River Bay National Historic Park** (www.nps.gov/sari; admission free) is the only documented place where Christopher Columbus washed ashore on US soil. Don't expect bells and whistles; the site remains undeveloped beach. The 700 acres surrounding the Salt River estuary is an ecological reserve. The best way to see its mangroves and egrets is by kayak with **Caribbean Adventure Tours** (☎778-1522; www.stcroixkayak.com; 2½hr tours US$45), located at Salt River Marina on the bay's west side; or with **Sea-Thru Kayak Adventures** (☎244-8696; www.seathrukayaksvi.com; 2hr tours US$50), which does its tours in über-cool clear kayaks. Paddling Salt River Bay at night, when the water glows with bioluminescence, is a St Croix highlight.

Sand seekers hit palm-fringed **Hibiscus Beach**, with good snorkeling and amenities, less than 2 miles west of Christiansted off Rte 75. **Cane Bay**, a long, thin strand along Rte 80 about 9 miles west of Christiansted, is also deservedly venerated. Cane Bay provides easy access to some of the island's best dives, and it's also the gateway into the rainforest's steep hills. The beach has several small hotels, restaurants, bars and the Cane Bay Dive Shop.

Sleeping

The lodgings here are more casual than glamorous. The Cane Bay properties have on-site restaurants.

Arawak Bay Inn at Salt River
B&B $$

(☎772-1684; www.arawakbaysaltriver.co.vi; 62 Salt River Rd; r incl breakfast US$140-160; ❄@🛜≋) The pick of the local litter for value, this peachy B&B has 14 bright rooms, each with different color schemes and decor. For those without a vehicle, it's isolated from the beaches and eateries, but the owners make amends by providing daily transportation to Christiansted and Cane Bay.

Waves at Cane Bay
HOTEL $$

(☎778-1805, 800-545-0603; www.cane baystcroix.com; North Shore Rd; r US$150-200; ❄🛜≋) The small, tidy Waves has pretty dang big rooms painted in tropical pastels. All 12 units have a balcony, kitchenette, cable TV and free wi-fi. But it's really all about location: you can snorkel or dive right off the rocks out front or lounge in the saltwater pool.

Cane Bay Reef Club
HOTEL $$

(☎778-2966, 800-253-8534; www.canebay.com; 114 North Shore Rd; r US$150-250; ❄🛜≋) This is good value because each of the nine rooms is like its own little villa overlooking the beach. The decor is dated but all suites include kitchens and private patios virtually hanging over the sea.

✗ Eating & Drinking

⌖TOP CHOICE Rowdy Joe's North Shore Eatery
INTERNATIONAL $$

(☎718-0055; North Shore Rd; mains US$9-15; �lunch & dinner; 🛜) Sit on the porch, and order off the blackboard menu. The chef strives for 'good mood food' using ingredients from St Croix's farms and fishermen. Dishes might include the Cubano pork sandwich, fish tacos or house-made pasta.

Eat @ Cane Bay
INTERNATIONAL $$

(☎718-0360; www.eatatcanebay.com; North Shore Rd; mains US$9-14; �lunch & dinner, brunch Sun, closed Tue) Located across from Cane Bay Beach, this place serves burgers that are a cut above the norm, along with wine and Belgian beers. The popular Sunday reggae brunch features eggs Benedict, crepes and bananas foster pancakes.

Frederiksted

St Croix's second-banana town is a motionless patch of colonial buildings snoring beside the sea. Other than the occasional boatload of visitors, it'll be you and that lizard sunning itself who will have the gritty outpost to yourselves. With its out-of-the-mainstream,

---

WORTH A TRIP

BUCK ISLAND REEF NATIONAL MONUMENT

For such a small land mass – 1 mile long by 0.5 miles wide – Buck Island draws big crowds. It's not so much what's on top but what's underneath that fascinates: an 18,800-acre fish-frenzied coral reef system surrounding the island, known as **Buck Island Reef National Monument** (www.nps.gov/buis).

The sea gardens and a marked underwater trail create captivating **snorkeling** on the island's east side. On land at pretty **Turtle Beach**, endangered hawksbill and green sea turtles come ashore. A **hiking trail** circles the island's west end and leads to an impressive observation point.

Most visitors glide here aboard tour boats departing from Kings Wharf in Christiansted, 5 miles to the west. Expect to pay US$70/90 (half/full day) per person, including snorkeling gear. Note that in winter, the trade winds blow hard at Buck Island, which can result in rough water for newbies to the mask and fins. Recommended operators include the following:

Big Beard's Adventures
BOAT TRIPS

(☎773-4482; www.bigbeards.com; Queen Cross St by Kings Wharf) Trips are aboard catamaran sailboats.

Caribbean Sea Adventures
BOAT TRIPS

(☎773-2628; www.caribbeanseaadventures.com; 59 Kings Wharf) Half-day trips are aboard a glass-bottom power boat; full-day trips are on a catamaran.

Teroro II
BOAT TRIPS

(☎773-3161; teroro@msn.com) A trimaran sailboat whose captain will entertain you completely; trips leave from Green Cay Marina, east of Christiansted.

laissez-faire ambience, Frederiksted is the center for gay life on St Croix.

◉ Sights & Activities

Frederiksted Pier & Waterfront Park   PARK
The palm-lined seafront has benches where you can sit and watch the cruise-ship scene. During quiet times (ie when cruise ships aren't here), snorkelers and divers gravitate to the pier's pilings, which attract an extensive collection of marine life, including schools of sea horses. The **Sunset Jazz Festival** (admission free; ◷6pm 3rd Fri of month) brings throngs of locals and visitors to the park.

Fort Frederik   FORT, MUSEUM
(admission US$3; ◷open when cruise ships in port) The deep red color of this fort at the foot of the pier is what most visitors remember about the little citadel. It's also where the island's slaves were emancipated in 1848. Exhibits inside explain the event.

Freedom City Cycles   CYCLING
(☏277-2433; www.freedomcitycycles.com; 2 Strand St; tours US$40) Pedal past sugar-plantation ruins and onward to Hams Bluff; more difficult rides bounce over rainforest trails. The shop is located a half block inland from the pier.

N2 The Blue   SNORKELING, DIVING
(☏772-3483; www.n2theblue.com) Specializes in west-end wreck dives and Frederiksted Pier snorkel trips; the shop is located across from the pier on the first side street next to the police station.

🛏 Sleeping

Frederiksted Hotel   HOTEL $$
(☏772-0500, 800-595-9519; www.frederiksted hotel.dk; 442 Strand St; r US$110-150; ✴@≋) This Danish-owned, bright-blue hotel sits right smack downtown. Four floors are built around a courtyard and small pool, and many rooms have patios overlooking the pier. The 36 units each have tiled floors and standard hotel-style furnishings, plus a refrigerator.

Sand Castle on the Beach   HOTEL $$
(☏772-1205, 800-524-2018; www.sandcastleonthe beach.com; 127 Estate Smithfield; r/ste incl breakfast from US$149/259; ✴🤏≋) Right on the beach about a mile south of Frederiksted, 21-room Sand Castle is one of the few gay- and lesbian-oriented hotels in the Virgin Islands.

The motel-like rooms come with kitchenettes; most have sea views.

🍴 Eating & Drinking

Polly's at the Pier   CAFE $
(☏719-9434; 3 Strand St; mains US$5-9; ◷breakfast & lunch; @🤏) Beloved by cruise-shippers, Polly's serves coffee, tea, sandwiches and omelets three doors down from the pier. It also scoops several flavors of local Armstrong's ice cream.

Coconuts on the Beach   TEX-MEX $$
(☏719-6060; www.coconutsonthebeach-stx.com; 72 LaGrange; mains US$8-15; ◷lunch & dinner) The casual beach bar serves nachos, jalapeño-spiced burgers and wraps. If nothing else, go for a drink and watch the sunset. It's about a five-minute walk north of town.

Blue Moon   CARIBBEAN, CAJUN $$
(☏772-2222; www.bluemoonstcroix.com; 7 Strand St; mains US$25-29; ◷lunch Tue-Fri, dinner Tue-Sat, brunch Sun) Considered one of the best restaurants on the island, Blue Moon dishes up Caribbean and Cajun cuisine in an atmospheric colonial warehouse. There's live jazz Wednesday and Friday nights and during Sunday brunch.

Turtles   SANDWICH SHOP $
(☏772-3676; www.turtlesdeli.com; 37 Strand St; mains US$7-10; ◷8:30am-5:30pm Mon-Sat) Chow hulking sandwiches on homemade bread, or sip a fine cuppa coffee, at beachfront tables under sea-grape trees.

Around Frederiksted

Many of the island's top sights surround Frederiksted. They are clustered north of town in the rainforest, and south along Centerline Rd.

RAINFOREST AREA

In the island's wet, mountainous northwest pocket, a thick forest of tall mahogany, silk cotton and white cedar trees grow. Technically, as only about 40in of rain fall here per year, the **Caledonia Rain Forest** is not a true 'rainforest.' No matter – it looks the part, with clouds, dripping trees and earthy aromas. Mahogany Rd (Rte 76) cuts through the spooky woods; it's twisty and pot-holed, so be careful.

Tucked into a steep hillside, about 20 minutes' drive from Frederiksted, is the unusual outdoor woodworking studio **St Croix**

Leap (☎772-0421; Rte 76, Brooks Hill; ☺8:30am-5pm Mon-Fri, 10am-4pm Sat). Here, master sculptor 'Cheech' leads a band of apprentice woodworkers in transforming chunks of fallen mahogany.

Deep in the rainforest is the **Montpellier Domino Club** (☎340-772-9914; ☺10am-5pm), an open-air West Indian bar-restaurant. Some folks come to drink the mamajuana (spiced rum), but the main attraction is the (nonalcoholic-) beer-guzzling pigs Hurricane Roger and Grunt.

Paul & Jill's Equestrian Stables (☎772-2880; www.paulandjills.com), 1.5 miles north of Frederiksted on Rte 63, offers trail rides that lead through hidden plantation ruins and the rainforest to hilltop vistas.

Hiking to **Hams Bluff** on the island's tip-top northwest corner unfurls views of sea-pounded cliffs; it's best to come with a guide (see p853).

Two ecologically minded lodgings have set up in the area:

🖉 **Mt Victory Campground** (☎772-1651, 866-772-1651; www.mtvictorycamp.com; Rte 58; campsites/equipped tents/cottages US$30/85/95) is located on a small working farm. The three perma-tents and two cottages are similar screened-in dwellings, each with a kitchen with cold-water sink, a propane stove and cooking utensils. There's no electricity, and guests share the solar-heated bathhouse. Cash only.

🖉 **Northside Valley** (☎772-0558; www.northsidevalley.com; 2 Estate Northside; villas per week US$1000-1500) is a step up, offering eight concrete-and-tile villas with private bathrooms and bamboo sheets, all washed using 'green' cleaning supplies. There is a one-week minimum stay. It's on the beach near Butler Bay.

CENTERLINE ROAD
Several sights lie south of Frederiksted on Centerline Rd (Rte 70).

Only a few of Whim Plantation's original 150 acres survive at **Estate Whim Plantation Museum** (☎772-0598; www.stcroixlandmarks.com; Centerline Rd; adult/child US$10/5; ☺10am-4pm Mon-Sat), but the grounds thoroughly evoke the colonial days when sugarcane ruled St Croix. Guided tours leave every 30 minutes, or wander by the crumbling stone windmill and chimney on your own. Don't forget to ask for the Landmarks Society's map to other ruins around the island.

To find out how the islands' popular elixir gets made, stop by **Cruzan Rum Distillery** (☎692-2280; www.cruzanrum.com; 3 Estate Diamond, Rte 64; adult/child $5/1; ☺9:30-11:30am & 1-4pm Mon-Fri) for a tour. The journey through gingerbread-smelling (from molasses and yeast), oak-barrel-stacked warehouses takes 20 minutes, after which you get to sip the good stuff. The factory is about 2 miles east of Whim Plantation.

Continuing east on Centerline Rd, you'll get to **St George Village Botanical Garden** (☎692-2874; www.sgvbg.org; Centerline Rd; adult/child $8/1; ☺9am-5pm). The 16-acre park built over a colonial sugar plantation does for the flora and fauna what Whim Plantation does for the grandeur of plantation days. More than 1500 native and exotic species grow on the grounds. Orchid-lovers, in particular, are in for a treat.

Captain Morgan Distillery (www.diageo.com; Rte 66), the makers of Captain Morgan Rum, are slated to open a LEED-certified visitors center in 2012. Diageo, the company that owns the brand, also owns Guinness, among other well-known booze, so expect an entertaining tour for the masses at the new facility.

UNDERSTAND THE US VIRGIN ISLANDS

History
Pirates & Powerbrokering

Folks have been living on the islands from as early as 2000 BC. The Taínos ruled the roost for a while, but the ruthless, seafaring Caribs eventually wiped them out.

Around this time Christopher Columbus sailed up to St Croix's Salt River Bay during his second trip to the Caribbean. It was 1493, and he gave the islands their enduring name: Santa Ursula y Las Once Mil Vírgenes, in honor of a 4th-century princess and her 11,000 maidens. Mapmakers soon shortened the mouthful to 'The Virgins.'

The islands remained under Spanish control until the English defeated the Spanish Armada in 1588. England, France and Holland were quick to issue 'letters of marque,' which allowed 'privateers' the rights to claim territory and protect those claims.

TOP USVI HISTORIC SITES

» Annaberg Sugar Mill Ruins, St John

» Fort Christiansvaern, St Croix

» Fort Frederik, St Croix

» Whim Plantation, St Croix

» Salt River Bay National Historic Park, St Croix

One king's privateer became every other king's pirate. Blackbeard (Edward Teach) operated in the Virgin Islands before 1720, with a collection of other rascals.

The Danes and English bickered over the islands, while each built vast sugar and tobacco plantations. The English held colonies on islands east of St John, while the Danes held St Thomas to the west. St John remained disputed territory. Finally, in 1717 the Danes sent a small but determined band of soldiers to St John and drove the British out. The Narrows, between St John and Tortola in the British Virgin Islands, became the border that has divided the eastern (first Danish, now US) Virgins from the British Virgins for more than 250 years.

Slavery & Liberation

The West Indies grew rich producing sugar and cotton for Europe. In pursuit of profits, the Danish West India and Guinea Company declared St Thomas a free port in 1724, and purchased St Croix from the French in 1733. By the end of the century, the number of African slaves on the islands exceeded 40,000.

Harsh living conditions and oppressive laws drove slaves to revolt. Meanwhile, sugar production in Europe and American tariffs on foreign sugar cut into the islands' profits. The deteriorating economy put everyone in a foul mood. Something had to give and it finally did in 1848, when Afro-Caribbeans on St Croix forced the legal end to slavery.

However, they remained in economic bondage. Life on the islands was dismal. Average wages for field workers were less than US$0.15 a day. A series of labor revolts left the plantation infrastructure in ruins.

USA Eyes the Prize

The USA, realizing the strategic value of the islands, negotiated with Denmark to buy its territories. The deal was almost done in 1867, but the US Congress choked at paying US$7.5 million (more than the US$7.2 million it had just paid for Alaska).

As WWI began in Europe, the USA grew concerned that German armies might invade Denmark and claim the Danish West Indies. Finally, the USA paid the Danes US$25 million in gold for the islands in 1917.

The US Navy then took control, which resulted in tensions with the local population. The USA tried to enforce Prohibition here, an unusual concept for an economy tied to the production, sale and distribution of rum. In 1931 President Herbert Hoover traveled to the Virgins, stayed for less than six hours and made a speech in which he declared, 'It was unfortunate that we ever acquired these islands.'

In 1934, however, President Franklin Delano Roosevelt visited and saw the potential that Hoover had missed. Soon, the USA instituted programs to eradicate disease, drain swamps, build roads, improve education and create tourism infrastructure.

Islanders received the right to elect their own governor in 1970. Though local politics brought its share of nepotism, cronyism and other scandals, the next four decades also brought unprecedented growth in tourism and raised the standard of living. Hurricane Marilyn took a chunk out of the islands in 1995, but they got back to business quickly thereafter.

Every once in a while, USVI citizens get a bee in their bonnet and seek greater self-determination through a Virgin Islands Constitution. They've tried and failed to ratify it four times during the last half century. A new draft – the fifth – is currently winding its way through the political process. Stay tuned.

Culture

The US Virgin Islands are a territory of the USA, and the islands participate in the political process by sending an elected, nonvoting representative to the US House of Representatives. All citizens of the USVI are US citizens (and have been since 1927) with one exception: they cannot vote in presidential elections.

Though the USVI wears a veneer of mainstream American culture, with conveniences such as shopping malls and fast food, West African culture is a strong and respected presence.

Since 1970 the population of USVI has quadrupled, although current growth has plateaued. Economic opportunities draw immigrants from other parts of the West Indies, along with US mainlanders who come to escape the politics and busyness of American life, or to retire in the sun. Tourism accounts for 80% of GDP and employment, and many locals work as hoteliers, restaurant owners, taxi drivers and shopkeepers.

Afro-Caribbeans (most of whom are descendants of former slaves) outnumber white by more than four to one and dominate the islands' political and professional arenas.

Violent crime has been on the rise, a consequence of increased drug trafficking in the territory. In 2010 the USVI saw a record 66 homicides committed, which is 10 more than the year prior. The struggling economy does not help matters.

Landscape & Wildlife

The Land

The US Virgins consist of about 50 islands, 40 miles east of Puerto Rico. They are the northernmost islands in the Lesser Antilles chain and, along with the British Virgin Islands, form an irregular string of islands stretching west to east. The one exception to this string is the USVI's largest island, St Croix, which lies 40 miles south.

The mountain slopes are dense subtropical forests. All of the timber is second or third growth; the islands were stripped for sugar, cotton and tobacco plantations in the colonial era. There are no rivers and very few freshwater streams. Coral reefs of all varieties grow in the shallow waters near the seashores.

Wildlife

Very few of the land mammals that make their home in the Virgin Islands are natives; most mammal species have been accidentally or intentionally introduced to the island over the centuries. Virtually every island has a feral population of goats and burros, and some islands have wild pigs, white-tailed deer, cattle, horses, cats and dogs. Other prevalent land mammals include mongooses and bats.

The islands are home to a few species of snake (none of which are poisonous), including the Virgin Island tree boa.

More than 200 bird species – including the official bird, the bananaquit – inhabit the islands.

Environmental Issues

The US Virgin Islands have long suffered from environmental problems, including deforestation, soil erosion, mangrove destruction and a lack of fresh water. During the 18th century logging operations denuded many of the islands to make room for plantations. The demise of the agricultural economy in the late 19th century allowed the islands to reforest, and in recent years locals (especially on St John) have begun several forest conservation projects.

But population growth and rapid urbanization continue to pose grave threats. If not for the desalination plants (which make fresh water out of sea water) the islands couldn't support even a quarter of their population, let alone visitors. When a hurricane strikes, power and desalination facilities shut down. Islanders with enough foresight and money keep rainwater cisterns for such emergencies, but folks without suffer.

Rising sea temperatures are another topic of concern, as they impact local reefs and cause coral bleaching. In 2005 a particularly 'hot' period killed about half of the USVI's coral.

Prior years of overfishing have put conch in a precarious situation. Currently, conch fishing is not allowed from July through September so stocks can replenish.

NAME THAT TUNE

You hear that? Reggae and calypso tunes blast from USVI vehicles and emanate from shops, restaurants and beach bars. *Quelbe* and fungi (*foonghee*, also an island food made of cornmeal) are two types of folk music. *Quelbe* blends jigs, quadrilles, military fife and African drum music, with *cariso* lyrics (often biting satire) from slave field songs. Fungi uses homemade percussion such as washboards, ribbed gourds and conch shells to accompany a singer. The best time to experience island music is during the 'jump up' parades and competitions associated with major festivals such as Carnival on St Thomas and St John, or at St Croix's Cruzan Christmas Fiesta.

The past decade has seen an increase in the level of awareness, resources and action dedicated to conservation efforts. Friends of the Virgin Islands National Park (www.friendsvinp.org) and USVI Department of Planning & Natural Resources (www.vifish andwildlife.com) are two groups working toward environmental preservation.

SURVIVAL GUIDE

Directory A–Z

Accommodations

The US Virgin Islands offer a wide range of lodging, including campgrounds, B&Bs, guesthouses, hotels, private villas and luxury resorts.

Peak season is winter, from mid-December through April, when prices are highest. It's best to book ahead at this time as rooms can be scarce. Some lodgings close in September, the heart of low season.

Be aware that while air-conditioning is widely available, it is not a standard amenity, even at top-end places. If you want it, be sure to ask about it when you book.

Rental accommodations are widely available, ranging towards the top end for costs (though you might find a few one-bed places for $250 per night). Try **McLaughlin Anderson Luxury Villas** (☑776-0635, 800-537-6246; www.mclaughlinanderson.com) and **Purple Pineapple** (☑305-396-1586; www.purplepineapple.com) for rentals. Also check **Vacation Rental by Owner** (www.vrbo.com) – many return USVI visitors say it provides the best results for the islands' resorts, where individual units can vary markedly.

In this chapter, prices listed are for peak-season travel and, unless stated otherwise, do not include taxes (typically 18%).

The price indicators used in accommodations listings are as follows:

$	budget	under US$75
$$	midrange	US$75 to US$200
$$$	top end	more than US$200

Activities

Diving and snorkeling are superb in the USVI, thanks to warm water temperatures and excellent visibility. Hiking is popular throughout Virgin Islands National Park on St John (p846); St Croix offers guided ecohikes (p853). Fishing and sailing charters are big business out of Red Hook, St Thomas.

Skim Caribbean (www.skimcaribbean.com) Skimboarding hot spots in the islands.

USVI Game Fishing Club (www.vigfc.com) Information on local conditions and regulations.

Virgin Islands Charter Yacht League (www.vicl.org) Lists charter boat companies and prices.

Business Hours

The list below provides 'normal' opening hours for businesses. Reviews throughout this chapter show specific hours only if they vary from these standards. Note, too, that hours can vary by season. Our listings depict peak season (December through April) operating times. Many places are closed on Sunday.

Banks 9am-3pm Mon-Thu, to 5pm Fri

Bars & pubs noon-midnight

General office hours 8am-5pm Mon-Fri

Restaurants breakfast 7-11am, lunch 11am-2pm, dinner 5-9pm daily; some open for brunch 10am-2pm Sun

Shops 9am-5pm Mon-Sat

Children

The USVI welcomes children, with opportunities for swimming, hiking and getting up close to sea creatures at Coral World Ocean Park. Family-friendly lodgings cluster on St Thomas' East End and St John's North Shore. Many resorts have children's programs and babysitting services.

On St John, **Island Baby VI** (www.islandbabyvi.com) rents out gear such as high chairs (US$60 per week), baby hiking backpacks (US$50 per week), baby monitors and much more, which can lighten your travel load considerably.

Embassies & Consulates

With the exception of those listed here, there are no foreign embassies or consulates in the USVI. The closest cache is in nearby San Juan, Puerto Rico.

Denmark (☑776-0656; www.dkconsulateusvi.com; Scandinavian Center, Havensight Mall, Bldg 3, Charlotte Amalie, St Thomas)

Sweden (☎774-6845; charlotteamalie@con sulateofsweden.org; 1340 Taarneberg, Charlotte Amalie, St Thomas)

Food

Price indicators in Eating listings in this chapter denote the cost of a main dish.

$	budget	under US$12
$$	midrange	US$12 to US$30
$$$	top end	more than US$30

Gay & Lesbian Travelers

While a fair number of islanders are gay, you're not likely to meet many who are 'out,' nor are you likely to see public displays of affection among gay couples.

St Croix is the most gay friendly of the islands, with Frederiksted the center of gay life, but overall there aren't many structured outlets for meeting. One exception is Sand Castle on the Beach, in Frederiksted.

Health

Pesky mosquitoes and no see 'ums (tiny sandflies) bite throughout the islands, so slather on insect repellent.

Tap water is safe to drink, unless specified otherwise.

Internet Access

Internet cafes cluster in the main tourist areas, often near marinas and cruise-ship docks. Access generally costs US$5 per half-hour. Wi-fi is widely available. Most lodgings have it for free in their public areas (though it is less common in-room), as do many restaurants and bars in the main towns.

Legal Matters

The blood-alcohol limit in the USVI is 0.08%. Driving under the influence of alcohol is a serious offense, subject to stiff fines and even imprisonment.

Open-container laws do not exist here, so you can walk around with drinks on the streets.

Maps

Many businesses offer free, fold-out road maps of the various islands and their main towns, which should suffice for driving trips. The widely available free tourist magazines *St Thomas/St John This Week* and *St Croix This Week* also have maps inside.

PRACTICALITIES

» **Electricity** 110 volts; North American–style plugs have two (flat) or three (two flat, one round) pins.

» **Newspapers & Magazines** The *VI Daily News* and *St Croix Avis* are the daily papers in the USVI. *St Thomas/St John This Week* and *St Croix This Week* are widely available free monthly (despite the name!) magazines.

» **Radio** Stations include WVGN (107.3FM), the NPR affiliate in St Thomas, and WSTX (970AM), island tunes and talk from St Croix.

» **Smoking** Lighting up isn't allowed in any indoor restaurants, bars and other public venues.

» **TV** Local TV stations include channels 8 (ABC) and 12 (PBS).

» **Weights & Measures** The islands use imperial weights and measurements. Distances are in feet and miles; gasoline is measured in gallons.

Money

The US dollar is used throughout the islands. Banks with ATMs hooked into worldwide networks (Plus, Cirrus, Exchange etc) are in the main towns.

A 15% to 20% tip is customary in restaurants; tip 10% to 15% in taxis and US$1 to US$2 per bag for hotel bellhops. A 10% to 20% tip is reasonable for dive boat operators and yacht crews.

Public Holidays

Islanders celebrate regional holidays (p872) as well as the following US public holidays and local holidays. Banks, schools and government offices close on these days.

Three Kings Day (Feast of the Epiphany) January 6

Martin Luther King Jr's Birthday Third Monday in January

Presidents' Day Third Monday in February

Transfer Day March 31

Holy Thursday Before Easter (in March or April)

Memorial Day Last Monday in May

Emancipation Day July 3

Independence Day (Fourth of July) July 4

Hurricane Supplication Day Fourth Monday in July

Labor Day First Monday in September

Columbus Day Second Monday in October

Liberty Day November 1

Veterans' Day November 11

Thanksgiving Day Fourth Thursday in November

Telephone

The phone system works like the US system.

All USVI phone numbers consist of a three-digit area code (⌀340), followed by a seven-digit local number. If you are calling from abroad, dial all 10 digits preceded by ⌀1. If you are calling locally, just dial the seven-digit number. For direct international calls, such as to Europe, dial ⌀011 + country code + area code + local phone number.

CELL PHONES

You should be able to use your cell phone on the islands, but be prepared for exorbitant roaming fees. It's difficult to find local SIM cards.

AT&T (www.att.com/wireless) and **Sprint** (www.sprint.com) are the islands' main service providers. If you use these companies at home, it's possible you may not have a roaming fee, but definitely check in advance.

Travelers with Disabilities

While the Americans With Disabilities Act holds sway in the USVI, facilities are not accessible to the same degree as they are in the US.

On St Thomas, **Accessible Adventures** (www.accessvi.com) provides island tours on a trolley suitable for visitors in wheelchairs. **Dial-A-Ride** (⌀776-1277) helps with transportation needs on the island.

On St John, **Concordia Eco-Tents** (www.maho.org) provides well-regarded accessible lodging.

Visas

Visitors from most Western countries do not need a visa to enter the USVI if they are staying less than 90 days.

This holds true as long as you can present a machine-readable passport and are approved under the **Electronic System for Travel Authorization** (ESTA; www.cbp.gov/esta). Note that you must register for ESTA

at least 72 hours before arrival, and there's a US$14 fee for processing and authorization.

If you do need a visa, contact your local embassy. The **US State Department** (www.travel.state.gov) has the latest information on admission requirements.

Volunteering

Friends of the Virgin Islands National Park (www.friendsvinp.org) Volunteer for trail or beach clean-ups on St John.

St Croix Environmental Association (www.stxenvironmental.org) It has programs (from US$35) where you can help count sea turtles.

Virgin Islands Sustainable Farm Institute (www.visfi.org) Stay on an organic farm in St Croix's rainforest and work in the fields; lodging is provided from US$35 per day.

Getting There & Away
Entering the US Virgin Islands

US citizens do not need a passport to visit the US Virgin Islands, but all other nationalities do. Entering the territory is straightforward: anyone arriving on a plane from the US mainland or Puerto Rico simply walks off and heads to their destination – there are no immigration procedures. But when departing the USVI, everyone must clear immigration and customs before boarding the plane. US citizens will be asked to show photo identification (such as a driver's license) and proof of citizenship (such as a birth certificate). If traveling to any other Caribbean country (besides Puerto Rico, which, like the USVI, is a US territory), US citizens must have a valid passport to re-enter the US.

Air

AIRPORTS

St Thomas has the main airport. St Croix's airport is smaller. Both airports are modern facilities with food concessions, car rentals and taxis; St Thomas' airport has ATMs.

Cyril E King Airport (STT; www.viport.com) On St Thomas.

Henry E Rohlsen Airport (STX; www.viport.com) On St Croix.

AIRLINES

Almost all flights to the USVI from outside the Caribbean either originate in or transit through the US (including Puerto Rico). American Airlines, Continental, Delta, Spirit Airlines, United and US Airways all fly to the USVI. Other airlines serving the region:

Air Sunshine (www.airsunshine.com) Serves San Juan and Tortola from St Thomas daily.

Cape Air (www.flycapeair.com) Serves San Juan from St Thomas and St Croix daily.

LIAT (www.liatairline.com) Daily flights to Antigua, Anguilla and St Kitts from St Thomas, and daily flights to St-Martin/Sint Maarten from St Croix.

Seaborne Airlines (www.seaborneairlines. com) Serves San Juan from St Thomas and St Croix daily.

Sea

CRUISE SHIP

Cruise ships are big business in the USVI, especially on St Thomas.

St Thomas

The island has two cruise-ship terminals, both of which bustle with taxis and shops. Tenders are not needed to get ashore.

Havensight The West Indian Company dock is the busiest of the two terminals, with big ships in every day; it's about a mile east of Charlotte Amalie.

Crown Bay The newer, secondary dock; it's located about a mile west of Charlotte Amalie.

St Croix

Ships call on sleepy Frederiksted a few times per week. The pier juts out from downtown, so tenders are not needed.

St John

It happens infrequently, but small vessels do call on St John. They anchor offshore in Pillsbury Sound and passengers take a tender in.

FERRY
USVI to BVI

There are excellent ferry connections linking St Thomas and St John with Tortola, Virgin Gorda and Jost Van Dyke. For trips between the USVI and BVI, a passport is required.

St Thomas/St John This Week magazine prints the full timetables, or check **VI Now** (www.vinow.com).

Ferries from Charlotte Amalie leave from the **Marine Terminal** (Waterfront Hwy) at downtown's western edge. Ferry companies include the following:

Inter-Island (☎340-776-6597; www.interisland boatservices.vi)

Native Son (☎284-495-4617; www.nativeson ferry.com)

Road Town Fast Ferry (☎284-494-2323; www.roadtownfastferry.com)

Smith's Ferry (☎284-494-4454; www. smithsferry.com)

Speedy's (☎284-495-5240; www.speedysbvi. com)

Ferries from Charlotte Amalie:

Road Town, Tortola 45 minutes, US$30 one way, several daily; Road Town Fast Ferry, Speedy's, Smith's, Native Son

Spanish Town, Virgin Gorda 90 minutes, US$40 one way, three days weekly; Speedy's

Ferries from Red Hook:

West End, Tortola US$25 to US$28 one-way, 35 minutes, four daily; Smith's, Native Son

Road Town, Tortola US$35 one-way, 45 minutes, 9pm night ferry Thursday to Sunday; Road Town Fast Ferry

Jost Van Dyke US$70 round-trip, 45 minutes, twice daily (except no services on Wednesday or Thursday); Inter-Island

Ferries from Cruz Bay:

West End, Tortola US$45 round-trip, 30 minutes, three daily; Inter-Island

Jost Van Dyke US$70 round-trip, 45 minutes, twice daily (except no services on Wednesday or Thursday); Inter-Island

USVI to Puerto Rico

Transportation Services (☎776-6282) operates a ferry twice a month from Charlotte Amalie's waterfront to Fajardo, Puerto Rico (round trip US$125, two hours). The schedule changes; call for details.

YACHT

Lots of yachts drift into the USVI. Many pull into American Yacht Harbor in Red Hook, St Thomas. The bars and restaurants there are good places to inquire about hitching a ride as a crew member.

Getting Around

Air

You have two choices for air travel within the USVI:

Cape Air (www.flycapeair.com) Flies between St Thomas' and St Croix's airports.

Seaborne Airlines (www.seaborneairlines. com) Flies seaplanes between the downtown harbors of Charlotte Amalie, on St Thomas, and Christiansted, on St Croix (one way US$80, 20 minutes). Flights depart at least once per hour for the convenient (no taxis needed!) ride. Be aware there's a baggage restriction of 30lb (16kg) and it costs US$1 per extra pound.

Boat

Frequent ferries run between the islands. *St Thomas/St John This Week* magazine prints the full timetables, or check **VI Now** (www. vinow.com).

ST THOMAS TO ST JOHN

From Red Hook Passenger ferries (US$6 one way, 20 minutes) run on the hour to Cruz Bay, between roughly 7am and midnight. They return from Cruz Bay on the hour, too.

Three different companies run car ferries between Red Hook and Enighed Pond beside Cruz Bay (round trip around US$50, 20 minutes), with sailings almost every hour between 6am and 7pm.

From Charlotte Amalie Passenger ferries (US$12 one way, 45 minutes) run three times a day from Charlotte Amalie's waterfront (at the foot of Raadet's Gade, *not* from the Marine Terminal), departing at 10am, 1pm and 5:30pm.

ST THOMAS TO ST CROIX

VI Seatrans (☑776-5494; www.goviseatrans.com) operates a passenger ferry (one way US$50, 90 minutes) between Charlotte Amalie's Marine Terminal and Christiansted's Gallows Bay, about 0.75 miles east of downtown. It sails twice on Friday and Saturday, and once on Sunday and Monday each way. Look for humpback whales during winter crossings.

ST THOMAS TO WATER ISLAND

The **Water Island Ferry** (☑690-4159; one-way US$5, 10min) departs roughly every hour from outside Tickle's Dockside Pub at Crown Bay Marina.

Bus

Vitran (fare US$1) operates air-conditioned buses over the length of St Thomas, St John and St Croix. Buses run daily between 5:30am and 7:30pm (approximately one bus per hour).

Car

Driving is undoubtedly the most convenient way to get around, as public transportation is limited and taxi fares add up in a hurry.

To rent a car in the USVI you generally need to be at least 25 years old, hold a valid driver's license and have a major credit card.

Cars cost between US$55 and US$85 per day. If you're traveling in peak season, it's wise to reserve a couple of months in advance, as supplies are limited. Major international car-rental companies have branches at the airports and sometimes at ferry terminals. See the Getting There & Around sections of each destination for local rental agencies.

ROAD CONDITIONS

Be prepared for challenging road conditions. Steep, winding roads are often the same width as your car, and the potholes can be outrageous.

Chickens, cows, goats and donkeys dart in and out of the roadway. Keep your eyes peeled for critters.

ROAD RULES

» Rule number one: drive on the left-hand side of the road!
» The steering wheel is on the left side.
» Seat-belt use is compulsory; children under age five must be in a car seat.
» Driving while using a hand-held cell phone is illegal (but ear pieces are permitted).

Taxi

All of the islands have taxis that are easily accessible in the main tourist areas. Most vehicles are vans that carry up to 12 passengers; sometimes they're open-air pickup trucks with bench seats and awnings. To hail one, stand by the side of the road and wave when the vehicle approaches.

Rates are set, with prices listed in the free tourist guides. You can also access rate sheets from **VI Now** (www.vinow.com).

Survival Guide

Directory A–Z

See the Directory A–Z sections in On the Road chapters for details specific to each island.

Accommodations

A wide range of accommodations awaits travelers in the Caribbean, from inexpensive guesthouses and good-value efficiency apartments (apartments with fridge and partial kitchen), to elaborate villas and luxury beachside resorts. And there are also plenty of midrange options in between.

'Private bath' in this book means the room has its own toilet and shower – it does not necessarily mean that it has a bathtub.

Prices

Each sleeping option has an indicative price category next to it (from **$** to **$$$**) – these correspond to the price of the room relative to that country's price breakdown (given in each chapter's directory). Note that not all islands have rooms in all price categories – many have no budget accommodations at all, while other islands are less expensive across the board.

Seasons

Throughout the book we've listed high-season rates unless otherwise noted. High season corresponds to mid-December to April; the low season is May to mid-December. Keep in mind that hotel rates can be up to 40% cheaper in the low season and in most places they'll fluctuate with tourist traffic.

Some hotels close for a month or so in late summer, usually around September. Some of the smaller hotels and guesthouses might even close down from June to September.

Camping

Although a good way to save money, camping is limited in the Caribbean and on some islands freelance camping is either illegal or discouraged – usually to protect nature or because of crime. Check with the local tourist office for rules and regulations.

There are a number of camping possibilities throughout the US Virgin Islands and on Puerto Rico. The former is well known for its affordable ecocampgrounds.

Guesthouses

The closest thing the Caribbean has to hostels, guesthouses are usually great value. Often in the middle of a town or village and rarely alongside a beach, they offer good opportunities for cultural immersion. Rooms usually have a bed and private bath and some have communal kitchens and living rooms. In some areas you can arrange private homestays with a local family. These are most readily available in Cuba, where they are known as casas particulares.

Hotels

Across the Caribbean, hotel rooms can range from humdrum to massive 1000-room resorts to glorious villas hovering over the sea. Islands often have clusters of one type of hotel. Aruba, for example, has resorts aimed at mass-market tourism, while nearby Bonaire has plenty of great-value resorts catering to divers.

All-Inclusive Resorts

Born in Jamaica and now prevalent across the Caribbean, all-inclusive resorts allow you to pay a set price and then nothing more once you arrive. You usually get a wristband that allows you free access to the hotel or resort's restaurants, bars and water-

BOOK YOUR STAY ONLINE

For more accommodations reviews by Lonely Planet authors, check out hotels.lonelyplanet.com/Caribbean. You'll find independent reviews, as well as recommendations on the best places to stay. Best of all, you can book online.

sports equipment. Many properties have jumped onto the 'all-inclusive' bandwagon, but don't necessarily supply the goods. Be sure to find out exactly what 'all-inclusive' includes. Questions to ask:

» What is the variety and quality of food available?

» How many meals are included?

» Are all drinks included?

» Is 'free alcohol' limited to wine with dinner?

» Are there lots of extra-charge options at mealtimes (steaks etc), meaning that the regular food is uninspiring?

» What activities are included (an extra charge for snorkeling gear is a sign of stinginess)?

Rental Accommodations

If you're traveling with your family or a large group, you might want to look into renting a villa. Villas are great because you have room to stretch out, do your own cooking and enjoy plenty of privacy. Rentals cost anywhere from US$600 per week for a basic villa with bedrooms, kitchen and living space, to US$15,000 per night for a beachside estate with staff. For even more, you can rent an island.

Agencies on the individual islands rent properties; the following rent villas throughout the region:

At Home Abroad (☑in the USA 212-421-9165; www.athomeabroadinc.com)

Caribbean Way (☑in the USA 514-393-3003, 877-953-7400; www.caribbeanway.com)

CV Travel (☑in the UK 020-7401-1010; www.cvtravel.co.uk)

Heart of the Caribbean (☑in the USA 262-783-5303, 800-231-5303; www.hotcarib.com)

Island Hideaways (☑in the USA 703-378-7840, 800-832-2302; www.islandhideaways.com)

Vacation Rentals By Owner (www.vrbo.com)

Wimco Private Villa Rentals (www.wimcovillas.com)

Business Hours

Standard opening hours for each island are given in the chapter directories.

Climate

For information on climate across the region, see p18, the charts on p870, and each island chapter.

Customs Regulations

All the Caribbean islands allow a reasonable amount of personal items to be brought in duty free, as well as an allowance of liquor and tobacco. Determining what you can take home depends on where you're vacationing and your country of origin. Check with your country's customs agency for clarification.

Notable customs regulations for each country are explained in the chapter directories.

ISLAND TIME

In the Caribbean life moves at a slow, loosely regimented pace. You'll often see signs in front of shops, bars and restaurants that say 'open all day, every day' and this can mean several things; the place could truly be open all day every day of the week, but don't count on it. If business is slow, a restaurant, shop or attraction might simply close. If a bar is hopping and the owner's having fun, it could stay open until the wee hours. If the rainy season is lasting too long, a hotel or restaurant might close for a month. If a shop owner has a hangover, doctor's appointment or date, or just needs a day off – hey mon, store's closed. In other words, hard and fast rules about opening times are hard to come by. The only consistent rule is that Sundays are sacred and 'open every day' generally translates to 'open every day except Sunday.'

Once you get in sync with local rhythms you'll see the concept of 'island time' as a blessing.

Electricity

The electric current varies across the islands. See individual chapter directories for details.

Embassies & Consulates

It's important to realize what your own embassy can and can't do to help you if you get into trouble. Generally speaking, it won't be much help in emergencies if the trouble you're in is remotely your own fault. Remember that you are bound by the laws of the country you are visiting. Your embassy will not be sympathetic if you end up in jail after committing a crime locally, even if such actions are legal in your own country.

In genuine emergencies you might get some assistance, but only if other channels have been exhausted. For example, if you need to get home urgently, a free ticket is exceedingly unlikely – the embassy would expect you to have insurance. If you have all your money and documents stolen, it

Freeport/Lucaya

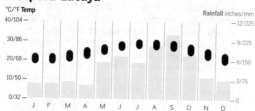

Kingston

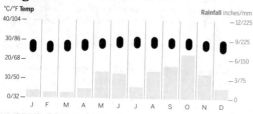

Port of Spain

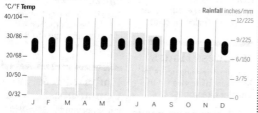

San Juan

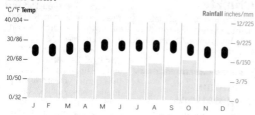

will assist with getting a new passport, but not a loan.

See the chapter directories for a list of foreign embassies in each region. Nations such as Australia, Canada, New Zealand and the US have embassies and consulates in the largest Caribbean countries. Check your government's foreign affairs website for locations.

Gay & Lesbian Travelers

Parts of the Caribbean are not particularly gay-friendly destinations and on many of the islands overt homophobia and machismo is prevalent.

Gay men and lesbians generally keep a low profile, and public hand-holding, kissing and other outward signs of affection are not commonplace. Jamaica unfortunately is a special case in terms of harassment (and worse) of gay people (see p562).

Still, there are several niches for gay travelers. Particularly friendly islands include Aruba, Bonaire, Curaçao, Cuba, Dominican Republic, Guadeloupe, Martinique, Puerto Rico, Saba, St-Martin/Sint Maarten and the US Virgin Islands.

See also p64 for information on gay and lesbian cruises.

Useful websites:

Damron (www.damron .com) The USA's leading gay publisher offers guides to world cities.

Spartacus International Gay Guide (www.spartacus world.com) A male-only directory of gay entertainment venues and hotels.

Insurance

It's foolhardy to travel without insurance to cover theft, loss and medical problems. Start by seeing what your own insurance covers; you may find that many aspects of travel in the Caribbean are covered, but there may be gaping holes.

There's a wide variety of policies – check the small print. Some policies specifically exclude 'dangerous activities', which can include scuba diving, motorcycling, adventure sports or even hiking. Some pay doctors or hospitals directly, but most require you to pay upfront, save the documentation and then claim later. Some policies also ask you to call back (reverse charges) to a center in your home country, where an immediate assessment of your problem is made. Check that the policy covers ambulances or an emergency flight home.

The policies handled by STA Travel and other student

travel agencies are usually good value. In the UK, the website **Money Supermarket** (www.moneysupermarket.com) does an automated comparison of 450 partner policies and comes up with the best for your needs.

Worldwide travel insurance is available at www.lonelyplanet.com/travel_services. You can buy, extend and claim online anytime – even if you're already on the road.

Internet Access

Internet access and wi-fi is generally easily found throughout most of the Caribbean. Only on more remote islands or in cheaper homestays or guesthouses will you be unlikely to find at least a computer you can use for internet access.

Throughout this book, the wireless icon (🛜) indicates if an establishment offers wi-fi.

Legal Matters

Due to the stereotype that pot-smoking is widespread in the Caribbean (it isn't), some visitors take a casual attitude about sampling island drugs.

Be forewarned that drug trafficking is a serious problem throughout the Caribbean and most officials have little to no tolerance of visitors caught using. Penalties vary throughout the islands, but getting caught smoking or possessing marijuana (or any illegal drug for that matter) can result in stiff jail sentences.

Money

For an overview of the main currencies used in the Caribbean, see p18. Specific currency and money details are given on the opening pages and in the directories of each chapter.

Note that at the time of writing, Curaçao and Sint Maarten used the Nether-

lands Antillean guilder (NAf/ANG) as official currency, but plans were being debated to switch to either US dollars, or use a new currency, the Caribbean guilder (CMg). A decision could be made by 2012, later or not at all. Check on the latest currency news before you travel; local prices for these islands are given in NAf where applicable.

ATMs & Credit Cards

ATMs are generally common on all but small islands, with the exception of Cuba, where there are special considerations. Many give out US dollars in addition to the local currency. Credit cards are widely accepted but watch for surcharges.

Cash

The US dollar is accepted almost everywhere, so it's not necessary to have local currency before you arrive. Carry smaller denominations to pay for taxis, street snacks or tips.

EXCHANGE RATES

	US$1	C$1	€1	UK£1
Aruban florin (Afl)	1.80	1.88	2.57	2.94
Bahamian dollar (BS$)	1.00	1.05	1.44	1.64
Barbadian dollar (B$)	2.00	2.10	2.87	3.28
Cayman Islands dollar (CI$)	0.82	0.86	1.18	1.35
Cuban convertible peso (CUC$)	1.00	1.05	1.44	1.64
Dominican peso (RD$)	37.60	39.48	54.09	61.80
Eastern Caribbean dollar (EC$)	2.70	2.83	3.88	4.44
Euro (€)	0.70	0.73	-	1.14
Haitian gourde (HTG)	40.35	42.37	58.04	66.37
Jamaican dollar (J$)	85.22	89.21	122.18	139.72
Netherlands Antillean guilder (NAf/ANG)	1.79	1.85	2.53	2.89
Trinidad & Tobago dollar (TT$)	6.35	6.67	9.13	10.44
US dollar (US$)	-	1.05	1.44	1.64

For the latest exchange rates see www.xe.com.

ISLAND SOVEREIGNTY

The islands by national affiliation (if an island is not mentioned here, it is an independent nation):

» British West Indies – Anguilla, Turks and Caicos, the Cayman Islands, Montserrat (an 'overseas territory') and British Virgin Islands (a crown colony) due to their affiliation with the UK.

» French West Indies – Includes Guadeloupe, St-Martin, St-Barthélemy and Martinique due to their status as départements d'Outre-mer (overseas départements) of France.

» Netherlands Antilles – Historically Aruba, Curaçao, Bonaire, Sint Maarten, Saba and Sint Eustatius. Aruba, Bonaire and Curaçao (often called the ABC Islands) are also known as the Leeward Netherlands Antilles. Note that the Netherlands Antilles has dissolved with some of the former members seeking tighter affiliation with the Netherlands (eg Bonaire).

» USA – Puerto Rico, US Virgin Islands

Tipping

Whether to tip, and how much, varies across the Caribbean. See the Money sections of the individual island directories for specifics.

Traveler's Checks

Traveler's checks are now uncommon and are inconvenient on all but a couple of islands (eg Jamaica).

Public Holidays

Regionwide standard public holidays:

New Year's Day January 1

Good Friday Friday before Easter, late March/early April

Easter Monday Monday after Easter, late March/early April

Whit Monday Eighth Monday after Easter

Christmas Day December 25

Boxing Day December 26

See individual chapters for additional island-specific holidays.

Safe Travel

In terms of individual safety and crime, the situation is quite varied in the Caribbean. It's hard to imagine more tranquil areas than Saba and Sint Eustatius, where most people don't even have locks on their doors; whereas walking the streets of Port of Spain (Trinidad) or Fort-de-France (Martinique) after dark can certainly be a risky venture, especially for women (see p874 for more information specific to female travelers).

In most areas there is a huge disparity between the income of locals and the (real or perceived) wealth of visitors. If you venture beyond the borders of the tourist areas, you may observe populations devastated by poverty, and a lack of medical supplies and clean water, in places like Jamaica and Haiti. Add to this the existence of drug production and trafficking and you can see why crime is a problem in some areas.

Any notable safety concerns for each country are given in the chapter directories. It's advisable to check your own government's travel advisories for the latest information.

Telephone

Overall, the telephone systems work relatively well throughout the Caribbean. You can make both local and long-distance calls from virtually all public phones; most use phonecards that often have very good rates. Coin phones are rare and internet calling is popular.

Avoid the credit-card phones found in airports, hotels and rather strategically outside some tourist bars, as they charge a steep US$2 per minute for local calls, US$4 to other Caribbean islands or the US, and as much as US$8 per minute to elsewhere. Many bear monikers like 'Global Phone' or 'Phone Home'. View the phone in your hotel room with the same suspicion you'd have of a person with a knife in a dark alley: rates can be extortionate.

Cell phones are widespread. Check the details of your contract before you turn on your smartphone, however, as data charges can be hefty. Many people buy a local SIM card.

See the chapter directories for details on local cell-phone carriers.

Time

» **Eastern Standard Time** (EST; five hours behind GMT) Bahamas, Turks and Caicos, Jamaica, the Cayman Islands, Cuba, Haiti, the Dominican Republic

» **Atlantic Standard Time** (AST; four hours behind GMT) All other islands

» Only the Bahamas, and Turks and Caicos observe Daylight Savings Time

Tourist Information

Travel information is often available by the kilo. Many free publications found in hotel lobbies are excellent and most islands have a tourist information center in the main town and offices at the airport. See individual country chapters for more details.

Travelers with Disabilities

Unfortunately, travel in the Caribbean is not particularly easy for those with physical disabilities. Overall there is little or no awareness of the need for easier access onto planes, buses or rental vehicles. One exception is Puerto Rico, where good compliance with the Americans Disabilities Act (ADA) means many sights and hotels have wheelchair accessibility.

Visitors with special needs should inquire directly with prospective hotels for information on their facilities. The larger, more modern resorts are most likely to have the greatest accessibility, with elevators, wider doorways and wheelchair-accessible baths.

While land travel may present some obstacles, cruises are often a good option for travelers with disabilities in the Caribbean. Many cruise lines can coordinate shore-based excursions in tour buses equipped for special needs.

Travelers with disabilities might want to get in touch with national support organizations in their home country. These groups commonly have general information and tips on travel and are able to supply a list of travel agents specializing in tours for visitors with special needs. Some resources:

Access-Able Travel Source (www.access-able .com) A US-based organization with a good website and links to international disability sites, newsletters, guidebooks, travel tips and cruise information.

Lonely Planet (www.lonely planet.com/thorntree) Share experiences on the Travellers with Disabilities branch of the Thorn Tree message board.

Radar (www.radar.org.uk) A UK-based advocacy organization providing general information on travel.

Society for Accessible Travel & Hospitality (www .sath.org) Lots of information for travelers with disabilities.

Visas

Passport and visa requirements vary from island to island; specific information is given in individual country chapters. There are revised passport regulations for US citizens returning from the Caribbean; see p875.

Volunteering

Many volunteer programs in the Caribbean mix holiday fun with good intentions, and include themes like 'learn to dive while saving the reef' (if only it were that easy). Some organisations don't provide a lot of value beyond the interesting experience for the traveler. Generally, the greater the time commitment, the greater opportunity volunteers will have to do something useful. Note that most volunteer organizations levy charges to take part in their programs.

The following organizations operate in the region. See also p523 for organizations working in Haiti.

Caribbean Volunteer Expeditions (www.cvexp .org) A US-based organization. Volunteers work on archaeology projects, artifact restoration and environmental preservation projects. Typically about US$900 per week, including accommodations, food and land transportation, but not airfare.

Global Volunteers (www .globalvolunteers.org) Long-time organizer of volunteer projects lasting up to 24 weeks or more. In Jamaica, a program rehabilitates houses in the Blue Mountains. Fees for a two-week stint are US$2000.

MANCHINEEL TREES

Manchineel trees grow on beaches throughout the Caribbean. The fruit of the manchineel, which looks like a small green apple, is poisonous. The milky sap given off by the fruit and leaves can cause severe skin blisters, similar to the reaction caused by poison oak. If the sap gets in your eyes, it can result in temporary blindness. Never take shelter under the trees during a rainstorm, as the sap can be washed off the tree and onto anyone sitting below.

Manchineel trees can grow as high as 40ft (12m), with branches that spread widely. The leaves are green, shiny and elliptical in shape. On some of the more visited beaches, trees will be marked with warning signs or bands of red paint. Manchineel is called *mancenillier* on the French islands and *anjenelle* on Trinidad and Tobago.

Greenforce Conservation Expeditions (www.green force.org) A UK-based organization specializing in wildlife conservation expeditions for gap-year and university students, who work with scientists to study the Andros reef system in the Bahamas. Cost is from £1550 for three weeks.

Habitat for Humanity (www.habitat.org) An international nonprofit, ecumenical Christian housing organization. Volunteers build simple, affordable housing for people in need. Costs vary, depending on the size and scope of the project. Active in the Dominican Republic, Haiti, and Trinidad and Tobago.

Healing Hands for Haiti (www.healinghandsforhaiti. org) Dedicated to bringing rehabilitation medicine to Haiti. You don't need a medical background to join a 10-day medical mission, which costs about US$1500, not including airfare.

Weights & Measures

Some Caribbean countries use the metric system, others use the imperial system, and a few use a confusing combination of both; check the country chapter directories for details. Within each country chapter, measurements are given in metric or imperial, depending on the system of measurement followed in that country.

Women Travelers

Although the situation varies between islands, machismo is alive and well. Men can get aggressive, especially with women traveling alone. On many islands local men have few qualms about catcalling, hissing, whistling, sucking their teeth or making kissy sounds to get female attention. While much of this is simply annoying, it can make women feel unsafe.

Like it or not, women will generally feel much safer if traveling with a male companion. Women traveling alone need to be sensible and careful – avoid walking alone after dark, heading off into the wilderness on your own, hitchhikiing or picking up male hitchhikers. Generally try to avoid any situation where you're isolated and vulnerable. Don't wear skimpy clothing when you're not on the beach – it will just garner you a lot of unwanted attention. Also note that 'harmless flirtation' at home can be misconstrued as a serious come-on in the Caribbean. It's also worth singling out Cuba as being a good place for solo women travelers.

See the individual chapters for specific details.

Work

The Caribbean has high unemployment rates and low wages, as well as strict immigration policies aimed at preventing foreign visitors from taking up work.

Generally the best bet for working is to crew with a boat or yacht. As boat hands aren't usually working on any one island in particular, the work situation is more flexible and it's easier to avoid hassles with immigration. Marinas are a good place to look for jobs on yachts; check the bulletin-board notices, strike up conversations with skippers or ask around at the nearest bar. Marinas in Miami and Fort Lauderdale are considered good places to find jobs, as people sailing their boats down for the season stop here looking for crew.

You can also look for jobs with a crew-placement agency such as UK-based **Crew Finders** (www.crewfinders .com) or US-based **Crew Seekers** (www.crewseekers .net).

the opening pages and the Directory sections in each chapter.

875

Transportation

GETTING THERE & AWAY

This chapter gives a broad overview about the many options for travel to the Caribbean and ways to get around once you are there. See the Getting There & Away sections in the relevant destination chapters for details specific to each island.

Flights and tours can be booked online at www.lonely planet.com/travel_services.

Entering the Caribbean Islands

Generally your passport is all that's required to enter most Caribbean islands (the exception is Cuba, although for most people this isn't a complex procedure). Fill out your entry form in black ink (some places such as Antigua are notoriously fussy) and have in mind the name of a hotel in case you are asked where you plan to stay, even if you plan to sort it out later.

You may be asked to show an onward air ticket (Barbados is known for this) or prove sufficient funds. On islands that ask for your length of stay, always pad the figure substantially so as to avoid having to extend the length of your stay, should the sun-kissed beaches and azure waters keep you there longer than you had planned.

Visa and document requirements vary by country. For specific information, see

US Travel Law

All US citizens traveling to the Caribbean will need a passport to re-enter the US if traveling by air. If traveling by sea (eg on a cruise ship), you will need a passport or a passport card to re-enter the US. The latter is essentially a wallet-sized US passport that is only good for land and sea travel between the US and Canada, Mexico and the Caribbean. In some circumstances you may only need a valid drivers' license but confirm this carefully with the cruise line.

The law does not affect the US state territories of Puerto Rico and the US Virgin Islands, which will continue to allow established forms of identification like valid driver's licenses.

Air

Airports & Airlines

It doesn't matter which island you fly into, touching down on Caribbean land is always a thrilling experience. Some islands, such as Saba, Montserrat or Sint Eustatius, have tiny runways, where small regional planes miraculously land on airstrips that don't look much longer than Band-Aids. When you fly into the Bahamas you feel like you're surely going to land in the ocean. Other islands, such as Dominica, look like vague

---

CLIMATE CHANGE & TRAVEL

Every form of transport that relies on carbon-based fuel generates CO_2, the main cause of human-induced climate change. Modern travel is dependent on aeroplanes, which might use less fuel per kilometer per person than most cars but travel much greater distances. The altitude at which aircraft emit gases (including CO_2) and particles also contributes to their climate change impact. Many websites offer 'carbon calculators' that allow people to estimate the carbon emissions generated by their journey and, for those who wish to do so, to offset the impact of the greenhouse gases emitted with contributions to portfolios of climate-friendly initiatives throughout the world. Lonely Planet offsets the carbon footprint of all staff and author travel.

THREE FLYING RECOMMENDATIONS

The authors of this book learned from experience three things you should remember:

» Try not to arrive on a regional flight in the afternoon when most of the North American and European flights arrive, swamping immigration and customs. We flew from Montserrat to Antigua: the flight was 15 minutes; the wait in immigration lines was 2½ hours.

» Keep anything essential you might need for a few days with you. Luggage often somehow misses your flight – even if you see it waiting next to the plane as you board. It may take days – if ever – to catch up with you.

» Check in early. Bring a book and snack and hang out. We saw people with confirmed seats repeatedly bumped after flights checked in full and their alternative was days later. Two hours is not bad if you're prepared for the wait. In many airports, you could check in early and then go someplace else like the incredibly fun beach bars near the Sint Maarten airport.

colonial outposts, surrounded by cane fields, dusty roads or mountains. Conversely, airports such as those in Barbados, Aruba and Sint Maarten are as big and modern as you could wish.

Airline and flight details for each country are listed in the chapter Getting There & Away sections. See also p51 for more information on air services in the Caribbean.

FROM NORTH AMERICA

Most major airlines in North America fly direct to the more popular islands in the Caribbean. In fact such service is so wide-spread that even places as tiny as Bonaire have nonstop service to major US cities. Generally however, getting to the Caribbean from US cities without hub airports will involve changing planes somewhere. American Airlines has major hubs for its extensive Caribbean service in Miami and San Juan, Puerto Rico.

Also note that service to the Caribbean is seasonal. An island that has, say, weekly nonstop flights from Chicago in January may have none at all in June.

FROM EUROPE

You can reach the Caribbean nonstop from Europe. Proving that old colonial ties

linger, airlines from the UK serve former British colonies like Barbados and Antigua; French airlines serve the French-speaking islands; and Dutch carriers fly to Aruba, Bonaire and Curaçao. There are no direct flights to the Caribbean from Australia, New Zealand or Asia – travelers fly via Europe or the US.

CHARTERS

Charter flights from the US, Canada, UK and Europe offer another option for getting to the islands. Fares are often cheaper than on regularly scheduled commercial airlines, but you usually have to depart and return on specific flights and you'll probably have no flexibility to extend your stay. Such flights also often come as part of packages that include stays in resorts.

Browse the sites below and check with a travel agent as they are usually the frontline sales force for these travel companies and their many competitors.

Apple Vacations (www.applevacations.com) From the US

Air Transat (www.airtransat.ca) From Canada

Funjet Vacations (www.funjet.com) From the US

Monarch (www.monarch.co.uk) From the UK

Thompson (www.thomson.co.uk) From the UK and elsewhere in Europe

Departure Tax

Some airports charge a departure that is *not* included in the price of the ticket. These can be rather costly; see the chapter directories for details.

Sea

The only way to reach the Caribbean by sea is on a cruise ship (or for a few lucky people on a yacht). See the Cruising chapter and individual island chapters for details.

GETTING AROUND

For a useful explanation of various terms used in the Caribbean for island groups, eg Windward and Leeward, see the Island Hopping chapter, p51.

Air

The Caribbean has an extensive network of airlines serving even the smallest islands.

For specific details see p51 and the Getting Around sections within each island chapter.

Bicycle

The popularity of cycling in the Caribbean depends on where you go. Several islands are prohibitively hilly, with narrow roads that make cycling difficult. On others, such as Cuba, cycling is a great way to get around. Many of the islands have bicycles for rent; for details see the chapter Getting Around sections.

Bike shops are becoming more common. Most ferries will let you bring bikes on board at no extra charge; regional airlines will likely charge a fee.

Boat

Ferries link some islands within the Caribbean, such as Guadeloupe, Dominica, Martinique and St Lucia. Generally they are preferable to flying for environmental and purely personal comfort reasons. Fast modern ferries are found in some countries such as St Vincent and the Grenadines.

Getting around the islands by yacht is a fantasy for many. Charters are generally quite easy. For details on island ferries and yacht charters, see p52.

Bus

Inexpensive bus service is available on most islands, although the word 'bus' has different meanings in different places. Some islands have full-size buses, while on others a 'bus' is simply a pickup truck with wooden benches in the back. Whatever the vehicle, buses are a good environmental choice compared to rental cars and they are excellent ways to meet locals. People are generally quite friendly and happy to talk to you about their island. Buses are also often the best way to hear the most popular local music

tracks, often at an amazingly loud volume.

Buses are often the primary means of commuting to work or school and thus are most frequent in the early mornings and from mid- to late afternoon. There's generally a good bus service on Saturday mornings, but Sunday service is often nonexistent.

Buses can get crowded. As more and more people get on, children move onto their parents' laps, kids share seats, people squeeze together and everyone generally accepts the cramped conditions with good humor. Whenever someone gets off the back of a crowded minivan, it takes on the element of a human Rubik's Cube, with seats folding up and everyone shuffling; on some buses there's actually a conductor to direct the seating.

For specific details on buses by island, see the chapter Getting Around sections.

Car & Motorcycle

Driving in the Caribbean islands can rock your world, rattle your brains and fray your nerves. At first. Soon, you'll get used to the chickens, goats, stray dogs and cows wandering the roadways. You'll get the hang of swerving like a maniac, of slowing for no reason, of using your horn to communicate everything from 'Hey, I'm turning right!' to 'Hey,

you're cute!' to 'Hey, [expletive] you!'

Driver's License

You'll need your driver's license in order to rent a car. On most of the former British islands, you'll also need to purchase a local driver's license (US$12 to US$20) when you rent a car, but you can do that by showing your home license and paying the fee.

Rental

Car rentals are available on nearly all of the islands, with a few exceptions (usually because they lack roads). On most islands there are affiliates of the international chains, but local rental agencies often have better rates. Or they may simply be more hassle. Always understand what rental insurance coverage your credit card or personal auto insurance provide, if any. Purchasing insurance from the rental company can add over US$10 a day to your bill and you may already be covered.

During the busy winter high season, reserve your car in advance, especially if you want an economy car. On many islands you need to be 25 years old to rent a car. Cars may be in good shape or they may be beaters, castoffs from another land sent to die an island death.

International rental agencies found across many islands in the Caribbean include **Avis** (www.avis.com), **Budget** (www.budget.com), **Dollar** (www.dollar.com),

---

ISLAND DRIVING

Offer a lift It's common courtesy on many islands to slow down and offer pedestrians a lift (and is considered obligatory on some). As well as putting you in good stead with the locals, the conversations can be fun.

Beware of goats! Keep an eye out for stray dogs, chickens and goats, all of which meander aimlessly on the island roads.

Europcar (www.europcar.com) and **Hertz** (www.hertz.com). See individual chapters for local agencies and further details.

Road Rules

Road rules vary by island; see the chapter Getting Around sections for details. In general note that driving conditions may be more relaxed than you are used to. And observe pleasant local habits such as giving others the right-of-way (especially pedestrians) even when you think it is yours.

What side of the road to drive on depends on the island, and this can prove particularly confusing if you're island-hopping and renting cars on each island. Adding to the confusion, some cars have steering columns on the opposite side of the car. As a rule, drivers stick to the following:

Left side of the road Anguilla, Antigua and Barbuda, Bahamas, Barbados, British Virgin Islands, Cayman Islands, Dominica, Grenada, Jamaica, St Kitts and Nevis, St Lucia, St Vincent, Trinidad and Tobago, Turks and Caicos, US Virgin Islands

Right side of the road Aruba, Bonaire, Cuba, Curaçao, Dominican Republic, Guadeloupe, Haiti, Martinique, Puerto Rico, Saba, St-Barthélemy, Sint Eustatius, St-Martin/Sint Maarten

Hitchhiking

Hitchhiking is an essential mode of travel on most islands, though the practice among foreign visitors isn't as common.

If you want to hitch a ride, stand by the side of the road and put your hand out. Be aware that this is also how locals flag taxis and since many private cars look like taxis, this can be confusing (note that most taxis have the letter 'H' – for Hire – on their front license plate). Foreign women traveling alone should not hitchhike (your want for a ride could be misconstrued as a want for something else). Men traveling alone should also be cautious. Though most drivers will happily give you a ride, others might see you as a target, especially if you're carrying around expensive luggage or camera equipment.

If you're driving a rental car, giving locals a lift can be a great form of cultural interaction and much appreciated by those trudging along the side of the road while – comparatively – rich foreigners whiz past.

Health

Recommended Vaccinations

At the time of writing there were no recommended vaccinations for the Caribbean. If you are traveling away from major resort areas or going to places such as Haiti, however, it is vital that you consult a travel medical clinic at least three weeks before departure to check whether vaccinations are needed. Also check the internet resources listed under Websites later in this chapter.

Medical Checklist

Recommended items for a personal medical kit:

» acetaminophen/paracetamol (eg Tylenol) or aspirin

» antibacterial ointment (eg Bactroban) for cuts and abrasions

» antihistamines (for hay fever and allergic reactions)

» antibacterial hand sanitizer (eg Purell)

» anti-inflammatory drugs (eg ibuprofen/Advil)

» DEET-containing insect repellent

» steroid cream or cortisone (for allergic rashes)

» sunscreen

Prevention is the key to remaining healthy while traveling abroad. Travelers who receive the recommended vaccinations for the destination and follow commonsense precautions usually come away with nothing more serious than a little diarrhea.

From a health point of view, the Caribbean is generally safe as long as you're reasonably careful about what you eat and drink. The most common travel-related diseases, such as dysentery and hepatitis, are acquired by consumption of contaminated food and water. Mosquito-borne illnesses aren't a significant concern on most of the islands, except during outbreaks of dengue fever.

Health standards in major resort islands, such as Barbados, Bermuda and the Cayman Islands, is high, and access to health care is good.

See the Health sections of the individual chapter directories for any relevant information specific to the island.

BEFORE YOU GO

Bring medications in their original containers and clearly labeled. A signed, dated letter from your physician describing all medical conditions and medications, including generic names, is also a good idea. If carrying syringes or needles, be sure to have a physician's letter documenting their medical necessity.

Insurance

If your health insurance does not cover you for medical expenses while abroad, consider supplemental insurance; travel agents and the internet are good places to start looking. Find out in advance if your insurance plan will make payments directly to providers or reimburse you later for overseas health expenditures.

Note that Cuba requires proof of medical insurance to enter the country. On remote islands, such as the Grenadines, you will require transport to more developed areas for any significant problem, so be sure your insurance covers medical transport and evacuation.

HEALTH ADVISORIES

It's always a good idea to consult your government's travel-health website before departure, if one is available:

» Australia (www.smartraveller.gov.au)

» Canada/US (www.cdc.gov/travel)

» UK (www.nhs.uk/nhsengland/Health careabroad)

Websites

There is a wealth of travel-health advice on the internet.

Centers for Disease Control & Prevention (CDC; www.cdc.gov) Has good general information.

MD Travel Health (www.mdtravelhealth.com) Provides travel health recommendations for every country.

World Health Organization (WHO; www.who.int/ith) Publishes a superb book called *International Travel & Health,* which is revised annually and is available online at no cost.

IN THE CARIBBEAN ISLANDS

Availability & Cost of Health Care

Acceptable health care is available in most major cities throughout the Caribbean, but may be hard to locate in rural areas. To find a good local doctor, your best bet is to ask the management of the hotel where you are staying or contact your local embassy.

Many doctors and hospitals expect payment in cash, regardless of whether you have travel-health insurance. If you develop a life-threatening medical problem, you'll probably want to be evacuated to a country with state-of-the-art medical care. Since this may cost tens of thousands of dollars, be sure you have insurance to cover this before you depart (see p879).

Many pharmacies are well supplied, but important medications may not be consistently available. Be sure to bring along adequate supplies of all your prescription drugs.

See the Health sections of the chapter directories for any relevant information specific to the country.

Infectious Diseases

You are unlikely to come down with an infectious disease in the Caribbean, especially if you are just visiting resorts and the most developed islands. Cruisers will find themselves sprayed with antibacterial hand sanitizer at every turn as the cruise lines seek to prevent mass viral outbreaks.

A few ailments to be aware of – by checking travel advisory websites before your trip – are as follows.

Dengue Fever

Dengue fever is a viral infection common throughout the Caribbean. Dengue is transmitted by *Aedes* mosquitoes, which bite mostly during the daytime and are usually found close to human habitations, often indoors. They breed primarily in artificial water containers, such as jars, barrels, cans, cisterns, metal drums, plastic containers and discarded tires. As a result, dengue is especially common in densely populated, urban environments.

Dengue usually causes flu-like symptoms, including fever, muscle aches, joint pains, headaches, nausea and vomiting, often followed by a rash. The body aches may be quite uncomfortable, but most cases resolve uneventfully in a few days. Severe cases usually occur in children aged under 15 who are experiencing their second dengue infection.

If you suspect you have dengue fever, seek out medical advice. There is no vaccine. The cornerstone of prevention is protection against insect bites.

Hepatitis A

Hepatitis A is the second-most-common travel-related infection (after traveler's diarrhea). The illness occurs throughout the world, but the incidence is higher in developing nations. It occurs throughout the Caribbean, particularly in the northern islands.

Hepatitis A is a viral infection of the liver that is usually acquired by ingesting contaminated water, food or ice, though it may also be acquired by direct contact with infected persons. Symptoms may include fever, malaise, jaundice, nausea, vomiting and abdominal pain. Most cases resolve without complications, though hepatitis A occasionally causes severe liver damage. There is no treatment.

The vaccine for hepatitis A is extremely safe and highly effective. If you get a booster six to 12 months later, it lasts for at least 10 years. You should get it before you go to any developing nation. Because the safety of the hepatitis A vaccine has not been established for pregnant women or children

---

HAITI

Many of Haiti's challenges are health related. Cholera, malaria and other maladies have caused problems. The recommendations in this chapter do not necessarily apply to Haiti, where a higher level of health vigilance is required. See p523 for more information and always check travel-health resources, such as those listed under Websites in this chapter, before travel to that country.

under the age of two, they should instead be given a gamma globulin injection, which temporarily boosts immunity.

HIV/AIDS

HIV/AIDS has been reported in all Caribbean countries. More than 2% of all adults in the Caribbean carry HIV, which makes it the second-worst-affected region in the world, after sub-Saharan Africa. The highest prevalence is reported in The Bahamas, Haiti, and Trinidad and Tobago. Most cases in the Caribbean are related to heterosexual contact, especially with sex workers. The exception is Puerto Rico, where the most common cause of infection is intravenous drug use. Be sure to use condoms for all sexual encounters. If you think you might visit a piercing or tattoo parlor, or if you have a medical condition that might require an injection, bring along your own sterile needles.

Schistosomiasis

A parasitic infection carried by snails and acquired by exposure of skin to contaminated freshwater, schistosomiasis has been reported in parts of the Dominican Republic, Guadeloupe, Martinique, Puerto Rico, Antigua and Barbuda, Montserrat and St Lucia. To find out whether or not schistosomiasis is present in the areas you'll be visiting, go to the World Health Organization's **Global Schistosomiasis Atlas** (www.who.int/wormcontrol/documents/maps/country/en).

Early symptoms may include fever, loss of appetite, weight loss, abdominal pain, weakness, headaches, joint and muscle pains, diarrhea,

TAP WATER

Tap water is safe to drink on some of the islands, but not on others. Unless you're certain that the local water is safe, you shouldn't drink it.

See the Health sections of the chapter directories for tap water safety. Note: if tap water is safe to drink – as it is on the major destination islands except for Cuba – then avoiding bottled water reduces the significant environmental impact of plastic water containers.

nausea and a cough, but most infections are asymptomatic at first.

When traveling in areas where schistosomiasis occurs, you should avoid swimming, wading, bathing or washing in bodies of freshwater, including lakes, ponds, streams and rivers. Toweling yourself dry after exposure to contaminated water may reduce your chance of getting infected, but does not eliminate it. Saltwater and chlorinated pools carry no risk of schistosomiasis.

Traveler's Diarrhea

In places where tap water is safe to drink – much of the Caribbean – your risk of diarrhea is not high. But in places where the tap water is suspect, take the usual precautions: eat fresh fruits or vegetables only if cooked or peeled; be wary of dairy products that might contain unpasteurized milk; and be highly selective when eating food from street vendors.

Environmental Hazards

A few things to watch out for:
» **Mosquito bites** Caribbean mosquitoes and other biting/stinging insects come in all

shapes and sizes, and are quite common. The biggest concern here, outside the few areas with malaria, is simply discomfort and hassle. Make certain you have a good insect repellent with at least 25% DEET (we tried 5% DEET and it just seems to encourage them). Brands such as Off! are easily found.

» **Rabies** Some islands do have rabies, so do as you would at home and avoid touching or petting strays.

» **Sea stingers** Spiny sea urchins and coelenterates (coral and jellyfish) are a hazard in some areas. If stung by a coelenterate, apply diluted vinegar or baking soda. Remove tentacles carefully, but not with bare hands. If stung by a stinging fish, such as a stingray, immerse the limb in water at about 115°F (45°C).

» **Sunburn** We are surprised we still have to write this: wear sunscreen with an SPF of at least 15 as the Caribbean sun is very strong and sunburn is common. Every day we see people who are as pink as lobsters and having their trips ruined because they didn't apply sunscreen, especially after time in the water.

WANT MORE?

For in-depth language information and handy phrases, check out Lonely Planet's *Latin American Spanish, French,* and *Dutch Phrasebooks* You'll find them at **shop.lonelyplanet.com**, or you can buy Lonely Planet's iPhone phrasebooks at the Apple App Store.

Language

The rich language environment of the greater Caribbean is testament to the diverse array of people that have come to call it home.

From a colonial past that saw the dying out of virtually all traces of indigenous languages, there is the legacy of English, French, Spanish, Dutch and Portuguese. Outside these predominant languages, perhaps the most notable influences can be traced back to the slaves brought to the islands from West Africa. European tongues, creoles, patois, local accents and pidgins contribute to the particular linguistic mix of each island.

To find out who speaks what where, see the opening pages of each On the Road chapter.

FRENCH

The French used in the Caribbean is flatter in intonation, with less of the traditional French lilting cadence. Also, speakers of Creole pay less attention to gender; anything or anyone can be *il* (the French word for 'he').

There are nasal vowels (pronounced as if you're trying to force the sound through the nose) in French, indicated in our pronunciation guides with o or u followed by an almost inaudible nasal consonant sound m, n or ng. Note also that air is pronounced as in 'fair', eu as the 'u' in 'nurse', ew as ee with rounded lips, r is a throaty sound, and zh is pronounced as the 's' in 'pleasure'.

Basics

Hello.	Bonjour.	bon·zhoor
Goodbye.	Au revoir.	o·rer·vwa
Excuse me.	Excusez-moi.	ek·skew·zay·mwa
Sorry.	Pardon.	par·don
Please.	S'il vous plaît.	seel voo play
Thank you.	Merci.	mair·see
Yes.	Oui.	wee
No.	Non.	non

What's your name?
Comment vous appelez-vous? — ko·mon voo za·play voo

My name is ...
Je m'appelle ... — zher ma·pel ...

Do you speak English?
Parlez-vous anglais? — par·lay·voo ong·glay

I don't understand.
Je ne comprends pas. — zher ner kom·pron pa

How much is it?
C'est combien? — say kom·byun

Accommodations

campsite	camping	kom·peeng
guesthouse	pension	pon·syon
hotel	hôtel	o·tel
youth hostel	auberge de jeunesse	o·berzh der zher·nes

Do you have a ... room?	Avez-vous une chambre ...?	a·vey·voo ewn shom·bre ...
single	à un lit	a un lee
double	avec un grand lit	a·vek ung gron lee

How much is it per ...?	Quel est le prix par ...?	kel ey le pree par ...
night	nuit	nwee
person	personne	pair·son

Numbers – French		
1	un	un
2	deux	der
3	trois	trwa
4	quatre	ka·trer
5	cinq	sungk
6	six	sees
7	sept	set
8	huit	weet
9	neuf	nerf
10	dix	dees

Eating & Drinking

What would you recommend?
Qu'est-ce que vous conseillez? — kes·ker voo kon·say·yay

Do you have vegetarian food?
Vous faites les repas végétariens? — voo fet ley re·pa vey·zhey·ta·ryun

I'll have ...	Je prends ...	zhe pron ...
Cheers!	Santé!	son·tay

I'd like the ..., please.	Je voudrais ..., s'il vous plaît.	zhe voo·drey ... seel voo pley
bill	l'addition	la·dee·syon
menu	la carte	la kart

breakfast	petit déjeuner	per·tee day·zher·nay
lunch	déjeuner	day·zher·nay
dinner	dîner	dee·nay

Emergencies

Help!
Au secours! — o skoor

Leave me alone!
Fichez-moi la paix! — fee·shay·mwa la pay

I'm lost.
Je suis perdu(e). (m/f) — zhe swee pair·dew

I'm ill.
Je suis malade. — zher swee ma·lad

Where are the toilets?
Où sont les toilettes? — oo son ley twa·let

Call ...!	Appelez ...!	a·play un ...
a doctor	un médecin	un mayd·sun
the police	la police	la po·lees

Question Words – French		
How?	Comment?	ko·mon
What?	Quoi?	kwa
When?	Quand?	kon
Where?	Où?	oo
Who?	Qui?	kee
Why?	Pourquoi?	poor·kwa

Transportation & Directions

Where's ...?
Où est ...? — oo ay ...

What's the address?
Quelle est l'adresse? — kel ay la·dres

Can you show me (on the map)?
Pouvez-vous m'indiquer (sur la carte)? — poo·vay·voo mun·dee·kay (sewr la kart)

One ... ticket (to Bordeaux), please.	Un billet ... (pour Bordeaux), s'il vous plaît.	um bee·yey ... (poor bor·do) seel voo pley
one-way	simple	sum·ple
return	aller et retour	a·ley ey re·toor

boat	bateau	ba·to
bus	bus	bews
plane	avion	a·vyon
train	train	trun

SPANISH

While Spanish in the Caribbean is mutually intelligible with European Spanish, there are some differences, as migration and indigenous languages have left their mark on local vocabulary and pronunciation.

Spanish vowels are generally pronounced short. Note that ow is pronounced as in 'how', kh as in the Scottish *loch* (harsh and guttural), rr is rolled and stronger than in English, and v is a soft 'b' (pronounced between the English 'v' and 'b' sounds).

Basics

Hello.	Hola.	o·la
Goodbye.	Adiós.	a·dyos
Excuse me.	Perdón.	per·don
Sorry.	Lo siento.	lo syen·to

Question Words – Spanish

How?	¿Cómo?	ko·mo
What?	¿Qué?	ke
When?	¿Cuándo?	kwan·do
Where?	¿Dónde?	don·de
Who?	¿Quién?	kyen
Why?	¿Por qué?	por ke

Please.	Por favor.	por fa·vor
Thank you.	Gracias.	gra·syas
Yes.	Sí.	see
No.	No.	no

What's your name?
¿Cómo se llama / ko·mo se ya·ma
Usted? (pol) / oo·ste
¿Cómo te llamas? (inf) / ko·mo te ya·mas

My name is ...
Me llamo ... / me ya·mo ...

Do you speak English?
¿Habla/Hablas / a·bla/a·blas
inglés? (pol/inf) / een·gles

I don't understand.
Yo no entiendo. / yo no en·tyen·do

How much is it?
¿Cuánto cuesta? / kwan·to kwes·ta

Accommodations

campsite	terreno de cámping	te·re·no de kam·peeng
guesthouse	pensión	pen·syon
hotel	hotel	o·tel
youth hostel	albergue juvenil	al·ber·ge khoo·ve·neel

Do you have a ... room?	¿Tiene una habitación ...?	tye·ne oo·na a·bee·ta·syon ...
single	individual	een·dee·vee·dwal
double	doble	do·ble

How much is it per ...?	¿Cuánto cuesta por ...?	kwan·to kwes·ta por ...
night	noche	no·che
person	persona	per·so·na

Eating & Drinking

What would you recommend?
¿Qué recomienda? / ke re·ko·myen·da

Do you have vegetarian food?
¿Tienen comida vegetariana? / tye·nen ko·mee·da ve·khe·ta·rya·na

| I'll have ... | Para mí ... | pa·ra mee ... |
| Cheers! | ¡Salud! | sa·loo |

I'd like the ..., please.	Quisiera ..., . por favor.	kee·sye·ra ... por fa·vor
bill	la cuenta	la kwen·ta
menu	el menú	el me·noo

breakfast	desayuno	de·sa·yoo·no
lunch	comida	ko·mee·da
dinner	cena	se·na

Emergencies

Help!
¡Socorro! / so·ko·ro

Go away!
¡Vete! / ve·te

I'm lost.
Estoy perdido/a. (m/f) / es·toy per·dee·do/a

I'm ill.
Estoy enfermo/a. (m/f) / es·toy en·fer·mo/a

Where are the toilets?
¿Dónde están los servicios? / don·de es·tan los ser·vee·syos

Call ...!	¡Llame a ...!	lya·me a ...
a doctor	un médico	oon me·dee·ko
the police	la policía	la po·lee·see·a

Transportation & Directions

Where's ...?
¿Dónde está ...? / don·de es·ta ...

What's the address?
¿Cuál es la dirección? / kwal es la dee·rek·syon

Can you show me (on the map)?
¿Me lo puede indicar (en el mapa)? / me lo pwe·de een·dee·kar (en el ma·pa)

Numbers – Spanish

1	uno	oo·no
2	dos	dos
3	tres	tres
4	cuatro	kwa·tro
5	cinco	seen·ko
6	seis	seys
7	siete	sye·te
8	ocho	o·cho
9	nueve	nwe·ve
10	diez	dyes

a ... ticket	un billete de ...	oon bee·ye·te ... de ...
one-way	ida	ee·da
return	de ida y vuelta	de ee·da ee vwel·ta
boat	barco	bar·ko
bus	autobús	ow·to·boos
plane	avión	a·vyon
train	tren	tren

DUTCH

While it isn't necessary to speak Dutch to get by on the islands of Saba, Sint Eustatius and Sint Maarten, these Dutch basics might help you make some new friends in the East Caribbean.

Note that aw is pronounced as in 'saw', eu as the 'u' in 'nurse', ew as 'ee' with rounded lips, oh as the 'o' in 'note', öy as the '-er y-' in 'her year' (without the 'r'), uh as the 'a' in 'ago', kh as in the Scottish loch (harsh and guttural), and zh as the 's' in 'pleasure'.

Basics

Hello.	Goedendag.	khoo·duh·dakh
Goodbye.	Dag.	dakh
Excuse me.	Pardon.	par·don
Sorry.	Sorry.	so·ree
Please.	Alstublieft. (pol)	al·stew·bleeft
	Alsjeblieft. (inf)	a·shuh·bleeft
Thank you.	Dank u/je. (pol/inf)	dangk ew/yuh

Yes.	Ja.	yaa
No.	Nee.	ney

What's your name?

Hoe heet u/je? (pol/inf)	hoo heyt ew/yuh

My name is ...

Ik heet ...	ik heyt ...

Haitian Creole

Here are a few basics to get you started in the predominant lingo of Haiti.

Good day.	Bonjou. (before noon)
Good evening.	Bonswa. (after 11am)
See you later.	Na wè pita.
Yes./No.	Wi./Non.
Please.	Silvouple.
Thank you.	Mèsi anpil.
Sorry./Excuse me.	Pàdon.
How are you?	Ki jan ou ye?
Not bad.	M pal pi mal.
I'm going OK.	M-ap kenbe.
What's your name?	Ki jan ou rele?
My name is ...	M rele ...
Do you speak English?	Eske ou ka pale angle?
I don't understand.	M pa konprann.
How much is it?	Konbyen?
I'm lost.	M pèdi.
Where is/are ... ?	Kote ... ?

GLOSSARY

ABCs – Aruba, Bonaire and Curaçao

agouti – short-haired rabbitlike rodent resembling a guinea pig with long legs; it has a fondness for sugarcane

Arawak – linguistically related tribes that inhabited most of the Caribbean islands and northern South America

bake – sandwich made with fried bread and usually filled with fish

bareboat – sail-it-yourself charter yacht usually rented by the week or longer

beguine – Afro-French dance music with a bolero rhythm that originated in Martinique in the 1930s; also spelled 'biguine'

bomba – musical form and dance inspired by African rhythms and characterized by call-and-response dialogues between musicians and interpreted by dancers; often considered as a unit with plena, as in bomba y plena

breadfruit – large, round, green fruit; a Caribbean staple that's comparable to potatoes in its carbohydrate content and is prepared in much the same way

BVI – British Virgin Islands

cabrito – goat meat

callaloo – spinachlike green, originally from Africa; also spelled 'kallaloo'

calypso – popular Caribbean music developed from slave songs; lyrics reflect political opinions, social views and commentary on current events

Carnival – major Caribbean festival; originated as a pre-Lenten festivity but is now observed at various times throughout the year on different islands; also spelled 'Carnaval'

casa particular – private house in Cuba that lets out rooms to foreigners

cassava – a root used since precolonial times as a staple of island diets, whether steamed, baked or grated into a flour for bread; also called 'yucca' or 'manioc'

cay – small island; comes from an Arawak word

cayo – coral key (Spanish)

chattel house – type of simple wooden dwelling placed upon cement or stone blocks so it can be easily moved

conch – large gastropod that, due to overfishing, is endangered; its chewy meat is often prepared in a spicy *Creole*-style sauce; also called *lambi*

cou-cou – creamy cornmeal and okra mash, commonly served with saltfish

Creole – person of European, or mixed black and European ancestry; local language predominantly a combination of French and African languages; cuisine characterized by spicy, full-flavored sauces and heavy use of green peppers and onions

dancehall – contemporary offshoot of reggae with faster, digital beats and an MC

dasheen – type of taro; the leaves are known as *callaloo*, while the starchy tuberous root is boiled and eaten like a potato

dolphin – a marine mammal; also a common type of white-meat fish (dolphinfish; sometimes called *mahimahi*); the two are not related, and 'dolphin' on any menu always refers to the fish

flying fish – gray-meat fish named for its ability to skim above the water, particularly plentiful in Barbados

fungi – semihard cornmeal pudding similar to Italian polenta that's added to soups and used as a side dish; also a Creole name for the music made by local scratch bands; 'funchi' on Aruba, Bonaire and Curaçao

gade – street (Danish)

gîte – small cottages for rent (French)

goat water – spicy goat-meat stew often flavored with cloves and rum

gommier – large native gum tree found in Caribbean rainforests

green flash – Caribbean phenomenon where you can see a green flash as the sun sets into the ocean

guagua – local bus; *gua-gua* in Dominican Republic

I-tal – natural style of vegetarian cooking practised by Rastafarians

irie – all right; used to indicate that all is well

jintero/a – tout or prostitute; literally 'jockey'

johnnycake – corn-flour griddle cake

jump-up – nighttime street party that usually involves dancing and plenty of rum drinking

lambi – see *conch*

limin' – hanging out, relaxing, chilling; also spelled 'liming'; from the Creole verb 'to lime'

mahimahi – see *dolphin*

mairie – town hall (French)

malecón – main street; literally 'sea wall'

manchineel – tree whose poisonous fruit sap can cause a severe skin rash; common on Caribbean beaches; called *mancenillier* on the French islands, and *anjenelle* on Trinidad and Tobago

manicou – opossum

mas camp – workshop where artists create Carnival costumes; short for 'masquerade camp'

mento – folk *calypso* music

mojito – cocktail made from rum, mint, sugar, seltzer and fresh lime juice

mountain chicken – legs of the crapaud, a type of frog found in Dominica

négritude – Black Pride philosophical and political movement that emerged in Martinique in the 1930s

Obeah – system of ancestral worship related to *Vodou* and rooted in West African religions

oil down – mix of breadfruit, beef, pork, *callaloo* and coconut milk

out islands – islands or *cays* that lie across the water from the main islands of an island group

Painkiller – popular alcoholic drink made with two parts rum, one part orange juice, four parts pineapple juice, one part coconut cream and a sprinkle of nutmeg and cinnamon

paladar – privately owned restaurant in Cuba serving reliable, inexpensive meals

panyards – place where steel pan is practiced in the months leading up to *Carnival*

parang – type of music sung in Spanish and accompanied by guitars and maracas; originated in Venezuela

pate – fried pastry of *cassava* or *plantain* dough stuffed with spiced goat, pork, chicken, *conch*, lobster or fish

pepperpot – spicy stew made with various meats,

accompanied by peppers and cassareep

plantain – starchy fruit of the banana family; usually fried or grilled like a vegetable

playa – beach (Spanish)

público – collective taxis; *publique* in Haiti

quelbe – blend of jigs, quadrilles, military fife and African drum music

rapso – a fusion of *soca* and hip-hop

reggaeton – mixture of hip-hop, reggae and *dancehall*

roti – curry (often potatoes and chicken) rolled inside flat bread

rumba – Afro-Cuban dance form that originated among plantation slaves during the 19th century; during the 1920s and '30s, the term 'rumba' was adopted in North America and Europe for a ballroom dance in 4/4

time; in Cuba today, 'to rumba' means 'to party'

salsa – Cuban music based on *son*

Santería – Afro-Caribbean religion representing the syncretism of Catholic and African beliefs

snowbird – North American, usually retired, who comes to the Caribbean for its warm winters

soca – energetic offspring of *calypso*; it uses danceable rhythms and risqué lyrics to convey pointed social commentary

son – Cuba's basic form of popular music, with African and Spanish elements

souse – dish made out of pickled pig's head and belly, spices and a few vegetables; commonly served with a pig-blood sausage called 'pudding'

steel pan – instrument made from oil drums or the music it produces; also

called 'steel drum' or 'steel band'

SVG – St Vincent and the Grenadines

Taíno – settled, Arawak-speaking tribe that inhabited much of the Caribbean prior to the Spanish conquest; the word itself means 'We the Good People'

taptap – local Haitian bus

timba – contemporary *salsa*

TnT – Trinidad and Tobago

USVI – US Virgin Islands

Vodou – religion practised in Haiti; a synthesis of West African animist spirit religions and residual rituals of the *Taíno*

zouk – popular French West Indies music that draws from the *beguine* and other French Caribbean folk forms

behind the scenes

SEND US YOUR FEEDBACK

We love to hear from travelers – your comments keep us on our toes and help make our books better. Our well-traveled team reads every word on what you loved or loathed about this book. Although we cannot reply individually to postal submissions, we always guarantee that your feedback goes straight to the appropriate authors, in time for the next edition. Each person who sends us information is thanked in the next edition – and the most useful submissions are rewarded with a free book.

Visit **lonelyplanet.com/contact** to submit your updates and suggestions or to ask for help. Our award-winning website also features inspirational travel stories, news and discussions.

Note: We may edit, reproduce and incorporate your comments in Lonely Planet products such as guidebooks, websites and digital products, so let us know if you don't want your comments reproduced or your name acknowledged. For a copy of our privacy policy visit lonelyplanet.com/privacy.

OUR READERS

Many thanks to the travelers who used the last edition and wrote to us with helpful hints, useful advice and interesting anecdotes:

Silje Abelsen, Scott Adams, Dean Alexander, Gunilla Bewert, Steve Brosnan, Brandon Bruce, Susan Burton, John Condon, Jerry Coyd, Sergio De Sousa, Amelie A Gagnon, Holly Hill, Darlene James, Martin Jennett, Jessica Johnson, Philip Johnston, Niels Juul, Megan Kelly, Kevin Krol, Jeff Mahler, Ignacio Morejon, Odell Prior, Trish Reid, Michael Ryan, Vic Sofras, Ivo Sotorp, Prammantioti Stavroula, Stanley Urban, Phil Vass

AUTHOR THANKS

Ryan Ver Berkmoes

Huge thanks go to the amazing team of authors who worked on this book. That we were able to produce this level of work when forced to travel to the Caribbean from our cold winter homes is extraordinary. Thanks to the in-house team, including Cat Craddock, Bruce Evans, Alison Lyall and Laura Crawford. On the road, big thanks to the island of Bequia for being so cool that it's my new favorite small island. And to old pals everywhere: humble thanks.

Jean-Bernard Carillet

Heaps of thanks to Catherine Craddock for her trust and to the editorial and cartography teams. Ryan, coordinating-author extraordinaire, deserves the thumbs up for his humor and support – a few beers await! In St Lucia, special thanks to Genevieve, Janique, Rhonda, Charkar, Jacques, Zaka and the staff at the St Lucia tourism board. In Paris, a heartfelt *désolé* to Celine L, who (unwillingly) shared my ups and downs while I was on the road. On the home-front, well-deserved *bisous* to my daughter Eva and Christine, who shared some of my Caribbean adventures a long time ago.

Nate Cavalieri

Thanks to the 'Dream Team' for the lengthy and heated discussion about desserts of the world and to my excellent colleagues at Lonely Planet. Thanks especially to Florence Chien, my favorite person.

Paul Clammer

Travel in Haiti is always an amazing experience, but my trips in 2010 were particularly humbling, seeing the aftermath of the earthquake and the fortitude of the Haitians. Special thanks to Michael, Walnes and the St Joe's family. Thanks also to Jacqualine Labrom, Emily Troutman, Landon Yarrington, Bette Gebrian, Tessa Lewis, Nat Segaren, Leah Page, Gabie Vincent and Thor Burnham.

Michael Grosberg

Rebecca Tessler, my heart, is always with me. Gracias to Isabel Rosario, Oscar Jr and his father and Pinky Rodriguez in Jarabacoa; Mark Fernandez and Tim Hall for their help in Puerto Plata; mountain biker Maximo Gomez; Mariam Matías and her brother David from Constanza; Steve McKenney from Luperon; chef Rafael Vasquez; Martin Pantallon in Santo Domingo. To Carly Neidorf for her support and presence. And of course to my co-author Kevin Raub, coordinating author Paul Clammer and commissioning editor Catherine Craddock and managing editor Bruce Evans.

Adam Karlin

Thanks: Julian and Alex for friendship, laughs and perspective, Steve and Roger for tons of valuable advice, Rachel for her companionship and constant support, every Jamaican who passed along a genuine smile and warmth, Ryan for heading this mammoth book – and big ups to Anna Kaminski for helping make this Jamaica chapter what it is.

Tom Masters

Many thanks to Rosemary Masters, who accompanied me on much of my travels for this book, and retained her good humor as I defected to research hotels or drove her down dirt tracks looking for obscure beaches: you're the best mother in the world, and I couldn't have hoped for a more inspirational parent. Many thanks also to all the folks who helped me along the way, to my Lonely Planet colleagues and the wonderful people of the Caribbean Islands.

Emily Matchar

Thanks to Robbin Whachell, Lyndah Wells, Lanelle Phillips, Harry Bahama, Kaybel Taylor and Erika and Ed Gates for their excellent Grand Bahama info. Thanks to Eugene at the Pineville Motel in Andros for sharing his vast local knowledge. Thanks to Katie and Grant at the Bimini Sands, for their great Bimini and Andros tips. Thanks to Laurie Costanza, my Loyalist Cays partner in crime. And thanks as always to Jamin Asay for being my companion in travel and life.

Brandon Presser

Once again too many names, too little space. Sincere thanks to Lynn Costenaro, Andries Bonnema, Grant Gilmore, Trudy Nixon, Sue Ricketts, Jean-Philippe, travel pal Greg and St Joanne. At Lonely Planet, thanks to Cat, RVB, and the rest of the exceptional publishing team.

Brendan Sainsbury

Thanks to all the untold bus drivers, weather forecasters, paladar owners, wandering troubadours and innocent bystanders who helped me during my research, In Cuba special thanks to Julio Muñoz, Rafael Requejo, Nilson Guilaré, Angel Rodríguez, Victor in Trinidad, Maité and Idolka in Morón, Norberto Hernández in Havana and the bloke at Ecotur in Bayamo. On the work-front, muchas gracias to co-author Luke Waterson and commissioning editor Catherine Craddock. On the home-front, well-deserved *besos* to wife, Liz and son, Kieran.

Andrea Schulte-Peevers

A heartfelt thank you to all those whose advice, support and insights were invaluable during the research of this book, particularly the irrepressible Carolanne Watson, the gracious Simonetta Di Barbora and film-maker par excellence David Lea. Special thanks to my colleague Ryan Ver Berkmoes for so generously sharing his expertise, to Cat Craddock for entrusting me with this gig and to Suki Gear for her many years of trust and support. Last but not least, a giant thank you to my Nascar-quality husband David for white-knuckling the islands' often hellish roads.

Polly Thomas

Huge thanks to Dexter Lewis for support beyond the call of duty; and to Skye Hernandez, Bess Hernandez and Dwayne Lewis for love, support and Aaron-related backup. Thanks also to Lucille Sylvester for coming up trumps where the Tourist Board didn't; to Brandon Presser for guiding lights; and Bruce Evans and Cat Craddock for their patience and editorial wisdom.

Karla Zimmerman

Mega-thanks to Lisa Beran and Tamara Beran Robinson for helping research the Painkillers and piña coladas. Thanks the following people for sharing their local knowledge: Don Near, Mr Frett, Dmitri at Magens Bay, Matthew Telesford and Bailey at Udder Delight. Extreme gratefulness to Lonely Planet's Ryan Ver Berkmoes, Cat Craddock and Bruce Evans for advice and patience. Thanks most of all to Eric Markowitz, the world's best partner-for-life, for ecocamping.

ACKNOWLEDGMENTS

Climate map data adapted from Peel MC, Finlayson BL & McMahon TA (2007) 'Updated World Map of the Köppen-Geiger Climate Classification', *Hydrology and Earth System Sciences*, 11, 163344.

BEHIND THE SCENES

THIS BOOK

This 6th edition of Lonely Planet's *Caribbean Islands* guidebook was researched and written by Ryan Ver Berkmoes (coordinating author), Jean-Bernard Carillet, Nate Cavalieri, Paul Clammer, Michael Grosberg, Anna Kaminski, Beth Kohn, Adam Karlin, Tom Masters, Brandon Presser, Kevin Raub, Emily Matchar, Tom Masters, Brendan Sainsbury, Andrea Schulte-Peevers, Polly Thomas, Luke Waterson and Karla Zimmerman. The 5th edition was researched and written by Ryan Ver Berkmoes (coordinating author), Amy C Balfour, Paul Clammer, Michael Grosberg, Scott Kennedy, Richard Koss, Josh Krist, Tom Masters, Jens Porup, Brandon Presser, Brendan Sainsbury, Ellee Thalheimer and Karla Zimmerman. This guidebook was commissioned in Lonely Planet's Oakland office, and produced by the following:

Commissioning Editors Kathleen Munnelly, Suki Gear, Catherine Craddock-Carrillo

Coordinating Editor Laura Crawford

Coordinating Cartographer Mark Griffiths

Coordinating Layout Designer Kerrianne Southway

Managing Editors Bruce Evans, Annelies Mertens

Managing Cartographer Alison Lyall

Managing Layout Designer Chris Girdler

Assisting Editors Andrew Bain, Carolyn Boicos, Jessica Crouch, Kim Hutchins, Asha Ioculari, Sarah Koel, Bella Li, Alan Murphy, Catherine Naghten, Di-anne Schallmeiner, Matty Soccio, Gina Tsarouhas, Jeanette Wall

Assisting Cartographers Ildiko Bogdanovits, Valeska Canas, Julie Dodkins, Joelene Kowalski, Andy Rojas

Cover Research Naomi Parker

Internal Image Research Sabrina Dalbesio

Thanks to Helen Christinis, Ryan Evans, Trent Paton, Martine Power, Averil Robertson, Gerard Walker, Juan Wanita

index

how to use this book

These symbols will help you find the listings you want:

◉ Sights	☝ Tours	🍷 Drinking
🏖 Beaches	🎉 Festivals & Events	☆ Entertainment
🏃 Activities	🛏 Sleeping	🛍 Shopping
🍷 Courses	🍴 Eating	ℹ Information/Transport

Look out for these icons:

TOP CHOICE	Our author's recommendation
FREE	No payment required
🍃	A green or sustainable option

Our authors have nominated these places as demonstrating a strong commitment to sustainability – for example by supporting local communities and producers, operating in an environmentally friendly way, or supporting conservation projects.

These symbols give you the vital information for each listing:

☏ Telephone Numbers	🕐 Opening Hours	P Parking	⊖ Nonsmoking	❄ Air-Conditioning	@ Internet Access
🛜 Wi-Fi Access	☰ Swimming Pool	🥗 Vegetarian Selection	📖 English-Language Menu	👪 Family-Friendly	🐾 Pet-Friendly
🚌 Bus	⛴ Ferry	Ⓜ Metro	Ⓢ Subway	⊖ London Tube	🚋 Tram	🚆 Train

Reviews are organised by author preference.

Map Legend

Sights
- Beach
- Buddhist
- Castle
- Christian
- Hindu
- Islamic
- Jewish
- Monument
- Museum/Gallery
- Ruin
- Winery/Vineyard
- Zoo
- Other Sight

Activities, Courses & Tours
- Diving/Snorkelling
- Canoeing/Kayaking
- Skiing
- Surfing
- Swimming/Pool
- Walking
- Windsurfing
- Other Activity/Course/Tour

Sleeping
- Sleeping
- Camping

Eating
- Eating

Drinking
- Drinking
- Cafe

Entertainment
- Entertainment

Shopping
- Shopping

Information
- Post Office
- Tourist Information

Transport
- Airport
- Border Crossing
- Bus
- Cable Car/Funicular
- Cycling
- Ferry
- Metro
- Monorail
- Parking
- S-Bahn
- Taxi
- Train/Railway
- Tram
- Tube Station
- U-Bahn
- Other Transport

Routes
- Tollway
- Freeway
- Primary
- Secondary
- Tertiary
- Lane
- Unsealed Road
- Plaza/Mall
- Steps
- Tunnel
- Pedestrian Overpass
- Walking Tour
- Walking Tour Detour
- Path

Boundaries
- International
- State/Province
- Disputed
- Regional/Suburb
- Marine Park
- Cliff
- Wall

Population
- Capital (National)
- Capital (State/Province)
- City/Large Town
- Town/Village

Geographic
- Hut/Shelter
- Lighthouse
- Lookout
- Mountain/Volcano
- Oasis
- Park
- Pass
- Picnic Area
- Waterfall

Hydrography
- River/Creek
- Intermittent River
- Swamp/Mangrove
- Reef
- Canal
- Water
- Dry/Salt/Intermittent Lake
- Glacier

Areas
- Beach/Desert
- Cemetery (Christian)
- Cemetery (Other)
- Park/Forest
- Sportsground
- Sight (Building)
- Top Sight (Building)

Polly Thomas

Grenada, Trinidad & Tobago Polly Thomas first traveled to the Caribbean aged 18, when she spent two months in Jamaica. This sparked an enduring love of the region, and more trips to Jamaica were followed by commissions to write guidebooks on Jamaica and Trinidad and Tobago. Since then, she has written about Antigua, St Lucia, Dominica, St Vincent and the Grenadines, Jamaica and TnT for various publications. She lives in Port of Spain, Trinidad, with her partner and child.

Karla Zimmerman

British Virgin Islands, US Virgin Islands During her island travels, Karla hiked past wild donkeys on St John, ate an embarrassing number of johnnycakes on St Thomas and felt no pain on Jost Van Dyke. She first bounced around the Virgins as a kid, and still remembers seeing the true-blue hue of Magens Bay on that initial visit. Karla is based in Chicago, where she writes for newspapers, magazines and websites. She has worked on several Lonely Planet guidebooks covering the USA, Canada, the Caribbean and Europe.

Read more about Karla at:
lonelyplanet.com/members/karlazimmerman

Contributing Authors

Anna Kaminski The Caribbean first captured Anna's imagination when she studied the history and literature of the region at the University of Warwick. She came to Jamaica in 2006, where she spent five months becoming acquainted with the city's ghettos and prisons while penning articles for the *Caribbean Times*. She is also a connoisseur of Jamaican cuisine. Anna contributed to the Jamaica chapter of this guidebook.

Beth Kohn Beth has loved Puerto Rico since her first trip, when she catapulted into a shimmering bio-bay and stayed up for hours listening to the coquí frogs. Her favorite experience this time was tramping up the south road of El Yunque. She is an author of many Lonely Planet guides and you can see more of her written and photographic work at www.bethkohn.com. Beth contributed to the Puerto Rico chapter of this guidebook.

Kevin Raub Kevin Raub grew up in Atlanta and started his career as a music journalist in New York. He worked for *Men's Journal* and *Rolling Stone* magazines, before taking up travel writing while ditching the States for Brazil. He has worked on many Lonely Planet guides and you can find him at www.kevinraub.net. Kevin contributed to the Dominican Republic chapter of this guidebook.

Luke Waterson Cruising the countryside in wheezing Cadillacs and Plymouths, smoking several dozen cigars, experiencing two drag shows, sinking numerous mojitos and learning some (tentative) salsa moves while researching this edition helped Luke fall in love with Cuba all over again. Travel-wise Luke's passions are Latin America, Eastern Europe and Britain: musings on his journeys can be found at www.lukewaterson.co.uk.

Michael Grosberg

Dominican Republic In addition to working on the last two *Dominican Republic & Haiti* guidebooks, Michael has visited the DR on other occasions, going back to his graduate school days when he was focusing on literature and culture of Latin America. Michael is based in Brooklyn, New York, and usually writes just down the street from several Dominican restaurants, where he gets his lunch. A reformed academic/journalist by trade, Michael has worked on over 15 Lonely Planet books.

Read more about Michael at:
lonelyplanet.com/members/michaelgrosberg

Adam Karlin

Jamaica Adam Karlin has always covered the edges of the Caribbean for Lonely Planet – Miami, New Orleans – and he jumped at the chance to travel deep into the heart of the region. In Jamaica he barreled down the road on taxis, watched a silly amount of beautiful sunsets, traded many stories for shots of overproof rum, tasted some truly sublime jerk and turned 30. Adam has worked on over two dozen guidebooks for Lonely Planet.

Read more about Adam at:
lonelyplanet.com/members/adamkarlin

Tom Masters

Guadeloupe, Martinique, Turks & Caicos Tom has been a long-time lover of all things Caribbean, particularly anything to do with diving, which he's done everywhere in the region. Having spent much of his childhood in France, covering Martinique and Guadeloupe was an obvious choice, while the diving in the Turks and Caicos was some of the best he's ever experienced. Tom also contributed to the Bahamas chapter. He lives in Berlin; find him online at www.tommasters.net.

Read more about Tom at:
lonelyplanet.com/members/tommasters

Emily Matchar

The Bahamas Emily's first trip to the Bahamas was inauspicious (let us never speak of Spring Break 2003 again, please!). But subsequent trips opened her eyes to the wonders of pink-sand beaches, blue holes and cracked conch. In fact, she's kind of annoyed that she's not on Eleuthera's Lighthouse Beach right now. When she's not globetrotting, Emily lives in Chapel Hill, North Carolina, and writes about culture for a number of magazines and newspapers. She's contributed to a dozen Lonely Planet guidebooks.

Read more about Emily at:
lonelyplanet.com/members/emilymatchar

Brandon Presser

Anguilla, Saba, Sint Eustatius, St-Barthélemy, St-Martin/Sint Maarten After diving through the deep blue off the coasts of six continents, and working at a marine life conservation center, Brandon was primed to take on the grueling task of hunting for hidden Caribbean treasure. These days Brandon spends his time trotting the globe as a full-time freelance travel writer. He's contributed to over 20 Lonely Planet titles from *Iceland* to *Thailand* and many '-lands' in between.

Read more about Brandon at:
lonelyplanet.com/members/brandonpresser

Brendan Sainsbury

Cuba Brendan is a British freelance writer who lives in British Columbia, Canada. He first visited Cuba in the 1990s and returned in 2002 to work as a travel guide leading cultural and cycling trips around the country. He authored his first Lonely Planet *Cuba* guide in 2006 with his then three-month-old son in tow. Since then he has produced three more *Cuba* guides, written countless Cuba-related newspaper articles, given live presentations and been interviewed by everyone from Rick Steves to *USA Today*.

Read more about Brendan at:
lonelyplanet.com/members/brendansainsbury

Andrea Schulte-Peevers

Antigua & Barbuda, St Kitts & Nevis, Dominica, Montserrat Andrea has traveled to some 65 countries, but she'll forever cherish the memory of swimming up a gorge to a waterfall in Dominica, and witnessing both the destruction and rebirth of an island in Montserrat. When she's not gallivanting around the globe, Andrea makes her home in Berlin. She's worked on more than 40 Lonely Planet titles and traces her passion for the Caribbean back to a trip to St Kitts and Nevis in the mid-1990s.

OUR STORY

A beat-up old car, a few dollars in the pocket and a sense of adventure. In 1972 that's all Tony and Maureen Wheeler needed for the trip of a lifetime – across Europe and Asia overland to Australia. It took several months, and at the end – broke but inspired – they sat at their kitchen table writing and stapling together their first travel guide, *Across Asia on the Cheap*. Within a week they'd sold 1500 copies. Lonely Planet was born.

Today, Lonely Planet has offices in Melbourne, London and Oakland, with more than 600 staff and writers. We share Tony's belief that 'a great guidebook should do three things: inform, educate and amuse'.

OUR WRITERS

Ryan Ver Berkmoes

Coordinating Author, Aruba, Barbados, Bonaire, Cayman Islands, Curaçao, St Vincent & the Grenadines Ryan Ver Berkmoes grew up in the beach town of Santa Cruz, California, and always feels at home with a little sand lodged in the cracks between his toes. He's written about beaches worldwide but still can never get over the stunningly turquoise Caribbean and the blindingly white beaches. It's a cliché, yes, but it's often remarkably spot on. As a journalist who has covered stories worldwide and experienced a lot of cultures, Ryan is still surprised at the diversity of people and places within the Caribbean. Follow him at www.ryan verberkmoes.com.

Read more about Ryan at:
lonelyplanet.com/members/ryanverberkmoes

Jean-Bernard Carillet

Diving & Snorkeling, St Lucia Paris-based journalist and photographer Jean-Bernard is a die-hard island lover, diving instructor and calypso dance aficionado. He has clocked up numerous trips to the Caribbean. In St Lucia he searched for the perfect beaches, the best dive sites, the most thrilling adventure tours, the best value accommodations and the most memorable views of the Pitons. Jean-Bernard has contributed to many Lonely Planet titles, in French and English, and coordinated Lonely Planet diving guides. He also writes for travel and dive magazines.

Nate Cavalieri

Puerto Rico, Sounds of the Caribbean Nate's favorite experiences on this research trip included scanning the waters for manatee from the lighthouse at Cabo Rojo and sharing a Medalla with an on-duty cop at a beach bonfire in Rincón. He's authored Lonely Planet guides on California, the US and Latin America, as well as covering Puerto Rico. He gets a bit of the island every day in his neighborhood, Brooklyn, New York.

Read more about Nate at:
lonelyplanet.com/members/natecavalieri

Paul Clammer

Haiti Sometime molecular biologist, tour leader and now travel writer, Paul would like to think that Haiti first came to his attention from reading Graham Greene's *The Comedians*, but secretly wonders if childhood viewings of *Live and Let Die* didn't also play their part. In the aftermath of the 2010 earthquake, Paul volunteered clearing rubble in Léogâne, before returning to research for this guidebook. His website is www.paulclammer.com.

Read more about Paul at:
lonelyplanet.com/members/paulclammer

OVER PAGE MORE WRITERS

Published by Lonely Planet Publications Pty Ltd
ABN 36 005 607 983
6th edition – Nov 2011
ISBN 978 1 74179 454 0
© Lonely Planet 2011   Photographs © as indicated 2011
10 9 8 7 6 5 4 3 2 1
Printed in China

Although the authors and Lonely Planet have taken all reasonable care in preparing this book, we make no warranty about the accuracy or completeness of its content and, to the maximum extent permitted, disclaim all liability arising from its use.